Understanding Session Border Controllers

Comprehensive Guide to Designing, Deploying, Troubleshooting, and Maintaining Cisco Unified Border Element (CUBE) Solutions

Kaustubh Inamdar, CCIE® Voice No. 42277
Steve Holl, CCIE® Collaboration No. 22739
Gonzalo Salgueiro, CCIE® No. 4541
Kyzer Davis, CCIE® Collaboration No. 54735
Chidambaram Arunachalam, CCIE® Collaboration No. 14809

Cisco Press

Understanding Session Border Controllers

Comprehensive Guide to Designing, Deploying, Troubleshooting, and Maintaining Cisco Unified Border Element (CUBE) Solutions

Kaustubh Inamdar, Steve Holl, Gonzalo Salgueiro, Kyzer Davis, Chidambaram Arunachalam

Published by:
Cisco Press

01 18

Library of Congress Control Number: 2018940999

ISBN-13: 978-1-58714-476-9
ISBN-10: 1-58714-476-X

Warning and Disclaimer

This book is designed to provide information about session border controllers for collaboration deployments. Every effort has been made to make this book as complete and as accurate as possible, but no warranty or fitness is implied.

The information is provided on an “as is” basis. The authors, Cisco Press, and Cisco Systems, Inc. shall have neither liability nor responsibility to any person or entity with respect to any loss or damages arising from the information contained in this book or from the use of the discs or programs that may accompany it.

The opinions expressed in this book belong to the author and are not necessarily those of Cisco Systems, Inc.

Trademark Acknowledgments

All terms mentioned in this book that are known to be trademarks or service marks have been appropriately capitalized. Cisco Press or Cisco Systems, Inc., cannot attest to the accuracy of this information. Use of a term in this book should not be regarded as affecting the validity of any trademark or service mark.

Special Sales

For information about buying this title in bulk quantities, or for special sales opportunities (which may include electronic versions; custom cover designs; and content particular to your business, training goals, marketing focus, or branding interests), please contact our corporate sales department at corpsales@pearsoned.com or (800) 382-3419.

For government sales inquiries, please contact governmentsales@pearsoned.com.

For questions about sales outside the U.S., please contact intlcs@pearson.com.

Feedback Information

At Cisco Press, our goal is to create in-depth technical books of the highest quality and value. Each book is crafted with care and precision, undergoing rigorous development that involves the unique expertise of members from the professional technical community.

Readers' feedback is a natural continuation of this process. If you have any comments regarding how we could improve the quality of this book, or otherwise alter it to better suit your needs, you can contact us through email at feedback@ciscopress.com. Please make sure to include the book title and ISBN in your message.

We greatly appreciate your assistance.

Editor-in-Chief: Mark Taub

Product Line Manager: Brett Bartow

Business Operation Manager, Cisco Press: Ronald Fligge

Executive Editor: Paul Carlstroem

Managing Editor: Sandra Schroeder

Development Editor: Eleanor C. Bru

Project Editor: Mandie Frank

Copy Editor: Kitty Wilson

Technical Editors: Esteban Valverde, David Hanes

Editorial Assistant: Vanessa Evans

Designer: Chuti Prasertsith

Composition: codemantra

Indexer: Erika Millen

Proofreader: Abigail Manheim

Americas Headquarters
Cisco Systems, Inc.
San Jose, CA

Asia Pacific Headquarters
Cisco Systems (USA) Pte. Ltd.
Singapore

Europe Headquarters
Cisco Systems International BV Amsterdam,
The Netherlands

Cisco has more than 200 offices worldwide. Addresses, phone numbers, and fax numbers are listed on the Cisco Website at **www.cisco.com/go/offices.**

About the Authors

Kaustubh Inamdar, CCIE Voice No. 42277, is an escalation point for the Multiservice teams of the Cisco Unified Communications Technical Assistance Center (TAC) in India. He has worked on numerous complex VoIP issues for Cisco partners and key customers. He is a subject matter expert in the area of real-time communications and has deep knowledge of the associated standards and protocols. He is also the co-inventor of five patents (pending) in diverse areas such as collaboration, security, machine learning, and cloud technologies.

Steve Holl, CCIE Collaboration No. 22739, manages a global engineering team that supports the Cisco Collaboration as a Service (CaaS) offering for Cisco's largest customers. Joining Cisco in 2005, he previously served as a team lead for voice solutions in the Global Technical Assistance Center (TAC). Steve graduated from the Rochester Institute of Technology with a bachelor of science in Applied Networking and System Administration, and he later completed a master's of engineering in Engineering Management at the University of Colorado Boulder. In addition to holding a CCIE since 2008, Steve is also an ITIL Expert, PMP, and Six Sigma Black Belt. In his spare time, he enjoys cooking with his wife, Jenn, playing loud guitar solos, and undertaking outdoor adventures.

Gonzalo Salgueiro, CCIE No. 4541, is a Principal Engineer at Cisco, working on several emerging technologies and the services opportunities they offer. Gonzalo has spent more than 20 years at Cisco, establishing himself as a subject matter expert, an innovator, and an industry thought leader in various technologies, including Collaboration, ML/AI, Cloud, and IoT.

Gonzalo is an established member of numerous industry organizations and is a regular presenter and distinguished speaker at a variety of technical industry conferences and Cisco events around the world. He currently holds various industry leadership roles, including serving as a member of the Board of Directors of the SIP Forum, co-chair of the INSIPID and SIPBRANDY IETF working groups, a member of the IoT Directorate in the IETF, and co-chair of the WebRTC Task Group, IPv6 Task Group, and FoIP Task Group in the SIP Forum. He is an active contributor to various industry organizations and standardization activities.

Gonzalo previously co-authored the Cisco Press books *IoT Fundamentals: Networking Technologies, Protocols, and Use Cases for the Internet of Things* as well as *Fax, Modem, and Text for IP Telephony*. He has also co-authored 25 IETF RFCs, 4 IEEE papers, 4 ITU contributions, and numerous industry and academic research papers on a variety of different technical topics. He is also co-inventor of 100+ patents (issued and pending) and has contributed to various interop and open source development efforts. Gonzalo received a master's degree in Physics from the University of Miami.

Kyzer Davis, CCIE Collaboration No. 54735, is an escalation point for the worldwide Multiservice teams of the Cisco Technical Assistance Center (TAC). He is the focal point for supporting, troubleshooting, and resolving complex solution-level problems involving Voice, Video, and Cloud portions of the Cisco Unified Collaboration product portfolio.

In addition to his work on this book, Kyzer has also authored numerous technical white papers on Cisco Collaboration configuration, architecture, and protocol design. In addition, he works with Learning@Cisco on strategy and content development for numerous Cisco certifications. Kyzer is a technology enthusiast and mentor who is always working on automation initiatives and dabbling with new and evolving technology in the lab. He also enjoys a mean barbecue.

Chidambaram (Arun) Arunachalam, CCIE No. 14809, is a Cisco Principal Engineer, responsible for resolving complex problems in large-scale collaboration networks. He works closely with engineering teams to drive solution-level serviceability requirements for end-to-end call signaling analysis in contact center environments and with industry experts for defining end-to-end SIP message logging capabilities (logme). He co-leads the Collaboration focus area within the TAC Technology office and is currently working on innovations such as Faster Cisco Support Experience (direct connection to engineer) and TAC Virtual Spaces (Webex Teams as a real-time communication channel for support engagements). He is a contributor to Wireshark and guides NCSU graduate students in developing Wireshark dissectors. His areas of interest include ease of doing business, talent development, and innovation.

About the Technical Reviewers

Esteban Valverde, CCIE No. 34305, is a senior engineer with 12 years of experience in networking and software development. In his current role, he is part of the Cisco Collaboration Escalation team of the Technical Assistance Center (TAC) in Research Triangle Park, North Carolina. His main focus is working with customers and Cisco Support Engineers on escalations that involve Cisco Unified Border Element (CUBE), Fax and Modems, Cisco Unified Communications Manager (CUCM), and Unified Contact Center Enterprise Deployments, as well as working closely with the Cisco Engineering team to enhance product serviceability and automating common troubleshooting tasks. During the past 6 years, he has specialized in troubleshooting complex issues for some of the largest VoIP Networks, and has provided technical leadership for some of the most critical worldwide Collaboration deployments. Esteban has developed and delivered all levels of training and documentation on the Cisco Unified Border Element to Cisco Technical teams. Before joining the Escalation team in 2012, Esteban worked as a Cisco Support Engineer in TAC for Switching and Voice Technologies. He holds a bachelor degree in Systems Engineering.

David Hanes, CCIE No. 3491, is a Principal Engineer in Cisco's Cloud Support Technical Assistance Center (TAC). Specializing in IoT, Cloud, and Collaboration technologies, he assists in escalated customer issues and the incubation of new products and solutions. David has authored various industry publications in his areas of expertise, including the Cisco Press books *IoT Fundamentals: Networking Technologies, Protocols, and Use Cases for the Internet of Things* and *Fax, Modem, and Text for IP Telephony*. He has spoken at industry conferences around the world and is a Cisco Live Hall of Fame Speaker. He has worked on various standardization efforts, including leading and participating in working groups with the SIP Forum and authoring and contributing to RFCs in the IETF. David has more than 20 patents (issued and pending) related to IoT, Collaboration, and other computer networking technologies. He holds a B.S. in Electrical Engineering from North Carolina State University.

Dedications

Kaustubh: I dedicate this book to my parents, Vijay and Suhasini, whose love, care, support, and warmth are more than I could ever ask for and whose way of life serves as a constant inspiration. I am truly grateful for every moment I spend with them.

I also dedicate this book to my wife, Isha, the love of my life. How I existed before I met her I will never know.

Steve: This book is foremost dedicated to my wife, Jenn, who maintains endless inspiration and patience to support and ensure priority for career and personal development, with the understanding that it also makes us better together.

I must also express endless gratitude to my mom, dad, and sister for the foundational motivation to pursue my interests and challenges. I cannot provide enough appreciation for the amazing extended support structure comprised of my extended family and friends throughout so many years.

Gonzalo: I dedicate this book to my loving family. To Becky, my wife, best friend, and biggest fan. Your unconditional love, support, and friendship serve as the bedrock for the amazing family and life we have built together. To our four incredible children, Alejandro, Sofia, Gabriela, and Mateo: You are truly the treasures in my life and make every day a wondrous and joy-filled adventure. I'm so fortunate to be the father of such amazing kids.

I also dedicate this book to my parents, Alberto and Elena, who have selflessly given everything and made countless personal sacrifices to make me the man I am today. This amazing life I lead is only possible because of your enduring love and kindness. I love you.

Kyzer: To my parents and grandparents, for encouraging me to always ask questions, explore new ideas, and expand my horizons by continuously striving to learn new topics throughout my career in information technology. Without their wisdom and guidance, I would not be where I am today.

Chidambaram: This book is dedicated to my parents Arunachalam and Muthayee, paternal grandparents Chidambaram and Valliammai, maternal grandparents Alagappan and Muthayee, Uncle Ramanathan and Aunt Seethalakshmi, who helped me truly understand the value of education and made huge efforts to provide the best possible education during my school and college days.

I also dedicate this to my wife, Haripriya, and our kids, Palaniappan and Sribala, whose love, flexibility, kind words, and happy faces make it possible to realize our dreams.

Acknowledgments

From the Author Team:

The collective author group would like to acknowledge and thank the following contributors:

Kyzer Davis: The rest of the author group would sincerely like to express our deepest appreciation for Kyzer's enthusiasm to join the book project late in the development stage, after already having provided technical review for most of the other chapters. He did an excellent job exceeding a significant challenge to turn around a large body of complex material in a very short timeframe to meet book deadlines and help us complete this publication.

Esteban Valverde and David Hanes: Thanks very much to both of you for the careful and thorough review of all the chapters to ensure that the content is accurate, useful, and consumable.

Arundeep Nagaraj: Thanks, Arundeep, for setting up the Cisco Unified Workforce Optimization lab that is used in Chapter 11.

Felipe Garrido: Thank you for reviewing the overall scope and layout of the book, including what content should be covered and ways to present it, and providing candid feedback based on what would be of value to readers. Thank you for listening and providing suggestions on the variety of examples discussed in this book.

Ben Wollak and Ramiro Amaya: Thanks to Ben Wollak for building the Collaboration Lab as a Service framework that is extensively used in Chapter 12 to illustrate the concepts using real-world deployment scenarios. Thanks to Ramiro Amaya for reviewing Chapter 12 even during his tight schedules with Cisco Live presentations. Ben's and Ramiro's contact center expertise was helpful in striking a balance between abstraction and specifics while discussing contact center concepts.

Divyang Mithaiwala and Ram Mohan: Thanks to both of you for providing CUBE feature-related clarifications in a very quick timeframe.

CUBE Engineering team: Thanks very much for building an amazing product and evolving the product based on the needs of our customers.

Customers and partners: Thanks for deploying Cisco solutions, sharing your business problems, co-innovating solutions, and being patient during the complex troubleshooting process. Day-to-day interactions with you enable us to learn and innovate, and it makes projects like this book possible.

Cisco Press: Finally, a thank you to everyone at Cisco Press for all the support with everything that happens after the technical words hit the page. We are grateful for all your efforts in making us look good!

From Kaustubh Inamdar:

I would like to thank my mentor and co-author, Gonzalo Salgueiro, for selflessly dedicating countless hours of his time to my personal and professional development. What started out as a simple email asking for guidance has evolved into one of the most valued relationships in my life. His body of work serves as an inspiration and as a professional benchmark for me.

I would like to thank my co-authors Steve Holl and Chidambaram Arunachalam for working with me on this publication; I'm honored to have co-authored this book with two individuals whose work helped me learn a great deal in my formative years as an engineer.

I would like to thank my former manager, Ajmal Hasan, who always inspired me to take on challenges and explore new frontiers. His personal investment in my successes and failures is a true testament to his greatness as a leader.

I would like to thank Sarthak Saxena and Roopa Jayaraman for their encouragement and support during this endeavor. I am truly indebted to them.

I would like to thank Hari Haran SM for providing his insights into the principles of audio and video conferencing and for helping me out with some of the illustrations.

I would like to thank Bopanna MS, Pawan Srivastava, Neeraj Nair, and Vinay Kumar Dharmaraj for their friendship and support over the years.

From Steve Holl:

First, I'd like to thank Kaustubh for his vision and inspiration to develop this publication. Without him, this publication simply would not exist, and I would not be an author. His breadth of knowledge and commitment to ensure that this is an encompassing body of work was a tireless effort of immense value.

Also, I am humbled to co-author a book alongside such a prestigious cast of engineers, who have all individually contributed greatly to the continued development of collaboration technologies to keep the technology evolving and to keep Cisco a relevant leader in the marketplace. Thank you for the friendship and professional mentorship that sums to over two decades.

To Russ Hardison: Thank you for your continued support over several years, allowing for professional development and presenting challenges, inspiration, and a platform from which to both innovate and inspire.

It is also essential to acknowledge the entire cast of the TAC Escalation team and CALO staff that took the time when I started Cisco to set the standard very high for the expectations on how to effectively solve problems. This guidance continues to serve as my benchmark on how to support and strive to delight Cisco customers.

Finally, a thanks to Michael Cho, who took a chance on a guy coming fresh out of college with only limited network knowledge, seeing something that he felt would be a positive contribution to Cisco Services.

From Gonzalo Salgueiro:

Thanks to Kaustubh Inamdar for bringing me into this project and allowing me to lead. As a mentor, your amazing growth and incessant desire to better yourself fills me with joy and comfort that the next generation is poised for greatness.

Thanks to all my co-authors for their dedication and passion for making this book a reality. Your knowledge and excellence were the reasons I recruited you.

I'd like to extend my sincere gratitude to the Customer Experience (CX) leadership team, especially Marc Holloman and Tom Berghoff. This book wouldn't have been possible without their unwavering encouragement, belief, and support.

A special note of thanks to my manager, Marc Holloman, for your daily leadership, kindness, friendship, and counsel. I appreciate all that you have done for me over the course of many years and allowing me the flexibility and freedom to innovate, teach, and inspire.

Thanks to Jonathan Rosenberg for writing the Foreword to this book. Your groundbreaking and pioneering body of work in SIP and real-time communications serves as an inspiration to us all.

From Kyzer Davis:

A big hearty thanks to the other authors of this book for allowing me to be a part of this publication. This is an amazing ensemble of talented individuals, and I am humbled to be included.

A midsize spirited thanks to Daniel Wallace, who cared for my dog, Cooper, while I tirelessly worked on content for this book.

Finally, a smaller, more personal thanks to Josh Meadows, Lyle Gardner, Daniel Peterson, Esteban Valverde, and Felipe Garrido for mentoring and sharing their personal knowledge across the numerous areas of information technology and topics of life.

From Chidambaram Arunachalam:

I would like to thank Gonzalo Salgueiro for giving me the great opportunity to contribute to this book and sharing authoring best practices throughout the journey. Thanks to my mentor, Carlos Pignataro, for teaching the concept of important versus urgent tasks and encouraging me to always get out of my comfort zone. Thanks to Marc Holloman for his continuous guidance, support, and encouragement in everything we do and always providing suggestions to overcome challenges.

Thanks to my teachers Mr. Varadhan Ramaswamy (E.R Higher Secondary School, Trichy India) and Dr. Yannis Viniotis and Dr. Mladen Vouk (both of NC State University) for their endless dedication to students and technology development.

Cisco is all about people, and the way it nourishes people to grow and accomplish great things is amazing. I am thankful to all my mentors and leaders—from day one, today, and in the future—Bryan Deaver, Keith Early, Gonzalo Salgueiro, Peng Mok, Wes Sisk, Rodney Dunn, Hazim Dahir, Edward Swenson, Bob Hoerauf, Manil Uppal, Scott Lawrence, Dan Bakely, Scott Veibell, and Raymond Castillo for sharing their deep knowledge and experience and sharing actionable feedback throughout my career.

Life has many ups and downs. My cousins Vasantha, Ramanathan, Annamalai, and Meenakshi, my sister Vallikannu, and my friends Senthilnathan and Alagappan have always been great sources of inspiration, motivation, and support. I am very thankful for their tremendous help over the years and for celebrating success together.

Contents at a Glance

Reader Services

Register your copy at www.ciscopress.com/title/ISBN for convenient access to downloads, updates, and corrections as they become available. To start the registration process, go to www.ciscopress.com/register and log in or create an account.* Enter the product ISBN 9781587144769 and click Submit. Once the process is complete, you will find any available bonus content under Registered Products.

*Be sure to check the box that you would like to hear from us to receive exclusive discounts on future editions of this product.

Contents

Icons Used in This Book

Laptop

Server/ Location

IP Phone

SIP Proxy

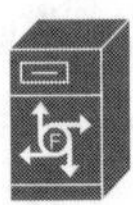
Cisco Server

Class 4/5 Switch

CUBE

Enterprise Network

Recording Server

Web Server

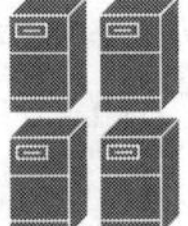
Registrar

Unity Connection

Universal Gateway

Media Mixer

Cloud

IP Communicator

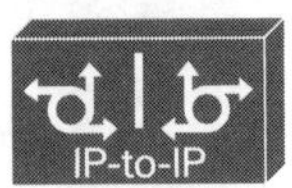

Cisco SBC Portfolio

Telepresence 500

PBX

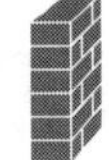
Firewall

Cisco ASA 5500

Switch

Virtual Router

Layer 3 Remote Switch

WAN

Router

ATA

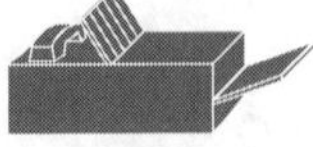
Fax

Command Syntax Conventions

The conventions used to present command syntax in this book are the same conventions used in the IOS Command Reference. The Command Reference describes these conventions as follows:

- **Boldface** indicates commands and keywords that are entered literally as shown. In actual configuration examples and output (not general command syntax), boldface indicates commands that are manually input by the user (such as a **show** command).
- *Italic* indicates arguments for which you supply actual values.
- Vertical bars (|) separate alternative, mutually exclusive elements.
- Square brackets ([ ]) indicate an optional element.
- Braces ({ }) indicate a required choice.
- Braces within brackets ([{ }]) indicate a required choice within an optional element.

Foreword

In the mid-1990s, I began work as a PhD student at Columbia University. These were the early days of the Internet—and it was far from a household name at that point. There was no Google, no Facebook, no Amazon. Email was the primary application for the Internet, used mostly by academics and universities. The Web had just been invented, and was gaining some buzz but was still mostly a toy. Indeed, most Internet technologies were still in the research category, and so I began my own research on a really new technology—voice over IP (VoIP). My PhD advisor, Henning Schulzrinne, was a new faculty member at Columbia. He had some crazy ideas about moving phone calls onto the Internet, and together we worked on this research technology called Session Initiation Protocol (SIP). Over the next few years, I worked on SIP as part of my dissertation, as well as writing many of the protocols, which became standardized in the Internet Engineering Task Force (IETF). The future of SIP was far from certain.

Fast forward 20 years, and SIP technology is now mainstream. It has become the foundation of modern telecommunications. It is built into most cell phones. It is the backbone for most telephone networks. It is how businesses connect their phone systems to the phone network. It facilitated the transition of telecommunications from hardware to software. That, in turn, shook up the entire industry. It caused some companies to eventually go out of business (Nortel, for example). Others, like Cisco Systems, took advantage of the technology transition and rose to market leadership. SIP technology has helped create thousands of new jobs, and it created entirely new industries along with it. One such industry is the Session Border Controller, or SBC, the subject of this book.

When we were first crafting the SIP protocol, we honestly had not anticipated the need for such devices, and they were not officially baked into the protocol. The official SIP specification makes no mention of SBCs; however, as SIP began to see widespread adoption, it became clear that the SIP interconnection between two administrative domains was complicated. We were seeing interoperability challenges. We were seeing quality problems. We were seeing security problems. A clear need emerged for an SIP component that could serve as a point of demarcation, allowing these problems to be addressed. And, the market responded. My startup company at the time, dynamicsoft, built one of the first Session Border Controllers, before the name had even stuck. Indeed, we called ours the Firewall Control Proxy. It was, unfortunately, not a commercial success. But others put their products forward, and a multivendor market ultimately emerged.

Today, this market is vibrant and mature, with many vendors offering solutions in this space. Cisco, with its CUBE product, is one of the leaders. Almost every VoIP deployment today has some form of SBC function at its edge. Indeed, anyone doing VoIP system architecture, operations, deployment or troubleshooting needs a solid understanding of SBCs.

I've had the pleasure of working with Gonzalo Salgueiro over the years. He's one of the leaders in SIP and related technologies in the industry. When he told me that he was writing a book on SBCs with a collection of other Cisco experts, I thought it was a fantastic idea. The industry needs engineers who are deeply skilled in this technology, and it's a skill which is hard to come by. This book addresses that need, providing a fabulous resource for people looking to work in this area. It provides great breadth as well as incredible depth in this space. It outlines all of the technical problems which SBCs are meant to address, and then goes into great detail on how to deploy Cisco technologies to solve those problems. It can be used for tutorial purposes, giving an overview, as well as providing a reference for active practitioners.

I hope you enjoy this book, and I'm sure it will teach you a lot about SBC technologies.

Dr. Jonathan Rosenberg

Chief Technology Officer, Collaboration, Cisco Systems

Lead Author, Session Initiation Protocol (SIP)

Figure Credits

Figure 5-46 Courtesy of Wireshark

Figure 7-18 Courtesy of Wireshark

Figure 7-19 Courtesy of Wireshark

Figure 7-20 Courtesy of Audacity Software, Inc.

Figure 7-21 Courtesy of Audacity Software, Inc.

Figure 7-22 Courtesy of Audacity Software, Inc.

Figure 8-3 Courtesy of VMware, Inc.

Figure 8-4 Courtesy of VMware, Inc.

Figure 10-34 Courtesy of Wireshark

Figure 10-35 Courtesy of Wireshark

Figure 11-29 Courtesy of Wireshark

Figure 11-30 Courtesy of Wireshark

Figure 14-5 Used by permission of ArcanaNetworks, Inc.

Multiple figures Courtesy of Wireshark

Introduction

Session border controllers (SBCs) provide essential functionality for integrating and utilizing features of a collaboration network deployment. This book was designed with a focus on utilizing these technologies in a production environment as effectively as possible. Industry leaders were consulted for technical accuracy throughout this book.

The end goal of this publication is to help professionals understand why an SBC should be deployed, when it is required, and how to manage the lifecycle of such a device from inception through the end of the device's lifecycle.

Who Should Read This Publication?

This publication is designed for unified communications engineers and technologists who want to implement SBCs, such as Cisco Unified Border Element (CUBE), into a collaboration solution.

This publication is targeted toward networking professionals who have foundational collaboration technology knowledge, similar to that defined by the CCNA (Cisco Certified Network Associate) Collaboration certification.

How This Book Is Organized

Chapter 1, "Laying the Groundwork": This chapter introduces the fundamental concepts that are important to understanding the application of an SBC. It provides an introduction to the SIP and H.323 protocols, as well as an overview of back-to-back user agents, SBCs, and CUBE in particular.

Chapter 2, "SBC Deployment Models": This chapter covers some of the common deployment types and options for SBCs to help further support the decision of whether an SBC is either useful or required for a deployment. This chapter also discusses high availability architectures for SBCs.

Chapter 3, "Call Routing": This chapter covers the concepts that must be understood for directing calls through an SBC. The various ways to dial and route a call are explained in this chapter, which describes concepts such as directory number, URI, and source-based call routing. The chapter also covers special topics related to call routing, such as how to reroute or translate numbers for calls, handle load balancing across next-hop devices, or support Multi-VRF deployments along with troubleshooting best practices using end-to-end call trace capabilities.

Chapter 4, "Signaling and Interworking": This chapter covers the features that allow an SBC to be used to interconnect different signaling technologies in real-time multimedia networks. It examines the many topics that surround SIP–SIP and SIP–H.323 interworking before, during, after, and outside session establishment. This chapter also covers topics such as Layer 3, Layer 4, supplementary services, ringback, and protocol extension interworking.

Chapter 5, "Media Processing": This chapter explains the various operations that are performed for the media portion of a call. It covers the details of RTP and RTCP in detail.

Chapter 6, "Secure Signaling and Media": This chapter starts by introducing the fundamental building blocks required to properly understand the many aspects of information security topics. The chapter then builds on these topics, discussing the applicable security protocols used by modern collaboration networks and applied to the signaling and media planes for data security assurance.

Chapter 7, "DTMF Interworking": This chapter discusses the various ways dual-tone multifrequency (DTMF) can be signaled, how DTMF traverses through SBCs, and the interworking mechanisms available to convert between different DTMF standards.

Chapter 8, "Scalability Considerations": This chapter outlines approaches to appropriately size an SBC deployment, license the deployment for the intended use, and control the finite resources of the platform effectively to prevent oversubscription or degradation of SBC service quality.

Chapter 9, "SIP Trunking for PSTN Access Through SBCs": This chapter explains some of the best practices in deploying SIP trunking services with SBCs and delves into the details of how enterprises establish an identity or a relationship with service provider networks. This chapter covers trunk registration, authentication, and troubleshooting of these integrations in detail.

Chapter 10, "Fax over IP (FoIP) on SBCs": This chapter describes the approaches for carrying fax over an IP network. It discusses how SBCs, and specifically CUBE, handle fax over IP.

Chapter 11, "Network-Based Call Recording": This chapter addresses the business requirements for call recording, the SIP recording architecture standard (SIPREC) as well as API-based call recording, and how to configure and troubleshoot call recording issues in CUBE deployments.

Chapter 12, "Contact Center Integration": This chapter discusses concepts for integrating an SBC into a contact center environment. The Cisco Unified Contact Center Enterprise is used as a working example of how an SBC can provide contact center integration. This chapter gives a detailed walkthrough of inbound, call transfer, courtesy callback, and call progress analysis call flows, along with techniques for troubleshooting common problems such as call disconnects.

Chapter 13, "Security Threat Mitigation": This chapter outlines the approaches across both policy and technical defense mechanisms to reduce the risk of attacks on collaboration systems where SBCs are deployed. The various types of security threats, how to design networks for security, and other SBC features that improve security of the environment are covered here.

Chapter 14, "Monitoring and Management": This final chapter describes a suggested approach for both monitoring and daily operational management of SBCs that have been deployed into a production service. This chapter shows how to improve service assurance of SBCs through monitoring for health and availability. This chapter also covers the concepts of access and configuration management.

Chapter 1

Laying the Groundwork

The field of communications has come a very long way since the introduction of the telephone in the 1800s by Alexander Graham Bell. Voice over IP (VoIP) traces its roots back to as early as the 1920s, when the first advancement in reproducing speech electronically and transmitting it over long distances was made. Decades later, in 1974, a significant milestone was achieved when the first voice datagram was transmitted over ARPANET, the precursor to the Internet. The year 1974 also saw another significant milestone in the history of the Internet: the introduction of Transmission Control Protocol (TCP), which would revolutionize the way information was transmitted over the Internet.

Experiments carried out in subsequent years adequately demonstrated the need to develop a more flexible protocol for the transmission of real-time traffic classes. This led to the introduction of User Datagram Protocol (UDP), which has gone on to become the default transport layer protocol for real-time applications.

The next big leap in the world of real-time communications occurred in 1995, when an Israeli company by the name of VocalTec pioneered the first widely available Internet phone. At that time, it was possible to make calls between two such phones over the Internet, but speech quality, reliability of connection establishment, and the overall user experience were huge hindrances in preventing VoIP technology from becoming the next big wave in telecommunications.

However, transmitting real-time traffic, like voice and video, over the Internet at a fraction of the cost incurred in circuit-switched networks was too exciting a prospect for equipment manufacturers to abandon. The introduction of broadband Internet, with its "always-on" capability, greatly improved connection reliability, voice quality, and the user experience. This seemed to be the inflection point at which VoIP went mainstream as corporations realized the immense cost benefits associated with this technology. Consequently, equipment manufacturers invested significant amounts of money and time in developing product lines with an abundance of features and customization options.

Over the next couple years, standards organizations such as the International Telecommunication Union Telecommunication Standardization Sector (ITU-T) and the

Internet Engineering Task Force (IETF) took up the task of developing and publishing standards related to VoIP. These standards have become the backbone protocols and enablers on which modern, real-time communications infrastructures operate today.

In the mid- to late 2000s, corporations began to make a concerted effort to modernize their communication infrastructures and migrate to Session Initiation Protocol (SIP) trunking in favor of the traditional public switched telephone network (PSTN) access methods, such as digital and analog circuits. Although it is immensely beneficial, SIP trunking for service provider access does come with its own set of challenges, including protocol interworking, toll fraud, perimeter defense, and NAT traversal. There was a need to mitigate these challenges and ensure that SIP trunking for service provider access was as seamless as traditional PSTN access methods. However, given the plethora of challenges with SIP trunking, it made little sense to deploy independent, functionally specific devices to cater to each one of these challenges. Enter session border controllers (SBCs). SBCs provide a very wide range of features that can be leveraged to overcome the challenges of SIP trunking and enable the seamless transfer of real-time information from one network to another.

Today SBCs are a necessity in deployments where real-time communications span network boundaries. This chapter and subsequent chapters describe the features commonly seen in SBCs and how these features play a pivotal role in ensuring smooth operations from the perspective of signaling, media, security, monitoring, and reporting. This chapter includes the following main topics:

- **Overview of SIP**—This section provides a brief history of SIP and describes its functional components, the different methods commonly used in SIP, and the process by which a call is set up and torn down.
- **Introduction to H.323**—This section covers H.323 basics, including the various components typically seen in H.323 networks and the flow for a typical H.323 call.
- **Introduction to SIP Trunking**—This section discusses the emergence of SIP trunking as a viable alternative to traditional methods of service provider peering and reviews the advantages of SIP trunking. This section concludes by describing a basic SIP trunking model.
- **Introduction to SDP**—This section examines Session Description Protocol (SDP) fundamentals and describes the offer/answer framework.
- **Overview of B2BUAs**—This section introduces the concept of back-to-back user agents (B2BUAs) and looks at the various classifications of B2BUAs.
- **Session Border Controllers**—This section defines session border controllers and provides a description of some of the common functions performed by SBCs.
- **Cisco Unified Border Element**—This section introduces Cisco's enterprise SBC: Cisco Unified Border Element (CUBE).

SIP trunking is a critical component of contemporary IP communications networks, and this chapter details the foundational concepts you need to understand before you can take a more in-depth look at this subject. By the end of this chapter, you will have a thorough understanding of SIP, H.323, the SDP offer/answer framework, B2BUAs, and the need for SBCs in real-time multimedia networks.

Overview of SIP

Session Initiation Protocol (SIP) forms the backbone of modern real-time communication networks. Over the years, SIP has been enhanced a great deal to include several usage paradigms that make it a very robust, multipurpose communication protocol. The following sections provide a brief overview of SIP.

Brief Introduction to and History of SIP

The SIP communications protocol is used for session setup, modification, and teardown. It is an application layer protocol that incorporates many elements of Hypertext Transfer Protocol (HTTP) and Simple Mail Transfer Protocol (SMTP). SIP is modular in design and can work in concert with many other protocols that are required to set up and support communication sessions, including the following:

- Real-Time Transport Protocol (RTP)
- Session Description Protocol (SDP)
- Resource Reservation Protocol (RSVP)
- Lightweight Directory Access Protocol (LDAP)

SIP was originally designed by Mark Handley, Henning Schulzrinne, Eve Schooler, and Jonathan Rosenberg in 1996, and it was standardized in 1999 as RFC 2543. The version of SIP standardized in RFC 2543 was 1.0. At the time of this writing, the current SIP version is 2.0, standardized as RFC 3261.

Operation

SIP works on the request/response framework and mirrors a model similar to HTTP, where there is a client/server exchange. A node that generates the request is called a user agent client (UAC), and a node that processes the request and sends out at least one response is called a user agent server (UAS). The concepts of a SIP transaction and a SIP dialog characterize the interaction between the UACs and UASs. A SIP transaction consists of a single request and all responses to that request, which may include zero or more provisional responses (1XX) and one or more final responses. A SIP dialog is a peer-to-peer relationship between user agents that exists for some time. A dialog can include multiple SIP transactions.

SIP commonly uses TCP or UDP as the transport protocol. For devices such as call agents, voice gateways, SIP proxies, and SBCs that typically handle several SIP sessions simultaneously, the transport layer protocol is usually UDP. Establishing and maintaining a connection involves a significantly larger overhead on TCP than on UDP. However, when SIP sessions have to traverse communication links that are prone to errors such as packet drops, it is better to use TCP as the transport layer protocol. Port number 5060 is typically used for SIP over UDP or TCP.

SIP messages exchanged between UACs and UASs carry a lot of information that could be misused if it fell into the hands of an attacker. For example, a SIP INVITE carries information that could reveal details of the network topology, the nature of the device originating or servicing the request, and details of the media stream(s), such as the IP addresses and port numbers. This is especially problematic when communication sessions span open networks. To prevent such attacks, it is possible to secure SIP signaling by using Transport Layer Security (TLS). The port number used for SIP over TLS is 5061.

Resources on a SIP network are identified by a uniform resource identifier (URI), which takes the following generic format:

```
sip:username:password@host:port
```

If the port is not specified, it defaults to 5060. For secure SIP transmission over TLS, an **s** is added to the end of **sip** to make it **sips:**

```
sips:username:password@host:port
```

As with a non-secure URI, if the port is not specified, a default one is used. In this case however, the default is 5061 instead of 5060.

SIP devices are referred to as user agents and can be devices such as IP phones, call servers, PDAs, gateways, and SBCs. The originator of a SIP request is called a UAC, and a device that processes the request is called a UAS. SIP includes several functional components, and interactions between user agents in real-world scenarios are in most cases more complex than generic client/server transactions. In order to understand the core tenets of SIP operation, you need to first understand the following functional components of SIP:

- **SIP proxy**—A SIP proxy is a device that is capable of performing call routing, authentication, authorization, address resolution, loop detection, and load balancing. A SIP proxy can be *stateless* or *stateful*; the fundamental difference between the two is whether they are aware of SIP transactions. A SIP transaction consists of a single request and all responses to that request, which may include zero or more provisional responses (1XX) and one or more final responses.

  A stateful proxy becomes aware of the state of a SIP transaction by creating a server transaction, client transaction, and a response context. By being transaction aware, it is capable of forking requests, retransmitting requests, and generating messages by itself. For example, a stateful SIP proxy can generate a SIP CANCEL message to all entities still processing a forked request after a final response has already been received.

  Stateless proxies, on the other hand, do not maintain transaction state; they transparently forward requests from the client to the server, and they send responses in the reverse direction. Once a request or a response is forwarded to the intended recipient, all details or transaction context of the message is purged. Consequently, stateless proxies cannot fork requests, retransmit requests, or generate messages on their own.

Proxies do not manipulate SIP message headers such as To, From, Call-ID, and so on. They do, however, include a Via header and a Record-Route header, and they decrement the Max-Forwards header value by one.

- **Redirect server**—A redirect server is a server that provides location services to user agents or proxies by replying to requests with the location or route to the host that ultimately services the request. This is desirable in situations where there is a need to build highly scalable servers that do not participate in a SIP transaction but simply help the proxy or user agent reach the host by sending a single message. Redirect servers reply to requests with a 3XX response in which the Contact header contains the URI of the location to the host. Figure 1-1 diagrams the operation of a SIP redirect server.

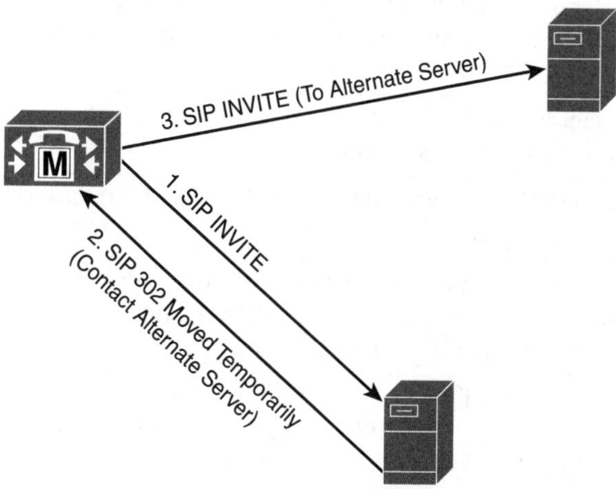

Figure 1-1 *Operation of a SIP Redirect Server*

- **Registrar server**—A registrar server is a server that accepts registration requests from user agents and creates a mapping between their address of record (AOR)—the public identifier of the user agent—and the user agent's location. Subsequently, this mapping between the user agent AOR and location is indexed and stored in a location server. More details about SIP registrar servers are provided in Chapter 9, "SIP Trunking for PSTN Access Through SBCs."
- **Location server**—A location server contains a mapping between a user agent's AOR and location; it need not be instantiated by a separate physical server and can be physically and logically co-located with the registrar server.
- **B2BUA**—B2BUAs are devices that have both UAC and UAS functionality and are capable of forwarding requests and processing them. SBCs are examples of B2BUAs. Over the course of this book, we discuss various aspects of SBCs in terms of session handling, media handling, security, monitoring, call routing, interworking, and deployment use cases.

SIP Messages

SIP messages are transmitted in plaintext. SIP messages can be requests or responses to requests. Table 1-1 lists SIP requests along with the purpose of each one.

Table 1-1 *SIP Requests*

SIP Request	Description
INVITE	A caller sends out this message to request another entity to join a SIP session.
ACK	This indicates that the client has received a final response to an INVITE request.
OPTIONS	This request queries the server for its capabilities.
BYE	This is used by the UAC to indicate to the server that it wishes to terminate the established SIP session. (Note that this request can be issued by the caller or the callee.)
CANCEL	This is used to cancel a pending request and can be sent only if the server has not replied with a final response.
REGISTER	A client uses REGISTER to register the address listed in the **To** header field with a SIP registrar server.
PRACK	This provisional acknowledgment is used to ensure that provisional responses are received reliably. For more details on the PRACK method, see Chapter 4, "Signaling and Interworking."
SUBSCRIBE	This creates a subscription for important event notification. For more details about the SUBSCRIBE method, see Chapter 7, "DTMF Interworking."
NOTIFY	This notifies the subscriber of the occurrence of an event. For more details about the NOTIFY method, see Chapter 7.
INFO	This allows the exchange of application-level information among communicating entities. Information is exchanged without affecting the state of the SIP transaction or dialog.
PUBLISH	This publishes an event to the server.
REFER	This instructs the recipient to contact another entity, using the information found in the REFER request.
UPDATE	This modifies the state of the session without changing the state of the dialog.
MESSAGE	This transports instant messages using SIP.

A SIP transaction begins with a request from a UAC to a UAS. The UAS begins processing the request as soon as it is received. The result of this processing depends on the nature of the request, the formatting of the request, the state of the server at the time the requesting was being serviced, and the general configuration and policies local to the server. In the case of devices such as SIP proxies, B2BUAs, and voice gateways, the result of processing a request could depend on downstream devices.

SIP servers are always required to respond with the results of request processing. SIP responses use the following formatting convention:

- The SIP version number (2.0 is the current SIP version number)
- A three-digit status code (for example, 404)
- A textual description (for example, Not Found)

The three-digit status code is an integer that communicates the outcome of request processing and is used for machine interpretation. The textual description, on the other hand, is for human observers and is useful in call failure debugging and call record interpretation. The first digit of the status code indicates the SIP response class; there are six classes in all (see Table 1-2). For additional details about these six classes of responses values, refer to RFC 2543.

Table 1-2 *Class of Response*

Class of Response	Meaning
1XX	Informational: The request has been received and is being processed.
2XX	Success: The request has been received, understood, and accepted.
3XX	Redirection: Further action needs to be taken to complete the request. For example, the UAC needs to contact another server that would process the request.
4XX	Client error: The request contains bad syntax (such as malformed headers) or could not be fulfilled at the server (for example, if the server could not find the number referenced in the requested URI).
5XX	Server error: A server failed to fulfill a valid request.
6XX	Global failure: The request could not be fulfilled at any server.

Breaking Down a SIP Call

Before diving into the details of how a communication session over SIP is established, it is important to first get a sense of how the initiator of a request—the UAC—forms the request and how the UAS ultimately processes the request. The following subsections take a detailed look at how SIP requests and responses are created.

Forming a Request

Standards-based SIP requires that a request contain at least the following header fields:

- Request-URI
- Via
- From
- To
- Call-ID
- Max-Forwards
- CSeq

Subsequent sections discuss these header fields in more detail, and subsequent chapters throughout this book introduce several other header fields used for specific applications. The header fields that appear in a request can vary depending on the type of request (refer to Table 1-4). For example, a SIP INVITE request would require additional header fields in comparison to a SIP REGISTER request. The following paragraphs briefly describe the mandatory SIP headers that appear in all requests:

- **Request-URI**—In general, each resource within a SIP network is identified by a URI, which is expressed either as a SIP URI or a SIPS URI (SIP Secure URI). Specifically, within the scope of a SIP request, the Request URI header identifies the resource that process the request.

Note In real-world networks, there could be several devices between the UAC and UAS, such as call agents, SIP proxies, and SBCs. While a proxy cannot alter the Request-URI header field, devices such as SBCs and call agents can modify and transform the Request-URI header field, if required by local policy or configuration.

- **Via**—This header field indicates the transport layer protocol used for exchanging SIP messages and the location to which responses have to be sent. For example, the following Via header field specifies UDP as the transport layer protocol and 10.1.1.1:5060 as the address/port pair for responses:

  ```
  Via: SIP/2.0/UDP 10.1.1.1:5060;branch=z9hG4bK2D1F9D1C08
  ```

  Also included in the Via header field is the **branch** parameter, which serves as an identifier for the SIP transaction created by any request and remains the same from the perspective of the UAC and the UAS. The **branch** parameter, which is unique across space and time, is valid until the termination of a SIP transaction. Subsequent requests that create new transactions must ensure that they generate new and unique values for this parameter. When a SIP proxy handles a request, such as a SIP INVITE, it inserts a Via header field before forwarding the request to the next hop. The next hop could be another proxy server or the eventual destination that processes the request. A request traversing proxies has more than one Via header field value.

- **From**—This header field indicates the logical identity of the user agent that initiates the request. The From header field carries the identity of the initiator of the request in the form of a URI. Optionally, this header field can also include the display name of the initiator. For media sessions established over SIP, the display name in the From header field serves as a caller ID assertion. Intermediary devices like SBCs usually transform the contents of the From header field. This might be required for a myriad of reasons, such as to enable interoperability across different SIP networks, provide topology abstraction, or make identity assertions. The From header field must carry a **tag** parameter. The significance of the **tag** parameter will be explained shortly.
- **To**—This header field usually identifies the logical entity that is supposed to process the request and is populated using a sip URI/SIPS URI or a tel URI. (tel URIs are explained in Chapter 3, "Call Routing.") The logical entity identified in the To header field may or may not be the actual UAS that processes the request. In fact, the entity identified in the To header field usually isn't the one to process the request when the request traverses several hops. Dialog-creating requests (such as SIP INVITE) must never carry a **tag** parameter in the To header field. Instead, the **tag** parameter is populated by the user agent that processes the request.
- **Call-ID**—This header field uniquely identifies all messages that belong to a SIP dialog; the SIP dialog in turn is uniquely identified by the combination of the Call-ID header, the From tag, and the To tag. A SIP dialog may contain several SIP transactions. The Call-ID header field value is created by the UAC and retained in messages sent by the UAS. The Call-ID must be unique across space and time. User agents must ensure that this header field is generated with sufficient entropy to ensure that there isn't any overlap with the Call-ID field of another SIP dialog. The Call-ID header field can sometimes carry the IP addressing information or domain name details of the initiating user agent, which might be undesirable in terms of topology abstraction. As discussed in subsequent sections, SBCs overcome this problem by overwriting the Call-ID header field value and preventing any internal network topology information from crossing network boundaries.
- **Max-Forwards**—This header field value limits the number of hops a request can traverse before it reaches its final destination. Every node that receives a request either partially or completely processes a SIP request. Partial processing could include running syntactical checks, adding header fields, or occasionally modifying a request before it is passed on to the next hop. Complete processing of the request, on the other hand, involves sending one or more of the six response classes listed in Table 1-2 after processing the request. Every node that partially processes the request decrements the Max-Forwards header field value by one before sending the request to the next hop. If a request is received at a user agent or a proxy that is not the final destination of the request, an explicit check is run on the value of the Max-Forwards header field. If it is 0, the request is rejected with a 483 Too Many Hops response. If it is a nonzero value, it is forwarded to the next hop.

- **CSeq**—This header field is used to order transactions within a dialog. It is formatted as follows:

  ```
  CSeq: <Sequence-Number> <Method>
  ```

  where ***Method*** is a SIP request (see Table 1-1).

The six header fields listed here are required for every type of SIP request. However, additional header fields might also be required, depending on the type of the SIP method (request). For example, a SIP INVITE requires additional header fields accompanying the six mandatory header fields to be efficiently processed by the UAS. For SIP INVITE, the following additional header fields are required:

- **Contact**—This header field provides a SIP or SIPS URI at which the user agent can be contacted for subsequent requests. For example, consider an audio call that is already established between a UAC and a UAS. Due to negotiated session policy or application interactions, the UAS might need to send a mid-session request to the UAC. To do so, it uses the SIP or SIPS URI indicated in the Contact header field. Note that the usage of the Contact header field is not restricted only to INVITE requests. This header field is also present in responses to the SIP INVITE and other SIP methods, when applicable.

- **Allow**—It is recommended for the Allow header field to be present within a SIP INVITE. This header field advertises the different SIP methods that can be invoked on the UAC within the scope of the dialog initiated by the SIP INVITE request. Parsing the Allow header field allows a UAS to understand the types of requests that can be sent to the UAC during the SIP dialog. For example, if the UAS wants to transmit dual-tone multifrequency (DTMF) information using the SIP INFO message, it can do so only if the UAC advertised support for the SIP INFO message is in the Allow header field of the INVITE. The following is an example of the Allow header field:

  ```
  Allow:INVITE,ACK,CANCEL,BYE,REGISTER,REFER,INFO,SUBSCRIBE,NOTIFY,PRACK,
  UPDATE,OPTIONS
  ```

  Though it is recommended for UACs to include the Allow header field in INVITE requests, there might be instances when this header field isn't included. In such cases, the UAS must not assume that the UAC does not support any method; rather, it must be interpreted as the unwillingness of the UAC to advertise what methods it supports. The UAS can go ahead and send requests that are required to further advance the communication session; however, if the method is unsupported by the UAC, these requests are rejected by using the 405 Method Not Allowed response.

- **Supported**—A UAC might use this header field to enumerate the various extensions to baseline SIP that it supports. A UAS might apply these extensions to baseline SIP when responding to the request. For example, if the UAC includes the **timer** extension in the Supported header field, it advertises support for SIP session refresh. The UAS might apply this extension to ensure session liveliness, as per the guidelines of RFC 4028.

- **Accept**—The UAC might include the Accept header field to indicate content types that are acceptable to it in responses to requests or in new requests within the dialog. This header field allows user agents to advertise support for various session description formats.

Although some of the header fields listed here are optional, they are nonetheless used ubiquitously across device types and vendors for initiating communication sessions over SIP. The following header fields might be added in SIP INVITE requests (but their exclusion does not deter the SIP session from proceeding smoothly):

- **Require**—When included in the SIP INVITE, this header field enumerates extensions to baseline SIP using option tags. Each option tag represents a SIP extension that the server must support in order to process the request. If the server cannot support a specific extension, the request is rejected with a 420 Bad Extension response.
- **Expires**—This header field might be added by a UAC to limit the validity of an invitation. Once a communication session is established, this header field value has no bearing on the amount of time for which the session can last. The usage of the Expires header field is method dependent. (As described in Chapter 9, this header field has a different purpose for the SIP REGISTER method.)

Table 1-3 summarizes the mandatory, method-dependent, and optional headers for a SIP INVITE. As mentioned previously, different SIP methods have different method-dependent and optional headers.

Table 1-3 *Classification of Headers in SIP INVITE Messages*

Header Fields	Requirement
Request-URI, Via, From, To, Call-ID, Max-Forwards, CSeq	Mandatory for all SIP messages
Contact, Allow, Supported, Accept	Required for INVITE messages and optional for other methods
Require, Expires	Optional for SIP INVITE messages

It is also possible for vendors to include proprietary header fields in the SIP INVITE request. If such a request happens to be processed by a device from the same vendor, the proprietary header field(s) is interpreted to enable additional functionality. For example, Cisco devices such as CUCM, voice gateways, and CUBE use the Call-Info header field in SIP INVITE messages (and corresponding responses) to advertise support for Cisco's proprietary method of DTMF relay or SIP unsolicited notify. (For more on this, see Chapter 7.) If a nonmandatory proprietary header cannot be understood by a UAS, it is dropped, and processing of the request continues as per the guidelines of RFC 3261.

Forming a Response

On receiving a SIP request, a UAS performs a host of checks to determine how to respond to the request. Figure 1-2 diagrams the logic executed on the server to process a request.

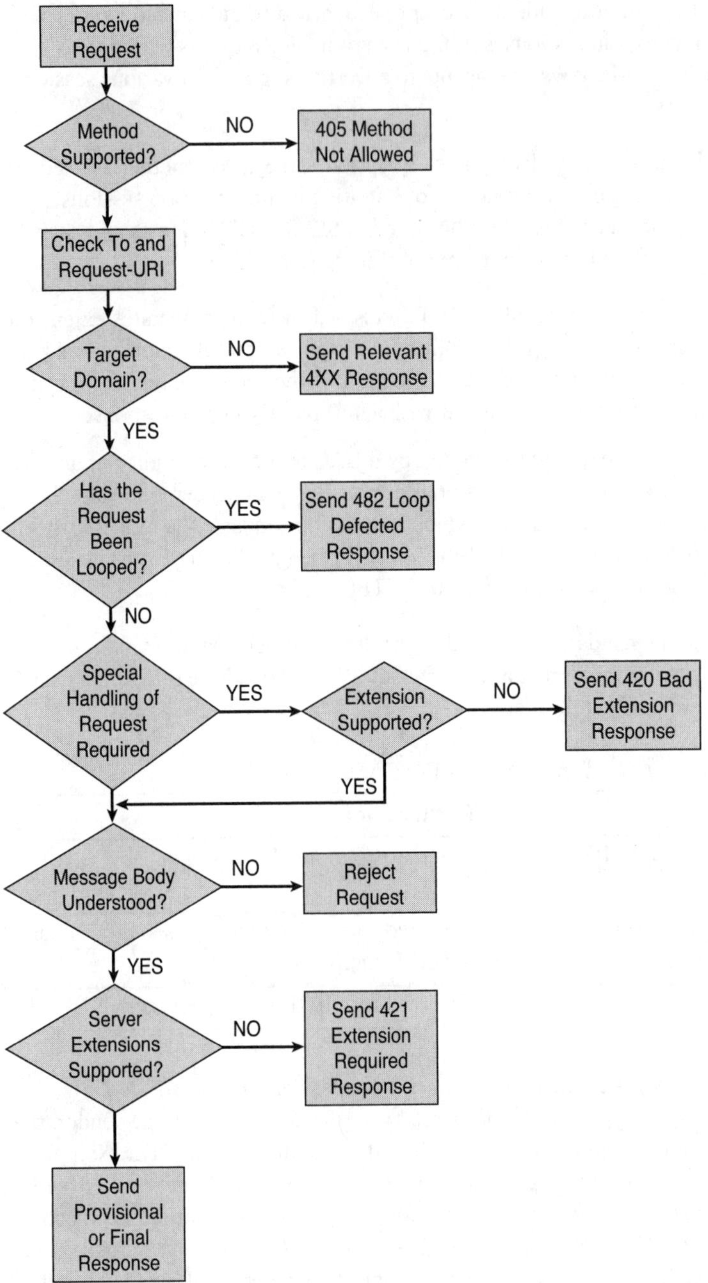

Figure 1-2 *SIP Request Processing Logic*

The first check executed at the UAS involves whether the SIP method is supported. SIP methods are nothing but requests that require a specific action to be executed at the server. The SIP requests listed in Table 1-1 are all examples of SIP methods. All SIP user agents that initiate and support calls support the SIP INVITE method; however, it is possible for a UAS to not extend support to all the methods listed in Table 1-1. If a UAS does not support a given SIP method, it responds to the corresponding request with a 405 Method Not Allowed response.

After inspecting whether the method is supported, the SIP UAS then proceeds to check various header fields in the request. The first header fields to be checked are the To and Request URI header fields. These header fields are checked for syntactical correctness and whether the UAS is indeed the node that is supposed to process the request. If either check fails, the request is rejected via the relevant 4XX class of responses.

The next check that is run is to verify whether the request has been looped—basically, whether the UAS has already processed exactly this request. Looping of requests is quite common in SIP networks, especially when nodes have improperly configured call routing. Call loops result in the UAS rejecting the request with a 482 Loop Detected response.

If a request is determined to be new, the UAS checks whether the client has requested special processing of the request by using the **Require** header field. This field specifies extensions to baseline SIP that facilitate specific application usage paradigms. These extensions are specified in the form of option tags in the Require header field. For example, the UAC might include the **100rel** option tag in an INVITE request to ensure that the server sends provisional responses (101 to 199 responses) reliably. In case a UAS does not support an option tag specified by the client, it rejects the request with a 420 Bad Extension response. (For more details on the **100rel** option tag, see Chapter 4.)

After the UAS verifies that it supports the extensions required by the client, the next check performed is to determine whether it understands the message body within the request. A request can carry a message body (typically utilizing SDP) that provides additional details about the request. If the UAS cannot interpret a message body within a request, it is rejected.

Finally, in certain cases, a UAS might require the client to support certain extensions to baseline SIP for the request to be successfully processed. For example, if the server requires that provisional responses be sent reliably when a SIP session is being set up, and the UAC does not include the **100rel** option tag in the Supported header field, it can reject an INVITE request with a 421 Extension Required response. A UAS should not use the 421 Extension Required response unless it truly cannot process the request using the constructs of baseline SIP.

Once all the checks are executed at the UAS, further processing of the request is strictly method dependent. For example, the same set of rules cannot be used to process an INVITE request and a REGISTER request. While processing a SIP INVITE, the following logic is applied:

- If the INVITE contains an Expires header field, the UAS must send a final response before the expiration interval. If it fails to do so, the request is rejected with a 487 Request Terminated response.

- The received INVITE might be a mid-dialog request (a Re-INVITE). Unless the server undergoes an unexpected restart, it maintains state information for all established dialogs. Mid-dialog requests are usually sent to modify session characteristics or ensure session freshness. For such requests, the processing rules of Section 12.2.2 of RFC 3261 are followed.

- A mid-dialog INVITE request received at the UAS might not match an existing dialog. This could be because of an unexpected server restart where all dialog contexts are purged, or it may be a result of incorrect request routing by downstream devices. Whatever the underlying cause, the guidelines of Section 12.2.2 of RFC 3261 are followed to handle such a situation.

If the SIP INVITE is not a mid-dialog request but rather is a dialog-creating request, the UAS is being invited to a communication session. When processing such a request, the UAS can either indicate progress, failure, or success of the request. Alternatively, the request could be redirected:

- **Progress**—If the UAS cannot immediately send a final response to the SIP INVITE, it can indicate some kind of progress to the request by sending a provisional response between 101 and 199. Commonly used progress indications include the SIP 180 Ringing and 183 Session Progress provisional responses. Provisional responses are classified as early dialog responses and require the UAS to populate the **tag** parameter of the To header field in the response. A provisional response is usually followed by a 200 OK final response or, in rare cases, a failure response.

- **Failure**—If the UAS is unable to accept the session invitation, a failure response is sent to the client. Processing of the request at the server may fail for a number of reasons. The server could be overloaded, in which case it sends a 503 Service Unavailable response, or it may be that the server could not locate the device specified in the Request URI, in which case it responds with a 404 Not Found response. Whatever the reason, the server will respond to the request with an error code that reflects the outcome of processing. The failure response might occasionally carry supplementary information to provide more granular details of the failure and to allow the client to augment the request, if applicable.

  As an example, if the server sends a 503 Service Unavailable response, it can also choose to include a Retry-After header field that provides the client a time after which the request may be retried. If the overloaded condition at the server clears after the specified time interval, the server might respond with a success response.

- **Success**—The session invitation being accepted at the UAS generates a 200 OK response. It is recommended that the 200 response includes the Allow, Supported, and Accept header fields. Inclusion of these header fields ensures that the server can advertise any extensions to baseline SIP that it supports without having to be explicitly probed, perhaps via a SIP OPTIONS message.

  Even if the SIP INVITE did not carry a SDP body, the server must include an SDP offer in the 200 OK response. If the INVITE carried an SDP offer, the UAS must include an SDP answer in the 200 OK response if it was not already included in a previous message, such as a 180 Ringing or a 183 Session Progress.

If an SDP body was included in a 18X message and then later in the 200 OK message, the SDP body and the originator version must be the same across both the messages. It is forbidden for the UAS to alter the contents of the SDP body between 18X and 200 OK messages. (The SDP originator version number is explained in greater detail later in this chapter, in the section "Introduction to SDP.")

200 OK responses to the SIP INVITE must be followed by a SIP ACK method. This ensures that the 200 OK response was delivered reliably.

- **Redirect**—A UAS can respond to INVITE requests with a redirect response (3XX). On receiving a redirect response, the client is required to execute an additional set of actions to complete the request. This usually entails the client parsing the Contact header field of the redirect response and sending the INIVTE to one or more URIs included in the Contact header field.

  When multimedia communication networks peer over SIP, more often than not, 3XX redirect responses are viewed as attempts at toll fraud attacks. Consequently, on receiving a 3XX response, many user agents tend to terminate the request completely instead of trying to further process the request.

Analyzing a Basic SIP Call

A SIP call begins when a UAC invites a UAS to a communication session. In real-world implementations, the two user agents might be separated over several hops. However, for the sake of simplicity, let's assume that the two user agents communicate directly with one another.

When inviting another user agent to a communication session, the UAC might be preconfigured with the exact location of the UAS. If not, its request might be ferried by a SIP proxy server to the intended UAS. Once the request is received at the UAS, the UAS allocates the necessary resources to process the request. As the request is being processed, the UAS might be required to send provisional responses. It must send a final response once the request is fully processed to alert the UAC of the outcome.

Based on the results of request processing, the server will respond with any one of the six classes of response codes listed in Table 1-2. Depending on the request, the UAS may respond with a provisional response class (1XX) followed by a final response class, or it may respond directly with a final response class. For example, when processing a SIP INVITE, the UAS typically sends a 100 Trying provisional response, followed by a final response. The provisional 100 Trying response alerts the UAC that the request is currently being processed, and a final response is expected shortly. It also serves as a mechanism to deter the UAC from sending subsequent copies of the same SIP INVITE.

Figure 1-3 demonstrates a SIP message exchange for establishing an audio call between Phone A and Phone B. A call agent, like Cisco's Unified Communication Manager (commonly known as CUCM), is the signaling focus for both phones and aids in the establishment of the communication session. The SIP call in Figure 1-3 can be broken down and analyzed as follows:

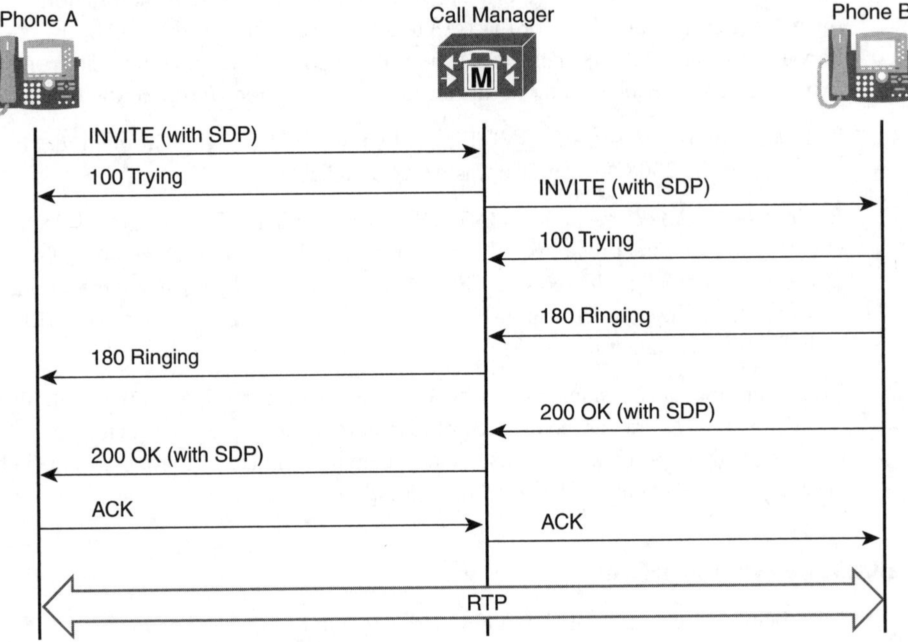

Figure 1-3 *Analyzing a Basic SIP Call*

Step 1. Phone A initiates a communication session with Phone B by sending a SIP INVITE to the CUCM. In this scenario, the CUCM functions as both the registrar server for the phones and their UAS for all outbound requests.

Step 2. Included in the SIP INVITE are several pieces of information that enable the transaction/dialog to progress smoothly. These pieces of information include several header field values in the SIP message. The SIP INVITE can be sent in one of two ways:

- With an SDP body
- Without an SDP body

If the SIP INVITE carries an SDP body, the call is classified as an "early offer" call. If an SDP body is not advertised in the SIP INVITE, the call is classified as a "delayed offer" call. As discussed shortly, SDP is used to encode the characteristics of a media session, such as the type of media stream(s) supported (for example, audio, video), the IP addresses and port numbers for the media stream(s), and the set of supported codecs for different media stream types.

Sending an early offer INVITE allows the UAC to enforce characteristics of the session up front by including its supported media stream types, the relevant media formats per media stream, and any SDP-based extensions. With delayed offer invites, the UAC has to tailor its session characteristics in accordance with the SDP body advertised by the UAS. The example shown in Figure 1-3 describes an early offer call.

Step 3. On receiving the SIP INVITE, the CUCM sends a 100 Trying response to Phone A. The 100 Trying response serves to inform Phone A that the INIVITE has been received, and processing is underway. After sending the 100 Trying response, the CUCM examines the Request URI in the received INVITE and does a database lookup. The database lookup is done to determine the location information (IP address and port) of Phone B. The location information for Phone B is present in the CUCM because it also functions as a registrar server. (More details on the SIP registration process can be found in Chapter 9.)

Step 4. On obtaining the location information of Phone B, a SIP INVITE is sent from the CUCM to Phone B. Phone B sends a 100 Trying response to the CUCM.

Step 5. After the request is completely processed at Phone B and it begins ringing, a 180 Ringing message is sent to the CUCM. The 180 Ringing message is then relayed from the CUCM to Phone A. At this stage, an audible ringback tone must be generated at Phone A. The ringback tone might be generated locally on the phone or might be generated by the CUCM. Alternatively, if Phone B wants to stream a custom ringback tone or preconnect announcement, it sends a 183 Session Progress message with an SDP body. This scenario, defined as "early media," allows Phone A to listen to media packets encapsulating custom ringback tones or preconnect announcements even before Phone B goes off-hook.

Step 6. Once Phone B is taken off-hook, a 200 OK response is sent to the CUCM, indicating that the call has been answered. Included in the 200 OK is an SDP body indicating the chosen media stream(s) and media codecs. The 200 OK response is then sent to Phone A. At this stage, the phones can begin to exchange media packets with one another. The 200 OK response must be followed by a SIP ACK sent end-to-end to indicate that the 200 OK response was reliably received.

At this stage, the SIP dialog is considered complete. You should note that the CUCM is only responsible for setting up the communication session but does not place itself in the path of the media packets.

Step 7. The SIP call terminates when one of the phones transmits a SIP BYE message.

Note In Figure 1-3, the CUCM functions as a signaling-only B2BUA wherein it manipulates only selected SIP header fields. B2BUAs are discussed in more detail later in this chapter.

Overview of H.323

H.323 is a communication protocol from the ITU-T. It is a VoIP call control protocol that allows for the establishment, maintenance, and teardown of multimedia sessions across H.323 endpoints. H.323 is a suite of specifications that controls the transmission of voice, video, and data over IP networks. The following are some of the H.323 specifications relevant to the subject matter laid out in this book:

- **H.225**—Handles call setup and teardown between H.323 endpoints and is also responsible for peering with H.323 gatekeepers via the Register Admission Status (RAS) protocol.
- **H.245**—Acts as a peer protocol to H.225 and is used to negotiate the characteristics of the media session, such as media format, the method of DTMF relay, the media type (audio, video, fax, and so on), and the IP address/port pair for media.
- **H.450**—Controls supplementary services between H.323 entities. These supplementary services include call hold, call transfer, call park, and call pickup.

H.323 Components

The H.323 protocols outlined in the previous section are utilized in the communications between H.323 components or devices. The following are the most common H.323 devices:

- **H.323 gateways**—H.323 gateways are endpoints that are capable of interworking between a packet network and a traditional POTS network (analog or digital). Since these H.323 endpoints can implement their own call routing logic, they are considered to be "intelligent" and as such operate in a peer-to-peer mode. H.323 gateways are capable of registering to a gatekeeper and interworking calls with a gatekeeper by using the RAS protocol.
- **H.323 gatekeepers**—H.323 gatekeepers function as devices that provide lookup services. They indicate via signaling to which endpoint or endpoints a particular called number belongs. Gatekeepers also provide functionality such as Call Admission Control and security. Endpoints register to the gatekeeper by using the RAS protocol.
- **H.323 terminals**—Any H.323 device that is capable of setting up a two-way, real-time media session is an H.323 terminal. H.323 terminals include voice gateways, H.323 trunks, video conferencing stations, and IP phones. H.323 terminals use H.225 for session setup, progress, and teardown. They also use H.245 to define characteristics of the media session such as the media format, the method of DTMF, and the media type.
- **Multipoint control units**—These H.323 devices handle multiparty conferences and is each composed of a multipoint controller (MC) and multipoint processor (MP). The MC is responsible for H.245 exchanges, and the MP is responsible for the switching and manipulation of media.

H.323 Call Flow

An H.323 call in its most basic form involves the following:

- Establishment of a TCP socket on port 1720 to initiate H.225 signaling with another H.323 peer. This assumes that there is no gatekeeper in the call flow. As defined in the previous section, gatekeepers assist in endpoint discovery and call admission.
- For an H.323 call, the H.225 exchange is responsible for call setup and termination, whereas the H.245 exchange is responsible for establishment of the media channels and their properties. In most cases, the establishment of two independent TCP connections is required: one for the H.225 exchange and the other for the H.245 exchange. To effectively bind the two, the TCP port number on which the answering terminal intends to establish an H.245 exchange is advertised in one of the H.225 messages. The port number can be advertised before the H.225 connect message is sent (for example, in an H.225 progress message) or when the H.225 connect message is sent.
- H.225 and H.245 exchanges can proceed on the same TCP connection, using a process called *tunneling*.
- Every H.245 message is unidirectional in the sense that it is used to specify the negotiation from the perspective of the sender of that H.245 message. For the successful establishment of a two-way real-time session, both H.323 terminals must exchange H.245 messages.

Figure 1-4 depicts a basic H.323 slow start call between two H.323 terminals. The calling terminal first initiates a TCP connection to the called terminal, using destination port 1720. Once this connection is established, H.225 messages are exchanged between the two terminals to set up the call. In order to negotiate parameters that define call characteristics such as the media types (for example, audio, video, fax), media formats, and DTMF types, an H.245 exchange has to ensue between the terminals.

In most cases, a separate TCP connection is established between the endpoints to negotiate an H.245 exchange; however, in some cases, as an optimization, H.245 messages are tunneled using the same TCP socket as H.225. When utilizing a separate TCP connection for H.245, the called terminal advertises the TCP port number over which it intends to establish an H.245 exchange. The ports used for the establishment of H.245 are ephemeral and are not dictated by the H.323 specification.

The H.245 exchange results in the establishment of the media channels required to transmit and receive real-time information. You should be aware that while Figure 1-4 highlights a slow start call, a variant to the slow start procedure, fast start, also exists. When fast start is negotiated with H.225, H.245 negotiations begin before the call connects.

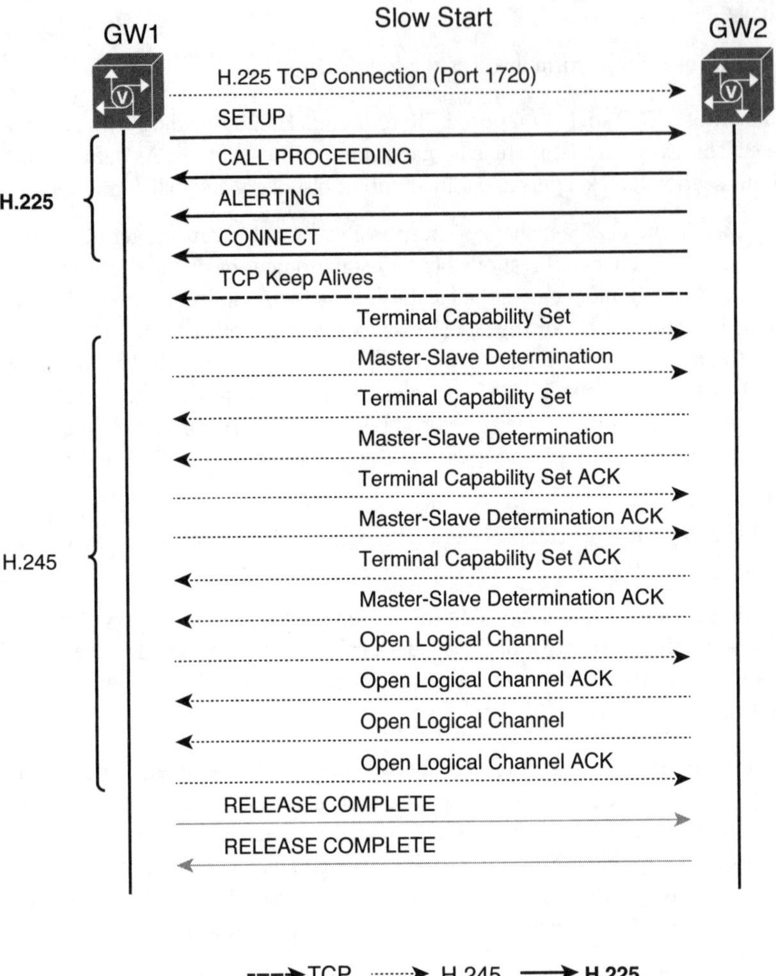

Figure 1-4 *Basic H.323 Call*

Introduction to SIP Trunking

Over the years, vendors have developed a plethora of device types that can be deployed in enterprise networks to enable rich collaboration experiences. These device types include call agents, voicemail servers, fax servers, conference controllers, recording servers, and sophisticated audio/video endpoints. With many of these devices being SIP capable, communication sessions between such device types have commonly occurred over SIP with RTP used as the media transmission protocol.

However, for communication sessions that spanned enterprise and service provider networks, end-to-end IP-based delivery of signaling and media had to be interrupted by devices such as voice gateways. This was because enterprises used traditional methods of interconnecting with service providers, such as digital or analog circuits. While digital circuits or analog lines have proven extremely useful in the past, these methods of interconnection were simply not sustainable from cost, scalability, flexibility, and reliability standpoints.

For example, the number of the T1/E1 Primary Rate Interface (PRI) bundles acquired by an enterprise dictated the number of simultaneous PSTN calls that could be made or received. If the enterprise grew in size, capital had to be invested in procuring additional voice gateways, PRI line cards, or at least additional PRI circuits. In addition, there were recurring costs incurred because of hardware wear and tear. These problems, coupled with a whole host of others, are contributed to the demise of TDM trunking.

As businesses began migrating their internal communication infrastructures to IP, service providers began to offer IP-based connectivity to enterprise customers. Some of the benefits afforded by IP-based connectivity to service providers include the following:

- **Reduced infrastructure costs**—Service providers no longer need to install special-purpose hardware at customer sites to deliver voice services. Enterprises can use broadband connections or dedicated links to peer with service provider networks directly.
- **Peering**—Service provider networks traditionally peered with each other over TDM connections. With IP-based connectivity, service providers can interact with one another over standards-based SIP. Peering directly over IP eliminates the need to maintain a costly TDM infrastructure, minimizes delays, and prevents the errors that would be introduced by malfunctioning hardware.
- **Competitive service pricing**—Enabling IP-based access allows service providers to aggregate multimedia traffic from several enterprise customers and pass it to downstream PSTN service providers. This happens at a fraction of the costs incurred when enterprises connect directly to the PSTN.

Just as with traditional TDM circuits that had a well-defined set of protocols providing the communication framework between terminals, IP-based trunking required a similar framework to enable seamless communication between multimedia networks. Baseline SIP was standardized as early as the year 2002, and with the IETF churning out RFCs for extensions to SIP over the next couple of years, SIP was the overwhelming choice as the communication protocol for IP-based trunking services. Enterprises also found it relatively easy to peer with service providers over SIP because several devices already deployed within the enterprise were SIP enabled.

Many organizations have understood the benefits of SIP trunking over traditional circuit-switched communication infrastructures and have made the move to deploying end-to-end, IP-based solutions with SIP trunking as the interconnect method between enterprise and service provider networks. Many studies over the years have indicated that the adoption of SIP trunking will grow with time and will eventually outnumber the traditional circuit-switched interconnect methods that are still present. Following are some of the advantages of SIP trunking:

- **Rapid ROI—**SIP trunking does not require a significant capital expenditure and provides all the features of traditional PBX integrations.
- **Reliability—**SIP trunking is reliable as it allows for the monitoring of trunk status and rerouting of calls in case of outages. Also, it doesn't face some of the hardware issues inherent in traditional TDM and analog lines.
- **Reduced call cost—**SIP trunking requires a single data path for the transmission of signaling and media, unlike PRI bundles, which require specialized hardware.
- **Mobility—**SIP trunking can help tie together mobile devices and remote workers by enabling a blend of on-premises and cloud-based services.
- **Scalability—**Unlike traditional POTS and PRI circuits, SIP trunking allows for highly scalable call volumes, especially when making use of high-compression encoding schemes. SIP trunking is not tied down by the hardware restrictions of PRI circuits that only allow a maximum of 23 or 30 simultaneous calls.

Table 1-4 lists the very basic requirements to enable a SIP trunking solution across communication networks. It is by no means exhaustive. Enterprise and service provider networks usually need more detailed sets of requirements. For example, these networks may require encryption of the signaling and communication channels, protection of the access network from denial-of-service (DoS) or distributed denial-of-service (DDoS) attacks, media translation from one payload format to another, protection of enterprise resources through Call Admission Control, NAT traversal, and protocol repair.

Table 1-4 *Basic Requirements for SIP Trunking*

Call Signal Protocol	SIP
Physical layer 3 connectivity	DSL, T1, Metro Ethernet, 3G, and so on
Encoding schemes	G.711, G.729, H.264, iLBC, and so on
Supplementary services	Call transfer, codec re-negotiation, and media format renegotiation
DTMF relay	RTP-NTE, raw inband DTMF, SIP NOTIFY, and SIP INFO
Monitoring	SIP OPTIONS

Many of these requirements have to be met and fulfilled at the network periphery—the ingress and egress points where traffic enters and leaves the network. Deploying individual devices to cater to a specific requirement such as enabling NAT traversal or thwarting DoS attacks is prohibitively expensive and increases complexity. Instead, there is a need to deploy a multifunctional, robust device that caters to many if not all of these requirements.

Over time, SBCs have evolved to become the enablers of SIP trunking for enterprise and service provider networks. From enabling features such as NAT traversal and perimeter defense to facilitating media payload translation and SIP message manipulation, SBCs are indispensable in a SIP trunking solution. This book discusses the role of SBCs in modern real-time communication networks in detail.

SIP Trunking Architectural Models

As enterprises move from traditional methods of interconnecting with service provider networks to SIP trunking solutions, they can choose to deploy a centralized, distributed, or hybrid SIP trunking model. Each deployment model has its own set of advantages and disadvantages. Which model is ultimately chosen depends largely on organizational needs and existing network topologies. Figure 1-5 details a logical SIP trunking deployment scenario between an enterprise network and a service provider network.

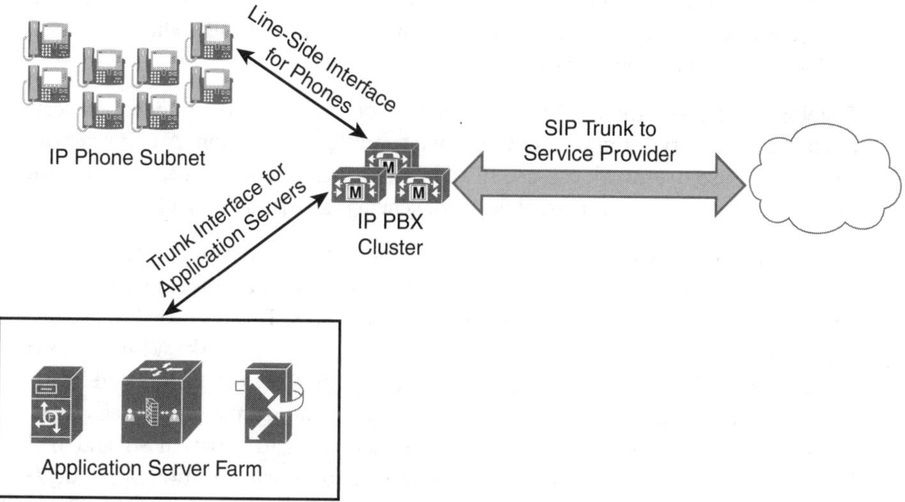

Figure 1-5 *Logical SIP Trunking Deployment*

In Figure 1-5 an IP PBX cluster provides a line-side interface to endpoints such as IP phones for registration, voice and video calls, messaging, and presence. The IP PBX cluster also provides a trunk-side interface to application servers. Application servers communicate with the IP PBX cluster using one of the common call control protocols (primarily SIP) and RTP. Application servers are usually hosted on physically distinct units and each provides a specific functionality, such as faxing, voicemail, conference hosting, recording, and so on.

A SIP trunk between the IP PBX cluster and the service provider network provides PSTN connectivity. Although the topology depicted in Figure 1-5 is sufficient to provide service provider access, a palette of practical difficulties hinder smooth operations of such a deployment. Some of these difficulties include the following:

- **Integrity and confidentiality attacks—**Allowing application traffic from within the enterprise over public networks can result in integrity and confidentiality attacks. An attacker can easily intercept signaling and media traffic for a communication session, record it, and possibly tamper with it.
- **Availability attacks—**Attackers over public networks can launch DoS or DDoS attacks aimed at robbing the IP PBX cluster of processing cycles. With the IP PBX cluster compromised, virtually the entire communications infrastructure within the enterprise is rendered useless.
- **Protocol repair—**In principle, SIP trunking is based on communicating entities adhering to SIP and its extensions to set up, sustain, and tear down communication sessions. However, RFCs tend to leave sufficient room for varying interpretations, invariably resulting in vendors having slightly different implementations of SIP and its extensions. This could potentially lead to unforeseen interoperability issues during a communication session.
- **Topology hiding—**Although IP PBX servers function as B2BUAs, they have a very restricted capability set in terms of enabling topology abstraction. An attacker over a public untrusted network can use IP addresses advertised in SIP header fields and SDP attributes to uncover internal network schemas and launch attacks.
- **NAT traversal—**A NAT traversal solution is required in a SIP trunking scenario to segregate the IP addressing space of traffic within the enterprise and the IP addressing space of traffic traversing public networks. This is needed to avoid unauthorized access of enterprise resources from a public network. With each server within an IP PBX cluster configured with a single, internally reachable IP address, a NAT traversal solution is required to enable reachability across public networks. Another problem is the presence of internal IP addresses and ports in SIP and SDP headers. The NAT traversal solution should also enable re-substitution of IP address and ports in application traffic. IP PBX servers usually don't have a native NAT traversal solution and require an intermediary to provide this functionality.

Implementers quickly realized the challenges of directly integrating IP PBX devices to service provider networks. They realized that there was a need for an intermediary device that abstracts fixes to these problems and provides seamless, secure service provider interworking, while at the same time allowing IP PBX servers to function without a major overhaul.

SBCs solved this requirement by weaving into the network fabric and abstracting all the complexities of interworking SIP, SDP, and RTP across different real-time networks. As described later in this chapter and elsewhere throughout this book, SBCs provide immense benefits in real-time communication networks.

With a SIP trunking solution, signaling and media traffic are transported end-to-end across the enterprise over IP. However, over the service provider networks, there are still dependencies on legacy time-division multiplexing (TDM) and Signaling System 7 (SS7) infrastructures. This is especially an issue when service providers have to interconnect with other service provider networks to ensure call completion. Figure 1-6 illustrates a SIP trunking architectural model from the enterprise and service provider perspective.

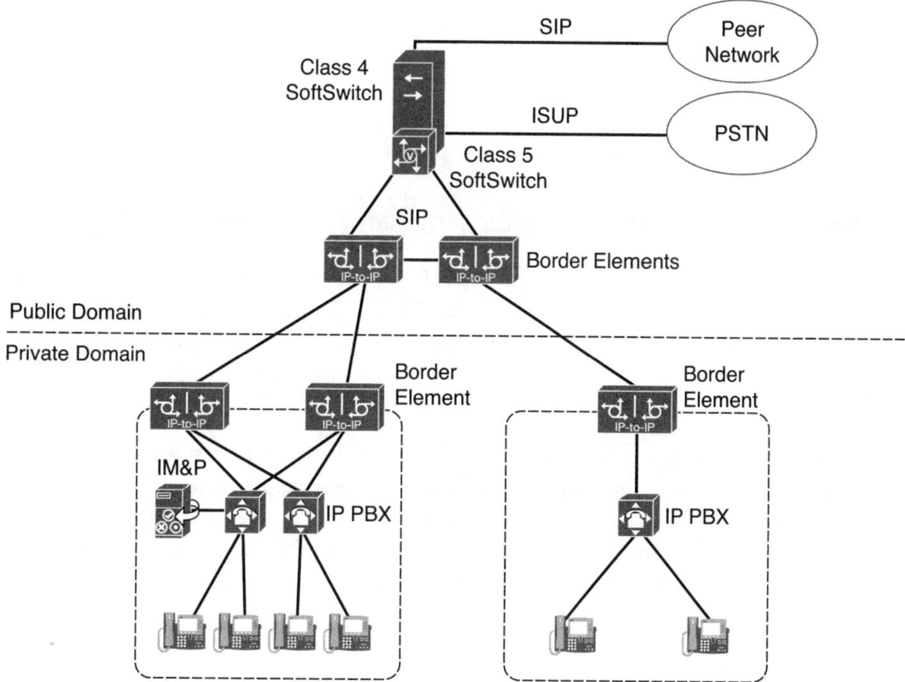

Figure 1-6 *SIP Trunking Architectural Model*

For service providers to properly interconnect with one another, certain network devices are necessary. Service provider networks typically have a combination of the following devices:

- Class 4 and Class 5 softswitches
- Service provider–grade SBCs

A *softswitch* is a device that is used to automatically route calls from one phone to another. A softswitch is classified according to the geographic area it serves and the set of features it implements. A Class 5 softswitch is responsible for routing calls over geographic areas that spans towns or cities, whereas a Class 4 softswitch is responsible for routing calls over larger geographic areas. To provide call routing services over large geographic areas, a Class 4 softswitch provides interconnection between different carrier networks over SIP or ISDN User Part (ISUP).

Features that are provided by most service providers to enterprise businesses include 911 calling, IVR services, annunciator services, music-on-hold, caller ID, and caller name. All these features are implemented within a Class 5 softswitch. Between the Class 5 softswitch and various enterprise networks in a geographic area, service provider–grade SBCs enable topology abstraction, Call Admission Control, NAT traversal, media interworking, protocol repair, and perimeter defense over the service provider network.

As shown in Figure 1-6, enterprise networks also have certain devices that are part of a SIP trunk implementation. These devices include the following:

- Enterprise-grade SBCs
- An IP PBX cluster
- Collaboration endpoints
- Application servers (IM&P, fax, voicemail, recording, and so on)

As described in more detail in Chapter 2, "SBC Deployment Models," several enterprises are beginning to offload the complexities of deploying, configuring, and maintaining on-premises IP PBX and application servers. Instead of these servers being hosted locally, the IP PBX and application servers are hosted in service provider networks. In this case, the only devices hosted on-premises for the enterprise are collaboration endpoints and SBCs.

Service providers typically offer their SIP trunking enterprise customers a standard set of features, such as audio calls, fax calls, and trunk monitoring. However, if businesses require a more detailed feature set—such as audio calls with codec variations, video calls, fax call with a specific switchover method, secure signaling and media services, and trunk redundancy—that can be provided at an additional cost.

Introduction to SDP

In the earlier days of Internet telephony, the process of setting up a call was really cumbersome and drawn out—very unlike the seamless call setup we experience today. To set up a communication session in the early days, participants had to do the following:

Step 1. The caller would bootstrap an audio or video application at a specific port number and IP address.

Step 2. The caller would inform the callee of the details of the port number and IP address over a PSTN line.

Step 3. The callee would fire up a local audio or video application and inform the caller of the IP address and port number on her end.

While this process was acceptable for the occasional calls made over packet networks for the purpose of research and demonstration, it clearly would not find acceptance if Internet telephony were to scale. Protocols were needed to set up, modify, and tear down communication sessions, and these protocols needed to provide enough information to allow participation within the communication session. SIP, as a call control protocol, is adept at setting up and tearing down communication sessions. However, it does not provide participants any information about the details of the communication session (for example, the media types supported and the IP/port pair for media). It has to work in concert with a peer protocol to facilitate advertisement and negotiation of media capabilities.

Session Description Protocol (SDP), originally defined in RFC 2327 (and later updated in RFC 4566), was designed to provide session details (such as the media types, media codec, and IP/port pair for media) and session metadata (such as the purpose of the session and the originator of the session) to participants. SDP is strictly a description protocol and is used in concert with higher-level protocols such as Session Announcement Protocol (SAP), Session Initiation Protocol (SIP), Media Gateway Control Protocol (MGCP), Real Time Streaming Protocol (RTSP), Multipurpose Internet Mail Extensions (MIME), and Hypertext Transfer Protocol (HTTP).

SDP is completely textual and rigid in terms of formatting. Unlike H.323, it does not use binary encoding, such as ASN.1. This was done deliberately so that it could be used in concert with a plurality of protocols and to ensure that malformed SDP bodies could be easily identified and discarded. The formatting of SDP bodies is mostly in UTF-8. SDP bodies contain a number of textual lines that are each either classified as a *field* or as an *attribute*. A field is separated from the next one by a carriage return/line feed (CRLF) sequence. The format of each field is as follows:

```
<type>=<value>[CRLF]
```

Attributes are the primary means of extending SDP. Over time, to enable several application usage paradigms and to enable smooth interoperability between communicating entities, many SDP attributes were defined and standardized. (At the time of this writing, there are a few new SDP attributes in the process of being standardized by the IETF.) Attributes can be of two types:

- **Property attributes**—These attributes are in the format **a=<*flag*>**. A property attribute conveys a simple Boolean meaning for media or the session.
- **Value attributes**—These attributes are in the format **a=<*attribute*>:<*value*>**. For example, the SDP **crypto** attribute is a value attribute.

The primary purpose of an SDP body is to always ensure that the participants are provided with sufficient information to join a communication session. Accordingly, SDP bodies are classified into three description levels:

- Session description
- Time description
- Media description

The session description consists of a number of fields and optional attributes that provide details around the session, such as the name of the session, the originator of the session, and bandwidth constraints for the session. The session description can optionally contain attributes as well.

Communication sessions can either be unbounded or bounded in time. SDP time descriptions specify when communication sessions are active by using the timing (**t=**) field. The timing field has the following format:

```
t=<start-time> <stop-time>
```

This field is self-explanatory: ***start-time*** and ***stop-time*** simply encode the time when the session starts and ends, respectively. ***start-time*** and ***stop-time*** are expressed in decimal representations of Network Time Protocol (NTP) time values in seconds since 1900. The encoding of the ***start-time*** and ***stop-time*** determines whether the communication session is bounded, unbounded, or permanent. A bounded session has a explicit ***start-time*** and ***stop-time***. An unbounded session does not have a ***stop-time***, whereas a permanent session does not have a ***start-time*** or ***stop-time***. The encoding of the timing field is useful for multicast communication sessions. For unicast sessions, the timing field must be encoded to specify a permanent session (**t=0 0**).

The media description section of SDP bodies provides sufficient detail about the media and transport characteristics of the communication session. This information is used by participants to join a multicast session or negotiate common capabilities for unicast sessions. The media description section includes the following information:

- The media types (for example, audio, video, application, image)
- The transport protocol (for example, RTP)
- The media formats for different media types (for example,G711, H.264)
- Optionally, the IP address and port pair for media.

Fields and attributes in SDP bodies can either be mandatory or optional. In either case, they must follow the rigid ordering structure shown in Table 1-5.

Table 1-5 *Fields and Attributes in SDP Bodies*

Field/Attribute	Description	Mandatory or Optional?
Session Description		
v=	Protocol version	Mandatory
o=	Originator and session identifier	Mandatory
s=	Session name	Mandatory
i=	Session information	Optional
u=	URI of description	Optional
e=	Email address	Optional
p=	Phone number	Optional
c=	Connection information; not required if included in all media	Optional
b=	Zero or more bandwidth information lines	Optional
z=	Time zone adjustments	Optional
k=	Encryption key	Optional
a=	Zero or more session attribute lines	Optional

Field/Attribute	Description	Mandatory or Optional?
Time Description		
t=	Time the session is active	Mandatory
r=	Zero or more repeat times	Optional
Media Description (if Present)		
m=	Media name and transport address	Mandatory
i=	Media title	Optional
c=	Connection information; optional if included at session level	Optional
b=	Zero or more bandwidth information lines	Optional
k=	Encryption key	Optional
a=	Zero or more media attribute lines	Optional

SDP fields and attributes can appear at two levels:

- Session level
- Media level

The session level section of SDP bodies provides default values for various fields that are to be used and interpreted. For example, if a user agent wants to use the same media connection IP address for all media streams within the session, it can encode an SDP body with a session-level description of media connection information. However, if further granularity is required on a per media stream basis, the user agent can encode an SDP body with one or several media-level descriptions. Example 1-1 is snippet of an SDP body carried within a SIP message. (The actual SIP message is omitted for brevity.)

Example 1-1 *SDP Body Carried Within a SIP Message*

```
v=0
o=CiscoSystemsSIP-GW-UserAgent 1597 5834 IN IP4 10.94.64.12
s=SIP Call
c=IN IP4 10.1.1.1
t=0 0
a=recvonly
m=audio 16590 RTP/AVP 8 101
a=rtpmap:8 PCMA/8000
a=rtpmap:101 telephone-event/8000
a=fmtp:101 0-15
a=ptime:20
m=video 51372 RTP/AVP 99
a=rtpmap:99 h263-1998/90000
```

The session-level description starts with the **v=** line and continues until the first media-level section. Every media-level section is identified by a **m=** line and continues until the next **m=** line or until the end of the SDP body. As shown in Example 1-1, the media connection IP address (**c=IN IP4 10.1.1.1)** has only a session-level description, and it spans the audio and video stream. In addition to having a media connection information field, the direction attribute (**a=recvonly**) is specified for both the audio and video media streams. Session-level descriptions serve as default values to be interpreted and used if no corresponding media-level description(s) is available.

Example 1-2 is a snippet of an SDP body where the direction attribute has a session-level description and a media-level description. You should be aware that certain SDP fields and attributes can be present concurrently at different levels of the SDP body. When this occurs, the media-level field or attribute overrides the session-level field or attribute. So, in the case of the direction attribute appearing twice in Example 1-2, the media-level description of the direction attribute is given higher precedence.

Example 1-2 *SDP Body with Session- and Media-Level Definitions for the Direction Attribute*

```
v=0
o=CiscoSystemsSIP-GW-UserAgent 1597 5834 IN IP4 10.94.64.12
s=SIP Call
c=IN IP4 10.1.1.1
t=0 0
a=recvonly
m=audio 16590 RTP/AVP 8 101
a=rtpmap:8 PCMA/8000
a=rtpmap:101 telephone-event/8000
a=fmtp:101 0-15
a=sendrecv
a=ptime:20
```

The Offer/Answer Framework

SDP was originally conceived as a way to describe multicast sessions over Mbone (short for *multicast backbone*). SDP scales really well for multicast, as there is a unified view of the session for all participants. For example, for multicast communication sessions, each participant requires a single media address and port to join a communication session. While SDP has the capability of describing unicast communication sessions, it is a slightly more challenging proposition than describing multicast sessions. For a unicast session between two participants, each participant has a localized view of the session; each participant has its own media IP address and port pair, its own set of supported media types, and its own set of supported codecs per media type. To obtain a complete view of a unicast session, the participants must exchange information elements and agree on a common set of parameters. The SDP offer/answer model, defined in RFC 3264, provides such a framework for information exchange and parameter negotiation. To get a better understanding of the offer/answer framework, it is important to first understand certain terms that are frequently referenced in subsequent sections:

- **Agent**—An entity involved in an offer/answer exchange
- **Answerer**—An agent that receives a session description that describes aspects of a plausible media communication session and responds with its own session description
- **Answer**—An SDP message sent from an answerer to an offerer
- **Offerer**—An agent that generates a session description to create or modify a session
- **Offer**—An SDP message sent by an offerer
- **Media Stream**—A single media instance in a communication session

Operation of the Offer/Answer Framework

The offer/answer exchange requires the existence of a stateful, higher-level protocol such as SIP that is capable of exchanging SDP bodies during call setup and/or modification. The protocol has to be stateful to maintain context around the exchange between an offerer and answerer, as there may be several SDP exchanges during the course of a call. It is important for the higher-level protocol to accurately map requests and responses.

Generating the SDP Offer and Answer

The SDP offer/answer model begins with one of the user agents constructing an SDP body according to the guidelines of RFC 4566. You should realize that the initiator of a communication session (the user agent that sends the SIP INVITE) need not always be the one constructing the SDP offer. For SIP delayed offer calls, the user agent being invited to a communication session is the one that constructs the SDP offer.

Regardless of which user agent constructs the offer, the SDP body must consist of a session description, time description, and media description section. This strict encoding format ensures that the peer user agent is provided sufficient information to participate in the communication session. The session description section contains all the mandatory fields (for example, **v**, **o**, **s**) as well as optional attribute values. For unicast sessions, the time description section must contain a timing field to indicate a permanent session (**t=0 0**). The media description section of the SDP offer can contain several media lines (**m=**), such that each media line corresponds to different media types or they correspond to the same media type or a combination of the two.

Each media line appearing in the SDP body must encode sufficient information about the media stream to convey the following:

- The media type of the stream (for example, audio, video, image)
- The transport port and IP address of the media stream
- The list of media formats per media stream

The format of any media line within an SDP body is as follows:

```
m=<media> <port> <proto> <fmt list>
```

The **<media>** subfield indicates the media type, such as audio, video, image, and so on. The possible set of media types that can be advertised in SDP bodies is maintained in the Media Type registry of the Internet Assigned Numbers Authority.

The **<port>** subfield is used to encode the port number on which media is expected. It is a common misconception that the port number encodes the port number from which media is sourced. For media transport protocols such as RTP, a peer protocol, Real-Time Transport Control Protocol (RTCP), allows participants to provide real-time media reception quality feedback. By default, RTCP is exchanged on the next higher port number following the RTP port number. If for some reason an application does not want to exchange RTCP on the next higher port number following RTP, it can explicitly indicate this by using the **a=rtcp** attribute. Example 1-3 demonstrates the use of the **a=rtcp** attribute in an SDP body.

Example 1-3 *SDP Body Demonstrating the Use of the* **a=rtcp** *Attribute*

```
v=0
o=CiscoSystemsSIP-GW-UserAgent 1597 5834 IN IP4 10.94.64.12
s=SIP Call
c=IN IP4 10.1.1.1
t=0 0
a=recvonly
m=audio 16590 RTP/AVP 8 101
a=rtcp:53020
a=rtpmap:8 PCMA/8000
a=rtpmap:101 telephone-event/8000
a=fmtp:101 0-15
a=sendrecv
a=ptime:20
```

The **<port>** subfield is useful only when interpreted and used in conjunction with the connection data (**c=**) field. Without the connection data field, the remote user agent is only aware of a port number and has no information about the remote IP address. The connection data field can be scoped to include a session-level or media-level definition.

The **<proto>** subfield identifies the transport protocol for media. For media encapsulated over RTP, this subfield is set to **RTP/AVP** or, optionally, to **RTP/SAVP** for secure RTP (SRTP).

The **<fmt list>** subfield specifies the media formats supported by the user agent generating the SDP body. The encoding of this subfield depends on the value of the **<proto>** subfield. If the **<proto>** field is either set to **RTP/AVP** or **RTP/SAVP**, this subfield includes a list of payload numbers (or sometimes only one payload number). For applications to discern the media format to which a given payload number corresponds, there is a list of payload number-to-media format mappings defined in the RTP audio/video profile. Table 1-6 lists a selection of these mappings for common audio codecs.

A comprehensive listing of the mappings of all payload numbers to media formats is maintained in an Internet Assigned Numbers Authority registry at https://www.iana.org/assignments/rtp-parameters/rtp-parameters.xhtml.

Table 1-6 *Mapping Between Payload Numbers and Media Formats for Common Audio Codecs*

Payload Type	Encoding Name	Clock Rate (Hz)
0	PCMU	8000
4	G723	8000
8	PCMA	8000
9	G722	8000
15	G728	8000
18	G729	8000

In the case of dynamic payload numbers (payload numbers between 96 and 127), there has to be an explicit mapping specified in the SDP body, using the **a=rtpmap** attribute. While it is not required to use the **a=rtpmap** attribute for static assignments already specified in the RTP audio/video profile, it seems to be the preferred formatting choice for most vendors.

To better explain this concept, see the sample SDP body provided in Example 1-4. The media line (**m=**) lists three static payload numbers: 0, 8, and 18. For a user agent that receives this SDP body, the interpretation of the static payload numbers 0, 8, and 18 is provided by the RTP audio/video profile and translates to PCMU, PCMA, and G729, respectively (refer to Table 1-6). Providing a mapping between these static payload numbers and their corresponding media formats via the **a=rtpmap** attribute is a redundant but nonetheless ubiquitous construct. For dynamic payload numbers, the a=**rtpmap** attribute is required to explicitly provide a binding to the media format.

Example 1-4 *SDP Body Demonstrating the Use of the* **a=rtpmap** *Attribute*

```
v=0
o=CiscoSystemsCCM-SIP 2828060 1 IN IP4 10.1.1.1
s=SIP Call
c=IN IP4 10.1.1.1
b=TIAS:64000
b=AS:64
t=0 0
m=audio 17236 RTP/AVP 0 8 18 101
a=rtpmap:0 PCMU/8000
a=rtpmap:8 PCMA/8000
a=rtpmap:18 G729/8000
a=rtpmap:101 telephone-event/8000
a=fmtp:101 0-15
```

The **a=fmtp** attribute shown in Example 1-4 is used to encode media format specific parameters. For example, while using named telephony events for transmission of DTMF events, the **a=fmtp** attribute can be used to specify the list of events (0–15) that can be transmitted between sender and receiver.

Media lines have their interpretations tightly coupled with the SDP direction attribute. A direction attribute can have a session-level scope or media-level scope. For unicast streams, the offerer can specify the directionality of a media stream by using the SDP direction attribute. Accordingly, a stream can be marked as **sendonly**, **recvonly**, **inactive**, or **sendrecv**. Table 1-7 summarizes the implications of the different ways in which the direction attribute can be encoded.

Table 1-7 *SDP Direction Attribute Description*

Direction Attribute	Direction of Media
sendonly	The sender wishes to only send media to its peer.
recvonly	The sender wishes to only receive media from its peer.
sendrecv	The sender wishes to send and receive media.
inactive	The sender wishes to set up the session but not transmit or receive media.

When the direction attribute has a **sendrecv** or **recvonly** value, it signifies the IP address and port number on which the sender would expect to receive media (RTP) from its peer. If the direction attribute is marked as **sendonly**, it indirectly signifies the IP address and port on which the sender (of the SDP) expects to receive RTCP. Typically, RTCP is received or sent on the next higher port than RTP.

As mentioned previously, the IP address and port listed in the SDP does not signify the source address and port for RTP packets. Instead, it signifies the address and port on which the sender expects to receive media.

If a user agent sets the direction attribute to **inactive**, it means that the user agent wants to simply establish a communication session without transmitting or receiving media. However, at a later time, the user agent can initiate a new SDP offer/answer exchange to update the direction attribute. Regardless of the value of the direction attribute, there is a continuous passage of RTCP traffic between communicating entities. While constructing an SDP body, if the user agent does not specify an explicit value for the direction attribute, it always defaults to **sendrecv**.

As mentioned earlier, the user agent constructing the SDP offer can include one or more media lines such that the media lines can correspond to the same media type, different media types, or a combination of the two. Conventionally, the offerer must use a valid, nonzero port number for each media line within the offer. This is because the use of port zero for a media line(s) within the offer has no useful semantics.

> **Note** At the time of this writing, the IETF is in the process of defining a new specification that allows applications to multiplex different media types over a single transport layer connection. This specification introduces a new SDP grouping framework extension called **BUNDLE** that defines useful semantics for an offerer to use zero as the port number for a media line(s) in the offer.

On receiving the offer, the answerer must construct an SDP body following the guidelines of RFC 4566: It must include a session description, a time description, and a media description. Even if there is absolute parity between the offer and the answer in terms of the media streams and media formats per stream, it is reasonable to assume that the answer will differ from the offer on certain aspects such as the IP address and port pair for media, support for SDP extensions, and so on. In such instances, the origin line (**o=**) of the answer must be different from that of the offer. The timing field in the answer must mirror the timing field in the offer. With regard to the media description, the constructed answer must follow several rules that are discussed in more detail in the following paragraphs.

While constructing the answer, the answerer must generate a response to each media line listed in the offer such that the number of media lines in the offer and answer must always be the same. If a given media type in the offer is not supported by the answerer, the corresponding media line must be rejected by the answer by setting the port number to zero. If an answerer rejects a media stream, there is no RTCP traffic exchanged for that media stream. Example 1-5 demonstrates an offer/answer exchange where the video media type is rejected by the answerer.

Example 1-5 *SDP Offer/Answer Exchange for Disabling Video*

```
Offer]
    v=0
    o=alice 2890844526 2890844526 IN IP4
    host.atlanta.example.com
    s=
    c=IN IP4 host.atlanta.example.com
    t=0 0
    m=audio 49170 RTP/AVP 0 8 97
    a=rtpmap:0 PCMU/8000
    a=rtpmap:8 PCMA/8000
    a=rtpmap:97 iLBC/8000
    m=video 51372 RTP/AVP 31 32
    a=rtpmap:31 H261/90000
    a=rtpmap:32 MPV/90000
```

```
[Answer]

  v=0
  o=bob 2808844564 2808844564 IN IP4
  host.biloxi.example.com
  s=
  c=IN IP4 host.biloxi.example.com
  t=0 0
  m=audio 49172 RTP/AVP 0 8
  a=rtpmap:0 PCMU/8000
  a=rtpmap:8 PCMA/8000
  m=video 0 RTP/AVP 31
  a=rtpmap:31 H261/90000
```

Note If there are no media formats in common for all streams, the entire offered session is rejected.

As discussed previously, an offerer can set the direction attribute (at the session level or media level) to **sendrecv**, **sendonly**, **recvonly**, or **inactive**. Table 1-8 highlights the different ways in which the direction attribute can be set in the answer.

Table 1-8 *Different Ways of Setting the Direction Attribute in the Answer.*

Direction Attribute in Offer	Direction Attribute in Answer
sendonly	recvonly/inactive
recvonly	sendonly/inactive
sendrecv	sendrecv/sendonly/recvonly/inactive
inactive	inactive

For streams that are marked as **recvonly** in the answer, the answer must contain at least one media format that was listed in the offer. In addition, the answerer may include media formats not listed in the offer that the answerer is willing to receive. This is useful in scenarios where the offerer proceeds to modify the communication session at a later stage and includes an updated media format list.

For streams that are marked as **sendonly** by the answerer, the answer must contain at least one media format that was listed in the offer. For streams marked as **sendrecv** in the answer, the answer must list at least one media format that it is willing to use for both sending and receiving media. In such a situation, the answer might also list media formats that were not a part of the offer. Again, this is useful in scenarios where the offerer proceeds to modify the communication session at a later stage and includes an updated media format list. For streams marked as **inactive** in the answer, the media format list in the answer mirrors that in the offer.

Note Media formats in the offer and answer are always listed in decreasing order of precedence, from left to right.

In terms of the payload numbers of media formats, the answer has to use the same payload numbers as the offer. It is also required for the answerer to use the **a=rtpmap** attribute for each media format to provide a payload number to the media format binding—regardless of whether the answer contains static or dynamic payload numbers. If a media format in the offer is described using the **a=fmtp** attribute, and that media format is echoed in the answer, the answerer must ensure the same **fmtp** parameters are listed.

Note The offer and answer can optionally include bandwidth and packetization interval attributes. For more on packetization intervals, see Chapter 5, "Media Processing."

Media lines marked as **sendonly** and **recvonly** by the offerer have a reverse interpretation when accepted by the answerer. For example, consider an offer where the audio media line is marked as **sendonly**. When accepted by the answerer, the same audio media line has to be marked as **recvonly**. This ensures that the offer/answer exchange concludes with both user agents converging on a unified view of the communication session. In this case, the offerer only transmits media packets, while the answerer only receives media packets. Of course, this assumes that the answerer does not set the stream as **inactive**.

Modifying a Session

During the course of a communication session, it is not uncommon for application interactions to require a modification of session characteristics. These modifications could include changing the media formats, changing the value of the direction attribute, adding new media streams, and removing existing media streams, among others. Nearly all aspects of a communication session can be modified. To effect a change or modification of session characteristics, the two user agents must engage in a new SDP offer/answer exchange. The high-level flow of modifying a communication session is depicted in Figure 1-7.

A user agent attempting to modify a communication session first constructs an updated SDP body whose content reflects the modifications required. These modifications could range from the trivial to the complex. Regardless of the degree of modification reflected in the SDP body, the user agent must increment the version number of the origin field (**o=**) by one. Example 1-6 highlights this concept.

The original SDP body in Example 1-6 contains the version number 5834. Sometime during the course of the communication session, the user agent requires changing the list of media formats and accordingly proceeds to construct and transmit an updated SDP body. The updated SDP offer has its version number incremented by one and a modified media format list in the audio media line.

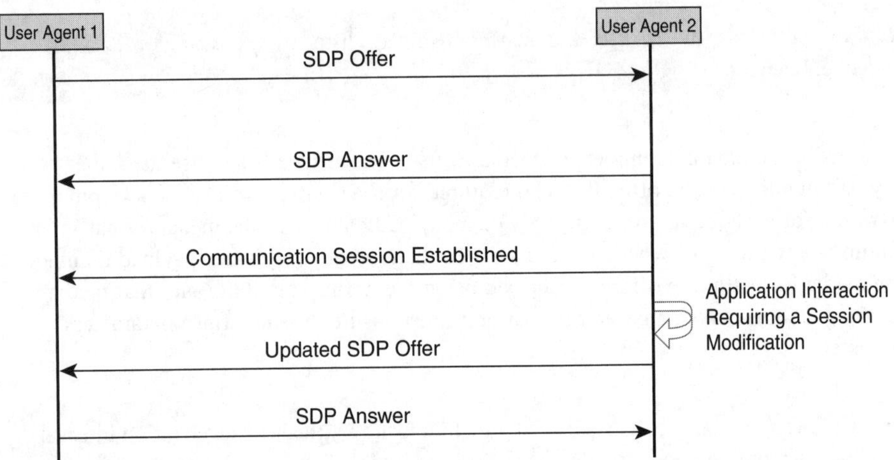

Figure 1-7 *Modifying a Communication Session by Using the SDP Offer/Answer Exchange*

Example 1-6 *Incrementing the SDP Originator Version Number*

```
Original SDP:

v=0
o=CiscoSystemsSIP-GW-UserAgent 1597 5834 IN IP4 10.94.64.12
s=SIP Call
c=IN IP4 10.1.1.1
t=0 0
a=recvonly
m=audio 16590 RTP/AVP 8 101
a=rtpmap:8 PCMA/8000
a=rtpmap:101 telephone-event/8000
a=fmtp:101 0-15
a=ptime:20
m=video 51372 RTP/AVP 99
a=rtpmap:99 h263-1998/90000


Modified SDP:


v=0
o=CiscoSystemsSIP-GW-UserAgent 1597 5835 IN IP4 10.94.64.12
s=SIP Call
```

```
c=IN IP4 10.1.1.1
t=0 0
a=recvonly
m=audio 16590 RTP/AVP 0
a=rtpmap:0 PCMA/8000
a=ptime:20
m=video 51372 RTP/AVP 99
a=rtpmap:99 h263-1998/90000
```

It is quite possible for a user agent to initiate a new SDP offer/answer exchange without changing the contents of the SDP body. While this exchange doesn't result in the modification of session characteristics, it could be used for reasons such as determining session freshness. If a new SDP body is identical to the previous SDP body, the version number must remain the same.

While generating an updated offer, the user agent must ensure that the number of media lines (**m=**) equals the number of media lines in the previous SDP body. In other words, if the previous SDP body had *N* media lines, the updated SDP body must contain at least *N* media lines. It is possible for the updated SDP body to contain more than *N* media lines, since this is required when adding a new media line.

Adding a Media Stream

It is possible to add new media streams to a session by appending the appropriate media lines to an existing SDP body. For example, if an audio-only communication session is established between two participants and one of the participants wants to escalate the session to include video, that participant appends a video media line (**m=video**) to the existing SDP body and sends an updated offer. User agents that want to add a media stream must always append media lines to existing ones. This ordering ensures that the peer user agent is able to gauge any new media line additions.

It is also possible to add a media stream to a communication session by activating a previously disabled media stream. Consider a scenario in which a user agent attempts to establish a communication session that includes audio and video media types. If the peer user agent does not support video, it rejects the video media line by setting the port to zero (see Example 1-5). During the course of the communication session, either user agent may decide to reuse the video media line slot to introduce a new media stream. The new media stream can have a video media type or any other valid media type. Example 1-7 demonstrates this process.

Example 1-7 *Adding a Media Stream*

```
Initial SDP Offer/Answer:

      [Offer]
      v=0
      o=alice 2890844526 2890844526 IN IP4 host.atlanta.example.com
      s=
      c=IN IP4 host.atlanta.example.com
      t=0 0
      m=audio 49170 RTP/AVP 0 8 97
      a=rtpmap:0 PCMU/8000
      a=rtpmap:8 PCMA/8000
      a=rtpmap:97 iLBC/8000
      m=video 51372 RTP/AVP 31 32
      a=rtpmap:31 H261/90000
      a=rtpmap:32 MPV/90000

     [Answer]

      v=0
      o=bob 2808844564 2808844564 IN IP4 host.biloxi.example.com
      s=
      c=IN IP4 host.biloxi.example.com
      t=0 0
      m=audio 49172 RTP/AVP 0 8
      a=rtpmap:0 PCMU/8000
      a=rtpmap:8 PCMA/8000
      m=video 0 RTP/AVP 31
      a=rtpmap:31 H261/90000

Updated SDP Offer/Answer Activating the Previously Disabled Media Line.

[Offer]
      v=0
      o=alice 2890844526 2890844526 IN IP4 host.atlanta.example.com
      s=
      c=IN IP4 host.atlanta.example.com
      t=0 0
      m=audio 49170 RTP/AVP 0 8 97
      a=rtpmap:0 PCMU/8000
      a=rtpmap:8 PCMA/8000
      a=rtpmap:97 iLBC/8000
      m=image 54322 udptl t38
      a=T38FaxVersion:0
      a=T38MaxBitRate:14400
```

```
      a=T38FaxRateManagement:transferredTCF
      a=T38FaxMaxBuffer:300
      a=T38FaxMaxDatagram:72
      a=T38FaxUdpEC:t38UDPRedundancy

[Answer]

      v=0
      o=bob 2808844564 2808844564 IN IP4 host.biloxi.example.com
      s=
      c=IN IP4 host.biloxi.example.com
      t=0 0
      m=audio 49172 RTP/AVP 0 8
      a=rtpmap:0 PCMU/8000
      a=rtpmap:8 PCMA/8000
      m=image 44322 udptl t38
      a=T38FaxVersion:0
      a=T38MaxBitRate:14400
      a=T38FaxRateManagement:transferredTCF
      a=T38FaxMaxBuffer:300
      a=T38FaxMaxDatagram:72
      a=T38FaxUdpEC:t38UDPRedundancy
```

In Example 1-7, the initial offer contains two media types: an audio media type and a video media type. On receiving this offer, the answerer disables the video media stream by setting the port to zero in the answer. At this stage, the communication session is established as an audio-only session. At some time during the communication session, one of the user agents (in this specific example, the user agent is the offerer) decides to set up a T.38 fax connection by reusing the previously disabled video media line to advertise the **image** media type (which corresponds to T.38 Fax Relay). The updated offer is accepted by the answerer, and the communication session escalates to fax.

Removing a Media Stream

A user agent can remove an existing media stream by constructing a new SDP body and setting the media port of the corresponding media stream to zero. When such an SDP body is received by the peer user agent, it is treated as a non-negotiable and explicit indication to disable a given media stream. Therefore, the peer user agent must construct an answer with the port for the media stream in question also set to zero.

Media streams that are deleted by an updated SDP offer/answer exchange cease to exchange RTP or RTCP traffic. Any resources allocated for such media streams can be de-allocated.

Modifying the Address, Port, Transport or Media Format

As mentioned earlier in this chapter, nearly every aspect of a communication session can be modified. The way in which media streams can be added and removed using the SDP offer/answer exchange is discussed in the previous section. During the course of a communication session, it may happen that a user agent discovers a new interface that is known to be more reliable than the current interface engaged in media transmission and reception. To ensure that the newly discovered, higher-priority interface takes over for media transmission and reception, the user agent has to construct an updated SDP offer in which the connection information field is modified to reflect the new interface identity. In most instances, a modification of the connection information field proceeds with a change in the port number(s) for a media line(s), and this is reflected in the update SDP offer.

Note There are several other scenarios that require modification of the media IP address and port. These include, but are not limited to, media redirection from one endpoint to another, call hold, and call resume.

Even after updating the connection information and port, a user agent must be prepared to receive media on the old IP address/port pair for a reasonable amount of time. This is because the peer user agent has to accept the updated SDP offer, proceed to process the changes, and then program its internal software subsystems accordingly. You should also be aware that it is possible for an answerer to update its own IP address/port pair in the answer to an updated offer.

When setting up a communication session, both participants converge on a media format using the SDP information that is exchanged. In addition, it is perfectly acceptable for a user agent to attempt to change the media format midsession. Intuitively, it has to do so by first constructing an updated SDP offer such that the media line(s) contains a completely new set of media formats (not present in the previous SDP) or a set of media formats that partially overlap with the previous SDP body. The offer can be rejected or accepted by the answerer. When accepted, the media format used is determined by the way in which the answer is encoded (refer to the section "Generating the SDP Offer and Answer," earlier in this chapter).

Overview of B2BUAs

B2BUAs are devices that have co-located UAC and UAS functionality. A B2BUA essentially functions as a UAS to one downstream device and a UAC to another downstream device. Figure 1-8 demonstrates the basic operation of a B2BUA.

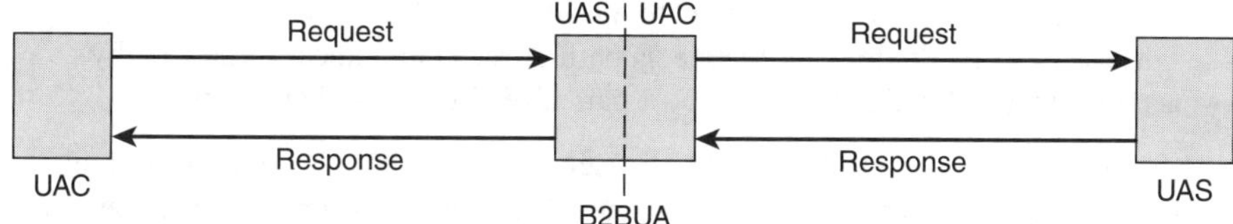

Figure 1-8 *Basic B2BUA Operation*

B2BUAs have operations defined in the media plane, the signaling plane, or both. The versatility of operations on either plane depends on the type of B2BUA in question, as there are several variants of such devices. An effort to standardize the definition and function of B2BUAs was carried out in the IETF STRAW (SIP Traversal Required for Applications to Work) Working Group. B2BUAs can be broadly classified as follows:

- **Signaling plane B2BUAs**—A signaling plane B2BUA is a device that operates exclusively in the signaling plane and has no operations defined in the media plane. For most modern deployments, SIP is the protocol of choice for session setup, modification, and teardown. Signaling plane B2BUAs are capable of modifying SIP header field values before requests and responses are transmitted to the next hop. Signaling plane B2BUAs are not placed in the media path on call establishment and therefore cannot manipulate RTP packet headers or payloads. Though signaling plane B2BUAs primarily modify SIP header field values, they can, in some instances, modify SDP bodies, too. The scope of modification of SDP bodies is, however, restricted to manipulating only the media format list; there is no change made to the IP address/port pair of SDP bodies.

  Signaling plane B2BUAs can further be categorized as follows:

  - **Proxy B2BUAs**—A proxy B2BUA, from a SIP perspective, behaves similarly to a SIP proxy. A proxy B2BUA maintains sufficient dialog context to enable it to generate messages by itself when required. For example, a proxy B2BUA is capable of tearing down a communication session by generating a SIP BYE. These devices do not modify SIP header fields such as To, From, and Contact (among others). The only headers that are modified by such B2BUAs are the Via and Record-Route header fields.

  - **Signaling-only B2BUAs**—A signaling-only B2BUA is a device that functions beyond the definition of a regular proxy and is capable of modifying headers such as To, From, and Contact. It is also capable of removing or modifying the Record-Route and Via headers. It is very likely that a request received on a signaling-only B2BUA is modified a great deal before it is forwarded to the next hop, based on the routing logic of the proxy.

  - **SDP-modifying signaling-only B2BUAs**—These B2BUAs function as signaling-only B2BUAs but are "SDP aware," in that they understand the semantics and syntax used in SDP. The operations of such B2BUAs on SDP bodies are extremely restricted and can possibly extend to modifying media format lists (codecs). These B2BUAs do not alter the media path of the communication session by modifying the media IP address/port pair advertised in the SDP body.

- **Media/signaling plane B2BUAs**—Media/signaling plane B2BUAs have operations that can span the signaling and media planes. They can modify not only SIP headers but also SDP bodies. In the media plane, these devices are capable of transforming RTP headers and RTP payloads. From an architectural perspective, given the broad scope of operations these devices can perform, they may be physically decomposed into separate components, such that one component handles signaling and another component handles media. To ensure that the two components are in synchronization with one another, there is a constant control dialog in place. A more fine-grained classification of such B2BUAs is as follows:
  - **Media Relays**—A media relay is a B2BUA that terminates media traffic (RTP and RTCP) and re-originates it toward the peer leg. Media relays only repackage Layer 3 and Layer 4 headers, and there are no modifications done to RTP headers or payloads. The default mode of operation for SBCs is the media relay mode.
  - **Media-aware B2BUAs**—A media-aware B2BUA functions in pretty much the same capacity as a media relay, but it has the ability to inspect and potentially modify the TCP or UDP payloads that encapsulate RTP and RTCP traffic. An example of a media-aware B2BUA is a device that multiplexes and demultiplexes RTP and RTCP on the same 5-tuple (source network address, destination network address, source port, destination port, and Layer 4 transport).
  - **Media termination B2BUAs**—A media termination B2BUA is capable of terminating media and transforming it a great deal before re-originating it on the peer call leg. Devices that perform transformation operations on media payloads, such as changing the media format from one representation to another (transcoding), changing the media payload from one packetization period to another, or changing DTMF from one in-band representation to another, are all examples of media termination B2BUAs.

SBCs are devices that function as media/signaling plane B2BUAs with the ability to perform a plethora of operations on the signaling and media planes. Depending on local policy and configuration, SBCs can flexibly oscillate between different variants of media/signaling plane B2BUAs.

Session Border Controllers

The adoption of SIP in real-time communication networks far outpaced the standardization activities carried out by the IETF. As a result, vendors had to resort to proprietary solutions to deal with commonly encountered problems. Many of these problems arose due to lack of interoperability between vendors, device types, and protocols. To enable interoperability and achieve the required functionality, vendors began implementing these proprietary solutions in network intermediaries that came to be known as session border controllers (SBCs). For a very long time, there was no consensus on what these devices could or should be able to do. In 2010, well after SBCs had already become an indispensable part of real-time networks, the IETF took up the task of defining the requirements of SIP-based SBCs. These requirements are officially documented in RFC 5853.

Traditionally, these devices are deployed at the network edge and serve as transit points for signaling and media traffic. Due to their placement at the network periphery, SBCs abstract several security services, such as access control, DoS detection and prevention, topology hiding, and protection of signaling and media traffic. They also enable features and services that are not present natively within endpoints, such as NAT traversal, transcoding, transrating, and DTMF interworking. SBCs also provide a wide variety of traffic management options, such as enforcing quality of service (QoS), enabling media recording, and restricting the choice of media formats.

Figure 1-9 depicts a high-level SBC architecture. There are two logical units: the signaling plane and the media plane. The signaling plane is responsible for handling call control protocols such as SIP and H.323, modifying protocol headers and bodies, maintaining dialog context, correlating dialogs, enforcing protocol-related timers, and determining session freshness. The media plane is responsible for handling RTP and RTCP traffic, allocating and de-allocating port pairs for media traffic, enabling transformation operations on media packet payloads, and general traffic management.

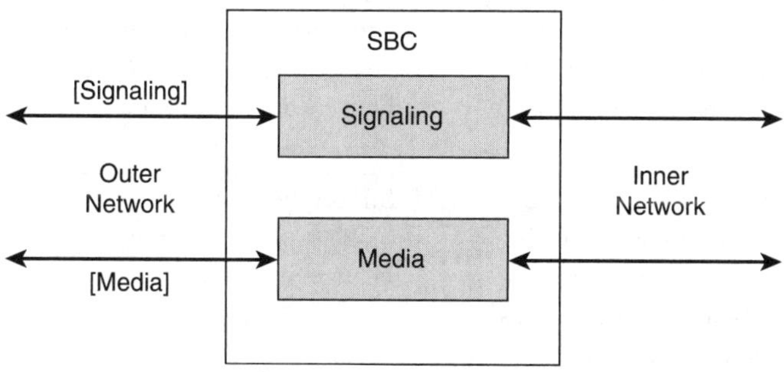

Figure 1-9 *High-Level SBC Architecture*

The media and signal planes may be part of the same physical unit, or they may be distributed across distinct physical units. Service provider–grade SBCs typically employ a distributed architecture wherein the media and signaling planes are part of physically distinct units. There is a continuous control dialog between these units to ensure that they are in synchronization with one another. Distributed architectures allow the signaling and media sessions to scale independently of one another. This is highly advantageous because the sheer volume of messaging, presence, call handling, and monitoring traffic on SBCs can place restrictions on the number of concurrent media sessions the SBCs can handle. Enterprise SBCs usually have a monolithic architecture that is restricted by hardware and software to allow an upper bound for the number of concurrent media or signaling sessions. If the either one of the logical planes reaches its upper bound, this effectively inhibits the other from reliably handling traffic.

The "inner network" and "outer network" in Figure 1-9 describe the role of an SBC as a border element in terms of handling signaling and media plane operations between logically or physically different networks. For example, an SBC can be deployed in peering mode to interconnect two service provider networks, or it can be deployed in access mode to interconnect an enterprise network and a service provider network.

SBCs versus Proxies

SBCs are B2BUAs that have operations defined in the media and signaling planes. While there isn't an IETF RFC that completely defines how an SBC should function, most SBCs, regardless of vendor and make, have evolved over the years to exhibit a consistent operational model. SIP proxies, on the other hand, have their operations defined in RFC 3261 (and supporting extensions). Table 1-9 demonstrates some of the high-level differences between SBCs and SIP proxies.

Table 1-9 *Operational Differences Between SBCs and SIP Proxies*

Operation	SBCs	SIP Proxies
Header manipulation	SBCs can modify headers such as To, From, Contact, and Call-ID. It is also possible for an SBC to introduce new headers into the SIP message.	SIP proxies add a Via header and optionally a Record-Route header, and the rest of the headers are left untouched.
SDP modification	SBCs are SDP aware in that they can interpret and understand the semantics of SDP. SBCs can also drastically transform SDP bodies from one call leg to another.	SIP proxies are not SDP aware and do not change SDP bodies.
Protocol interwork	SBCs are capable of interworking completely different protocols to set up, modify, and tear down communication sessions.	SIP proxies are only capable of working on the SIP protocol.
Terminating SIP sessions	SBCs are context aware and generate protocol messages on their own accord. For example, during prolonged periods of media inactivity, an SBC can tear down a communication session by generating a SIP BYE on either call leg.	Stateful proxies are context aware; however, they should not be able to terminate communication sessions by themselves.

Figure 1-10 illustrates the operation of an SBC on a SIP INVITE message.

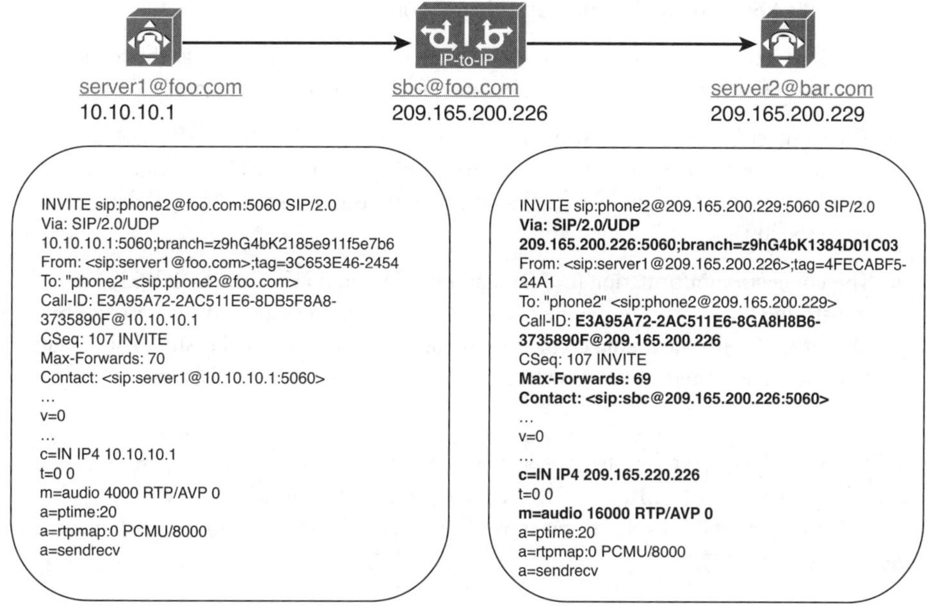

Figure 1-10 *An SBC Handling a SIP INVITE*

In Figure 1-10, an SBC functions as an intermediary between two SIP servers that are attempting to establish a communication session on behalf of two endpoints. (The endpoints are not depicted in the figure.) The incoming SIP INVITE from SIP server 1 has an enclosed SDP body and thus is an early-offer INVITE. Given that SBCs function as media/signaling plane B2BUAs, they tend to transform SIP message headers and SDP bodies significantly before forwarding the message to the next hop. This transformation on SIP header fields and SDP bodies is done for several reasons, such as security, ensuring dialog completion, influencing the media characteristics of the call, and interworking signaling/media plane mismatches. In Figure 1-10, the SBC transforms the following SIP headers and SDP field/attributes:

- The Via header is transformed to overwrite the IP address of SIP server 1 (10.10.10.1), with the IP address of the SBC (209.165.200.226). This is done to ensure topology abstraction (which is explained shortly) and ensure that reverse signaling within the SIP transaction traverses the SBC.
- The Call-ID header field is replaced with a new Call-ID header field before the message is forwarded to the next hop. This is because the SBC functions as a B2BUA and terminates and re-originates signaling. Creating a new Call-ID header field implicitly creates a new SIP dialog between the SBC and SIP server 2. In certain instances, but not always, the Call-ID header field might contain the IP address or domain name of the node that originated the message. If this header field were left

untouched, it could lead to internal or sensitive topology information leaking into another network, which is not always desirable. By transforming the Call-ID header field, the SBC can provide topology abstraction.

- The Max-Forwards header field is decremented by one to ensure that the request can traverse a finite number of devices before a final response is received.
- The Contact header is transformed to overwrite the IP address of SIP server 1 (10.10.10.1) with the IP address of the SBC (209.165.200.226). This is done to ensure topology abstraction and ensure that any new transactions with the SIP dialog traverse the SBC.
- The connection information (**c=**) field and media line (**m=**) of the SDP body are transformed to overwrite the media connection IP address and port advertised by SIP server 1 with the media connection IP address and port of the SBC. This ensures that media (RTP and RTCP) flows through the SBC on call establishment.

> **Note** Figure 1-10 is a very simplistic representation of the transformation operations that could be carried out by SBCs on SIP messages and SDP bodies. In real-world implementations, an SBC is likely to transform SIP messages and SDP headers to a much greater extent.

Figure 1-11 illustrates the operation of a SIP proxy on a SIP INVITE message.

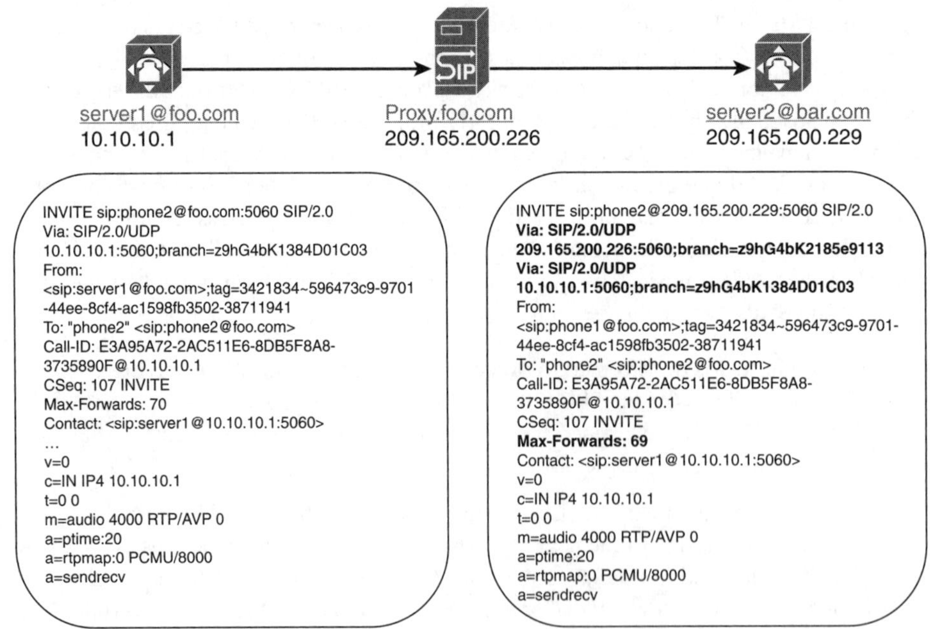

Figure 1-11 *A SIP Proxy Handing a SIP INVITE*

In Figure 1-11 a SIP proxy is placed between two SIP servers attempting to establish a communication session on behalf of two endpoints. (The endpoints are not illustrated in the figure.) The incoming SIP INVITE from SIP server 1 has an enclosed SDP body and thus is an early-offer INVITE. A SIP proxy performs a limited set of transformation operations on the SIP message but leaves the SDP body untouched. The SIP proxy transforms the following SIP header fields:

- A new SIP Via header field is inserted above any existing Via header fields. This ensures that reverse signaling within the SIP transaction traverses the proxy.
- The Max-Forwards header field is decremented by one to ensure that the request can traverse a finite number of devices before a final response is received.

Note A SIP proxy can optionally add a Record-Route header field if it is to be included in all messages within the scope of the dialog. For more details about SIP proxies, see Chapter 3.

Common SBC Functions

As media and signaling are made to flow across network boundaries, many interoperability issues could arise. For example, different vendors might have varying interpretations of protocol standards, or different vendors might implement incompatible protocol extensions, or at a more basic level, different vendors might not be able to agree on a media format. In addition, when communication infrastructures are accessible over unprotected networks like the Internet, a whole host of security issues need to be addressed, including perimeter defense, confidentiality and integrity attacks, toll fraud, and availability attacks, to name a few. To enable seamless communication between real-time networks, an effective, application-aware NAT traversal solution is often required.

Instead of deploying devices to individually cater to the various requirements, a better, more flexible and economically viable option is to deploy an SBC. SBCs are multipurpose devices with a wide span of operations on media, signaling, security, reporting, monitoring, traffic management, and perimeter defense.

It might not always be necessary to enable all the features provided by an SBC. For example, if an SBC is used to interconnect two internal, real-time enterprise networks, it is unlikely that there would be a need to enable topology abstraction, perimeter defense, and secure media and signaling. A select list of SBC features are discussed in the following sections.

Topology Abstraction

SBCs are deployed at the edges of enterprise or service provider networks. An SBC is essentially the last hop when signaling or media transits from one network to another. SIP messages include several header fields that could potentially expose details of the internal network schema. This is undesirable as attackers or competitors can leverage this information to mount DoS or toll fraud attacks. SBCs assist in minimizing or completely preventing such attacks when they rewrite the IP address or host name information present in headers such as To, From, Via, Contact, and Call-ID. The IP address or host name information in these headers is modified to reflect the local SBC IP address or host name. Any malicious actors examining SIP messages to uncover internal topology information would only find the SBC's local IP address or host name. Subsequently, if DoS or toll fraud attacks are targeted toward the SBC, they can be easily thwarted.

NAT Traversal

A NAT traversal solution is required when signaling and media are exchanged between networks where there is a need to create a mapping between internal and external IP addresses. For real-time communication sessions, common NAT traversal solutions such as TURN (Traversal Using Relays Around NAT), STUN (Session Traversal Utilities for NAT), and ICE (Interactive Connectivity Establishment) are expensive and not commonly found across all device types. SBCs offer a flexible alterative to this problem by functioning as the public interface for all outbound traffic from the enterprise. Due to their ability to terminate and re-originate signaling and media, SBCs ensure the smooth passage of traffic between public and private networks.

DoS and Overload Protection

Call processing servers that are accessible over public networks or that have their access routes breached can easily fall prey to availability or DoS attacks. Such attacks can be mounted by sending an unusually high number of SIP requests to the target server or by sending a large number of malformed SIP messages. The CPU cycles expended in processing such significant traffic volumes quickly move the server to an "overloaded" state, where it is incapable of processing requests in a timely manner. SBCs natively have intrusion detection and prevention systems that build models of legitimate, acceptable traffic patterns and malicious traffic patterns. Whenever there is a surge in malicious traffic patterns beyond a certain threshold, SBCs can raise high-severity alarms or begin discarding traffic without passing it to the application layer.

Legitimate spikes in call volume may occur in some instances. For example, during a natural disaster, call servers might have to process significantly more call volume than usual. Such a spike in call volume can result in the expeditious movement of call servers to an overloaded state. SIP as a call control protocol provides little protection against these types of scenarios. The most common method for an overloaded server to attempt to throttle down the rate and number of requests is the 503 Server Unavailable response. While this is a very reactive approach that sets in when the damage is already underway, it is often accompanied by other problems, such as on/off semantics and load amplification. *On/off semantics* basically refers to the condition in which a requestor is simply notified about whether the request can be processed. If the request cannot be processed, the requestor is not provided with supporting information about how the request can be completed, such as alternate server(s), a specific time when the server is expected to recover, and so on. *Load amplification* refers to a condition in which all servers on the network start moving to an overloaded state because of large-scale and frequent redirection of requests.

SBCs can not only protect call servers from processing an overwhelmingly large number of requests, they can also proactively indicate resource availability to downstream servers well ahead of the onset on an overloaded condition. This allows downstream servers to engineer traffic volumes in accordance with resource availability on the SBC. Given that overload control is a significant problem in core SIP networks, the IETF has standardized a proactive method to solve this problem via the constructs of the RFCs in the concluded SIP Overload Control (SoC) working group. Details about these methods are provided in Chapter 8, "Scalability Considerations."

Fixing Capability Mismatches

When interconnecting two real-time communication networks, more often than not, there is a significant chance of encountering interoperability issues. For example, the two networks might support different call control protocols, different extensions within the same call control protocol, different media encoding formats, different media format packetization periods, different methods of DTMF relay, different media encryption schemes, different IP addressing versions, and so on. Many of the endpoints initiating and terminating communication sessions don't natively have the ability to address such problems. Intermediaries such as SBCs exert control over media and session traffic to ensure that it is engineered to a format acceptable to the communicating entities. Accordingly, capability mismatches in communication sessions can be broadly classified as signaling plane mismatches and media plane mismatches, as discussed in the following sections.

1. Signaling Plane Mismatches

SBCs are capable of interconnecting two networks that implement different call control protocols. Without SBCs or some other device to effectively translate messages from one call control protocol to another (for example, SIP to H.323 and vice versa), it would be impossible for such networks to interconnect with one another. While protocol interworking is extremely useful in establishing communication sessions, there cannot be an exhaustive translation of all the constructs of one call control protocol to another. Consequently, communication sessions that are established as a result of protocol interworking might not have the same rich, in-call experience that would be available if the protocol were the same end-to-end.

Over the years, baseline SIP, defined in RFC 3261, has been refined a great deal, and several extensions to the protocol have been standardized. Many of these extensions, while they do address real problems, have not found wide adoption across the industry. In some scenarios, real-time networks implement and support different extensions to SIP. To avoid interoperability issues or to avoid call failure because certain extensions are not implemented end-to-end, a common practice is to deploy SBCs to do the job of protocol repair between two networks. There are also scenarios in which different vendors interpret and implement standards differently. This is largely because standards can sometimes be open to varying interpretations. Even in such scenarios, SBCs have sufficient constructs to normalize such differences and allow smooth session setup and teardown.

SIP, which is used in an overwhelmingly large number of real-time network deployments, can function over UDP or TCP. Most deployments prefer SIP over UDP, but some use SIP over TCP for increased reliability. SBCs, because of their ability to terminate and re-originate signaling, can interwork SIP over different transport layer protocols.

2. Media Plane Mismatches

With the SBC setting up communication sessions across different real-time networks, there always exists the possibility of interoperability issues arising in the media plane. Interoperability issues in the media plane are primarily attributed to incompatible media formats, media packetization intervals, media security schemes and incompatible methods of in-band DTMF relay. From the perspective of fixing interoperability issues in the media plane, SBCs offer the following:

- **Media encryption:** When communication sessions span network boundaries and cross over to untrusted public networks, it is necessary to avoid integrity and confidentiality attacks; this is done by cryptographically securing signaling and media traffic. SBCs can be used to encrypt signaling and media leaving the enterprise network and to decrypt signaling and media being received by the enterprise network.

- **DTMF handling:** DTMF tones can be transmitted out-of-band, using call control protocol messages, or in-band, within the media stream. With out-of-band mechanisms, the method of DTMF relay is largely dictated by the call control protocol. For example, if SIP is used to set up, modify, and tear down a communication session, the methods of DTMF relay could include SIP NOTIFY, SIP INFO, and SIP KPML. Among these different variants of SIP DTMF relay, there might not be ubiquitous consensus on how digit information needs to be encapsulated. There are also scenarios in which you might need to interwork between in-band and out-of-band mechanisms of DTMF relay for the same call. To enable a flexible framework on DTMF interworking for a myriad of scenarios, SBCs are commonly used.

- **Media format interworking:** Different networks might enforce different media formats for a given media type. As discussed earlier in this chapter, the list of media formats might overlap between the offerer and answerer. In this case, the highest-preference common media format is chosen. However, if there are no common media formats between the networks, the communication session will fail to set up. To avoid such a situation, the SBC can be configured to transcode from one media format to another. In addition, even if there is a common media format across communicating networks, each network might require a different packetization period. In such situations, the SBCs can also be used to transform media formats from one packetization period to another.

3. IPv4-to-IPv6 Interworking

Due to the near exhaustion of the IPv4 address space, IPv6 adoption is seeing a steady increase. For communication networks that use different IP addressing versions, SBCs can be used to provide translation services at the network layer and at the application layer.

Cisco Unified Border Element

Cisco Unified Border Element (CUBE) is Cisco's offering in the enterprise SBC space. Cisco CUBE is a feature-rich product that has all the offerings of a conventional SBC and can fit into a number of deployment scenarios based on scale, required SBC functionality, and the traffic profile. CUBE provides network administrators with tremendous flexibility in terms of monitoring, reporting, security, configuration, and traffic management.

CUBE can be deployed on several different platforms, depending on the required functionality and scale of operations. More details about different deployment models and platform options are provided in Chapter 2. Architecturally, CUBE can have a monolithic architecture, with the signaling plane and media plane (and accompanying subsystems) part of the same physical unit, or it can have a distributed architecture, in which case the signaling and media planes are part of distinct physical units. From a very high level, the following subsystems work in concert with one another to enable CUBE's rich feature set:

- **SIP/H.323 protocol stack**—This, along with related subsystems, instantiates the CUBE signaling plane. The protocol stack takes care of all protocol-related operations.
- **RTP stack**—The RTP stack represents the media plane of CUBE. The media plane is responsible for numerous operations, such as allocating and de-allocating ports for RTP and RTCP traffic, detecting and discarding phantom media packets, working with the cryptographic subsystems for encryption and decryption of media packets, transforming media payloads from one media format to another or one packetization period to another, and in-band DTMF handling.
- **Call routing logic**—On CUBE platforms, this unit is logically represented by dial peers. Several supporting constructs—such as SIP profiles, server groups, dial peer groups, pattern maps, and translation rules—assist in the call routing process.
- **Transport logic**—This unit includes the stacks for UDP, TCP, and TLS.

Given that SBCs are deployed as border elements, it is important for these devices to implement a wide array of security features. Some of the security features offered by CUBE include cryptographic protection of media and signaling, toll fraud prevention, SIP silent discard, zone-based firewalls, Call Admission Control, and traffic filtering through access lists. No single software unit implements these diverse security constructs; rather, they are implemented by several subsystems working in concert with one another. Throughout this book, the various features of CUBE are discussed in more detail.

Summary

This chapter provides an introduction to the common call control protocols deployed on SBCs: SIP and H.323. This chapter also provides a brief introduction to SIP trunking. It also covers SDP and various nuances of the offer/answer exchange, as well as B2BUAs and their various classifications. This chapter introduces SBCs and their use in IP-based multimedia networks. The chapter concludes with an introduction to CUBE, Cisco's offering in the enterprise SBC space.

References

RFC 3261, "SIP: Session Initiation Protocol," https://tools.ietf.org/html/rfc3261

RFC 3264, "An Offer/Answer Model with the Session Description Protocol (SDP)," https://tools.ietf.org/html/rfc3264

RFC 4566, "SDP: Session Description Protocol," https://tools.ietf.org/html/rfc4566

RFC 5853, "Requirements from Session Initiation Protocol (SIP) Session Border Controller (SBC) Deployments," https://tools.ietf.org/html/rfc5853

RFC 8079, "Guidelines for End-to-End Support of the RTP Control Protocol (RTCP) in Back-to-Back User Agents (B2BUAs)," https://tools.ietf.org/html/rfc8079

RFC 7092, "A Taxonomy of Session Initiation Protocol (SIP) Back-to-Back User Agents," https://tools.ietf.org/html/rfc7092

SIP Trunking by Hattingh et al. (Cisco Press)

Chapter 2

SBC Deployment Models

Chapter 1, "Laying the Groundwork," outlines the fundamentals of multimedia communications protocols and also explores some of the basic capabilities of session border controllers (SBCs). This chapter covers some of the common deployment types and options for SBCs to further support the decision of whether an SBC is useful or required for a deployment.

Once it has been determined that an SBC should be deployed in an environment, an organization can follow several implementation strategies to support the various needs of features, availability, hardware, and scalability.

This chapter is composed of the following main sections, which support the decision and design of an SBC implementation:

- **Purposeful Deployments**—This section discusses integrations and use cases that drive the general use and need for SBCs to be deployed in communications networks.
- **CUBE Deployment Options**—This section discusses deployment options specific to Cisco Unified Border Element (CUBE) and covers the various hardware and software platforms that CUBE can be deployed upon.
- **Multi-VRF Support on CUBE**—CUBE with multi-VRF support allows for virtual segmenting as a way of separating networks. This section discusses use cases and caveats with this type of deployment that are common with service provider environments.
- **SBC High Availability**—There are various options for designing high availability with SBCs to ensure that SBC services remain available during impacting events. This section addresses both general internal resilience within SBCs and resilience of external peers that the SBC is integrating with. This section also discusses high availability solutions specific to CUBE.

At the conclusion of this chapter, you will be able to adequately scope a CUBE design and will understand the purpose and features of CUBE, including options for multitenancy and device resilience.

Purposeful Deployments

Various driving factors in a business make it either a good practice or a requirement to deploy SBCs, based on the nature of the integrations. This section outlines some scenarios that call for deployment of SBCs.

Deployments can be split into two types—*external integrations* and *internal integrations*—depending on whether the SBCs are inside or outside the administrative boundary of the network. The majority of integrations aim to leverage some or all of the four main goals of SBCs: providing session control, security, interworking, and demarcation.

Some common SBC integrations are logically represented in Figure 2-1.

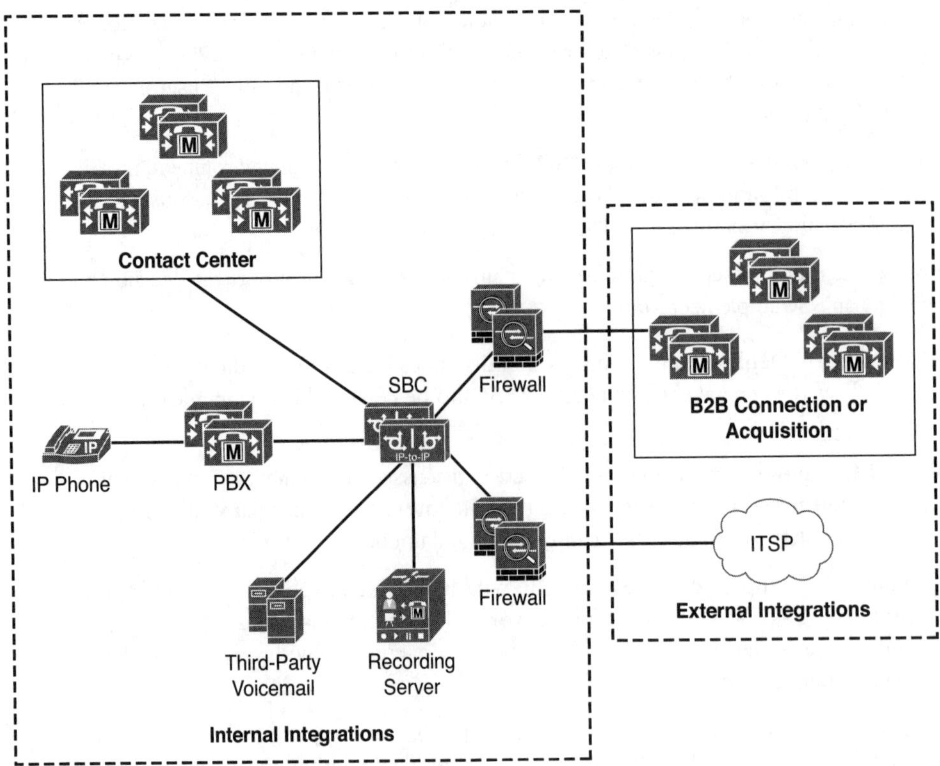

Figure 2-1 *Common SBC Integrations*

External Integrations

With an external integration, an SBC is placed at the edge of the administrative network, to integrate the communications services residing in the local network with another network that is outside local administrative control. Examples of external integrations are connecting an enterprise communications deployment to a service provider for PSTN access or to another company's communications service.

Caution When performing external integrations, information security needs to be top of mind. Following security best practices is essential throughout this entire process. Any integrations with untrusted networks or with exposure to the Internet should be implicitly untrusted. Refer to Chapter 6, "Secure Signaling and Media," for further information on secure protocols, and Chapter 13, "Security Threat Mitigation," for best practices on security threat mitigations.

Integrating for PSTN Access

Perhaps the most common driving factor for deployment of SBCs is to support the integration of an internal communications network with an external Internet telephony service provider (ITSP). Because integrating with an ITSP requires extending communication paths to another entity, interoperability and security must be considered during the planning and deployment of such an integration. Placing an SBC at the edge between these entities allows for the insertion of additional capabilities that provide additional security and flexibility.

For example, an SBC can provide sophisticated quality of service (QoS) marking to ensure that media quality is optimized for network edge traversal, as well as provide *call admission control* (CAC) to ensure that committed resources are available and not overrun. Integration with ITSPs may also require that SIP messaging be modified for interoperability, and an SBC can offer this through a process of modifying SIP message content through *SIP normalization*. An SBC can provide the capability of *transcoding* between two different codecs if there is a mismatch in codec offerings between the two sides for a presented call flow, and can also provide interworking between diffferent dual-tone multifrequency (DTMF) specifications. SBCs also allow for improved security, with features such as toll fraud protection and interworking between secure and unsecure media.

Integrations with Mergers and Acquisitions

With a merging of two company entities, there is a chance that the internal dial plan of a communication network may overlap between the two entities. An example of this would be if Company A deployed internal directory numbers 1001 through 4999 and allowed users to short-dial each other by dialing only the four-digit extension. These four-digit extensions would have no relevance outside Company A's administrative boundary as they are logically unique within Company A.

Now given the Company A deployment, consider a scenario where Company A purchases 100-user Company B. Company B also has extensions 1000 through 1999 deployed for its users. After the acquisition, there may be a desire for Company A to call Company B directly by using short-dialing. However, there is no mechanism to discern in what instances a call to extension 1001 should be routed to Company A's call processing server or to Company B's call processing server. This challenge is called *dial plan overlap*. Deployment of an SBC can solve this problem, as an SBC has the capability to translate between Company A's and Company B's calling and called party numbers, providing a way to minimize or eliminate dial plan changes on each of the company's central call processing servers.

Considering that communication to the acquired company may be across a WAN and deployed with a different vendor's solution, the other advantages of SBCs—such as QoS, CAC, SIP normalization, and security—may also be desired or necessary in this type of integration.

Internal Integrations

Aside from the placement of SBCs at boundaries to external networks, there is also often a need to deploy an SBC within the administrative boundary of a network. Scenarios arise where the benefits of an SBC are either desired or required for integration of other applications, solutions, or features within the same internal communications network. Some examples where SBCs would be deployed for internal integrations would be for third-party application integration, a contact center, or media recording solutions. These situations are discussed in the following sections.

Integrating with Third-Party Appliances

The challenge with third-party appliances is that an appliance's behavior may not adhere to the same standards and requirements that another vendor has implemented for communication signaling or media support. Implementing CUBE between disparate vendors or products allows for flexibility with normalizing signaling and media between both vendors, and it also provides a means to convert media types (such as SRTP to RTP) or codecs (such as G.729 to G.722). As a result, an SBC may be inserted between two unified communication solutions (such as between two different IP PBXs) or between an IP PBX and a VoIP-to-PSTN gateway to provide features such as security or signaling normalization.

Contact Center Integration

SBCs are commonly deployed in contact center environments, standing in as entry points (*ingress gateways*) for calls coming into the contact center from an ITSP and/or as egress gateways for calls being delivered out to customers or remote agents. SBCs provide interworking, demarcation, and security services between the PSTN and the contact center. (This is similar to the PSTN integration for SBCs use case mentioned earlier.) A high-level contact center integration is shown in Figure 2-2.

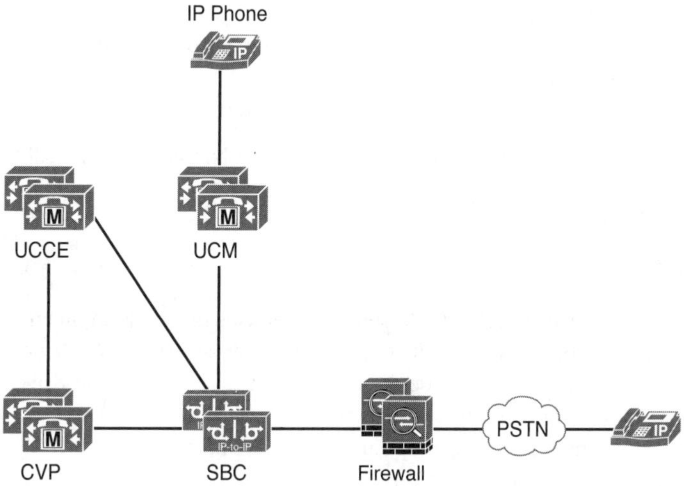

Figure 2-2 *SBC in Cisco Contact Center for Ingress/Egress and PBX Integration*

In addition to being used as ingress or egress gateways, Cisco Unified Border Element can be deployed in contact center environments between Unified CM and Unified CVP. CUBE supports survivability in the event that the core contact center components are unavailable, and it also integrates with the SIP dialer to support the Cisco Outbound Option dialer that is a part of Cisco Contact Center Enterprise.

The nuances of contact center integration are explored in great detail in Chapter 12, "Contact Center Integration."

Call Recording Integration

In some scenarios, the recording of calls is either desired for supporting business functions (such as quality assurance of agents in a contact center) or for supporting compliance and regulations. CUBE can invoke and support the recording of calls by forking media and signaling to a recording server, as shown in Figure 2-3.

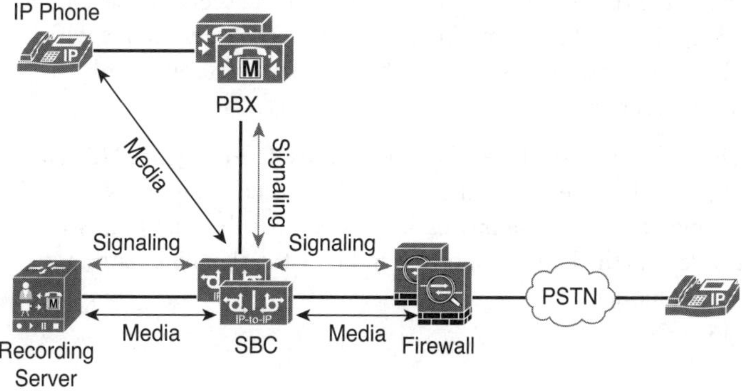

Figure 2-3 *SBC Integration with an IP PBX for Call Recording*

CUBE supports both network-based call recording and the SIP Recording (SIPREC) specification. These scenarios require deployment of an external recording server, which receives the metadata information for the call being recorded and also stores the associated recorded media of the call. Voice and video are both supported recording options.

This type of integration is covered in further detail in Chapter 11, "Network-Based Call Recording."

Line-Side Integrations

As more services continue to transition to being hosted off-premises in the cloud, in an increasing number of deployments, collaboration endpoints register across the WAN or Internet to the call processing system. In these deployments, some scenarios might drive a need for an intermediary device to perform some manipulation of the traffic between the call processing system and the registering endpoints. Line-side integrations can be deployed for both internal and external integrations.

A typical scenario for this type of integration is where the signaling traffic traverses a Network Address Translation (NAT) boundary, and the device performing NAT is performing as an application-level gateway (ALG) to fix up the address/port information by translating between inside and outside addresses. (This behavior is defined in RFC 6314.) The specific challenge here, as demonstrated in Figure 2-4, can be accomplished with most firewalls or routers today without the need for an SBC.

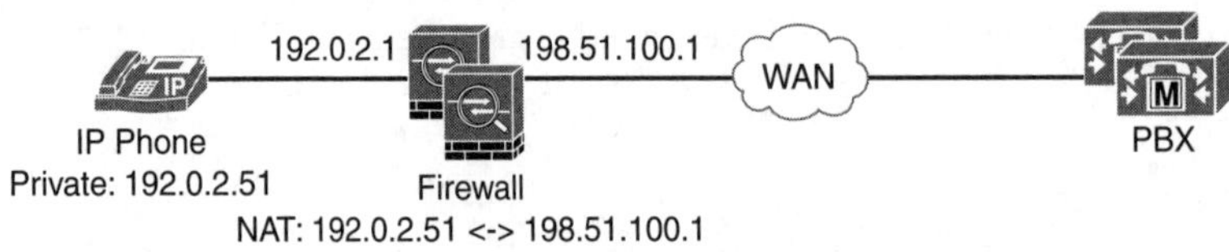

Figure 2-4 *Basic NAT/ALG integration Without an SBC*

Often, though, more is required of an intermediary device to manipulate signaling than NAT ALG is capable of performing. NAT ALG only has the ability to manipulate the address and port information in the signaling. What is to be done in scenarios where the SIP messages from the endpoint need some modification in order to interoperate with the processing server? This is often seen in scenarios that involve registering third-party endpoints to a call processing server.

In these scenarios, much as an SBC is deployed for a back-to-back user agent (B2BUA) between two SIP servers, there is a need for a line-side B2BUA to help interwork the signaling between the endpoint and the call processing system that the endpoint is registering to. Figure 2-5 depicts the logical topology and how the signaling paths are modified in this deployment model.

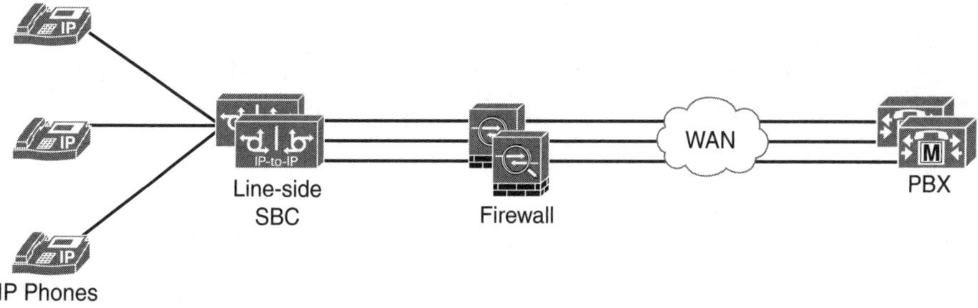

Figure 2-5 *Line-Side Integration with an SBC*

CUBE supports a line-side B2BUA in two different variants:

- **Cisco Unified Communications Manager (CUCM) line-side support**—This allows for IP endpoints on different logical networks to connect over the WAN or Internet to CUCM.
- **Line-side B2BUA**—This deployment is offered in NanoCUBE, targeting deployments of small remote sites where endpoints are registering to cloud services. NanoCUBE features are discussed in the section "CUBE Deployment Options," later in this chapter.

For a more detailed look at the details and configuration for line-side CUBE configurations, see Chapter 9, "SIP Trunking for PSTN Access Through SBCs."

CUBE Deployment Options

CUBE is the SBC offering from Cisco Systems. CUBE provides session management, interworking, demarcation, and security for collaborative communication between devices or across an administrative network boundary.

Note It is worth mentioning that Cisco also has another product called Cisco Expressway that offers a different set of capabilities for collaborative communication across a network edge. Expressway supports communication services that need to traverse a firewall and is often deployed in scenarios that involve integrating with public Internet connections.

In addition to providing session control at the edge for voice and video, much as CUBE does, Expressway offers support for instant messaging and presence edge traversal, as well as integration of CUCM with WebEx Teams to provide hybrid services.

Expressway may be desired for a deployment where other capabilities are needed, such as extensible messaging and presence Protocol (XMPP) traversal, that are not possible with CUBE. However, note that Expressway does not support the entire feature set of CUBE either. Some features available with CUBE but not Expressway include media forking for call recording and multi-VRF support.

Because Expressway uses a different operating system and methodology than CUBE, details on Expressway are not covered in this book. See the "Collaboration Edge" section in *Cisco Preferred Architecture for Enterprise Collaboration* for more details on Expressway capabilities and designs.

The following sections cover the various platforms and physical hardware for which CUBE is available.

Supported Platforms

As of the publication of this book, CUBE capabilities are offered on the hardware platforms listed in Table 2-1. It is important to note that as new hardware models come out, this information is subject to change. Please consult the *Cisco Unified Border Element Data Sheet* or the "Supported Platforms" section in the *Cisco Unified Border Element Configuration Guide* for current details on these deployment options.

Table 2-1 *Supported Platforms for CUBE*

Platform	Model	Operating System
Cisco Integrated Services Generation 2 Router (ISR G2)*	Cisco 2900 Series Cisco 3900 Series	IOS
Cisco 4000 Series Integrated Services Router (ISR G3)	Cisco 4321 Cisco 4331 Cisco 4351 Cisco 4431 Cisco 4451	IOS XE
Cisco Aggregated Services Router (ASR)	ASR 1001-X ASR 1002-X ASR 1004 with RP2 ASR 1006 with RP2	IOS XE
Cisco Cloud Services Router (CSR)	CSR 1000V series	IOS XE

* The ISR G2 was announced as end-of-life in 2016, with the last day of software support in 2020 and the last day of hardware support in 2022.

Note Which model to choose from the platform list mostly depends on features/capabilities as well as the scalability of the platform. This section discusses the architectural and feature differences between the platforms. The following chapters discuss foundational topics that impact the platform scale, and Chapter 8, "Scalability Considerations," discusses how the various platforms and models scale.

There is also a stripped-down CUBE implementation called NanoCUBE. NanoCUBE deployments are intended for interconnection with ITSPs for small sites that have direct ITSP connections and for small sites where endpoints are peered to cloud providers, such as for integration of Cisco endpoints into the Broadsoft Cloud PBX.

NanoCUBE can run on the following platforms:

- Cisco 881
- Cisco 886
- Cisco 887
- Cisco 888
- Cisco 892FSP
- Cisco 897VA
- Cisco SPIAD2901
- Cisco SPIAD2911

NanoCUBE also has enhanced some functionality certified for specific use with some popular cloud-hosted solutions that target small businesses. NanoCUBE performs as a *line-side B2BUA*, where SIP phones register through NanoCUBE out through the edge to the cloud-premises service. This type of deployment provides additional flexibility with SIP interoperability that cannot be provided by traditional firewalls performing NAT SIP ALG due to CUBE's ability to provide tasks such as SIP normalization and DTMF interoperability. As a result, NanoCUBE is beneficial where deploying standard CUBE hardware at every site is not financially feasible due to the cost of the hardware compared to the size of the user base being supported at the deployment site. NanoCUBE has a stripped-down capability set that does not include support for the following standard CUBE features:

- Transcoding/transrating
- Video or TelePresence
- H.323 Gatekeeper
- High availability
- SIP message forking to multiple dial peers
- SRTP on any listed platforms other than the 89x models

Hardware Appliance versus Virtualization

With Cisco CSR deployments, Cisco offers virtualization of the routing software that traditionally needed to be run on dedicated Cisco router hardware. For the CSR, IOS XE is run in virtualized software instances directly on the top of a virtualization infrastructure. Running CUBE on a CSR is referred to as either *Virtual CUBE* or *vCUBE.*

Deployment of the CSR 1000V is supported on the following platforms:

- Virtualization platforms:
  - VMware ESXi
  - Red Hat KVM
  - Citrix XenServer
  - Microsoft Hyper-V
- Cloud-provided virtualization platforms:
  - Microsoft Azure
  - Amazon Web Services (EC2)

Deployment of the CSR 1000V on these virtualization platforms creates an abstraction of the hardware dependencies and opens up support of the underlying hardware that can be used for running CSR 1000V on a nearly endless list of hardware. For more information on the supported hardware that the virtualization platforms that can be used, refer to the documentation that corresponds to each of the desired virtualization platforms. The only minimum hardware restrictions are either Intel Nehalem (2008 release) or AMD Barcelona (2007 release) CPUs of at least 2.0 GHz or better and Gigabit Ethernet interfaces.

The advantage of deploying on virtualized instances is mainly portability. Taking advantage of virtualization, CSR instances can be migrated to different hosts in the event of hardware failure. Virtualization also allows for rapid deployment through the use of cloning or templates, allowing for new instances of CSR to be stood up very quickly and potentially auto-provisioned, without waiting for dedicated hardware router appliances to be shipped to the data center.

Virtualization also allows for better compartmentalization, as dedicated CSR instances can be stood up within the existing virtualization environment. This can allow for per-customer deployments to have their own CSR and CUBE instances without the need to directly procure additional hardware, rack space, power, and cooling resources. This is also advantageous when it is not possible to isolate instances by using *virtual route forwarding* (VRF). (Multi-VRF deployments are discussed later in this chapter.)

Note Even though the CSR can run on a virtualized platform, it is important to take note of the underlying hardware requirements for the CSR instance. Each CSR instance that is deployed requires vCPUs, memory, and disk space. These requirements correlate to underlying hardware needs, such as additional blades or server hosts, as the oversubscription of physical CPU cores is not a supported deployment model with the CSR.

If virtually discrete CUBE instances are not a requirement for sizing and segmentation, leveraging multiple VRF instances with a common CSR (or physical) CUBE instance may be preferred over deploying multiple CSR instances. This is because a multi-VRF deployment with the same CSR does not require additional vCPUs, whereas a multiple-CSR instance does.

The main disadvantage of CUBE virtualization is that the virtual instances do not have the performance scalability provided by dedicated hardware appliance routers. (Scalability of platforms is discussed further in Chapter 8.)

Further, vCUBE does not support the following features that are available with hardware appliance deployments:

- H.323-SIP interworking
- Digital signal processor (DSP) registration and transcoding (see Chapter 5, "Media Processing")
- Noise reduction (NR), acoustic shock protection (ASP), and audio gain
- Call progress analysis (see Chapter 12)
- H.323 Gatekeeper

Platform Feature Comparison

Expanding on the differences between virtualized and dedicated hardware deployments for CUBE, there are also some differences in feature support within the various hardware offerings on which CUBE is supported. Table 2-2 provides a comparison of the feature support differences across the various platform deployments.

Table 2-2 *Platform Comparison for CUBE Features*

Feature	Cisco ASR 1000 Series	Cisco ISR G2 Series	Cisco ISR 4000 Series	Cisco CSR 1000V Series
In-box redundancy	X			
High availability implementation	X	X*	X	X
DSP card	X	X	X	
Transcoder registered to CUCM (SCCP)		X**	X**	
Transcoding (registered with LTI)	X**	X**	X**	
Noise reduction and ASP	X	X	X	
Call progress analysis (CPA)	X	X	X	
Unified SRST colocation with CUBE		X	X***	
RTP/SRTP interworking	X	X**	X	X

Feature	Cisco ASR 1000 Series	Cisco ISR G2 Series	Cisco ISR 4000 Series	Cisco CSR 1000V Series
Co-resident VXML gateway		X		
Co-resident TDM trunks		X**	X**	

*Requires using HSRP instead of redundancy groups.

**Requires DSP hardware.

***Support on these platforms begins with IOS XE 16.7.1.

On all the CUBE platforms, the CUBE feature set is enabled under **voice service voip** with the command **mode border-element license capacity** ***max-current-sessions***. ***max-current-sessions*** defines the number of concurrent calls the platform has been entitled to (see Chapter 8). The status of the CUBE feature set on the platform can be validated with the command **show cube status**. Example 2-1 demonstrates the use of these commands.

Example 2-1 *Configuration and Validation of CUBE Feature Status*

```
cube1(config)# voice service voip
cube1(conf-voi-serv)# mode border-element license capacity 100
cube1(conf-voi-serv)# end
cube1# show cube status
CUBE-Version : 12.0.0
SW-Version : 16.6.1, Platform ISR4451-X/K9
HA-Type : none
Licensed-Capacity : 100
```

The version of CUBE specified in the output in Example 2-1 is directly tied to the version of IOS that is running but provides a more friendly version number to align specifically with CUBE's feature documentation.

IOS versus IOS XE

CUBE can be deployed on either Cisco IOS or Cisco IOS XE, depending on the underlying hardware platform. IOS deployment has been phased out on newer CUBE platforms but is still present in the industry and also provides a foundation for talking about the advantages that have come with more recent IOS XE deployments.

On the ISR, call control signaling and forwarding of packets such as RTP media are done within the same CPU. As a result, performance and scale are impacted as the two tasks compete for the same resources.

With IOS XE (as run on the ISR 4000, ASR, and CSR), signaling processing is supported by a different CPU than is RTP media forwarding. This reduces contention, as the time-sensitive packet forwarding of media traffic is not competing against signal processing tasks. Further, IOS is a *monolithic operating system*, so all processes run within the same CPU and memory pool. If an issue arises with one function in IOS, that issue can impact all other processes on the device as well, potentially causing the entire device to crash. IOS XE has a modular design based on a Linux kernel, so separate functions can run as separate processes. This offers additional protection in the event of a misbehaving process, helping prevent other discrete processes from impacting the entire system.

The modular design of IOS XE also allows for better use of multiple-core processors by allowing separate processes to run on separate cores. The current architecture for IOS XE has three discrete modules: the route processor (which contains the IOS daemon), the embedded services processor (for forwarding/data plane inclusive of encryption tasks), and the shared port adapter interface processor (which provides discovery, bootstrapping, and initialization of physical interfaces). This hardware architecture is demonstrated in Figure 2-6.

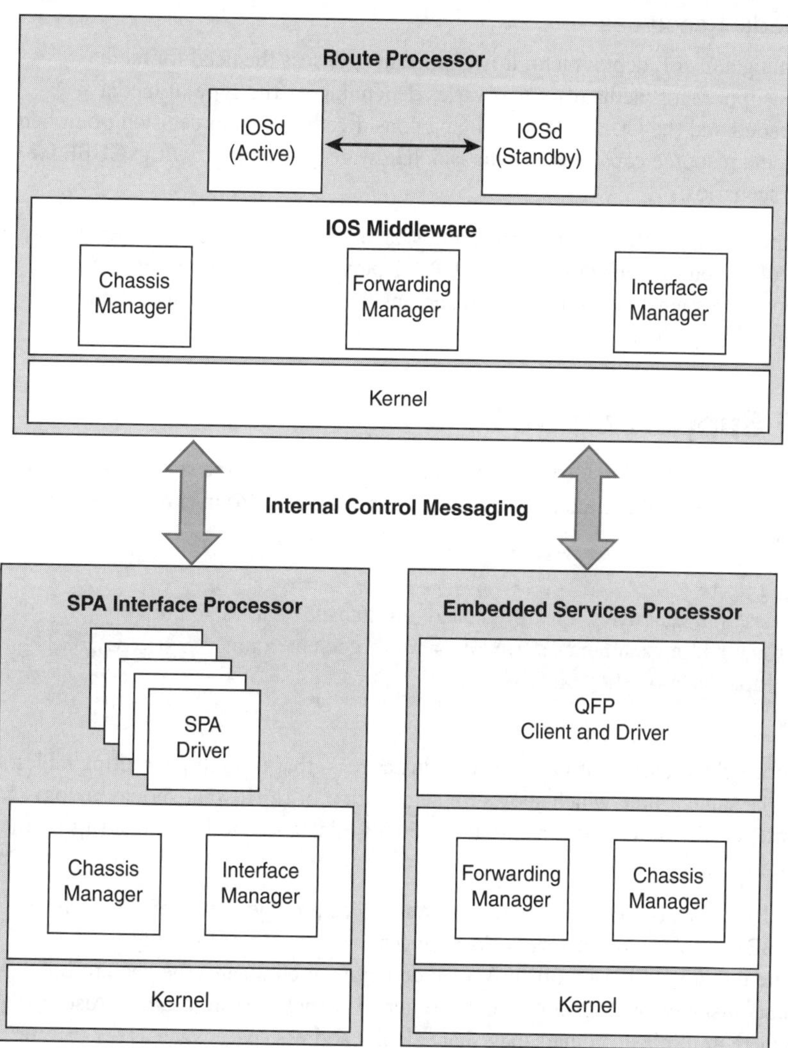

Figure 2-6 *IOS XE Process Architecture*

As a result of the enhancements provided by IOS XE over IOS, IOS XE is the current strategic operating system for Cisco routing platforms and CUBE. IOS XE offers more expansive support of new features than IOS.

Note Fortunately for those who have been administering IOS platforms since before the advent of IOS XE, the majority of CLI commands and configurations are common across IOS and IOS XE. When discussing configuration examples in this book, any differences across the platforms are noted.

Planning for Media Resources

When designing a CUBE deployment, it is important to assess the need for media resources, as support for media resources varies depending on the type of media resources needed and the CUBE platform being considered. The main decision point here regarding media resource capabilities is the lack hardware DSP support with vCUBE for transcoding scenarios.

Media resources (for example, DSPs, transcoders) are a complex topic, discussed in Chapter 5. For the purpose of designing a CUBE deployment, it is important to determine what media resource types are needed and ensure that they are available in the platform that is being chosen.

Multi-VRF Support on CUBE

Thanks to multi-VRF support, CUBE offers features that allow for the segmentation and administrative ease of integration and operation for multiple environments on the same CUBE instance.

Note As discussed in Chapter 9, a feature called multitenancy allows you to configure unique SIP parameters for each tenant's trunk in a converged environment where CUBE is terminating multiple tenants' SIP trunks.

CUBE supports the presence of multiple VRF instances—that is, multiple routing tables residing on the same router, which allows for segregation of traffic that should be logically separate. CUBE allows for a maximum of 54 VRF instances to be co-resident on the same CUBE instance.

Multi-VRF deployments are useful in hosted and service provider environments, where a single CUBE supports multiple network instances that should not logically be able to communicate directly with each other. A VRF deployment eliminates the need to host each customer instance on a separate CUBE router or virtual vCUBE instance. Also, for scenarios where multiple customers may share similar address space (such as the private address space), VRF allows for the same IP address to be assigned to multiple interfaces on the router, as long as the interfaces are in different VRF instances. This allows for additional flexibility in deployments where changing IP address schemes may not be a factor that can be easily influenced.

On CUBE, one VRF can be associated with multiple interfaces, but an interface (or subinterface) can be associated with only a single VRF (see Figure 2-7).

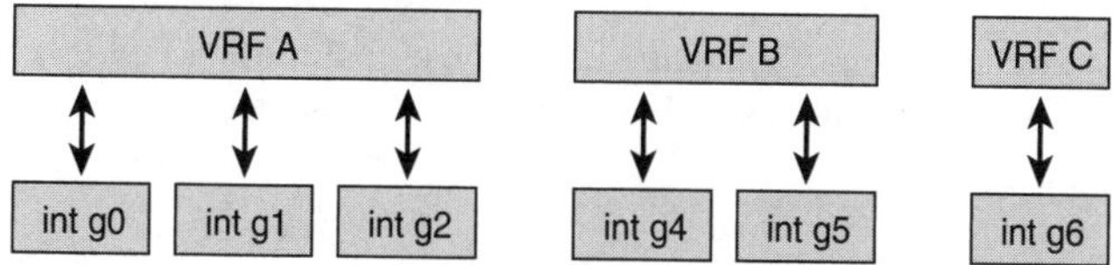

Figure 2-7 *VRF-to-Interface Mapping Logic*

Multi-VRF requires that the dial peers be bound to a specific interface. This associated interface then has a VRF assigned to it. The binding allows for a dial peer to be associated with a VRF instance of that bound interface. Calls coming in an interface bound to a VRF then restrict the criteria for matching of the inbound dial peer to only those peers that are associated with the VRF of the interface on which the call has been received. Once potential dial-peer matches have been filtered to match the VRF the call arrived on, the inbound dial-peer matching process proceeds, with the standard inbound dial-peer matching procedure. This is explored further in Chapter 3, "Call Routing."

It is important to note that the default behavior with multi-VRF CUBE allows for a call coming in VRF A to be routed to VRF B. There is no default constraint to prevent call routing between different VRF instances with a multi-VRF CUBE deployment. If this behavior is desired, *dial-peer groups* are used to provide control over what VRF instances can communicate to others from a call routing perspective. This concept is discussed in Chapter 3, after the foundations of the basic configuration for multi-VRF and dial peers have been presented.

Multi-VRF does have some restrictions you need to be aware of. It does not support the following features:

- The single-VRF feature (one VRF for all CUBE voice traffic), otherwise known as VRF-Aware, must be disabled to support Multi-VRF with the command **no voice vrf** ***vrf-name***.
- H.323-to-SIP and H.323-to-H.323 calls are not supported.
- It is not possible to deploy multi-VRF with Cisco Unified Communications Manager Express (CME) or Cisco Unified Survivability Remote Site Telephony (SRST) on the same box as CUBE.
- Multi-VRF does not support IPv6.
- Multi-VRF does not support TDM connections.
- Multi-VRF does not support media flow-around (see Chapter 5) deployment.
- Multi-VRF does not support media anti-tromboning (see Chapter 5).

A caveat to also consider is that domain name system (DNS) resolution from CUBE cannot be directed out a specific VRF instance. In scenarios where destinations are specified (with the **session target** command) as DNS addresses instead of IP addresses, there is a need to resolve the DNS name to an IP address through resolution of the service (DNS SRV) record. When multi-VRF is deployed, DNS resolution uses the global routing table instead of the VRF instance specific to the outbound dial peer chosen. This means the DNS server being used for name resolution is contacted using the global routing table, and that DNS server must have entries for all DNS addresses that are referenced by dial peers bound to specific VRF instances.

Multi-VRF Configuration

To configure a VRF instance, first a VRF instance needs to be defined with a unique (case-sensitive) name and *route distinguisher*. This is done with the following command:

```
ip vrf vrf-name
   rd route-distinguisher
```

The ***route-distinguisher*** is either in the format of an autonomous system (AS) number and an arbitrary number (for example, *xxx:y*), or an IP address and arbitrary number (for example, *A.B.C.D:y*). The idea behind the arbitrary number is to suffix the item so that it is not common across the different tenants on the device (such as in cases where multiple customers are using the same private IP space 10.1.1.1/24). The suffix of the arbitrary number ensures that the two physically different networks terminating on the same physical device with the same IP space can be uniquely identified. This is discussed further in Section 4.1 of RFC 4364.

The previously defined VRF is then applied to an interface:

```
interface interface-id
 ip address ip-address subnet-mask
 ip vrf forwarding vrf-name
```

Note If an IP address is already configured on the interface, when you use the **ip vrf forwarding** *vrf-name* command, it removes the IP address from the interface and requires it to be reentered.

Before testing or sending traffic through the VRF instances, it is recommended that the router be rebooted after the VRF configuration is completed under an interface.

Further, if global SIP interface binding is added or modified in respect to a VRF, then SIP services need to also be restarted after the change is made. The following sequence of commands is used to restart the SIP process for this:

```
voice service voip
 sip
  call service stop
  no call service stop
```

These commands fail if there are active calls. To forcefully shut down the call service, including any active calls, the shutdown can be forced with the **forced** modifier, as shown here:

```
voice service voip
 sip
  call service stop forced
  no call service stop
```

The final step is to bind the signaling and media for the dial peer(s) that are intended to be used for this VRF to the interface that has already been assigned to the VRF. Binding control traffic to a different interface than media traffic is not supported when using VRF instances. The configuration for performing this binding is provided with the following commands:

```
dial-peer voice tag voip
 voice-class sip bind control source-interface interface-id
 voice-class sip bind media source-interface interface-id
```

Example 2-2 shows these configurations used together on two discrete VRF instances of a CUBE deployment, named **vrf1** and **vrf2**.

Example 2-2 *Configuration for Dial Peers with Multi-VRF Deployments*

```
ip vrf vrf1
 rd 1:1

interface GigabitEthernet1
 ip vrf forwarding vrf1
 ip address 192.0.2.1 255.255.255.0

dial-peer voice 100 voip
 voice-class sip bind control source-interface GigabitEthernet1
 voice-class sip bind media source-interface GigabitEthernet1

ip vrf vrf2
 rd 2:2

interface GigabitEthernet2
 ip vrf forwarding vrf2
 ip address 198.51.100.1 255.255.255.0

dial-peer voice 200 voip
 voice-class sip bind control source-interface GigabitEthernet2
 voice-class sip bind media source-interface GigabitEthernet2
```

> **Note** If you are using server groups (discussed later in this chapter) with multi-VRF deployments, it is important to make sure all destinations defined in the server group are routable from the outbound VRF. This is because the outbound dial peer is bound to a specific interface that is associated to a specific VRF.

If desired, port ranges for RTP and RTCP media can be assigned for each specific VRF by using the following command in the **voice service voip** sub-configuration:

```
media-address voice-vrf vrf-name port-range min-port max-port
```

Overlap of the port ranges with VRF instances is allowed, and if configured that way, those VRF instances will share the pool of available overlapping ports to whichever VRF needs it next.

SBC High Availability

When designing and operating an environment to support collaboration technologies, it is important to have a design that accounts for the possibility of various failures, and to also have resilience for continuous operation in such conditions. This section covers the various techniques for ensuring the availability that is expected or required for a particular business purpose.

When looking at high availability for SBC environments, the following general topics should be accounted for:

- **Hardware resiliency**—Multiple hardware modules are used in the same physical SBC instance, to allow for another module to take over service if there is hardware failure on a module. This may entail items such as processors, interfaces, power supplies, hard drives, or fans.
- **Clustering**—Multiple physical device instances are used to allow for another device to assume service responsibilities in the event of a device failure.

A general networking practice is to consider having resilience at multiple layers, when it is cost-effective and technically feasible to do so. Consider the following components when designing for resilience through an SBC network:

- **Interface resilience**—Ensure that a cabling path on a device has more than one physical connection, ideally through a diverse neighboring device, to protect against physical cabling failure. This concept should also apply to any WAN circuits that the design depends on.
- **Drive resilience**—Where possible and applicable in the SBC, ensure that the file system has resiliency. This could be provided through a RAID configuration for server-based SBCs, or also through deployment of a resilient storage array.

- **Module resilience**—Any critical components may need to be redundant where physically possible. Consider device resilience when module resilience is not feasible for critical components. However, it is important to assess for the impacts of the differences between intra-box and inter-box failover.
- **Device resilience**—Device resilience can be accomplished through clustering of device instances, presenting virtual addresses across multiple devices or chassis. Virtual addressing can be provided by HSRP, VRRP, and DNS, as well as other solutions within the applications' dial plans that allow for multiple devices/paths to be defined.
- **Geographic diversity**—Where possible and supported by the design, having a geographically diverse cluster of SBCs is ideal in the event of widespread failure in a physical location.
- **Provider diversity**—As with geographic diversity, where possible, consider having diversity of multiple providers for WAN circuits, PSTN providers, or ITSPs so that an issue with a single provider (which may affect multiple locations) doesn't result in a total outage for the dependent service.
- **Call routing resilience**—Where specific devices or paths may be unavailable, consider building in resilience at the call routing layer within the applications to account for alternate paths when there is signaling failure. This could be backup paths that route calls out another location or circuit type in the event of a failure or timeout in the primary call routing path.

When deciding where to invest in resiliency, it is important to note at the various layers of the service infrastructure that there are many layers of resiliency. Such layers of resilience must be accounted for to understand the overall impacts to the service when a component/device fails. The impacts of a failure differ depending on the type of component that is failing. Some components have failover mechanisms that are completely transparent to the service, whereas other component failovers may result in temporary degradation or disruption to the service. Specific items to consider when designing for availability of an SBC and understanding potential impacts of a failure include understanding the following:

- Is call signaling preserved after a failover?
- What are the impacts to SIP Re-INVITEs for existing calls during a failure?
- What are the impacts to SIP OPTIONS keepalives during the failure?
- Is media for active calls preserved after a failover?
- What is the recovery time between failure detection and the ability for the standby component to take on new services?
- What is the impact to overall capacity of the platform in the various failure scenarios?
- If signaling isn't preserved with a failover, how are calls cleared after completion?

The options for high availability in SBCs are highly dependent on the product design; as a result, the options for designing highly available SBCs vary greatly from one SBC vendor to another. This section covers the options that are available specifically for the CUBE product to provide both internal and external resiliency. Regardless of the specifics that will be demonstrated for CUBE, many of these notions may also conceptually apply across other SBC products and vendors.

Before outlining the high availability types, a few components of the Cisco ASR architecture need to be explained first:

- **Route processor (RP)**—The route processor is where the SIP signaling traffic is processed for call setup, application of per-session policies, and teardown.
- **Embedded services processor (ESP)**—This processor handles the processing for the network data plane. This includes the baseline packet handling flows across interfaces, allowing packet flows to maintain the defined line rates for interfaces. RTP media flows through the embedded services processor after the call is set up.
- **IOS daemon (IOSd)**—This is a logical instance of the IOS firmware that runs as a discrete software process instance within IOS XE.

Three types of high availability are available in CUBE deployments:

- **Intra-box redundancy**—This is the ability for certain components in a physical device to provide resilience upon failure so that the device can still provide service. This includes route processor, service processor, and software process (IOSd) redundancy. The two methods for this are route processor redundancy (RPR) and stateful switchover (SSO).
- **Inter-box redundancy**—This is the ability for two physical boxes to be virtually clustered in an active/standby mode so that one router can assume responsibility in the event that the primary device fails. This function is performed thought either Hot Standby Router Protocol (HSRP) or redundancy groups (RGs).
- **External resiliency**—This involves concepts that allow for resilience of the external peers that an SBC is connecting with so that service isn't disrupted if a single peer has an issue. This approach encompasses call routing resilience through means such as multiple trunk configurations and concepts of virtual addresses such as HSRP addresses and DNS SRV records.

When designing for high availability with CUBE, consider that the decisions you make may affect how the hardware scales for sizing. (Consult Chapter 8 "Scalability Considerations," for more information on sizing decisions.)

The options for redundancy capabilities vary based on both the series and the model of the hardware CUBE is running on. Table 2-3 shows the current redundancy supports for CUBE platforms as of the time of this publication.

Table 2-3 *Redundancy Capabilities for CUBE*

Family	Series	Intra-Box Redundancy		Inter-Box Redundancy	
		RPR	SSO	HSRP	Redundancy Groups
ISR G2	2900			X	
	3900			X	
ISR 4400	4000				X
ASR	1001		X (software)		X
	1002		X (software)		X
	1004		X (software)		X
	1006	X	X (hardware)		X
CSR	1000v				X

Because the ASR 1006 supports multiple route processors, intra-box SSO is provided only by using hardware redundancy through two route processors—and not through software redundancy. Also, inter-box and intra-box redundancy cannot coexist; only one of the two redundancy methods (either intra-box or inter-box) must be chosen and used for the deployment. If using inter-box redundancy with the ASR 1006, only one route processor is used in each chassis.

For all the CUBE redundancy modes that are discussed further in this chapter, only SIP calls are supported.

Note CUBE supports high availability of calls where DSP resources with SIP-to-SIP calls have been invoked—in both intra-box and inter-box failover scenarios.

The following prerequisites apply for high availability to function with DSP-invoked calls:

- DSP resources must be registered by using the local transcoding interface (LTI). See Chapter 5 "Media Processing," for more details on LTI configuration.
- Identical DSPs must be used on both the active and standby devices. Card quantity and density must match, and and the cards must be installed in the same slot/sub-slot.
- The **dspfarm** configurations must match between the primary and standby devices.

The following features are not supported in high availability scenarios where DSPs are invoked for the affected calls:

- SDP passthrough calls
- Transrated calls (see Chapter 5)
- Call progress analysis (see Chapter 12)
- Noise reduction and acoustic shock protection
- Media resources registered by using SCCP (see Chapter 5)

Checkpointing for Stateful Failover

To support stateful failover between components in a CUBE environment, the communication of state between the active and standby components is performed through a process called *checkpointing*.

Checkpointing supports SDP messages up to 6000 bytes and with up to 6 media lines (for example, **m=audio** and **m=video** lines) in the SDP. Checkpointing also supports media forked calls for call recording, as long as media is flowing through CUBE.

When checkpointing across two physical chassis, checkpointing is done across the data plane and through a dedicated LAN connection.

The following restrictions exist with checkpointing:

- Calls that are handled by a non-default session application (TCL/VXML) through the presence of the **service** command under a dial peer will not be checkpointed until after the call has been connected on both legs.
- Some checkpoint data in supported conditions may not have been sent from the active to the standby device before the failure, due to the inherent time required to process, transmit, and consume the call state data across the redundancy pair. This can be seen especially during times when the call is in the middle of a signaling transaction. In such scenarios, preservation of the states of these calls cannot be guaranteed.

The risk of a call not being checkpointed is that after failover, the new active router may not be aware of the state of the call. Media may still be preserved and routed through the new active device, but signaling states may not be maintained. This can pose issues such as the external peers expecting responses to SIP session refresh re-INVITEs or a call in the middle of a transaction dialog expecting a response. When signaling states aren't maintained, there is also no external ability to know when the call is disconnected by the endpoints. These calls are cleared through the process of media inactivity, where the device detects when media are no longer still flowing for the call and then tears down the call. If media inactivity is not configured or is not relevant for calls such as media flow-around, the call entries stay in the CUBE active call list until they are manually cleared, and they continue to count toward active call counts and consume memory. These 'hung' calls can be cleared by an administrator with the following command:

```
clear call voice causecode q850-value id call-id
```

The *call-id* used in the command is obtained from the output of **show call active voice compact**, as shown in Example 2-3.

Example 2-3 *Using* **show call active voice compact** *to Obtain the Call ID* **redundancy states** *Output*

```
CUBE# show call active voice compact
A/O FAX T Codec type Peer Address IP R:
Total call-legs: 2
126523 ANS T74411 g711ulaw VOIP P4085551234 192.0.2.50:18724
126524 ORG T74411 g711ulaw VOIP P1001 198.51.100.50.:21284
```

In Example 2-3, the call ID **126523** is highlighted; it represents a call from **4085551234**, as indicated by the **Peer Address** parameter.

The highlighted **T74411** value is the amount of time, in seconds, that the call has been active, which in this case is 74,411 seconds—or over 20 hours. The duration is a valuable parameter for identifying potentially hung call legs, given the assumption that real calls over a long duration such as 24 hours is atypical.

It is wise to check for any hung call entries after a high-availability event has been detected through monitoring. (See Chapter 14, "Monitoring and Management," for more information on proactively monitoring these types of events.) If these calls aren't cleared, the system will continue to consider them as active calls, which may affect decisions made by CAC, RSVP, and any other features that make decisions based on active call statistics.

Intra-box redundancy

Intra-box redundancy, also called in-box redundancy, is the ability for a single chassis to survive a software or hardware failure, specifically of the route processor. Before discussing the details of this, it is important to explore the key differences between the two failover types.

Types of Failover

There are two methods for providing intra-box redundancy across multiple processes within a box:

- Route processor redundancy (RPR)
- Stateful switchover (SSO)

With RPR, the standby route processor or software process does not maintain state synchronization. During a failure, the system switches to the standby instance. Active protocol state information is not passed to the secondary instance in this implementation, so any dynamic routing information and signaling states are lost.

SSO is an alternative to RPR. SSO allows for resilience in the event of a route processor failure or IOS failure within the same box. Line card, protocol, and application state information are synchronized from the active instance to the standby instance. For SSO to function, *redundancy pairs* must be defined. Upon a failure, switchover to the standby route processor is performed in a matter of seconds. There is no transit packet loss during this process because transit packets are handled by the forwarding plane (FP), which is part of the embedded services processor described earlier.

Note When software is being upgraded on the route processors, there is a period of time during which there is a software difference between the two route processors. If there is a version mismatch of software during a failure event, SSO cannot be performed, and the failover method used is downgraded to RPR, regardless of the SSO configuration.

Synchronization for SSO

To ensure the ability for states to be passed across the pairs in the redundancy pair for which SSO is enabled, the configuration needs to stay synchronized between the two instances. This is initially done through a *bulk synchronization*, and then it is maintained through *incremental synchronizations*.

Bulk synchronization is performed during initial configuration of SSO. The active route processor performs chassis discovery to determine the types of modules, cards, and interfaces present, and it also parses the configuration file. The active route processor then passes this data to the standby route processor and instructs the standby to perform the same initialization. Once this is complete, any configuration changes made on the active route processor are synchronized to the standby route processor.

Note Making configuration changes directly on the standby instance of the redundancy pair is not supported. All new configuration must be performed on the active instance.

To manually force a switchover, the **reload** command should not be used. Instead, use **redundancy force-switchover** to perform a manual switchover to the other device before performing disruptive actions such as reloading.

Upon system startup, the configuration from the active route processor is pushed over to the backup configuration. This overwrites the existing configuration on the backup system. The configuration is pushed to the other side during the following scenarios, which trigger bulk synchronization:

- When any of the following commands are executed:
  - `copy system:running-config nvram:startup-config`
  - `copy running-config startup-config`
  - `write memory`
  - `copy filename nvram:startup-config`
- **SNMP SET** of **ccCopyEntry** in the **CISCO_CONFIG_COPY** MIB is used
- The system configuration is saved by using the **reload** command
- The system configuration is saved following entry of a forced switchover command
- The standby router completes a reload

When the bulk synchronization is complete, incremental synchronizations then occur, based on the following events:

- Updates to routing protocol information
- Interface status changes
- Commands being entered from the active route processor

- Cisco Express Forwarding (CEF) updates to the forwarding information base (FIB)
- Chassis state changes such as line card insertion and removal

Note The synchronization of counters and statistics from the active route processor to the standby are not supported due to the performance issues with the rate of change and sheer amount of status data. This should be considered if monitoring appliances are polling standby nodes for statistics or when observing such statistics for calls that have been preserved from a failover.

Intra-Box Redundancy Options for ASR Platforms

Intra-box redundancy allows for providing resilience within a single chassis for failures. This feature is currently available only on CUBE for the ASR and is not available for the ISR and CSR platforms.

For the ASR platforms that don't support two separate route processors modules (1001, 1002, 1004), stateful failover can still be performed in software. Because IOS XE supports IOSd running as a separate process, two instances of IOSd can run on the same route processor in the chassis. If the active IOS process fails, the standby IOSd process can take over processing responsibilities. These redundancy methods are shown in Figure 2-8.

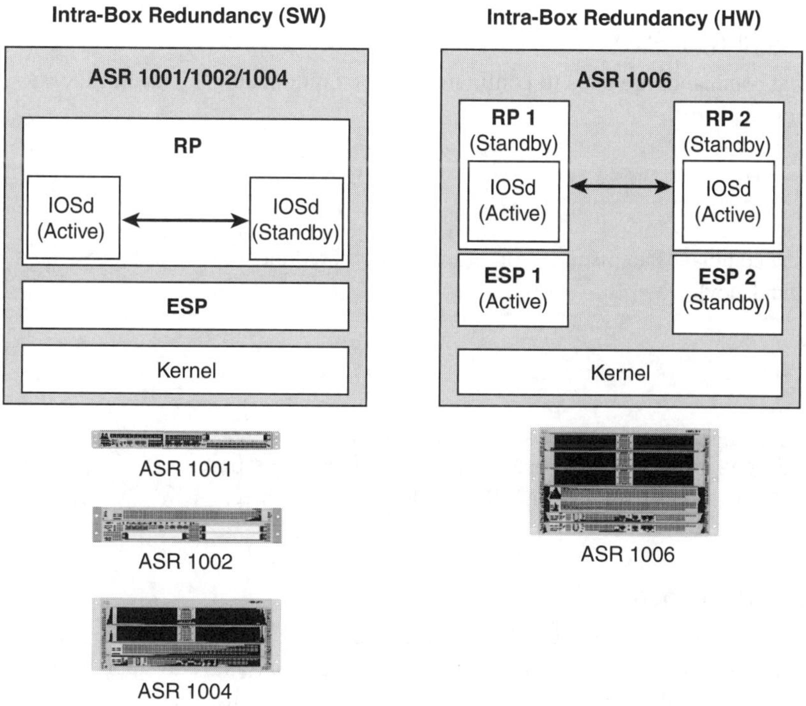

Figure 2-8 *Hardware and Software Redundancy for ASR 1000 Devices*

As opposed to the software redundancy approach noted above, intra-box hardware resilience is supported through the presence of a secondary route processor in the chassis for platforms that support it. The ASR 1006 is the only platform at the time of this publication to be supported by CUBE with this type of redundancy.

When there is a second route processor in a chassis, the secondary route processor is in a hot-standby state, and SSO or RPR is provided across this hardware redundancy between the primary and secondary processors. In the event that the active processor becomes unavailable, the secondary processor in the chassis takes over and maintains state in the conditions that SSO/RPR is documented to support.

The following capabilities are not supported during SSO scenarios of intra-box redundancy for redundancy pairs:

- SDP pass-thru (see Chapter 4, "Signaling Interworking")
- Alternative Network Address Types (ANAT) (see Chapter 5)
- SRTP-to-RTP interworking (see Chapter 6)
- SRTP pass-through (see Chapter 6)
- Resource Reservation Protocol (RSVP) (see Chapter 8)
- Call escalation and de-escalation of video capabilities in REFER consumption mode (see Chapter 12)

Configuration of RPR or SSO

The following commands are used to configure intra-box redundancy by using RPR (stateless redundancy):

```
redundancy
 mode rpr
```

The following commands are used to configure intra-box redundancy by using SSO (stateful redundancy):

```
redundancy
 mode sso
```

> **Note** For hardware redundant platforms, the standby route processor reloads when redundancy is initially configured by using the commands shown here.

Troubleshooting Redundancy

The first step when troubleshooting failover issues is to ensure that the hardware and software configurations between the two instances are identical. This only applies to platforms with hardware redundancy (ASR 1006), but it is important that they match; otherwise, synchronization will fail between the route processors.

Example 2-4 shows the output of **show redundancy states** after SSO is enabled but before a manual reboot is performed to complete the redundancy setup. Notice the **DISABLED** state for the peer.

Example 2-4 show redundancy states *Output*

```
CUBE1# show redundancy states
       my state = 13 -ACTIVE
     peer state = 1  -DISABLED
           Mode = Simplex
           Unit = Primary
        Unit ID = 48

Redundancy Mode (Operational) = Non-redundant
Redundancy Mode (Configured)  = sso
Redundancy State              = Non Redundant
     Maintenance Mode = Disabled
    Manual Swact = disabled (system is simplex (no peer unit))
 Communications = Down      Reason: Simplex mode

   client count = 109
 client_notification_TMR = 30000 milliseconds
           RF debug mask = 0x0
```

After a manual reboot of each device, the output of **show redundancy states** transitions to the states shown in Example 2-5, respectively being **ACTIVE** for the local state and **STANDBY HOT** for the device's peer's state.

Example 2-5 show redundancy states *After Reboot*

```
CUBE1# show redundancy states
       my state = 13 -ACTIVE
     peer state = 8  -STANDBY HOT
           Mode = Duplex
           Unit = Primary
        Unit ID = 48

Redundancy Mode (Operational) = sso
Redundancy Mode (Configured)  = sso
Redundancy State              = sso
     Maintenance Mode = Disabled
    Manual Swact = enabled
 Communications = Up

   client count = 109
 client_notification_TMR = 30000 milliseconds
           RF debug mask = 0x0
```

The application clients that support updating SSO can also be observed with **show redundancy clients**, as demonstrated in the abbreviated output displayed in Example 2-6.

Example 2-6 *Output of* **show redundancy clients**

```
Router# show redundancy clients
 clientID = 0        clientSeq = 0       RF_INTERNAL_MSG
 clientID = 29       clientSeq = 60      Redundancy Mode RF
 clientID = 139      clientSeq = 62      IfIndex
 clientID = 25       clientSeq = 69      CHKPT RF
 clientID = 1340     clientSeq = 90      ASR1000-RP Platform
 clientID = 1501     clientSeq = 91      Cat6k CWAN HA
 clientID = 78       clientSeq = 95      TSPTUN HA
 clientID = 305      clientSeq = 96      Multicast ISSU Conso
...
 clientID = 136      clientSeq = 290     IPSEC RF Client
 clientID = 130      clientSeq = 291     CRYPTO RSA
 clientID = 148      clientSeq = 296     DHCPv6 Relay
 clientID = 4000     clientSeq = 303     RF_TS_CLIENT
 clientID = 4005     clientSeq = 305     ISSU Test Client
 clientID = 93       clientSeq = 309     Network RF 2 Client
 clientID = 205      clientSeq = 311     FEC Client
 clientID = 141      clientSeq = 319     DATA DESCRIPTOR RF C
 clientID = 4006     clientSeq = 322     Network Clock
 clientID = 225      clientSeq = 326     VRRP
 clientID = 65000    clientSeq = 336     RF_LAST_CLIENT
```

Finally, the **show redundancy history** command is useful for determining why a switchover event has occurred (for example, a standby route processor being reset). This command should be entered from the newly active route processor. It has verbose output from each of the clients registered to SSO for having redundancy available but is useful output for Cisco support to use in diagnosing behavior. Example 2-7 shows an example of this output.

Example 2-7 *Abbreviated* **show redundancy history** *Output*

```
CUBE1# show redundancy history
...
01:01:09 RF_STATUS_OPER_REDUNDANCY_MODE_CHANGE(406) FMANRP CXSC RF Client(1348)
  op=7 rc=0
01:01:09 RF_STATUS_OPER_REDUNDANCY_MODE_CHANGE(406) Flow Metadata(255) op=7 rc=0
01:01:09 RF_STATUS_OPER_REDUNDANCY_MODE_CHANGE(406) RSVP SYNC(24112) op=7 rc=0
01:01:09 RF_EVENT_SLAVE_STATUS_DONE(523) Slave(3) op=406 rc=7
01:01:09 RF_STATUS_OPER_REDUNDANCY_MODE_CHANGE(406) Last Slave(65000) op=7 rc=0
01:01:09 RF_EVENT_SLAVE_STATUS_DONE(523) Last Slave(65000) op=7 rc=0
```

```
01:01:09 RF_STATUS_PEER_COMM(401) op=1 rc=0
01:01:09 RF_STATUS_PEER_COMM(401) First Slave(0) op=1 rc=0
01:01:09 RF_STATUS_PEER_COMM(401) Slave(3) op=1 rc=0
01:01:09 RF_EVENT_SLAVE_STATUS_DONE(523) First Slave(0) op=401 rc=1
01:01:09 RF_STATUS_PEER_COMM(401) Redundancy Mode RF(29) op=1 rc=0
01:01:09 RF_STATUS_PEER_COMM(401) IfIndex(139) op=1 rc=0
01:01:09 RF_STATUS_PEER_COMM(401) CHKPT RF(25) op=1 rc=0
01:01:09 RF_STATUS_PEER_COMM(401) Event Manager(77) op=1 rc=0
```

Inter-Box Redundancy

CUBE also supports inter-box redundancy (sometimes also referred to as box-to-box redundancy), in which state information is passed to a separate box. The ASR, CSR, and ISR G3 platforms support inter-box redundancy through the means of *redundancy groups*. Alternatively, the ISR G2 supports this capability through HSRP, which is discussed in the next section.

Note Geo-redundancy is not supported for inter-box redundancy. Both boxes must reside on the same Layer 2 network segment and within the same physical data center. The routers must also be identical models and hardware configurations, running the same version and software configuration.

It is important to note that inter-box redundancy cannot be enabled if intra-box redundancy is configured. For platforms where intra-box redundancy is supported, a decision must be made about whether intra-box or inter-box redundancy is desired. Inter-box redundancy offers more diverse protection over failures, as there is a completely separate hardware router acting as a standby. The disadvantages of inter-box redundancy are the cost of an additional router and introduction of some additional complexity for monitoring and management.

CUBE High Availability with HSRP

CUBE does not support the redundancy group configuration when deployed on the ISR G2, but it can still take advantage of CUBE high availability and media preservation as long as HSRP is configured.

HSRP leverages a virtual IP address that has primary and standby associations to two different devices. The status of what device is in active mode and what device is in standby mode is communicated through multicast. In an HSRP pair, if any interface on the active device goes down, the active device marks itself as inactive, and the standby device is promoted to an active state.

Figure 2-9 shows a basic HSRP configuration. In this diagram, **192.0.2.50** is the virtual IP address that would be presented to the remote SIP peers. Each CUBE also has a unique physical IP address, provisioned on the same network as the virtual HSRP IP address.

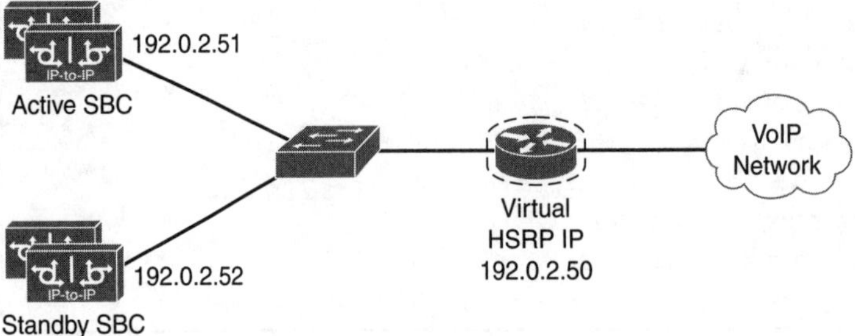

Figure 2-9 *HSRP for CUBE Resiliency*

When using HSRP for CUBE resiliency, the following caveats should be noted:

- There is no configuration synchronization between the two routers. Configuration replication must be done manually, but configurations should be identical across both routers in the HSRP pair, except for items exclusive to each individual device (such as the physical IP address configuration, which must be different on each device).
- Both routers should have identical hardware configuration.
- Both routers should have identical software loads.
- Only SIP–SIP call flows are supported.
- SIP transport must either be UDP–UDP or UDP–TCP.
- Only IPv4 addresses are supported.
- SIP must be bound to the virtual HSRP IP.
- Loopback interfaces are not supported.

Note that with HSRP, signaling states are not preserved after a failover, so supplementary services will not function for the preserved calls. This includes the following features:

- SIP session refresh (Re-INVITE)
- Video media stream
- Hold/resume
- Transfer
- Conference
- DTMF interworking (see Chapter 7)
- SIP–TLS (see Chapter 6)
- RSVP (see Chapter 8)

- STUN (see Chapter 13)
- RTP–SRTP conversion (see Chapter 6)
- Fax/modem (see Chapter 10, "Fax over IP (FoIP) and Modem")

The following section walks through the configuration of CUBE redundancy, using the topology for high availability outlined in Figure 2-10 as the basis for the deployment.

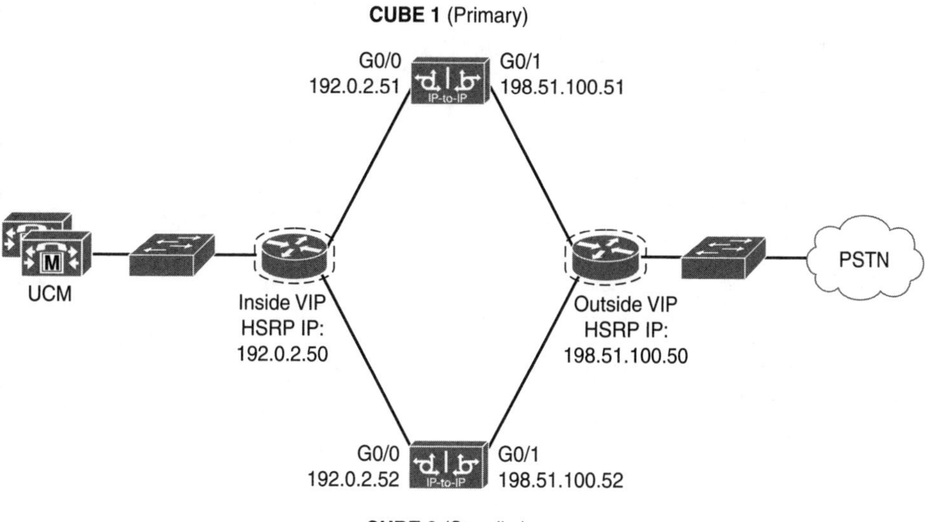

Figure 2-10 *Topology for CUBE High Availability*

Single-Interface Redundancy Configuration

The configuration provided in Example 2-8 is applied to each router of the intended redundancy pair to enable redundancy for CUBE.

Example 2-8 *CUBE Redundancy Configuration*

```
voice service voip
  redundancy
redundancy inter-device
  scheme standby SB
```

Next, HSRP is configured on each device. The configuration in Example 2-9 is for the first router. This can be repeated if multiple HSRP IP addresses across multiple interfaces on the same box are desired.

Example 2-9 *HSRP Configuration for the Primary CUBE*

```
ipc zone default
  association 1
    no shutdown
    protocol sctp
      local-port 5000
        local-ip 192.0.2.51
        exit
      remote-port 5000
        remote-ip 192.0.2.52

track 2 ip interface GigabitEthernet0/1

interface GigabitEthernet0/0
 ip address 192.0.2.51 255.255.255.0
 duplex auto
 keepalive
 speed auto
 standby delay minimum 30 reload 60
 standby version 2
 standby 0 ip 192.0.2.50
 standby 0 preempt
 standby 0 priority 50
 standby 0 track 2 decrement 10
 standby 0 name SB
```

Example 2-9 includes the following commands and parameters:

- **ipc zone default**—Enables interprocess communication (IPC), which allows for communication and synchronization of information across the redundancy pair and enters the sub-configuration for the protocol.
- **association 1**—Defines a unique instance with an identifier of **1** for association, for which sub-parameters will be defined.
- **protocol sctp**—Indicates to use Stream Control Transmission Protocol (SCTP) and enters the sub-configuration for the protocol.
- **local-port 5000**—Configures the local source port to be used for SCTP communication. This should match the port used on the remote router's remote port.
- **local-ip 192.0.2.51**—Defines the local IP address for the device to be used for communicating to the remote devices. This corresponds to the local physical interface from which SCTP traffic will source. A virtual IP address cannot be used. Up to two addresses can be defined, but they must be in the global VRF table.

- **remote-port 5000**—Configures the device's listening port for SCTP and is used for the communication that is coming from the remote device in the high availability pair. It should match the local port defined on the remote router.
- **remote-ip 192.0.2.52**—Defines the IP address of the remote device in the pair. If two addresses are defined here, they need to correspond to the same physical device and cannot be virtual IP addresses.
- **track 2 ip interface GigabitEthernet0/1**—Defines object group **2** for status tracking and associates GigabitEthernet0/1 to group 2. This allows for the HSRP group that will be defined with **standby 0** to watch the **GigabitEthernet0/1** interface as well. If **GigabitEthernet0/1**'s status is degraded, it also impacts the device's HSRP priority related to **GigabitEthernet0/0** (HSRP group **0**).
- **keepalive**—Enables the keepalive function, which sends messages across the connection to test the ability of the device to reach the shared Ethernet bus. These messages are sent every 10 seconds by default, with 5 retries before marking down. This process does not test remote connectivity to a peer but just integrity of the Ethernet adapter and wire.
- **standby delay minimum 30 reload 60**—Defines the time before initializing HSRP. This example sets the preemption delay to 30 seconds before becoming active again (applicable in situations when it should be promoted back to active). Specifically for a reload event, the device doesn't become active in the HSRP pair until 60 seconds after the interface link has restored. The default timer is no delay for preemption.
- **standby version 2**—Defines HSRP to be version 2, which offers communication enhancements over version 1. HSRP version 2 is more robust than version 1 due to enhancement such as advertising timer values, and as a result version 2 should be preferred in all scenarios where the software supports it.
- **standby 0 ip 192.0.2.50**—Defines HSRP group **0** and virtual IP address **192.0.2.50** for HSRP. This should be the same on the remote device.
- **standby 0 preempt**—Enables HSRP preemption for group **0**. This results in the device with the lower priority always being the active router when available. Preemption results in an additional switchover after the previously active router returns to availability, after previously being unavailable. When preemption is not enabled, when the old active route returns to availability, it will not force switchover until the currently active router becomes unavailable.
- **standby 0 priority 50**—Defines the local priority for HSRP to be **50** for HSRP group **0**. Higher values have preference.
- **standby 0 track 2 decrement 10**—Tells the HSRP group to watch the status of interface object group **2** that was defined earlier. For each interface in the HSRP group that goes down, the priority of the device will be decremented by the specified value, which in this case is **10**. Consider where this group has multiple interfaces; the priority for HSRP would be 50 (as defined in the **standby 0 priority 50** command

described in prior), but if one interface on this device goes down, the group's priority would decrease to 40 and become less desirable. If a second interface also went down, it would diminish to 30. This mechanism ensures that a router with more active interfaces is more desirable during contention for the primary HSRP role.

- **standby 0 name SB**—Defines a logical name for the standby group for ease of identification of the purpose. This name cannot be reused on other standby groups on the same router.

The configuration is then repeated on the second CUBE in the HSRP pair, as shown in Example 2-10.

Example 2-10 *HSRP Configuration for a Secondary CUBE*

```
ipc zone default
  association 1
    no shutdown
    protocol sctp
      local-port 5000
        local-ip 192.0.2.52
        exit
      remote-port 5000
        remote-ip 192.0.2.51

track 2 interface GigabitEthernet0/1

interface GigabitEthernet0/0
 ip address 192.0.2.52 255.255.255.0
 duplex auto
 keepalive
 speed auto
 standby delay minimum 30 reload 60
 standby version 2
 standby 0 ip 192.0.2.50
 standby 0 preempt
 standby 0 priority 50
 standby 0 track 2 decrement 10
 standby 0 name SB
```

Next, the media inactivity timeout should be configured on both gateways. Although the default is just RTP inactivity detection, the **all** keyword here changes such behavior, so that inactivity detection is performed with both RTP and RTCP. This ensures that sessions are cleared when RTP and RTCP are no longer being received from the remote peer for the media stream to indicate that the call is no longer active. This is important for clearing stale calls after call preservation, where signaling can no longer properly tear down a call.

By default, the gateway enables only RTP media silence detection for 20 minutes. Similarly, an RTCP timer is used, as there are scenarios where RTP may legitimately not be sent (for example, a call to voicemail or a conference call put on mute when voice activity detection [VAD]) is enabled). In these scenarios, although no RTP is sent, RTCP is still transmitted and used to keep the call considered alive. Therefore, it is generally beneficial to change the behavior to account for both RTP and RTCP media detection by using the command **media-inactivity-criteria all**. RTCP inactivity detection is not enabled by default but can be enabled and will consider an inactive call when no RTCP has been received for the defined timer duration. This expiration time is defined as the RTCP report transmission interval (**ip rtcp report interval**) multiplied by the number of missed RTCP messages (**timer receive-rtcp**).

If choosing to only use RTP media detection (or where **all** is used but there are devices that don't support RTCP), it is suggested that the **receive-rtp** timer for RTP be set to a high value above the maximum expectation of a call (for example, possibly 8 or 24 hours). Inactivity based on the RTCP-only criteria should be used only in an environment where there is confidence that all endpoints transmitting media support transmission of RTCP.

With the configuration in Example 2-11, a call would be disconnected when both of these criteria are met:

- No RTP has been received within 1 hour.
- No RTCP is received within 25 seconds (that is, 5000 ms × 5 seconds)

The RTP and RTCP timeout values can be appropriately tuned to best suit the call behavior in the supported deployment. This media inactivity configuration is provided in Example 2-11.

Example 2-11 *Configuring a Media Inactivity Timer*

```
ip rtcp report interval 5000
gateway
  media-inactivity-criteria all
  timer receive-rtp 3600
  timer receive-rtcp 5
```

Finally, dial peers are bound to the interface that HSRP has been configured for, as shown in Example 2-12.

Example 2-12 *Binding to the HSRP Interface*

```
dial-peer voice 1 voip
  voice-class sip bind control source-interface GigabitEthernet0/0
  voice-class sip bind media source-interface GigabitEthernet0/0
```

After these configurations have been made, both routers must first have their configurations saved, and then need to be reloaded. The reload must be performed before the CUBE pair will honor the HSRP configuration to service resilience. The configuration is saved and reloaded with execution of these commands:

```
copy running-config startup-config
reload
```

After the reboot of each device in the pair, the two devices in the HSRP pair can now communicate with each other through HSRP multicast packets to 224.0.0.2 to share state and current HSRP priority. The device with the higher priority will have preference. In the event of a tie, the device with the higher physical IP address will take priority. If preemption is defined, the device will take over the active role either immediately or potentially after a defined time delay. If preemption is not defined, the device may have higher priority but will not take over again until there is another significant event in which the current active router has a disruption.

Piecing together all the relevant commands shown so far, Example 2-13 shows the entire relevant configuration for high availability on the primary CUBE using HSRP, and Example 2-14 shows the configuration for the secondary CUBE.

Example 2-13 *Full High Availability Configuration for HSRP on the Primary CUBE*

```
voice service voip
  redundancy
redundancy inter-device
  scheme standby SB

ipc zone default
 association 1
  no shutdown
  protocol sctp
   local-port 5000
    local-ip 192.0.2.51
    exit
   remote-port 5000
   remote-ip 192.0.2.52

track 2 ip interface GigabitEthernet0/1

interface GigabitEthernet0/0
 ip address 192.0.2.51 255.255.255.0
 duplex auto
 keepalive
 speed auto
 standby delay minimum 30 reload 60
```

```
 standby version 2
 standby 0 ip 192.0.2.50
 standby 0 preempt
 standby 0 priority 50
 standby 0 track 2 decrement 10
 standby 0 name SB

ip rtcp report interval 5000
gateway
  media-inactivity-criteria all
  timer receive-rtp 86400
  timer receive-rtcp 5

dial-peer voice 1 voip
  voice-class sip bind control source-interface GigabitEthernet0/0
  voice-class sip bind media source-interface GigabitEthernet0/0
```

Example 2-14 *Full High Availability Configuration for HSRP on the Secondary CUBE*

```
voice service voip
  redundancy
redundancy inter-device
  scheme standby SB

ipc zone default
  association 1
    no shutdown
    protocol sctp
      local-port 5000
        local-ip 192.0.2.52
        exit
      remote-port 5000
        remote-ip 192.0.2.51

track 2 ip interface GigabitEthernet0/1

interface GigabitEthernet0/0
 ip address 192.0.2.52 255.255.255.0
 duplex auto
 keepalive
 speed auto
 standby delay minimum 30 reload 60
 standby version 2
```

```
 standby 0 ip 192.0.2.50
 standby 0 preempt
 standby 0 priority 50
 standby 0 track 2 decrement 10
 standby 0 name SB

ip rtcp report interval 5000
gateway
 media-inactivity-criteria all
 timer receive-rtp 86400
 timer receive-rtcp 5

dial-peer voice 1 voip
 voice-class sip bind control source-interface GigabitEthernet0/0
 voice-class sip bind media source-interface GigabitEthernet0/0
```

Troubleshooting High Availability

When troubleshooting high availability implementations, the first step is to ensure that the hardware configurations of the primary and secondary CUBEs are identical. Also, ensure that all relevant configuration is mirrored between the two CUBEs. Although there are individual configuration elements that must be different between the two configurations, such as each device's physical interface IP addresses, all CUBE-specific configuration, including **voice service voip** and **dial-peers**, should match across the two CUBE instances. This concept is especially critical to maintain with the HSRP deployment, as there is no automatic method to synchronize configurations across the devices.

Two useful commands for validating the status of redundancy are **show redundancy inter-device** and **show redundancy states**. If the output of **show redundancy inter-device** shows the pending scheme as **(Will not take effect until next reload)**, as shown in Example 2-15, the router still needs to be reloaded for the configuration to take effect.

Example 2-15 *Redundancy Status Before Reload*

```
CUBE1# show redundancy inter-device
Redundancy inter-device state: RF_INTERDEV_STATE_INIT
Pending Scheme: Standby (Will not take effect until next reload)
Pending Groupname: SB
Scheme: <NOT CONFIGURED>
Peer present: UNKNOWN
Security: Not configured
```

After the router is reloaded, the group state changes to **Init** on the standby router, as shown in Example 2-16.

Example 2-16 *Redundancy Status After Reload*

```
CUBE1# show redundancy inter-device
Redundancy inter-device state: RF_INTERDEV_STATE_PNC_NO_HSRP
Scheme: Standby
Groupname: SB Group State: Init
Peer present: UNKNOWN
Security: Not configured

CUBE1# show redundancy states
my state = 3  -NEGOTIATION
peer state = 13 -ACTIVE
Mode = Duplex
Unit ID = 0

Maintenance Mode = Disabled
Manual Swact = disabled (this unit is still initializing)
Communications = Up

client count = 14
client_notification_TMR = 30000 milliseconds
RF debug mask = 0x0
```

During the process of a switchover during an HSRP state change, when a standby router is in the process of becoming active, the status shown in Example 2-17 may be observed, where there is no peer unity detected.

Example 2-17 *Redundancy Status During Switchover*

```
CUBE1# show redundancy inter-device
Redundancy inter-device state: RF_INTERDEV_STATE_ACT
Scheme: Standby
Groupname: SB Group State: Active
Peer present: RF_INTERDEV_PEER_NO_COMM
Security: Not configured

CUBE1# show redundancy states
my state = 13 -ACTIVE
peer state = 1  -DISABLED
Mode = Simplex
Unit ID = 0

Maintenance Mode = Disabled
Manual Swact = disabled (system is simplex (no peer unit))
Communications = Up

client count = 14
client_notification_TMR = 30000 milliseconds
RF debug mask = 0x0
```

After the switchover but before the routers have exchanged *hello* status messages, the status is **RF_INTERDEV_PEER_NO_COMM**, as shown in Example 2-18.

Example 2-18 *Redundancy Output After Switchover and Before Hello*

```
CUBE1# show redundancy inter-device
Redundancy inter-device state: RF_INTERDEV_STATE_ACT
Scheme: Standby
Groupname: SB Group State: Active
Peer present: RF_INTERDEV_PEER_NO_COMM
Security: Not configured
```

After the exchange of hello status messages, the status changes to **RF_INTERDEV_PEER_COMM**, as shown in Example 2-19.

Example 2-19 *Redundancy Output After Switchover and After Hello*

```
CUBE1# show redundancy inter-device
Redundancy inter-device state: RF_INTERDEV_STATE_ACT
Scheme: Standby
Groupname: SB Group State: Active
Peer present: RF_INTERDEV_PEER_COMM
Security: Not configured

CUBE1# show redundancy states
my state = 13 -ACTIVE
peer state = 8  -STANDBY HOT
Mode = Duplex
Unit ID = 0

Maintenance Mode = Disabled
Manual Swact = disabled (peer unit not yet in terminal standby state)
Communications = Up

client count = 14
client_notification_TMR = 30000 milliseconds
RF debug mask = 0x0
```

The status of the HSRP state for the redundancy pair can be validated with the **show standby brief** command. Example 2-20 shows this command and its output on both active and standby devices.

Example 2-20 *Validating HSRP Status with* **show standby brief**

```
CUBE1# show standby brief
                     P indicates configured to preempt.
                     |
Interface    Grp  Pri P State   Active     Standby      Virtual IP
Gi0/0        0    50    Active  local      192.0.2.52   192.0.2.50

CUBE2# show standby brief
                     P indicates configured to preempt.
                     |
Interface    Grp  Pri P State   Active        Standby  Virtual IP
Gi0/0        0    50    Standby 192.0.2.51    local    192.0.2.50
```

After a switchover has taken place, the command **show voice high-availability summary** can be used to validate checkpointing, observe media inactivity, and determine what calls have preserved.

The total count of preserved calls is validated with the abbreviated output shown in Example 2-21. This output demonstrates a total of 150 active calls, with 70 calls active before the failover and preserved post-failover.

Example 2-21 *Validating Preserved Calls by Using* **show voice high-availability summary**

```
CUBE2# show voice high-availability summary
======== Voice HA DB INFO ========
Number of calls in HA DB: 100
Number of calls in HA sync pending DB: 50
Number of calls in HA preserved session DB: 70
...
```

Example 2-21 shows counts for the following call states:

- **Number of calls in HA DB**—These calls have entries in both the primary and standby devices and should be preserved during a failover event.
- **Number of calls in HA sync pending DB**—These calls have recently undergone a state change that has not synchronized to the standby router, and as a result they may not be preserved during a failover event.
- **Number of calls in HA preserved session**—These calls are not native to this device and were set up on the other device in the high availability pair that failed over during a high availability event. As a result, these calls are currently in

preservation mode. These calls would either be expected to be cleared after the call is completed through the detection of media inactivity, or they might instead be manually cleared by an administrator.

As demonstrated in the abbreviated output in Example 2-22, 70 calls have been cleared by media inactivity and disconnected.

Example 2-22 *Validating Preserved Call Count with Media Inactivity*

```
CUBE-2# show voice high-availability summary
...
======== Voice HA COUNTERS ========
Total number of checkpoint requests sent (Active): 171
Total number of checkpoint requested received (Standby): 70
Total CREATE received on Standby: 70
Total MODIFY received on Standby: 0
Total DELETE received on Standby: 0
Media Inactivity event count: 70
...
```

CUBE High Availability with Redundancy Groups

With the ASR, CSR, and ISR G3, a redundancy group allows for a pair of routers to share a virtual IP address. One router is active, and the other is in standby mode in regards to responding to the virtual IP address.

Redundancy groups behave very similarly to HSRP. With a redundancy group, there is communication from the control interface between both routers through *hello* and *keepalive* messages to determine the status and active member. A switchover can be triggered by any of the following: lack of a response to a hello message for the group, an event (such as a tracked interface going down) that changes the active device's priority to be lower than the standby device's priority, or the active router's priority falling below a specific threshold.

Configuration and call states are synchronized across the active and standby devices continually through checkpointing. This information is sent from the active router to the standby router using the data interface. The process of checkpointing requires a dedicated physical interface between the active and standby devices. This interface can only be used for checkpointing purposes, and it cannot have a VRF instance assigned to it. The use of a cross-over cable to directly connect the CUBE pair is not supported because a reboot will cause the link to go down on both routers. As a result, a LAN switch much be used to connect the two CUBEs in the pair (see Figure 2-11).

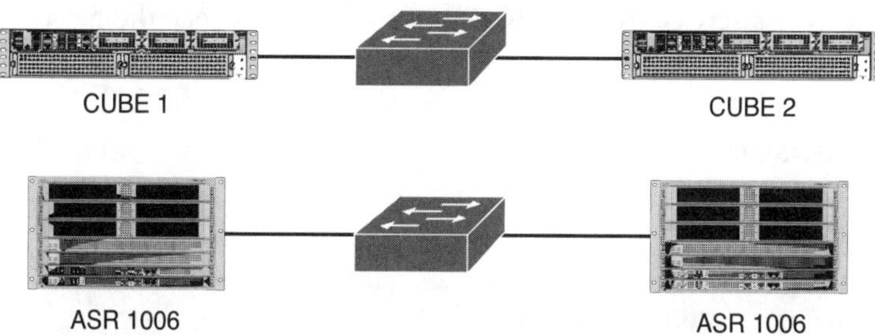

Figure 2-11 *Back-to-Back Connectivity for Redundancy Groups*

The default behavior when high availability is triggered is for the router to automatically reload. This allows for states to be cleared on the device that incurred the issue triggering the high availability event so that devices in the pair don't go out of synchronization. This helps prevent split-brain mode between the states across the two boxes after a failure.

If this auto-reload behavior is not desired, it can be disabled in favor of using protection modes. In this scenario, when auto-reload is disabled, the device does not restart but instead enters **PROTECTED** mode, where the following happens for this non-active box in the pair:

- Checkpointing is disabled
- Incoming call processing is disabled
- Bulk sync configuration requests between the pair are disabled

In order to transition the router out of the **PROTECTED** state, the router must be manually rebooted by an administrator.

The protected mode is useful in scenarios where administrators do not want the primary router to automatically reboot during the condition that triggers a failover to the second CUBE. A router in protected mode turns off CUBE high availability and checkpointing but still allows other services, such as routing and firewalls, to perform. The administrator can then control the timing of the reboot during reactive notification of the event and can perform manual intervention to reload.

A risk with protected mode is that there is no resilience in place after a failover event takes place upon first occurrence of the disruption. Service resilience will not be maintained for a subsequent event on the then-active router, until the non-active router (which is now in protected mode) is manually rebooted. Put in other words, when protected mode is enabled, the redundancy pair is in a single point of failure after first failure, until manual recovery action is taken on the standby router.

Due to the need for manual intervention with this design after a failure, it is suggested that protected mode be configured only when it is known that there would be additional detriment to non-voice services running over the top of the router pair during an unplanned reload of the primary side.

Redundancy Group Configuration

Figure 2-12 shows the topology for the redundancy group configuration that will be used to support the configuration examples for redundancy groups.

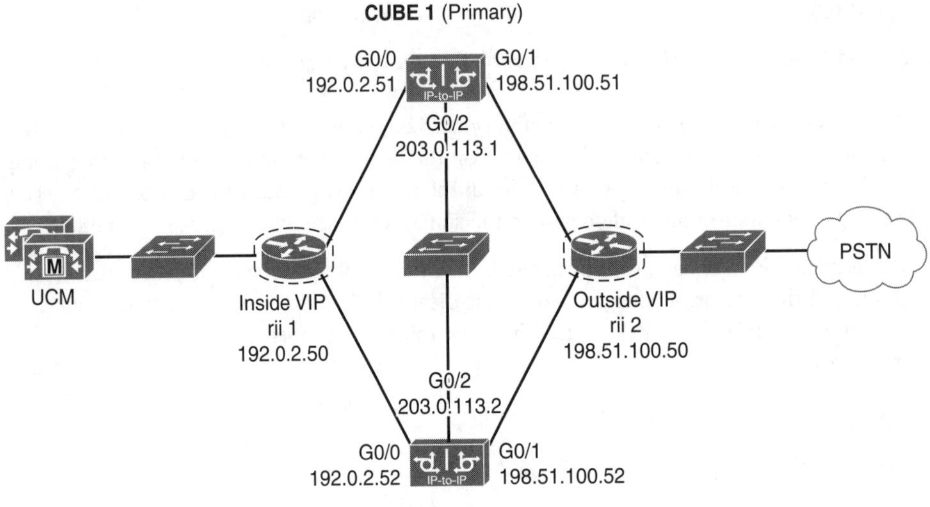

Figure 2-12 *Topology for CUBE High Availability by Using Redundancy Groups*

First, two separate redundancy groups are configured on the applicable inside and outside interfaces, as shown in Example 2-23.

Example 2-23 *Redundancy Group Interface Configuration*

```
interface GigabitEthernet0/0
  redundancy rii 1
  redundancy group 1 ip 192.0.2.50 exclusive

interface GigabitEthernet0/1
  redundancy rii 2
  redundancy group 1 ip 198.51.100.50 exclusive
```

The network interfaces are then configured for state tracking, as shown in Example 2-24.

Example 2-24 *Configuring Interface State Tracking*

```
track 1 interface GigabitEthernet 0/0 line-protocol
track 2 interface GigabitEthernet 0/1 line-protocol
```

Then redundancy mode is configured by disabling RPR/SSO redundancy and enabling application redundancy. A redundancy group is defined, and it is bound to the desired interface that is dedicated for the back-to-back connection to the other CUBE. The interface state tracking defined in the last step is also applied here. This portion of the configuration is demonstrated in Example 2-25.

Example 2-25 *Configuring Application Redundancy*

```
redundancy
 mode none
 application redundancy
 group 1
  name ha
  priority 100 failover threshold 75
  timers delay 30 reload 60
  control GigabitEthernet 0/2 protocol 1
  data GigabitEthernet 0/2
  track 1 shutdown
  track 2 shutdown
```

Note CUBE high availability is supported on interfaces with VRF instances assigned for any interface other than the peer link to the standby CUBE. The peer link interface cannot have any VRF assigned.

High availability is enabled for CUBE by associating the previously configured redundancy group, as shown in Example 2-26.

Example 2-26 *Enabling High Availability for CUBE*

```
voice service voip
 redundancy-group 1
```

Appropriate dial peers should then be bound to the desired interface that now has the high availability configuration, as shown with Example 2-27.

Example 2-27 *Binding the High Availability Interface to a Dial Peer*

```
dial-peer voice 1 voip
 voice-class sip bind control source-interface GigabitEthernet0/0
 voice-class sip bind control media-interface GigabitEthernet0/0
dial-peer voice 2 voip
 voice-class sip bind control source-interface GigabitEthernet0/1
 voice-class sip bind control media-interface GigabitEthernet0/1
```

Finally, it is a good practice to enable a media inactivity timer with this implementation, as shown in Example 2-28.

Example 2-28 *Media Inactivity Configuration*

```
ip rtcp report interval 5000
gateway
  media-inactivity-criteria all
  timer receive-rtp 86400
  timer receive-rtcp 5
```

With this configuration, the implementation forces a reload of the router when it transitions away from being the active router in the redundancy group. To disable the self-reload and use protected mode instead, you can use the commands shown in Example 2-29.

Example 2-29 *Disabling Self-reload for High Availability*

```
voice service voip
 no redundancy-reload
```

The entire configuration then needs to be replicated on the standby router, with the only deviation being that the IP addresses assigned to the interface are different addresses (but still on the same subnet).

The following examples show the consolidated configuration for high availability on both the active (see Example 2-30) and standby (see Example 2-31) CUBEs. The configurations define two redundancy groups (**rii 1** and **rii 2**). Notice that the only difference between the two configurations is the IP address assigned to the physical interface.

Example 2-30 *Full High Availability Configuration for the Primary CUBE with Redundancy Groups*

```
interface GigabitEthernet0/0
  redundancy rii 1
  redundancy group 1 ip 192.0.2.50 exclusive
  ip address 192.0.2.51 255.255.255.0
```

```
interface GigabitEthernet0/1
  redundancy rii 2
  redundancy group 1 ip 198.51.100.50 exclusive
  ip address 198.51.100.51 255.255.255.0
interface GigabitEthernet0/2
  ip address 203.0.113.1 255.255.255.0

track 1 interface GigabitEthernet 0/0 line-protocol
track 2 interface GigabitEthernet 0/1 line-protocol

redundancy
 mode none
 application redundancy
 group 1
  name ha
  priority 100 failover threshold 75
  timers delay 30 reload 60
  control GigabitEthernet 0/2 protocol 1
  data GigabitEthernet 0/2
  track 1 shutdown
  track 2 shutdown

voice service voip
 redundancy-group 1

dial-peer voice 1 voip
 voice-class sip bind control source-interface GigabitEthernet0/0
 voice-class sip bind control media-interface GigabitEthernet0/0
dial-peer voice 2 voip
 voice-class sip bind control source-interface GigabitEthernet0/1
 voice-class sip bind control media-interface GigabitEthernet0/1

ip rtcp report interval 5000
gateway
  media-inactivity-criteria all
  timer receive-rtp 86400
  timer receive-rtcp 5
```

Although the parameters here are similar to those for HSRP, the following differences in the configuration for redundancy groups should be noted:

- **redundancy rii 1**—Specifies the redundancy interface identifier (RII) for the interface. This must match on the interface on the other side of the redundancy group.
- **redundancy group 1 ip 192.0.2.50 exclusive**—Associates the interface with **rii 1**.
- **redundancy**—Enables redundancy configuration mode.

- **mode none**—Disables redundancy mode (for example, RPR/SSO), which is required for using application redundancy.
- **application redundancy**—Enables application redundancy mode and enters the sub-configuration.
- **group 1**—Specifies a redundancy group instance with an identifier of **1** and enters the sub-configuration mode.
- **name ha**—Specifies an optional name to be used as a description.
- **priority 100 failover threshold 75**—Defines the initial priority of the router as **100** and the threshold at which to trigger a failover as **75**. Higher priorities take preference.
- **timers delay 30 reload 60**—Defines the duration of delay before taking over the role as a primary as **30** seconds after a triggering event and **60** seconds if specifically triggered by a reload event.
- **control GigabitEthernet 0/2 protocol 1**—Specifies the control interface to be used for the redundancy group.
- **data GigabitEthernet 0/2**—Specifies the data interface to be used with the redundancy group.
- **track 1 shutdown**—Enables object tracking and tells the router to fail over during a status change on the object group. The alternative is to use the parameter **decrement** and define the value by which to reduce the priority when the interface goes down.
- **track 1 interface GigabitEthernet 0/0 line-protocol**—Defines the object tracking group **1** to watch for and trigger upon line-protocol changes to interface **interface GigabitEthernet 0/0**.

Example 2-31 shows the configuration for the secondary device.

Example 2-31 *Full High Availability Configuration for the Secondary CUBE with Redundancy Groups*

```
interface GigabitEthernet0/0
 redundancy rii 1
 redundancy group 1 ip 192.0.2.50 exclusive
 ip address 192.0.2.52 255.255.255.0

interface GigabitEthernet0/1
 redundancy rii 2
 redundancy group 1 ip 198.51.100.50 exclusive
 ip address 198.51.100.52 255.255.255.0

interface GigabitEthernet0/2
 ip address 203.0.113.2 255.255.255.0
```

```
track 1 interface GigabitEthernet 0/0 line-protocol
track 2 interface GigabitEthernet 0/1 line-protocol

redundancy
 mode none
 application redundancy
 group 1
  name ha
  priority 100 failover threshold 75
  timers delay 30 reload 60
  control GigabitEthernet 0/2 protocol 1
  data GigabitEthernet 0/2
  track 1 shutdown
  track 2 shutdown

voice service voip
 redundancy-group 1

dial-peer voice 1 voip
 voice-class sip bind control source-interface GigabitEthernet0/0
 voice-class sip bind control media-interface GigabitEthernet0/0
dial-peer voice 2 voip
 voice-class sip bind control source-interface GigabitEthernet0/1
 voice-class sip bind control media-interface GigabitEthernet0/1

ip rtcp report interval 5000
gateway
  media-inactivity-criteria all
  timer receive-rtp 86400
  timer receive-rtcp 5
```

Troubleshooting Redundancy Groups

The output of **show sip-ua handoff stats** helps in validating the number of calls that have been handed off successfully to the new active instance after a failover event. This command also demonstrates the number of calls that were not successful in handoff, as shown in Example 2-32.

Example 2-32 show sip-ua handoff stats *After a Failover Event*

```
CUBE1# show sip-ua handoff stats
Total Calls Handed Off        = 1
Successful Call Hand offs     = 1
Un-Successful Call Hand offs = 0
```

In addition, the output of **show voice high-availability rf-client** provides useful information about the current state of the high availability pair. Example 2-33 shows output from the primary instance, and Example 2-34 shows output for the standby instance.

Example 2-33 **show voice high-availability rf-client** *Output from the Active CUBE*

```
CUBE1# show voice high-availability rf-client
FUNCTIONING RF DOMAIN: 0x2
-----
RF Domain: 0x0
Voice HA Client Name: VOIP RF CLIENT
Voice HA RF Client ID: 1345
Voice HA RF Client SEQ: 128
My current RF state ACTIVE (13)
Peer current RF state DISABLED (1)
Current VOIP HA state [LOCAL / PEER] :
        [(ACTIVE (13) / UNKNOWN (0)]
-----
RF Domain: 0x2 [RG: 1]
Voice HA Client Name: VOIP RG CLIENT
Voice HA RF Client ID: 4054
Voice HA RF Client SEQ: 448
My current RF state ACTIVE (13)
Peer current RF state STANDBY HOT (8)
Current VOIP HA state [LOCAL / PEER] :
        [(ACTIVE (13) / PROTECTED (7)]
```

Example 2-34 **show voice high-availability rf-client** *Output from the Standby CUBE*

```
CUBE2# show voice high-availability rf-client
RF Domain: 0x0
Voice HA Client Name: VOIP RF CLIENT
Voice HA RF Client ID: 1345
Voice HA RF Client SEQ: 128
My current RF state ACTIVE (13)
Peer current RF state DISABLED (1)
Current VOIP HA state [LOCAL / PEER] :
        [(ACTIVE (13) / PROTECTED (0)]
-----
RF Domain: 0x2 [RG: 1]
Voice HA Client Name: VOIP RG CLIENT
Voice HA RF Client ID: 4054
Voice HA RF Client SEQ: 448
My current RF state STANDBY HOT (8)
Peer current RF state ACTIVE (13)
Current VOIP HA state [LOCAL / PEER] :
        [PROTECTED (7) / ACTIVE (13)]
```

External Resiliency

The sections of this chapter on high viability have explored the design and architecture to allow for resilience within the SBC or CUBE component itself. While providing resilience within the SBC is an important part of providing a highly available service, it is also critical that the SBC's external integrations be configured for resiliency.

When integrating with external peers, there are a few options for providing external resilience to the remote peer. There are two main approaches:

- **Using multiple trunks**—You can use alternate paths to the destination through the configuration of multiple call routes.
- **Using virtual address**—You can use a virtual IP address that logically represents multiple disparate destinations, such as through HSRP or through a DNS SRV record.

These concepts of providing resilience across multiple external destinations are further explored in the following sections.

External Peer Resilience with CUBE with Multiple Trunks

The simplest form of resilience for external peers is to configure multiple outbound call routes that are either logically or physically diverse. This helps ensure that if one of the peers goes down, there is still a route available to the intended destination of the call. Functionally, this is achieved by having outbound call routing configured with more than one external peer. When using multiple routes for a call, the multiple paths can either be all active, with the load distributed across the peers, or in an active/standby configuration.

When designing for high availability, it may also be desired to have diversity across providers for the multiple call routes. Special care should be taken when looking at failure points of the potential routes to ensure interface, circuit, provider, or geographic resilience. The decision on when to implement these layers of resilience is typically driven by if the resilient solution is cost-effective, or if resilience is required by the business services for compliance and/or service availability.

External Peer Resilience with CUBE with Multiple Dial Peers

For CUBE, outbound resilience involves configuring multiple dial peers that handle the same destination pattern. In Example 2-35, **dial-peer 1** is the primary route, and calls will only be sent out **dial-peer 2** if **dial-peer 1** becomes unavailable, such as through an **OPTIONS** keepalive.

Example 2-35 *Configuration for Resilience Through a Secondary Dial Peer*

```
dial-peer voice 1 voip
 destination-pattern 9T
 session target ipv4:192.0.2.50
 preference 1

dial-peer voice 2 voip
 destination-pattern 9T
 session target ipv4:192.0.2.51
 preference 2
```

The configuration shown in Example 2-35 routes all calls to **dial-peer 1**, as long as **dial-peer 1** is active.

Whether IOS attempts to route a call to a less-preferred dial peer depends on the call failure reason for the attempt out the first call. By default, IOS does not hunt on user busy (cause value 17) and no answer (19). The default hunt behavior for each cause code can be validated by consulting the default state of the command(s):

```
voice hunt cause-code
```

Dial peer hunting can be forced for all cause code scenarios with the following command:

```
voice hunt all
```

Note When defining multiple dial peers to offer resilience with external peers, it is important for the SBC to be able to mark the route unavailable as soon as it is capable of being detected as no longer providing service availability.

A method of marking a trunk unavailable is by using a SIP OPTIONS ping, as discussed later in this section.

Load balancing calls across multiple peers can be done by assigning equal preferences for destination patterns (see Example 2-36). Spreading the load across multiple devices reduces the failure domain in the event of an impacting event.

Example 2-36 *Configuration for Load Balancing Across Multiple Dial Peers*

```
dial-peer voice 1 voip
 destination-pattern 9T
 session target ipv4:192.0.2.50
 preference 1

dial-peer voice 2 voip
 destination-pattern 9T
 session target ipv4:192.0.2.51
 preference 1
```

A combination of these two techniques can also be deployed if there is a desire for a hybridization of both active/standby and load-balanced resiliency.

To observe or validate proper dial-peer matching when configured with multiple paths, the dial-peer selection can be observed in real time with **debug voice dialpeer inout**, as shown in Example 2-37.

Example 2-37 *Sample Output of* **debug voice dialpeer inout**

```
Oct  8 16:48:43.616: //-1/xxxxxxxxxxxx/DPM/dpMatchPeersCore:
   Calling Number=, Called Number=4085551234, Peer Info Type=DIALPEER_INFO_SPEECH
Oct  8 16:48:43.629: //-1/xxxxxxxxxxxx/DPM/dpMatchPeersCore:
   Match Rule=DP_MATCH_DEST; Called Number=4085551234
Oct  8 16:48:43.642: //-1/xxxxxxxxxxxx/DPM/dpMatchPeersCore:
   Result=Success(0) after DP_MATCH_DEST
Oct  8 16:48:43.642: //-1/xxxxxxxxxxxx/DPM/dpMatchSafModulePlugin:
   dialstring=NULL, saf_enabled=0, saf_dndb_lookup=0, dp_result=0
Oct  8 16:48:43.642: //-1/xxxxxxxxxxxx/DPM/dpMatchPeers:
   Result=SUCCESS(0)
   List of Matched Outgoing Dial-peer(s):
     1: Dial-peer Tag=1
     2: Dial-peer Tag=102
Oct  8 16:48:43.643: csimSetupPeer peer type(2), destPat(4085551234), matched(10),
  target()
Oct  8 16:48:43.684: //-1/xxxxxxxxxxxx/CCAPI/ccCallSetupRequest:
   Destination=, Calling IE Present=FALSE, Mode=0,
   Outgoing Dial-peer=1, Params=0x7FA9FFF00438, Progress Indication=NULL(0)
```

External Peer Resilience with CUBE with a Server Group

Fortunately, CUBE has a construct that allows for better flexibility than defining multiple dial peers to provide resilient destinations. It is possible to define a server group, as shown in Example 2-38:

Example 2-38 *Defining a Server Group*

```
voice class server-group 100
 ipv4 192.0.2.50 preference 1
 ipv4 192.0.2.51 preference 2

dial-peer voice 1 voip
 session server-group 100
```

As with dial peer preference values, multiple peers with an equal preference are chosen at random when they are an equal outbound match.

Further details on dial-peers, matching logic, and server groups are discussed in Chapter 3, "Call Routing."

External Peer Resilience with Virtual Addresses

The approach of using a unique dial peer for each potential target for all call route scenarios may not be tenable. Take the example of a large CUCM cluster, where there may be multiple (up to eight) servers that handle call processing in a cluster. In addition, a complex dial plan may have many outbound destination patterns to each cluster of servers. This becomes challenging from an administrative standpoint due to the large number of dial peers that need to be managed.

Fortunately, it is possible to provide virtual destinations with a unified logical address across multiple physical destinations. The two approaches for this are by either using a virtual IP address, or by using a DNS SRV record as defined in RFC 2782.

External Peer Resilience with Virtual IP Addresses

Look again at Figure 2-9, shown earlier in this chapter. In this figure, a virtual HSRP address 192.0.2.50 is configured for presentation, in front of the two physically separate CUBE instances that are addressed 192.0.2.51 and 192.0.2.52. If an external device routes calls to this pair of CUBEs, the route is configured to point to the virtual HSRP. This way, 192.0.2.50 is just virtually pointing to 192.0.2.51 in a normal state. If 192.0.2.51 goes down, 192.0.2.50 is still responsive because it is answered by the physical device assigned 192.0.2.52. The same concept of peering to a virtual IP address applies to other industry-standard approaches that provide inter-device IP resiliency, such as the open standard Virtual Router Redundancy Protocol (VRRP) that is defined in RFC 5798.

External Peer Resilience with a DNS SRV Record

A DNS SRV record is a special entry in a DNS server that allows for resolution of a specific service record for a domain name to resolve to another DNS A record or IP address. A common use for this is to define a generic domain name, such as **example.com**, where there is an underlying SRV record that resolves any requests for the SIP service for **example.com** to go to **mysipproxy.example.com**.

Destinations for call routes, such as through a session target in a dial peer, can point to a DNS SRV record. This provides external resilience of the destination for the routed call. SRV records are discussed further in Chapter 3, "Call Routing."

Summary

This chapter outlines the various deployments that drive the need for SBC integrations. It covers the various CUBE deployment options, including the software and hardware options currently available as of this publication, and notes the significant differences in feature sets across the assorted platforms.

This chapter also explores some design concepts that allow for multitenancy through the use of multi-VRF instances on a single CUBE instance, and it also outlines the various methods to design and configure a highly available SBC service.

This chapter provides the information you need in order to make decisions on whether and where an SBC should be used. It also describes the product offerings within the CUBE suite to support the capability and resilience needs of the intended communication network.

This chapter concludes the introduction section on SBCs. The following chapters explore the architecture, capabilities, and design for SBCs and specifics that pertain to CUBE.

References

- RFC 5798, "Virtual Router Redundancy Protocol (VRRP) Version 3 for IPv4 and IPv6," https://tools.ietf.org/html/rfc5798.
- RFC 6314, "NAT Traversal Practices for Client-Server SIP," https://tools.ietf.org/html/rfc6314.
- RFC 27824, "A DNS RR for Specifying the Location of Services (DNS SRV)," https://tools.ietf.org/html/rfc2782.
- "Call Processing: Unified CM Cluster Services," *Cisco Collaboration System 11.x Solution Reference Network Designs (SRND)*, https://www.cisco.com/c/en/us/td/docs/voice_ip_comm/cucm/srnd/collab11/collab11/callpros.html?bookSearch=true.
- "Cisco Preferred Architecture for Enterprise Collaboration 11.6, CVD," https://www.cisco.com/c/en/us/td/docs/solutions/CVD/Collaboration/enterprise/11x/116/collbcvd.html.
- Telecommunication Standardization Sector of ITU, "Series H: Audiovisual and Multimedia Systems. Infrastructure of Audiovisual Services—Systems and Terminal Equipment for Audiovisual Services. Packet-Based Multimedia Communications Systems (Recommendation H.323 12/09)," https://www.itu.int/rec/T-REC-H.323-200912-I/en.

Chapter 3

Call Routing

Taking advantage of a digital assistant ("Siri, call Cisco TAC") is now an easy way to call family, friends, and businesses. Though this engagement may seem simple, a plethora of technical operations are happening in the background to make this call routing magic occur. This chapter provides insights into how SBCs play a role in routing calls across enterprise and service provider networks.

This chapter consists of the following sections:

- **Dialing and Routing a SIP Call**—This section introduces dialing concepts based on telephone number and uniform resource identifiers (URIs). It also takes a detailed protocol-level look at how a SIP call originates and routes across SIP devices.
- **Call Routing Types**—This section discusses the differences between three types of call routing mechanisms: directory numbers, URIs, and the call request source.
- **Next-Hop Determination**—This section explores how SBCs choose the next hop after the call routing decision has been made.
- **Next-Hop Availability Check**—This section presents the need to proactively monitor the availability status of the next-hop devices to avoid call setup delays. It also shows how the SIP OPTIONS request can be leveraged to determine availability status.
- **End-to-End Call Trace**—This section describes how the Session-ID header field simplifies troubleshooting of complex call flows that traverse multiple devices.
- **CUBE Call Routing Mechanisms**—This section applies theoretical concepts in practice, using CUBE as an SBC example. This section explains the inner workings of CUBE, covering topics such as the dial peer matching process, translation profiles, call rerouting techniques, multitenant deployments, and dial peer optimization. Best practices and troubleshooting approaches are discussed using real-world scenarios.

Dialing and Routing a SIP Call

The most common way to place a call is to dial the telephone number associated with the entity the caller wishes to reach. The ITU-T E.164 standard defines the numbering structure that is used to assign unique telephone numbers to global subscribers and services. Each number can have a maximum of 15 digits, and the first 1 to 3 digits are used to identify the country in which the subscriber is located. The remaining digits are the national significant number (NSN), which consists of the national destination code (commonly referred to as the area code) and the subscriber number (see Figure 3-1).

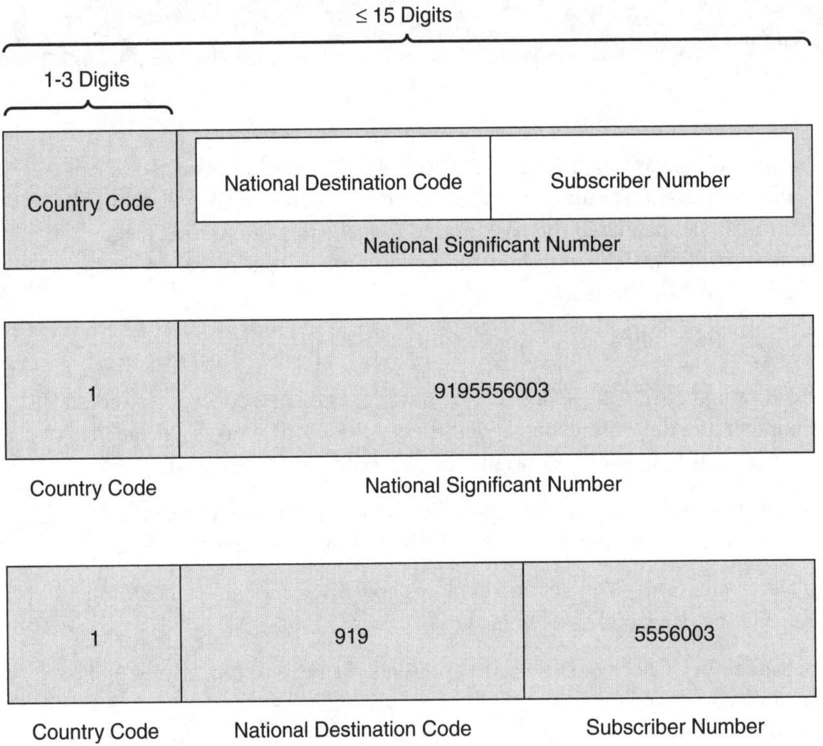

Figure 3-1 *E.164 Telephone Number Format and Example*

A SIP endpoint initiates a call by sending an INVITE request with the To and Request-URI header fields set to the SIP URI of the called entity. Example 3-1 shows the first line of a SIP INVITE message, beginning with the SIP method type (INVITE), followed by Request-URI, and ending with the SIP version (SIP/2.0).

Example 3-1 *SIP INVITE Message*

```
INVITE sip:14083926001@cl2-cucm-sub1.entcomp1.com;user=phone SIP/2.0
Via: SIP/2.0/TCP 10.118.58.68:55093;branch=z9hG4bK3cb3039b
From: "9193925002" <sip:9193925002@cl2-cucm-sub1@entcomp1.com>;
  tag=f45c89b76b25000b60fc9d5d-68bf7669
To: sip:14083926001@cl2-cucm-sub1@entcomp11.com
Call-ID: f45c89b7-6b250005-51d3d65a-2a9dd8ae@10.118.58.68
Max-Forwards: 70
Session-ID: 27e1afaa00105000a000f45c89b76b25;remote=00000000000000000000000000000000
Date: Sat, 25 Nov 2017 07:51:08 GMT
CSeq: 101 INVITE
User-Agent: Cisco-CSF
Contact: <sip:a1bc444e-89f9-dff1-da5e-f53872bbe521@10.118.58.68:55093;
  transport=tcp>;+u.sip!devicename.ccm.cisco.com="JabberClient1";video;bfcp
Expires: 180
Accept: application/sdp
Allow: ACK,BYE,CANCEL,INVITE,NOTIFY,OPTIONS,REFER,REGISTER,UPDATE,SUBSCRIBE,INFO
Remote-Party-ID: "9193925002" <sip:9193925002@cl2-cucm-sub1@entcomp1.com>;
  party=calling;id-type=subscriber;privacy=off;screen=yes
Allow-Events: kpml,dialog
```

The SIP URI consists of a user portion and a host portion. When the user initiates a call by dialing a telephone number, the SIP endpoint sets the user portion to the dialed telephone number, as shown in Figure 3-2. The host portion of the SIP URI is set to the host name or IP address of the SIP registrar where the caller's SIP endpoint is registered.

An alternative URI scheme is to use the tel URI to represent the telephone number of the called party. This approach avoids the need to specify the host portion. The telephone number could be a globally unique E.164 number routable across the PSTN (for example, 9193925002), as shown in Figure 3-2, a private number routable only within an enterprise (for example, 25002), or a number that has a local context (for example, emergency number 911, directory assistance number 411). RFC 3966 defines how the tel URI is formatted to represent the different types of numbers. The plus (+) character at the start of the telephone number indicates that the given number is a globally unique number (for example, **tel:+19193925002**), whereas the value of the URI parameter **phone-context** indicates the context in which a private number or a local number is valid (for example, **tel:25002;phone-context=entcomp1.com**). The hyphen (-) symbol is a visual separator to help easily read and remember the numbers (for example, **tel:+1-919-392-5002**); it is ignored in the call routing decision process.

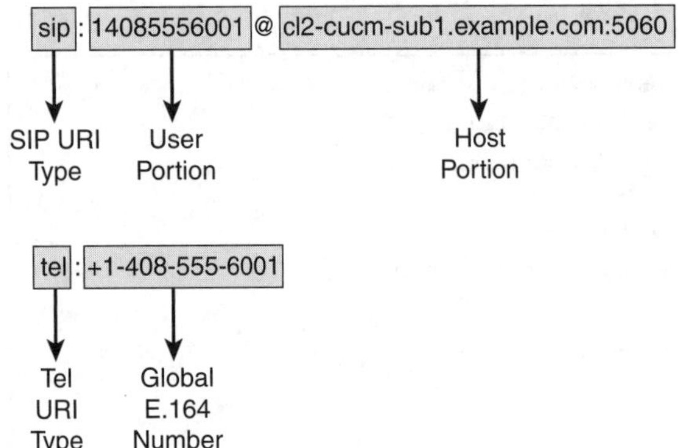

Figure 3-2 *sip and tel URIs for Telephone Number–Based Calling*

When a caller places an in-country call without specifying the country code (for example, 919-555-6003), the national destination code (919) of the telephone number is used in the initial call routing process to select the target SIP trunk, and the country code is implicitly the same country of the caller. In contrast, when a caller places an international call (for example, +1-919-555-6003), the country code (+1) is explicitly defined, and it plays a key role in the initial call routing decision.

With the introduction of end-to-end IP communications, people can now initiate audio and video calls just by specifying the URI of the called person. The URI is very similar to an email address format (that is, *username@domain*), as shown in Figure 3-3. In this case, the user portion of the SIP or SIPS (Secure SIP) URI is set to the called party's username in replacement of a telephone number, and the host portion is set to the domain name that corresponds to the destination entity.

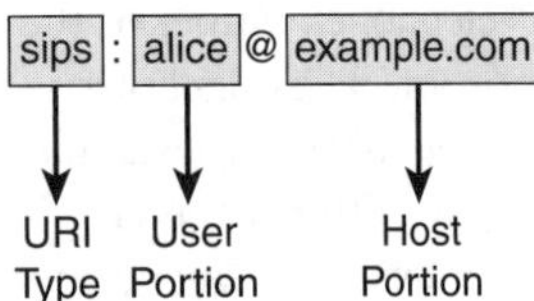

Figure 3-3 *sip URI for URI-Based Calling*

SIP INVITE Request Forwarding

Routing a SIP call is analogous to routing an IP packet: Each network device in the IP routing path analyzes the IP packet header content (such as the destination IP address), determines the next network hop, and forwards the packet to the next hop. When routing a SIP call, each call control device in the call routing path looks at the SIP INVITE's header field content (that is, the Request-URI), determines the next call signaling hop, and forwards the SIP INVITE request to the next hop.

The next hop of the SIP INVITE request is either a SIP intermediary or a final destination device. The intermediary could be one of the following:

- **SIP proxy—**Looks up the call routing table and forwards the request to the next hop.
- **Back-to-back user agent (B2BUA)—**Processes the incoming SIP INVITE and originates a new SIP INVITE request toward the final destination device. An SBC is an example of a B2BUA.
- **SIP gateway—**Processes the incoming SIP INVITE and originates a new call across the PSTN network, across analog or digital TDM circuits.

The final destination device for the SIP INVITE request could be one of the following:

- **SIP endpoint—**The IP phone used by the called party.
- **Application server—**The server that provides services such as voicemail, call recording, and fax.

Each SIP proxy that processes and forwards an incoming SIP request to the next hop adds a Via header field containing its transport address information. If one or more Via header fields already exist in the SIP request, the new Via header field is inserted at the top of the existing stack of Via header field. The Via header field stack has complete signaling path information when the SIP request reaches the final destination.

SIP INVITE Response Routing

The final destination SIP device terminates the SIP request, processes the request, and sends a final or provisional response to the transport address indicated in the topmost Via header field. The topmost Via header field contains the previous hop's transport address. When the response is received at a subsequent downstream SIP device, it first validates whether the response belongs to a request that it had sent earlier by comparing the transport address in the topmost Via header field to its own transport address and by performing additional checks, using header fields like CSeq. If the validation is successful, it strips off the topmost Via header field and then forwards the SIP response to the next downstream device indicated in the transport address of the new topmost Via header field. This process is repeated by each intermediary in the call signaling path until the SIP response traverses its way back to the SIP device that originated the SIP request. Figure 3-4 illustrates the processing of SIP requests and responses at SIP endpoints, proxies, and B2BUAs.

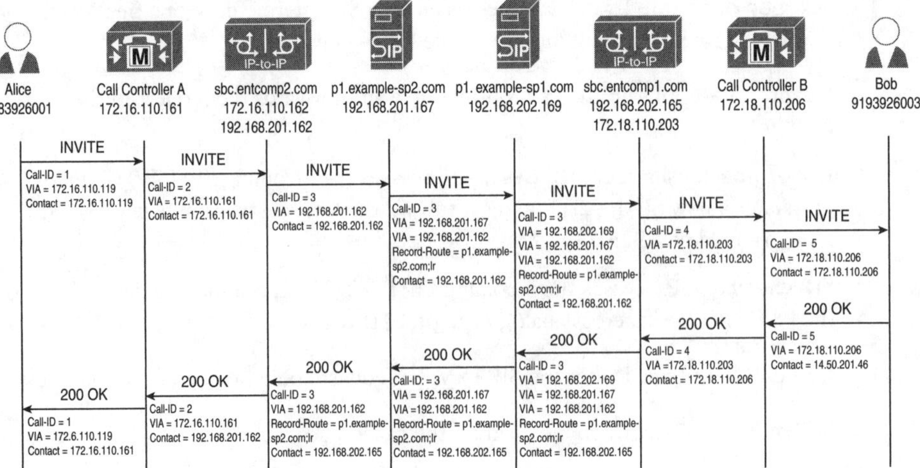

Figure 3-4 *Via and Record-Route Via Header Field Processing*

In Figure 3-4, Alice and Bob belong to two different enterprise companies, entcomp1 and entcomp2. Alice's SIP endpoint is registered to a SIP registrar within her company, and Bob's SIP endpoint is registered to a SIP registrar within his company. This example explains the routing procedure of a call originated from Alice (4083926001) to Bob (9193926003), where each company's registrar is an instance of Cisco Unified Communications Manager (CUCM).

CUCM also acts as the signaling plane back-to-back user agent (B2BUA, discussed in Chapter 1, "Laying the Groundwork"), meaning that it terminates the incoming SIP session from Alice's endpoint (Call-ID 1), makes a call routing decision, and originates an outgoing SIP session to the SBC (Call-ID 2). The B2BUA functionality enables the call controller to maintain the incoming SIP session and deliver supplementary services such as call hold, call transfer, and call forward by connecting the inbound SIP session to different destinations.

The SBC receives the SIP INVITE, makes a call routing decision, and routes the call across a SIP trunk to the SIP proxy of the service provider SP2 (p1.example-sp2.com). The SBC also acts as a media/signaling plane B2BUA (discussed in Chapter 1) and handles two call legs (Call-ID 2 and Call-ID 3) for the outbound external call. The SIP INVITE with Call-ID 3 traverses across p1.example-sp2.com and arrives at the proxy of service provider SP1 (p1.example-sp1.com), where entcomp1's company's telephone numbers are managed.

Each proxy adds its transport address information as a new topmost Via header field in the SIP INVITE and forwards to the next hop. The p1.example-sp1.com proxy delivers the SIP INVITE to the SBC of entcomp1 company (sbc.entcomp1.com), which terminates and re-originates a new SIP session (Call-ID 4) to the appropriate call controller (cl2-cucm-sub1.entcomp1.com) that manages registration of Bob's endpoint. The call controller functioning as SIP registrar and B2BUA originates the SIP INVITE (Call-ID 5) to Bob's endpoint.

Examples 3-2 through 3-6 show the content of the SIP INVITE request as it travels from Call Controller A in entcomp2 company to Call Controller B in entcomp1 via the SBCs and SIP proxies. (The message body of the SIP message is not shown for brevity.)

There are three individual SIP dialogs, each with its own Call-ID in this message sequence. The first dialog is between CUCM and SBC at entcomp2, the second dialog is between the SBCs at entcompl and entcomp2, and the third dialog is between the SBC and CUCM at entcomp1. Examples 3-3, 3-4, and 3-5 show how the Via header field is inserted at each hop as the SIP INVITE traverses from one SBC to another. Also, the Max-Forwards header field value is decremented at each hop. The purpose of this header field is to prevent an infinite call routing loop. When a SIP device gets an INVITE with Max-Forwards equal to 0 and the request needs to be sent to the next hop, it stops further forwarding and sends a 483 Too Many Hops as a final response.

Example 3-2 *SIP INVITE from CUCM to sbc.entcomp2.com*

```
INVITE sip:9193926003@sbc.entcomp2.com:5060 SIP/2.0
Via: SIP/2.0/TCP 172.16.110.161:5060;branch=z9hG4bK12b7b1dc851
From: <sip:4083926001@172.16.110.161>;tag=4662~4118cad0-3694-4ab3-9a80-
  dbb0d63408f3-23946266
To: <sip:9193926003@sbc.entcomp2.com>
Date: Fri, 01 Dec 2017 02:55:29 GMT
Call-ID: 1579ec00-a201c4a1-10a-a1caa8c0@172.16.110.161
Supported: timer,resource-priority,replaces
Min-SE:  1800
User-Agent: Cisco-CUCM12.0
Allow: INVITE, OPTIONS, INFO, BYE, CANCEL, ACK, PRACK, UPDATE, REFER, SUBSCRIBE,
  NOTIFY
Cseq: 101 INVITE
Expires: 180
Allow-Events: presence, kpml
Supported: X-cisco-srtp-fallback,X-cisco-original-called
Call-Info: <sip:172.16.110.161:5060>;method="NOTIFY;Event=telephone-
  event;Duration=500"
Call-Info: <urn:x-cisco-remotecc:callinfo>;x-cisco-video-traffic-class=DESKTOP
Session-ID: 000078f800105000a000000c298ea018;remote=00000000000000000000000000000000
Cisco-Guid: 0360311808-0000065536-0000000103-2714413248
Session-Expires:  1800
P-Asserted-Identity: <sip:4083926001@172.16.110.161>
Remote-Party-ID: <sip:4083926001@172.16.110.161>;party=calling;screen=yes;
  privacy=off
Contact: <sip:4083926001@172.16.110.161:5060;transport=tcp>;video;audio;
  +u.sip!devicename.ccm.cisco.com="JabberClient1";bfcp
Max-Forwards: 69
Content-Length: 0
```

Example 3-3 *SIP INVITE Terminated and Re-originated from sbc.entcomp2.com to p1.example-sp2.com*

```
INVITE sip:9193926003@entcomp1.com:5060 SIP/2.0
Via: SIP/2.0/TCP 192.168.201.162:5060;branch=z9hG4bK7D142
Max-Forwards: 68
To: <sip:9193926003@entcomp1.com>
From: <sip:4083926001@192.168.201.162>;tag=13D088E2-4BA
Contact: <sip:4083926001@192.168.201.162:5060;transport=tcp>
Expires: 180
Remote-Party-ID: <sip:4083926001@192.168.201.162>;party=calling;screen=yes;
  privacy=off
Call-ID: E1821D77-D57911E7-8249B2A0-6E96DC16@192.168.201.162
CSeq: 101 INVITE
Content-Length: 0
Date: Fri, 01 Dec 2017 02:55:10 GMT
Supported: timer,resource-priority,replaces,sdp-anat
Min-SE: 1800
Cisco-Guid: 0360311808-0000065536-0000000103-2714413248
User-Agent: Cisco-SIPGateway/IOS-15.6.1.S4
Allow: INVITE, OPTIONS, BYE, CANCEL, ACK, PRACK, UPDATE, REFER, SUBSCRIBE, NOTIFY,
  INFO, REGISTER
Timestamp: 1512096910
Allow-Events: telephone-event
Session-Expires: 1800
```

Example 3-4 *SIP INVITE Received by p1.example-sp1.com with a Record-Route Header field*

```
INVITE sip:9193926003@192.168.202.169:5060;transport=tcp SIP/2.0
Via: SIP/2.0/TCP 192.168.201.167:5060;branch=z9hG4bKRzUwlcSQ3rMWDN01cODE+Q~~50
Via: SIP/2.0/TCP 192.168.201.162:5060;branch=z9hG4bK7D142
Max-Forwards: 67
Record-Route: <sip:rr$n=sp2-network@p1.example-sp2.com:5060;transport=tcp;lr>
To: <sip:9193926003@entcomp1.com>
From: <sip:4083926001@192.168.201.162>;tag=13D088E2-4BA
Contact: <sip:4083926001@192.168.201.162:5060;transport=tcp>
Expires: 180
Remote-Party-ID: <sip:4083926001@192.168.201.162>;party=calling;screen=yes;
  privacy=off
Call-ID: E1821D77-D57911E7-8249B2A0-6E96DC16@192.168.201.162
CSeq: 101 INVITE
```

```
Content-Length: 0
Date: Fri, 01 Dec 2017 02:55:10 GMT
Supported: timer,resource-priority,replaces,sdp-anat
Min-SE: 1800
Cisco-Guid: 0360311808-0000065536-0000000103-2714413248
User-Agent: Cisco-SIPGateway/IOS-15.6.1.S4
Allow: INVITE, OPTIONS, BYE, CANCEL, ACK, PRACK, UPDATE, REFER, SUBSCRIBE, NOTIFY,
  INFO, REGISTER
Timestamp: 1512096910
Allow-Events: telephone-event
Session-Expires: 1800
```

Example 3-5 *SIP INVITE from p1.example-sp1.com to sbc.entcomp1.com*

```
INVITE sip:9193926003@192.168.202.165:5060;transport=tcp SIP/2.0
Via: SIP/2.0/TCP 192.168.202.169:5060;branch=z9hG4bKuqikwX.Yw24UpUvmEEXmdQ~~47
Via: SIP/2.0/TCP 192.168.201.167:5060;branch=z9hG4bKRzUwlcSQ3rMWDN01cODE+Q~~50
Via: SIP/2.0/TCP 192.168.201.162:5060;branch=z9hG4bK7D142
Max-Forwards: 66
Record-Route: <sip:rr$n=sp2-network@p1.example-sp2.com:5060;transport=tcp;lr>
To: <sip:9193926003@entcomp1.com>
From: <sip:4083926001@192.168.201.162>;tag=13D088E2-4BA
Contact: <sip:4083926001@192.168.201.162:5060;transport=tcp>
Expires: 180
Remote-Party-ID: <sip:4083926001@192.168.201.162>;party=calling;screen=yes;
  privacy=off
Call-ID: E1821D77-D57911E7-8249B2A0-6E96DC16@192.168.201.162
CSeq: 101 INVITE
Content-Length: 0
Date: Fri, 01 Dec 2017 02:55:10 GMT
Supported: timer,resource-priority,replaces,sdp-anat
Min-SE: 1800
Cisco-Guid: 0360311808-0000065536-0000000103-2714413248
User-Agent: Cisco-SIPGateway/IOS-15.6.1.S4
Allow: INVITE, OPTIONS, BYE, CANCEL, ACK, PRACK, UPDATE, REFER, SUBSCRIBE, NOTIFY,
  INFO, REGISTER
Timestamp: 1512096910
Allow-Events: telephone-event
Session-Expires: 1800
```

Example 3-6 *SIP INVITE Terminated and Re-originated from sbc.entcomp1.com to CUCM*

```
INVITE sip:9193926003@cl2-cucm-sub1.entcomp1.com:5060 SIP/2.0
Via: SIP/2.0/TCP 172.18.110.203:5060;branch=z9hG4bK4C18B4
Remote-Party-ID: <sip:4083926001@172.18.110.203>;party=calling;screen=yes;
  privacy=off
From: <sip:4083926001@172.18.110.119>;tag=F3C835D2-16F7
To: <sip:9193926003@cl2-cucm-sub1.entcomp1.com>
Date: Fri, 01 Dec 2017 02:55:29 GMT
Call-ID: EC66D137-D57911E7-81559A97-7107F84E@172.18.110.203
Supported: timer,resource-priority,replaces,sdp-anat
Min-SE:  1800
Cisco-Guid: 0360311808-0000065536-0000000103-2714413248
User-Agent: Cisco-SIPGateway/IOS-16.6.1
Allow: INVITE, OPTIONS, BYE, CANCEL, ACK, PRACK, UPDATE, REFER, SUBSCRIBE, NOTIFY,
  INFO, REGISTER
CSeq: 101 INVITE
Timestamp: 1512096929
Contact: <sip:4083926001@172.18.110.203:5060;transport=tcp>
Expires: 180
Allow-Events: telephone-event
Max-Forwards: 65
Session-ID: 49d42eda7be25e6a8f16b8bae1710bb1;remote=00000000000000000000000000000000
Session-Expires:  1800
Content-Length: 0
```

When Bob answers the call, Bob's endpoint builds the final 200 response and then sends it to Call Controller B. The response is then sent to sbc.entcomp1.com. Upon receipt of this response, sbc.entcomp1.com has the media information to send and receive media from Bob's endpoint. It then builds an outgoing 200 response by copying all the Via header fields from the incoming SIP INVITE request (Call-ID 3) and sets its external IP address (192.168.202.165) as the media address in the Session Description Protocol (SDP) section of the 200 response. It sends the 200 response to the transport address in the topmost Via header field, which is the IP address of the example-sp1 proxy (192.168.202.169).

The p1.example-sp1.com proxy processes the incoming response, removes the topmost Via header field, validates that the transport address in the removed Via header field is its own address, and sends the response to the transport address present in the current topmost Via header field. The p1.example-sp2.com proxy receives and forwards the response to entcomp2 company's SBC in a similar manner. This completes the traversal of SIP 200 response for the SIP INVITE (Call-ID 3). Now both SBCs have each other's IP addresses and port numbers and can transmit bidirectional media.

The SBCs sbc.entcomp1.com and sbc.entcomp2.com share their call signaling address using the Contact header field in the SIP request and response. This header field contains the SIP URI to be used to send subsequent SIP requests within the same dialog.

The sbc.entcomp2.com builds a new 200 OK response for the corresponding internal SIP session (Call-ID 2) with the media connection address set to its internal IP address (172.16.110.162) facing the Call Controller A; it then encodes this address in the SDP body of the 200 response and forwards it to the call controller. Upon receipt of the 200 OK response from the SBC, the call controller builds an outgoing 200 OK response for the inbound SIP dialog (Call-ID 1) and sends it to the originating endpoint. Now Alice's endpoint has the IP address and port number of the entcomp2's SBC, allowing for the media streams to be sent and received.

SIP Record-Route and Route Header Fields

SBCs at entcomp1 and entcomp2 directly exchange SIP requests to acknowledge the final response, keep the call on hold, resume the call, or disconnect the call. SIP proxies may not stay engaged in the call signaling path after the initial call setup process. In scenarios where the call path needs to be enforced to persist through a proxy device, such as for ensuring accountability for billing, a Record-Route header field in the SIP INVITE request is used. This header field is used to inform all upstream and downstream devices to include the SIP proxy in the call signaling path.

There are two types of request routing: strict routing and loose routing. *Strict routing*, defined in RFC 2543, is a process in which a SIP proxy sets the Request-URI to the SIP(S) URI of the next hop. RFC 3261 recommends *loose routing*, in which the Request-URI header field continues to represent the URI of the target destination as the request traverses one or more proxies and the proxy uses the topmost Route header field value to determine the next hop.

When a proxy receives a request, it validates the request, determines the request targets, makes a copy of the received request for each target, updates the Request-URI in the request copy with the URI of the target, decrements the Max-Forwards header field value by one, inserts a Record-Route header field if it wishes to be in the signaling path of future requests for the dialog created by this request, and inserts Route header field if the local policy requires the request to be routed across a given set of proxies prior to reaching the final destination.

The proxy then checks the topmost Route header field value in the request copy. If this Route header field value doesn't have the **lr** parameter, the proxy performs the strict routing process, in which it inserts the Request-URI value as the last value of Route header fields present in the request and replaces the Request-URI portion of the request with the topmost Route header field value and removes this topmost Route header field value. Basically, it sets the Request-URI to the SIP URI of the next hop. The proxy uses the Request-URI to determine the address, port, and transport type of the next hop and forwards the request to it. If the topmost Route header field value in the request copy has the **lr** parameter, the proxy performs the loose routing process in which the Request-URI remains unchanged, and it uses the topmost Route header field value to determine the address, port, and transport type of the next hop and forwards the request to it.

When the SIP device needs to send a subsequent SIP request within the same dialog, the Request-URI is set to the SIP URI of the target destination, and then the SIP URIs of the proxies to be visited are added to the SIP request as a sequence of Route header fields. The device sends the request to the call signaling address of the first proxy in the route list.

Example 3-4 shows a scenario in which the p1.example-sp2.com proxy inserts a Record-Route header field in the SIP INVITE, which is carried all the way to sbc.entcomp1.com and then returned back in the SIP 200 response all the way back to sbc.entcomp2.com. The origination and destination SIP devices retrieve the SIP URI of the proxies provided in the Record-Route header fields and store them as a list of routes in their internal memory. Subsequent requests and responses within this dialog are routed such that they traverse the proxies in the stored list.

Examples 3-7 through 3-11 show the content of the SIP 200 OK response as it travels from Call Controller B in entcomp1 company to Call Controller A in entcomp2 via the SBCs and SIP proxies. Examples 3-8, 3-9, and 3-10 show how the Via header field is processed and removed at each hop as the SIP 200 response traverses from one SBC to another. Note that some of the messages have a Via header field with multiple values concatenated instead of an individual Via header field for each value, which is indeed a valid SIP header field format. (The SDP body of the messages in Examples 3-7 through 3-11 is not shown for brevity.)

Example 3-7 *200 OK Response from CUCM to sbc.entcomp1.com*

```
SIP/2.0 200 OK
Via: SIP/2.0/TCP 172.18.110.203:5060;branch=z9hG4bK4C18B4
From: <sip:4083926001@172.18.110.119>;tag=F3C835D2-16F7
To: <sip:9193926003@cl2-cucm-sub1.entcomp1.com>;tag=71599~154a292d-1558-48b6-9155-
  e3e49acd9216-44381281
Date: Fri, 01 Dec 2017 02:55:29 GMT
Call-ID: EC66D137-D57911E7-81559A97-7107F84E@172.18.110.203
CSeq: 101 INVITE
Allow: INVITE, OPTIONS, INFO, BYE, CANCEL, ACK, PRACK, UPDATE, REFER, SUBSCRIBE,
  NOTIFY
Allow-Events: presence, kpml
Supported: replaces
Server: Cisco-CUCM11.5
Call-Info: <urn:x-cisco-remotecc:callinfo>;x-cisco-video-traffic-class=DESKTOP
Supported: X-cisco-srtp-fallback
Supported: Geolocation
Session-Expires:  1800;refresher=uas
Require:  timer
Session-ID: 8c8c368da411d8df347e57996aa71600;remote=49d42eda7be25e6a8f16b8bae1710bb1
P-Asserted-Identity: <sip:9193926003@172.18.110.206>
Remote-Party-ID: <sip:9193926003@172.18.110.206>;party=called;screen=yes;privacy=off
Contact: <sip:9193926003@172.18.110.206:5060;transport=tcp>;DeviceName="SEP1C17D340
  848C"
Content-Type: application/sdp
Content-Length: 413
```

Example 3-8 *200 OK Response from sbc.entcomp1.com to p1.example-sp1.com*

```
SIP/2.0 200 OK
Via: SIP/2.0/TCP 192.168.202.169:5060;branch=z9hG4bKuqikwX.Yw24UpUvmEEXmdQ~~47,SIP/
  2.0/TCP 192.168.202.167:5060;branch=z9hG4bKRzUwlcSQ3rMWDN01cODE+Q~~50,SIP/2.0/TCP
  192.168.202.162:5060;branch=z9hG4bK7D142
From: <sip:4083926001@192.168.202.162>;tag=13D088E2-4BA
To: <sip:9193926003@entcomp1.com>;tag=F3C83616-307
Date: Fri, 01 Dec 2017 02:55:29 GMT
Call-ID: E1821D77-D57911E7-8249B2A0-6E96DC16@192.168.202.162
Timestamp: 1512096910
CSeq: 101 INVITE
Allow: INVITE, OPTIONS, BYE, CANCEL, ACK, PRACK, UPDATE, REFER, SUBSCRIBE, NOTIFY,
  INFO, REGISTER
Allow-Events: telephone-event
Remote-Party-ID: <sip:9193926003@192.168.202.165>;party=called;screen=yes;
  privacy=off
Contact: <sip:9193926003@192.168.202.165:5060;transport=tcp>
Record-Route: <sip:rr$n=sp2-network@p1.example-sp2.com:5060;transport=tcp;lr>
Supported: replaces
Supported: sdp-anat
Server: Cisco-SIPGateway/IOS-16.6.1
Session-ID: 8c8c368da411d8df347e57996aa71600;remote=49d42eda7be25e6a8f16b8bae1710bb1
Session-Expires:  1800;refresher=uas
Require: timer
Supported: timer
Content-Type: application/sdp
Content-Disposition: session;handling=required
Content-Length: 255
```

Example 3-9 *200 OK Response from p1.example-sp1.com to p1.example-sp2.com*

```
SIP/2.0 200 OK
Via: SIP/2.0/TCP 192.168.202.167:5060;branch=z9hG4bKRzUwlcSQ3rMWDN01cODE+Q~~50,
  SIP/2.0/TCP 192.168.202.162:5060;branch=z9hG4bK7D142
Record-Route: <sip:rr$n=sp2-network@p1.example-sp2.com:5060;transport=tcp;lr>
To: <sip:9193926003@entcomp1.com>;tag=F3C83616-307
From: <sip:4083926001@192.168.202.162>;tag=13D088E2-4BA
Contact: <sip:9193926003@192.168.202.165:5060;transport=tcp>
Require: timer
Remote-Party-ID: <sip:9193926003@192.168.202.165>;party=called;screen=yes;
  privacy=off
Call-ID: E1821D77-D57911E7-8249B2A0-6E96DC16@192.168.202.162
CSeq: 101 INVITE
```

```
Content-Length: 255
Date: Fri, 01 Dec 2017 02:55:29 GMT
Timestamp: 1512096910
Allow: INVITE, OPTIONS, BYE, CANCEL, ACK, PRACK, UPDATE, REFER, SUBSCRIBE, NOTIFY,
  INFO, REGISTER
Allow-Events: telephone-event
Supported: replaces
Supported: sdp-anat
Supported: timer
Server: Cisco-SIPGateway/IOS-16.6.1
Session-ID: 8c8c368da411d8df347e57996aa71600;remote=49d42eda7be25e6a8f16b8bae1710bb1
Session-Expires: 1800;refresher=uas
Content-Type: application/sdp
Content-Disposition: session;handling=required
```

Example 3-10 *200 OK Response from p1.example-sp2.com to sbc.entcomp2.com*

```
SIP/2.0 200 OK
Via: SIP/2.0/TCP 192.168.202.162:5060;branch=z9hG4bK7D142
Record-Route: <sip:rr$n=sp2-network@p1.example-sp2.com:5060;transport=tcp;lr>
To: <sip:9193926003@entcomp1.com>;tag=F3C83616-307
From: <sip:4083926001@192.168.202.162>;tag=13D088E2-4BA
Contact: <sip:9193926003@192.168.202.165:5060;transport=tcp>
Require: timer
Remote-Party-ID: <sip:9193926003@192.168.202.165>;party=called;screen=yes;
  privacy=off
Call-ID: E1821D77-D57911E7-8249B2A0-6E96DC16@192.168.202.162
CSeq: 101 INVITE
Content-Length: 255
Date: Fri, 01 Dec 2017 02:55:29 GMT
Timestamp: 1512096910
Allow: INVITE, OPTIONS, BYE, CANCEL, ACK, PRACK, UPDATE, REFER, SUBSCRIBE, NOTIFY,
  INFO, REGISTER
Allow-Events: telephone-event
Supported: replaces
Supported: sdp-anat
Supported: timer
Server: Cisco-SIPGateway/IOS-16.6.1
Session-ID: 8c8c368da411d8df347e57996aa71600;remote=49d42eda7be25e6a8f16b8bae1710bb1
Session-Expires: 1800;refresher=uas
Content-Type: application/sdp
Content-Disposition: session;handling=required
```

Example 3-11 *200 OK Response from sbc.entcomp2.com to CUCM*

```
SIP/2.0 200 OK
Via: SIP/2.0/TCP 192.168.202.161:5060;branch=z9hG4bK12b7b1dc851
From: <sip:4083926001@192.168.202.161>;tag=4662~4118cad0-3694-4ab3-9a80-
  dbb0d63408f3-23946266
To: <sip:9193926003@sbc.entcomp2.com>;tag=13D0895E-1055
Date: Fri, 01 Dec 2017 02:55:10 GMT
Call-ID: 1579ec00-a201c4a1-10a-a1caa8c0@192.168.202.161
CSeq: 101 INVITE
Allow: INVITE, OPTIONS, BYE, CANCEL, ACK, PRACK, UPDATE, REFER, SUBSCRIBE, NOTIFY,
  INFO, REGISTER
Allow-Events: telephone-event
Remote-Party-ID: <sip:9193926003@192.168.202.162>;party=called;screen=yes;privacy=off
Contact: <sip:9193926003@192.168.202.162:5060;transport=tcp>
Supported: replaces
Supported: sdp-anat
Server: Cisco-SIPGateway/IOS-15.6.1.S4
Session-Expires:  1800;refresher=uas
Require: timer
Supported: timer
Content-Type: application/sdp
Content-Disposition: session;handling=required
Content-Length: 255
```

When the SIP device needs to send the next SIP request within the same session, the Request-URI is set to the SIP URI of the target destination, and then the SIP URIs of the proxies to be visited are added to the SIP request as a sequence of Route header field. The device sends the request to the call signaling address of the first proxy in the route list. In the example being discussed, sbc.entcomp2.com has only one SIP URI in the Route list, so it sends the ACK request to the transport address of p1.example-sp2.com and includes a Route header field. The proxy p1.example-sp2.com receives the request and looks up the topmost Route header field value and determines that it is its own SIP URI. As a result, it removes the topmost Route header field and sends the request to either the SIP URI of the next Route header field (if present) or to the final destination's URI, as shown in Figure 3-5.

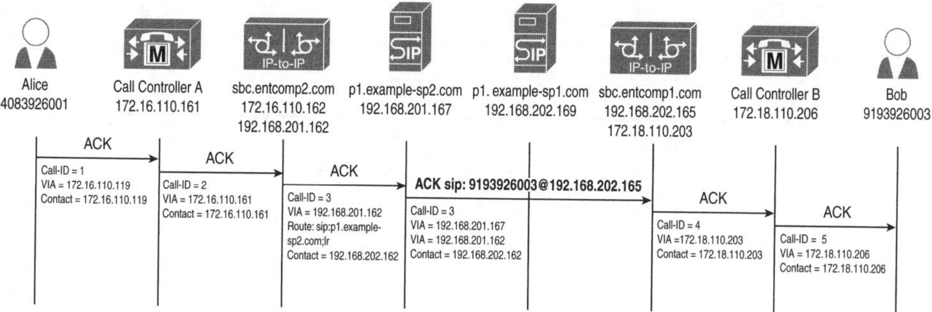

Figure 3-5 *Signaling Path of an ACK Request When Record-Route Is Used*

Examples 3-12 through 3-15 show the content of the SIP ACK request as it travels from call controller in entcomp2 company to call controller in entcomp1 via the SBCs and SIP proxies. Example 3-13 shows the **Route** header field inserted by sbc.entcomp2.com in the SIP request sent to p1.example-sp2.com proxy. This Route header field is processed and removed by p1.example-sp2.com and is no longer present in the SIP ACK forwarded to sbc.entcomp1.com as shown in Example 3-14. (The SDP body of the messages in Examples 3-12 through 3-15 is not shown for brevity.)

Example 3-12 *SIP ACK Request from CUCM to sbc.entcomp2.com*

```
ACK sip:9193926003@192.168.201.162:5060;transport=tcp SIP/2.0
Via: SIP/2.0/TCP 172.16.110.161:5060;branch=z9hG4bK12c21a33d9e
From: <sip:4083926001@172.16.110.161>;tag=4662~4118cad0-3694-4ab3-9a80-
  dbb0d63408f3-23946266
To: <sip:9193926003@sbc.entcomp2.com>;tag=13D0895E-1055
Date: Fri, 01 Dec 2017 02:55:29 GMT
Call-ID: 1579ec00-a201c4a1-10a-a1caa8c0@172.16.110.161
User-Agent: Cisco-CUCM12.0
Max-Forwards: 70
CSeq: 101 ACK
Allow-Events: presence, kpml
Session-ID: 000078f800105000a000000c298ea018;remote=62183134705badd6f462c9273bab4662
Content-Type: application/sdp
Content-Length: 229
```

Example 3-13 *SIP ACK Request from sbc.entcomp2.com to p1.example-sp2.com*

```
ACK sip:9193926003@192.168.202.165:5060;transport=tcp SIP/2.0
Via: SIP/2.0/TCP 192.168.201.162:5060;branch=z9hG4bK7E3E7
From: <sip:4083926001@192.168.201.162>;tag=13D088E2-4BA
To: <sip:9193926003@entcomp1.com>;tag=F3C83616-307
Date: Fri, 01 Dec 2017 02:55:10 GMT
Call-ID: E1821D77-D57911E7-8249B2A0-6E96DC16@192.168.201.162
Route: <sip:rr$n=sp2-network@p1.example-sp2.com:5060;transport=tcp;lr>
Max-Forwards: 70
CSeq: 101 ACK
Allow-Events: telephone-event
Content-Type: application/sdp
Content-Length: 255
```

Example 3-14 *SIP ACK Request from p1.example-sp2.com to sbc.entcomp1.com*

```
ACK sip:9193926003@192.168.202.165:5060;transport=tcp SIP/2.0
Via: SIP/2.0/TCP 192.168.201.167:5060;branch=z9hG4bKRzUwlcSQ3rMWDN01cODE+Q~~51
Via: SIP/2.0/TCP 192.168.201.162:5060;branch=z9hG4bK7E3E7
Max-Forwards: 69
To: <sip:9193926003@entcomp1.com>;tag=F3C83616-307
From: <sip:4083926001@192.168.201.162>;tag=13D088E2-4BA
Call-ID: E1821D77-D57911E7-8249B2A0-6E96DC16@192.168.201.162
CSeq: 101 ACK
Content-Length: 255
Date: Fri, 01 Dec 2017 02:55:10 GMT
Allow-Events: telephone-event
Content-Type: application/sdp
```

Example 3-15 *SIP ACK Request from sbc.entcomp1.com to CUCM*

```
ACK sip:9193926003@172.18.110.206:5060;transport=tcp SIP/2.0
Via: SIP/2.0/TCP 172.18.110.203:5060;branch=z9hG4bK4D206D
From: <sip:4083926001@172.18.110.119>;tag=F3C835D2-16F7
To: <sip:9193926003@cl2-cucm-sub1.entcomp1.com>;tag=71599~154a292d-1558-48b6-9155-
  e3e49acd9216-44381281
Date: Fri, 01 Dec 2017 02:55:29 GMT
Call-ID: EC66D137-D57911E7-81559A97-7107F84E@172.18.110.203
Max-Forwards: 70
CSeq: 101 ACK
Allow-Events: telephone-event
Session-ID: 49d42eda7be25e6a8f16b8bae1710bb1;remote=8c8c368da411d8df347e57996aa71600
Content-Type: application/sdp
Content-Length: 240
```

If the Record-Route header field isn't inserted by p1.example-sp2.com, then sbc.entcomp2.com sends the ACK request directly to sbc.entcomp1.com (192.168.202.165), as shown in Figure 3-6.

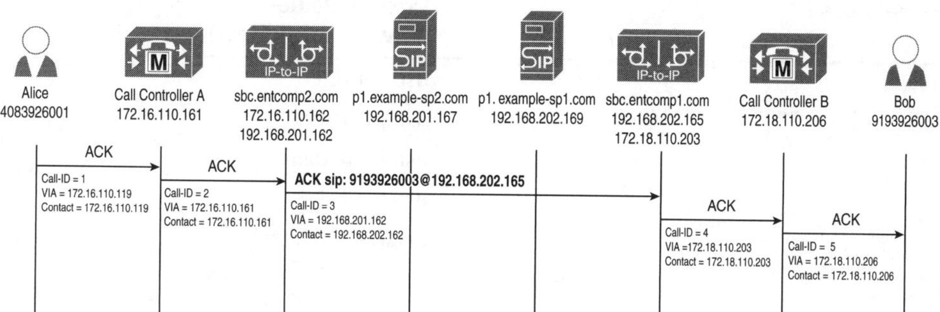

Figure 3-6 *Signaling Path of ACK Request When Record-Route Is Not Used*

The media stream associated with this call takes the path Alice's endpoint → sbc.entcomp2.com → sbc.entcomp1.com → Bob's endpoint. This bypasses the proxies in the service provider network.

Call Routing Types

The call routing process involves the logic of determining the next signaling hop for a given call. SBCs offer a high degree of configuration flexibility for the call routing decision process. Network administrators can use one or more call routing types to accommodate end-user dialing habits. This may include the use of telephone number transformations to send the correct calling and called number patterns expected by service providers and peer-to-peer business entities.

Call routing approaches can be categorized into different types based on which specific information in the incoming SIP INVITE is used to make the call routing decision:

- Directory number of the called person or system
- SIP URI of the called party (user, domain, or both of the SIP URI)
- IP address or host name of the previous-hop device
- Origination and destination trunk group
- Carrier identification code

RFC 4412 introduces the concept of preferential call treatment during emergency situations. The origination endpoint indicates the resource prioritization requested for a given call by using the Resource-Priority header field, whose value is a combination of the given namespace and the priority value defined within that namespace. RFC 4412 refers to five commonly used namespaces, which are listed in Table 3-1. An SBC typically passes through the Resource-Priority header field in the SIP INVITE and uses this value to determine whether it needs to route or reject incoming calls in time of network congestion or high system utilization.

Table 3-1 *Namespace and Priority Values Used in the Resource-Priority Header Field Value*

Namespace	Priority Values (Lowest to Highest)
DSN (Defense Switched Network)	dsn.routine dsn.priority dsn.immediate dsn.flash dsn.flash-override

Namespace	Priority Values (Lowest to Highest)
DRSN (Defense Red Switched Network)	drsn.routine drsn.priority drsn.immediate drsn.flash drsn.flash-override drsn.flash-override-override
Q.735 (Multi-Level Precedence and Preemption)	q735.4 q735.3 q735.2 q735.1 q735.0
ETS (Government Emergency Telecommunications Service)	ets.4 ets.3 ets.2 ets.1 ets.0
WPS (Wireless Priority Service)	wps.4 wps.3 wps.2 wps.1 wps.0

Directory Number–Based Routing

Directory number–based routing is the most commonly deployed mechanism for routing calls originated by SIP telephony endpoints and gateways. SIP gateways take the called number received in an analog or digital TDM call leg and map it to the user portion of the Request-URI header field of a SIP INVITE.

An SBC that receives this call parses the directory number (DN) of the called party present in the user portion of the Request-URI of the incoming SIP INVITE and applies any configured called number transformations. An example of this would be converting a direct-inward-dial number (9195556003) to an extension (56003). These number transformations can be performed by any device along the call signaling path that is consuming the call messaging. After the transformation process, the called DN is used as a key to look up call routing table to determine the next-hop device. This destination device could be a SIP proxy, a SIP gateway, a SIP B2BUA, or another SBC.

URI-Based Routing

URI-based routing has gained popularity with the widespread use of instant and persistent messaging applications. Each user in an instant messaging application is assigned an email address-like identity (for example, bob@entcomp1.com and alice@entcomp2.com). End users can easily transition from messaging to audio/video communication channel in a couple of clicks. SBCs provide the option to configure call routing based on the user part, the host part, or the entire pattern of the SIP URI.

For example, Alice (alice@entcomp2.com) starts the conversation with Bob by sending an instant message to Bob (bob@entcomp1.com). Alice then switches to a multimedia communication channel by clicking the Call button on her endpoint, which triggers the messaging client to initiate a call by sending a SIP INVITE with Request-URI set to **sip:bob@entcomp1.com** or **sips:bob@entcomp1.com**. The call controller to which Alice is registered routes the call to the SBC at entcomp2 company.

The SBC at **entcomp2** receives the SIP INVITE but is unaware of end users within entcomp1 company, and hence it cannot route the call based on the user portion of the Request-URI of the SIP INVITE. Instead, it parses the domain name from the host part of the SIP URI and uses it as a key to look up the call routing table and determine that the next signaling hop is entcomp1's SBC. This process of using the domain name to route calls, referred to as *domain-based call routing*, is the primary technique used to route URI-based outbound calls from one enterprise to another.

The SBC at **entcomp1** company receives the SIP INVITE from SBC at entcomp2, retrieves the SIP URI of the destination user from the Request-URI, and uses the user portion, the host portion, or the entire SIP URI pattern based on the configuration to determine the next hop. The call gets routed to Bob's endpoint and gets answered by Bob, and both users are connected in an audio/video call in addition to the instant messaging channel.

Source-Based Routing

Call routing decisions can also be made based on the criteria of the source of the call. SBCs can identify the source of an incoming SIP INVITE by using SIP Via header fields. The topmost Via header field in a SIP INVITE contains the transport address (the IP address or host name) of the previous signaling hop, and the bottommost Via header field contains the transport address of the device that originated the SIP session. Many of the SBCs in the industry provide the ability to use the IP address or host name of the previous signaling hop in the call routing process, in addition to the destination user's SIP URI.

This mechanism allows for the ability to filter call routing based on the source of the call, allowing for restricting or differentiated treatment of a call based on its source. For example, a service provider can ensure that a specific customer's calls are only routed to specific destinations.

This approach can be useful in scenarios where calls from certain sources, such as calls from agents in a contact center, need to be sent down a specific call signaling path different from the ones used by other calls.

Trunk Group–Based Routing

SIP gateways that accept calls from TDM trunks and originate SIP calls across SIP trunks can be configured to include information about the origination TDM trunk group in which the call was received. This information is inserted in the Contact header field of the SIP INVITE request sent by the origination SIP TDM gateway, as specified in RFC 4904.

SIP proxies can be configured to use origination trunk group information in the SIP INVITE during the call routing lookup process to determine the next hop and also to identify the destination trunk group through which the destination SIP TDM gateway must route the call. SIP proxies insert the destination trunk group information in the Request-URI header field of the SIP INVITE prior to forwarding the request to the next hop. SBCs are typically configured to pass through the origination and destination trunk groups. They can also be configured to route a call based on the source and destination trunk group information. Example 3-16 shows a SIP INVITE of a call that was originated from trunk group TG1 at ingress-gw.entcompl.com, as indicated in the Contact header field, and that is being routed to the destination trunk group TG2 at egress-gw.entcomp1.com, as specified by the **tgrp** and **trunk-context** SIP URI parameters of the Request-URI.

Example 3-16 *SIP INVITE with Origination and Destination Trunk Group Details*

```
INVITE sip:4083926001;tgrp=TG2;trunk-context=egress-gw.entcomp1.com@entcomp1.com
  SIP/2.0
Via: SIP/2.0/TCP 172.18.110.197:5060;branch=z9hG4bK27c45a2d0eb
Via: SIP/2.0/TCP 172.18.110.206:5060;branch=z9hG4bK27c45a2d0eb
Via: SIP/2.0/TCP 172.18.110.83:5060;branch=z9hG4bK27c12345
From: <sip:9193925020@ingress-gw.entcomp1.com>;tag=66278~154a292d-1558-48b6-9144-
  e3e49acd9216-44381219
To: <sip:4083926001@entcomp1.com>
Date: Sat, 23 June 2018 20:05:34 GMT
Call-ID: 855b2300-a1912987-c0-ce6e1456@172.18.110.83
Supported: timer,resource-priority,replaces
Min-SE:  1800
Allow: INVITE, OPTIONS, INFO, BYE, CANCEL, ACK, PRACK, UPDATE, REFER, SUBSCRIBE,
  NOTIFY
CSeq: 101 INVITE
Expires: 180
Session-Expires:  1800
Contact: <sip:9193925020;tgrp=TG1;trunk-context=ingress-gw.entcomp1.com@ingress-gw.
  entcomp1.com>
Max-Forwards: 68
Content-Length: 0
```

Carrier-Based Routing

The Carrier Identification Code (CIC) URI parameter was introduced in RFC 4694 to address the Number Portability (NP) use case, which enables routing of toll-free telephone numbers and routing of numbers that have been moved from one carrier to another.

When an end user originates a call to a toll-free number, a SIP network node in the subscriber's carrier/service provider performs a database lookup in the number portability database (NPDB) to find the ID of the carrier/service provider that serves the toll-free number. This ID is inserted in the Request-URI header field of the SIP INVITE request using the **cic** URI parameter.

SIP intermediaries such as SIP proxies and SBCs route the call based on the **cic** parameter until the call reaches the service provider identified in the **cic** parameter. The SIP network nodes within the destination service provider route the call based on the user portion of the SIP URI (that is, the toll-free number). Example 3-17 shows a SIP INVITE that corresponds to a call to 1-800-123-4567 that is serviced by a carrier whose identification code is 1234.

Example 3-17 *SIP INVITE with Carrier Identification Code*

```
INVITE sip:18001234567;cic=1234@example.com SIP/2.0
Via: SIP/2.0/TCP 172.18.110.206:5060;branch=z9hG4bK27c45a2d0eb
From: <sip:9193925002@172.18.110.206>;tag=66278~154a292d-1558-48b6-9166-e3e-
  49acd9216-44381219
To: <sip:18001234567;cic=1234@example.com>
Date: Sat, 23 June 2018 21:18:34 GMT
Call-ID: 855b2300-a1912987-c0-de6e1456@172.18.110.206
Supported: timer,resource-priority,replaces
Min-SE:  1800
Allow: INVITE, OPTIONS, INFO, BYE, CANCEL, ACK, PRACK, UPDATE, REFER, SUBSCRIBE,
  NOTIFY
CSeq: 101 INVITE
Expires: 180
Session-Expires:  1800
Contact: <sip:9193925002@172.18.110.206:5060;transport=tcp>
Max-Forwards: 69
Content-Length: 0
```

Next-Hop Determination

At the end of the call routing decision process, an SBC has one of the following parameters to establish communication with the next hop:

- IP address
- Host name

- Service domain
- Server group

The following sections discuss these parameters.

IP Address

In the most straightforward hop determination method, the SBC's call routing table is configured with the next hop's IPv4 or IPv6 address, protocol (for example, UDP, TCP, TLS), and port number. In the case of TCP and TLS, the SBC sets up the required connection and sends the INVITE across this connection, whereas in the case of UDP, the SBC sends the SIP INVITE as a connectionless UDP message.

Many SBCs also offer the ability to define a list of next-hop servers with IPv4 or IPv6 addresses and ports. SBCs can be configured to send SIP requests to the servers in a specified order. The order of server selection from the list can vary; common approaches include top-down selection from the list, selection based on a set weight, random selection, and round-robin selection.

Host Name

Specifying the next hop by providing its host name avoids the need to update the call routing table when the next-hop device is physically or virtually moved to another IP network space. SBCs use Domain Name System (DNS) to resolve the host name and determine the corresponding IP address. When the IP address of the next hop changes, the administrator of that next hop just needs to update DNS server entries, and no changes are required in the SBC configuration. This host name approach is commonly used in implementations due to the ease of administration. For example, Cisco CUBE could be configured to use the host names of individual call processing nodes of a CUCM cluster as next-hop devices for inbound calls to the enterprise and to use the host names of service provider proxies for outbound external calls.

Example 3-18 shows two types of DNS records configured in a DNS server (bind9) running in an Ubuntu Linux machine. The **A** record is used to define the mapping between IPv4 address and host name. The **AAAA** record is used to define the mapping between IPv6 address and host name.

Example 3-18 *DNS A and AAAA Resource Records*

```
cl2-cucm-pub    IN    A       172.18.110.205
cl2-cucm-sub1   IN    A       172.18.110.206
cl2-cucm-sub2   IN    A       172.18.110.207
cl2-cucm-pub    IN    AAAA    2001:db8:cafe:1:0:FFFF:8012:6ecd
cl2-cucm-sub1   IN    AAAA    2001:db8:cafe:1:0:FFFF:8012:6ece
cl2-cucm-sub2   IN    AAAA    2001:db8:cafe:1:0:FFFF:8012:6ecf
```

DNS SRV

A DNS Network Authority Pointer (NAPTR, RFC 2915) and service resource record (SRV) are useful when the SBC administrator doesn't know the exact IP address, protocol, and port number to be used for communicating with the next hop. With DNS SRV, an SBC's call routing table is configured with only the domain name of the next-hop device. A dynamic lookup is then performed on the domain name by an SBC to determine the address(es) that is responsible for processing the call requests for that specified domain.

NAPTR resource records provide information about the list of services such as SIP, H.323, and email that are available in a given domain. Example 3-19 shows three NAPTR records for the domain name example-sp1.com, with each of them pointing to SIP services indicated by **SIP+D2T** (SIP TCP service) and **SIP+D2U** (SIP UDP service). Each entry also has an associated DNS SRV value for each service, represented by the prefixes **_sip._tcp.** and **_sip._udp.** for each TCP and UDP entry respectively. Following is the list of NAPTR service field values applicable for SIP services:

- **SIP+D2U**—SIP over UDP
- **SIP+D2T**—SIP over TCP
- **SIP+D2S**—SIP over Stream Control Transmission Protocol (SCTP)
- **SIPS+D2T**—Secure SIP over Transport Layer Security (TLS)
- **SIPS+D2S**—Secure SIP over SCTP

Example 3-19 *DNS NAPTR and SRV Resource Records*

```
;Name             class type   order preference flags service    regexp replacement
example-sp1.com.  IN    NAPTR  10    50         "S"   "SIP+D2T"  ""     _sip._tcp.
                                                                        example-
                                                                        sp1.com.

example-sp1.com.  IN    NAPTR  20    50         "S"   "SIP+D2U"  ""     _sip._udp.
                                                                        example-
                                                                        sp1.com.

example-sp1.com.  IN    NAPTR  30    50         "S"   "SIPS+D2T" ""     _sips._tcp.
                                                                        example-
                                                                        sp1.com.



;_serv._proto.name           class type priority weight port host
_sip._tcp.example-sp1.com.   IN    SRV  10       20     5060 p1.example-sp1.com.
_sip._tcp.example-sp1.com.   IN    SRV  20       20     5060 p2.example-sp1.com.
_sip._udp.example-sp1.com.   IN    SRV  10       20     5060 p1.example-sp1.com.
_sip._udp.example-sp1.com.   IN    SRV  20       20     5060 p2.example-sp1.com.
_sips._tcp.example-sp1.com.  IN    SRV  10       20     5061 p1.example-sp1.com.
_sips._tcp.example-sp1.com.  IN    SRV  20       20     5061 p2.example-sp1.com.
```

Tip Wondering why the host name and SRV names end with a period (.)? If the period is not specified, the name is not fully qualified to the root domain. When the name isn't fully qualified, the DNS server automatically appends the server's domain name in an attempt to fully qualify the domain name.

For example, configuring **p1.example-sp1.com** sets the host name value to **p1.example-sp1.com.example-sp1.com**, whereas configuring **p1.example-sp1.com.** avoids the automatic domain name appending and properly sets the host name value to **p1.example-sp1.com**.

The SBC that is configured with a domain name (for example, example-sp1.com) as the next hop initiates a NAPTR query for the domain name and receives NAPTR resource records as a response, as shown in Figure 3-7. Each record has a **class**, an **order**, a **preference**, **flags**, a regular expression (**regexp**), and a **replacement** parameter. The SBC creates a list of records sorted in ascending order according to the **order** parameter value (for example, the record with the lowest-order value is the most preferred). Multiple records with the same order value are sorted using the preference, and then the regexp and replacement parameter values are used to find a matching record. A record is matched if it either has a replacement value or it matches the regexp value. The input value is replaced with the value in the **replacement** parameter. The complete NAPTR algorithm is documented in Section 4 of RFC 2915.

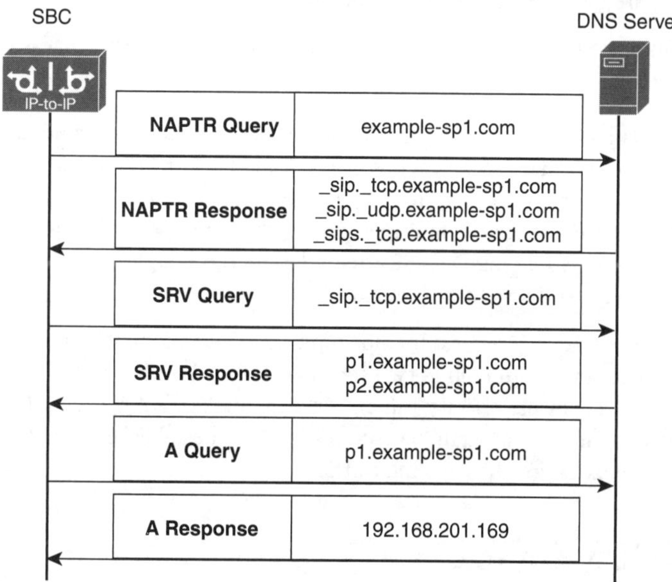

Figure 3-7 *DNS Lookup Process to Determine the Next Hop's Transport Information*

The **flag** value in the matched record is used to determine the next step:

- S—Initiate a DNS SRV lookup.
- A—Initiate an A, AAAA, or A6 lookup.
- U—Output is a URI, and a lookup is not required.

In the example shown in Figure 3-7, the SBC processes the NAPTR response and selects the record with the lowest **order** value (**10**) and a non-empty replacement parameter. It then replaces the input value **example-sp1.com** with **_sip._tcp.example-sp1.com** and sends a DNS SRV query for **_sip._tcp.example-sp1.com**.

DNS SRV records provide information about the host names and port numbers of the servers offering a given service. The DNS SRV record format, which is defined in RFC 2782, is as follows:

```
_Service._Proto.Name TTL Class SRV Priority Weight Port Target
```

The fields in the SRV format are defined as follows:

- **_Service**—The name of the service
- **_Proto**—The transport protocol used to communicate with the server
- **Name**—The domain name
- **TTL**—The Time to Live parameter, in seconds, which is used to determine how long the record can cached by the DNS client
- **Class**—DNS SRV resource records, which belong to resource record class INTERNET (**IN**) and are identified using code type SRV (**22**)
- **Port and Target**—Indicate the host name and the port number of the server that is providing the service

The **Priority** and **Weight** parameters play a key role in load balancing incoming requests across the servers and indicating which servers act as primary and backup. The record with the lowest priority value is the most preferred. If the service application administrator wants to load balance the requests across multiple servers, the **Priority** parameter is set to the same value in the corresponding DNS SRV records, and the **Weight** parameter values are set according to request distribution percentage.

When an SBC sends a DNS SRV query request for sip._tcp.example-sp1.com, it receives p1.example-sp1.com and p2.example-sp1.com as two servers offering this service. It prefers p1.example-sp1.com (the lowest priority value), performs an A or AAAA record lookup to determine the IP address of p1.example-sp1.com, and then establishes a TCP connection on port 5060 to exchange SIP signaling traffic.

Next-Hop Availability Check

SIP devices support three transport protocols: UDP, TCP, and SCTP. The retransmission mechanism that is used when there is no response to an INVITE from the next hop depends on the transport protocol chosen for use. TCP and SCTP provide reliable message delivery, whereas UDP does not. As a result, retransmissions for SIP messages are handled at the transport layer (OSI Layer 4) for TCP and SCTP, but the SIP application layer is responsible for retransmission of the SIP messages when UDP is used. This is shown in Figure 3-8.

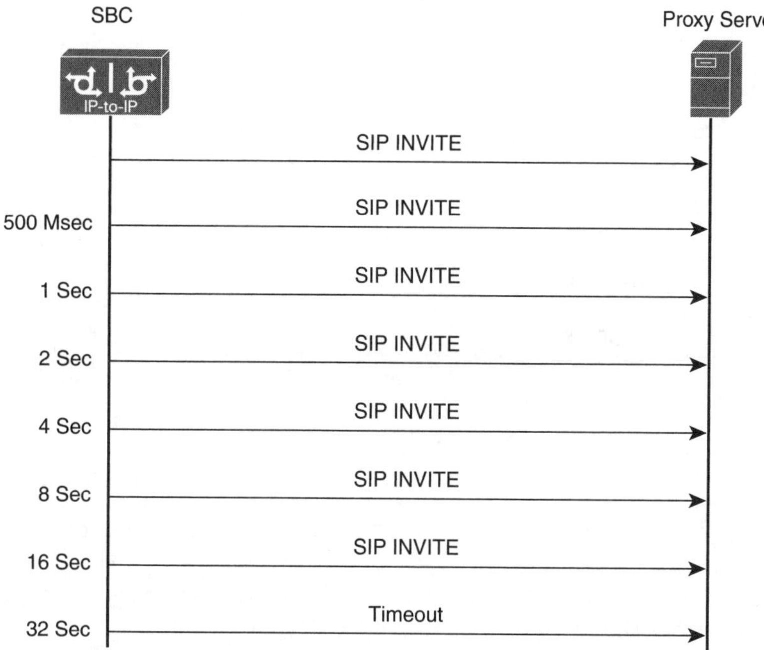

Figure 3-8 *Retransmission Process for SIP INVITE over UDP*

According to the procedure defined in Section 17.1.1 of RFC 3261 and using the recommended default timer values, an SBC re-sends the first SIP INVITE at time T1 (500 ms) and waits for a time duration of 2 × T1 (1000 ms) for a response. After 1000 ms, if there is still no response, another INVITE is sent, and the waiting time is doubled again, to 2000 ms (2 × 1000). This process repeats, with the waiting time doubled at each retransmission, until total waiting time has reached 64 × T1 (32 seconds). 32 seconds is a very long time to determine that the next hop is unavailable to process an incoming request—a long enough delay to result in a noticeable degradation of the caller's user experience.

SIP devices that use TCP as the transport protocol delegate the retransmission handling to the transport layer and also specify a maximum connection establishment wait time for the TCP stack. Section 5 of RFC 6298 describes the TCP retransmission process, in which unacknowledged TCP segments are re-sent using an exponential back-off algorithm by doubling the retransmission interval at each retry. Figure 3-9 shows an example of Cisco Unified Border Element (CUBE) initiating a TCP connection by sending a TCP SYN packet with SIP INVITE message in the payload. When it doesn't get a response, it re-sends the TCP SYN packet after 2 seconds. The next retransmission would happen at an elapsed time of 6 seconds (4 seconds after the previous SYN). Since the CUBE SIP application has set a maximum connection wait time of 5 seconds, the connection times out prior to the second retransmission. Even though next-hop unavailability with TCP is determined in a shorter time (5 seconds) compared to UDP (32 seconds), 5 seconds may still present an observable delay for a user making a call.

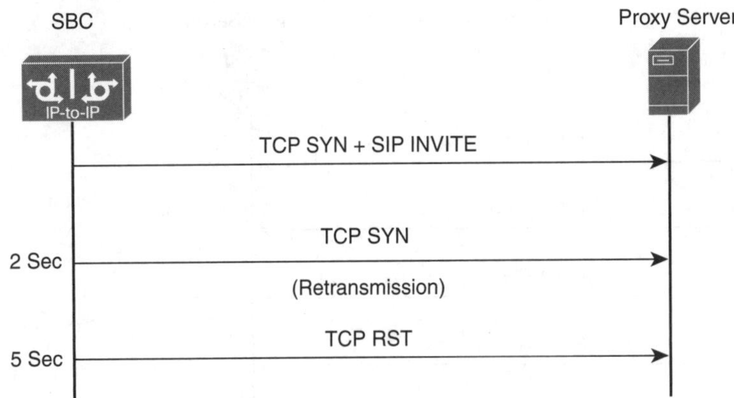

Figure 3-9 *Retransmission Process for SIP INVITE over TCP*

> **Note** It is completely valid to send data in the initial TCP SYN packet even before the TCP connection is established. This is explained in Section 3.4 of RFC 793, which requires the TCP connection receiver to buffer the data and deliver it to the receiving application after the connection is established.

SBCs leverage two primary mechanisms to proactively monitor and identify next hops that aren't available so that they can be excluded in the call routing decision process without relying on timeouts from TCP/UDP retransmission. The first mechanism, called out-of-band SIP OPTIONS (OOB SIP OPTIONS) ping, uses SIP signaling to determine whether the SIP stack at the next hop is active and available to accept incoming requests. The second mechanism, called ICMP ping, checks network connectivity to the next hop. It is recommended to use the OOB SIP OPTIONS ping mechanism as it provides availability verification at the SIP application level instead of verifying network connectivity up through OSI Layer 3 and also due to the fact that ICMP ping packets may be blocked in the network path.

SIP OPTIONS Ping

The SIP OPTIONS request was originally designed to query the capabilities of a SIP server such as a proxy server, a B2BUA, or an endpoint. It allows the originating SIP device to understand the next-hop capabilities prior to initiating a SIP INVITE request. This helps in structuring the INVITE message such that it uses only signaling and media-related functionalities that are supported by the next hop. For example, if the next hop doesn't support SIP PRACK (provisional acknowledgment), then it can avoid requesting reliable provisional response functionality by not including the **100rel** option (RFC 3262) in the Supported or Require header field of the SIP INVITE request sent to the next hop.

An interesting fact about OPTIONS is that the response code sent by the device processing the OPTIONS request is the same response code as if the request were a SIP INVITE. This enables the usage of OPTIONS to also check the call processing status of the next hop. The industry has since leveraged this response to extend the usage of OPTIONS to check the next-hop availability status at the SIP application layer level.

SBCs can be configured to periodically send SIP OPTIONS to next-hop devices. If there is no response for the SIP OPTIONS, then the next hop is considered to be down and is excluded from the call routing decision process. SBCs typically change the next-hop status back to active once they receive a 2XX or 4XX response. Though the use of SIP OPTIONS as a keepalive mechanism hasn't been standardized, an IETF draft (draft-jones-sip-options-ping-02) proposes guidelines about this process, such as using 503 Service Unavailable as a response to SIP OPTIONS to indicate that the server is unable to process additional requests.

Example 3-20 shows a SIP OPTIONS message received by CUBE from a CUCM subscriber node and its corresponding 200 response, with the SDP body containing CUBE's media capabilities. The example also shows the SIP OPTIONS sent by CUBE to one of the call processing nodes in the CUCM cluster and the 200 OK response received.

Example 3-20 *SIP OPTIONS Request and Response*

```
39396382: Jun 24 16:02:34.078 UTC: //-1/xxxxxxxxxxxx/SIP/Msg/ccsipDisplayMsg:
Received:
OPTIONS sip:cube1.entcomp1.com:5060 SIP/2.0
Via: SIP/2.0/TCP 172.18.110.205:5060;branch=z9hG4bK7f3602e9b1
From: <sip:172.18.110.205>;tag=791723988
To: sip:cube1.entcomp1.com
Date: Sun, 24 Jun 2018 16:02:34 GMT
Call-ID: 73ce80-b2f1c09a-39-cd6e12ac@172.18.110.205
User-Agent: Cisco-CUCM11.5
CSeq: 101 OPTIONS
Contact: sip:172.18.110.205:5060;transport=tcp
Max-Forwards: 0
Content-Length: 0


39396538: Jun 24 16:02:34.087 UTC: //-1/xxxxxxxxxxxx/SIP/Msg/ccsipDisplayMsg:
Sent:
SIP/2.0 200 OK
Via: SIP/2.0/TCP 172.18.110.205:5060;branch=z9hG4bK7f3602e9b1
From: <sip:172.18.110.205>;tag=791723988
To: <sip:cube1.entcomp1.com>;tag=A7928DE5-25A5
```

```
Date: Sun, 24 Jun 2018 16:02:34 GMT
Call-ID: 73ce80-b2f1c09a-39-cd6e12ac@172.18.110.205
Server: Cisco-SIPGateway/IOS-16.6.1
CSeq: 101 OPTIONS
Allow: INVITE, OPTIONS, BYE, CANCEL, ACK, PRACK, UPDATE, REFER, SUBSCRIBE, NOTIFY,
  INFO, REGISTER
Allow-Events: telephone-event
Accept: application/sdp
Supported: timer,resource-priority,replaces,sdp-anat
Content-Type: application/sdp
Content-Length: 381

v=0
o=CiscoSystemsSIP-GW-UserAgent 3801 2582 IN IP4 172.18.110.203
s=SIP Call
c=IN IP4 172.18.110.203
t=0 0
m=audio 0 RTP/AVP 18 0 8 9 4 2 15 3
c=IN IP4 172.18.110.203
m=image 0 udptl t38
c=IN IP4 172.18.110.203
a=T38FaxVersion:0
a=T38MaxBitRate:9600
a=T38FaxRateManagement:transferredTCF
a=T38FaxMaxBuffer:200
a=T38FaxMaxDatagram:320
a=T38FaxUdpEC:t38UDPRedundancy


39400514: Jun 24 16:03:43.174 UTC: //1457971/000000000000/SIP/Msg/ccsipDisplayMsg:
Sent:
OPTIONS sip:cl2-cucm-sub2.entcomp1.com:5060 SIP/2.0
Via: SIP/2.0/TCP 172.18.110.203:5060;branch=z9hG4bK19F7D112F
From: <sip:172.18.110.203>;tag=A7939BCB-68D
To: sip:cl2-cucm-sub2.entcomp1.com
Date: Sun, 24 Jun 2018 16:03:43 GMT
Call-ID: 7CFE87-76FF11E8-B668E1BE-18C7C14D@172.18.110.203
User-Agent: Cisco-SIPGateway/IOS-16.6.1
Max-Forwards: 70
CSeq: 101 OPTIONS
Contact: sip:172.18.110.203:5060;transport=tcp
Content-Length: 0
```

```
39400528: Jun 24 16:03:43.177 UTC: //1457971/000000000000/SIP/Msg/ccsipDisplayMsg:
Received:
SIP/2.0 200 OK
Via: SIP/2.0/TCP 172.18.110.203:5060;branch=z9hG4bK19F7D112F
From: <sip:172.18.110.203>;tag=A7939BCB-68D
To: <sip:cl2-cucm-sub2.entcomp1.com>;tag=674253297
Date: Sun, 24 Jun 2018 16:03:43 GMT
Call-ID: 7CFE87-76FF11E8-B668E1BE-18C7C14D@172.18.110.203
Server: Cisco-CUCM11.5
CSeq: 101 OPTIONS
Allow: INVITE, OPTIONS, INFO, BYE, CANCEL, ACK, PRACK, UPDATE, REFER, SUBSCRIBE,
  NOTIFY
Content-Length: 0
```

An important distinction between a SIP OPTIONS message and an INVITE message is the Request-URI header field. SIP OPTIONS does not have the user part of the SIP or SIPS Request-URI header field. In Example 3-20, Request-URI **sip:cl2-cucm-sub2.entcomp1.com: 5060** contains only the host part of the SIP URI. The Allow header field in the response lists the SIP methods supported by the device. SIP endpoints use the message body of the response to indicate the list of supported codecs.

End-to-End Call Trace

Troubleshooting complex call flows like call transfers and abnormal call disconnects in SIP networks is time-consuming and has a direct impact on issue resolution time. Due to the number of call hops present in a collaboration network, network administrators and support engineers spend significant time collecting and analyzing logs from different SIP devices in the call signaling path to diagnose issues.

The simple call from Alice to Bob shown in Figure 3-10 traverses six SIP devices before it reaches Bob. This end-to-end call consists of five SIP Call-IDs, one from each of the following:

- Alice's endpoint to call controller A in entcomp2 company
- Call controller A to sbc.entcomp2.com
- sbc.entcomp2.com to sbc.entcomp1.com
- sbc.entcomp1.com to call controller B in entcomp1 company
- Call controller B to Bob's endpoint

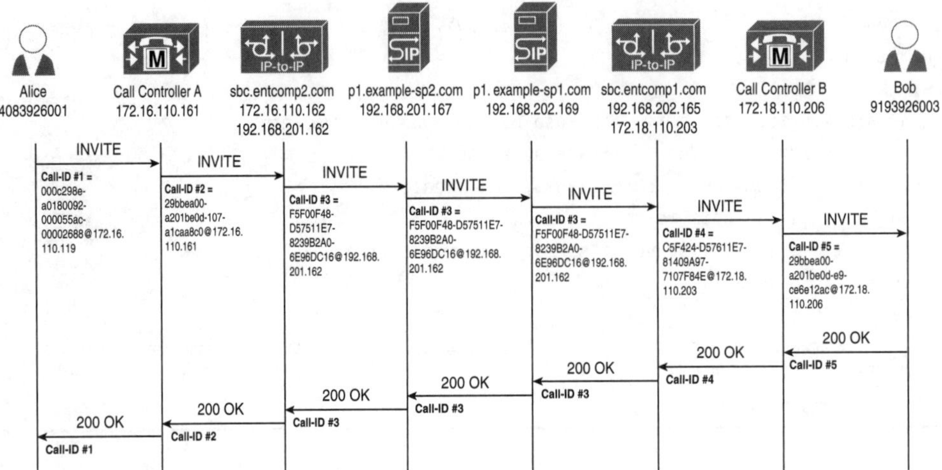

Figure 3-10 *Call-IDs Used in a Basic SIP Call Flow*

While troubleshooting a call disconnect, support teams need to collect and analyze the logs from the various call processing devices to determine whether a call disconnect is initiated by an internal device or if the disconnection initiated from an external source, such as a service provider. This analysis is performed by getting the calling party number, the called party number of the disconnected call, and the timestamp of the problem occurrence and then manually finding the corresponding Call-IDs associated with the disconnected call in each SIP device through which the call has traversed. The Call-IDs are identified by searching the calling party number in the From header field and called party number in the To header field of the SIP INVITE and then stitched together to form an end-to-end call signaling trace. If there are any calling or called party number transformations applied, then those must also be taken into account while finding the individual Call-IDs. This manual stitching of Call-IDs to visualize the end-to-end call flow is where network and support engineers spend a significant amount of time.

If analysis shows that an abnormal disconnect is not triggered by any of the internal devices, then the support team engages the service provider to troubleshoot further by providing the calling number, the called party number, and the problem occurrence timestamp. This process is then repeated by the service provider's support team and may lead to diagnosis even further upstream in the call flow.

One may observe that it could ease troubleshooting to have a single identifier shared by all call legs that is passed end-to-end across the various call signaling components—and perhaps even retained when traversing other disparate networks, such as those of service providers. To address this need, RFC 7989 defines a unique end-to-end identifier named Session-ID that allows calls to be tracked across devices and network boundaries.

Session-ID

Session-ID is a header field that is added by the SIP device that originates a multimedia session (audio, video, fax and so on). This field is passed across SIP proxies and B2BUAs along the call signaling path to the destination SIP device. Once a Session-ID header field is added in the initial SIP INVITE, it is also added in the corresponding responses of that INVITE request and also in all subsequent requests and responses in that session. This enables tracking of all messages corresponding to the end-to-end call across multiple devices using a single unique global identifier.

Local and Remote UUID

Session-ID is not just a static identifier that is generated at the time of session initiation and maintained throughout the session. Instead, it gets updated whenever a new participant is added to the session.

Session-ID is made up of two universally unique identifiers (UUIDs), each consisting of 32 alphanumeric characters (0–9, a–f): the local UUID and the remote UUID. Each endpoint participating in a session generates its own UUID and maintains a reference to the remote endpoint's UUID. When an endpoint sends a SIP request or response message within a dialog, it adds the {local-uuid, remote-uuid} pair value as the Session-ID header field value. The first UUID in the Session-ID header field value always represents the local UUID and the UUID present in the "remote" parameter represents the remote UUID. For example, dce94db12ae05513ab05e1346c29dcdd is the local UUID, and 8c8c368da411d8df347e57996aa71588 is the remote UUID for the Session-ID header field shown at the bottom of Figure 3-11.

Let's consider a scenario in which the endpoints of two users, Foo and Bob, are registered to the same call controller B, as shown in Figure 3-11. When Foo's endpoint sends the first SIP INVITE in a dialog, it generates a new local UUID dce94db12ae05513ab-05e1346c29dcdd for itself, but it doesn't know the UUID of the remote endpoint and hence sets the remote UUID to nil, which is represented as a string of 32 zeros. The Session-ID header is set to the {local-uuid, remote-uuid} pair value {dce94db12ae05513a-b05e1346c29dcdd, 00000000000000000000000000000000}.

When Bob's endpoint (remote endpoint) receives the first SIP INVITE in a dialog, it copies the local UUID value dce94db12ae05513ab05e1346c29dcdd from the Session-ID header field in the received request and stores it as its remote UUID. It also generates a UUID 8c8c368da411d8df347e57996aa71588 for itself and stores it as the local UUID. It sends its {local-uuid, remote-uuid} pair value of {8c8c368da411d8df347e57996aa71588, dce94db12ae05513ab05e1346c29dcdd} in the provisional and final responses (180 Ringing, 200 OK) to the SIP INVITE.

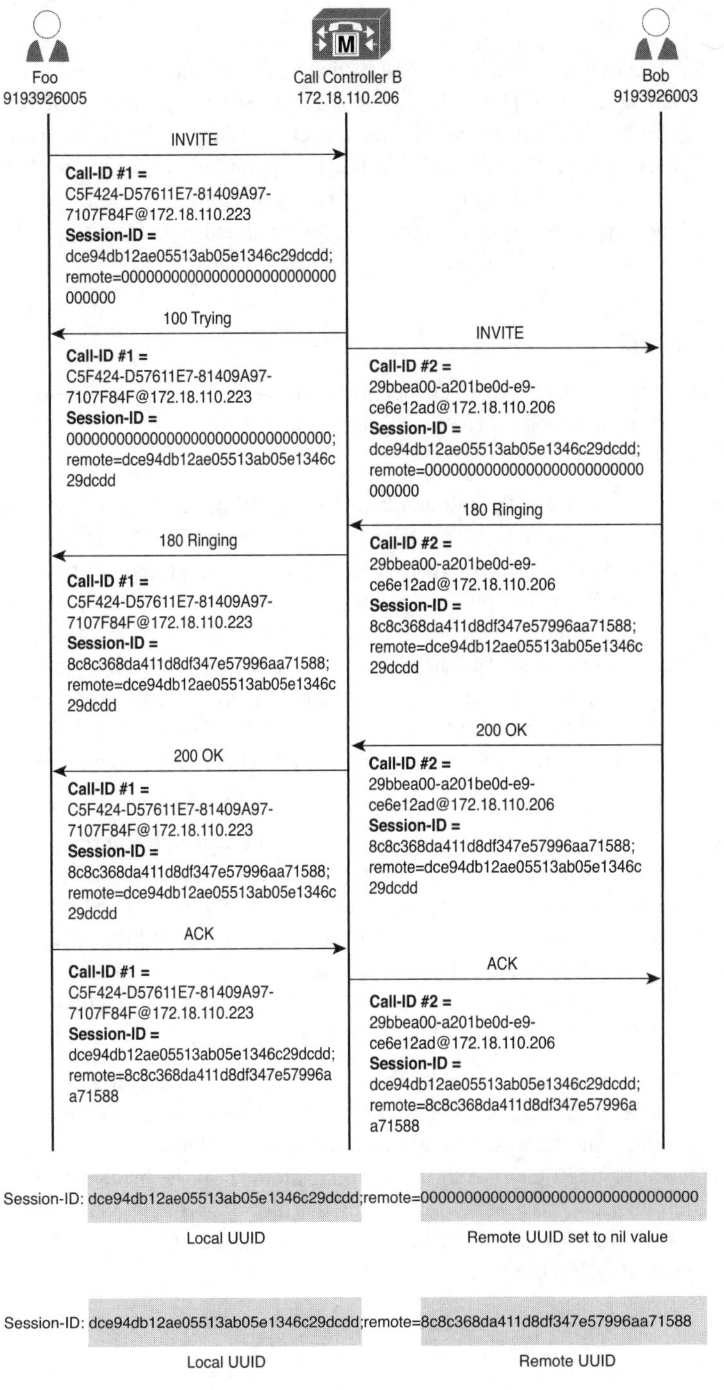

Figure 3-11 *Session-ID Header Field with Local and Remote UUIDs*

When Foo's endpoint (the origination endpoint) receives the response to the SIP INVITE, it learns the remote endpoint's UUID from the local UUID value 8c8c368da411d8df3 47e57996aa71588 present in the Session-ID header field in the received response and updates its remote UUID from nil to the learned value. Its {local-uuid, remote-uuid} pair is now updated from {dce94db12ae05513ab05e1346c29dcdd, 0000000000000000000000 0000000000} to {dce94db12ae05513ab05e1346c29dcdd, 8c8c368da411d8df347e57996 aa71588} and is sent as the Session-ID header field value in subsequent requests, such as ACK, as shown in Figure 3-11. Whenever an endpoint receives a SIP request and response with a different remote UUID, it updates the remote UUID value in its {local-uuid, remote-uuid} pair and uses it in subsequent requests and responses within that dialog and related dialogs such as call transfer call legs.

Call controller B in Example 3-11 acts as an intermediary and primarily passes the Session-ID header field from one call leg to another. When sending the 100 Trying message to Foo's endpoint, the call leg between the call controller and Bob is yet to be set up, and hence it sets the local UUID to nil and the remote UUID to the value received in the SIP INVITE message for the {local-uuid, remote-uuid} pair of the call leg between itself and Foo. This pair has the value {00000000000000000000000000000000, dce94db12ae05513a-b05e1346c29dcdd} and is sent as the Session-ID header field in the 100 Trying message. After receiving the 180 response from Bob's endpoint, it learns the UUID value of Bob's endpoint and updates the {local-uuid, remote-uuid} value from {000000000000000000000 00000000000, dce94db12ae05513ab05e1346c29dcdd} to {8c8c368da411d8df347e57996 aa71588, dce94db12ae05513ab05e1346c29dcdd} and forwards the 180 response with the updated Session-ID header field value. Section 7 of RFC 7989 is a good reference on how Session-ID header field are processed by SIP intermediaries. SIP intermediaries that do not support Session-ID may either pass through the header field without any change to Session-ID value or drop the header field prior to forwarding the request to next hop. A network engineer troubleshooting a call between Foo and Bob can track all the SIP messages that belong to this end-to-end session just by using the local UUID of Foo's endpoint, which is present in all SIP messages exchanged within the dialogs that are part of this session. This eliminates the need to use per-dialog SIP Call-IDs to visualize the end-to-end call flow.

RFC 7989 also provides the provision for SIP intermediaries to generate UUIDs on behalf of the devices that do not have Session-ID support. For example, when an SBC receives a SIP INVITE without the Session-ID header field from the service provider in the inbound call leg, it can generate a local UUID and insert a Session-ID header field in the SIP INVITE sent to the next hop across the outbound call leg. An example of this technique for a call from 4083926001 to 9193926003 is shown in Example 3-21, in which the SBC receives a SIP INVITE without Session-ID from the service provider in the inbound call leg with call-ID **F5F00F48-D57511E7-8239B2A0-6E96DC16@192.168.202.162**. It generates a local UUID **dce94db12ae05513ab05e1346c29dcee**, sets the remote UUID to a null value of **00000000000000000000000000000000**, and inserts the Session-ID header field in the SIP INVITE sent to the next hop across the outbound call leg with call-ID **C5F424-D57611E7-81409A97-7107F84E@172.18.110.203**.

Example 3-21 *SBC Generating Local UUID and Inserting Session-ID in the Outbound Call Leg*

```
Received:
INVITE sip:9193926003@192.168.202.165:5060;transport=tcp SIP/2.0
Via: SIP/2.0/TCP 192.168.202.169:5060;branch=z9hG4bKuqikwX.Yw24UpUvmEEXmdQ~~45
Via: SIP/2.0/TCP 192.168.202.167:5060;branch=z9hG4bKRzUwlcSQ3rMWDN01cODE+Q~~48
Via: SIP/2.0/TCP 192.168.202.162:5060;branch=z9hG4bK771EBF
Max-Forwards: 66
To: <sip:9193926003@entcomp1.com>
From: <sip:4083926001@192.168.202.162>;tag=13B6D7E2-10EC
Contact: <sip:4083926001@192.168.202.162:5060;transport=tcp>
Expires: 180
Remote-Party-ID: <sip:4083926001@192.168.202.162>;party=calling;screen=yes;
  privacy=off
Call-ID: F5F00F48-D57511E7-8239B2A0-6E96DC16@192.168.202.162
CSeq: 101 INVITE
Content-Length: 0
Date: Fri, 01 Dec 2017 02:27:07 GMT
Supported: timer,resource-priority,replaces,sdp-anat
Min-SE: 1800
Cisco-Guid: 0700180992-0000065536-0000000100-2714413248
User-Agent: Cisco-SIPGateway/IOS-15.6.1.S4
Allow: INVITE, OPTIONS, BYE, CANCEL, ACK, PRACK, UPDATE, REFER, SUBSCRIBE, NOTIFY,
  INFO, REGISTER
Timestamp: 1512095227
Allow-Events: telephone-event
Session-Expires: 1800

Sent:
INVITE sip:9193926003@cl2-cucm-sub1.entcomp1.com:5060 SIP/2.0
Via: SIP/2.0/TCP 172.18.110.203:5060;branch=z9hG4bK4312D7
Remote-Party-ID: <sip:4083926001@172.18.110.203>;party=calling;screen=yes;
  privacy=off
From: <sip:4083926001@172.18.110.119>;tag=F3AE8472-15DE
To: <sip:9193926003@cl2-cucm-sub1.entcomp1.com>
Date: Fri, 01 Dec 2017 02:27:25 GMT
Call-ID: C5F424-D57611E7-81409A97-7107F84E@172.18.110.203
Supported: timer,resource-priority,replaces,sdp-anat
Min-SE:  1800
Cisco-Guid: 0700180992-0000065536-0000000100-2714413248
User-Agent: Cisco-SIPGateway/IOS-16.6.1
Allow: INVITE, OPTIONS, BYE, CANCEL, ACK, PRACK, UPDATE, REFER, SUBSCRIBE, NOTIFY,
  INFO, REGISTER
```

```
CSeq: 101 INVITE
Timestamp: 1512095245
Contact: <sip:4083926001@172.18.110.203:5060;transport=tcp>
Expires: 180
Allow-Events: telephone-event
Max-Forwards: 65
Session-ID: dce94db12ae05513ab05e1346c29dcee;remote=00000000000000000000000000000000
Session-Expires:  1800
Content-Length: 0
```

The SIP device that terminates the SIP session extracts the local UUID in the incoming SIP INVITE and stores it as the remote UUID. It then generates a local UUID and inserts a Session-ID header field into provisional and final SIP responses. If the termination endpoint doesn't have Session-ID capability, the call controller can generate the Session-ID in the SIP response on behalf of the termination endpoint, much the way it generates the Session-ID in the SIP request on behalf of the origination endpoint.

Example 3-22 shows a 180 SIP response received by the SBC that corresponds to the outbound SIP INVITE shown in Example 3-21. The local UUID **dce94db12ae05513ab05e1346c29dcee** generated by the SBC in the SIP INVITE is returned as the remote UUID in the 180 response, and the termination endpoint's UUID **8c8c368da411d8df347e57996aa71577** is presented as the local UUID.

Example 3-22 *SIP Response with Session-ID Header Field Containing Local and Remote UUIDs*

```
SIP/2.0 180 Ringing
Via: SIP/2.0/TCP 172.18.110.203:5060;branch=z9hG4bK4312D7
From: <sip:4083926001@172.18.110.119>;tag=F3AE8472-15DE
To: <sip:9193926003@cl2-cucm-sub1.entcomp1.com>;tag=71576~154a292d-1558-48b6-9155-
  e3e49acd9216-44381277
Date: Fri, 01 Dec 2017 02:27:25 GMT
Call-ID: C5F424-D57611E7-81409A97-7107F84E@172.18.110.203
CSeq: 101 INVITE
Allow: INVITE, OPTIONS, INFO, BYE, CANCEL, ACK, PRACK, UPDATE, REFER, SUBSCRIBE, NOTIFY
Allow-Events: presence
Server: Cisco-CUCM11.5
Call-Info: <urn:x-cisco-remotecc:callinfo>;x-cisco-video-traffic-class=DESKTOP
Supported: X-cisco-srtp-fallback
Supported: Geolocation
Session-ID: 8c8c368da411d8df347e57996aa71577;remote=dce94db12ae05513ab05e1346c29dcee
P-Asserted-Identity: <sip:9193926003@172.18.110.206>
Remote-Party-ID: <sip:9193926003@172.18.110.206>;party=called;screen=yes;privacy=off
Contact: <sip:9193926003@172.18.110.206:5060;transport=tcp>
Content-Length: 0
```

Figure 3-12 shows a subsection of the end-to-end call flow in Figure 3-10, from the perspective of sbc.entcomp1.com. It depicts a scenario in which SIP devices in entcomp2 company do not support Session-ID. In this scenario, the SIP messages received from the service provider proxy p1.example-sp1.com do not have the Session-ID header field, but all the messages sent and received by the SBC on the internal network side of the entcomp1 company have the Session-ID header field. This call can then be traced by just using the SBC's local UUID **dce94db12ae05513ab05e1346c29dcee** within the logs of the SBC, the call controller, and Bob's endpoint. (100 Trying messages have been omitted from Figure 3-12 for brevity.)

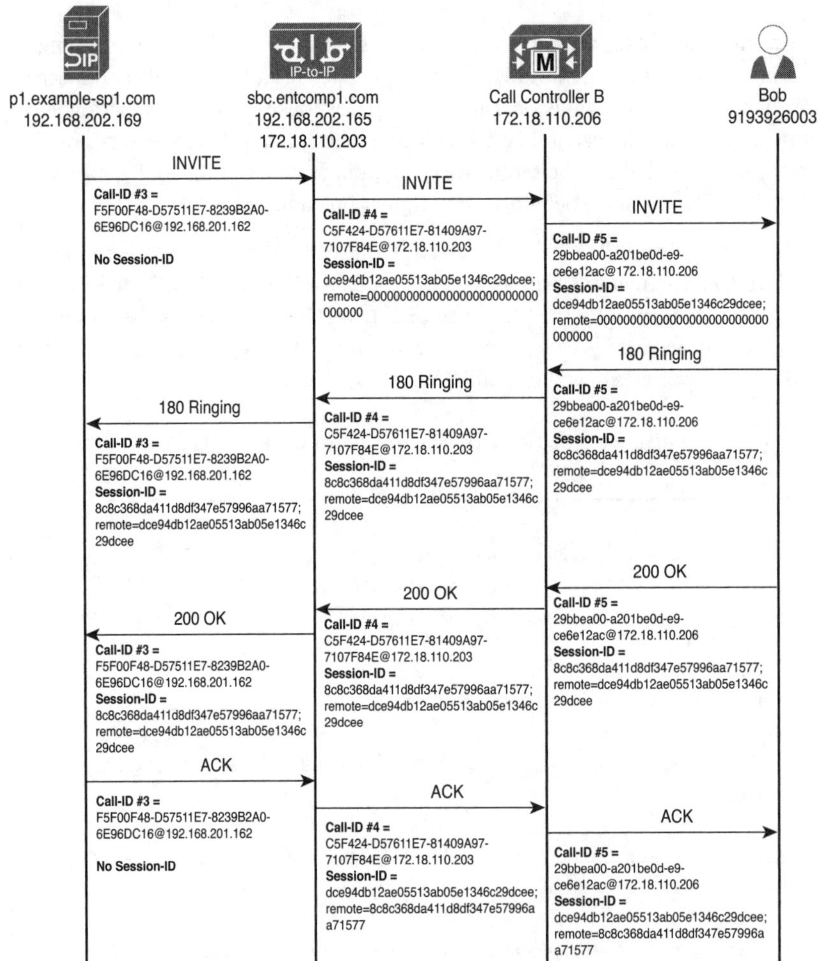

Figure 3-12 *End-to-End Call Trace Using Session-ID*

Tip A 100 Trying message contains a Session-ID header field with local UUID set to a nill value and a remote UUID set to the local UUID that is extracted from the received SIP INVITE.

The Session-ID concept becomes more useful in complex call flows such as call transfers and conference calls that involve multiple participants and several call legs. Imagine a scenario in which Bob (9193926003) transfers the initial call with Alice (4083926001) to another user, Foo (9193926005). Bob's endpoint would use its same local UUID **8c8c368da411d8df347e57996aa71577** from the initial call with Alice (Call-ID 5) for the transfer call to Foo. (Section 10.2 and 10.3 in RFC 7989 provide a detailed look at the call transfer call flow using Session-ID.)

The Session-ID provides a simple and elegant way for call analysis tools to correlate the initial incoming call with all the subsequent call transfers. This can be accomplished by performing the following steps to provide an end-to-end call trace visualization from the presence of a Session-ID:

Step 1. Get the calling number, the called party number, or the SIP URI and timestamp of the call of interest.

Step 2. Identify the corresponding SIP INVITE and retrieve the local UUID.

Step 3. Build a UUID list, beginning with the identified local UUID.

Step 4. Search the logs collected from all relevant SIP devices for all messages that have the local UUID.

Step 5. Process all the matching messages, extract the remote UUIDs from those messages, and add them to the UUID list.

Step 6. Search the SIP device logs again to find messages that have UUIDs that were recently added to the UUID list in step 5.

Step 7. Repeat steps 5 and 6 until no new UUIDs are identified in the matching messages.

Step 8. Put together all the matching messages in a call ladder diagram format to display the end-to-end call trace.

CUBE Call Routing Mechanisms

CUBE offers a number of features to configure call routing according to business needs. It is essential to understand how the features work so you can choose them appropriately to optimize the configuration management and operations. CUBE deployed at the edge of an enterprise network plays the role of an SBC, routing both inbound calls from external callers and outbound calls originated by internal users and applications. CUBE can also be configured to apply different call signaling handling and routing mechanisms when supplementary services such as call transfer and call forward are invoked.

Dial Peers

A *dial peer* is a basic configuration object in Cisco IOS and IOS XE that contains information about the call signaling element's peer and is used for call routing purposes. The peer could either be a previous hop from which CUBE receives a call or a next hop to which CUBE sends a call.

POTS and VoIP are the two dial peer types commonly used in devices running Cisco IOS and IOS XE software. POTS dial peers contains communication details for TDM-based call signaling peers such as ISDN switches and analog voice devices. VoIP dial peers contain details of IP-based call signaling peers such as proxies, B2BUAs, gateways, and gatekeepers. Because CUBE processes only IP-to-IP calls, this chapter focuses primarily on concepts relevant to VoIP dial peers.

VoIP dial peers contain the following information to be used while communicating with a peer:

- **VoIP signaling protocol**—Such as SIP or H.323
- **Signaling peer address**—Such as the IPv4/IPv6, DNS, or ENUM address of peer
- **Transport layer protocol**—Such as TCP or UDP
- **Media capabilities**—Such as the audio/video codecs and DTMF capabilities to be advertised (for example, G.711, G.729)
- **Inbound matching criteria**—Such as the calling or called party URI to match for inbound calls on an inbound dial peer
- **Outbound matching criteria**—Such as the called party URI to match for outbound calls to route out to the specified next hop
- **URI transformations**—Changes to be applied to the calling or called party numbers
- **Protocol related configuration parameters** to communicate or interoperate with the peer such as enabling or disabling reliable provisional responses (rel1xx).

Inbound and Outbound Dial Peers

Every SIP-to-SIP call that gets successfully connected using CUBE has two call legs. The first call leg, referred to as the *inbound call leg*, represents the signaling connection between the previous hop and CUBE. The second call leg, referred to as the *outbound call leg*, represents the signaling connection between CUBE and the next hop.

When a new call arrives, CUBE looks up the list of configured dial peers and selects the closest match to be associated with the inbound call. This selected dial peer, an inbound dial peer, is used to identify any calling/called party transformations and list of media capabilities to be used for this incoming call leg. Once an inbound dial peer is matched, CUBE then looks up the list of configured dial peers again—but this time to find the next hop. The lookup process uses called party information, such as the directory number or URI, as the lookup key. This ultimately selected dial peer is called an outbound dial peer, and the configuration is used to establish how to reach the next hop and what capabilities can be offered in the outbound call leg. Figure 3-13 shows a visual representation of the dial peer and call legs used for a call from 4083926001 to 9193926003.

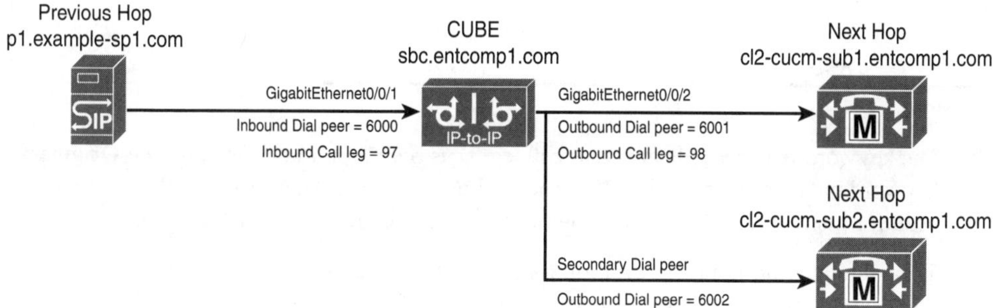

Figure 3-13 *Dial Peers and Call Legs Used to Process an Inbound Call*

The command **show call active voice brief** provides useful information about each active voice call leg in CUBE. Example 3-23 shows a snippet of this command's output for this call.

Example 3-23 *Output of* **show call active voice brief**

```
cube1#show call active voice brief
...
0    : 97 4088217210ms.1 (02:27:25.370 UTC Fri Dec 1 2017) +1100 pid:6000 Answer
  4083926001 active
 dur 00:00:44 tx:2168/433600 rx:2172/434096 dscp:0 media:0 audio tos:0xB8
  video tos:0x0
 IP 192.168.202.162:8218 SRTP: off rtt:4ms pl:0/0ms lost:0/0/0 delay:0/0/0ms
  g711ulaw TextRelay: off Transcoded: No ICE: Off
 media inactive detected:n media contrl rcvd:n/a timestamp:n/a
 long duration call detected:n long duration call duration:n/a timestamp:n/a
 LostPacketRate:0.00 OutOfOrderRate:0.00
 LocalUUID:dce94db12ae05513ab05e1346c29dcee
 RemoteUUID:8c8c368da411d8df347e57996aa71577
 VRF:
0    : 98 4088217230ms.1 (02:27:25.390 UTC Fri Dec 1 2017) +1050 pid:6001 Originate
  9193926003 active
 dur 00:00:44 tx:2172/434096 rx:2168/433600 dscp:0 media:0 audio tos:0xB8
  video tos:0x0
 IP 14.50.201.46:17876 SRTP: off rtt:3ms pl:0/0ms lost:0/0/0 delay:0/0/0ms g711ulaw
  TextRelay: off Transcoded: No ICE: Off
 media inactive detected:n media contrl rcvd:n/a timestamp:n/a
 long duration call detected:n long duration call duration:n/a timestamp:n/a
 LostPacketRate:0.00 OutOfOrderRate:0.00
```

```
 LocalUUID:8c8c368da411d8df347e57996aa71577
 RemoteUUID:dce94db12ae05513ab05e1346c29dcee
 VRF:

Telephony call-legs: 0
SIP call-legs: 2
...
Total call-legs: 2
```

The keyword **Answer** indicates that call leg **97** is the inbound call leg, and the **Originate** keyword indicates that call leg **98** is the outbound call leg. These call leg IDs are only used for internal reference within the platform but are unique for each call leg.

The parameter **pid** is an abbreviation for *peer ID*, and its value is set to the dial peer tag associated with the call leg. Using the output from Example 3-23, it can be observed that dial peers 6000 and 6001 are selected by CUBE as inbound and outbound dial peers for the given call. The configuration of these dial peers along with dial peer 6002 is shown in Example 3-24. Dial peer 6002 is used as second outbound dial peer if the call routing across 6001 is not successful.

The SIP IP-to-IP call functionality needs to be explicitly enabled by using the command **allow connections sip to sip** for the platform to route SIP-to-SIP calls. Address hiding ensures that SIP messages sent to the service providers on the external network interface do not contain internal IP address information. For example, when CUBE receives a SIP REFER from the internal call controller and the **address-hiding** command is enabled, CUBE replaces the internal IP address in the Refer-To header field with an external IP address prior to sending the SIP REFER to the service provider. The **ip name-server** command specifies the DNS server IP address to be used for DNS A, AAAA, and SRV record lookups for the next-hop determination during the call routing process.

Example 3-24 *Inbound and Outbound Dial Peer Configuration for DN-Based Call Routing*

```
ip domain lookup
ip name-server 172.18.110.106

voice service voip
 address-hiding
 mode border-element license capacity 100
 allow-connections sip to sip

dial-peer voice 6000 voip
 description "Inbound dial-peer for Agent phone calls"
 video codec h264
 session protocol sipv2
 session transport tcp
```

```
 incoming called-number 9193926...
 voice-class sip bind control source-interface GigabitEthernet0/0/1
 voice-class sip bind media source-interface GigabitEthernet0/0/1
 dtmf-relay rtp-nte
 codec g711ulaw
!
dial-peer voice 6001 voip
 description "Outbound dial-peer for Agent phone calls"
 preference 0
 destination-pattern 9193926...
 video codec h264
 session protocol sipv2
 session target dns:cl2-cucm-sub1.entcomp1.com
 session transport tcp
 voice-class sip options-keepalive up-interval 65 down-interval 25 retry 3
 voice-class sip bind control source-interface GigabitEthernet0/0/2
 voice-class sip bind media source-interface GigabitEthernet0/0/2
 dtmf-relay rtp-nte
 codec g711ulaw
!
dial-peer voice 6002 voip
 description "Outbound dial-peer for Agent phone calls"
 preference 1
 destination-pattern 9193926...
 video codec h264
 session protocol sipv2
 session target dns:cl2-cucm-sub2.entcomp1.com
 session transport tcp
 voice-class sip options-keepalive up-interval 65 down-interval 25 retry 3
 voice-class sip bind control source-interface GigabitEthernet0/0/2
 voice-class sip bind media source-interface GigabitEthernet0/0/2
 dtmf-relay rtp-nte
 codec g711ulaw
!
```

In Example 3-24, dial peer 6000 is defined as the inbound dial peer for calls destined to 10-digit directory numbers beginning with 9193926. This is specified using the **incoming called-number** ***<called number pattern>*** command. Similarly, dial peers 6001 and 6002 are defined as primary and secondary outbound dial peers, using the **destination-pattern** ***<called number pattern>*** command. The called number pattern is a string of digits along with optional regular expression (regex) characters. Table 3-2 shows the most commonly used regex characters in dial peers for SIP trunks. Note that Cisco IOS and IOS XE software supports only a subset of regex characters for called and calling number pattern.

Table 3-2 *Commonly Used Regex Characters for Called and Calling Number Patterns*

Regex Character	Description	Example
. (period)	Matches any one of the digits and characters 0–9, A–F, and, #.	**9193926...** Matches 10-digit directory numbers beginning with a 9193936 prefix.
[ ] (brackets)	Indicates a list that is allowed to match a single digit or character. The character "-" inside the brackets indicates a range. A range is a sequence of characters enclosed in the brackets; only alphanumeric characters 0–9 and A–F are allowed in the range.	**919392600[079]** Matches the 10-digit directory numbers 9193926000, 9193926007, and 9193926009. **919392600[0-9]** Matches 10-digit directory numbers from 9193926000 to 9193926009.
+ (plus symbol)	Indicates that the preceding digit occurred one or more times. The plus symbol, when present as the first character in the value of the *destination-pattern* command, represents an E.164 number.	**2600[0-9]+** Matches directory numbers such as 26000, 26001 to 26009, 260000, and so on. **+19193926009** Matches the E.164 number +19193926009.
? (question mark)	Indicates that the preceding digit occurred zero or one times.	**26000?** Matches the directory numbers 2600 and 26000.
$ (dollar sign)	Matches the end of the input string.	**3926...$** Matches seven-digit numbers beginning with 3926000 to 3926999.
T (interdigit timeout)	A Cisco IOS router configured as a TDM gateway waits to collect additional digits until the expiration of the interdigit timeout. In the case of CUBE, all digits of the called party number are received in the SIP INVITE at the same time, and hence T is used as to match any string of digits of 0 or more in length.	**9T** Matches directory numbers of all lengths and starting with the digit 9 (for example, 9, 911, and 9911).

Regex Character	Description	Example
^ (circumflex)	When used inside brackets, it indicates that the digit following ^ will not be considered a match. When used as the first character in the regex pattern, it indicates that the matched string begins with the alphanumeric character that follows ^.	**1[^8][^0][^0].......** Matches 11-digit numbers beginning with a 1, except for 1800 numbers. **^2...$** Matches 4-digit numbers that begin with 2.
( ) (parentheses)	Indicates a sequence of digit and character patterns that are grouped and matched together.	**9193926(0[1-9])0** Matches the 11-digit numbers 9193926010, 9193926020, 9193926030, 9193926040, 9193926050, 9193926060, 9193926070, 9193926080, and 9193926090 but not 9193926000.

Table 3-3 describes the parameters configured in inbound dial peer 6000.

Table 3-3 *Inbound Dial Peer Configuration Parameters*

Parameter Description	Parameter Value	Relevant Command
VoIP signaling protocol	Use SIP to communicate with the signaling peer.	**session protocol** *sipv2*
Signaling peer address	None. This is an inbound dial peer and hence CUBE will use the IP address and port number in the topmost Via header field of the received SIP INVITE to send SIP responses to the peer as defined in Section 18.2.2 of RFC 3261.	N/A
IP transport protocol	Use TCP to send SIP messages to this peer.	**session transport** *tcp*
Audio codec	Use G.711μ law codec for calls from this peer.	**codec** *g711ulaw*
Video codec	Use H.264 video codec for calls from this peer.	**video codec** *h264*
DTMF relay	Use out-of-band DTMF relay mechanism defined in RFC 2833 (RTP-NTE).	**dtmf-relay** *rtp-nte*

Parameter Description	Parameter Value	Relevant Command
Calling or called party number, URI of inbound calls that needs to use this dial peer as the inbound dial peer	Calls with 10-digit called party number beginning with 9193926 can use this dial peer as inbound dial peer. The . is a regular expression wildcard to represent any digit 0–9, A–F.	**incoming called-number** *9193926...*
Called party number or URI of outbound calls that needs to use this dial peer as outbound dial peer to reach the next hop	Not applicable. This is an inbound dial peer.	N/A
Calling and called number or URI transformations to be applied	None. (Transformations are discussed in the next section.)	N/A
Protocol-related configuration parameters to communicate or interop with the peer	Use the IP address associated with Gig 0/0/1 as the source IP address while sending signaling messages (SIP) packets to the peer. Gig 0/0/1 is the interface connected to the external network that is used to reach the service provider.	**voice-class sip bind control source-interface** *GigabitEthernet0/0/1*
Protocol-related configuration parameters to communicate or interop with the peer	Use the IP address associated with Gig 0/0/1 as the source address while sending media (audio, video, DTMF) packets to the peer.	**voice-class sip bind media source-interface** *GigabitEthernet0/0/1*

Table 3-4 describes the parameters configured in outbound dial peer 6001.

Table 3-4 *Primary Outbound Dial Peer Configuration Parameters*

Parameter Description	Parameter Value	Relevant Command
Preference of the dial peer when multiple outbound dial peers are matched	Use this dial peer as the first option in the outbound dial peer selection process. The preference value ranges from 0 to 10, with 0 being the highest priority.	**preference** *0*
VoIP signaling protocol	Use SIP to communicate with the signaling peer.	**session protocol** *sipv2*

Parameter Description	Parameter Value	Relevant Command
Signaling peer address	The next-hop signaling peer is the first subscriber of the CUCM cluster. The subscriber's host name is specified as cl2-cucm-sub1.entcomp1.com. Use the default port 5060 for UDP and TCP and 5061 for TLS. The DNS server specified by the **ip name-server** command is used to perform DNS lookup. The next hop can also be specified as an IPv4 or IPv6 address.	**session target** *dns:cl2-cucm-sub1.entcomp1.com* Example: **session target** *ipv4:172.18.110.206*
IP transport protocol	Use TCP to send SIP messages to this peer.	**session transport** *tcp*
Audio codec	Use G.711µ law codec for calls from this peer.	**codec** *g711ulaw*
Video codec	Use H.264 video codec for calls from this peer.	**video codec** *h264*
DTMF relay	Use out-of-band DTMF relay mechanism as defined in RFC 2833 (RTP-NTE).	**dtmf-relay** *rtp-nte*
Calling or called party number, URI of inbound calls that needs to use this dial peer as the inbound dial peer	Not applicable. This is an outbound dial peer.	N/A
Called party number or URI of outbound calls that needs to use this dial peer as the outbound dial peer to reach the next hop	Calls with 10-digit called party number beginning with 9193926 can use this dial peer as the outbound dial peer. The . represents any digit 0–9, A–F.	**destination-pattern** *9193926...*
Calling and called number or URI transformations to be applied	None. (Transformations are discussed in the next section.)	N/A

Parameter Description	Parameter Value	Relevant Command
Protocol-related configuration parameters to communicate or interop with the peer	Use the IP address associated with Gig 0/0/2 as the source IP address while sending signaling messages (SIP) packets to the peer. Gig 0/0/2 is the interface connected to the internal network.	**voice-class sip bind control source-interface** *GigabitEthernet0/0/2*
Protocol-related configuration parameters to communicate or interop with the peer	Use the IP address associated with Gig 0/0/2 as the source address while sending media (audio, video, DTMF) packets to the peer.	**voice-class sip bind media source-interface** *GigabitEthernet0/0/2*

Table 3-5 describes only the parameters configured in secondary outbound dial peer 6002 that are different from dial peer 6001.

Table 3-5 *Secondary Outbound Dial Peer Configuration Parameters*

Parameter Description	Parameter Value	Relevant Command
Preference of the dial peer when multiple outbound dial peers are matched	Use this dial peer as the second option in the outbound dial peer selection process but having a preference less desirable than that in Table 3-4.	**preference** *1*
Signaling peer address	The next-hop signaling peer is the second subscriber of the CUCM cluster. The subscriber's host name is cl2-cucm-sub2.entcomp1.com.	**session target** *dns:cl2-cucm-sub2.entcomp1.com*

Inbound Dial Peer Matching Rules

Having the knowledge of how CUBE selects inbound and outbound dial peers is very beneficial for troubleshooting call routing issues. The inbound dial peer has multiple criteria for the selection process. The SIP URI is extracted from the topmost Via, From, To, and Request-URI header fields, as are the directory numbers (calling and called party) to make a decision. The algorithm for matching these rules is shown in Table 3-6.

Table 3-6 *Match Rules Used for Inbound Dial Peer Selection*

Order of Preference	Match Rules	Values Extracted from Incoming SIP INVITE	Command Used to Specify the Match Pattern in the Inbound Dial Peer
1	SIP URI of previous hop	SIP URI in topmost VIA header field	**incoming uri via** *voice-class-uri-identifier*
2	Request-URI	SIP URI in Request-URI	**incoming uri request** *voice-class-uri-identifier*
3	SIP URI of the called device	SIP URI in To header field	**incoming uri to** *voice-class-uri-identifier*
4	SIP URI of the calling device	SIP URI in From header field	**incoming uri from** *voice-class-uri-identifier*
5	Called party number	User part of SIP URI in Request-URI header field	**incoming called-number** *called-number-pattern* **incoming called e164-pattern-map** *e164-pattern-map-voice-class-tag-number*
6	Calling party number	User part of SIP URI in From header field	**answer-address** *calling-number-pattern* **incoming calling e164-pattern-map** *e164-pattern-map-voice-class-tag-number*
7	Calling party number	User part in SIP URI in From header field	**destination-pattern** *called-number-pattern*

Each dial peer in CUBE can be configured with one or more of the commands in the fourth column of Table 3-6. The dial peer lookup is performed by the Cisco IOS call control API (CCAPI) software component. The first dial peer whose configured **incoming uri** pattern matches the value present in the incoming SIP INVITE according to the match rules order is selected as the inbound dial peer. The SIP URI match pattern is specified using the **voice class uri** command and is referenced by the **incoming uri** command.

A sample configuration for SIP URI-based call routing from the entcomp2.com domain to the entcomp1.com domain is shown in Example 3-25. Two SIP URI patterns are defined using the **voice class uri** commands with the names **entcomp1** and **entcomp2**, which match SIP URIs that have the host portion set to entcomp1.com and entcomp2.com, respectively. The command **incoming uri from** *entcomp2* under dial peer 8000 indicates that this dial peer is used as inbound dial peer for all inbound SIP calls, with the host portion of the SIP URI in the From header field matching entcomp2.com.

SIP URI-based dialing is not enabled by default; it is enabled only if the command **voice-class sip call-route url** is configured either in the inbound dial peer or at the global level.

Example 3-25 *Inbound and Outbound Dial Peer for SIP URI-Based Call Routing*

```
voice class uri entcomp1 sip
 host entcomp1.com

voice class uri entcomp2 sip
 host entcomp2.com

dial-peer voice 8000 voip
 description "Inbound dial-peer for SIP URI Calls"
 video codec h264
 session protocol sipv2
 session transport tcp
 incoming uri from entcomp2
 voice-class sip call-route url
 voice-class sip bind control source-interface GigabitEthernet0/0/1
 voice-class sip bind media source-interface GigabitEthernet0/0/1
 voice-class sip requri-passing
 dtmf-relay rtp-nte
 codec g711ulaw
 no vad

dial-peer voice 8001 voip
 description "Outbound dial-peer for SIP URI calls"
 preference 0
 video codec h264
 session protocol sipv2
 session target dns:cl2-cucm-sub1.entcomp1.com
 session transport tcp
 destination uri entcomp1
 voice-class sip localhost dns:entcomp1.com
 voice-class sip bind control source-interface GigabitEthernet0/0/2
 voice-class sip bind media source-interface GigabitEthernet0/0/2
 voice-class sip requri-passing
 dtmf-relay rtp-nte
 codec g711ulaw
 no vad

dial-peer voice 8002 voip
 description "Outbound dial-peer for SIP URI calls"
 preference 1
 video codec h264
 session protocol sipv2
 session target dns:cl2-cucm-sub2.entcomp1.com
```

```
session transport tcp
destination uri entcomp1
voice-class sip localhost dns:entcomp1.com
voice-class sip bind control source-interface GigabitEthernet0/0/2
voice-class sip bind media source-interface GigabitEthernet0/0/2
voice-class sip requri-passing
dtmf-relay rtp-nte
codec g711ulaw
no vad
```

If an inbound dial peer is not found using the URI-based match rules, then the dial peers configured with called party number patterns using the command **incoming called-number** *pattern* are considered. The dial peer whose pattern matches the called party number of the inbound SIP INVITE is selected.

If no inbound dial peers are found even after using the called party number, the CCAPI attempts to match incoming dial peers based on the calling party number of the inbound call. The calling party number is matched against the string specified in the **answer-address** *pattern* of dial peers. If there is still no match, the CCAPI continues to use the calling party number as the lookup key but looks up dial peers that are configured with **destination-pattern** *pattern*. The number pattern in **answer-address** supports the same set of wildcard characters shown in Table 3-2. The calling party number is also referred to as the automatic network identification (ANI).

The searching process is complete when a matching dial peer is found, and the call is processed based on the parameters defined under the matched dial peer. If there are multiple dial peers that match the incoming call's called or calling party number or URI, then the dial peer with the pattern that has the most specific match (typically matching the longest length) is selected. If there are multiple dial peer matches even with the longest match, the dial peer that appears first in the CUBE's configuration is used as the inbound dial peer.

The system **dial peer 0** is used as the inbound dial peer if none of the configured dial peers match the URI and directory number parameters of the incoming call. It is not recommended to rely on dial peer 0 for incoming dial peer matches, as it has restricted media capabilities (for example, no DTMF relay), and the parameters under it cannot be changed.

Example 3-26 is a snippet of **debug voip dialpeer default** and **debug voip ccapi inout** output collected for the call from 4083926001 to 9193926003. It shows selected inbound dial peer 6000 and the parameters **cisco-ani** and **dest** of the inbound call leg passed to set up the outbound call leg.

Example 3-26 *Debug Output for Inbound Dial Peer Matching*

```
178160: Dec  1 02:27:25.373: //-1/C461DB800000/DPM/dpAssociateIncomingPeerCore:
   Result=Success(0) after DP_MATCH_INCOMING_DNIS; Incoming Dial-peer=6000
...
178168: Dec  1 02:27:25.374: //-1/C461DB800000/CCAPI/cc_api_display_ie_subfields:
   cc_api_call_setup_ind_common:
   cisco-username=4083926001
   ----- ccCallInfo IE subfields -----
   cisco-ani=4083926001
   cisco-anitype=0
   cisco-aniplan=0
   cisco-anipi=0
   cisco-anisi=1
   dest=9193926003
   cisco-desttype=0
   cisco-destplan=0
   cisco-rdie=FFFFFFFFFFFFFFFF
   cisco-rdn=
   cisco-rdntype=0
   cisco-rdnplan=0
   cisco-rdnpi=-1
   cisco-rdnsi=-1
   cisco-redirectreason=-1   fwd_final_type =0
   final_redirectNumber =
   hunt_group_timeout =0

178169: Dec  1 02:27:25.375: //-1/C461DB800000/CCAPI/cc_api_call_setup_ind_common:
   Interface=0x7F8694ACD1C8, Call Info(
   Calling Number=4083926001,(Calling Name=)(TON=Unknown, NPI=Unknown,
    Screening=User, Passed, Presentation=Allowed),
   Called Number=9193926003(TON=Unknown, NPI=Unknown),
   Calling Translated=FALSE, Subscriber Type Str=Unknown, FinalDestinationFlag=TRUE,
   Incoming Dial-peer=6000, Progress Indication=NULL(0), Calling IE Present=TRUE,
   Source Trkgrp Route Label=, Target Trkgrp Route Label=, CLID Transparent=FALSE),
    Call Id=97
```

Outbound Dial Peer Matching Rules

Given the variety of configuration options, dial peer matching rules may seem complex at the first glance. Listing the CUBE deployment scenarios and then looking at applicable matching rules for each deployment helps make the learning process easier. The following outbound matching scenarios are currently possible:

- **Basic**—CUBE deployed to connect with a service provider, SIP call controller, or IP PBX using SIP trunks for a small number of directory numbers or directory number ranges

- **Advanced**—CUBE integrated with a service provider, SIP call controller, or IP PBX but with a large number of directory number ranges and hence requiring a large number of dial peers
- **ILS**—CUBE deployed to connect two CUCM clusters participating in the Cisco-proprietary Interlookup Cluster Service (ILS) across a SIP trunk
- **Multi-VRF**—CUBE configured to support Multiple Virtual Routing and Forwarding (VRF) instances
- **Service provider**—CUBE deployed within a service provider network and used to route calls from one service provider peer to another, referred to as *source-based routing*

The call routing for basic deployment can be accomplished by using a simple configuration consisting only of **destination uri** and **destination-pattern** commands. Table 3-7 lists the outbound dial peer matching rules order for this scenario.

Table 3-7 *Match Rules Used for Outbound Dial Peer Selection*

Order of Preference	Match Rules	Value Extracted from Incoming SIP INVITE	Command Used to Specify Match Value in Outbound Dial Peer
1	Request-URI	SIP URI in Request-URI	**destination uri** *voice-class-uri-identifier*
2	Called party number	User part of SIP URI in Request-URI header field	**destination-pattern** *called-number-pattern* **destination e164-pattern-map** *voice-class-tag-number*
3	Calling party number	User part of the URI in From header field	**destination calling e164-pattern-map** *e164-pattern-map-voice-class-tag-number*

Note In order to make it easier to understand, the inbound and outbound dial peer match rules shown in Tables 3-6 and 3-7 do not show rules that are related to the Carrier-ID parameter. The Carrier-ID parameter is added by Cisco SIP gateways and CUBE when the voice source group feature is configured and is included as the **x-route-tag** parameter value in the VIA header field. This is different from the CIC discussed earlier in this chapter. The following is an example of using the Carrier-ID parameter:

```
Via: SIP/2.0/TCP 172.18.110.203:5060;x-route-tag="cid:1234@172.18.110.203";branch=z9
hG4bK1C32B241C
```

After the inbound dial peer lookup process, CUBE performs the transformations for the calling and called numbers and applies protocol modifications (for example, using

SIP profiles) configured in the dial peer. If SIP URI-based dialing is configured with the **voice-class sip call-route url** command in the inbound dial peer, CUBE extracts the Request-URI and tries to find a matching outbound dial peer with the **destination uri** command. The SIP URI match pattern is defined using **voice class uri** and is associated with the **destination uri** command.

For the URI dialing configuration shown in Example 3-25, the command **destination uri entcomp1** under dial peers 8001 and 8002 indicates that these dial peers are used as outbound dial peers for SIP calls with the host portion of the Request-URI matching entcomp1.com. The dial peer 8001 with **preference 0** routes the call to the primary CUCM subscriber, and dial peer 8002 with **preference 1** routes the call to a secondary CUCM subscriber.

If SIP URI-based routing is not enabled, then those dial peers configured with called party number patterns through the use of **destination-pattern** *pattern* are considered. The dial peer whose pattern matches the called party number of the outbound SIP INVITE is selected. If there are multiple dial peers that match the incoming call's called party number, then the dial peer with the pattern that matches the longest number of digits is selected. Calls that do not match any outbound dial peers are disconnected by CUBE with SIP response code 404 Not Found.

CUBE builds the outbound SIP INVITE based on the selected outbound dial peer parameters. First, it determines the next-hop IP address, port number, and transport protocol by using the **session target** command, as shown in Table 3-8. The next-hop reachability can be defined in multiple ways—with the IPv4/IPv6 address, host name, or domain name. When applicable, CUBE performs DNS lookup to resolve the host names and domain names to IP addresses, as described in "Next-Hop Determination" section, earlier in this chapter.

Table 3-8 *Next-Hop Reachability Configuration in Outbound Dial Peers*

Next-Hop Reachability Type	Command	Example
IPv4	**session target** *ipv4:ip-address*	**session target** *ipv4:172.18.110.206*
IPv6	**session target** *ipv6:ip-address*	**session target** *ipv6:2001:DB8:CAFE:1:0:FFFF:8012:6ECE*
Host name	**session target** *dns:host-name*	**session target** *dns:cl2-cucm-sub1.entcomp1.com*
Domain name	**session target** dns:*domain name*	**session target** *dns:example-sp1.com*

The SIP INVITE message body is then formed by including SDP parameters such as audio, video, and DTMF relay capabilities along with the media IP address and port number. The call signaling source address and media address are set to the IP address assigned to the interfaces specified in the **voice class sip bind control** and **voice class sip bind media** commands, respectively. If the control and media source interface are not explicitly configured under the outbound dial peer or globally under **voice service voip** SIP mode, CUBE selects the best source interface, based on what interface will be used for reaching the next hop, as determined by performing a lookup in the local IP routing table. The best source interface can be identified using **show ip route** *<next-hop IP address>*.

Example 3-27 is another snippet of **debug voip dialpeer default** and **debug voip ccapi inout** output collected for the call from 4083926001 to 9193926003. It shows the list of matching outbound dial peers and the first dial peer, 6001, selected to route the call.

Example 3-27 *Debug Output for Outbound Dial Peer Matching*

```
178516: Dec  1 02:27:25.387: //-1/C461DB800000/DPM/dpMatchPeersMoreArg:
   Result=SUCCESS(0)
   List of Matched Outgoing Dial-peer(s):
     1: Dial-peer Tag=6001
     2: Dial-peer Tag=6002
178517: Dec  1 02:27:25.387: //147711/C461DB800000/CCAPI/ccCallSetupRequest:
   Destination=, Calling IE Present=TRUE, Mode=0,
   Outgoing Dial-peer=6001, Params=0x7F869EAEE9B8, Progress Indication=NULL(0)
...


178522: Dec  1 02:27:25.387: //147711/C461DB800000/CCAPI/cc_api_display_ie_
  subfields:
   ccCallSetupRequest:
   cisco-username=4083926001
   ----- ccCallInfo IE subfields -----
   cisco-ani=4083926001
   cisco-anitype=0
   cisco-aniplan=0
   cisco-anipi=0
   cisco-anisi=1
   dest=9193926003
   cisco-desttype=0
   cisco-destplan=0
   cisco-rdie=FFFFFFFFFFFFFFFF
   cisco-rdn=
   cisco-rdntype=0
   cisco-rdnplan=0
   cisco-rdnpi=-1
   cisco-rdnsi=-1
   cisco-redirectreason=-1   fwd_final_type =0
   final_redirectNumber =
   hunt_group_timeout =0
```

```
178523: Dec  1 02:27:25.387: //147711/C461DB800000/CCAPI/ccIFCallSetupRequestPrivate:
   Interface=0x7F8694ACD1C8, Interface Type=3, Destination=, Mode=0x0,
   Call Params(Calling Number=4083926001,(Calling Name=)(TON=Unknown, NPI=Unknown,
     Screening=User, Passed, Presentation=Allowed),
   Called Number=9193926003(TON=Unknown, NPI=Unknown), Calling Translated=FALSE,
   Subscriber Type Str=Unknown, FinalDestinationFlag=TRUE, Outgoing Dial-peer=6001,
     Call Count On=FALSE,
   Source Trkgrp Route Label=, Target Trkgrp Route Label=, tg_label_flag=0,
     Application Call Id=)
```

Tip The commands **show dialplan number** *called-party-number* and **show dialplan uri** *called-uri* can be used to find the list of matching outbound dial peers for a given called number or URI, as shown in this example:

```
cube1#show dialplan number 9193926003
Macro Exp.: 9193926003

VoiceOverIpPeer6001
    peer type = voice, system default peer = FALSE, information type = voice,
    description = `"Outbound dial-peer for Agent phone calls"',
    tag = 6001, destination-pattern = `9193926...',
    voice reg type = 0, corresponding tag = 0,
...
cube1#
```

The dial peer matching process for the advanced and Multi-VRF deployments is discussed later in this chapter, in the "Dial Peer Optimization" section. URI-based routing and multitenant routing are discussed later in this chapter.

Translation Profiles

CUBE provides the ability to transform the calling and called party numbers of inbound and outbound calls. It can also translate the redirect numbers in call forwarding scenarios, as well as serve as a mechanism for blocking calls to and from undesired numbers. This section provides an overview of the functionality and its configuration, using real-world use cases.

Cisco IOS and IOS XE software provide a generic capability to configure voice translation rules. Each rule has a match pattern and a replace pattern. A set of up to 100 rules are grouped together in a specific order (highest-priority first) under a configuration object called **voice translation-rule.** Voice translation rules are associated to **voice translation-profile** in order to apply the translation rules to called, calling, and redirect numbers. Voice translation profiles are then configured under one or more dial peers to apply the transformations. A rule can be applied for either inbound or outbound peer matches or both.

The match and replace patterns are regex patterns defined in the same format as the regex patterns used in Stream Editor (SED, a non-interactive command-line text editor from GNU). The patterns begin and end with a forward slash (/) character. In addition to digits 0–9 and A–F, all the common regex wildcard characters are supported, including these:

```
. [ ] * ? + ^ $
```

A defined subset of digits in the match pattern can also be grouped together by using escaped open **\(** and closed **\)** parentheses to define a *backreference*. The groups are automatically numbered based on their occurrence within the pattern. The first group in the match pattern is referenced as **\1** in the replace pattern, the second group is referenced as **\2**, and so on. This grouping concept is very powerful and allows you to extract specific portions from an input string and use that information in the output string.

The following sections describe four use cases to help you understand how to apply voice translation rules for practical purposes:

- **Called number transformation**—Transforms a 10-digit DID number to a 5-digit DN
- **Calling number transformation**—Transforms a calling party number for outbound calls
- **Redirect number transformation**—Transforms a 5-digit internal DN present in the SIP Diversion header field to a full 10-digit DID
- **Call blocking**—Drops calls that originate from a specific number without routing to their intended destination

> **Caution** For brevity, all the upcoming configuration examples discussed in this chapter do not explicitly show the audio, video, and DTMF relay capability–related commands under the dial peers. All configurations referenced in this chapter use the G.711μ law audio codec, H.264 video codec, RTP-NTE, DTMF relay, and TCP as the SIP transport protocol. Please make sure to add the relevant configuration commands similar to the ones shown below in real-world CUBE deployments:

```
dial-peer voice 8000 voip
 video codec h264
 session transport tcp
 dtmf-relay rtp-nte
 codec g711ulaw
 no vad
```

Called Number Transformation

The objective of the example shown in Figure 3-14 is to convert the called party number of incoming calls received across the SIP trunk from a 10-digit direct-inward-dial (DID) number range to a 5-digit internal directory number (DN) before routing the call to the call controller within the enterprise.

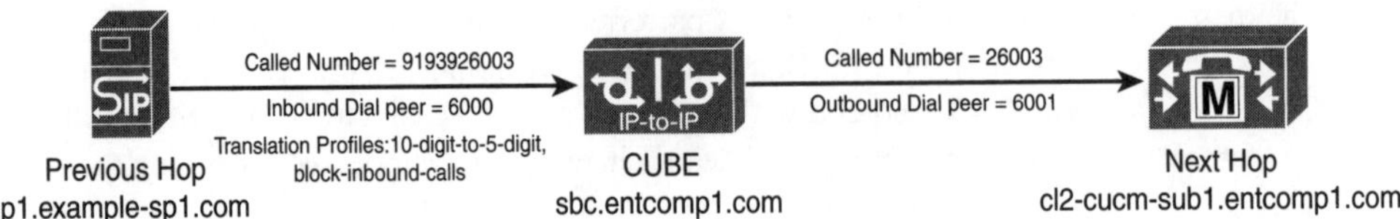

Figure 3-14 *Called Number Transformation for an Inbound Call*

The following steps outline how to strip the leading five digits off of the DIDs that come in for the range 9193926000 through 9193926999:

Step 1. Create a voice translation rule that matches the 10-digit DID range of interest. The last 5 digits are grouped in the match pattern and is backreferenced as **\1** in the replace pattern. The replaced string after the translation contains only the last 5 digits.

Step 2. Create a voice translation profile that applies the translation rule to the called party number using the **translate** called command.

Step 3. Apply the translation profile in the inbound dial peer 6000, which is used to handle incoming calls from the service provider across the SIP trunk. The **incoming** keyword in the **translation-profile incoming** command indicates that transformation is applied for calls received by this dial peer. Example 3-28 shows the relevant configuration snippet.

Example 3-28 *Voice Translation Profile for Called Party Number Transformation*

```
voice translation-rule 2
 rule 1 /^91939\(2....\)/ /\1/

voice translation-profile 10-digit-to-5-digit
 translate called 2

dial-peer voice 6000 voip
 description "Inbound dial-peer for Agent phone calls"
 translation-profile incoming 10-digit-to-5-digit
 session protocol sipv2
 incoming called-number 9193926...
 voice-class sip bind control source-interface GigabitEthernet0/0/1
 voice-class sip bind media source-interface GigabitEthernet0/0/1
```

It is a best practice to test voice translation rules before applying them to dial peers. This can be done by using the **test voice translation-rule** *ruleset-number input-value* command, as shown in Example 3-29.

Example 3-29 *Voice Translation Rule Verification*

```
cube1# test voice translation-rule 2 9193926003
Matched with rule 1
Original number: 9193926003    Translated number: 26003
Original number type: none      Translated number type: none
Original number plan: none      Translated number plan: none
```

The output of **debug voip ccapi inout** and **debug voice translation** can be used to verify whether transformation is applied correctly after matching the inbound dial peer by viewing the transformed called party number that is used to look up the outbound dial peer, as shown in Example 3-30.

Example 3-30 *Voice Translation Profile Verification for Called Number Transformation*

```
6181495: Dec 26 02:19:52.640: //-1/400D59800000/CCAPI/cc_api_call_setup_ind_common:
   Interface=0x7F8694ACD1C8, Call Info(
   Calling Number=4083926001,(Calling Name=)(TON=Unknown, NPI=Unknown,
     Screening=User, Passed, Presentation=Allowed),
   Called Number=9193926003(TON=Unknown, NPI=Unknown),
   Calling Translated=FALSE, Subscriber Type Str=Unknown, FinalDestinationFlag=TRUE,
   Incoming Dial-peer=6000, Progress Indication=NULL(0), Calling IE Present=TRUE,
   Source Trkgrp Route Label=, Target Trkgrp Route Label=, CLID Transparent=FALSE),
     Call Id=147487

...

6181521: Dec 26 02:19:52.642: //-1/400D59800000/RXRULE/regxrule_profile_translate_
  internal: number=9193926003 type=unknown plan=unknown numbertype=called
6181522: Dec 26 02:19:52.642: //-1/400D59800000/RXRULE/regxrule_profile_match_
  internal: Matched with rule 1 in ruleset 2
6181523: Dec 26 02:19:52.642: //-1/400D59800000/RXRULE/regxrule_profile_match_
  internal: Matched with rule 1 in ruleset 2
6181524: Dec 26 02:19:52.643: //-1/400D59800000/RXRULE/sed_subst: Successful substi-
  tution; pattern=9193926003 matchPattern=91939(2....) replacePattern=\1 replaced
  pattern=26003
6181525: Dec 26 02:19:52.643: //-1/400D59800000/RXRULE/regxrule_subst_num_type:
  Match Type = none, Replace Type = none Input Type = unknown
6181526: Dec 26 02:19:52.643: //-1/400D59800000/RXRULE/regxrule_subst_num_plan:
  Match Plan = none, Replace Plan = none Input Plan = unknown
6181527: Dec 26 02:19:52.643: //-1/400D59800000/RXRULE/regxrule_profile_translate_
  internal: xlt_number=26003 xlt_type=unknown xlt_plan=unknown
6181528: Dec 26 02:19:52.643: //147487/400D59800000/CCAPI/ccCallProceeding:
   Progress Indication=NULL(0)
6181529: Dec 26 02:19:52.643: //147487/400D59800000/CCAPI/ccCallSetupRequest:
   Destination=, Calling IE Present=TRUE, Mode=0,
   Outgoing Dial-peer=6002, Params=0x7F869EAEE9B8, Progress Indication=NULL(0)
...
```

```
6181534: Dec 26 02:19:52.643: //147487/400D59800000/CCAPI/cc_api_display_ie_
  subfields:
   ccCallSetupRequest:
   cisco-username=4083926001
   ----- ccCallInfo IE subfields -----
   cisco-ani=4083926001
   cisco-anitype=0
   cisco-aniplan=0
   cisco-anipi=0
   cisco-anisi=1
   dest=26003
   cisco-desttype=0
   cisco-destplan=0
 ...

6181535: Dec 26 02:19:52.643: //147487/400D59800000/CCAPI/ccIFCallSetupRequestPrivate:
   Interface=0x7F8694ACD1C8, Interface Type=3, Destination=, Mode=0x0,
   Call Params(Calling Number=4083926001,(Calling Name=)(TON=Unknown, NPI=Unknown,
     Screening=User, Passed, Presentation=Allowed),
   Called Number=26003(TON=Unknown, NPI=Unknown), Calling Translated=FALSE,
   Subscriber Type Str=Unknown, FinalDestinationFlag=TRUE, Outgoing Dial-peer=6002,
     Call Count On=FALSE,
   Source Trkgrp Route Label=, Target Trkgrp Route Label=, tg_label_flag=0,
     Application Call Id=)
```

Calling Number Transformation

The example shown in Figure 3-15 sets the calling party number for all service provider–bound calls (from within the enterprise) to the main number of the enterprise: 9193926000. Certain service providers enforce the requirement to have the assigned number as the calling party number of all outbound calls in order to further route the call upstream toward the called party.

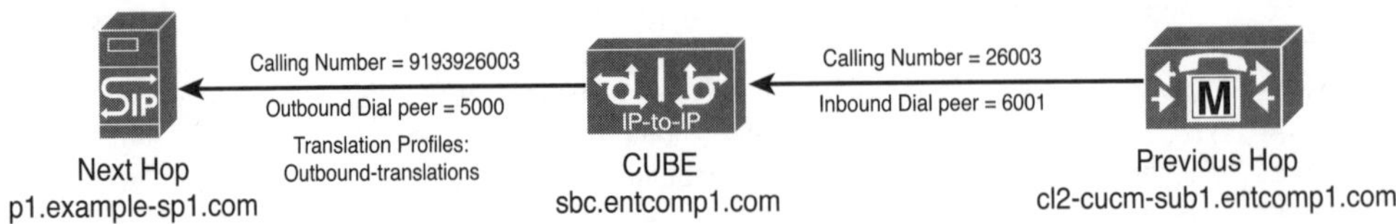

Figure 3-15 *Calling Number Transformation for an Outbound Call*

The following steps outline how to translate the calling party number from the 5-digit directory extension number to a 10-digit main number assigned to the caller's company:

Step 1. Create a voice translation rule with match pattern **/^2....$/** to match the internal directory number and then replace it with the specific **/9193926000/** pattern. The characters ^ and $ are used to indicate that the match pattern begins with the digit 2 and ends after exactly five digits. The **$** ensures that only 5-digit internal directory numbers match this pattern.

Step 2. Associate the translation rule to a translation profile by using the **translate calling** command to apply the rule to the calling party number.

Step 3. Apply the translation profile under the outbound dial peer 5000, which is used to route calls to number beginning with a **[2-9].........** pattern. The **outgoing** keyword in the **translation-profile outgoing** command implies that the transformation is applied only to calls originated from this dial peer. The corresponding configuration is shown in Example 3-31.

Step 4. Use **test voice translation-rule**, as demonstrated in Example 3-32, to ensure that the configured rule performs the expected translation.

Example 3-31 *Voice Translation Profile for Calling Party Number Transformation*

```
voice translation-rule 1
 rule 1 /^2....$/ /9193926000/

voice translation-profile outbound-translations
 translate calling 1

dial-peer voice 5000 voip
 description "Outbound dial-peer for external calls"
 translation-profile outgoing outbound-translations
 destination-pattern [2-9].........
 session protocol sipv2
 session target ipv4:192.168.202.164
 incoming called-number 9193925...
 voice-class sip bind control source-interface GigabitEthernet0/0/1
 voice-class sip bind media source-interface GigabitEthernet0/0/1
```

Example 3-32 *Voice Translation Rule Verification*

```
cube1#test voice translation-rule 1 26003
Matched with rule 1
Original number: 26003      Translated number: 9193926000
Original number type: none    Translated number type: none
Original number plan: none    Translated number plan: none
cube1#
```

The output of **debug voip ccapi inout** and **debug voice translation**, as shown in Example 3-33, can be used to verify whether the translation profile is applied to the correct dial peer and ensure that calling party transformation is happening properly.

Example 3-33 *Voice Translation Profile Verification for Calling Number Transformation*

```
6181819: Dec 26 02:42:59.788: //-1/7AC4C1000000/DPM/dpMatchPeersMoreArg:
   Result=SUCCESS(0)
   List of Matched Outgoing Dial-peer(s):
     1: Dial-peer Tag=5000
6181820: Dec 26 02:42:59.788: //-1/7AC4C1000000/RXRULE/regxrule_translate_exist_
  internal: no rule for callback-number number
6181821: Dec 26 02:42:59.788: //-1/7AC4C1000000/RXRULE/regxrule_profile_translate_
  internal: number=26003 type=unknown plan=unknown numbertype=calling
6181822: Dec 26 02:42:59.788: //-1/7AC4C1000000/RXRULE/regxrule_profile_match_
  internal: Matched with rule 1 in ruleset 1
6181823: Dec 26 02:42:59.788: //-1/7AC4C1000000/RXRULE/regxrule_profile_match_
  internal: Matched with rule 1 in ruleset 1
6181824: Dec 26 02:42:59.788: //-1/7AC4C1000000/RXRULE/sed_subst: Successful
  substitution; pattern=26003 matchPattern=^2....$ replacePattern=9193926000
  replaced pattern=9193926000
6181825: Dec 26 02:42:59.788: //-1/7AC4C1000000/RXRULE/regxrule_subst_num_type:
  Match Type = none, Replace Type = none Input Type = unknown
6181826: Dec 26 02:42:59.788: //-1/7AC4C1000000/RXRULE/regxrule_subst_num_plan:
  Match Plan = none, Replace Plan = none Input Plan = unknown
```

Redirect Number Transformation

This example supports scenarios where an internal extension 26003 is set to forward all incoming calls to an external number. The external number is reachable through the SIP trunk between CUBE and the service provider, but when the call is forwarded, the diversion extension is presented as an abbreviated 5-digit number in the Diversion header field (see RFC 5806) to the service provider.

Translation patterns can help with this condition by normalizing the abbreviated extension present in the Diversion header field to a fully qualified number, as service providers typically reject From or Diversion header fields that are not fully qualified numbers.

In this example, the user in entcomp2 company 4083926001 calls 9193926003. CUBE transforms the called party number to a 5-digit extension number 26003 and routes the call to CUCM. The call to extension 26003 gets forwarded to 9193927003 due to the Call Forward All configuration. CUCM originates the outbound call to 9193927003 across CUBE. The outbound SIP INVITE to the provider has a SIP Diversion header field with the diversion extension set to the internal extension (**26003**) instead of DID (**9193926003**), as shown in Example 3-34.

The goal of this translation is to change the original called party number to 9193926003 to ensure that the service provider recognizes the DID number and doesn't reject the outbound forwarding call.

Example 3-34 *SIP INVITE to the Call Forward Destination with an Incorrect Diversion Value*

```
INVITE sip:9193927003@192.168.202.164:5060 SIP/2.0
Via: SIP/2.0/TCP 192.168.202.165:5060;branch=z9hG4bK25B2A1C32
Remote-Party-ID: <sip:4083926001@192.168.202.165>;party=calling;screen=yes;
  privacy=off
From: <sip:4083926001@172.18.110.119>;tag=787CA218-1F08
To: <sip:9193927003@192.168.202.164>
Date: Tue, 26 Dec 2017 21:22:25 GMT
Call-ID: B42D0151-E9B911E7-B9369A97-7107F84E@192.168.202.165
Supported: timer,resource-priority,replaces,sdp-anat
Min-SE:  1800
Cisco-Guid: 3704816640-0000065536-0000000004-3463320236
User-Agent: Cisco-SIPGateway/IOS-16.6.1
Allow: INVITE, OPTIONS, BYE, CANCEL, ACK, PRACK, UPDATE, REFER, SUBSCRIBE, NOTIFY,
  INFO, REGISTER
CSeq: 101 INVITE
Timestamp: 1514323345
Contact: <sip:4083926001@192.168.202.165:5060;transport=tcp>
Expires: 180
Allow-Events: telephone-event
Max-Forwards: 63
Diversion: <sip:26003@192.168.202.165>;privacy=off;reason=unconditional;screen=yes
Session-ID: 61443b30f06c5c95894d23de262aa73b;remote=00000000000000000000000000000000
Session-Expires:  1800
Content-Length: 0
```

The following steps outline how to translate the diversion number from an internal extension to a fully qualified number:

Step 1. Create a voice translation rule with match pattern **/^\(2....\)$/** to match and group the internal directory number. The pattern **/919392\1/** is used as the replace pattern, and it adds the prefix **919392** to the matched 5-digit string. The **\1** in the replace pattern is the backreference to the first group.

Step 2. Because the outbound dial peer 5000 is already configured with a translation profile named **outbound-translations** to perform calling party number transformation (use case 2), update this translation profile with the **redirect-called** command and the reference translation rule created in step 1. The **redirect-called** command shown in Example 3-35 refers to the rule to translate the original called party number, and **redirect-target** refers to the rule to translate the call forward destination number.

Step 3. Use the output of **debug voip ccapi inout**, **debug voip dialpeer default**, **debug voice translation**, and **debug ccsip message** to view the translation processing that modifies the SIP Diversion header field. Example 3-36 is a debug snippet with key lines highlighted to show the outbound dial peer used, matching and replacement of the redirect called number, and SIP INVITE with the translated redirecting number.

Example 3-35 *Voice Translation Profile for Redirect Called Number Transformation*

```
voice translation-rule 4
 rule 1 /^\(2....\)$/ /91939\1/

voice translation-profile outbound-translations
 translate calling 1
 translate redirect-called 4

dial-peer voice 5000 voip
 description "Outbound dial-peer for external calls"
 translation-profile outgoing outbound-translations
 destination-pattern [2-9].......
```

Example 3-36 *Voice Translation Profile Verification for Calling Number Transformation*

```
6187673: Dec 26 21:16:42.273: //-1/10615E800000/DPM/dpMatchPeersMoreArg:
   Result=SUCCESS(0)
   List of Matched Outgoing Dial-peer(s):
     1: Dial-peer Tag=5000
...
6187687: Dec 26 21:16:42.273: //-1/10615E800000/RXRULE/regxrule_profile_translate_
  internal: number=26003 type=unknown plan=unknown numbertype=redirect-called
6187688: Dec 26 21:16:42.273: //-1/10615E800000/RXRULE/regxrule_profile_match_
  internal: Matched with rule 1 in ruleset 4
6187689: Dec 26 21:16:42.273: //-1/10615E800000/RXRULE/regxrule_profile_match_
  internal: Matched with rule 1 in ruleset 4
6187690: Dec 26 21:16:42.273: //-1/10615E800000/RXRULE/sed_subst: Successful
  substitution; pattern=26003 matchPattern=^(2....)$ replacePattern=91939\1 replaced
  pattern=9193926003
.......
.......
6187715: Dec 26 21:16:42.275: //154516/10615E800000/SIP/Msg/ccsipDisplayMsg:
Sent:
INVITE sip:9193927003@192.168.202.164:5060 SIP/2.0
Via: SIP/2.0/TCP 192.168.202.165:5060;branch=z9hG4bK25B10102D
Remote-Party-ID: <sip:4083926001@192.168.202.165>;party=calling;screen=yes;
  privacy=off
From: <sip:4083926001@172.18.110.119>;tag=787763BE-1354
To: <sip:9193927003@192.168.202.164>
Date: Tue, 26 Dec 2017 21:16:42 GMT
Call-ID: E7598E64-E9B811E7-B9149A97-7107F84E@192.168.202.165
...
Diversion: <sip:9193926003@192.168.202.165>;privacy=off;reason=unconditional;
  screen=yes
Session-ID: f538138405505557b8f647ab3cbf8b07;remote=00000000000000000000000000000000
Session-Expires:  1800
Content-Length: 0
```

Call Blocking

This example demonstrates how to block all calls coming in from 4083927001 and send call reject (**21**) as the disconnect cause code through the use of a translation profile. The same procedure can be used to block a range of numbers by using a regex pattern that matches the numbers of interest. The following configuration steps outline how to block inbound calls based on the calling party number:

Step 1. Create a voice translation rule that matches the number to be blocked and use the keyword **reject** to specify that this is a call block rule. There is no replace pattern for call block rules.

Step 2. Associate the translation rule with a translation profile by using the **translate calling** command to apply the call blocking rule to the calling party number.

Step 3. Configure the translation profile in the inbound dial peer 6000 used to handle incoming calls from the service provider across the SIP trunk. The **incoming** keyword in the **call-block translation-profile incoming** command indicates that transformation is applied for calls received by this dial peer. Example 3-37 shows the relevant configuration snippet. The call reject cause code (**21**) is defined as the call disconnect cause code with the command **call-block disconnect-cause incoming call-reject**.

Step 4. Use the **test voice translation-rule** command to ensure that the configured rule blocks the numbers of interest. Example 3-38 demonstrates this, for this example.

Example 3-37 *Voice Translation Profile for Call Blocking*

```
voice translation-rule 3
 rule 1 reject /4083927001/

voice translation-profile block-inbound-calls
 translate calling 3

dial-peer voice 6000 voip
 description "Inbound dial-peer for Agent phone calls"
 translation-profile incoming 10-digit-to-5-digit
 call-block translation-profile incoming block-inbound-calls
 call-block disconnect-cause incoming call-reject
```

Example 3-38 *Voice Translation Rule Verification*

```
cube1#test voice translation-rule 3 4083927001
4083927001 blocked on rule 1
cube1#
```

The output of **debug voip ccapi inout**, **debug voice translation**, and **debug ccsip message** can be used to verify call block behavior and the corresponding call disconnect cause code. CUBE sends a 403 Forbidden final response with the Reason header field set to Q.850 cause code 21 when blocking a call, as shown in Example 3-39.

Example 3-39 *Voice Translation Profile Verification for Call Blocking*

```
6183160: Dec 26 16:21:35.084: //-1/D59700800000/CCAPI/cc_api_call_setup_ind_common:
   Interface=0x7F8694ACD1C8, Call Info(
   Calling Number=4083927001,(Calling Name=)(TON=Unknown, NPI=Unknown,
     Screening=User, Passed, Presentation=Allowed),
   Called Number=9193926003(TON=Unknown, NPI=Unknown),
   Calling Translated=FALSE, Subscriber Type Str=Unknown, FinalDestinationFlag=TRUE,
   Incoming Dial-peer=6000, Progress Indication=NULL(0), Calling IE Present=TRUE,
   Source Trkgrp Route Label=, Target Trkgrp Route Label=, CLID Transparent=FALSE),
     Call Id=152787
...
6183177: Dec 26 16:21:35.086: //-1/D59700800000/RXRULE/regxrule_match: Matched a
  call block rule; number=4083927001 rule precedence=1
6183178: Dec 26 16:21:35.086: //-1/D59700800000/RXRULE/regxrule_profile_block_
  internal: Matched with rule 1 in ruleset 3
...
6183182: Dec 26 16:21:35.086: //152787/D59700800000/CCAPI/ccCallDisconnect:
   Cause Value=21, Call Entry(Responsed=TRUE, Cause Value=21)
6183183: Dec 26 16:21:35.087: //152787/D59700800000/SIP/Msg/ccsipDisplayMsg:
Sent:
SIP/2.0 403 Forbidden
Via: SIP/2.0/TCP 192.168.202.169:5060;branch=z9hG4bKuqikwX.
  Yw24UpUvmEEXmdQ~~101,SIP/2.0/TCP 192.168.202.167:5060;branch=z9hG4bKRzUwlcSQ3rMWDN
  01cODE+Q~~148,SIP/2.0/TCP 192.168.202.162:5060;branch=z9hG4bKDEE28
From: <sip:4083927001@192.168.202.162>;tag=976FADE8-1D84
To: <sip:9193926003@entcomp1.com>;tag=7769330A-D4C
Date: Tue, 26 Dec 2017 16:21:35 GMT
Call-ID: 5A160E01-E98F11E7-838BB2A0-6E96DC16@192.168.202.162
Timestamp: 1514305155
CSeq: 101 INVITE
Allow-Events: telephone-event
Server: Cisco-SIPGateway/IOS-16.6.1
Reason: Q.850;cause=21
Session-ID: 4156ba8ac0865023bd733da1a9472423;remote=6eeda7cdf20c516ba0f337c2a081883e
Content-Length: 0
```

Dial Peer Optimization

The configuration discussed earlier in this chapter for number transformations uses dial peers that each have one destination pattern and one session target configured. This approach requires one dial peer for each combination of called number pattern and next-hop combination. For example, a network administrator of a company with a DID range 919392000 through 9193922010 and a CUCM cluster with three call-processing subscribers would need to configure two dial peers to route the inbound calls from CUBE to each subscriber in the UCM cluster. The first dial peer has the destination pattern **919392200[0-9]$**, and the second dial peer has the destination pattern **9193922010$**. This results in a total of six dial peers—two peers for each of the three subscribers to handle one unique DID range.

Figure 3-16 shows a sample network topology in which CUBE is deployed at the central site to handle inbound calls to the enterprise. The enterprise has four sites with unique DID ranges and IP phones at each site, registered to a CUCM cluster with three call-processing subscriber nodes available. A network administrator would need to configure 24 dial peers (6 per unique DID range) to correctly route inbound external calls from the service provider to CUCM.

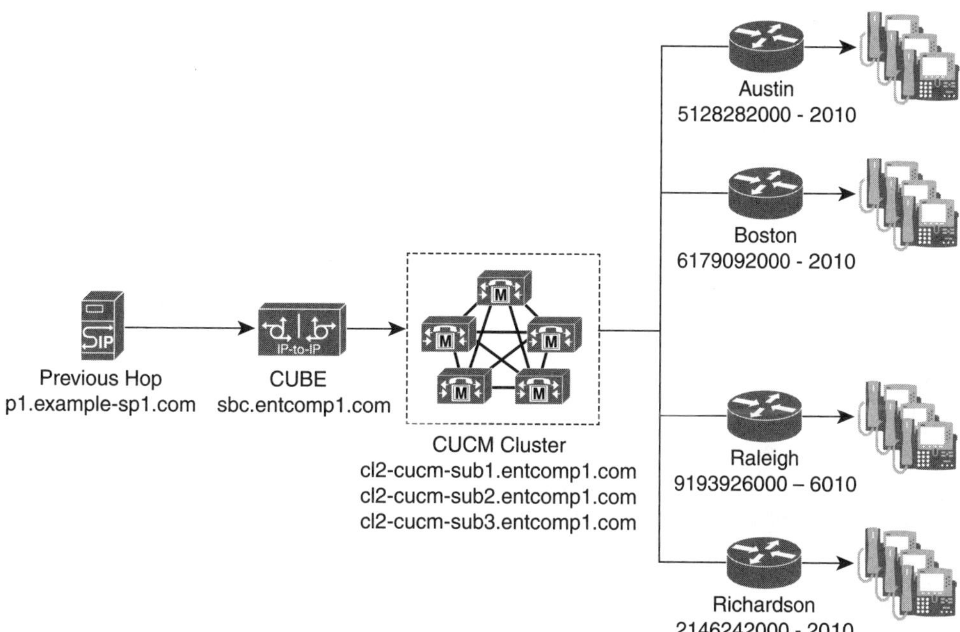

Figure 3-16 *Central Site UC Deployment Model with Five Node CUCM Cluster and Four Sites*

Configuration management takes more time and is subject to human errors as the number of dial peers increases as the dial plan grows in size and/or complexity. This also impacts the time it takes to troubleshoot call failures as a support engineer would need to identify the relevant dial peers from a large set of dial peers.

The interesting item is that except for the **destination-pattern** and **session target** parameters, most of the other parameters (for example, the audio codec, the DTMF relay capabilities, the SIP OPTIONS keepalive) in the 24 dial peers are the same across the peers. To significantly reduce the number of necessary dial peers, there is an option to configure multiple destination patterns and multiple session targets in the same dial peer. This is done through the use of E.164 pattern maps and server groups.

E.164 Pattern Map

The E.164 pattern map enables multiple E.164 patterns to be grouped together as a logical entity for reference. This map is assigned a tag that can be referenced to match called and calling party numbers as part of the inbound and outbound dial peer selection process.

Example 3-40 shows how the **voice class e164-pattern-map** command is defined to group all the DID ranges for the four sites shown in Figure 3-16. The syntax for the pattern in the **e164** command is the same as the syntax used in the **destination-pattern** command.

Example 3-40 *E.164 Pattern Map Configuration*

```
voice class e164-pattern-map 1
  e164 2146242010
  e164 5128282010
  e164 6179092010
  e164 9193926010
  e164 214624200[0-9]
  e164 512828200[0-9]
  e164 617909200[0-9]
  e164 919392600[0-9]

voice class e164-pattern-map 2
 url ftp://ftp.entcomp1.com/e164-patterns.txt

dial-peer voice 5003 voip
 description "Inbound dial-peer for incoming external calls"
 translation-profile outgoing outbound-translations
 destination-pattern [2-9].........
 session protocol sipv2
 session target ipv4:192.168.202.164
 incoming called e164-pattern-map 1
 voice-class sip bind control source-interface GigabitEthernet0/0/2
 voice-class sip bind media source-interface GigabitEthernet0/0/2


dial-peer voice 6003 voip
 description "Outbound dial-peer for incoming external calls to CUCM"
 huntstop
```

```
session protocol sipv2
session transport tcp
session target ipv4:172.18.110.206
destination e164-pattern-map 1
voice-class sip options-keepalive profile 1
voice-class sip bind control source-interface GigabitEthernet0/0/2
voice-class sip bind media source-interface GigabitEthernet0/0/2
```

The command **destination e164-pattern-map** *tag* is used in outbound dial peers to specify the list of called number patterns. The **destination-pattern** (used for a single pattern) and **destination e164-pattern-map** (used for multiple patterns) commands have the same match order of preference in the outbound dial peer selection process.

Similarly, the command **incoming called e164-pattern-map** *tag* is used in inbound dial peers to specify the list of called number patterns. The **incoming called-number** (used for single pattern) and **incoming called e164-pattern-map** (used for multiple patterns) commands have the same match order of preference in the inbound dial peer selection process.

The command **answer-address** *calling-number-pattern* defines a single calling number pattern in the inbound dial peer. The multi-pattern equivalent of **answer-address** is **incoming calling e164-pattern** *tag*, which defines a list of calling number patterns instead of just one.

To make configuration management even simpler, the list of patterns can also be read from a text file. The text file has one pattern per line and can be stored locally or retrieved from a remote location such as a TFTP, FTP, or HTTP server. The file location is specified with **voice class e164-pattern-map** and the **url** parameter, as shown in Examples 3-40 and 3-41. The patterns are loaded at the time of initial URL configuration, when the router is reloaded, and can also be manually loaded using the command **voice class e164-pattern-map load.** Network engineers can use **show voice class e164-pattern-map** to validate the current list of patterns grouped under the map.

Example 3-41 *Loading and Verifying E.164 Patterns from a File*

```
cube1#voice class e164-pattern-map load 2
url ftp://ftp.entcomp1.com/e164-patterns.txt loaded successfully

All e164 patterns are valid

cube1#
cube1#show voice class e164-pattern-map 2

e164-pattern-map 2
----------------------------------------
```

```
  It has 8 entries
  It is populated from url ftp://ftp.entcomp1.com/e164-patterns.txt .
  Map is valid.

E164 pattern
-------------------
2146242010
5128282010
6179092010
9193926010
214624200[0-9]
512828200[0-9]
617909200[0-9]
919392600[0-9]
cube1#

cube1#more e164-patterns.txt
2146242010
5128282010
6179092010
9193926010
214624200[0-9]
512828200[0-9]
617909200[0-9]
919392600[0-9]

cube1#
```

Server Group

As the name suggests, *server groups* provide the ability to combine multiple next-hop servers into a logical group and reference the group tag in the outbound dial peers. For example, all the call-processing subscriber nodes of a CUCM cluster can be listed in **server-group 1**. Each server can be assigned a **preference** that is used to determine the order within the server group in which CUBE attempts to send an outbound INVITE to establish a call. The command **hunt-scheme round-robin** can also be used instead of the **preference** command to have CUBE automatically load balance outbound calls across the given set of servers.

Example 3-42 shows the optimized inbound and outbound dial peer configuration for the centralized CUBE deployment model shown in Figure 3-16. The list of called number patterns to match the enterprise DID range is configured as an E.164 pattern map tagged with ID 1. Three subscribers from the CUCM cluster are listed together in the **voice class server-group** command. A separate **voice class sip-options-keepalive** profile is configured and associated with the outbound dial peer 6003 to monitor the status of the elements defined within the server group.

Example 3-42 *Optimized Inbound and Outbound Dial Peer Configuration*

```
voice class e164-pattern-map 1
  e164 2146242010
  e164 5128282010
  e164 6179092010
  e164 9193926010
  e164 214624200[0-9]
  e164 512828200[0-9]
  e164 617909200[0-9]
  e164 919392600[0-9]



voice class server-group 1
 ipv4 172.18.110.206 port 5060 preference 1
 ipv4 172.18.110.207 port 5060 preference 2
 ipv4 172.18.110.205 port 5060 preference 3

voice class sip-options-keepalive 1
 down-interval 25
 up-interval 65
 retry 3
 transport tcp

dial-peer voice 5003 voip
 description "Inbound dial-peer for incoming external calls"
 translation-profile outgoing outbound-translations
 destination-pattern [2-9].........
 session protocol sipv2
 session target ipv4:192.168.202.164
 incoming called e164-pattern-map 1
 voice-class sip bind control source-interface GigabitEthernet0/0/2
 voice-class sip bind media source-interface GigabitEthernet0/0/2



dial-peer voice 6003 voip
 description "Outbound dial-peer for incoming external calls to CUCM"
 huntstop
 session protocol sipv2
 session transport tcp
 session server-group 1
 destination e164-pattern-map 1
 voice-class sip options-keepalive profile 1
 voice-class sip bind control source-interface GigabitEthernet0/0/2
 voice-class sip bind media source-interface GigabitEthernet0/0/2
```

Inbound dial peer 5003 is configured with **incoming called e164-pattern-map** instead of the **incoming called-number** command, and outbound dial peer 6003 is configured with **destination e164-pattern-map** instead of the **destination-pattern** command. The outbound dial peer is associated with the server group using the command **session server-group** instead of the **session target** command. The optimized configuration reduces the number of outbound dial peers from 24 to 1 for the deployment scenario described in Figure 3-16.

Tip You may notice that CUBE does not send SIP OPTIONS messages to the elements in the server group when the command **voice-class sip option-keepalive up-interval 65 down-interval 35 retry 3** is configured with **dial-peer voice 6003**. This is because the option of directly specifying SIP OPTIONS parameters in a dial peer with a server group configuration is not supported. Instead, the SIP out-of-dialog **OPTIONS keepalive profile** must be configured via **voice class sip-options-keepalive** and then referenced in the outbound dial peer that contains the server group configuration for the keepalive mechanism to work correctly.

Multiple dial peers can share this same keepalive profile. The keepalive profile feature consolidates the sending of SIP OPTIONS messages such that only one SIP OPTIONS message is sent to each next hop, even if the same hop is specified as the target destination across multiple dial peers, either using the **session target** command or as an element in a server group.

The commands **show dial-peer voice summary**, **show voice class server-group**, and **show voice class sip-options-keepalive** can be used to view a high-level configuration summary of the configured dial plan and to also check the operational status of the next-hop servers defined in the server group. This is demonstrated in Example 3-43. If all the elements in the server group are determined to be down through the SIP OPTIONS mechanism, then all dial peers associated with that server group are busied out. The parameters **map** and **SESS-SVR-GRP** in the output of **show dial-peer voice summary** provide the E.164 pattern map tag and the server group tag associated with a given dial peer. The **show voice class sip-options-keepalive** command provides an overall keepalive status for each dial peer, as well as for each element in the associated server group.

Example 3-43 show *Commands to Review Optimized Dial Peer Configuration*

```
cube1#show dial-peer voice summary
dial-peer hunt 0
            AD                                  PRE  PASS  SESS-SER-GRP\  OUT
TAG    TYPE  MIN  OPER PREFIX    DEST-PATTERN   FER  THRU  SESS-TARGET
  STAT PORT  KEEPALIVE  VRF
6003  voip  up   up              map:1            0  syst  SESS-SVR-GRP: 1
  active     NA
5003  voip  up   up              [2-9].......   0  syst  ipv4:192.168.202.164      NA
 For server-grp details please execute command:show voice class server-group
  <tag_id>

cube1#show voice class server-group 1
```

```
Voice class server-group: 1
 AdminStatus: Up         OperStatus: Up
 Hunt-Scheme: preference     Last returned server:
 Description: "CUCM Subscriber Nodes"
 Total server entries: 3

 Pref   Type   IP Address                              IP Port
 ----   ----   ----------                              -------
 1      ipv4   172.18.110.206                          5060
 2      ipv4   172.18.110.207                          5060
 3      ipv4   172.18.110.205                          5060

-------------------------------------

cube1#show voice class sip-options-keepalive 1
Voice class sip-options-keepalive: 1         AdminStat: Up
 Description:
 Transport: tcp         Sip Profiles: 0
 Interval(seconds) Up: 65         Down: 25
 Retry: 3

  Peer Tag         Server Group    OOD SessID      OOD Stat         IfIndex
  --------         ------------    ----------      --------         -------
  6003             1                               Active           38

  Server Group: 1          OOD Stat: Active
   OOD SessID       OOD Stat
   ----------       --------
   1                Active
   2                Active
   3                Active

 OOD SessID: 1                  OOD Stat: Active
  Target: ipv4:172.18.110.206:5060
  Transport: tcp                Sip Profiles: 0

 OOD SessID: 2                  OOD Stat: Active
  Target: ipv4:172.18.110.207:5060
  Transport: tcp                Sip Profiles: 0

 OOD SessID: 3                  OOD Stat: Active
  Target: ipv4:172.18.110.205:5060
  Transport: tcp                Sip Profiles: 0

------------------------------------------------------
```

URI-Based Dialing

Enterprises that are directly connected across the Internet via CUBE can enable URI dialing so that users can place calls using the SIP URI of the called party instead of using a telephone number. Figure 3-17 shows a sample deployment in which two enterprises, entcomp1 and entcomp2, are connected across a SIP trunk using CUBE. Alice can place a call to Bob by dialing bob@entcomp1.com, and Bob can place a call to Alice by dialing alice@entcomp2.com.

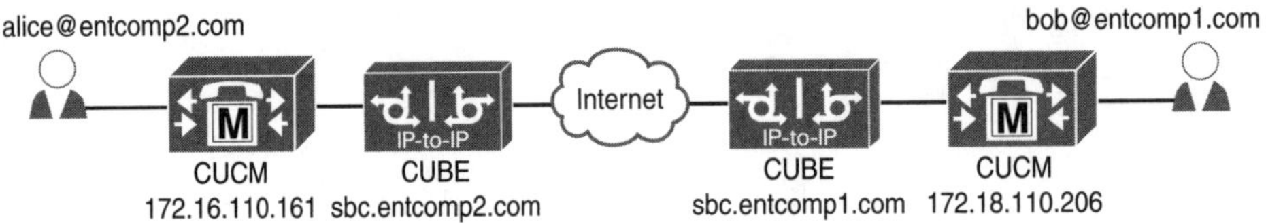

Figure 3-17 *URI-Based Dialing Across Enterprises Connected via CUBE*

As discussed earlier in this chapter, URI-based dial peer matching rules (through the **incoming uri** and **destination uri** commands) have higher preference than the DN-based dial peer match rules in the inbound and outbound dial peer selection process. When introducing URI-based dialing, care should be taken to not cause the existing DN-based dialing to no longer function properly. CUBE's *domain-based call routing* configuration is the most suitable approach for enabling URI dialing. A sample configuration is shown in Example 3-44.

Example 3-44 *Inbound and Outbound Dial Peer for SIP URI-Based Call Routing*

```
voice class uri entcomp1 sip
 host entcomp1.com

voice class uri entcomp2 sip
 host entcomp2.com

dial-peer voice 8000 voip
 description "Inbound dial-peer for SIP URI Calls"
 session protocol sipv2
 incoming uri from entcomp2
 voice-class sip call-route url
 voice-class sip bind control source-interface GigabitEthernet0/0/1
 voice-class sip bind media source-interface GigabitEthernet0/0/1

dial-peer voice 8001 voip
 description "Outbound dial-peer for SIP URI calls"
 session protocol sipv2
```

```
session server-group 1
destination uri entcomp1
voice-class sip bind control source-interface GigabitEthernet0/0/2
voice-class sip bind media source-interface GigabitEthernet0/0/2
voice-class sip requri-passing
```

The **voice class uri** command supports URI matching using the user portion, host portion, or a regex pattern against the full *user@domain* value. The configuration in this example consists of two **voice class uri** patterns, entcomp1 and entcomp2, to specify a match for the host part of the SIP URI. The command **incoming uri from** *entcomp2* chooses dial peer 8000 as the inbound dial peer for all calls where the **From** header field contains entcomp2.com as the domain name (that is, calls originated by users in entcomp2 company). By default, CUBE extracts only the user part of the Request-URI header field and then uses it as a key to find an outbound dial peer match. For URI dialing, you need to make CUBE consider the entire Request-URI as the lookup key in the outbound dial peer process. The command **voice-class sip call-route url** in the inbound dial peer instructs CUBE to consider the entire Request-URI for call routing purposes.

The command **destination uri** *entcomp1* under dial peer 8001 chooses this dial peer as the outbound dial peer for all calls where the Request-URI contains entcompl.com as the host name. Another important command is **voice-class sip requri-passing**, as present in the outbound dial peer, which overrides CUBE's default behavior of setting the host name in the Request-URI to the next hop's IP address or host name. When this command is configured, the Request-URI (bob@entcomp2.com) as received in the inbound SIP INVITE is sent as it is in the outbound SIP INVITE instead of getting changed to bob@172.18.110.206. Example 3-45 shows the output of **show call active voice brief** collected during an active call dialed using the SIP URI mechanism. Note that bob@entcomp1.com and alice@entcomp2.com are shown as called and calling party URIs instead of telephone numbers.

Example 3-45 **show call active voice brief** *Output for SIP URI-Based Dialing*

```
cube1#show call active voice brief
Total call-legs: 2
0     : 160865 2117380754ms.1 (00:02:56.211 UTC Thu Dec 28 2017) +1070 pid:8000
  Answer alice active
 dur 00:00:17 tx:886/177200 rx:887/177400 dscp:0 media:0 audio tos:0xB8 video
  tos:0x0
 IP 192.168.202.162:8516 SRTP: off rtt:3ms pl:0/0ms lost:0/0/0 delay:0/0/0ms
  g711ulaw TextRelay: off Transcoded: No ICE: Off
 media inactive detected:n media contrl rcvd:n/a timestamp:n/a
 long duration call detected:n long duration call duration:n/a timestamp:n/a
 LostPacketRate:0.00 OutOfOrderRate:0.00
 LocalUUID:5563f6f49d165d0fb5a82035e75011f2
```

```
RemoteUUID:8c8c368da411d8df347e57996aa12703
VRF:
0     : 160866 2117380764ms.1 (00:02:56.221 UTC Thu Dec 28 2017) +1050 pid:8001 Orig-
  inate sip:bob@entcomp1.com active
 dur 00:00:17 tx:887/177400 rx:886/177200 dscp:0 media:0 audio tos:0xB8 video
  tos:0x0
 IP 14.50.201.46:30484 SRTP: off rtt:3ms pl:0/0ms lost:0/0/0 delay:0/0/0ms g711ulaw
  TextRelay: off Transcoded: No ICE: Off
 media inactive detected:n media contrl rcvd:n/a timestamp:n/a
 long duration call detected:n long duration call duration:n/a timestamp:n/a
 LostPacketRate:0.00 OutOfOrderRate:0.00
 LocalUUID:8c8c368da411d8df347e57996aa12703
 RemoteUUID:5563f6f49d165d0fb5a82035e75011f2
 VRF:
...
```

The output of **debug voip ccapi inout**, **debug ccsip message**, and **debug voip dialpeer default** can be used to view the domain-based routing operation. The Request-URI bob@entcomp1.com is passed from the inbound call leg to the outbound call leg without any modifications, as shown in Example 3-46.

Example 3-46 *Debug Output Showing Inbound Dial Peer Matching Using SIP URI*

```
6356507: Dec 28 00:02:56.206: //-1/xxxxxxxxxxxx/SIP/Msg/ccsipDisplayMsg:
Received:
INVITE sip:bob@entcomp1.com SIP/2.0
Via: SIP/2.0/TCP 192.168.202.162:5060;branch=z9hG4bK13717BB
Remote-Party-ID: <sip:alice@entcomp2.com>;party=calling;screen=yes;privacy=off
From: <sip:alice@entcomp2.com>;tag=9E3C52FA-1A86
To: <sip:bob@entcomp1.com>
Date: Thu, 28 Dec 2017 00:00:30 GMT
Call-ID: F4088E5C-EA9811E7-84E9B2A0-6E96DC16@entcomp2.com
...

6356750: Dec 28 00:02:56.214: //-1/73C2BD800000/DPM/dpMatchPeersCore:
   Match Rule=DP_MATCH_DEST_URI; URI=sip:bob@entcomp1.com
6356751: Dec 28 00:02:56.214: //-1/73C2BD800000/DPM/dpMatchPeersCore:
   Result=Success(0) after DP_MATCH_DEST_URI
6356752: Dec 28 00:02:56.214: //-1/73C2BD800000/DPM/dpMatchSafModulePlugin:
   dialstring=, saf_enabled=1, saf_dndb_lookup=1, dp_result=0
6356753: Dec 28 00:02:56.214: //-1/73C2BD800000/DPM/dpMatchPeersMoreArg:
   Result=SUCCESS(0)
```

```
  List of Matched Outgoing Dial-peer(s):
     1: Dial-peer Tag=8001



6356760: Dec 28 00:02:56.215: //160865/73C2BD800000/CCAPI/ccIFCallSetupRequest
  Private:
   Interface=0x7F8694ACD1C8, Interface Type=3, Destination=, Mode=0x0,
   Call Params(Calling Number=alice,(Calling Name=)(TON=Unknown, NPI=Unknown,
     Screening=User, Passed, Presentation=Allowed),
   Called Number=sip:bob@entcomp1.com(TON=Unknown, NPI=Unknown), Calling
     Translated=FALSE,
   Subscriber Type Str=Unknown, FinalDestinationFlag=TRUE, Outgoing Dial-peer=8001,
     Call Count On=FALSE,
   Source Trkgrp Route Label=, Target Trkgrp Route Label=, tg_label_flag=0,
     Application Call Id=)


6356996: Dec 28 00:02:56.222: //160866/73C2BD800000/SIP/Msg/ccsipDisplayMsg:
Sent:
INVITE sip:bob@entcomp1.com SIP/2.0
Via: SIP/2.0/TCP 172.18.110.203:5060;branch=z9hG4bK273C1D84
Remote-Party-ID: <sip:alice@172.18.110.203>;party=calling;screen=yes;privacy=off
From: <sip:alice@172.18.110.203>;tag=7E35F079-1CDD
To: <sip:bob@entcomp1.com>
Date: Thu, 28 Dec 2017 00:02:56 GMT
Call-ID: 4AB288C1-EA9911E7-91189A97-7107F84E@172.18.110.203
...
```

Call Routing in Multitenant Environments

Network virtualization enables you to deliver individualized routing and forwarding services to multiple tenants or customers using a single SBC instance. This is made possible by the Virtual Routing and Forwarding (VRF) feature, which allows multiple routing table instances to be run on the same device, with each VRF instance associated to an individual tenant. The book *IP Routing on Cisco IOS, IOS XE, and IOS XR* (Cisco Press) is a good reference for VRF-related routing concepts.

As discussed in Chapter 2, "SBC Deployment Models," CUBE has been enhanced to be Multi-VRF aware: It can identify the VRF of the SIP messages and RTP packets received on any interface of the router and can send Unified Communications (UC) traffic across all the VRF instances configured in the router. The source VRF in which a call is received is also taken into consideration during the call routing decision process. The Multi-VRF capability extends CUBE's usage to multitenant environments in which the network traffic of each customer can be isolated from other customers and service providers through VRF instances.

Service providers offering managed UC services using Cisco Hosted Collaboration Solution (HCS) can leverage the Multi-VRF capability to centralize SIP trunks for multiple customers.

Figure 3-18 shows an example of a scenario in which a service provider uses a CUBE device (sbc.example-hcs.com) to aggregate SIP trunks from two CUCM clusters that are dedicated to two customers, Customer-1 and Customer-2.

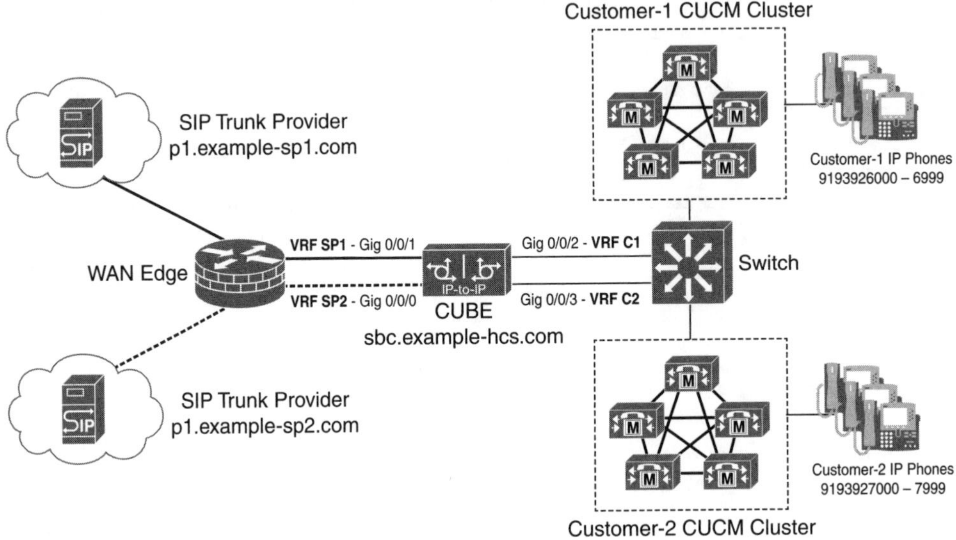

Figure 3-18 *Multi-VRF CUBE Deployment in HCS Solution to Centralize SIP Trunks*

This provider gives customers the option to choose from multiple SIP trunk carriers. Customer-1 has chosen SIP trunk provider SP1, whereas Customer-2 has chosen SP2. VRF is used as a network segmentation technique to keep the Customer-1, Customer-2, SP1, and SP2 traffic in isolated virtual network segments. SIP devices in a customer VRF (C1) cannot directly communicate with a SIP server in another customer VRF (C2) and the service provider VRF instances (SP1, SP2) because there is no direct route between the virtual network segments. Only CUBE performs the interworking function to route calls and send/receive RTP packets between the customer and service provider VRF instances.

Example 3-47 shows the configuration related to the VRF definition and assignment of interfaces to the four VRF instances used in Figure 3-18. Customer-1's CUCM cluster has a SIP trunk pointing to CUBE's IP address 172.18.110.203 in VRF C1, and Customer-2's CUCM cluster has a SIP trunk pointing to CUBE's IP address 172.19.110.203 in VRF C2. Note that for configuration consistency purposes, the same IP address 172.18.110.203 could also be assigned as the CUBE IP address in the Customer-2 VRF (C2). This is possible because the IP addresses in VRF C1 and C2 do not overlap as they are in separate virtual routing table instances.

Example 3-47 *VRF Definition and Interface Assignment*

```
ip vrf SP1
 rd 100:1
!
ip vrf SP2
 rd 200:1
!
ip vrf C1
 rd 300:1
!
ip vrf C2
 rd 400:2
!
interface GigabitEthernet0/0/0
 description "Interface for SP2 traffic"
 ip vrf forwarding SP2
 ip address 192.168.201.165 255.255.255.0
!
interface GigabitEthernet0/0/1
 description "Interface for SP1 traffic"
 ip vrf forwarding SP1
 ip address 192.168.202.165 255.255.255.0
 negotiation auto
!


interface GigabitEthernet0/0/2
 description "Interface for Customer-1 traffic"
 ip vrf forwarding C1
 ip address 172.18.110.203 255.255.255.0
!
interface GigabitEthernet0/0/3
 description "Interface for Customer-2 traffic"
 ip vrf forwarding C2
 ip address 172.19.110.203 255.255.255.0
```

Dial Peer Selection in Multi-VRF Environments

The key change to the inbound dial peer selection process for Multi-VRF scenarios is the filtering of configured dial peers to include only dial peers are that are associated with the source VRF in which CUBE received the SIP INVITE for the incoming dial peer match. The filtering mechanism leverages the **voice-class sip bind control** command to identify dial peers that are bound to the interfaces that are part of the source VRF. After filtering, CUBE continues with selection of a specific dial peer, using URI, called number, and calling number information, as shown in Figure 3-19.

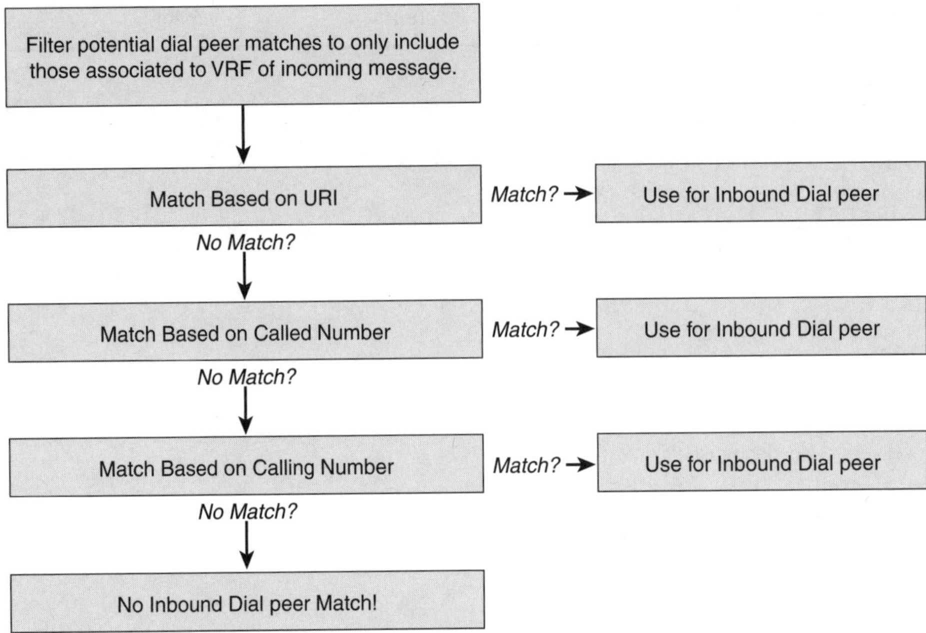

Figure 3-19 *Inbound Dial Peer Selection in Multi-VRF Scenarios*

Example 3-48 shows the configuration used to route inbound calls from the service provider to the customer tenants. Dial peer 6000 is bound with Gig0/0/1, which belongs to VRF SP1. Similarly, dial peer 9000 is bound with Gig0/0/0, which belongs to VRF SP2. When CUBE receives a SIP INVITE from SP1 to Customer-1 DID number 9193926003 via Gig0/0/1, it looks up the dial peers that are associated with Gig0/0/1 to filter applicable dial peers for VRF SP1. It finds 6000 and then proceeds with the dial peer selection process and chooses this dial peer as the inbound dial peer since it matches the called number matching rule defined by the **incoming called-number 9193926...** command.

Example 3-48 *Inbound Call Routing Configuration in a Multitenant Environment*

```
voice class server-group 1
 ipv4 172.18.110.206 port 5060 preference 1
 ipv4 172.18.110.207 port 5060 preference 2
 description "Customer-1 CUCM Subscriber Nodes"

voice class server-group 2
 ipv4 172.19.110.206 port 5060 preference 1
 ipv4 172.19.110.207 port 5060 preference 2
 description "Customer-2 CUCM Subscriber Nodes"

dial-peer voice 6000 voip
 description "Inbound DP for inbound calls from SP1 to Customer-1"
```

```
 session protocol sipv2
 incoming called-number 9193926...
 voice-class sip bind control source-interface GigabitEthernet0/0/1
 voice-class sip bind media source-interface GigabitEthernet0/0/1


dial-peer voice 6003 voip
 description "Outbound DP for inbound calls from SP1 to Customer-1"
 huntstop
 session protocol sipv2
 session server-group 1
 destination-pattern 9193926...
 voice-class sip options-keepalive profile 1
 voice-class sip bind control source-interface GigabitEthernet0/0/2
 voice-class sip bind media source-interface GigabitEthernet0/0/2
!

dial-peer voice 9000 voip
 description "Inbound DP for inbound calls from SP2 to Customer-2"
 session protocol sipv2
 incoming called-number 9193927...
 voice-class sip bind control source-interface GigabitEthernet0/0/0
 voice-class sip bind media source-interface GigabitEthernet0/0/0

dial-peer voice 9003 voip
 description "Outbound DP for inbound calls from SP2 to Customer-2"
 huntstop
 session protocol sipv2
 session server-group 2
 destination-pattern 9193927...
 voice-class sip options-keepalive profile 1
 voice-class sip bind control source-interface GigabitEthernet0/0/3
 voice-class sip bind media source-interface GigabitEthernet0/0/3
!
```

CUBE then looks up an outbound dial peer by using the normal outbound dial peer selection process, using match rules defined by the **destination uri**, **destination-pattern**, and **destination e164-pattern-map** commands described earlier. The source VRF is not used as a criterion to select the outbound dial peer, which means the selected outbound dial peer may or may not belong to the source VRF. In other words, CUBE by default permits routing of calls across different VRF devices. In Example 3-47, dial peer 6003 associated to a different VRF (C1) gets selected, and CUBE performs inter-VRF call routing. This can be verified with output from the **show call active voice brief** and **show voip rtp connection** commands, which displays the VRF associated with each call leg and RTP stream (see in Example 3-49).

Example 3-49 show call active voice brief *and* show voip rtp connection *for Inter-VRF Calls*

```
cube1#show call active voice brief
...
Total call-legs: 2
0    : 314 2511910ms.1 (22:51:18.968 UTC Fri Dec 29 2017) +1100 pid:6000 Answer
  4083926001 active
 dur 00:00:21 tx:1077/215400 rx:1079/215496 dscp:0 media:0 audio tos:0xB8 video
  tos:0x0
 IP 192.168.202.162:8550 SRTP: off rtt:3ms pl:0/0ms lost:0/0/0 delay:0/0/0ms
  g711ulaw TextRelay: off Transcoded: No ICE: Off
 media inactive detected:n media contrl rcvd:n/a timestamp:n/a
 long duration call detected:n long duration call duration:n/a timestamp:n/a
 LostPacketRate:0.00 OutOfOrderRate:0.00
 LocalUUID:059b7677d7ed54e3be3b8115f8014a73
 RemoteUUID:8c8c368da411d8df347e57996aa16818
 VRF: SP1
0    : 315 2511930ms.1 (22:51:18.988 UTC Fri Dec 29 2017) +1070 pid:6003 Originate
  9193926003 active
 dur 00:00:21 tx:1079/215496 rx:1077/215400 dscp:0 media:0 audio tos:0xB8 video
  tos:0x0
 IP 14.50.201.46:22634 SRTP: off rtt:4ms pl:0/0ms lost:0/0/0 delay:0/0/0ms g711ulaw
  TextRelay: off Transcoded: No ICE: Off
 media inactive detected:n media contrl rcvd:n/a timestamp:n/a
 long duration call detected:n long duration call duration:n/a timestamp:n/a
 LostPacketRate:0.00 OutOfOrderRate:0.00
 LocalUUID:8c8c368da411d8df347e57996aa16818
 RemoteUUID:059b7677d7ed54e3be3b8115f8014a73
 VRF: C1
...
cube1#show voip rtp connection
VoIP RTP Port Usage Information:
Max Ports Available: 19999, Ports Reserved: 101, Ports in Use: 2
Port range not configured
                                           Min   Max   Ports     Ports     Ports
Media-Address Range                        Port  Port  Available Reserved  In-use
--------------------------------------------------------------------------------
Global Media Pool                          8000  48198 19999     101       2
--------------------------------------------------------------------------------
VoIP RTP active connections :
No. CallId dstCallId  LocalRTP RmtRTP   LocalIP          RemoteIP         MPSS   VRF
1    314    315        8016     8550     192.168.202.165  192.168.202.162  NO     SP1
2    315    314        8018     22634    172.18.110.203   14.50.201.46     NO     C1
Found 2 active RTP connections
```

An interesting issue arises for outbound calls from the customer tenants to the SIP trunk providers. Assume that there are two outbound dial peers, 6004 and 9004, one each for routing long-distance calls via SP1 and SP2, respectively, with both dial peers configured with the same destination pattern **[2-9].........** When a user in Customer-1 calls 4083926001, the network administrator needs to ensure that CUBE always routes the call via dial peer 6004 (associated with SP1 VRF) and not via dial peer 9004 (associated with SP2 VRF). Note that customer C1 has chosen service provider SP1, so all outbound calls need to go via dial peer 6004.

The default outbound dial peer selection process could select either of these dial peers, and it is not 100% certain that CUBE will always choose 6004 for the outbound call. This ambiguity, illustrated in Figure 3-20, can be resolved by using dial peer groups, as discussed in the next section.

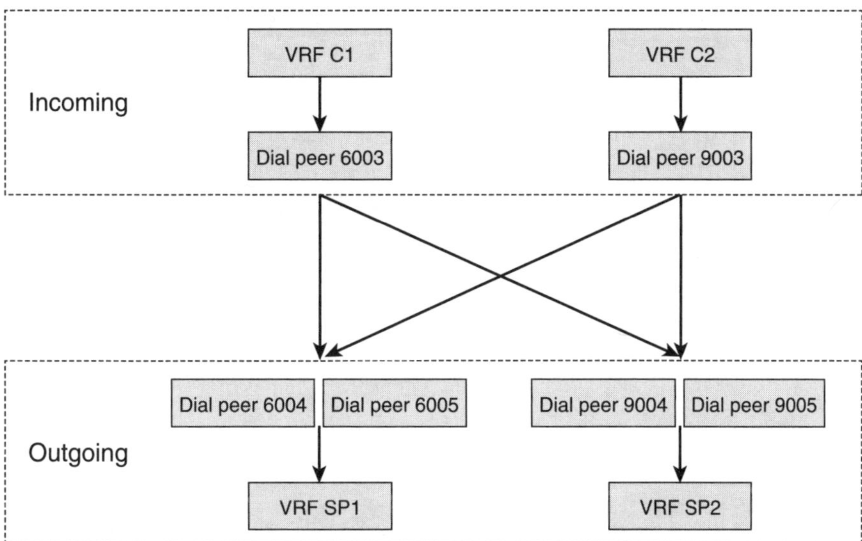

Figure 3-20 *Outbound Dial Peer Selection Ambiguity in Multi-VRF Scenarios*

Dial Peer Groups (DPGs)

With a *dial peer group*, a network administrator can explicitly specify a list of outbound dial peers that can be used for an incoming call. If there is a **destination dpg** configured under the incoming dial peer, then CUBE does not apply the regular outbound dial peer selection process. The **voice class dpg** *group-tag* command is used to define the grouping of outbound peers, and it is referenced under an inbound dial peer using **destination dpg** *group-tag*. This concept can be applied in multitenant CUBE deployments to steer the incoming calls from a specific tenant to a specific service provider.

For the Multi-VRF example discussed previously, the outbound dial peers 6004 and 6005 that are used to route calls to proxies p1.example-sp1.com and p2.example-sp1.com can be grouped under a dial peer group 1 and specified as **destination dpg** *1* under the dial peer 6003, as shown in Figure 3-21 and in Example 3-50.

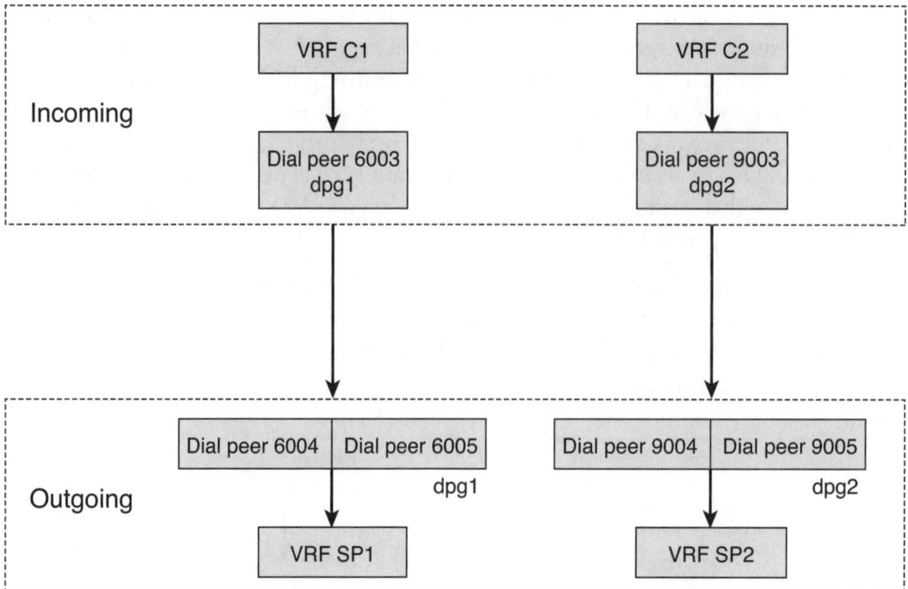

Figure 3-21 *Outbound Dial Peer Selection Using Dial Peer Groups*

Example 3-50 *Dial Peer Group Configuration*

```
ip name-server 192.168.201.106

voice class dpg 1
 description "Outbound dial-peers for external calls originated from C1"
 dial-peer 6004 preference 1
 dial-peer 6005 preference 2
!
voice class dpg 2
 description "Outbound dial-peers for external calls originated from C2"
 dial-peer 9004 preference 1
 dial-peer 9005 preference 2

voice class e164-pattern-map 3
  e164 011T
  e164 [2-9].........
 !

dial-peer voice 6003 voip
 description "Inbound dial-peer for external calls originated from C1"
 session protocol sipv2
```

```
 session transport tcp
 session server-group 1
 destination dpg 1
 destination e164-pattern-map 1
 incoming called e164-pattern-map 3
 voice-class sip options-keepalive profile 1
 voice-class sip bind control source-interface GigabitEthernet0/0/2
 voice-class sip bind media source-interface GigabitEthernet0/0/2

!
dial-peer voice 6004 voip
 description "Multi-VRF: Outbound dial-peer for outgoing LD calls via SP1"
 session protocol sipv2
 session target dns:p1.example-sp1.com
 destination e164-pattern-map 3
 incoming called-number 9193925...
 voice-class sip bind control source-interface GigabitEthernet0/0/1
 voice-class sip bind media source-interface GigabitEthernet0/0/1

!
dial-peer voice 6005 voip
 description "Multi-VRF: Outbound dial-peer for outgoing Int. calls via SP1"
 session protocol sipv2
 session target dns:p2.example-sp1.com
 destination e164-pattern-map 3
 incoming called-number 9193925...
 voice-class sip bind control source-interface GigabitEthernet0/0/1
 voice-class sip bind media source-interface GigabitEthernet0/0/1

!
dial-peer voice 9003 voip
 description "Inbound dial-peer for external calls originated from C2"
 session protocol sipv2
 session server-group 2
 destination dpg 2
 destination e164-pattern-map 1
 incoming called e164-pattern-map 3
 voice-class sip options-keepalive profile 1
 voice-class sip bind control source-interface GigabitEthernet0/0/2
 voice-class sip bind media source-interface GigabitEthernet0/0/2
!
dial-peer voice 9004 voip
 description "Multi-VRF: Outbound dial-peer for outgoing LD calls via SP2"
```

```
 session protocol sipv2
 session target dns:p1.example-sp2.com
 destination e164-pattern-map 3
 voice-class sip bind control source-interface GigabitEthernet0/0/2
 voice-class sip bind media source-interface GigabitEthernet0/0/2

!
dial-peer voice 9005 voip
 description "Multi-VRF: Outbound dial-peer for outgoing Int. calls via SP2"
 session protocol sipv2
 session target dns:p2.example-sp2.com
 destination e164-pattern-map 3
 incoming called-number 9193925...
 voice-class sip bind control source-interface GigabitEthernet0/0/2
 voice-class sip bind media source-interface GigabitEthernet0/0/2
```

Dial peer 6003 gets selected as the inbound dial peer for external long-distance and international calls originated by users in Customer-1. This peer is selected because it is bound with the Gig0/0/2 through which the SIP INVITE was received, and it also has **incoming called e164-pattern-map 3**, which matches the long-distance and international E.164 number patterns. This configuration excludes the usage of dial peers 9004 and 9005 as outbound dial peers for calls using dial peer 6003 as the inbound dial peer and hence avoids routing Customer-1 calls across SP2. CUBE tries to route calls through the first dial peer specified in the **destination dpg**, 6004, and then through 6005 if the call setup through **6004** is not successful. CUBE uses the global routing table to reach the DNS server (192.168.201.106) for domain name and DNS SRV lookup.

Tip Even though the **destination-pattern** and **destination e164-pattern map** commands of the outbound dial peers that are part of the dial peer group aren't used for the outbound dial peer selection process, one of these two commands is still necessary in order to have the operational status of the outbound dial peer to be in the UP state. You should therefore configure a valid **destination-pattern** or **destination e164-pattern map** command in the dial peer group members.

The debug output of **debug voip ccapi inout**, **debug voip dialpeer default**, and **debug ccsip info** can be used to view the source VRF identification, inbound dial peer selection, and use of the destination dial peer group to route the call.

The command **show vrf tableid** provides the internal VRF ID assigned by Cisco IOS/IOS XE for the user-defined VRF names and is useful for interpreting the debug output. Example 3-51 shows debug output in which Cisco IOS/IOS XE identifies VRF ID 2 (C1) as the source VRF, matches 6003 as the inbound dial peer, and selects 6004 as the outbound dial peer from the destination dial-group 1.

Example 3-51 *Debug Output for Dial Peer Group–Based Call Routing*

```
cube1#show vrf tableid
VRF Name                          Tableid              Address Family
C1                                0x00000002           ipv4 unicast
C2                                0x00000003           ipv4 unicast
Mgmt-intf                         0x00000001           ipv4 unicast
Mgmt-intf                         0x1E000001           ipv6 unicast
SP1                               0x00000004           ipv4 unicast
SP2                               0x00000005           ipv4 unicast
cube1#

cube1#show log
2281709: Jan  1 00:02:21.548: //-1/000000000000/SIP/Function/resolve_sig_ip_address_
  to_bind:
2281710: Jan  1 00:02:21.548: //-1/xxxxxxxxxxxx/SIP/Info/verbose/512/ccsip_get_vrf_
  from_sip_bind: vrfid 0 for tag 0, sip_vrfid 0, voice_vrfid 0
2281711: Jan  1 00:02:21.548: //-1/000000000000/SIP/Info/info/8192/resolve_sig_ip_
  address_to_bind: VRF id = 0
2281712: Jan  1 00:02:21.548: //-1/000000000000/SIP/Info/info/8192/resolve_sig_ip_
  address_to_bind: VRF id = 2

2281817: Jan  1 00:02:21.554: //-1/029749000000/DPM/dpAssociateIncomingPeerCore:
   Calling Number=26003, Called Number=4083926001, Voice-Interface=0x0,
   Timeout=TRUE, Peer Encap Type=ENCAP_VOIP, Peer Search Type=PEER_TYPE_VOICE,
   Peer Info Type=DIALPEER_INFO_SPEECH
2281818: Jan  1 00:02:21.554: //-1/029749000000/DPM/dpAssociateIncomingPeerCore:
   Result=Success(0) after DP_MATCH_INCOMING_DNIS; Incoming Dial-peer=6003


2282301: Jan  1 00:02:21.578: //-1/029749000000/DPM/dpMatchPeersCore:
   Calling Number=, Called Number=4083926001, Peer Info Type=DIALPEER_INFO_SPEECH
2282302: Jan  1 00:02:21.578: //-1/029749000000/DPM/dpMatchPeersCore:
   Outbound Destination DPG Group Request; Destination DPG=1
2282303: Jan  1 00:02:21.578: //-1/029749000000/DPM/dpMatchPeersCore:
   Result=SUCCESS(0) after DestDPGroup
2282305: Jan  1 00:02:21.578: //-1/029749000000/DPM/dpMatchPeersMoreArg:
   Result=SUCCESS(0)
   List of Matched Outgoing Dial-peer(s):
     1: Dial-peer Tag=6004
     2: Dial-peer Tag=6005


2282312: Jan  1 00:02:21.579: //22009/029749000000/CCAPI/ccIFCallSetupRequestPrivate:
```

```
Interface=0x7FB63C103DD8, Interface Type=3, Destination=, Mode=0x0,
Call Params(Calling Number=26003,(Calling Name=)(TON=Unknown, NPI=Unknown,
  Screening=User, Passed, Presentation=Allowed),
Called Number=4083926001(TON=Unknown, NPI=Unknown), Calling Translated=FALSE,
Subscriber Type Str=Unknown, FinalDestinationFlag=TRUE, Outgoing Dial-peer=6004,
  Call Count On=FALSE,
Source Trkgrp Route Label=, Target Trkgrp Route Label=, tg_label_flag=0,
  Application Call Id=)
```

Dial Peer Provisioning Policies

The default outbound dial peer selection process uses only the called number and Request-URI to look up a matching dial peer. The objective of a dial peer provisioning policy is to empower CUBE network administrators with additional flexibility to customize the call routing decision process based on the attributes received in the incoming SIP message. Attributes that can be used as criteria include the SIP URI from the topmost Via header field, the topmost Diversion header field, and the Referred-By, From, and To header field. These all supplement the commonly used Request-URI header field, called number, and calling number attributes for routing.

The command **voice class dial-peer provision-policy** *policy-tag* specifies the provisioning rules (that is, which information should be used as lookup keys to find the outbound dial peer). Each lookup option can contain one or two attributes and is also assigned a preference. If CUBE isn't able to find a matching dial peer using the first preferred lookup key combination, it will use the next preferred lookup combination. The provisioning policy is applied to the inbound dial peer using the command **destination provision-policy** *policy-tag*. If none of the lookup combinations match an outbound dial peer, CUBE returns a 404 Not Found response (unassigned number) to the incoming SIP INVITE.

Table 3-9 lists the first attribute keywords that can be configured in the provisioning policy, with the corresponding second attribute options available. The **uri** keyword in Table 3-9 refers to the Request-URI header field in the SIP INVITE. When the second attribute is specified, only the outbound dial peers that match both attributes are selected. In other words, the second attribute forms a logical AND clause between the first and second attributes, not an OR clause.

Table 3-9 *Dial Peer Provisioning Policy Attributes*

First Attribute	Second Attribute
diversion	**from**, **referred-by**, **to**, **uri**, or **via**
from	**diversion**, **referred-by**, **to**, **uri**, or **via**
referred-by	**diversion**, **from**, **to**, **uri**, or **via**
to	**diversion**, **referred-by**, **from**, **uri**, or **via**
uri	**diversion**, **referred-by**, **to**, **from**, **via**, or **carrier-id**

First Attribute	Second Attribute
via	diversion, referred-by, to, uri, or from
called	calling or carrier-id
calling	called
carrier-id	called or uri

Source-based call routing is one of the use cases that can be realized using this dial peer provisioning policy. Figure 3-22 shows a CUBE enterprise deployment in which the enterprise entcomp1 has chosen to use different service providers for different internal organizations. Calls originating from the contact center CUCM cluster are routed via SP1, whereas calls originating from the corporate CUCM cluster are routed via SP2.

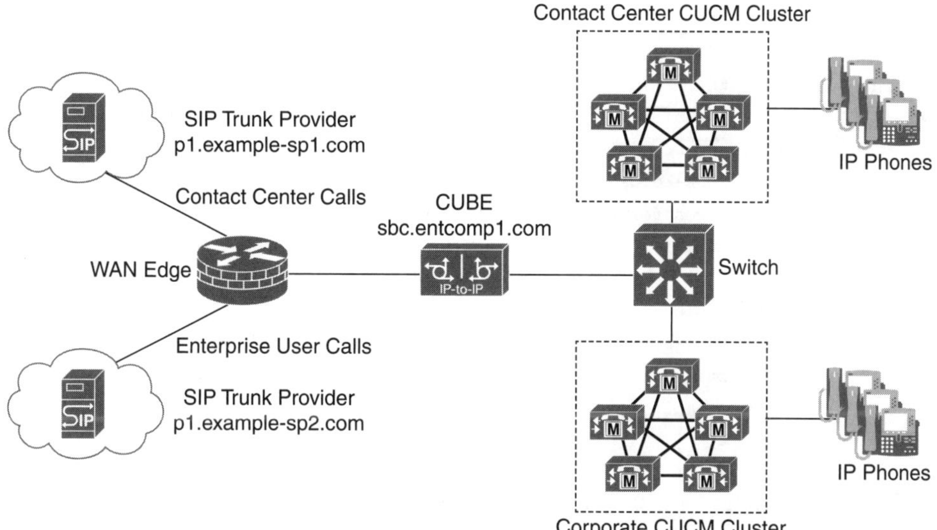

Figure 3-22 *Differentiated Call Routing Experience Using Source-Based Call Routing*

Example 3-52 shows a sample configuration for source-based call routing. **voice class uri** with tag ID **3** defines the regex pattern to match the host portion of the Via header fields coming from the contact center CUCM subscriber nodes 172.18.110.205, 172.18.110.206, and 172.18.110.207. The **voice class e164-pattern-map** tag ID **3** defines the destination patterns that match long-distance and international calls. The e164-pattern-map 3 is used to specify inbound dial-peer match rule under dial peer 6010 with the **incoming called e164-destination-map** command. This command makes 6010 the inbound dial peer for all long-distance and international calls received by CUBE. **voice class dial-peer provision-policy** with tag ID **1** specifies the Via URI and called number as the two separate rules for the outbound dial peer selection. The dial peer provision policy is associated with the inbound dial peer 6010 through the **destination provision-policy** command.

Example 3-52 *Inbound and Outbound Dial Peers for Source-Based Call Routing*

```
voice class e164-pattern-map 3
  e164 011T
  e164 [2-9].........

voice class uri 3 sip
 host 172\.18\.110\.20[567]

voice class dial-peer provision-policy 1
 preference 1 via
 preference 2 called

dial-peer voice 6010 voip
 description "Inbound dial-peer for LD and Int. calls from entcomp1 clusters"
 session protocol sipv2
 session server-group 1
 destination e164-pattern-map 1
 destination provision-policy 1
 incoming called e164-pattern-map 3
 voice-class sip options-keepalive profile 1
 voice-class sip bind control source-interface GigabitEthernet0/0/2
 voice-class sip bind media source-interface GigabitEthernet0/0/2
!
dial-peer voice 6011 voip
 description "Outbound dial-peer for Contact Center calls to SP1"
 session protocol sipv2
 session target dns:example-sp1.com
 session transport tcp
 destination uri-via 3
 voice-class sip bind control source-interface GigabitEthernet0/0/1
 voice-class sip bind media source-interface GigabitEthernet0/0/1
```

When CUBE selects 6010 as the inbound dial peer, it uses the dial peer provision policy to identify the lookup key types to be used for the outbound dial peer selection process. As shown in Example 3-53, CUBE uses the SIP URI in the topmost Via header field (172.18.110.206) to look up as per the first rule in dial peer provision policy 1. It finds 6011 as the matching outbound dial peer and sends the outbound INVITE to the next hop configured in dial-peer 6011.

The output of the commands **debug voip ccapi inout**, **debug voip dialpeer default**, and **debug ccsip message** can be used to view the execution of the dial peer provisioning policy in action.

Example 3-53 *Debug Output for Source-Based Call Routing*

```
2672375: Jan  1 15:51:19.661: //-1/xxxxxxxxxxxx/SIP/Msg/ccsipDisplayMsg:
Received:
INVITE sip:4083926001@cube1.entcomp1.com:5060 SIP/2.0
Via: SIP/2.0/TCP 172.18.110.206:5060;branch=z9hG4bK4e735cd733
From: <sip:26003@172.18.110.206>;tag=12695~154a292d-1558-48b6-9155-e3e-
  49acd9216-26380056
To: <sip:4083926001@cube1.entcomp1.com>
Date: Mon, 01 Jan 2018 15:51:19 GMT
Call-ID: 9a3e7b00-a4a158f7-41-ce6e12ac@172.18.110.206



2672393: Jan  1 15:51:19.663: //-1/9A3E7B000000/CCAPI/cc_api_call_setup_ind_common:
   Interface=0x7FB63C103DD8, Call Info(
   Calling Number=26003,(Calling Name=)(TON=Unknown, NPI=Unknown, Screening=User,
     Passed, Presentation=Allowed),
   Called Number=4083926001(TON=Unknown, NPI=Unknown),
   Calling Translated=FALSE, Subscriber Type Str=Unknown, FinalDestinationFlag=TRUE,
   Incoming Dial-peer=6010, Progress Indication=NULL(0), Calling IE Present=TRUE,
   Source Trkgrp Route Label=, Target Trkgrp Route Label=, CLID Transparent=FALSE),
     Call Id=32600

2672437: Jan  1 15:51:19.665: //-1/9A3E7B000000/DPM/dpMatchDestDPProvPolicy:
   Calling Number=, Called Number=4083926001, DPProvPolicy=1
2672438: Jan  1 15:51:19.665: //-1/9A3E7B000000/DPM/dpMatchDestDPProvPolicy:
   Result=Success(0) after DP_MATCH_DEST_VIA_URI
2672441: Jan  1 15:51:19.665: //-1/9A3E7B000000/DPM/dpMatchPeersMoreArg:
   Result=SUCCESS(0)
   List of Matched Outgoing Dial-peer(s):
     1: Dial-peer Tag=6011

2672448: Jan  1 15:51:19.666: //32600/9A3E7B000000/CCAPI/ccIFCallSetupRequestPrivate:
   Interface=0x7FB63C103DD8, Interface Type=3, Destination=, Mode=0x0,
   Call Params(Calling Number=26003,(Calling Name=)(TON=Unknown, NPI=Unknown,
     Screening=User, Passed, Presentation=Allowed),
   Called Number=4083926001(TON=Unknown, NPI=Unknown), Calling Translated=FALSE,
   Subscriber Type Str=Unknown, FinalDestinationFlag=TRUE, Outgoing Dial-peer=6011,
     Call Count On=FALSE,
   Source Trkgrp Route Label=, Target Trkgrp Route Label=, tg_label_flag=0,
     Application Call Id=)
```

```
2672460: Jan  1 15:51:24.671: //32601/9A3E7B000000/SIP/Msg/ccsipDisplayMsg:
Sent:
INVITE sip:4083926001@example-sp1.com:5060 SIP/2.0
Via: SIP/2.0/TCP 192.168.202.165:5060;branch=z9hG4bK5697239
Remote-Party-ID: <sip:26003@192.168.202.165>;party=calling;screen=yes;privacy=off
From: <sip:26003@192.168.202.165>;tag=E1A70A3-24FF
To: <sip:4083926001@example-sp1.com>
Date: Mon, 01 Jan 2018 15:51:24 GMT
Call-ID: 71725332-EE4211E7-977EAB27-C5AF3C32@192.168.202.165
```

Call Rerouting

The simplest way to provide resiliency for external peers is to configure multiple outbound call routes that are either logically or physically diverse. This helps ensure that if one of the peers goes down, there is still a route available to the intended destination of the call. Functionally, this is achieved by having outbound call routing configured to more than one external peer. When a call has multiple routes, the multiple paths can either be all active, with the load distributed across the peers, or in an active/standby configuration.

When designing for high availability, it may also be desirable to have diversity across providers for the multiple call routes. Special care should be taken when looking at failure points of the potential routes to ensure that there is interface, circuit, provider, or geographic resiliency when it is either cost-effective or required by the business services and compliance.

Rerouting Criteria

Whether CUBE attempts to reroute a call depends on the call failure reason for the attempt of the first call. By default, CUBE does not hunt on user busy (cause value **17**), invalid number (**28**), or unassigned number (**1**). The default hunt behavior for each cause code can be validated by consulting the default state of this command:

```
voice hunt cause-code
```

The **show sip-ua map sip-pstn** command output is a useful reference for viewing how the SIP response codes, such as 500 and 503, are mapped to Q.850 disconnect cause codes. Example 3-54 shows a small snippet highlighting the mapping of SIP 503 response code to Q.850 cause code 38 (network out of order), which is enabled for voice call hunting by default. The command **set sip-status** *<400-699 SIP response code>* **pstn-status** *<1-127 cause code>* in **sip-ua** configuration mode can be used to override the default mapping.

Example 3-54 *Mapping of SIP Response Codes to Call Disconnect Cause Codes*

```
cube1#show sip-ua map sip-pstn
The SIP Status code to PSTN Cause mapping table:-

SIP-Status    Configured          Default
              PSTN-Cause           PSTN-Cause
......
404                1                 1
......
500               41                41
501               79                79
502               27                27
503               38                38
......
cube1#s
```

Reroute Mechanisms

Alternate call routing paths can be defined through multiple mechanisms, such as dial peer hunting, server groups, and DNS SRV.

Dial Peer Hunting

Having multiple outbound dial peers that handle the same destination patterns—using methods such as **destination-pattern**, **destination e164-pattern-map**, or **destination uri**—is one way of configuring outbound resiliency in CUBE. In Example 3-55, dial peer 6001 is the primary route, and calls will be sent out dial peer 6002 only if dial peer 6001 becomes unavailable, such as through the means of OPTIONS keepalive or in failure scenarios such as the first dial peer being deemed appropriate for hunting to the next dial peer.

Example 3-55 *Configuration for Resiliency Through a Secondary Dial Peer*

```
dial-peer voice 6001 voip
 destination-pattern 9193926...
 session target dns:cl2-cucm-sub1.entcomp1.com
 preference 1

dial-peer voice 6002 voip
 destination-pattern 9193926...
 session target dns:cl2-cucm-sub1.entcomp1.com
 preference 2
```

In Example 3-55, the configuration routes all calls to peer 6001, as long as peer 6001 is active.

Note When defining multiple dial peers to offer resiliency with external peers, keep in mind that it is important for the SBC to be able to mark the route unavailable as soon as it is capable of being detected as no longer providing service availability. One way to mark a trunk unavailable is by using SIP OPTIONS ping.

If there is a desire to loadbalance calls across multiple peers, it can be done by having equal preferences for destination patterns. Spreading the load across multiple devices reduces the failure domain in the event of an impacting event. This is demonstrated in Example 3-56.

Example 3-56 *Configuration for Load Balancing Across Multiple Dial Peers*

```
dial-peer voice 6001 voip
 destination-pattern 9193926...
 session target dns:cl2-cucm-sub1.entcomp1.com
 preference 1

dial-peer voice 6002 voip
 destination-pattern 9193926...
 session target dns:cl2-cucm-sub1.entcomp1.com
 preference 1
```

Finally, note that a combination of these techniques can also be deployed, for example, if there is a desire for a hybridization of active/standby and load-balanced resiliency.

To observe or validate proper dial peer matching when configured with multiple paths, the dial peer selection can be observed in real time with **debug voip dialpeer inout**, provided by Example 3-57.

Example 3-57 *Debug Output Showing Selected Outbound Dial Peers*

```
6182775: Dec 26 02:52:12.897: //-1/C461DB800000/DPM/dpMatchPeersCore:
   Calling Number=, Called Number=9193926003, Peer Info Type=DIALPEER_INFO_SPEECH
6182776: Dec 26 02:52:12.897: //-1/C461DB800000/DPM/dpMatchPeersCore:
   Match Rule=DP_MATCH_DEST; Called Number=9193926003
6182777: Dec 26 02:52:12.897: //-1/C461DB800000/DPM/dpMatchPeersCore:
   Result=Success(0) after DP_MATCH_DEST
6182778: Dec 26 02:52:12.897: //-1/C461DB800000/DPM/dpMatchSafModulePlugin:
   dialstring=9193926003, saf_enabled=1, saf_dndb_lookup=1, dp_result=0
6182779: Dec 26 02:52:12.897: //-1/C461DB800000/DPM/dpMatchPeersMoreArg:
   Result=SUCCESS(0)
   List of Matched Outgoing Dial-peer(s):
     1: Dial-peer Tag=6001
     2: Dial-peer Tag=6002
6182780: Dec 26 02:52:12.897: //147711/C461DB800000/CCAPI/ccCallSetupRequest:
   Destination=, Calling IE Present=TRUE, Mode=0,
   Outgoing Dial-peer=6001, Params=0x7F869EAEE9B8, Progress Indication=NULL(0)
```

Server Groups

Using a *server group* is another way to configure resilient destinations and allows for better flexibility than defining multiple dial peers. The configuration details are discussed earlier in this chapter, in the section "Dial Peer Optimization." Multiple peers with an equal preference are chosen at random when they are an equal outbound match.

Note Only five servers can be listed in a server group. Consider using DNS SRV records if distributing across more than five nodes for a destination.

HSRP Virtual IP Addresses

Hot Standby Routing Protocol (HSRP), discussed in Chapter 2, provides the ability to have a unified logical address across multiple physical destinations. Figure 3-23 shows an example of a deployment in which a virtual HSRP address 172.18.110.200 is configured, across two physically separate CUBE instances addressed 172.18.110.203 and 172.18.110.204.

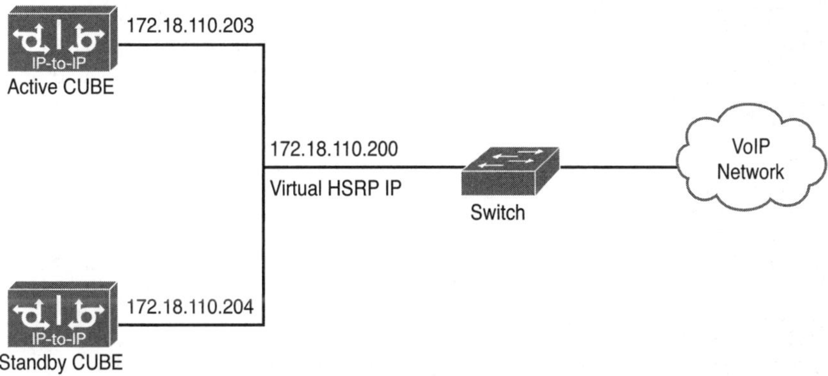

Figure 3-23 *Outbound Resiliency Using HSRP Virtual IP*

If an SBC were pointing call routes to this pair of CUBEs, the route would be configured to point to the virtual HSRP. This way, 172.18.110.200 is just virtually pointing to 172.18.110.203 in a normal state. If 172.18.110.203 goes down, 172.18.110.200 is still responsive though being answered by the physical device assigned 172.18.110.204. The same concept of peering to a virtual IP address applies to other industry approaches that provide inter-device IP resiliency, such as the open standard Virtual Router Redundancy Protocol (VRRP) that is defined in RFC 5798.

DNS SRV

CUBE supports rerouting of calls across the SIP servers resolved via DNS SRV lookup. DNS SRV is a special entry in a DNS server that allows for resolution of a specific service record for a domain name to resolve to another DNS A record or IP address. A common use for this is to define a generic domain name such as example-sp1.com where there is an underlying SRV record that resolves any requests for the SIP service for example-sp1.com to go to p1.example-sp1.com and p2.example-sp2.com.

There are two solutions for where a DNS SRV may be defined. One approach is to configure the SRV record on an external DNS server, where that DNS server is trusted to be a highly available and resilient service. The configuration on CUBE to refer DNS resolution requests to an external DNS server can be done with the commands shown in Example 3-58.

Example 3-58 *Configuration for External DNS to Resolve DNS SRV*

```
ip domain-lookup
ip name-server 172.18.110.106
ip name-server 172.18.110.107
```

The advantage with the approach shown in Example 3-58 is that the SRV configuration is centralized in the external DNS server cluster, and changes to that SRV record need to be made in only one place. The disadvantage is that the SRV lookup is dependent upon external connectivity to the DNS server, which, depending on the network design, might be a critical failure point, such as in scenarios where the DNS server is located on a remote network.

Note DNS lookups are implemented in the SIP stack, using a blocking API. This means that only one DNS query is placed at a time. While a DNS query is being performed by the SIP stack, subsequent DNS queries are placed in a queue. The queued queries will not get responses until the active DNS query has been relinquished, after which the next DNS query in the stack will be attempted.

The caveat here is that if the DNS server is slow or unresponsive, the timeout of the DNS query may take a significant amount of time (the default is three attempts with 3-second timeouts for each attempt, for a total of 9 seconds before failure), which may result in subsequent calls timing out for call signaling transactions.

The timers associated with this behavior can be tuned with the commands **ip domain timeout** and **ip domain retry.**

Another approach is to define the DNS SRV records locally on the device that is looking up the DNS SRV record for resolution. For CUBE, this is done by defining the SRV records on IOS and then pointing CUBE to itself as the source for DNS. When this is done, DNS resolution is no longer dependent on any external DNS and ensures the ability to resolve the virtual SRV records if the external corporate or service provider's DNS server is not available. This also prevents the situation mentioned in the previous note about DNS queries blocking subsequent calls from occurring, as long as all session targets for peers are defined as local DNS entries on CUBE.

To configure local SRV records, first the DNS service is enabled on CUBE with the command **ip dns server**, and then it is associated to the CUBE DNS server with the command **ip name-server** *CUBE-ip address*. DNS lookup is then enabled with **ip domain-lookup**. The syntax for a SRV entry is as follows:

```
ip host hostname srv priority weight port target-server-hostname
```

Lower values for the priority field in an SRV record have preference and will be attempted first. If multiple entries contain the same priority value, they will be load-balanced based on the percentage defined by the weight. All weights within the priority are added up and then compared as a percentage. For human readability, it is easiest to define numbers as a percentage by using a range of 1 through 99. RFC 2782 also recommends using a value of 0 when not loadbalancing across other hosts so that it is intuitive that the host isn't intended for balancing any load.

If the host chosen within the lowest priority value is unavailable, it will skip other hosts with that same priority and then attempt the next lowest priority.

The host name being defined in a lookup will appear with the *service identifier* preceding the domain name. The following are some common identifiers used with CUBE:

- **_sip._udp.example.com**—SIP over UDP
- **_sip._tcp.example.com**—SIP over TCP
- **_sips._tcp.example.com**—Secure SIP (TLS)

SRV records are then added for the services desired, as shown in Example 3-59 for SIP TCP and SIP TLS.

Example 3-59 *Configuration for DNS SRV Entries*

```
ip dns server
ip domain-lookup
ip name-server 172.18.110.203

ip host _sip._tcp.example-sp1.com srv 10 50 5060 p1.example-sp1.com
ip host _sip._tcp.example-sp1.com srv 20 50 5060 p2.example-sp1.com

ip host _sips._tcp.example-sp1.com srv 10 50 5061 192.168.202.169
ip host _sips._tcp.example-sp1.com srv 20 50 5061 192.168.202.170
```

In Example 3-59, the target server can either be a host name or an IP address. If specifying local entries with a host name as the target for an SRV entry, there also need to be definitions for the name-to-IP resolution of that specific host name. This is shown in Example 3-60.

Example 3-60 *Configuration for Local DNS A Record*

```
ip host p1.example-sp1.com 192.168.202.169
ip host p2.example-sp1.com 192.168.202.170
```

Note When accepting inbound calls from the trunk defined with the SRV record, ensure that calls from the explicit hosts are permitted in **ip address trusted list**. IOS does not permit the hosts that are resolved with SRV when a session target is defined for a SRV. See Chapter 13, "Security Threat Mitigation," for more details on the trust list feature in CUBE.

DNS resolution of an SRV record can be tested with the commands shown in Example 3-61.

Example 3-61 nslookup *for SRV Record*

```
linux$ nslookup
> server 172.18.110.203
> set type=srv
> _sip._tcp.example-sp1.com

Non-authoritative answer:
_sip._tcp.example-sp1.com        service = 10 50 5060 p1.example-sp1.com
_sip._tcp.example-sp1.com        service = 20 50 5060 p2.example-sp1.com
```

When a dial peer configured with **session target dns:example-sp1.com** is selected as the outbound dial peer, CUBE performs DNS SRV lookup and routes the call to p1.example-sp1.com as it has a lower priority value of 10. If p1.example-sp1.com isn't reachable or available to process the SIP INVITE, CUBE routes the call to p2.example-sp1.com, which has the next lowest priority value of 20.

Troubleshooting Call Setup Failures

The most common symptoms of call routing issues are the lack of ring-back, delayed ring-back, and hearing special information tones (SIT) (for example, reorder or no circuit tones) when an end user places a call. Depending on the level of call routing redundancy deployed, an end user may not notice call setup failures when the calls to specific SIP servers aren't correctly established, as the call may get routed via the alternate path without impact to the end-user experience. As a result, in addition to addressing user-reported problems, it is also a good practice to proactively monitor abnormal call disconnect cause codes from call detail records, as discussed in Chapter 14, "Monitoring and Management." This approach will help avoid the potential for widespread call setup failures and minimize the impact on other call-processing elements due to increased call volume or load.

The key troubleshooting objective for support engineers is to quickly isolate which device in the call signaling path is contributing to the delayed call setup or call setup failure. Support engineers can review the configuration and operational status of the contributing device, collect diagnostics data, and enable any additional debugging (if needed) to find the root cause. The first step in accomplishing this objective is to get a clear understanding of the problem by answering a series of questions, as shown in Table 3-10.

Table 3-10 *Gaining an Understanding of a Problem*

Question Type	Sample Questions
What	What is the symptom experienced by the end user? Is the issue observed in inbound or outbound calls or both? What is the expected call signaling flow and call routing path for the given scenario?
Who	Which users are experiencing the issues? What are the calling and called party numbers or the URI for the calls of interest? Where are the impacted users located (that is, site, city, country)?
When	When was the problem first observed? Is the problem happening upon every call attempt, or is it intermittent? If intermittent, how often? Is it possible to re-create the problem? Have there been any recent configuration changes?

The second step is to assess what type of diagnostics data are readily available in call signaling devices across the path. The output of **show** commands in CUBE can be used to do a quick first-level analysis.

The command **show call history voice brief** provides details of recent calls, along with the calling, called number, inbound and outbound dial peer, and disconnect cause codes. This command has options to filter the output based on calling number, called number, session ID, and call leg ID. By default, CUBE stores 100 entries in a call history table and retains each entry for 15 minutes. The number of entries and retention time can be modified by using the commands **call-history-mib max-size** and **call-history-mib retain-timer**.

Example 3-62 shows information about recent outbound calls placed from 26003 (an internal extension) to 4083926001 via CUBE. The first call with call legs 38665 and 38666 was connected successfully and was disconnected with **normal call clearing (16)**. The second call (call legs 40293 and 40294) to the same destination, placed about

5 hours after the initial call, experienced call failure, as indicated by a **destination out of order (27)** cause code. This second call used the same set of dial peers, 6010 and 6011, as the first call.

Example 3-62 show call history voice brief *Output for a Given Called Number*

```
cube1#show call history voice brief called-number 4083926001
...
Telephony call-legs: 0
SIP call-legs: 4
H323 call-legs: 0
Call agent controlled call-legs: 0
Total call-legs: 4

0    : 38666 315138330ms.102 (13:41:32.949 UTC Tue Jan 2 2018) +1660 +4980 pid:6011
  Originate 4083926001
 dur 00:00:03 tx:161/32200 rx:158/31600 10  (normal call clearing (16)) dscp:0
  media:0 audio tos:0xB8 video tos:0x88
 IP 192.168.202.162:8678 SRTP: off rtt:0ms pl:0/0ms lost:0/0/0 delay:0/0/0ms
  g711ulaw TextRelay: off Transcoded No
  media inactive detected:n media contrl rcvd:n/a timestamp:n/a
  long duration call detected:n long dur callduration :n/a timestamp:n/a

 LostPacketRate:0.00 OutOfOrderRate:0.00
 LocalUUID:dfbf7775c44b53ae9f7ae1c85e8545da
 RemoteUUID:8c8c368da411d8df347e57996aa24606


0    : 38665 315138320ms.101 (13:41:32.939 UTC Tue Jan 2 2018) +1670 +4970 pid:6010
  Answer 26003
 dur 00:00:03 tx:158/31600 rx:161/32200 10  (normal call clearing (16)) dscp:0
  media:0 audio tos:0xB8 video tos:0x88
 IP 14.50.201.46:32160 SRTP: off rtt:0ms pl:0/0ms lost:0/0/0 delay:0/0/0ms g711ulaw
  TextRelay: off Transcoded No
  media inactive detected:n media contrl rcvd:n/a timestamp:n/a
  long duration call detected:n long dur callduration :n/a timestamp:n/a

 LostPacketRate:0.00 OutOfOrderRate:0.00
 LocalUUID:8c8c368da411d8df347e57996aa24606
 RemoteUUID:dfbf7775c44b53ae9f7ae1c85e8545da

0    : 40294 335933780ms.117 (19:28:08.397 UTC Tue Jan 2 2018) +-1 +40 pid:6011
  Originate 4083926001
 dur 00:00:00 tx:0/0 rx:0/0 1B  (destination out of order (27)) dscp:0 media:0 audio
  tos:0x0 video tos:0x0
 IP 0.0.0.0:0 SRTP: off rtt:0ms pl:0/0ms lost:0/0/0 delay:0/0/0ms g711ulaw
  TextRelay: off Transcoded No
```

```
 media inactive detected:n media contrl rcvd:n/a timestamp:n/a
 long duration call detected:n long dur callduration :n/a timestamp:n/a

LostPacketRate:0.00 OutOfOrderRate:0.00
LocalUUID:
RemoteUUID:
0     : 40293 335933770ms.118 (19:28:08.387 UTC Tue Jan 2 2018) +-1 +50 pid:6010
 Answer 26003
dur 00:00:00 tx:0/0 rx:0/0 1B  (destination out of order (27)) dscp:0 media:0 audio
 tos:0x0 video tos:0x0
IP 0.0.0.0:0 SRTP: off rtt:0ms pl:0/0ms lost:0/0/0 delay:0/0/0ms g711ulaw
 TextRelay: off Transcoded No
 media inactive detected:n media contrl rcvd:n/a timestamp:n/a
 long duration call detected:n long dur callduration :n/a timestamp:n/a

LostPacketRate:0.00 OutOfOrderRate:0.00
LocalUUID:8c8c368da411d8df347e57996aa25149
RemoteUUID:00000000000000000000000000000000
```

The next step is to enable and collect relevant debugging for further call signaling analysis, if needed. It is recommended to always start with very basic debugging and then increase debug/log levels as further details are needed. Debugging can be manually enabled or automatically enabled, collected, and transferred to an FTP server using diagnostic signatures (discussed in Chapter 14). Cisco TAC–authored diagnostic signatures for call routing issues are available in the Diagnostic Signature Lookup Tool from Cisco.com.

The final step is to analyze the collected data. For this example, it is known that the issue is not related to dial peer matching, as the same dial peers are used in working and not working scenarios. The engineer needs to identify which next hop was selected and the corresponding SIP messages exchanged to determine the next actionable step. **debug ccsip message** and **debug ccsip info** will provide this information from the Cisco IOS SIP stack. **debug ccsip feature** *<feature>* can be used to further limit the output of **debug ccsip info. debug ccsip feature control** results in only call control related debug information being printed.

Example 3-63 provides outputs from **debug voip ccapi inout**, **debug ccsip message**, and **debug ccsip info** for illustration purposes. Typically, debug logs contain information about other calls that were being established during the same time. The debugging associated with a given call of interest can be identified by using the call leg ID and call reference ID at the beginning of the debug output line. The lines that start with **//40293/0EA019800000** are associated with inbound call leg 40293, and the lines that start with **//40294/0EA019800000** are associated with outbound call leg 40294.

Example 3-63 *CUBE Debug Output of a SIP Call Failure*

```
2755808: Jan  2 19:28:08.381: //-1/xxxxxxxxxxxx/SIP/Msg/ccsipDisplayMsg:
Received:
INVITE sip:4083926001@cube1.entcomp1.com:5060 SIP/2.0
Via: SIP/2.0/TCP 172.18.110.206:5060;branch=z9hG4bK68467cea08
From: <sip:26003@172.18.110.206>;tag=15777~154a292d-1558-48b6-9155-e3e-
  49acd9216-26380077
To: <sip:4083926001@cube1.entcomp1.com>
Date: Tue, 02 Jan 2018 19:28:08 GMT
Call-ID: ea01980-a4b1dd48-53-ce6e12ac@172.18.110.206

2755971: Jan  2 19:28:08.387: //-1/0EA019800000/CCAPI/cc_api_call_setup_ind_common:
   Interface=0x7FB63C103DD8, Call Info(
   Calling Number=26003,(Calling Name=)(TON=Unknown, NPI=Unknown, Screening=User,
     Passed, Presentation=Allowed),
   Called Number=4083926001(TON=Unknown, NPI=Unknown),
   Calling Translated=FALSE, Subscriber Type Str=Unknown, FinalDestinationFlag=TRUE,
   Incoming Dial-peer=6010, Progress Indication=NULL(0), Calling IE Present=TRUE,
   Source Trkgrp Route Label=, Target Trkgrp Route Label=, CLID Transparent=FALSE),
     Call Id=40293

2756010: Jan  2 19:28:08.389: //40293/0EA019800000/CCAPI/ccCallSetupRequest:
   Calling Number=26003(TON=Unknown, NPI=Unknown, Screening=User, Passed,
     Presentation=Allowed),
   Called Number=4083926001(TON=Unknown, NPI=Unknown),
   Redirect Number=, Display Info=
   Account Number=26003, Final Destination Flag=TRUE,
   Guid=0EA01980-0001-0000-0000-0053CE6E12AC, Outgoing Dial-peer=6011


2756061: Jan  2 19:28:08.391: //40294/0EA019800000/SIP/Info/verbose/5120/ccsip_call_
  setup_request: Session target or outbound proxy configured
2756062: Jan  2 19:28:08.391: //-1/xxxxxxxxxxxx/SIP/Info/verbose/5120/sipSPIGetOut-
  boundHostAndDestHostPrivate: CCSIP: target_host : example-sp1.com target_port : 5060

2756177: Jan  2 19:28:08.394: //-1/xxxxxxxxxxxx/SIP/Info/notify/8192/sip_dns_type_
  srv_query: TYPE SRV query for _sip._tcp.example-sp1.com and type:1
2756178: Jan  2 19:28:08.395: //-1/xxxxxxxxxxxx/SIP/Info/info/8192/sip_dns_type_srv_
  query: Server Name p1.example-sp1.com
Priority 10 Weight 30 Port 5060
2756179: Jan  2 19:28:08.395: //-1/xxxxxxxxxxxx/SIP/Info/info/8192/sip_dns_type_srv_
  query: Server Name p2.example-sp1.com
Priority 10 Weight 20 Port 5060

2756182: Jan  2 19:28:08.396: //-1/xxxxxxxxxxxx/SIP/Info/notify/8192/sip_dns_type_a_
  query: TYPE A query successful for p1.example-sp1.com
```

```
2756184: Jan  2 19:28:08.396: //-1/xxxxxxxxxxxx/SIP/Info/info/8192/sip_dns_type_srv_
  query: IP Address of p1.example-sp1.com is:

2756185: Jan  2 19:28:08.396: //-1/xxxxxxxxxxxx/SIP/Info/info/8192/sip_dns_type_srv_
  query: 192.168.202.169

2756241: Jan  2 19:28:08.399: //40294/0EA019800000/SIP/Msg/ccsipDisplayMsg:
Sent:
INVITE sip:4083926001@example-sp1.com:5060 SIP/2.0
Via: SIP/2.0/TCP 192.168.202.165:5060;branch=z9hG4bK749417B7
Remote-Party-ID: <sip:26003@192.168.202.165>;party=calling;screen=yes;privacy=off
From: <sip:9193926000@192.168.202.165>;tag=14073872-1A45
To: <sip:4083926001@example-sp1.com>
Date: Tue, 02 Jan 2018 19:28:08 GMT
Call-ID: E5AA71B8-EF2911E7-B5A3AB27-C5AF3C32@192.168.202.165
Supported: timer,resource-priority,replaces,sdp-anat
Min-SE:  1800
Cisco-Guid: 0245373312-0000065536-0000000083-3663320236
User-Agent: Cisco-SIPGateway/IOS-16.6.1
Allow: INVITE, OPTIONS, BYE, CANCEL, ACK, PRACK, UPDATE, REFER, SUBSCRIBE, NOTIFY,
  INFO, REGISTER
CSeq: 101 INVITE
...
2756261: Jan  2 19:28:08.437: //40294/0EA019800000/SIP/Msg/ccsipDisplayMsg:
Received:
SIP/2.0 502 No More Routes or Policies To Advance
Via: SIP/2.0/TCP 192.168.202.165:5060;branch=z9hG4bK749417B7
To: <sip:4083926001@example-sp1.com>;tag=dsaae91cd4
From: <sip:26003@192.168.202.165>;tag=14073872-1A45
Call-ID: E5AA71B8-EF2911E7-B5A3AB27-C5AF3C32@192.168.202.165
CSeq: 101 INVITE
Content-Length: 0

2756290: Jan  2 19:28:08.438: //40294/0EA019800000/CCAPI/cc_api_call_disconnected:
   Cause Value=27, Interface=0x7FB63C103DD8, Call Id=40294
...
```

Analysis of the CUBE debug log shows that it receives a SIP INVITE from 172.18.110.206 (the CUCM subscriber node) to establish a call from extension 26003 to 4083926001. It matches the outbound dial peer 6011, resolves the next-hop domain name example-sp1.com using DNS SRV and A record lookups, and selects p1.example-sp1.com (192.168.202.169, proxy server in service provider network) as the next hop. It originates a SIP INVITE with a new Call-ID, **E5AA71B8-EF2911E7-B5A3AB27-C5AF3C32@192.168.202.165**, and CSeq 101 to the next hop. Call-ID and CSeq are used to identify SIP responses that correspond to the given SIP INVITE. The SIP request and the corresponding responses will maintain the same Call-ID and CSeq values. CUBE receives 502 as a final error response instead of 200 OK and disconnects the call with the corresponding Q.850 cause code **destination out of order (27)**. Based on this analysis, the call routing issue has been isolated to be triggered outside the entcomp1 enterprise network. The next step would be to engage the service provider or the support team of the called company to investigate why the call processing server is not able to route the call to the called user.

The commands **show host** and **show host vrf** *vrf-name* are useful for quickly viewing the mapping between DNS host names and DNS SRV-to-IP address mapping. If there is a problem resolving the DNS records, enable the commands **debug ip dns view**, **debug ip domain**, and **debug ccsip error** to get insights into the root cause.

Troubleshooting Tools

Analyzing SIP messages from multiple devices is a tedious task when done manually using text editors. Thanks to tools such as Wireshark and TranslatorX, there is a simple way to visually analyze SIP messages in packet capture files using Wireshark and device log files (for example, CUCM, CUBE) using TranslatorX.

Figure 3-24 shows a snapshot of the SIP packets that correspond to the debug output in Example 3-63. It is advisable to use network packet capture to view signaling messages exchanged between CUBE and a service provider in high-call-volume environments to avoid performance impacts on CUBE due to debug enablement. The packets relevant to the call are filtered using the following Wireshark filter:

```
sip.to.user == 4083926001
```

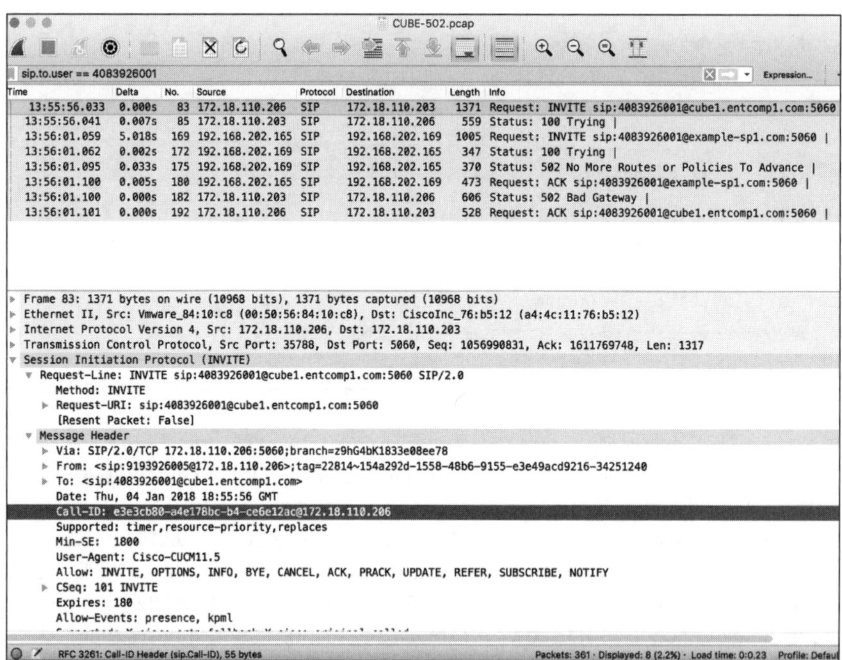

Figure 3-24 *Filtering Relevant SIP Messages Using Wireshark Filters*

The specific call of interest can also be found using these additional Wireshark filters:

```
sip.to.user contains "26001"
sip.from.user == 9193926005
sip.from.user contains "26005"
```

After finding the SIP INVITE for the call of interest, expand the **Message Header** section, select the **Call-ID** header field, and right-click and choose **Apply as Filter > Selected** to view all the SIP messages that belong to this SIP call.

To view the message in graphical form, select **Telephony > VoIP Calls** or **Telephony > SIP Flows** from the Wireshark toolbar menu. This shows the list of calls in the Wireshark PCAP file. Selecting multiple calls of interest and clicking the **OK** button renders the call flow in a ladder diagram, which helps in expediting the issue isolation process (see Figure 3-25) by providing a visually pleasing representation of the call.

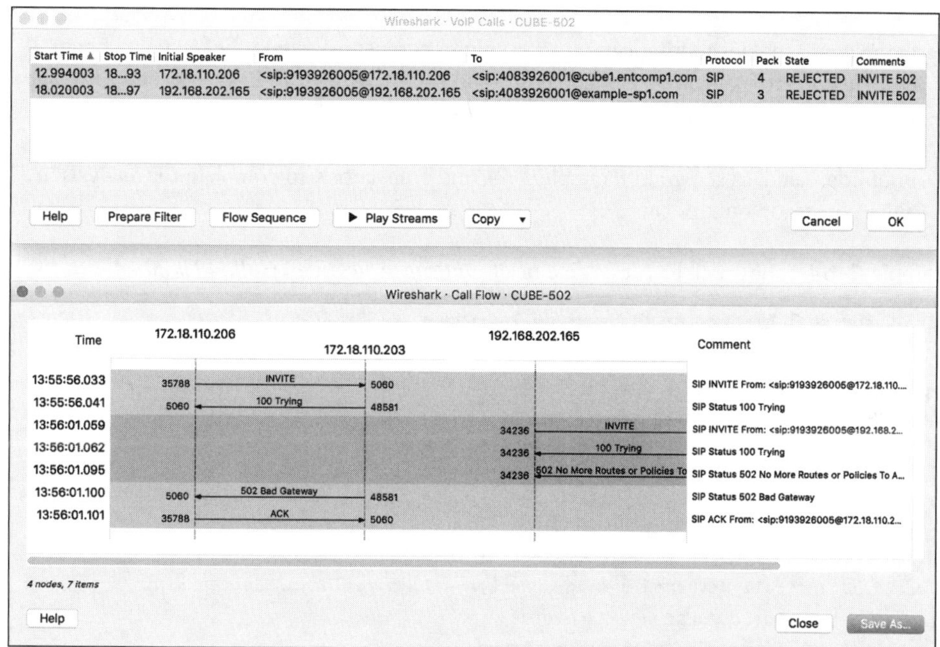

Figure 3-25 *Visual Representation of SIP Call Flow Using Wireshark*

The combination of **Session-ID** and visual **Call Trace Analysis** tools is very useful in troubleshooting complex call flows such as call transfers. The following filters in Wireshark can be applied to filter the SIP messages for a given end-to-end session:

- sip.session-ID
- sip.session-ID.local_uuid
- sip.session-ID.remote_uuid

Consider the scenario shown in Figure 3-26. The caller 4083926001 is first connected to an internal user 9193926005, who then transfers the call to 9193926006. There are tens of SIP messages exchanged between CUBE, CUCM, and Jabber endpoints.

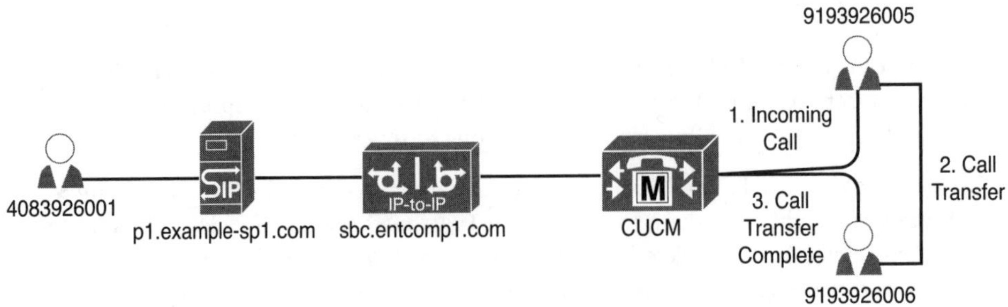

Figure 3-26 *Transfer of an Incoming Call*

In the past, troubleshooting call transfer failures took substantial time as support engineers needed to manually stitch an end-to-end call by using Call-IDs between CUBE and CUCM, CUCM and endpoint 1, and CUCM and endpoint 2 by using the sip.Call-ID Wireshark filter. Now engineers can use Session-ID values in the **show call history voice brief** command, as shown in Example 3-64, and TranslatorX to complete the analysis in a much shorter amount of time.

Example 3-64 **show call history voice brief** *Output for a Given Called Number*

```
cube1#show call history voice brief called-number 9193926005
...
0     : 46588 400297960ms.1 (13:20:52.581 UTC Wed Jan 3 2018) +2060 pid:6010 Origi-
  nate 9193926005 connected
 dur 00:01:11 tx:2670/533696 rx:2665/532312 dscp:0 media:0 audio tos:0xB8 video
  tos:0x88
 IP 10.82.182.130:24586 SRTP: off rtt:24ms pl:0/0ms lost:0/0/0 delay:0/0/0ms
  g711ulaw TextRelay: off Transcoded: No ICE: Off
 media inactive detected:n media contrl rcvd:n/a timestamp:n/a
 long duration call detected:n long duration call duration:n/a timestamp:n/a
 LostPacketRate:0.00 OutOfOrderRate:0.00
 LocalUUID:11a1eb5f00105000a000f45c89b76b25
 RemoteUUID:9972c895a8fc5f6fa70d405abb2e3549
 VRF:
0     : 46587 400297950ms.1 (13:20:52.571 UTC Wed Jan 3 2018) +2080 pid:6000 Answer
  4083926001 connected
 dur 00:01:11 tx:2664/532264 rx:2674/534344 dscp:0 media:0 audio tos:0xB8 video
  tos:0x88
```

```
IP 192.168.202.162:8986 SRTP: off rtt:23ms pl:0/0ms lost:0/0/0 delay:0/0/0ms
 g711ulaw TextRelay: off Transcoded: No ICE: Off
media inactive detected:n media contrl rcvd:n/a timestamp:n/a
long duration call detected:n long duration call duration:n/a timestamp:n/a
LostPacketRate:0.00 OutOfOrderRate:0.00
LocalUUID:9972c895a8fc5f6fa70d405abb2e3549
RemoteUUID:11a1eb5f00105000a000f45c89b76b25
VRF:
```

In Example 3-64, the **LocalUUID** in the outbound call leg is the local UUID of the remote peer, and the **RemoteUUID** is the UUID of CUBE. The UUID of the peer changes as the call gets transferred to different destinations, whereas CUBE's UUID **9972c895a8fc5f6fa70d405abb2e3549** remains the same. Support engineers can open the CUCM-detailed SDI traces and log files containing the CUBE debug information (**show log** output) in TranslatorX and then input CUBE's UUID in the **Search** field at the top right of the main window. Figure 3-27 shows the filtered messages.

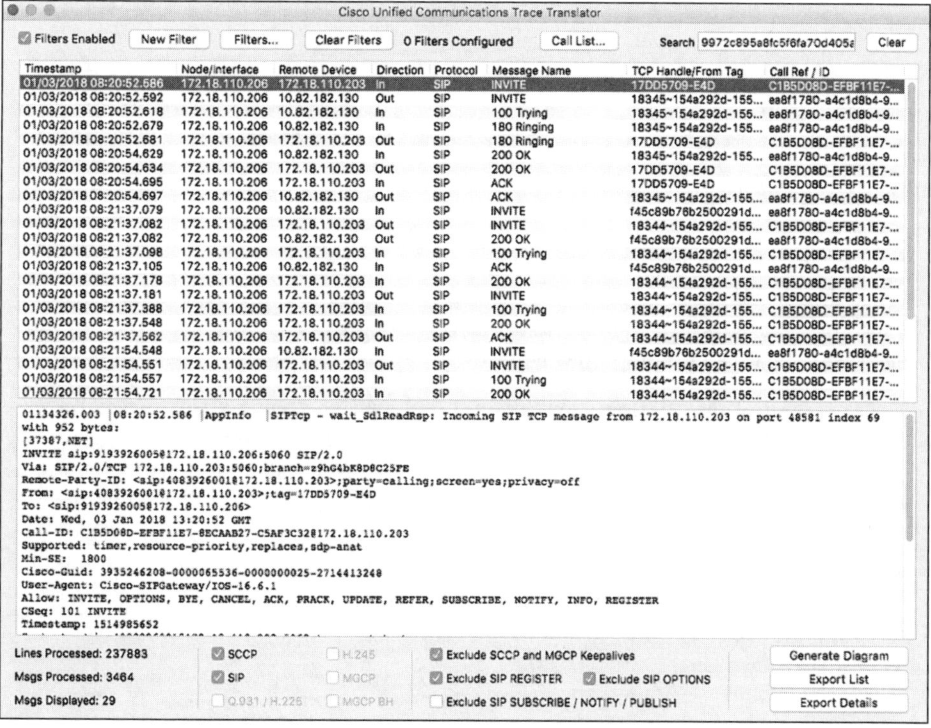

Figure 3-27 *TranslatorX: Messages That Match CUBE's UUID*

If you select the first message and then select **Filter > Add to Filter From Selected Message > SIP Session**, TranslatorX automatically finds all the related Call-IDs associated with the selected INVITE message, using the local and remote UUIDs, and then dynamically builds and applies a filter, as shown in Figure 3-28. An additional Session-ID filter **386b802500105000a000f45c89b76b25** is manually added to the existing filter list. This is the local UUID used in the SIP INVITE sent by 9193926005 to set up a call with 9193926006.

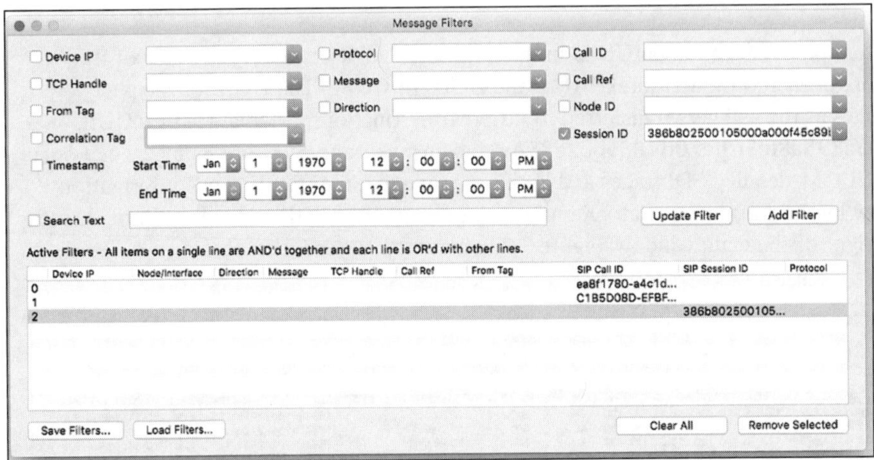

Figure 3-28 *TranslatorX: Dynamically Built Call-ID Filters and a Session-ID Filter*

You can click the **Generate Diagram** button in the main window (refer to Figure 3-27) to see the filtered messages in call ladder diagram format, shown in Figure 3-29. When a specific message is clicked in the visual view, the entire content of the message of the message is displayed in a pop-up window.

Visual analysis of the call flow shows that the call transfer attempt wasn't successful because of a 404 Not Found (unassigned number) message received as a response when 9193926005 called 9193926006. This is due to an incorrect calling search space configuration in CUCM for the line 9193926005. After the configuration is fixed to address this misconfiguration, a call is reattempted, and new logs are collected. The ladder diagram for the same call flow, with the Session-ID filter enabled, is shown in Figure 3-30 for this working call. For the sake of brevity, only the SIP messages that correspond to the call setup between 9193926005 and 9193926006 and subsequent call transfer using SIP REFER are shown here.

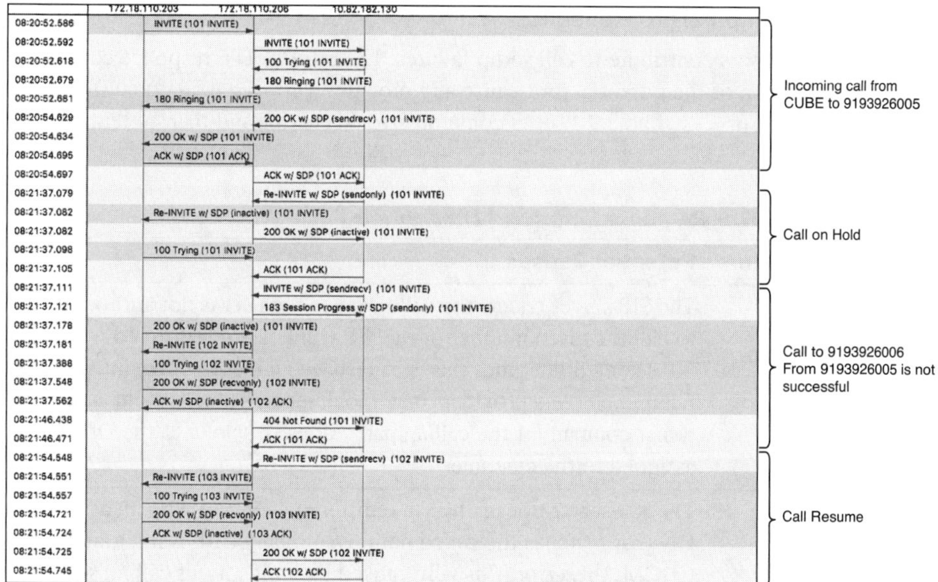

Figure 3-29 *TranslatorX: End-to-End Call Flow for the Nonworking Transfer Scenario*

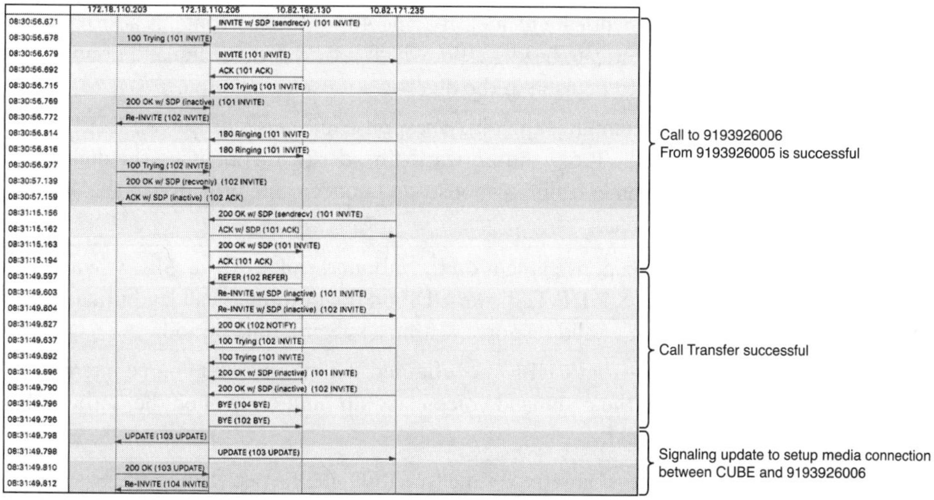

Figure 3-30 *TranslatorX: End-to-End Call Flow for the Working Call Transfer Scenario*

Common Call Setup Failure Reasons

A variety of factors contribute to call setup failures. The SIP INVITE response code is a good indication of the potential root cause and provides a good starting point for the troubleshooting process. Table 3-11 lists common error scenarios and their potential causes.

Table 3-11 *SIP Error Response Codes and Description*

SIP Response Code	Potential Causes
403 Forbidden	The SIP server rejects the call because the user is not authorized to call the given number or the SIP trunk is not registered with the SIP server. Sometimes this is caused by an incorrect calling party number. Service providers may block incoming calls from a customer company if the calling party doesn't belong to the DID range assigned to the customer.
404 Not Found	The SIP server doesn't have a registered endpoint with an assigned DN that matches the called number. When CUBE is integrated with CUCM, this error is usually caused by an incorrect calling search space setting in the CUCM SIP trunk configuration. It could also be the result of no valid outbound dial peer match at CUBE.
407 Proxy Authentication Required	The proxy in the service provider network challenges the SBC to authenticate its identity. The 407 response contains a Proxy-Authenticate header field, which provides the realm and nonce value to be used in the digest response calculation. SBC computes the digest response and re-sends the SIP INVITE with the Proxy-Authorization header field containing the digest username, realm, response, and nonce value provided in the 407 response.
408 Request Timeout	This response is sent on the inbound call leg by an SBC when it has sent a SIP INVITE over UDP on the outbound call leg but hasn't gotten a valid response within a specific time period. Ensure that CUBE is configured with the correct source interface, using the command **voice-class sip bind control** on the outbound dial peer.

422 Session Interval Too Small	The session refresh time (see RFC 4028) specified by the Session-Expires header field in the SIP INVITE message is smaller than the value acceptable by the server processing the SIP INVITE request. This value can be modified in CUBE by using the **session-expires** parameter in the following command:
	
	`voice service voip`
	` sip`
	`   min-se minimum-time session-expires refresh-time`

SIP Response Code	Potential Causes
480 Temporarily Unavailable	The called party is unavailable to accept the call.
483 Too Many Hops	A call routing loop occurs due to misconfiguration. When this happens, an incoming call is sent back to the originating SIP server due to incorrect **destination-pattern** or **session target** commands in outbound dial peers.
486 Busy Here	The called party is talking to another person and hence is not able to accept the given call.
487 Request Terminated	This response doesn't indicate an error. When a user places a call but hangs up before the call gets connected, the user's endpoint sends a SIP CANCEL request to cancel the SIP INVITE request. The SIP server processing the INVITE request terminates the session by sending a 487 Request Terminated response.
488 Media Not Acceptable Here	A media codec mismatch (such as an unsupported audio, video, or fax codec) occurs.
500 Internal Server Error	A generic server level error occurs. Check the SIP Warning header field in the SIP response to get more details about the internal error. It could be due to reasons such as a lack of transcoding resources, the maximum number of connections being reached, or the defined call spike threshold being reached. This error is also observed when CUBE's SIP stack is unable to handle specific sequences of SIP messages.
502 No More Routes or Policies To Advance	The SIP proxy server has tried all configured routes to send the SIP INVITE to the next hop, but none of them have been successful.
503 Service Unavailable	Either the SIP server doesn't support the requested transport protocol or the service is taken offline for maintenance purposes. For example, a service provider may not support SIP over TCP. This can also be observed when the next hop is not reachable. **debug ip tcp transactions** and **debug ccsip transport** provide useful details about the connection setup for SIP over TCP calls.

Summary

This chapter introduces the different ways of dialing and routing a SIP call through an SBC. Directory number, URI, and source-based call routing are discussed. CUBE is used as an example in this chapter to illustrate the call routing mechanisms.

This chapter explains the inner workings of CUBE's call routing decision, using dial peer matching rules. A detailed overview of CUBE's call routing capabilities covers items such as number translations, call rerouting, dial peer optimization techniques, Multi-VRF support, dial peer groups, and customized call routing using dial peer provisioning policies.

This chapter explores concepts related to configuring and troubleshooting call routing issues using solution-level serviceability capabilities such as Session-ID based end-to-end call trace, show commands, debugging, and visualization tools. These useful techniques allow you to reduce the time spent troubleshooting call routing issues across SBC environments.

References

E.164, "The International Public Telecommunication Numbering Plan," https://www.itu.int/rec/T-REC-E.164-201011-I/en

RFC 1035, "Domain Names—Implementation and Specification," https://tools.ietf.org/html/rfc1035

RFC 2782, "A DNS RR for Specifying the Location of Services (DNS SRV)," https://tools.ietf.org/html/rfc2782

RFC 2833, "RTP Payload for DTMF Digits, Telephony Tones and Telephony Signals," https://tools.ietf.org/html/rfc2833

RFC 2915, "The Naming Authority Pointer (NAPTR) DNS Resource Record," https://tools.ietf.org/html/rfc2915

RFC 3261, "SIP: Session Initiation Protocol," https://tools.ietf.org/html/rfc3261

RFC 3262, "Reliability of Provisional Responses in the Session Initiation Protocol (SIP)," https://tools.ietf.org/html/rfc3262

RFC 3966, "The tel URI for Telephone Numbers," https://tools.ietf.org/html/rfc3966

RFC 4028, "Session Timers in the Session Initiation Protocol (SIP)," https://tools.ietf.org/html/rfc4028

RFC 4412, "Communications Resource Priority for the Session Initiation Protocol (SIP)," https://tools.ietf.org/html/rfc4412

RFC 4694, "Number Portability Parameters for the "tel" URI," https://tools.ietf.org/html/rfc4694

RFC 4904, "Representing Trunk Groups in tel/sip Uniform Resource Identifiers (URIs)," https://tools.ietf.org/html/rfc4904

RFC 5798, "Virtual Router Redundancy Protocol (VRRP) Version 3 for IPv4 and IPv6," https://tools.ietf.org/html/rfc5798

"Using OPTIONS to Query for Operational Status in the Session Initiation Protocol," https://tools.ietf.org/html/draft-jones-sip-options-ping-02

RFC 5806, "Diversion Indication in SIP," https://tools.ietf.org/html/rfc5806

RFC 6298, "Computing TCP's Retransmission Timer," https://tools.ietf.org/html/rfc6298

RFC 7989, "End-to-End Session Identification in IP-Based Multimedia Communication Networks," https://tools.ietf.org/html/rfc7989

"Voice Translation Rules," https://www.cisco.com/c/en/us/support/docs/voice/call-routing-dial-plans/61083-voice-transla-rules.html

Cisco CallManager Fundamentals, 2nd ed., by Alexander et al. (Cisco Press)

IP Routing on Cisco IOS, IOS XE, and IOS XR: An Essential Guide to Understanding and Implementing IP Routing Protocols, by *Edgeworth* et al. (Cisco Press)

"Wireshark," https://www.wireshark.org

"TranslatorX," https://www.translatorx.org/

"Diagnostic Signatures Lookup Tool," https://cway.cisco.com/tools/dslt

Chapter 4

Signaling and Interworking

SBCs are often the demarcation point between many different real-time multimedia networks. When interconnecting two real-time communication networks, more often than not, there is a significant chance of encountering interoperability issues. For example, the two networks might support different call control protocols, different extensions within the same call control protocol, different media encoding formats, different media format packetization periods, different methods of dual-tone multifrequency (DTMF) relay, different media encryption schemes, or different IP addressing versions.

Many of the endpoints initiating and terminating communication sessions don't natively have the ability to address interoperability situations that may arise. Intermediary devices, such as SBCs, exert control over media and session traffic to ensure that it is engineered to a format acceptable to the communicating entities on separate networks.

The different types of interworking that an SBC may perform are often split into two different operational planes: the media plane and the signaling plane. The *media plane* handles the interworking of real-time multimedia data such as media formats, media encoding, DTMF types, and media encryption schemes. Media plane interworking is further discussed in Chapters 5, "Media Processing," 6, "Secure Signaling and Media," and 7, "DTMF Interworking." This chapter focuses on the signaling plane and the types of interworking an SBC must be equipped to handle. This chapter includes the following sections:

- **SIP–SIP Interworking—**This section provides a comprehensive analysis of the different types of SIP interworking, including different types of session establishment, extensions, signaling exchanges, and mid-call session modifications from the perspective of an SBC.
- **SIP Header Interworking** and **SIP Normalization—**These sections cover how to use an SBC to manipulate, modify, and manage SIP messaging headers and the message body on an SBC.

- **Transport and Protocol Interworking**—This section dives into new and existing Layer 4 and Layer 3 protocol interworking scenarios used by modern SBCs.
- **Supplementary Services**—This section discusses the signaling exchanges that are used to enhance sessions and add features to new and existing sessions.
- **SIP–H.323 Interworking**—This section provides a quick summary detailing how an SBC can facilitate the interworking of different VoIP session establishment protocols.

This chapter details the most common interworking scenarios an SBC may encounter on the signaling plane. It provides real-world interworking examples and describes ways that such scenarios can be accomplished. In addition, the interworking samples are coupled with relevant configuration examples and debugging examples from Cisco's SBC, CUBE.

SIP–SIP Interworking

The most common SBC deployment utilizes SIP as the signaling protocol to connect different networks. In this type of scenario, an SBC acts as a back-to-back user agent (B2BUA). Being a B2BUA, the SBC has co-located user agent client (UAC) and user agent server (UAS) functionality. This is very useful for SIP interworking as it allows the SBC to receive and send SIP messages from either perspective during a session. The B2BUA can maintain two separate SIP dialogs and interwork any events that occur on one dialog with the participant of the other dialog and vice versa.

The following sections cover the many different interworking options available for SIP–SIP SBCs.

Early Offer and Delayed Offer Interworking

An early offer call is initiated when a UAC advertises its media capabilities in the Session Description Protocol (SDP) of the first INVITE of a SIP dialog. On the other hand, a delayed offer is the opposite. When a UAC is initiating a delayed offer call, there is no message body containing SDP in the initial INVITE of the SIP dialog. In a delayed offer scenario, the UAC answers the offer from the UAS. During either a delayed offer or early offer call, the UAS may respond with the SDP body in a provisional or final response.

Take, for example, the signaling detailed in Figure 4-1. The UAC has sent an INVITE with SDP body as the offer, which indicates that this is an early offer call. The UAS sends a provisional response with SDP (183 with SDP). At this point, audio channels can be opened up between the UAC and UAS. This is commonly referred to as *early media*. Early media is very important for things like in-band ringback reception and service messages that may need to be delivered to a session participant. It is important to note that in this scenario, the offer/answer is *not* complete. A final response with the SDP body (200 OK) may still be sent from the UAS to indicate a true answer to the early offer. That being said, if the provisional response is received with reliability, the offer/answer could be complete, and the final response does not need to contain SDP. (The section

"Reliable Handling and Interworking of Provisional Responses," later in this chapter, provides more information about this scenario.)

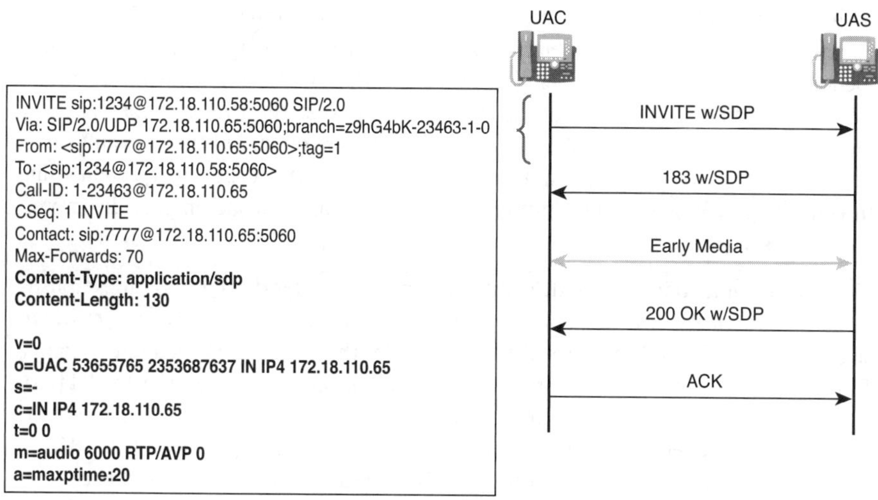

UAC
UAS
INVITE sip:1234@172.18.110.58:5060 SIP/2.0
Via: SIP/2.0/UDP 172.18.110.65:5060;branch=z9hG4bK-23463-1-0
From: <sip:7777@172.18.110.65:5060>;tag=1
To: <sip:1234@172.18.110.58:5060>
Call-ID: 1-23463@172.18.110.65
CSeq: 1 INVITE
Contact: sip:7777@172.18.110.65:5060
Max-Forwards: 70
Content-Type: application/sdp
Content-Length: 130
v=0
o=UAC 53655765 2353687637 IN IP4 172.18.110.65
s=-
c=IN IP4 172.18.110.65
t=0 0
m=audio 6000 RTP/AVP 0
a=maxptime:20
INVITE w/SDP
183 w/SDP
Early Media
200 OK w/SDP
ACK

Figure 4-1 *Early Offer Session Between a UAC and a UAS*

Figure 4-2 details a session in which a UAC has sent an INVITE without SDP. The UAS sends a provisional response without SDP (180 Ringing) and then a final response with SDP (200 OK). This is now the offer for the session, and the UAC is required to provide an answer, usually in the form of an ACK with SDP. After this, the offer/answer is complete, and bidirectional media is established.

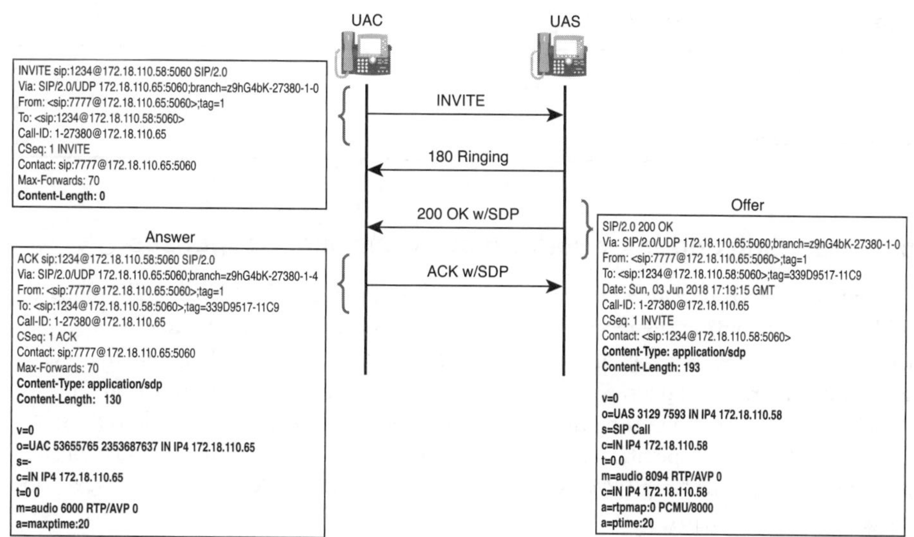

Figure 4-2 *Delayed Offer Session Between a UAC and a UAS*

One problem that occurs with delayed offer is the potential for audio clipping. The device answering with a 200 OK final response may begin transmitting audio immediately. Because the session is not established until there is an answer to the offer (200 OK with SDP), the UAC may not hear audio until the answer to the offer (ACK with SDP) is processed by the UAS. Depending on how long this exchange takes, some audio may be lost. Another possible problematic scenario is that the UAS may respond with a provisional response containing SDP (183 with SDP). Because the UAC has not shared any media information with the UAS, no audio channels are open. This means things like ringback and service messages may not be delivered to the UAC. (The "Reliable Handling and Interworking of Provisional Responses" section, later in this chapter, provides more details on this scenario.)

An SBC must be able to interwork delayed offer and early offer during session establishment so that the offer/answer is completed properly on all legs of a call. Normally, when sending an offer, SBCs tend to mirror the type of offer they receive on the ingress call leg. That is, if the SBC received an early offer INVITE, it sends an early offer INVITE to the peer call leg. Similarly, if the SBC receives a delayed offer INVITE, it sends a delayed offer INVITE to the peer call leg. However, in certain scenarios, especially when SBCs peer with service provider networks, it might be required to always send early offer INVITEs. In such scenarios, the default behavior would have to be modified through configuration to ensure successful interworking. Example 4-1 shows how to modify this behavior on CUBE and always send early offer.

Tip CUBE cannot send delayed offer on an outbound call leg if early offer is received on the inbound call leg. Early offer is always sent in this scenario.

Example 4-1 *Forcing Early Offer Globally*

```
voice service voip
 sip
  early-offer forced
```

Reliable Handling and Interworking of Provisional Responses

A *provisional response acknowledgement*, better known as a *PRACK*, is a SIP request used to reliably confirm the receipt of a provisional 1xx-level response. PRACK is defined in RFC 3262 as a way to mirror the reliability seen with INVITE, 200 OK, and ACK. Some Internet Telephony Service Providers (ITSPs) and other devices require a PRACK exchange before cutting through ringback or service messages. In addition, some SIP RFCs indicate that specific signaling exchanges cannot be completed unless a reliable message exchange involving PRACK has occurred. This chapter details one such scenario in the "Update" section.

Take, for example, a scenario outlined in Figure 4-3, where a UAC has sent an early offer INVITE to an upstream UAC, and there are many different network hops in between. This UAS sends an 18x message with SDP to the UAC with the intent that it will be sending media to the UAC. Due to some unforeseen circumstances, the 18x message is dropped in transit across one of the network hops and does not make it to the UAC. The UAS does not know that this was dropped and begins sending packets to the UAC. From the perspective of the UAC, which did not receive the 18x message, these packets may be dropped as they are not part of the SIP current dialog. Had the 18x message been sent with reliability in mind, the UAS would know for sure if the 18x was received and processed by the UAC.

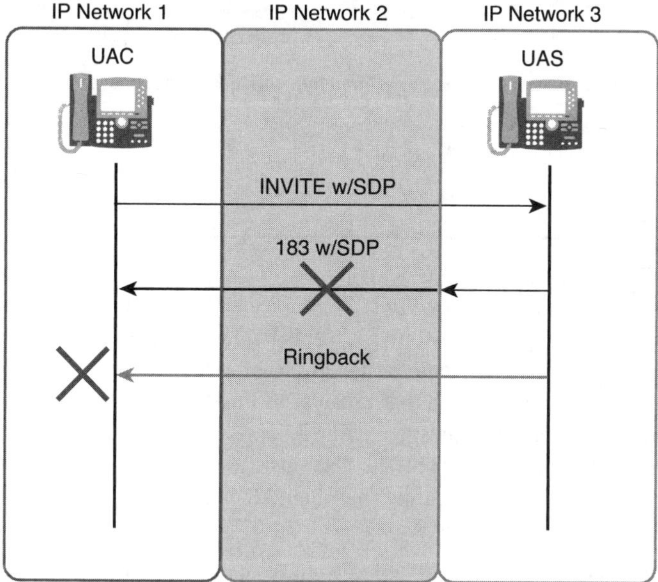

Figure 4-3 *Unreliable Provisional Response Across Different Network Hops*

A UAC advertises the ability to support PRACK by including the tag **100rel** in the Supported header of a SIP INVITE. This can be observed in Example 4-2. RFC 3262 dictates that the only SIP request type that can advertise the support for PRACK is that of a SIP INVITE. In addition, the use of advertising support for PRACK in a re-INVITE is not often seen because mid-call re-INVITEs rarely have provisional responses, which would require the use of reliability. Finally, in addition to having a Supported header, a UAC may also advertise PRACK support and necessity by sending the **100rel** tag in the Require header.

Example 4-2 *Sample INVITE with PRACK Support*

```
INVITE sip:7777@172.18.110.58:5060 SIP/2.0
Via: SIP/2.0/TCP 172.18.110.48:5060;branch=z9hG4bK3a34b28097e
From: <sip:1024@172.18.110.48>;tag=22968~1992ce86-77ac-43a7-91b7-
  90778966a9f5-30207629
To: <sip:7777@172.18.110.58>
Call-ID: 82535500-b00171fb-80-306e12ac@172.18.110.48
Supported: 100rel,timer,resource-priority,replaces
Min-SE:  1800
Allow: INVITE, OPTIONS, INFO, BYE, CANCEL, ACK, PRACK, UPDATE, REFER, SUBSCRIBE,
  NOTIFY
CSeq: 101 INVITE
Expires: 180
Session-ID: 1aaee55200105000a0000c75bd110ca4;remote=00000000000000000000000000000000
Session-Expires:  1800
Contact: <sip:1024@172.18.110.48:5060;transport=tcp>
Max-Forwards: 69
Content-Length: 0
```

Because this UAC has advertised the ability to support PRACK, the UAS receiving this request can send a provisional response reliably if it wants to. The reception of a Supported header with **100rel** *does not* require the UAS to send a response reliably. These items are only informing the UAS that it can send PRACK if it deems it necessary. In the same vein, a UAS cannot request a reliable response if the UAC has not advertised support for PRACK in the INVITE. The UAC instead may send a 421 Extension Required response to the UAC, indicating that the UAS expects the UAC to support PRACK.

If the UAS wants to send a provisional response reliably, it must include the **100rel** tag within the Require SIP header of the provisional response. Including this header and tag requires a PRACK from the UAC, and failure to return a PRACK results in session termination because the UAS does not consider the provisional response to have been handled properly by the UAC. The message will also contain an RSeq header with a numeric value for later use by the PRACK message. Example 4-3 details a 180 Ringing message sent from the UAS requesting a reliable confirmation by the UAC.

Tip PRACK cannot be sent for a 100-level provisional response such as a 100 Trying response. All other numbered responses 101 through 199 can be sent reliably.

Example 4-3 *A 180 Ringing Response Expecting PRACK*

```
SIP/2.0 180 Ringing
Via: SIP/2.0/TCP 172.18.110.48:5060;branch=z9hG4bK3a34b28097e
From: <sip:1024@172.18.110.48>;tag=22968~1992ce86-77ac-43a7-91b7-90778966a9f5-
  30207629
To: <sip:7777@172.18.110.58>;tag=512A088-1C36
Call-ID: 82535500-b00171fb-80-306e12ac@172.18.110.48
CSeq: 101 INVITE
Require: 100rel
RSeq: 3322
Allow: INVITE, OPTIONS, BYE, CANCEL, ACK, PRACK, UPDATE, REFER, SUBSCRIBE, NOTIFY,
  INFO, REGISTER
Remote-Party-ID: <sip:7777@172.18.110.58>;party=called;screen=no;privacy=off
Contact: <sip:7777@172.18.110.58:5060;transport=tcp>
Content-Length: 0
```

Upon reception of a provisional response with a Require **100rel** header, the UAC must respond with a PRACK to inform the UAS of message reception. The PRACK message includes the RAck header, which contains the value from the RSeq header of the message, requiring reliability in addition to the method that is copied from the CSeq of that same response being acknowledged. Example 4-4 details the PRACK in response to Example 4-3.

Example 4-4 *Sample PRACK for the 180 Ringing Response*

```
PRACK sip:7777@172.18.110.58:5060;transport=tcp SIP/2.0
Via: SIP/2.0/TCP 172.18.110.48:5060;branch=z9hG4bK3a42384a9bf
From: <sip:1024@172.18.110.48>;tag=22968~1992ce86-77ac-43a7-91b7-90778966a9f5-
  30207629
To: <sip:7777@172.18.110.58>;tag=512A088-1C36
Call-ID: 82535500-b00171fb-80-306e12ac@172.18.110.48
CSeq: 102 PRACK
RAck: 3322 101 INVITE
Max-Forwards: 70
Content-Length: 0
```

Upon reception of the PRACK, the UAS sends a 200 OK with the CSeq of the PRACK to confirm its reception. At this point, the PRACK process is complete, and the rest of the session establishment occurs normally. Figure 4-4 details the entire PRACK exchange, starting with the first request and ending with the 200 OK.

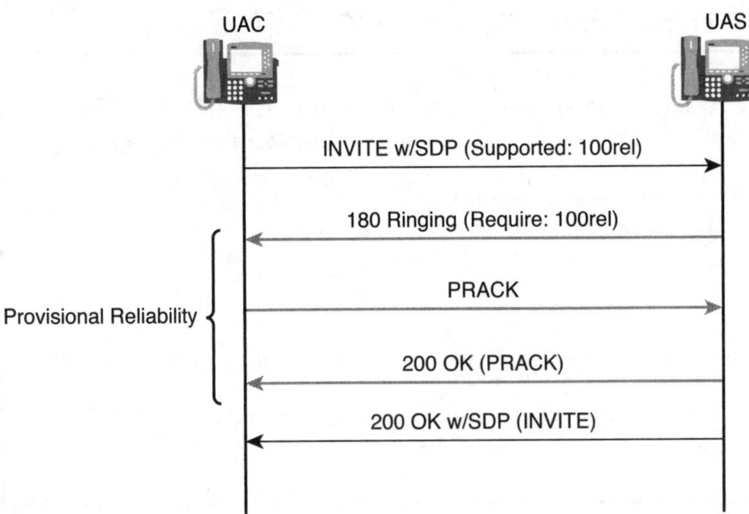

Figure 4-4 *Full PRACK Exchange Between a UAC and a UAS*

CUBE supports PRACK by default, without the need for configuration. If a device advertises PRACK in an INVITE, then CUBE will request reliability of provisional responses on that call leg. CUBE will always advertise PRACK capabilities for egress SIP INVITEs, regardless of the PRACK support on the inbound call leg. This is due to PRACK being a per–call leg mechanism, meaning that one call leg on an SBC may have a PRACK exchange occur while the other call leg does not have a PRACK exchange. Figure 4-5 shows an example of the asynchronous nature of PRACK on an SBC.

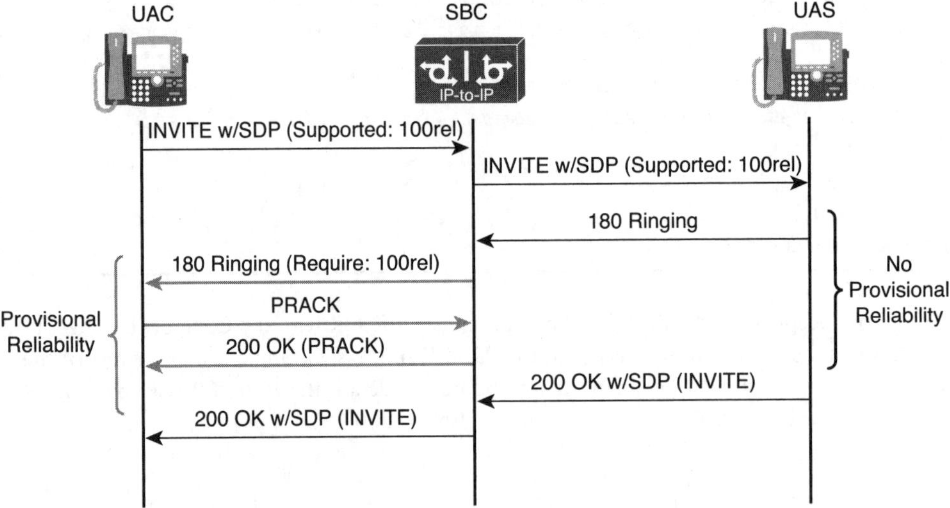

Figure 4-5 *Asynchronous PRACK Exchange Across an SBC*

PRACK support on CUBE can be disabled by adding the command shown in Example 4-5. Alternatively, Example 4-6 details how CUBE can be configured to require PRACK and advertise **Require: 100rel** in the outbound INVITE requests. The command can be returned to the default by either issuing one of the commands shown in Example 4-7.

Example 4-5 *Disabling PRACK Support on CUBE*

```
voice service voip
 sip
  rel1xx disable
```

Example 4-6 *Requiring PRACK Support on CUBE*

```
voice service voip
 sip
  rel1xx require 100rel
```

Example 4-7 *Defaulting PRACK Support on CUBE*

```
voice service voip
 sip
  no rel1xx
! or
voice service voip
 sip
  rel1xx supported 100rel
```

Ringback and Provisional Response Interworking

You have probably heard the expression "I'll give you a ring." In this expression, the term *ring* stems from the sound a telephony device makes when a caller is placing a call to somebody and the call is presented to that device. The phone being rung plays an audible ringtone aloud in attempt to notify the owner of the telephone that she is receiving a call. While the called telephone is ringing aloud, the caller hears an audible signaling tone.

A *ringback tone*, also referred to simply as a *ringback*, is a sequence of call progress tones played to the caller initiating a phone call. These call progress tones inform the caller that the called party telephone is ringing. The absence of ringback is cause for concern, and the caller should assume that the called party is not actually ringing or that the devices handling the call are not handling the call properly.

Call progress tones are a generic term that refers to many different tones that occur during a call. Call progress tones include the dial tone, the busy signal, the call waiting tone, and the ringback tone. Call progress tones vary from country by country. For example, the U.S. call progress tone consists of 2 seconds of ringing followed by 4 seconds of silence, resulting in 6 seconds per ring cycle, as defined in the ITU E.180 specification. European ringback follows the European Telecommunication Standards Institute (ETSI) ETS 300 512 specification. It involves 1 second of ringing followed by 4 seconds of silence, resulting in a ring cycle of 5 seconds. (For further information about country-specific ringback tones, consult the applicable telecommunications standards that a specific country adheres to.) Figure 4-6 details a side-by-side waveform comparison of various types of ringback.

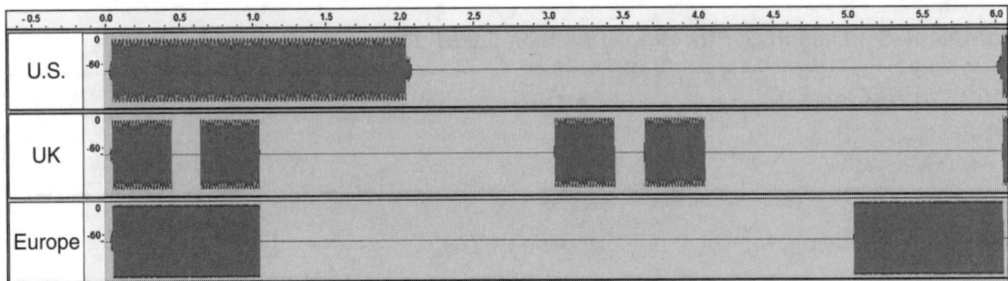

Figure 4-6 *U.S., UK, and European Ringback Waveforms*

Ringback is present in almost every phone call made by a phone, whether it is a cellphone, land line, soft client, or IP phone. This technique of alerting a caller dates back to the inception of telephony systems. It is crucial that an SBC have the ability to facilitate ringback interworking so that the calling party knows the call is progressing, the call has been delivered to the remote device, and an end device is actually ringing.

During session establishment involving an SBC, ringback may be played from one of three sources. The first is a remote device, usually special-purpose equipment on a service provider network or, in some rare scenarios, the end device that is actually being called. In this scenario, a unidirectional audio channel is established from the called party to the calling party, and ringback is played out over this channel. In this scenario, the ringback played is specific to the country of the device providing ringback through the established audio channel. Figure 4-7 details where a remote device plays ringback to the SBC and calling party.

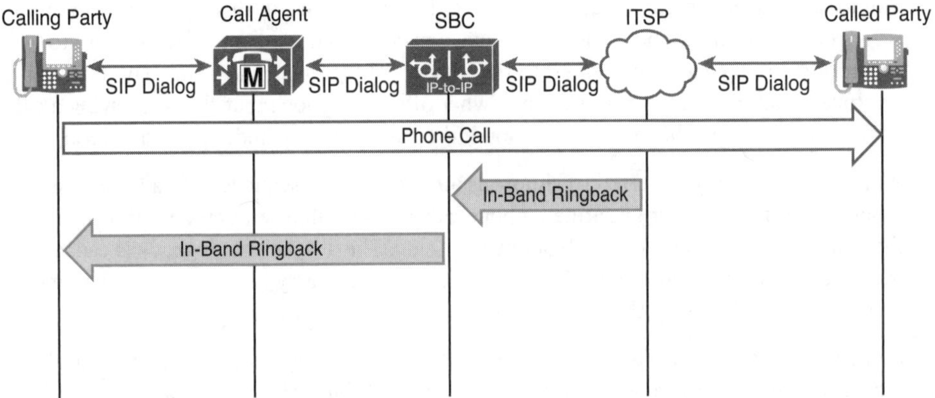

Figure 4-7 *Ringback Generated from Special Provider Equipment*

The second method, which is the least common method, involves the called device signaling the inability to play ringback over a backward audio channel and an SBC taking care of providing ringback to the calling party. This signaling sent to the SBC may include additional information about what type of ringback to play. It could include the cadence, frequency, country type, and so on. At present, there is no standard specifying this extra data for SIP. Thus an SBC may play a ringback tone based on the configuration or administrative policies of the SBC. Figure 4-8 details the aforementioned scenario of an SBC being used to provide ringback.

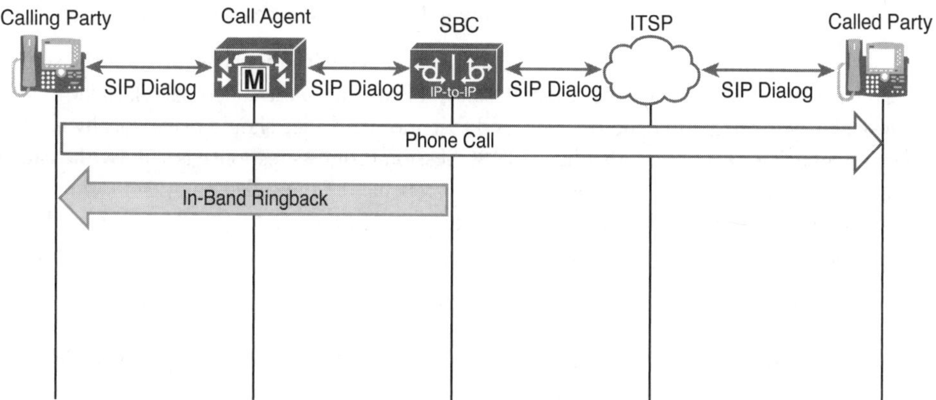

Figure 4-8 *Ringback Generated from an SBC*

The last method for generating ringback is for the called device to signal the inability to play ringback to the SBC. If the SBC is unable to introduce locally generated ringback tones, it may proxy this indication back to the calling party. The call agent responsible for the calling device would receive this message and understand that this response means the called party is ringing but cannot play ringback. Thus the call agent would generate local ringback to the caller or instruct the endpoint to play ringback to the caller. This ringback is usually the type local to the device, unless specified otherwise in the signaling received. Figure 4-9 shows this scenario, with a call agent in charge of playing ringback to the calling party device.

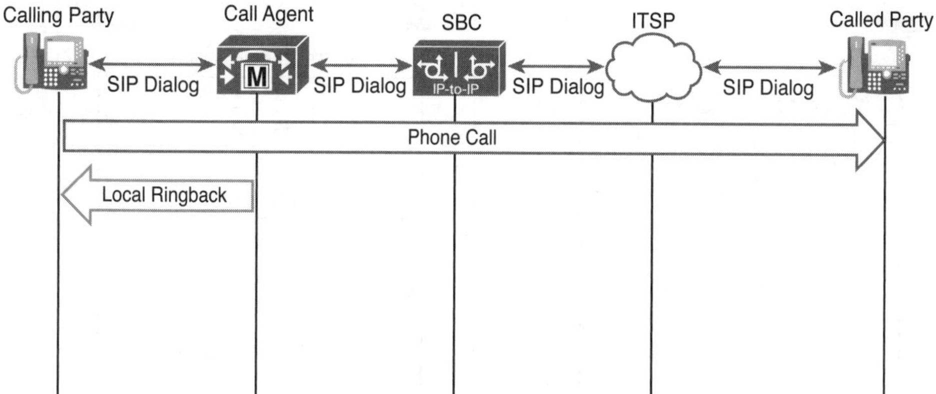

Figure 4-9 *Ringback Generated Locally by a Call Agent*

In the context of a SIP call, call alerting (with the called party in the ringing state) is signaled using the SIP 180 Ringing or 183 Session Progress provisional responses. When a call is attempted, it may take the called party several seconds—or maybe even a few minutes—to answer the call. Before the call is connected, the called party may choose to send either zero, one, or more provisional responses. The 18x (180 or 183) provisional responses serve as an indication to play a ringback tone to the calling party. The specific type of the 18x provisional response usually indicates the source of the ringback tone.

A 180 Ringing response is sent by the called party, or a device that is negotiating call setup on behalf of the called party (for example, an IP PBX local to the called party), to indicate the inability to stream in-band ringback and that another device should play a locally generated ringback tone. On the other hand, a 183 Session Progress response is sent by the called party, or a device that is negotiating call setup on behalf of the called party (for example, an IP PBX local to the called party), to indicate that the ringback tone will be generated in-band from the called party or special access equipment on the service provider network.

For the ringback tone to be generated from the called side, two conditions must be met:

- An audio channel from the called party to the calling party must be established.
- Information must be provided about the IP address and port pair on which the calling party is expecting to receive media.

The first condition is fulfilled by the called party, including an SDP body in the 183 Session Progress response. The second condition is met only when the SDP body encoding the media characteristics of the calling party is made available. If an early offer call is sent and a 183 with SDP is received, then early media can be cut through for ringback. If a delayed offer call is sent and a 183 with SDP is received, then a PRACK with SDP should be exchanged to enable early media ringback and audio session establishment for ringback. Figure 4-10 details the different permutations of 183 with SDP and early and delayed offer.

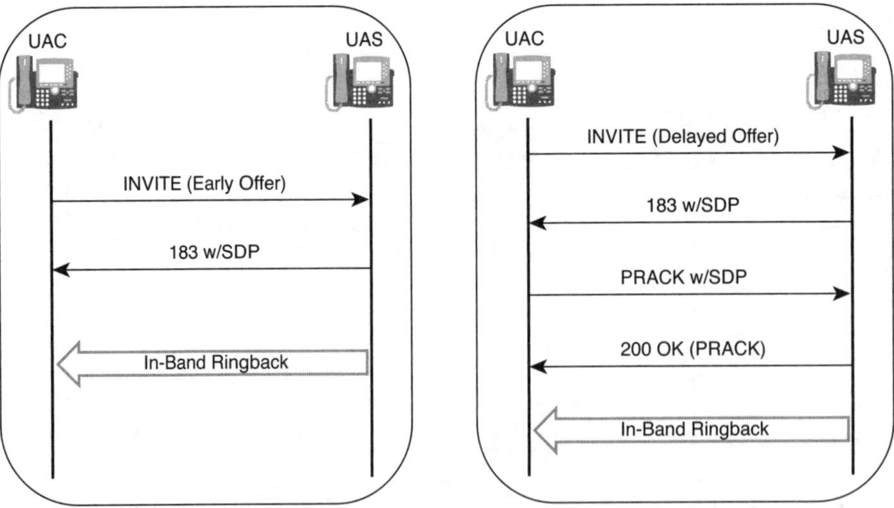

Figure 4-10 *Sample In-Band Ringback Scenarios Between a UAC and a UAS*

A problem arises from the fact that RFC 3261 does not define which 18x ringback responses should contain SDP. Although this is not defined, it is normal to see a 183 with SDP for in-band ringback and use the 180 Ringing message without SDP to signal the inability to play in-band ringback. In rare circumstances, a 180 with SDP or a 183 without SDP may be observed. Thus it is generally accepted that a device is attempting to establish an audio channel for ringback if it sends either 18x message with SDP, while the absence of SDP indicates the inability to provide ringback, and local ringback interworking is required.

In most scenarios, an SBC simply forwards the received 18x response from the in-leg to the out-leg, without the need for extra configuration. However, SBCs that are equipped with digital signal processors (DSPs) may perform 18x interworking by receiving the 18x response without SDP and inserting a DSP while also adding an SDP body, for the purpose of generating ringback toward the calling party. The egress message may be 18x with SDP and result in an audio stream opened in the backward direction from the SBC to the calling party, as shown in Figure 4-11.

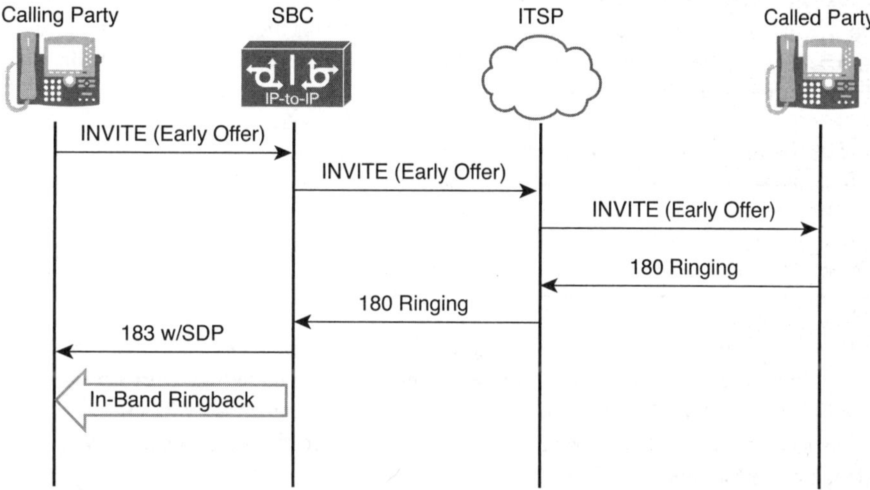

Figure 4-11 *An SBC Converting a 180 Ringing to a 183 with SDP*

> **Tip** CUBE does not support the interworking of an inbound 18x provisional response without SDP into an outbound 18x provisional response with SDP. This also includes the dynamic insertion of a DSP for the purpose of ringback.

Another problem that can arise is that there may be no upper bound on how many provisional response messages can be sent during session establishment. This includes the number of duplicate provisional responses and the sending of different types of provisional responses. In addition, RFC 3261 does not set any guidelines for the handling and interpretation of multiple different types of provisional responses within the same dialog. Should an SBC place preference on a provisional response with SDP for ringback, or should it honor the first or last provisional responses received? Due to this issue, an SBC may be equipped with its own logic in regard to the handling of multiple provisional responses, including those of different types. One example of this logic would be to block, disregard, or filter specific types of provisional responses so that only specific occurrences of provisional responses are sent on the other side of the SBC. CUBE allows an administrator to define different types of 18x messages based on the presence or absence of SDP, as shown in Example 4-8.

Example 4-8 *18x Blocking on CUBE*

```
voice service voip
 sip
  block {180 | 181 | 183} sdp {present | absent}
```

Another example of local logic in regard to provisional response handling is changing the messages received on one call leg into another type for the egress call leg. This can be observed if CUBE receives a 180 response with SDP. This message is converted, by default, into a 183 Session in Progress with SDP unless the command **send 180 sdp** is enabled, as shown in Example 4-9.

Example 4-9 *Enable the Sending of 180 with SDP*

```
voice service voip
 sip
  send 180 sdp
```

Finally, in addition to blocking, modifying, or filtering specific messages, CUBE can be configured to disable early media for 18x responses containing SDP with **sip-ua**, as shown in Example 4-10. Be aware that when you add this command, the UAS may not be able to successfully deliver ringback or services messages to the UAC, which may result in silence during session establishment.

Example 4-10 *Disabling 180 Early Media*

```
sip-ua
 disable-early-media 180
```

When troubleshooting ringback issues, it is always important to look at the SIP signaling exchanged in **debug ccsip messages**. Then you need to attempt to answer the following questions:

- What type of 18x response is received?
- Does the remote party provide ringback, or is that device expecting another device to play ringback on its behalf?
- Does the SBC properly forward this message from one call leg to another?
- If an 18x with SDP is received, is the early media session being properly opened through a valid offer/answer?
- If this session is being opened properly, does the remote device actually send RTP packets from the defined IP and port in the SDP of the 18x with SDP? (To verify this information, a packet capture can be collected and reviewed.)
- In situations where ringback is delayed before being received, are there protocol errors, UDP retransmissions, or erroneous call hunting (which leads to delay in the signaling that is ultimately sent to the called device)? (You can best troubleshoot delays in ringback on CUBE by enabling **debug ccsip messages** and **debug voip ccapi inout**.)

Table 4-1 can assist with troubleshooting ringback and provisional response interworking on CUBE.

Table 4-1 *CUBE 18x Interworking*

Received Message	Sent Message	Command Needed?
180 Ringing no SDP	180 Ringing no SDP	Default behavior
180 Ringing with SDP	183 Session in Progress with SDP	Default behavior
180 Ringing with SDP	180 Ringing with SDP	**send 180 sdp**
183 Session in Progress no SDP	183 Session in Progress no SDP	Default behavior
183 Session in Progress with SDP	183 Session in Progress with SDP	Default behavior
180 Ringing no SDP	None	**block 180 sdp absent**
180 Ringing with SDP	None	**block 180 sdp present**
183 Session in Progress no SDP	None	**block 183 sdp absent**
183 Session in Progress with SDP	None	**block 183 sdp present**

Signal Forking

Often a phone number or other identifiers may be shared across different devices. Take, for example, a shared line that is on two different IP phones and a soft client. When a call is presented to the call agent responsible for these devices, the SIP session may be forked (that is, split into two sessions), with a separate INVITE request sent to all the aforementioned devices. The device performing the forking in the previous example is often referred to as the *forking proxy*. This device is responsible for forking a single, received

SIP INVITE into multiple egress SIP INVITEs that are sent to their respective destination (see Figure 4-12). The aforementioned SIP proxy is considered a stateful proxy because it remains aware of the overall session and can cancel redundant transactions.

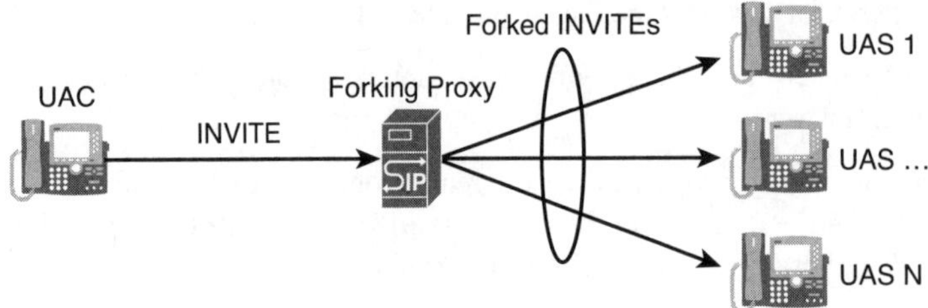

Figure 4-12 *Forking Proxy Sending Multiple Requests to Upstream User Agents*

A similar example is a scenario in which a service provider receives a request and extends the SIP session to multiple downstream ITSP SIP servers by forking the request. This could be done by the stateful SIP forking proxy for a number of reasons, including load balancing requests to available servers or decreasing the time it takes to perform call routing and failure retries by sending the request to all the potential next-hop destinations at the same time. The ITSP may then use local logic to determine which of the SIP dialogs to continue the session with, and it may cancel all other outstanding SIP dialogs.

The devices receiving the forked INVITE may generate provisional responses, which are sent to the forking proxy and the UAC. This means the UAC may receive multiple provisional responses from the forking proxy for each forked session. Each provisional response from the forking proxy to the UAC would contain a unique tag on the To header. This unique tag allows the UAC to distinguish the different SIP dialogs. The handling of multiple provisional responses is covered earlier in this chapter, in the section "Ringback and Provisional Response Interworking." Figure 4-13 details a scenario in which multiple 18x responses are received for a single call through a forking proxy

Any of the devices presented the call by the forking server may send a final response indicating a failure (4xx, 5xx, 6xx) or an attempt to answer (200 OK). The signaling proxy may take the first final response to connect the session and send it to the UAC, or the signaling proxy may use local logic and wait for multiple responses before sending its choice of final response to the UAC. The response sent to the UAC will contain a tag on the To header, indicating the dialog in which the session is being established. If the signaling proxy is stateful, it may send a CANCEL request to the other forked sessions as a session is being established with another UAS. Figure 4-13 also displays the session establishment between the UAC and UAS 1 through the stateful forking proxy, which then removes the other UAS sessions by sending a CANCEL request.

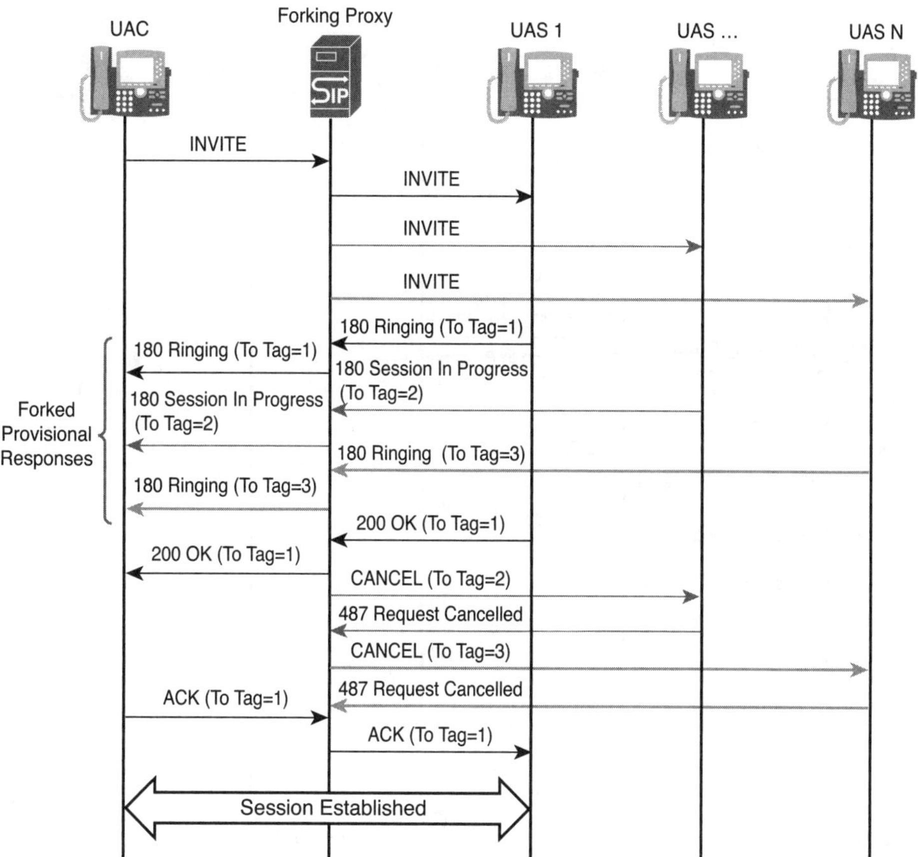

Figure 4-13 *Ladder Diagram Depicting Forking for Multiple UAs*

RFC 6228 defines the use of a 199 response when signaling forking is being used. It allows a forking proxy to update the UAC when a dialog has been terminated. This is often in the response format 199 Early Dialog Terminated. A UAC advertises its ability to process 199 responses by sending the extension **199** in the Supported header.

Figure 4-14 details a scenario like one in Figure 4-13 in which a UAC has extended an INVITE to a forking proxy, which sends an INVITE to different UASs. Each UAS responds with a provisional response, and the forking proxy sends the responses to the UAC with a different tag on the To header to indicate which dialogs they belong to. UAS 1 responds with a 503 Service Unavailable message, and the forking proxy sends a 199 Early Dialog Terminated with the tag of the dialog that is being terminated. The UAC may then clear the dialog and free up any allocated resources for that dialog.

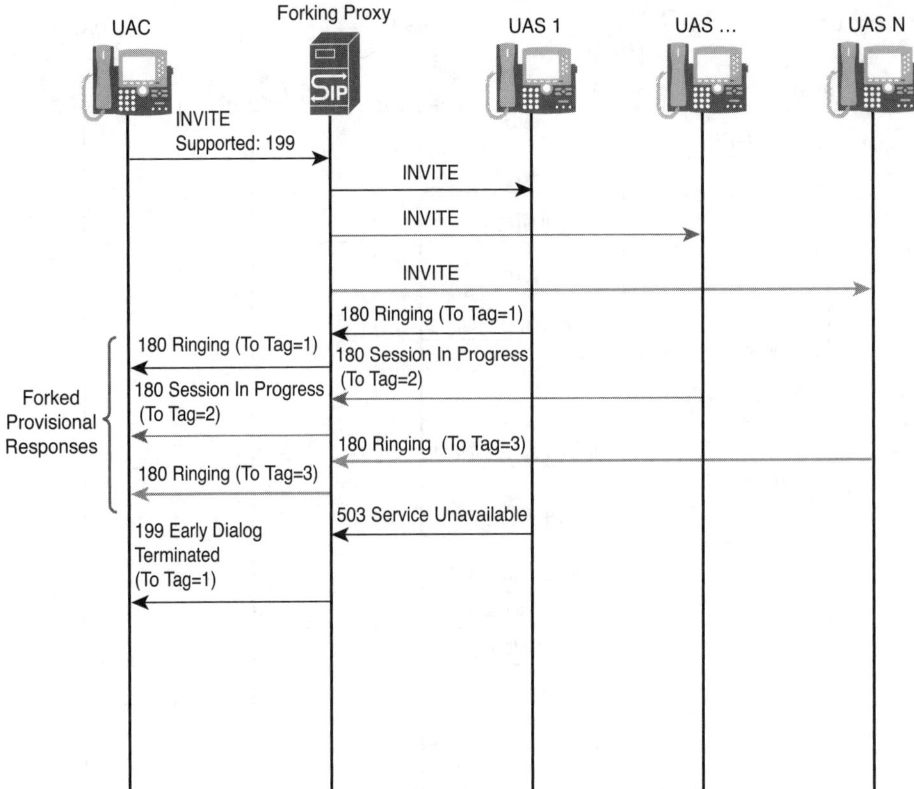

Figure 4-14 *199 Response Sent upon Failure on a Forked SIP Dialog*

An SBC may act as a forking proxy in some scenarios, or it may directly interface with a forking proxy, such as a call agent or an ITSP device. One scenario where an SBC may act as a forking proxy is if it is performing call recording functions. The SBC may fork a session between the desired user agent and a recording server. (This is further discussed in depth in the Chapter 11, "Network-Based Call Recording.") If the SBC is interfacing with an upstream forking proxy, it may be required to interwork multiple provisional responses and keep track of multiple SIP dialogs. The SBC may choose one of two actions when performing this interworking:

- Forward all events to the peer call leg.
- Process the events on behalf of the peer call leg and forward only the need-to-know information to the peer call leg.

The first method is similar to what happens in Figure 4-13. The main difference is that there is now an SBC between the UAC and the forking proxy. The second method is shown in Figure 4-15. In this scenario, an SBC is tasked with interworking forked signaling between a UAC and a forking proxy in the ITSP network. The SBC chooses to process the forked signaling on behalf of the UAC and sends only the need-to-know information through to the peer call leg. The information on the peer call leg uses a unique tag on the To header that is different from those of the forked responses. This means it does not matter which forked provisional responses are received or which dialog receives a final 200 OK response. The SBC converts or consumes provisional responses, and it converts the 200 OK received for any dialog into a new 200 OK response with the appropriate tag on the To header for the peer call leg. The UAC interfacing with the SBC would be none the wiser that forking has taken place upstream beyond the SBC.

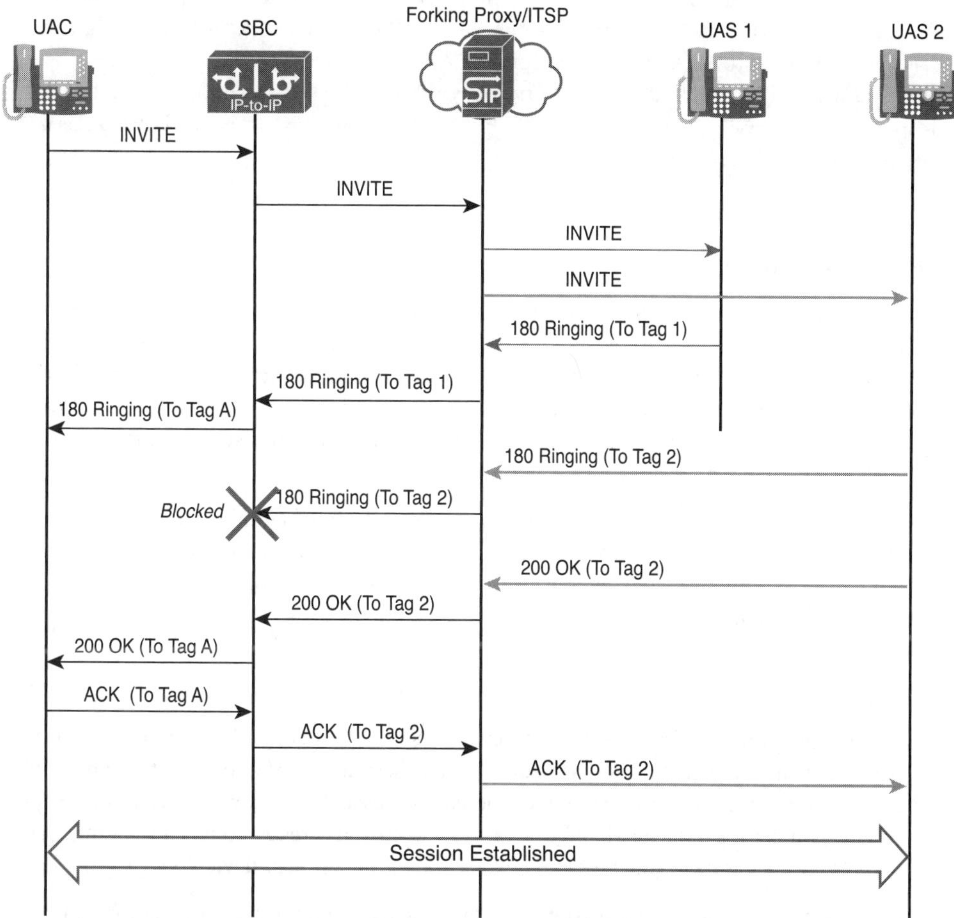

Figure 4-15 *An SBC Interworking Forked Provisional Responses*

Although CUBE does not support the constructs of RFC 6228 in regard to the 199 forking tag, it does support the handling of multiple provisional responses due to upstream forking conditions. CUBE takes an approach similar to what is described earlier for forking SBC operations. When CUBE receives multiple forked provisional responses, they are transparently passed through to the peer call leg by default. Using techniques described earlier in this chapter, in the "Ringback and Provisional Response

Interworking" section, an administrator may block redundant provisional responses from being passed from one call leg to another. If a 200 OK for a request is received that contains a To header tag that is different from the original To header tag on the provisional response, CUBE may send an UPDATE on the peer call leg before sending the 200 OK to the peer endpoint. This UPDATE allows CUBE to notify the peer endpoint that signaling forking has occurred.

> **Tip** In older versions of IOS and IOS XE, this behavior requires that UPDATE capabilities be available on that call leg. In later versions, such as IOS XE 16.6 and later, this behavior has been reworked to exclude the need for UPDATE before transmitting the 200 OK for the forked signaling. If a 500 Internal Server Error is observed due to a forked provisional response and 200 OK combination on CUBE, be sure to verify whether the UPDATE is negotiated on the peer call leg.

Mid-call Signaling

When a session is established, additional signaling exchanges may be required to maintain or modify a session. These post-session establishment messages are referred to as *mid-call signaling*. Mid-call signaling includes actions like caller ID updates, modification of session media parameters, and determinations of session freshness. In addition to the previous signaling exchanges, mid-call signaling also includes supplementary services, such as call hold, call resume, and call transfer.

An SBC is responsible for ensuring that these mid-call signaling messages are appropriately handled on both SIP dialogs. The following sections detail some of the most common mid-call signaling exchanges as well as how an SBC interworks the different types of mid-call signaling that can occur with these signaling exchanges.

Hold/Resume

"Let me put you on hold while I check on this item." You frequently hear this sentence from customer care centers. What occurs in such scenarios is that one party momentarily disrupts the bidirectional flow of media by pressing a softkey (typically the Hold softkey) on her local device. Bidirectional flow of media is resumed when the same party presses another softkey (or the same Hold softkey) on her local device.

Because any participant in a session can place the call on hold, the terms *holder* and *holdee* are often used to define participants of a hold scenario. The holder is the participant who initiates the call hold event, and the holdee is the person being placed on hold. Placing a call on hold in most modern IP-based telephony systems typically consists of the following sequence of events:

Step 1. One party places the call on hold by pressing a softkey (such as the Hold softkey) or keying in a specific system-defined sequence of keys.

Step 2. The indication of call hold is communicated by the call control protocol over the signaling channel.

Step 3. Bidirectional flow of media is disrupted between the participants.

Step 4. Usually, when the call is placed on hold, a new media session is established between a streaming server and the holdee. This streaming server is commonly referred to as a music-on-hold server, and it streams hold music or prerecorded announcements. Because a new media session is initiated between the holdee and the music-on-hold server, the holdee doesn't have to listen to dead air until the call is resumed.

Step 5. When the holder is ready to resume a bidirectional media session, he presses the call hold softkey or keys in a specific system-defined sequence of keys.

Step 6. The indication to remove the call from hold and resume the communication session is communicated by the call control protocol over the signaling channel. This results in terminating the media stream between the music-on-hold server and the holdee and creating a new media session (or reusing the previous one) between the holder and holdee.

This process is diagrammatically depicted in Figure 4-20, later in this chapter. Before we get to that, we need to discuss each part of this process in detail.

With SIP, the endpoints involved in the call are either the holder or holdee. An SBC has the privilege of being both a holder and holdee, although it is very rare for an SBC to initiate a hold event without first receiving a hold event from another device. The main goal for the SBC is to interwork hold and resume events so that media is terminated, redirected, and reestablished properly for all parties and call legs. Failure to do this properly may result in problematic one-way audio situations, no-way audio situations, or even undesired call terminations.

There is no explicit SIP header field that indicates call hold and call resume. Rather, SIP has to be used in concert with SDP to indicate call hold and resume. While there isn't unanimous consensus on the exact semantics of SIP and SDP for call hold and call resume, most vendors follow the guidelines of RFC 3264 and 6337. The predominant method of indicating call hold and call resume is to use SIP re-INVITEs and to format the SDP media direction attribute (a=) and connection data information (c=) fields.

A holder can indicate its desire to place the call hold by appropriately modifying the media direction attribute (a=) or/and connection data information field (c=) of the SDP body enclosed within the SIP re-INVITE. There are distinct ways in which a call can be placed on hold:

- A call can be placed on hold without any music.
- A call can be placed on hold such that the holdee hears music on hold.

The first scenario involves the holdee hearing silence, which is commonly referred to as "dead air," when the call is placed on hold. This is achieved when the holder sends a SIP re-INVITE such that the direction media attribute of the SDP is set to a=inactive. As per the guidelines of RFC 3264, when the direction media attribute in the SDP offer is set to a=inactive, the SDP answer must mirror the same value of the direction attribute (that is, it has to be set as a=inactive). Setting the media direction attribute to a=inactive in the offer and answer ensures that there is no media sent or received. A second method by which the holder can achieve the same outcome is by setting the connection data information field to all zeros (c=0.0.0.0). This not only results in suspension of any media exchange between the calling party and the called party, it also results in termination of any RTCP traffic. Therefore, this alternative is not always the best. Figures 4-16 and 4-17 diagram these alternatives for hold with no music. There are certain scenarios in which these methods are used together—that is, the SDP of the re-INVITE has the media direction attribute set to a=inactive and the connection data information field set to 0.0.0.0.

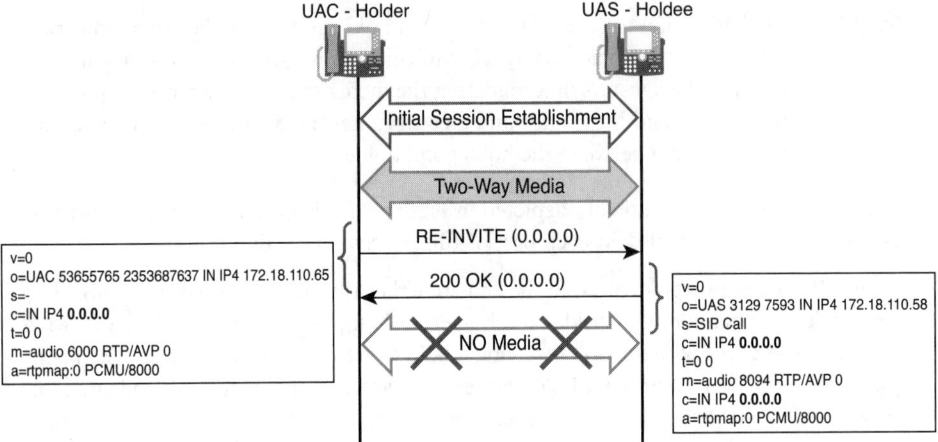

Figure 4-16 *Hold with No Media—0.0.0.0*

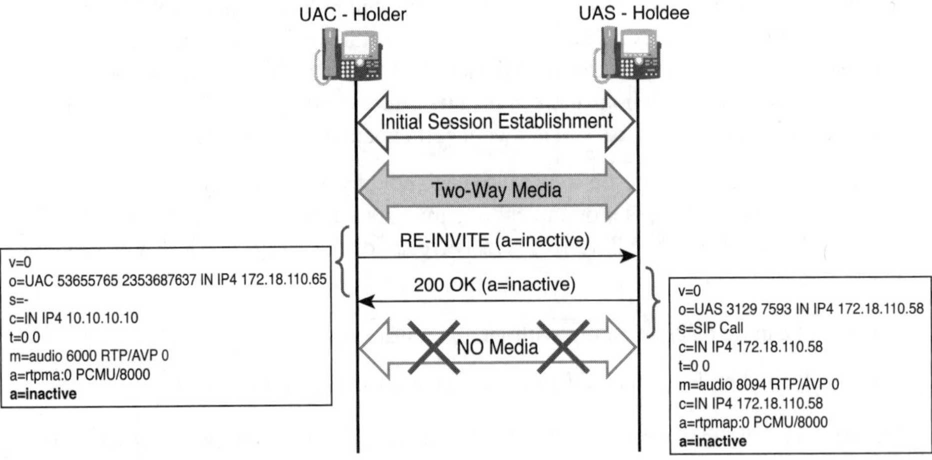

Figure 4-17 *Hold with No Media—a=inactive*

The second scenario (refer to Figure 4-17), which is preferred by enterprises, involves the holdee listening to hold music or prerecorded messages for the duration of the hold sequence. This scenario is achieved when the holder sends a SIP re-INVITE such that the media direction attribute in the SDP offer is set to a=sendonly. Assuming that the holdee sets the media direction attribute to a=recvonly in the SDP answer, a unidirectional media channel that terminates on the holdee is established. In real-world scenarios, the hold music or announcements are usually streamed from a standalone device to the holdee endpoint. Therefore, to effectively stream hold music or announcements, it is required for the holder to first break the media stream between itself and the holdee and establish another media stream between the music-on-hold server and the holdee. To break the media stream, the holder might engage in an initial offer/answer exchange that sets the connection data information field to all zeros (c=0.0.0.0). After this, a subsequent offer/answer exchange is initiated to establish another media stream between the music-on-hold server and the holdee. This exchange often establishes unidirectional one-way media from the MOH server to the holdee through media direction attributes of a=sendonly and a=recvonly. Figure 4-18 diagrams this process.

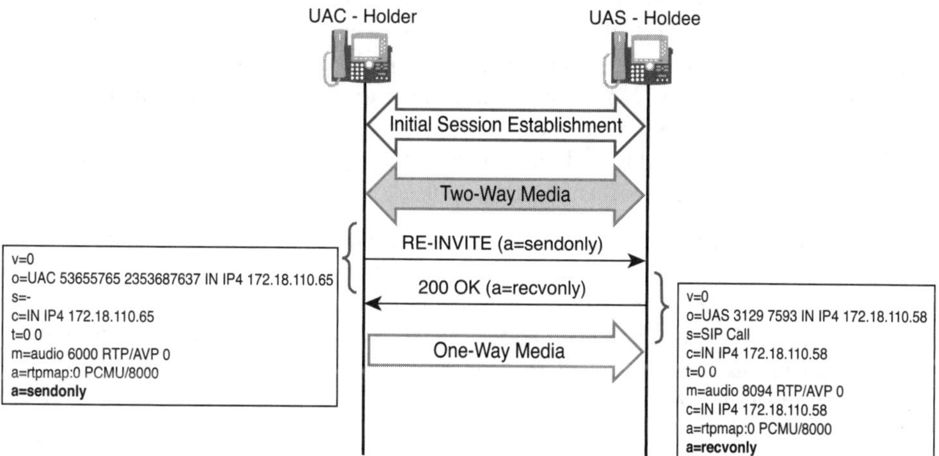

Figure 4-18 *Hold with Unidirectional Media—a=sendonly*

To resume a held call, the holder must initiate another offer/answer exchange to reestablish the media stream between itself and the holdee. If music-on-hold is being streamed, the holder may first send a re-INVITE in an attempt to remove the media session with the music-on-hold server and the holdee. This re-INVITE may set the connection data information field to all zeros (c=0.0.0.0) and send a media direction attribute of a=inactive. Once the music-on-hold stream has been removed, another re-INVITE is sourced from the holder; it contains the media information of the holder and sets the media direction to a=sendrecv. The holdee returns his own media information, and if he also responds with a media direction attribute of a=sendrecv, bidirectional media is reestablished.

There is currently no standard that defines the procedures to be followed by SBCs or B2BUAs to reliably handle call hold and resume. Nonetheless, vendors of such devices must embed sufficient logic in software to ensure that such events are handled reliably, without negatively impacting the call experience. Broadly, SBCs handle call hold/resume events in one of two ways:

- Passing across SIP re-INVITE sequences end to end with minimal modification
- Abstracting hold/resume events from the holdee

In the first method, SIP re-INVITES and responses that: break the media stream between the holder and holdee, establish a media stream between the music-on-hold server and the holdee, and reestablish the media stream between holder and holdee on call resume are passed across from the holder network to the holdee network with minimal modification. These modifications typically include overwriting the IP addresses advertised in the SIP header fields and the SDP bodies of SIP re-INVITEs and responses. Figure 4-20 demonstrates this.

In the second method, the SBC completely abstracts hold/resume exchanges by the holder by handling such exchanges locally. This method may lead to interoperability issues and unexpected behavior when a peer device expects to be notified of such events. On the other hand, a peer device may not be properly equipped to handle specific types of hold/resume events, and as a result, cause audio problems during or after the hold/resume. Thus, this method can be employed to solve this type of interoperability issues by not advertising hold/resume events to the peer device. The benefits and drawbacks behind the application of this method by an SBC are highly dependent on the peer devices capability sets and local network variables.

Using CUBE and Cisco Unified Communication Manager (CUCM) as an example, this chapter details a sample hold/resume event signaled by a CUCM registered endpoint. CUCM uses a mixture of the hold methods defined in the previous section when advertising a hold event. Figure 4-19 covers the topology for the following hold/resume event. It should also be noted that CUCM will also take on the role of the MOH server for this example session.

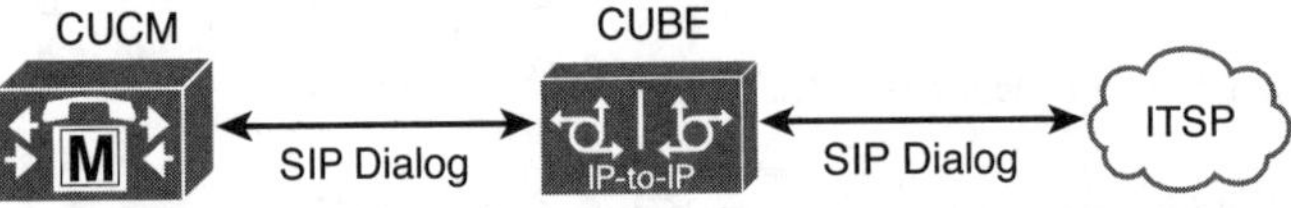

Figure 4-19 *CUCM, SBC, and ITSP Topology*

After a call is established, a user can press the hold button or softkey on her device to initiate a hold event. CUCM then modifies the established media stream by sending a SIP re-INVITE with the media direction attribute set to a=inactive and the connection data information field set to c=0.0.0.0. Example 4-11 shows the SIP signaling for this event between CUBE and CUCM. CUBE forwards the re-INVITE for modifying the media stream to the peer call leg and waits for a response on that call leg before sending an answer to CUCM. After a response is received on the peer call leg, CUBE answers the re-INIVTE with a 200 OK message that contains the media direction attribute a=inactive as an answer to the re-INVITE offer, but CUBE chooses to sends its local IP address rather than respond with c=0.0.0.0 in both the global and local connection data information SDP lines.

Example 4-11 *Signaling with Audio Set to Inactive and 0.0.0.0 Advertised*

```
Received:
INVITE sip:7777@172.18.110.58:5060;transport=tcp SIP/2.0
CSeq: 102 INVITE

v=0
o=CiscoSystemsCCM-SIP 25337 2 IN IP4 172.18.110.48
s=SIP Call
c=IN IP4 0.0.0.0
b=TIAS:64000
b=AS:64
t=0 0
m=audio 22018 RTP/AVP 0 101
a=rtpmap:0 PCMU/8000
a=inactive
a=rtpmap:101 telephone-event/8000
a=fmtp:101 0-15

[...The same information occurs on the other call leg...]

Sent:
SIP/2.0 200 OK
CSeq: 102 INVITE

v=0
o=CiscoSystemsSIP-GW-UserAgent 5020 5458 IN IP4 172.18.110.58
s=SIP Call
c=IN IP4 172.18.110.58
t=0 0
m=audio 8066 RTP/AVP 0 101
c=IN IP4 172.18.110.58
a=inactive
a=rtpmap:0 PCMU/8000
a=rtpmap:101 telephone-event/8000
a=fmtp:101 0-16
```

After the media stream is successfully disabled through the SDP offer/answer exchange end to end, CUCM sends a delayed offer re-INVITE soliciting the SBC and, ultimately, the holdee for its media capabilities (which are subsequently encoded in the 200 OK response). After receiving the peer SDP, CUCM sends an ACK with SDP with the media direction attribute set to a=sendonly and the connection data information encoding the

IP address of a music-on-hold server. Example 4-12 shows the delayed offer exchange between CUCM and CUBE for music-on-hold insertion. (Music-on-hold is detailed in the "Music on Hold" section, later in this chapter.) Again, this SIP transaction takes place end to end. When this SIP transaction concludes, the call is on hold, and the holdee hears music-on-hold audio. This continues until the user desires to take the call off hold. In addition, because the music-on-hold media resource does not need to receive media but only send media, CUCM allocates a dummy port of 4000 for sourcing media from the music-on-hold resource.

Example 4-12 *Negotiating Unicast Music-on-Hold*

```
Sent:
SIP/2.0 200 OK
CSeq: 103 INVITE

v=0
o=CiscoSystemsSIP-GW-UserAgent 5020 5459 IN IP4 172.18.110.58
s=SIP Call
c=IN IP4 172.18.110.58
t=0 0
m=audio 8066 RTP/AVP 0 101 19
c=IN IP4 172.18.110.58
a=rtpmap:0 PCMU/8000
a=rtpmap:101 telephone-event/8000
a=fmtp:101 0-16
a=ptime:20

Received:
ACK sip:7777@172.18.110.58:5060;transport=tcp SIP/2.0
CSeq: 103 ACK

v=0
o=CiscoSystemsCCM-SIP 25337 3 IN IP4 172.18.110.48
s=SIP Call
c=IN IP4 172.18.110.48
t=0 0
m=audio 4000 RTP/AVP 0
a=X-cisco-media:umoh
a=ptime:20
a=rtpmap:0 PCMU/8000
a=sendonly
```

When the end user is ready to take the call off hold, he presses the button or softkey again to resume the call; CUCM sends another re-INVITE with the media direction attribute set to a=inactive and the connection data information field set to 0.0.0.0. This results in the de-allocation of the media resource for music-on-hold. Finally, CUCM sends a delayed offer re-INIVTE, soliciting the SBC and ultimately the holdee for their capabilities (which are subsequently encoded in the 200 OK response). Finally, the CUCM reconnects audio to the endpoint and sends an ACK with SDP, which reopens bidirectional media. Figure 4-20 illustrates the entire hold/resume process and multiple transactions in the SIP dialog that takes place between CUCM and CUBE.

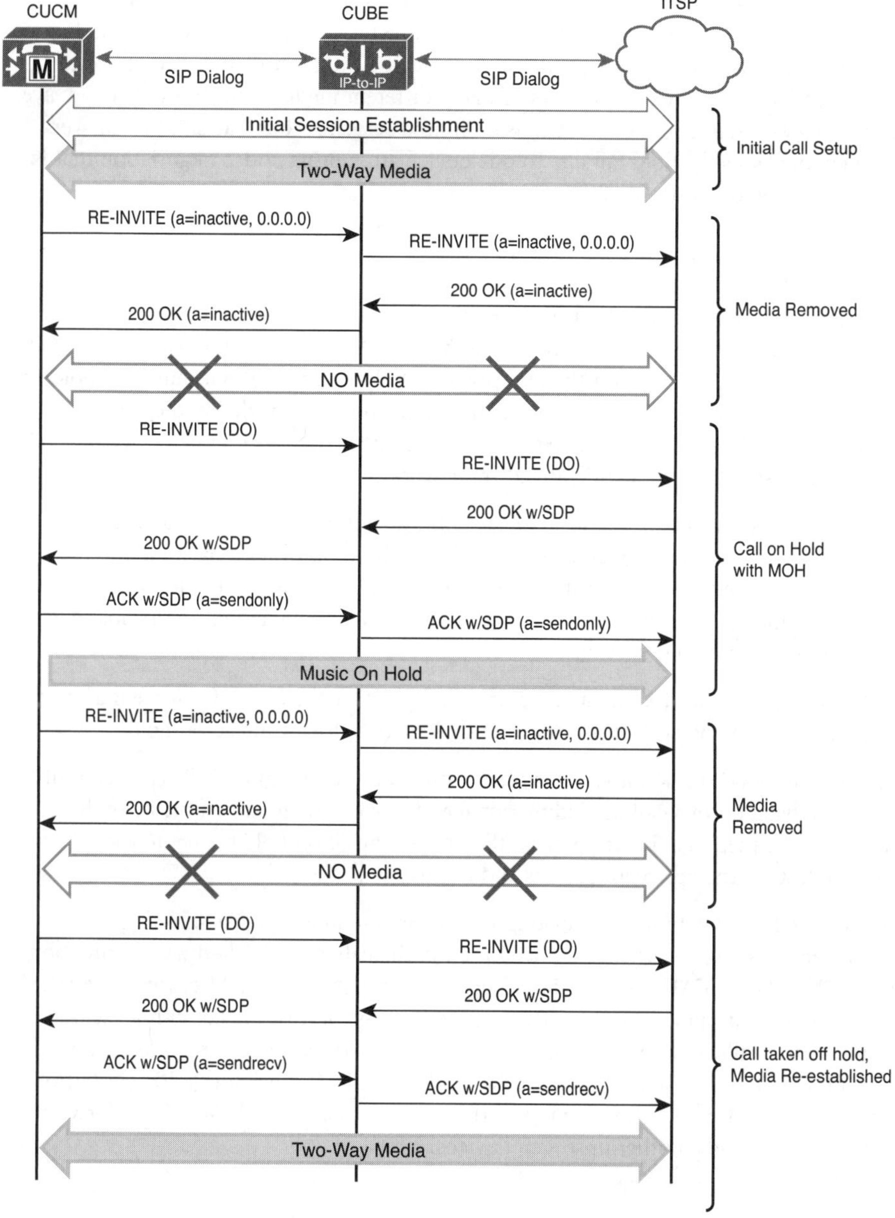

Figure 4-20 *Full Hold Resume and Music-on-Hold Signaling on CUCM, CUBE, and ITSP*

When troubleshooting hold/resume issues, it is best to use **debug ccsip messages, debug ccsip error**, and **debug voip ccapi inout** on an SBC. Because there will be upward of 20 SIP messages per dialog, it is recommended to use an application like TranslatorX to assist in visualizing the different events of the mid-call signaling. You can break up the different events into their own respective SIP transactions for further diagnosis (for example, initial call establishment, media inactive, music-on-hold establishment, music-on-hold de-allocation, media recommencement). By using this method, troubleshooting can be focused on specific parts of the hold/resume process and can facilitate finding if something may have gone awry during that specific transaction. It is also important to remember that the process consists of many different media changes and may involve negotiating different codecs for the music-on-hold server. Ask and attempt to answer the question: Does the hold fail due to one device attempting codec negotiation that is unsupported by other devices?

Music-on-Hold

The previous section briefly discusses the concept of music-on-hold and how it applies within the concept of hold events. Music-on-hold itself is an audio file played to a holdee from a music-on-hold server for the duration of a hold event. Without music-on-hold, the holdee would experience silence, or dead air, for the duration of the hold event. Many consider complete silence undesirable from the perspective of user experience, and therefore music-on-hold is a widely deployed framework.

The audio file for music-on-hold can be anything an administrator or organization desires, from simple beeps or a music file to live radio or informational announcements, such as prerecorded sales information, stock prices, or even the current weather forecast. This information is delivered over the unicast audio stream opened up in the hold event discussed in the previous section.

There are two methods for streaming music-on-hold over a network from the music-on-hold server to the holdee: unicast music-on-hold and multicast music-on-hold.

Unicast music-on-hold is not very different from audio for a regular call. The main difference is that a normal call has bidirectional audio, while with unicast music-on-hold, audio/RTP flows in one direction, from the unicast music-on-hold source to the SBC and from the SBC to the upstream devices and ultimately to the holdee.

Examples 4-11 and 4-12 in the previous section feature unicast music-on-hold establishment between CUBE and CUCM. First, the call is established with bidirectional audio. Then the CUCM sets the established audio stream inactive. After this the CUCM renegotiates media and inserts the IP and codecs of the unicast music-on-hold server. Figure 4-20 details how an SBC negotiates the same information on the other call leg or consumes the mid-call signaling. After the hold and unicast music-on-hold negotiation is complete, the RTP packets received from the unicast music-on-hold server are forwarded to the next hop and all other upstream devices.

Multicast music-on-hold is slightly more complicated in its implementation than its unicast counterpart. The SIP signaling for the call establishment, hold, and multicast music-on-hold negotiation follows the same sequence as a unicast music-on-hold session, but the semantics of how SDP is encoded in the offer/answer and the way music-on-hold is served up by the network differ.

Note If CUCM is involved, the Cisco-proprietary SDP media attribute a=X-cisco-media:mmoh will be observed rather than a=X-cisco-media:umoh.

Tip A device advertising a multicast address in SDP will always send a=sendonly in the SDP, as per RFC 3264. The answer to this offer should always mirror the offer for example, the answer may contain media direction attributes the same as those of the offer (a=sendonly).

The complexity of multicast music-on-hold mainly derives from the underlying requirements of multicast. The first is that the SBC and LAN/WAN must be properly configured for IP multicast capabilities in order to route multicast traffic properly. In addition, the SBC must join the multicast group specified in the SDP of the hold event and receive multicast RTP packets. The music-on-hold server must also join this multicast group and will send multicast RTP, which is then replicated to all participants of the multicast session.

The second item is the inability of devices over the service provider network to join multicast groups scoped within an enterprise. Thus, an SBC must be able to convert the received multicast RTP into unicast RTP for transmission to the service provider network. CUBE only requires a few configuration lines to enable multicast-to-unicast conversion. These commands are detailed in Example 4-13. Figure 4-21 illustrates a CUBE receiving multicast RTP packets from a multicast music-on-hold audio source and then converting them into unicast RTP packets to be sent for transport over the ITSP network.

Example 4-13 *Multicast Music-on-Hold–to–Unicast Music-on-Hold Conversion Commands*

```
!
ip multicast-routing distributed
!
ccm-manager music-on-hold
!
interface GigabitEthernet0/0/0.249
 ip pim sparse-dense-mode
!
```

> **Tip** Underlying LAN and network infrastructure configuration to facilitate Multicast PIM on Layer 3 devices and IGMP multicast for Layer 2 devices are not covered in this book. In addition, the type of PIM configured on the CUBE interface is dependent on the type of LAN multicast implementation.

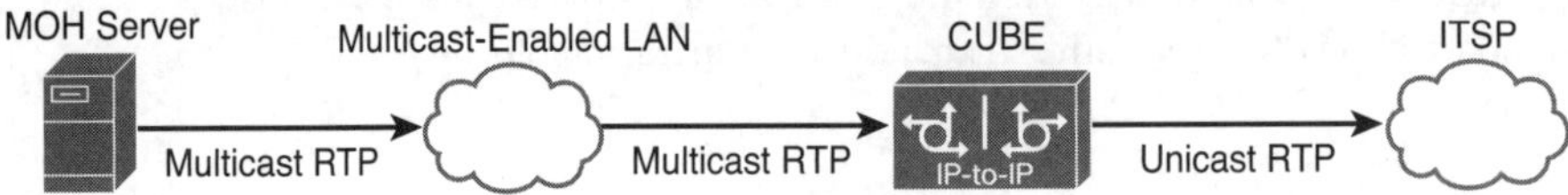

Figure 4-21 *Multicast Music-on-Hold–to–Unicast Music-on-Hold Conversion on CUBE*

Troubleshooting unicast music-on-hold or multicast music-on-hold issues always starts with verifying the signaling involved in setting up the unicast music-on-hold or multicast music-on-hold session by running **debug ccsip messages** and **debug ccm-manager music-on-hold all**. This can be coupled with **show** commands like **show call active voice compact** and **show voip rtp connections**, which display RTP connections between the CUBE and the music-on-hold server or multicast IP specified in the SIP signaling. Both IOS and IOS XE use the command **show ccm-manager music-on-hold**, which displays music-on-hold packets replicated from the ingress call leg to the egress call leg. IOS XE can use the command **show platform hardware qfp active feature sbc mmoh global**, which shows multicast music-on-hold packets received and passed to the ccm-manager application. Finally, using a Packet Capture (PCAP) is a great way to determine if packets are being received from a music-on-hold server or multicast IP on the ingress CUBE interface.

> **Tip** With IOS XE, an IP PIM command must be defined on both the ingress and egress Layer 3 interface, or the multicast music-on-hold–to–unicast music-on-hold conversion will not occur. Without an IP PIM command on the egress interface, the output of **show ccm-manager music-on-hold** will display 0 packets received, and the output of **show platform hardware qfp active statistics drop** will show the multicast music-on-hold RTP packets dropped with the reason "**UnconfiguredIpv4Fia**".

Call Transfer

Applications like interactive voice response (IVR), contact center scripts, and even end telephone users need the ability to transfer a call to a different destination without the other party hanging up or being disconnected. An SBC must not inhibit the transfer process and may even be required to perform interworking so that the call transfer can be seamlessly completed.

A call transfer differs from a call forward in that it takes place *after* a session is established, and the bulk of the signaling to facilitate a transfer takes place in the mid-call signaling. There are a few different ways to complete a transfer. The following sections define these transfer types. For more information on call forwarding, see the "Call Forwarding" section, later in this chapter.

Note The terms *transferor*, *transferee*, and *transfer target* are used to define the parties involved in a call transfer. The *transferor* is the person or device initiating a transfer, and the *transferee* is the person being transferred to a new destination. Finally, the *transfer target* is the new destination to which the transferee will be connected when the transfer is completed by the transferor. These terms are illustrated in Figure 4-22.

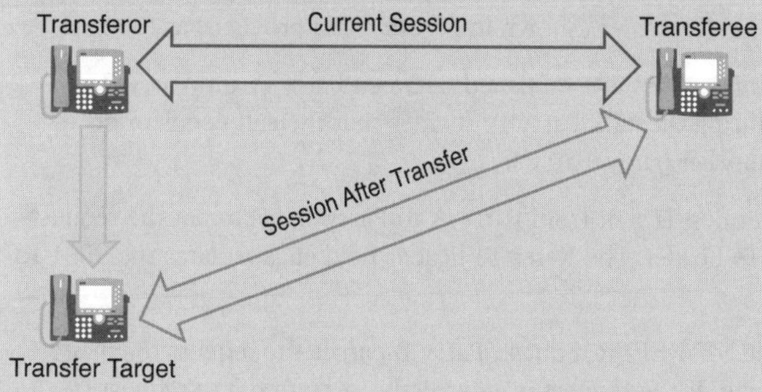

Figure 4-22 *Transferor, Transferee, and Transfer Target Illustrated*

REFER

The SIP REFER method was defined and standardized in RFC 3515 to provide a framework for call transfers in SIP networks. Over the years, several modifications have been made to the implementation of the SIP REFER method to fit a variety of application usages. This section provides an overview of the basic implementation of the SIP REFER method outlined in RFC 3515.

A user agent (*transferor*) attempting to transfer a call (to the *transfer target*) does so by sending a SIP REFER request to the *transferee*. Included in the SIP REFER request is information on how the transferee can reach the transfer target; this information is encapsulated in the Refer-To header field (see Example 4-14). For a REFER request to be sent, there needs to be an established, active communication session between the transferor and transferee. The REFER request is sent on the same SIP dialog as the established communication session to ensure that the request is delivered to the intended recipient, can be correctly co-related by the transferee to the existing communication session, and is from an authorized source.

Example 4-14 *Sample REFER and the Refer-To Header*

```
REFER sip:b@atlanta.example.com SIP/2.0
Via: SIP/2.0/UDP agenta.atlanta.example.com;branch=z9hG4bK2293940223
To: <sip:b@atlanta.example.com>
From: <sip:a@atlanta.example.com>;tag=193402342
Call-ID: 898234234@agenta.atlanta.example.com
CSeq: 93809823 REFER
Max-Forwards: 70
Refer-To: sip:alice@atlanta.example.com
Contact: sip:a@atlanta.example.com
Content-Length: 0
```

The SIP REFER method for call transfer (Shown in Figure 4-23) proceeds as follows:

Step 1. A communication session is established between Party A and Party B. At some time during the call, Party A decides that the call needs to be transferred to another party, Party C.

Step 2. A SIP REFER request is sent from Party A to Party B, such that the request carries a Refer-To header. The Refer-To header field encapsulates the SIP URI of Party C.

Step 3. On receiving the SIP REFER request, Party B parses the request to ensure correct formatting. If the request is incorrectly formatted, the request is rejected, with an appropriate error code. For example, if the REFER request carries zero or more than one Refer-To header field, it is rejected with a 400 Bad Request response.

Step 4. Assuming that the request is correctly formatted, Party B sends a 202 Accepted response to Party A. This response also results in the establishment of an implicit SIP subscription between Party A and Party B, and the aim of the subscription is for Party B to notify Party A of the status of processing the REFER request.

Step 5. Immediately after sending a 202 Accepted response, Party B sends a SIP NOTIFY request to Party A. In parallel, it attempts to create a communication session with Party C, using the URI specified in the Refer-To header field of the REFER request.

Step 6. The results of the attempt to establish a communication session with Party C are encapsulated in subsequent NOTIFY messages sent from Party B to Party A. If Party B succeeds in establishing a communication session with Party C, it sends a SIP NOTIFY with the SIP response status line SIP/2.0 200 OK. If the attempt is unsuccessful, it sends a SIP NOTIFY with a SIP response status line of either SIP/2.0 503 Service Unavailable or SIP/2.0 603 Declined.

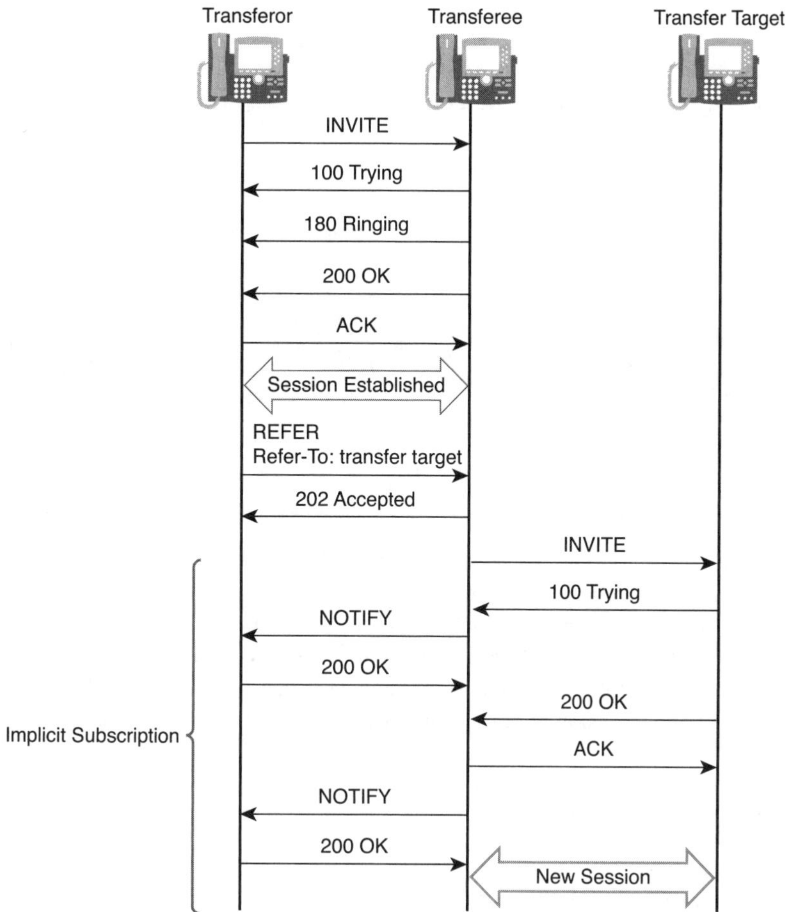

Figure 4-23 *High-Level REFER Overview*

A detailed account of the SIP SUBSCRIBE/NOTIFY framework is provided in Chapter 7, "DTMF Interworking." Note that the implicit subscription created by the REFER request can either be explicitly or implicitly terminated by the transferor (Party A) at any time. Termination of the subscription should not negatively impact the outcome of REFER processing by the transferee (Party B). SIP NOTIFY messages sent by the transferee to the transferor indicate the outcome of request processing at the transferee. Every NOTIFY message must contain a message body of type message/sipfrag and include an Event header field with the tag value refer. Example 4-15 displays a SIP NOTIFY with a message body containing SIP/2.0 100 Trying to let the transferor know the request is being processed.

Example 4-15 *Sample SIP NOTIFY with a 100 Trying sipfrag Body*

```
NOTIFY sip:a@atlanta.example.com SIP/2.0
Via: SIP/2.0/UDP agentb.atlanta.example.com;branch=z9hG4bK9922ef992-25
To: <sip:a@atlanta.example.com>;tag=193402342
From: <sip:b@atlanta.example.com>;tag=4992881234
Call-ID: 898234234@agenta.atlanta.example.com
CSeq: 1993402 NOTIFY
Max-Forwards: 70
Event: refer
Subscription-State: active;expires=(depends on Refer-To URI)
Contact: sip:b@atlanta.example.com
Content-Type: message/sipfrag;version=2.0
Content-Length: 20

SIP/2.0 100 Trying
```

When the transfer is answered, the device handling the REFER sends one last NOTIFY specifying the 200 OK. This final NOTIFY contains the SIP header Subscription-State: terminated;reason=noresource to indicate that this is the final NOTIFY, and the REFER process is complete. Example 4-16 displays a SIP NOTIFY with a message body containing SIP/2.0 200 OK, indicating to the transferor that the REFER has been processed completely, and a session with the transfer target has been established.

Example 4-16 *Sample NOTIFY with a 200 OK sipfrag Body*

```
NOTIFY sip:a@atlanta.example.com SIP/2.0
Via: SIP/2.0/UDP agentb.atlanta.example.com;branch=z9hG4bK9323394234
To: <sip:a@atlanta.example.com>;tag=193402342
From: <sip:b@atlanta.example.com>;tag=4992881234
Call-ID: 898234234@agenta.atlanta.example.com
CSeq: 1993403 NOTIFY
Max-Forwards: 70
Event: refer
Subscription-State: terminated;reason=noresource
Contact: sip:b@atlanta.example.com
Content-Type: message/sipfrag;version=2.0
Content-Length: 16

SIP/2.0 200 OK
```

Often the transferor, transferee, and transfer target are on different networks. In such scenarios, there may be many different devices, such as a call agent and an SBC, involved in the session. In such a scenario, the REFER is sent from the transferor to other signaling devices involved in the session. These devices can take one of two actions with a received REFER request:

- The device can act on behalf of the transferee and attempt to establish a session with the transfer target defined in the Refer-To header of the REFER request.
- The device may pass the REFER request from one call leg to the peer call leg without acting on the REFER request.

The first method of REFER handling, detailed previously, is often referred to as *REFER consumption*. In this scenario, an SBC consumes the REFER request, as shown in Figure 4-24, and takes action on the provided URI in the Refer-To header. If the Refer-To header contains a SIP URI, the SBC extends an INVITE between itself and the user agent identified in the Refer-To header in an attempt to establish a session. This is the most common implementation of SIP REFER handling on an SBC.

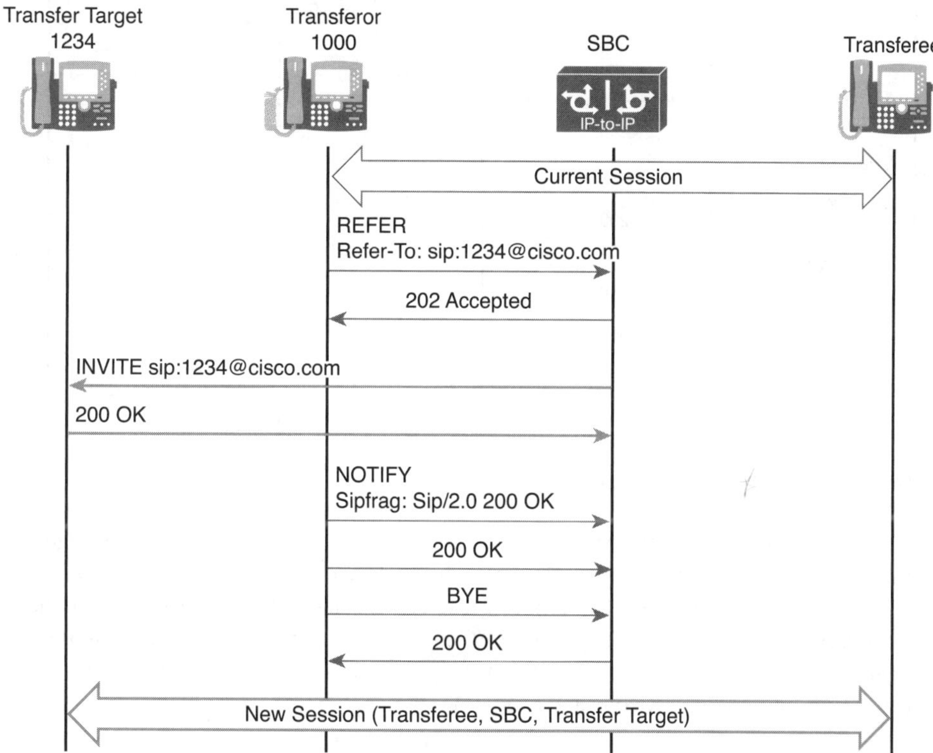

Figure 4-24 *REFER Consumption on an SBC*

The second method is for an SBC to perform a passthrough of the REFER so that a downstream device can take further action on the REFER request. This method can be used to potentially remove the SBC from further signaling after the transfer is complete. This is often used when transferring an off-net PSTN party to another off-net PSTN party. Both the transfer target and the transferee are not on the network the SBC is responsible for, so the SBC may be dropped from the signaling. This is shown in Figure 4-25.

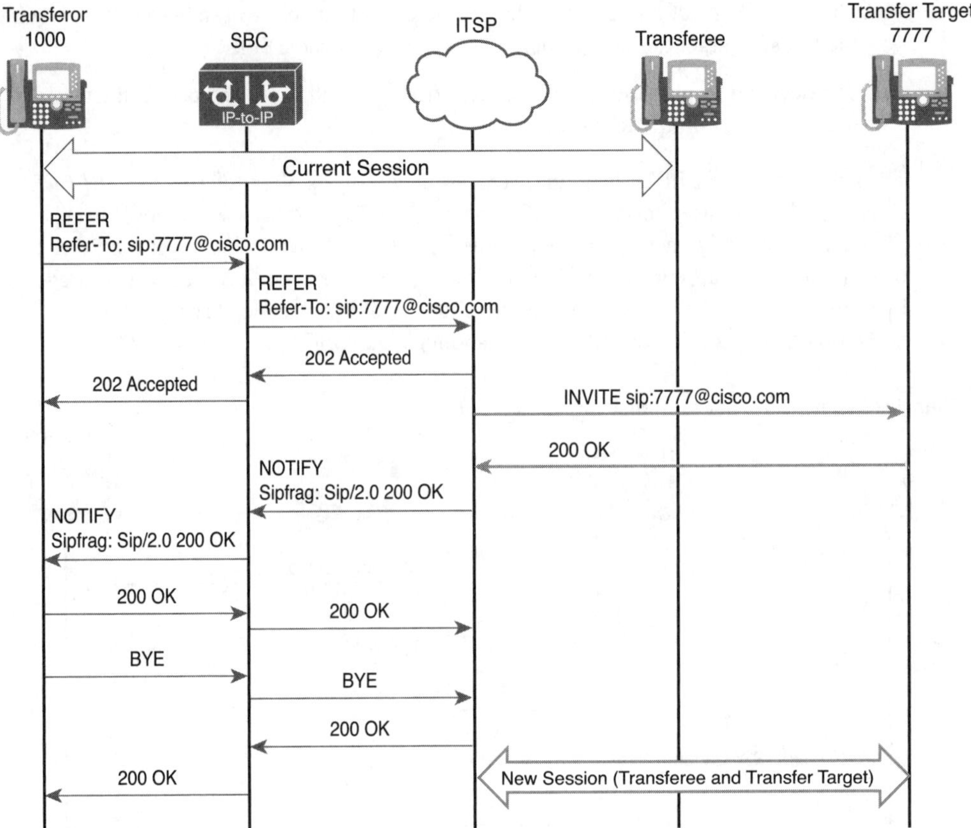

Figure 4-25 *REFER Passthrough on an SBC*

CUBE can be configured to either consume or pass across a received REFER message. Using the configuration example in Example 4-17, when a REFER is received at CUBE, CUBE does not process the REFER but instead creates an egress REFER with the same information and sends it to the peer hop. When the REFER transfer is complete in this scenario, CUBE is no longer involved in the call. Most ITSPs do not support REFER-based transfers, so REFER consume is often used.

Example 4-17 *CUBE REFER Passthrough Configuration*

```
voice service voip
 supplementary-service sip refer
 no supplementary-service media-renegotiate
 sip
  referto-passing
```

Example 4-18 shows how to configure CUBE to consume and completely process the REFER request. When this method is employed, CUBE parses the user portion of the request URI in the Refer-To header. This is used as the key for performing a dial peer lookup. When the dial peer matching logic is satisfied, an outbound INVITE is sent to the session target defined on the dial peer. When the REFER is complete, the CUBE is still involved in the signaling and session. The transferor who sent the REFER is removed, and the session now involves the transferee, CUBE, and the transfer target. This is the scenario most often seen and further discussed in Chapter 12, "Contact Center Integration." The supplementary service command for media renegotiation is included to allow CUBE to renegotiate end-to-end media capabilities when consuming the REFER and establishing the new session call leg.

Example 4-18 *CUBE REFER Consumption Configuration*

```
voice service voip
 no supplementary-service sip refer
 supplementary-service media-renegotiate
 sip
  no referto-passing
```

As mentioned earlier in this section, there have been a number of enhancements to the REFER method defined by RFC 3515. RFC 3892 defined a new header, Referred-By, for use in REFER-based transfer scenarios. The user agent originating a REFER request may include a single Referred-By header, which has the following format:

```
Referred-By: <sip-uri>;cid="<content-id>"
```

The optional cid= portion of the Referred-By header references the Content-ID from the MIME message body, which should contain the same token as the CID value in the Referred-By header. This is formatted as follows and may be encrypted using S/MIME:

```
Content-ID: <content-id>
```

A user agent processing a REFER containing a Referred-By header may include the Referred-By header within the SIP INVITE request sent to the refer target indicated in the Refer-To header. The use of the Referred-By header allows the refer target to parse the SIP URI provided and authenticate the call transfer by using local logic. For example, say that there is an established session between Alice and Bob. Bob attempts to transfer Alice to a refer target, Josh. The Referred-By header would state that Bob is the one referring Alice to Josh. Josh may have in place logic that rejects a call transfer if Bob is the referring party, and this is communicated to Josh by the content of the Referred-By header.

The use of a Referred-By header is entirely optional and not required for a successful REFER-based transfer to complete. However, a device may require that a Referred-By header be present to satisfy local logic and permit session establishment. In this scenario, a 429 Provide Referrer Identity may be sent in response to a REFER/INVITE that does not contain a Referred-By header.

As mentioned earlier in this section, when a REFER is accepted, an implicit subscription occurs between the transferor and transferee. During this implicit subscription, NOTIFY messages are sent to convey information to the transferor about the state of the ongoing REFER call transfer. RFC 4488 modifies the implicit subscription of the REFER process and allows the device originating a REFER to request that the creation of an implicit subscription be avoided. This is done by sending the SIP header Refer-Sub and a value of false, as shown here:

```
Refer-Sub: false
```

The device handling a REFER would also send the same Refer-Sub: false header and value in the 202 Accepted response to indicate that there will not be an implicit subscription and ultimately no NOTIFY messages sent for this REFER request. The device handling the REFER request may want to create an implicit subscription, and thus the 202 Accepted may contain Refer-Sub: true and result in an implicit subscription with NOTIFY messages exchanged for the REFER call transfer. In addition, the use of the tag norefersub may be included in the Supported header of SIP requests to convey the support for REFER request handling without an implicit subscription.

RFC 7614 further modifies the implicit subscription used in REFER and allows the use of an explicit subscription, as defined by RFC 6665. A device originating a REFER advertises the desire to use an explicit subscription for the REFER process by sending the tag explicitsub within the Require header of the SIP REFER request. This format is as follows:

```
Require: explicitsub
```

If the device handling the REFER accepts the use of explicit subscription for notification during the REFER processing, the 202 Accepted Response will contain the Refer-Events-At header with a SIP URI of the event server. This header is as follows:

```
Refer-Events-At: <sip:1234@example.com>
```

The value of the Refer-Events-At header is often the same as the address of the device currently processing the REFER. The RFC 6665 subscription method is then utilized to set up a subscription session between the event server and the UA that originated the REFER. (The SIP subscription process is outlined in Chapter 7.)

RFC 7614 also defines another method for removing the implicit subscription from the REFER process: by sending a Require header with the tag **nosub**. This differs from the norefersub tag proposed by RFC 4488 as the norefersub extension only suggests that no implicit subscription be created. However, ultimately the choice of tag is up to the device in charge of processing the REFER request. With RFC 7614, the device sending the REFER requires that no implicit subscription be created by sending Require: nosub within the REFER request. The differences between RFC 4488 and RFC 7614 in regard to disabling the implicit subscription are discussed in RFC 7647.

RFC 5368 modifies REFER in that a user agent may send a REFER that contains multiple SIP URIs in which the device handling a REFER may attempt to extend a session invitation. This is done by sending a Require header with the tag multiple-refer. The Refer-To header is then augmented with a content ID pointer that defines a URI list within the message body as resource-lists+xml content. SIP URI lists are further defined in RFCs 4826, 5363, and 5364. REFER requests using RFC 5368 must also adhere to the methods defined in RFC 4488 so that there is no implicit subscription created between the device processing the REFER and the device originating the REFER request. Example 4-19 details a REFER request with multiple refer URIs encoded within the SIP resource-lists+xml message body.

Example 4-19 *Sample REFER with Multiple Refer Targets in the Message Body*

```
REFER sip:conf-123@example.com;gruu;opaque=hha9s8d-999a  SIP/2.0
Via: SIP/2.0/TCP client.chicago.example.com;branch=z9hG4bKhjhs8ass83
Max-Forwards: 70
To: "Conference 123" <sip:conf-123@example.com>
From: Carol <sip:carol@chicago.example.com>;tag=32331
Call-ID: d432fa84b4c76e66710
CSeq: 2 REFER
Contact: <sip:carol@client.chicago.example.com>
Refer-To: <cid:cn35t8jf02@example.com>
Refer-Sub: false
Require: multiple-refer, norefersub
Allow: INVITE, ACK, CANCEL, OPTIONS, BYE, REFER, SUBSCRIBE, NOTIFY
Allow-Events: dialog
Accept: application/sdp, message/sipfrag
Content-Type: application/resource-lists+xml
Content-Disposition: recipient-list
Content-Length: 362
Content-ID: <cn35t8jf02@example.com>

<?xml version="1.0" encoding="UTF-8"?>
<resource-lists xmlns="urn:ietf:params:xml:ns:resource-lists"
        xmlns:xsi="http://www.w3.org/2001/XMLSchema-instance">
  <list>
    <entry uri="sip:bill@example.com" />
    <entry uri="sip:joe@example.org" />
    <entry uri="sip:ted@example.net" />
  </list>
</resource-lists>
```

Note This chapter does not discuss out-of-dialog (OOD) REFER messages.

Hold and re-INVITE

Another method of call transfer, primary used by call agents, is achieved by using SIP re-INVITEs. During a call transfer that utilizes re-INVITEs, the original media stream may be temporarily suspended while the re-INVITEs transfer is being processed. When the call transfer is complete, the media stream is reestablished between the transferee and the transfer target.

To initiate the hold and re-INVITE transfer process, the transferor presses a button or soft-key, which places the transferee on hold. While the transferee is on hold, the transferor can initiate a call transfer by dialing the number of a transfer target. After dialing the transfer target number, the transferor can complete the transfer in one of a few ways.

The first method is termed an *unattended transfer*, or *blind transfer*, which means the call is sent to the transfer target, and when the transfer target answers, audio is connected between the transferee and the transfer target. The transferor is dropped from the session before the transfer target is connected. Ringback may be played to the transferee rather than music-on-hold in this scenario. Because the call is already connected, a 18x message is not sent, but rather a third-party media resource is required to play ringback to the transferee. Figure 4-26 details a blind transfer from Phone A to Phone B for a call through a call agent.

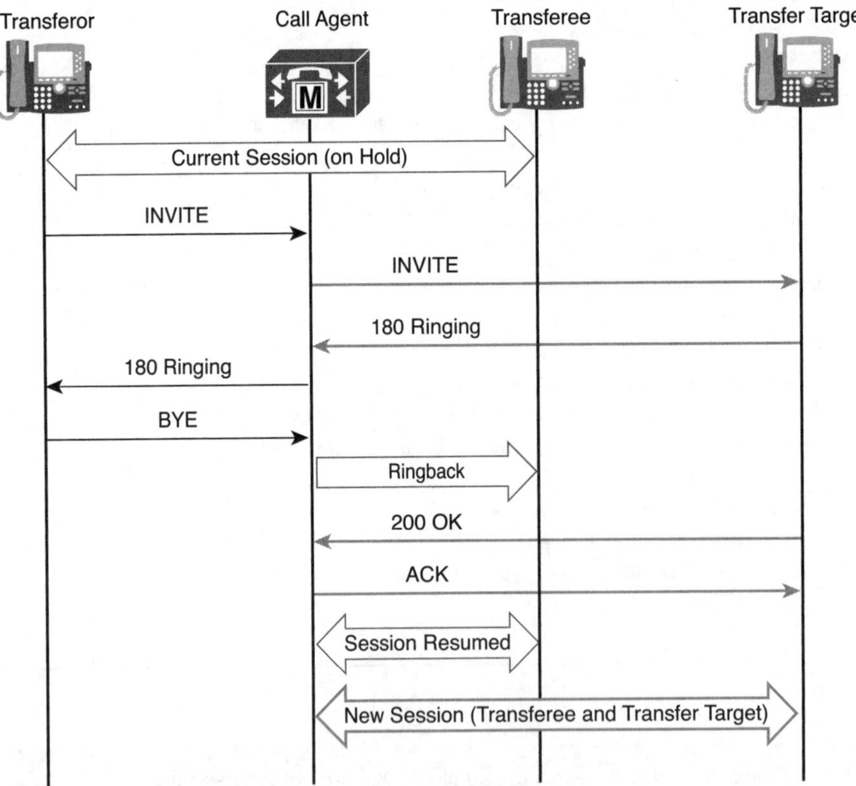

Figure 4-26 *A Blind Transfer*

The second method is called a *consult transfer*, or *attended transfer*. The transferor places the transferee on hold, and music-on-hold is played. The transferor then dials a transfer target. The transfer target answers, and audio is cut through between the transferor and the transfer target. These two parties may communicate over the established audio channel before the transferor completes the transfer. Upon completion, the transferee is taken off hold, the transferor is removed, and audio is negotiated between the transfer target and the transferee. The transferor also has the option of conferencing all three parties together so that the transferee, transferor, and transfer target can speak. At this point, any party can leave the conference. Figure 4-27 details a consult transfer from Phone A to Phone B for a call through a call agent.

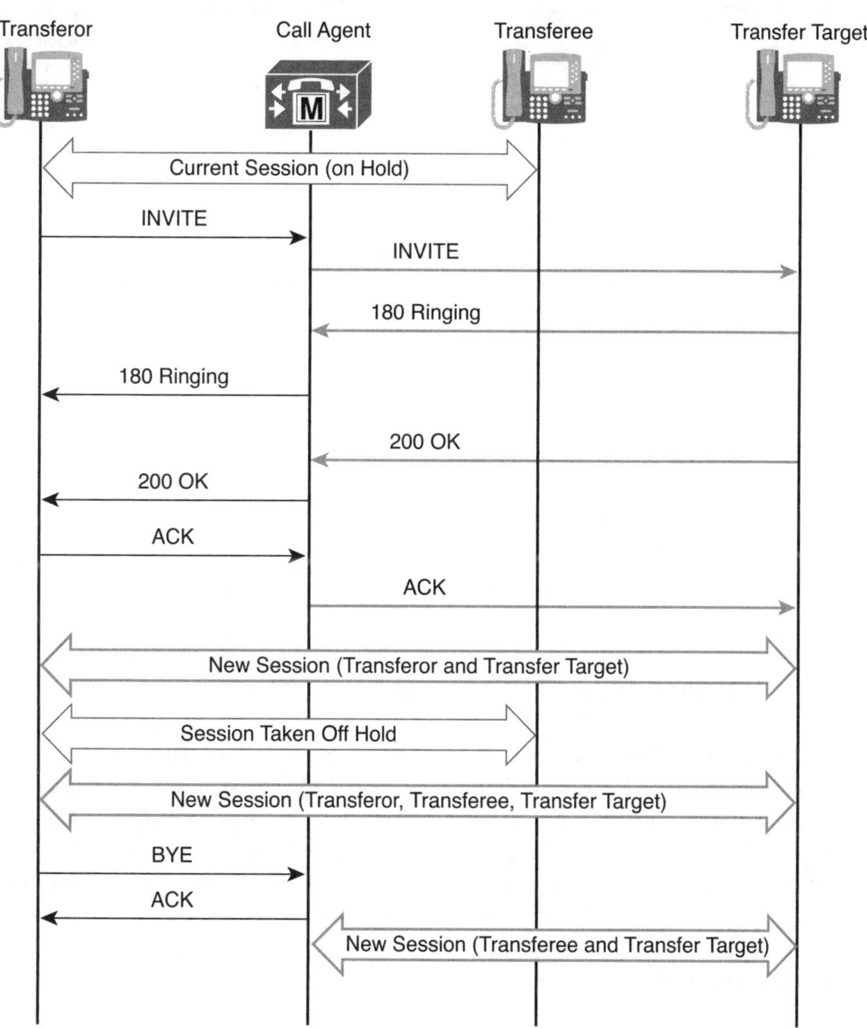

Figure 4-27 *A Consult Transfer*

For these transfer methods, the call agent responsible for the endpoints usually takes care of inviting the transfer target to the session as well as for the hold and resume the transferee experiences and also for the bridging together of media for the transfer target, transferee, and transferor. From the SBC's perspective, a re-INVITE-based transfer makes use of two different call dialogs. The first SIP dialog is the original call between the transferor and the transferee. The second is a new SIP dialog between the call agent, on behalf of the transferor, and the transfer target. Figure 4-28 details a hold and re-INVITE transfer that involves a PSTN participant and an SBC.

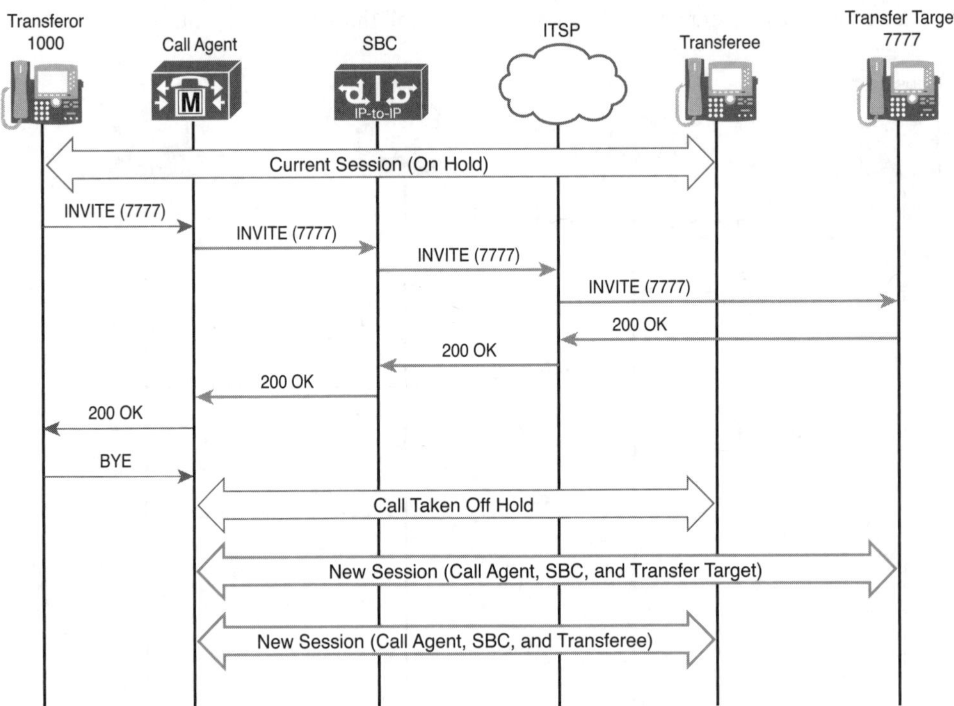

Figure 4-28 *A re-INVITE Transfer Through an SBC*

One problem that arises with the scenario outlined in Figure 4-28 is that the call agent and SBC are still involved in the signaling due to the re-INVITE being sourced from the call agent and sent to the SBC. The only party that is removed is the transferor endpoint. In addition, it is possible for the call agent and SBC to remain involved in the media for the session after the transfer. This can lead to undesired resource allocation on the media plane. The preferred method of performing a transfer is to use the REFER method, which allows SIP devices to remove themselves from further signaling and media plane interworking after the transfer.

BYE Also

BYE Also is a deprecated form of transfer that was replaced by the REFER method in RFC 3515. REFER is a much better approach to transfer than BYE Also as it decouples the transfer from the BYE, allowing greater functionality and control over a transfer. The use of BYE Also is not widely adopted, but it is supported by CUBE. With BYE Also, the transferor sends a BYE, which indicates that the session will be terminated between the SBC and that user agent. The BYE contains an Also header, which specifies the URI of the transfer target in which CUBE should attempt to establish a communication session and complete the call transfer (see Example 4-20).

Example 4-20 *Sample BYE Also Message*

```
Received:
BYE sip:1234@172.18.110.58 SIP/2.0
Via: SIP/2.0/UDP 172.18.110.65:5060;branch=z9hG4bK-636-1-4
From: <sip:7777@172.18.110.65>;tag=1
To: <sip:1234@172.18.110.58>;tag=66EEFF-6E5
Call-ID: 7073BEF9-5D5411E8-8309B2BC-296D212F@172.18.110.58
CSeq: 2 BYE
Contact: sip:7777@172.18.110.65:5060
Max-Forwards: 70
Also: <sip:1231231234@10.10.10.10:5060>
Content-Length: 0
```

UPDATE

The SIP UPDATE method, defined in RFC 3311, provides a way for a SIP user agent to modify session characteristics before the call is answered. The SIP UPDATE method is similar to the SIP re-INVITE method, but the main difference is that the SIP UPDATE can be used to modify session characteristics before a session is established, while a SIP re-INVITE cannot do this. Table 4-2 covers the differences between the two method types.

Table 4-2 *Comparison of re-INVITE and UPDATE Request Methods*

	re-INVITE	UPDATE
Can be sent before session establishment?	No	Yes
Can be sent after session establishment?	Yes	Yes*
Requires immediate answer?	No	Yes
Must require SDP offer/answer exchange?	Yes	No

* Note that the SIP UDPATE method can also be used to update session characteristics after a session is established. However, it is recommended that SIP re-INVITEs be used in such scenarios instead.

A device advertises its capability to support the SIP UPDATE method by specifying this method in the Allow header (see Example 4-21). This can be in a request or in a response. In addition, an UPDATE may or may not contain SDP. Updates without SDP usually modify session characteristics such as the caller ID and session timers, whereas UPDATEs with SDP directly modify the session's media attributes.

Example 4-21 *An Allow Header with the UPDATE Method Specified*

```
INVITE sip:7777@172.18.110.58:5060 SIP/2.0
Via: SIP/2.0/TCP 172.18.110.48:5060;branch=z9hG4bK59c13d0833e
From: <sip:1234@172.18.110.48>;tag=30489~1992ce86-77ac-43a7-91b7-90778966a9f5-
  30207788
To: <sip:7777@172.18.110.58>
Call-ID: 990bdd00-b041b14b-f2-306e12ac@172.18.110.48
Supported: timer,resource-priority,replaces
Min-SE:  1800
Allow: INVITE, OPTIONS, INFO, BYE, CANCEL, ACK, PRACK, UPDATE, REFER, SUBSCRIBE,
  NOTIFY
CSeq: 101 INVITE
Expires: 180
Session-Expires:  1800
Contact: <sip:1234@172.18.110.48:5060;transport=tcp>
Max-Forwards: 70
Content-Length: 0

SIP/2.0 183 Session Progress
Via: SIP/2.0/TCP 172.18.110.48:5060;branch=z9hG4bK59c13d0833e
From: <sip:1234@172.18.110.48>;tag=30489~1992ce86-77ac-43a7-91b7-
  90778966a9f5-30207788
To: <sip:7777@172.18.110.58>;tag=66EF7A-1E33
Call-ID: 990bdd00-b041b14b-f2-306e12ac@172.18.110.48
CSeq: 101 INVITE
Allow: INVITE, OPTIONS, BYE, CANCEL, ACK, PRACK, UPDATE, REFER, SUBSCRIBE, NOTIFY,
  INFO, REGISTER
Contact: <sip:7777@172.18.110.58:5060;transport=tcp>
Content-Length: 0
```

A SIP UPDATE request may be sent by any participant in a session. However, there are specific guidelines related to when it is and is not appropriate to send a SIP UPDATE. These are broken down into three key scenarios:

- If the original offer *does* contain a session media description (early offer) and this offer is answered reliably by a PRACK exchange (as described earlier in this chapter, in the section "Reliable Handling and Interworking of Provisional Responses"), then an UPDATE may be sent for session description modification. Figure 4-29 details an early offer call in which a UAS has sent a 183 with SDP. The PRACK is exchanged, and the offer/answer has been completed reliably. However, the UAC wants to change the aspects of the media session. Because the call is not yet answered by the UAS with a final response, the UAS sends an UPDATE with SDP. The UAS responds with a 200 OK with SDP. This can continue as many times as needed until a final response to the INVITE is processed. If the offer is not answered reliably with PRACK, only an UPDATE without SDP can be processed for this session.

- If the original offer *does not* contain any offer (delayed offer), then an UPDATE for session media modification cannot be processed unless an answer/offer PRACK exchange occurs. In this scenario, the provisional response (such as a 183 with SDP) would contain an offer, and the PRACK with SDP would contain the answer. If the aforementioned offer/answer is been completed, only an UPDATE without SDP can be processed for this session.
- UPDATEs for session media modification may be utilized after the initial INVITE transaction has been completed, as long as there are no outstanding offers (re-INVITE or UPDATE) awaiting answers. If there is an outstanding transaction awaiting an answer to an offer and an UPDATE is received, this solicits a 491 response. Similarly, if there is an outstanding transaction in which the device receiving the UPDATE is in the process of generating an answer, the response must be a 5xx-level response with a Retry-After header. This is the same response code and behavior observed if a device attempts to send an UPDATE before a previous UPDATE, of any kind, has been answered with a 200 OK.

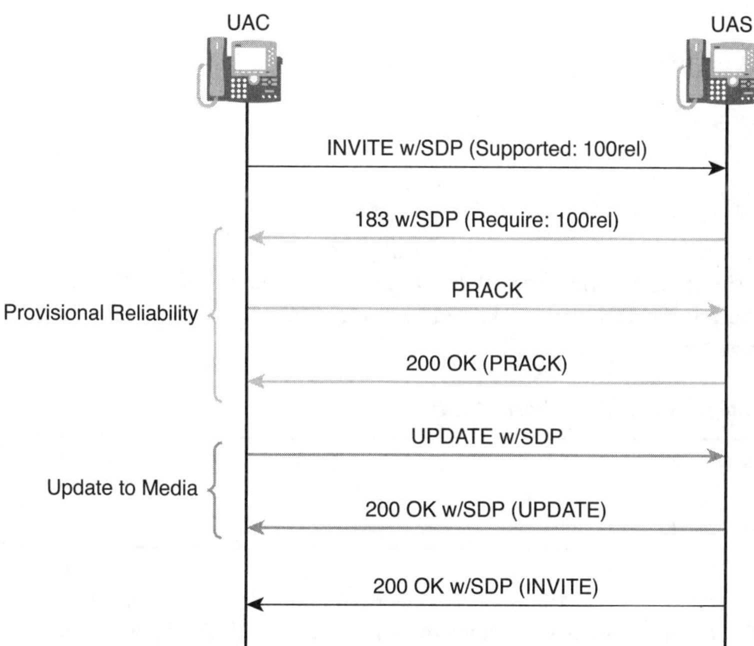

Figure 4-29 *PRACK and UPDATE Between a UAC and a UAS*

One problem that arises in the scenario of updating a session description before a call is connected has to do with the asymmetrical nature of PRACK. Because PRACK is a per-call leg mechanism, from the perspective of an SBC, a reliable provisional response might be exchanged on one call leg and not on the other. This scenario is depicted in Figure 4-30. In this scenario, it is valid for the device on Call Leg A to send an UPDATE with SDP to the SBC. The SBC would either need to respond to the UPDATE on behalf of Call Leg B or return a 491 Request Pending message back to Call Leg A because it is unable to pass the UPDATE with SDP to Call Leg B.

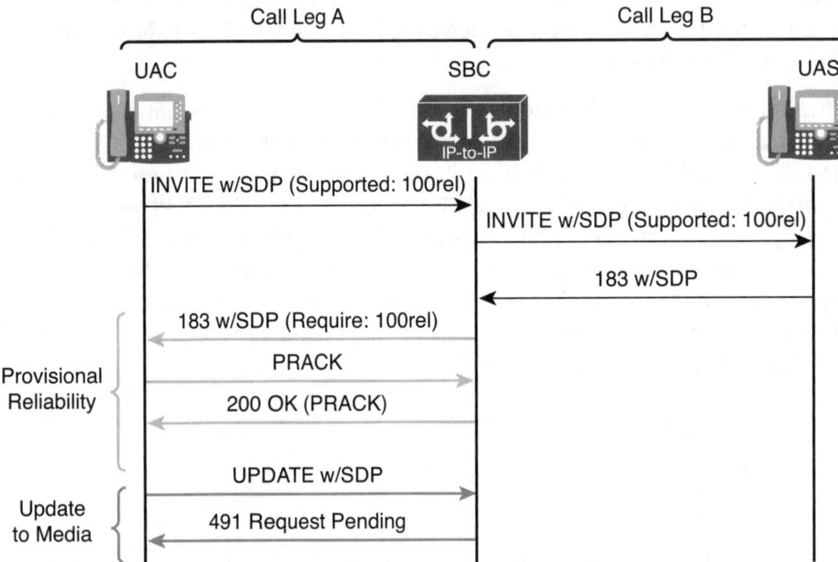

Figure 4-30 *Asymmetric PRACK, UPDATE, and 491 Responses*

For such scenarios, SBCs can be configured to locally consume SIP UPDATEs without passing the request to the peer call leg. From the perspective of CUBE, local consumption of SIP UPDATEs can be achieved by configuring an **early-media update block**, as demonstrated in Example 4-22.

Example 4-22 *Configuring a CUBE Early Media Update Block*

```
voice service voip
 sip
  early-media update block
```

As mentioned in the introduction to this section, UPDATEs are commonly used to modify caller ID when a remote device transfers a call or when additional parties are added to the call. This can be done at any time during a session and does not require any prerequisite signaling exchanges, such as PRACK. Most SBCs forward these types of UPDATEs on the peer call leg by default. It is common to observe this method of UPDATE in conjunction with the call transfer events discussed in the "Call Transfer" section, earlier in this chapter. When a device transfers from one party to another, often the caller ID of the new participant is sent in an UPDATE to the other participants in the session. By default, CUBE passes through mid-call UPDATEs for caller ID changes. The passing of these messages may lead to additional SIP traffic being sent to the service provider, which also increases bandwidth on the network and could even lead to race conditions when an UPDATE is not expected. Thus the default behavior of passing caller ID updates can be changed by removing the default command, as shown in Example 4-23.

Example 4-23 *Disabling CUBE Update Caller ID*

```
voice service voip
 sip
  no update-callerid
```

Session Refresh

It is quite common for a communication session established over SIP to span several intermediary devices, such as call agents, SIP proxies, and SBCs. In such scenarios, it is vital that requests and corresponding responses be transmitted reliably and in a timely manner end to end to ensure that the state of the communication session is synchronized across all devices in the call path. Consider a situation in which a communication session is established across the topology depicted in Figure 4-31.

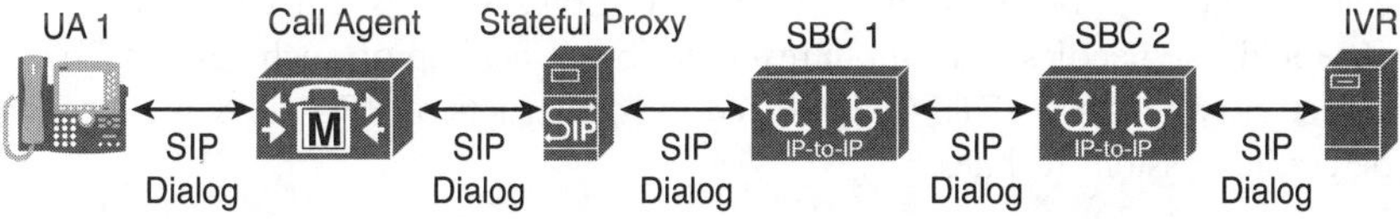

Figure 4-31 *Topology with UA, Call Agent, Stateful Proxy, SBCs, and an IVR*

The IVR device is capable of only triggered disconnects. That is, it can terminate a communication session only when it receives SIP BYE requests and not of its own accord. Referring to Figure 4-32, which uses the aforementioned topology, if the caller decides to end the communication session, it transmits a SIP BYE or an equivalent indication. This indication is transmitted across all devices along the call path such that it is received at the IVR. The IVR then acknowledges this request, leading to the termination of the communication session.

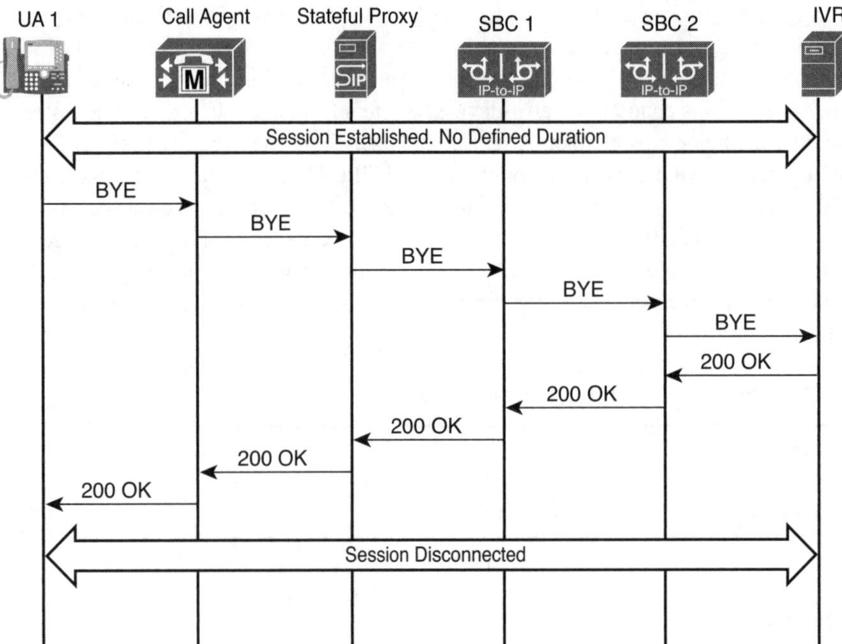

Figure 4-32 *Diagram Detailing a BYE Sent to All Participants in the Session*

Figure 4-33 details a scenario in which the indication to disconnect the communication session (SIP BYE) is lost in transit or is not processed properly on one of the downstream devices due to a transient condition and as a result the state of the session is not synchronized end to end. This leads devices along the call path that haven't received the indication for call disconnect to believe that the communication session is still active. Such a situation would also needlessly result in resources being held up on such devices. To overcome such situations, the IETF standardized the constructs of RFC 4028 as a mechanism to determine session freshness.

RFC 4028 defines many different terms, such as a *session interval*, which is conveyed in the Session-Expires SIP header. This header conveys the maximum time a session is considered active or fresh. After this timer expires, the session is timed out, and all devices that have agreed upon the session interval disconnect the session. This disconnection is called a *session expiration*. The *minimum timer* is carried in the Min-SE SIP header and is used to convey the lowest possible value for the session interval. To modify or extend a previously agreed-upon session interval, a *session refresh* must occur; it is carried out by the predetermined refresher. Figure 4-34 defines a sample of a session interval being negotiated between a UAC and a UAS. The following sections break down this signaling exchange, using Figure 4-34 as a starting point.

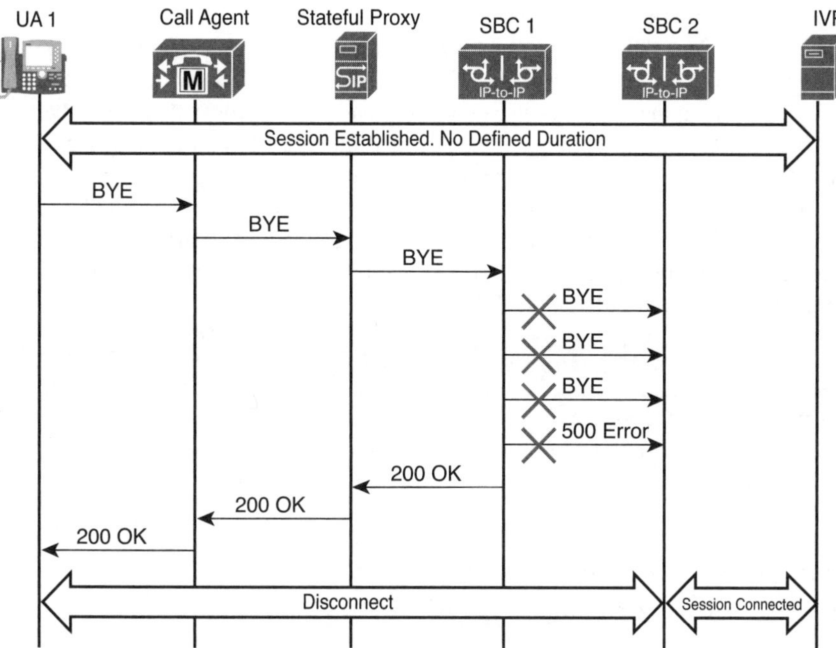

Figure 4-33 *Diagram Detailing a Transient Condition in Which BYE Is Not Received by All Session Participants*

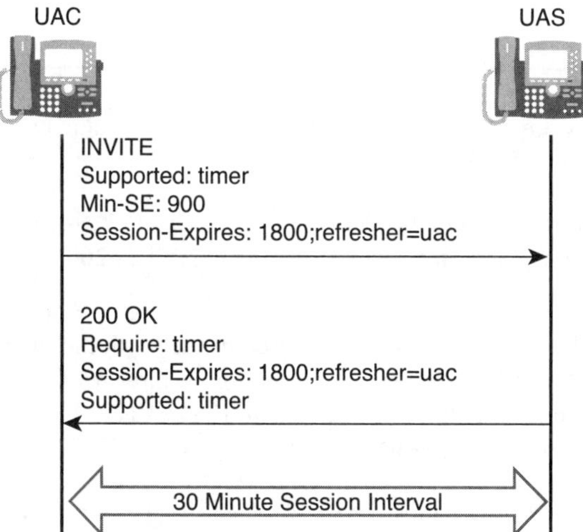

Figure 4-34 *Session Timer Negotiation Between a UAC and a UAS*

If a UAC wants to engage in a new session with a session interval, it must first include the timer extension in the Supported SIP header. A Session-Expires header may also be included in the initial INVITE request, indicating a proposed maximum session interval.

It is important to note that the Session-Expires header sent by the UAC is an offer and a proposed timer. Thus this value may not reflect the final timer value negotiated for the session. The timer extension may be included in the Require header to indicate that the UAC is requesting that the UAS also support a session timer to participate in the session. If the UAC wants to convey a minimum session interval, the UAC may include the Min-SE timer. Finally, if the UAC wants, it may indicate that it would like to play the role of refresher for this session by adding the tag ;refresher=uac to the Session-Expires header. If the UAC would like to leave this decision up to the UAS, it may omit this tag from the Session-Expires header. A sample INVITE request for a new session requesting a session interval is detailed in Example 4-24.

Example 4-24 *Sample INVITE with Session Interval Information*

```
INVITE sip:7777@172.18.110.58:5060 SIP/2.0
Via: SIP/2.0/TCP 172.18.110.48:5060;branch=z9hG4bK3a34b28097e
From: <sip:1024@172.18.110.48>;tag=22968~1992ce86-77ac-43a7-91b7-
  90778966a9f5-30207629
To: <sip:7777@172.18.110.58>
Call-ID: 82535500-b00171fb-80-306e12ac@172.18.110.48
Supported: 100rel,timer,resource-priority,replaces
Min-SE: 900
Allow: INVITE, OPTIONS, INFO, BYE, CANCEL, ACK, PRACK, UPDATE, REFER, SUBSCRIBE,
  NOTIFY
CSeq: 101 INVITE
Expires: 180
Session-Expires: 1800;refresher=uac
Max-Forwards: 69
```

The UAS or midstream proxy receiving a request with a proposed session interval may perform one of many actions, including the following:

- If the device handling a request with a Require header contains the timer extension but does not support session timers or the timer extension, it may send a 420 Bad Extension response.
- If the device handling a request that only contains a Supported header with the timer extension and no Session-Expires header, it may include a Session-Expires header with its own proposed session value in the 200 OK response to the INVITE. The UAC may then answer this session interval offer in the ACK.
- If the device handling a request contains a Supported header with the timer extension and a Session-Expires header with a value, it may generate a 200 OK response without a Session-Expires header (as long as there is not a Require timer header present). By doing this, the UAS indicates that there is no defined session interval for the session.

- Alternatively, if the device handling a request contains a Supported header with the timer extension and a Session-Expires header with a value, the device may include a Session-Expires with a value equal to or lower than the value contained in the Session-Expires header sent by the UAC. This value cannot be lower than the Min-SE header value indicated by the UAC if the header was present.
- Finally, as shown in Figure 4-35, if the value of the Session-Expires header is lower than the desired minimum session expiration for the device, it may send a 422 Session Interval Too Small response. The 422 response must contain a Min-SE header specifying the minimum timer allowed by the server rejecting the message. The UAC may attempt to increase the timer and try the request again or try another UAS, using local logic.

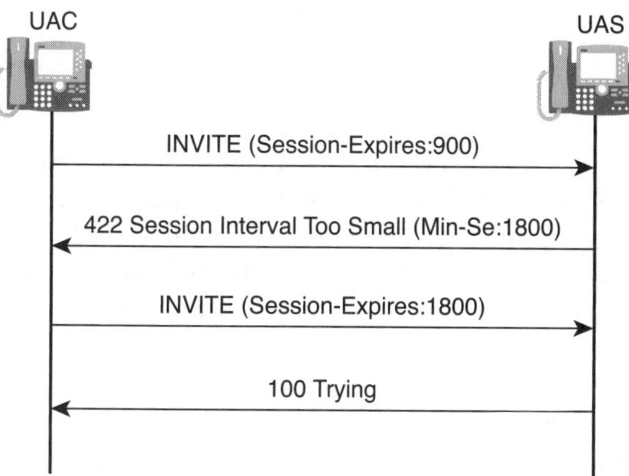

Figure 4-35 *422 Response to a Request Containing a Session Timer That Is Too Small*

The minimum for any session interval is 90 seconds. In addition, when no Min-SE header is present, the assumed value is 90 seconds. It is recommended that you avoid small session timers in order to avoid oversaturating the network with session refresh messages. The recommended session refresh timer is 1800 seconds (that is, 30 minutes).

Tip The Min-SE header cannot be sent in any numbered response except the 422.

Continuing with the previous example, defined in Example 4-24, let's now examine a response to that offer in Example 4-25. The UAS has confirmed that it will support a session interval by responding with a Session-Expires header containing a value equal to or less than the offer but not less than the Min-SE in the previous offer. A Supported header with the timer extension is mandatory when the UAS is sending a Session-Expires answer. Finally, the Require header with a timer extension is sent when the UAS is selecting the UAC as the designated session refresher. This is indicated by the tag ;refresher=uac on the Session-Expires header. (More details about this tag can be found in the paragraphs following Example 4-25.)

Example 4-25 *Establishing a Successful Session Timer*

```
Sent:
SIP/2.0 200 OK
Via: SIP/2.0/TCP 172.18.110.48:5060;branch=z9hG4bK3a34b28097e
From: <sip:1024@172.18.110.48>;tag=22968~1992ce86-77ac-43a7-91b7-
  90778966a9f5-30207629
To: <sip:7777@172.18.110.58>;tag=512A088-1C36
Call-ID: 82535500-b00171fb-80-306e12ac@172.18.110.48
CSeq: 101 INVITE
Allow: INVITE, OPTIONS, BYE, CANCEL, ACK, PRACK, UPDATE, REFER, SUBSCRIBE, NOTIFY,
  INFO, REGISTER
Server: Cisco-SIPGateway/IOS-15.3.3.S
Require: timer
Session-Expires: 1800;refresher=uac
Supported: timer
```

This section previously detailed that the refresher tag can be sent in the Session-Expires header by either the UAC or the UAS. This tag indicates the desired refresher for the session but is ultimately defined and required in the answer/response from the UAS. Table 4-3 defines the different permutations and how the value of this tag is derived when the Supported header in the request contains or does not contain a timer extension and/or the refresher value is or is not present in the initial request.

Table 4-3 *UAS Refresher Response Permutation*

UAC Supports Timer Extension?	Refresher Parameter Value in the Request?	Refresher Parameter Value in the Response?
No	None, value not present	;refresher=uas
No	;refresher=uac	Not permitted by the RFC
No	;refresher=uas	Not permitted by the RFC
Yes	None, value not present	;refresher=uac or ;refresher=uas
Yes	;refresher=uac	;refresher=uac
Yes	;refresher=uas	;refresher=uas

After a session has been established with a defined session interval and a designated session refresher, the timer starts for the session. At some point during the session—normally the midway point, as per the RFC 4028 recommendation—the designated refresher sends either a re-INVITE or an UPDATE, which operates exactly the same as in the earlier examples in this section. Only a 200 OK response to a session refresh request can extend the session. Failure to properly negotiate this session refresh can lead to premature call failure at the session refresh interval rather than the session timer expiration. One example of this type of failure would be the refresher modifying the SDP through the session refresh. If this modification is not accepted by the other devices in the session, the call can be terminated on the spot. Figure 4-36 shows both a successful session refresh and a refresh that fails due to the session refresh being rejected.

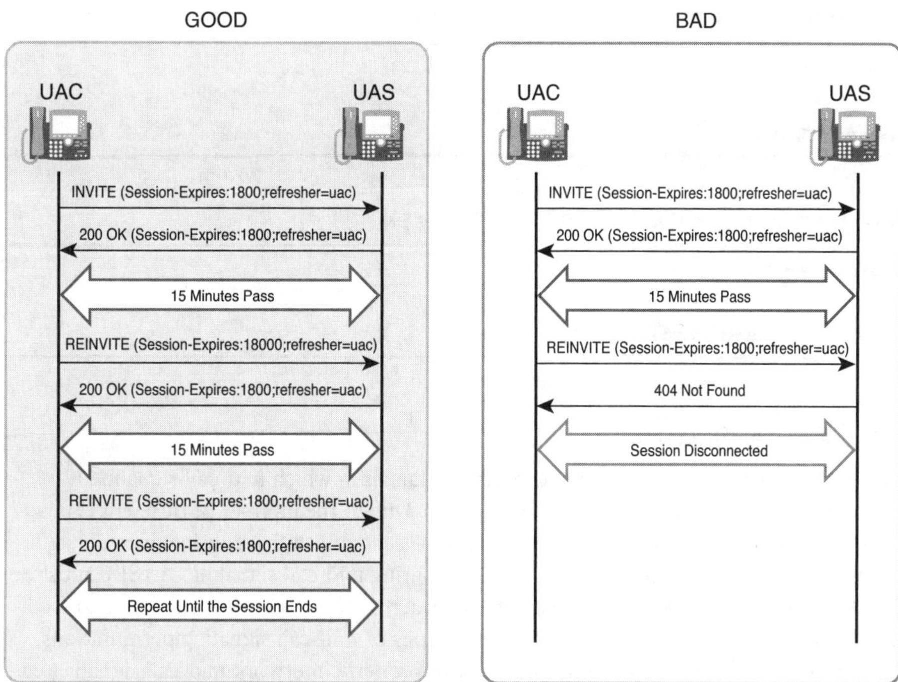

Figure 4-36 *Good and Bad Session Refresh Attempts Between a UAC and a UAS*

The inclusion of a session timer is entirely optional. The absence of a Session-Expires header means the user agent wants the session to be infinite, or without a definite end. The Session-Expires header can be removed mid-call during a session refresh, which results in further session refreshing being disabled because the new session timer is now infinite.

> **Tip** Any mid-call signaling UPDATE or re-INVITE sent for a purpose other than a session refresh may also contain session timer parameters. Completing these offers/answers will also refresh the session if they occur as per the specifications defined in the RFC.

It is very important for an SBC to have the ability to interwork and pass session refreshes on all call legs requiring that the session timer be updated. Failure to comply can lead to call failures and premature disconnects. It may also be possible for an SBC to have one call leg without a session timer and another call leg with a session timer. An SBC must be able to maintain session timers across different SIP dialogs in order to avoid session timeout events and unwanted session termination.

CUBE can facilitate session interval interworking across different call legs by default without any configuration. CUBE does not select itself as the designated session refresher unless the command shown in Example 4-26 is enabled. In addition, the Min-SE and Session-Expires timer can be configured on CUBE if something outside the default value is required, as show in in Example 4-27.

Example 4-26 *Configuring a CUBE Session Refresh*

```
voice service voip
 sip
  session refresh
```

Example 4-27 *Configuring a CUBE Session Timer*

```
voice service voip
 sip
  min-se 1800 session-expires 1800
```

Managing Mid-call Signaling

The previous sections discuss many different instances in which mid-call signaling is required for established communication sessions. Due to the number of different types of mid-call signaling needed and methods used to accomplish these tasks, there is a possibility of interoperability events occurring during mid-call signaling. An SBC must be able to handle complex mid-call signaling events across many different call legs and facilitate signaling interworking for many different types of mid-call signaling permutations and combinations. An SBC lacking the ability to properly interwork mid-call signaling can lead to vendor interoperability, call failures, and session establishment issues.

By default, CUBE interworks and passes through all mid-call signaling from one call leg to another. However, in many cases, passing across all mid-call signaling messages end-to-end is a hindrance. Reducing the number of mid-call signaling messages end to end often promotes smooth interoperability across device types and networks.

CUBE provides the ability to consume all mid-call signaling and handle such signaling locally instead of passing it across to the peer call leg. This flavor of mid-call call signaling is activated using the **midcall-signaling block** command. This command can be configured in different submodes of CUBE, as demonstrated in Figure 4-37.

While handling all mid-call signaling natively presents a drastic improvement in terms of reducing the number of message exchanges end to end and speeding up transaction establishment times, it may lead to unexpected behavior and call failures as well. Consider a situation in which two video-capable endpoints establish an audio-only session across an SBC by using **midcall-signaling block**. With this command, neither of these devices would be able to escalate the audio-only session into an audio and video session. This is due to the fact that CUBE blocks any and all mid-call signaling. The re-INVITE for video escalation would be consumed by CUBE and result in a failure of that particular operation.

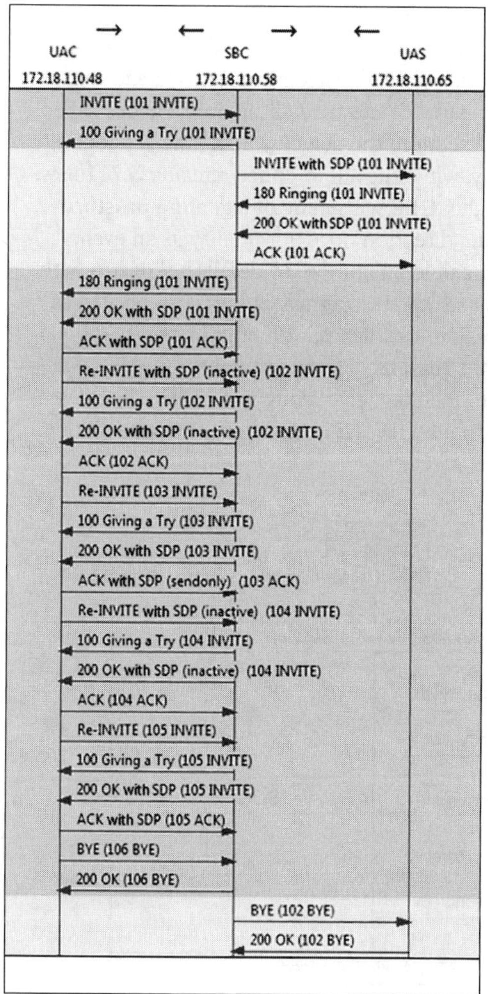

Figure 4-37 *CUBE Blocking All Mid-call Signaling*

Tip Session refresh messages can also be blocked by the **midcall-signaling block** command. It is best to avoid using this command if session interval timers are being used as these are required to keep a session established.

To provide the flexibility of natively handling most mid-call signaling while at the same time passing across certain mid-call signaling transactions that need to be transmitted end to end, CUBE provides the **midcall-signaling passthru media-change** command. With this command in place, only mid-call signaling transactions that alter the media characteristics of the communication session are passed through. These characteristics include codec changes and addition and modification of media types (for example, audio, video, image) to the communication session.

Changes to the media direction attribute (a=) and the connection data information field (c=) of the SDP do not qualify as sufficient conditions to pass across the message end to end. This is the case, for example, if a session is established between two endpoints with bidirectional G.711ulaw audio and one party places the call on hold. As described earlier in this chapter, in the "Hold/Resume" section, the device placing the session on hold may send a re-INVITE with a=sendonly, while the audio codec remains G.711ulaw. This re-INVITE would not be passed through CUBE with **midcall-signaling passthru media-change** present as the change in media direction does not qualify as an event that needs to be passed through to the peer call leg. Figure 4-38 details a scenario with **midcall-signaling passthru media-change** in which the original call was established as a G.711ulaw audio-only session, and the session was then put on hold briefly before returning. This hold is blocked because of the reasons defined previously in this paragraph. Finally, the session is escalated to include video along with audio. Because CUBE considers this a valid media change, the re-INVITE is passed to the peer call leg.

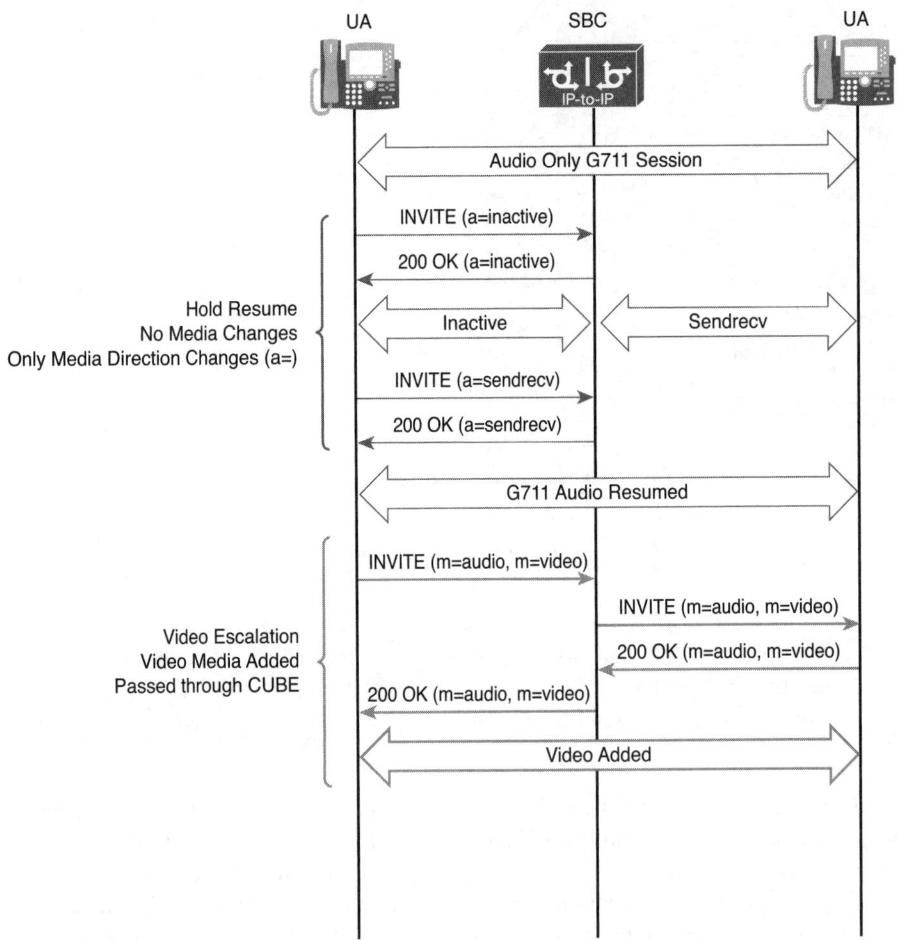

Figure 4-38 *CUBE Passing Mid-call Signaling with Media Changes*

SIP Header Interworking

A SIP header has the following format:

```
Header: Value
```

The contents of *Value* in a SIP header can be almost anything. The goal of a SIP header is to carry data and provide the data in a consumable manner to the next-hop application, which handles the parsing of the SIP message. Many RFCs pertaining to SIP define required and optional SIP headers; in addition, there are vendor-proprietary headers and custom application headers. From an SBC's perspective, it is nearly impossible to incorporate support for parsing, understanding, and interpreting every possible SIP header in existence.

RFC 3261 details a small list of required headers for every SIP request or SIP response. However, most SBCs have a list of additional supported headers considered mandatory to handle SIP messages and session establishment. All headers outside this list are unsupported and may be dropped when creating additional requests and responses during session establishment. There is a problem here: Every SBC vendor or service provider may have a slightly different list of mandatory headers that need to be present for a session to complete successfully with another device.

Sometimes specific headers need to be passed seamlessly across an SBC, oftentimes without modification. Alternatively, there may arise a situation in which a specific header should not be sent across an SBC because the inclusion of a specific header may cause the upstream device to handle a session incorrectly, terminate a call prematurely, or behave in some other undesired fashion. This means the ability of an SBC to interwork headers from many different device types is of paramount importance. The Cisco.com document "Configurable Pass-Through of SIP INVITE Parameters" details the supported mandatory and supported non-mandatory headers on CUBE.

Table 4-4 details many of the most common SIP headers that need to be interworked through CUBE. These headers are so important that each has its own CLI command for passing the header. The opposite form of the same command removes the header from being passed through CUBE if received on a call leg.

Table 4-4 *Common SIP Headers*

SIP Header	Command to Pass Through	Default Behavior
Remote-Party-ID	**sip-ua** **remote-party-id**	Passed
P-Asserted-ID	**voice service voip** **sip** **asserted-id pai**	Dropped
P-Preferred-ID	**voice service voip** **sip** **asserted-id ppi**	Dropped

SIP Header	Command to Pass Through	Default Behavior
Diversion	voice service voip sip no privacy-policy strip diversion	Passed
History-Info	voice service voip sip no privacy-policy strip history-info	Passed
Refer-To	voice service voip sip referto-passing	Passed

Tip The command **header-passing** is often mistakenly configured on CUBE, although this command has no bearing on any SIP–SIP header interworking. This command is used to allow the passing of SIP headers to IOS-based TCL applications, which otherwise do not have access to such information.

In addition to the explicit CLI commands for the specific headers detailed in Table 4-4, CUBE has the ability to configure passthrough of any unsupported SIP header, as shown in Example 4-28. If a more refined approach is desired, rather than passing every unsupported header, an administrator can define a list of unsupported headers that can be passed by using the commands shown in Example 4-29.

Example 4-28 *Passthrough of Unsupported SIP Headers*

```
voice service voip
 sip
  pass-thru headers unsupp
```

Example 4-29 *Defined List of Unsupported Headers*

```
!
voice class sip-hdr-passthrulist 1
 passthru-hdr MyCustomHeader
 passthru-hdr-unsupp
!
voice service voip
 sip
  pass-thru headers 1
```

Even more granularity is possible through the use of SIP profiles and SIP copylist, which allow the addition of custom headers and the manipulation of not only SIP headers but anything in a SIP message. The next section dives into this topic.

SIP Normalization

SIP normalization is the concept of a user agent manipulating SIP headers, header data, or SDP attributes. The need to modify portions of a SIP message may arise from a number of different scenarios, such as formatting header fields to the preference of upstream devices, adding proprietary data to a SIP message, or modifying received SIP messages to enable smooth processing.

The content of a SIP message, including the SIP headers and message bodies (for example, SDP), is plaintext data. As a result, SIP profiles use regular expressions (regex) to match portions of a SIP message and modify the matched portions to meet an administrator's needs. This process is similar to the translation rules and profiles discussed in Chapter 3, "Call Routing." The big difference is that a SIP profile is not constrained to just a phone number.

For example, a message received from a device may contain a SIP header that is malformed or incorrectly formatted; processing such a message could lead to unexpected behavior. SIP normalization is an effective tool in modifying such messages and ensuring that they are correctly formatted before processing.

SIP normalization is heavily used by SBCs due to the fact that an SBC's primary function is to integrate and interwork many separate networks. These disparate networks usually have vastly different capability sets in terms of supporting SIP standards. A few ways SIP normalization can be achieved include LUA scripting, TCL scripting, IOS SIP profiles, and SIP editor. Although different SBCs offer different methods for performing SIP normalization, the end goal is always the same: to provide the administrator a means of modifying or reformatting SIP messages.

SIP normalization is usually broken down into two main categories: preprocessing normalization and postprocessing normalization. Figure 4-39 displays both forms of SIP normalization and details the flow of operations for each. With preprocessing normalization, the following events occur:

Step 1. The SIP message is received by the SBC as an IP packet.

Step 2. The SIP message is extracted from the IP packet and passed on to the SIP application.

Step 3. The SIP application performs the required preprocessing normalization, based on locally configured policies.

Step 4. The normalized message is passed on to the SIP stack, where the message is then interpreted for processing.

Step 5. Based on the results of processing, further action is performed. This could include immediately sending a response, passing the message to the peer call leg, or formulating a new request.

With postprocessing normalization, the following events occur:

Step 1. The SIP stack performs local logic, such as forming a new request or handling a message from the peer call leg.

Step 2. New SIP message data is created, and existing data from the peer leg may be added to the newly created SIP message. This message is then passed to the SIP application.

Step 3. The SIP application performs the required postprocessing normalization, based on locally configured policies.

Step 4. The normalized SIP message is encapsulated for transport over the LAN as an IP packet.

Step 5. The IP packet containing the SIP message is put on the wire and sent to the next hop.

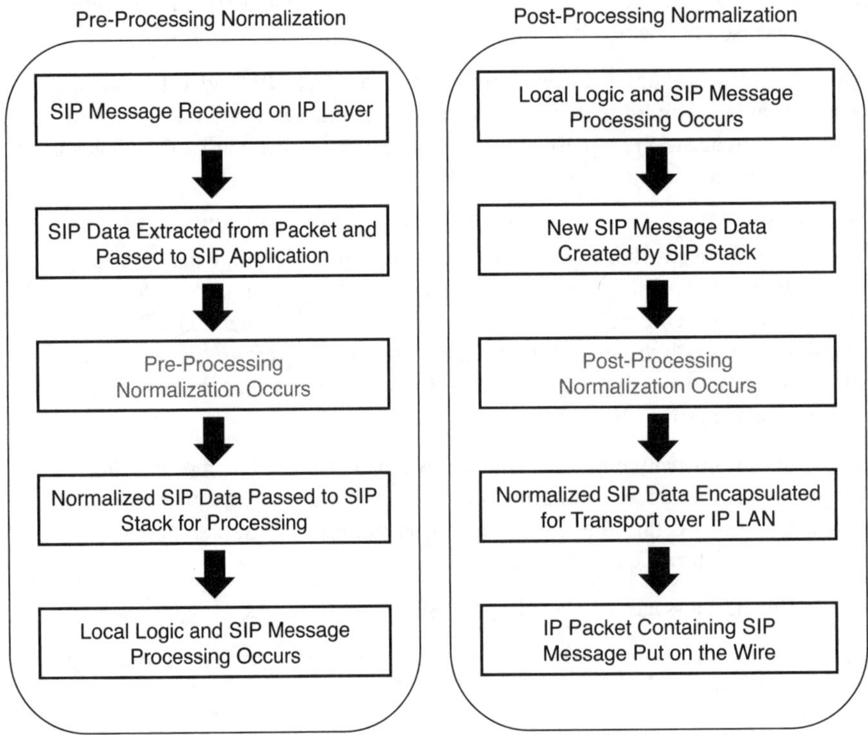

Figure 4-39 *Pre- and Postprocessing SIP Normalization*

The following sections detail the different types of SIP profiles provided by CUBE. The next section also includes some common scenarios an administrator may encounter that require configuration of SIP normalization on CUBE.

SIP Profile Configuration

A SIP profile is configured by defining **voice class sip-profiles** *profile-id*, where *profile-id* is a numeric identifier for the configured SIP profile. An administrator would add statements to the SIP profile. Each statement consists of a request or a numbered response, the specific message being modified, a header type, and the actual header name. With a

SIP profile, an administrator can modify, add, or remove SIP message data. Example 4-30 and Table 4-5 show the command syntax used to configure a SIP profile for SIP header or SDP modification.

Example 4-30 *SIP Profile Syntax Used for Header Modification*

```
!
voice class sip-profiles profile-id
 {request | response} message {sip-header | sdp-header} header-to-modify modify
  "value-to-match" "value-to-replace"
!
```

Table 4-5 *SIP Profile Modification Syntax*

Argument	Function
request	Specifies to run this SIP profile statement only against a SIP request method.
response	Specifies to run this SIP profile statement only against numbered SIP responses.
message	Defines the SIP request or response message to run this SIP profile statement against. Defining ANY here runs against all requests or responses.
sip-header	Modifies SIP headers, including the SIP request URI (**SIP-Req-URI**) and SIP status line (**SIP-StatusLine**).
sdp-header	Modifies the SDP body of the SIP message body.
header-to-modify	Defines the actual SIP header or SDP field to modify.
modify	Specifies that the SIP profile will be performing a modification.
value-to-match	Specifies a regular expression statement that is used to match a portion of the desired header or SDP attribute.
value-to-replace	Specifies the desired modification output of the match.

SIP profiles can also be used to add proprietary headers to SIP messages. This is done through the **ADD** statement within a SIP profile. The ability to add custom headers was introduced in IOS 15.5(2)T and IOS XE 3.13S. Example 4-31 and Table 4-6 show the command syntax for adding a SIP header or SDP value to a SIP message.

Example 4-31 *SIP Profile Syntax Used for Adding Headers*

```
!
voice class sip-profiles profile-id
 {request | response} message {sip-header | sdp-header} header-to-add add
  "value-to-add"
!
```

Table 4-6 *SIP Profile Addition Syntax*

Argument	Function
request	Specifies to run this SIP profile statement only against a SIP request method.
response	Specifies to run this SIP profile statement only against numbered SIP responses.
message	Defines the SIP request or response message to run this SIP profile statement against. Defining ANY here runs against all requests or responses.
sip-header	Modifies SIP headers, including the SIP request URI (**SIP-Req-URI**) and SIP status line (**SIP-StatusLine**).
sdp-header	Modifies the SDP body of the SIP message body.
header-to-add	Defines a new SIP header name that will be added.
add	Specifies that this statement will be adding a value.
value-to-add	Specifies the defined value to add to the SIP message as a newline.

A SIP profile can also be used to remove a value from a SIP message. This is a very powerful way of dropping headers that may be causing interworking issues. Example 4-32 and Table 4-7 detail the command syntax for header removal.

Example 4-32 *SIP Profile Syntax Used for Removing Headers*

```
!
voice class sip-profiles profile-id
 {request | response} message {sip-header | sdp-header} header-to-remove remove
!
```

Table 4-7 *SIP Profile Removal Syntax*

Argument	Function
request	Specifies to run this SIP profile statement only against a SIP request method.
response	Specifies to run this SIP profile statement only against numbered SIP responses.
message	Defines the SIP request or response message to run this SIP profile statement against. Defining ANY here runs against all requests or responses.
sip-header	Modifies SIP headers, including the SIP request URI (SIP-Req-URI) and SIP status line (SIP-StatusLine).
sdp-header	Modifies SDP body of the SIP Message Body.

Argument	Function
header-to-remove	Defines a new SIP header name that will be removed.
remove	Specifies that this statement will be removing a value.

Once a SIP profile has been defined, it is then applied to the global configuration under **voice service voip** and the **SIP** subsection, which allows for the profile to be run against any SIP message, regardless of the dial peers used. Global application of SIP profiles is also useful when an administrator needs to manipulate SIP messages that do not use dial peers (for example, SIP REGISTER messages, OOD OPTIONS messages). SIP profiles can also be applied to voice class tenant configurations or dial peers for more granular control of SIP messages on a per-call basis.

The different levels of profile application are shown in Example 4-33. One thing to keep in mind is the order of operations for SIP profiles and that SIP profiles defined on a dial peer/tenant take precedence over a global SIP profile when they are modifying the same item.

Example 4-33 *Different SIP Profile Application Levels*

```
! Global Application
!
voice service voip
 sip
  sip-profiles 1
!

! Tenant Application
!
voice class tenant 1
 sip-profiles 1
!

! Dial-peer Application
!
dial-peer voice 1 voip
 voice-class sip profiles 1
!
```

Outbound SIP Profiles

Outbound SIP profiles are the most common type of SIP profile used in CUBE deployments. These SIP profiles follow the postprocessing normalization process defined earlier in this chapter (refer to Figure 4-39). This modification occurs *after* call routing decisions are made and *before* the SIP message is placed on the wire and sent to the next hop as an IP packet. This modification can be applied to both SIP requests and responses as well as SIP headers and an SDP body.

A common use case of outbound SIP profiles is the need to add or modify a SIP Diversion header sent in an egress SIP INVITE for authentication by an upstream device such as a proxy or an ITSP. The SIP profile in this use case would be added to the outbound dial peer so that CUBE can modify the egress INVITE before actually sending the message to the user agent requiring the header. Example 4-34 details the configuration for the addition of a Diversion header. This method can be used when no Diversion header is received on the other call leg. Example 4-35 shows the modification performed by CUBE that takes place in this scenario.

Example 4-34 *Adding a Diversion Header to an Egress INVITE*

```
!
voice class sip-profiles 777
 request INVITE sip-header Diversion add "Diversion: <sip:1234@example.com>"
!
dial-peer voice 777 voip
 destination-pattern 7777
 session protocol sipv2
 session target ipv4:172.18.110.65
 voice-class sip profiles 777
 codec g711ulaw
```

Example 4-35 details a set of debugs for the configuration shown in Example 4-31. Notice the outbound dial peer match of 777. This is where the outbound SIP profile is applied. Thus the addition of the new header occurs when the SIP profile is executed on the SIP INVITE request. The new SIP message containing the added header is then put on the wire and sent on the network.

Example 4-35 *Debugs for Adding a Diversion Header*

```
May 19 21:05:57.762: //125/6B6A2E000000/CCAPI/ccCallSetupRequest:
   Guid=6B6A2E00-0001-0000-0000-001A306E12AC, Outgoing Dial-peer=777


May 19 21:05:57.762: //-1/xxxxxxxxxxxx/SIP/Info/info/64/sipSPISetSipProfilesTag:
  voice class SIPProfiles tag is set : 777
May 19 21:05:57.763: //-1/xxxxxxxxxxxx/SIP/Info/info/64/sip_profiles_application_
  change_sip_headers:  New header added to the SIP message : Diversion: <sip:1234@
  example.com>


May 19 21:05:57.764: //126/6B6A2E000000/SIP/Msg/ccsipDisplayMsg:
Sent:
INVITE sip:7777@172.18.110.65:5060 SIP/2.0
[..Truncated for brevity..]
Diversion: <sip:1234@example.com>
```

The previous two examples detail a situation in which a Diversion header is not present on the ingress SIP messaging. If a Diversion header is received on the ingress call leg, CUBE passes the Diversion header through to the outbound call leg. Example 4-36 details how to modify a Diversion header that was received and passed through CUBE. Example 4-37 details the received Diversion header field, CUBE SIP profile modification, and egress SIP message after modification. A good rule to remember is that a modification always occurs on a header that is present either by default or by being passed from one call leg to another.

Example 4-36 *Modifying a Diversion Header in an Egress INVITE*

```
!
voice class sip-profiles 888
 request INVITE sip-header Diversion modify "sip:(.*)>" "sip:1234@example.com>"
!
dial-peer voice 888 voip
 destination-pattern 7777
 session protocol sipv2
 session target ipv4:172.18.110.65
 voice-class sip profiles 888
 codec g711ulaw
```

Example 4-37 details the debugs for the configuration in Example 4-36. Notice that the outbound dial peer match occurs on dial peer 888, where the outbound SIP profile is applied. Because you receive an inbound SIP request with a Diversion header, this is going to be passed through CUBE and included in the outbound SIP request. The SIP profile is then able to modify that header because it will be present in the outbound request. The final SIP message containing the modification is then put on the wire and sent across the network.

Example 4-37 *Debugs for Modifying a Diversion Header*

```
Sent:
INVITE sip:7777@172.18.110.48:5060 SIP/2.0
[..Truncated for brevity..]
Diversion: <sip:1024@172.18.110.48>;privacy=off;reason=unconditional;screen=yes
May 19 21:13:27.416: //147/77A2BB000000/CCAPI/ccCallSetupRequest:
   Guid=77A2BB00-0001-0000-0000-001D306E12AC, Outgoing Dial-peer=888
May 19 21:13:27.417: //-1/xxxxxxxxxxxx/SIP/Info/info/64/sipSPISetSipProfilesTag:
  voice class SIPProfiles tag is set : 888


May 19 21:13:27.418: //-1/xxxxxxxxxxxx/SIP/Info/info/64/sip_profiles_application_
  modify_remove_header: Header before modification : Diversion: <sip:1024@172.18.110
  .48>;privacy=off;reason=unconditional;screen=yes
May 19 21:13:27.418: //-1/xxxxxxxxxxxx/SIP/Info/info/64/sip_profiles_application_
  modify_remove_header: Header after modification : Diversion: <sip:1234@example
  .com>;privacy=off;reason=unconditional;screen=yes


Sent:
INVITE sip:7777@172.18.110.65:5060 SIP/2.0
[..Truncated for brevity..]
Diversion: <sip:1234@example.com>;privacy=off;reason=unconditional;screen=yes
```

A common misconception is that an outbound SIP profile can only be applied to an outbound dial peer. This is not the case. The term *outbound SIP profile* references the direction of SIP messaging that needs modification. For example, an administrator may need to modify an outbound SIP message on an inbound call leg. This is achieved by applying the defined SIP profile to an inbound dial peer that is anchored to the call leg where you need to modify outbound SIP messaging.

An example of this use case would be an administrator changing a 100 Trying message sent from CUBE to a 100 Giving a Try message. The 100 Trying response is always sent after CUBE matches an inbound dial peer, and because this is an egress SIP message, from CUBE to the previous hop, this is where you would apply an outbound SIP profile. Example 4-38 details the configuration needed to perform outbound SIP message modification on an inbound dial peer, and Example 4-39 details the outbound SIP 100 Provisional response and the outbound SIP profile modification, which is applied to this egress message. All of this is done by applying an outbound SIP profile to an inbound dial peer.

Example 4-38 *Outbound SIP Profile on an Inbound Dial Peer*

```
!
voice class sip-profiles 164
 response 100 sip-header SIP-StatusLine modify "100 Trying" "100 Giving a Try"
!
dial-peer voice 222 voip
 description INBOUND DIAL-PEER
 session protocol sipv2
 incoming called-number 7777
 voice-class sip profiles 164
 dtmf-relay rtp-nte
 codec g711ulaw
```

Example 4-39 details the debugs for the configuration in Example 4-38. Notice the inbound dial peer match of 222. This is where the outbound SIP profile is defined. CUBE attempts to send a 100 Trying response to the previous hop in order to let that UAC know that it is currently processing the message. Because you have an outbound SIP profile, it is first executed against the 100 Trying message. The message matches the statement and changes the value of the status line to 100 Giving a Try. The message is then put on the wire and sent across the network.

Example 4-39 *Debugs from an Outbound SIP Profile on an Inbound Dial Peer*

```
May 19 21:00:49.005: //-1/B33C85800000/CCAPI/cc_api_call_setup_ind_common:
   Incoming Dial-peer=222, Progress Indication=NULL(0), Calling IE Present=TRUE,


May 19 21:00:49.004: //-1/xxxxxxxxxxxx/SIP/Info/info/64/sipSPISetSipProfilesTag:
  voice class SIPProfiles tag is set : 164
May 19 21:00:49.005: //109/B33C85800000/SIP/Info/info/64/sip_profiles_application_
  modify_stat_line: Status-Line before modification : SIP/2.0 100 Trying
May 19 21:00:49.005: //109/B33C85800000/SIP/Info/info/64/sip_profiles_application_
  modify_stat_line: Status-Line after modification : SIP/2.0 100 Giving a Try
```

```
Sent:
SIP/2.0 100 Giving a Try
Via: SIP/2.0/TCP 172.18.110.48:5060;branch=z9hG4bK3ce13e40fa2
From: <sip:1024@172.18.110.48>;tag=23232~1992ce86-77ac-43a7-91b7-
  90778966a9f5-30207641
To: <sip:7777@172.18.110.58>
Call-ID: b33c8580-b0019080-a4-306e12ac@172.18.110.48
CSeq: 101 INVITE
Content-Length: 0
```

Inbound SIP Profiles

Like their outbound counterpart, inbound SIP profiles are used to manipulate aspects of a SIP message, including SIP headers and the SDP body. The syntax of an inbound SIP profile is exactly the same as that of an outbound SIP profile; the main differences between them are in their use and application.

Inbound SIP profiles modify ingress messages on CUBE globally or for each dial peer. Just as with outbound SIP profiles, an administrator can apply an inbound SIP profile to an inbound or outbound dial peer. Inbound SIP profiles allow an administrator to modify a SIP message *before* CUBE processes the message. This gives an administrator great flexibility in modifying SIP messages and SDP bodies of inbound traffic before that traffic is actually processed by CUBE.

Inbound SIP profile support must be enabled globally before the feature can be used on a SIP message (see Example 4-40).

Example 4-40 *Enabling Inbound SIP Profile Support*

```
voice service voip
 sip
  sip-profiles inbound
```

When inbound SIP profile support is enabled, an administrator can start the process of defining a SIP profile. When the definition of the desired SIP profile is complete, it is applied to either global configuration or dial peers by postfixing the keyword **inbound** to the normal **sip-profile** command, as shown in Example 4-41.

Example 4-41 *Applying an Inbound SIP Profile*

```
! Global Application
!
voice service voip
 sip
  sip-profiles 555 inbound
!
```

```
! Dial-peer Application
!
dial-peer voice 555 voip
 voice-class sip profiles 555 inbound
!
```

Examples 4-42 and 4-43 show an inbound SIP profile being used to convert a received Date header in a SIP INVITE from EST to GMT. RFC 3261 explicitly states that Date headers must be in the GMT format, and the reception of a nonstandard Date header would cause this call to fail. An administrator can use an inbound SIP profile to perform the desired modification on the Date header before the CUBE application processes the message and, as a result, avoid undesired session termination.

Example 4-42 *Configuring an Inbound SIP Profile*

```
voice service voip
 sip
  sip-profiles inbound
!
voice class sip-profiles 111
 request ANY sip-header Date modify "EST" "GMT"
!
dial-peer voice 1 voip
 session protocol sipv2
 incoming called-number 1234
 voice-class sip profiles 111 inbound
 codec g711ulaw
```

Example 4-43 details the debugs for the configuration in Example 4-39. Here we see a received INVITE with a Date header containing the problematic EST value. An inbound dial peer match occurs, and the inbound SIP profile defined on that dial peer is triggered. As a result, the EST is changed to GMT. This is all done before the SIP message is parsed by the SIP stack, thus circumventing the failure that may have occurred without the manual change to this header.

Example 4-43 *Debugs for an Inbound SIP Profile*

```
Received:
INVITE sip:1234@172.18.110.58:5060 SIP/2.0
Via: SIP/2.0/UDP 172.18.110.65:5060;branch=z9hG4bK-16095-1-0
From: <sip:7777@172.18.110.65:5060>;tag=1
To: sut <sip:1234@172.18.110.58:5060>
Call-ID: 1-16095@172.18.110.65
CSeq: 1 INVITE
Contact: sip:7777@172.18.110.65:5060
```

```
Max-Forwards: 70
Supported: timer
Date: Fri, 25 May 2018 21:01:13 EST
Session-Refresh: 1800;refresher=uac
Subject: Performance Test
Content-Type: application/sdp
Content-Length:   130

v=0
o=user1 53655765 2353687637 IN IP4 172.18.110.65
s=-
c=IN IP4 172.18.110.65
t=0 0
m=audio 6000 RTP/AVP 0
a=maxptime:20

May 25 21:07:12.568: //-1/xxxxxxxxxxxx/SIP/Info/verbose/64/ccsip_inbound_profile_
  populate_callinfo_in_ccb: Dial-peer 1 is used for inbound profiles config
May 25 21:07:12.568: //-1/xxxxxxxxxxxx/SIP/Info/info/64/sipSPISetSipProfilesTag:
  voice class SIP Profiles inbound tag is set : 111
May 25 21:07:12.568: //-1/xxxxxxxxxxxx/SIP/Info/info/64/sip_profiles_application_
  modify_remove_header: Header before modification : Date: Fri, 25 May 2018 21:01:13
  EST
May 25 21:07:12.568: //-1/xxxxxxxxxxxx/SIP/Info/info/64/sip_profiles_application_
  modify_remove_header: Header after modification : Date: Fri, 25 May 2018 21:01:13
  GMT
```

SIP Copylist

A SIP copylist is a special type of SIP profile that allows CUBE to copy contents from a SIP header as a variable that is stored in memory for later use. The value of this variable can then be used in an outbound SIP profile to manipulate SIP message data.

A SIP copylist can be used to expand on the Diversion header example previously demonstrated in the discussion of outbound SIP profiles. The application of a copylist within this example allows the modification statements to use a variable rather than statically defined data. Subsequently, this variable acts as a placeholder for a large number of potential patterns. Example 4-44 shows a sample configuration in which the copylist will copy the user in the From header URI of the ingress INVITE. CUBE then store that value as variable **u01**. Then, by referencing this variable in the outbound SIP profile statement, the outbound SIP profile can be made to operate with potentially limitless patterns, as long as the patterns follow a specific syntax allowing the regex to properly match. When the outbound SIP profile executes its logic, it inserts the data from the variable **u01**. Example 4-45 displays the entire process and debugs for the full copylist scenario.

Example 4-44 *SIP Copylist Example for a Diversion Header*

```
!
voice class sip-copylist 2
 sip-header From
!
dial-peer voice 2 voip
 voice-class sip copy-list 2
!
voice class sip-profiles 888
 request INVITE peer-header sip From copy "<sip:(.*)@" u01
 request INVITE sip-header Diversion modify "sip:(.*)>" "sip:\u01@example.com>"
!
dial-peer voice 888 voip
 voice-class sip profiles 888
!
```

Example 4-45 shows the debugs from CUBE for the configuration shown in Example 4-44. Here you can see a received INVITE with the From header containing user 1027. An inbound dial peer match occurs, and the SIP copylist is applied. You can see that the SIP copylist executes and successfully matches the value of 1027, as you would expect. This value is then stored as variable **u01** for later use. Outbound dial peer matching occurs, and the SIP profile defined on that dial peer is executed. The value from the **u01** variable is then subsisted in the SIP profile, which means 1027 is now placed in the Diversion header. Finally, you see the outbound SIP INVITE and modified Diversion header sent to the next hop, and it contains the 1027 value copied from the inbound INVITE's From header.

Example 4-45 *Debugs for the SIP Copylist for a Diversion Header*

```
Received:
INVITE sip:7777@172.18.110.58:5060 SIP/2.0
Via: SIP/2.0/TCP 172.18.110.48:5060;branch=z9hG4bK3e82ddee05f
From: <sip:1027@172.18.110.48>;tag=23337~1992ce86-77ac-43a7-91b7-
  90778966a9f5-30207669

May 19 21:37:58.510: //-1/E46B84800000/CCAPI/cc_api_call_setup_ind_common:
   Incoming Dial-peer=2, Progress Indication=NULL(0), Calling IE Present=TRUE,

May 19 21:37:58.512: //201/E46B84800000/CCAPI/ccCallSetupRequest:
   Guid=E46B8480-0001-0000-0000-0020306E12AC, Outgoing Dial-peer=888

May 19 21:37:58.513: //-1/xxxxxxxxxxxx/SIP/Info/info/64/sipSPISetSipProfilesTag:
  voice class SIPProfiles tag is set : 888
May 19 21:37:58.513: //-1/xxxxxxxxxxxx/SIP/Info/info/64/sip_profiles_prefix_slash_
  in_copy_var_val: ret_dst: 1027
```

```
May 19 21:37:58.513: //202/E46B84800000/SIP/Info/info/64/sip_profiles_application_
  peer_copy_pattern: SIP Profiles COPY variable: u01 val: 1027
May 19 21:37:58.514: //-1/xxxxxxxxxxxx/SIP/Info/info/64/sip_profiles_application_
  modify_remove_header: Header before modification : Diversion: <sip:1024@172.18.110
  .48>;privacy=off;reason=unconditional;screen=yes
May 19 21:37:58.514: //202/E46B84800000/SIP/Info/info/64/sip_profiles_check_and_get_
  variables_in_replace_pattern: Node found: COPY variable: u01 val: 1027
May 19 21:37:58.514: //202/E46B84800000/SIP/Info/info/64/sip_profiles_check_and_get_
  variables_in_replace_pattern: substituted_replace_pattern : sip:1027
May 19 21:37:58.514: //202/E46B84800000/SIP/Info/info/64/sip_profiles_check_and_get_
  variables_in_replace_pattern: configured_replace_pattern : @example.com>
May 19 21:37:58.514: //202/E46B84800000/SIP/Info/info/64/sip_profiles_check_and_
  get_variables_in_replace_pattern: Final substituted_replace_pattern : sip:1027@
  example.com>
May 19 21:37:58.514: //-1/xxxxxxxxxxxx/SIP/Info/info/64/sip_profiles_application_
  modify_remove_header: Header after modification : Diversion: <sip:1027@example
  .com>;privacy=off;reason=unconditional;screen=yes


May 19 21:37:58.514: //202/E46B84800000/SIP/Msg/ccsipDisplayMsg:
Sent:
INVITE sip:7777@172.18.110.65:5060 SIP/2.0
[..Truncated for brevity..]
Diversion: <sip:1027@example.com>;privacy=off;reason=unconditional;screen=yes
```

Tip SIP copylist stores the variable data from the SIP message only until the next egress SIP message is sent. After the egress message is sent, the contents of the variable are flushed.

Common SIP Profiles

An administrator may need to modify the URI of a SIP header to meet specific formatting requirements of the next hop. Example 4-46 shows how to modify the user portion, the host portion, or the entire URI. This modification can be used for any SIP header and is not limited to the Contact header.

Example 4-46 *Modifying the User, Host, or Entire URI in a SIP Header*

```
! User
!
voice class sip-profiles 1
 request ANY sip-header Contact modify "sip:(.*)@" "sip:7777@"
!
```

```
! Host
!
voice class sip-profiles 2
 request ANY sip-header Contact modify "@10.10.10.10>" "@example.com>"
!

! Modify the full URI, Both User and Host
!
voice class sip-profiles 3
 request ANY sip-header Contact modify "sip:(.*)>" "sip:7777@example.com>"
!
```

A situation may arise in which an administrator needs to modify the received caller name in a SIP header. Normally this would happen if a caller ID (CLID) name of **Anonymous** or **Unknown** is being received in a SIP message. The caller ID name is displayed in a SIP message as a quoted string between the specific header and the SIP URI, as shown here:

```
From: "MY CLID NAME" <sip:1234@10.10.10.10>
```

Example 4-47 demonstrates a way to match everything in the quotes within the content of the From header. The modification statement produces "TEST CLID" as the output in the From header content.

Example 4-47 *Modifying the Caller ID Name*

```
voice class sip-profiles 123
 request INVITE sip-header From modify "\".*\"" "\"TEST CLID*\""
```

Tip The command **clid strip** can be defined under a dial peer to remove the caller ID name if removal rather than modification is desired.

This chapter previously defined many different ways an UPDATE can be utilized to change aspects of a session. From caller ID updates to media description updates and even session refresh updates, the possibilities are endless. However, if an administrator does not want to advertise update capabilities on CUBE for a specific call leg, the code in Example 4-48 can be used to remove the UPDATE extension from the Allow header. The result of this SIP profile is that the SIP messages sent do not contain the UPDATE entry in the Allow header. Thus, a device receiving the message should not send an UPDATE to this SBC any reason.

Example 4-48 *Removing UPDATE Advertisement on CUBE*

```
voice class sip-profiles 200
 request ANY sip-header Allow-Header modify ", UPDATE" ""
 response ANY sip-header Allow-Header modify ", UPDATE" ""
```

There may arise a situation in which sending one of the hold methods defined in the hold/resume section may produce issues with a remote device. Example 4-49 defines different methods of modifying the audio media attributes for a=sendonly or a=inactive and replacing them with a=sendrecv. The use of a pipe character (|) is the regex OR method and essentially presents a list of alternatives. Thus, the statement is looking for either audio direction attribute (a=) in parentheses, and if either is present, the modification will take place.

In addition, Example 4-49 details how to change the connection address that is all zeros, 0.0.0.0, to a real IP address. This can be defined for both requests and responses, depending on the direction of messaging that needs to be modified. An administrator could replace 10.10.10.10 with the desired IP address.

Example 4-49 *Hold/Resume or Audio Interop with a Provider*

```
voice class sip-profiles 300
 request ANY sdp-header Audio-Attribute modify "(a=sendonly|a=inactive)"
  "a=sendrecv"
 request ANY sdp-header Audio-Connection-Info modify "0.0.0.0" "10.10.10.10"
 response ANY sdp-header Audio-Attribute modify "(a=sendonly|a=inactive)"
  "a=sendrecv"
 response ANY sdp-header Audio-Connection-Info modify "0.0.0.0" "10.10.10.10"
```

Example 4-50 shows how to insert the option **user=phone** into any To header within a SIP request or response. This example also details the concept of a set. Each set in regex is a grouping of data within a pair of parentheses. In Example 4-50, the SIP profile is grabbing everything between the < and > characters and storing it as set 1. The **\1** is a back reference that allows IOS or IOS XE to call the data from the set 1 that was previous stored. Up to nine unique sets can be used within a SIP profile. The data in a set correlates with the order in which the data appears in a **match** statement.

Example 4-50 *Modifying a To Header with Sets*

```
voice class sip-profile 400
 request ANY sip-header To modify "<(.*)>" "<\1;user=phone>"
 response ANY sip-header To modify "<(.*)>" "<\1;user=phone>"
```

Later versions of CUBE allow a user to define a rule tag on a SIP profile. This capability was added to allow for the definite ordering of SIP profile statements and to facilitate quicker modification of statements. Without a rule tag, an administrator must first delete the statement and then add it back; otherwise, the statement is duplicated and placed at the end of the current list of statements. Example 4-51 details a simple SIP profile with rule tags. This example also shows the modification of a SIP header into its shorthand form.

Example 4-51 *A SIP Profile with Three Rules*

```
voice class sip-profiles 1234
 rule 1 request INVITE sip-header From modify "From:" "f:"
 rule 2 request INVITE sip-header To modify "To:" "t:"
 rule 3 request INVITE sip-header Contact modify "Contact:" "m:"
```

The commands **voice sip sip-profiles downgrade** and **voice sip sip-profiles upgrade** can be used to either remove or add the rule statements from previously configured SIP profiles. Example 4-52 shows the use of these commands.

Example 4-52 *Dynamic Rule Tag*

```
CUBE# voice sip sip-profiles upgrade
CUBE# show run | s 1234
voice class sip-profiles 1234
 rule 1 request INVITE sip-header From modify "From:" "f:"
 rule 2 request INVITE sip-header To modify "To:" "t:"
 rule 3 request INVITE sip-header Contact modify "Contact:" "m:"

CUBE# voice sip sip-profiles downgrade
CUBE# show run | s 1234
voice class sip-profiles 1234
 request INVITE sip-header From modify "From:" "f:"
 request INVITE sip-header To modify "To:" "t:"
 request INVITE sip-header Contact modify "Contact:" "m:"
```

Tip It is important to note that if rule tags are being used and an administrator downgrades IOS to a version where rules tags are not present, the SIP profile will be lost. The rule tag command was introduced in IOS 15.5(2)T and IOS XE 3.15S. It is recommended to issue the **voice sip sip-profiles downgrade** command before downgrading software versions.

Troubleshooting SIP Profiles

SIP profiles allow for granular control over SIP messages, but improper configuration can lead to incorrect formatting of SIP messages, SIP headers, or SDP. Always refer to the applicable RFCs when manipulating any SIP messages to avoid violating the standard formatting of a header and causing undesired call failures. If a modified SIP message is no longer RFC compliant, an upstream device may respond with a 400 Bad Request or another 4xx client-level error indicating that the modification is not accepted.

Use the following debugs to triage and troubleshoot SIP profile configuration and configuration issues:

```
debug ccsip messages
debug ccsip info
debug ccsip feature sip-profile
debug voip ccapi inout
```

You can also leverage the Cisco SIP-Profile Test tool (see https://cway.cisco.com/tools/SipProfileTest) to test SIP profiles without the need to make any changes to a device or perform test calls.

As shown in Figure 4-40, to use this tool, you input the SIP message you would like to modify, along with the proposed SIP profile. The tool then runs the SIP profile against the SIP message provided and displays the output before and after modification, highlighting the items that were modified or added.

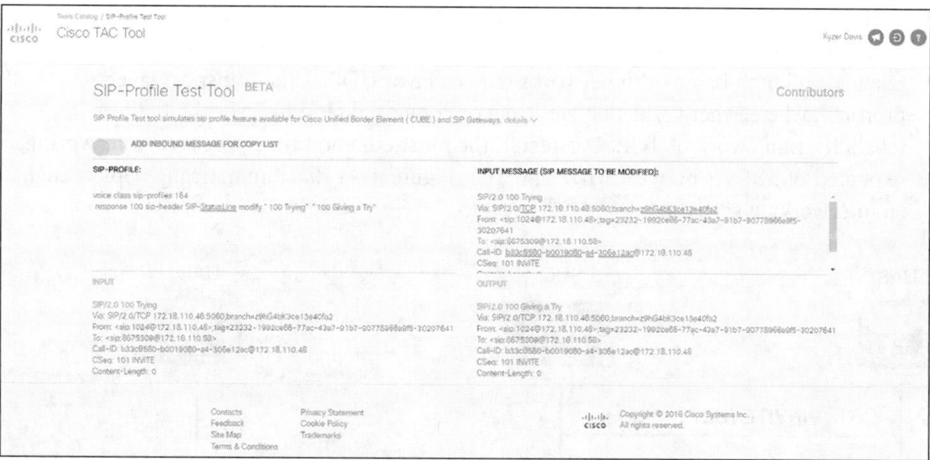

Figure 4-40 *The SIP-Profile Test Tool*

Transport and Protocol Interworking

The previous sections of this chapter discuss how to manage SIP–SIP interworking, including SIP mid-call signaling, header manipulation, SIP message normalization, and other items specific to SIP session establishment. These are all Layer 7 items, actions, and behaviors performed by an SBC. Diving deeper into the Open Systems Interconnection

(OSI) stack, next we take a look at Layer 3 and Layer 4 interworking on SBCs. This section includes the following interworking examples:

- Transport layer interworking between different transport layer protocols
- IP interworking between networks that implement different IP versions
- ICE interworking

Layer 4 Transport Interworking

RFC 3261 specifies that any device handling SIP *must* have mandatory support for UDP and TCP as transport protocols for SIP. In addition, SIP can be transported over SCTP and multicast UDP. However, the use of SCTP is not widely adopted, and the most common implementations of SIP use unicast UDP. Additional security can be provided over TCP by using TLS to encrypt the contents of a SIP message and strengthen security on a per-hop basis. TLS as a transport mechanism is further discussed in Chapter 6, "Secure Signaling and Media." In addition to these transport methods, newer standards, such as RFC 7118, detail the use of the WebSockets protocol as a transport mechanism for SIP, although adoption of this method has been relatively slow.

Due to the per-hop nature of transport protocols and the fact that SBCs are often deployed between two real-time networks that might require the use of different transport layer protocols, SBCs need to be able perform Layer 4 interworking. Fast, reliable, and high-bandwidth networks tend to favor UDP as the transport layer protocol, whereas networks that are lossy or congested tend to favor the built-in reliability framework of TCP. As a result, the most common transport layer interworking expected of SBCs is between UDP and TCP. Figure 4-41 diagrammatically depicts such an interworking scenario.

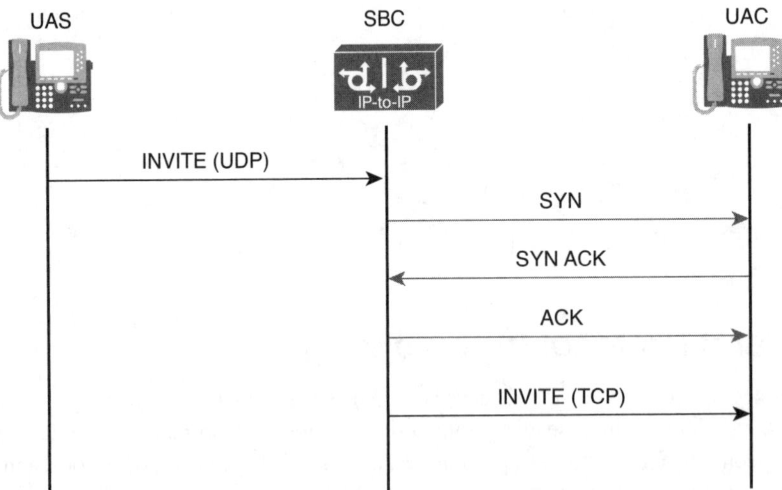

Figure 4-41 *UDP and TCP Transport Interworking on an SBC*

When selecting the transport protocol, it is important to understand the advantages and disadvantages that each transport protocol offers with regard to SIP. An administrator must also take into account additional network requirements that may be in play, such as LAN and WAN requirements and other devices, such as firewalls. Table 4-8 compares TCP and UDP when SIP is the application data being transmitted.

Table 4-8 *Comparison of UDP and TCP Protocols*

Feature or Capability	UDP	TCP
Connection type	Connectionless.	Established after a three-way handshake. TCP also provides periodic keepalives between nodes.
Transport reliability	No reliability or confirmation that a message was received.	TCP ACK is required for every received segment.
Error handling	Requires SIP message retransmission, wait timers, and retries before a timeout occurs.	If the initial three-way handshake is not successful, the device can immediately try another destination, thus greatly increasing failover times. TCP retransmissions can occur if no ACK is received for a particular segment. In addition, if a socket closes prematurely, a device can disconnect the session.
Message size limit	Dependent on the MTU. Larger messages may be fragmented and require re-assembly.	No fragmentation.
Processing and memory overhead	Small when dealing with large numbers of SIP sessions.	Slightly larger as there is more messaging per SIP session. As the number of sessions grows, the overhead increases.*
Security	DTLS can be employed to encrypt UDP traffic. DTLS is normally used by SRTP and not SIP traffic.	TLS can be employed to encrypt SIP signaling.

* TCP streams can be reused if a socket is still open between two endpoints.

CUBE, like most other SBCs, supports the reception of SIP messages through Unicast UDP, TCP, and TLS by default, without any need for any additional configuration. The command **show sip-ua status** can be used to view active transports over which CUBE is listening for connections (see Example 4-53). The commands that enable CUBE to handle inbound SIP traffic over UDP, TCP, or TLS are enabled by default under the **sip-ua** section of the configuration, as shown in Example 4-54. It is recommended that you *not* disable these commands.

Example 4-53 show sip-ua status *Detailing Listening Transports*

```
CUBE# show sip-ua status
SIP User Agent Status
SIP User Agent for UDP : ENABLED
SIP User Agent for TCP : ENABLED
SIP User Agent for TLS over TCP : ENABLED
```

Example 4-54 show run all *with the Commands for Listening Transports*

```
CUBE# show run all | i sip-ua
sip-ua
 transport udp
 transport tcp tls
 transport tcp
```

For egress connections, UDP is enabled by default at the global and dial peer levels. TCP is configurable globally or per dial peer, as shown in Example 4-55. UDP connections sourced from CUBE always use a random ephemeral port as the source for the UDP session. Some devices or firewalls may require that UDP SIP traffic be sourced from SIP port 5060. This can be accomplished by adding the command shown in Example 4-56.

Example 4-55 *Configuring CUBE Outbound Transport*

```
voice service voip
 sip
  session transport tcp
!
dial-peer voice 1 voip
 session transport tcp
```

Example 4-56 *Configuring CUBE Connection Reuse*

```
sip-ua
 connection-reuse
```

TCP connections with CUBE are always sourced from a random ephemeral port. There is no command to make TCP source from 5060, as there is with UDP. Instead, CUBE makes use of the built-in connection reuse behavior offered by TCP. If a TCP connection is already open between CUBE and another device, CUBE reuses that connection for sending SIP messages even if they are for a different SIP session. This behavior is displayed in Figure 4-42.

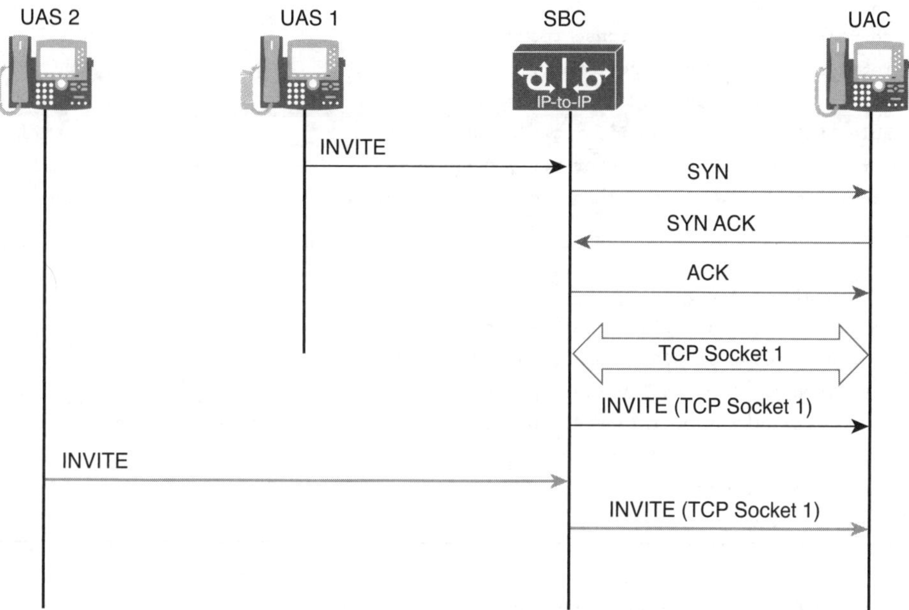

Figure 4-42 *Reusing a TCP Socket for Multiple Requests*

With UDP as the transport protocol, the only two restrictions on the size of a SIP message are the maximum size of a datagram packet (65,535) and the maximum transmission unit (MTU) size of a network path. As a result, when using UDP, a large SIP message with lots of SIP headers and a verbose message body may be fragmented due the aforementioned MTU size. It may not be desirable to fragment SIP packets, and thus RFC 3261 states, "If a request is within 200 bytes of the path MTU, or if it is larger than 1300 bytes and the path MTU is unknown, the request MUST be sent using...congestion controlled transport protocol, such as TCP." CUBE supports dynamic protocol switching through the command **transport switch udp tcp** can be defined globally or on dial-peers as **voice-class sip transport switch udp tcp**.

Because UDP is connectionless, SIP requests and responses that do not receive a response will be retransmitted the default number of times specified with command **show sip-ua retry**. The retransmission rate is also defined using **show sip-ua timers**.

These timers and retry values are configurable through **sip-ua**, as shown in Examples 4-57, 4-58, and 4-59. It is best practice to follow the values outlined in the RFC 3261 table "A Table of Timer Values."

Example 4-57 show sip-ua retry *and* show sip-ua timers

```
CUBE# show sip-ua retry
SIP UA Retry Values
invite retry count = 6    response retry count = 6
bye retry count    = 10   cancel retry count   = 10
prack retry count  = 10   update retry count    = 6
reliable 1xx count = 6    notify retry count   = 10
refer retry count  = 10   register retry count = 6
info retry count   = 6    subscribe retry count = 6
options retry count = 6

CUBE# show sip-ua timers
SIP UA Timer Values (millisecs unless noted)
trying 500, expires 180000, connect 500, disconnect 500
prack 500, rel1xx 500, notify 500, update 500
refer 500, register 500, info 500, options 500, hold 2880 minutes
, registrar-dns-cache 3600 seconds
tcp/udp aging 5 minutes
tls aging 60 minutes
```

Example 4-58 retry *Commands Under* sip-ua

```
CUBE# show run all | include sip-ua
sip-ua
 retry invite 6
 retry response 6
 retry bye 10
 retry cancel 10
 retry prack 10
 retry update 6
 retry rel1xx 6
 retry notify 10
 retry refer 10
 retry info 6
 retry register 6
 retry subscribe 6
 retry keepalive 6
 retry options 6
```

Example 4-59 timers *Commands Under* sip-ua

```
CUBE# show run all | include sip-ua
sip-ua
 timers trying 500
 timers expires 180000
 timers connect 500
 timers connection aging tls 60
 timers connection aging 5
 timers disconnect 500
 timers prack 500
 timers update 500
 timers rel1xx 500
 timers notify 500
 timers refer 500
 timers hold 2880
 timers info 500
 timers register 500
 timers keepalive down 30
 timers keepalive active 120
 timers dns registrar-cache 3600
 timers options 500
```

When troubleshooting transport interworking with CUBE, always verify the configuration present. If debugs are needed, you can use **debug ccsip messages**, **debug ccsip transport**, and **debug ccsip error** for analysis. If TCP is the transport mechanism, you can use **debug ip tcp transactions** to detail the TCP session establishment. In addition to using debugs, using a packet capture (PCAP) is a great way to see what messages are being exchanged.

Common transport troubleshooting scenarios include the following:

- An outbound dial-peer is matched, but no SIP message is sent. If TCP is being used, there could be a problem establishing the TCP session. Use **debug ip tcp transactions** or a PCAP for errors in the TCP handshake.
- SIP messages sent from CUBE are not getting responses. If UDP is being used, one of a few items is likely occurring. First, the message may not be making it to the remote server because of a potential network issue, assuming that the packet has been put on the wire. The second possibility is that the message is making it to the server, and the server is responding. There is a chance that this response is blocked or dropped by the network, and thus it does not make it back to the originator. In this scenario, the server is receiving the messages from CUBE and generating responses. The responses may not be making it back across the network to CUBE due to network conditions or devices in the network path. If the SIP response is too large, the message may be fragmented due to MTU mismatches somewhere in the network on

the way back to the source. If the source is not configured to reassemble fragmented packets with the command **ip virtual-reassembly in**, then this message could be dropped at Layer 3 before making it back to the Layer 7 CUBE application. It should be noted that an application may set the Don't Fragment (DF) bit inside the UDP packet to 1 rather than to 0, to indicate that it does not want the UDP message to be fragmented. Although this is great in theory, it does not stop a network device on the Layer 3 path from simply discarding a packet that is larger than the path MTU.

- TCP socket errors may occur, such as the socket send being blocked, handshake failures, a large number of retransmissions, erroneous restarts, or remote closures. There is a chance that some device in the network, such as a firewall, may be intercepting and blocking or closing TCP connections between two SIP devices. There is also a possibility of undesired WAN or LAN network conditions, such as loss or high round-trip time (RTT) that adversely affect the TCP connection.

These are only a handful of troubleshooting scenarios that can be encountered when working with the transport layer. For most of the scenarios detailed in the previous section, it is best to troubleshoot using Wireshark to analyze a packet capture taken simultaneously at the source and destination UAC and UAS. Then a comparison of the sent/received SIP messages and transport signaling can be performed. This can be repeated at different points in the network until the problematic hop is identified.

Layer 3 IP Interworking

Because SIP is a voice over IP (VoIP) protocol, it runs on Layer 3 IP networks. The implementation of IP routing that is required is determined by the underlying network requirements specifying where an SBC will exist. Some deployments with an SBC may require only a few static routes, while others may require that a fully autonomous routing protocol, such as BGP, be deployed. The network connection with an ITSP may be a direct point-to-point Ethernet connection or a serial connection, or an SBC may be required to peer over a WAN connection mechanism such as MPLS. On the LAN side, the same complexities or more may exist. In addition, advanced IP routing techniques such as Virtual Route Forwarding (VRF) may be required. These are a few of the reasons it is recommended to confirm an SBC's Layer 3 capabilities against your existing or proposed network requirements.

In terms of IP networking protocols, using IPv4 is the most common method of working with SIP on Layer 3 IP networks. The benefits and drawbacks of IPv4 should be well-known by most networking engineers in this day and age, but further info on the topic of IPv4 as a protocol can be found in the Cisco Press book *IP Routing on Cisco IOS, IOS XE, and IOS XR: An Essential Guide to Understanding and Implementing IP Routing Protocols*. This section details how SIP works with IPv4. Example 4-60 shows a sample IPv4 SIP message inside an IPv4 packet, taken from Wireshark. In this example, you can see that the SIP headers and the SIP body use IPv4 addresses where applicable.

Example 4-60 *IPv4 Packet from Wireshark*

```
Internet Protocol Version 4, Src: 172.18.110.58, Dst: 172.18.110.65
    0100 .... = Version: 4
    .... 0101 = Header Length: 20 bytes (5)
    Differentiated Services Field: 0x68 (DSCP: AF31, ECN: Not-ECT)
    Total Length: 1179
    Identification: 0x0001 (1)
    Flags: 0x00
    Fragment offset: 0
    Time to live: 255
    Protocol: UDP (17)
    Header checksum: 0x8248 [validation disabled]
    Source: 172.18.110.58
    Destination: 172.18.110.65
    [Source GeoIP: Unknown]
    [Destination GeoIP: Unknown]
User Datagram Protocol, Src Port: 61188 (61188), Dst Port: 5060 (5060)
Session Initiation Protocol (INVITE)
    Request-Line: INVITE sip:7777@172.18.110.65:5060 SIP/2.0
    Message Header
        Via: SIP/2.0/UDP 172.18.110.58:5060;branch=z9hG4bK02352
        From: <sip:1024@172.18.110.58>;tag=610B74F-1A77
        To: <sip:7777@172.18.110.65>
        Call-ID: B3ECF320-594011E8-A134DF13-E535538@172.18.110.58
        Supported: 100rel,timer,resource-priority,replaces,sdp-anat
        Min-SE:  1800
        User-Agent: Cisco-SIPGateway/IOS-16.8.1
        Allow: INVITE, OPTIONS, BYE, CANCEL, ACK, PRACK, UPDATE, REFER, SUBSCRIBE,
  NOTIFY, INFO, REGISTER
        CSeq: 101 INVITE
        Timestamp: 1526585907
        Contact: <sip:1024@172.18.110.58:5060>
        Expires: 180
        Allow-Events: telephone-event
        Max-Forwards: 68
        Session-ID: 7187a2a300105000a0000c75bd110ca4;remote=
  00000000000000000000000000000000
        Content-Type: application/sdp
        Content-Disposition: session;handling=required
        Content-Length: 217
```

```
   Message Body
       Session Description Protocol
           Session Description Protocol Version (v): 0
           Owner/Creator, Session Id (o): CiscoSystemsSIP-GW-UserAgent 4133 1623 IN
 IP4 172.18.110.58
           Session Name (s): SIP Call
           Connection Information (c): IN IP4 172.18.110.58
           Time Description, active time (t): 0 0
           Media Description, name and address (m): audio 8002 RTP/AVP 0 19
           Connection Information (c): IN IP4 172.18.110.58
           Media Attribute (a): rtpmap:0 PCMU/8000
           Media Attribute (a): rtpmap:19 CN/8000
           Media Attribute (a): ptime:20
```

Although it is somewhat uncommon, it is also possible to employ IPv6 and SIP with an SBC. The SBC can either run in dual-stack mode, meaning it supports both IPv4 and IPv6, or run in IPv6-only mode. Example 4-61 shows a sample IPv6 SIP message (detailed in RFC 5118). Here you can see that each SIP header that contains an IPv6 address must be wrapped in brackets ([]), leading zeros are dropped, and consecutive groups of zeros are condensed to a double colon (::). IPv6 addresses in the SDP do not require the wrapping of brackets as delimiters, as shown by the connection data information (c=), which also indicates the protocol as **IP6**.

Example 4-61 *Sample IPv6 SIP INVITE*

```
INVITE sip:user@[2001:db8::10] SIP/2.0
To: sip:user@[2001:db8::10]
From: sip:user@example.com;tag=81x2
Via: SIP/2.0/UDP [2001:db8::20];branch=z9hG4bKas3-111
Call-ID: SSG9559905523997077@hlau_4100
Contact: "Caller" <sip:caller@[2001:db8::20]>
CSeq: 8612 INVITE
Max-Forwards: 70
Content-Type: application/sdp
Content-Length: 268

v=0
o=assistant 971731711378798081 0 IN IP6 2001:db8::20
s=Live video feed for today's meeting
c=IN IP6 2001:db8::20
t=3338481189 3370017201
m=audio 6000 RTP/AVP 2
a=rtpmap:2 G726-32/8000
m=video 6024 RTP/AVP 107
a=rtpmap:107 H263-1998/90000
```

If an SBC is IPv6-only capable, its operation is similar to that of an SBC that is IPv4-only capable as both call legs would implement and expect the same IP addressing scheme. The real challenge arises when an SBC interconnects two networks that implement different IP addressing schemes—specifically when one implements IPv4 and the other implements IPv6. The ability to interwork IPv4 and IPv6 signaling and media for different call legs through a B2BUA or SBC is not defined by any RFC. RFC 6157 does detail IPv4/IPv6 SIP proxies, but this is not the same as a B2BUA, which is the category an SBC falls under. As a result, the implementation, features, and restrictions surrounding this topic may vary by SBC vendor.

First, the SBC would need to run in dual-stack mode in this scenario. Second, the SBC must have the capability to understand, decode, and build both IPv4 and IPv6 SIP signaling packets as well as IPv4 and IPv6 RTP media packets, assuming that media is flowing through the SBC. Figure 4-43 details an SBC interworking IPv4 and IPv6 signaling and media in dual-stack mode.

Figure 4-43 *IPv4 and IPv6 Interworking on an SBC*

As an SBC, CUBE runs on the established Cisco ASR, ISR, and CSR platforms. These platforms allow CUBE to make full use of the underlying IOS and IOS XE routing infrastructure available for those platforms. In addition, CUBE supports the three different modes of operation when it comes to Layer 3 SIP interworking: IPv4-only, IPv6-only, and dual-stack modes. The default configuration for CUBE is to accept and send IPv4. Additional commands are required to enable IPv6 or dual-stack modes with CUBE. Example 4-62 shows the commands necessary to enable dual-stack support on CUBE. An optional preference can be given to either IPv4 or IPv6, using the command **protocol mode ipv4 | ipv6 | dual-stack[preference {ipv4 | ipv6}]**. The command **show sip-ua status** is used to confirm which mode CUBE is running, as shown in Example 4-63. SDP supports both IPv4 and IPv6 by default, with no extra configuration needed.

Example 4-62 *Dual-Stack Configuration for CUBE*

```
voice service voip
 shutdown forced
 sip
  call service stop forced
!
sip-ua
 protocol mode dual-stack
!
```

```
voice service voip
 no shutdown
 sip
  no call service stop
```

Tip CUBE does not allow for protocol mode changes unless the SIP service is fully shut down. The **forced** portion of the commands **shutdown** and **call service stop** will result in CUBE dropping any active SIP session on CUBE.

Example 4-63 **show sip-ua status** *Confirming Dual-Stack Operation*

```
CUBE# show sip-ua status
[..Truncated for brevity..]
protocol mode is dual-stack, preference is ipv4
SDP application configuration:
[..Truncated for brevity..]
 Network types supported: IN
 Address types supported: IP4 IP6
```

Tip Alternative Network Address Translation (ANAT) is automatically enabled when CUBE is configured in dual-stack mode. To disable ANAT, issue the command **no anat** under **voice service voip** and the **SIP** subsection.

To configure a dial peer with an IPv6 session target, the IPv6 format **session target ipv6:[ipv6-address]:port** must be used, which includes wrapping the IPv6 address in brackets ([]) as a delimiter. The port is optional, just as with IPv4 session targets. Example 4-64 shows how to configure an IPv6 session target. Signaling and media binding can also be used in dual-stack mode. The operation is the same as with IPv4, in which the IPv4 or IPv6 address of the interface specified is used. If ANAT is desired, the interface specified in the **bind** statement must be configured with IPv4 and IPv6 addresses. If the desired interface is configured with more than one IPv6 address, the **bind** command can be augmented to specify an exact IPv6 address. (This is also detailed in Example 4-64.)

Example 4-64 *Sample IPv6 Dial Peer*

```
dial-peer voice 999 voip
 destination-pattern 9T
 session protocol sipv2
 session target ipv6:[2001:DB8:0:0:8:800:200C:417A]:5060
 voice-class sip bind control source-interface Gig0/0/0 ipv6-address
  2001:DB8:0:1::FFFF
 voice-class sip bind media source-interface Gig0/0/0 ipv6-address
  2001:DB8:0:1::FFFF
```

Example 4-65 details a dual-stack CUBE offering both an IPv4 and IPv6 in the SDP body, while the rest of the SIP message headers use IPv6 addresses. (Chapter 5 provides further information about ANAT.)

Example 4-65 *Sample IPv6 SIP INVITE with ANAT*

```
INVITE sip:6000@[2001:DB8:C18:2:217:59FF:FEDE:8898]:5060 SIP/2.0
Via: SIP/2.0/UDP [2001:DB8:C18:2:223:4FF:FEAC:4540]:5060;branch=z9hG4bK15D1013
From: <sip:1001@[2001:DB8:C18:2:223:4FF:FEAC:4540]>;tag=5EAE624-253A
To: <sip:6000@[2001:DB8:C18:2:217:59FF:FEDE:8898]>
Call-ID: FB05CC74-B08E11E1-82C1F4DD-5665AA1B@2001:DB8:C18:2:223:4FF:FEAC:4540
Supported: timer,resource-priority,replaces,sdp-anat
Min-SE: 1800
Allow: INVITE, OPTIONS, BYE, CANCEL, ACK, PRACK, UPDATE, REFER, SUBSCRIBE, NOTIFY,
  INFO, REGISTER
CSeq: 101 INVITE
Contact: <sip:1001@[2001:DB8:C18:2:223:4FF:FEAC:4540]:5060>
Expires: 180
Allow-Events: telephone-event
Max-Forwards: 69
Content-Type: application/sdp
Content-Length: 443
v=0
o=CiscoSystemsSIP-GW-UserAgent 7132 4992 IN IP6 2001:DB8:C18:2:223:33FF:FEB1:B440
s=SIP Call
t=0 0
a=group:ANAT 1 2
m=audio 16712 RTP/AVP 18 0 19
c=IN IP6 2001:DB8:C18:2:223:4FF:FEAC:4540
a=mid:1
a=rtpmap:18 G729/8000
a=fmtp:18 annexb=no
a=rtpmap:0 PCMU/8000
a=rtpmap:19 CN/8000
m=audio 16714 RTP/AVP 18 0 19
c=IN IP4 9.44.30.14
a=mid:2
a=rtpmap:18 G729/8000
a=fmtp:18 annexb=no
a=rtpmap:0 PCMU/8000
```

Tip IETF Draft *draft-klatsky-dispatch-ipv6-impact-ipv4-03* details many different problematic scenarios that may arise with IPv4 and IPv6 SIP interworking.

Interworking Protocol Extensions

As indicated so far, an SBC lies at the edges of disparate networks that may support a host of different SIP extensions. An SBC may be employed in a scenario where one network does not support a particular extension but another network requires that extension to establish a session.

One of the most popular SIP extensions is Interactive Connectivity Establishment (ICE). ICE is discussed in depth in Chapter 5, but at this point, it is important to consider that an SBC may need to interwork ICE and non-ICE networks. An example of this scenario would be a public network that requires ICE to facilitate NAT traversal. The SIP message sent to the SBC might contain the **Require: ice** tag, and thus the SBC must be equipped to handle this requested. On the other call leg, such as to an enterprise LAN, an SBC may not be required to perform any NAT traversal mechanisms. This scenario would require that the SBC perform ICE and non-ICE interworking as well as media interworking for the LAN devices that do not require ICE. Figure 4-44 displays an SBC performing ICE interworking with a public network and a local LAN. This is the most common scenario for deploying ICE with an SBC or a B2BUA. ICE interworking with a B2BUA is further discussed in RFC 7584.

Figure 4-44 *ICE and Non-ICE Interworking on an SBC*

Supplementary Services

In telephony, *supplementary services* are features that allow a device, a user, or an endpoint to enhance a phone call in some way. These are items that usually occur in addition to the act of placing and receiving phone calls. They can take place during session establishment, after session establishment, or even outside a session altogether. Most supplementary services are provided by the call agent/server responsible for endpoint registration and call control rather than an SBC. That being said, they often involve an SBC, so an SBC must be able to handle specific signaling required to successfully complete the actions of the supplementary service. In addition, not all supplementary services are offered by every vendor. For example, Vendor A may have a set of supplementary services that its endpoints can perform, while vendor B may have a subset of these services but may include some proprietary services that only its endpoints can utilize. This makes listing all the available supplementary services very difficult.

However, there are some basic, universal supplementary services that have been adopted by most telephony vendors. These services may have been included in or have their own industry standards, although it is not required. Most endpoints support the ability to perform a hold/resume during a call, forward a call from one phone to another, transfer an established call from one phone to another, join together multiple calls into a conference, illuminate message waiting indicators, and perform call waiting functions, such as call barge, call paging, and many more.

The previous sections of this chapter detail supplementary services such as hold, resume, and transfer as they occur during mid-call signaling, after a session is established. The following sections detail a few key supplementary services that take place either during session establishment or outside of an established session (that is, out-of-dialog OOD events).

Call Forwarding

Consider the following scenarios:

- A receptionist steps out for lunch and may be required to forward his phone, temporarily, to a different phone to cover for the calls that come in during that time.
- A user will be out of the office traveling and would like to send all calls destined for her desk phone to her cell phone.
- A user was unable to answer his device, and the call is sent to a voicemail application, so that the caller can leave a message for the called party.

In these scenarios, the devices are performing basic call forwarding. The first and second scenarios describe call forward all (CFWALL), and the third scenario describes a call forward no answer (CFWNOAN). There are also additional scenarios that trigger call forwarding, such as when the endpoint is busy on another call or when the endpoint is temporarily unregistered from its call agent.

While the basic idea of call forwarding may appear simple, SIP signaling requires methods of handling these scenarios in a way that allows a session to be established with the new device in which the call was forwarded to rather than the one originally called. It is important to note that all these scenarios take place before a call is established and the offer/answer is complete. This means they differ from a call transfer in terms of how a call agent and SBC must handle them.

The most common method of handling call forwarding is with the use of a 3xx SIP message sent in response to the initial INVITE. The most common type of message used is the 302 Moved Temporarily SIP response. Upon reception of a 302 Moved Temporarily message, an SBC should retry a new request (INVITE) to the address specified in the Contact header. Figure 4-45 displays a call from the PSTN through an SBC that is sent to IP Phone A. This phone is forwarded to a different number, and the INVITE receives a 302 response. The SBC then has the option to disconnect the session or send a new request to the defined forward target, as seen in the contact header through a new INVITE.

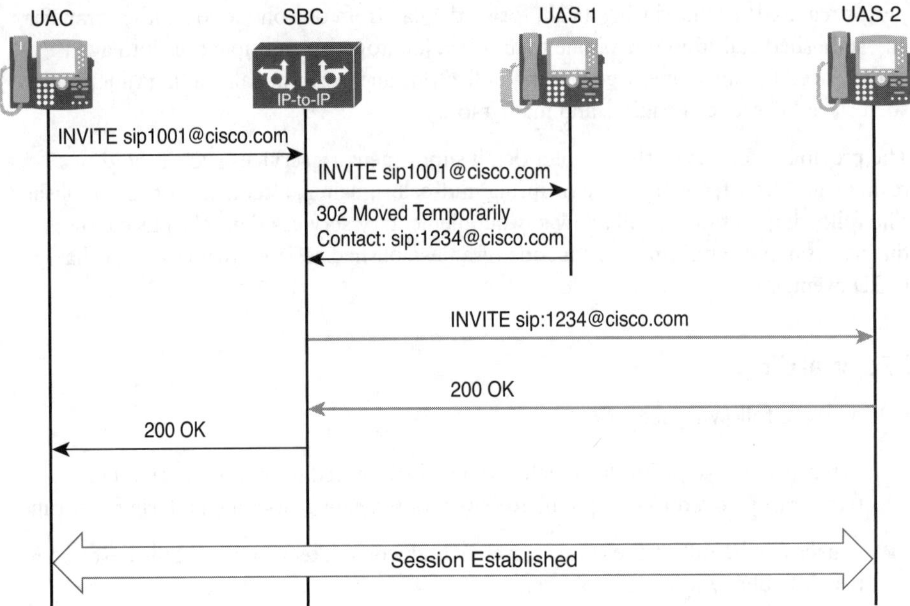

Figure 4-45 *SIP Messaging for 302 Moved Temporarily*

Chapter 13, "Security Threat Mitigation," provides more information about the security considerations surrounding the use of a 3xx message during session establishment. The command shown in Example 4-66 needs to be defined if an administrator would like CUBE to handle a 302 Moved Temporarily response; if this command is not defined, CUBE will not attempt to route to the 302 message's specified Contact header.

Example 4-66 *Enabling CUBE to Process a 302 Moved Temporarily Message*

```
voice service voip
 no notify redirect ip2ip
```

Message Waiting Indicator (MWI)

A message waiting indicator (MWI) is a light, an icon, or a sound on an IP endpoint that is used to signify that there is a new message waiting in a user's voicemail box. An MWI message is not usually sent by an SBC but rather is sent by a voicemail server. However, an SBC may be employed to interwork SIP signaling between the voicemail server and the call agent responsible for an IP endpoint. This means that because the SBC is in the signaling path between the voicemail server and call agent, it may be responsible for forwarding an MWI message that it receives to a specific destination.

With SIP, MWI messages normally take the form of SIP NOTIFY messages, as shown in Example 4-67. Such a NOTIFY message may be part of an existing subscription that follows the RFC 6665 SUBSCRIBE process. This process is defined in Chapter 7 for DTMF messages, such as SIP-KPML, which also use the same SIP subscription-based method. Although subscription-based MWI notification does exist, the most common implementation of MWI with SIP uses the concept of unsolicited NOTIFY, which means the SIP NOTIFY message is sent without any dialog or existing subscription. Such events are often defined as OOD events.

An SBC interworking voicemail application and call agents must be able to interwork MWI, or users will never know they have voicemail messages. In Example 4-67 you can see that the NOTIFY message for MWI will contain an Event header with the type message-summary. The message body of a NOTIFY message containing MWI will be defined with **Content-Type application/simple-message-summary**. Common values in this message body are the **Message-Waiting yes** or **no** value and the **Voice-Message** section, which indicates the total number of unread messages, the total number of old messages, and possibly also the number of unread urgent messages and the total number of urgent messages in parenthesis. Optional message body sections may exist, such as **Fax-Message**, **Message-Account**, and even vendor-proprietary headers.

Example 4-67 *Sample MWI SIP NOTIFY Message*

```
NOTIFY sip:1234@172.18.110.58:5060 SIP/2.0
Via: SIP/2.0/UDP 172.18.110.65:5060;branch=z9hG4bK-8381-1-0
From: <sip:7777@172.18.110.65:5060>;tag=1
To: <sip:1234@172.18.110.58:5060>
Call-ID: 1-8381@172.18.110.65
CSeq: 101 NOTIFY
Max-Forwards: 70
User-Agent: VOICEMAIL
Event: message-summary
Contact: sip:7777@172.18.110.65:5060
Content-Type: application/simple-message-summary
Content-Length:   110

Messages-Waiting: yes
Voice-Message: 1/3 (0/1)
Fax-Message: 0/0 (0/0)
Message-Account: sip:1234@cisco.com
```

Continuing with the example shown in Example 4-67, you can decode the format for the **Voice-Message** entry in the message body. These values convey the following:

- 1 Unread New Message
- 3 Read Old Messages
- 0 Unread New Urgent Message
- 1 Read Old Urgent Message

CUBE has the ability to pass through MWI events using the configuration shown in Example 4-68. Without this configuration, CUBE rejects MWI NOTIFY messages with the SIP response 481 Call Leg/Transaction Does Not Exist. The **voice-class sip-event** is used to define the type of event to pass. In the case of MWI, the event type is **message-summary**, according to RFC 3842. This is then configured globally through **voice service voip** and the **SIP** subsection. With this in place, CUBE can match a NOTIFY event for MWI with the type of event that should be passed through. CUBE then routes NOTIFY messages based on a basic dial peer check to find out where the user is located. The session target on this dial peer is where the NOTIFY should be sent. A 200 OK to the NOTIFY message ends the dialog.

Example 4-68 *CUBE MWI Passthrough Configuration*

```
!
voice class sip-event 1
 event message-summary
!
voice service voip
 sip
  pass-thru subscribe-notify-events 1
!
dial-peer voice 1 voip
 destination-pattern 1234
 session protocol sipv2
 session target ipv4:172.18.110.48
 incoming called-number 1234
```

Example 4-69 shows the debug output from **debug ccsip message** and **debug ccsip info** for the configuration provided in Example 4-68. Here you survey a SIP NOTIFY for MWI being sent to CUBE. CUBE then confirms that this is a NOTIFY that does not belong to any existing subscriptions. After this, CUBE checks for any configured passthrough lists and compares the received message event against the configured list. This results in a positive match, and CUBE then attempts to route the NOTIFY using an applicable dial peer for the user portion of the request URI. CUBE finds dial peer 1 suitable and sends the NOTIFY to the session target on that dial peer. If the match on the event does not occur, CUBE sends a 481 Call/Transaction Does Not Exist because there is no existing SIP subscription for this NOTIFY message.

Example 4-69 *CUBE MWI Passthrough Debugs*

```
Received:
NOTIFY sip:1234@172.18.110.58:5060 SIP/2.0
Via: SIP/2.0/UDP 172.18.110.65:5060;branch=z9hG4bK-8381-1-0
From: <sip:7777@172.18.110.65:5060>;tag=1
To: <sip:1234@172.18.110.58:5060>
Call-ID: 1-8381@172.18.110.65
CSeq: 101 NOTIFY
Max-Forwards: 70
```

```
User-Agent: VOICEMAIL
Event: message-summary
Contact: sip:7777@172.18.110.65:5060
Content-Type: application/simple-message-summary
Content-Length:   110

Messages-Waiting: yes
Voice-Message: 1/1 (0/0)
Fax-Message: 0/0 (0/0)
Message-Account: sip:1234@cisco.com

May 30 22:55:29.741: //-1/xxxxxxxxxxxx/SIP/Info/verbose/8192/ccsip_asnl_send_event_
   to_app: collecting route params for Unsol notify
May 30 22:55:29.741: //-1/xxxxxxxxxxxx/SIP/Info/info/128/is_sip_pass_through_config-
   ured_for_sn_event:
 Trying to find the event list for tag 1
May 30 22:55:29.741: //-1/xxxxxxxxxxxx/SIP/Info/info/128/is_sip_pass_through_config-
   ured_for_sn_event:
 Found it!!

Sent:
NOTIFY sip:1234@172.18.110.48:5060 SIP/2.0
Via: SIP/2.0/UDP 172.18.110.58:5060;branch=z9hG4bKBDB1A6E
From: <sip:7777@172.18.110.58>;tag=203509FB-613
To: <sip:1234@172.18.110.48>
Call-ID: EFA4A4C9-639211E8-B2CAB53D-61A2CAEA@172.18.110.58
CSeq: 101 NOTIFY
Max-Forwards: 70
Date: Wed, 30 May 2018 22:52:17 GMT
User-Agent: Cisco-SIPGateway/IOS-16.7.1
Event: message-summary
Subscription-State: terminated
Contact: <sip:7777@172.18.110.58:5060>
Content-Type: application/simple-message-summary
Content-Length: 112

Messages-Waiting: yes
Voice-Message: 1/1 (0/0)
Fax-Message: 0/0 (0/0)
Message-Account: sip:1234@cisco.com
```

Joins/Replaces

RFC 3911 details the use of SIP join to facilitate supplementary services such as barge-in or call center monitoring. The basic concept of a join in a SIP call is to add a participant to an already established two-party session. The concept is similar to a conference call, which is normally coordinated by call agents responsible for local endpoints rather than an SBC. A device advertises support for join functionality by sending the "join" extension in the Supported SIP header. The syntax of the Join header is as follows:

```
Join: <call-id>;from-tag=<from-tag>;to-tag=<to-tag>
```

Mid-call signaling, such as a call to transfer through REFER or the supplementary service call pickup between shared lines, may make use of the SIP replaces concept. Replaces is defined in RFC 3891 as a way to replace an existing session between a UAC and a UAS with new session involving a new endpoint. Consider the example provided in Figure 4-46, which involves a call through an SBC from the PSTN to an IP phone of a secretary. This secretary is tasked with answering any calls for the office and the boss. As a result, the boss's phone and the secretary's phone share a phone line. This means that any call to that line rings both phones. The secretary answers, and the session is established with her phone. At this point, she realizes it is a call the boss was expecting. The secretary can put the call on hold, and the boss may resume the call from his phone.

In this scenario, the session is established between the PSTN participant and the secretary's phone. When the call is put on hold, the boss is able to press the resume button and retrieve the call. What occurs in the background is that the boss's phone sends a SIP INVITE with a Replaces header. The Replaces header contains information about the other session (the secretary's)—such as the **Call-ID**, **To-Tag**, and **From-Tag**—which this INVITE attempts to replace. At this point, the other session between the PSTN and secretary is tore down, and a new session is established between the boss's phone and the PSTN participant.

The following is the format for the Replaces header:

```
Replaces: <call-id>;to-tag=<to-tag>;from-tag=<from-tag>
```

Figure 4-46 details a simple example of the Replaces header in action. There are numerous uses for the Replaces header, all mostly dependent on the call agent's or the collaboration system's usage. An SBC may be required to perform this functionality if a request is sent containing the Replaces header. A device signals the ability to perform replaces by indicating the extension in the Supported header. CUBE supports replaces by default. To disable replaces functionality, you use the commands in Example 4-70.

Example 4-70 *CUBE Replacing the Support Configuration*

```
voice service voip
 sip
  no supplementary-service sip handle-replaces
```

Note CUBE does not support the join functions defined in RFC 3911.

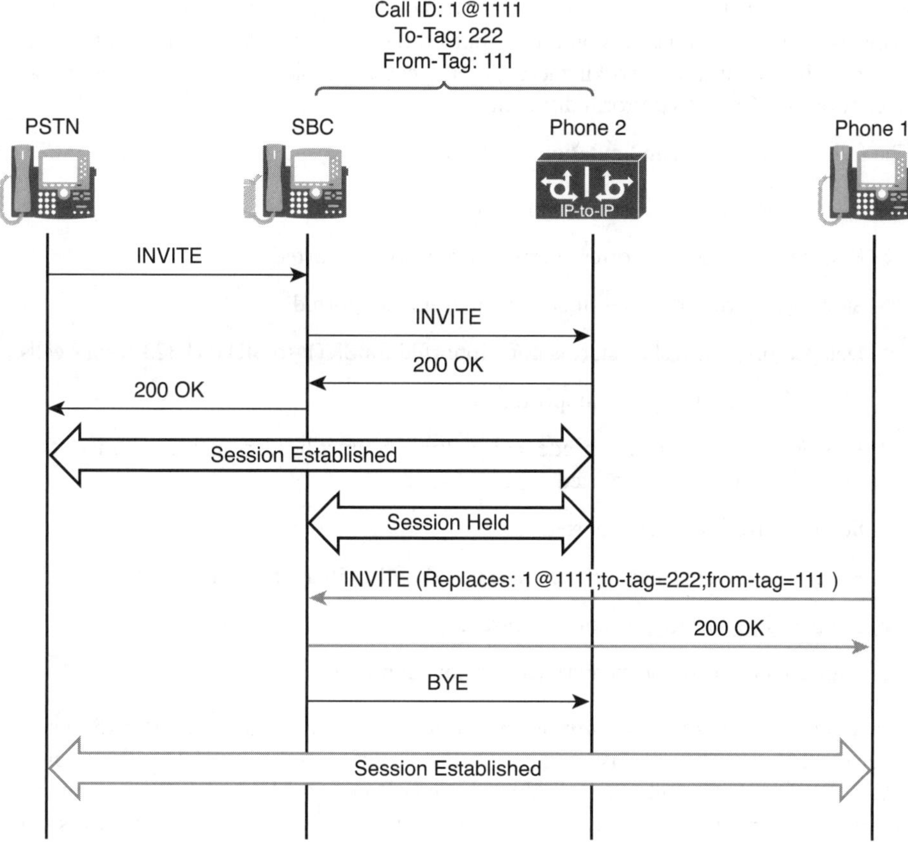

Figure 4-46 *A Replaces Scenario Between an SBC and Various UAs*

SIP–H.323 Interworking

Because an SBC is an IP-to-IP gateway, it may be required to interwork different Layer 7 VoIP signaling protocols. The most common is SIP and H.323 interworking. H.323 is often used between LAN instances of different vendor call control equipment and is rarely used to trunk with a service provider. H.323 itself can be broken down into two different protocols that together make up the majority of the H.323 suite: H.225 and H.245. When comparing these to SIP, H.225 is the most similar in the sense that it handles the session establishment. H.245 is often compared to the SDP in a SIP message body because both SDP and H.245 have the purpose of defining the media characteristics of a session.

Because SIP and H.323 have vastly different protocols with different approaches to the many aspects surrounding session establishment, there are a number of limitations. As a result of the complex interworking logic, every vendor's implementation of SIP-to-H.323 interworking is likely to perform differently.

The following are the main limitations with CUBE:

- The use of voice class codecs is not supported.
- Fast start with delayed offer interworking is not supported.
- Slow start with early offer interworking is not supported.
- Delayed offer with slow start is not supported for SRTP-to-SRTP H.323-to-SIP calls.
- Media flow-around is not supported.
- Passing multiple diversion headers or multiple contact headers in 302 messages to the H.323 leg is not supported.
- Session refresh is not supported.
- SIP-to-H.323 supplementary services based on H.450 are not supported.
- LTI-based transcoding is not supported.
- Transcoding for supplementary calls is not supported.

The terms *fast start* and *slow start* are similar to early offer and delayed offer, discussed earlier in this chapter. With fast start, the media characteristics of an H.323 session are established before the call is answered by the remote device. This is done by tunneling the H.245 open logical channel (OLC) messages within the H.225 setup. Fast start is only compatible with SIP early offer.

H.323 slow start is similar to delayed offer in the sense that the media is established later in the session and often when the call is answered. This is done by sending H.245 a set of terminal capability set (TCS) and OLC messages separate from the H.225 messages. These are sent in both directions and also involve an ACK message for the response. Slow start is only compatible with SIP delayed offer.

If CUBE receives an H.323 fast start message, the egress messaging is early offer, and in the same vein, if CUBE receives a slow start message, the egress signaling is delayed offer. In addition, CUBE sends the appropriate signaling type for egress signaling depending on whether delayed offer or early offer messaging was received on the SIP call leg. Figure 4-47 shows a sample call through an SBC that uses slow start on the H.323 leg and delayed offer on the SIP leg.

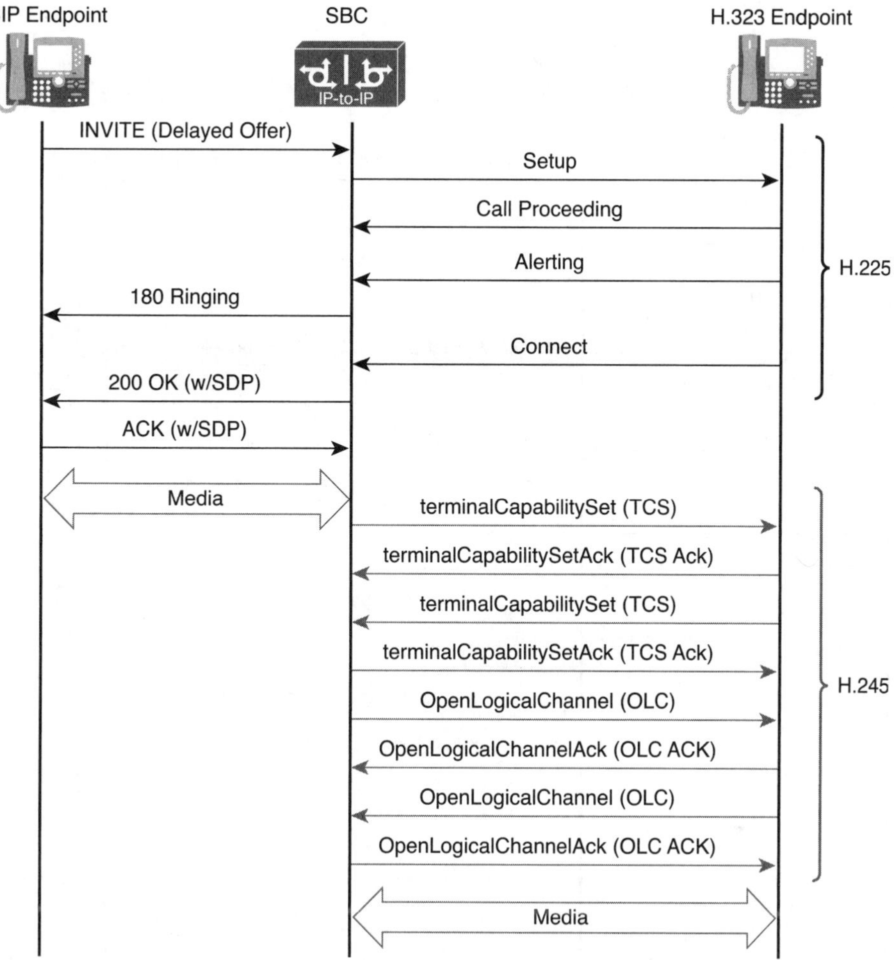

Figure 4-47 *H.323 Slow Start and SIP Delayed Offer Call on an SBC*

Figure 4-48 shows a sample call through an SBC that uses fast start on the H.323 leg and early offer on the SIP leg.

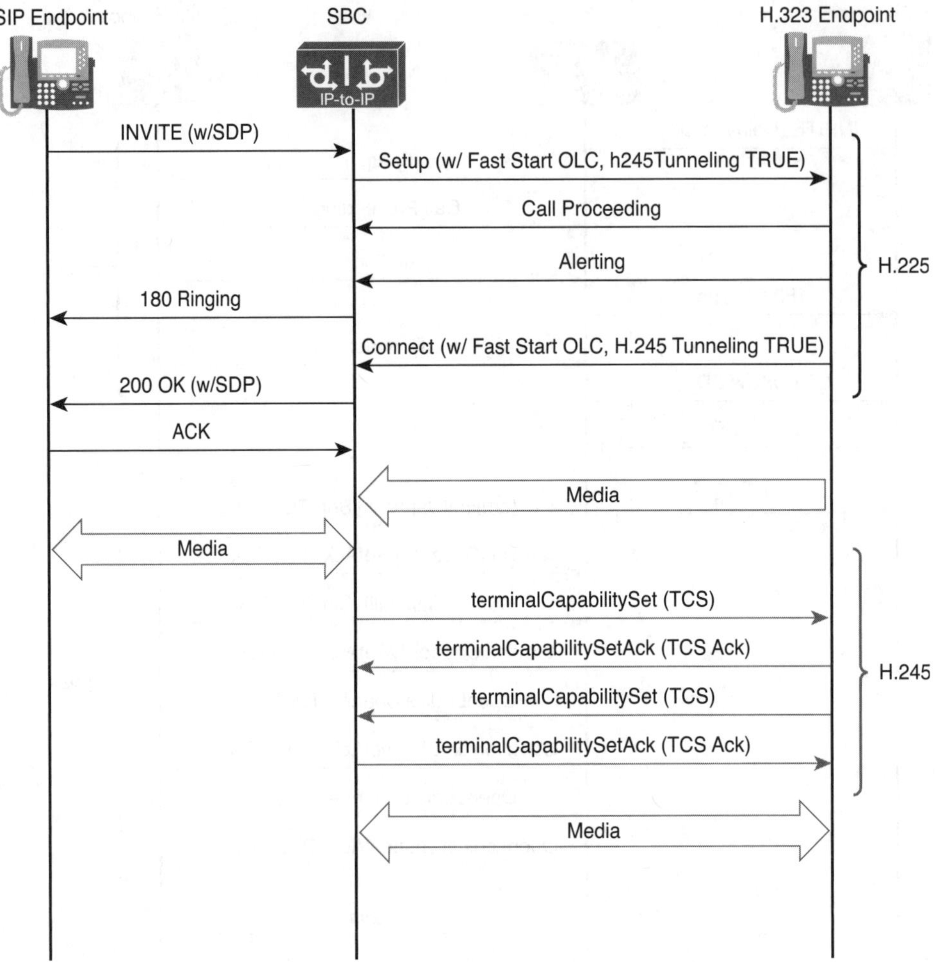

Figure 4-48 *H.323 Fast Start and SIP Early Offer Call on an SBC*

Troubleshooting SIP–H.323 Interworking

When troubleshooting SIP-to-H.323 interworking on an SBC, it is always good to get debugging information. The following list can be used as starting point for these protocols.

SIP:

```
debug ccsip messages
debug ccsip error
```

Call control API and signaling interworking:

```
debug voip ccapi inout
```

H.323:

```
debug h225 asn1
debug h245 asn1
```

H.323 uses the ASN.1 markup format, which is much more verbose than SIP. As a result, it is recommended to increase the logging buffer in order to avoid losing messages. This can be done with the command **logging buffer 1000000 debug**. Always look at the type of signaling used on the two sides of the call to ensure that they are compatible. H.323 mainly runs over TCP, so it is important to verify TCP socket establishment with **debug ip tcp transactions** or a PCAP.

Summary

This chapter covers many different types of interworking scenarios that an SBC may encounter on the signaling plane at the application layer. This includes interworking of different VoIP protocols, extensions, and even header/message body manipulation or modification. This chapter also details the vital role an SBC plays in many different types of supplementary services and call signaling scenarios occurring during, after, or even outside session establishment.

In addition to covering Layer 7 application interworking, this chapter also discusses Layer 4 transport interworking and Layer 3 IP interworking from the perspective of SBCs.

References

RFC 768, "User Datagram Protocol," https://tools.ietf.org/html/rfc768

RFC 793, "Transmission Control Protocol," https://tools.ietf.org/html/rfc793

RFC 3261, "SIP: Session Initiation Protocol," https://tools.ietf.org/html/rfc3261

RFC 3262, "Reliability of Provisional Responses in the Session Initiation Protocol (SIP)," https://tools.ietf.org/html/rfc3262

RFC 3264, "An Offer/Answer Model with the Session Description Protocol (SDP)," https://tools.ietf.org/html/rfc3264

RFC 3265, "Session Initiation Protocol (SIP)-Specific Event Notification," https://tools.ietf.org/html/rfc3265

RFC 3311, "The Session Initiation Protocol (SIP) UPDATE Method," https://tools.ietf.org/html/rfc3311

RFC 3515, "The Session Initiation Protocol (SIP) Refer Method," https://tools.ietf.org/html/rfc3515

RFC 3665, "Session Initiation Protocol (SIP) Basic Call Flow Examples," https://tools.ietf.org/html/rfc3665

RFC 3842, "A Message Summary and Message Waiting Indication Event Package for the Session Initiation Protocol (SIP)," https://tools.ietf.org/html/rfc3842

RFC 3891, "The Session Initiation Protocol (SIP) 'Replaces' Header," https://tools.ietf.org/html/rfc3891

RFC 3892, "The Session Initiation Protocol (SIP) Referred-By Mechanism," https://tools.ietf.org/html/rfc3892

RFC 3911, "The Session Initiation Protocol (SIP) 'Join' Header," https://tools.ietf.org/html/rfc3911

RFC 3960, "Early Media and Ringing Tone Generation in the Session Initiation Protocol (SIP)," https://tools.ietf.org/html/rfc3960

RFC 4028, "Session Timers in the Session Initiation Protocol (SIP)," https://tools.ietf.org/html/rfc4028

RFC 4488, "Suppression of Session Initiation Protocol (SIP) REFER Method Implicit Subscription," https://tools.ietf.org/html/rfc4488

RFC 4826, "Extensible Markup Language (XML) Formats for Representing Resource Lists," https://tools.ietf.org/html/rfc4826

RFC 5118, "Session Initiation Protocol (SIP) Torture Test Messages for Internet Protocol Version 6 (IPv6)," https://tools.ietf.org/html/rfc5118

RFC 5363, "Framework and Security Considerations for Session Initiation Protocol (SIP) URI-List Services," https://tools.ietf.org/html/rfc5363

RFC 5364, "Extensible Markup Language (XML) Format Extension for Representing Copy Control Attributes in Resource Lists," https://tools.ietf.org/html/rfc5364

RFC 5368, "Referring to Multiple Resources in the Session Initiation Protocol (SIP)," https://tools.ietf.org/html/rfc5368

RFC 5589, "Session Initiation Protocol (SIP) Call Control—Transfer," https://tools.ietf.org/html/rfc5589

RFC 5768, "Indicating Support for Interactive Connectivity Establishment (ICE) in the Session Initiation Protocol (SIP)," https://tools.ietf.org/html/rfc5768

RFC 5853, "Requirements from Session Initiation Protocol (SIP) Session Border Control (SBC) Deployments," https://tools.ietf.org/html/rfc5853

RFC 5923, "Connection Reuse in the Session Initiation Protocol (SIP)," https://tools.ietf.org/html/rfc5923

RFC 6157, "IPv6 Transition in the Session Initiation Protocol (SIP)," https://tools.ietf.org/html/rfc6157

RFC 6228, "Session Initiation Protocol (SIP) Response Code for Indication of Terminated Dialog," https://tools.ietf.org/html/rfc6228

RFC 6337, "Session Initiation Protocol (SIP) Usage of the Offer/Answer Model," https://tools.ietf.org/html/rfc6337

RFC 6665, "SIP-Specific Event Notification," https://tools.ietf.org/html/rfc6665

RFC 7118, "The WebSocket Protocol as a Transport for the Session Initiation Protocol (SIP)," https://tools.ietf.org/html/rfc7118

RFC 7584, "Session Traversal Utilities for NAT (STUN) Message Handling for SIP Back-to-Back User Agents (B2BUAs)," https://tools.ietf.org/html/rfc7584

RFC 7614, "Explicit Subscriptions for the REFER Method," https://tools.ietf.org/html/rfc7614

RFC 7647, "Clarifications for the Use of REFER with RFC 6665," https://tools.ietf.org/html/rfc7647

RFC 7984, "Locating Session Initiation Protocol (SIP) Servers in a Dual-Stack IP Network," https://tools.ietf.org/html/rfc7984

draft-klatsky-dispatch-ipv6-impact-ipv4-03, "Interoperability Impacts of IPv6 Interworking with Existing IPv4 SIP Implementations," https://tools.ietf.org/html/draft-klatsky-dispatch-ipv6-impact-ipv4-03

H.225, "Call Signalling Protocols and Media Stream Packetization for Packet-Based Multimedia Communication Systems," https://www.itu.int/rec/T-REC-H.225.0-200912-I/en

H.245, "Control Protocol for Multimedia Communication," https://www.itu.int/rec/T-REC-H.245/en

E.180, "Technical Characteristics of Tones for the Telephone Service," https://www.itu.int/rec/T-REC-E.180-199803-I/en

"Various Tones Used in National Networks (According to ITU-T Recommendation E.180)," https://www.itu.int/ITU-T/inr/forms/files/tones-0203.pdf

ETS 300 512, "European Digital Cellular Telecommunications System (Phase 2); Procedure for Call Progress Indications (GSM 02.40)," http://www.etsi.org/deliver/etsi_i_ets/300500_300599/300512/01_60/ets_300512e01p.pdf

"Delayed Offer to Early Offer Translation for SIP Calls," https://www.cisco.com/c/en/us/td/docs/ios/voice/cube/configuration/guide/vb_8241.html

"Delayed-Offer to Early-Offer," https://www.cisco.com/c/en/us/td/docs/ios-xml/ios/voice/cube/configuration/cube-book/voi-cube-do-eo.pdf

"SIP Profiles," https://www.cisco.com/c/en/us/td/docs/ios-xml/ios/voice/cube_fund/configuration/xe-3s/cube-fund-xe-3s-book/voi-sip-param-mod.html

"Multicast Music-on-Hold Support on Cisco UBE," https://www.cisco.com/c/en/us/td/docs/ios-xml/ios/voice/cube_proto/configuration/15-mt/cube-proto-15-mt-book/voi-multicast-moh.html

"Dynamic Refer Handling," https://www.cisco.com/c/en/us/td/docs/ios-xml/ios/voice/cube_sip/configuration/15-mt/cube-sip-15-mt-book/voi-cub-sip-dyn-refer-handling.html

"Configuring SIP Call-Transfer Features," https://www.cisco.com/c/en/us/td/docs/ios-xml/ios/voice/sip/configuration/15-mt/sip-config-15-mt-book/voi-sip-call-transfer.html

"Mid-call Signaling Consumption," https://www.cisco.com/c/en/us/td/docs/ios-xml/ios/voice/cube/configuration/cube-book/voi-cube-midcall-reinvite.html

"Nano CUBE SUBSCRIBE-NOTIFY Passthrough," https://www.cisco.com/c/en/us/td/docs/ios-xml/ios/voice/cube_nano/configuration/15-mt/nanocube-config-15-mt-book/voi-nanocube-subscribe-notify.html

H.323-to-SIP Interworking on CUBE," https://www.cisco.com/c/en/us/td/docs/ios-xml/ios/voice/cube/configuration/cube-book/h323-to-sip.html

"H.323 to SIP Interworking," https://www.cisco.com/c/en/us/td/docs/routers/asr1000/configuration/guide/sbcu/2_xe/sbcu_2_xe_book/sbc_hsp.pdf

"Configurable Pass-Through of SIP INVITE Parameters," https://www.cisco.com/c/en/us/td/docs/ios-xml/ios/voice/cube_sip/configuration/15-mt/cube-sip-15-mt-book/voi-conf-pass-thro.html

"Configuring Support for Dynamic REFER Handling on the Cisco UBE," https://www.cisco.com/c/en/us/td/docs/ios-xml/ios/voice/cube_sip/configuration/xe-3s/cube-sip-xe-3s-book/voi-cub-sip-dyn-refer-handling.pdf

"Achieving SIP RFC Compliance," https://www.cisco.com/c/en/us/td/docs/ios-xml/ios/voice/sip/configuration/15-mt/sip-config-15-mt-book/voi-sip-rfc.html

"SIP Profiles," https://www.cisco.com/c/en/us/td/docs/ios-xml/ios/voice/cube/configuration/cube-book/voi-sip-param-mod.html

"VoIP for IPv6," https://www.cisco.com/c/en/us/td/docs/ios-xml/ios/voice/cube/configuration/cube-book/voi-cube-voip-ipv6.pdf

"ICE-Lite Support on CUBE," https://www.cisco.com/c/en/us/td/docs/ios-xml/ios/voice/cube/configuration/cube-book/voi-cube-ice-lite.html

"Nano CUBE SUBSCRIBE-NOTIFY Passthrough," https://www.cisco.com/c/en/us/td/docs/ios-xml/ios/voice/cube_nano/configuration/15-mt/nanocube-config-15-mt-book/voi-nanocube-subscribe-notify.html

Chapter 5

Media Processing

IP networks form the foundation for exchanging voice and video packets. There has to be a set of rules and procedures to provide an overarching framework for transmission of real-time media information between participants in a communication session. Real-Time Transport Protocol (RTP) was developed for precisely this reason, and it has seen overwhelming acceptance across the industry. RTP and many of its extensions have been built and standardized over many years to fit a myriad of different situations.

SBCs are devices that have operations defined in both the media and signaling planes, with the ability to transform signaling and media and to strongly influence session characteristics. Over the years, SBCs have been developed and installed in real-time multimedia networks to "fix" some of the inherent interoperability challenges seen when attempting to establish multimedia sessions across network boundaries.

This chapter talks about the various media plane operations that are performed by SBCs and also discusses certain considerations that need to be taken into account with media handling by SBCs.

This chapter includes the following sections:

- **Real-Time Transport Protocol—**This section provides an introduction to Real-Time Transport Protocol (RTP) and explains how RTP packets are formatted.
- **Real-Time Transport Control Protocol—**This section covers Real-Time Transport Control Protocol (RTCP) as a peer protocol to RTP and discusses various RTCP packet types.
- **SBC Handling of RTP and RTCP—**This section discusses how SBCs handle RTP and RTCP traffic, as well as the different considerations that arise when SBCs manipulate RTP and RTCP packets.

- **Symmetric and Asymmetric RTP/RTCP**—This section covers the symmetric and asymmetric properties of RTP.
- **DSP-Based RTP Handling on SBCs**—This section covers the various RTP/RTCP manipulation operations that can be carried out by digital signal processors (DSPs).
- **Media Anti-tromboning**—This section covers how media loops are created on SBCs and discusses techniques for mitigating such media loops.
- **Alternate Network Address Types**—This section covers how SBCs can work with multiple address types (IPv4 and IPv6) when setting up a communication session.
- **Solving NAT Traversal Challenges**—This chapter covers the basics of Network Address Translation (NAT), the problems NAT introduces in real-time media transmission, and some of techniques that can help overcome these problems.
- **Troubleshooting RTP**—This section includes diagnostic commands, debugging snippets, and a general methodology for troubleshooting media-related issues on SBCs, using CUBE as an example.

By the end of this chapter, you will have a thorough understanding of RTP and RTCP, how SBCs handle and modify RTP and RTCP traffic, and a general approach for troubleshooting RTP issues on SBCs.

Real-Time Transport Protocol

Real-Time Transport Protocol (RTP), originally defined in RFC 1889 and superseded by RFC 3550, provides a framework for the end-to-end transport of voice and video. RTP typically operates over UDP/IP and provides built-in loss detection, receiver feedback, source identification, important event indications, and sequencing. RTP has a peer protocol, Real-Time Control Protocol (RTCP), that provides media reception feedback for the related RTP stream. RTCP is discussed in further detail in the following section.

Central to the operation of RTP is the concept of an RTP session. An RTP *session* is a group of participants interacting over RTP, such that a given participant may be a part of several different RTP sessions at the same time. For example, a pair of endpoints could have both an audio RTP session and a video RTP session active between them. An RTP session is identified by the combination of a network address and port pair on which traffic is sent and received. Different ports may be used for RTP and RTCP for each session.

An RTP session can be either unicast (one-to-one communication between a pair of participants) or multicast (one-to-many communication to participants). Before exploring various other topics discussed in this and subsequent chapters, it is important to first take a close look at the RTP packet format.

RTP Packet Format

An RTP packet consists of two parts: an RTP header and an RTP payload (with optional padding). Figure 5-1 shows the RTP packet format.

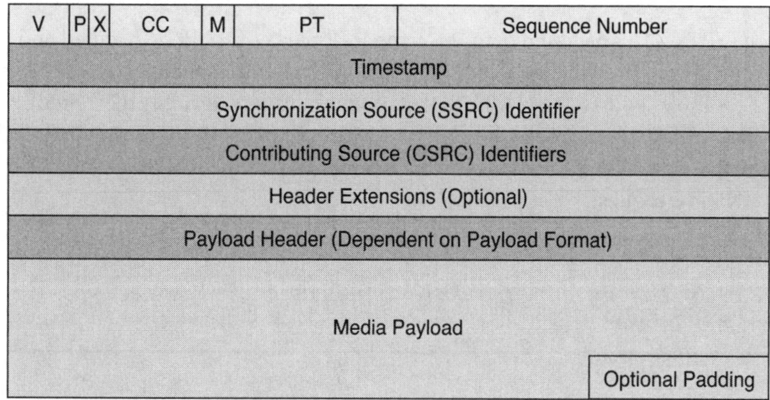

Figure 5-1 *RTP Packet Format*

Descriptions of the various fields appearing in the RTP header are listed:

- **Version (V)**—This header field specifies the RTP version in use. The current version at the time of this publication is 2.
- **Padding (P)**—This single-bit header field, when set to 1, indicates that there are additional octets appended to the RTP payload. These additional octets are not a part of the payload and are primarily inserted to ensure that certain encryption algorithms always work on fixed-size blocks of data.
- **Extension (X)**—This single-bit field indicates the presence of an RTP header extension. RTP header extensions are required to carry additional media session information that cannot be encoded within the standard RTP headers or payload. Typical examples of this include the RTP header extensions for audio level information of RTP samples, as defined in RFC 6464. Although header extensions are not commonly implemented, it is important for the specification to have such accommodation for these rare cases.
- **CSRC count (CC)**—This field identifies the number of CSRC identifiers that follow the fixed header field. CSRCs are explained further later in this section.
- **Marker bit (M)**—This header filed is used to designate important events during the media session. For example, the marker bit might designate the start of a new DTMF event. This usage can be observed when using named telephony events for DTMF transmission. (See Chapter 7, "DTMF Interworking," for more details.) Yet another usage of the M field is when the payload format changes during a media session. For example, a media session might negotiate G.711 as the audio codec and begin transmission of RTP packets back and forth. Sometime during the course of the communication session, an application interaction might cause the audio codec to change

to G.729 (a change that is accompanied by a corresponding Session Description Protocol [SDP] offer/answer exchange), the first RTP packet encoded with a G.729 payload has the marker bit set. Setting of the marker bit indicates the occurrence of a significant event (such as a transition from G.711 to G.729) from the perspective of the media stream.

- **Payload type (PT)**—This field indicates how the RTP packet should be handled and interpreted at the receiver. Payload type values are correlated to specific payload formats (for example, PCMU, G.729, H.264) through the use of RTP profiles. From the perspective of SIP, this correlation is carried within the SDP body of the offer/answer exchange. Consider Example 5-1, which demonstrates the SDP body of a typical SIP INVITE request.

Example 5-1 *SDP Body Demonstrating the Correlation Between the Payload Type, Payload Format, and RTP Profile*

```
INVITE sip:2222@192.0.2.1:5060 SIP/2.0
Via: SIP/2.0/UDP 192.0.2.2:5060;branch=z9hG4bK531305
Remote-Party-ID: <sip:1111@192.0.2.2>;party=calling;screen=no;privacy=off
From: <sip:1111@192.0.2.2>;
To: <sip:2222@192.0.2.1>;tag=53A7B00-628
Date: Sat, 04 Feb 2017 07:11:33 GMT
Call-ID: 5113703A-E9E911E6-815DDB64-68BBC9B8@192.0.2.66
!
!
! Omitted for brevity
!
Content-Type: application/sdp
Content-Length: 221

v=0
o=CiscoSystemsSIP-GW-UserAgent 7031 5812 IN IP4 192.0.2.2
s=SIP Call
c=IN IP4 192.0.2.2
t=0 0
m=audio 16512 RTP/AVP 0
c=IN IP4 192.0.2.61
a=rtpmap:0 PCMU/8000
a=ptime:20
```

In the Example 5-1, the payload number advertised is **0**, the RTP profile is **RTP/AVP**, and the **rtpmap** attribute provides a mapping between the payload number (**0**) and the payload format (G.711µ). The RTP/AVP profile (audio/video profile), defined in RFC 3551, is the most commonly used profile; it defines several static assignments of payload numbers to payload formats. Table 5-1 lists some of these static assignments.

Table 5-1 *Payload Type-to-Format Mapping for RTP/AVP*

Payload Type	Encoding Name	Clock Rate (Hz)
0	PCMU	8000
4	G723	8000
8	PCMA	8000
9	G722	8000
15	G728	8000
18	G729	8000

The RTP profile is also useful in providing the clock rate for predefined static assignments. The payload formats are responsible for determining how information is encapsulated in the RTP packet, such as specifying what is present in the RTP header and the RTP payload.

Note Dynamic assignments of payload types to formats are also possible, in which case this mapping has to be explicitly specified with the SDP **rtpmap** attribute.

- **Sequence number—**The sequence number is a 16-bit field that increases sequentially for each RTP packet sent from the sender to the receiver. It is through this 16-bit field that RTP provides its built-in loss-detection mechanism. Packets are assumed to have been dropped during transit if the receiver notices a break in the RTP sequence numbers of received packets. Figure 5-2 depicts a scenario where the receiver experiences packet loss in a real-time communication session.

  The RTP sequence number is always chosen randomly and does not start from zero. From the randomly chosen offset of the first RTP packet, successive RTP packets have incrementally increasing sequence numbers. A random sequence number value is usually chosen for the initial RTP packet to protect against known plaintext security attacks.

Note A common misconception about the sequence number is that it assists the receiver in determining the order in which the packets are played out, but this is an incorrect assumption. The order in which packets are played out at the receiver is dependent on the RTP timestamp header field, described next.

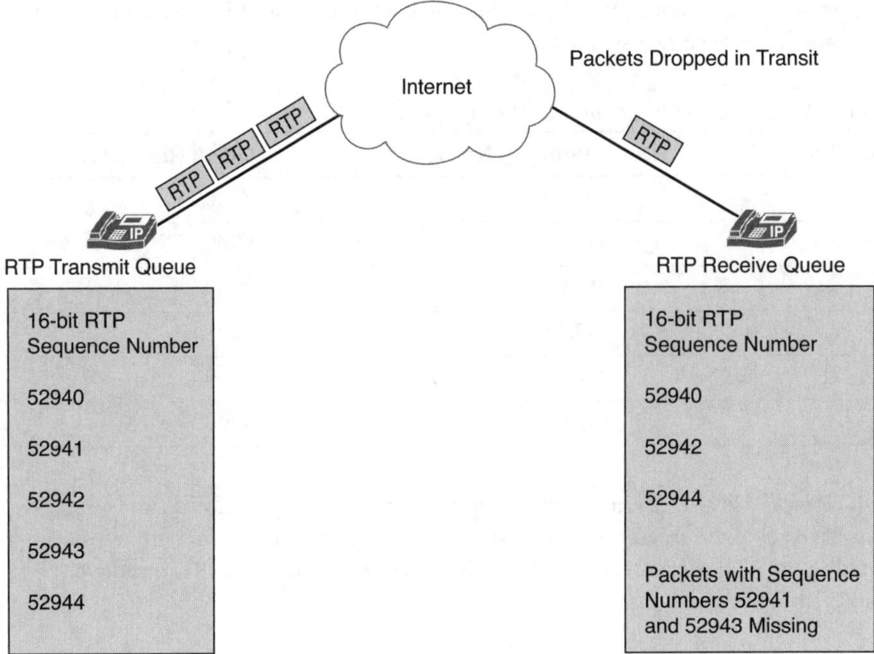

Figure 5-2 *RTP Packet Loss During a Real-Time Communication Session*

- **Timestamp**—The timestamp header field is a 32-bit value that designates the sampling instant of the first octet of the media payload in the RTP packet. The sampling instant is derived from a media clock that increases linearly and monotonically in time. The rate at which this clock advances is dependent on the payload format and can sometimes drastically vary based on the media format. The timestamp field is used at the receiver to decide the order in which packets are played out. The timestamp header field value in the first packet is randomly chosen and advances at a rate specified by the payload format (refer to Table 5-1).
- **Synchronization source (SSRC)**—This 32-bit field serves as an identifier of a participant in an RTP session. The SSRC values must always be chosen randomly by participants in an RTP session because each RTP session has its own unique SSRC space. If one or more participants in an RTP session have the same SSRC value (which is possible because these values are chosen randomly), a collision occurs. Collisions are resolved by having the endpoints send an RTCP BYE packet, followed by choosing a new random SSRC value. For participants that are part of multiple RTP sessions at the same time (for example, both an audio and video session), the SSRC values have to be unique across those multiple sessions. Some of the scenarios that might cause the SSRC to change during the course of a communication session include the following:
  - Application restarts
  - SSRC collisions
  - Changes in the RTP transport address (network address and port pair)

- **Contributing source (CSRC)**—There are often scenarios in real-time communication sessions in which participants stream media directly to an intermediary device such as a mixer. The mixer is responsible for combining streams from various participants and sending over the resultant media stream to one or more receivers. Because the mixer is part of the RTP session, it has its own SSRC value that is used when it transmits RTP packets. The number of sources that contribute to the resultant output of the mixer is captured in the CC field of the RTP packet. The individual SSRCs of the contributing sources are captured in the CSRC blocks. Note that not all RTP packets contain this header field, as it is only used when combining streams from various sources. This forms a part of the optional RTP header.

  The usage of the CSRC header field is shown in Figure 5-3.

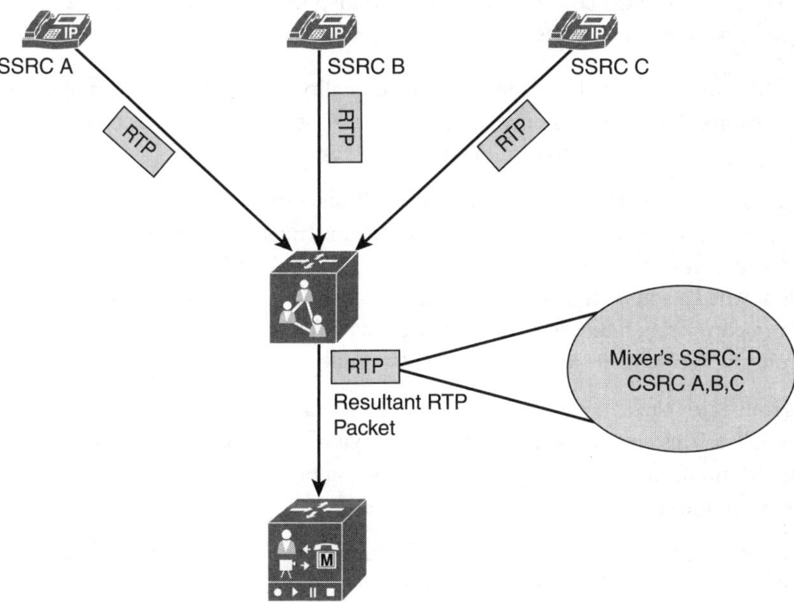

Figure 5-3 *Usage of the CSRC Header Field by a Mixer*

- **Payload header**—The presence of this optional header is based on the requirements of the payload format that is negotiated.
- **Media payload**—This forms the actual media that is framed by the RTP packet. Its contents are governed by the payload format that is used.

Note For UDP and similar transport layer protocols, applications are required to use an even port number for RTP.

RTP Enhancements

Over the years, as RTP has found ubiquitous adoption in real-time environments, the protocol has been greatly enhanced through several peer IETF standards. These enhancements have increased the robustness and operation of the protocol to fit into the emerging areas and applications of real-time communications. Support for these various RTP enhancements is signaled through the SDP body.

Real-Time Transport Control Protocol

As discussed in the previous section, RTP defines a framework for real-time transfer of audio and video media between senders and receivers in an RTP session. The RTP framework also defines a peer protocol called Real-Time Transport Control Protocol (RTCP) and includes the following functions:

- It allows receivers to provide periodic reception quality feedback to senders by using receiver reports. These reports enable senders to take stock of network characteristics, and possibly alter their transmission patterns, as required.
- RTCP defines a transport-level identifier called the canonical name (CNAME) that serves as the common identifier for all media streams transmitted by a source. This is especially useful in cases when a source changes its SSRC during a communication session or when a source transmits multiple streams simultaneously. It also assists the receiver in correlating multiple streams to a given participant and in achieving media synchronization across the multiple streams transmitted by the participant.
- RTCP requires all participants to exchange reports, regardless of whether they are active senders. This ensures that there is a global view of the RTP session. RTCP provides useful diagnostics and gives each participant an estimate of the number of members in the RTP session.
- RTCP can optionally be used to transmit additional information in terms of participant identity, email, and location information.

Given that all participants must stream RTCP traffic, transmission must be periodic and designed in such a way that it does not overrun session bandwidth. This is especially true for RTP sessions that have a large number of participants; if RTCP traffic were to be exchanged at the same rate as RTP, there would be bandwidth contention and a potential for lost data. As a result, RTCP traffic must always be allocated a fraction or percentage of total session bandwidth. The recommended percentage of bandwidth allocation for RTCP is 5%, with active senders allocated one-quarter of the total RTCP bandwidth. This ensures that required reports, such as those for media synchronization, are successfully delivered in a timely manner, without competing against RTP for bandwidth.

RTCP defines five different packet types that are used for different scenarios. All the RTCP packet types use the common format shown in Figure 5-4.

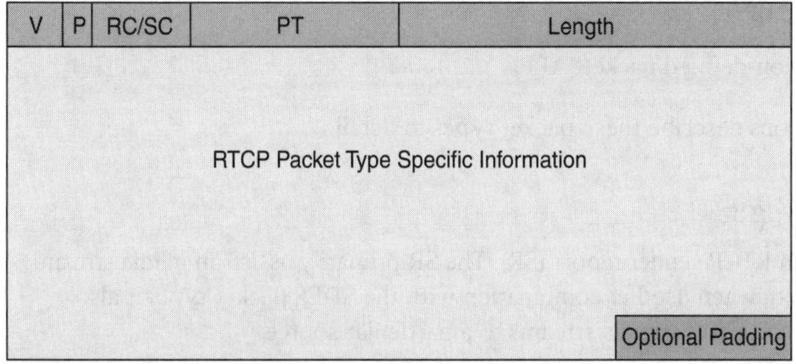

Figure 5-4 *Common RTCP Packet Format*

The following fields are included in the common RTCP packet format:

- **Version (V)**—Specifies the version number, which correlates to the same version as RTP, currently 2.
- **Padding (P)**—When set, this bit indicates that the packet contains additional data octets toward the end of the packet. This is primarily required when encryption ciphers require fixed-size blocks of data.
- **Receiver count/source count (RC/SC)**—This header field is used to provide the count of receiver reports or source description (SDES) items included in the RTCP packet.
- **Packet Type (PT)**—The encoding in this header field defines the RTCP type. Different RTCP packet types are described in the next section.
- **Length**—This header field denotes the length of the packet following the common header. This field is expressed in 32-bit words and can have a value of 0. A value of 0 indicates an empty packet that just contains the 4-byte common header.

All RTCP packets must be sent as *compound* RTCP packets, which include a combination of different RTCP packet types that follow a very strict ordering scheme.

RTCP Packet Types

There are five different RTCP packet types, which serve different purposes in a communication session:

- RTCP sender report (SR)
- RTCP receiver report (RR)
- RTCP source description (SDES)

- RTCP goodbye (BYE)
- RTCP application-defined packet (APP)

The following sections describe these packet types in detail.

RTCP Sender Report (SR)

Figure 5-5 shows an RTCP sender report (SR). The SR primarily assists in media stream synchronization, and, when used in combination with the SDES packet type, it also assists receivers in correlating media streams to a particular source.

V	P	RC	PT=200	Length
Reporter SSRC				
NTP Timestamp				
RTP Timestamp				
Sender's Packet Count				
Sender's Octet Count				
Zero/One or More Receiver Report Blocks				

Figure 5-5 *RTCP Sender Report Format*

RTCP sender reports are sent by sources that have recently transmitted media and are identified by a packet type value of 200. An active sender also includes reception statistics for all the other sources from which it has received media packets. The reception statistics are encoded as RTCP receiver report (RR) blocks, such that each block corresponds to a source from which media was received.

The receiver count (RC) header field in the RTCP sender report packet captures the number of receiver report blocks included. If media hasn't been received from any source, there are no receiver report blocks included in the compound RTCP packet, and the RC header field is set to 0.

The Reporter SSRC of the packet sender encodes the SSRC of the source that transmits the RTCP SR packet, and it is a 32-bit field. Following this is a 64-bit Network Time Protocol (NTP) timestamp field. The time in this field is expressed in NTP format, which is the number of seconds that have elapsed since January 1, 1900. This field indicates the time when the RTCP SR packet was sent.

The 32-bit RTP timestamp header field follows this, and it encodes the same time as the NTP timestamp header field discussed previously but is expressed in RTP timestamp format. The NTP timestamp and RTP timestamp header fields are used by the receiver to synchronize the media clocks of the different streams from a sender, allowing for synchronization of offset audio and video media streams (lip sync).

Following the RTP timestamp field are the sender's packet count and the sender's octet count. The sender's packet count captures the total number of RTP data packets transmitted by the sender from the start of the session up through transmission of the RTCP SR packet. The sender's octet count header field captures the total number of data octets sent since the start of the RTP session, up through transmission of the RTCP SR packet. The octet count does not take into account the RTP headers and padding, and is only concerned with the number of octets that are sent using the RTP packet payload.

Note The sender's packet count and sender's octet count header field values are reset if the SSRC changes for a sender during the RTP session. SSRC values can change if there is an SSRC collision detected or if the sender changes its media type during an RTP session.

Sender reports can also be used to get an estimate of the average payload size of RTP data packets transmitted by a sender and the network throughput available.

RTCP Receiver Report (RR)

RTCP receiver reports are used to report transmission statistics to the senders from which RTP media packets are received. The format of an RTCP receiver report is diagrammed in Figure 5-6. The *packet type* header field in an RTCP RR packet is set to 201, and the number of reports blocks present in a particular RTCP RR is captured in the RC header field.

V	P	RC=1	PT=201	Length
SSRC of Sender				
SSRC of Source_N				
Loss Fraction			Cumulative Number of Packets Lost	
Extended Highest Sequence Number Received				
Interarrival Jitter				
LSR				
DLSR				

Figure 5-6 *RTCP Receiver Report Format*

The identity of the sender of an RTCP RR packet is captured by using the *SSRC of packet sender* header field. The RTP sender for which statistics are being reported is indicated by the *SSRC of source_N* header field. It is possible for a single participant in an RTP session to receive RTP packets from multiple sources, in which case reception statistics have to be reported for each source. A total of 31 reception reports are possible per RTCP RR packet. If there are more than 31 sources to report on, multiple RTCP RR compound packets must be leveraged.

The *fraction lost* header field captures the fraction of RTP media packets lost from a particular source since the transmission of the previous SR or RR packet. This value is expressed as a fixed-point number, with the binary point at the left edge of the field. The fraction is calculated by dividing the number of packets lost by the number of packets expected. During an RTP session, it is not uncommon to come across packet duplicates, in which case the number of packet received would be more than the number of packets actually expected. This results in the number of packets lost (to be described next) being represented as a negative value. In such scenarios, the fraction lost header field is instead set to 0.

The *cumulative number of packets lost* header field is a 24-bit signed integer that denotes the number of packets received subtracted from the number of packets expected. The number of packets expected is defined as the extended last sequence number received subtracted from the initial sequence number received. In case of packet duplicates, the number of packets lost header field will carry a negative value.

The *extended highest number sequence number received* is a 32-bit header field value, where the lower 16 bits indicate the highest sequence number received in an RTP media packet from a given source. The higher 16 bits indicate the number of times the sequence numbering in RTP media has wrapped around from 65535 (maximum value) to 0 (minimum value).

> **Note** The sequence number in RTP packets is a 16-bit field, which means RTP packets from a source can carry distinct sequence numbers for a maximum of 65,535 packets (2^{16} packets). After crossing this maximum value, the sequence number has to wrap around to 0. Wrapping of RTP sequence numbers is fairly common and occurs for conversations that extend a duration beyond 21 minutes 50 seconds (assuming a codec packetization rate of 50 packets per second). It is for this reason that sequence numbers cannot be used to uniquely identify packets within an RTP session. To account for this, a 32-bit sequence number is commonly used, where the lower 16 bits encode the RTP sequence number of a packet, and the upper 16 bits encode the number of times the sequence number space has wrapped around to zero.

The *inter-arrival jitter* field provides an estimate of the statistical variance of the RTP media packet inter-arrival time. This header field is measured in timestamp units and expressed as a signed integer.

The *last SR timestamp* (*LSR*) header field captures the middle 32 of the 64 bits received in the NTP timestamp header field of the previous SR packet to which this RR block corresponds. If there haven't been any RTCP SR packets received from the source, this field is set to 0.

The *delay since last SR* (*DSLR*) header field is a 32-bit field expressed in units of 1/65536 seconds that calculates the delay between receiving the last SR packet from a source (to which this RR block corresponds) and sending this RR block. If no SR packet has been received yet from the corresponding source, this header field is set to 0.

RTCP receiver reports are commonly used to provide reception quality feedback to senders in real time. Senders can then use these reports to alter their transmission patterns. RTCP reports are also used by third-party monitoring applications to gauge the overall media quality of sessions from a local, regional, or global perspective.

RTCP Source Description (SDES) Packet

The RTCP SDES packet is primarily used to provide a persistent participant identifier that spans SSRC changes and system restarts. In addition to providing a persistent identifier, it also provides information such as the participant name, email address, location, and telephone number. The common SDES packet format, is diagrammed in Figure 5-7, carries the packet type 202. SDES packets contain zero or more chunks, the exact count of which is captured in the SC header field value.

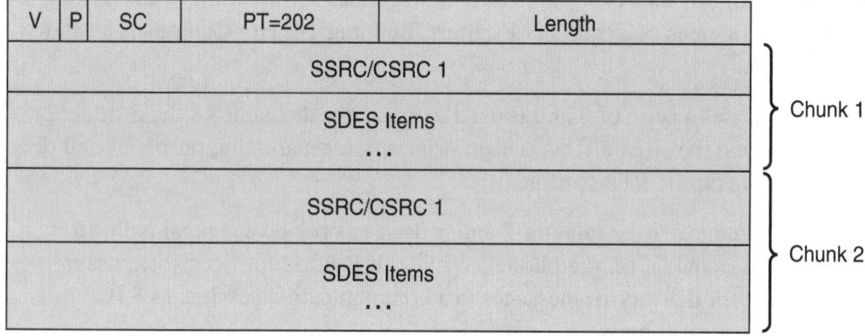

Figure 5-7 *SDES Common Packet Format*

Each item chunk begins with the SSRC of the sender, followed by a string of entries in the format shown in Figure 5-8. The *type* header field conveys the type of the SDES RTCP packet, and the *length* header field encodes (as UTF-8) the number of octets of text present.

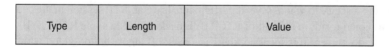

Figure 5-8 *SDES Item Format*

The *CNAME SDES* item carries a type value of 1 and is the only mandatory SDES packet that must be sent by all implementations. This packet provides a persistent transport-level identifier for the participant, known as the CNAME. The CNAME of a participant is expected to stay the same across SSRC changes and system restarts, and it is expected to be unique in an RTP session or a group of related RTP sessions. The CNAME header field value is derived algorithmically using the format *user@host* or just *host* when the username is unavailable. The CNAME is essential for a receiver to identify and synchronize media streams that originate from a given source.

The *NAME SDES* item carries a type value of 2 and is required to provide the name of a participant. This is usually populated by a user and can be in a format as desired by the user (for example, **John Doe**). The NAME SDES item can be used by applications to populate conference rosters as participants join. This SDES item should not be considered unique among all participants in a communication session.

The EMAIL SDES item carries a type value of 3 and is used to convey the email of the participant in RFC 2822 format (for example, John.Doe@example.com). The email of the participant is expected to remain persistent during the course of an RTP session.

The *PHONE SDES* item carries a type value of 4 and reflects the phone number of the participant in international format.

The *LOC SDES* item carries a type value of 5 and encodes the location of the participants with varying degrees of detail. For example, **Building 14, HQ Campus** is a valid encoding.

The *TOOL* item carries a type of 6 and is used to advertise the name of the product or application generating the stream. This is used primarily for marketing purposes and does not have any bearing on the RTP session.

The *NOTE SDES* item carries a value of 7 and is used to provide a general indication such as a status (for example, **on the phone**). While this is good for occasional usage, it must not be used for delivery of messages in a communication session, as RTCP is exchanged too infrequently between participants.

The *PRIV SDES* item carries a value of 8 and is used for experimental purposes.

RTCP Goodbye Packet (BYE)

The RTCP BYE packet is transmitted whenever a participant leaves an RTP session or whenever an SSRC collision is detected. There are certain timing considerations that participants need to take into account while transmitting RTCP BYE messages to prevent congestion. Consider a scenario where several participants leave an RTP session at around the same time; this could result in a flood of RTCP BYE packets and in some RTCP BYE messages being lost. To prevent this scenario, there is a back-off algorithm provided with RTCP BYE transmission.

The format of the RTCP BYE packet is depicted in Figure 5-9; it has the packet type value 203. The SC header field captures the number of SSRC/CSRC identifiers present in this RTCP BYE packet. There is an optional 8-bit field that captures the number of octets present in the following header field, reserved for the purpose of specifying a reason for leaving. The reason for leaving header field provides a textual description of why the source decided to leave the RTP session. An example encoding of this header field could be **camera not operational**.

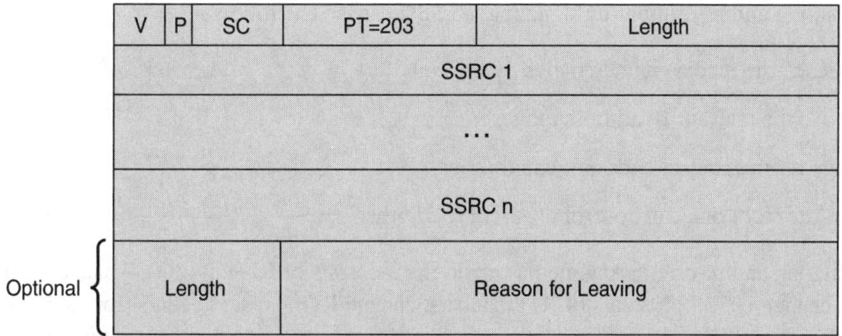

Figure 5-9 *RTCP Goodbye Packet Format*

RTCP APP Packet (APP)

The RTCP APP packet, also known as the application-defined RTCP packet, allows for application-specific extensions. This packet type is primarily used to exchange proprietary information. As newer application-specific extensions are developed and tested sufficiently, they may evolve to become valid RTCP packet types.

Note As highlighted earlier, for UDP and similar transport layer protocols, applications must use an even port number for RTP and the next higher (odd) port number for RTCP.

SBC Handling of RTP and RTCP

Chapter 1, "Laying the Groundwork," provides a brief introduction to SBCs and touches on some of the functional aspects of these devices. While SBCs are tremendously flexible and important in modern multimedia networks, there is a wide range in terms of how SBCs handle RTP and RTCP traffic. SBCs function as back-to-back user agents (B2BUAs), by both terminating and re-originating media and signaling. This behavior is diagrammed in Figure 5-10.

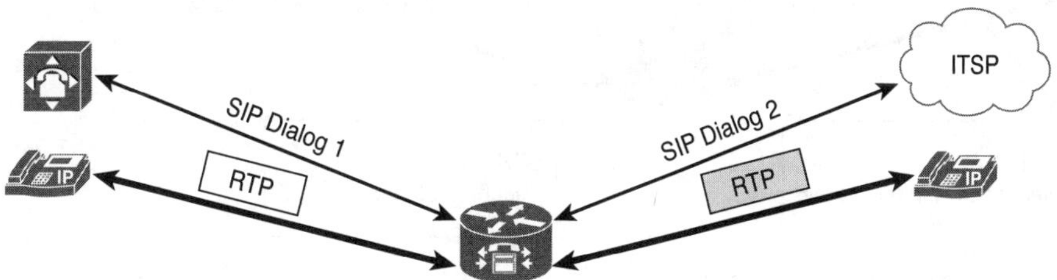

Figure 5-10 *SBC Operation on Media and Signaling*

By terminating and re-originating signaling, an SBC can do the following:

- Influence the media characteristics of the call
- Expose the relevant IP address ranges
- Bridge mismatches in endpoint capabilities
- Translate from one call control protocol to another

By terminating and re-originating media traffic that consists of RTP and RTCP packets, an SBC can change UDP/IP headers of RTP packets, change RTP packet headers (for example, SSRC, sequence numbers, timestamps), and perform translation operations on the RTP packet payloads. Changing RTP headers or RTP payloads midpath disrupts the end-to-end nature of RTP, and endpoints remain unaware of the presence of the SBC within the communication session. This could lead to issues when RTCP reports are exchanged between endpoints, as described in the following paragraphs.

Consider the sample topology diagrammed in Figure 5-11, where Endpoints A and B set up a communication session and begin transmitting media packets with each other through an SBC. As a matter of local policy, the SBC might change the SSRC and sequence numbers of media packets as they are exchanged back and forth between Endpoint A and Endpoint B. This could lead to issues when RTCP sender reports, receiver reports, or SDES CNAME packets are exchanged end-to-end without SBC intervention/manipulation, resulting in references to SSRCs or sequence numbers being introduced by the SBC instead of the values from actual endpoints.

For example, if Endpoint B were to send an RTCP compound packet with a sender report and a receiver report block, the SSRC and extended highest sequence number header field (in the RR) would incorrectly reference the SSRC and sequence numbering introduced by the SBC. The header field values in such RTCP packets would make little sense when interpreted by Endpoint A and would cause issues in collating statistics of the session.

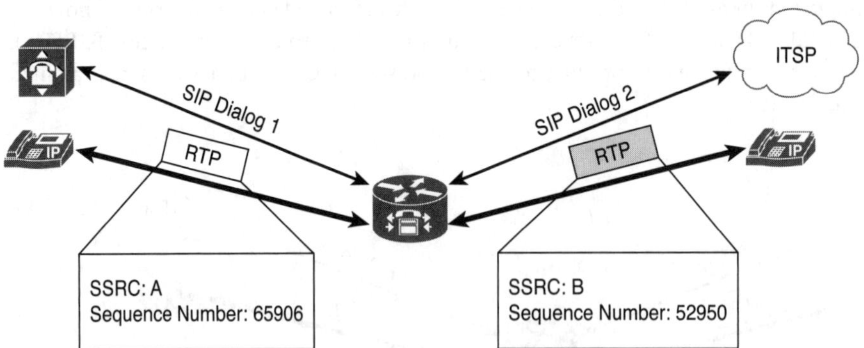

Figure 5-11 *SBCs Changing SSRCs and Sequence Numbers of RTP Packets*

While making use of RTCP as a general feedback mechanism for packet retransmission (as defined in RFC 4585), the SSRC of the RTCP packet sender and the SSRC of the source from which retransmission is required is included in the RTCP feedback packet.

Also included in the RTCP packet are sequence numbers of media packets for which retransmissions are requested. With an SBC altering the sequence numbering of packets, it is very possible that an end-to-end RTCP feedback message from one endpoint to another may reference the sequence numbers introduced by the SBC and not by the endpoint itself. This would lead to a breakdown of the overall RTCP feedback framework. This scenario is diagrammed in Figure 5-12.

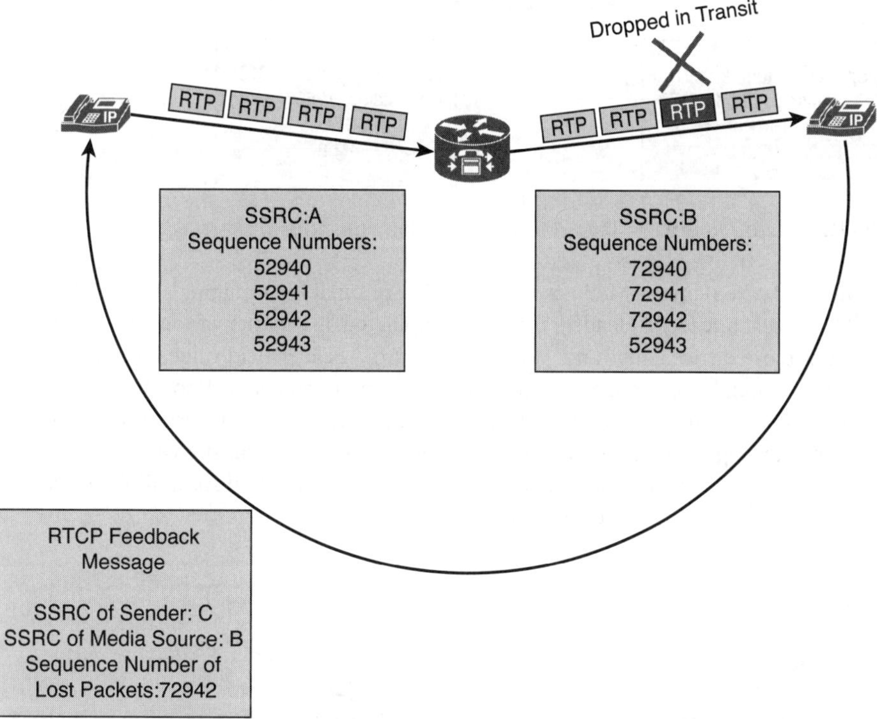

Figure 5-12 *RTCP Feedback Messages Using SBCs*

As a result of the scenario described earlier, it is essential for SBCs to ensure that any operations that span the header fields or payloads of RTP packets don't negatively impact the RTCP framework. In general, SBCs must ensure that whatever changes are made to RTP headers and payloads are accounted for in RTCP messages. This can either be done by having the SBC rewrite RTCP packet header field values or by simply terminating and re-originating RTCP packets for each individual call leg.

To understand how SBCs can influence RTP and RTCP traffic, here we revisit the Chapter 1 discussion on the different types of B2BUAs:

- **Media relays**—Media relays transparently forward RTP and RTCP traffic from one call leg to the other without looking into the RTP/RTCP packet headers and payloads. This means that SSRC identifiers, sequence numbering, timestamps, and RTP payloads are untouched across the entire end-to-end path. Most SBCs function this way, and some of the problems described in the previous paragraph don't apply to media relays. Figure 5-13 diagrams a media relay.

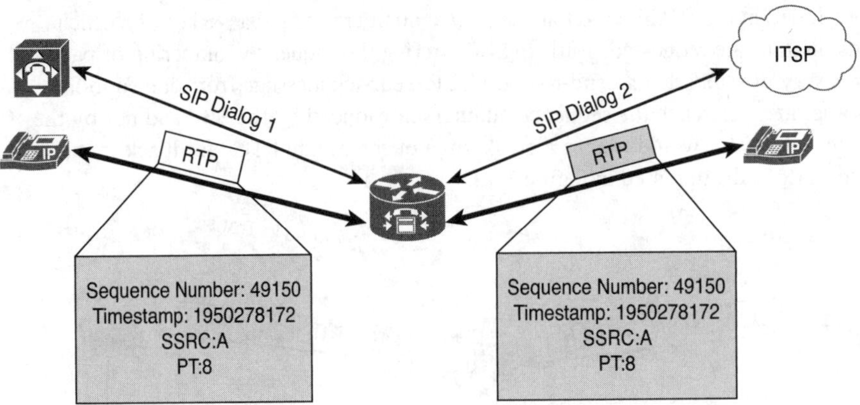

Figure 5-13 *Media Relay*

- **Media-aware relays**—Media-aware B2BUAs are capable of manipulating RTP and RTCP packet headers. Headers may be manipulated as a matter of local security policy, as these devices might not want to pass across header field values such as SSRC, sequence numbers, and CNAME transparently from one network to another. This is especially true in the case of the CNAME header field, as it can carry the identity of the participant in **user@host** format. Media-aware relays must ensure that whatever changes are made to RTP packet headers are compensated for in RTCP packets. Figure 5-14 diagrams a media-aware relay.

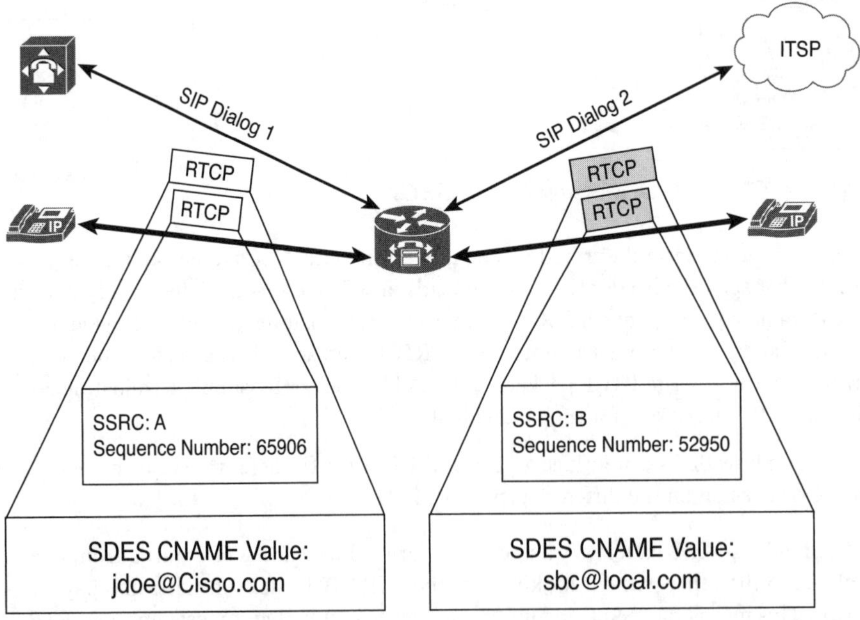

Figure 5-14 *Media-Aware Relay*

- **Media terminators**—Media terminators are capable of performing operations on the RTP packet header fields and payloads. Payload operations could include transcoding from one media-encoding scheme to another, transrating from one packetization period to another, or encrypting payloads using a cipher. While performing operations on RTP packet payloads, appropriate RTP and RTCP headers have to be manipulated by the B2BUA. For example, when transrating RTP packets from one packetization period to another for a given RTP session, the number of packets received and sent on the SBC can vary greatly over time. Therefore, RTP headers cannot just be transparently passed from one call leg to another without due manipulation by the SBC on the RTP and packet headers.

There have to be similar changes made to the RTCP packet headers as well. For example, consider the same transrating scenario as before. Because packet counts would likely differ greatly over time across both call legs, the SBC has to ensure that RTCP sender and receiver reports are changed a great deal before being forwarded. Figure 5-15 diagrams a media terminator.

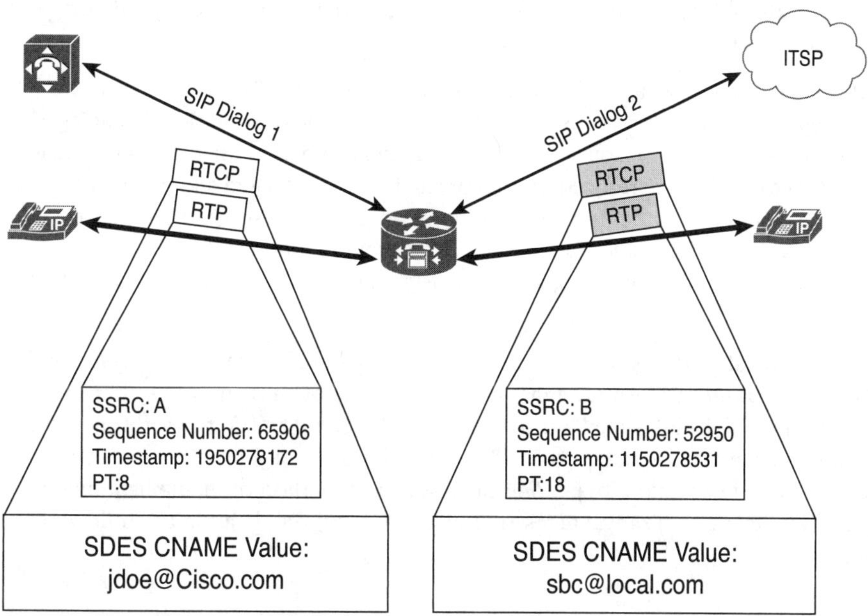

Figure 5-15 *Media Terminator*

SBCs tend to oscillate operational modes between media relays, media-aware relays, and media terminators, based on the configuration and dynamic requirements of each situation. For example, there could be a simple G.711 audio call traversing the SBC, in which case the SBC operates like a media relay transparently passing RTP packets without header or payload manipulations from one call leg to another.

Due to application interactions on one of the user agents, a dynamic request to change the codec to G.729 can be made over SIP and SDP. The SBC might be configured to invoke a transcoder and interwork G.729 and G.711, in which case it needs to overwrite RTP headers and RTCP headers and rework RTP payloads. This situation requires the SBC to no longer function as just a media relay, so the SBC then begins functioning as a media terminator. SBCs have these dynamic operational states built in to software logic to ensure that the end-to-end nature of RTP and RTCP is preserved across a myriad of scenarios.

Another factor that weighs in heavily on media plane operations is the negotiation of RTP- and RTCP-based extensions during session setup. Several extensions to RTP and RTCP have been standardized over the years to introduce additional functionality and increase the robustness of these peer protocols. Some examples of these are explicit SSRC indication in SDP (RFC 5576) and RTCP-based feedback mechanisms (RFC 4585). Given that SBCs are in the path of RTP and RTCP traffic, it is important that these extensions be supported by the SBC to ensure that the RTP/RTCP framework is kept intact. If an SBC is unable to extend support to an RTP/RTCP extension, it has to influence the SDP negotiation by rejecting support for such an extension.

In addition to terminating and re-originating standard RTP and RTCP traffic, there are several media-based features on SBCs that enable a multitude of operations spanning specialized media handling, monitoring, reporting, and troubleshooting. Certain media-based features on SBCs are realized in software and can be activated and deactivated with simple commands. Other features require the additional presence of specialized hardware, such as a DSP, in addition to the required configuration. Before discussing various media-related features on SBCs, it is extremely important to first get a sense of how they handle media traffic.

The two principal methods of media handling on SBCs are *media flow-through* and *media flow-around*. A close examination of the names of these modes ought to reveal how an SBC handles media traffic: Either RTP/RTCP traffic flows through the SBC from one network segment to another, or it flows directly between endpoints in a communication session, bypassing the SBC. Each method of media handling has unique advantages and disadvantages, and discussed in more detail in the following sections.

Media Flow-Around

Media flow-around refers to the passage of RTP and RTCP traffic directly between endpoints in a communication session, completely bypassing the SBC. The SBC is in the signaling path and is responsible for session setup/modification/teardown; however, the SBC manipulates the SDP in such a way so as to allow direct passage of RTP between the endpoints. Figure 5-16 diagrams a typical media flow-around call on an SBC.

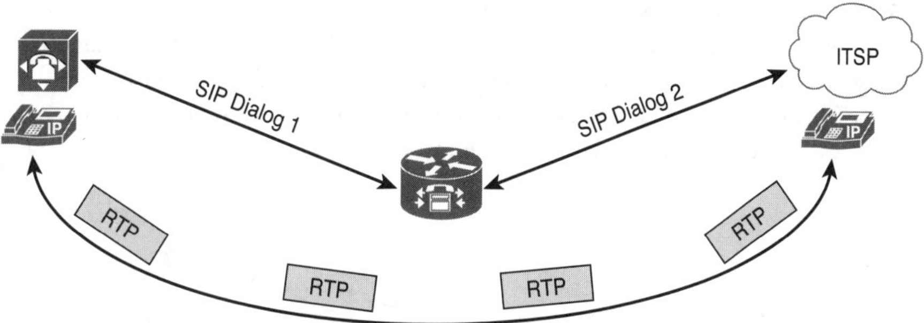

Figure 5-16 *Media Flow-Around Call*

Media flow-around calls ensure that the SBC participates only in call setup, modification, and teardown and does not handle any media traffic; this affords greater CPU and memory cycles and increases the overall throughput. With RTP and RTCP flowing directly between endpoints, the media path is akin to a point-to-point call, without any potential RTP/RTCP header or payload manipulation by intermediary devices.

Enabling media flow-around, where RTP/RTCP traffic bypass the SBC, is strictly deployment specific and must be configured after due consideration, knowledge, and analysis of some of the limitations of an SBC in media flow-around mode.

Note Many SBCs (including CUBE) have the ability to dynamically fall back from media flow-around to media flow-through mode based on the SDP offer/answer exchange. For example, as a communication session is being set up, if the user agents cannot converge on a common encoding scheme, the call falls back to a media flow-through call to allow passage of the audio packets through the SBC. This ensures that the SBC can perform transcoding before sending out RTP traffic.

Media Flow-Through

Media flow-through refers to the passage of RTP and RTCP traffic through an SBC on session setup and modification (possibly by using midcall codec and media format changes) until the call is terminated. With RTP and RTCP traffic traversing the SBC, it is possible to perform several operations on media traffic that span RTP header manipulation, RTP payload manipulation to real-time diagnostics, and reporting.

Decisions can be made dynamically during session setup to provide the appropriate handling of RTP, including whether the SBC needs to function in media relay mode, transparently passing RTP/RTCP headers and payloads from one call leg to the other, or whether it needs to function as a media terminator and invoke a transcoder.

Figure 5-17 depicts a typical media flow-through call where RTP and RTCP traverse the SBC. While media flow-through calls place processing overhead on the SBC for handling and possibly transforming RTP packets, it remains the default mode of operation for most SBCs. The ability of an SBC to perform a rich array of features on media is one of the reasons it is so common in modern communication networks.

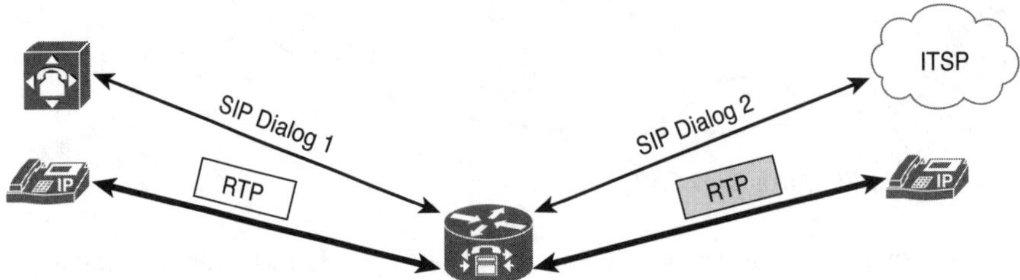

Figure 5-17 *Media Flow-Through Call*

One of the greatest advantages of having SBCs serve as an intermediary device in a communication session that spans disparate networks is their ability to bridge capability mismatches that occur in the media plane. They also perform a myriad of operations on the media plane, such as RTP forking, generating highly customizable and granular call quality metrics, and spoofing RTCP traffic. All these feature sets are only made available when media traffic traverses the SBC.

Due to the advantages of increased flexibility with media flowing through the SBC, media flow-through is the preferred and more common deployment for most SBCs.

Configuration for Media Handling

This section deals with configuration for media handling on SBCs, using CUBE as an example. The configuration and diagnostic **show** commands are specific to Cisco IOS/IOS XE software.

Media flow-around can be configured either in global mode or in dial-peer configuration mode by using the **media** command. Table 5-2 provides the arguments to the **media** command.

Table 5-2 *Arguments to the* media *Command*

Command	Argument	Meaning
media [flow-around | flow-through]	flow-around	Configures the CUBE to operate in media flow-around mode.
	flow-through	Configures the CUBE to operate in media flow-through mode.

Note The default mode of operation on CUBE is media flow-through. As a result, there isn't a need to explicitly configure **media flow-through** at the global or dial-peer level when this mode of operation is intended.

Example 5-2 demonstrates the configuration of media flow-around in the global configuration mode, which means that media flow-around applies to all calls traversing CUBE.

Example 5-2 *Configuring Media Flow-Around in Global Configuration Mode*

```
CUBE(config)# voice service voip
CUBE(conf-voi-serv)# media flow-around
```

Example 5-3 demonstrates the configuration of media flow-around in dial-peer configuration mode.

Note Both of the dial peers must be configured for media flow-around; otherwise, the call is a media flow-through call.

Example 5-3 *Configuring Media Flow-Around in Dial-Peer Mode*

```
dial-peer voice 1703 voip
 incoming called-number 14085553471
 session protocol sipv2
 voice-class codec 1
 no vad
 dtmf-relay rtp-nte
 media flow-around
 fax protocol t38 ls-redundancy 0 hs-redundancy 0 fallback pass-through g711ulaw

dial-peer voice 1803 voip
 destination-pattern 14085553471
 session protocol sipv2
 session target ipv4:192.0.2.1
 voice-class codec 1
 no vad
 dtmf-relay rtp-nte
 media flow-around
 fax protocol t38 ls-redundancy 0 hs-redundancy 0 fallback pass-through g711ulaw

! Or, alternatively...
!
```

```
CUBE(config)#voice class media 1
CUBE(config-class)# media flow-around

dial-peer voice 1703 voip
incoming called-number 14085553471
session protocol sipv2
voice-class codec 1
no vad
dtmf-relay rtp-nte
voice-class media 1
fax protocol t38 ls-redundancy 0 hs-redundancy 0 fallback pass-through g711ulaw

dial-peer voice 1803 voip
destination-pattern 14085553471
session protocol sipv2
session target ipv4:192.0.2.1
voice-class codec 1
no vad
dtmf-relay rtp-nte
voice-class media 1
fax protocol t38 ls-redundancy 0 hs-redundancy 0 fallback pass-through g711ulaw
```

Note If media flow-around is enabled globally (in **voice service voip** mode), all calls are handled as media flow-around calls, unless explicitly overridden in dial-peer configuration mode with the **media flow-through** command.

Verification of whether calls are handled in media flow-through or media flow-around can be done in real time by using **show** commands or reactively by analyzing call logs. Understanding how CUBE handles RTP is extremely important while troubleshooting audio-related issues such as one-way or no-way audio. For example, consider the sample topology shown in Figure 5-18, where CUBE interconnects an enterprise network and a service provider network over the public Internet. To ensure that there is minimal scope for network attacks mounted from the Internet, direct IP connectivity between the two networks is disabled.

In the network topology diagrammed in Figure 5-18, CUBE can successfully establish the communication session between the media endpoints. However, the communication session is set up to ensure direct passage of RTP and RTCP traffic between the endpoints, completely bypassing CUBE. Given that there is no IP reachability between the communicating endpoints, routing of RTP and RTCP traffic directly between the endpoints is impossible. The lack of IP reachability between the communicating endpoints manifests as no-way audio, wherein the call connects fine, but either participant hears silence.

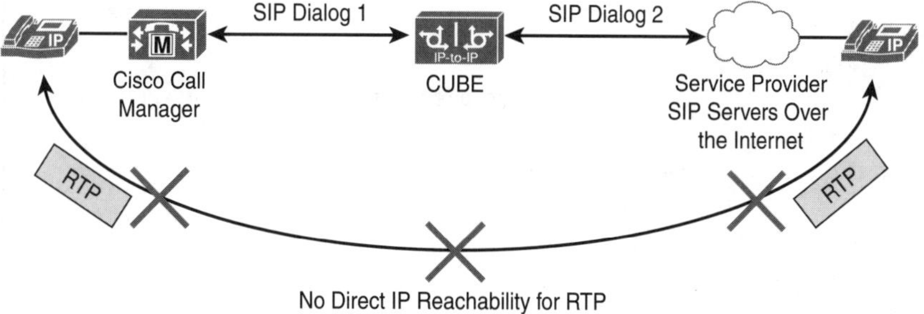

Figure 5-18 *No-Way Audio in a Media Flow-Around Call*

To verify the media flow mode for calls in real time, the **show sip calls** and **show voip rtp connections** commands are highly useful. The **show sip calls** command provides some useful information about the SIP session and its corresponding media session. Example 5-4 provides sample output of the **show sip calls** command when the call is in media flow-around mode.

Example 5-4 *Sample Output of the* **show sip calls** *Command*

```
CUBE-2# show sip calls
Total SIP call legs:2, User Agent Client:1, User Agent Server:1
SIP UAC CALL INFO
Call 1
SIP Call ID                 : 3F3B5FFA-F90E11E6-80BCBCE3-29A73B59@192.0.2.195
   State of the call        : STATE_ACTIVE (7)
   Substate of the call     : SUBSTATE_NONE (0)
   Calling Number           : 408345
   Called Number            : 4082000
!!! Omitted for brevity

Media Mode                  : flow-around
   Media Stream 1
     State of the stream      : STREAM_ACTIVE
     Stream Call ID           : 21696
     Stream Type              : voice+dtmf (1)
     Stream Media Addr Type   : 1
     Negotiated Codec         : g711ulaw (160 bytes)

!!! Omitted for brevity

Options-Ping    ENABLED:NO    ACTIVE:NO
   Number of SIP User Agent Client(UAC) calls: 1
```

```
SIP UAS CALL INFO
Call 1
SIP Call ID                  : 3EA098A0-F90E11E6-88ECD9BE-3B16EEBB@192.0.2.196
   State of the call         : STATE_ACTIVE (7)
   Substate of the call      : SUBSTATE_NONE (0)
   Calling Number            : 408345
   Called Number             : 4082000

!!! Omitted for brevity
   Media Mode                : flow-around
   Media Stream 1
     State of the stream        : STREAM_ACTIVE
     Stream Call ID             : 21695
     Stream Type                : voice+dtmf (0)
     Stream Media Addr Type     : 1
     Negotiated Codec           : g711ulaw (160 bytes)
!!! Omitted for brevity
Options-Ping    ENABLED:NO    ACTIVE:NO
   Number of SIP User Agent Server(UAS) calls: 1
```

For media flow-through calls, the **Media Mode** attribute of the **show sip calls** command is set to **flow-through** instead of **flow-around.**

The **show voip rtp connections** command is useful for displaying both the number of active RTP sessions on CUBE and the number of available RTP ports and the IP address/ RTP port details of RTP sessions. Example 5-5 provides sample output of the **show voip rtp connections** command for a media flow-through call.

Example 5-5 *Sample Output of the* **show voip rtp connections** *Command*

```
CUBE-2# show voip rtp connections
VoIP RTP Port Usage Information:
Max Ports Available: 8091, Ports Reserved: 101, Ports in Use: 2
                                        Min    Max    Ports
! Omitted for brevity
VoIP RTP active connections :
No. CallId     dstCallId  LocalRTP RmtRTP      LocalIP          RemoteIP        MPSS
1     2182        2183        16452     16496    192.0.2.195      192.0.2.196     NO
2     2184        2183        16454     24522    192.0.2.195      192.0.2.223     NO

! Omitted for brevity
```

The **show voip rtp connections** command does not display any output for media flow-around calls, as RTP packets bypass CUBE and hence are not relevant for that deployment type.

Generic RTP and RTCP Handling by SBCs

Now that a clear distinction has been made between media flow-through and media flow-around on SBCs, it is important to understand how an SBC handles RTP and RTCP in the context of being a B2BUA. The concept of a media relay is briefly discussed earlier; recall that a media relay functions as an intermediary device that passes RTP traffic from one call leg to another without any transformation of the RTP headers or payloads. For simple calls that do not require any DSP involvement, an SBC functions as a media relay, passing across RTP packet headers and payloads from one call leg to another, without any manipulation. Its operation is similar to what is diagrammed in Figure 5-13.

For calls that require RTP packets to be transformed in some way before being forwarded out to the peer call leg (for example, transcoding, transrating, encryption), an SBC functions as a media terminator. *Media terminators* manipulate RTP packet headers and payloads. The operation of an SBC as a media terminator is akin to the behavior diagrammed in Figure 5-15. By functioning as a media terminator, an SBC can transform RTP packet headers (such as the SSRC, sequence numbers, and timestamps), as well as the RTP payloads.

For simple calls that do not require DSPs, the media relay behavior of an SBC is also applied to RTCP. This means that sender reports, receiver reports, and SDES packets are sent without any transformation from one call leg to another. In the case of calls that require DSPs to manipulate RTP packets, however, an SBC overwrites various header fields in the RTCP reports.

Assisted RTCP on SBCs

RTCP traffic is extremely useful in a communication session as it provides reception quality feedback, assists in synchronization of the media clock with a common reference, and enables correlation between different media streams transmitted by an endpoint. In addition, RTCP is vital in providing a global view of the communication session, and it can be used to analyze transient or permanent faults in the network. Despite the huge value RTCP brings to a communication session, certain endpoints do not support the generation of RTCP traffic. This could be challenging in networks where RTCP reports are relied upon for monitoring media quality status.

Another use case for RTCP traffic is to serve as a keepalive mechanism and validate session liveliness because RTCP packets are exchanged at fixed intervals, regardless of whether actual RTP media are exchanged for the duration of interest.

In scenarios where endpoints are incapable of generating RTCP traffic, there might be moments in a call during which no media are transmitted from either or both of the endpoints (for example, when a call is put on hold). To ensure that the session stays alive during these scenarios, an SBC can be configured to generate RTCP reports on behalf of the endpoints. This allows for validating that the session is still active.

The assisted RTCP feature on SBCs can either generate RTCP packets that are very generic, such that a packet contains a single receiver report and an SDES CNAME item, or detailed RTCP packets that encapsulate true session statistics. The assisted RTCP feature on CUBE provides a very generic RTCP report at periodic intervals, and it therefore cannot be used to determine reception statistics. This serves purely as a means to ensure that RTCP traffic is generated at defined time intervals to keep the session alive.

Configuration of Assisted RTCP

The configuration for assisted RTCP is provided in Example 5-6.

Example 5-6 *Sample Configuration of Assisted RTCP*

```
CUBE-2# conf t
CUBE-2(config)# voice service voip
CUBE-2(conf-voi-serv)#rtcp keepalive
CUBE-2(conf-voi-serv)# exit
CUBE-2(config)#ip rtcp report interval 5000
```

The assisted RTCP feature is activated by using the **rtcp keepalive** and **ip rtcp report interval <duration>** commands. The periodicity of assisted RTCP reports can be set to an appropriate duration ranging from 1 to 65535 milliseconds by using the **ip rtcp report interval** command.

Symmetric and Asymmetric RTP/RTCP

Although RTP and RTCP can both run over TCP (RFC 4571), the de facto choice of the transport protocol for RTP-/RTCP-based applications is UDP. UDP as a protocol isn't inherently bidirectional, which means that the UDP port allocated by the transport layer for transmitting traffic does not also need to be the same port that receives the traffic for the media session. It is possible to use two different ports: one to transmit RTP and another to receive RTP for the same session. This UDP directionality property is illustrated in Figure 5-19.

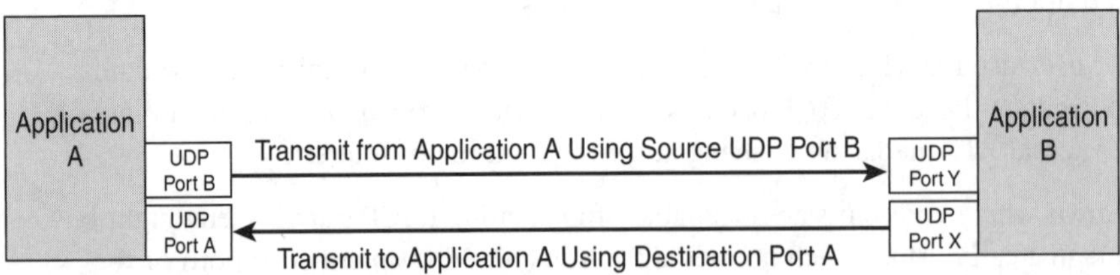

Figure 5-19 *UDP Directionality*

For both RTP and RTCP, if an endpoint receives RTP/RTCP on IP address X and UDP port x (denoted by *X:x*) and uses the same IP address and UDP port to transmit RTP (*X:x*), it is called a *symmetric endpoint*. Conversely, if an endpoint receives RTP/RTCP on IP address X and UDP port x (*X:x*) and transmits using a different IP address and/or UDP port, it is called an *asymmetric endpoint*. These concepts are diagrammatically illustrated in Figure 5-20 and Figure 5-21.

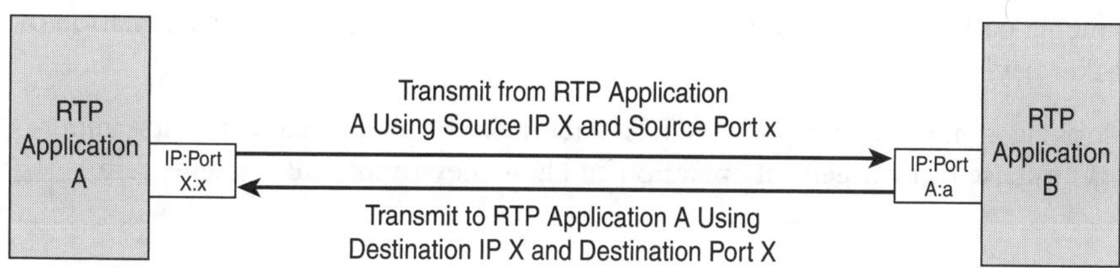

Figure 5-20 *Symmetric RTP*

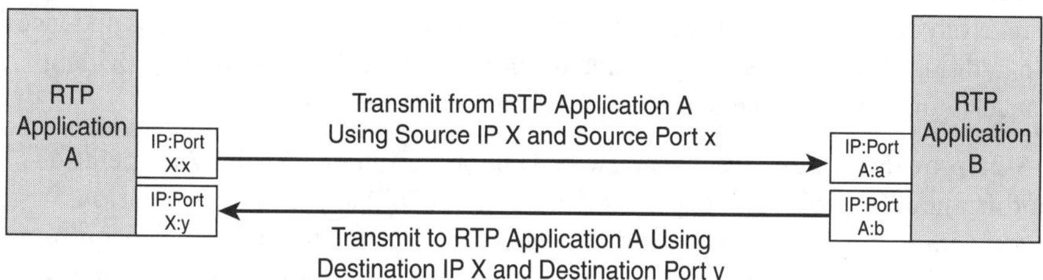

Figure 5-21 *Asymmetric RTP*

The RTP specification in RFC 3550 places no restriction on endpoints to either use symmetric RTP or asymmetric RTP; whether symmetric RTP is used is largely a matter of how the endpoint is designed. Using asymmetric RTP has certain implications in real-world deployments, especially when RTP traverses through intermediary devices such as media relays or devices performing NAT. Devices such as voice gateways and SBCs may drop asymmetric RTP packets, viewing them as a security threat, which results in one or no-way audio. If there is a presence of asymmetric media in a solution, full support of the behavior should be carefully considered for all devices in the media path.

RFC 3550 and accompanying standards don't specify an explicit port range for RTP/RTCP traffic. RTP and RTCP can typically use UDP ports from 1024 to 65535. Port numbers below 1024 aren't typically used for RTP-/RTCP-based applications because UNIX operating systems use these ports for privileged processes. Depending on the platform, CUBE uses the port range 8000 to 42801 (IOS XE-based devices) or the port range 16384 to 32767 (IOS-based devices).

DSP-Based RTP Handling on SBCs

As signaling and RTP sessions traverse an SBC, it is not uncommon for the media legs of a call to have vastly differing capabilities in terms of potential codecs supported, codec packetization periods, methods of DTMF, methods of faxing, and media payload encryption schemes. To effectively overcome these differences in the media plane, SBCs usually invoke specialized hardware in the form of DSPs. A DSP is inserted in a media path so that it can perform real-time manipulation and transformation of RTP packet payloads.

Before looking at how DSPs manipulate RTP packets in the media plane, it is first important to get a sense of their general operation and how they fit into SBC architecture.

Overview of DSPs on SBCs

DSPs are an extremely vital component of traditional media gateways that interconnect IP networks with analog and digital circuits. DSPs are responsible for translating voice signals received on traditional analog and digital circuits to RTP packet payloads and vice versa. In addition, DSPs are also responsible for manipulating signal strength, providing echo cancelation, enabling tone detection, and handling fax/modem calls.

Figure 5-22 provides a high-level overview of DSP operation on an SBC. All operations that modify the RTP payload manipulation are done in DSP logic. These operations may include transforming payloads from one encoding scheme to another, transforming the packetization period from one duration to another, or converting between raw in-band DTMF tones and named telephony events. The RTP stacks on SBCs are responsible for stripping off RTP headers before the contents of the media payload are sent to the DSP for manipulation. Once transformed, the media payload is sent back to the RTP stack, where is it packaged into the standard RTP packet format, as diagrammed in Figure 5-22.

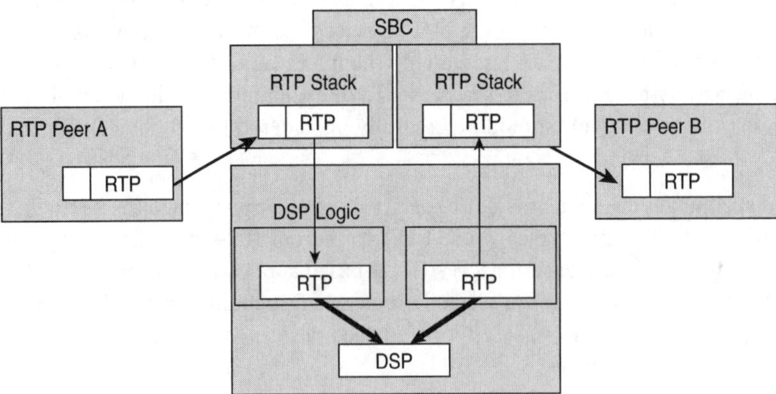

Figure 5-22 *DSP Operation on SBCs*

The placement or removal of DSPs is done dynamically, based on the media capabilities negotiated on a per-call-leg basis. Figure 5-23 depicts the dynamic placement and removal of DSPs on SBCs, based on the capabilities negotiated on a per-call-leg basis.

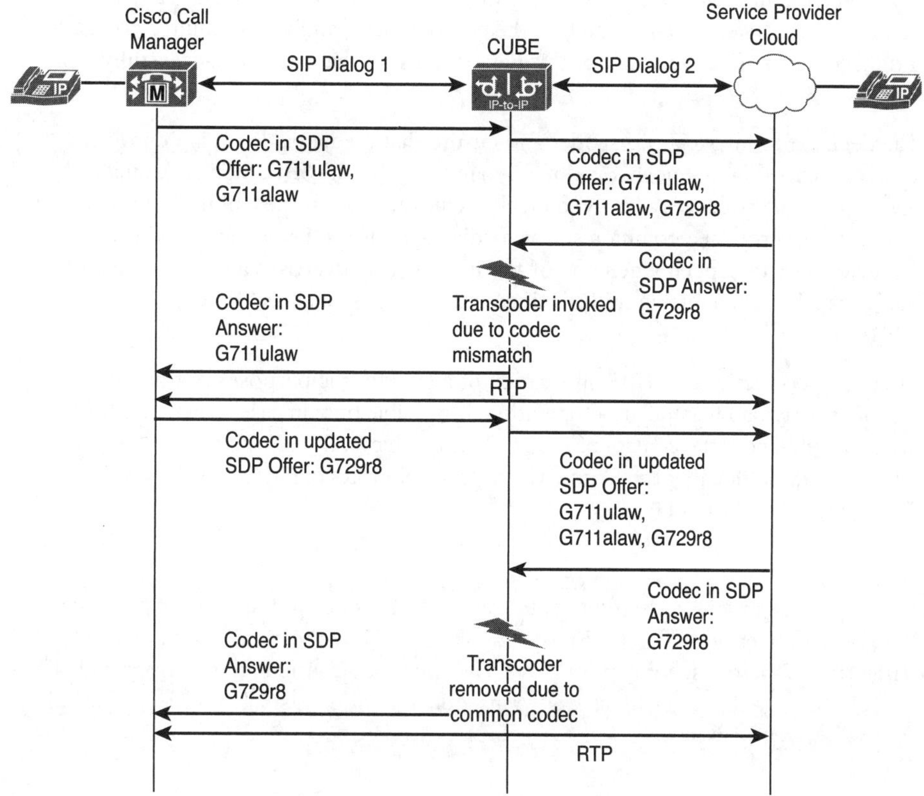

Figure 5-23 *Dynamic DSP Placement and Removal on SBCs*

The following sections describe some of the specific operations performed by DSPs on SBCs, the inherent need for such operations, the required configuration, and troubleshooting guidelines.

Transcoding

Transcoding refers to the process of changing one media encoding scheme to another or, in the context of this discussion, transforming one codec to another for a given media type, such as audio or video. Although transcoding can be performed with software, an inherent delay in software processing of audio usually results in a preference of transcoding being performed on discrete DSP hardware to reduce the latency and performance impact.

The need for a transcoder is realized in real time whenever there isn't a common set of media capabilities between the two call legs. For example, consider the sample call flow depicted in Figure 5-23. The two endpoints support a non-overlapping set of audio codecs. Given this mismatch in the audio codecs, an SBC is required to insert a transcoder to effectively bridge this gap and ensure that the call successfully completes.

The decision to invoke a transcoder and ensure that media payloads are converted from one encoding to another is done dynamically by the SBC. Similarly, once invoked, a transcoder may be dynamically removed later in the call if the user agents reconverge on a common set of media capabilities. Dynamically removing a transcoder can happen when one of the user agents advertises an updated list of media capabilities by using midcall signaling messages, such as SIP REINVITEs or UPDATEs.

From the perspective of CUBE, invocation of a DSP for the purposes of transcoding (or for any payload manipulation operation) is possible only in cases where the DSP is exclusively under the control of CUBE. This is achieved by registering a transcoding profile through either the Skinny Client Control Protocol (SCCP) or the Local Transcoding Interface (LTI).

Note One common misconception about transcoder functionality is that the presence of DSPs or a transcoder profile on CUBE is sufficient to achieve the required functionality. This isn't true as the transcoding profile on CUBE might be configured to register with a Cisco CallManager cluster, in which case transcoder operation is solely under the control of the CallManager cluster.

The following sections discuss the configuration required on CUBE to register transcoder profiles and the diagnostic commands required to verify transcoder functionality. The configuration and diagnostic commands are specific to IOS/IOS XE software running on CUBE and cannot be applied across all SBCs.

Skinny Client Control Protocol (SCCP) Transcoder

Figure 5-24 provides a high-level SCCP-based transcoding architecture.

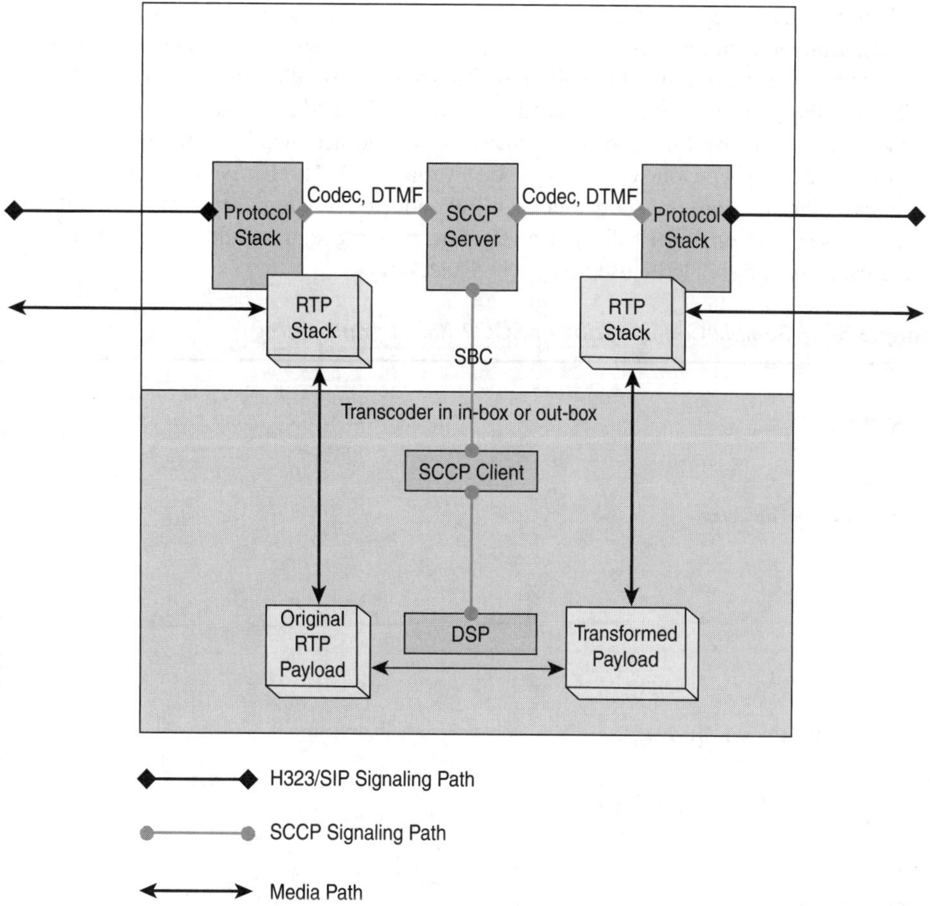

Figure 5-24 *SCCP-Based Transcoding Architecture on CUBE*

SCCP transcoding can be achieved by either locating DSPs on the same physical device that functions as CUBE (*in-box transcoding*) or on a separate device (*out-of-box transcoding*). The required configuration to ensure that SCCP-based transcoders register to CUBE can be broadly broken down into the following steps:

Step 1. Enable the required DSP resources for transcoding.

Step 2. Configure a transcoding profile with the required list of codecs.

Step 3. Enable the SCCP application on CUBE.

Step 4. Enable CUBE to function as the SCCP server.

These four basic steps are segregated into Sections 1, 2, 3, and 4 in the configuration snippet provided in Example 5-7. Before diving into a configuration example, however, it is important to understand the different flavors of transcoding available on CUBE. Transcoding can either be G.711-based or universal. *G.711-based transcoding* refers to the process of converting from G.711 µlaw/alaw to another encoding and vice versa. With this transcoding type, one call leg must be a variant of G.711. *Universal transcoding* refers to the ability to transcode between any codec pairs, without the restriction of having to use G.711 on either call leg. Universal transcoding requires additional DSP processing capacity and should be used only when necessary.

Example 5-7 *Sample Configuration of SCCP-Based Transcoding*

```
!
! Section 1
!
voice-card 0
 dsp services dspfarm
!
!


!
! Section 2
!
dspfarm profile 10 transcode
!
! -----------> for g711 to any
!
 codec g711ulaw
 codec g711alaw
 codec ilbc
 codec g723r63
 codec g723r53
 codec g729ar8
 codec g729abr8
 maximum sessions 10
 associate application SCCP
 no shutdown


dspfarm profile 20 transcode universal
!
! -------------> for Any to Any
!
 codec g711ulaw
 codec g711alaw
 codec ilbc
```

```
 codec g723r63
 codec g723r53
 codec g729ar8
 codec g729abr8
 maximum sessions 20
 associate application SCCP
 no shutdown
!
! Section 3
!

interface GigabitEthernet0/0
 ip address 209.165.200.225 255.255.255.224
 duplex auto
 speed auto
 media-type rj45
!
!
sccp local GigabitEthernet0/0
sccp ccm 209.165.200.225 identifier 1  version 7.0
sccp
!
sccp ccm group 1
 associate ccm 1 priority 1
 associate profile 20 register UNIVERSAL
 associate profile 10 register PCMXCODE
!
!
!
! Section 4
!
telephony-service
 ip source-address 209.165.200.225  port 2000
 sdspfarm units 2
 sdspfarm transcode sessions 12
 sdspfarm tag 1 UNIVERSAL
 sdspfarm tag 2 PCMXCODE
 max-ephones 1
 max-dn 1
 create cnf-files
```

Note While configuring transcoding profiles, the G.729r8 codec is not present by default. It has to be configured manually.

Note By default, **dspfarm** profiles are shut down. They have to be manually activated by issuing the **no shutdown** command.

The configuration snippet provided in Example 5-7 is segregated into four sections to show how to systematically configure an SCCP-based transcoder. The **maximum sessions** count specified under transcoding profiles **10** and **20** dictates the maximum number of G.711-based or universal transcoding sessions that can be handled at any given time. The **telephony-service** configuration is mandatory to ensure that the CUBE functions as an SCCP server and allows for transcoder profile registrations locally. The **sdspfarm units** command under **telephony-service** specifies the maximum number of **dspfarm** profiles that can register to CUBE. The **sdspfarm transcode sessions** command specifies the maximum number of transcoding sessions allowed by CUBE and is platform dependent.

Note An out-of-box transcoding solution is achieved when physical DSP resources are located on a separate device and register to CUBE by using SCCP. The configuration required is similar to Example 5-7, but the configuration highlighted in Sections 1, 2, and 3 must be done on the device that houses the DSPs. Only the configuration in Section 4 is required on CUBE to ensure that it functions as an SCCP server.

With the configuration complete, to verify whether the transcoder has successfully registered to CUBE, the **show dspfarm profile <*tag*>** command is used. Example 5-8 demonstrates the output of this command for a successful transcoder registration that has the profile identifier **40.**

Example 5-8 *Sample Output of the* **show dspfarm profile <tag>** *Command*

```
CUBE-2# show dspfarm profile 20
Dspfarm Profile Configuration

 Profile ID = 20, Service = TRANSCODING, Resource ID = 3
 Profile Description :
 Profile Service Mode : Non Secure
 Profile Admin State : UP
 Profile Operation State : ACTIVE
 Application : SCCP   Status : ASSOCIATED
 Resource Provider : FLEX_DSPRM   Status : UP
 Total Number of Resources Configured : 20
 Total Number of Resources Available : 20
 Total Number of Resources Out of Service : 0
 Total Number of Resources Active : 0
 Codec Configuration: num_of_codecs:7
 Codec : g723r53, Maximum Packetization Period : 60
Codec : g723r63, Maximum Packetization Period : 60
 Codec : ilbc, Maximum Packetization Period : 120
```

```
Codec : g711ulaw, Maximum Packetization Period : 30
Codec : g711alaw, Maximum Packetization Period : 30
Codec : g729ar8, Maximum Packetization Period : 60
Codec : g729abr8, Maximum Packetization Period : 60
```

With SCCP-based transcoding, the number of RTP streams per call increases from two to four. This increase in the total number of RTP streams per call—by a factor of two—can deplete the number of UDP ports available for other RTP sessions on CUBE. To optimize the number of RTP streams for transcoded calls and bring them in line with the regular calls, high-density transcoding can be used. Figure 5-25 demonstrates the difference in operation between a regular SCCP-based transcoder and a high-density SCCP-based transcoder. With high-density transcoding, media packet flow occurs directly to and from the logical RTP unit within the transcoder, without flowing through the RTP stack on CUBE. (Compare this figure against Figure 5-24 to see the difference.)

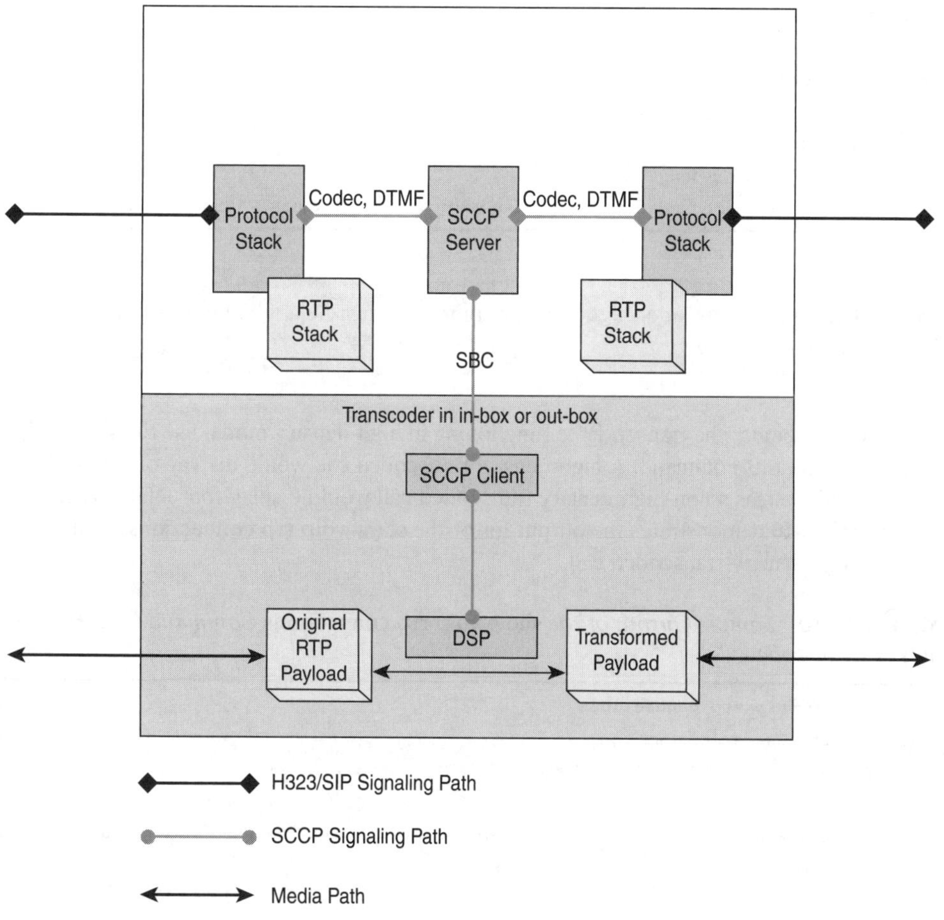

Figure 5-25 *High-Density SCCP Transcoding*

Using the **media transcoder high-density** command enables high-density transcoding on CUBE. Example 5-9 provides a configuration snippet for high-density transcoding.

Example 5-9 *Sample Configuration for High-Density Transcoding*

```
dial-peer voice 1703 voip
incoming called-number 14085553471
session protocol sipv2
voice-class codec 1
no vad
dtmf-relay rtp-nte
media transcoder high-density
fax protocol t38 ls-redundancy 0 hs-redundancy 0 fallback pass-through g711ulaw

dial-peer voice 1803 voip
destination-pattern 14085553471
session protocol sipv2
session target ipv4:192.0.2.1
voice-class codec 1
no vad
dtmf-relay rtp-nte
media transcoder high-density
fax protocol t38 ls-redundancy 0 hs-redundancy 0 fallback pass-through g711ulaw
```

Note The **media transcoder high-density** command must be applied to both the incoming and outgoing dial peers.

To verify whether the transcoder is functioning in high-density mode, use the **show voip rtp connections** command. A high-density transcoded call would display only two RTP sessions, whereas a non-high-density transcoded call would display four RTP sessions. Example 5-10 demonstrates the output for of the **show voip rtp connections** command for a high-density transcoded call.

Example 5-10 *Sample Output of the* **show voip rtp connections** *Command for a High-Density Transcoded Call*

```
CUBE-2# show voip rtp connections
VoIP RTP Port Usage Information:
Max Ports Available: 8091, Ports Reserved: 101, Ports in Use: 2
                                       Min   Max   Ports     Ports     Ports
Media-Address Range                    Port  Port  Available Reserved  In-use
```

```
----------------------------------------------------------------------------
Global Media Pool                        16384 32766 8091      101        2
----------------------------------------------------------------------------
VoIP RTP active connections :
No. CallId     dstCallId  LocalRTP RmtRTP    LocalIP          RemoteIP       MPSS
1      2182       2183       16452     16496     192.0.2.195   192.0.2.196    NO
2      2184       2183       16454     24522     192.0.2.195   192.0.2.223    NO
Found 2 active RTP connections
```

As shown the snippet presented in Example 5-10, the number of RTP sessions on CUBE for a high-density transcoded call is two, which is equal to the number of RTP sessions for regular calls. For regular SCCP transcoded calls, the number of RTP sessions increases from two to four. This is demonstrated in Example 5-11.

Example 5-11 *Sample Output of the* **show voip rtp connections** *Command for a Regular SCCP-Based Transcoded Call*

```
CUBE-2# sh voip rtp connections
VoIP RTP Port Usage Information:
Max Ports Available: 8091, Ports Reserved: 101, Ports in Use: 4
                                         Min    Max    Ports      Ports      Ports
Media-Address Range                      Port   Port   Available Reserved   In-use
----------------------------------------------------------------------------
Global Media Pool                        16384 32766 8091      101        4
----------------------------------------------------------------------------
VoIP RTP active connections :
No. CallId     dstCallId   LocalRTP RmtRTP    LocalIP          RemoteIP       MPSS
1      2203       2204       16456     16500     192.0.2.195    192.0.2.196    NO
2      2204       2203       16458     27292     192.0.2.195    192.0.2.223    NO
3      2205       2206       16460     2000      192.0.2.195    192.0.2.197    NO
4      2207       2206       16462     2000      192.0.2.195    192.0.2.198    NO
Found 4 active RTP connections
```

Note The **media transcoder high-density** command is not available on IOS XE-based platforms. Cisco development has made a concerted effort to encourage the adoption of LTI-based transcoding on newer platforms.

Local Transcoding Interface (LTI) Transcoder

Although SCCP-based transcoding was originally the way to register a transcoder, it was built on the top of a signaling protocol designed for endpoint communication. As a result, the protocol has complex signaling and many lines of configuration to enable the functionality. LTI transcoding offers an elegant and compact alternative to SCCP-based transcoding, making use of internal APIs to manage DSP resources. LTI-based transcoding is vastly simpler to configure and easier to troubleshoot, and it enables high-density transcoding by default.

Example 5-12 provides a configuration snippet for LTI transcoding.

Example 5-12 *Sample Configuration for LTI Transcoding*

```
dspfarm profile 10 transcode
!
! ------------> for g711 to any
!
 codec g711ulaw
 codec g711alaw
 codec ilbc
 codec g723r63
 codec g723r53
 codec g729ar8
 codec g729abr8
 maximum sessions 10
 associate application CUBE
 no shutdown
!
dspfarm profile 20 transcode universal
!
--------------> for Any to Any
!
 codec g711ulaw
 codec g711alaw
 codec ilbc
 codec g723r63
 codec g723r53
 codec g729ar8
 codec g729abr8
 maximum sessions 20
 associate application CUBE


 no shutdown
```

Note While configuring transcoding profiles, the G.729r8 codec is not present by default. It has to be configured manually.

Note By default, **dspfarm** profiles are shut down. They have to be manually activated by issuing the **no shutdown** command.

A simple comparison of Example 5-12 and Example 5-7 reveals the simplicity brought in by LTI transcoding on CUBE. Once LTI transcoding is configured, the **show dspfarm profile** ***<tag>*** command can be used to verify whether the LTI-based transcoder(s) are associated to CUBE. Example 5-13 demonstrates the expected output of the command for a scenario where the transcoder has successfully associated to CUBE.

Example 5-13 *Sample Output of the* **show dspfarm profile <tag>** *Command to Verify LTI Transcoder Association*

```
CUBE# show dspfarm profile 20
Dspfarm Profile Configuration
 Profile ID = 20, Service =Universal TRANSCODING, Resource ID = 1
 Profile Description :
 Profile Service Mode : Non Secure
 Profile Admin State : UP
 Profile Operation State : ACTIVE
 Application : CUBE   Status : ASSOCIATED
 Resource Provider : FLEX_DSPRM   Status : UP
 Number of Resource Configured : 20
 Number of Resources Out of Service : 0
 Number of Resources Active : 0
 Codec Configuration: num_of_codecs:7
 Codec : g723r53, Maximum Packetization Period : 60
 Codec : g723r63, Maximum Packetization Period : 60
 Codec : ilbc, Maximum Packetization Period : 120
 Codec : g711ulaw, Maximum Packetization Period : 30
 Codec : g711alaw, Maximum Packetization Period : 30
 Codec : g729ar8, Maximum Packetization Period : 60
 Codec : g729abr8, Maximum Packetization Period : 60
```

Table 5-3 details some of the differences between SCCP and LTI transcoding on CUBE.

Table 5-3 *Differences Between LTI and SCCP Transcoding*

Feature	SCCP Transcoding	LTI Transcoding
Control over DSP resources	The SCCP protocol stack controls DSP allocation and deallocation	DSPs are controlled by using internal APIs. Dependency on the SCCP protocol stack is removed.
Out-of-box transcoding	SCCP-based transcoding allows physical DSPs to be located on a separate box, as long as these DSPs register to the SCCP server stack on CUBE.	LTI transcoding does not support out-of-box transcoding.
High-density transcoding	High-density transcoding has to be configured explicitly (see Example 5-9). The example reference was previously incorrect. I changed it to reflect the correct reference.-Kaustubh	High-density transcoding is enabled by default.
Configuration	The configuration is verbose, as it has four logical sections.	The configuration is extremely simplified, as it does not use the SCCP/Call Manager Express (CME) architecture.

Transcoding remains one of the most important features offered by SBCs as they peer with networks that have different media capabilities. While it is possible to exercise strict control over the media characteristics of voice and video calls traversing the SBC—mostly by testing a myriad of different call flow scenarios and configuring devices appropriately—there are certain scenarios in which the use of transcoders is unavoidable. For example, in a communication session that is established between two endpoints that have absolutely no overlapping media capabilities in terms of the media formats, mode of in-band DTMF relay or media encryption schemes, an SBC will have to place a transcoder within the media path to achieve interoperability.

Transrating

Real-time networks transmit voice and video data over RTP such that each individual RTP packet contains a fixed-size payload that serves as an information unit. Within the RTP payload are the voice and video samples that are encoded and decoded at the sender and receiver applications, respectively. The time duration of media that is encoded within these payloads, known as the **packetization period**, can vary on a per-codec basis. For example, G.711-encoded streams can have packetization periods that vary from 5 milliseconds to 40 milliseconds.

Table 1 in RFC 3551 highlights the default packetization periods to be used by RTP-based applications for a myriad of codecs. Table 5-4 provides a few selected examples.

Table 5-4 *Default Packetization Periods of Common Audio Codecs*

Codec	Default Packetization Period (in milliseconds)
G723	30
G722	20
G729	20
PCMU	20
PCMA	20

The default packetization periods for different codecs merely serve as a recommendation and can be overridden when needed. Consider the network topology diagrammed in Figure 5-26, in which an SBC peers with a service provider and an enterprise network and such that G.729 is the codec used end-to-end. Between the enterprise network and SBC is a WAN link that is used to carry data and real-time traffic.

Consider that every RTP packet sent requires a predefined amount of header data. As a result, more packets sent per second result in more header data being sent, amounting to a higher consumption of bandwidth. As a result, increasing the packetization period may be desirable to reduce the amount of bandwidth from the resulting IP/UDP/RTP header.

A risk of increased packetization times is the increased latency required for the sampling of audio and an increased loss of audio content during packet loss, which results in a decrease in the ability to conceal the packet loss effect to the listener.

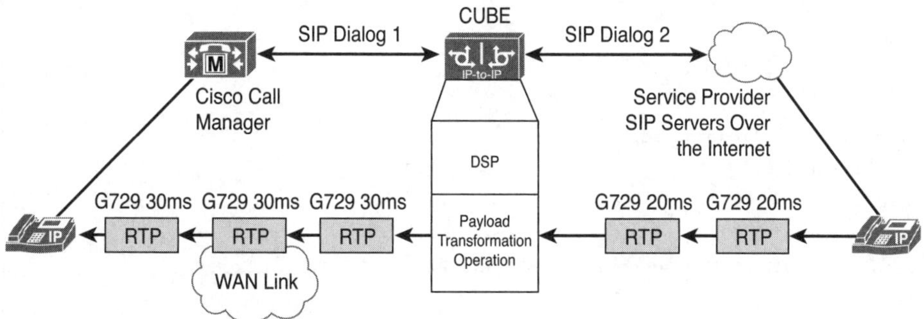

Figure 5-26 *Transrating on SBCs*

RTP sessions are subject to fixed and variable delays in packet transmission. With transrating, the only factor directly influenced is the packetization delay, which is the amount of time taken to encode the payload of the RTP packet.

Transrating can increase or decrease the packetization delay, depending on the amount of voice and video data encoded in RTP packet payloads. Increasing the packetization period (and hence delay) results in packets with large media payloads but decreases the overall number of packets that traverse the network.

Decreasing the packetization period means the media payloads are smaller, resulting in the packets being placed on the network much sooner and decreasing the likelihood of voice quality issues. The downside to this is the unnecessary and costly increase in overall bandwidth utilization. A decrease in the packetization period has no effect on the size of the RTP/UDP/IP headers, as packetization operations are specific to RTP payloads.

In RTP sessions that are set up using SIP and SDP, the packetization period is advertised using the **ptime** and **maxptime** attributes. The **ptime** attribute specifies the length of media within a packet, expressed in milliseconds, whereas the **maxptime** attribute specifies the maximum amount of media that can be encapsulated in a packet, also expressed in milliseconds. While setting up a communication session between RTP peers, in the ensuing offer answer exchange, if the **ptime** attribute is included in the SDP body by the offeror or answerer, it indicates the desired packetization interval that the offeror or answerer would expect to receive. Example 5-14 highlights the use of the **ptime** attribute in SDP.

Example 5-14 *Using the SDP* **ptime** *Attribute to Indicate the Desired Packetization Interval*

```
INVITE sip:2222@192.0.2.1:5060 SIP/2.0
Via: SIP/2.0/UDP 192.0.2.2:5060;branch=z9hG4bK531305
Remote-Party-ID: <sip:1111@192.0.2.2>;party=calling;screen=no;privacy=off
From: <sip:1111@192.0.2.2>;
To: <sip:2222@192.0.2.1>;tag=53A7B00-628
Date: Sat, 04 Feb 2017 07:11:33 GMT
Call-ID: 5113703A-E9E911E6-815DDB64-68BBC9B8@192.0.2.2
!
!
! Omitted for brevity
!
Content-Type: application/sdp
Content-Length: 221

v=0
o=CiscoSystemsSIP-GW-UserAgent 7031 5812 IN IP4 192.0.2.2
s=SIP Call
c=IN IP4 192.0.2.2
t=0 0
m=audio 16512 RTP/AVP 0
c=IN IP4 192.0.2.61
a=rtpmap:0 PCMU/8000
a=ptime:20
```

The **ptime** (or **maxptime**) attribute is encoded in SDP using the following format:

```
a=ptime:<packet time>
a=maxptime:<maximum packet time>
```

The numeric value specified in the attribute denotes the value, in milliseconds, of the desired packetization time or maximum possible packetization time, depending on whether the **ptime** or **maxptime** attribute is used. If the **ptime** attribute is not specified in the SDP, the default packetization period for the codec applies. (See Table 5-4 for a selected representation and Table 1 in RFC 3551 for further details.)

For any device that functions as an RTP source, media can potentially be encoded using different codecs and packetization periods. Consider the case of a phone supporting multiple codecs, such as PCMU, PCMA, G.729, G.722, and G.723; the phone might be configured to expect these codecs at different packetization rates. For example, the phone may need to see PCMU/PCMA packetized at 20 ms, whereas it might require G.723 packetized at 30 ms. This presents a peculiar problem when encoding this preference using the SDP **ptime** attribute: The **ptime** attribute cannot be used to provide the desired packetization period on a per-codec basis; rather, it applies to the entire media line, which could have a plurality of codecs. Example 5-15 demonstrates such an encoding.

Example 5-15 *Multiple Audio Codecs Advertised with the Same* **ptime**

```
m=audio 62052 RTP/AVP 18 4 8 101
a=rtpmap:18 G729/8000/1
a=rtpmap:4 G723/8000
a=fmtp:4 annexa=no;bitrate=5.3
a=rtpmap:8 PCMA/8000/1
a=rtpmap:101 telephone-event/8000
a=fmtp:101 0-15
a=sendrecv
a=ptime:20
```

Example 5-15 specifies a **ptime** value of 20 ms, which is applicable for all the codecs. This could easily cause issues if the device that encodes the SDP in Example 5-12 expects G.723 packets with a packetization period of 30 ms.

There have been attempts in the past to solve this problem by allowing for a more granular encoding of codec characteristics; however, due to lack of industry consensus, these approaches are not widely adopted, and using them may result in interoperability issues. While using the **ptime** attribute remains a recommendation, failure to receive media packets that adhere to the expected packetization rate can manifest in audio playback issues. For this reason, there may be a requirement to transrate codecs from one packetization rate to another.

From the perspective of SBCs, transrating can be a fairly common requirement as SBCs function as B2BUAs and abstract endpoint capabilities by breaking the end-to-end nature of SIP and SDP. Transrating can also be deliberately introduced by using configuration to increase packetization periods and efficiently utilize bandwidth.

Transrating on CUBE

Transrating on CUBE is achieved by using DSP resources that are configured as transcoder profiles. Using SCCP transcoders and using LTI transcoders are both viable options, and the procedure to register transcoding profiles remains exactly the same as described in the earlier section on transcoding.

Due to the challenges with representing multiple **ptimes** across a codec list in the SDP specification, using a suite of codecs with the **voice-class codec** command is not supported while transrating on CUBE. To ensure successful transrating, the call leg on which transrating occurs (where the codec is converted from one packetization period to another) must be configured to use a single codec with the packetization period explicitly configured.

Figure 5-26 demonstrates a transrating scenario where CUBE peers with the service provider and enterprise networks. The service provider network sends and expects G.729 packets with a packetization period of 20 ms, whereas the enterprise network sends and expects a packetization period of 30 ms. If CUBE were to function as a media relay, just passing RTP packets between the enterprise and service networks that have disparate packetization times, this could result in audio playback issues. Instead, packets are redirected to the DSP for appropriate treatment before they are forwarded. This results in CUBE functioning as a media terminator. Refer to the section "SBC Handling of RTP and RTCP," earlier in this chapter, for more details.

Example 5-16 provides a configuration snippet for transrating on CUBE, where CUBE is configured to transrate G.729 between 20 ms and 30 ms.

Example 5-16 *Sample Configuration for Transrating*

```
dspfarm profile 20 transcode universal
 codec g711ulaw
 codec g711alaw
 codec ilbc
 codec g723r63
 codec g723r53
 codec g729ar8
 codec g729abr8
 maximum sessions 2
 associate application CUBE
 no shutdown
!
!
```

```
dial-peer voice 1703 voip
description towards service provider
incoming called-number 14085553471
session protocol sipv2
codec g729r8
!
! Service provider sends and receives G729 at 20ms

!
no vad
dtmf-relay rtp-nte
fax protocol t38 ls-redundancy 0 hs-redundancy 0 fallback pass-through g711ulaw
!
!
dial-peer voice 1803 voip
description towards enterprise
destination-pattern 14085553471
session protocol sipv2
session target ipv4:192.0.2.1
codec g729r8 bytes 30 fixed-bytes
!
! G729 hardcoded to use 30 ms
!
no vad
dtmf-relay rtp-nte
fax protocol t38 ls-redundancy 0 hs-redundancy 0 fallback pass-through g711ulaw
```

Note When transrating non-G.711–based codecs, a universal transcoding profile is required.

Note While configuring transcoding profiles, the G.729r8 codec is not present by default. It has to be configured manually.

Note By default, **dspfarm** profiles are shut down. You must manually activate them by issuing the **no shutdown** command.

Media Anti-Tromboning

Media anti-tromboning is a method of detecting and mitigating hairpinned media (RTP) on intermediary devices such as SBCs. Media anti-tromboning is also known as *media handoff*, *media release*, or *anti-hairpinning*. Media anti-tromboning allows the number of media sessions on SBCs to scale by saving bandwidth and processing cycles on media streams that are being sent back to the same destination to which they arrive. Figure 5-27 depicts a scenario that leads to hairpinned media on SBCs.

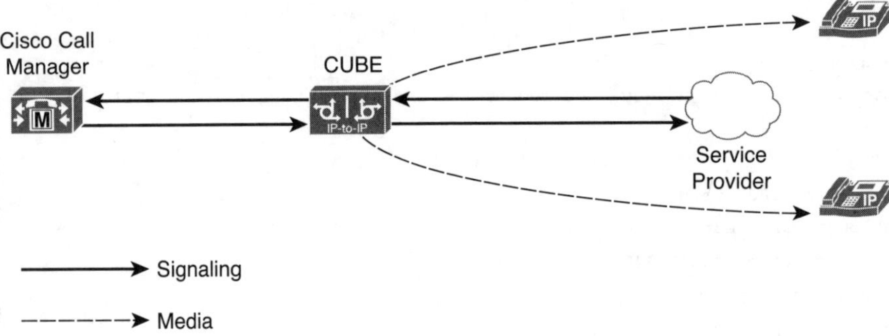

Figure 5-27 *Media Loop on SBCs*

In Figure 5-27, an SBC peers with enterprise and service provider networks, such that the caller and callee are part of the same network. The call may begin with the caller intending to reach a phone in the enterprise network; however, due to certain conditions (for example, call forward, call transfer), the ultimate destination might be a phone in the same network as the caller.

When the final media session is set up between the caller and callee, RTP packets flow from the service provider network to the SBC, and they are then routed back to the service provider network. This scenario isn't optimal, as it needlessly contributes to bandwidth consumption and, even worse, requires the SBC to allocate resources for handling of RTP packets. For devices like SBCs that are overloaded with a rich feature set, many of which are exercised simultaneously, this could mean a drastic reduction in overall processing power and efficiency.

SBCs detect and preempt media hairpins by identifying SIP transactions or dialogs that would contribute to hairpinned media—usually by examining transactions or dialogs that reuse SDP bodies of other ongoing transactions or dialogs. SDP reuse is typically seen in calls that are forwarded back to the same network from which they came or in calls that are transferred back to the same network from which they came. Figure 5-28 demonstrates the process by which media hairpins are detected. In this particular example, the call arrives from the service provider network and routes through the SBC to the IP PBX. Because of the call-forward configuration on the IP PBX, the call is routed back to the service provider network by the SBC.

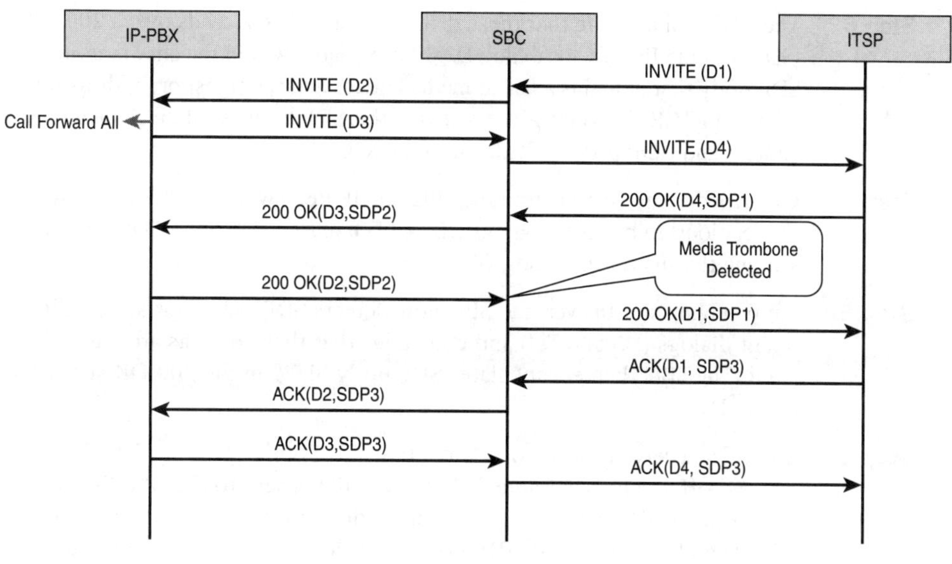

Figure 5-28 *Media Hairpin Detection on SBCs*

The process of media-loop detection can be summarized as follows:

Step 1. A phone over the service provider network tries to reach a phone registered to the enterprise IP PBX.

Step 2. A delayed offer SIP INVITE is received on the SBC, identified by the SIP dialog D1. The SBC sends a new SIP INVITE within the scope of a new SIP dialog, D2, to the IP PBX.

Step 3. The phone registered to the IP PBX is configured to forward all calls to another phone over the service provider network. Because of this, the IP PBX initiates a third SIP dialog, D3, and sends an SIP INVITE to the SBC.

Step 4. At this point in time, the SBC is unaware that the dialogs D1, D2, and D3 are related; therefore, it sends over a new SIP INVITE to the service provider within the scope of yet another SIP dialog, D4.

Step 5. The answer is received from the service provider with an SIP 200 OK message. Encapsulated within the 200 OK message SDP body is SDP1, which has the list of media codecs and the transport address for RTP and RTCP. The transport address in this SDP body would include an IP address and UDP port local to the service provider network.

Step 6. The SBC, still unaware that these dialogs are all related, sends over a 200 OK (SDP2) to the IP PBX for dialog D3. Encapsulated within the answer is an SDP body that contains a list of media codecs and the transport address for RTP and RTCP. The transport address in this SDP body would include an IP address and UDP port that is local to the SBC.

Step 7. On receiving the answer from the SBC, the IP PBX, which is already aware of the relationship between dialogs D2 and D3, reuses SDP body SDP2 when sending the answer for dialog D2.

Step 8. On receiving the answer, the SBC now detects SDP reuse across two different dialogs (D3 and D4) and concludes that these dialogs are interrelated. The SBC then encapsulates SDP body SDP1 in the 200 OK sent for dialog D1.

Step 9. The ACK received for dialog D1 contains SDP body SDP3 (which is a delayed offer call). The same SDP body SDP3 is sent to the IP PBX within the scope of dialog D2. The transport address in this SDP body would include an IP address and UDP port that is local to the service provider network.

Step 10. The IP PBX reuses SDP3 when sending an ACK for dialog D3. SDP body SDP3 is reused again when the SBC sends the ACK for dialog D4.

On identifying transactions/dialogs that contribute to media hairpins, the SBC manipulates the SDP presented toward the destination network by removing itself completely from the media path. Figure 5-29 diagrammatically depicts such a scenario.

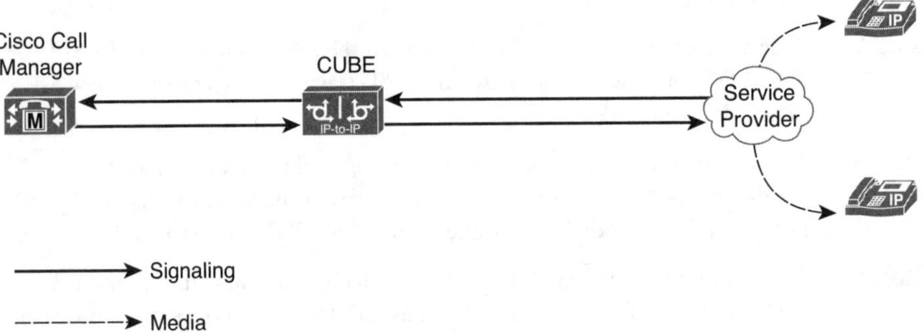

Figure 5-29 *Media Hairpin Avoidance on SBCs*

Media anti-tromboning can be configured on CUBE by using the **media anti-trombone** command in global or dial-peer configuration mode. Example 5-17 provides a configuration snippet of media anti-tromboning on CUBE.

Example 5-17 *Configuration Snippet of Media Anti-Tromboning on CUBE*

```
voice service voip
no ip address trusted authenticate
address-hiding
dtmf-interworking standard
mode border-element
media anti-trombone
allow-connections sip to sip
```

The **media anti-trombone** command can also be used at the dial-peer level, in which case it has to be configured on all dial peers that are expected to handle the tromboned call. Note that when a media hairpin is identified, CUBE removes itself out of the media path by dynamically moving the call to a media flow-around call.

Because anti-tromboning creates a scenario similar to media flow-around, functions that require media to traverse CUBE (for example, transcoding, transrating, SRTP–RTP interworking) would not be available for the call. Due to this caveat, it is important to ensure that media anti-tromboning is configured only in cases where interworking is not required.

It is worth pointing out that several service providers implement a security mechanism wherein they begin transmission of media packets only after first receiving media packets from the remote peer. This is done to ensure that resources in the media plane are not allocated for fraudulent communication sessions. However, this security feature presents a problem for calls whose media paths are optimized with **media anti-tromboning**, as the caller and callee are both in the service provider network. Because the enterprise network is completely removed from the media path as a result of optimized signaling, it is impossible for media packets to be sourced from within the enterprise. This is a catch-22 situation that manifests as no-way audio for calls. It is therefore highly recommended to carry out thorough testing before implementing media anti-tromboning.

Note Even without media anti-tromboning configured, certain call flows lead to the caller and callee being on the same network (for example, calls that involve off-net-to-off-net transfers, calls where the forwarded-to destination is an off-net entity). For such call flows, the problem highlighted in the previous paragraph might be applicable (depending, of course, on the security policy implemented by the service provider). However, because such call flows still retain the enterprise network within the media path, media packets can be injected by the enterprise to trigger the service provider to start exchanging packets. With Cisco CallManager-based networks, this is achieved by using a media termination point (MTP) within the call flow.

Alternative Network Address Types

In networks where both IPv4 and IPv6 are deployed, there may be a need to have devices operate in *dual*-stack mode. A device in this mode device is aware of both IPv4 and IPv6 address spaces. This presents a challenge when user agents enabled for dual-stack encode Session Description Protocol (SDP) bodies for a communication session. SDP bodies provide details of an impending communication session or alter the characteristics of an already existing communication session. Some of the details provided by SDP bodies include the following:

- The different types of media streams in a communication session (audio, video, fax)
- The different codec types per media stream
- The supported extensions for RTP/RTCP
- The network address and port pair for exchanging RTP and RTCP

SDP allows for only one network address to be advertised for each media stream. For SIP user agents that are dual-stacked, this means the user agent can advertise either only the IPv4 or the IPv6 address. However, it is useful to have the ability to offer a set of network address (IPv4 and IPv6) when communicating with a peer that supports only an IPv4-centric or an IPv6-centric addressing scheme. This is because many times there is no real way of knowing the addressing preferences of remote peers beforehand.

Alternative Network Address Type (ANAT), defined in RFC 4091, resolves this problem by allowing an SIP user agent to encode a pair of network addresses in the SDP body. Depending on the ability of the remote peer, it can either choose to communicate media over IPv4 or IPv6. ANAT groups together multiple media lines (**m=**) that all correspond to a single logical media stream, using the semantics outlined in RFC 3388. Example 5-18 demonstrates a sample SDP body using ANAT, which encodes an IPv4/IPv6 network address pair for a single audio stream.

Example 5-18 *Sample SDP Body for ANAT*

```
v=0
o=bob 280744730 28977631 IN IP4 host.example.com
s=
t=0 0
a=group:ANAT 1 2
m=audio 25000 RTP/AVP 0
c=IN IP6 2001:DB8::1
a=mid:1
m=audio 22000 RTP/AVP 0
c=IN IP4 192.0.2.1
a=mid:2
```

In Example 5-18, the two **m=** lines correspond to a single logical audio media stream, such that the audio media stream can be established to exchange RTP over IPv6 or IPv4. The preference of a specific addressing scheme for establishing media is encoded using the *media stream identification*, or **mid**, attribute. In Example 5-18, IPv6 addressing is given first preference (**a=mid:1**), and IPv4 addressing is given second preference (**a=mid:2**).

When receiving an offer that uses ANAT, the receiver must use the addressing that it understands and set the remaining **m=** lines to zero. For example, if a receiver that is only IPv4 capable receives the SDP offer as in Example 5-18, it generates an answer similar to the one in Example 5-19.

Example 5-19 *SDP Answer with ANAT*

```
v=0
o=bob 280744730 28977631 IN IP4 host.example.com
s=
t=0 0
a=group:ANAT   2
m=audio 0 RTP/AVP 0
c=IN IP6 2001:DB8::2
a=mid:1
m=audio 22004 RTP/AVP 0
c=IN IP4 192.0.2.2
a=mid:2
```

In Example 5-19, the receiver accepts the media line (**m=**) with IPv4 addressing by advertising a valid media port of 22004 in the answer, and it rejects the media line with IPv6 addressing by setting the port to 0.

Support for ANAT is advertised by using the **sdp-anat** tag. An offeror includes this tag in the SIP **Require:** header field, whereas a receiver includes this tag in the SIP **Supported:** header field.

Example 5-20 provides a sample configuration for enabling ANAT on CUBE.

Example 5-20 *Sample ANAT Configuration on CUBE*

```
voice service voip
 sip
  anat

sip-ua
 protocol mode dual-stack preference ipv6
```

With this configuration in place, the CUBE generates an SDP offer with IPv6 and IPv4 network addresses, such that the IPv6 network address is given first preference in the SDP encoding (**a=mid:1**). Similarly, if the administrator wishes to attribute first preference to IPv4 addressing, the last line in Example 5-20 can be replaced with the following:

```
protocol mode dual-stack preference ipv4
```

Note When configuring ANAT on CUBE, the CUBE must be dual-stacked with IPv4 and IPv6 interfaces.

Although ANAT supports advertisement of multiple *network* address types, it does not allow an endpoint/user agent to advertise multiple *transport* addresses. This is often required when endpoints wish to establish reliable communication sessions across Network Address Translation (NAT) boundaries. Interactive Connectivity Establishment (ICE) provides the semantics and framework for endpoints to advertise multiple transport addresses. ICE is discussed in the next section.

Solving NAT Traversal Challenges

As a result of the limited number of public IPv4 addresses (roughly 4.29 billion total addresses), network implementations started to deploy Network Address Translation (NAT) as a way around the need for directly assigning public addresses to devices. In NAT deployments, a NAT device allows for the translation between a pair of IP addresses and ports.

Typical deployments leverage NAT when using a reserved private address pool (typically the RFC 1918 address spaces 10.0.0.0/8, 172.16.0.0/12, and 192.168.0.0/16) within a local network. Because many companies can all use this internal RFC 1918 address space, these addresses have no meaning to the external world, as they are no longer unique on the outside global scale. These addresses are only locally significant within the private network; service providers don't even typically permit advertising for routes that correspond to these address ranges.

When devices with these internal addresses need to communicate with the outside world, they require the assistance of a device that can perform NAT.

How NAT Works

A NAT device builds a dynamic mapping that translates the device's internal address and port to an external address and port. The benefit here is that instead of requiring an external address for every host, external addresses only need to be provisioned on the NAT boundary devices that sit on the edge of the network. NAT typically works on the premise of *port overload*, which operates on the assumption that each internal host doesn't need to use all 65535 ports for external communication at once, and the available pool of 65535 ports on the external IP can be dynamically shared for use with multiple internal hosts on an as-needed basis. Figure 5-30 demonstrates this basic NAT construct.

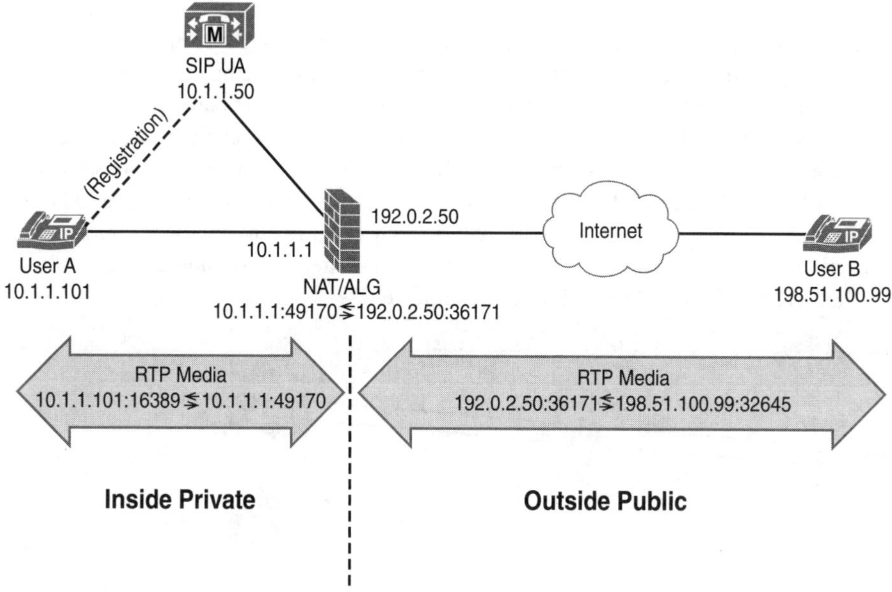

Figure 5-30 *Generic NAT Topology*

There are four general methods of performing NAT:

- **Full cone (one-to-one)**—An internal address and internal port pair are mapped to an external address and external port pair (for example, **intAddr:intPort–extAdd:extPort**). As depicted in Figure 5-31, once the mapping is created by the first outbound packet from the internal host, any external host can communicate to the internal host by sending traffic to **extAdd:extPort**.
- **Address-restricted cone**—An internal address and internal port pair are mapped to an external address and external port pair (for example, **intAddr:intPort–extAdd:extPort**). As demonstrated in Figure 5-32, external hosts can only communicate to the internal host through **extAdd:extPort** if the internal host has already sent a packet to that external host's IP address. Consider a scenario where 10.1.1.1:1025–192.0.2.50:2112 is built so that the inside host can talk to external host 192.51.100.50. 198.51.100.99 cannot reach 10.1.1.1:1025 through 192.0.2.50:2112 until 10.1.1.1:1025 has sent a legitimate packet to 198.51.100.99 on any port.
- **Port-restricted cone**—An internal address and internal port pair are mapped to an external address and external port pair (for example, **intAddr:intPort–extAdd:extPort**). External hosts can communicate to the internal host through **extAdd:extPort** only if the internal host has already sent a packet to that external host's IP address and port pair, as demonstrated in Figure 5-33. Consider a scenario where 10.1.1.1:1025–192.0.2.50:2112 is built so that the inside host can talk to external host 192.51.100.50. 198.51.100.99 can only reach 10.1.1.1:1025 through 192.0.2.50:2112 by sending it from the same source port that 10.1.1.1:1025 has already used to communicated with 198.51.100.99.

- **Symmetric (bidirectional)**—An internal address and internal port pair are mapped to an external address and external port pair (for example, **intAddr:intPort–extAdd:extPort**), where the external address and port pair are used only for that specific communication to the external host's address and port pair. Other external hosts cannot use the same external address and port pair to communicate to the inside host. This is visually represented in Figure 5-34. Consider a scenario where 10.1.1.1:1025–192.0.2.50:2112 is built so that the inside host can talk to external host 192.51.100.50:90125. 198.51.100.99 cannot reach 10.1.1.1 through 192.0.2.50:2112 under any circumstance. 10.1.1.1:1025 must first initiate an outbound connection to 198.51.100.99 for that host pair to communicate.

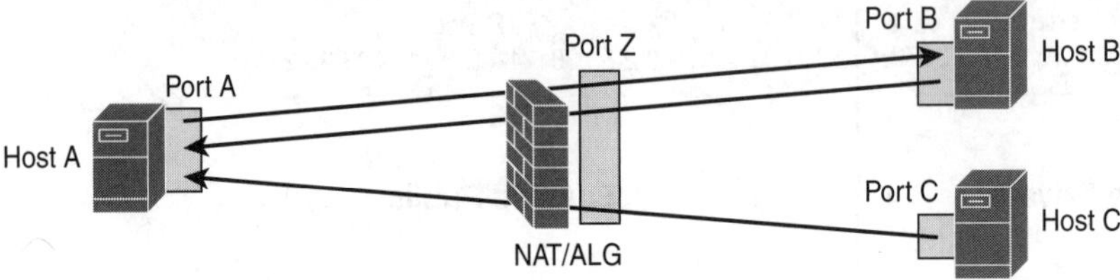

Figure 5-31 *Full-Cone NAT*

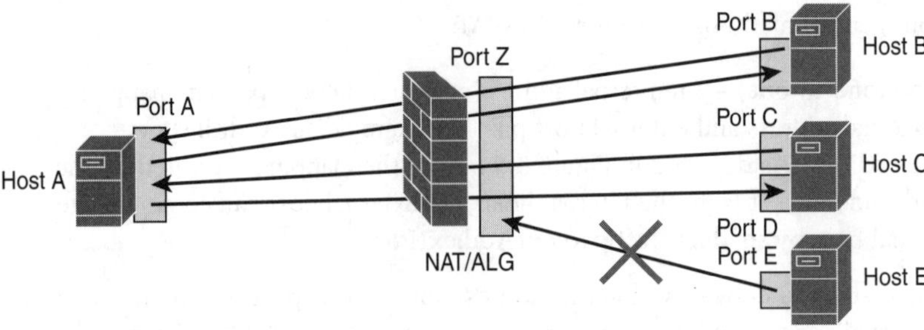

Figure 5-32 *Address-Restricted Cone NAT*

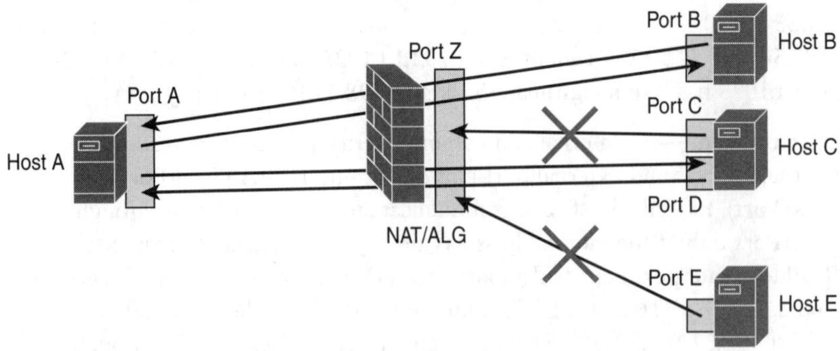

Figure 5-33 *Port-Restricted Cone NAT*

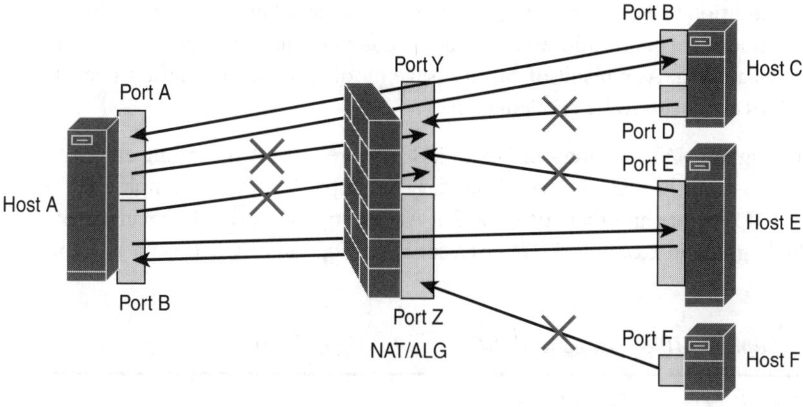

Figure 5-34 *Symmetric NAT*

As a result of the restrictive nature of symmetric NAT, it is the most common deployment for the security preference, yet it presents the most challenge for dynamic application traversal.

Problems with Real-Time Collaboration over NAT

Although NAT solves the problem of IPv4 address exhaustion, it presents challenges when real-time media communication traverses these NAT boundaries. Recall from earlier in this chapter that the IP address and port for a media exchange are inserted into the call signaling so that the endpoints know where to send media traffic. When this signaling communication of media addresses traverses a NAT boundary, the address and port information need to be changed so that external hosts are presented with the external address and port pair, and the internal host is presented with the internal address and port pair of the NAT translation.

There are currently four common approaches for addressing this challenge of media traversal over NAT boundaries:

- Application-level gateway (ALG) fixup
- Session Traversal Utilities for NAT (STUN)
- Traversal Using Relays Around NAT (TURN)
- Interactive Connectivity Establishment (ICE)

ALG Fixup

The first approach to solving the challenge of NAT was using application-level gateways (ALGs) to do application-level packet inspection and modify addresses at the NAT boundary between public and private addresses for call signaling protocols.

With ALG, in addition to NAT converting the Layer 3 (IP) and Layer 4 (TCP/UDP) headers between inside and outside addresses, it also needs to change any addresses or ports within the call signaling. As a result of this message modification, the relevant packet checksum values also need to be recalculated.

Consider the original NAT topology in Figure 5-30, where **User A** is sending an outbound SIP INVITE to **User B** through the NAT boundary. Example 5-21 and Example 5-22 represent the INVITE before and then after the SIP ALG fixup. Modified fields in the SIP packet are highlighted in Example 5-22 for easier identification of what has been modified by the ALG.

Example 5-21 *Sample SIP Message with SDP Before ALG Fixup*

```
INVITE sips:userB@198.51.100.99 SIP/2.0
Via: SIP/2.0/TLS 10.1.1.50:5061;branch=z9hG4bK74bf9
Max-Forwards: 70
From: userA <sips:userA@10.1.1.50>;tag=1234567
To: userB <sips:userB@198.51.100.99>
Call-ID: 12345600@10.1.1.50
CSeq: 1 INVITE
Contact: <sips:userA@10.1.1.50;gr>
Allow: INVITE, ACK, CANCEL, OPTIONS, BYE, REFER, NOTIFY
Supported: replaces, gruu
Content-Type: application/sdp
Content-Length: [omitted]

v=0
o=userA 2890844526 2890844526 IN IP4 10.1.1.101
s=
c=IN IP4 10.1.1.101
t=0 0
m=audio 49170 RTP/AVP 0
a=rtpmap:0 PCMU/8000
```

Example 5-22 *Sample SIP Message with SDP After ALG Fixup*

```
INVITE sips:userB@198.51.100.99 SIP/2.0
Via: SIP/2.0/TLS 192.0.2.50:5061;branch=z9hG4bK74bf9
Max-Forwards: 70
From: userA <sips:userA@192.0.2.50>;tag=1234567
To: userB <sips:userB@198.51.100.99>
Call-ID: 12345600@192.0.2.50
CSeq: 1 INVITE
Contact: <sips:userA@192.0.2.50;gr>
Allow: INVITE, ACK, CANCEL, OPTIONS, BYE, REFER, NOTIFY
Supported: replaces, gruu
```

```
Content-Type: application/sdp
Content-Length: [omitted]

v=0
o=userA 2890844526 2890844526 IN IP4 192.0.2.50
s=
c=IN IP4 192.0.2.50
t=0 0
m=audio 36171 RTP/AVP 0
a=rtpmap:0 PCMU/8000
```

At the time of this publication, using ALG is still the most common approach for solving this NAT traversal challenge, though with the recent increase in proprietary signaling protocols and WebRTC applications, this approach is slowly falling out of favor and being replaced by the other approaches discussed later in this section.

Limitations of ALG for NAT Fixup

One limitation of ALG for fixing up NAT addresses is that the device performing NAT needs to be aware of the signaling protocol. This does not pose a major issue when the call signaling protocol being used is an open standard such as SIP and H.323, as many NAT devices have the capability for application-level inspection and fixup of SIP and H.323 traffic that traverses the device. The NAT device will look for traffic on those specified call signaling ports and then modify the IP address and port information found in the signaling messages (such as the SDP) to be the public address that corresponds to the active NAT translation entry for that communication flow. NAT poses a challenge when proprietary protocols traverse a NAT boundary, though, as the ALG would need to understand the proprietary protocol in order to fix up the media addresses.

Another limitation is that if call signaling is encrypted as it traverses a NAT boundary, then there is not a possibility for this content to be modified. As a result, the addresses presented in the SDP need to be modified into public addresses before the SDP is sent, which means the problem needs to be solved by using methods other than ALG.

STUN

Simple Traversal of UDP through NATs (STUN), defined in RFC 5389, is a client/server protocol that allows an endpoint to discover its public IP address and the type of NAT used between itself and its peer media connection. The STUN client typically runs from the endpoint behind the inside (and potentially private) NAT address space and transmits a *binding request* out to a public STUN server on the Internet. STUN communication defaults to port 3478 for TCP and UDP and 5349 for STUNS (STUN over TLS). A client can determine the STUN server to use automatically, based on a DNS lookup of the SRV record (for example, _stun._udp.example.com, _stun._tcp.example.com, _stuns._tcp.example.com).

The STUN specification allows an endpoint that is behind a NAT to discover its public address, as seen by the STUN server. To do this, the endpoint (which functions as a client) transmits a *STUN binding* request to the STUN server and expects a response containing its public address and port. Each STUN message (request or response) follows a strict formatting structure. The format of a STUN message is diagrammed in Figure 5-35.

0	0	STUN Message Type	Message Length
Magic Cookie			
Transaction ID (96 Bits)			
Type			Length
Value (Variable)			

Figure 5-35 *STUN Message Format*

Every STUN message contains a fixed 20-byte header followed by optional attributes. The two most significant bits of a STUN message are always set to 0. The next header field, *STUN message type,* identifies the STUN method and the message class. RFC 5389 defines only a single method, the STUN binding method, and four message classes:

- Request
- Success response
- Failure response
- Indication

All four message classes are used within the scope of the STUN binding method. A client always sources a STUN binding request toward the server. Depending on the ability of the server to process the request, it can respond with a success response or a failure response. An indication can be sent either by the client or the server; however, an indication does not trigger a response.

The message length header field indicates the length of the STUN message, not including the 20-byte fixed header. The magic cookie header field always takes the fixed value **0x2112A442** in network byte order. The transaction ID header field is a 96-bit header field that is used to uniquely distinguish STUN transactions at the client and server. Conceptually, the usage of the transaction ID is similar to the usage of the Call-ID header field in SIP messages. Following the transaction ID header field are zero, one or more attributes. The STUN specification defines several attributes used for different scenarios.

STUN attributes are Type-Length-Value (TLV) encoded. Each STUN attribute must terminate on a 32-bit boundary. The **type** value of an attribute is divided into two spaces. Attributes with type values between 0x0000 and 0x7FFF are called *comprehension-required* attributes. A STUN agent (client or server) needs to understand comprehension-required attributes to successfully process a message. Attributes with type values between 0x8000 and 0xFFFF are called *comprehension-optional* attributes. A STUN agent (client or server) can ignore these attributes if it does not understand them.

The length header field contains the length of the value part of the attribute, in bytes. Because attributes must terminate on 32-bit boundaries, it is possible for a STUN agent to add padding bits to the value field. While encoding the value of the length attribute, the padded bits are ignored.

The client sends a STUN binding request to the server (either over UDP, TCP, or TLS over TCP). As the message makes its way to the STUN server, it may pass through intervening NAT devices. Each NAT device transforms the source transport address (source IP address and port) of the request. Finally, when the request arrives at the STUN server, it runs a series of checks to determine the validity and formatting of the request. If no errors are found, the STUN server sends a success response. Included in the response are the client's IP address and port, as seen by the STUN server after NAT processing.

The success response carries the public address and port of the client in the **MAPPED-ADDRESS** attribute. To protect any NAT/ALG boundaries from translating the address returned in the STUN response, the STUN response contains an additional field, **XOR-MAPPED-ADDRESS**, which is a hash of the public address created by performing an exclusive or (XOR) function between the public address and a key called a *magic cookie*. The client can then use this XORed address to determine whether the public address has been changed as a result of any deep packet inspection.

Once the client has its outside IP address and port, the STUN server's has accomplished its responsibility, and it is no longer in the signaling or media path. No call state is maintained by the STUN server. As a result of the lightweight implementation of STUN, free public STUN servers are available for use, though they should be used only in scenarios where the STUN server's service level doesn't need to be guaranteed.

Due to the lightweight nature of STUN, it can be leveraged quickly for a media negotiation. Figure 5-36 depicts the logical communication of negotiating addresses between two NATed hosts for media transmission through STUN.

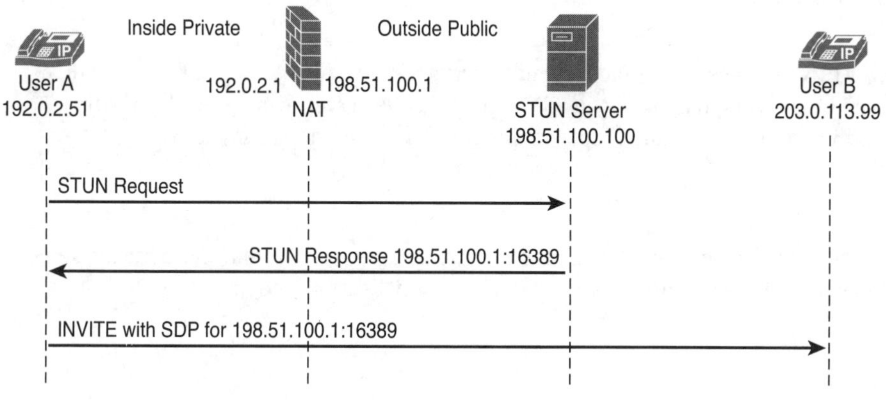

Figure 5-36 *Signaling for STUN*

Limitations of STUN

The original deployment of STUN supported only UDP flows, but it has been enhanced and now allows for TCP support as well as communication over TLS.

STUN cannot be used to solve the challenge of symmetric NAT traversal, though, because the port mapping that is used for the STUN communication is a different translation mapping than would be used for the communication from the local endpoint to the remote endpoint.

Due to symmetric NAT being the most popular NAT implementation in large network deployments, STUN is not sufficient to ensure end-to-end communication of a media stream between the clients. This has resulted in further development of solutions over the top of STUN.

TURN

In situations in which a direct communication path cannot be established between communicating entities, it may be necessary for an intermediary to function as a traffic relay. The TURN specification, defined in RFC 5766, allows a host behind a NAT (called a TURN client), to use the services of a TURN server as a traffic relay. The TURN server is used to relay traffic to and between the TURN client and other hosts, called *peers*. To be able to do this, the client discovers a TURN server and creates a TURN *allocation*. The TURN allocation allows the TURN server to provide the client with a *relayed transport address* that is subsequently used by the client and its communication peer to exchange traffic.

Due to the TURN server proxying media, TURN introduces extra administrative complexities, similar to the concerns that arise when deploying an SBC that is relaying media. As a result, bandwidth and resource requirements need to be considered with TURN servers. Due to these administrative needs and added expense, it is uncommon to find public TURN servers available for use. Products that leverage TURN typically have their own servers deployed on the Internet for their specific product or service's implementation.

Note TURN operates on the same default ports as STUN. Also as with STUN, a TURN server can be discovered by using an SRV record. TURN servers can be resolved with _turn._udp.example.com, _turn._tcp.example.com, or _turns._tcp.example.com.

Note The client has to communicate the relayed transport port to its peer by using some out-of-band mechanism. This is typically done using ICE, described in RFC 5128.

A TURN allocation logically consists of the following state information:

- A relayed transport address
- An identifier called **5-tuple** that consists of the client's IP address and port, the server's IP address and port, and the transport protocol over which TURN messages are exchanged (UDP)
- Authentication information
- The validity of the allocation
- A list of bindings or permissions

The TURN framework is set into motion by a client discovering a TURN server and then transmitting a TURN allocate request over UDP. Included in the TURN allocate request is the mandatory **REQUESTED-TRANSPORT** attribute. This attribute specifies the transport protocol to be used between the TURN server and the communication peer of the client. Optionally, the client might include the **LIFETIME** attribute to specify the time duration for which the allocation is active. For real-time traffic such as RTP and RTCP traffic, it is required for the TURN server to allocate an even port for RTP and a separate (next higher) port for RTCP. In such situations, the client includes the **EVEN-PORT** attribute and sets the **R** bit in this attribute to 1. There are other optional attributes that can be included in the TURN allocate request as well.

Note When RTP and RTCP are multiplexed on the same port, it is not required for the client to request an additional port reservation for RTCP traffic on the TURN server.

As the allocate request makes its way to the server, the source address and port are transformed by intervening NAT devices. When the allocate request is received at the server, the source address and port of the request, as seen by the server, is called the *server-reflexive* transport address. On receiving the allocate request, as a matter of local policy on the server, the request might need to be authenticated by the client. In such scenarios, the long-term credential mechanism of STUN is used. Consequently, all messages from the client must use this authentication information.

The server then runs a series of checks to determine the validity and formatting of the request. If these checks pass, the server creates the allocation and replies with a success response. Included in the response are the following attributes:

- An **XOR-RELAYED-ADDRESS** attribute encapsulates the relayed transport address allocated by the server.
- A **LIFETIME** attribute specifies the amount of time for which the allocation is valid. Although the client might suggest the amount of time for which an allocation is valid (by including the **LIFETIME** attribute in the request), it is the server that ultimately decides this value.

- A **RESERVATION-TOKEN** attribute is included if the client requested an additional port reservation for RTCP.
- An **XOR-MAPPED-ADDRESS** attribute encapsulates the server-reflexive transport address of the client.

The default amount of time for which allocations remain active is 10 minutes. However, a TURN server can specify any other value in the **LIFETIME** attribute of the response. Clients must refresh allocations before they expire; this is done by sending a refresh request containing a **LIFETIME** attribute.

Application data can be exchanged by using *send and data STUN* indications. However, because of the large overhead associated with the formatting of these STUN messages, they are not conducive to real-time communications. As an alternative, TURN specifies an alternate packet format known as a *ChannelData* message. This packet format does not use the STUN header format; instead, it uses a 4-byte header that includes a header field called the channel number. This header field is bound to the peer to which the client communicates. The binding between the communication peer and the channel number is done by the *ChannelBind* request.

ChannelBind requests are always initiated by clients, and they are either used to bind a communication peer (of the client) to a channel or to refresh existing channel bindings. A channel binding consists of the following:

- A channel number
- The communication peer transport address
- The lifetime of the binding

When the TURN server sends a success response to the ChannelBind request, the client and server can begin exchanging ChannelData messages.

Note The ChannelBind message is a STUN-formatted message. However, the ChannelData message is not STUN formatted.

Figure 5-37 and 5-38 show the formats of the ChannelBind and ChannelData messages.

	0 0 Request		Message Length
	Magic Cookie		
	Transaction ID (96 Bits)		
Channel Number	0X000C		4-Bytes
	Channel Number		RFFU=0
XOR-PEER-ADDRESS	XXXXXXXX	Family	X-Port
	X-Address (Variable)		

Figure 5-37 *Format of the ChannelBind Message*

Figure 5-37 shows the high-level format of a ChannelBind message. The message contains a standard STUN header followed by two attributes:

- The Channel Number attribute
- The XOR-PEER-ADDRESS attribute

The Channel Number attribute contains the type value **0x000C**. The length of this attribute is fixed at 4 bytes. The Value header field (refer to Figure 5-35) is subdivided into the channel number and reserved for future use (RFFU) header fields. The channel number header field encodes the channel number and can take values between 0x4000 and 0X7FFF. The RFFU header field is ignored and has no purpose.

The XOR-PEER-ADDRESS attribute provides the XOR mapped address of the remote communication peer. Upon successfully processing a ChannelBind request, the TURN server creates a binding between the channel number and a communication peer.

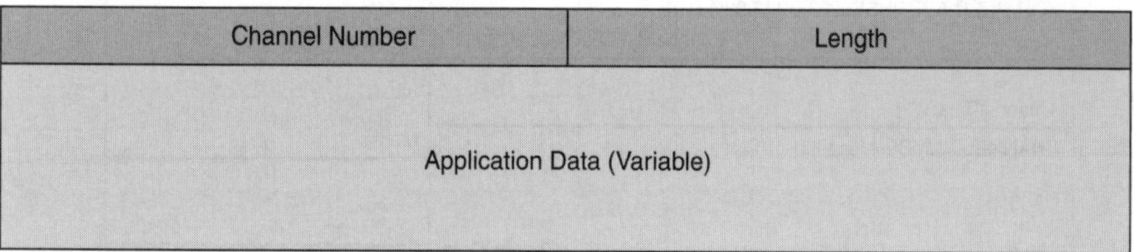

Figure 5-38 *Format of the ChannelData Message*

Figure 5-38 shows the high-level format of a ChannelData message. The channel number encodes a channel for which a successfully binding was previously created. The length header field encodes in bytes the length of the encapsulated application data.

Figure 5-39 shows the exchange between User A (TURN client) and the TURN server for the creation of an allocation. This allocation is subsequently used to exchange real-time traffic between User A and User B. Figure 5-39 shows the following process:

Step 1. An allocate request is sent to the TURN server to create a TURN allocation.

Step 2. If digest authentication is enabled, the request is rejected with an **Allocate error response** and reason code **401 (Unauthorized)**.

Step 3. The client transmits another allocate request, this time with digest authentication included for a username, with the appropriate credential hash.

Step 4. The server runs a series of checks to determine the validity and formatting of the request. If these checks pass, the server creates the allocation and replies with a success response. Included in the response are the **XOR-RELAYED-ADDRESS**, **LIFETIME**, and **XOR-MAPPED-ADDRESS** attributes. Optionally, if the client requested the TURN server to allocate an additional port for RTCP, a **RESERVATION-TOKEN** is included in the response as well.

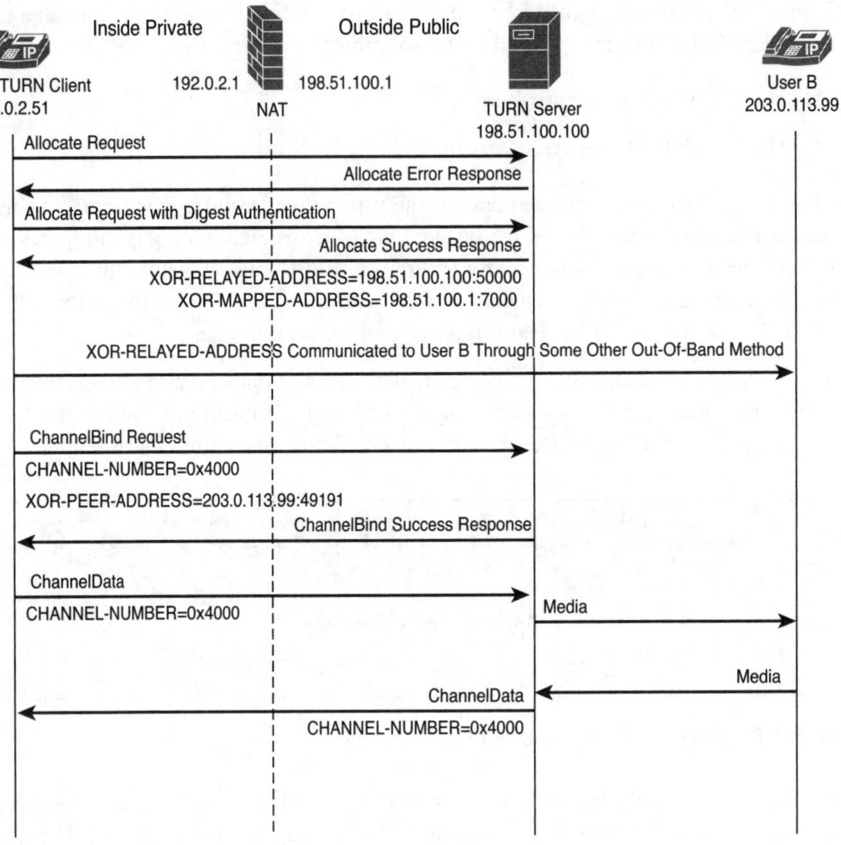

Figure 5-39 *Signaling for TURN*

Step 5. The client communicates the XOR-RELAYED-ADDRESS of the TURN allocation (in this case, **192.0.2.15:50000**) to its communication peer by some out-of-band mechanism. This is typically done using the procedures spelled out in RFC 5128, such as ICE.

Step 6. When the TURN address is exchanged, media still does not flow through the TURN server until permissions are properly set and the media channels are bound. All data through the TURN server will be dropped until these tasks are accomplished.

Step 7. A ChannelBind Request is sent from User A to the TURN server. The ChannelBind request attempts to create a mapping between channel number 0x4000 and User B (203.0.113.99:49191).

Step 8. The channel bind is acknowledged with a ChannelBind success response.

Step 9. Data is now sent from User A to the TURN server through a ChannelData message. As demonstrated in Figure 5-39, the ChannelData message encapsulates application data.

Step 10. The TURN server receives the ChannelData message and de-encapsulates it to send the media stream to User B.

Step 11. Reverse media traffic sent from User B is encapsulated by the TURN server in a ChannelData message, such that the same channel number (for which a binding is created in step 7) is referenced.

Limitations of TURN

TURN servers need to be able to proxy media. This means there are requirements for administering the bandwidth, CPU and packet forwarding resources, and the address capacity of the server.

Security of the media traversing the proxy must also be considered if the media's payload is not already encrypted through means such as SRTP. In these conditions, where unencrypted media is being forwarded through the TURN server, it is important for the TURN server to be a trusted entity. TURN should be integrated by using TLS over TCP when not implementing SRTP to ensure that the TURN server is not being impersonated by an attacker, which otherwise could result in a man-in-the-middle attack for media eavesdropping. See Chapter 13 for more information on these types of eavesdropping attacks.

ICE

Protocols that use the offer/answer framework do not work reliably with NAT. This is primarily because these protocols carry the IP addresses and ports of media sources and sinks within messages. Constructs like STUN and TURN have limitations, too, as discussed in previous sections. To provide a comprehensive NAT traversal solution, the IETF developed and standardized the Interactive Connectivity Establishment (ICE) framework in RFC 5245. ICE is not a standalone protocol; rather, it is a framework that leverages several other protocols, such as SIP, SDP, TURN, and STUN, to achieve a seamless NAT traversal solution. This section provides a very high-level overview of ICE. The detailed and intricate nuances of ICE are not included in this section.

In a typical ICE deployment, there are two endpoints (also known as agents) that intend to establish a communication session. The two agents engage in an offer/answer exchange to converge on a plurality of parameters for the communication session, such as the media types, the media formats, and the address and port information for the exchange of RTP and RTCP. However, because these agents might be behind NAT devices or might not have enough information about their network topologies, there is no guarantee of bidirectional transmission of media. ICE provides a framework in which the communicating agents are guaranteed to discover a pair of transport addresses for communication.

ICE begins with the calling agent gathering a set of candidate transport addresses (IP address and port pair with UDP as the transport layer protocol). These candidate transport addresses can be of the following types:

- **Host address(s)**—The transport address of a directly connected interface or NIC (If the host is multihomed, it may gather several host transport addresses.)

- **Server-reflexive address—**A transport address on the public side of the NAT
- **Relayed address—**A relayed transport address

An ICE agent typically uses STUN and TURN to gather reflexive and relayed candidates. If using only STUN, the agent can gather only a server-reflexive address. If using TURN, the agent can gather a server-reflexive address and a relayed address.

Once candidate transport addresses are gathered, the agent prioritizes the candidates from highest to lowest priority. The gathered transport addresses are then encoded in SDP and transmitted to the remote agent (in concert with a call control protocol such as SIP). On receiving the offer, the peer agent performs the same step of gathering different transport addresses and prioritizing them from highest to lowest priority. The list of gathered transport addresses is sent to the initiating agent in the SDP answer.

At this time, both agents have a list of all local and remote transport addresses. Each agent then proceeds to pair up these candidates to form *candidate pairs*. The candidate pairs are sorted according to their priority values and inserted into a checklist.

Note Candidate pair priority is computed according to the guidelines of Section 5.7.2 of the ICE specification.

Note An independent checklist is maintained for each media stream of the communication session.

After candidate pairs are ordered according to their priority, *connectivity checks* are scheduled for each candidate pair. A connectivity check is a two-way STUN request/response transaction to validate bidirectional reachability. The STUN request/response transactions to verify connectivity are always sent on the same ports that would eventually be used to transmit media. Figure 5-40 diagrams this process.

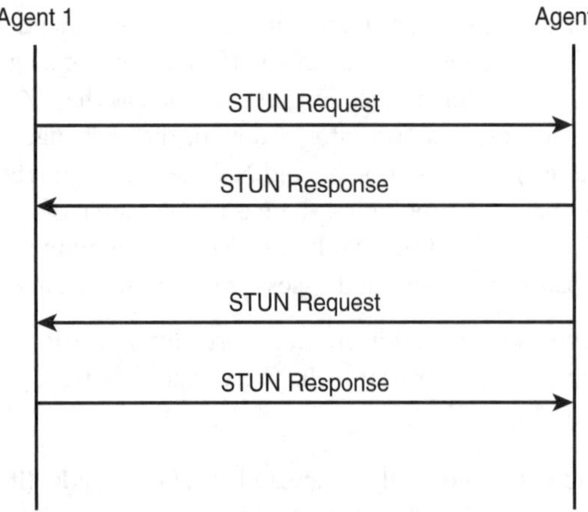

Figure 5-40 *ICE Connectivity Check*

With ICE, it is expected that several connectivity checks will fail. For example, a connectivity check between a local host candidate and a remote host candidate is unlikely to succeed if either both or one of the agents are behind NAT devices. Every connectivity check that succeeds results in the candidate pair being placed into a list called a valid list. A valid list is maintained for each media stream of the communication session.

ICE assigns one of the agents the *controlling agent* role and assigns the other agent the *controlled agent* role. When valid pairs (candidate pairs placed in the valid list) are constructed as a result of successful connectivity checks, the controlling agent can decide which candidate pair is "nominated" as the one to be used for media transmission. The nomination process can occur in two ways:

- Regular nomination
- Aggressive nomination

In regular nomination, the controlling agent waits for a predefined number of checks to successfully conclude before it nominates a candidate pair. A candidate pair is nominated by initiating a second STUN request/response transaction for that candidate pair such that the controlling agent includes the **USE-CANDIDATE** attribute. The controlling agent can nominate several valid candidate pairs, but the one with the highest priority is chosen for media transmission.

In aggressive nomination, the controlling agent includes the **USE-CANDIDATE** attribute in the first STUN request/response transaction of candidate pairs. This method has the benefit of gathering nominated pairs much more quickly that regular nomination. However, if connectivity checks for higher-preference candidate pairs take longer to complete, there could be a number of transient selections before ICE stabilizes.

Note The controlling agent is the originating party of the call unless it is an ICE-Lite implementation (described in the next section), in which the side that is not an ICE-Lite implementation decides the candidates for use.

Figures 5-41 and 5-42 diagram the regular and aggressive nomination processes.

The initial offer/answer exchange between the two agents includes a candidate (IP address and port) for each media stream; these candidates are called *default candidates*. It is recommended that an agent use a relayed candidate as its default candidate. If there are no relayed candidates, it is recommended that an agent use a server-reflexive candidate. If there are no server-reflexive candidates or if the server-reflexive candidate is the same as the host candidate (which is possible if an agent is not behind a NAT device), then the host candidate is used as the default candidate.

After the initial offer/answer exchange, the ICE state machine begins execution to determine a set of candidate pairs for media transmission. If the highest-priority candidate pair as discovered by ICE is different from the default candidate pair, there is a subsequent SDP offer/answer exchange to update the transport addresses for media.

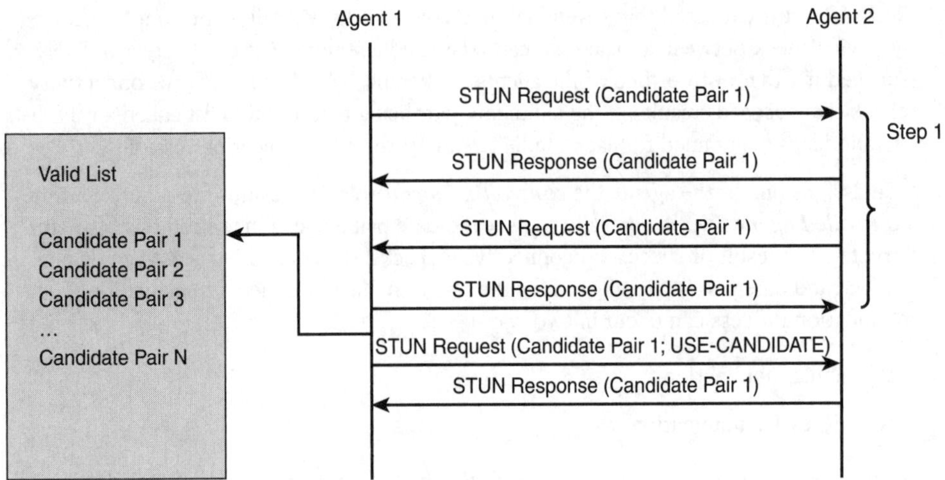

Figure 5-41 *ICE Regular Nomination*

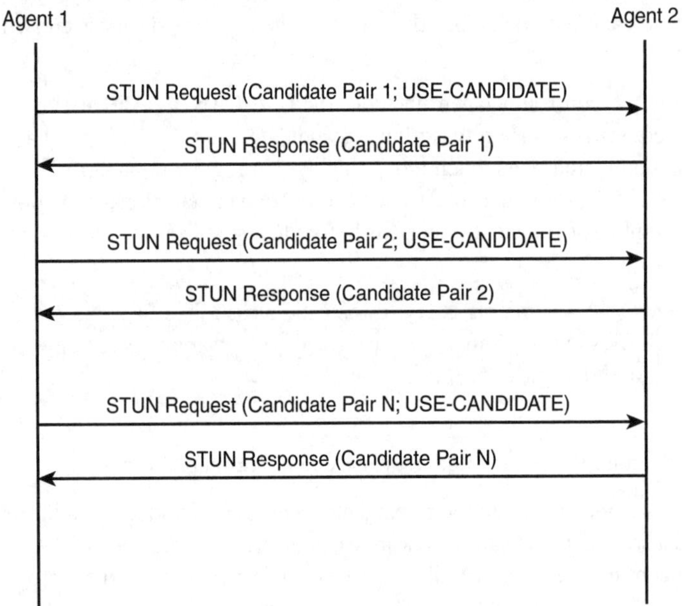

Figure 5-42 *ICE Aggressive Nomination*

ICE defines several new SDP attributes. A sample SDP body carrying ICE attributes is provided in Example 5-23.

Example 5-23 *SDP Containing ICE Candidates*

```
v=0
o=jdoe 2890844526 2890842807 IN IP4 10.0.1.1
s=
c=IN IP4 192.0.2.3
t=0 0
a=ice-pwd:asd88fgpdd777uzjYhagZg
a=ice-ufrag:8hhY
m=audio 45664 RTP/AVP 0
b=RS:0
b=RR:0
a=rtpmap:0 PCMU/8000
a=candidate:1 1 UDP 2130706431 10.0.1.1 8998 typ host
a=candidate:2 1 UDP 1694498815 192.0.2.3 45664 typ srflx raddr 10.0.1.1 rport 8998
a=candidate:3 1 udp 25108223 203.0.113.11 58779 typ relay raddr 198.51.100.3 rport  54761
```

Note **ice-ufrag** and **ice-pwd** are attributes whose values are used in STUN's short-term credential mechanism for connectivity checks.

The parameters from the **a=candidate** line in the SDP found in Example 5-23 are defined as follows:

- **2**—The foundation, a unique identifier for each candidate.
- **1**—The component ID, which is **1** for RTP and **2** for RTCP.
- **udp**—The transport type to be used for the candidate.
- **1694498815**—The priority of the component. Higher priorities have preference.
- **192.0.2.3**—The component's IP address.
- **45664**—The component's port.
- **typ srflx**—The type of candidate. Options are **host** (local candidate), **srflx** (address directly discovered by a STUN request), **prflx** (address discovered indirectly during an ICE candidate connectivity check), and **relay** (TURN server).
- **raddr**—The related address for the candidate. For reflexive hosts, this would be the IP address of the requesting agent. If the candidate is relayed, this is equal to the mapped address in the allocate response that provided the client with that relayed candidate.
- **rport**—The related port for the candidate, following the same criteria as for **raddr**.

Consider the deployment shown in Figure 5-43. Agent A is a private communication endpoint resident behind a NAT device. Agent B is an endpoint on the public Internet. Both of these devices have access to the same SIP server and STUN server. The NAT device has an endpoint-independent mapping property and an address-dependent filtering property. To establish a communication session assisted by ICE, the following events occur:

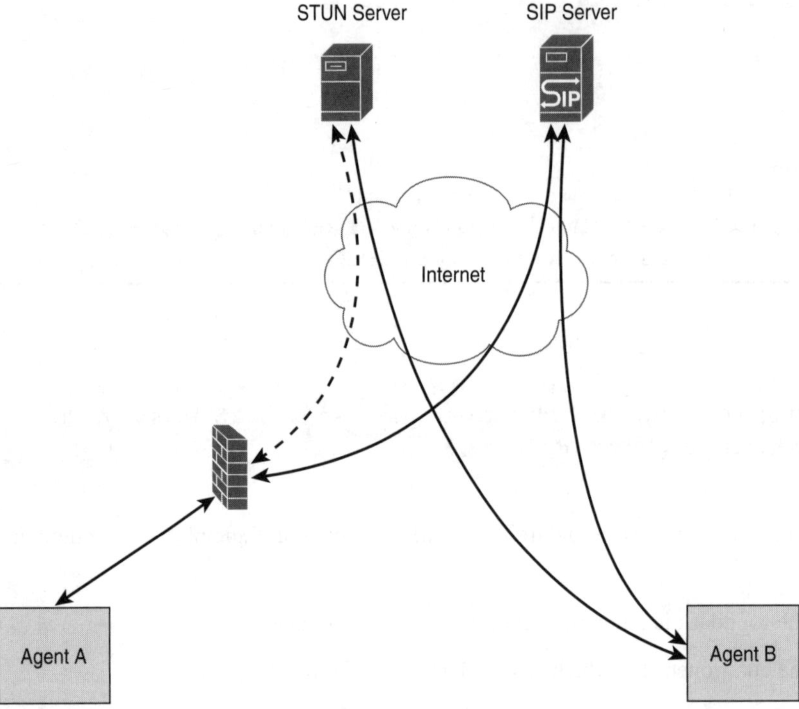

Figure 5-43 *Demonstration of the ICE Framework*

Step 1. Agent A gathers candidates. Local candidates for Agent A include its host candidate derived from a locally attached interface and a server-reflexive candidate. To obtain the server-reflexive candidate, Agent A sends a STUN binding request from its host candidate.

Step 2. The STUN server receives the request, creates a binding, and responds with a success response. Included in the response are the **MAPPED-ADDRESS** and **XOR-MAPPED ADDRESS** attributes of Agent A.

Step 3. Agent A prioritizes candidates. As per the priority calculation guidelines of the ICE specification, the host candidate is given a higher preference value than the server-reflexive candidate. The preference of the host candidate is 2130706431, and the preference of the server-reflexive candidate is

1694498815. The host candidate is assigned a foundation of 1, and the server-reflexive candidate is assigned a foundation of 2.

Step 4. Agent A encodes an SDP offer, using the semantics of ICE, and transmits the resulting offer to Agent B. The default candidate for media will be the server-reflexive candidate. This occurs despite the host candidate having a higher preference, as the probability of successfully transmitting and receiving on a mapped interface (server-reflexive) is higher than the probability on a host interface.

The SDP body is provided in Example 5-24.

Example 5-24 *SDP Encoding of Agent A*

```
v=0
o=jdoe 2890844526 2890842807 IN IP4 10.0.1.1
s=
c=IN IP4 192.0.2.3
t=0 0
a=ice-pwd:asd88fgpdd777uzjYhagZg
a=ice-ufrag:8hhY
m=audio 45664 RTP/AVP 0
b=RS:0
b=RR:0
a=rtpmap:0 PCMU/8000
a=candidate:1 1 UDP 2130706431 10.0.1.1 8998 typ host
a=candidate:2 1 UDP 1694498815 192.0.2.3 45664 typ srflx raddr 10.0.1.1 rport 8998
```

Step 5. Agent B receives the offer and begins gathering its own candidates. It derives a host candidate from a directly attached interface and subsequently uses the host candidate to obtain its service-reflexive address. Because Agent B is not behind a NAT device, its server-reflexive address is the same as its host address.

Step 6. Agent B calculates the priority for its host candidate. Because the calculation is guided by the recommendations of the ICE specification, its priority is the same as that of the host candidate of Agent A. Agent B then chooses a foundation of 1 for the host candidate and transmits the SDP answer. The SDP answer is provided in Example 5-25.

Step 7. Based on the candidates advertised in the SDP offer/answer exchange, both agents pair candidates. The ICE specification requires that any agent replace its server-reflexive candidate with the host candidate (from which the server-reflexive candidate was derived). This process is called *pruning candidate pairs*. Therefore, Agent A ends up having only one candidate pair: its local host candidate and Agent B's local host candidate. Agent B, on the other hand, ends up having two candidate pairs: its local host candidate and Agent A's server-reflexive candidate and its local host candidate and Agent A's local host candidate. Candidate pair priorities are calculated, and checklists are formed.

Example 5-25 *SDP Encoding of Agent B*

```
v=0
o=bob 2890844526 2890842844 IN IP4 192.0.2.1
s=
c=IN IP4 192.0.2.1
t=0 0
a=ice-pwd:asd88fgpdd777uzjYhagZg
a=ice-ufrag:8hhY
m=audio 3478 RTP/AVP 0
b=RS:0
b=RR:0
a=rtpmap:0 PCMU/8000
a=candidate:1 1 UDP 1694498815 192.0.2.1 3478 typ host
```

Step 8. Agent B attempts a connectivity check between its local host candidate and Agent A's local host candidate. (This candidate pair is assigned a higher pair priority, as per the algorithm specified in the ICE specification.) This check fails straightaway.

Step 9. Agent A attempts a connectivity check for the only candidate pair it has. Because this setup uses ICE's aggressive nomination process, Agent A includes the **USE-CANDIDATE** attribute in the STUN binding request. The STUN binding response from Agent B carries the server-reflexive address of Agent A. Because the check succeeds, Agent A adds this candidate pair to the *valid list*. Also, because the **USE-CANDIDATE** flag was included in the request and there are no more media streams, Agent A's ICE processing is complete, and Agent A is now ready to start sending media.

Step 10. Agent B generates its own check (called a *triggered check*) in response to the connectivity check that succeeded in step 9. This check is a STUN request/response transaction from the local candidate of Agent B to the server-reflexive candidate of Agent A. When the check succeeds, this candidate pair is added to the **list list** of Agent B. Note that there are no more checks for Agent B to initiate, as the candidate pair discovered in the previous step matches the one signaled in the SDP body of Agent A. ICE processing is now complete for Agent B as well, and Agent B is ready to transmit media.

This entire process is diagrammed in Figure 5-44.

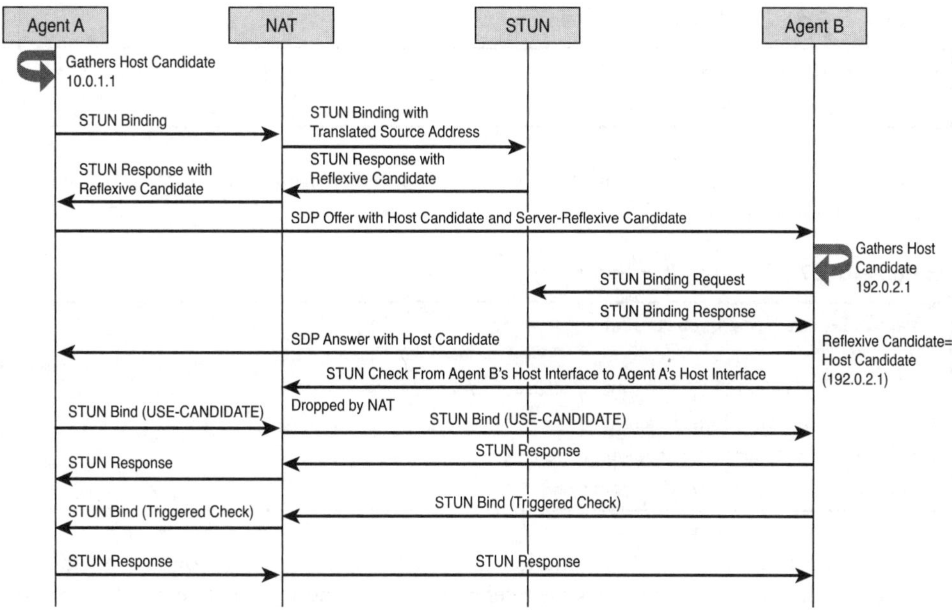

Figure 5-44 *Demonstration of the ICE Framework*

ICE-Lite

For ICE to work properly, both sides need to support the ICE implementation. In scenarios where a device is always directly attached to a public Internet interface, the device does not need to gather a candidate list, as the local candidates will always be a better option than using STUN or TURN. As a result, ICE-Lite agents only include local (host) candidates.

ICE-Lite agents do not perform connectivity checks, but they need to respond to connectivity checks originating from the remote ICE-enabled agent. When using ICE-Lite, the parameter **a=ice-lite** is present in the SDP. In scenarios where one side is a full ICE implementation and the other is an ICE-Lite implementation, the full agent takes the role of the controlling agent to initiate the connectivity check and ultimately select the candidate to be used for the media session. When two Lite implementations are communicating, no connectivity checks are sent, so to reconcile a potential mismatch in candidate selection, a media renegotiation through a RE-INVITE transaction after media selection is required.

ICE-Lite on CUBE

At the time of this publication, CUBE supports only an ICE-Lite implementation. This implementation inserts local candidates in the SDP for outbound dial-peer matches on CUBE. Inbound ICE candidates are processed if they are present in the incoming SDP offer.

ICE-Lite configuration on CUBE is demonstrated in Example 5-26.

Example 5-26 *ICE-Lite Configuration on CUBE*

```
voice class stun-usage 1
 stun usage ice lite
```

Overall statistics for ICE negotiations can be observed with **show voip ice global-stats**, as shown in Example 5-27.

Example 5-27 *Viewing ICE Summary Statistics*

```
CUBE# show voip ice global-stats

Interactive Connectivity Establishment(ICE) global stats:
Total Rx Stun BindingRequests          : 43
Total Tx Stun BindingSuccessResponses: 43
Total Tx Stun BindingErrorResponses   : 0
```

Details on an active call ICE negotiation can be observed with **show voip ice instance call-id**, where the **call-id** matches the reference found in **show call active**. Example 5-28 shows the details for the ICE candidate checks for a call where an ICE candidate was successfully negotiated.

Example 5-28 *Verifying ICE Candidates*

```
CUBE# show voip ice instance call-id 25

Interactive Connectivity Check(ICE) Instance details:
Call-ID is 25
Instance is 0x7FC617FC0508
Overall ICE-State is COMPLETED
LocalAgent's mode is ICE-CONTROLLED
RemoteAgent's mode is ICE-CONTROLLING
m-line:1
---------
ICE-State: ACTIVE
NominatedPairs:
LocalIP 198.51.100.107   port 8000  type host    RemoteIP 192.0.2.137  port 2326  type host

m-line:2
---------
ICE-State: ACTIVE
NominatedPairs:
LocalIP 198.51.100.107   port 8002  type host    RemoteIP 192.0.2.137  port 2328  type host
LocalIP 198.51.100.107   port 8003  type host    RemoteIP 192.0.2.137  port 2329  type host
```

```
m-line:3
---------
ICE-State: ACTIVE
NominatedPairs:
LocalIP 198.51.100.107   port 8036   type host    RemoteIP 192.0.2.137  port 2454   type host

m-line:4
---------
ICE-State: ACTIVE
NominatedPairs:
LocalIP 198.51.100.107   port 8004   type host    RemoteIP 192.0.2.137  port 2330   type host
LocalIP 198.51.100.107   port 8005   type host    RemoteIP 192.0.2.137  port 2331   type host

m-line:5
---------
ICE-State: ACTIVE
NominatedPairs:
LocalIP 198.51.100.107   port 8038   type host    RemoteIP 192.0.2.137  port 2332   type host

Total Rx STUN Bind Req 22
Total Tx STUN Bind Succ Resp 22
Total Tx STUN Bind failure resp 0
```

The following features are not supported on CUBE with ICE-Lite:

- IPv6
- ANAT
- ANAT–ICE interworking
- Media anti-tromboning
- High availability support for video calls
- Transparent codec
- SDP pass-through
- Media flow-around
- Resource Reservation Protocol (RSVP)
- SIP-to-TDM gateway support
- Media termination points (MTPs)
- VXML and TCL scripts

Troubleshooting RTP

Troubleshooting RTP issues on SBCs is similar to troubleshooting any other issue on SBCs: It requires a well-informed, structured approach of gathering details related to the problem, verifying the configuration, running diagnostics, and, ultimately, reaching a conclusion on the probable causes of failure. RTP issues generally manifest as one of the following situations:

- One-way audio
- No-way audio
- Audio quality issues
- Call establishment failures

In scenarios where the communicating endpoints cannot converge on a common set of media codecs and there isn't the possibility of transcoding, call establishment failures occur. However, applying a new configuration or modifying an existing configuration can rectify these failures.

Example 5-29 provides a snippet of SIP messages exchanged between user agents that cannot converge on a common set of media codecs.

Example 5-29 *SIP Message Exchange Resulting in Codec Mismatch*

```
Sent:
INVITE sip:Alice@example.com SIP/2.0
Via: SIP/2.0/UDP 192.0.2.2:5060;branch=z9hG4bK13DDC569
From: <sip:Bob@example1.com>;tag=805CEE6C-84
To: <sip:Alice@example.com>
Call-ID: 3D8BCD24-DDF911E5-A6DD8141-723D6149@192.0.2.2
///Truncated for brevity///

v=0
o=CiscoSystemsCCM-SIP 174369 1 IN IP4 192.0.2.2
s=SIP Call
c=IN IP4 192.0.2.2
t=0 0
m=audio 28280 RTP/AVP 0 101
a=rtpmap:0 PCMU/8000
a=ptime:20
a=rtpmap:101 telephone-event/8000
a=fmtp:101 0-15

Received:
SIP/2.0 488 Not Acceptable Here
```

```
Via: SIP/2.0/UDP 192.0.2.2:5060;branch=z9hG4bK13DDC569
From: <sip:Bob@example1.com>;tag=805CEE6C-84
To: <sip:Alice@example.com>;tag=5msm434m
Call-ID: 3D8BCD24-DDF911E5-A6DD8141-723D6149@192.0.2.2
Timestamp: 1456736225
CSeq: 101 INVITE
Reason: Q.850;cause=16;text="normal call clearing"
```

In Example 5-29, the calling user agent tries to establish a communication session with G.711 μlaw as the audio codec; however, the destination user agent does not support this codec and rejects the request with a **488 Not Acceptable Here** response. Call establishment failures related to codec negotiation can be rectified by altering the configuration on CUBE to present an acceptable list of codecs on either call leg. CUBE, by default, works on the principle of *codec filtering*, wherein the set of media codecs advertised in the incoming offer serves as a template for advertising the set of codecs in the outgoing offer. Figure 5-45 depicts codec filtering on CUBE.

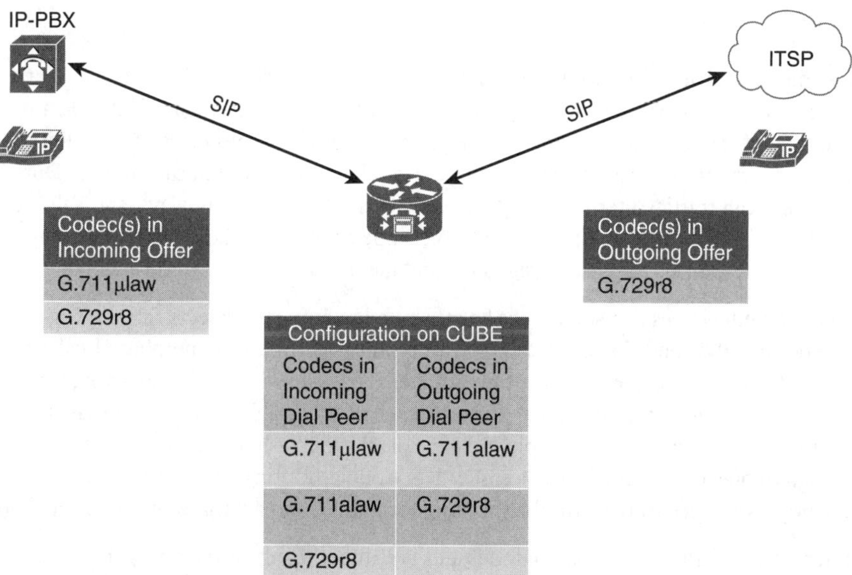

Figure 5-45 *Codec Filtering on CUBE*

In Figure 5-45, the incoming offer advertises codecs G.711 μlaw and G.729r8. The outgoing offer on CUBE is constructed after applying codec filtering—the process of converging on a common set of codecs across both call legs. As a result, the outgoing offer advertises only G.729r8 instead of the entire suite of codecs configured in the outgoing dial peer. This behavior on CUBE can lead to scenarios in which requests are rejected because of codec negotiation failures. To override this behavior on CUBE, the **voice-class codec <*tag*> offer all** command is used under the specific dial peer. This command ensures that the entire suite of codecs configured under a dial peer is advertised, regardless of the list of advertised codecs in the incoming offer.

Note It is advisable to locally register a transcoding profile on CUBE when deciding to override codec filtering on CUBE.

For media issues that are related to either call quality or one-way/no-way media, before jumping in to collect debugging information, diagnostic command outputs, and packet captures, it is advisable to gather more details around the issue first:

- Does it occur for every single call?
- Does it occur during a specific time of the day?
- Does it happen intermittently? If so, what is the frequency of occurrence?
- Does it depend on the direction of the call?
- Does it affect users on the enterprise network or the service provider network or both?

For a media issue that occurs for every single call, the issue could be related to configuration, software defects, or malfunctioning hardware. If the issue presents itself during a specific time of the day, it is extremely unlikely to be a result of misconfiguration. Rather, it could be related to the processing load of devices along the communication path. During hours of high-call traffic, intermediary devices such as SBCs, voice gateways, and call proxies could handle call traffic volumes close to their operational thresholds, often resulting in processing delays, dropped packets (signaling and media), and decreased throughput.

Intermittent media issues can sometimes be attributed to software defects that are triggered under specific conditions; for example, after processing a certain number of calls, the transcoder logic on an SBC could pass through media packets without manipulating the payloads. Depending on the frequency of occurrence of the problem, the appropriate troubleshooting mechanism(s) may be deployed. In general, troubleshooting intermittent issues with a high frequency of occurrence is easier than troubleshooting issues that occur very infrequently, as a wider array of troubleshooting techniques and alternatives may be applied.

The intermittent nature of media-related issues is a direct result of the "trigger" of such issues not being readily apparent. For example, consider a case in which users report choppy audio for all calls during a specific time of the day. On further investigation, it could be revealed that calls have choppy audio only during peak business hours. By co-relating other variables, such as the number of calls, average CPU utilization, and average memory utilization during peak hours, it may be determined that the numbers of calls serviced by CUBE exceed system-defined thresholds. Thus, the root cause or the trigger of the problem may be determined to be platform sizing as opposed to any issue that is specific to media handling on CUBE. Often while troubleshooting intermittent media issues, it is advisable to try to uncover the underlying trigger by co-relating dependent variables as opposed to adopting a brute-force approach.

Media issues related to the directionality of a call can result from variations in the communication paths, the endpoints involved in the communication session, or misconfiguration.

After specific details about an issue are gathered, run through the configuration, placing emphasis on sections that have a bearing on RTP or media. On CUBE, these include the following:

- Dial peers
- Media flow mode
- Presence of media resources
- Interface(s) to which RTP is bound

Each one of these sections has a direct bearing on eventual media plane operations: The dial peers might be incorrectly configured to advertise codecs that result in call establishment failures. The media flow mode might be incorrectly configured to media flow-around, resulting in no-way audio calls. Media resources might be required to transcode or transrate calls. RTP could be bound to an incorrect interface because of the **voice-class sip bind media source-interface <*interface*>** command, resulting in one-way or no-way audio calls.

When the configuration looks to be correct, begin using generic **show** commands when the call is active. These **show** commands provide details about the dial peers used by calls, the codec that is negotiated, the IP addresses involved in the RTP session, and whether packets are being dropped. The following commands are most useful when troubleshooting media-based issues on CUBE:

- **show call active voice brief**—The output of this command provides several important information elements, such as the dial peers matched for the call, the remote RTP IP address and port, and the number of RTP packets received and transmitted per call leg. Example 5-30 shows an example of the output of the **show call active voice brief** command.

Example 5-30 *Output of the* **show call active voice brief** *Command*

```
CUBE# show call active voice brief


3929 : 80875 -2107718356ms.1 (13:54:01.161 UTC Mon Nov 28 2016) +1160 pid:10 Answer
  408345 active
 dur 00:00:30 tx:1516/242560 rx:1467/234560 dscp:0 media:0 audio tos:0xB8 video
  tos:0x0
 IP 192.0.2.1:53310 SRTP: off rtt:0ms pl:0/0ms lost:0/0/0 delay:0/0/0ms g711ulaw
  TextRelay: off Transcoded: No ICE: Off
 media inactive detected:n media contrl rcvd:n/a timestamp:n/a
 long duration call detected:n long duration call duration:n/a timestamp:n/a
 LostPacketRate:0.00 OutOfOrderRate:0.00
 VRF: NA
```

```
3929 : 80876 -2107718346ms.1 (13:54:01.171 UTC Mon Nov 28 2016) +1140 pid:20
 Originate 2001 active
 dur 00:00:30 tx:1467/234560 rx:1516/242560 dscp:0 media:0 audio tos:0xB8 video
  tos:0x0
 IP 192.0.2.2:8012 SRTP: off rtt:0ms pl:0/0ms lost:0/0/0 delay:0/0/0ms g711ulaw
  TextRelay: off Transcoded: No ICE: Off
 media inactive detected:n media contrl rcvd:n/a timestamp:n/a
 long duration call detected:n long duration call duration:n/a timestamp:n/a
 LostPacketRate:0.00 OutOfOrderRate:0.00
 VRF: NA

Telephony call-legs: 0
SIP call-legs: 2
H323 call-legs: 0
Call agent controlled call-legs: 0
SCCP call-legs: 0
Multicast call-legs: 0
Total call-legs: 2
```

In Example 5-30, **pid** represents the dial-peer ID for a given call leg. **IP** represents the remote IP address and port, and **tx/rx** are counters for the number of packets sent/received for a given call leg. If the command is keyed in succession several times during a call, the counters for **tx/rx** are expected to increase, signifying a continuous passage of RTP packets. However, if the counters remain static as the call progresses, this indicates an issue with regard to RTP transmission that typically manifests as one-way or no-way audio.

Note On the IOS XE platform to collate real-time statistics using the **show call active voice brief** command, it is required to enable **media bulk-stats** under **voice service voip** mode.

- **show voip rtp connections**—The output of this command provides the IP addresses and ports of active RTP sessions on CUBE. The output of this command doesn't provide anything beyond what the **show call active voice brief** command already provides, but, it is compact and can be used for a quick lookup of RTP session details. The output to this command is provided earlier in this chapter, in Example 5-5.

The previously listed commands are useful if media-related issues occur in real time, but in scenarios where the issue is highly intermittent, the administrator can make use of the **show call history voice** command. This command displays a call history table that contains a list of calls handled by CUBE. The number of calls displayed in the table can be controlled with the **dial-control-mib max-size** command. The default number of entries is 50. By default, records are retained for 15 minutes, after which they are purged.

To increase the amount of time for which these records are maintained, **dial-control-mib retain-timer** can be used. The output of this command displays useful information such as the duration of the call, the disconnect cause code, the number of packets sent and received, and the number of packets lost. Example 5-31 demonstrates the output of the **show call history voice** command.

Example 5-31 *Output of the* **show call history voice** *Command*

```
CUBE# show call history voice

GENERIC:
SetupTime=176833940 ms (23:21:44.943 pdt Sat Nov 4 2017)
//Truncated for brevity//
DisconnectCause=10
DisconnectText=normal call clearing (16)
ConnectTime=176835610 ms (23:21:46.613 pdt Sat Nov 4 2017)
DisconnectTime=176898230 ms (23:22:49.233 pdt Sat Nov 4 2017)
CallDuration=00:01:02 sec
CallOrigin=1
ReleaseSource=2
ChargedUnits=0
InfoType=speech
TransmitPackets=3122
TransmitBytes=499520
ReceivePackets=3129
ReceiveBytes=500640
VOIP:
ConnectionId[0x54E647AE 0xC12811E7 0x8A23E016 0x56D87008]
IncomingConnectionId[0x54E647AE 0xC12811E7 0x8A23E016 0x56D87008]
CallID=23
SessionId=0
CallReferenceId=0
CallServiceType=Unknown
RTP Loopback Call=FALSE
RemoteIPAddress=10.106.118.199
RemoteUDPPort=23368
RemoteSignallingIPAddress=10.106.118.199
RemoteSignallingPort=5060
RemoteMediaIPAddress=10.106.118.226
RemoteMediaPort=23368
SRTP = off
TextRelay = off
Fallback Icpif=0
Fallback Loss=0
Fallback Delay=0
```

```
RoundTripDelay=0 ms
SelectedQoS=best-effort
tx_DtmfRelay=rtp-nte
FastConnect=FALSE

AnnexE=FALSE

Separate H245 Connection=FALSE

H245 Tunneling=FALSE

//Truncated for brevity//
GapFillWithSilence=0 ms
GapFillWithPrediction=0 ms
GapFillWithInterpolation=0 ms
GapFillWithRedundancy=0 ms
//Truncated for brevity//
ReceiveDelay=0 ms
LostPackets=0
EarlyPackets=0
LatePackets=0
VAD = disabled
CoderTypeRate=g711ulaw
CodecBytes=160
cvVoIPCallHistoryIcpif=0
MediaSetting=flow-through
AlertTimepoint=176834000 ms (23:21:45.005 pdt Sat Nov 4 2017)
CallerName=
CallerIDBlocked=False
OriginalCallingNumber=5081004
OriginalCallingOctet=0x0
OriginalCalledNumber=4082001
OriginalCalledOctet=0x0
//Truncated for brevity//
CPA Call History Parameters
  CPA Event Status: DISABLE
 RTCP TransmitPackets=0
 RTCP ReceivePackets=0
```

The listed **show** commands provide a general overview of the media characteristics of a call, including what codec is used, the IP addresses and port numbers involved, and whether packets are transmitted bidirectionally. It is possible for packets to be dropped at an interface; if this interface is directly involved in the transmission of RTP, these packet drops could manifest as one-way audio, no-way audio, or audio calls with choppy voice. To rule out any interface drops, the **show interface [interface-type] [slot]** command may be used.

When using commands such as **show voip rtp connections** and **show call active voice brief** to determine the peer IP addresses that participate in media transmission, it is generally a good practice to verify IP reachability from CUBE to those peers. IP reachability can be verified by running real-time checks such as ICMP pings or by examining the routing table on CUBE.

While **show** commands are extremely useful in deriving useful real-time information, they are limited in scope when troubleshooting complicated or intermittent RTP-related problems. For example, there could be cases in which RTP packets relayed to CUBE don't have any audio samples in the payload, or an abrupt change in the sequence number or the timestamp header field might lead to playout issues at the receiving end. For troubleshooting issues that are related to the operating principle of RTP as a protocol, it is advisable to capture network packets and use third-party applications such as Wireshark for analysis.

Once a packet capture file is loaded into Wireshark, several functions can be carried out with regard to analyzing RTP streams—from going through the headers of individual RTP packets to analyzing the characteristics of a particular RTP session. If there happen to be issues in the RTP stream, such as a large number of packets missing or arriving significantly late, going through the RTP stream analysis on Wireshark will be helpful. To analyze a particular RTP stream on Wireshark, use the following procedure:

Step 1. Load the capture file into Wireshark.

Step 2. Navigate to **Telephony > RTP > Show All Streams** (or **RTP Streams** for Wireshark version 2.0 and later).

Step 3. Choose the relevant stream from the ones displayed in the dialog window and click **Analyze.**

This procedure opens a new window that displays the RTP stream details, such as the average jitter, the number of RTP packets lost, and the number of sequencing errors. If there happen to be packets that arrive late or are lost, the problem may manifest as an audio quality issue such as choppy or garbled audio. Figure 5-46 provides a snapshot from Wireshark of a stream experiencing packet loss.

Another useful construct when troubleshooting audio issues is to play out the audio stream to check for problems. For example, enterprise users might complain of poor-quality audio for calls traversing CUBE. It is very likely that all RTP streams coming in from the service provider network have lost packets or have late-arriving packets.

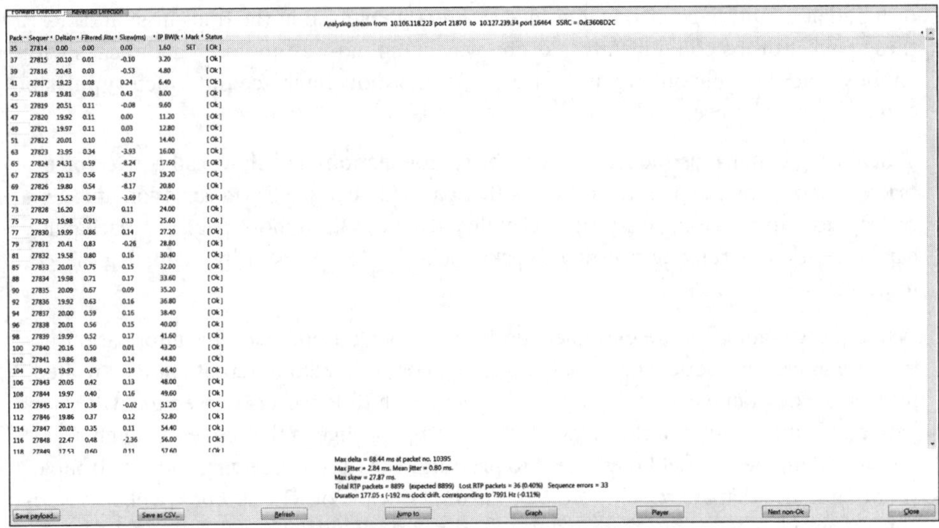

Figure 5-46 *Snapshot of an RTP Stream Experiencing Packet Loss*

Just analyzing and playing out the RTP stream from the service provider could help an administrator pinpoint the problem. To play out an audio stream on Wireshark, navigate to the dialog box that provides a snapshot of the relevant RTP stream (refer to Figure 5-46). Once there, click **Player > Decode > Play** (or **Play Streams** in newer versions of Wireshark). Wireshark then plays out the audio stream as received on CUBE before any kind of processing and represents the true stream of audio from the transmitter.

> **Note** Wireshark is optimized to decode only G.711 streams. For streams using high-compression codecs such as G.729, additional software is required; such streams cannot be decoded natively in Wireshark.

Audio quality issues may also arise on CUBE due to CPU or memory resources being exceeded. If there are persistent audio quality problems (or call setup times that take unreasonably long), it is a good idea to check the CPU and memory profile by using the **show process cpu sorted** and **show process memory sorted** commands. For a historical CPU usage profile over 72 hours, the **show process cpu history** can be used.

In summary, the best bet in understanding the cause of media issues it to obtain details about the issue through a statistical or an actual representation, and then using that representation to diagnose towards a root cause.

Summary

This chapter discusses the various aspects of RTP as a protocol for the real-time transmission of media. It also introduces RTCP, the peer protocol to RTP. The discussion extends into summarizing the operation of RTP and RTCP on SBCs. The chapter also discusses various media-based features supported by SBCs, such as transcoding and transrating. The chapter discusses the challenges posed by NAT for real-time communications and commonly implemented NAT traversal solutions. The final section discusses some generic approaches to troubleshooting media-related issues.

References

- RFC 2198, "RTP Payload for Redundant Audio Data," https://tools.ietf.org/html/rfc2198.
- RFC 2833, "RTP Payload for DTMF Digits, Telephony Tones and Telephony Signals," https://tools.ietf.org/html/rfc2833.
- RFC 3261, "SIP: Session Initiation Protocol," https://tools.ietf.org/html/rfc3261.
- RFC 3388, "Grouping of Media Lines in the Session Description Protocol (SDP)," https://tools.ietf.org/html/rfc3388.
- RFC 3550, "RTP: A Transport Protocol for Real-Time Applications," https://tools.ietf.org/html/rfc3550.
- RFC 4091, "The Alternative Network Address Types (ANAT) Semantics for the Session Description Protocol (SDP) Grouping Framework," https://tools.ietf.org/html/rfc4091.
- RFC 4571, "Framing Real-Time Transport Protocol (RTP) and RTP Control Protocol (RTCP) Packets over Connection-Oriented Transport," https://tools.ietf.org/html/rfc4571.
- RFC 5245, "Interactive Connectivity Establishment (ICE): A Protocol for Network Address Translator (NAT) Traversal for Offer/Answer Protocols," https://tools.ietf.org/html/rfc5245.
- RFC 5389, "Session Traversal Utilities for NAT (STUN)," https://tools.ietf.org/html/rfc5389.
- RFC 5766, "Traversal Using Relays Around NAT (TURN): Relay Extensions to Session Traversal Utilities for NAT (STUN)," https://tools.ietf.org/html/rfc5766.
- RFC 7092, "A Taxonomy of Session Initiation Protocol (SIP) Back-to-Back User Agents," https://tools.ietf.org/html/rfc7092.
- RFC 8079, "Guidelines for End-to-End Support of the RTP Control Protocol (RTCP) in Back-to-Back User Agents (B2BUAs)," https://tools.ietf.org/html/rfc8079.

Chapter 6

Secure Signaling and Media

Every day, all around the world, people create millions of media sessions for exchanging data. These sessions may be established using email, web pages, instant messaging, or even phone calls. The types of data exchanged in these media sessions is endless but may be in the form of files, audio, video, images, and text. More often than not, the parties involved in these sessions expect that the data they are exchanging is free from observation or manipulation by third-party entities with malicious intent. These privacy concerns lead to security implementations that are used in the signaling and media planes to ensure that the session establishment and the resulting media stream are free from third-party intervention and inspection.

This chapter covers the following topics pertaining to security on the signaling and media planes:

- **Understanding Secure Technologies**—This section provides a crash course on the various foundational aspects of information security required to achieve a proper understanding of the security protocols detailed throughout this chapter.
- **Establishing Secure Sessions**—This section provides an in-depth analysis of the protocols and processes used to provide security at the signaling and media planes.
- **SBC Signaling and Media Security**—This section discusses the different ways SBCs put the various signaling and media security protocols to use.
- **Alternative Security Methods**—This section provides a brief overview of additional and alternative security methods available for signaling and media plane operations.

Understanding Secure Technologies

Information security is an ever-expanding field of technology. Parties with malicious intent are always trying to find exploits and circumvent current security constructs, while security experts continue to create new, stronger, and better security mechanisms, techniques, and protocols in hopes of staying one step ahead of hackers. Different security experts have fundamentally different views on and approaches to solving the same information security problems. As a result, there isn't one all-encompassing protocol that can be used to secure a network or data on a network; rather, it's important to understand a set of core information security concepts because the different protocols and solutions to everyday problems are created around these concepts.

These are the core information security concepts which pertain to data:

- **Confidentiality**—Data must remain private and secure from prying eyes. In the world of information security, encryption protocols are used to secure data both at rest and in transit.
- **Data integrity**—Data must not be changed, modified, corrupted, or altered by a malicious third party either at rest or in transit. There are many different ways to ensure that data has not been modified by unauthorized parties, but one of the most common mechanisms is through the use of a one-way hashing program that produces a message authentication code.
- **Availability**—Data and devices that provide access to data must remain available. Denial of service, data corruption, and erasure of data can all compromise availability. High availability, redundant pathing through load balancing, distributed denial of service (DDoS) protection, and secure disaster recovery backups are methods of ensuring that data remains available at all times.

In addition to these three core concepts, three more core concepts are often used to extend information security for people or devices that handle data:

- **Non-repudiation**—Parties must always be accountable for the actions performed. Checks must be in place so that consistent logging is performed and so a party cannot later deny accessing, modifying, or deleting data.
- **Authentication**—Parties must be able to prove, with a high degree of certainty, that they are who they claim to be. Without authentication, a malicious party could use impersonation to gain unwarranted access to data or the network.
- **Authorization**—Parties must be authorized to perform actions they are attempting. This often goes hand-in-hand with authentication. Although a party is authenticated, that party should have a limited scope in terms of what he or she is authorized to do within an information system. Authorization greatly reduces the potential attack surface. The *principle of least common privilege* says that a party must have access to the information and resources required to perform the necessary tasks and that access control restrictions must be placed on anything outside those actions.

Malicious parties commonly attempt to gain undesired access to systems or data by exploiting vulnerabilities in security protocols. These vulnerabilities let an attacker circumvent the security put in place and fundamentally undermine everything the security protocol provides. In addition, security protocols should attempt to reduce the number of different ways a party can potentially employ an exploit. The ways a party can employ an exploit are referred to as *attack vectors*, and the sum of all potential attack vectors is referred as the *attack surface*. One attack vector is a man-in-the-middle (MITM) attack. With this type of attack, a third party eavesdrops on a conversation between two people or devices by intercepting traffic as it is sent and received. If this data is not encrypted, an attacker has full access to review and potentially make changes. MITM attacks are a large problem that the core security concepts aim to prevent.

The following sections detail the different building blocks and key protocols used to secure multimedia collaboration networks at the signaling plane and the media plane. The core focus of this chapter is securing signaling and media across SBCs. Although the scope of this chapter is limited to SBCs, many of the topics discussed here also apply to other devices in the collaboration ecosystem. The contents of this chapter are referenced in Chapter 13, "Security Threat Migration," which covers applicable use cases, with the aim of mitigating various types of security attacks targeted at SBCs.

Encryption and Decryption

Encryption refers to the act converting plaintext into a format that only authorized parties can view or access. *Decryption* refers to turning encrypted data into plaintext. Both of these actions are aided with the help of a *key*, as discussed in depth later in this chapter. Encryption and decryption of data are the backbone of most cryptographic protocols discussed in this chapter.

Encrypting data at rest means encrypting data stored on a hard drive, while encrypting data in transit involves securing data as it is sent/received across different network segments. These network segments may lie on your own network or LAN. Alternatively, these network segments might lie in public networks such as the Internet or a service provider uplink. In either scenario, data must be securely encrypted so that if unauthorized third parties get hold of said data, they cannot view the contents of the data.

Example 6-1 shows a very basic example of encryption and decryption. Alice has a plaintext file containing the characters abcde. Alice encrypts this data by applying a rotational/substitution cipher, also known as a Caesar cipher (named after Julius Caesar). In short, a *cipher*, commonly referred to as an *algorithm*, is a set of steps used to encrypt or decrypt data. The cipher is aided by a *key*, which is used in the computation of the cipher. In this case, Alice chooses the key 2. Using the Caesar cipher and key, Alice is able to manually change the data in the text file into ciphertext. *Ciphertext* is the resulting output after the key and cipher have been applied. In this example, the cipher and key are used on each value of the original text. The a is shifted two letters and becomes c, the b is shifted two letters and becomes d, and so on until all the data is encrypted as ciphertext. At this point, the original data is encrypted. Alice may now give the key and data to Bob, who can then decrypt the ciphertext cdefg back into its plaintext form for consumption.

Example 6-1 *A Very Basic Example of a Cipher*

```
Plain Text: abcde
Cipher: Rotational
Key: 2
Cipher Text: cdefg
```

The encryption method used in Example 6-1 is not very secure, and a hacker could crack the key and cipher very quickly. In the real world, encryption protocols are far more complex, require stronger inputs (keys), and ultimately are much more secure. The following sections detail these inputs and various techniques used to encrypt the data we use every day.

Symmetric and Asymmetric Keys

Keys play a large role in encryption and decryption of digital data. They therefore often have their own algorithms, which are used to compute the key from various given inputs. Keys also come in a variety of different sizes, and the term *key space* is used to refer to all possible permutations of a key. The larger the key space, the more resilient the key to a brute-force attack by a computer. Keep in mind that a larger key, while more secure, does require more computing resources. Therefore, after a certain size, the security advantages are not great enough to justify the computing resources needed. Next-generation encryption (NGE) standards state that key sizes less than 1024 bits should be avoided, and 2048 bits is the current standard for keys. Cryptographic keys can be broadly classified into two categories:

- **Symmetric keys**—With symmetric keys, the same key is used to encrypt data and decrypt data. Take, for example, the locks on the front door of your home. You can create copies of your key and distribute them to other people, who can then lock and unlock the door, while you can still use your key to lock and unlock the same door. The key shared in Example 6-1 is considered a symmetric key because Alice and Bob use the same key to encrypt and decrypt the data.

- **Asymmetric keys**—Asymmetric keys are two separate keys that serve different purposes: One key can be used to encrypt, and the other key can be used to decrypt. If we apply the concept of asymmetric keys to a lock, we can think of a lock with two differently shaped key holes; because the keys are shaped differently, each can fit only into its respective keyhole. You use one of the keys to lock the door, and the other key must be used to unlock the door. Neither key can use the other's keyhole. Exactly how the magic between keys occurs is not required to understand the contents of this chapter. You just need to know that the two keys are mathematically associated, which is what facilitates the asymmetry.

  Asymmetric keys are commonly used in public key infrastructure (PKI) and facilitate public key cryptography, where one key, the public key, is available, and the other key, the private key, is kept secret and never known to anybody except for the key holder. As you may have guessed, asymmetric keys are far more complex than symmetric keys, and this means they offer more security. However, this security comes with the cost of additional computational resources, such as CPU and memory. Thus asymmetric keys such as an RSA key pair, discussed later in this chapter, are often used to secure small amounts of data or aid in the process of securely negotiating symmetric keys which are then used to secure large amounts of bulk data.

Block and Stream Ciphers

As mentioned earlier in this chapter, a *cipher* is an encryption algorithm used in conjunction with a key, multiple keys, and other inputs to encrypt plaintext data into encrypted ciphertext. Many different types of cipher specifications are used to encrypt data, including Advanced Encryption Standard (AES), Data Encryption Standard (DES), Triple DES (3DES), Blowfish, Twofish, Rivest Cipher 4 (RC4), International Data Encryption Algorithm (IDEA), and Camelia. All these encryption ciphers aim to provide a way to secure data and ensure confidentiality.

Ciphers can be split into two different categories, based on their operational mode: block and stream. A *stream* cipher runs against every bit of plaintext data, converting it on the fly into ciphertext by using a symmetric keystream. The *keystream* is a set of pseudorandom or random characters, each of which is mathematically computed against the bit of plaintext data. The result of this computation is a bit of ciphertext. Stream ciphers are very efficient when presented with minimal computing resources. *Block ciphers*, on the other hand, convert entire sections (blocks) of plaintext data into ciphertext. An example of a common block cipher is AES-256, which can encrypt a block of 256 bits into ciphertext by performing a computation on the entire block of plaintext, using a symmetric key. One small problem with block ciphers occurs when they are presented with a data set that is smaller than their block size. For example, if AES-256 were required to encrypt a block of 192 bits, it would need to add 64 bits of padding to allow for proper computation in the cipher algorithm.

Data Integrity Verification

Hashing refers to the process of generating unique output based on an input, often called a message authentication code (MAC). This output of a hashing operation will always be the same, based on the input, and so changing the input results in a different output. Hashing also operates on the principle of *collision avoidance*. This means that for every unique input, there is an equally unique output, and two unique inputs should never return the same hash value. This can be useful for cryptographic integrity checks, as discussed shortly.

Common hashing protocols are Message Digest 5 (MD5) and Secure Hash Algorithm (SHA). Many others exist, but in this section, we focus on SHA-256. The process of creating a hash is useful for signing data, providing integrity checks, and outputting data at a consistent length. For example, SHA-256 takes any input and always outputs a 32-byte hash. This hash is in hex, and each hex value actually represents 8 bits in the hash ($32 \times 8 = 256$), which is how we derive the 256 bits in SHA-256. Example 6-2 shows a hash being generated on a few different inputs. The first is the test input **abc**, which is used to confirm that the hashing program is actually returning proper outputs. Remember that two different devices performing a hash on the same input will always return the same output. You can therefore check the publicly available NIST.gov hash result for the input abc. In this case, it matches, thus confirming that the hashing program is functioning correctly. The next example shows the input **A short sentence**, which outputs a 32-byte hash. The final input is much longer and also outputs a 32-byte hash.

Example 6-2 *Examples of SHA-256 Being Run on Multiple Inputs*

```
root@linux-server:~$ echo -n abc | sha256sum
ba7816bf8f01cfea414140de5dae2223b00361a396177a9cb410ff61f20015ad  -

root@linux-server:~$ echo -n A short sentence | sha256sum
c42f2dc9dc063f6c3d06496a68f9a2a7f74586d008ff55e13a0247c98c6c7485  -

root@linux-server:~$ echo -n A really long sentence that is not of consistent length
  or an input which may be variable in length | sha256sum
2da03b0070baba8a9e2aa01820272e9c03e6894e1f4ac1d95accd27c20dbc1c6  -
```

In Example 6-3, you can see a hash being run on a Linux text file created with the contents abc. Say that you want to copy this file to another device, such as a Windows desktop, using FTP. To confirm that nothing has been inadvertently changed in transit, you can compute the hash again on the Windows machine (see Example 6-4). The hash output provided by different programs may introduce spaces every two characters, as shown in Example 6-4. If you manually remove the spaces, you can confirm that the two hashes are identical, which means the data has not been modified.

Example 6-3 *Generating a SHA-256 Hash Value on Linux*

```
Linux:
root@linux-server:~$ more test.txt
abc
root@linux-server:~$ sha256sum test.txt
edeaaff3f1774ad2888673770c6d64097e391bc362d7d6fb34982ddf0efd18cb  test.txt
```

Example 6-4 *Generating a SHA-256 Hash Value on Windows*

```
Windows:
C:\> CertUtil -hashfile test.txt SHA256
SHA256 hash of file test.txt:
ed ea af f3 f1 77 4a d2 88 86 73 77 0c 6d 64 09 7e 39 1b c3 62 d7 d6 fb 34 98 2d df
  0e fd 18 cb
CertUtil: -hashfile command completed successfully.
```

The following is the Linux command syntax shown in Example 6-2 through 6-4:

- **echo**—Outputs the input text to the terminal.
- **-n**—Removes a newline (**\n**) from the echo output. If it is included, this newline is included with hash computation and thus changes the value. To properly generate a hash using echo, the newline must be omitted.
- **sha256sum**—Computes the hash on the input using SHA-256.
- **more**—Reads out contents of an existing file to the terminal.

The following is the Windows command syntax shown in Example 6-4:

- **CertUtil**—This built-in Windows utility allows for viewing, creation, and management of certificates.
- **-hashfile**—This command is used to compute a hash against a specific file.
- **SHA256**—This computes a hash using SHA-256.

If two different devices perform a hash on abc and return the same output hash, why can't the input be derived from the output hash? First, hashing is not meant to securely encrypt data. You must remember that its purpose is to allow devices to perform data validation and integrity checks. Second, the input value *can* be derived from the output hash. Take, for example, the simple math equation 300 + 300 = 600. 300 + 300 would be the input, and 600 would be the output. Given the input, it is easy for multiple devices to calculate an output. But given only the output, it is much more difficult, but not impossible, for a device to calculate the actual input. In the real world, hashing operates with a much more complex algorithm for generating output hashes, which renders it impractical to attempt to reverse a one-way hash.

If the device receiving a piece of data is relying on the hash to be sent with the data, then an attacker could easily circumvent the data integrity provided by the hash. To do this, the attacker would simply intercept the data, remove the hash, change the data, compute a new hash to include with the data, and send it on. The device receiving this data and hash would not know if the hash was created by the MITM or the originator of the data. To add additional security to the data integrity and verification process, hashes can be combined with secret keys to compute an output that can be derived only if a party had access to the key. This type of message authentication code is called a *hashed message authentication code* (*HMAC*) when a symmetric shared-secret key is used; it is referred to as a *digital signature* when asymmetric keys such as a public/private key pair are used with the hash. Digital signatures offer non-repudiation because the creator of the hash can be confirmed by the public/private key pair used to encrypt and decrypt the hash.

For example, as shown in Figure 6-1, say that Bob creates a piece of data and calculates a hash on that data set. Then he uses his private key with the hash to create a digital signature. Bob then uses this new digital signature as a way to "sign" the data and confirm the authenticity of the contents. This data with the signature can then be passed indirectly over a network to Alice. When Alice receives this data, she will remove Bob's signature and compute her own hash of the data set. Alice can then decode Bob's signature by using Bob's public key. It decrypts, thus confirming that the signature was created by Bob because only Bob's private key could have created that signature. Alice's hash is compared to the hash in the decoded signature provided on the data by Bob. If Alice's computed hash equals Bob's hash from the signature, then Alice knows that the data has not been modified in transit. Remember that even if even one bit changes in the data, the hash will not be the same when Alice performed her hash calculation. In addition, a MITM attacker cannot intercept this data, change the contents, and compute a new hash without knowing the private key required to create an authentic-looking signature.

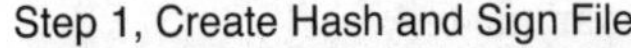

Step 2, Transfer File

Step 3, Compute Hash and Verify Signature

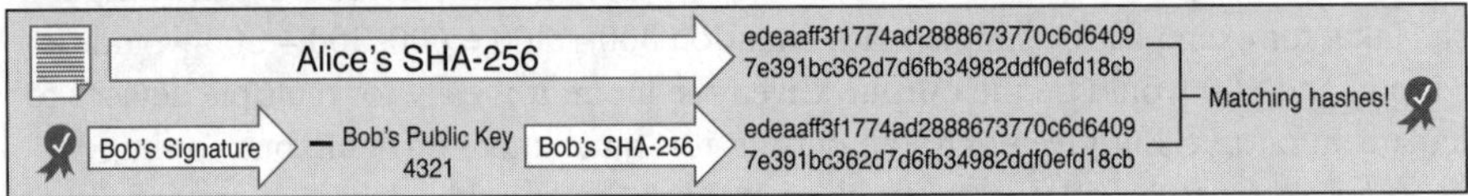

Figure 6-1 *Digital Signature Creation Process*

Hashing, message authentication codes, and digital signatures are used in conjunction with other cryptography protocols that work together to secure data. As indicated in this section, a hash may be referred to as a signature or a fingerprint, and it can be implemented by signing the data. This signature is a hash computed against the given data set, which may be a packet, the contents of a packet, digital certificates, or other data inputs. Hashing is used in digital certificates, Transport Layer Security (TLS), and many other protocols discussed later in this chapter.

Public Key Cryptography

Public key cryptography refers to the technology protocols, standards, and best practices related to the use of public and private keys for cryptography. Most of how public key cryptography operates is explained in the original Public-Key Cryptography Standards (PKCS) published by RSA Security Inc. Presently, most of these standards have been incorporated into or translated directly to IETF RFCs. It would be possible to spend days writing about all the different aspects of public key cryptography. However, for the sake of brevity, this chapter breaks the topic of public key cryptography into a few fundamental areas required to understand the latter topics of this chapter:

- **Key agreement**—The process of agreeing on a shared-secret key used in encryption and decryption of data
- **Public key encryption**—The use of public/private keys for transport of a shared-secret key from one party to another
- **Digital certificates**—An authentication mechanism for verifying peers communicating in a key agreement session

Key Agreement

Key agreement is a process in which two parties agree on the key that will be used for encryption and decryption of data. Different types of key agreement techniques exist, including pre-shared keys, passwords, and shared-secret keys. Shared-secret symmetric keys are often used with public key cryptography to encrypt data. Diffie-Hellman is one of the most widely used key agreement methods because it allows two parties to anonymously compute a shared-secret symmetric key using asymmetric data.

For example, say that Bob needs to send a highly sensitive piece of data to Alice. Bob would like to encrypt this data during transport so that only Alice can view it upon receipt. As discussed earlier in this chapter, Bob needs a cryptographic key to encrypt the data, and Alice needs the key to decrypt the data. Rather than use a pre-shared key, Bob elects to use Diffie-Hellman to create a key with Alice that is just for this document. With Diffie-Hellman at the helm for key agreement, both parties can independently calculate a symmetric key used for the encryption and decryption of data. Figure 6-2 illustrates the Diffie-Hellman key agreement between Bob and Alice.

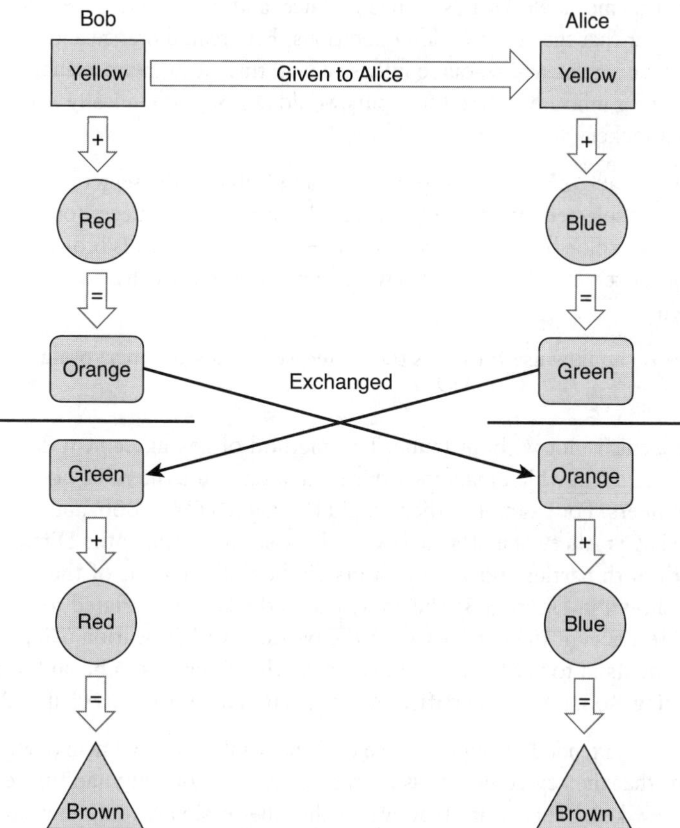

Figure 6-2 *Illustration of the Diffie-Hellman Handshake*

It must be stressed that Diffie-Hellman uses very complex mathematical operations that involve exponentially large numbers. While this is great for security, due to the mathematical intensity, it is a computationally expensive operation for applications and devices. This complexity also means that the process would be very hard to understand without majorly simplifying it. Thus this figure and explanation use colors instead of exponential numbers and color mixtures rather than mathematical computations. Examining Figure 6-2, you can see exactly what will happen between Bob and Alice as they accomplish a Diffie-Hellman key agreement:

Step 1. Bob starts by picking a color, yellow, which he then publicly shares with Alice.

Step 2. Alice chooses a secret color, known only to her (and you: blue), and Bob chooses a secret color, known only to him (and you: red), and then the two of them each mix the secret color with the public color chosen by Bob. Bob's red mixes with yellow to become orange, and Alice's blue mixes with yellow to create green.

Step 3. Alice and Bob then publicly exchange the newly combined color between themselves. This means Bob sends orange to Alice, and Alice sends green to Bob. Remember that the computation operations that created orange and green are very complex and resource intensive, and this means reverse engineering the color mixture to find the inputs would not be economically feasible for an attacker.

Step 4. After receiving each other's colors, both Alice and Bob mix the secret color they previously selected into the color received from his or her peer. Bob mixes his secret color, red, into Alice's green mixture, which yields brown. Alice mixes her secret color, blue, into the orange mixture, which also yields brown.

Step 5. Alice and Bob can now use brown as the shared-secret key for encrypting their data.

Diffie-Hellman, while great, is not without faults. This method of key agreement is susceptible to MITM attacks in which malicious third parties assume the roles of actual communication peers. For example, Alice would think a MITM is Bob, and Bob would think a MITM is Alice. The attacker would be able to complete the Diffie-Hellman exchange with both parties and would ultimately be in the middle of the encrypted session, as shown in Figure 6-3. The MITM uses the keys negotiated to encrypt, decrypt, and re-encrypt the data between the parties. Authentication using digital certificates can be used to verify that Bob is really who he claims to be and not an attacker impersonating Bob. (Digital certificates are discussed later in this chapter.)

Diffie-Hellman can also be extended through the use of Ephemeral Diffie-Hellman (DHE) keys. *Ephemeral* means that the key computed is for the current session only, and future sessions will compute new keys. This means that even if this one session is compromised, a MITM would need to be part of the next session as well in order to compromise that session. No material from the first session can compromise future sessions. This concept, known as *perfect forward secrecy* (*PFS*), is a large part of most public key cryptography protocols.

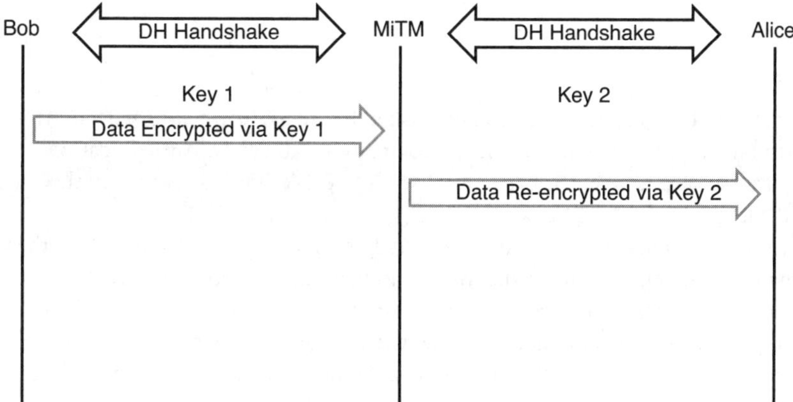

Figure 6-3 *A MITM Attack on the Diffie-Hellman Handshake*

Public Key Encryption

Originally defined in RFC 2313 and later updated in RFC 8017, the Rivest, Shamir, Adleman (RSA) cryptography specification details a type of private and public keys often used during authentication and symmetric key exchange between two parties. In this case, the public/private key pair is referred to as an *RSA key pair*. RSA key pairs are considered asymmetrical keys in the sense that they are two different keys, and each serves a different purpose. When creating an RSA key pair, you are provided with two values:

- **RSA public key**—This key can be distributed widely to any party. A public key is used to encrypt data and verify signatures. The RSA public key cannot be used to compute the private key. The public key is shared with third parties by use of digital certificates, as discussed in the next section.
- **RSA private key**—This key must remain secret to the owner at all times. A private key is used to decrypt data and provide signatures. If the private key is compromised, the entire RSA key pair should be revoked.

Because the RSA keys are asymmetric, they are not actually used for bulk data encryption. As discussed earlier in this chapter, asymmetric keys are often used to assist with computing a symmetric key that will be used for mass data encryption. In the case of RSA, the public keys can be used to encrypt data in transit, like premaster secret keys and other inputs that will be used to independently compute the master session keys. This reduces the ability for a MITM to intercept data exchanged between two parties, as discussed earlier with Diffie-Hellman. That being said, RSA can be used alongside Diffie-Hellman as a layered approach to key management and public key encryption. RSA key pairs are discussed further later in this chapter.

Digital Certificates

A *digital certificate* is an electronic document issued by a *certificate authority* (*CA*) that is used to bind a public key to a device, a company, or an entity. Authentication is the main purpose of digital certificates. As discussed earlier in this chapter, in the "Key Agreement" section, a MITM can easily impersonate a party in a session and thus gain access to the computation of a shared-secret key such as the one discussed for the Diffie-Hellman key agreement handshake. By employing digital certificates, each session participant can authenticate the party that is providing a public key. This is done through the *digital signature* assigned to the certificate, and it allows the receiver to verify that the sender is who he or she says he or she is and that the public key belongs to that person.

CAs are in charge of providing and revoking digital certificates. CAs usually operate in a hierarchy, as shown in Figure 6-4. The topmost CA, referred to as the *root CA*, signs other certificates by using the *root certificate*. The certificate your device or application owns is called the *identity certificate*, and it is signed directly by a root CA or by an *intermediate CA*. An identity certificate is the lowest certificate in the chain of trust. There may be more than one intermediate CA or none, mainly depending on the CA you choose to sign your certificate.

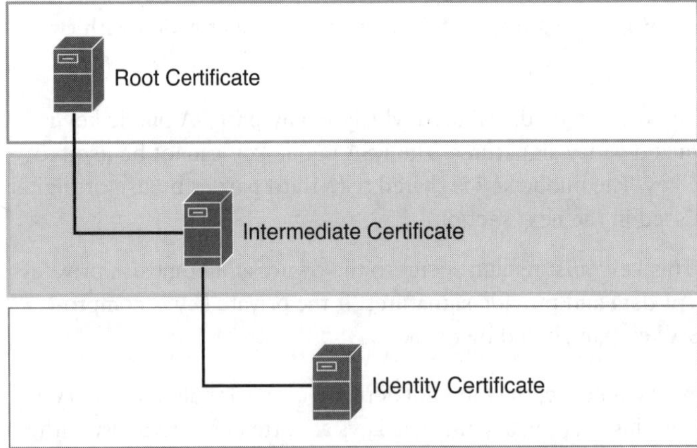

Figure 6-4 *Certificate Hierarchy of Root, Intermediate, and Identity Certificates*

Figure 6-5 shows a root CA signing the certificate of an intermediate CA, which then signs an identity certificate for an application or a device. The certificate chain is flipped upside down in this figure to better illustrate the fact that the issuer's name on the identity certificate references the intermediate CA's certificate name. The issuer's signature on the identity certificate references the intermediate CA's private key, which was used to sign the identity certificate. The public key from the CA's certificate can be used to confirm the signature on the identity certificate. Similarly, the issuer's name on the intermediate CA's certificate references the root CA's name and the signature on the intermediate CA's certificate, which was signed using the root CA's private key. This signature can be verified by using the public key from the root CA's certificate. The root CA would sign its own certificate using its own private key as it is the topmost CA in the chain of trust. The root CA's public key can be used to verify the signature on the root CA's certificate. A root CA certificate is very similar to a self-signed certificate, where a device signs its own certificate by using its private key, and the issuer references itself.

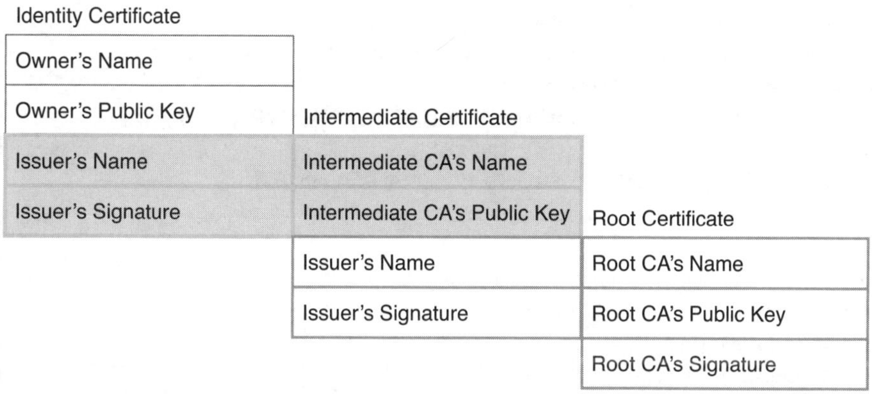

Figure 6-5 *Certificate Chain of Root, Intermediate, and Identity Certificates*

In order to have a certificate provided by a CA, you must first generate a certificate signing request (CSR). CSRs, defined in PKCS #10 and RFC 2986, contain all the important information a CA would need to issue a digital certificate, including the distinguished name of the requestor, the public key of the requestor, and other optional attributes. Example 6-5 shows the creation and subsequent viewing of a CSR from a Linux server. Here you can see the creation of a new RSA key pair consisting of 2048 bits, which is done using the command **openssl req -newkey rsa:2048**. The key is then sent to a file by adding **-keyout key.pem** to the previous command. Finally, the CSR is output to a file with **-out csr.pem**. The system then asks for basic items that are required and optional in the CSR and that will be bundled into the CSR.

Example 6-5 *Creating a CSR in Linux Using OpenSSL*

```
root@linux-server:~/openssl$ openssl req -newkey rsa:2048 -keyout key.pem -out csr.pem
Generating a 2048 bit RSA private key
.............................+++
..................................+++
writing new private key to 'key.pem'
Enter PEM pass phrase: *****
Verifying - Enter PEM pass phrase: *****
-----
You are about to be asked to enter information that will be incorporated
into your certificate request.
What you are about to enter is what is called a Distinguished Name or a DN.
There are quite a few fields but you can leave some blank
For some fields there will be a default value,
If you enter '.', the field will be left blank.
-----
Country Name (2 letter code) [AU]: US
State or Province Name (full name) [Some-State]: North Carolina
Locality Name (eg, city) []: Raleigh
Organization Name (eg, company) [Internet Widgits Pty Ltd]: Cisco Systems
Organizational Unit Name (eg, section) []: TAC
Common Name (e.g. server FQDN or YOUR name) []: cube.cisco.com
Email Address []: root@cisco.com

Please enter the following 'extra' attributes
to be sent with your certificate request
A challenge password []: .
An optional company name []: .
```

You can view the contents of the CSR by using the commands shown in Example 6-6. The command **openssl req -text -noout -verify -in csr.pem** displays the output of the CSR in text output, and the command **more csr.pem** displays the output of the CSR in Base64 encoded output. The Base64 output is given to the CA. As you can see, all the items entered above are present in the CSR, and the encryption is RSA, with SHA-256 used for signing. Base64 and Privacy-Enhanced Mail (PEM) format always begin and end with the values **-----BEGIN <something> -----** and **-----END <something> -----**.

Example 6-6 *Viewing a CSR That Has Been Created by OpenSSL*

```
root@linux-server:~/openssl$ openssl req -text -noout -verify -in csr.pem
verify OK
Certificate Request:
    Data:
        Version: 1 (0x0)
```

```
        Subject: C = US, ST = North Carolina, L = Raleigh, O = Cisco Systems, OU =
  TAC, CN = cube.cisco.com, emailAddress = root@cisco.com
        Subject Public Key Info:
            Public Key Algorithm: rsaEncryption
                RSA Public-Key: (2048 bit)
                Modulus:
                    00:ed:cc:0e:67:d6:18:ee:f0:f7:f2:b5:1c:0a:ad:
                    [..Truncated for Brevity..]
                    dd:ce:be:6e:51:fa:0a:98:61:c1:10:be:9d:bd:47:
                    29:f3
                Exponent: 65537 (0x10001)
        Attributes:
            a0:00
    Signature Algorithm: sha256WithRSAEncryption
         22:f6:44:18:48:44:68:29:c6:0d:68:4e:04:59:1a:c5:8c:9f:
         [..Truncated for Brevity..]
         b0:6f:a4:12:cb:21:5f:64:d3:e3:fe:96:fe:2e:80:e1:dc:f8:
         87:d0:ac:97

root@linux-server:~/openssl$ more csr.pem
-----BEGIN CERTIFICATE REQUEST-----
MIIC3zCCAccCAQAwgZkxCzAJBgNVBAYTAlVTMRcwFQYDVQQIDA5Ob3J0aCBDYXJv
[..Truncated for Brevity..]
EsshX2TT4/6W/i6A4dz4h9Cslw==
-----END CERTIFICATE REQUEST-----
```

The CSR generated by a device or an application is then provided to your CA of choice, which works to verify your identity, company, and other information provided using different out-of-band methods. When the out-of-band methods are completed successfully, the CA will compute a hash against your certificate and sign the hash with its private key to produce a digital signature. This signature is then placed on the certificate the CA provides back. The certificate that you receive follows the X.509v3 format, defined in Section 4.2 of RFC 5280, which consists of the following fields:

- **Serial Number**—Specifies a unique identifier that is placed on the certificate, which the CA uses to track the certificate. It is also used in certificate revocation lists, discussed later in this chapter.
- **Issuer**—Specifies the distinguished name of the CA that issues the certificate.
- **Not Before**—Specifies the start of validity for a certificate. If the current date is before this date, the certificate is not yet valid.
- **Not After**—Specifies the end of validity for a certificate. If the current date is after this date, the certificate is no longer valid.

- **Subject**—Contains the entity's distinguished name (DN), which is tied to the certificate.
- **Key Usage**—Specifies the use cases for this certificate. These may vary, based on the signing service selected with the CA.
- **Extended Key Usage**—Indicates one or more purposes for which this certificate can be used.
- **Public Key**—Specifies the public key for the entity in which this certificate belongs.
- **Signature Algorithm**—Specifies the algorithm used by the issuer to sign this certificate.
- **Signature**—Contains the signature of the CA that signed this certificate.

An administrator may receive a certificate from a CA in a number of different types of certificate file formats. Depending on how you plan to upload a certificate, conversion from one file type to another may be required. This can be accomplished using a variety of third-party tools, such as OpenSSL. Table 6-1 details the differences in these file formats.

Table 6-1 *Formatting of Various Certificate File Type Extensions*

File Type Extension	Description
.der, .cer	Binary-encoded certificate. There can be one per file, and copy and paste cannot be used.
.pem, .cer, .crt, .key	Base64-encoded ASCII files. More than one certificate is used per file, and copy and paste can be used. This is the most common type of certificate format.
.p7b, .p7c	Base64-encoded ASCII based on PKCS #7. Does not contain private keys.
.pfx, .p12	Binary-encoded certificate chain. May contain private keys. May also be password protected.
.csr	Certificate signing request based on PKCS #10.

Example 6-7 show the output of a CA signed identity certificate based on the CSR generated in Example 6-6. The root certificate is shown in Example 6-8. This output was generated by either downloading or converting the received certificate chain into a .cer format, where each file contains one certificate in the chain. Then the command **openssl x509 -in <*filename*> -text -noout** is run against each file. The Windows utility equivalent command to view similar output is **CertUtil <*filename*>**. Both of these commands output the contents of the certificate in text form.

Example 6-7 *Viewing an X.509 Identity Certificate Using OpenSSL*

```
root@linux-server:~/openssl$ openssl x509 -in identity.cer -text -noout
Certificate:
    Data:
        Version: 3 (0x2)
        Serial Number:
            28:00:00:00:21:3e:9f:fa:35:0f:a3:27:95:00:00:00:00:00:21
        Signature Algorithm: sha256WithRSAEncryption
        Issuer: CN = WIN-4NQ4D0URE7B-CA
        Validity
            Not Before: Jun 20 20:31:58 2018 GMT
            Not After : Jun 20 20:41:58 2019 GMT
        Subject: C = US, ST = North Carolina, L = Raleigh, O = Cisco Systems, OU =
  TAC, CN = cube.cisco.com, emailAddress = root@cisco.com
        Subject Public Key Info:
            Public Key Algorithm: rsaEncryption
                RSA Public-Key: (2048 bit)
                Modulus:
                    00:ed:cc:0e:67:d6:18:ee:f0:f7:f2:b5:1c:0a:ad:
                    [..Truncated for Brevity..]
                    dd:ce:be:6e:51:fa:0a:98:61:c1:10:be:9d:bd:47:
                    29:f3
                Exponent: 65537 (0x10001)
        X509v3 extensions:
            X509v3 Subject Key Identifier:
                33:F7:1B:96:BE:20:2A:CC:DC:4C:B6:E4:BD:84:1B:A5:0F:E6:E0:D3
            X509v3 Authority Key Identifier:
                keyid:75:96:F1:89:74:DC:69:B2:28:95:93:F4:70:AE:F5:86:82:48:48:F1

            X509v3 CRL Distribution Points:


                Full Name:
                  URI:file:////WIN-4NQ4D0URE7B/CertEnroll/WIN-4NQ4D0URE7B-CA.crl


            Authority Information Access:
                CA Issuers - URI:file:////WIN-4NQ4D0URE7B/CertEnroll/WIN-
  4NQ4D0URE7B_WIN-4NQ4D0URE7B-CA.crt


            X509v3 Basic Constraints: critical
                CA:FALSE
    Signature Algorithm: sha256WithRSAEncryption
         82:4a:02:47:8a:44:b0:3c:f5:92:1f:41:1b:4a:d4:06:a5:64:
         [..Truncated for Brevity..]
         77:12:0d:0b:7f:27:8e:73:f3:84:66:84:a8:fa:ad:65:2b:df:
         0f:1a:49:6c
```

Example 6-8 *Viewing an X.509 Root CA Certificate in OpenSSL*

```
root@linux -server:~/openssl$ openssl x509 -in root.cer -text -noout
Certificate:
    Data:
        Version: 3 (0x2)
        Serial Number:
            2a:0d:89:87:97:df:c6:98:4f:b2:78:81:53:8d:e4:5f
        Signature Algorithm: sha256WithRSAEncryption
        Issuer: CN = WIN-4NQ4D0URE7B-CA
        Validity
            Not Before: Apr 18 22:11:37 2017 GMT
            Not After : Apr 18 22:21:37 2022 GMT
        Subject: CN = WIN-4NQ4D0URE7B-CA
        Subject Public Key Info:
            Public Key Algorithm: rsaEncryption
                RSA Public-Key: (2048 bit)
                Modulus:
                    00:96:f8:a6:4e:0f:b1:f3:78:02:aa:05:a8:23:0e:
                    [..Truncated for Brevity]
                    7b:cc:7c:ae:3c:62:16:7b:7b:dc:c5:dc:35:61:46:
                    78:8b
                Exponent: 65537 (0x10001)
        X509v3 extensions:
            X509v3 Key Usage:
                Digital Signature, Certificate Sign, CRL Sign
            X509v3 Basic Constraints: critical
                CA:TRUE
            X509v3 Subject Key Identifier:
                75:96:F1:89:74:DC:69:B2:28:95:93:F4:70:AE:F5:86:82:48:48:F1
            1.3.6.1.4.1.311.21.1:
                ...
    Signature Algorithm: sha256WithRSAEncryption
         11:f7:5f:a8:3f:56:8f:88:2b:96:d2:1e:98:ef:6b:75:5e:5c:
         [..Truncated for Brevity]
         79:ef:07:28:24:15:8a:73:c5:f6:2b:db:51:e8:90:88:de:71:
         31:ba:79:1e
```

A CA maintains a certificate revocation list (CRL), which you can see referenced in the extensions in Example 6-7. This can be used by the party receiving the certificate to verify whether the CA has revoked the certificate, thus rendering it invalid. Revocation checks should be enforced, and CAs frequently update CRLs. One example of a revocation may occur if the private key is compromised. In this scenario, the owner of the private key asks the CA to revoke the certificate.

Let's put the various pieces of digital certificates into action. Say that Bob has created an RSA key pair and needs to receive an encrypted document for business from Alice. He needs to send Alice his public key so that she can use the public key to encrypt the document for transit. However, Alice does not know Bob well enough to verify his identity and trust his public key. Therefore, Bob elects to use a third-party CA to vouch for his identity. He creates a CSR and sends it off to the CA, which performs verification checks that pass. The CA returns a digital certificate confirming Bob's identity and binding the public key to his identity. Bob can then send this digital certificate to Alice. Alice elects to verify that the certificate belongs to Bob by confirming with the CA that this certificate is valid (assuming that Alice trusts the CA that issues Bob's certificate, of course). Now that Alice has Bob's public key and has verified using a third party that Bob is who he claims to be, she may encrypt the data by using the public key. Bob receives this data and can decrypt it by using the private key.

The following section details a similar handshake between two parties using various handshake protocols that run over UDP and TCP. These protocols combine all the topics covered thus far to allow for secure application data to be sent and received from two parties.

Secure Sockets Layer (SSL) and Transport Layer Security (TLS)

Secure Sockets Layer (*SSL*) is a security protocol that evolved through three main versions: 1.0, 2.0, and 3.0. SSL 1.0 was never released to the public, and 2.0 and 3.0 were released in 1995 and 1996, respectively. *Transport Layer Security* (*TLS*) was based on the SSL 3.0 standard. TLS 1.1 was standardized in 2006, and TLS 1.2 followed in 2008. The original SSL 3.0 is detailed in the historical RFC 6101 and was formally prohibited under RFC 7568, while SSL 2.0 was prohibited under RFC 6176. Someone who references SSL is most likely referencing TLS—and more specifically TLS 1.2, which is the most widely adopted version of the standard defined by RFC 5246.

TLS operates on top of a reliable transport protocol such as TCP or SCTP and makes use of the public key cryptography and other core security concepts detailed earlier in this chapter. TLS is used to provide encryption for application traffic such as HTTP using HTTPS between a TLS client and TLS server. TLS performs a multistep handshake that is used to agree on encryption protocols and hashing algorithms, perform authentication, and compute session keys.

TLS is split into a few well-defined layers and sections. First, the *Record Protocol* is responsible for a number of different items, including data transmission, and handles the following processes:

Step 1. Receives data from the higher-level clients

Step 2. Fragments the data into manageable blocks

Step 3. Compresses the data, if desired

Step 4. Applies the message authentication code for integrity

Step 5. Encrypts the data

Step 6. Transmits the results

When the Record Protocol is responsible for data reception, it performs the following actions:

Step 1. Receives data from transport

Step 2. Decrypts the data

Step 3. Verifies the hash

Step 4. Decompresses, if required

Step 5. Re-assembles any fragments

Step 6. Delivers the data to higher-level clients

> **Tip** Packets must be sent to the transport layer in the same order in which they were processed by the Record Protocol.

The higher-level clients mentioned in the previous section are as follows:

- **Handshake Protocol**—This protocol performs the higher-level TLS handshake and exchange of messaging between the client and server. Data is sent and received from the Record Protocol.
- **Alert Protocol**—This protocol is responsible for signaling problematic notifications with the TLS handshake, which can fall into two categories: fatal or warning. Fatal alert messages result in immediate session termination, while when warning messages occur, a session may be able to be established normally.
- **Change Cipher Spec Protocol**—This protocol exists purely to signal the transition between plaintext and ciphertext.
- **Application Data Protocol**—Encryption, decryption, fragmentation, reassembly, and optional compression occur at this layer and are carried out by the Record Protocol.

Together the Record Protocol and higher-level client protocols work to establish and complete a TLS handshake between a TLS client and TLS server. The TLS handshake can be accomplished in two different modes of operation. The first is one in which only the server is authenticated during the handshake process. This is referenced as a *basic, one-way, TLS handshake*. The second method involves authenticating both the client and the server. This is commonly referenced as a *client-authenticated, two-way, TLS handshake*. A basic handshake may be useful to email clients that only need to confirm the validity of a server, while a client-authenticated handshake may be useful for collaboration products and protocols such as the Session Initiation Protocol

(SIP), where each device that wants to participate in a session needs to authenticate the other's identity.

The TLS handshake steps can also vary based on the type of key agreement protocol being used by the two participants in the handshake. RSA, RSA Ephemeral, Diffie-Hellman, and DHE each produce a slightly different TLS handshake. RFC 5246 outlines each of these different handshakes in great detail. This chapter discusses one handshake that contains the majority of the messages that may be observed in the other types of handshakes. Figure 6-6 details a client-authenticated TLS 1.2 handshake between a TLS client and TLS server that uses DHE and RSA.

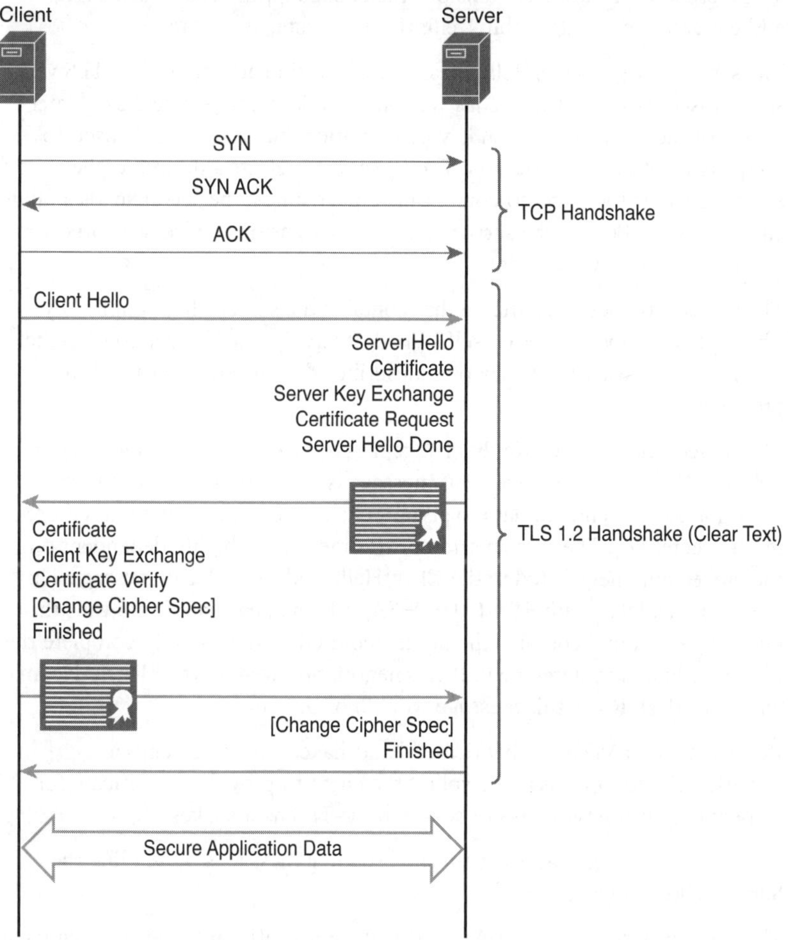

Figure 6-6 *An Illustration of a TLS 1.2 Client-Authenticated Two-Way Handshake*

The following events occur during the TLS 1.2 handshake detailed in Figure 6-6:

Step 1. A TCP handshake occurs between the client and the server. It consists of the normal SYN, SYN ACK, and ACK. If the TCP handshake does not complete, the session errors out here.

Step 2. The client sends a ClientHello message to the server. This message contains a TLS version, a random number field used later as one of the inputs in session key computation, and a session ID used to uniquely identify a TLS session. The client also indicates the list of cipher suites it supports. (More on cipher suites follows this example.) Finally, this message includes a list of compression methods and various extensions the client supports, such as message authentication code algorithms, elliptic curve data, and more.

Step 3. The server sends a ServerHello message, which similarly contains a TLS version chosen based on the client's version, a random number field used later as one of the inputs in session key computation, and a session ID used to uniquely identify a TLS session. The server also selects a desired cipher suite from the list. If there are no compatible cipher suites, the server sends a failure Alert message. Finally, the server selects the extensions it also supports from the list provided by the client.

Step 4. The server provides a certificate that contains the server's RSA public key. This certificate may either be self-signed or CA signed. The section "Digital Certificates," earlier in this chapter, describes digital certificates and their properties.

Step 5. The server sends a ServerKeyExchange message, which is transmitted soon after the Certificate message. This message is sent only when a certificate does not contain enough data to allow a client to compute the required premaster secret key. The transmission of this message is highly dependent on the cipher suite negotiated in the ClientHello and ServerHello messages. In this example, DHE with RSA (DHE_RSA) is being negotiated, and thus this message is sent and contains the inputs required to successfully complete the Diffie-Hellman key agreement. If this negotiation were normal Diffie-Hellman with RSA (DH_RSA), this message would not be sent.

Step 6. Because this is a client-authenticated handshake, the server sends a CertificateRequest message to solicit the client to provide a certificate for inspection. This message is not sent in basic TLS handshakes.

Step 7. The server indicates that it has finished sending messages by sending the ServerHelloDone message.

Step 8. The client processes the server's certificate and verifies its validity using local logic. If there are any errors with the certificate, the TLS handshake may fail here with an Alert message sent by the client.

Step 9. The client provides a certificate that contains the client's RSA public key. This certificate may either be self-signed or CA signed. The section "Digital Certificates" provides more details about digital certificates and their properties.

Step 10. The client sends a ClientKeyExchange message. This message is sent even in a basic TLS handshake, and it contains the premaster secret key encrypted with the server's public key. If an ephemeral key agreement protocol is being used, this will contain the ephemeral public keys.

Step 11. The client may send a CertificateVerify message after a ClientKeyExchange message. This message contains a signature that is a concatenation of all handshake messages exchanged thus far. This signature provides explicit verification of the client certificate.

Step 12. The client sends a ChangeCipherSpec message, which contains no data and has a length of 1 byte. This message is used to indicate to the other party that the session will transition from unencrypted to encrypted using the agreed-upon cipher specs.

Step 13. The client sends a ClientFinished message to indicate that the key exchange and authentication process was successful. This message also contains a hashed version of the entire TLS handshake until this point. The server verifies this hash against its own computed message authentication code. If this check does not succeed, the handshake fails and the connection drops.

Step 14. The server processes the received client certificate and verifies its validity by using local logic.

Step 15. The server responds with its own ChangeCipherSpec message, which indicates the same as the previous ChangeCipherSpec message.

Step 16. The server sends a ServerFinished message to indicate that the TLS handshake is complete. At this point, any application data sent between the client and server is encrypted using the negotiated session keys.

Tip The TLS handshake is considered a *lockstep cryptographic handshake*, which means it must be performed in a very specific order. Deviation from this order results in an error.

When RSA is being used for key agreement *and* authentication, the client generates a 48-byte premaster secret and encrypts this secret using the public key from the server's certificate. This is then sent to the server in the aforementioned ClientKeyExchange message. Alternatively, if DH or DHE is being used for key agreement, the value derived from the DH handshake is used as the 48-byte premaster secret by stripping leading zeros from the DH key. In the case of DHE, the ServerKeyExchange message contains the public values required by the client to independently compute the premaster, while the ClientKeyExchange message contains public values required for the server to independently negotiate the same premaster secret. If regular DH is used for key agreement, the ClientKeyExchange message contains the value NULL, and the ServerKeyExchange message is not used in the handshake.

For all key agreement methods, the same process is used to create the master secret key, which is also 48 bytes in length. This involves the use of the client and server random values from the Hello messages in conjunction with the premaster secret key. The master key derived from this process is then split into the following keys in the following order:

- **Client Write MAC key**—Used by the server to authenticate data written by the client.
- **Server Write MAC key**—Used by the client to authenticate data written by the server.
- **Client Write Encryption key**—Used by the server to encrypt data written by the client.
- **Server Write Encryption key**—Used by the client to encrypt data written by the server.
- **Client Write Initialization Vector (IV) key**—Used by the server for AEAD ciphers. Not required for all handshakes.
- **Server Write Initialization Vector (IV) key**—Used by the client for AEAD ciphers. Not required for all handshakes.

As mentioned in steps 2 and 3 above, a cipher suite is agreed upon between a client and server. This cipher suite is a bundle of different cryptographic elements that is used to greatly speed up the handshake process. There are many different cipher suites, and all of them are maintained by the Internet Assigned Numbers Authority (IANA), at https://www.iana.org/assignments/tls-parameters/tls-parameters.xhtml.

Let's quickly examine the following cipher suite in order to understand the purpose it serves in the TLS handshake:

```
TLS_ECDHE_RSA_WITH_AES_256_GCM_SHA384
```

We can decode this cipher suite as follows:

- **TLS (Transport Layer Security)**—Defines the type of suite this is for. All TLS 1.2 cipher suites start with TLS.
- **ECDHE (Elliptic-Curve Diffie-Hellman Ephemeral)**—Acts as part of the key management, which is used to compute a shared-secret key pair over insecure mediums. The *Ephemeral* portion means that this is temporary and thus will change per session.
- **RSA – (Rivest, Shamir, Adleman)**—Defines the private/public asymmetric key protocol to be used for this session.
- **AES256 – (Advanced Encryption Standard)**—Defines the bulk data encryption (block cipher) and symmetric key mechanism that will be used to encrypt the application data.
- **GCM = (Galois/Counter Mode)**—Provides a type of symmetric key cryptography that extends the encryption functionality with AES.
- **SHA384 – (Secure Hashing Algorithm)**—A hashing/message authentication code algorithm used for data integrity checks.

TLS 1.3 (RFC 8446) is the replacement for TLS 1.2 (RFC 5246) and older versions of TLS and SSL. TLS 1.3 aims to improve security and reduce the overall time it takes for handshakes to negotiate. First, TLS 1.3 removes support for many legacy, insecure, and obsolete features, such as SHA-1, RC4, DES, 3DES, AES-CBC, and MD5. Second, TLS 1.3 removes the key agreement methods and signature algorithms from being negotiated using cipher suites and negotiates them securely later in the handshake. Due to the changes to the structure of cipher suites, TLS 1.2 and TLS 1.3 cipher suites are incompatible. Finally, the TLS 1.3 handshake has been completely reworked from the ground up. Figure 6-7 details a TLS 1.3 1-RTT client-authenticated two-way handshake.

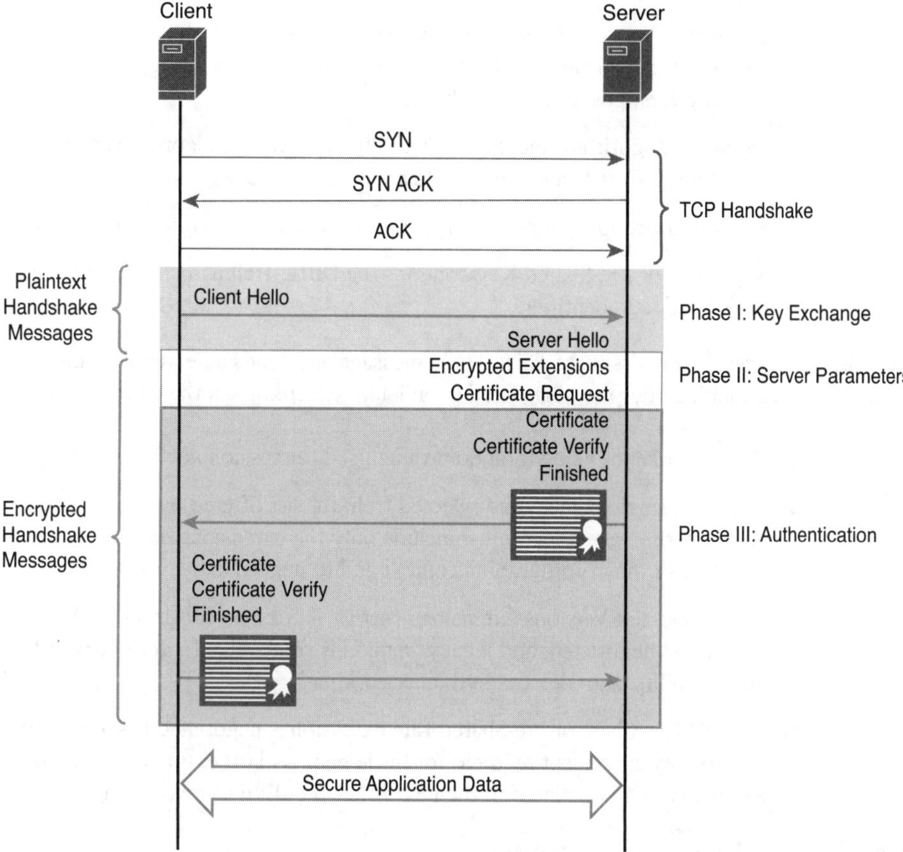

Figure 6-7 *An Illustration of a TLS 1.3 Client-Authenticated Two-Way Handshake*

Just like the TLS 1.2 handshake, a TCP 3-way handshake occurs between the TLS client and server. If it does not complete successfully, the TLS handshake is not initiated. Going through the TLS 1.3 handshake in Figure 6-7, we can see that observe the following phases and events occur:

Phase I: Key Exchange (Unencrypted)

Step 1. The TLS client initiates the handshake by sending a ClientHello message. This message contains a random number field that is used later for session key computation. In TLS 1.3, version negotiation occurs using the Supported Versions extension. However, the legacy TLS 1.2 version is still retained in the legacy_version field for backward compatibly, in case the server turns out to be a TLS 1.2 node. The client also sends a set of TLS 1.3–formatted cipher suites (for example, TLS_AES_128_GCM_SHA256, which is a mandatory cipher suite in TLS 1.3). This message also contains a set of Diffie-Hellman key shares and/or a pre-shared key. Finally, any TLS 1.3 extensions and other optional extensions the client supports may be included. The mandatory TLS 1.3 extensions include the following:

- Supported Versions is used for negotiating TLS 1.3 and above versions between the TLS client and server. At the time of this writing, TLS 1.3 is the only version supported in this extension.
- Signature Algorithms indicates which digital signature algorithms may be used within Certificate and CertificateVerify messages.
- Supported Groups is required if Diffie-Hellman will be used for key exchange.
- Key Share or Pre-Shared Key contains the Diffie-Hellman key share or the pre-shared key identifier.

Step 2. The server processes the ClientHello message and sends a ServerHello message that includes the negotiated parameters selected from the ClientHello:

- The server sends its own random value used for session key computation.
- There is a single cipher suite selected from the list offered by the client. In addition, the ServerHello must include only the extensions that are required to establish the cryptographic context and to negotiate the version.
- The Supported Versions extension is set to TLS 1.3 to confirm that TLS 1.3 will be negotiated, and legacy_version is set to TLS 1.2 for backward compatibility with devices in the network path.
- The DH Key Share or Pre-Shared Key extension is negotiated based on the type of key agreement required for the session. All other non-cryptographic extensions are negotiated in the next EncryptedExtensions message.

Phase II: Server Parameters (Encrypted)

Step 1. The exchange of the ServerHello and ClientHello messages in the previous phase is all that is required to establish the *handshake traffic keys*, which are used to encrypt the rest of the handshake messages from here on. The server then sends an EncryptedExtensions message, which contains any extension that was not required to establish the cryptographic context for the handshake traffic keys. These extensions, being encrypted, mean that a MITM cannot properly deduce what extensions are being negotiated, which greatly improves the security afforded by TLS. A few examples of items that may be in the EncryptedExtensions message are the server name, maximum fragment length, client certificate type, server certificate type, and use_srtp (for SRTP-DTLS). For a full list of TLS extensions, refer to the IANA-maintained document on available TLS extensions.

Step 2. Because this a client-authenticated handshake, the server solicits the client to send a certificate by sending a CertificateRequest message. This is an optional message and is not sent in basic one-way TLS handshakes. The signature_algorithms extension must be sent with this message to identify the type of certificate the server expects to receive.

Phase III: **Authentication (Encrypted)**

Step 1. At this point the server sends a Certificate message, which contains the server's public key. This certificate may either be self-signed or CA signed. The section "Digital Certificates," earlier in this chapter, provides more details about digital certificates and their properties. If pre-shared keys are being used, the server does not send a Certificate message.

Step 2. The Certificate message is always followed by a CertificateVerify message, which contains a signature of the entire TLS handshake thus far, including the certificate. This signature is created using the private key that pairs with the public key in the certificate and the negotiated signature algorithm in the TLS 1.3 extensions exchanged in the Hello messages. If pre-shared keys are being used, the server does not send a CertificateVerify message.

Step 3. The server sends a Finished message that contains an HMAC of the entire handshake thus far. This provides key confirmation, binds the endpoint's identity to the exchanged keys, and in PSK mode also authenticates the handshake.

Step 4. The client performs authentication checks on the previous three messages. If they pass, the client sends its own Certificate, as the server has requested a certificate using the CertificateRequest message, a CertificateVerify message (which always accompanies a Certificate message in TLS 1.3), and a Finished message containing an HMAC of the entire TLS handshake from the client's perspective.

Step 5. The server performs similar authentication checks on the Certificate, CertificateVerify, and Finished messages from the client. Assuming that these pass, the resulting application data may be encrypted using the *application traffic session keys* negotiated by the TLS 1.3 handshake. Remember that this is not the same as the handshake traffic key that was used to encrypt the TLS handshake messages after the Hello message exchange.

Another significant change in TLS 1.3 is the inclusion of a zero round-trip-time (0-RTT) TLS handshake. If two clients have already negotiated a TLS session in the past and have a pre-shared key (PSK), the client may send a ClientHello message and encrypted application data termed *early data*. This is useful in HTTPS connections between a client's browser and HTTPS server. It dramatically reduces the time it takes to start sending application data from a client to a server. However, it must be noted that the 0-RTT handshake trades speed for security. That means the 0-RTT method is not as secure as a full TLS 1.3 1-RTT handshake. These security drawbacks involve PFS due to the use of the PSK, which could be compromised, putting future sessions in jeopardy, and replay protection, which could potentially be abused in a 0-RTT handshake. Figure 6-8 details a 0-RTT handshake between a client and server that previously established a session and then resumed the session. At the start of the session, the client sends early data due to a PSK being exchanged between this client and server in the previous session. It must be noted that 0-RTT sessions use the PSK method of TLS handshake, which does not exchange certificates between client and server—hence their absence from the figure.

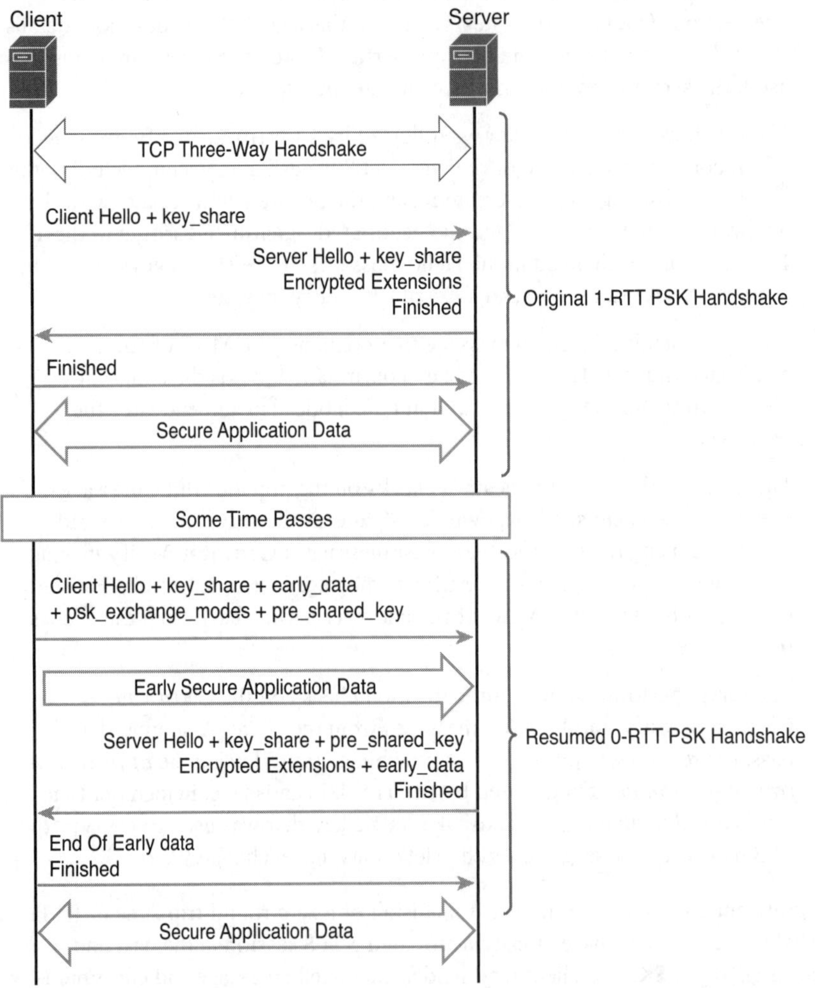

Figure 6-8 *An Illustration of a Resumed Session Between Two Peers Using a 0-RTT TLS 1.3 Handshake*

A few of the major differences between TLS 1.2 and TLS 1.3 in regard to the initial TLS handshake are defined in Table 6-2.

Table 6-2 *A High-Level Comparison of TLS 1.2 and TLS 1.3*

Item	TLS 1.2	TLS 1.3
Encryption of handshake message	None; all handshake messages are in plaintext	Handshake messages after the ServerHello message are encrypted using the handshake keys
Use of the ChangeCipherSpec message during the handshake	Yes	No, this was completely removed from TLS 1.3
PFS requirement	No	Yes, using EDH keys
TLS version negotiation	Client/Server Hello messagesversion renegotiation permitted	Now completed using the supported_versions extension. Version renegotiation forbidden
Allows for compression negotiation in Hello message	Yes	No, compression was removed from TLS 1.3; the value is set to NULL in the Hello messages
Key agreement in cipher suite	Yes	No, now in TLS 1.3 Extensions: ■ key_share ■ pre_shared_key ■ psk_key_exchange_modes
Signature algorithm in cipher suite	Yes	No, now in TLS 1.3 Extensions: ■ signature_algorithms ■ signature_algorithms_cert
Session ID for session resumption	Yes	No
Number of signaling round trips	Two	Zero or one, with one being default

Datagram Transport Layer Security (DTLS)

Datagram Transport Layer Security (DTLS) aims to provide the same level of application security as TLS but over unreliable transport mechanisms such as UDP. DTLS is defined in RFC 6347 and follows the same naming conventions used in TLS to avoid confusion. DTLS is functionally identical to TLS except in areas in which TLS does not have facilities to handle scenarios such as packet loss or reordering of UDP packets.

The main additions to DTLS to solve problems presented by UDP are as follows:

- DTLS does not allow for stream ciphers; block ciphers must be used for encryption.
- DTLS adds explicit sequence numbers to packets, which allows for the queuing of messages that are received out of order.
- DTLS defines retransmission timers if a message does not receive a response.
- DTLS defines a new HelloVerifyRequest message sent in response to a ClientHello message.
- DTLS allows for fragmentation of handshake messages over multiple UDP packets if required by the path MTU.
- DTLS also employs DoS countermeasures, using a stateless cookie technique.

Figure 6-9 outlines a full client-authenticated DTLS handshake between a client and a server.

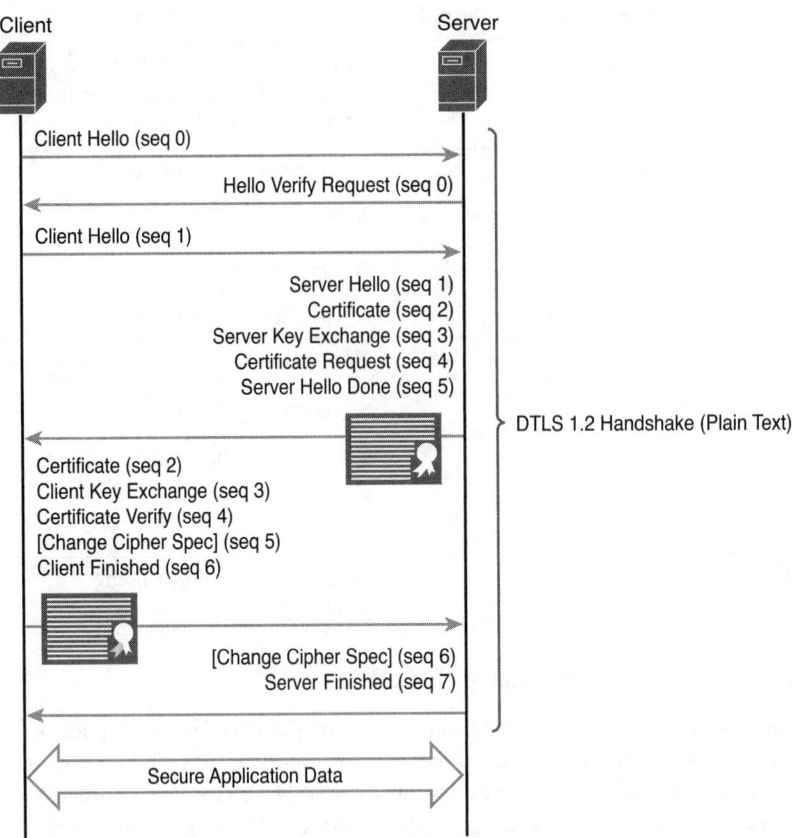

Figure 6-9 *An Illustration of a DTLS Handshake*

Due to the number of items that are exactly the same as TLS, the following analysis of the DTLS handshake discusses only items that are unique to DTLS:

- Notice that every message contains an explicit sequence number. Every new message from a particular party in the DTLS handshake should increment the sequence number by one.
- The client sends a ClientHello message exactly the same as described earlier in this chapter, in the section "Secure Sockets Layer (SSL) and Transport Layer Security (TLS)." This first ClientHello message is used to solicit a HelloVerifyRequest message from the server. If the HelloVerifyRequest message is not received, the client may wait for the retransmit timer to expire and then send a new ClientHello message with the same sequence number. This message contains an empty Cookie field.
- The server receive the ClientHello message normally and thus sends a HelloVerifyRequest message that contains a DTLS version and a cookie. The cookie is calculated based on the information provided in the ClientHello message.
- Upon reception of the HelloVerifyRequest message, the client sends exactly the same ClientHello message to the server except that it increments the sequence number by one and includes the cookie value received in the Hello Verify Request message.
- The server sends a ServerHello message that increments the sequence number and a DTLS version that is the same as the HelloVerifyRequest message sent earlier.
- The rest of the DTLS handshake occurs exactly the same as for TLS but with the sequence number added to every message.

Within collaboration and IP telephony, DTLS sees the most use when coupled with Secure Real-Time Transport Protocol (SRTP). DTLS for use with SIP has also been proposed, but there is no formal standard. DTLS with SRTP is discussed later in this chapter, in the "Secure Media" section.

Tip At the time of this book's publication, DTLS 1.3 has not been ratified into an official RFC. Thus the most recent version is DTLS 1.2.

Secure/Multipurpose Internet Mail Extensions (S/MIME)

Multipurpose Internet Mail Extensions (*MIME*) is used to extend message bodies of protocols such as HTTP, SMTP, and SIP. MIME allows for the following actions to be performed on a message body:

- Standardize the conveyance of character sets within message bodies using a character set (**;charset=**) tag applied to a Content-Type header, which allows devices to convey whether any non-default character sets are to be applied to the content. The following is a sample Content-Type header:

```
text/plain; charset=us-ascii
```

- Establish different formats for non-textual message bodies using the Content-Type header. These include application, text, image, audio, video, message, and multipart. The following is a sample Content-Type header:

```
application/sdp
```

- Allow conveyance of multiple-part message bodies through the use of multipart content types, which make use of a boundary tag added to the Content-Type header. This allows a message body to carry and convey multiple types of data in one message as the data is separated by the unique boundary defined in the header **boundary=***tag*. The following is a sample Content-Type header:

```
multipart/alternative;boundary=boundary42
```

SIP incorporates all the MIME attributes laid out in RFC 2046 and allows for SIP messaging to convey these items within the SIP message body. Example 6-9 details a sample MIME message body carried by a SIP message. You can see a SIP message with multiple message bodies, each of which is a different type of data. The first is SDP for negotiating media, and the second is Cisco proprietary Call Progress Analysis (CPA) data. The fact that this message body contains different data types is conveyed in the SIP message header Content-Type: Multipart/mixed. The actual description of each message is carried in the message body, and each data set in the message body is separated using a boundary defined in the Content-Type header. This example has the boundary boundary=uniqueBoundary. The first message body contains a nested Content-Type header, which conveys the application/SDP type and the different pieces of SDP for this message. Next is another unique boundary and a second message body of the type application/x-cisco-cpa, as well as the message body parameters for this message body. Notice that the message body types are different; this is what the Multipart/mixed portion of the Content-Type header indicates. The message body closes with a unique boundary that also ends with two dashes: --. This signals the end of the SIP message body.

Example 6-9 *Sample Signaling and Message Body for MIME Data*

```
INVITE sip:889197447009@10.0.1.83 SIP/2.0
[..Truncated for Brevity..]
Content-Type: Multipart/mixed;boundary=uniqueBoundary
Content-Length: 608

--uniqueBoundary
Content-Type: application/sdp
Content-Disposition: session;handling=required
```

```
v=0
o=UAC 2884 2524 IN IP4 172.19.155.41
s=SIP Call
c=IN IP4 172.19.155.41
t=0 0
m=audio 19994 RTP/AVP 0
a=rtpmap:0 PCMU/8000

--uniqueBoundary
Content-Type: application/x-cisco-cpa
Content-Disposition: signal;handling=optional

Events=FT,Asm,AsmT,Sit,Piano
CPAMinSilencePeriod=608
CPAAnalysisPeriod=2500
CPAMaxTimeAnalysis=5000
CPAMaxTermToneAnalysis=30000
CPAMinValidSpeechTime=112

--uniqueBoundary--
```

Note Call Progress Analysis (CPA) is discussed further in Chapter 12, "Contact Center Integration."

As you can imagine, MIME is a very robust protocol with many use cases. The ability to carry and convey different types of message bodies in one message is a very useful feature. This chapter only goes over the very basics of MIME so that we can cover *Secure Multipurpose Internet Mail Extensions* (*S/MIME*).

S/MIME is an extension of MIME that allows MIME to perform a host of security-related features related to message bodies carried by HTTP, SMTP, and SIP. The following are some of these features:

- Message bodies are compressed by encoding the message body as Base64 content. This does not offer any security advantages but rather allows for applications to significantly reduce the size of messages containing very large message bodies. This is conveyed using the **compressed-data** content protocol type tag.
- Message bodies are encrypted so that the contents are secure and confidential, and so their integrity is protected. This is conveyed using the **enveloped-data** content protocol type tag.

- Digital signatures provide a way of authenticating the contents of a message body. This is conveyed using the **signed-data** content type protocol tag. Signatures may also be conveyed using the content types **application/pkcs7-signature** and **multipart/signed.**

In Example 6-10 you can see a SIP message carrying S/MIME data that is both encrypted and signed. The Content-Type header in the SIP message indicates that this is a multipart/signed message with the protocol **application/pkcs7-signature.** The signature uses SHA-1, as per the **micalg** tag, and a unique boundary of **boundary42** is assigned for the message bodies. Examining the first message body, you can see that there is encrypted text based on the **Content-Type** header of this message body containing **enveloped-data**, and you know that the content is encoded as Base64 data. This encrypted data could be any type of data the application requires to be encrypted. Thus Example 6-10 contains the message body from Example 6-11 as encrypted data. Inspecting the second message body, you can see that it carries a Base64 encoded SHA-1 signature of the previous message body containing the encrypted data. This is conveyed through the Content-Type **application/pkcs7-signature.**

Example 6-10 *Sample Signaling and Message Body for S/MIME Data*

```
INVITE sip:bob@biloxi.com SIP/2.0
[..Truncated for Brevity..]
Content-Type: multipart/signed;protocol="application/pkcs7-signature"; micalg=sha1;
  boundary=boundary42
Content-Length: 568

--boundary42
Content-Type: application/pkcs7-mime; smime-type=enveloped-data;name=smime.p7m
Content-Transfer-Encoding: base64
Content-Disposition: attachment; filename=smime.p7m;handling=required
Content-Length: 231

[..Encrypted Base64 Message Body here..]

--boundary42
Content-Type: application/pkcs7-signature; name=smime.p7s
Content-Transfer-Encoding: base64
Content-Disposition: attachment; filename=smime.p7s;handling=required

[..Base64 Digital Signature on the previous message body here..]

--boundary42--
```

Example 6-11 *The Encrypted Message Body from Example 6-10*

```
Content-Type: application/sdp

v=0
o=UAC 2884 2524 IN IP4 172.19.155.41
s=SIP Call
c=IN IP4 172.19.155.41
t=0 0
m=audio 19994 RTP/AVP 0
a=rtpmap:0 PCMU/8000
```

You may be wondering how the device receiving the SIP message in Example 6-10 decrypts the first message body to reveal the contents. Either a Diffie-Hellman handshake may occur and/or RSA keys may be exchanged between the parties through digital certificates. These key agreement and exchange processes used in S/MIME follow the same steps shown earlier in this chapter.

Although it is not required, it is recommended to perform both encryption and authentication by signing the encrypted data, as shown in Example 6-10. This provides better security than plaintext data plus signing or encrypted data plus no signing. An attacker could easily circumvent either of those methods by either changing the plaintext data and then computing a new signature or by removing the encrypted data and replacing it with a new set of encrypted data.

While S/MIME offers a robust approach to encrypting message bodies of SIP messages—rather than the entire SIP message, as seen with TLS—it is not widely adopted in the industry for SIP and sees more use with HTTP and SMTP. S/MIME also has additional drawbacks with SIP that revolve around intermediary devices that perform changes to message body parameters. One such example would involve a SIP Application Layer Gateway (ALG) device that needs to perform translations on SDP IPs and ensure that private IPs are translated to public IPs. With the encryption afforded by S/MIME, these ALG devices may not be able to perform their duties. With the advent of modern technologies such as ICE, this may not pose a large problem, but it is a problem. Normal insecure MIME, however, does see far more adoption by the industry and has many applications not defined in this book. (For more information on S/MIME and potential uses, please refer to RFCs 5751 and 3261. For further reading on MIME, refer to RFCs 2045, 2046, and 3261.)

Establishing Secure Sessions

Devices in real-time multimedia networks that handle audio, video, text, and images must be able to secure their data and conform to the core concepts and security topics defined at the start of this chapter. These devices are not limited to SBCs; the concepts and protocols mentioned in the following sections are also applicable to any user agent that wishes to utilize SIP with TLS to secure the signaling plane and SRTP to secure the media plane.

These devices include IP PBXs, call agents, SIP proxies, SBCs, IP phones, softphones, fax servers, email servers, voicemail applications, and service provider equipment.

Secure Signaling

Session Initiation Protocol (SIP) is the most common signaling protocol used for establishing media sessions between different parties, often on different networks. SIP is a plaintext protocol that is transmitted over many different transport protocols. SIP messages may contain many of the following items in the message body or headers:

- Phone numbers
- Employee names or usernames
- Email addresses
- Passwords
- IP addresses
- Device hostnames
- Media IP address/port pairs

A company may not want these items to be in public records or viewable by third-party eyes. Chapter 4, "Signaling and Interworking," details many different ways an SBC can interwork SIP traffic at the transport layer (Layer 4). The two main methods of transport for SIP are TCP and UDP. By combining TLS with TCP, a device can ensure that the SIP application layer traffic is securely encrypted when being transmitted across a single insecure network hop. The SIP message data is considered Layer 7 application data and is transmitted after the TLS handshake has completed. Figure 6-10 details a SIP session encrypted using a TCP TLS 1.2 handshake.

In Figure 6-10, you can see that a TCP handshake occurs and then leads to a TLS handshake, as described earlier in this chapter, in the section "Secure Sockets Layer (SSL) and Transport Layer Security (TLS)." Note that the TLS handshake is client authenticated, and both parties participating in the session must exchange certificates. When the TLS handshake completes, Layer 7 SIP application traffic is encrypted and exchanged between the user agent client (UAC) and user agent server (UAS). Also note that TLS is a per-hop protocol, so these steps occur for every call leg in which security is required.

Sending encrypted SIP traffic is often called *Secure SIP* (*SIPS*). Examining the INVITE in Example 6-12, you can see that the request URI is formatted with **sips:** and the Via header contains **SIP/2.0/TLS** as the transport protocol. Finally, the port used for Secure SIP is 5061 rather than 5060, which is used for normal insecure SIP signaling. The rest of the message formatting and signaling exchange follow normal operational procedures.

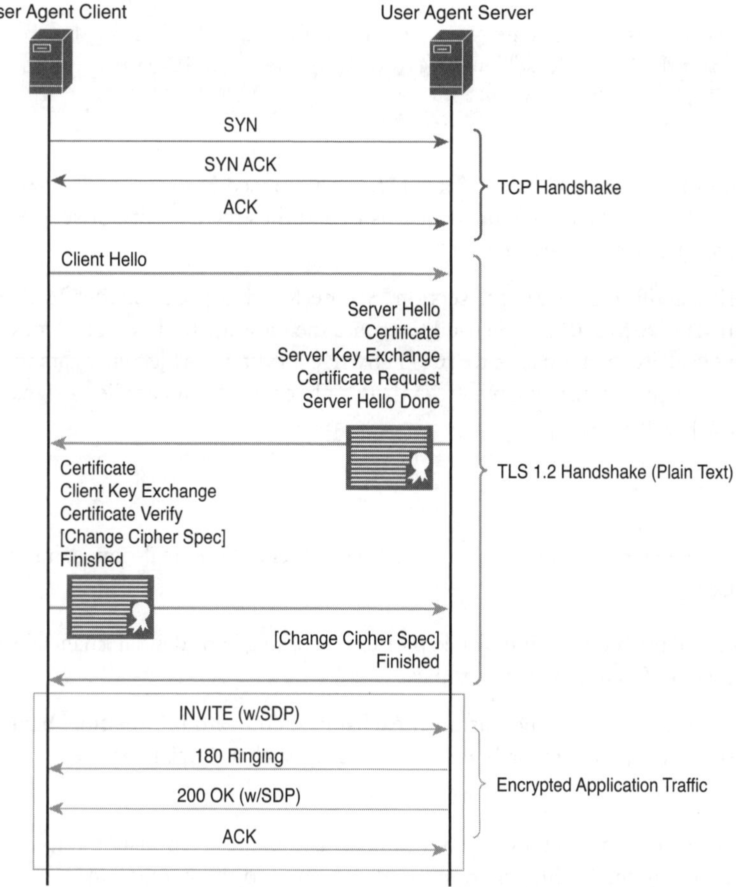

Figure 6-10 *An Illustration of a SIP-TLS Client-Authenticated Two-Way TLS 1.2 Handshake*

Example 6-12 *Sample Signaling for SIP-TLS INVITE with SIPS URI Structure*

```
INVITE sips:1234@172.18.110.48:5061 SIP/2.0
Via: SIP/2.0/TLS 172.18.110.58:5061;branch=z9hG4bK850D
From: <sips:1000@172.18.110.58>;tag=1A2D1D1C-727
To: <sips:1234@172.18.110.48>
Call-ID: F52F8DEB-741511E8-ABA8A48C-614FCA40@172.18.110.58
Allow: INVITE, OPTIONS, BYE, CANCEL, ACK, PRACK, UPDATE, REFER, SUBSCRIBE, NOTIFY,
  INFO, REGISTER
CSeq: 101 INVITE
Contact: <sips:1000@172.18.110.58:5061>
Expires: 180
Max-Forwards: 69
Content-Length: 0
```

Tip The **sips:** URI scheme is not mandatory for Secure SIP-TLS sessions. If an upstream device does not support the SIPS URI scheme, a 416 Unsupported URI Scheme response may be received.

Secure SIP for transport over UDP by way of DTLS was proposed in RFC Draft *draft-jennings-sip-dtls-05*, but it failed to gain a consensus, and thus the majority of secure SIP signaling exchanges occur using TCP TLS.

As discussed earlier in this chapter, in the section "Secure/Multipurpose Internet Mail Extensions (S/MIME)," S/MIME can be used to secure the message body of a SIP message. This may be used as an alternative to TCP-TLS SIP encryption, which encrypts the entire SIP message, including headers, while S/MIME only encrypts and applies a signature to the SIP message body.

Secure Media

Let's briefly look at a few real-world scenarios that occur every day in real-time communication networks:

- A conference call proceeds with multiple parties discussing confidential financial results or other confidential business topics.
- A customer care center agent and customer exchange credit card information, bank account information, and personally identifiable items such as Social Security numbers.

These scenarios involve items that are of high value to companies responsible for handling the data. If any of this information found its way into the wrong hands, it could spell disaster. With normal, insecure media, all it takes is one packet capture on the network path between the two participants in a session, and the audio can be played back by a third party that was should not have access to the contents of the session.

Real-Time Transport Protocol (RTP) is a media plane protocol that carries multimedia packets that may contain the aforementioned sensitive data. Secure Real-Time Transport Protocol (SRTP) works to encrypt the media payload of RTP packets and to provide confidentiality to multimedia sessions. SRTP also provides optional authentication over the media payload and packet headers through the use of an authentication tag. In addition, SRTP incorporates anti-replay protection into the protocol's operation. SRTP was officially drafted as a standard by the IETF in 2004, under RFC 3711. The creators of SRTP refer to it conceptually as a "bump in the stack" due to the fact that SRTP operates briefly between the application layer and the transport layer. SRTP is responsible for both encryption and decryption of the audio payload within an RTP or SRTP packet. The RTP packet format is illustrated in Figure 6-11.

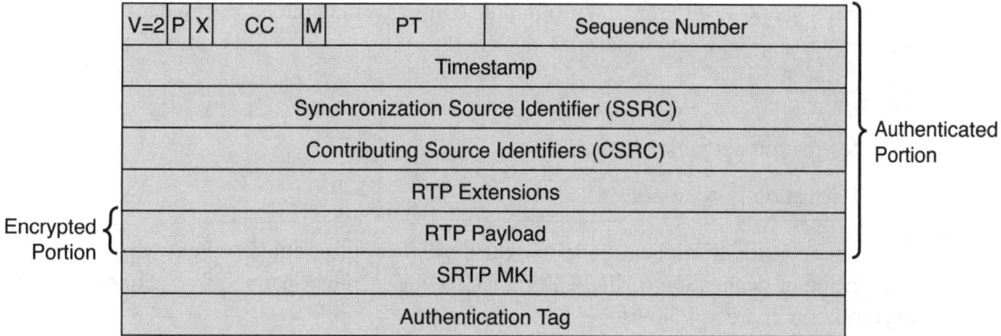

Figure 6-11 *The Structure of an SRTP Packet*

Except in a few key areas, the format of an SRTP packet is exactly the same as the format of an RTP packet (discussed in Chapter 5, "Media Processing"). In Figure 6-11, notice the following entries that differ from those of an RTP packet:

- **RTP Payload**—The entire RTP media payload is now encrypted, but the rest of the packet headers are in plaintext. This includes RTP header extensions, payload types, and other identifiers. These items are left unencrypted so that if actions such as header compression are required, devices can perform this operation on the headers. In addition, some devices in the media path may need access to the contents of these headers to successfully handle the RTP packets. The encrypted SRTP payload may be larger than the original RTP payload because encryption mechanisms may apply padding to properly encrypt the data.
- **SRTP Master Key Identifier (MKI)**—This field is optional but because there may be multiple RTP streams in a communication session, the MKI can be used as a way to uniquely identify the master key used to generate the session keys. (Master keys, MKI, and session keys are discussed later in this section.) Finally, the MKI is useful when SRTP needs to perform a re-key.
- **Authentication Tag**—This field carries message authentication data such as a hash of the RTP packet. The authenticated portion of the packet does not include the SRTP MKI but does include everything else. Although the authentication tag is not mandatory, it is nonetheless recommended for implementations to use these tags because certain RTP header field values such as the synchronization source identifier (SSRC) and sequence number are used in the encryption process. Without authentication, an attacker could modify these values, thus causing the SRTP process to malfunction.

There could be multiple media streams (for example, audio and video) within a communication session. With SRTP, each media stream is provided a unique security association called the *cryptographic context*. The cryptographic context includes the cryptographic algorithms, keying material, and other parameters that allow the smooth operation of the

SRTP framework. A different cryptographic context is maintained per media stream and identified using the following triplet identifier:

- SSRC
- Destination network address
- Destination port number

It is important for an application to use the correct cryptographic context while encrypting or decrypting traffic. The transform-independent parameters included in the crypto context are as follows:

- **Roll Over Counter (ROC)**—SRTP makes use of a rollover counter (ROC) that starts at zero and counts how many times the SRTP sequence number (SEQ) has rolled over the value 65,535. The ROC starts at 0 and never resets for the duration of the entire SRTP media session, even if a re-key has occurred.
- **SRTP Packet Index**—The ROC is used in computing the SRTP packet index, which is applied in calculating the session keys.
- **s_l**—The receiver maintains a value termed s_l, which is simply a 16-bit number that defines the highest received RTP sequence number. The s_l value is used in conjunction with the ROC to create the window replay list (discussed later in this chapter).
- **Encryption Cipher**—This is the encryption algorithm that will be used for the media stream. The particular encryption cipher that will be used for a given media stream is negotiated using SRTP cipher suites, as discussed later in this section.
- **Authentication Algorithm**—This is the authentication algorithm that will be used for the media stream. The particular authentication algorithm that will be used for a given media stream is negotiated using SRTP cipher suites, as discussed later in this section.
- **Replay List**—The replay list is used in the sliding window anti-replay technique for SRTP. It is a list of SRTP packets received and authenticated.
- **MKI Indicator**—This is a simple 0 or 1 value that indicates whether an MKI is being used for this media stream.
- **MKI Length**—Assuming that an MKI is in use, the MKI length is defined by this value.
- **MKI Value**—Again, assuming that an MKI is being used, the actual MKI value is stored within this value.
- **Master Key**—This is the secret master SRTP key that will be used to derive the session keys for this particular media stream.
- **Master Key Packet Counter**—This value in the cryptographic context counts the number of packets encrypted using a particular master key. The sequence number

and ROC together place a limitation on how many SRTP packets can be created using a specific session key. This limit is 2^48, as the SEQ is 16 bits and the ROC is 32 bits. For SRTCP the limit is 2^31 packets. When the SRTP/SRTCP limit is reached (or even before the limit is reached), a re-key must occur, which will generate a new master key, which in turn creates a new set of session, authentication, and salt keys. These new keys allow for another set of SRTP/SRTCP packets to be encrypted, up to the maximum defined by the algorithm. It is important to note that the ROC does not reset to zero after a re-key has occurred.

- **Master Salt**—The SRTP master key is an optional random value provided by the key management protocol that allows for greater entropy in the SRTP session key creation process. This value may be public and is recommended but not required.
- n_e—This value determines the length of the session keys used for encryption.
- n_a—This value specifies the length of the session keys used for authentication.
- **Key Derivation Rate**—This is the rate at which a pseudo-random function is applied to the master key. This is optional and carries the default value 0.
- **From, To Pairing**—If an MKI is not being used, the master key is identified by the unique 48-bit From, To packet index value pairing. The default From value is the first observed packet, and the default To value is one that does not exceed the maximum upper bound on the lifetime of the master key and master key packet counter.

In addition to the transport-independent parameters just listed, there are also transform-dependent parameters, which avoid complexity of interworking many different security algorithms. These parameters for the crypto context are as follows:

- **Block Cipher Mode**—This is the block cipher being used and the operational mode.
- **Block Size of Ciphers**—This is the bit size of the block cipher being used.
- **Session Encryption Key**—This is the key that will be used for encrypting the media payload.
- **Session Encryption Key Length**—This is the length of the session encryption key.
- **Session Salt Key**—This is an input used in conjunction with the session encryption key for encrypting the media payload.
- **Session Salt Key Length**—This is the length of the session salt key.
- **Data for the Initialization Vectors (IV)**—This is used with AED ciphers where IV data is required.
- **Authentication Algorithm**—This is the authentication algorithm that will be used.
- **Session Authentication Key**—This is the session authentication key used to create authentication tags for SRTP packets.

- **Session Authentication Key Length**—This is the length of the session authentication key.
- **Authentication Tag Length**—This is the length of the output authentication tag when one is generated.
- **SRTP Prefix Length**—This is the length of the SRTP keystream prefix.

As mentioned earlier, SRTP uses the packet index to protect against packet replay. *Packet replay* is the concept of injecting previously sent packets into an existing stream. The SRTP window size can be negotiated to a higher value by the key management protocol but by default SRTP defines a sliding window of 64 packets. This means that received packets that have an index higher than the current SRTP window or within the window but that are not already received are valid, while packets lower than the current window or duplicate packets inside the current window are dropped due to the anti-replay mechanism of SRTP. The term *sliding window* originates from the fact that the values in the window are always changing because the SRTP packet index increases with every successfully received and authenticated packet. Figure 6-12 illustrates the SRTP sliding window technique.

Anti-Replay List	Action
N – 1	Dropped
Window N	Accepted
...	Accepted
N + 63	Accepted
N + 64	Not Received Yet

Sliding Window

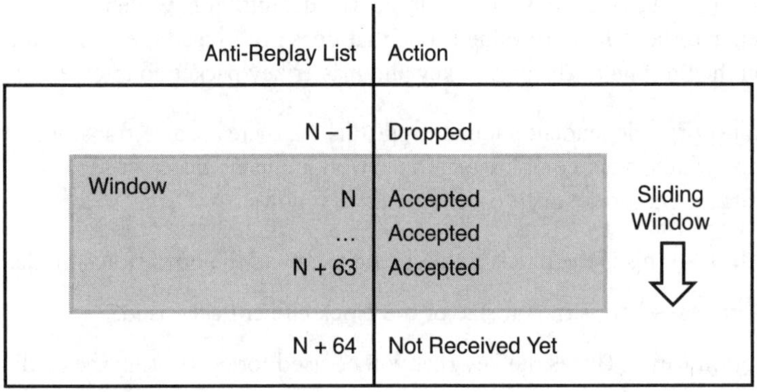

Figure 6-12 *A Sample Illustration of the SRTP Sliding Window Technique*

As mentioned earlier in this chapter, SRTP uses cipher suites to uniquely identify the encryption cipher and authentication algorithm that will be used for a cryptographic context. The concept of a cipher suite in SRTP is very similar to the usage defined earlier in this chapter. Cipher suites in SRTP use the following format:

```
AES_256_CM_HMAC_SHA1_80
<encryption_cipher>_<authentication_algorithm>
```

The negotiation of SRTP cipher suites takes place through the key management protocol, which is discussed later in this chapter. As with TLS cipher suites, SRTP cipher suite registration is available at https://www.iana.org/assignments/sdp-security-descriptions/sdp-security-descriptions.xhtml.

RFC 3711 also defines Secure Real-Time Transport Control Protocol (SRTCP) to go along with SRTP. A sample packet format is detailed in Figure 6-13.

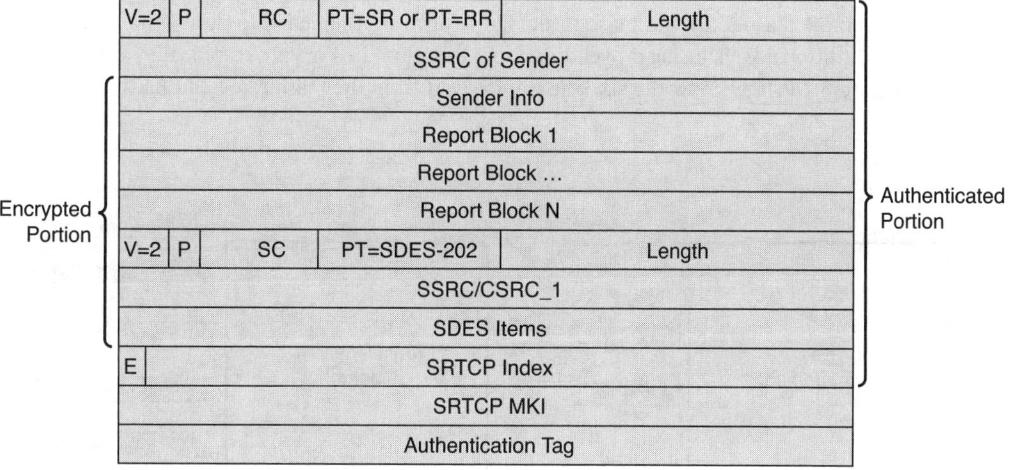

Figure 6-13 *The SRTCP Packet Structure*

Similarly to the SRTP packet, SRTCP follows the same format as RTCP except in the following key areas:

- The encrypted portion consists of the RTCP compound packet.
- The E flag is a 1-bit value that indicates whether the SRTCP packet is encrypted or unencrypted. The value 1 indicates encrypted, and the value 0 indicates unencrypted.
- The SRTCP Index field is a 31-bit counter that facilitates an explicit sequence number for the SRTCP packets. This index starts at 0 and increases. The index must never be set to 0 again for the duration of the session.
- The Authentication Tag field is run on every portion of the SRTCP packet excluding the SRTCP MKI. This is required for SRTCP because these packets may exert control over the RTP stream. One such method of control is the RTCP BYE packet, which can be used to tear down an RTP media session. Without authentication, an attacker could modify the contents of an SRTCP packet in a way that could disconnect the media session.
- SRTCP MKI is an optional field that for all intents and purposes is the same as the SRTP MKI field.

SRTCP uses the same cryptographic context parameters as SRTP except that SRTP does not contain a ROC or the s_l value. This is because the SRTP index is an explicit value carried with the authenticated SRTCP packet. In addition, the anti-replay for SRTCP would be a separate list. Finally, SRTCP maintains a separate counter for the master key, even if the master key is shared with SRTP, so that applications can count the number of SRTCP packets processed using the encryption keys created with a specific master key.

SRTP relies on an external key management protocol, discussed later in this chapter, to obtain the master key and master salt. These keys are then used to derive the following additional keys (using a pseudorandom function) in a cryptographically secure way. Figure 6-14 shows how the six keys are derived from the master key and master salt.

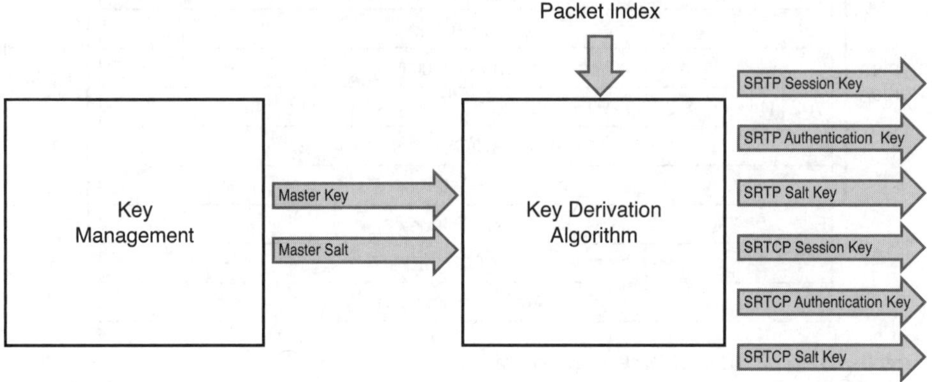

Figure 6-14 *An Illustration of the SRTP Key Derivation Process*

The session and salting keys for RTP and RTCP are used in payload encryption and decryption, while the authentication keys for RTP and RTCP are used to calculate and validate the message authentication tags of RTP and RTCP packets. While encrypting and decrypting packets, the SRTP framework ensures that a unique keystream is generated for each packet by using the following along with the session key:

- SRTP packet index
- SSRC of the RTP packet
- The salting key

While the encryption and decryption process is designed to generate a unique keystream for each packet, there is a possibility of the same keystream being generated across different media streams in a communication session. This could happen, for example, when the master key and master salt are shared across different media streams and the media streams happen to use the same SSRC (because the SSRC is randomly chosen) and packet index. However, RTP and RTCP have a built-in mechanism for resolving such SSRC collisions.

The following steps provide a high level view of what occurs when a device or an application needs to process an SRTP packet (see also RFC 3711):

Step 1. The cryptographic context associated with the media steam is identified by using the triplet identifier <*SSRC*, *destination address*, *destination port*>.

Step 2. The packet index is determined using the ROC and the highest sequence number available in the cryptographic context.

Step 3. The master key and master salt are determined.

Step 4. The session keys and session salt are determined.

Step 5. Encryption of the RTP packet payload occurs, with a combination of the session key, index, SSRC, and session salt. The inclusion of the SSRC and index ensures that a unique keystream is generated for each packet.

Step 6. If an MKI is being used, it is inserted into the SRTP packet.

Step 7. If authentication is being used, SRTP calculates the authentication tag over the encrypted RTP payload and the RTP headers.

Step 8. The newly created SRTP packet is passed to the transport layer for submission on the network.

When SRTP receives a packet, it performs the following steps:

Step 1. The cryptographic context associated with the media steam is identified by using the triplet identifier *<SSRC, destination address, destination port>*.

Step 2. The packet index is determined by using the ROC and the highest sequence number available in the cryptographic context.

Step 3. The master key and master salt are determined.

Step 4. The session keys and session salt are determined.

Step 5. The SRTP protocol receives an SRTP packet from the transport layer.

Step 6. The received SRTP packet index is checked against the locally maintained replay list to verify that the packet is not a duplicate or a potential packet replay attack.

Step 7. If the SRTP packet is accepted, the packet contains an authentication tag. This tag is verified by comparing a locally created authentication tag against the one received.

Step 8. The SRTP packet payload is decrypted.

Step 9. The ROC and s_l values in the replay list are updated.

Step 10. If an MKI was present in the packet, it is removed.

Step 11. If an authentication tag was present in the packet, it is removed.

Secure Media Key Management Protocols

As you may have noticed while reading the "Secure Media" section of this chapter, SRTP relies heavily on an external *key management protocol*. SRTP uses inputs such as a cipher suite, master key, master salt, and MKI to compute session keys, encrypt data, and structure packets. Although there are many different protocols that detail key management for SRTP, they can be broken down into two main categories:

- **Signaling plane key management**—These key management protocols use the signaling plane to establish the cryptographic context and provide keying material to SRTP.
- **Media plane key management**—These key management protocols use the media plane to establish a cryptographic context and provide keying material to SRTP. Although these protocols don't rely on the signaling plane for the establishment of the cryptographic context, the signaling plane might be leveraged for authentication and for establishing a binding with the media plane.

While the approach and operation of each key management protocol varies, they all solve the same problem of providing the required information to SRTP so that the media sessions can be encrypted. RFC 7201 discusses many of the key management protocols used in the industry. The main key management protocols are discussed in the following sections.

SDP Security (SDES)

SIP is used in concert with SDP to facilitate the setup of multimedia streams. SDP provides a simple framework for negotiating many parameters required for multimedia image, audio, video, and application sessions. SDP can also be used to establish the required SRTP keying material and other parameters, through the use of *Session Description Protocol Security Descriptions* (*SDES*) media attributes.

SDES follows the offer/answer SIP model, in which one side offers a list of supported SDP cryptographic parameters within the media attribute **a=crypto.** In addition, the user agent declares a specific master key and master salt for that media attribute. The device generating the answer selects a cryptographic parameter from the provided list, thus determining the options that will be used. The response also includes a declaration of the master key and master salt that will be used by that user agent. Figure 6-15 details the format for SDP entries that are used in the offer/answer.

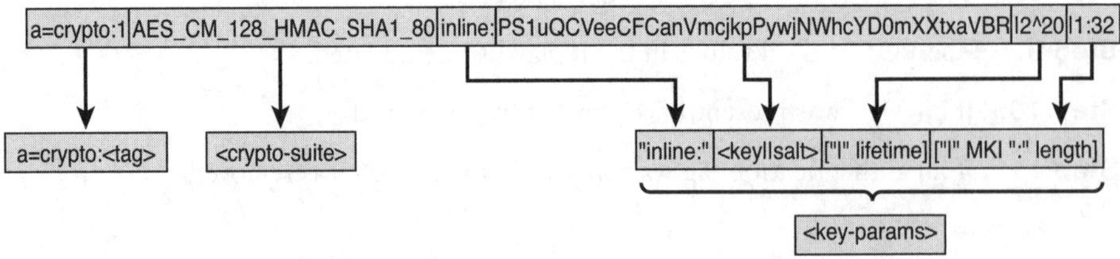

Figure 6-15 *An Illustration of the a=crypto SDP Media Attribute*

We can decode this format as follows:

- ***<tag>***—Designates that this cryptographic SDP attribute is a unique nonzero numeric tag. This tag is an identifier for this cryptographic SDP attribute as there may be more than one cryptographic attribute present in an offer. The tag must be unique across all media sessions in the SDP. The tag also indicates a preference order for the UA creating the offer.
- ***<crypto-suite>***—References one of the crypto suites defined in RFCs 4568, 5669, 6118, and 7714. The crypto suite is used to negotiate the encryption authentication mechanism that will be used for the SRTP session. In this example, we see AES Counter Mode (CM) with a bit length of 128 for the encryption protocol. The authentication protocol is using HMAC SHA-1 (80 rounds).
- ***<key-params>***—Has a few different sections, the first being the inline key method, followed by a Base64-encoded value that contains the master key and master salt. In addition, an optional lifetime definition can be included, which indicates the number of packets that can be encrypted using the session keys calculated from this master key. This maximum lifetime value may be equal to or lower than the maximum lifetime defined by SRTP. If desired, an MKI value and length may be defined. The MKI is the master key identifier used in the SRTP packet to identify this specific master key. The MKI is also given a length, in bytes (for example, this example contains a master key of 1 that is 32 bytes long).
- **[*<session-params>*]**—Specifies optional parameters that may be included. These include items such as key derivations rate, window size hint, and many more. These are not shown in the figure, but a full list can be found by reviewing Section 6.3 of RFC 5648 or by consulting the IANA SDP security description registrations.

Note SDES **a=crypto** media attributes must be declared per session media level and not included at a global level in the offer/answer SDP.

Example 6-13 shows a SIP message that contains an SDP offer. Here you can see a media description (**m=**) that contains the RTP profile value **RTP/SAVP**, which references the fact that the device originating this request is attempting to establish a secure audio session using SRTP. Also note the four different cryptographic SDP attributes, each containing a crypto suite and Base64-encoded master key/salt. The numeric order of the tags indicates this UAC's preference order for the cryptographic parameters. The UAC originating this request and SDP body has not elected to define the key parameters for an MKI, and thus no MKI will be used for these sessions. Because the optional master lifetime value is not included as a key parameter, it is assumed that the default value for the master lifetime of the SRTP packets is 2^48.

Example 6-13 *A Sample SDES Offer Carried by a SIP INVITE*

```
INVITE sip:7777@172.18.110.58:5061 SIP/2.0
Via: SIP/2.0/TLS 172.18.110.48:5061;branch=z9hG4bK493b2a4183
[..Truncated for Brevity..]
Content-Type: application/sdp
Content-Length: 1310

v=0
o=UAC 215 1 IN IP4 172.18.110.48
s=SIP Call
c=IN IP4 14.50.214.75
b=TIAS:64000
b=AS:64
t=0 0
m=audio 24180 RTP/SAVP 0 8
a=crypto:1 AEAD_AES_256_GCM
  inline:1g3E3aHfT5qdI5OHNKgqW6fWaF/A8fk6GD56Ex4JrpTLElcvVqfzaKmYAQ8=
a=crypto:2 AEAD_AES_128_GCM inline:5UFp0Tttp6MZzTDPlxSvUAP+VTqy10EhzGyIBA==
a=crypto:3 AES_CM_128_HMAC_SHA1_80 inline:js4G8xmC0OM1bLB6vpfM7jt/72SyoABCOhhR/v2f
a=crypto:4 AES_CM_128_HMAC_SHA1_32 inline:js4G8xmC0OM1bLB6vpfM7jt/72SyoABCOhhR/v2f
a=rtpmap:0 PCMU/8000
a=rtpmap:8 PCMA/8000
```

Example 6-14 continues with the offer/answer and shows an answer. The UAS answering the response selects the third cryptographic SDP attribute. The UAS then sends its own Base64-encoded master key and master salt, which the UAC will use to compute the SRTP session key used to encrypt the RTP payload of the negotiated SRTP packets.

Example 6-14 *A Sample SDES Answer to the Previous Offer*

```
SIP/2.0 200 OK
Via: SIP/2.0/TLS 172.18.110.48:5061;branch=z9hG4bK493b2a4183
[..Truncated for Brevity..]
Content-Type: application/sdp
Content-Length: 334

v=0
o=UAS 6398 1910 IN IP4 172.18.110.58
s=SIP Call
c=IN IP4 172.18.110.58
t=0 0
m=audio 8016 RTP/SAVP 0
c=IN IP4 172.18.110.58
a=rtpmap:0 PCMU/8000
a=crypto:3 AES_CM_128_HMAC_SHA1_80 inline:LQR0H2XowHOYVWzxsZLmZfRtQDfKHDgY91jIgU3t
```

Figure 6-16 illustrates the full offer/answer exchange between a client and a server. The INVITE carries the SDP with the applicable crypto suites and Base64-encoded master key and salt, along with the optional key parameters and session parameters. The server sends an answer in the 200 OK with SDP and selects a desired crypto suite from the list. The server's Base64-encoded master key and salt are then sent in the SDP back to the client, along with the optional key parameters and session parameters. If the server does not support SRTP or any of the crypto parameters provided in the offer, a 488 Not Acceptable Media might be observed.

Notice that in both Example 6-13 and Example 6-14, the Base64-encoded master key and master salt are sent over SIP as plaintext SDP values. This means that if a MITM were to get hold of that specific session's establishment, the MITM could decode the contents of any in-transit SRTP packets. This counteracts the efforts made to secure the media stream. Thus it is very important that the SIP signaling layer be encrypted using methods like TLS, which can encrypt the SIP application traffic, or S/MIME, which can encrypt the SIP message body.

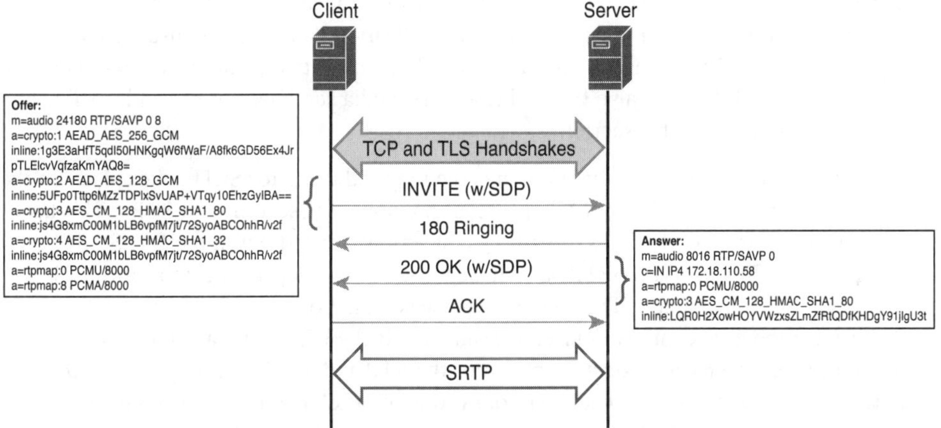

Figure 6-16 *SDES Offer and Answer Illustrated*

When the cryptographic context is established in the signaling plane using constructs such as SDES, it is impossible to determine the SSRC of the participating nodes as the SSRC is generated on the fly and randomly by RTP applications. Therefore, correctly invoking a cryptographic context using SDES involves the concept of late binding, in which the SSRC of the first SRTP packet received is used to bind the cryptographic context.

The other values of the cryptographic context are the destination network address, which is surmised from the address in the connection media attribute (**c=**), and the destination port number gathered from the media attribute (**m=**). SDES does not define any method of signaling the ROC or sequence number for a session. This is because the ROC always starts at 0, and the sequence number's starting value is selected by the SSRC source.

Finally, SDES defines that the master key used in negotiation is required to be unique for each session in order to avoid keystream reuse and circumvent two-time padding.

Although SDES does not support the negotiation of one-to-many media sessions, there is a chance that a user agent might receive an answer from multiple devices due to the forking of the original request by upstream devices. These answers may choose different IP and port combinations, along with different ciphers and crypto parameters. In addition, this increases the probability of an SSRC collision. These together can cause a lot of problems with SRTP operations and lead to a variety of security problems. Thus to handle this scenario, SDES suggests that if multiple answers are received, an offer in the form of an UPDATE with new keys, a new port, and if possible a new media IP address should be sent.

DTLS-SRTP

As discussed earlier in this chapter, DTLS is a delta of TLS for use with UDP as a transport. DTLS is specifically geared toward UDP and aims to solve problems that TCP-TLS is not equipped to cover. DTLS sees practicable application as a key management protocol for use with SRTP (insecure Layer 7 application data that may use UDP as a transport). DTLS-SRTP is heavily used in WebRTC, where it is required by the standard. That being said, DTLS can also be used to secure media sessions negotiated by SIP user agents, as discussed in this section.

The DTLS-SRTP handshake that negotiates the required items for SRTP takes place on the media plane rather than the signaling plane, as previously observed with SDES. This handshake may occur multiple times due to the restrictions spelled out in the DTLS-SRTP specification. First, a DTLS-SRTP handshake must occur independently for both RTP and RTCP. Second, a unique DTLS-SRTP handshake must occur for each unique source and destination port combination. This means that if the UDP ports are symmetric, two different DTLS handshakes occur for each of the RTP and RTCP streams. If the UDP ports being used are asymmetric, then four different DTLS handshakes need to occur to ensure proper encryption for each of the inbound and outbound RTP and RTCP streams. In addition to the previous two operational modes, RTP and RTCP may be multiplexed over the same UDP port, which means only one DTLS-SRTP handshake needs to occur to secure both. The recommended method of operations is to use symmetric source and destination port pairs for RTP and RTCP. The aforementioned items hold true for every individual media stream that requires security.

Tip When multiplexing occurs, a receiver is required to demultiplex the received packets in order to know what they represent. If the first byte of a packet is a 0 or 1, it is a STUN packet. If the value is between 20 and 63, the packet is DTLS. If the value is between 128 and 191, the packet is RTP or RTCP.

Figure 6-17 shows a single full DTLS-SRTP handshake as it occurs at the media plane to establish the keying material required for an SRTP session between Alice and Bob.

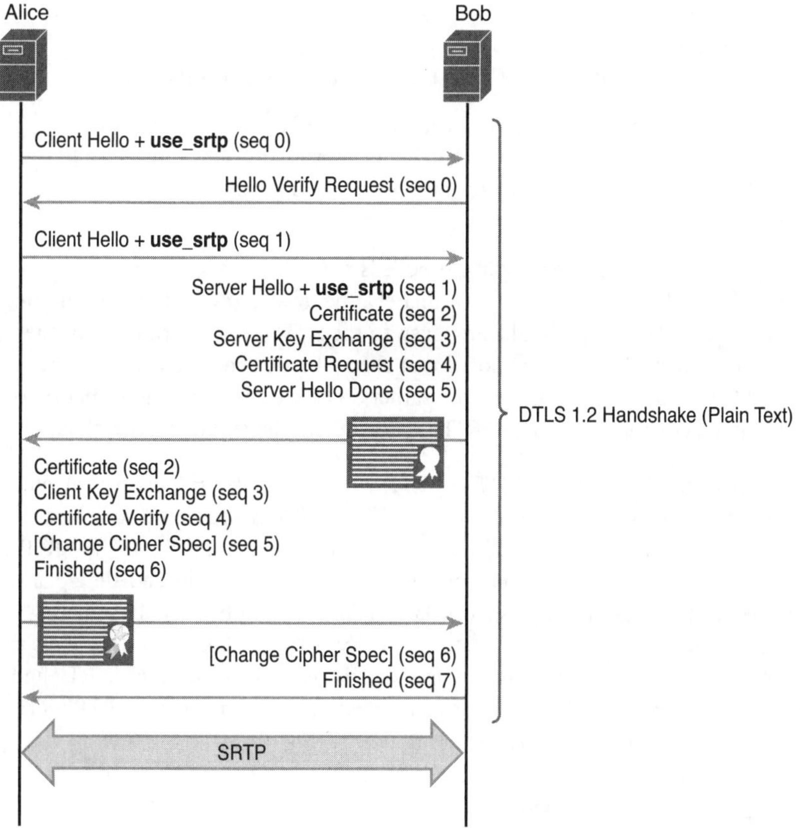

Figure 6-17 *An Illustration of the SRTP-DTLS Handshake Between Alice and Bob*

As you may have observed, most of the DTLS handshake in Figure 6-17 is the same as the DTLS handshake detailed in Figure 6-9, earlier in this chapter. The following occurs between Alice and Bob:

Step 1. Alice assumes the role of TLS client and starts the DTLS handshake by sending a ClientHello message with a sequence number of 0. The DTLS-SRTP specification mandates that the ClientHello message used for SRTP include the extension **use_srtp**. The **extension_data** portion also contains SRTP cipher suites, which aid in the process of negotiating the SRTP encryption keys and authentication mechanism. These cipher suites are formatted as follows: **SRTP_AES128_CM_HMAC_SHA1_80.** The cookie field in this message is empty.

Step 2. Bob, assuming the role of the TLS server, responds to the ClientHello message by sending a HelloVerifyRequest message set with the sequence number 0. This message is sent to acknowledge the response of the ClientHello message and stop retransmission by the client. The HelloVerifyRequest message contains a cookie, which is calculated based on the information provided in the received ClientHello message.

Step 3. Alice sends another ClientHello message with an incremented sequence number and the same data as the previous ClientHello message, except it now includes the cookie received from the HelloVerifyRequest message.

Step 4. If the server, Bob, is willing to accept and use SRTP for this session, the ServerHello response also includes the **use_srtp** extension and a selected SRTP cipher suite. The sequence number in this message is incremented by one.

Step 5. The rest of the DTLS handshake proceeds normally, as you would expect in a TLS or DTLS 1.2 handshake. Ultimately, the master key and master salt created by the DTLS handshake are given to the SRTP protocol to encrypt the media packets. It should be noted that the audio does not actually use the DTLS application data packets but rather SRTP packets. More information on the key derivation for DTLS-SRTP is provided at the end of this section.

While the key management portion of DTLS-SRTP, which produced the master key and master salt, occurs on the media plane, the use of DTLS-SRTP is signaled through an SDP offer/answer exchange on the signaling plane. This is done to bind the DTLS-SRTP handshake that will occur on the media plane with the operations of the signaling plane. Figure 6-18 shows a SIP session established between Alice and Bob. This SIP signaling negotiated a single audio stream that will occur directly between Alice and Bob. Thus the DTLS-SRTP handshake occurs there. Assuming that this session has symmetric RTP and RTCP ports for audio, only two DTLS handshakes need to occur: one for the RTP/SRTP stream and one for the RTCP/SRTCP stream.

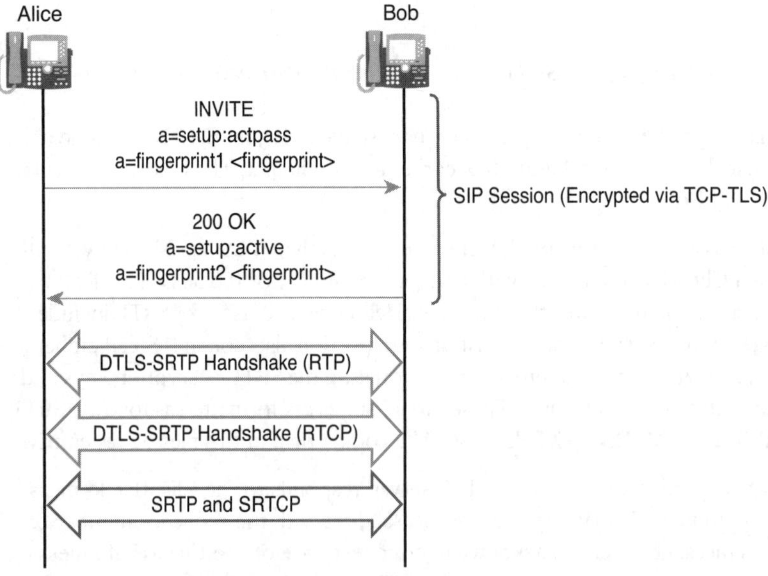

Figure 6-18 *An Illustration of the SRTP-DTLS Handshake at the Signaling Plane*

In Example 6-15, which shows is the INVITE request observed in Figure 6-18, you can see that there is an offer sent in an INVITE from Alice to Bob. The first item is a media attribute setup entry, **a=setup**, with the value of **actpass**. This is the setup parameter that must be sent in the initial offer. The next item is the media attribute containing a fingerprint and SHA-1 hash. This hash reflects the hash of the certificate that will be used in the DTLS handshake. Bob may use it to perform additional verification of the certificate that was presented to him during the DTLS-SRTP handshake. Alice also sends a list of transport protocols in the **a=tcap** media attribute. This holds the values **UDP/TLS/RTP/SAVP** and **RTP/AVP**, which indicate that the offer can support media profiles of DTLS-SRTP (UDP/TLS/RTP/SAVP) or normal insecure RTP (RTP/AVP). The transport protocol header is accompanied by a potential configuration media attribute (**a=pcfg**). This is used to associate and tie together different media attributes within the SDP body and present a potential configuration in the offer. This SIP session is also encrypted using TCP-TLS for added security and confidentiality, which prevents a MITM from tampering with the fingerprint values generated from the certificate. TCP-TLS could be replaced by the methods defined in RFC 8224 or with S/MIME encryption of the SDP message body.

Example 6-15 *A Sample DTLS-SRTP Offer Carried by a SIP INVITE*

```
INVITE sip:bob@example.com SIP/2.0
To: <sip:bob@example.com>
From: "Alice" <sip:alice@example.com>;tag=843c7b0b
Via: SIP/2.0/TLS ua1.example.com;branch=z9hG4bK-0e53sadfkasldkfj
Contact: <sip:alice@ua1.example.com>
Call-ID: 6076913b1c39c212@REVMTEpG
CSeq: 1 INVITE
Allow: INVITE, ACK, CANCEL, OPTIONS, BYE, UPDATE
Max-Forwards: 70
Content-Type: application/sdp
Content-Length: 285

v=0
o=- 1181923068 1181923196 IN IP4 ua1.example.com
s=example1
c=IN IP4 ua1.example.com
a=setup:actpass
a=fingerprint: SHA-1 4A:AD:B9:B1:3F:82:18:3B:54:02:12:DF:3E:5D:49:6B:19:E5:7C:AB
t=0 0
m=audio 6056 RTP/AVP 0
a=sendrecv
a=tcap:1 UDP/TLS/RTP/SAVP RTP/AVP
a=pcfg:1 t=1
```

Bob receives Alice's INVITE and has the capability to negotiate DTLS-SRTP. As a result, the response (shown in Example 6-16) contains the selected potential configuration media attribute (**a=pcfg**) in addition to the media line containing the selected media profile **UDP/TLS/RTP/SAVP**. Last but not least, Bob sends a fingerprint computed from the certificate that will be sent later in the DTLS handshake. Alice stores this for later verification checks when that part of the DTLS handshake is reached. The setup media attribute **a=setup** is now set to **active** in the response, confirming SRTP-DTLS.

Example 6-16 *A Sample DTLS-SRTP Answer to the Offer in Example 6-15*

```
SIP/2.0 200 OK
To: <sip:bob@example.com>;tag=6418913922105372816
From: "Alice" <sip:alice@example.com>;tag=843c7b0b
Via: SIP/2.0/TLS ua1.example.com;branch=z9hG4bK-0e53sadfkasldkfj
Call-ID: 6076913b1c39c212@REVMTEpG
CSeq: 1 INVITE
Contact: <sip:bob@ua2.example.com>
Content-Type: application/sdp
Content-Length: 254

v=0
o=- 6418913922105372816 2105372818 IN IP4 ua2.example.com
s=example2
c=IN IP4 ua2.example.com
a=setup:active
a=fingerprint: SHA-1 FF:FF:FF:B1:3F:82:18:3B:54:02:12:DF:3E:5D:49:6B:19:E5:7C:AB
t=0 0
m=audio 12000 UDP/TLS/RTP/SAVP 0
a=acfg:1 t=1
```

At the end of the offer/answer exchange shown in Figure 6-18, Example 6-15, and Example 6-16, Alice and Bob perform the DTLS-SRTP handshake shown in Figure 6-17. This is repeated the required number of times to compute the master key and master salt for each set of unique source and destination RTP and RTCP port pairs negotiated by the SIP signaling. The SRTP master key and master salt themselves are derived from the DTLS master secret in conjunction with the TLS extractor defined in RFC 5705. This means DTLS-SRTP can compute four separate SRTP keys from one DTLS master secret, as there is one master key/salt set used by the client, and another master key/salt set is used by the server. The SRTP application uses the following keys to create the SRTP session keys defined in the "Secure Media" section of this chapter:

- Client SRTP master key
- Server SRTP master key
- Client SRTP master salt
- Client SRTP master salt

Note Although the client generates a master key and salt, these are only used to decrypt packets from the server. The same is true for the server.

DTLS-SRTP maintains the SRTP cryptographic context and determines SSRC by attempting to decrypt a received SRTP packet, using a quartet of destination IP/port and source IP/port. If the decryption is successful, the SSRC is added to the table maintained by the protocol. This is similar to late binding, which is discussed earlier in this chapter, in the "SDP Security (SDES)" section. If DTLS-SRTP already knows the SSRC for the incoming packet and has a value in the table, it simply decodes the packet using that cryptographic context. If SRTP-DTLS cannot decode the packet using any known or unknown cryptographic context or table quartets, the packet is silently discarded.

Zimmermann RTP (ZRTP)

Zimmermann RTP (ZRTP) is an approach to SRTP key management that shares a few similarities with DTLS-SRTP, discussed in the previous section. One similarity between the two is that the key management handshake occurs on the media plane rather than on the signaling plane. Another similarity is that the ZRTP packets used for key management are multiplexed on the same IP and port that RTP and SRTP use. However, unlike DTLS-SRTP, ZRTP does not require that anything be done on the signaling plane to signal the use of ZRTP as a key management protocol. This is a stark contrast to SDES, where the entirety of the key management process takes place on the signaling plane. That being said, although it is not required, optional ZRTP SDP attributes do exists and can be used to provide a logical binding between the media and signaling planes.

While DTLS-SRTP makes use of the entire DTLS handshake has relies heavily on public key infrastructure (PKI), ZRTP makes use of DHE or pre-shared keys and does not rely on PKI. The use of DHE means that ZRTP can maintain PFS for all ZRTP–SRTP sessions, with minimal implementation and computational overhead. In addition, ZRTP uses key continuity, where ZRTP clients may cache pieces of the previous ZRTP session that are used in future ZRTP DHE key computations between the same participants. The concept of key continuity means that if an MITM attack did not capture the previous session between Alice and Bob, they won't know this additional variable used for ZRTP DHE key computation in the new session.

ZRTP uses a short authentication string (SAS) for additional session authentication; this replaces the PKI authentication used by other key management protocols. This value is calculated based on the DHE handshake or pre-shared key and is presented in some fashion to the users of the session. This SAS is then read aloud by both parties. After this, the two parties can use their own judgment to confirm whether the SAS matches. This allows the humans to make a judgment about whether an MITM attack is occurring. The SAS verification may also be completed by applications, without human intervention, by way of signing the SAS and providing the signature within the encrypted Confirm messages (covered later in this chapter).

Note ZRTP allows PKI to be used to augment the security features offered by the protocol but does not define any PKI usage parameters within the scope of RFC 6189.

Figure 6-19 shows a full ZRTP session between Alice and Bob. Using this illustration as a guide, in this section we dive into the different pieces that make up the ZRTP handshake. Note that this ZRTP handshake uses DHE rather than PSK.

Note This section provides a higher-level overview of ZRTP. For a deeper dive into the operational procedures and security afforded by ZRTP, see RFC 6189.

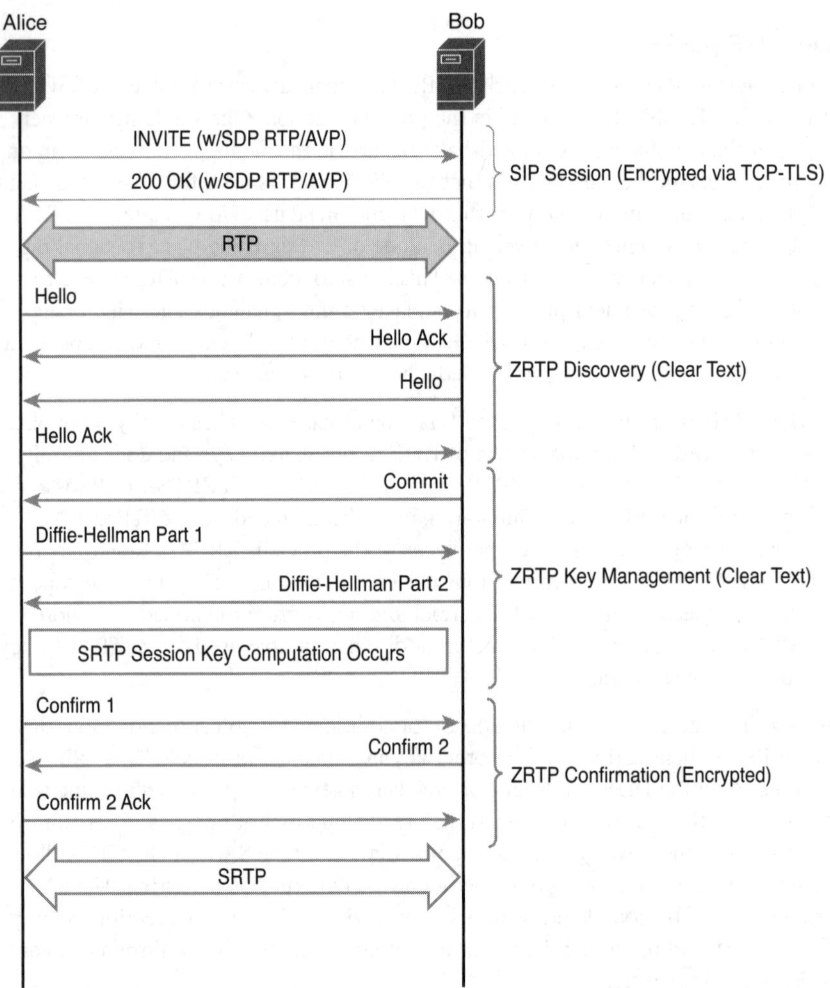

Figure 6-19 *An Illustration of a High-Level ZRTP Handshake Between Alice and Bob*

The first piece of important information observed in Figure 6-19 is the fact that the SIP signaling does not negotiate any security parameters. In fact, insecure RTP using the RTP/AVP profile is negotiated and established between the two parties. The SIP signaling may be encrypted using TCP-TLS, but this has no bearing on the ZRTP operation and thus is omitted for brevity.

ZRTP does not define when the start of a ZRTP discovery phase occurs, but it does state that the Hello messages are usually sent at the very start of an RTP session. This means that a user agent may sent a ZRTP Hello message the moment it has received an offer or answer with SDP. The ZRTP Hello message contains the ZRTP version (1.10) and ZRTP configuration options, such as a client identifier for identifying the vendor and software release of the ZRTP software being used. Other values include the signature-capable flag for identifying whether an endpoint can support digital signatures, a MITM flag used to identify whether a PBX/B2BUA is involved in the session, and a passive flag for indicating if the device can initiate a switch to secure communication using a Commit message or can only respond to Commit messages. The Hello messages also include is a 96-bit random ZRTP ID (ZID) that is unique to the ZRTP application. Finally, the various types of hashing algorithms, authentication types, encryption schemes, key agreement types, and SAS types are sent in the Hello message. The Hello message is then authenticated by computing a hash on the entire contents of the Hello message, and this is placed in the message authentication code field.

These Hello messages solicit a Hello Ack response to acknowledge the reception of the Hello message and stop retransmission. Because ZRTP uses UDP for the transport, the Hello messages are susceptible to packet loss, and thus these messages are mainly used to confirm the reception of the Hello message. If there is no Hello Ack received for a Hello message, a ZRTP client may employ retry counters and wait timers before sending another Hello message. If the user agent does not receive a response to the Hello message, it may retransmit 20 times before discovery fails and no further ZRTP messages are exchanged. Figure 6-19 shows that both Alice and Bob have exchanged Hello and Hello Ack messages, completing the ZRTP discovery phase of the handshake. A Commit message may be sent in place of a Hello Ack by the initiator; this message also stops Hello retransmissions.

Tip Either device may send the first Hello message during ZRTP discovery.

ZRTP key management for SRTP session key computation may occur either directly after the ZRTP discovery completes or when initiated by the user of a ZRTP application. The first method is preferred and allows ZRTP applications to escalate the insecure media session into a secure media session immediately after completing the discovery phase. However, the second method exists to emulate the behavior of specific types of endpoints, which have a Go Secure button that the user may click to signal to the application a desire to encrypt the session. At this point, the ZRTP application starts the key management handshake. Both of these methods use the same messaging shown in Figure 6-19. One of the two devices takes the role of initiator and sends a Commit message, which kicks off the key management exchange. Before sending the Commit message, the initiator computes its DHE key pair. The Commit message sent by the initiator contains the user's ZID and ZRTP options for hashing algorithms, authentication types, encryption schemes, key agreement types, and SAS types selected from the Hello message.

Because both parties may take the role of initiator, there is a chance of commit contention. When this occurs, if both PSK and DH are exchanged, DH must be selected, and the PSK commit must be discarded. If both commits contain the PSK method, the commit without a MITM flag is used, and the other commit is discarded. In the case of two DH commits, the commit with the lowest hashed value of initiator must be discarded. Finally, if both commits are non-DH modes, the lowest nonce value must be discarded. In Figure 6-19 there is no commit contention, and thus Bob takes the role of initiator, and Alice takes the role of responder.

The recipient of the Commit message will compute his or her own DHE key pair and start the first part of the Diffie-Hellman process by sending a Diffie-Hellman Part 1 (DHPart1) message. The initiator completes the Diffie-Hellman handshake and sends the Diffie-Hellman Part 2 (DHPart2) message. After the exchange of these messages, the applications compute the SRTP session key based on the DHE handshake. (See the "Key Agreement" section of this chapter for the operational aspects of Diffie-Hellman.)

Once the calculation has completed, the party who received the DHPart2 message sends a Confirm1 message. The initiator sends a Confirm2 after receiving the Confirm 1 message, indicating the DHE handshake completed successfully. The party receiving Confirm 2 must send a Confirm2Ack message to finish the confirmation handshake and stop retransmission of the Confirm 2 message. The Confirm messages are encrypted using the DHE keys negotiated in the last phase and carry information such as the session message authentication code and various flags, such as the disclosure (D), allow clear (A), SAS verified (V), and PBX enrollment (E). When the confirmation handshake is complete, the media session may be encrypted, and SRTP is exchanged between Alice and Bob.

In both the PSK and DHE ZRTP handshake modes, the participants create the following keys, which are used to encrypt and decrypt packets:

Note The initiator uses initiator keys to encrypt packets and responder keys to decrypt packets. The reverse is true for the responder.

- **srtpkeyi**—The SRTP initiator master key used by the initiator's SRTP application to derive SRTP session keys
- **srtpsalti**—The SRTP initiator master salt, which is used by the initiator's SRTP application to derive SRTP session keys
- **srtpkeyr**—The SRTP responder master key, used by the responder's SRTP application to derive SRTP session keys

- **srtpsaltr**—The SRTP responder master key, used by the responder's SRTP application to derive SRTP session keys
- **mackeyi**—The initiator message authentication code key used by ZRTP for authentication purposes
- **mackeyr**—The responder message authentication code key used by ZRTP for authentication purposes
- **zrtpkeyi**—The initiator ZRTP key used to encrypt the confirm messages
- **zrtpkeyr**—The responder ZRTP key used to encrypt the confirm messages

As mentioned previously, ZRTP does not rely on the signaling plane for any key management parameters; sessions start as insecure media sessions and then escalate to secure media sessions. This means the SIP user agents involved in establishing the session have no knowledge of whether a session is actually secure. This could pose a problem such as the signaling plane attempting key management using SDES while the application may actually attempt to use ZRTP for key management. Where applications and SIP user agents support multiple key management protocols, it is recommended to implement the ZRTP hash SDP media attribute (**a=zrtp-hash**). This attribute can be used alongside other SIP-SDP key management protocols and through the offer/answer model, can allow the signaling plane to know which key management protocol was selected for the session. Example 6-17 shows a sample ZRTP hash SDP media attribute.

Example 6-17 *A Sample Message Body Containing the* ***a=zrtp-hash*** *Media Attribute*

```
v=0
o=bob 2890844527 2890844527 IN IP4 client.biloxi.example.com
s=
c=IN IP4 client.biloxi.example.com
t=0 0
m=audio 3456 RTP/AVP 97 33
a=rtpmap:97 iLBC/8000
a=rtpmap:33 no-op/8000
a=zrtp-hash:1.10 fe30efd02423cb054e50efd0248742ac7a52c8f91bc2df881ae642c371ba46df
```

In Example 6-17 you can see that the media attribute is set to RTP/AVP instead of RTP/SAVP, which is due to the way ZRTP operates. Sessions establish as RTP and escalate to SRTP using the ZRTP handshake. Next is the ZRTP hash media attribute. This contains the ZRTP version and a hash that is calculated based on the ZRTP Hello message that will be sent from this client. Because the ZRTP handshake is performed for each media stream, it is not valid to place a ZRTP hash at the global SDP level. By including the hash, the signaling plane has knowledge of the SRTP key management protocol for the session as well as a method to authenticate the first ZRTP Hello packet and prevent false media packets from being inserted by third parties.

Tip Multiple ZRTP hashes may be present in the SDP body, one for each media stream, or zero may be present due to the fact that the ZRTP hash SDP attribute is completely optional for ZRTP protocol operation.

SBC Signaling and Media Security

Earlier sections of this chapter discuss the various security protocols that network devices can use to ensure that application data is secure and that it conforms to the core security concepts defined in the introduction to this chapter. The scope is then narrowed, as described earlier in this chapter, using security protocols and techniques that handle the session establishment and transmission of real-time media.

So far this chapter has discussed security topics in terms of a point-to-point or peer-to-peer connection between two devices (for example, Alice and Bob, a simple client and server relationship). This is done due to the fact that the majority of these protocols are not used for end-to-end encryption but rather are used for per-hop encryption. In the real world, Alice and Bob would rarely communicate directly. There may exist a whole host of different devices that interface with Alice and Bob on the signaling and media path. For example, Figure 6-20 shows an example of a networking topology that may exist in the real world. Alice exists on the network of Company A, and her device is registered to a centralized call agent that interfaces with an SBC for access to the service provider. This service provider interfaces with many others but, most importantly, it interfaces with Service Provider 2, which has a path to Company B's SBC. The SBC then interfaces with Bob's IP PBX and ultimately Bob's endpoint.

Security is only as strong as its weakest link. This means every one of the network hops discussed in Figure 6-20 would need to perform or apply security to the session on the signaling plane and media established between Alice and Bob. Otherwise, an attacker could simply perform an attack on the insecure network portion and thus circumvent the security in place on every other network hop. In addition, every hop in the session may use a slightly different security approach in terms of encryption techniques, handshakes, key management, and even transport mechanisms. As discussed earlier in this chapter, there are quite a few ways to secure signaling and media.

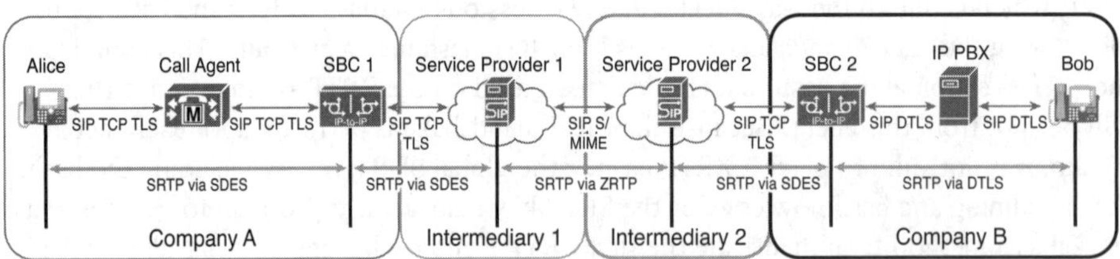

Figure 6-20 *A Sample End-to-End Topology for Security Spanning Multiple Networks*

The remaining sections of this chapter focus on how an SBC employs security at the media and signaling planes. In addition, the remaining sections provide relevant configuration examples and debug samples from Cisco's SBC, CUBE.

SBC Signaling Plane Security

An SBC, being a back-to-back user agent (B2BUA), has co-located user agent client (UAC) and user agent server (UAS) functionality. This affords an SBC the ability to perform security interworking at the signaling plane, which is very beneficial when different network segments and SIP applications require specific security protocols or standards for securing application data. An SBC may be used to interwork the differences between these two devices. The number of potential interworking scenarios is large, but they can be broken down into a few broad categories. The following are some examples of ways an SBC may need to perform signaling plane security interworking:

- Interworking of plaintext (insecure) SIP signaling to encrypted SIP signaling (for example, between SIP and SIPS)
- Interworking the same type of security protocol but with slightly different implementation standards (for example, TLS 1.2 and TLS 1.3)
- Interworking two types of encrypted secure signaling that are using different security protocols (for example, DTLS and TLS)
- Interworking different SRTP key management protocols that use the signaling plane (for example, SDES and DTLS-SRTP)

Due to the large number of possible interworking permutations, it is not possible for SBC vendors to support every type of security protocol and standard that exists. Thus it is crucial that an administrator review the applicable documentation and material provided by a vendor to verify whether the vendor's SBC will meet the interworking requirements posed by the network and any network the SBC may need to interface with.

Cisco's SBC, CUBE, natively supports SIP and SDP session encryption using TCP-TLS standards up to TLS 1.2, along with the latest TLS cipher suites for next-generation encryption and authentication. Cisco CUBE also leverages the deep security features available in IOS and IOS XE for many different operations, such as TLS handshakes, public key cryptography, and certificate management.

IOS and IOS XE have a certificate management feature called trustpoints. A *trustpoint* is a configuration item that contains certificates of CAs trusted by a device as well as the identity certificate for the device. Trustpoints are the backbone of cryptography in IOS and are used for a wide range of protocols, such as TLS, HTTPS, DMVPN, IPSec, IKE, and Secure SMTP. In this section we focus purely on the application of trustpoints for SIP TCP-TLS handshakes.

The following is a high-level overview of the steps required to configure signaling plane security and SIP TCP-TLS on CUBE when using a self-signed certificate:

Step 1. Define an RSA key pair and any additional settings required for the RSA keys.

Step 2. Create a trustpoint for CUBE and define all the applicable parameters that identify this device and associate the RSA key pair.

Step 3. Generate a self-signed certificate. Because this is a self-signed certificate, the certificate is created by IOS, and you only need to exchange the newly created self-signed certificate with other parties that the CUBE will peer with.

Step 4. Import additional self-signed or root CA certificates provided by peer devices that CUBE will communicate with.

Step 5. Associate the trustpoint containing the self-signed identity certificate for CUBE to the SIP application.

Step 6. Enable outbound TCP-TLS transport for SIP sessions with peer applications.

The following is a high-level overview of the steps required to configure signaling plane security and SIP TCP-TLS on CUBE when using a CA-signed certificate:

Step 1. Define an RSA key pair and any additional settings required for the RSA keys.

Step 2. Create a trustpoint for CUBE and define all the applicable parameters that identify this device and associate the RSA key pair.

Step 3. Generate a CSR.

Step 4. Provide the CSR to a CA and receive a CA-signed certificate.

Step 5. Import the CA-signed certificate and certificate chain to the original trustpoint used to create the CSR.

Step 6. Import additional self-signed or root CA certificates provided by peer devices that CUBE will communicate with.

Step 7. Associate the trustpoint containing the CA-signed certificate for CUBE to the SIP application.

Step 8. Enable outbound TCP-TLS transport for SIP sessions with peer applications.

In order to get started with security on CUBE, an administrator must first define an RSA key pair that will create the private and public key used in the TLS handshake and later configuration steps. Using the command detailed in Example 6-18, you can generate an RSA key pair for general purpose usage with a modulus of 2048 and the label CUBE. This key is exportable in the event that you need to import to another CUBE. One example of a situation in which you might need to import RSA keys is with CUBE high availability, discussed in Chapter 8, "Scalability Considerations." The two devices may share the same certificates and FQDN, and thus the RSA keys need to be the same on both devices in the CUBE high availability pair. It is not possible to make an RSA key pair exportable after the key is created. In the event that you create a non-exportable

RSA key and need to export, you need to delete the entire key and create a new one that is exportable. This renders any certificate created using that key pair invalid, as the keys are regenerated during this step.

Example 6-18 *Configuring an RSA Key Pair on CUBE*

```
cube(config)# crypto key generate rsa general-keys modulus 2048 label CUBE exportable
The name for the keys will be: CUBE

% The key modulus size is 2048 bits
% Generating 2048 bit RSA keys, keys will be exportable...
[OK] (elapsed time was 0 seconds)
```

To confirm whether an RSA key pair has already been created or other information about the RSA keys, you can use the command **show crypto key mypubkey rsa** (see Example 6-19). This **show** command details the different aspects of the RSA key process configured in Example 6-18.

Example 6-19 *Verifying the RSA Key Pair Created in Example 6-18*

```
cube# show crypto key mypubkey rsa
% Key pair was generated at: 17:41:28 EDT Jun 24 2018
Key name: CUBE
Key type: RSA KEYS
 Storage Device: not specified
 Usage: General Purpose Key
 Key is exportable. Redundancy enabled.
 Key Data:
  30820122 300D0609 2A864886 F70D0101 01050003 82010F00 3082010A 02820101
  [..Truncated for Brevity..]
```

As mentioned earlier in this chapter, in the section "Public Key Cryptography," you need a certificate that contains the public RSA key you just created. CUBE supports both self-signed and CA-signed certificates. Example 6-20 shows how to begin to configure a self-signed certificate on CUBE. It involves configuring a trustpoint and specifying the information for this device that should be included in the certificate. When all the information is entered, the trustpoint is then enrolled, and IOS generates an output certificate based on the commands present in the trustpoint. The command **crypto pki enroll** ***<trustpoint-label>*** enrolls the trustpoint based on the enrollment configured. In this case, the certificate is self-signed, so IOS asks a few questions of the administrator and generates a self-signed certificate. To export this certificate for import on other devices, you can use the command **crypto pki export** ***<trustpoint-label>*** **pem terminal**, which displays the trustpoint certificate in Base64-encoded PEM format inside the terminal for easy copying and pasting.

Example 6-20 *Creating a Self-Signed Certificate on CUBE*

```
cube# show run | section trustpoint CUBE-SELF
crypto pki trustpoint CUBE-SELF
 enrollment selfsigned
 fqdn cube.cisco.com
 subject-name CN=cube.cisco.com
 revocation-check none
 rsakeypair CUBE

cube(config)# crypto pki enroll CUBE-SELF
% Include the router serial number in the subject name? [yes/no]: no
% Include an IP address in the subject name? [no]: no
Generate Self Signed Router Certificate? [yes/no]: yes

Router Self Signed Certificate successfully created

cube(config)# crypto pki export CUBE-SELF pem terminal
% Self-signed CA certificate:
-----BEGIN CERTIFICATE-----
MIIDPjCCAiagAwIBAgIBATANBgkqhkiG9w0BAQUFADA4MRcwFQYDVQQDEw5jdWJl
[..Truncated for Brevity..]
oONBAqqXF0rq5RgVuNvJMTk4
-----END CERTIFICATE-----
```

The commands on the trustpoint in Example 6-20 are as follows:

- **crypto pki trustpoint <*trustpoint-label*>**—Creates a unique entry and trustpoint label for the configuration items being defined.
- **enrollment selfsigned**—Defines that this trustpoint will be enrolled using the self-signed method. Other options include **terminal, url**, **pkc12**, and more. (The **terminal** method is discussed later in this chapter.)
- **fqdn cube.cisco.com**—Defines an optional FQDN to be included with the certificate.
- **subject-name CN=cube.cisco.com**—Defines the distinguished name for the certificate. This can contain any of the valid X.509v3 comma-separated parameters discussed in the "Digital Certificates" section, earlier in this chapter. For the sake of simplicity, this example defines only the common name (CN), which is the FQDN of this CUBE.
- **revocation-check none**—Defines the revocation checks and CRL parameters for the certificate. For simplicity, this example waives revocation checks, but in a real configuration, it is advised to define a CRL and perform checks using the CRL option.
- **rsakeypair CUBE**—Applies the RSA key pair created in Example 6-18 to this trustpoint.

Other optional parameters can be defined on a trustpoint. Items not shown in the example that may be useful for configuration include the following:

- **hash**—Defines the hash algorithm used for the trustpoint. Values include **MD5**, **SHA1**, **SHA256**, **SHA384**, and **SHA512**.
- **subject-alt-name**—Includes an alternative X.509v3 subject name in the certificate.
- **ip-address a.b.c.d**—Includes an IP address in the certificate.

To view the configuration and verify the certificate created during enrollment, you use the **show** command in Example 6-21. Here you can see everything about the certificate created in Example 6-20.

Example 6-21 *Verifying a Self-Signed Certificate Created by CUBE*

```
cube# show crypto pki certificates CUBE-SELF
Router Self-Signed Certificate
  Status: Available
  Certificate Serial Number (hex): 01
  Certificate Usage: General Purpose
  Issuer:
    hostname=cube.cisco.com
    cn=cube.cisco.com
  Subject:
    Name: cube.cisco.com
    hostname=cube.cisco.com
    cn=cube.cisco.com
  Validity Date:
    start date: 17:56:24 EDT Jun 24 2018
    end   date: 19:00:00 est Dec 31 2019
  Associated Trustpoints: CUBE-SELF
```

Self-signed certificates may not offer the level of authentication required for some applications or public devices, and CA-signed certificates may be required. Using the configuration example in Example 6-22, you can generate a CSR that is then provided to a CA. Notice that the command set on the trustpoint is exactly the same as the previous self-signed example. The only difference is that here you are enrolling this certificate using the terminal, and you output a Base64 PEM-formatted CSR. The command **crypto pki enroll** ***<trustpoint-label>*** enrolls the trustpoint based on the enrollment configured. Because the configuration is terminal PEM, IOS knows that you want to create a CSR, and it starts asking the administrator various questions required to build the CSR. When this is complete, the CSR can be displayed in the terminal.

Example 6-22 *Creating a CSR on CUBE*

```
cube# show run | section trustpoint CUBE-CA
crypto pki trustpoint CUBE-CA
 enrollment terminal pem
 fqdn cube.cisco.com
 subject-name CN=cube.cisco.com
 revocation-check none
 rsakeypair CUBE

cube(config)# crypto pki enroll CUBE-CA
% Start certificate enrollment ..

% The subject name in the certificate will include: CN=cube.cisco.com
% The subject name in the certificate will include: cube.cisco.com
% Include the router serial number in the subject name? [yes/no]: no
% Include an IP address in the subject name? [no]: no
Display Certificate Request to terminal? [yes/no]: yes
Certificate Request follows:

-----BEGIN CERTIFICATE REQUEST-----
MIICnjCCAYYCAQAwODEXMBUGA1UEAxMOY3ViZS5jaXNjby5jb20xHTAbBgkqhkiG
[..Truncated for Brevity..]
NKa+1BrK+ekwN5vF1R0XrelY1LGOwErja+nZJbbg1rHDWgUae49ubVoMzgnUDali
-----END CERTIFICATE REQUEST-----

---End - This line not part of the certificate request---
```

An administrator would take the CSR PEM output provided by IOS and give it to a CA. Together the CA and administrator might work to verify the identity, and after some back and forth, a CA signed certificate is returned. Depending on the type of certificate provided, additional conversion may be required. (Refer to Table 6-2 earlier in this chapter for information on certificate file formats.) In this example, say that you have received two certificates in .cer format. The first is the root CA's certificate used to sign the CSR, and the second is the actual identity certificate created from the CSR. Because .cer is a Base64 PEM-formatted certificate file format, you can copy and paste this certificate directly into the IOS terminal. (To see certificates displayed in .cer format, refer to the "Public Key Cryptography" section of this chapter, specifically Example 6-7 and Example 6-8.)

You need to authenticate the trustpoint you used to create the CSR, using the root CA's certificate, as shown in Example 6-23. This is done using the command **crypto pki authenticate *<trustpoint-label>***. IOS then solicits you to enter the Base64 PEM data and press Enter; it then displays the fingerprint or hash of the certificate. You need to compare this hash carefully and verify that it matches the hash provided by the CA. If the hashes match, you can accept the question and should be greeted with a success message. Next you must import the identity certificate into the same trustpoint. This is done using the command **crypto pki import *<trustpoint-label>* certificate**. IOS again solicits for input, and this time you input the Base64 PEM data for the identity certificate provided by the CA. IOS performs a behind-the-scenes check to verify that the imported certificate matches the CA certificate you just used to authenticate the trustpoint, among other checks. If this succeeds, the trustpoint contains the full hierarchy of the CA signed certificate and the identity certificate created by the CSR (refer to Example 6-22).

Example 6-23 *Importing a Signed Certificate Hierarchy Based on the Previous CSR Signed by a Third-Party CA*

```
cube(config)# crypto pki authenticate CUBE-CA

Enter the base 64 encoded CA certificate.
End with a blank line or the word "quit" on a line by itself

-----BEGIN CERTIFICATE-----
MIIEETCCAvmgAwIBAgIUdMN1ikNsecmwGSMou06FfSiC2oEwDQYJKoZIhvcNAQEL
[..Truncated for Brevity]
RJ1CQfhf8/ZLw3hj/gw1ARIgHEeL6s3fT2sdeVCHZJOmgbetOg==
-----END CERTIFICATE-----

Certificate has the following attributes:
       Fingerprint MD5: A9B91A03 DC4F6AAC 29F3AD75 F016F5B9
      Fingerprint SHA1: A72BEAC1 2CA6AF06 96F0BAF2 A4485688 A1EDB02D

% Do you accept this certificate? [yes/no]: yes
Trustpoint CA certificate accepted.
% Certificate successfully imported

cube(config)# crypto pki import CUBE-CA certificate

Enter the base 64 encoded certificate.
End with a blank line or the word "quit" on a line by itself

-----BEGIN CERTIFICATE-----
MIIDRTCCAi0CAgMJMA0GCSqGSIb3DQEBCwUAMIGXMQswCQYDVQQGEwJVUzEXMBUG
[..Truncated for Brevity]
kTVLfwHBrd54/xOpM8F0jwFAnl3b5Pd5SA==
-----END CERTIFICATE-----

% Router Certificate successfully imported
```

Again, to verify specific certificates surrounding a trustpoint, you use the command **show crypto pki certificates** ***<trustpoint-label>***. Example 6-24 shows that this one trustpoint, which is configured in Example 6-23, contains both the root CA certificate and the identity certificate. All the details surrounding these certificates can be gathered from this command output.

Example 6-24 *Verification of the Imported Certificate Hierarchy*

```
cube# show crypto pki certificates CUBE-CA
Certificate
  Status: Available
  Certificate Serial Number (hex): 0309
  Certificate Usage: General Purpose
  Issuer:
    cn=root-ca.cisco.com
    ou=Root CA
    o=Third Party Certificate Authority Ltd
    l=Raleigh
    st=North Carolina
    c=US
  Subject:
    Name: cube.cisco.com
    hostname=cube.cisco.com
    cn=cube.cisco.com
  Validity Date:
    start date: 18:12:03 EDT Jun 24 2018
    end   date: 18:12:03 EDT Jun 24 2019
  Associated Trustpoints: CUBE-CA

CA Certificate
  Status: Available
  Certificate Serial Number (hex): 74C3758A436C79C9B0192328B8EE857D2882DA81
  Certificate Usage: General Purpose
  Issuer:
    cn=root-ca.cisco.com
    ou=Root CA
    o=Third Party Certificate Authority Ltd
    l=Raleigh
    st=North Carolina
    c=US
  Subject:
    cn=root-ca.cisco.com
    ou=Root CA
    o=Third Party Certificate Authority Ltd
    l=Raleigh
    st=North Carolina
    c=US
  Validity Date:
    start date: 18:08:42 EDT Jun 24 2018
    end   date: 18:08:42 EDT Jun 21 2028
  Associated Trustpoints: CUBE-CA
```

Note that Example 6-23 details a certificate hierarchy with no intermediate certificate. Due to the limitations of IOS trustpoints, a single trustpoint can contain only one CA certificate and one identity certificate. If there were one or more intermediate certificates present in the certificate chain, the following actions would need to occur:

Step 1. Create a new, unique trustpoint (for example, **crypto pki trustpoint ROOT-CA**) that contains the root CA's certificate. You simply specify **enrollment terminal pem** and use **crypto pki authenticate *<trustpoint-label>*** to import the Base64 root CA's certificate. The CLI asks the same questions shown in Example 6-23. If the process is successful, this trustpoint now contains the root CA certificate.

Step 2. Use the same **crypto pki authenticate** command on the trustpoint that you used to generate the CSR. Instead of authenticating using the root CA's certificate, though, authenticate using the intermediate CA's certificate. IOS performs a check and finds that the intermediate CA certificate you just authenticated is actually verified and signed by the trustpoint, **ROOT-CA**, created in step 1.

Step 3. Import the identity certificate, using the same **crypto pki import CUBE-CA certificate** command. This step is similar to what is shown in Example 6-23.

If this three-step process is completed successfully, you now have the entire certificate chain—including the root, intermediate, and identity certificates—configured. The first trustpoint, ROOT-CA, created in step 1, contains the root CA certificate, and the second trustpoint, CUBE-CA, contains the intermediate CA and the identity certificates. Example 6-25 shows the entire process.

Example 6-25 *Importing a Root, Intermediate, and Identity Certificate with CUBE*

```
cube# show run | section trustpoint
crypto pki trustpoint ROOT-CA
 enrollment terminal pem
 revocation-check none
!
crypto pki trustpoint CUBE-CA
 enrollment terminal pem
 subject-name CN=cube.cisco.com
 revocation-check none
 rsakeypair CUBE

cube(config)# crypto pki authenticate ROOT-CA


Enter the base 64 encoded CA certificate.
End with a blank line or the word "quit" on a line by itself

-----BEGIN CERTIFICATE-----
[..Truncated for Brevity]
-----END CERTIFICATE-----
```

```
Certificate has the following attributes:
       Fingerprint MD5: C955FC74 7AABC184 D8A75DE7 3C9E7218
      Fingerprint SHA1: 3A99FF61 1E9E6C7B D0E567A9 96D882F5 2279C534

% Do you accept this certificate? [yes/no]: yes
Trustpoint CA certificate accepted.
% Certificate successfully imported

cube(config)# crypto pki authenticate CUBE-CA

Enter the base 64 encoded CA certificate.
End with a blank line or the word "quit" on a line by itself

-----BEGIN CERTIFICATE-----
[..Truncated for Brevity]
-----END CERTIFICATE-----

Certificate has the following attributes:
       Fingerprint MD5: 4F765697 ECCC8052 CFB720D8 FC6C60A8
      Fingerprint SHA1: 3682BF36 CEF3698B A8AA149A 16EC0D1E B068E722
Certificate validated - Signed by existing trustpoint CA certificate.

Trustpoint CA certificate accepted.
% Certificate successfully imported

cube(config)# crypto pki import CUBE-CA certificate

Enter the base 64 encoded certificate.
End with a blank line or the word "quit" on a line by itself

-----BEGIN CERTIFICATE-----
[..Truncated for Brevity]
-----END CERTIFICATE-----

% Router Certificate successfully imported
```

You might need to create a trustpoint and authenticate other third-party CA certificates because IOS may need to validate incoming certificates provided to CUBE during the TLS handshake. IOS performs a verification check on received certificates by looking at all available trustpoints with certificates in an attempt to find an applicable match. If the certificate received during the handshake does not have a trustpoint entry, the certificate cannot be validated, and the handshake fails. If the other party is using self-signed certificates, the self-signed identity certificate needs to have a trustpoint entry configured on CUBE. If the other party is using CA-signed certificates, CUBE only requires that the root CA certificate in the chain of trust have a trustpoint entry. Consult with the vendor of the peer equipment for information about what types of certificates it is using and/or what CA was used to sign the device's certificate so that the applicable CA can be authenticated using an IOS trustpoint. For testing secure connections in this chapter, CUBE peers with Cisco Unified Communications Manager (CUCM) for test calls. As a result, Example 6-26 shows an imported self-signed certificate provided by CUCM. The command **crypto pki authenticate <*trustpoint-label*>** is used to import the certificate provided by CUCM.

Example 6-26 *Importing a CUCM Self-Signed Certificate as a CUBE Trustpoint*

```
cube# show run | section trustpoint CUCM
crypto pki trustpoint CUCM
 enrollment terminal
 revocation-check none

cube(config)# crypto pki authenticate CUCM
[..Truncated for Brevity..]

cube# show crypto pki certificates CUCM
CA Certificate
  Status: Available
  Certificate Serial Number (hex): 4CDC1D11BF500BCFBAE373D76A875D79
  Certificate Usage: General Purpose
  Issuer:
    l=cisco
    st=cisco
    cn=CUCM-12
    ou=cisco
    o=cisco
    c=US
  Subject:
    l=cisco
    st=cisco
    cn=CUCM-12
    ou=cisco
    o=cisco
    c=US
  Validity Date:
    start date: 11:37:17 EDT Mar 20 2018
    end   date: 11:37:16 EDT Mar 19 2023
  Associated Trustpoints: CUCM
  Storage: nvram:cisco#5D79CA.cer
```

Now that you have configured either a self-signed or CA-signed certificate for CUBE, you must associate the trustpoint containing the certificate with the SIP application. This can be done in two different ways, as shown in Example 6-27: An administrator can configure a default trustpoint used for all SIP TCP-TLS communication or can define a trustpoint based on the remote IP address range for the SIP TCP-TLS connection.

Note These **sip-ua** commands only instruct the SIP application what trustpoint and subsequently what certificate to *send* during a SIP TCP-TLS handshake. These commands have no bearing on the lookup and verification of *received* certificates during the SIP TCP-TLS handshake.

Example 6-27 *Setting the Trustpoint for CUBE to Use When Answering TLS Certificate Requests*

```
! Default
sip-ua
 crypto signaling default trustpoint CUBE-CA
!
! Per-device trustpoints
sip-ua
 crypto signaling remote-addr 172.18.110.48 255.255.255.255 trustpoint CUBE
!
```

Once you have associated a trustpoint with the SIP application, all that remains to do is to enable TLS as an egress transport, as shown in Example 6-28. By default, CUBE attempts to accept and establish inbound TCP-TLS connections, without the need for any configuration. The command in Example 6-28 only specifies that CUBE should attempt to initiate TCP-TLS connections when originating SIP messaging. Like the other transport commands, this can be enabled globally or at the dial peer level. In addition, there is no configuration required for CUBE to interwork insecure transports such as TCP/UDP to TCP-TLS, which means CUBE can receive TCP-TLS and send UDP/TCP or vice versa.

Example 6-28 *Enabling TLS on CUBE Globally and for Each Dial Peer*

```
! Global
voice service voip
 sip
  session transport tcp tls
!
! Per Dial-peer
dial-peer voice 11 voip
 destination-pattern 1024
 session protocol sipv2
 session target ipv4:172.18.110.48
 session transport tcp tls
 codec g711ulaw
 no vad
!
```

By default, CUBE does not configure the SIPS URI scheme defined in RFC 3261. Most devices can perform Secure SIP using TCP-TLS without this URI scheme. However, if required, the commands in Example 6-29 can be used to change the egress messaging scheme. Remember to always confirm support for the URI scheme before enabling the SIPS URI scheme.

Example 6-29 *Enabling SIPS URI Scheme on CUBE*

```
voice service voip
 sip
  url sips
```

Now that you have configured signaling plane security for the SIP messaging, the following section explores how to configure media plane security.

SBC Media Plane Security

When dealing with media plane operations, an SBC may operate in a few different modes, including Media Relay, Media Aware, and Media Termination. B2BUA media relays terminate and re-originate media traffic, while media termination B2BUAs do the same and also perform transformations on the media traffic. With media plane security using SRTP, these are the main operations required for an SBC to perform media plane interworking between different call legs. An SBC that operates on the media plane should perform the following actions to facilitate media plane security:

- An SBC should interface with the signaling protocol responsible for SRTP key management. RTP packets are encrypted and decrypted based on SRTP session keys derived from the master key and master salt provided by the key management protocol.
- In working with the key management protocol, which may be different for each call leg, the SBC may need to perform media plane interworking even when both call legs negotiate SRTP. This may be the case when each call leg has negotiated different SRTP keying information, using the key management protocol. Thus an SBC may be required to decrypt an SRTP packet received on one call leg by using the keying information from that call leg and re-encrypting the packet using the keying information negotiated on the peer call leg.
- In the same vein, an SBC may be required to interwork RTP and SRTP, depending on the media types negotiated by the signaling plane and key management protocols.

There is no standard for exactly how an SBC should go about achieving these three points, and thus it is recommended to consult the applicable vendor documentation for SRTP and key management protocols supported and capabilities surrounding SRTP–SRTP interworking and SRTP–RTP interworking at the media plane. As an SBC, CUBE can perform all these items with only a few lines of CLI programming. The majority of the hard work is done behind the scenes by the CUBE application.

Tip CUBE only supports SDES as a key management protocol for SRTP. Furthermore, SDES is automatically enabled when SRTP is enabled.

To enable SRTP on CUBE for all IOS versions and IOS XE versions prior to 16.5.1, you use the commands shown in Example 6-30. Just as with most other commands, these commands can be applied globally or per dial peer. This configuration example enables SRTP while also allowing transparent pass-through of unsupported SRTP crypto parameters received using SDP. Finally, you define the SRTP authentication algorithms to be used. The only supported algorithms in these versions are SHA1-80 and SHA1-32.

Example 6-30 *Enabling SRTP on CUBE*

```
! Global
voice service voip
 srtp
 srtp pass-thru
 sip
  srtp-auth sha1-80 sha1-32
!
! Dial-Peer
dial-peer voice 1 voip
 srtp
 srtp pass-thru
 voice-class sip srtp-auth sha1-80 sha1-32
!
```

If CUBE is running IOS XE version 16.5.1 or later, you use the slightly different commands shown in Example 6-31. This configuration can be used to define the SRTP cipher suites supported by CUBE with a **voice class srtp-crypto** command. Note that this step is optional, and all the cipher suites listed are supported by default. This configuration can be used to limit CUBE's SRTP negotiation to specific cipher suites and avoid negotiating the older, legacy, AES/SHA-1 variants. SRTP is then enabled globally or per dial peer, and the crypto suite, if defined, is associated. Finally, you allow for unsupported cipher suites received in SDP to be transparently passed by CUBE.

Example 6-31 *Enabling SRTP on CUBE*

```
! Define SRTP Crypto Suites
voice class srtp-crypto 1
 crypto 1 AEAD_AES_256_GCM
 crypto 2 AEAD_AES_128_GCM
 crypto 3 AES_CM_128_HMAC_SHA1_80
 crypto 4 AES_CM_128_HMAC_SHA1_32
!
! Global
```

```
voice service voip
 srtp
 srtp pass-thru
 sip
  srtp-crypto 1
!
! Dial-peer
dial-peer voice 1 voip
 srtp
 srtp pass-thru
 voice-class sip srtp-crypto 1
!
```

As stated earlier, CUBE can work with the SIP application and key management protocol SDES to negotiate SRTP keying material on both legs of the call when SRTP is enabled. CUBE can also interwork SRTP-to-SRTP media sessions with different keying material without the need for additional configuration. However, if you want to interwork RTP and SRTP, some configuration may be required, depending on the hardware being used for CUBE. Table 6-3 shows which platforms support SRTP–RTP interworking natively.

Table 6-3 *A Comparison of Cisco Voice Gateway Platforms and Their Respective SRTP–RTP Interworking Capabilities*

Platform	Model	OS	Native Support for SRTP–RTP Interworking?
Cisco Integrated Services Router Generation 2 (ISR G2)*	Cisco 2900 Series Cisco 3900 Series	IOS	No
Cisco 4000 Series Integrated Services Router (ISR G3)	Cisco 4321 Cisco 4331 Cisco 4351 Cisco 4431 Cisco 4451	IOS XE	Yes
Cisco Aggregated Services Router (ASR)	ASR 1001-X ASR 1002-X ASR 1004 with RP2 ASR 1006 with RP2	IOS XE	Yes
Cisco Cloud Services Router (CSR)	CSR 1000V series	IOS XE	Yes

* The ISR G2 was announced as end-of-life in 2016, with the last day of software support in 2020 and last day of hardware support in 2022.

For the platforms that support SRTP–RTP interworking natively, no configuration is required; however, for the platforms that do not support native interworking, the configurations in Example 6-32 can be used to perform the interworking by using a hardware PVDM/DSP. The hardware DSP must first be configured with DSP farm capabilities. Then a security transcoding DSP farm is defined. You can define the codecs and maximum number of sessions, and then the DSP farm is associated to the CUBE application and enabled using the **no shutdown** command. CUBE can now use this DSP farm and the underlying hardware to support SRTP–RTP interworking.

Example 6-32 *Sample Configuration for IOS LTI–Based SRTP–RTP Interworking Using a Secure Transcoder*

```
!
voice-card 0
 dspfarm
 dsp services dspfarm
!
dspfarm profile 1 transcode security
 codec g729abr8
 codec g729ar8
 codec g711alaw
 codec g711ulaw
 maximum sessions 10
 associate application CUBE
 no shutdown
!
```

Best-Effort SRTP and SRTP Fallback

In a perfect world, once SRTP is configured correctly, it works flawlessly with any peer device you need to communicate with. However, with the number of variables surrounding key management protocols and external variables—such as the capability sets of the various endpoints or intermediary devices in a session—this may not always hold true. Failures to negotiate SRTP using the different key management protocols can be grouped into two different categories:

- **All-or-nothing**—If SRTP negotiation fails, the session fails.
- **Best-effort SRTP**—Key management protocols attempt to negotiate SRTP, but in the event that this fails, the session can fall back to regular, insecure RTP. This is also called *SRTP fallback*.

Depending on company policy and/or external regulations, it may be required to outright fail a call if SRTP is not negotiated for the media. The negotiation of SRTP in this scenario is considered all-or-nothing. The majority of key management protocols using the signaling plane support this method. With SDES, a device may want SRTP through the conveyance of RTP/SAVP in the SDP. If an upstream device does not support SRTP, then a 488 Not Acceptable Media response may result, and the session fails.

However, sometimes it may be required for calls to connect even if SRTP negotiation fails or an upstream device does not support SRTP. This is known as *best-effort SRTP*, or *SRTP fallback*. Best-effort SRTP is achieved by using key management protocols such as ZRTP, which first set up as RTP and then attempt to "switch over" to SRTP by using the ZRTP handshake. The ZRTP handshake may fail for a number of reasons, but the session remains active and does not fail. Similarly, as discussed earlier in this chapter, the potential configuration parameters defined using RFC 5939 can be used to advertise support for RTP (RTP/AVP), SRTP (RTP/SAVP), and DTLS-SRTP (UDP/TLS/RTP/SAVP) in an offer and include their preferred choice for media plane operations. The user agent on the other side can then choose from the potential configurations provided and form a response. This means the session could set up as secure or insecure, based on the offer/answer, and circumvent failures where security is considered best effort and not mandatory. The potential configuration parameters need not apply only to DTLS-SRTP, the topics of RFC 5939 and 6871, but could be extended for use with SDES which also negotiates SRTP keying material using the SDP.

Always confirm with the SBC vendor and other third-party vendors exactly which method of SRTP negotiation is supported. In addition, ensure that the SBC and devices you plan to deploy conform to the security standards required for your organization when it comes to SRTP and RTP negotiation.

As discussed earlier in this chapter, CUBE supports SRTP on the media plane and SDES as the key management protocol on the signaling plane. SDES does not explicitly define any methods of achieving best-effort SRTP, and CUBE does not support RFC 5939 or 6871 due to a number of factors, such as vendor adoption rate. Thus Cisco does not support best-effort SRTP with third-party devices. However, CUBE does support a Cisco proprietary form of best-effort SRTP called SRTP fallback, which can be used between compatible Cisco devices such as CUCM devices. Example 6-33 shows the commands required to enable SRTP fallback with CUCM. Like the other SRTP commands, these commands can be configured globally or per dial peer.

Example 6-33 *Sample Configuration for SRTP Fallback on CUBE*

```
! Global
voice service voip
 srtp fallback
 sip
  srtp negotiate cisco
!
! Dial-peer
dial-peer voice 11 voip
 destination-pattern 1024
 session protocol sipv2
 session target ipv4:172.18.110.48
 voice-class sip srtp negotiate cisco
 srtp fallback
 codec g711ulaw
 no vad
```

Both of the commands detailed in Example 6-33 are required for CUBE to fall back. Operationally, with these commands enabled, CUBE sends the proprietary supported header extension **X-cisco-srtp-fallback**. The SDP contains the normal RTP/SAVP and SDES crypto attributes, indicating that CUBE would like to negotiate SRTP. When this is configured, the response to the offer may contain RTP/AVP, indicating that the session will use regular, insecure RTP rather than SRTP, as per the original offer.

Hardening SBC Security

The world of information security is ever-changing and rarely remains stationary. New security protocols and best practices are constantly being developed, and older protocols undergo continuous testing and scrutiny in attempts to verify if there are undesired vulnerabilities in the protocols' operation or logic. If a security testing group finds a vulnerability, then the vulnerability is published, and the security experts patch the vulnerability. If the patch requires a significant deviation from the original scope or functionality of the protocol, a new protocol may be created, and the old protocol is then considered legacy. Examples of this can be observed with protocols like SHA-1, TLS 1.0, all versions of SSL, and DES. These protocols where great when they were first introduced, but vulnerabilities were discovered as time progressed and additional probing occurred. As a result, each of these protocols has been replaced by a new stronger and more secure standard—SHA-1 with SHA-2/SHA-3, TLS 1.0 with TLS 1.2/1.3, and DES with AES. The replaced protocols in this case are considered legacy security protocols.

Using legacy security protocols puts you or your system at a major risk and should be avoided at all costs. That being said, many security devices have legacy protocols enabled by default, in an attempt to provide backward capability with devices that might not have implemented the latest security protocols. It is a good idea to audit the devices in your network and confirm the lowest common security protocols needed for interoperability and disable anything that is not required. This practice of disabling legacy protocols, commonly referred to as *hardening*, reduces the attack surface by removing potential attack vectors.

Chapter 13 covers many SBC hardening best practices, but this chapter covers a few of the key hardening concepts that pertain to the signaling and media planes.

Because TLS 1.0 and TLS 1.1 are considered legacy, security policy may require disabling these protocols and setting TLS 1.2 as a minimum. Doing so will thwart downgrade attacks during session establishment and offer better overall session security. The commands shown in Example 6-34 can be used to set a static TLS version for CUBE SIP TLS sessions. Note that when you define a static value, CUBE refuses to negotiate any TLS version other than the one specified. Always confirm that peer devices support a proposed TLS version before configuring a static value in order to avoid undesired connection terminations. If no configuration is defined, CUBE accepts and receives the different TLS versions and interworks them independently per call leg.

Example 6-34 *The Command to Set the Minimum TLS Version on CUBE*

```
sip-ua
 transport tcp tls v1.2
```

As discussed earlier in this chapter, in the section "Secure Sockets Layer (SSL) and Transport Layer Security (TLS)," numerous TLS cipher suites are registered with the IANA. You might want to control what suites are offered by CUBE during the TLS handshake in order to avoid negotiating legacy protocols and provide better security for the session. You can use the information in Table 6-4 to understand which cipher suites are supported on CUBE. The strict ciphers are sent only when the value **strict-cipher** is post-fixed to the **sip-ua crypto signaling** command (refer to Example 6-27). The same goes for ECDSA ciphers with the command post-fix **ecdsa-cipher**.

Table 6-4 *TLS Cipher Suites and Their Respective* **sip-ua crypto** *Commands*

Type	Command Syntax	TLS 1.2 Cipher Suite
Default ciphers	**crypto signaling default trustpoint** *<trustpoint-label>*	TLS_RSA_WITH_RC4_128_MD5 TLS_RSA_WITH_AES_128_CBC_SHA TLS_DHE_RSA_WITH_AES_128_CBC_SHA1 TLS_ECDHE_RSA_WITH_AES_128_GCM_SHA256 TLS_ECDHE_ECDSA_WITH_AES_128_GCM_SHA256 TLS_ECDHE_RSA_WITH_AES_256_GCM_SHA384 TLS_ECDHE_ECDSA_WITH_AES_256_GCM_SHA384
Strict ciphers	**crypto signaling default trustpoint** *<trustpoint-label>* **strict-cipher**	TLS_RSA_WITH_AES_128_CBC_SHA TLS_DHE_RSA_WITH_AES_128_CBC_SHA1 TLS_ECDHE_RSA_WITH_AES_128_GCM_SHA256 TLS_ECDHE_RSA_WITH_AES_256_GCM_SHA384
ECDSA ciphers	**crypto signaling default trustpoint** *<trustpoint-label>* **ecdsa-cipher**	TLS_ECDHE_ECDSA_WITH_AES_128_GCM_SHA256 TLS_ECDHE_ECDSA_WITH_AES_256_GCM_SHA384

The same concept for TLS cipher suites applies to SRTP, which also uses cipher suites. You can use the values in Table 6-5 to understand which SRTP cipher suites are supported on CUBE and in what release they were added. Always confirm the cipher suites supported between devices to avoid undesired failures when no compatible cipher suites are available and SRTP pass-through is not configured. (The commands shown in Example 6-30 and Example 6-31 can be used to control which cipher suites are offered during SRTP session establishment.)

Table 6-5 *SRTP Cipher Suite Support Version Mapping*

IOS Version	Cipher Suite
15.4(1)T/S and older	AES_CM_128_HMAC_SHA1_32
15.4(1)T/S	AES_CM_128_HMAC_SHA1_80
15.6(1)T/S (SRTP pass-through)	AEAD_AES_128_GCM AEAD_AES_256_GCM
16.5.1 (native IOS support)	AEAD_AES_128_GCM AEAD_AES_256_GCM

IOS XE offer a single command, **cc-mode**, that can be enabled on CUBE to enforce the latest security best practices defined by the Federal Information Processing Standards (FIPS) and Common Criterial (CC). At the time of this writing, the **cc-mode** command, when enabled, enforces the ISO-IEC 15408 and FIPS 140-2 standards. This includes the following items for TLS, SRTP, and NTP:

TLS requirements:

- Older versions of TLS/SSL are disabled, and TLS 1.1 is the minimum negotiable version.
- The minimum size for RSA keys is set to 2048, with 3072 suggested.
- The minimum length for Diffie-Hellman keys is set to 256.
- SHA-256 or higher must be used, and SHA-384 is recommended.
- Elliptic-curve restrictions of **NID_X9_62_prime256v1**, **NID_secp384r1**, and **NID_secp521r1** are set.
- TLS ClientHello message is restricted to curves of **secp256r1**, **secp384r1**, and **secp521r1**.
- The CA flag in self-signed or subordinate certificates must be **TRUE** when attempting to authenticate with an IOS trustpoint.
- Peer certificates must contain the Extended Key Usage value **clientAuth**.
- Alternate subject name verification is enabled by default.
- CUBE sends the distinguished name (DN) of the certificate it expects to receive from a peer in the TLS certificate request. This is configured using the command in Example 6-35, which pairs local and peer IOS trustpoints with a remote IP address or subnet range.

Example 6-35 *Configuration for Distinguished Name Mapping with TLS Certificate Requests*

```
crypto pki trustpoint CUBE
!
crypto pki trustpoint CUCM
!
sip-ua
 crypto signaling remote-addr 10.10.10.10 255.255.255.255 trustpoint CUBE client-vtp CUCM
```

SRTP requirements:

- SRTP pass-through and fallback are disallowed.
- SDP pass-through is disallowed.
- **AES_CM_128_HMAC_SHA1_80** is the only configurable SRTP cipher suite.
- SRTP keys carried by SDES are no longer printed to the logging terminal, debugs, or files.

NTP requirements:

- Only NTP versions 3 and 4 are configurable.
- NTP broadcast cannot be configured.
- NTP multicast cannot be configured.

The **cc-mode** command offers significant security hardening, all in one convenient place. However, it is recommended to confirm that all other devices CUBE will be required to peer with also support the items just listed before enabling the command. Doing so without proper confirmation could lead to undesired outages or other problems.

Note The **cc-mode** command is not supported on all IOS XE platforms.

IOS XE 16.6 and later versions offer default encryption of the storage and persistent key material stored in the router's non-volatile random-access memory (NVRAM). This is done automatically on upgrade and enabled using the command **service private-config-encryption**, which can be viewed in **show run all** output. When a CUBE is running IOS XE 16.6 or higher, if an administrator wants to downgrade the IOS XE version, the command should be removed before the downgrade, using **no service private-config-encryption**, and the configuration should be saved. Doing this decrypts the encrypted items stored in NVRAM. If this step is not performed, older versions of IOS XE will not be able to decrypt the encrypted files. This ultimately result in IOS XE deleting the encrypted items, which may contain RSA key pairs used for SSH, TLS, and other security procedures.

Many companies offer a method to subscribe to or manually check for security vulnerability notifications. These notifications often include details about the vulnerability and what software version offers a fix for the specific vulnerability. Staying up to date with the latest software means you have the latest security patches, as well as the latest security protocols. Routine software upgrades and security patches are part of the hardening process. To check for vulnerabilities with IOS and IOS XE, see https://tools.cisco.com/security/center/softwarechecker.x.

Troubleshooting Signaling and Media Security

Troubleshooting secure signaling and media issues may seem like a daunting task, but if you systematically break down the process into bite-size pieces, it becomes much more manageable. First, remember that security is an additional layer on top of the operations of insecure session establishment at the media and signaling planes between two user agents. Before applying security to the signaling plane or the media plane, you need to first confirm that the underlying foundation used for session and media establishment is sound. If session establishment does not work without security, this must be addressed before you layer on additional variables.

If you are enabling security on an insecure CUBE or troubleshooting a configuration that was previously working and security is already applied, remember to break the security operations into well-defined steps for troubleshooting. Take, for example, signaling plane security through protocols such as TCP-TLS. At a high level, the following must occur:

Step 1. Layer 3 network paths must be available in both directions to facilitate the handshake and transmission of messages between both devices on the IP network. ICMP **ping** and **traceroute** commands can be leveraged to check the Layer 3 path on the network. **show** commands such as **show ip route** and **show ip cef a.b.c.d** can be used to confirm that routing table entries and the local configuration are correct.

Step 2. A three-way TCP handshake must complete between the two user agents. **debug** commands such as **debug ip tcp transaction** or packet captures can show exactly what is negotiated and whether there are problems with a TCP handshake. **show** commands such as **show tcp brief** can be examined to check the state of TCP connections. TCP socket closures, retransmissions, and even other network devices, such as firewalls, may impede the TCP three-way handshake.

Step 3. A multistep TLS handshake must complete before it is possible to negotiate the keys required to transmit encrypted application data. This step includes endpoint authentication using digital certificates. You can use the **debug** commands listed in Table 6-6 to examine the TLS handshake for potential failures. Packet captures can provide the same information, and a packet capture can also be used to examine the certificates used during the TLS handshake. You can use the **show** commands listed in Table 6-6 to examine

TLS connections, failure reasons, certificate information, and trustpoint confirmation items. TLS handshakes often fail due to incompatible versions, cipher suites, and authentication failures due to problems with the certificate exchange.

Step 4. The SIP applications send and receive SIP messages over the encrypted application channels provided by TLS. You can use normal CUBE **debug** commands, such as **debug ccsip messages** and **debug voip ccapi inout**, to check for failures. If you don't observe any SIP messages exchanged, chances are one of the steps above is encountering a failure of some kind. You can use **show** commands such as **show call active voice compact**, **show call active voice brief**, and **show sip-ua calls** to gather information about session establishment. If the failure is occurring at this step, it may not be related to security at all!

Table 6-6 *CLI Commands That Can Be Used for Troubleshooting Security on CUBE*

Purpose	debug Commands	show Commands
IP routing	N/A	**show ip cef a.b.c.d** **show ip route**
TCP connections	**debug ip tcp transactions** **debug ip tcp packet**	**show tcp brief**
TLS connections	**debug crypto pki messages** **debug crypto pki transactions** **debug crypto pki validation** **debug crypto pki api** **debug crypto pki callback** **debug ssl openssl error** **debug ssl openssl msg** **debug ssl openssl states** **debug ssl openssl ext**	**show crypto pki trustpoints** **show crypto pki certificates** **show crypto key mypubkey rsa** **show sip-ua connections tcp tls detail**
SIP session establishment	**debug ccsip error** **debug ccsip messages** **debug ccsip transport** **debug voip ccapi inout**	**show sip-ua calls** **show call active voice compact** **show call active voice brief** **show dial-peer voice summary**

When it comes to SRTP, remember that it is best practice to also configure SIP TCP-TLS; otherwise, the SDES crypto keys are exchanged publicly. With TCP-TLS, this means the preceding steps also need to occur successfully before SRTP media is established. CUBE uses SDES as the key management protocol, which is carried in the SDP message body in encrypted SIP packets. If the problem is only with media negotiation, you should focus on the offer/answer that is needed to establish the required SRTP keying material. You can use the **debug** and **show** commands listed in Table 6-6 to find out if there is a problem with the offer/answer. SRTP negotiation issues are usually attributed to incompatible cipher suites or other incompatible parameters in the crypto media attribute SDP value.

With any troubleshooting or debugging effort, understanding how each step successfully operates and what should occur within each step greatly reduces the time it takes to find and resolve a problem. Refer to the examples and figures for a TLS handshake in the section "Secure Sockets Layer (SSL) and Transport Layer Security (TLS)," earlier in this chapter. You can use information from that section and the upcoming debug snippets, which show successful secure session establishment between CUBE and CUCM, using SIP TCP-TLS. Compare and contrast these outputs with the non-working scenario in order to find the point of deviation. The debugs gathered from this session are all from Table 6-6, and the CUBE configuration used is exactly the same as the configuration covered earlier in this chapter, in the "SBC Signaling and Media Security" section.

Example 6-36 shows a SIP application stating that it is required to perform TLS over TCP with the CUCM IP address 172.18.110.48 on port 5061. The transport layer generates a local random TCP port, sends a SYN, and transitions to SYNSENT. Upon reception of the SYN ACK, the ACK is sent, and the connection is established (**ESTAB**).

Example 6-36 *A Sample TCP Handshake from Debugs*

```
Jul  1 20:56:33.572: //-1/xxxxxxxxxxxx/SIP/Transport/sipCreateConnInstance: Cre-
  ated new initiated conn=0x7FD3DF5DD390, connid=-1, addr=172.18.110.48, port=5061,
  local_addr=, transport=TLS Over TCP, vrfid = 0
Jul  1 20:56:33.573: TCP: Random local port generated 15089, network 1
Jul  1 20:56:33.573: TCP: sending SYN, seq 3852058976, ack 0
Jul  1 20:56:33.573: TCP0: state was CLOSED -> SYNSENT [15089 -> 172.18.110.48(5061)]
Jul  1 20:56:33.577: TCP0: state was SYNSENT -> ESTAB [15089 -> 172.18.110.48(5061)]
```

Example 6-37 shows the SIP application initiating the TLS handshake. It begins by selecting the IOS trustpoint CUBE-CA that was defined using **sip-ua**. The certificate in the trustpoint is validated, and the handshake starts. CUBE assumes the role of TLS client and sends the ClientHello message. CUCM responds with a ServerHello message and sends a certificate. CUBE parses the certificate and begins the lookup process. CUBE finds a suitable trustpoint to validate the CUCM certificate, and thus the process succeeds. After CUBE has validated CUCM's certificate, CUCM sends ServerKeyExchange, CertificateRequest, and ServerHelloDone messages. CUBE sends a certificate and ClientKeyExchange message along with a ChangeCipherSpec message and finally a Finished message. CUCM works to validate the certificate provided by CUBE (though this is not shown in Example 6-37). This is a CA-signed certificate, so CUCM must trust the root CA that signed the certificate. This succeeds, and CUCM sends

ChangeCipherSpec and Finished messages. At this point, the TLS handshake between CUBE and CUCM has completed successfully.

Example 6-37 *A Sample TLS Handshake Shown by Debugs*

```
Jul  1 20:56:33.578: //-1/xxxxxxxxxxxx/SIP/Transport/sip_tls_initiate_handshake:
Jul  1 20:56:33.578: CRYPTO_PKI: (A088F) Session started - identity selected (CUBE-CA)
Jul  1 20:56:33.578: CRYPTO_PKI(Cert Lookup) issuer="cn=root-ca.cisco.com,ou=Root
  CA,o=Third Party Certificate Authority, Ltd,l=Raleigh,st=North Carolina,c=US"
  serial number= 03 09

Jul  1 20:56:33.579: Handshake start: before/connect initialization
Jul  1 20:56:33.580: >>> TLS 1.2 Handshake [length 0072], ClientHello

Jul  1 20:56:33.973: <<< TLS 1.2 Handshake [length 003E], ServerHello
Jul  1 20:56:33.974: <<< TLS 1.2 Handshake [length 03B7], Certificate
Jul  1 20:56:33.991: CRYPTO_PKI: (A0890) Adding peer certificate
Jul  1 20:56:33.991: CRYPTO_PKI: Added x509 peer certificate - (941) bytes
Jul  1 20:56:33.991: CRYPTO_PKI(Cert Lookup) issuer="l=cisco,st=cisco,cn=CUCM-12,
  ou=cisco,o=cisco,c=US" serial number= 4C DC 1D 11 BF 50 0B CF BA E3 73 D7 6A 87 5D 79
Jul  1 20:56:33.992: CRYPTO_PKI: (A0890)chain cert was anchored to trustpoint CUCM,
  and chain validation result was: CRYPTO_VALID_CERT
Jul  1 20:56:33.992: CRYPTO_PKI: (A0890) Validation TP is CUCM
Jul  1 20:56:33.992: <<< TLS 1.2 Handshake [length 014D], ServerKeyExchange
Jul  1 20:56:34.304: <<< TLS 1.2 Handshake [length 002A], CertificateRequest
Jul  1 20:56:34.305: <<< TLS 1.2 Handshake [length 0004], ServerHelloDone

Jul  1 20:56:34.305: >>> TLS 1.2 Handshake [length 0353], Certificate
Jul  1 20:56:34.318: >>> TLS 1.2 Handshake [length 0046], ClientKeyExchange
Jul  1 20:56:34.853: >>> TLS 1.2 Handshake [length 0108], CertificateVerify
Jul  1 20:56:34.854: >>> TLS 1.2 ChangeCipherSpec [length 0001]
Jul  1 20:56:34.855: >>> TLS 1.2 Handshake [length 0010], Finished

Jul  1 20:56:35.104: <<< TLS 1.2 ChangeCipherSpec [length 0001]
Jul  1 20:56:35.104: <<< TLS 1.2 Handshake [length 0010], Finished

Jul  1 20:56:35.104: Handshake done: SSL negotiation finished successfully
```

Now that the TCP and TLS handshakes have completed, SIP application data can be sent. Example 6-38 shows that CUBE creates a message with the SDP body containing SDES crypto parameters indicating that CUBE would like to use SRTP for this call. Notice the supported header containing **X-cisco-srtp-fallback**. This lets CUCM know that if the endpoint does not support SRTP, the session can always fall back to regular, insecure RTP. The CUCM endpoint does support SRTP, and thus the response contains a chosen crypto suite, and the offer/answer is complete. This call is connected with G.711ulaw SRTP.

Example 6-38 *A Sample Offer/Answer SDES Exchange Observed in Debugs*

```
Jul  1 20:56:35.105: //49859/12267281A50F/SIP/Msg/ccsipDisplayMsg:
Sent:
INVITE sip:1024@172.18.110.48:5061 SIP/2.0
Via: SIP/2.0/TLS 172.18.110.58:5061;branch=z9hG4bK222422
From: <sip:1234@172.18.110.58>;tag=33AF819A-15F3
To: <sip:1024@172.18.110.48>
Call-ID: 12275CBD-7CA811E8-A515EAC4-328F74C4@172.18.110.58
Supported: 100rel,timer,resource-priority,replaces,sdp-anat,X-cisco-srtp-fallback
User-Agent: Cisco-SIPGateway/IOS-16.8.1
Allow: INVITE, OPTIONS, BYE, CANCEL, ACK, PRACK, UPDATE, REFER, SUBSCRIBE, NOTIFY,
  INFO, REGISTER
CSeq: 101 INVITE
Contact: <sip:1234@172.18.110.58:5061;transport=tls>
Allow-Events: telephone-event
Max-Forwards: 69
Session-ID: acdf32654fc05d308c589333f35a4116;remote=00000000000000000000000000000000
Content-Type: application/sdp
Content-Disposition: session;handling=required
Content-Length: 535

v=0
o=CiscoSystemsSIP-GW-UserAgent 545 7449 IN IP4 172.18.110.58
s=SIP Call
c=IN IP4 172.18.110.58
t=0 0
m=audio 8066 RTP/SAVP 0
c=IN IP4 172.18.110.58
a=crypto:1 AEAD_AES_256_GCM inline:2L12cD4LnbNBCZE3ShiiM4TzA8TzrZgSv9xiUTk52w19jO3L
  5J5OYOfT71U=
a=crypto:2 AEAD_AES_128_GCM inline:AjB7+GyzhUOYJghROekrwTodvF/TEEUG+hRdEw==
a=crypto:3 AES_CM_128_HMAC_SHA1_80 inline:HFuTuoXD+FuukA3VnVbNcW9/NRTTrCqNJ92h2awy
a=crypto:4 AES_CM_128_HMAC_SHA1_32 inline:k4P3wWhEm4+h/J5bZFUfyNpLrWO1Q70eRI/eOKxL
a=rtpmap:0 PCMU/8000
a=ptime:20

Jul  1 20:56:36.469: //49859/12267281A50F/SIP/Msg/ccsipDisplayMsg:
Received:
SIP/2.0 200 OK
Via: SIP/2.0/TLS 172.18.110.58:5061;branch=z9hG4bK222422
From: <sip:1234@172.18.110.58>;tag=33AF819A-15F3
To: <sip:1024@172.18.110.48>;tag=18759~1992ce86-77ac-43a7-91b7-90778966a9f5-30026826
Call-ID: 12275CBD-7CA811E8-A515EAC4-328F74C4@172.18.110.58
CSeq: 101 INVITE
```

```
Allow: INVITE, OPTIONS, INFO, BYE, CANCEL, ACK, PRACK, UPDATE, REFER, SUBSCRIBE,
  NOTIFY
Server: Cisco-CUCM12.0
Supported: X-cisco-srtp-fallback
Supported: Geolocation
Session-ID: 7885062900105000a0000c75bd110ca4;remote=acdf32654fc05d308c589333f35a4116
Contact: <sip:1024@172.18.110.48:5061;transport=tls>;+u.sip!devicename.ccm.cisco.
  com="SEP0C75BD110CA4"
Content-Type: application/sdp
Content-Length: 323

v=0
o=CiscoSystemsCCM-SIP 18759 1 IN IP4 172.18.110.48
s=SIP Call
c=IN IP4 14.50.214.75
b=TIAS:64000
b=AS:64
t=0 0
m=audio 27856 RTP/SAVP 0 101
a=crypto:1 AEAD_AES_256_GCM inline:NlrB4ZQUKNleBwIt2CLkHYNAe6c/UJDwlvJ3BzVYbuNgbGyb
  PN3/9kbaFOo=
a=rtpmap:0 PCMU/8000
a=rtpmap:101 telephone-event/8000
a=fmtp:101 0-15
```

By using commands like **show call active voice brief** and **show voip rtp connections** during an active call, you can quickly see the state of the session at the signaling and media planes. Example 6-39 shows a call using dial peer 1 for inbound and dial peer 11 for outbound. SRTP is enabled on the egress call leg, and CUBE is performing SRTP-to-RTP interworking. This is an IOS XE 4451-X, and thus this is done natively. These outputs also provide valuable information for determining the media IP address and ports negotiated during session establishment.

Example 6-39 *Verification of an Active Secure Session on CUBE*

```
cube# show call active voice brief
36F7 : 49858 867053120ms.1 (16:56:33.575 EDT Sun Jul 1 2018) +2900 pid:1 Answer 1234
  active
 dur 00:00:11 tx:532/106400 rx:0/0 dscp:0 media:0 audio tos:0xB8 video tos:0x0
 IP 172.18.110.65:6000 SRTP: off rtt:0ms pl:0/0ms lost:0/0/0 delay:0/0/0ms g711ulaw
  TextRelay: off Transcoded: No ICE: Off
 media inactive detected:n media contrl rcvd:n/a timestamp:n/a
 long duration call detected:n long duration call duration:n/a timestamp:n/a
 LostPacketRate:0.00 OutOfOrderRate:0.00
```

```
 LocalUUID:acdf32654fc05d308c589333f35a4116
 RemoteUUID:7885062900105000a0000c75bd110ca4
 VRF: NA

36F7 : 49859 867053120ms.2 (16:56:33.575 EDT Sun Jul 1 2018) +2900 pid:11 Originate
  1024 active
 dur 00:00:11 tx:0/0 rx:532/114912 dscp:0 media:0 audio tos:0xB8 video tos:0x0
 IP 14.50.214.75:27856 SRTP: on rtt:0ms pl:0/0ms lost:0/0/0 delay:0/0/0ms g711ulaw
  TextRelay: off Transcoded: No ICE: Off
 media inactive detected:n media contrl rcvd:n/a timestamp:n/a
 long duration call detected:n long duration call duration:n/a timestamp:n/a
 LostPacketRate:0.00 OutOfOrderRate:0.00
 LocalUUID:7885062900105000a0000c75bd110ca4
 RemoteUUID:acdf32654fc05d308c589333f35a4116
 VRF: NA

cube# show voip rtp connections
VoIP RTP active connections :
No. CallId     dstCallId  LocalRTP RmtRTP   LocalIP          RemoteIP        MPSS  VRF
1     49858      49859      8064     6000     172.18.110.58  172.18.110.65 NO    NA
2     49859      49858      8066     27856    172.18.110.58  14.50.214.75  NO    NA
Found 2 active RTP connections
```

As an alternative to using the command in Example 6-38, you can use the command **show sip-ua calls** or, more specifically, **show sip-ua called-number <*number*>** to view similar information about the session. The output in Example 6-40 includes many valuable items that can be used when troubleshooting issues.

Example 6-40 *Further Verification of the Same Active Secure Session on CUBE*

```
cube# show sip-ua calls called-number 1024
Total SIP call legs:5, User Agent Client:1, User Agent Server:4
SIP UAC CALL INFO
Call 1
SIP Call ID                : 12275CBD-7CA811E8-A515EAC4-328F74C4@172.18.110.58
   State of the call       : STATE_ACTIVE (7)
   Substate of the call    : SUBSTATE_NONE (0)
   Calling Number          : 1234
   Called Number           : 1024
   Called URI              : sip:1024@172.18.110.48:5061
   Bit Flags               : 0xC04018 0x90000100 0x80
   CC Call ID              : 49859
   Local UUID              : 7885062900105000a0000c75bd110ca4
```

```
Remote UUID              : acdf32654fc05d308c589333f35a4116
Source IP Address (Sig ): 172.18.110.58
Destn SIP Req Addr:Port : [172.18.110.48]:5061
Destn SIP Resp Addr:Port: [172.18.110.48]:5061
Destination Name         : 172.18.110.48
Number of Media Streams : 1
Number of Active Streams: 1
RTP Fork Object          : 0x0
Media Mode               : flow-through
Media Stream 1
  State of the stream        : STREAM_ACTIVE
  Stream Call ID             : 49859
  Stream Type                : voice-only (0)
  Stream Media Addr Type     : 1
  Negotiated Codec           : g711ulaw (160 bytes)
  Codec Payload Type         : 0
  Negotiated Dtmf-relay      : inband-voice
  Dtmf-relay Payload Type    : 0
  QoS ID                     : -1
  Local QoS Strength         : BestEffort
  Negotiated QoS Strength    : BestEffort
  Negotiated QoS Direction : None
  Local QoS Status           : None
  Media Source IP Addr:Port: [172.18.110.58]:8066
  Media Dest IP Addr:Port    : [14.50.214.75]:27856
  Local Crypto Suite         :  AEAD_AES_256_GCM (
                                AEAD_AES_256_GCM
                                AEAD_AES_128_GCM
                                AES_CM_128_HMAC_SHA1_80
                                AES_CM_128_HMAC_SHA1_32 )
  Remote Crypto Suite        :  AEAD_AES_256_GCM
```

You can use the command **show sip-ua connections tcp tls brief** or **show sip-ua connections tcp tls detail** to view statistics about the active and problematic SIP TCP TLS connections. In the output in Example 6-41, you can see one active TLS connection with the CUCM server. If there were any failures with the client/server handshakes or remote closures, you would see values here. Running this command before and after a problematic test call might yield valuable information about the step at which the problem is occurring.

Example 6-41 *Verification of TCP-TLS Socket Connections on CUBE*

```
cube# show sip-ua connections tcp tls detail
Total active connections      : 1
No. of send failures          : 0
No. of remote closures        : 0
No. of conn. failures         : 0
No. of inactive conn. ageouts : 0
TLS client handshake failures : 0
TLS server handshake failures : 0

Remote-Agent:172.18.110.48, Connections-Count:1
  Remote-Port Conn-Id Conn-State  WriteQ-Size Local-Address TLS-Version
  =========== ======= =========== =========== ============= ===========
         5061       3 Established           0             -     TLSv1.2
```

If you have gathered a packet capture for the call in Example 6-41, you can use Wireshark filters like those shown in Example 6-42 to explore the packet capture. The values in the filters are from the **debug** and **show** commands from the previous examples for this test call. Remember that because the application data is encrypted, you cannot view the SIP messages in the packet capture. The same goes for the SRTP that you captured. Attempting to play the audio from SRTP packets using Wireshark will not yield anything of value as the RTP payload is encrypted by the SRTP protocol.

Example 6-42 *Sample Wireshark Filters for the Previous Session*

```
tcp.srcport == 15089
ip.addr == 172.18.110.48
ssl
udp.port == 8066
```

Alternative Security Methods

As discussed at the very beginning of this chapter, security experts can take many different approaches to solve the same security problems and keep data safe, secure, and out of the reach of malicious third parties. As an alternative to the security topics discussed in this chapter, techniques like VPNs, DMVPNs, and IPSec can be leveraged to establish secure tunnels between a hub and spoke. Application data like SIP signaling and RTP can be securely transmitted in these encrypted tunnels.

Summary

This chapter explores the core concepts and various building blocks that security experts use to build security protocols. It also examines these security protocols in terms of signaling and media plane operations. This chapter looks at how an SBC uses all the techniques discussed to ensure that signaling and media are safe, secure, and away from prying eyes. This chapter also discusses the best way to triage and troubleshoot security issues that may be encountered on a network. The chapter closes with an in-depth examination of a secure call between CUBE and CUCM.

References

RFC 1421, "Privacy Enhancement for Internet Electronic Mail: Part I: Message Encryption and Authentication Procedures," https://tools.ietf.org/html/rfc1421

RFC 2045, "Multipurpose Internet Mail Extensions (MIME) Part One: Format of Internet Message Bodies," https://tools.ietf.org/html/rfc2045

RFC 2046, "Multipurpose Internet Mail Extensions (MIME) Part Two: Media Types," https://tools.ietf.org/html/rfc2046.

RFC 2246, "The TLS Protocol Version 1.0," https://tools.ietf.org/html/rfc2246

RFC 2511, "Internet X.509 Certificate Request Message Format," https://tools.ietf.org/html/rfc2511

RFC 2986, "PKCS #10: Certification Request Syntax Specification Version 1.7," https://tools.ietf.org/html/rfc2986

RFC 3261, "SIP: Session Initiation Protocol," https://tools.ietf.org/html/rfc3261

RFC 3711, "The Secure Real-time Transport Protocol (SRTP)," https://tools.ietf.org/html/rfc3711

RFC 4346, "The Transport Layer Security (TLS) Protocol Version 1.1," https://tools.ietf.org/html/rfc4346

RFC 4567, "Key Management Extensions for Session Description Protocol (SDP) and Real Time Streaming Protocol (RTSP)," https://tools.ietf.org/html/rfc4567

RFC 4568, "Session Description Protocol (SDP) Security Descriptions for Media Streams," https://tools.ietf.org/html/rfc4568

RFC 4572, "Connection-Oriented Media Transport over the Transport Layer Security (TLS) Protocol in the Session Description Protocol (SDP)," https://tools.ietf.org/html/rfc4572

RFC 5246, "The Transport Layer Security (TLS) Protocol Version 1.2," https://tools.ietf.org/html/rfc5246

RFC 5280, "Internet X.509 Public Key Infrastructure Certificate and Certificate Revocation List (CRL) Profile," https://tools.ietf.org/html/rfc5280

RFC 5630, "The Use of the SIPS URI Scheme in the Session Initiation Protocol (SIP)," https://tools.ietf.org/html/rfc5630

RFC 5705, "Keying Material Exporters for Transport Layer Security (TLS)," https://tools.ietf.org/html/rfc5705

RFC 5751, "Secure/Multipurpose Internet Mail Extensions (S/MIME) Version 3.2 Message Specification," https://tools.ietf.org/html/rfc5751

RFC 5763, "Framework for Establishing a Secure Real-time Transport Protocol (SRTP) Security Context Using Datagram Transport Layer Security (DTLS)," https://tools.ietf.org/html/rfc5763

RFC 5764, "Datagram Transport Layer Security (DTLS) Extension to Establish Keys for the Secure Real-time Transport Protocol (SRTP)," https://tools.ietf.org/html/rfc5764

RFC 5939, "Session Description Protocol (SDP) Capability Negotiation," https://tools.ietf.org/html/rfc5939

RFC 6101, "The Secure Sockets Layer (SSL) Protocol Version 3.0," https://tools.ietf.org/html/rfc6101

RFC 6188, "The Use of AES-192 and AES-256 in Secure RTP," https://tools.ietf.org/html/rfc6188

RFC 6189, "ZRTP: Media Path Key Agreement for Unicast Secure RTP," https://tools.ietf.org/html/rfc6189

RFC 6347, "Datagram Transport Layer Security Version 1.2," https://tools.ietf.org/html/rfc6347

RFC 6871, "Session Description Protocol (SDP) Media Capabilities Negotiation," https://tools.ietf.org/html/rfc6871

RFC 7201, "Options for Securing RTP Sessions," https://tools.ietf.org/html/rfc7201

RFC 7714, "AES-GCM Authenticated Encryption in the Secure Real-time Transport Protocol (SRTP)," https://tools.ietf.org/html/rfc7714

RFC 7879, "DTLS-SRTP Handling in SIP Back-to-Back User Agents," https://tools.ietf.org/html/rfc7879

RFC 8017, "PKCS #1: RSA Cryptography Specifications Version 2.2," https://tools.ietf.org/html/rfc8017

RFC 8446, "The Transport Layer Security (TLS) Protocol Version 1.3," https://tools.ietf.org/html/draft-ietf-tls-tls13-28

draft-jennings-sip-dtls-05, "Session Initiation Protocol (SIP) over Datagram Transport Layer Security (DTLS)," https://tools.ietf.org/html/draft-jennings-sip-dtls-05.html

"Guide for Conducting Risk Assessments," https://nvlpubs.nist.gov/nistpubs/legacy/sp/nistspecialpublication800-30r1.pdf

"Guide to Data-Centric System Threat Modeling," https://csrc.nist.gov/csrc/media/publications/sp/800-154/draft/documents/sp800_154_draft.pdf

"Metrics of Security," https://ws680.nist.gov/publication/get_pdf.cfm?pub_id=917850

"Glossary of Key Information Security Terms," https://nvlpubs.nist.gov/nistpubs/ir/2013/nist.ir.7298r2.pdf

"Session Description Protocol (SDP) Security Descriptions," https://www.iana.org/assignments/sdp-security-descriptions/sdp-security-descriptions.xhtml

"Transport Layer Security (TLS) Parameters," https://www.iana.org/assignments/tls-parameters/tls-parameters.xhtml

"Introduction to Information Security," https://www.us-cert.gov/sites/default/files/publications/infosecuritybasics.pdf

"Cryptographic Standards and Guidelines: Examples with Intermediate Values," https://csrc.nist.gov/projects/cryptographic-standards-and-guidelines/example-values

"Secure Hash Algorithm," https://csrc.nist.gov/csrc/media/projects/cryptographic-standards-and-guidelines/documents/examples/sha_all.pdf

"Next Generation Encryption," https://www.cisco.com/c/en/us/about/security-center/next-generation-cryptography.html

"Chapter: Cisco IOS XE PKI Overview Understanding and Planning a PKI," https://www.cisco.com/c/en/us/td/docs/ios-xml/ios/sec_conn_pki/configuration/xe-16-6/sec-pki-xe-16-6-book/sec-pki-overview.html

"SIP-to-SIP Connections on a Cisco Unified Border Element," https://www.cisco.com/c/en/us/td/docs/ios/voice/cube/configuration/guide/15_2/vb_gw_15_2_book/vb-gw-sipsip.html#wp1459104%0A

"Chapter: Configuring SIP Support for SRTP," https://www.cisco.com/c/en/us/td/docs/ios-xml/ios/voice/sip/configuration/15-mt/sip-config-15-mt-book/voi-sip-srtp.html

"Chapter: SRTP-SRTP Interworking," https://www.cisco.com/c/en/us/td/docs/ios-xml/ios/voice/cube/configuration/cube-book/srtp-srtp-interworking.html

"TLS 1.2 Configuration Overview Guide," https://www.cisco.com/c/en/us/td/docs/voice_ip_comm/uc_system/TLS/TLS-1-2-Configuration-Overview-Guide.html

"TLS 1.2 Compatibility Matrix for Cisco Collaboration Products," https://www.cisco.com/c/en/us/td/docs/voice_ip_comm/uc_system/unified/communications/system/Compatibility/TLS/TLS1-2-Compatibility-Matrix.html

Chapter 7

DTMF Interworking

At some point, you have heard a prerecorded prompt requesting some information, perhaps a credit card number or an employee number. After a couple of presses on the keypad, you magically get the information you were looking for or are connected to a human agent. The underlying framework that enables this seamless transfer of information is known as *dual-tone multifrequency* (*DTMF*).

With the advent of voice over IP (VoIP), reliable transmission of keypad button presses end to end became somewhat of a problem, as audio codecs were not optimized for carrying DTMF tones without bringing in a degree of distortion. There was need to engineer a new way of reliably transmitting DTMF. This solution aimed to factor in all the complexities of modern real-time networks.

Fortunately, the industry (led by the IETF and ITU-T) came up with several methods of DTMF relay that have demonstrably worked well in real-time networks. This chapter provides an introduction to the various common methods of DTMF relay available today and extends the discussion to include the role of SBCs in DTMF relay.

This chapter is composed of the following main sections:

- **Introduction to DTMF Relay**—This section provides a very brief introduction to DTMF relay.
- **Variants of DTMF Relay**—This section details the various methods of DTMF relay used in real-time communication networks.
- **DTMF Relay on SBCs**—This section discusses how SBCs enable DTMF interworking and translation in real time.
- **Configuring and Troubleshooting DTMF Relay**—This section discusses configuration and troubleshooting of DTMF on SBCs, using CUBE as an instantiation.

Introduction to DTMF Relay

In the 1960s, Bell Labs introduced DTMF to the public under the trademarked name Touch Tone. It was a means for consumers to utilize tones to convey numeric signaling information. This proved to be a viable alternative to the rotary dial phones that were in use at the time.

DTMF employs a combination of two tones, a high-frequency tone and low-frequency tone interleaved to represent a digit on the keypad (0–9, *, #) or a letter (A–D). A device that supports DTMF has a keypad layout in the form of a 4×4 matrix, such that each row represents the low-frequency tone component and each column represents the high-frequency tone component of the signal. Figure 7-1 illustrates the 4×4 grid used in DTMF signal transmission.

	1209 Hz	1336 Hz	1477 Hz	1633 Hz
697 Hz	1	2	3	A
770 Hz	4	5	6	B
852 Hz	7	8	9	C
941 Hz	*	0	#	D

Figure 7-1 *4×4 DTMF Grid*

In the network topology diagrammed in Figure 7-2, a caller over a standard PSTN network dials in to an enterprise network, where the call is routed to an on-premises interactive voice response (IVR) system. When the call is connected, the IVR system might play a prompt soliciting the caller to enter the extension number of the person she wishes to speak to. The caller then enters the extension number through a series of keypad digit presses. Each digit press is a DTMF tone and is conveyed end to end from the caller to the IVR system. Over standard PSTN networks, DTMF information is transmitted as standard signals; over IP networks, DTMF is either transmitted along the signaling plane (as application protocol messages) or the media plane (within media or RTP packets). The process of transmitting digit information over IP networks—either in-band (within the media plane), out-of-band (signaling plane), or a combination of both over different call segments and usually in a mutually exclusive capacity—is called *DTMF relay*.

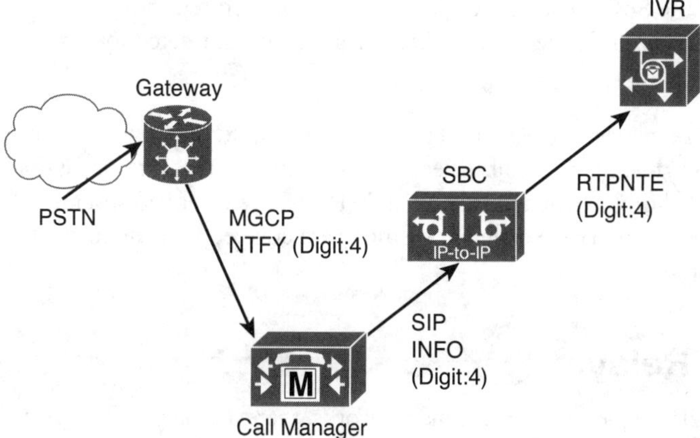

Figure 7-2 *Sample Network Topology for DTMF*

The transmission of signals using DTMF over TDM and analog networks is extremely reliable; however, transmission of DTMF over VoIP networks isn't so straightforward. Again consider the network topology illustrated in Figure 7-2. The different segments of the call flow negotiate different methods of DTMF:

- **MGCP gateway to call agent**—Out-of-band DTMF over the MGCP signaling channel.
- **Call agent to SBC**—Out-of-band DTMF over SIP INFO.
- **SBC to IVR system**—In-band DTMF over named telephony events

Note The concepts out-of-band and in-band and different methods of DTMF are explained in detail in subsequent sections of this chapter.

With this very simple call flow, several issues that could arise might hamper the successful transmission of DTMF from the PSTN gateway to the IVR, including the following:

- While detecting user input from the PSTN, the digital signal processors (DSPs) on the gateway might be unsuccessful in suppressing the tones from flowing into the audio stream. This could lead to dual representations of DTMF being transmitted to the destination—one over the signaling channel and another within the audio stream.
- Even if the MGCP segment of the call correctly relays digits out of band to the call agent and the call agent is successful in relaying digits to the SBC by using SIP INFO, the SBC might be incapable of converting SIP INFO to RTP–NTE, which would cause complete DTMF transmission failure on the last leg of the call.

- A software defect on the SBC could cause transmission of named telephony to violate the operating procedures defined in RFC 2833, leading to digit detection issues on the IVR system.

These are just a few basic examples of the myriad problems that could occur while transmitting digits over the IP segment(s) of a call. To ensure reliability of DTMF transmission over IP networks, standards bodies such as the IETF and ITU-T have designed several different methods of DTMF relay. These different methods are covered in detail in subsequent sections of this chapter.

Variants of DTMF Relay

Regardless of the scale and complexity of real-time networks, there are only two ways in which DTMF can be relayed over a given call leg:

- **In-band**—In-band DTMF relay refers to the transmission of tones within the RTP (media) stream.
- **Out-of-band**—Out-of-band transmission relies on the signaling channel to transmit DTMF information.

Both methods have merits and issues, and as with many other things in VoIP, the best choice of DTMF relay is implementation dependent and has a scope that spans the entire network end to end, as opposed to being restricted to a few devices or network segments.

In-Band DTMF Relay

Transmission of DTMF tones within the media stream is referred to as *in-band DTMF relay*. Most of the codecs used in VoIP networks were designed and optimized for human speech, and their encoding and decoding algorithms don't work well with raw dual-frequency tones. This is especially true with high-compression codecs such as G.729 that sufficiently distort tones so that they cannot be accurately reproduced at the receiving application.

It is precisely for this reason that the IETF took up the task of devising a way to reliably transmit tones within the media stream, which subsequently led to the standardization of named telephony events in RFC 2833 (which has since been superseded by RFC 4733). There are two ways DTMF tones can be transmitted within the media stream:

- Named telephony events
- Raw in-band tones

Named Telephony Events

RFC 2833 defines a payload format and specification for the transmission of DTMF tones within the media stream using named telephony events. This specification convincingly overcomes some of the known limitations of transmitting DTMF tones using a standard audio codec. The improvements provided by named telephony events over standard audio codecs for the transmission of DTMF include the following:

- Decoupling of DTMF tones with the audio codec ensures transmission success even when using high-compression codecs such as G.729.
- Defining a separate RTP payload format permits redundancy in DTMF digit transmission while maintaining a low transmission bit rate.
- Certain tones (such as the ANSAM tone for modem calls) have phase reversals. These phase reversals cannot be accurately transported as audio packets over an IP network. Using named telephony events to represent such tones greatly simplifies the process.
- Newer devices can relay DTMF information as named telephony events as opposed to actually generating tone pairs for digits.

The named telephony event (NTE) payload is carried in standard RTP packets such that the same sequence number and time stamp space are utilized for both audio-coded packets and NTE packets.

Note Further discussions in this chapter use the term *NTE packet* to designate an RTP packet that carries an NTE payload.

Three different types of packets are sent per event in the NTE scheme:

- A packet to designate the start of the DTMF event. The start packet always has the RTP marker (M) bit set to 1.
- Refresh or update packets that are sent every 50 milliseconds until the end of the event.
- Three redundant packets that designate the end of the event. End packets always have the end (E) bit in the NTE payload set to 1.

The three different types of packets described are for a single event or DTMF digit, and they all have the same RTP time stamp. The sequence number in each successive NTE packet increases by one. Figure 7-3 diagrams the RTP packet format with an NTE payload.

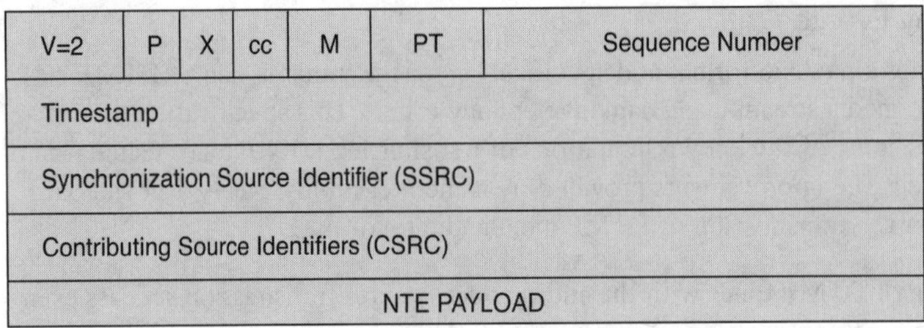

Figure 7-3 *RTP Packet Format with an NTE Payload*

The payload format for named telephony events is illustrated in Figure 7-4.

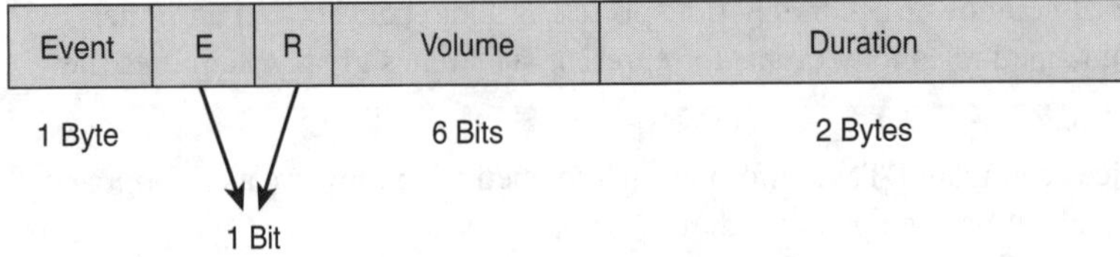

Figure 7-4 *Payload Format for Named Telephony Events*

The following fields appear within the payload:

- **Event** This is a number between 0 and 255 (inclusive), where each number designates a specific event, as outlined in RFC 2833 and RFC 4733. However, for DTMF, the event IDs can take a number between 0 and 15. Table 7-1 lists the digit and alphabetic assignments corresponding to numeric values between 0 and 15.

Table 7-1 *DTMF Named Events*

DTMF Event	Event Code
0	0
1	1
2	2
3	3
4	4
5	5
6	6
7	7
8	8

DTMF Event	Event Code
9	9
*	10
#	11
A	12
B	13
C	14
D	15

Letters A through D are for military application and are not typically used in commercial applications.

- **End (E) bit**—When this bit value is set to 1, it designates the end of the DTMF event; it is imperative that this bit not be set to 1 for packets that either designate the start of the event or refresh packets that are sent every 50 milliseconds.
- **Volume**—For DTMF digits and other events that can be represented as tones, this field describes the power level of the tone, expressed in dBm0 after dropping the sign. Power levels range from 0 to –63 dBm0. The range of valid DTMF is from 0 to –36 dBm0.
- **Duration**—This field designates, in time stamp units, the duration of the DTMF event. The time stamp field in any RTP packet for a given event indicates the instant when the event started, while the Duration field in any NTE packet for a given event indicates how long the event has lasted.
- **R bit**—This a reserve bit and currently does not have any defined function.

Note There are scenarios in which the time stamp can change within the span of a single event; this occurs when the event lasts for more than 8 seconds.

Given that named telephony events are carried within the media stream along with audio-encoded packets, the receiving application distinguishes these packets from standard audio packets by using the payload number and payload format. For NTE packets, the payload numbers chosen are dynamic and can vary between 96 and 127. For communication sessions set up using SIP in concert with SDP, the payload number for named telephony events is advertised by each user agent within the corresponding SDP body. Example 7-1 provides an SDP snippet that advertises a dynamic payload of 101 for NTE DTMF.

Example 7-1 *SDP Advertisement of Named Telephony Events*

```
// SIP message omitted for brevity//
v=0
o=CiscoSystemsSIP-GW-UserAgent 1597 5834 IN IP4 10.94.64.12
s=SIP Call
c=IN IP4 10.1.1.1
t=0 0
a=recvonly
m=audio 17389 RTP/AVP 8 101
a=rtpmap:8 PCMA/8000
a=rtpmap:101 telephone-event/8000
a=fmtp:101 0-15
a=ptime:20
```

As it stands, using named telephony events is the preferred method of DTMF relay in service provider and enterprise networks. There are, however, certain considerations that arise when DTMF is relayed by using named telephony events, as explained later in this chapter, in the section "Configuring and Troubleshooting DTMF Relay."

Raw In-Band Tones

Raw in-band DTMF refers to the transmission of raw tones within the media stream. Unlike named telephony events, for which there is a specialized payload format for DTMF, raw in-band DTMF encodes tone frequencies within the standard RTP payload. As mentioned earlier, audio codecs have their algorithms optimized for speech and don't work optimally to transmit DTMF tones. Using high-compression codecs for transmission of DTMF tones will almost certainly impede DTMF transmission due to significant tone distortion.

Some of the inherent disadvantages of using raw in-band DTMF are as follows:

- Lack of codec optimization for transmission of DTMF.
- No native support for redundancy while transmitting DTMF tones (unlike NTE, which has built-in redundancy). If redundancy has to be achieved, it will be through a redundant RTP stream using the constructs of RFC 2198. This leads to increased complexity and bandwidth utilization.
- Lack of diagnostics for troubleshooting. Because these tones are carried as raw tones within the audio codec, the only way to troubleshoot DTMF transmission is by decoding the audio stream using specialized software.
- Non-ubiquitous adoption across devices and vendors.

There are still some service providers that use this method of DTMF transmission, despite the obvious perils and limitations. Figure 7-5 diagrammatically depicts the end-to-end transmission of NTE and raw in-band DTMF.

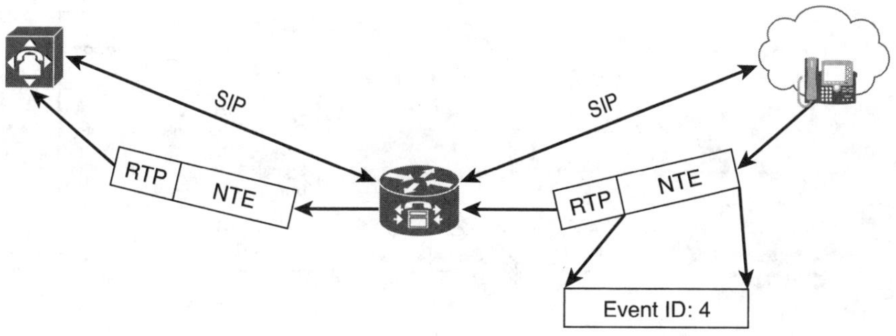

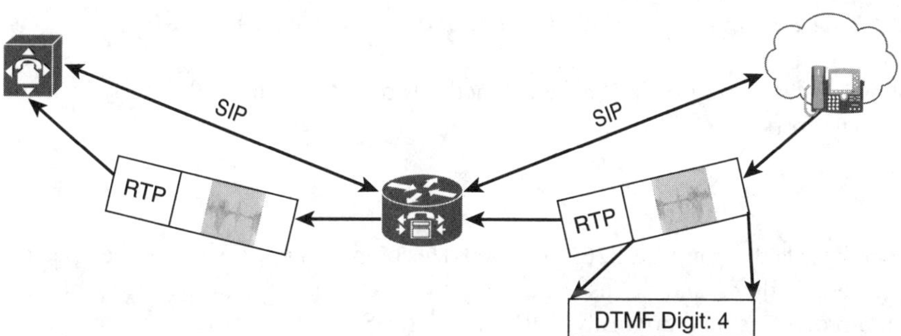

Figure 7-5 *End-to-End Transmission of NTE and Raw In-Band DTMF*

Out-of-Band DTMF Relay

Out-of-band DTMF relies on the signaling channel to communicate digit presses. Call control protocols such as SIP and H.323 have specialized mechanisms and extensions for communicating DTMF information. These mechanisms and extensions are discussed in detail in the sections that follow. With this method of DTMF relay, notifications for digit presses traverse the signaling path, which could include call agents and stateful proxies, among other devices. On the other hand, in-band DTMF relay uses the media path and is relayed directly between the participants of an RTP session. Figure 7-6 depicts the difference in path characteristics of in-band and out-of-band DTMF.

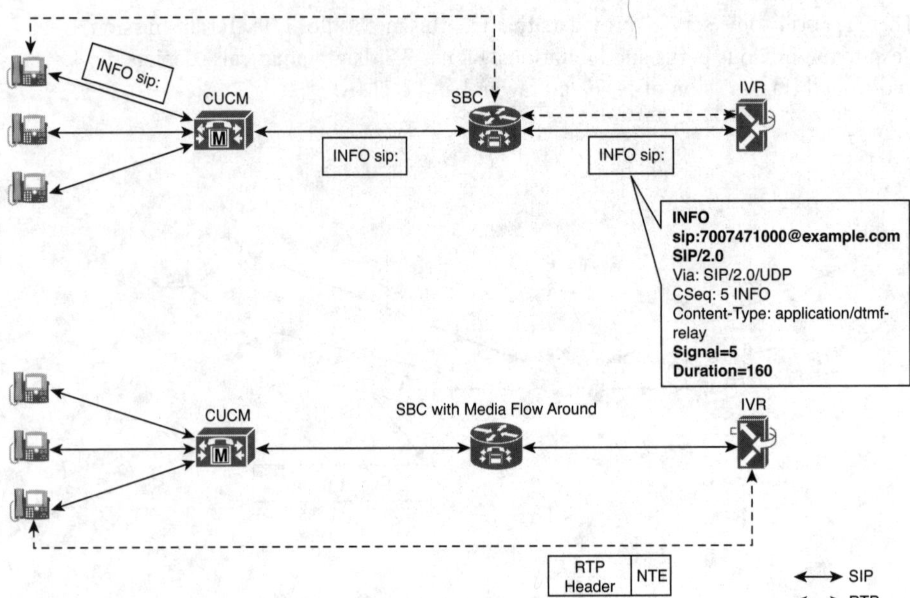

Figure 7-6 *Difference in Path Traversed by In-Band and Out-of-Band DTMF*

The following subsections discuss different methods of out-of-band DTMF relay in SIP and H.323 networks.

SIP INFO

The procedures laid out in RFC 3261 and several accompanying RFCs define the operating principles, methods, and extensions that make SIP a robust multipurpose communication protocol. Defined originally in RFC 2976, the SIP INFO method was one such extension to SIP, designed to allow exchange of application-level information along the signaling path.

The information that could be transmitted using SIP INFO was varied and in a way limitless, as it could be tailor made for any application usage. For example, a vendor could leverage SIP INFO to transmit resource availability information or billing information or even proprietary information. Over the years, SIP INFO has evolved into a convenient way to communicate application information spanning a broad spectrum of use cases, including the following:

- DTMF transmission
- QSIG encapsulation
- Fast video update requests
- Billing

Originally, application information could be carried in INFO message bodies or in specific SIP headers; the drawback of this approach was the lack of semantics on how specific application-level information is transmitted. For example, with DTMF, without a clear set of rules indicating how DTMF digits are transmitted from one node to another, does the application indicate digit presses in the INFO message headers or the body? If included in the body, what parameters should be used?

In an effort to standardize what information could be transmitted using INFO messages and the semantics of how that application-level information is delivered, RFC 6086 was developed. RFC 6086 allows for the creation of "info packages" that dictate the content and semantics of the information transmitted between applications; that is, different info packages can be designed to transmit different application-level information such as DTMF, billing, or resource availability information.

At the time of this writing, there is no standardized method for transmitting DTMF information using the guidelines of RFC 6086. All implementations that choose to transmit DTMF using SIP INFO do so using the guidelines of RFC 2976.

Support for the SIP INFO method is advertised in the SIP Allow header field of SIP requests and responses. The INFO method is a request and has to be answered by a 200 OK response. The streaming of a SIP INFO message does not create a new SIP dialog between user agents. Rather, it is sent on the existing dialog created by a SIP INVITE message.

Example 7-2 shows a sample SIP INFO message for DTMF digit 1, with a duration of 160 milliseconds.

Example 7-2 *Debug CCSIP Message Output for a SIP INFO Message*

```
INFO sip:2143302100@10.1.1.1 SIP/2.0
Via: SIP/2.0/UDP 10.1.1.2:5060
From:  <sip:9724401003@10.1.1.2>;tag=43
To:  <sip:2143302100@10.1.1.1>;tag=9753.0207
Call-ID: 984072_15401962@172.80.2.100
CSeq: 25634 INFO
Supported: 100rel
Supported: timer
Content-Length: 26
Content-Type: application/dtmf-relay
Signal= 1
Duration= 160
```

Notice in Example 7-2 that the content type is specified as **application/dtmf-relay**. In some implementations, it can also be encoded as **application/dtmf**, though the former variant is more popular.

SIP KPML

Defined in RFC 4730, SIP Key Press Markup Language (KPML) is used to monitor key presses. Before describing the working of SIP KPML in the transmission of DTMF, it is important to understand the underlying framework governing its operation. SIP KPML works on the subscribe/notify framework, which involves a subscriber and a notifier. The subscriber is a user agent that sends a subscription for event updates or state information to the notifier, and the notifier is a user agent that notifies the subscriber of any state change or observed events.

To receive event notifications from another user agent, the subscriber sends a SIP SUBSCRIBE message with an Event header; the contents of this header indicate the set of events for which for notifications are solicited. The Event header includes at most a single value, which corresponds to the name of the event package for which notifications are requested. Event packages are SIP extensions that build on top of the subscribe/notify framework of RFC 6665 to fit a specific usage paradigm. Several event packages are standardized as RFCs, and KPML is the one for DTMF.

Once a SUBSCRIPTION request has been accepted, the notifier sends a SIP NOTIFY message to communicate observed events or changes in state information, such that it includes the same event package specified in the SUBSCRIBE request. Figure 7-7 describes the exchange between user agents that support the subscribe/notify framework.

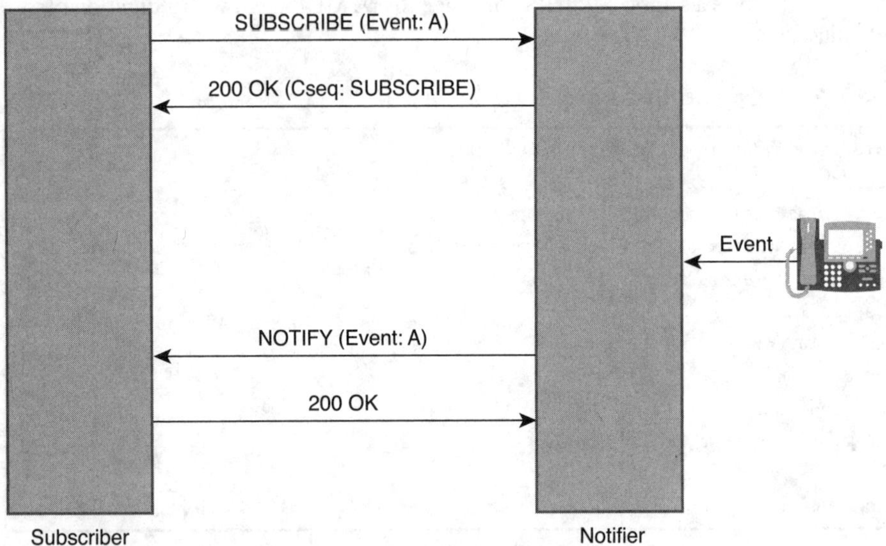

Figure 7-7 *SIP Subscribe/Notify Framework*

Each event package that is used in the subscribe/notify framework specifies a set of rules that operationally and syntactically define headers, message bodies, and information exchanged in a SUBSCRIBE or NOTIFY transaction. Support for this framework can be indicated in any of the following ways:

- With the SUBSCRIBE method in the **Allow** header field of SIP requests and responses
- In the **Allow-Events** header field
- Using the methods parameter of the **Contact** header

Each accepted subscription is active for a specific duration of time and has to be refreshed by the subscriber. The duration for which the subscription remains active is defined by the Expires header field value. The subscriber must refresh a subscription before it expires by sending a new SUBSCRIBE message. Figure 7-8 depicts the subscription refresh process.

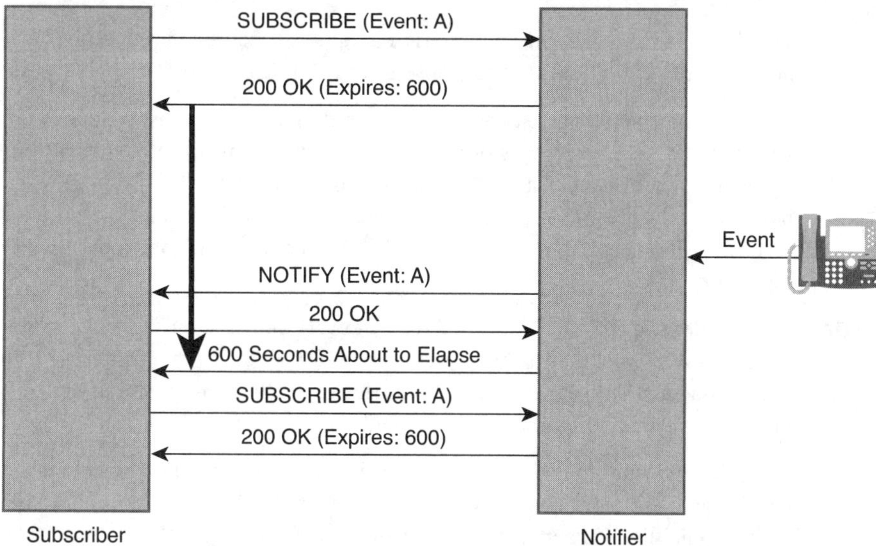

Figure 7-8 *Refreshing Subscriptions*

A user agent can unsubscribe from state or event notifications by sending a SUBSCRIBE message with the Expires header field value set to 0. Once the subscriber terminates a subscription, the notifier must not send further NOTIFY requests carrying event or state information.

While sending a SIP NOTIFY to the subscriber, the notifier must include the same event package as specified in the SUBSCRIBE request, along with the current state of the subscription, which can take one of three values:

- **Active**—Indicates that the SUBSCRIBE request has been accepted
- **Pending**—Indicates that there is insufficient policy or administrative information to accept or deny the subscription
- **Terminated**—Indicates that the subscription has terminated, and no new notifications will be sent

Drawing from the concepts discussed, the operation of the subscribe/notify framework can be summarized as follows:

Step 1. A user agent that requires event or state information updates from another entity (the notifier) and sends a SIP SUBSCRIBE request, referencing a specific event package in the Event header field.

Step 2. On receiving the SIP SUBSCRIBE request, assuming that the notifier understands the event package specified in the Event header field, a 200 OK is sent in response to the SUBSCRIBE request. A SIP SUBSCRIBE is a dialog-creating request and need not always exist within a dialog established by an INVITE/200 OK exchange.

Step 3. The duration for which the subscription is valid is specified in the Expires header of the 200 OK sent in response to the SUBSCRIBE request.

Step 4. As soon as the subscription has been accepted, the notifier must send a SIP NOTIFY message, regardless of whether it has any event or state information to communicate at the instant the subscription was accepted. If it does not have any event or state information to communicate at the instant the subscription was accepted, it sends a SIP NOTIFY message with an empty message body.

Step 5. The notifier triggers a SIP NOTIFY request every time there is a change in state information or an observed event. The NOTIFY message must contain the same Event header field value as the SUBSCRIBE request and must include the Subscription-State header field value.

Step 6. The subscriber must ensure that subscriptions are refreshed in a timely manner. If the subscriber does not wish to receive any further event notifications, it can explicitly terminate the subscription at any time.

As mentioned earlier in this chapter, SIP KPML, defined in RFC 4730, uses the subscribe/notify framework to report digit presses by using Extensible Markup Language (XML) documents known as KPML. XML documents are exchanged in the bodies of the SUBSCRIBE and NOTIFY messages. In a SUBSCRIBE message, the XML document serves to specify the digits or pattern(s) of interest, whereas in the NOTIFY message, it specifies the actual patterns or digits collected.

The operational principles of SIP KPML are governed by the kpml event package, which has to be included as an event package in every SUBSCRIBE and NOTIFY message used in the KPML framework.

There are two categories of KPML subscriptions, and they differ in the duration for which subscriptions are kept alive:

- One-shot subscriptions
- Persistent subscriptions

A one-shot subscription terminates as soon as a pattern match occurs and a NOTIFY message is sent (the Subscription-State header value is set to terminated). For further pattern match notifications, a new SUBSCRIBE dialog has to be initiated. Figure 7-9 diagrams one-shot subscriptions.

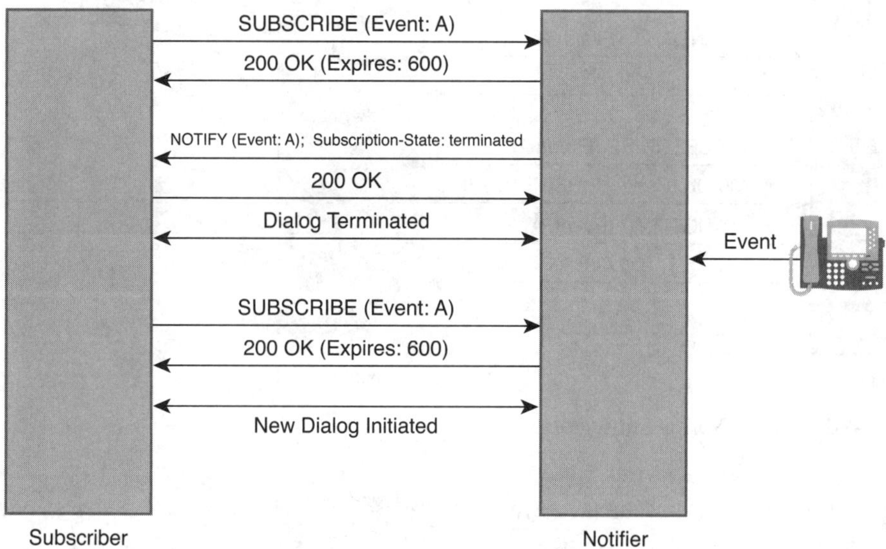

Figure 7-9 *One-Shot Subscriptions*

Persistent subscriptions remain active until explicitly terminated, regardless of whether a pattern match is indicated with a SIP NOTIFY message. Persistent subscriptions have two further variants: single-notify and continuous-notify subscriptions. A single-notify subscription sends a NOTIFY message on a pattern match but buffers or withholds further notifications until a new subscription is received (on the same dialog). Figure 7-10 diagrams persistent single-notify subscriptions.

A continuous-notify subscription sends notifications every time there is a pattern match. Figure 7-11 demonstrates the exchange and subscription state of a persistent continuous subscription.

KPML documents sent in SIP SUBSCRIBE messages indicate patterns of interest for an application. Each KPML document contains a **<pattern>** element; embedded within this element are a series of **<regex>** elements that indicate individual digit maps. The use of multiple **<regex>** elements within a KPML document is required when user input can match a plurality of potential patterns, such as user input dialing while dialing numbers within the scope of the North American Numbering Plan (NANP).

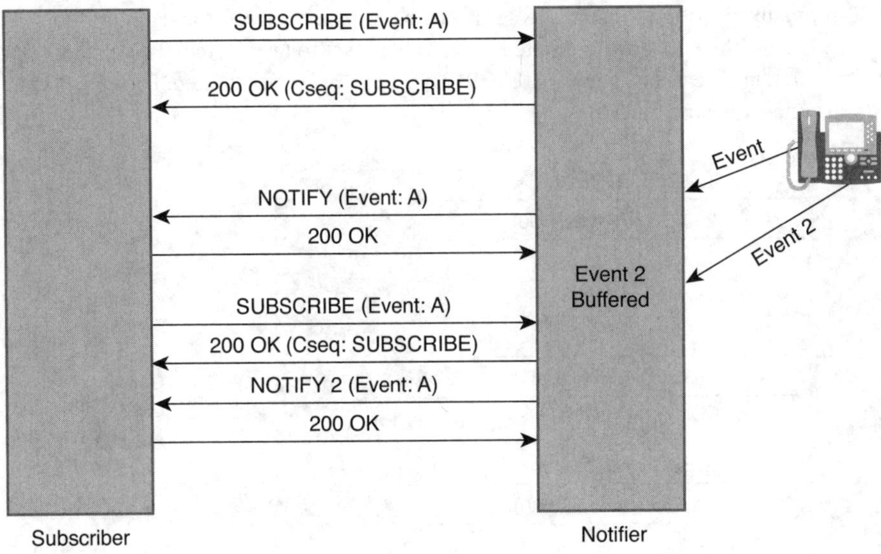

Figure 7-10 *Single-Notify Subscriptions*

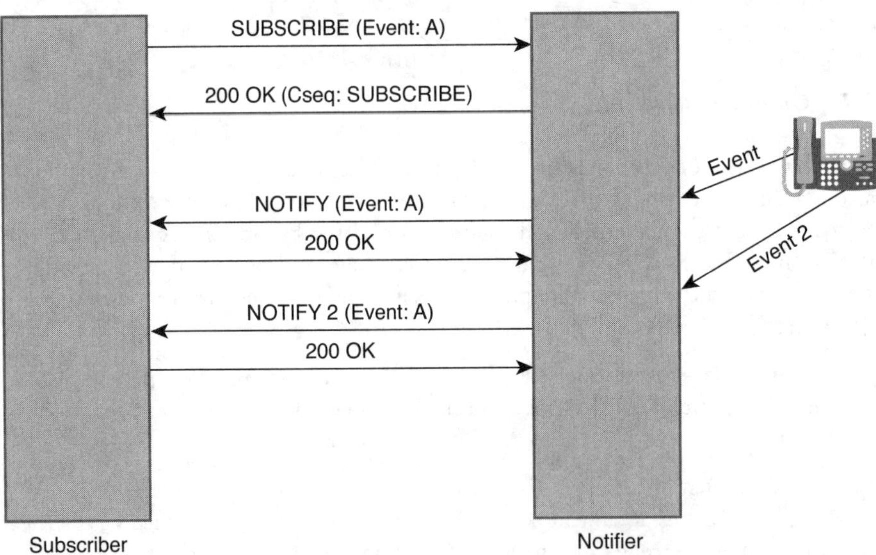

Figure 7-11 *Continuous Subscription*

Note KPML is extensively used to indicate digits pressed while dialing a phone number and is not restricted to reporting only DTMF information. Many of Cisco's IP phones use KPML to indicate the dial string while initiating a call.

However, from the perspective of DTMF, a single **<regex>** element suffices, as the events to be reported are restricted to the ones indicated in Table 7-1.

Example 7-3 provides a sample KPML document snippet that solicits DTMF event notification.

Example 7-3 *KPML Document Snippet*

```
<?xml version="1.0" encoding="UTF-8" ?>\n
        <kpml-request xmlns="urn:ietf:params:xml:ns:kpml-request" xmlns:xsi="http://
  www.w3.org/2001/XMLSchema-instance" xsi:schemaLocation="urn:ietf:params:xml:ns:
  kpml-request kpml-request.xsd" version="1.0">\n
        \n
          <pattern interdigittimer="7260000" persist="persist">\n
            <regex tag="dtmf">[x*#ABCD]</regex>\n
          </pattern>\n
        \n
        </kpml-request>\n
        \r\n
```

In Example 7-3, the **<pattern>** element encloses the digit map against which DTMF event notifications are sent. The actual digit map string is included in the **<regex>** element. For the notifier to distinguish between persistent and one-time subscriptions (described previously), the **persist** attribute of the **<pattern>** element is used. The **persist** attribute can take one of the following values:

- **one-shot**—Indicates one-shot subscriptions
- **single-notify**—Indicates single-notify subscriptions
- **persist**—Indicates continuous-notify subscriptions

In the case of DTMF, subscriptions are always persistent, as it does not make sense to send a new SIP SUBSCRIBE message for each DTMF digit within a call.

The **interdigittimer** attribute is used when the notifier transmits dial-string information. However, in the case of DTMF notification, this timer isn't of consequence and is set to a sufficiently high value.

As mentioned earlier, endpoints can use KPML to transmit dialed number information, in which case the number of patterns indicated in **<regex>** elements would range from a few potential dial strings to many. For the NANP, there would have to be at least the following patterns for dial string information:

- [2–9]x{6}—For local dialing
- [2–9]x{2}[2–9]x{6}—For national dialing
- 011x{15}—For international dialing
- 911—For emergencies

Patterns specified in KMPL use digit regex (DRegex), and the mapping from DRegex to POSIX ERE is provided is Table 7-2.

Table 7-2 *Digit Regex (DRegex) to POSIX ERE Mapping*

DRegex	POSIX ERE
*	*
.	*
x	[0–9]
xc	[0–9]c

When a multitude of patterns are specified in a subscription and the subscriber wants to know which particular digit map was matched, it can include the **tag** attribute in each **<regex>** element. When there is a match at the notifier for a specific digit map, the notifier includes the appropriate tag in the NOTIFY message that has the KPML report. Example 7-3 uses the **dtmf** tag in the **<regex>** element and is operationally redundant as there is only a single digit map specified for DTMF patterns.

Example 7-4 provides a snippet of a SIP NOTIFY message that is sent in response to a DTMF event.

Example 7-4 *SIP NOTIFY Message Sent in Response to a DTMF Event*

```
NOTIFY sip:10.1.1.1:5060;transport=tcp SIP/2.0
Via: SIP/2.0/TCP 10.1.1.1:5060;branch=z9hG4bK624B9
Call-ID: BE08917-8EB011E6-80F0A8E6-417953E@10.106.118.195
!! Message truncated for brevity!!
Event: kpml
Subscription-State: active
Content-Type: application/kpml-response+xml
Content-Length: 113
Message Body
    <?xml version="1.0" encoding="UTF-8"?><kpml-response version="1.0"
  code="200" text="OK" digits="1" tag="dtmf"/>\r\n
```

In Example 7-4, a notification is received for a DTMF event. Within the body of the SIP NOTIFY message is embedded a KPML document is also known as a *KPML report*. A KPML report for DTMF includes the following mandatory and optional attributes:

- **code** (mandatory)
- **text** (mandatory)
- **digit** (optional)
- **tag** (optional)

The **code** and **text** attributes are mandatory and must be a part of every KPML report, regardless of whether digits are reported. For example, when the KPML subscription terminates, the KPML report contains the body specified in Example 7-5. The **digit** attribute is used to specify the specific digit matched against the digit map included in the KPML body of the SUBSCRIBE request. As mentioned earlier, the **tag** attribute is used to distinguish between multiple potential patterns.

Example 7-5 is a snippet of the SIP NOTIFY message sent in response to a subscription termination.

Example 7-5 *SIP NOTIFY Message Sent in Response to a Subscription Termination*

```
NOTIFY sip:5081003@10.1.1.1:5060 SIP/2.0
Via: SIP/2.0/UDP 10.10.1.1.1:5060;branch=z9hG4bK6BE90
Call-ID: FB1F0711-8EAF11E6-93C5BE68-C696A51A@10.106.118.196
Event: kpml
Subscription-State: terminated
Content-Type: application/kpml-response+xml
Content-Length: 109
    Message Body
        <?xml version="1.0" encoding="UTF-8"?><kpml-response version="1.0"
  code="487" text="Subscription Expired"/>\r\n
```

As demonstrated in Example 7-5, the **code** and **text** attributes are different from what is reported in Example 7-4.

SIP Notify

The out-of-band methods of DTMF relay discussed so far are widely adopted in SIP-based networks; however, from the perspective of the amount of information disseminated, there are a few shortcomings. For example, in the case of SIP INFO, it is impossible to determine when the DTMF event actually began. In addition, many vendors use default event duration values for DTMF that fail to accurately capture the actual event duration. In the case of SIP KPML, digit notifications sent in the KPML report capture only the actual digit event, without providing much detail around how long the digit press event lasted, which could lead to issues when these tones have to be reproduced on a POTS interface (such as an ISDN circuit) or converted to another DTMF encoding scheme.

The section "SIP KPML," earlier in this chapter, provides an introduction to the SIP subscribe/notify framework, in which SIP NOTIFY messages are used to transmit specific event notifications or changes in state information. However, for notifications to be sent from one user agent to another, there always has to be an explicit, approved subscription in place (set up by the SIP SUBSCRIBE method). SIP NOTIFY, sometimes called "unsolicited NOTIFY" tweaks this framework by sending notifications for events such as DTMF and message-waiting indicators (MWIs) without an explicit subscription in place. This is a Cisco proprietary implementation and is not standardized in any IETF RFC.

The unsolicited notify framework borrows heavily from the framework standardized in RFC 2833/4733 by reusing and slightly tweaking the payload format highlighted earlier, in Figure 7-4. The use of this payload format provides the following benefits:

- It provides an explicit means of indicating when the DTMF event begins (by not setting the E bit).
- It allows for sending incremental updates that accurately capture the event duration.
- It can explicitly signal the end of the event, if the E bit is set.

Unsolicited notify cannot be negotiated with SDP or by using custom event packages such as KPML. Support for unsolicited notify is indicated with the Call-Info header field value; it is advertised in the SIP INVITE message and reciprocated by the answering side in a 18X/200 response. Example 7-6 provides a sample snippet of unsolicited notify negotiation between a UAS and a UAC.

Example 7-6 *Debug CCSIP Message Snippet for Unsolicited Notify Negotiation*

```
      INVITE sip:4082000@10.1.1.1:5060 SIP/2.0
      Via: SIP/2.0/UDP 10.1.1.2:5060;branch=z9hG4bKBC3516C
      !!! Message truncated for brevity!!!
      CSeq: 101 INVITE
      Contact: <sip:5081003@10.1.1.2:5060>
      Call-Info: <sip:10.1.1.2:5060>;method="NOTIFY;Event=telephone-
event;Duration-2000"
      Expires: 180
      Allow-Events: telephone-event



      SIP/2.0 180 Ringing
      Via: SIP/2.0/UDP 10.1.1.2:5060;branch=z9hG4bKBC3516C7
      CSeq: 101 INVITE
      Contact: <sip:4082000@10.1.1.1:5060>
      Call-Info: <sip:10.1.1.1:5060>;method="NOTIFY;Event=telephone-
event;Duration=2000"
      Content-Length: 0
```

Note The UAS can indicate support for unsolicited notify in the 200 OK message as well.

While negotiating bidirectional support for unsolicited notify through the exchange of the Call-Info header, the Duration header field value is of significant interest as it does not indicate the default value for all DTMF events in the dialog. Rather, it indicates the amount of time between successive NOTIFY messages sent for a single DTMF event.

It has already been established that unsolicited notify borrows heavily from the framework of RFC 2833/4733, using a similar payload structure and operating principle for DTMF event indication. The major difference between the two is that RFC 2833/4733 sends the payload within RTP packets, while unsolicited notify uses the SIP NOTIFY method body to encode the payload in binary.

The payload format for SIP NOTIFY/unsolicited notify is diagrammed in Figure 7-12.

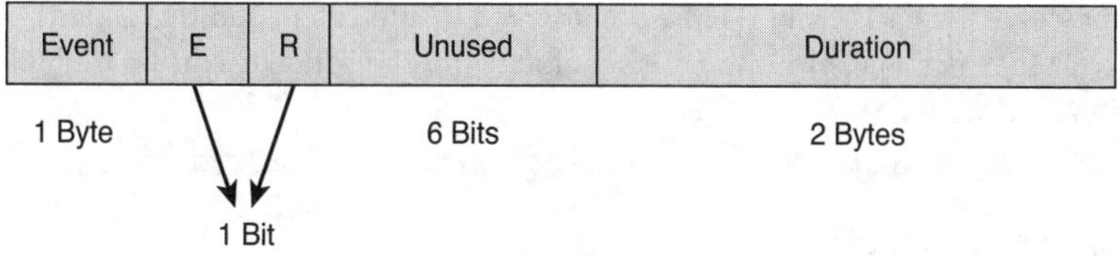

Figure 7-12 *Payload Format of an Unsolicited SIP NOTIFY*

The payload format for SIP NOTIFY is strikingly similar to that of named telephony events, with the exception of the Volume field and the way the Duration field is expressed. The Volume field is left undefined in the case of SIP NOTIFY, primarily because it is an out-of-band method of DTMF relay. The Duration field is measured in milliseconds in the case of SIP NOTIFY instead of in time stamp units.

In addition to using a similar payload format for the transmission of DTMF events, unsolicited notify also uses three packet types per DTMF event:

- Start packet
- Refresh packet(s)
- End packet

The operational summary of unsolicited notify for DTMF is as follows:

- As soon as DTMF stimulus is detected, a start SIP NOTIFY message is sent, such that the payload Duration field value mirrors the duration negotiated in the Call-Info header of the INVITE–18X/200 exchange. Because this is an out-of-band method of DTMF transmission, the M bit (found only in the RTP packet headers) cannot be set to 1. Instead, the E bit is set to 0, indicating that the event is in progress.
- If the actual DTMF event is of shorter duration than what was specified in the Duration field value of the start NOTIFY message, another NOTIFY is sent, with the E bit set to 1, indicating the end of the DTMF event. In addition, the Duration field value is updated to indicate the actual event duration. For example, if the start NOTIFY message was sent with a duration of 2000 milliseconds and the actual DTMF event lasted 800 milliseconds, then an end NOTIFY message (with the E bit set) is sent with an updated Duration field value of 800 milliseconds.

- If the actual DTMF event lasts longer than what was specified in the Duration field value of the start NOTIFY message, then a refresh NOTIFY message is sent such that the Duration field value is updated to reflect twice the negotiated duration in the Call-Info header field. The frequency with which the refresh NOTIFY messages are sent is dictated by a timer whose expiration time is the same as that of the negotiated duration in the Call-Info header field.
- Regardless of whether the actual event duration exceeds the duration of the start NOTIFY message, the end of the DTMF event has to be indicated, and this is done in an end NOTIFY message with the E bit set along with the actual event duration in the Duration field value.

H.245 Alphanumeric and Signal

While most IP-based voice and video networks today heavily use SIP for session setup, modification, and termination, it is not uncommon to find certain networks still operating with H.323 as the call control protocol. From the perspective of DTMF, H.323 uses two methods standardized in the H.245 specification:

- **H.245 Alphanumeric**—H.245 Alphanumeric transports the ASCII representation of DTMF events from one H.323 terminal to another. It is an out-of-band DTMF transmission method that uses the H.245 signaling channel. One major drawback of this method of DTMF transmission is the inability to indicate the actual event duration.
- **H.245 Signal**—H.245 Signal is another means of transmitting DTMF information over the signaling channel; it improves upon the framework of H.245 Alphanumeric by indicating the accurate event duration.

Note H.323 can also use NTE for DTMF relay.

DTMF Relay on SBCs

SBCs play a vital role in bridging capability mismatches between IP-based multimedia networks. Capability mismatches may arise for a myriad of reasons; for example, the two networks might enforce different audio and video codecs; use different signaling protocols for session setup, modification, and teardown; or use different baseline security schemes. Instead of deploying independent, functionally specific devices to individually cater to all these scenarios, it makes practical and economic sense to pack all required functionality reliably into a single device. SBCs efficiently achieve this requirement by influencing the negotiation of session characteristics and, if needed, playing the role of translator.

One of the most common capability mismatches in multimedia networks arises when the mode (that is, in-band or out-of-band) and method (for example, INFO, KPML, NOTIFY, NTE) of DTMF transmission is not the same end to end from the sending application to the receiving application. Such a mismatch easily translates to a critical outage for businesses; consider the example of a caller dialing into a contact center and being unable to navigate through an automated attendant with digit input to reach a specific department for immediate resolution of a problem.

The following sections discuss DTMF interworking principles on SBCs, using CUBE as an instantiation. Given that all the methods of DTMF (with the exception of raw in-band DTMF) are standardized either by the IETF or the ITU-T, their operating principles are preserved across vendors and device types. There could be extremely subtle variations in the way DTMF interworking occurs on different SBCs, but these variations don't override the general framework discussed in the following subsections.

The feature-rich DTMF library on CUBE enables seamless DTMF interworking between networks that implement different schemes of DTMF relay. Subsequent subsections outline the constructs available on CUBE to achieve this functionality, the configuration required to allow seamless DTMF interworking, and some of the restrictions that administrators have to take into consideration while deploying CUBE solutions.

In-Band DTMF Relay on SBCs

As discussed in the previous section, there are two methods of in-band DTMF relay:

- Named telephony events
- Raw in-band DTMF

CUBE supports both these methods of in-band DTMF relay. Which method is ultimately negotiated depends on the SDP offer/answer exchange and the configuration on CUBE.

Named Telephony Events on SBCs

The DTMF library on SBCs is capable of generating named telephony events inline with the procedures laid out in RFC 2833. SBCs provide implementers the flexibility of interworking different methods of DTMF relay with named telephony events. While establishing a media session, the characteristics of the session—such as the media type (audio, video), codec, and method of DTMF relay—are determined by the SDP offer/answer framework and advertisement of certain SIP header field values. With an SBC acting as a mediator that strongly influences session characteristics, it is imperative that the configuration be correctly rolled out.

Example 7-7 provides the configuration required to enable named telephony events as the method of DTMF on a particular call leg.

Example 7-7 *Dial Peer Configuration for Named Telephony Events*

```
Dial-peer voice 1703 voip
destination-pattern +19193923266
session protocol sipv2
session target ipv4:10.1.1.1
incoming called-number .
voice-class codec 1
dtmf-relay rtp-nte
no vad
```

For a given communication session that is set up and sustained by an SBC, a minimum of two call legs must exist. It is possible for the call legs to have drastically varying media capabilities. The following sections detail how SBCs usually interwork NTE with different methods of DTMF.

Named Telephony Events–Named Telephony Events

When both call legs are set up and negotiated to use named telephony events as the method of DTMF, the SBC functions as a DTMF switch, terminating and transparently passing named telephony event packets from one call leg to another. As depicted in Figure 7-3, named telephony event packets are RTP packets that have a specialized payload for carrying information such as DTMF.

As named telephony events are passed from one call leg to another, the following RTP header values are retained across the call legs:

- Synchronization source (SSRC)
- RTP sequence number
- Time stamp
- Marker (M) bit value

Note Passing named telephony event packets without modification would likely not be true when the SBC functions as a media terminator and performs payload manipulation operations such as transcoding and transrating. When functioning as a media terminator, the SBC would introduce its own SSRC and sequence numbering space. Refer to Chapter 5, "Media Processing," for more about the different modes of operation of an SBC.

In addition to the RTP headers being passed from one call leg to another, the contents of the various NTE fields are also passed from one call leg to another. These fields include the following:

- The event or DTMF digit
- The value of the end (E) bit
- The volume
- The duration

Named telephony events use dynamic payload numbers between 96 and 127, and the intended payload number is advertised in the SDP offer/answer exchange. Although the payload number 101 is most commonly used for NTE, it is perfectly valid to make use of any payload number between 96 and 127. From the perspective of SBCs, as a media session is being set up, the two user agents may advertise different payload numbers for NTE; for example, consider the scenario diagrammed in Figure 7-13, where the enterprise network advertises payload number 101 for NTE and the service provider advertises payload number 110.

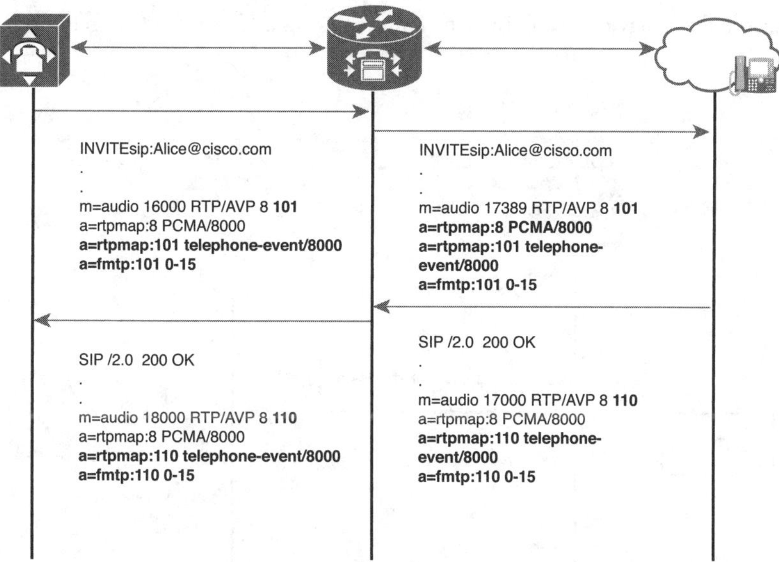

Figure 7-13 *Asymmetric Payload Number Negotiation for NTE*

When negotiating different payload numbers for NTE, the two call legs are asymmetric with respect to NTE. The asymmetric property can apply to voice and video codecs as well, but this is very rare. The ability of CUBE to interwork asymmetric payload numbers for DTMF occurs by default, with no additional configuration required. To instead allow the communication peers to handle asymmetric payload interworking, the **asymmetric payload** command may be used.

Table 7-3 details the arguments to the **asymmetric payload** command.

Table 7-3 *Arguments to the* **asymmetric payload** *Command*

Argument	Meaning
dtmf	Specifies that the asymmetric payload support is for DTMF only.
dynamic-codecs	(Optional) Specifies that the asymmetric payload support is for dynamic codec payloads only.
full	(Optional) Specifies that the asymmetric payload support is for both DTMF and dynamic codec payloads.
system	(Optional) Specifies that the asymmetric payload uses the global value.

The **dynamic codecs** argument is used if the voice or video codec across call legs uses different payload numbers. This command can also be applied at the dial peer level.

Figure 7-14 shows the behavior of an SBC when interworking different payload numbers for NTE.

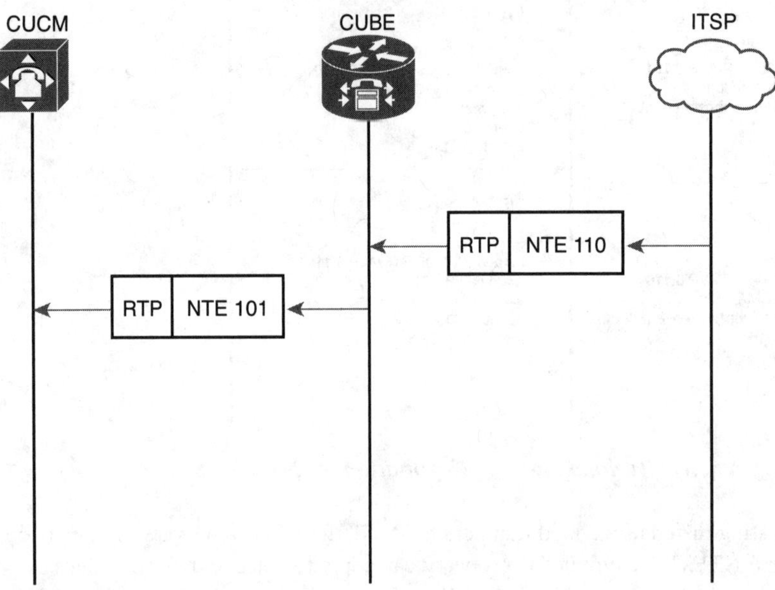

Figure 7-14 *Interworking Different NTE Payloads*

Note While interworking asymmetric payload numbers for NTE, all the RTP and NTE payload header field values remain the same across call legs:

- Synchronization source (SSRC)
- RTP sequence number
- Time stamp
- Marker (M) bit value
- The event or DTMF digit
- The value of the end (E) bit
- The volume
- The duration

SIP NOTIFY–Named Telephony Events

SIP NOTIFY or unsolicited notify is a Cisco proprietary method for transmission of DTMF and therefore is not widely adopted across the industry. There are two possible interworking scenarios for NTE and SIP NOTIFY: SIP NOTIFY to NTE and NTE to SIP NOTIFY.

Drawing from the prior discussion on the operating principles of SIP NOTIFY and named telephony events, the process of translating from SIP NOTIFY to NTE on CUBE involves the following:

- The initial SIP NOTIFY message is received, with the Duration field set to the value negotiated with the Call-Info header during call setup.
- Until CUBE doesn't receive the SIP NOTIFY end-of-event message (with the E bit set), CUBE does not trigger named telephony event generation on the peer leg.
- Although SIP NOTIFY can accurately encode event duration, CUBE does not retain the event duration while generating NTE packets on the peer leg. A default duration of 800 milliseconds is used for the named telephony events when interworking with SIP NOTIFY, regardless of the duration encoded in the end SIP NOTIFY message. (Remember that the end or final SIP NOTIFY message encodes the actual/true event duration.) This is primarily done to ensure that DTMF events using NTE do not overflow an upper duration threshold.

While converting from NTE to SIP NOTIFY for DTMF, CUBE enforces the following logic:

- As soon as an NTE start packet is received (with the M bit set), a SIP NOTIFY is generated, and the Duration field reflects the value negotiated in the Call-Info header field.

- No further SIP NOTIFY messages are sent until the end-of-event indication is received over the NTE leg.
- When the end-of-event NTE packet is received, CUBE generates a SIP NOTIFY with the E bit set to indicate the end of event, and it updates the Duration field to reflect a value of 140 milliseconds.
- Even in this mode of interworking, the accurate digit duration is not passed, and CUBE ends up using default values.

Note While interworking named telephony events and SIP NOTIFY, CUBE does not follow the general operational procedures of SIP NOTIFY in terms of sending refresh packets that update the Duration header field value.

SIP INFO–Named Telephony Events

When interworking SIP INFO and NTE, CUBE successfully converts SIP INFO DTMF indications to NTE packets. However, the reverse conversion of NTE to SIP INFO is not possible. On receiving a SIP INFO message with a specific DTMF digit in the message body, CUBE triggers the generation of named telephony event packets on the peer leg for that DTMF digit. The named telephony event packets specify a duration of 800 milliseconds for the DTMF digit, regardless of the duration of the DTMF event specified using the SIP INFO message.

H.245 Signal and H.245 Alphanumeric–Named Telephony Events

When SBCs interwork SIP and H.323 networks, bidirectional interworking of NTE and H.245 Alphanumeric/Signal is possible. Between the two variants of H.323 DTMF relay, H.245 Alphanumeric is incapable of capturing the DTMF event duration and is just an event indication over the H.245 signaling channel. On the other hand, H.245 Signal does encode the event duration, using the **Signal** parameter, which includes two attributes:

- **signalType**—Captures the DTMF event
- **duration**—Captures the event duration

While interworking H.245 Alphanumeric and named telephony events, the use case is trivial, and CUBE generates named telephony event packets with a duration of 800 milliseconds. In the reverse scenario, when converting from named telephony events to H.245 Alphanumeric, the H.245 Alphanumeric message is sent as soon as NTE packets are detected, regardless of whether the event is still in progress on the NTE leg of the call.

While interworking H.245 Signal and named telephony events, as soon as the H.245 Signal message with digit information is received, CUBE triggers named telephony event generation on the peer leg. In the reverse scenario, where CUBE converts named telephony events to H.245 Signal events, the H.245 Signal message is generated immediately on receipt of the NTE packets. Due to the built-in redundancy of NTE, which uses the start, refresh, and end packets, the H.245 Signal message is usually sent long before the end NTE packet is received, in which case an H.245 Signal message with an event duration of 4000 milliseconds is sent first. This is then followed by an H.245 Signal message with a **signalUpdate** parameter with the default duration of 160 milliseconds, once the end NTE packet is received on the peer leg. Example 7-8 provides a **debug h245 asn1** snippet from CUBE, demonstrating the use of the **signalUpdate** parameter.

Example 7-8 *H.245 Signal Snippet for DTMF*

```
value MultimediaSystemControlMessage ::= indication : userInput : signal :
    {
      signalType "5"
      duration 4000
    }



value MultimediaSystemControlMessage ::= indication : userInput : signalUpdate :
    {
      duration 160
      rtp
      {
        logicalChannelNumber 1
      }
    }
```

Note The **logicalChannelNumber** parameter is a mandatory parameter for sending a signalUpdate message and is used to correlate the RTP stream to which the update maps.

When interworking named telephony events with H.245 Signal/Alphanumeric, there could be dual representations of the same digit, one using NTE within the RTP stream and the other over the H.323 signaling channel using H.245 Alphanumeric/Signal messages. This is obviously not desirable as it invariably leads to DTMF detection failure on the receiving application. To avoid this, CUBE can be configured to suppress NTE digits and ensure that DTMF information is only propagated using the signaling channel. Example 7-9 demonstrates the required configuration.

Example 7-9 *Dial Peer Configuration for NTE Suppression Over the H.323 Call Leg*

```
dial-peer voice 99 voip
 /// Omitted for brevity///
 dtmf-relay rtp-nte digit-drop
```

The **digit-drop** argument to the **dtmf-relay** command can only be used along with named telephony events (**dtmf-relay rtp-nte**) and is applicable only for SIP–H.323 calls.

SIP KPML–Named Telephony Events

If the offer/answer exchange between an SBC and its communication peers results in the negotiation of SIP KPML on one call leg and named telephony events on another, the SBC must interwork SIP KPML and named telephony events for DTMF transmission. As discussed previously, SIP KPML requires an explicit, approved SIP subscription to be in place before any information about DTMF can be conveyed between communicating nodes. The following is an operational summary of interworking SIP KPML to named telephony events:

- On the call leg that negotiates SIP KPML, the SBC sends a SIP SUBSCRIBE request with the Event header field set to kpml and the Expires header field set to a nonzero value.
- The communication peer sends a SIP SUBSCRIBE request with the Event header set to kpml and the Expires header field set to a nonzero value.
- If either peer accepts the subscription request of the other, each peer must send a SIP NOTIFY message as soon as the subscription is accepted. The SIP NOTIFY message has to be sent regardless of whether there is any DTMF information to be conveyed at the time.
- DTMF information is conveyed to the SBC through a SIP NOTIFY message with the Event header field set to kpml and the message body carrying an XML document with the details of the digit pressed. (For details on the formatting of such a message, refer to Example 7-4.)
- Because KPML does not convey any information about the duration of a DTMF event, SBCs that are interworking KPML to named telephony events tend to use a predefined duration for NTE packets generated on the peer call leg. From the perspective of CUBE, this duration is hard-coded to 800 milliseconds.
- When the call terminates, the SBC and its KPML peer must explicitly terminate the subscription. This is done by either peer sending a SIP SUBSCRIBE with the Expires header field set to 0.

The following is an operational summary of interworking named telephony events to SIP KPML:

- On the call leg that negotiates SIP KPML, the SBC sends a SIP SUBSCRIBE request with that the Event header field set to kpml and the Expires header field set to a nonzero value.

- The communication peer sends a SIP SUBSCRIBE request with the Event header set to kpml and the Expires header field set to a nonzero value.
- If either peer accepts the subscription request of the other, each peer must send a SIP NOTIFY message as soon as the subscription is accepted. The SIP NOTIFY message has to be sent regardless of whether there is any DTMF information to be conveyed at the time.
- When the SBC receives DTMF information encoded in NTE packets, it **sends** a SIP NOTIFY message on the peer call leg, with the Event header set to **kpml** and the body of the message carrying an XML document. The XML body specifies the DTMF digit pressed. (For details on the formatting of such a message, refer to Example 7-4.)
- When the call terminates, the SBC and its KPML peer must explicitly terminate the subscription. This is done by either peer sending a SIP SUBSCRIBE with the Expires header field set to 0.

Support for RFC 4733

RFC 4733 iterates over RFC 2833 to provide enhancements for the reliable transmission of DTMF tones. At a high level, the operational differences between RFC 4733 and 2833 include the following:

- NTE packet transmission must begin with a valid duration specified in the Duration field.
- Refresh packets must be sent at regular intervals, and the recommended inter-packet duration is 50 milliseconds.

According to RFC 2833, it was possible to send start NTE packets with the Duration field set to 0, and each NTE packet (start, refresh, and end packets) corresponding to single events could be sent in a single burst without properly accounting for inter-packet transmission timing. This could cause issues on certain receiving applications in terms of buffering the various NTE packets for a given DTMF event and accurately reproducing the tone.

CUBE supports RFC 4733–compliant packets in the following DTMF interwork scenarios:

- NTE↔NTE
- SIP NOTIFY↔NTE
- SIP INFO→NTE

Note NTE, in the context of this discussion, refers to packets generated in compliance with RFC 4733.

Note In the three scenarios listed, notice the directionality arrows; SIP INFO to NTE is unidirectional, which means CUBE cannot convert NTE packets to SIP INFO messages.

Figure 7-15 illustrates the logical flow of events when interworking SIP INFO to RFC 4733.

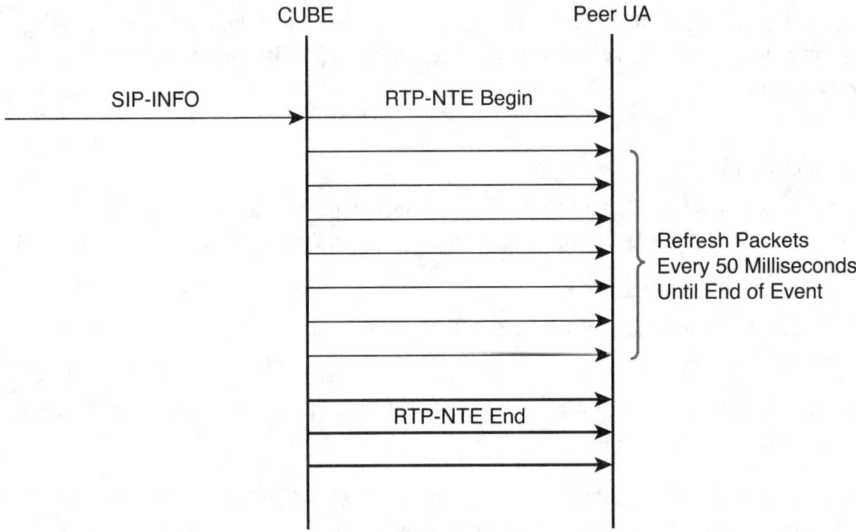

Figure 7-15 *CUBE DTMF Interworking for SIP INFO to RFC 4733*

When interworking SIP INFO to NTE (RFC 4733), the sequence of events is as follows:

Step 1. As soon as a SIP INFO message is received, a start NTE packet is sent on the peer leg. To ensure the start NTE packet complies with the recommendations of RFC 4733, the duration field is set to 1. There is only a single start NTE packet, and the M bit is set to 1.

Step 2. Refresh packets are generated every 50 milliseconds until the end of the DTMF event is reached. The duration of the DTMF event is dictated by the value of the Duration header field of the received SIP INFO message.

Step 3. CUBE terminates the NTE event by sending three end NTE packets.

Figure 7-16 illustrates the sequence of events when interworking SIP NOTIFY to RFC 4733.

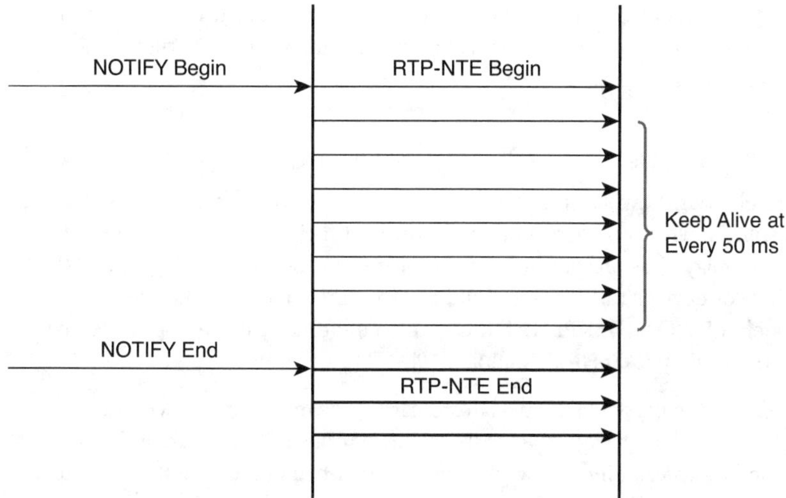

Figure 7-16 *CUBE DTMF Interworking for SIP NOTIFY to RFC 4733*

When interworking SIP NOTIFY to NTE (RFC 4733), the sequence of events is as follows:

Step 1. As soon as the initial SIP NOTIFY is received, CUBE generates a start NTE packet on the peer call leg. The start NTE packet has its M bit set to 1. The value of the Duration header is set to 1.

Step 2. Refresh packets are generated every 50 milliseconds until the final SIP NOTIFY message (with the E bit set to 1) is received. On receiving the final SIP NOTIFY, CUBE generates three end NTE packets.

Step 3. If for some reason the final SIP NOTIFY message is not received before the expiration of the duration interval specified in the initial SIP NOTIFY message, CUBE generates end NTE packets by itself.

The reverse interworking scenario, NTE to SIP NOTIFY, is the same as outlined previously. While interworking RFC 4733–compliant NTE on both call legs, CUBE acts as a pure "DTMF switch," passing events transparently from one call leg to another.

To configure CUBE to generate RFC 4733–compliant packets when interworking with SIP INFO and SIP NOTIFY, the **dtmf-interworking standard** command is used. This command can be used either at the global level or at the dial peer level.

> **Note** Regardless of whether the **dtmf-interworking standard** command is configured at a global or dial peer level, the dial peer corresponding to the call leg that generates NTE events must have **dtmf-relay rtp-nte** configured.

Although RFC 4733 iterates over RFC 2833 and provides some very useful enhancements, most devices deployed across real-time media networks still use the constructs of RFC 2833 for named telephony events.

Raw In-Band DTMF on SBCs

While there are obvious drawbacks to the transmission of DTMF as raw tones within the audio stream, some service providers around the world still choose this as the de facto method of DTMF relay. This presents a lot of problems in real-world deployments as most applications or devices that consume and transmit DTMF do so either using the signaling channel (SIP NOTIFY, KPML, INFO, and so on) or by using an optimized payload format in the audio packets (for example, RTE-NTE).

SBCs usually require the presence of specialized hardware while working with raw in-band DTMF, or they may have certain restrictions in terms of the different DTMF schemes that can be successfully interworked with raw in-band tones. CUBE can detect and generate raw in-band DTMF tones under these specific conditions:

- CUBE has a locally registered transcoder such that the transcoder can be invoked for interworking named telephony events to raw in-band DTMF and vice versa.
- Named telephony events must be negotiated on the peer call leg as the method of DTMF relay.
- The call leg on CUBE that negotiates raw in-band DTMF must use G.711ulaw/alaw as the audio codec.

A transcoder is required in this scenario because it has a built-in library of audio tones that indexes different frequency pair combinations as DTMF tones. When the transcoder is invoked for a call, all audio packets traversing CUBE for that call are made to flow through the transcoder, which picks up raw DTMF tones in the audio stream and converts them to NTE packets on the peer leg. When a conversion from named telephony events to raw DTMF tones is required, the transcoder receives the NTE packets and injects raw DTMF tones into the peer audio stream. Figure 7-17 diagrammatically illustrates the transcoder operation involved in converting raw DTMF tones to NTE.

The second condition refers to the fact that CUBE can only interwork raw in-band DTMF tones and named telephony events. It is not possible for CUBE to convert raw in-band tones to a DTMF relay method that uses the signaling channel to indicate digit presses (SIP NOTIFY, INFO, KPML, and so on).

It is, of course, possible to allow raw DTMF tones to pass through CUBE unaltered, using the RTP stream. However, most applications and devices such as IVR systems would not be able to discern these raw tones from the audio stream as they are optimized to work with explicit DTMF indications—either using NTE or the signaling plane.

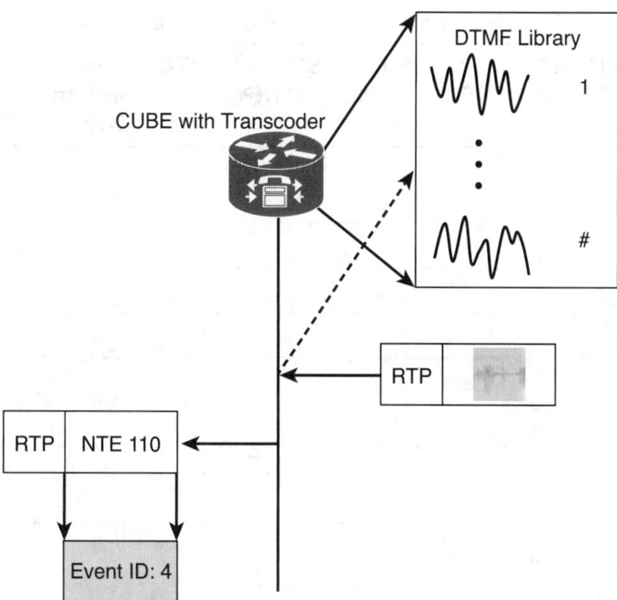

Figure 7-17 *Transcoder Operation on Raw In-Band DTMF Tones*

The third condition, which involves enforcing the encoding scheme to use G.711ulaw/alaw, is meant ensure that the tones are not distorted because of a high compression codec leading to detection failures on the transcoder.

Out-of-Band DTMF Relay on SBCs

The different methods of out-of-band DTMF relay and their operation have been detailed in previous sections of this chapter. A large majority of VoIP vendors today implement their DTMF transactions using named telephony events. The adoption and implementation of out-of-band methods of DTMF relay are on a steep decline in modern VoIP networks.

However, to successfully interwork DTMF with legacy equipment, it is required for devices to remain backward compatible with these methods of DTMF. This is especially true for SBCs, as they serve as the rendezvous point between two multimedia networks with varying characteristics.

Tables 7-4 through 7-7 summarize CUBE's ability to interwork different methods and modes of DTMF.

Table 7-4 summarizes the DTMF interworking capability set of CUBE when operating in media flow-through mode. (Refer to Chapter 5 to get a better understanding of media flow-through.)

Table 7-4 *CUBE–DTMF Interworking Capabilities for Media Flow-Through Mode*

	H.245 Alphanumeric	H.245 Signal	SIP INFO	SIP KPML	SIP NOTIFY	NTE	Raw In-Band DTMF
H.245 Alphanumeric	✓			✓	✓	✓	
H.245 Signal		✓		✓	✓	✓	
SIP INFO						✓	
SIP KPML	✓	✓		✓		✓	
SIP NOTIFY	✓	✓			✓	✓	
NTE	✓	✓		✓	✓	✓	✓*
Raw In-band DTMF						✓*	✓

* Designates the presence of a locally registered transcoder.

Table 7-5 summarizes the DTMF interworking capability set of CUBE when operating in media flow-around mode. (Refer to Chapter 5 to get a better understanding of media flow-around.)

Table 7-5 *CUBE–DTMF Interworking Capabilities for Media Flow-Around Calls*

	H.245 Alphanumeric	H.245 Signal	SIP INFO	SIP KPML	SIP NOTIFY	NTE	Raw In-Band DTMF
H.245 Alphanumeric	✓						
H.245 Signal		✓					
SIP INFO			✓				
SIP KPML				✓			
SIP NOTIFY					✓		
NTE						✓	✓*
Raw In-band DTMF						✓*	✓

* Designates the presence of a locally registered transcoder.

Note Interworking NTE↔NTE in media flow-around mode indicates the passage of NTE (and RTP) packets directly between endpoints, effectively bypassing CUBE. If there is a mismatch in the NTE payload number between the two call legs, the call falls back to media flow-through mode.

Note If it is required to interwork raw in-band DTMF and NTE, a transcoder locally registered to CUBE has to be invoked, in which case the call will function in media flow-through mode.

Table 7-6 summarizes the DTMF interworking capability set of CUBE when a high-density transcoder is placed in the call (refer to Chapter 5).

Table 7-6 *CUBE–DTMF Interworking Capabilities for Calls When a High-Density Transcoder Is Invoked*

	H.245 Alphanumeric	H.245 Signal	SIP INFO	SIP KPML	SIP NOTIFY	NTE	Raw In-Band DTMF
H.245 Alphanumeric	✓			✓	✓		
H.245 Signal		✓		✓	✓		
SIP INFO			✓				
SIP KPML	✓	✓		✓			
SIP NOTIFY	✓	✓			✓		
NTE				✓		✓	✓*
Raw In-band DTMF						✓*	✓

* Designates the presence of a locally registered transcoder.

Table 7-7 summarizes the DTMF interworking capability set of CUBE when interworking secure and non-secure media.

Table 7-7 *CUBE–DTMF Interworking Capabilities for SRTP-RTP Calls*

	H.245 Alphanumeric	H.245 Signal	SIP INFO	SIP KPML	SIP NOTIFY	NTE	Raw In-Band DTMF
H.245 Alphanumeric							
H.245 Signal							
SIP INFO			✓				

	H.245 Alphanumeric	H.245 Signal	SIP INFO	SIP KPML	SIP NOTIFY	NTE	Raw In-Band DTMF
SIP KPML				✓			
SIP NOTIFY					✓		
NTE						✓	✓*
Raw In-band DTMF						✓*	✓

* Designates the presence of a locally registered transcoder.

If any operations are required on the media stream, such as transcoding audio packets from one encoding scheme to another or transrating codecs from one packetization period to another, CUBE has to operate in media flow-through mode. As a general rule, any interworking required on CUBE in the media plane is possible only in media flow-through mode. With media flow-around, media bypasses CUBE and is exchanged directly between the endpoints. Endpoints such as phones, voicemail servers, and media servers are usually incapable of performing any manipulation of media payloads. From the perspective of DTMF interworking in media flow-around mode, there are some limitations that come to the forefront for in-band methods of DTMF relay, including named telephony events and raw in-band tones.

Because media does not flow through CUBE, it is not possible to achieve the following in media flow-around mode:

- Any out-of-band method to named telephony events and vice versa
- Named telephony events to raw in-band DTMF and vice versa
- Interworking dynamic payload numbers for named telephony events (asymmetric NTE)

During session setup, if there is a mismatch detected in DTMF capabilities—for example, if one call leg requires SIP-NOTIFY and other requires named telephony events—the call will dynamically fall back to a flow-through call. This ensures the passage of media through CUBE for scenarios that require interworking.

Configuring and Troubleshooting DTMF Relay

This section discusses the configuration and troubleshooting of DTMF relay on SBCs with CUBE as an instantiation. Rolling out configuration for DTMF relay on an SBC is obviously vendor and platform dependent and varies from one SBC to another.

From the perspective of troubleshooting, given that all methods of DTMF have been standardized by either the IETF or the ITU-T (with the exception of raw in-band tones), all vendors converge on a common set of rules and procedures for relaying DTMF.

Depending on whether the mode of DTMF is in-band or out-of-band, packet captures or signaling logs can be examined to isolate the scope of a problem, regardless of the vendor or SBC platform. CUBE as an SBC has a few constructs in software that aid in troubleshooting DTMF relay, and all of them are discussed in the subsections that follow. However, the general rule of thumb while troubleshooting DTMF is to first understand the expected behavior of a specific method of DTMF relay or interworking scenario and then examine the available logs or captures.

The configuration of DTMF relay on CUBE is handled exclusively at the dial peer level on a per–call leg basis. Chapter 3, "Call Routing," discusses the call routing logic of CUBE in detail, with every call logically anchored to an incoming call leg and an outgoing call leg.

DTMF configuration on CUBE is enabled by using the **dtmf-relay** command, and the argument(s) to this command determine the different methods of DTMF relay supported and advertised for a particular call leg. Table 7-8 lists and describes the arguments to the **dtmf-relay** command.

Table 7-8 *Arguments to the* **dtmf-relay** *Command*

Argument	Meaning
h245-alphanumeric	Forwards DTMF tones by using the H.245 Alphanumeric user input indication method. Supports tones 0–9, *, #, and A–D.
h245-signal	Forwards DTMF tones by using the H.245 Signal user input indication method. Supports tones 0–9, *, #, and A–D.
rtp-nte	Forwards DTMF tones by using RTP with the NTE payload type.
digit-drop	Passes digits out of band and drops in-band representation of digits.
sip-info	Forwards DTMF tones using SIP INFO messages. This keyword is available only if the VoIP dial peer is configured for SIP.
sip-kpml	Forwards DTMF tones using SIP KPML over SIP SUBSCRIBE/NOTIFY messages. This keyword is available only if the VoIP dial peer is configured for SIP.
sip-notify	Forwards DTMF tones using SIP NOTIFY messages. This keyword is available only if the VoIP dial peer is configured for SIP.

The following subsections discuss the configuration required on CUBE to enable a specific method of DTMF relay and the considerations to be taken into account while troubleshooting DTMF issues.

Configuring and Troubleshooting Named Telephony Events

NTE is a means by which DTMF digits are received and transmitted within the audio stream using a specialized payload format (refer to Figures 7-2 and 7-3). NTE as a method of DTMF relay has seen overwhelming adoption over the years by several vendors in the enterprise and service provider space.

Configuring Named Telephony Events

Several considerations need to be taken into account when configuring named telephony events for a specific call flow, including the following:

- Does NTE have to be enabled end to end, or is interworking required?
- If NTE has to be enabled end to end, is there a need to interwork the payload type?
- If interworking is required, is the interworking operation valid on CUBE? (Refer to Tables 7-4 through 7-7.)
- Is the call a media flow-through or a media flow-around call?

After factoring in all the different considerations and determining that NTE is the correct mode of DTMF operation, the appropriate configuration is applied to the different dial peers. Example 7-10 provides a sample configuration to enable end-to-end DTMF relay using NTE. In this example, dial peer 10 specifies the media and session characteristics between CUBE and a Cisco CUCM cluster, whereas dial peer 20 specifies the media and session characteristics between CUBE and a SIP service provider network.

Example 7-10 *End-to-End NTE DTMF Relay Configuration on CUBE*

```
Dial-peer voice 10 voip
  description towards CUCM
  destination-pattern +19193923266
  session protocol sipv2
  session target ipv4:10.1.1.1
  incoming called-number .
  voice-class codec 1
  voice-class sip bind-media source-interface gigabitEthernet 0/0
  voice-class sip bind-control source-interface gigabitEthernet 0/0
  dtmf-relay rtp-nte
  no vad
```

```
Dial-peer voice 20 voip
  description towards ITSP
  destination-pattern +1[2-9]..[2-9]......
  session protocol sipv2
  session target ipv4:10.1.1.2
  incoming called-number +191939232..
  voice-class codec 1
  voice-class sip bind-media source-interface gigabitEthernet 0/1
  voice-class sip bind-control source-interface gigabitEthernet 0/1
  dtmf-relay rtp-nte
  no vad
```

Troubleshooting Named Telephony Events

Troubleshooting named telephony event issues on SBCs can range from the trivial to the complex. In any case, a systematic and informed approach is needed to methodically break down a problem from a multitude of possibilities to a small subset and ultimately get to the root of the issue. In the world of troubleshooting, it is rare to come across two issues that are identical. There are almost always external factors that add uniqueness and significantly differentiate one problem from another.

The following sections describe approaches that can be used while troubleshooting DTMF relay on CUBE.

Verification of Configuration and Signaling

CUBE provides an administrator tremendous flexibility in terms of attributing unique session characteristics to different call flows using dial peers. On a given CUBE device, there could be a large number of dial peers to account for different number ranges or multimedia networks.

When troubleshooting NTE DTMF on CUBE, the first step is to determine whether the correct dial peers are matched (and, by extension, whether the correct method of DTMF relay is enforced for a call). The dial peers that are matched for a call can be determined in a number of ways, the most convenient being either by enabling debugging or issuing **show** commands in real time.

Example 7-11 provides a **debug voip ccapi inout** debug output snippet to demonstrate the dial peers matched for a call.

Example 7-11 *A Snippet of* **debug voip ccapi inout** *Demonstrating Dial Peer Matching*

```
Nov 24 19:16:10.839: //-1/4B14BD5F8337/CCAPI/cc_api_display_ie_subfields:
   cc_api_call_setup_ind_common:
   cisco-username=2001
   ----- ccCallInfo IE subfields -----
   cisco-ani=2001
   cisco-anitype=0
   cisco-aniplan=0
   cisco-anipi=0
   cisco-anisi=0
   dest=2001
///Truncated for brevity

Nov 24 19:16:10.839: //-1/4B14BD5F8337/CCAPI/cc_api_call_setup_ind_common:
   Interface=0x3F81F118, Call Info(
   Calling Number=2001,(Calling Name=)(TON=Unknown, NPI=Unknown, Screening=Not
  Screened, Presentation=Allowed),
   Called Number=2001(TON=Unknown, NPI=Unknown),
   Calling Translated=FALSE, Subscriber Type Str=Unknown, FinalDestinationFlag=TRUE,
   Incoming Dial-peer=10, Progress Indication=NULL(0), Calling IE Present=TRUE,

///Truncated for brevity


Nov 24 19:16:10.843: //68389/4B14BD5F8337/CCAPI/cc_api_display_ie_subfields:
   ccCallSetupRequest:
   cisco-username=2001
   ----- ccCallInfo IE subfields -----
   cisco-ani=2001
   cisco-anitype=0
   cisco-aniplan=0
   cisco-anipi=0
   cisco-anisi=0
   dest=2001

/// Truncated for brevity

Nov 24 19:16:10.843: //68389/4B14BD5F8337/CCAPI/ccIFCallSetupRequestPrivate:
   Interface=0x3F81F118, Interface Type=3, Destination=, Mode=0x0,
   Call Params(Calling Number=2001,(Calling Name=test)(TON=Unknown, NPI=Unknown,
  Screening=Not Screened, Presentation=Allowed),
   Called Number=2001(TON=Unknown, NPI=Unknown), Calling Translated=FALSE,
   Subscriber Type Str=Unknown, FinalDestinationFlag=TRUE, Outgoing Dial-peer=20,
  Call Count On=FALSE,
```

Example 7-12 provides sample output of the **show call active voice brief** command when the call is active. In addition to displaying the dial peers matched for the call, the **show call active voice brief** command also provides some useful metadata in terms of the IP address and port pair for RTP, the number of RTP packets sent and received, and the duration of the RTP session.

Example 7-12 *Output of* **show call active voice brief** *Demonstrating Dial Peers Matched*

```
3929 : 80875 -2107718356ms.1 (13:54:01.161 UTC Mon Nov 28 2016) +1160 pid:10 Answer
  408345 active
 dur 00:00:30 tx:1516/242560 rx:1467/234560 dscp:0 media:0 audio tos:0xB8 video
  tos:0x0
 IP 10.1.1.1:53310 SRTP: off rtt:0ms pl:0/0ms lost:0/0/0 delay:0/0/0ms g711ulaw
  TextRelay: off Transcoded: No ICE: Off
 media inactive detected:n media contrl rcvd:n/a timestamp:n/a
 long duration call detected:n long duration call duration:n/a timestamp:n/a
 LostPacketRate:0.00 OutOfOrderRate:0.00
 VRF: NA

3929 : 80876 -2107718346ms.1 (13:54:01.171 UTC Mon Nov 28 2016) +1140 pid:20
  Originate 2001 active
 dur 00:00:30 tx:1467/234560 rx:1516/242560 dscp:0 media:0 audio tos:0xB8 video
  tos:0x0
 IP 10.1.1.2:8012 SRTP: off rtt:0ms pl:0/0ms lost:0/0/0 delay:0/0/0ms g711ulaw
  TextRelay: off Transcoded: No ICE: Off
 media inactive detected:n media contrl rcvd:n/a timestamp:n/a
 long duration call detected:n long duration call duration:n/a timestamp:n/a
 LostPacketRate:0.00 OutOfOrderRate:0.00
 VRF: NA

Telephony call-legs: 0
SIP call-legs: 2
H323 call-legs: 0
Call agent controlled call-legs: 0
SCCP call-legs: 0
Multicast call-legs: 0
Total call-legs: 2
```

After examining the debug output or **show** command output and ensuring that the correct dial peers are matched, you need to examine the negotiation between CUBE and peer user agents/terminals. It is insufficient to just configure NTE as the method of DTMF on the dial peer; the ensuing offer/answer exchange between CUBE and its peer user agents must confirm bidirectional support for NTE using the SDP bodies.

Example 7-13 provides a snippet of an SDP body that advertises support for named telephony events.

Example 7-13 *A User Agent (CUBE or Its Peer) Advertising Support for NTE Using SDP*

```
// SIP message omitted for brevity//
v=0
o=CiscoSystemsSIP-GW-UserAgent 1597 5834 IN IP4 10.94.64.12
s=SIP Call
c=IN IP4 10.1.1.1
t=0 0
a=recvonly
m=audio 17389 RTP/AVP 8 101
a=rtpmap:8 PCMA/8000
a=rtpmap:101 telephone-event/8000
a=fmtp:101 0-15
a=ptime:20
```

While examining which dial peers are matched for a call and looking at the SIP or SDP exchange between CUBE and its peer user agents, it is advisable to enable debugging rather than rely on **show** commands. This is because debugging provides a much broader and better picture of the logical sequence of events from call initiation to establishment. If there is high call volume, however, it is better to rely on **show** commands, if applicable.

Debugging

The next step in troubleshooting named telephony events is to enable NTE-specific debugging on CUBE and determine if CUBE successfully relays named telephony events from one call leg to another (if NTE is negotiated end to end) or whether it is able to convert between different DTMF representation schemes on one call leg to named telephony events on the other call leg.

Tip It is highly advisable to read through Tables 7-4 to 7-7 to understand the possible DTMF relay combinations on CUBE before proceeding to debugging DTMF relay issues. It is likely that the two call legs on CUBE might be set up in a way that is not conducive for end-to-end DTMF relay. For example, if one call leg negotiates SIP KPML and the other call leg negotiates SIP NOTIFY, there is little reason to spend time analyzing the debugs in detail.

To debug named telephony events, the following commands can be enabled:

- **debug voip rtp session named-events**
- **debug voip rtp packet**

debug voip rtp session named-events is specialized to debug named telephony events, while **debug voip rtp packet** provides the details of all the RTP packets traversing CUBE, regardless of whether these packets are audio/video packets or named telephony event packets. It is not advisable to enable **debug voip rtp packet** in production environments because the output is extremely verbose and could lead to CPU spikes in a short amount of time.

Note **debug voip rtp session named-events** is optimized for any named telephony event packet. Drawing from our earlier discussion of named telephony events, these events can use packets with payload numbers ranging from 96 to 127 and can be used for several telephony events like ANSAM tone indication and carrying redundant payloads for audio packets among others.

Tip Always enable debug time stamp with millisecond level granularity while troubleshooting NTE issues. The following command can be used: **service time stamps debug datetime localtime msec.**

Example 7-14 illustrates a snippet of **debug voip rtp session named-events** for the digit 2 in the receive direction (NTE packets arriving on CUBE). Example 7-15 illustrates the same thing but for NTE packets leaving CUBE.

Example 7-14 *Snippet of* **debug voip rtp session named-events** *for Digit 2 in the Receive Direction*

```
        s=VoIP d=DSP payload 0x62 ssrc 0x107A780F sequence 0x8 timestamp 0xAFA0
<<<Rcv> Pt:98      Evt:2        Pkt:0A 00 00
        s=VoIP d=DSP payload 0x62 ssrc 0x107A780F sequence 0x9 timestamp 0xAFA0
<<<Rcv> Pt:98      Evt:2        Pkt:0A 00 00
        s=VoIP d=DSP payload 0x62 ssrc 0x107A780F sequence 0xA timestamp 0xAFA0
<<<Rcv> Pt:98      Evt:2        Pkt:0A 00 00
        s=VoIP d=DSP payload 0x62 ssrc 0x107A780F sequence 0xB timestamp 0xAFA0
<<<Rcv> Pt:98      Evt:2        Pkt:0A 01 90
        s=VoIP d=DSP payload 0x62 ssrc 0x107A780F sequence 0xC timestamp 0xAFA0
<<<Rcv> Pt:98      Evt:2        Pkt:84 03 20
        s=VoIP d=DSP payload 0x62 ssrc 0x107A780F sequence 0xD timestamp 0xAFA0
<<<Rcv> Pt:98      Evt:2        Pkt:84 03 20
        s=VoIP d=DSP payload 0x62 ssrc 0x107A780F sequence 0xE timestamp 0xAFA0
<<<Rcv> Pt:98      Evt:2        Pkt:84 03 20
```

Example 7-15 *Snippet of* **debug voip rtp session named-events** *for Digit 2 in the Send Direction*

```
s=DSP d=VoIP payload 0x62 ssrc 0x107A780F sequence 0x8 timestamp 0xAFA0
Pt:98      Evt:2         Pkt:0A 00 00  <Snd>>>
s=DSP d=VoIP payload 0x62 ssrc 0x107A780F sequence 0x9 timestamp 0xAFA0
Pt:98      Evt:2         Pkt:0A 00 00  <Snd>>>
s=DSP d=VoIP payload 0x62 ssrc 0x107A780F sequence 0xA timestamp 0xAFA0
Pt:98      Evt:2         Pkt:0A 00 00  <Snd>>>
s=DSP d=VoIP payload 0x62 ssrc 0x107A780F sequence 0xB timestamp 0xAFA0
Pt:98      Evt:2         Pkt:0A 01 90  <Snd>>>
s=DSP d=VoIP payload 0x62 ssrc 0x107A780F sequence 0xC timestamp 0xAFA0
Pt:98      Evt:2         Pkt:84 03 20  <Snd>>>
s=DSP d=VoIP payload 0x62 ssrc 0x107A780F sequence 0xD timestamp 0xAFA0
Pt:98      Evt:2         Pkt:84 03 20  <Snd>>>
s=DSP d=VoIP payload 0x62 ssrc 0x107A780F sequence 0xE timestamp 0xAFA0
Pt:98      Evt:2         Pkt:84 03 20  <Snd>>>
```

Example 7-14 provides a debug snippet of named telephony events for NTE packets received on CUBE. The debug definition of every NTE packet begins with the s=DSP field and ends with the Pkt field. Therefore, every NTE packet is defined by two lines of output in the debug. Among the various fields displayed in the debug output, the following are of significance:

- **Pt**—This field indicates the payload number for named telephony events and can be a number between 96 and 127. Which payload number is ultimately used for NTE transmission depends on the SDP offer/answer exchange between CUBE and its peer user agent.
- **Evt**—This field indicates the actual DTMF event and can take any of the values specified in Table 7-1.
- **Pkt**—This field is a hexadecimal summary of the named telephony event payload structure depicted in Figure 7-4. This field is extremely useful in determining how many start packets, refresh packets, and end packets are present for a given NTE DTMF digit on CUBE and the total duration of the event. The first two hexadecimal digits of the Pkt field are used to depict the following headers of the NTE payload:
  - Event
  - End (E) bit
  - Reserved (R) bit
  - Volume
- **<<<Rcv>**—This tag in the debug output signifies that the NTE event is received on CUBE.

The last four hexadecimal digits in the debug output are used to encode the Duration field of the NTE payload.

In the snippet in Example 7-14, there are three start packets, one refresh packet, and three end packets for DTMF digit 2. A start packet is displayed in the first two lines of the debug output and ends with the Pkt field. If lines representing successive NTE packets for the same event reuse the same Pkt value, they signify redundant packets. In Example 7-14, there are a total of three start packets (refer to lines 1–6).

> **Note** Start NTE packets can also be identified by enabling **debug voip rtp packet** in conjunction with **debug voip rtp session named-events.** All start NTE packets in the debug output will have the M bit indication. Example 7-16 illustrates a snippet of three start NTE packets.

Example 7-16 *Start NTE Packets*

```
 s=VoIP d=DSP payload 0x62 ssrc 0x107A780F sequence 0x8 timestamp 0xAFA0
<<<Rcv> Pt:98     Evt:2        Pkt:0A 00 00
RTP(8): fs rx s=10.106.120.15(16384), d=10.106.106.106(32544), pt=98, ts=AFA0,
  ssrc=107A780F, marker=1

 s=VoIP d=DSP payload 0x62 ssrc 0x107A780F sequence 0x9 timestamp 0xAFA0
<<<Rcv> Pt:98     Evt:2        Pkt:0A 00 00
RTP(9): fs rx s=10.106.120.15(16384), d=10.106.106.106(32544), pt=98, ts=AFA0,
  ssrc=107A780F, marker=1


 s=VoIP d=DSP payload 0x62 ssrc 0x107A780F sequence 0xA timestamp 0xAFA0
<<<Rcv> Pt:98     Evt:2        Pkt:0A 00 00
RTP(10): fs rx s=10.106.120.15(16384), d=10.106.106.106(32544), pt=98, ts=AFA0,
  ssrc=107A780F, marker=1
```

The fourth packet in Example 7-14 depicts a refresh packet. For NTE, successive refresh packets would have their Duration fields incremented by a constant factor. The Refresh packet in this example has a duration of 50 milliseconds. The calculation of the Duration value is done using the logic illustrated in Example 7-17.

Example 7-17 *Calculation of NTE Duration from **debug voip rtp session named event** Output*

```
 (Decimal value of duration header field  * 1 sec)/ Sampling rate
```

The decimal value of the Duration header is obtained after converting the hexadecimal representation (01 90) to decimal, which in this case is 400. The sampling rate defaults to 8000 samples unless explicitly specified in the SDP body.

When this logic is applied to all the NTE packets received on CUBE in Example 7-14, you can see that the start packets have a duration of 0, and the refresh packet has a duration of 50 milliseconds. The end packets have a duration of 100 milliseconds. The end packets are identified when the first two hexadecimal digits in the Pkt field are toggled (because these packets all have the E bit set to 1 in the NTE payload); in Example 7-14, all packets beginning with 84 instead of 0A are end NTE packets.

The very same logic is used in interpreting NTE packets that are sent from CUBE. The only difference is that the **<<<Rcv>** tag is replaced by the **<Snd>>>** tag. This is depicted in Example 7-15.

> **Note** When NTE packets are transmitted end to end on CUBE, the debug output contains a mixture of **<<<Rcv>** and **<Snd>>>** packets. However, the two types of packets are segregated into Examples 7-14 and 7-15 for your convenience.

> **Note** On IOS XE–based platforms, the **debug voip rtp session named events** command cannot be used to troubleshoot named telephony events. This is primarily because of the reworked software architecture on these platforms. An administrator must rely on packet capture for troubleshooting NTE.

Packet Capture

If all the troubleshooting constructs laid out so far have been exhausted and there are still reports of failure for NTE DTMF transmission or reception, the next logical approach is to verify whether the NTE packets are put on the wire toward the intended destination. Several approaches can be used to obtain a packet capture (for example, embedded packet capture, traffic export, spanning the switch port, remote span) and determine whether NTE packets egress out the CUBE or ingress into the CUBE.

When a packet capture has been obtained, applications such as Wireshark that are highly optimized for VoIP traffic may be used to dig into the details of the call. Figure 7-18 provides a screenshot of a Wireshark capture where the filter **rtpevent** is used to identify all NTE packets in the call.

Figure 7-19 provides an expanded view of an NTE packet, as seen on Wireshark. The expanded view of NTE packets on Wireshark displays the values encoded for various fields in the RTP header and NTE payload.

```
Filter: rtpevent                                   Expression... Clear Apply Save

Protocol    Length   Info
RTP EVENT       44 Payload type=RTP Event, DTMF Five 5
RTP EVENT       44 Payload type=RTP Event, DTMF Five 5
RTP EVENT       44 Payload type=RTP Event, DTMF Five 5
RTP EVENT       44 Payload type=RTP Event, DTMF Five 5
RTP EVENT       44 Payload type=RTP Event, DTMF Five 5
RTP EVENT       44 Payload type=RTP Event, DTMF Five 5
RTP EVENT       44 Payload type=RTP Event, DTMF Five 5
RTP EVENT       44 Payload type=RTP Event, DTMF Five 5
RTP EVENT       44 Payload type=RTP Event, DTMF Five 5
RTP EVENT       44 Payload type=RTP Event, DTMF Five 5
RTP EVENT       44 Payload type=RTP Event, DTMF Five 5
RTP EVENT       44 Payload type=RTP Event, DTMF Five 5
RTP EVENT       44 Payload type=RTP Event, DTMF Five 5
RTP EVENT       44 Payload type=RTP Event, DTMF Five 5
RTP EVENT       44 Payload type=RTP Event, DTMF Five 5
RTP EVENT       44 Payload type=RTP Event, DTMF Five 5
RTP EVENT       44 Payload type=RTP Event, DTMF Five 5
RTP EVENT       44 Payload type=RTP Event, DTMF Five 5
RTP EVENT       44 Payload type=RTP Event, DTMF Five 5 (end)
RTP EVENT       44 Payload type=RTP Event, DTMF Five 5 (end)
RTP EVENT       44 Payload type=RTP Event, DTMF Five 5 (end)
```

Figure 7-18 *NTE Packets on Wireshark*

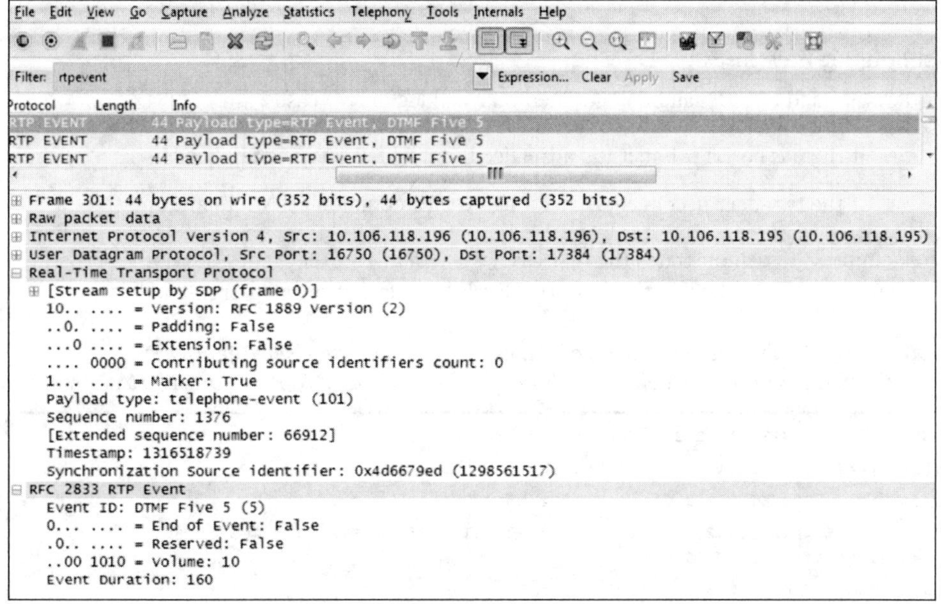

Figure 7-19 *NTE Packet Payload on Wireshark*

When the source and destination IP addresses are verified, it can be concluded that packets are on the wire. However, confirming that packets leave CUBE or arrive on CUBE does not conclusively eliminate the chances of DTMF relay failure. Unforeseen issues could still be contributing to failure, including the following:

- Changing the SSRC of RTP packets during NTE transmission without setting the M bit
- Sending NTE packets in a burst so that the receiving application does not have sufficient time to buffer these packets and re-create the tone duration
- Sending NTE packets with a payload value (96 to 127) that is not in line with the SDP negotiation

It is always best to eliminate as many potential failures as possible by validating the configuration, collecting debugs, and, if needed, confirming by using packet captures. If there is still failure, then it is best to involve the different vendors and jointly troubleshoot the issue.

Configuring and Troubleshooting Raw In-Band DTMF

This chapter has discussed in detail the inherent shortcomings of transmitting DTMF as raw tones in the audio stream. However, to ensure DTMF interoperability with certain service providers and ensure end-to-end reliable tone transmission, there are constructs available on CUBE for raw in-band DTMF configuration and troubleshooting.

Configuring Raw In-Band DTMF

Raw in-band DTMF can be negotiated on a call leg in two cases:

- If there is no DTMF method advertised in the SDP body or SIP headers
- If the two peer user agents cannot agree on a common DTMF method

Example 7-18 demonstrates the first case, where a given user agent does not advertise support for an explicit method of DTMF relay, either out-of-band or in-band.

Example 7-18 *Snippet of* **debug ccsip messages** *Where the User Agent Does Not Advertise Support for an Explicit Method of DTMF in the SDP Body or SIP Headers*

```
INVITE sip:6473230@10.1.1.1:5060;transport=tcp SIP/2.0
Via: SIP/2.0/TCP 10.1.1.2:5060;branch=z9hG4bK3B5DCE8B
From: <sip:550956@10.1.1.2>;tag=B3DF27E8-1CDB
To: "Alice" <sip:6473230@10.1.1.1>;tag=29201101~f0b14648-6a7f-4e83-9266-
  40281d5627f6-191705821
Date: Wed, 16 Nov 2016 08:31:01 GMT
Call-ID: fabf0b80-82c1193c-ae256e-cf09640a@10.1.1.2

///Truncated for brevity///

Supported: timer,resource-priority,replaces,sdp-anat
User-Agent: Cisco-SIPGateway/IOS-15.4.3.M4
```

```
Allow: INVITE, OPTIONS, BYE, CANCEL, ACK, PRACK, UPDATE, REFER, NOTIFY, REGISTER
CSeq: 103 INVITE
Content-Type: application/sdp
Content-Length: 194

v=0
o=CiscoSystemsSIP-GW-UserAgent 2771 2656 IN IP4 10.1.1.1
s=SIP Call
c=IN IP4 10.1.1.2
t=0 0
m=audio 20368 RTP/AVP 0
c=IN IP4 10.1.1.2
a=rtpmap:0 PCMU/8000
a=sendrecv
```

In Example 7-18, there is no explicit method of DTMF advertised (NOTIFY, INFO, KPML, or NTE), and therefore the method of DTMF relay negotiated will be raw in-band DTMF.

For the second case, two user agents may be unable to agree on a common method of DTMF relay. For example, one user agent may be only capable of supporting named telephony events, while its peer may be able to do only SIP KPML.

On a given call leg, if there is no common method of DTMF negotiated between CUBE and its peer user agent, that call leg will end up using raw in-band tones for DTMF transmission and reception. To enforce the use of raw in-band DTMF on a particular call leg, the dial peer that corresponds to that call leg must not have any method of DTMF relay defined. Example 7-19 provides the required dial peer configuration to enforce raw in-band DTMF on a given call leg

Example 7-19 *Dial Peer Configuration to Enforce Raw In-Band Tone Usage*

```
Dial-peer voice 20 voip
  description towards ITSP
  destination-pattern +1[2-9]..[2-9]......
  session protocol sipv2
  session target ipv4:10.1.1.2
  incoming called-number .
  voice-class codec 1
  voice-class sip bind-media source-interface gigabitEthernet 0/1
  voice-class sip bind-control source-interface gigabitEthernet 0/1
  no dtmf-relay
  no vad
```

Using raw in-band DTMF end to end almost always leads to problems because most endpoints are incapable of either generating raw in-band tones or detecting raw in-band tones. Instead, they are optimized to work with DTMF using NTE or the signaling channel. Therefore, a middle box like CUBE is needed to act as the DTMF translator. CUBE can interwork NTE and raw in-band tones if the following criteria are satisfied:

- A transcoder registered to CUBE is invoked.
- Peer call legs are set up for named telephony events.
- The call leg that negotiates raw in-band tones uses G.711ulaw/alaw as the audio codec.

Note Interworking raw in-band DTMF is possible only with NTE on CUBE.

The configuration of transcoders that locally register to CUBE is explained in detail in Chapter 5.

Troubleshooting Raw In-Band DTMF

With raw in-band tones, the scope for troubleshooting DTMF transmission and reception is extremely narrow because tones are encoded within standard audio packets. There are, however, certain preliminary checks that can be done while a call is active to verify if CUBE is correctly configured to handle interworking between NTE and raw in-band tones.

Negotiation of Raw In-Band DTMF and G.711

To confirm that one of the call legs has negotiated raw in-band DTMF and is using G.711 as the audio codec, you can use the **show sip calls** command when the call is active. You can use the same command to ensure that the peer call leg uses NTE for DTMF. Example 7-20 provides a snippet of this command.

Example 7-20 *Output of* **show sip calls**

```
CUBE-2#sh sip calls
Total SIP call legs:2, User Agent Client:1, User Agent Server:1
SIP UAC CALL INFO
Call 1
SIP Call ID                : 795E2093-B61A11E6-85F5A8E6-417953E@10.106.118.195
   State of the call       : STATE_ACTIVE (7)
   Substate of the call    : SUBSTATE_NONE (0)
   Calling Number          : 408345
```

```
   Called Number            : 2001
   Called URI               : sip:2001@10.106.118.199:5060
   Bit Flags                : 0xC04018 0x90000100 0x80
   CC Call ID               : 9459
   Source IP Address (Sig ): 10.106.118.195
   Destn SIP Req Addr:Port : [10.106.118.199]:5060
   Destn SIP Resp Addr:Port: [10.106.118.199]:5060
   Destination Name         : 10.106.118.199
   Number of Media Streams : 1
   Number of Active Streams: 1
   RTP Fork Object          : 0x0
   Media Mode               : flow-through
   Media Stream 1
     State of the stream      : STREAM_ACTIVE
     Stream Call ID           : 9459
     Stream Type              : voice+dtmf (1)
     Stream Media Addr Type   : 1
     Negotiated Codec         : g711ulaw (160 bytes)
     Codec Payload Type       : 0
     Negotiated Dtmf-relay    : rtp-nte
     Dtmf-relay Payload Type  : 101
     QoS ID                   : -1
     Local QoS Strength       : BestEffort
     Negotiated QoS Strength  : BestEffort
     Negotiated QoS Direction : None
     Local QoS Status         : None
     Media Source IP Addr:Port: [10.106.118.195]:17418
     Media Dest IP Addr:Port  : [10.106.118.223]:30820


Options-Ping    ENABLED:NO    ACTIVE:NO
   Number of SIP User Agent Client(UAC) calls: 1

SIP UAS CALL INFO
Call 1
SIP Call ID                 : 689BC631-B61A11E6-BA5FD9BE-3B16EEBB@10.106.118.196
   State of the call        : STATE_ACTIVE (7)
   Substate of the call     : SUBSTATE_NONE (0)
   Calling Number           : 408345
   Called Number            : 2001
   Called URI               : sip:2001@10.106.118.195:5060
   Bit Flags                : 0x8C4401C 0x10000100 0x4
   CC Call ID               : 9458
```

```
   Source IP Address (Sig ): 10.106.118.195
   Destn SIP Req Addr:Port : [10.106.118.196]:5060
   Destn SIP Resp Addr:Port: [10.106.118.196]:63540
   Destination Name        : 10.106.118.196
   Number of Media Streams : 1
   Number of Active Streams: 1
   RTP Fork Object         : 0x0
   Media Mode              : flow-through
   Media Stream 1
     State of the stream      : STREAM_ACTIVE
     Stream Call ID           : 9458
     Stream Type              : voice-only (0)
     Stream Media Addr Type   : 1
     Negotiated Codec         : g711ulaw (160 bytes)
     Codec Payload Type       : 0
     Negotiated Dtmf-relay    : inband-voice
     Dtmf-relay Payload Type  : 0
     QoS ID                   : -1
     Local QoS Strength       : BestEffort
     Negotiated QoS Strength  : BestEffort
     Negotiated QoS Direction : None
     Local QoS Status         : None
     Media Source IP Addr:Port: [10.106.118.195]:17416
     Media Dest IP Addr:Port  : [10.106.118.196]:16818


Options-Ping    ENABLED:NO    ACTIVE:NO
   Number of SIP User Agent Server(UAS) calls: 1
```

Invocation of Transcoder

A locally registered transcoder (either LTI or SCCP based) must be invoked to successfully interwork NTE and raw in-band tones. The sample output in Example 7-21 provides a snippet of the **show dspfarm dsp active** command that demonstrates the insertion of a transcoder into a call.

Example 7-21 *Output of* show dspfarm dsp active

```
CUBE-2#sh dspfarm dsp active
SLOT    DSP VERSION  STATUS CHNL USE    TYPE    RSC_ID BRIDGE_ID PKTS_TXED PKTS_RXED

0       1   40.2.0   UP     1    USED   xcode   1      9459      1478      1491
0       1   40.2.0   UP     1    USED   xcode   1      9458      1488      1487
```

Packet Capture

Unlike with conventional methods of DTMF relay that have specialized debugs to discern DTMF information, raw in-band DTMF has an extremely restricted set of options for troubleshooting. Because these tones are well concealed within the payloads of regular audio packets, the only option to uncover these raw tones and dive into tone characteristics—such as the actual DTMF digit, the duration of the digit, and spacing between consecutive digits—is to extract the audio stream from a packet capture and subject the stream to over-the-top analysis using a specialized application such as Audacity.

To start off, the audio steam is identified within a packet capture using an application like Wireshark. Once it is identified, the stream payload is saved in "raw" format. The audio stream is then imported in raw format and into audio recording and editing software such as Audacity, where the stream is normalized to use the characteristics outlined in Table 7-9.

Table 7-9 *Stream Characteristics While Importing into Audacity*

Parameter	Value
Encoding	ulaw or alaw, depending on the codec negotiated
Byte Order	No endienness
Channels	1 channel mono
Start Offset	0 bytes
Amount to Import	100%
Sample Rate	8000 samples

Once the audio stream is imported, you should be able to see distinct visible spikes on the audio waveform, which denote DTMF digits (see Figure 7-20).

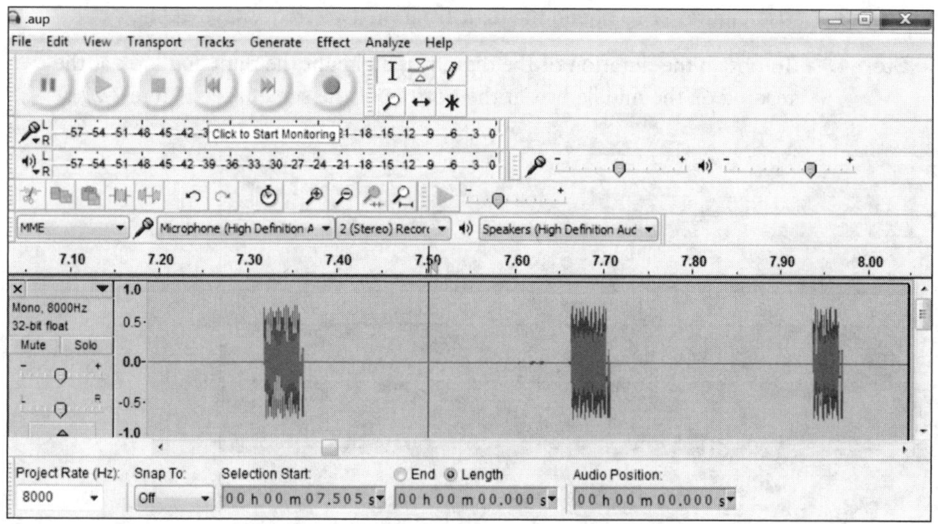

Figure 7-20 *Audio Waveform with In-Band DTMF Digits*

In an application like Audacity, to determine the actual digits and their corresponding tone duration, follow these steps:

Step 1. Highlight any of the DTMF tones (which appear as spikes) and select **Analyze > Plot Spectrum**. Notice that there are two distinct spikes, which represent the two tones making up a DTMF digit.

Step 2. Hover the mouse cursor at the apex of each spike and note the frequency reading in the Peak field. Do the same for the second spike. The combination of the two readings will give you the actual DTMF digit, as shown in Figure 7-21 (which shows digit 4, a combination of 770 Hz and 1209 Hz).

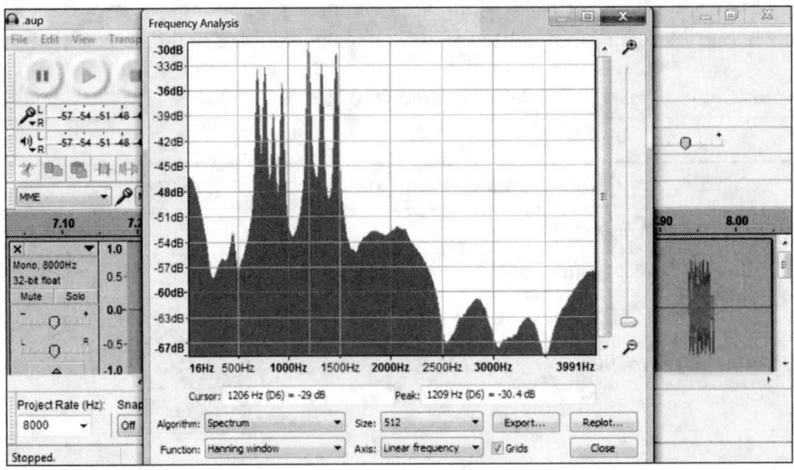

Figure 7-21 *Determining the Frequencies of Each Individual DTMF Digit*

Step 3. Use Figure 7-1 to obtain the digit from the two frequency readings.

Step 4. To obtain the duration of the digit, just highlight the digit and look at the reading on the middle box at the bottom of the screen (see Figure 7-22).

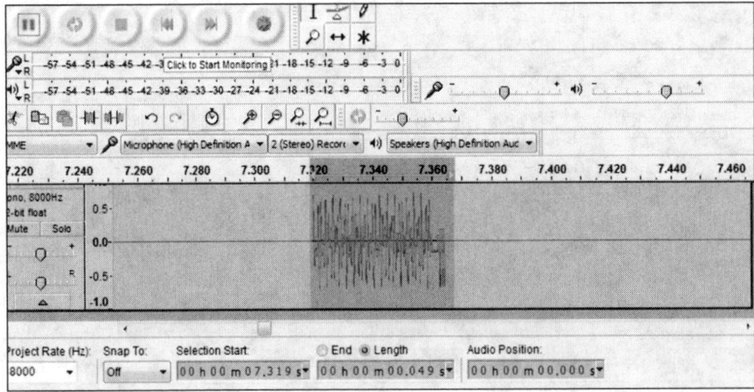

Figure 7-22 *Determining the Duration of a DTMF Digit*

Configuring and Troubleshooting SIP KPML, SIP NOTIFY, and SIP INFO

As has already been established, SIP KPML, SIP INFO, and SIP NOTIFY are out-of-band methods of DTMF relay that are transmitted over the SIP signal channel. It is extremely convenient to troubleshoot DTMF relay issues for out-of-band methods because they can be easily identified as SIP messages in a call trace.

Configuring SIP KPML, SIP NOTIFY, and SIP INFO

The configuration for the SIP KPML, SIP INFO, and SIP NOTIFY methods of DTMF is pretty straightforward and is applied to the dial peer. Example 7-22 provides a sample configuration of a dial peer for these three methods of DTMF relay. It is, of course, possible to configure any one of these methods individually on a dial peer.

Example 7-22 *Dial Peer Configuration for SIP NOTIFY, SIP KPML, and SIP INFO*

```
Dial-peer voice 20 voip
  description towards ITSP
  destination-pattern +1[2-9]..[2-9]......
  session protocol sipv2
  session target ipv4:10.1.1.2
  incoming called-number .
  voice-class codec 1
  voice-class sip bind-media source-interface gigabitEthernet 0/1
  voice-class sip bind-control source-interface gigabitEthernet 0/1
  dtmf-relay sip-notify sip-kpml sip-info
  no vad
```

Note When multiple methods of out-of-band DTMF relay are configured and negotiated, the method that is configured first takes precedence. For example, if SIP KPML and SIP INFO is configured with NTE, NTE takes precedence. If SIP NOTIFY and NTE are configured, whatever appears first in the configuration takes precedence.

Note You can enable SIP KPML, SIP NOTIFY, and SIP INFO only after configuring **session protocol sipv2** on the dial peer.

Troubleshooting SIP KPML, SIP NOTIFY, and SIP INFO

Troubleshooting out-of-band DTMF is extremely convenient and does not involve the detailed and often-complicated constructs used for NTE or raw in-band DTMF troubleshooting. A simple analysis of the **debug ccsip message** output suffices in determining whether there is DTMF failure.

After you confirm that the required configuration is in place, you can analyze the SIP traces on CUBE to uncover potential problems with regard to out-of-band DTMF relay. (For details on how the different methods of out-of-band DTMF relay are advertised, negotiated, and work, refer to the sections that discuss SIP INFO, SIP KPML, and SIP NOTIFY, earlier in this chapter.)

Configuring and Troubleshooting H.245 Alphanumeric and H.245 Signal

Although almost every modern VoIP network chooses SIP over H.323 as a call control protocol for session setup, modification, and teardown, there are still several legacy networks that work on H.323. From the perspective of DTMF, the configuration for H.323 is also done at the dial peer level, and there are three potential methods for DTMF relay:

- H.245 Signal
- H.245 Alphanumeric
- Named telephony events

Configuring H.245 Alphanumeric/Signal

You can configure H.323 dial peers for DTMF relay by either specifying the **h245-alphanumeric**, **h245-signal**, or **rtp-nte** argument to the **dtmf-relay** command. Example 7-23 shows a dial peer configured for H.245 Alphanumeric.

Example 7-23 *Dial Peer Configuration for H.245 Alphanumeric*

```
Dial-peer voice 20 voip
  description towards CUCM
  destination-pattern +1[2-9]..[2-9]......
  session target ipv4:10.1.1.2
  incoming called-number .
  voice-class codec 1
  dtmf-relay h245-alphanumeric
  no vad
```

Troubleshooting H.245 Alphanumeric and H.245 Signal

For a call being set up over H.323, to verify which method of the DTMF relay is negotiated, you examine the H.245 Terminal Capability Set (TCS) message. The contents of the TCS message would be different while advertising support for H.245 Alphanumeric/Signal and NTE. Example 7-24 provides a snippet of the TCS messages when negotiating H.245 Alphanumeric/Signal and NTE, respectively.

Example 7-24 *Debug H.245 Snippet for DTMF Negotiation over H.323*

```
value MultimediaSystemControlMessage ::= request : terminalCapabilitySet :
    {

/// truncated for brevity

              capabilityTableEntryNumber 3
           capability receiveAndTransmitDataApplicationCapability :
           {
                          {
           capabilityTableEntryNumber 5
           capability receiveAndTransmitUserInputCapability : basicString : NULL
         },



value MultimediaSystemControlMessage ::= request : terminalCapabilitySet :

/// truncated for brevity
              capabilityTableEntryNumber 3
           capability receiveAndTransmitDataApplicationCapability :
           {
                     {
           capabilityTableEntryNumber 4
           capability receiveAndTransmitUserInputCapability : dtmf : NULL
         }
  }


value MultimediaSystemControlMessage ::= request : terminalCapabilitySet :

/// truncated for brevity
        {
           capabilityTableEntryNumber 34
           capability receiveRTPAudioTelephonyEventCapability :
           {
             dynamicRTPPayloadType 101
             audioTelephoneEvent "0-16"
           }
         },
```

In Example 7-24, **basicString:NULL** refers to H.245 Alphanumeric, and **dtmf:NULL** refers to H.245 Signal.

With the call set up, the output of **debug h245 asn1** is analyzed to examine DTMF relay over the H.323 call leg. Example 7-25 provides a **debug h245 asn1** debug output snippet for the H.245 Alphanumeric and H.245 Signal scenarios, respectively:

Example 7-25 *Output of* **debug h245 asn1** *for H.245 Alphanumeric and H.245 Signal*

```
value MultimediaSystemControlMessage ::= indication : userInput :
alphanumeric
 :
"5"

value MultimediaSystemControlMessage ::= indication : userInput :
signal
 :              {
               signalType "5"
               duration 4000
             }
```

Note Cisco RTP, which is the method of DTMF on IOS, is not discussed in this chapter as its use has long been deprecated, and it has seen very little adoption in VoIP networks globally.

Summary

This chapter discusses the various methods of DTMF relay available in VoIP networks today from a standardization and operational perspective. It also discusses the role of SBCs in DTMF interplay.

References

RFC 3261, "SIP: Session Initiation Protocol," https://tools.ietf.org/html/rfc3261

RFC 2198, "RTP Payload for Redundant Audio Data," https://tools.ietf.org/html/rfc2198

RFC 2833, "RTP Payload for DTMF Digits, Telephony Tones and Telephony Signals," https://tools.ietf.org/html/rfc2833

RFC 4730, "A Session Initiation Protocol (SIP) Event Package for Key Press Stimulus (KPML)," https://tools.ietf.org/html/rfc4730

RFC 2976, "The SIP INFO Method," https://tools.ietf.org/html/rfc2976

RFC 6086, "Session Initiation Protocol (SIP) INFO Method and Package Framework," https://tools.ietf.org/html/rfc6086

RFC 4733, "RTP Payload for DTMF Digits, Telephony Tones, and Telephony Signals," https://tools.ietf.org/html/rfc4733

Recommendation H.323, "Packet-Based Multimedia Communication Systems," https://www.itu.int/rec/T-REC-H.323

Recommendation H.225, "Call Signalling Protocols and Media Stream Packetization for Packet-Based Multimedia Communications Systems," https://www.itu.int/rec/T-REC-H.225.0

Recommendation H.245, "Control Protocol for Multimedia Communication," https://www.itu.int/rec/T-REC-H.245

Chapter 8

Scalability Considerations

The previous chapters provide background on the foundational topics related to SBCs, and this chapter can proceed to a meaningful discussion of the approaches to sizing and scaling SBCs for a desired implementation. This chapter discusses the following major topics as they pertain to scalability and sizing considerations for SBCs:

- **Platform Sizing—**This section outlines the factors and constraints that dictate decisions around how to size the SBC platform for the desired environment. Specific sizing guidelines for CUBE are provided for the various supported platforms.
- **Licensing—**Because many vendors have implemented licensing mechanisms that are coupled to the quantity of SBC nodes and/or call capacity of the platform, licensing considerations and procedures are discussed in this section.
- **Oversubscription Prevention Techniques—**The final section of this chapter covers the general recommendations and techniques for preventing oversubscription of SBC-resources—including the RFCs for SIP overload control and Call Admission Control (CAC) techniques to control the use of finite system resources.

Though the topics in this chapter cover vendor-neutral concepts and approaches, note that a substantial amount of this topic is vendor and platform specific. When deploying an SBC, in considering sizing and licensing, be sure to consult design and deployment references specific for that vendor and platform. Also, given that sizing is tightly bound to the hardware available at the time, the platform-specific data in this chapter is subject to change as the publication ages. Please consult the Cisco Unified Border Element Data Sheet for the most recent information specific to these topics for CUBE.

This chapter covers the factors you need to understand to appropriately size an SBC deployment, license the deployment for the intended use, and control the finite resources of the platform effectively to prevent oversubscription or degradation of SBC service quality.

Platform Sizing

This section outlines the basic concepts involved in appropriately sizing an SBC platform for an environment. First, the general concepts around how vendors size SBCs are outlined, along with how to monitor and validate a platform's capability to operate within the existing capacity. Then, as sizing recommendations are inherently vendor and platform specific, this section also covers the specific sizing guidelines for CUBE.

General Scalability Concepts

Sizing of SBCs is usually governed by two main constraints: calls per second and concurrent calls. These statistics determine the call density capability of the SBC platform but alone are not enough to determine the SBC footprint needed for a deployment. In addition to understanding the capability of the platform, the call behavior of the user base and the nature of how the infrastructure devices communicates between each other for the intended call flows must also be understood to determine the overall SBC deployment needs.

The following sections cover how to determine the maximum SBC call size capability, as well as how to design for the capacity needs of the user base supported by the SBC service.

Calls per Second and Messages per Second

Calls per second (CPS) is a measurement of the number of attempted calls that are coming into the platform for setup at any given time. It is typically determined based on the number of inbound call setup requests for new discrete calls within a defined measurement period, typically a single second. The processing of call setup requests is demanding on the platform's resources. Current SBC platforms support a wide range of only a few CPS to more than 1000 CPS, depending on the platform hardware and processing capability.

Different call signaling protocols and different call flow types affect the extent to which the incoming call processing is affected. With a typical standard SIP call, there are a total of 14 messages (7 on each call leg) at a minimum. With early-offer calls, this increases to 9 messages per leg due to the addition of the PRACK transaction. Invoking supplementary call services such as call transfers, hold and resume, conferencing, or mid-call session refresh also increases the count of messages per call that need to be processed. As a result of a call having a variable number of messages, messages per second is a more ideal parameter for anticipating the capability of a platform; however, most vendors currently size SBCs based on CPS values instead of documenting messages-per-second capabilities.

Tip In complex call flows, such as for customer care (contact center) environments, the number of messages for a single call may increase by a factor of 3, to around 20 messages per call leg. This is due to the increase in call redirections and media renegotiations through the life of a single call.

When sizing for environments with a high density of complex call flows, it is worthwhile to consider the delta in message counts against the standard of 7 messages per leg and account for this extra processing. For example, if a standard call flow for the target environment has 21 messages per leg instead of 7, unless the vendor also has guidelines for message-per-second support on its platforms, it would be prudent to reduce the recommended CPS that the platform recommends by a factor of 3 to account for the extra messaging.

Most vendors run benchmark tests to define these guidelines and have a standard call flow type that is tested across the platform. Call density is then increased until the platform reaches a specific threshold of CPU and memory utilization that is deemed at the threshold of being acceptable. Although the CPU utilization can theoretically get to 99.99...% before it starts blocking messages and resulting in performance degradation, general practice is to keep CPU around a maximum average of 75% and peaks below 90%. Some SBC vendors also deploy techniques to block or deprioritize lower-priority tasks when resources get scarce, which may entail rejecting calls at a specific CPU threshold. Cisco IOS starts rejecting calls when the 5-second CPU value exceeds 98%.

The configuration of additional call features has the potential to impact and reduce the CPS from the benchmark tests. Consider that there may be some impact to the CPS capability when enabling features such as the following:

- Security features (for example, SRTP, TLS, IPsec, access lists, firewall, intrusion detection)
- Authentication, authorization, and accounting (AAA) lookups
- Gatekeeper requests
- Voice XML (VXML) or TCL scripts attached to calls
- CAC or Resource Reservation Protocol (RSVP)
- SIP normalization
- Media forking (such as call recording)
- Simple Network Management Protocol (SNMP) polling/logging or call detail record (CDR) reporting
- Multi-VRF (virtual routing and forwarding) support

Therefore, although vendors can provide guidelines on CPS for the platform, CPU should be monitored in the actual environment to understand actual behavior and identify conditions where CPU utilization could be causing impacts to SBC performance. The root concept is to understand if there are tasks that are waiting on availability of the CPU to process; although CPU utilization has high correlation to this condition, it is often not the best measurement to observe when application processes are waiting for system resources.

An alternative way to measure CPU performance is to observe the system load, which is the count of the active processes that are running or waiting. A system load value that is greater than the total number of CPU cores on the platform indicates that processes are waiting for a CPU to be available and creating latency.

Figure 8-1 provides a conceptual example of a system load of three on a four-core system. In this example, the system has an overall processing capacity of four simultaneous processes (one per core), yet there is only a system need for processing three processes. So, for this example, the instantaneous system load is three (all currently processing), against the overall capable capacity of four parallel processes. If four concurrent processes are exceeded, processes will have to wait in queue for processing. To put this another way, the system load is currently performing at 75% of the overall capacity in this example and, consequently, not introducing any additional delay due to queueing for processing time.

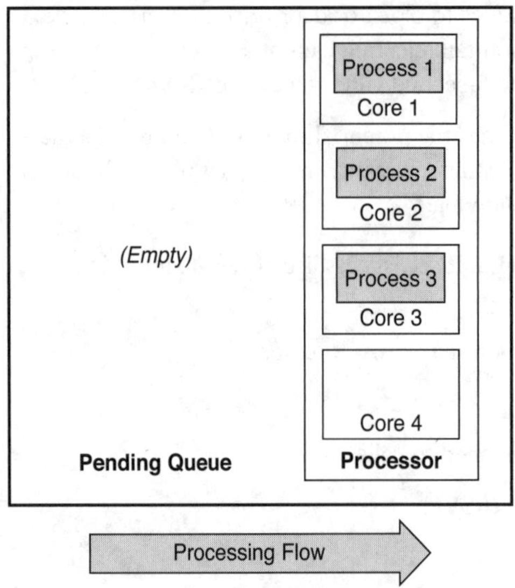

Figure 8-1 *Visual Demonstration of Underutilized System Load*

Now consider another example, where the same four-core system has more items to process within the same moment of time. In Figure 8-2, the system is processing four active processes, so there are not any more available cores to use. As a result, three additional processes are ready to be processed yet have to wait in the queue. A system load is the total of currently processing tasks plus those in the pending queue, so the system load here is measured as seven. Given that the system has only four cores, the system is currently being overloaded by 75% (100% – 7/4). This overload percentage is mathematically derived by subtracting 1 by the division of the system load and the number of cores, and representing as a percentage.

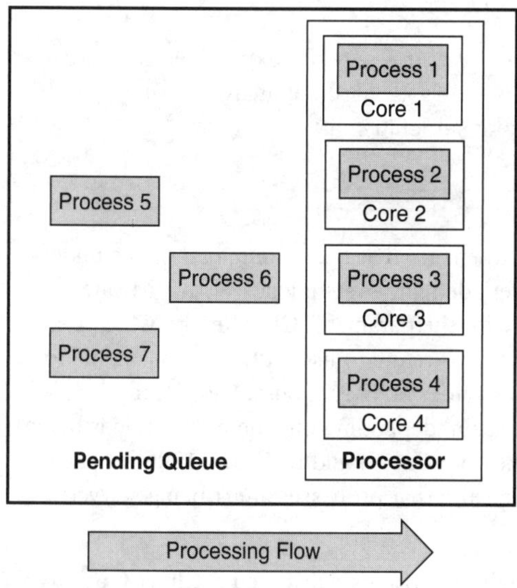

Figure 8-2 *Visual Demonstration of System Load Being Exceeded*

The instantaneous values are not the most meaningful measurements (and calculating them is not practical). What is more important is how quickly processes are entering and leaving the queue and CPU. Therefore, system load is often measured as an average of the values over a period of time and often represented as a decimal.

On Linux platforms (a common deployment platform for various SBC vendors), system load is measured with commands such as the **uptime** command, as shown in Example 8-1.

Example 8-1 *Output of the* **uptime** *Command on Linux to Measure System Load*

```
linux$ uptime
23:25  up 14:52, 2 users, load averages: 2.32 2.34 2.42
```

The highlighted values in Example 8-1 represent the 1-minute, 5-minute, and 15-minute averages of CPU load, respectively. This output was taken on an eight-core system and demonstrates that the system is operating under sufficient load, at about 30% of capacity (2.42 / 8).

> **Note** The system load value in the **uptime** command measures system load instead of CPU load. As a result, it also takes storage wait into account, so processes that are waiting due to high-storage input/output (I/O) are also observed here. This should be considered when troubleshooting high-system load, as the root cause may be poor storage I/O instead of a CPU throughput issue.
>
> Also, some vendors that base the SBC on a Linux platform may not expose the standard Linux CLI commands such as **uptime** to administrators. If these commands are not available on Linux-based SBCs, consult the vendor's documentation for equivalent means to identify the system load.

In virtual environments, it is also important to ensure that the system load of the underlying compute infrastructure is running under adequate system load. With VMware ESXi environments, CPU load be observed with the parameter **CPU Ready**, which is a measurement of times when a virtual machine was ready to use CPU but was unable to be scheduled due to underlying host CPU resources not being busy. CPU Ready is represented in either a percentage or a time duration, depending on where the value is being observed. VMware suggests that the CPU Ready value should be below 1000 ms (also sometimes represented as a value of 5%) to ensure that processes aren't being starved from CPU resources.

CPU Ready can be observed on ESXi through the options **Advanced > Chart Options > CPU > Real Time > Ready** under the virtual machine in vCenter. Figure 8-3 shows this output represented as a percentage, and Figure 8-4 shows the output represented as a duration of time:

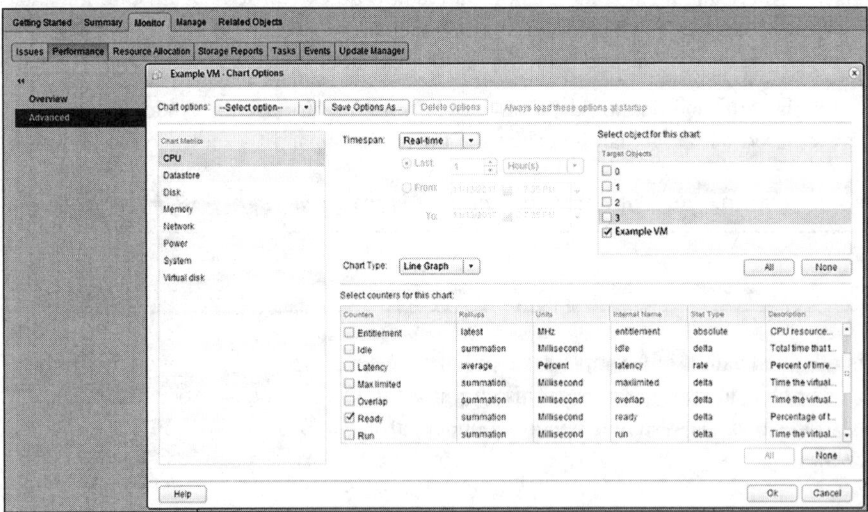

Figure 8-3 *Enabling CPU Ready Parameter in vCenter Chart Options*

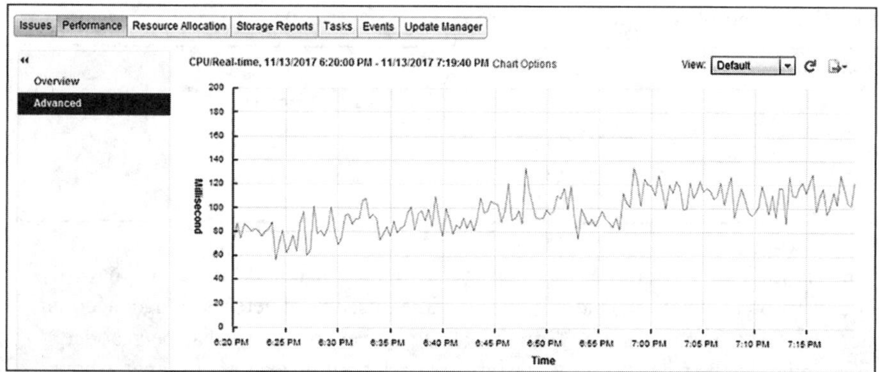

Figure 8-4 *Observing CPU Ready Values for System Load on ESXi Environments*

Monitoring of the CPU Ready value is especially important in virtual environments where a decision has been made to oversubscribe the virtual CPU (vCPU) allocation over the physical CPU cores (pCPUs) available. It is important to note that not all vendors support conditions where vCPUs are oversubscribed above a direct 1:1 relationship of vCPU to pCPU.

Concurrent Calls

Concurrent calls refers to the number of calls that are active on a platform at any given time. Depending on the platform, CPU may still be leveraged for forwarding of packets once a call is set up, but the typical significant constraint with the number of concurrent calls that a platform supports at once is the amount of available memory on the platform. Once the calls are already set up (as governed by the CPU constraints that impact CPS), the constraint shifts to the memory component. Memory is used to support both maintenance of the call state information and packet forwarding of the media stream. Note that many specialized SBC hardware platforms forward the majority of media plane packets in hardware to lessen the strain of packet forwarding on the CPU. The codec complexity and number of RTP and RTCP streams per call are main factors that dictate how many concurrent calls can be supported across the platform.

On Linux-based platforms, extra memory is used to cache information that is commonly read from disk. As a result, it is common to observe slow growth in used memory, but this should not be considered a memory leak, as the memory can be freed up again when needed. Instead of observing the used memory percentage, which includes the memory used by cache, the amount of memory used by cache should be ignored. On Linux-based platforms, available memory exclusive of the cache can be observed with the command **free -m**, as shown in Example 8-2.

Example 8-2 *Output of* **free -m** *to Observe Memory Utilization*

```
linux$ free -m
             total       used       free     shared buffers     cached
   Mem:  12286456   11715372     571084          0   81912    6545228
-/+ buffers/cache:    5088232    7198224
  Swap:  24571408      54528   24516880
```

Some recent Linux distributions (anything with **procps-3.3.10** and higher) will have a modified version of the command output, where the used parameter no longer accounts for the cache used by the system. With this change, a new parameter has been added, which is similar to the free count for **-/+ buffers/cache** but instead approximates how much memory would still be used by applications while still sparing a minimum amount of utilization for cache. Therefore, the **available** field provides a more real-word estimate of how much memory is available for applications than does **free -/+ buffers/cache.** The output of **free -m** with the **available** field is demonstrated in Example 8-3.

Example 8-3 *Changed Output of* **free -m** *to Observe Available Memory*

```
linux$ free -m
              total        used        free      shared  buff/cache   available
Mem:           3553        1192         857          16        1504        2277
Swap:          3689           0        3689
```

In addition to memory constraints that govern the concurrent call capacity, the concurrent call number is also potentially governed by any hard limits that may be placed on the platform (such as maximum calls supported). This limit may be platform or hardware specific, but it may also be restricted by the licensing of the platform permitting a specific maximum of concurrent calls.

Finally, if DSP resources are needed for transcoding, transrating, or interworking scenarios, then the total capacity of how many of these sessions can be supported must also be taken into account when determining the overall concurrent call capacity of the platform. Consult vendor-specific documentation to determine the total capacity of the available DSPs for the various scenarios where they may need to be invoked.

Call Traffic Engineering

Understanding only the capability of the platform is not enough to appropriately size an SBC environment. It is also important to understand the call volume of the overlaying user base that is consuming the SBC service.

The expected values of CPS and concurrent calls that will be seen in a call environment are largely based on two factors:

- **Busy hour call attempts (BHCAs)**—The quantity of call attempts made within the busiest hour of the day
- **Average handle time (AHT)**—The average time that a user is on a call, determined by the difference in time between call setup and final disconnect of the call

These values vary depending on the underlying nature of the user base that is placing and receiving calls. There is also an interaction effect between the two values, as the length of a call also dictates how many calls a user can potentially place in an hour. For instance, a manufacturing warehouse is likely to place fewer calls than a corporate office, and both will generally handle fewer calls than a customer care center. As a result, these different environments will result in different BHCAs based on the underlying worker types. Most non-contact center enterprises average between 1 and 2 BHCAs per user. When BHCA behavior is unknown, 4 BHCAs is a good value to use for non-contact center environments to account for unknowns. Contact center environments may be anywhere from 5 to 30 BHCAs per user. Contact center environments that see above 30 BHCAs per user are atypical, and as a result would require custom attention to sizing.

AHT values also vary based on the underlying work being performed. As a result, a contact center for a service desk handling password resets may be significantly lower than the AHT for a corporate office where employees are joining several hour-long conference calls in a day. The generally accepted practice in the industry for call traffic engineering is to use 3 minutes for AHT. Lower AHT values will be more demanding on the call infrastructure, so if it is known that a user base fields very short calls, this may be reduced to 90 seconds or substituted with the actual known AHT values that have been observed. Industry surveys show that the general average handling time is closer to somewhere between 7 and 15 minutes; therefore, using a 3-minute AHT as a standard for most deployments will help account for fluctuations and unknowns in call behavior as it is more aggressive than the reality generally seen in deployments.

When sizing for an SBC deployment, it is important to understand what the BHCA and AHT values are for the targeted environment. Usually, call detail records are available from the current call system, which can be leveraged to calculate the actual values for the environment. Actual values for BHCA and AHT should be used whenever possible to avoid invalid assumptions.

If previous values for call volume are not available, consider using the values listed in Table 8-1 as a starting point.

Table 8-1 *BHCA, AHT, and Concurrent Call Suggested Values*

Scenario	BHCA per User	Concurrent Calls (% of user base)	AHT
Low demand	>1	10%	3 minutes
Average enterprise	1.5	20%	3 minutes
High demand*	4	33%	3 minutes
Contact center	5–30	60–90%	3 minutes

* Consider using this specification when actual values are unknown to reduce the risk of the deployment sizing not being adequate.

In addition to understanding the characteristics discussed to this point, it is also important to understand how the call behavior corresponds to the type of calls the SBC will be handling. Not all calls considered for the concurrent call ratios may be going through the SBC deployed, based on the nature of how the calls route and for what call paths the SBC is intended to be deployed. Consider whether internal calls will still be routed across the SBC deployment and how SBCs distributed across different sites or regions may affect the call volume relevant for the SBC deployment.

Case Study: Sizing a Generic SBC

This section provides an example of an SBC deployment with the following requirements:

- Contact center integration
- 5 SIP-to-SIP calls per second
- 200 concurrent calls
- 10% of calls requiring transcoding between G.711 and G.729
- No expectation of additional capacity growth
- SBC high availability with stateful failover
- Geo-resiliency of SBC service across data centers

The following steps can be taken to appropriately size this SBC based on the requirements listed:

Step 1. Identify the vendor specification for calls per second and concurrent calls supported for the vendor's platform(s).

Step 2. Include any additional call volume that may either be anticipated for future growth or for a risk buffer as a precaution against unanticipated factors.

Step 3. Assess the CPS requirements for the targeted deployment. Also consider that if there is a significant presence of complex call flows, the increased SIP messaging per call may reduce the vendor's baseline guidelines on CPS.

Step 4. Factor in any additional features or supplementary services that may further reduce sizing based on vendor's guidance and adjust accordingly. Refer to the list in the section "Calls per Second and Messages per Second," earlier in this chapter, for some potential examples.

Step 5. Select a platform that meets the minimum requirements for both calls per second and concurrent calls, as determined in steps 1–4.

Step 6. Assess whether any other features are needed on the SBC that may exist only on some subset of the platform offerings to ensure that the target platform meets the functional needs of the deployment.

Step 7. If providing a design with local resiliency, account for the additional hardware needs to support local high availability of the SBC service.

Step 8. If providing a design with geo-resiliency, replicate the design in a second data center. Then account for this resiliency with the call routing design of these other components to provide geo-resiliency in the event that the SBC in one of the data centers becomes unavailable.

Based on the requirements, the SBC platform(s) to be selected for the deployment of this case study must meet a total of 5 SIP-to-SIP calls per second and 200 concurrent calls. There is a desire to be able to handle all the call-processing needs on a single active device, avoiding the need for external devices to load balance across multiple active SBCs.

The vendor chosen for this case study guides CPS only for standard SIP calls. Because this deployment is for a contact center, the vendor's CPS requirements must be adjusted to better reflect the message density in the contact center environment. As a result, the base requirement of 5 CPS will be adjusted by a factor of three to account for the three-fold increase in per call SIP messaging in this contact center environment. Therefore, this environment will be sized against vendor guidelines for a platform that supports 15 CPS even though only an anticipated maximum of 5 CPS will be observed on this contact center platform.

Due to 10% of the calls requiring a transcoder, DSPs will also be needed. As a result, based on DSP calculations to support 20 high-complexity transcoding sessions for this platform, a hardware DSP module with 64 channels is selected for purchase with each chassis.

No additional features, such a SRTP or Multi-VRF routing, are needed for this deployment, so further adjustments to sizing are not needed at this point. Given the requirements for high availability, each data center would get two of the vendor's medium-class chassis, so one device in a pair can perform as a warm standby. This design would then be replicated in an additional data center to provide geo-resiliency, resulting in a total of four devices being purchased to support these deployment requirements.

Because the concurrent call volume required is much less than the platform can handle, no additional memory expansions would be needed on these devices for this scenario.

The sizing of this platform doesn't allow for any additional growth with the incoming call rate of 15 CPS, but it allows for 60% growth of transcoding resource needs and 93% growth of concurrent calls.

After these SBCs are deployed, utilization of CPU, memory, and media resources will be monitored and logged. The goal of this monitoring is to validate that the capacity assumptions from the original requirements are met and that the router is performing adequately based on the actual load across the platform for this specific production environment.

Monitoring thresholds will then be defined for the resource capacities, such that if demand on the router grows unexpectedly over time and consistently crosses above 75% for system load or memory utilization, administrators will be notified to purchase additional resources for handling the growth in demand.

CUBE Sizing

Many of the general sizing concepts outlined in the previous section also dictate how CUBE deployments are sized for call environments. This section describes the various items that may constrain CUBE's call volume capability.

General CUBE Platform Sizing

With CUBE, the number of concurrent sessions and calls-per-second capability depend on the underlying platform. IOS-XE platforms where the signaling and media planes are discrete (such as the ASR series) allow for significantly higher CPS capability than platforms with monolithic processing. The improved performance is due to the platform's use of separate hardware for handling of call signaling from the hardware for forwarding of established call's media streams.

Sizing of the virtual CUBE environments (that is, vCUBE on the CSR 1000v) is dependent upon the CPU and DRAM provisioning.

For the most up-to-date information on CUBE sizing, consult the current Cisco Unified Border Element Data Sheet.

The following are some items to keep in mind when sizing CUBE for a deployment:

- CPS capability decreases for more complex call flows where more messages per second need to be processed.
- Media forking for call recording reduces the maximum sessions and CPS by the number of multiple sessions per call leg (for example, 5 calls being recorded to a single server would be considered a total of 10 sessions).
- Multi-VRF support increases processing overhead in proportion to the number of VRFs configured.
- Enabling the call monitoring feature slightly reduces the platform's maximum concurrent call volume.

Media Resource Sizing for CUBE

In situations where media resources need to be invoked, the DSP resources may become a constraint before the platform's call limitations are reached for concurrent calls.

When a transcoder (for converting between two mismatched codecs or transrating between two packetization/payload rates) is needed on CUBE, physical DSPs are required. As a result, when sizing a CUBE platform, it is important to properly size for the number of DSPs on the platform. Each platform has a different capable DSP density based on both the number of DSP slots available and the type of DSPs for the platform. Different DSP types may also support different densities for each codec. For either of these scenarios, the MTPs should be registered to UCM as a transcoder; this is a minor difference from when solving for transrating to UCM where a hardware MTP is configured. CUBE only supports registration of a transcoder resource and not a hardware MTP resource for the use of transrating.

Note that in situations where transcoding sessions may be reached before CUBE's concurrent session limit is reached, the platform will still support the remainder of calls to reach the concurrent session limit as non-transcoder-invoked calls, as long as the latter is permissible by the needs of the call flow.

Tip DSP calculation can be done with the online DSP Calculator at Cisco.com. Due to the complexities of calculating DSP densities across the various DSP platforms and codec scenarios, it is recommended to leverage this tool to determine details of the underlying DSP hardware.

Before outlining the DSP density capabilities on platforms, a key concept of codec complexity must be discussed. It takes various processing power to encode and decode the various codecs, so codecs have been categorized into three general complexity buckets for ease of calculation. Each DSP platform may vary in terms of the complexity with which it treats each specific codec that it supports. Codec complexity is categorized as low, medium, and high. Enabling secure RTP codecs may also influence the complexity associated to the codec of interest.

In addition to considering codec complexity, it is important to understand the DSP type and quantities that each CUBE platform supports to appropriately determine the DSP capacity of a platform. Each CUBE platform supports different models of DSPs, and the various models differ in their capacity. Likewise, the various CUBE platforms also have varying numbers of DSP slots, and the number of slots influences the total number of DSPs that can be supported on the platform. Consult the router platform and DSP data sheets for more information on the current options.

Figure 8-5 shows a hypothetical router chassis with three DSP slots to house three DSP cards. The diagram demonstrates how a DSP card can be loaded in many permutations, based on the total capacity supported by a DSP. This example shows that these DSP card types could support 20 G.729 calls, 43 G.711 calls, or a combination thereof, such as 18 G.729 calls and 4 G.711 calls on a DSP. Note that there can be some unused DSP capacity, depending on how the different permitations of the codecs and quantities fit against the DSP's available capacity.

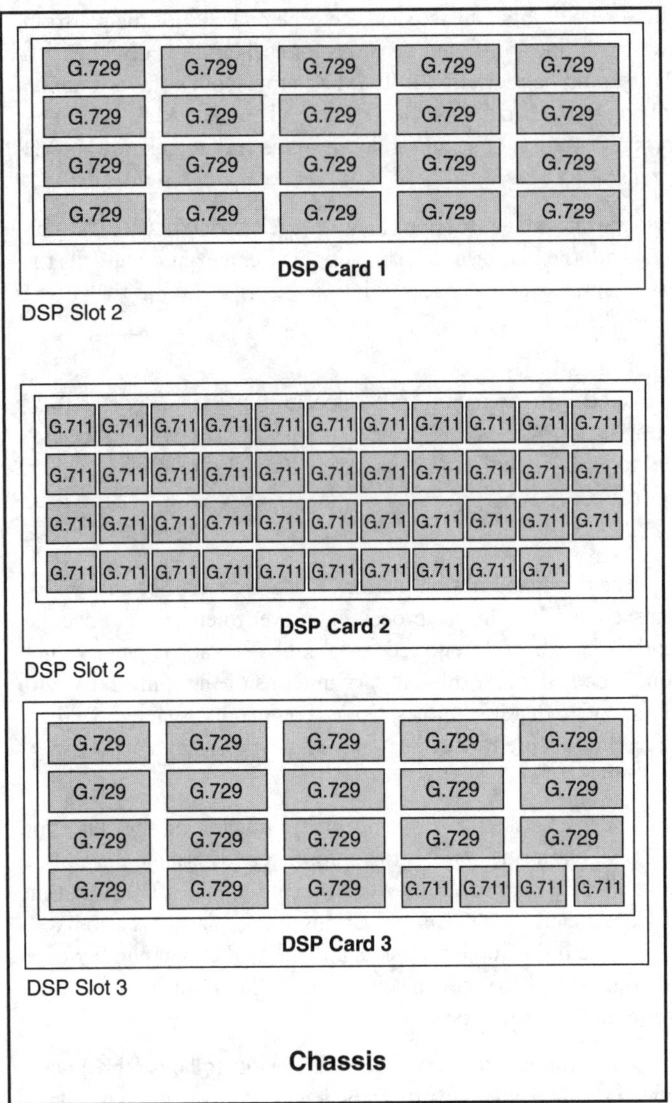

Figure 8-5 *DSP Capacity with Mixed Codecs*

When codec complexity or the call density that is supported for a DSP platform is not known, it can be verified with the **show voice dsp capabilities** command shown in Example 8-4.

Example 8-4 *Output of* **show voice dsp capabilities** *to Validate DSP Codec Density*

```
CUBE# show voice dsp capabilities slot 0 dsp 2

DSP Type: SP2600 -43
Card 0 DSP id 2 Capabilities:
Credits 645, G711Credits 15, HC Credits 32, MC Credits 20,
FC Channel 43, HC Channel 20, MC Channel 32,
Conference 8-party credits:
G711 58, G729 107, G722 129, ILBC 215
Secure Credits:
Sec LC Xcode 24, Sec HC Xcode 64,
Sec MC Xcode 35, Sec G729 conf 161,
Sec G722 conf 215, Sec ILBC conf 322,
Sec G711 conf 92,
Max Conference Parties per DSP:
G711 88, G729 48, G722 40, ILBC 24,
Sec G711 56, Sec G729 32,
Sec G722 24 Sec ILBC 16,
Voice Channels:
g711perdsp = 43, g726perdsp = 32, g729perdsp = 20, g729aperdsp = 32,
g723perdsp = 20, g728perdsp = 20, g723perdsp = 20, gsmperdsp = 32,
gsmefrperdsp = 20, gsmamrnbperdsp = 20,
ilbcperdsp = 20, modemrelayperdsp = 20
g72264Perdsp = 32, h324perdsp = 20,
m_f_thruperdsp = 43, faxrelayperdsp = 32,
maxchperdsp = 43, minchperdsp = 20,
srtp_maxchperdsp = 27, srtp_minchperdsp = 14, faxrelay_srtp_perdsp = 14,
g711_srtp_perdsp = 27, g729_srtp_perdsp = 14, g729a_srtp_perdsp = 24,
```

The output from Example 8-4 has the following important components:

- **Credits 645**—These are the total MIPS (machine instructions per second) processing cycles for the DSP, which correspond to the total density of processing that the DSP can support.
- **G711Credits 15**—These are the number of credits used for a single G.711 call, also referred to as flex complexity (FC), which in this case is 15 credits per call.
- **HC Credits 32**—High-complexity codecs use 32 credits on this DSP platform.
- **MC Credits 20**—Medium-complexity codecs use 20 credits on this DSP platform.
- **FC Channel 43**—This is the total number of flex calls supported on the entire DSP (or channel), which is the number of FC calls that can fit on the DSP. This is the same as calculating the codec complexity (15 for FC on this DSP) into the total number of credits (645) for the DSP.

- **HC Channel**—This is the same as the **FC Channel** but for high-complexity codecs. (that is, 645 / 32 = 20 high-complexity calls for each channel.)
- **Sec HC Xcode 64**—Transcoding to a high-complexity SRTP codec takes 64 credits. (The encryption requires more DSP processing than that of a normal high-complexity call.)
- **g711perdsp = 43**—This is the list of each codec supported on the platform and the total calls supported by the platform. These are the same values as for **Channel**, listed earlier in the output, but now listed for each specific codec to help when the complexity is not known for a coded with a specific DSP type.

Note When sizing for a hardware transcoder, the values from the command in Example 8-4 are used to determine the complexity of the codec of interest. When sizing for a transcoder, the codec complexity of the highest-complexity codec should be used to determine the transcoding density.

For instance, with the DSP type shown in Example 8-4 (SP2600, which is a PVDM3), if a hardware transcoder is invoked for a G.711-to-G.711, then both legs are G.711, and hence the credits for a low-complexity codec are consumed. In contrast, if a hardware transcoder is used for a G.711-to-G.726 call, the transcoder will use credits neccessary for processing a medium-complexity codec due to G.726 processing requiring medium complexity. Similarly, when transcoding G.729 to either G.711 or G.722 on this DSP platform, it would would use high complexity due to G.729 being a high complexity codec.

Troubleshooting Scalability Issues

To validate that there aren't capacity issues on CUBE, there are three key components to observe:

- CPU utilization and system load
- Memory utilization
- Media resource rejection

The troubleshooting methodologies for these items are described in the subsequent subsections.

CPU Utilization and System Load

It is important to monitor the CPU and system load on a platform to ensure that the calls per second and message processing are not putting the system in a situation where message processing is degraded. The goal is to keep average CPU processing below a 75% average. Monitoring of CPU through SNMP is discussed at length in Chapter 14, "Monitoring and Management."

As mentioned earlier in this chapter, though, CPU utilization does not provide the most accurate measurement of load on a platform for processing. System load is a measurement that expresses the system load and any processes that are getting starved, and it more accurately reflects system processing performance than CPU utilization. With IOS-XE platforms (discussed in Chapter 2, "SBC Deployment Models"), system load can be observed with the command shown in Example 8-5.

Example 8-5 *Validation of System Load on IOS-XE*

```
Router# show platform software status control-processor brief | section Load
Load Average
 Slot  Status  1-Min  5-Min 15-Min
  RP0 Healthy   0.25   0.30   0.44
  ESP0 Healthy   0.01   0.05   0.02
  SIP0 Healthy   0.15   0.07   0.01
```

In Example 8-5, note the presence of a discrete entry for each processing module (for example, RP0, ESP0, SIP0).

The target values for system load will depend upon how many processing cores are available for each of the different control processor types. Target system load values should not peak above the number of cores available to the specific processing module. When system load values are greater than the number of processing cores, the system is experiencing load where the platform cannot process as fast as there is demand. Such scenarios result in some amount of performance degradation, as processes are waiting in a queue to be processed. The number of cores on a module can be found by referencing the corresponding data sheet for that module.

Example 8-6 provides an example that demonstrates excessive load for both the 1- and 5-minute averages. This example is from a platform with two cores for RP0, two cores for ESP0, and two cores for SIP0. Therefore, the target average load value to prevent processing latency is to keep each of these values below the number of cores (2). Highlighted values represent excessive load.

Example 8-6 *Excessive System Load on IOS-XE*

```
Router# show platform software status control-processor brief | section Load
Load Average
 Slot  Status  1-Min  5-Min 15-Min
  RP0 Healthy   1.25   1.30   3.44
  ESP0 Healthy   3.01   2.05   1.02
  SIP0 Healthy   1.15   2.07   1.01
```

It is advisable to log the system load values to a central monitoring appliance so that the system load can be trended and correlated to busy call periods in the network. System load trends should be periodically reviewed for the peak system load values, with the CPS or messages per second being observed during that period of time. It is also important to set a threshold to alert administrators if the system load is peaking above the number of cores on the platform to raise awareness when there may be degradation in platform performance. These monitoring concepts are discussed further in Chapter 14. Table 8-2 lists examples of OIDs for system load on IOS-XE.

Table 8-2 *OIDs Corresponding to System Load for IOS-XE*

Time Interval	Module	OID
1-minute	RP0	1.3.6.1.4.1.9.9.109.1.1.1.1.24.2
	ESP0	1.3.6.1.4.1.9.9.109.1.1.1.1.24.3
	SIP0	1.3.6.1.4.1.9.9.109.1.1.1.1.24.4
5-minute	RP0	1.3.6.1.4.1.9.9.109.1.1.1.1.25.2
	ESP0	1.3.6.1.4.1.9.9.109.1.1.1.1.25.3
	SIP0	1.3.6.1.4.1.9.9.109.1.1.1.1.25.4
15-minute	RP0	1.3.6.1.4.1.9.9.109.1.1.1.1.26.2
	ESP0	1.3.6.1.4.1.9.9.109.1.1.1.1.26.3
	SIP0	1.3.6.1.4.1.9.9.109.1.1.1.1.26.4

Because system load is highly correlated to the CPS and messages per second on the platform, it is often beneficial to understand where the CPS value is peaking on the platform.

CUBE has a useful command, **show call history stats cps**, that can be used to identify details on the CPS occurring up to the last 72 hours on the platform (see Example 8-7).

Example 8-7 *Sample Output of* **show call history stats cps** *to Observe Max CPS*

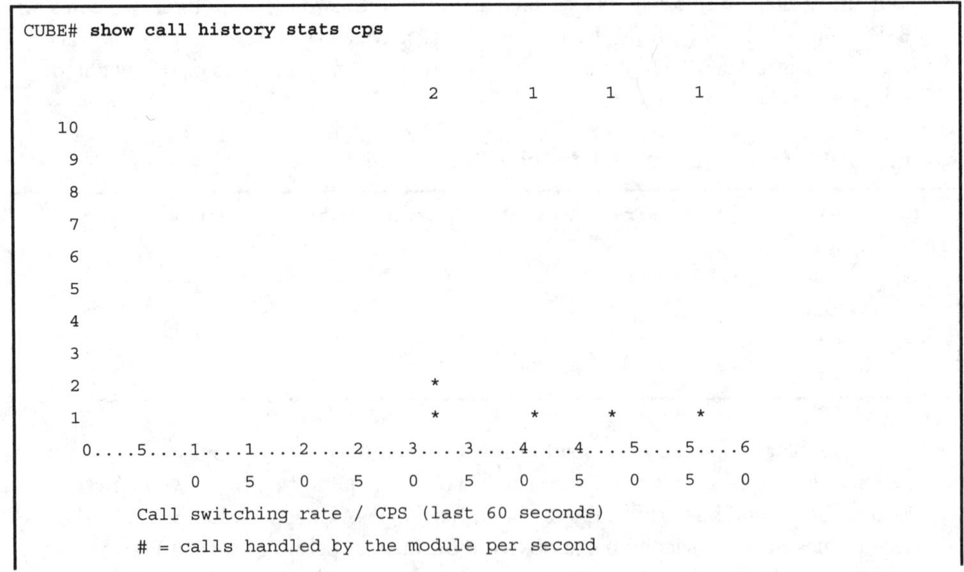

```
CUBE# show call history stats cps

                                     2        1      1       1
   10
    9
    8
    7
    6
    5
    4
    3
    2                                *
    1                                *        *      *       *
     0....5....1....1....2....2....3....3....4....4....5....5....6
               0    5    0    5    0    5    0    5    0    5    0
          Call switching rate / CPS (last 60 seconds)
          # = calls handled by the module per second
```

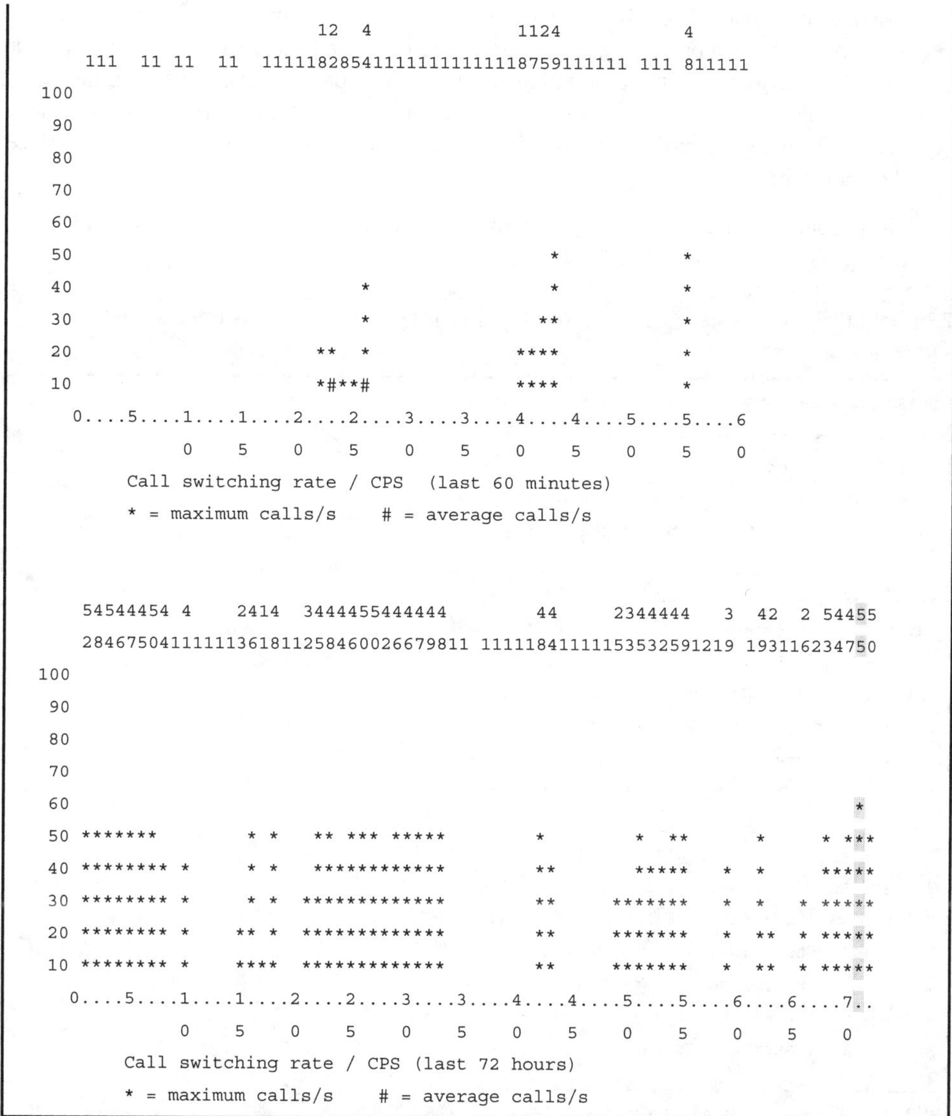

```
                         12 4            1124           4
    111  11 11  11  1111182854111111111118759111111 111 811111
100
 90
 80
 70
 60
 50                                         *           *
 40                         *               *           *
 30                         *              **           *
 20                      ** *            ****           *
 10                      *#**#           ****           *
   0....5....1....1....2....2....3....3....4....4....5....5....6
             0    5    0    5    0    5    0    5    0    5    0
        Call switching rate / CPS  (last 60 minutes)
        * = maximum calls/s    # = average calls/s


    54544454 4    2414  3444455444444        44     2344444   3  42  2 54455
    28467504111111361811258460026679811 11111841111153532591219 193116234750
100
 90
 80
 70
 60                                                                       *
 50 *******        * *   ** *** *****        *        *  **      *     * ***
 40 ******** *     * *   ************        **       *****   *  *     *****
 30 ******** *     * *  *************        **     *******   *  *   * *****
 20 ******** *    ** *  *************        **     *******   *  **  * *****
 10 ******** *    ****  *************        **     *******   *  **  * *****
   0....5....1....1....2....2....3....3....4....4....5....5....6....6....7..
             0    5    0    5    0    5    0    5    0    5    0    5    0
        Call switching rate / CPS (last 72 hours)
        * = maximum calls/s    # = average calls/s
```

Tip Because the y-axis represents only 10% intervals, the actual values for the peaks in the output in Example 8-7 are written horizontally in the x-axis above the chart. For example, the peak value for 71 hours ago was 55 and has been highlighted for reference, as shown in the second to last column in the third chart.

The output in Example 8-7 is useful for understanding the peak values for CPS, but it has a 72-hour limitation on history. Alternatively, the command **show call history watermark cps table** provides absolute timestamps for the top five peak values, across four intervals of time since the last router reload (all-time). The titles of the sections are somewhat misleading: They represent the previous 60 seconds, 60 minutes, 72 hours, and all-time (since the last router reload).

The output shown in Example 8-8 demonstrates a peak CPS of 63 calls per second during **Thu, 26 Oct 2017 17:16:21 GMT.**

Example 8-8 *Example Output for* **show call history watermark cps table** *to Observe Times of Peak CPS*

```
CUBE# show call history watermark cps table
==============================================
   Calls Per Second / CPS
==============================================
------- The WaterMark Table for Second --------
______________________________________________
Value : 2, ts : [Wed, 01 Nov 2017 13:59:28 GMT]
Value : 1, ts : [Wed, 01 Nov 2017 13:59:19 GMT]
Value : 1, ts : [Wed, 01 Nov 2017 13:59:12 GMT]
Value : 1, ts : [Wed, 01 Nov 2017 13:59:04 GMT]
Value : 0, ts : [Wed, 01 Nov 2017 13:59:29 GMT]
==============================================
------- The WaterMark Table for Minute-------
______________________________________________
Value : 43, ts : [Wed, 01 Nov 2017 13:17:24 GMT]
Value : 55, ts : [Wed, 01 Nov 2017 13:15:20 GMT]
Value : 26, ts : [Wed, 01 Nov 2017 13:34:39 GMT]
Value : 42, ts : [Wed, 01 Nov 2017 13:18:24 GMT]
Value : 23, ts : [Wed, 01 Nov 2017 13:37:28 GMT]
==============================================
------- The WaterMark Table for Hour --------
______________________________________________
Value : 55, ts : [Sun, 29 Oct 2017 14:15:24 GMT]
Value : 54, ts : [Wed, 01 Nov 2017 11:00:00 GMT]
Value : 53, ts : [Sun, 29 Oct 2017 18:00:30 GMT]
Value : 52, ts : [Wed, 01 Nov 2017 13:10:40 GMT]
Value : 50, ts : [Wed, 01 Nov 2017 07:20:00 GMT]
==============================================
```

```
------- The WaterMark Table for All-Time-------
______________________________________________
Value : 63, ts : [Thu, 26 Oct 2017 17:16:21 GMT]
Value : 61, ts : [Fri, 01 Sep 2017 18:02:03 GMT]
Value : 58, ts : [Fri, 20 Oct 2017 13:01:36 GMT]
Value : 58, ts : [Fri, 15 Sep 2017 12:13:41 GMT]
Value : 56, ts : [Mon, 18 Sep 2017 06:10:20 GMT]
==============================================
```

Finally, although CPS is the typical means by which SBC vendors size platforms, processing is more determined by the overall message processing count. CUBE also has a way to uncover the average and peak SIP messages per second, through the respective commands **show sip-ua history stats message-rate** and **show sip-ua history watermark message-rate table**. The structure of these commands' output is identical to that found in Example 8-8, except for representing the message rate histroy instead of CPS history.

The values for the commands used in Examples 8-7 and 8-8 are also exposed with SNMP through **cvCallVolumeStatsHistory**, and the parent OIDs of interest are shown in Table 8-3.

Table 8-3 *SNMP OIDs for CUBE Call Volume Statistics*

SNMP Object	OID
cvCallRateStatsTable	1.3.6.1.4.1.9.9.63.1.4.3.1
cvSipMsgRateStatsTable	1.3.6.1.4.1.9.9.63.1.4.3.5
cvSipMsgRateWMTable	1.3.6.1.4.1.9.9.63.1.4.3.9
cvCallRateWMTable	1.3.6.1.4.1.9.9.63.1.4.3.6

Each of the OIDs from Table 8-3 have child attributes that offer maximum and average values for the defined interval.

Memory Utilization

In addition to observing processing load, it is important to continually monitor memory utilization of a CUBE platform. Memory is important for two main reasons: to identify whether the concurrent call capacity is encroaching on the limit of the platform, and to detect the presence of memory leaks.

Much as when monitoring or troubleshooting CPU and system load issues, it is useful to monitor and trend memory utilization with network management software. Trends in memory utilization are useful for identifying times when memory utilization is exceptionally high.

For classic IOS platforms, **show memory statistics history** can be used to observe a historical trend up through 3 days. The two main items of interest are the average memory utilization and ensuring that available memory does not become starved. Example 8-9 provides an example of output from this command.

Example 8-9 *Output of* show memory statistics history

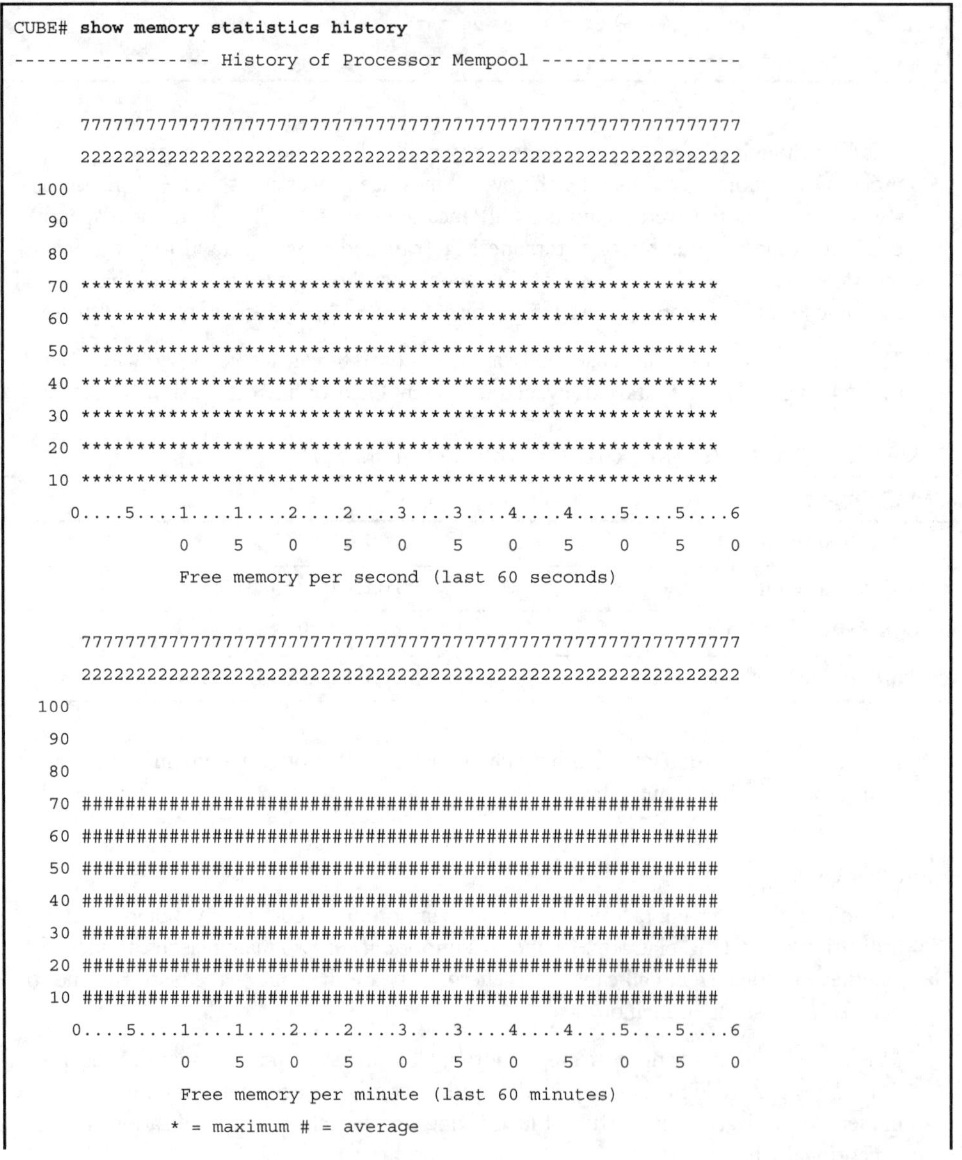

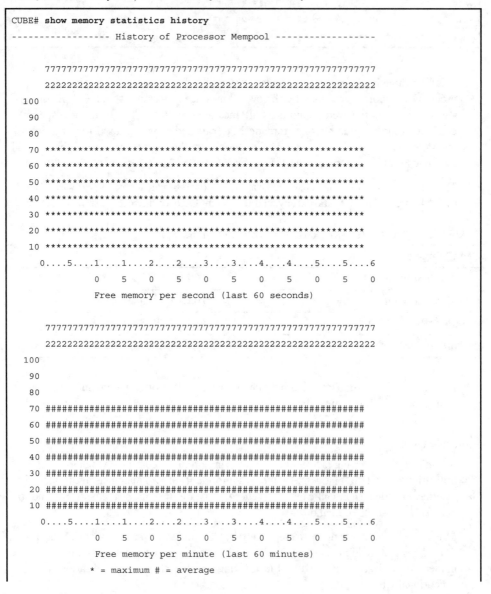

```
CUBE# show memory statistics history
----------------- History of Processor Mempool -----------------

      777777777777777777777777777777777777777777777777777777777777
      222222222222222222222222222222222222222222222222222222222222
  100
   90
   80
   70 **********************************************************
   60 **********************************************************
   50 **********************************************************
   40 **********************************************************
   30 **********************************************************
   20 **********************************************************
   10 **********************************************************
     0....5....1....1....2....2....3....3....4....4....5....5....6
               0    5    0    5    0    5    0    5    0    5    0
               Free memory per second (last 60 seconds)

      777777777777777777777777777777777777777777777777777777777777
      222222222222222222222222222222222222222222222222222222222222
  100
   90
   80
   70 ##########################################################
   60 ##########################################################
   50 ##########################################################
   40 ##########################################################
   30 ##########################################################
   20 ##########################################################
   10 ##########################################################
     0....5....1....1....2....2....3....3....4....4....5....5....6
               0    5    0    5    0    5    0    5    0    5    0
               Free memory per minute (last 60 minutes)
              * = maximum # = average
```

```
    777777777777777777777777777777777777777777777777777777777777777777777777
     222222222233333333333333334444444444444444455555555555555566666666666666667777
100
 90
 80                                        **#############################
 70 ######################################################################
 60 ######################################################################
 50 ######################################################################
 40 ######################################################################
 30 ######################################################################
 20 ######################################################################
 10 ######################################################################
    0....5....1....1....2....2....3....3....4....4....5....5....6....6....7..
              0    5    0    5    0    5    0    5    0    5    0    5    0
                  Free memory per hour (last 72 hours)
                  * = maximum # = average
```

Remember that Linux-based platforms handle memory differently. Consumed memory is used as cache, and this cache is discarded or reduced later, when other applications need to utilize that memory space. As a result, with IOS-XE, it is not useful to observe memory utilization the same way as mentioned earlier, as memory reserved for cache is still potentially available memory for use when needed.

For IOS-XE, instead of monitoring utilized memory, you can use the command **show platform software status control-processor brief** to observe the instantaneous committed memory utilization. Example 8-10 shows abbreviated output of this command, which is obtained by suffixing the parameter **| section Memory**.

Example 8-10 *Viewing Committed Memory for IOS-XE*

```
CUBE# show platform software status control-processor brief | section Memory
Memory (kB)
 Slot   Status    Total      Used(Pct)       Free (Pct)       Committed (Pct)
 RP0    Healthy   3874504    2188404 (56%)   1686100 (44%)    2155996 (56%)
 ESP0   Healthy    969088     590880 (61%)    378208 (39%)     363840 (38%)
 SIP0   Healthy    471832     295292 (63%)    176540 (37%)     288540 (61%)
```

The output in Example 8-10 shows the committed memory (that is, the amount of utilized memory minus the memory used for temporary cache), which cannot be relinquished and repurposed for other needs. In other words, the committed memory is the memory that the system needs for current operations. Example 8-10 shows that 23% of the **ESP0** memory (calculated as the difference between 61% and 38%) is being used for temporary cache.

When trending this memory construct across time, the SNMP OIDs shown in Tables 8-4 through 8-6 are useful.

Table 8-4 *OIDs for Committed Memory (***cpmCPUMemoryHCCommitted***)*

Module	OID
RP0	1.3.6.1.4.1.9.9.109.1.1.1.1.29.2
ESP0	1.3.6.1.4.1.9.9.109.1.1.1.1.29.3
SIP0	1.3.6.1.4.1.9.9.109.1.1.1.1.29.4

Functional memory that is available would be the difference between the total available on the platform and **cpmCPUMemoryHCCommitted.** To convert the raw values for committed memory from above into the percentage utilized, the committed memory utilization can be compared against the sum of the used and free memory (effectively comparing committed memory against the total memory on the platform). The corresponding OIDs for used and free memory are outlined in Tables 8-5 and 8-6.

Table 8-5 *OIDs for Memory Used, Inclusive of Temporary Cache (***cpmCPUMemoryHCUsed***)*

Module	OID
RP0	1.3.6.1.4.1.9.9.109.1.1.1.1.17.2
ESP0	1.3.6.1.4.1.9.9.109.1.1.1.1.17.3
SIP0	1.3.6.1.4.1.9.9.109.1.1.1.1.17.4

Table 8-6 *OIDs for Memory Available but Not Being Used (***cpmCPUMemoryHCFree***)*

Module	OID
RP0	1.3.6.1.4.1.9.9.109.1.1.1.1.19.2
ESP0	1.3.6.1.4.1.9.9.109.1.1.1.1.19.3
SIP0	1.3.6.1.4.1.9.9.109.1.1.1.1.19.4

When troubleshooting potential scalability issues on a platform, it is important to observe the utilized (IOS) or committed (IOS-XE) memory on the platform to ensure that there is enough available memory for the platform to perform adequately. From the perspective of CUBE scalability, if used memory (IOS) or committed memory (IOS-XE) utilization approaches the physical available limit, the concurrent call volume being handled across the platform should be decreased.

Media Resource Capacity

It is often not possible to anticipate the number of calls that will need media resources in an actual call environment, as the need to transcode or transrate calls often depends upon external factors that may be intermittent from the remote side of the integration. For example, it is not uncommon for calls across CUBE to an ITSP with exactly the same calling and called numbers to intermittently offer different codecs, determined by the call path taken in the ITSP cloud for each call instance. As a result, it is likely necessary to monitor and tune the media resources available when production call load on the system is observed. From this, the percentage of calls that need media resources can be observed and then used as a benchmark to scale as demand changes the overall call volume across the SBC.

Utilization of media resources can be observed in real time with the command **show dspfarm all.** Example 8-11 shows output of this command, with active sessions for a transcoder (profile 3).

Example 8-11 *Validating Active Media Resource Utilization with* **show dspfarm all**

```
Cube1# show dspfarm all
Dspfarm Profile Configuration

 Profile ID = 3, Service = TRANSCODING, Resource ID = 3
 Profile Service Mode : Non Secure
 Profile Admin State : UP
 Profile Operation State : ACTIVE
 Application : CUBE   Status : ASSOCIATED
 Resource Provider : FLEX_DSPRM   Status : UP
 Total Number of Resources Configured : 2
 Total Number of Resources Available : 1
 Total Number of Resources Out of Service : 0
 Total Number of Resources Active : 1
 Codec Configuration: num_of_codecs:5
 Codec : g729r8, Maximum Packetization Period : 60
 Codec : g711ulaw, Maximum Packetization Period : 30
 Codec : g711alaw, Maximum Packetization Period : 30
 Codec : g729ar8, Maximum Packetization Period : 60
 Codec : g729abr8, Maximum Packetization Period : 60

SLOT   DSP VERSION  STATUS CHNL USE   TYPE    RSC_ID BRIDGE_ID PKTS_TXED PKTS_RXED

0/1     1  46.2.0   UP     1    USED  xcode   1      13        0         5
0/1     1  46.2.0   UP     N/A  FREE  xcode   4      -         -         -


Total number of DSPFARM DSP channel(s) 2
```

Some of the statistics shown in Example 8-11 are also available through SNMP. Tables 8-7 and 8-8 outline the applicable OIDs for these statistics for overall and profile-specific utilization of media resources.

Table 8-7 *SNMP OIDs for Overall Media Resource Utilization*

Object	OID	Description
cdspTotAvailTranscodeSess	1.3.6.1.4.1.9.9.86.1.7.1	Total configured transcoder sessions across all profiles on the platform
cdspTotUnusedTranscodeSess	1.3.6.1.4.1.9.9.86.1.7.2	Total unused transcoder sessions across all profiles on the platform

Table 8-8 *SNMP OIDs for Profile-Specific Media Resource Utilization*

Object	OID	Description
cdspTranscodeProfileMax-ConfSess	1.3.6.1.4.1.9.9.86.1.6.3.1.2	Maximum configured trans-coding sessions per profile
cdspTranscodeProfileMax-AvailSess	1.3.6.1.4.1.9.9.86.1.6.3.1.3	Current available transcoding sessions per profile

Tip The profile-specific OIDs use the profile number as the suffix of the OID.

When media resources deplete, CUBE fails with a Q.850 cause value of 47 (**Resource unavailable, unspecified**). It is therefore useful to monitor when calls fail with this cause code on CUBE. The robust way to perform this is to observe cause values through centralized CDR collection from CUBE.

The command **show h323 gateway cause-code** can be used to quickly observe whether there is an increase in the number of call failure codes caused by a lack of media resources. Example 8-12 shows output for this command, which is available for use with H.323 calls through CUBE.

Example 8-12 *Output of* **show h323 gateway cause-code** *for Observing Media Resource Failure*

```
CUBE# show h323 gateway cause-code

CAUSE CODE STATISTICS AT 01:40:25

DISC CAUSE CODE            FROM OTHER PEER      FROM H323 PEER
16 normal call clearing    66                   4976
31 normal, unspecified     1                    0
34 no circuit              31                   0
41 temporary failure       3                    0
44 no requested circuit    13                   0
47 no resource             3                    17
```

In Example 8-12, the local CUBE has run out of media resources 17 times, and one of its remote peers has run out of media resources 3 times. The former would be remediated by adding more resources for this CUBE, whereas the latter would need to be addressed by the administrator of the remote peer.

For SIP gateways, presence of calls that have failed with a cause value 488 can be observed in the output of **show sip-ua statistics**, as shown in Example 8-13.

Example 8-13 *Output of* **show sip-ua statistics** *to Validate Calls Failed with Cause Value 488*

```
CUBE# show sip-ua statistics
SIP Response Statistics (Inbound/Outbound)
    Informational:
      Trying 0/0, Ringing 0/0,
      Forwarded 0/0, Queued 0/0,
      SessionProgress 0/0
     Success:
      OkInvite 0/0, OkBye 0/0,
      OkCancel 0/0, OkOptions 0/0,
      OkPrack 0/0, OkPreconditionMet 0/0,
      OkSubscribe 0/0, OkNOTIFY 0/0,
      OkInfo 0/0, 202Accepted 0/0
      OkRegister 12/49
     Redirection (Inbound only except for MovedTemp(Inbound/Outbound)) :
      MultipleChoice 0, MovedPermanently 0,
      MovedTemporarily 0/0, UseProxy 0,
      AlternateService 0
      Client Error:
      BadRequest 0/0, Unauthorized 0/0,
      PaymentRequired 0/0, Forbidden 0/0,
      NotFound 0/0, MethodNotAllowed 0/0,
      NotAcceptable 0/0, ProxyAuthReqd 0/0,
      ReqTimeout 0/0, Conflict 0/0, Gone 0/0,
      ReqEntityTooLarge 0/0, ReqURITooLarge 0/0,
      UnsupportedMediaType 0/0, BadExtension 0/0,
      TempNotAvailable 0/0, CallLegNonExistent 0/0,
      LoopDetected 0/0, TooManyHops 0/0,
      AddrIncomplete 0/0, Ambiguous 0/0,
      BusyHere 0/0, RequestCancel 0/0,
      NotAcceptableMedia 0/13, BadEvent 0/0,
      SETooSmall 0/0
     Server Error:
      InternalError 0/0, NotImplemented 0/0,
      BadGateway 0/0, ServiceUnavail 0/0,
      GatewayTimeout 0/0, BadSipVer 0/0,
```

```
      PreCondFailure 0/0
    Global Failure:
      BusyEverywhere 0/0, Decline 0/0,
      NotExistAnywhere 0/0, NotAcceptable 0/0
      Miscellaneous counters:
      RedirectRspMappedToClientErr 0
SIP Total Traffic Statistics (Inbound/Outbound)
      Invite 0/0, Ack 0/0, Bye 0/0,
      Cancel 0/0, Options 0/0,
      Prack 0/0, Comet 0/0,
      Subscribe 0/0, NOTIFY 0/0,
      Refer 0/0, Info 0/0
      Register 49/16
Retry Statistics
      Invite 0, Bye 0, Cancel 0, Response 0,
      Prack 0, Comet 0, Reliable1xx 0, Notify 0
      Register 4, Subscribe 0
SDP application statistics:
Parses: 0, Builds 0
Invalid token order: 0, Invalid param: 0
Not SDP desc: 0, No resource: 0
Last time SIP Statistics were cleared: <never>
```

The counters from this command can be reset with **clear sip-ua statistics**.

Similar to observing the count of no resource conditions with the command in Example 8-13, the count of no resource conditions can be monitored with 1.3.6.1.4.1.9.9.152.1.2.4.50 (**cSipStatsClientNoAcceptHereOuts**) for SIP calls.

> **Tip** The scenario described here is distinct from scenarios where calls are failing with cause value 65 (**Bearer capability not implemented**). Cause value 65 is indicative of a codec mismatch, where dial-peer configuration does not present a codec match, and a transcoder is not configured on the system to handle such mismatch.

Cause codes and CDR failure monitoring are discussed further in Chapter 14, "Monitoring and Management."

Licensing

The majority of software is copyrighted by the manufacturer, and ownership of the software remains with the software publishing vendor. The right to use the software is extended to the consumer through an end-user license agreement (EULA). A mechanism to account for the deployment instances of the product is especially important for vendors that reuse copyrighted or open source code from other vendors and need to account for the usage and potential royalties of reselling those capabilities.

The industry has shifted toward more virtualization of appliances, and functionality that used to be performed on purchased hardware appliances can now be installed as virtual software instances. With the flexibilities of virtualization and ease of software instance portability, there is now a greater need for software vendors to govern the extent to which their software can be deployed. This control is accomplished through software licensing, with the specific aim of accounting for and controlling the number of instances of a piece of software that are running, as well as sometimes also controlling the capacity supported by each instance.

General Licensing Considerations

Although the licensing behavior across vendors varies greatly, this section outlines some of the common areas where an SBC may require licensing. In many SBC implementations, it is an important requirement to consider licensing as part of SBC procurement, design, and deployment.

Licensing types can generally be grouped into three categories:

- **Base license**—A general license for the base capabilities on a specific instance.
- **Feature license**—A license with the ability to enable specific restricted features.
- **Capacity license**—A license that dictates the capacity or number of instances of a feature that are supported on the device. This may refer to licensing limitations for concurrent calls, calls per second, or utilization of special features for which the vendor has chosen to apply licensing limitations.

The most common and basic licensing is to require a license for each SBC instance that is deployed in the environment, which entitles the SBC to run a certain foundational capability as either a single instance or for the cluster. Such licenses may also allow for a certain amount of call capacity before enforcing a restriction at a specific capacity.

Some additional features may then be licensed á la carte, such as special optional features or codecs that require royalties. With SBCs, it is common to also license based on capacity. Some vendors, for example, implement a maximum number of concurrent calls or calls per second to be handled on the SBC.

> **Note** Licensing is as much a tracking mechanism as it is a sales vehicle for a software vendor. When a license is required for a feature or function, it does not always imply that there is a cost associated to acquire the license. Some vendors may make licenses of these capabilities or features available at no cost to the consumer. For example, this practice is observed in scenarios where the vendor does not wish to extend any extra price to the consumer for a feature, yet still account for the quantity of the install base of the feature, to support tracking of royalty payments to upstream suppliers.

Across the various vendors' current SBC platforms, the following features require additional licensing (for at least one vendor) to be acquired before the features are enabled:

- Media forking/call recording
- Video support
- Transcoding
- Specific codec support (for example, G.722)
- Secure RTP (SRTP)
- IPv6 support
- Load balancing
- Quality of service (QoS)
- ENUM support
- Denial-of-service (DoS) detection
- High availability

This is not intended to be an exhaustive list of all features that could be licensed by a vendor, but it demonstrates some of the advanced features for which licensing may be required. Vendor-specific documentation should be consulted during the SBC design phase to ensure that the cost and acquisition of the needed features for the SBC deployment are appropriately considered.

Some vendors may also alternatively or additionally implement licensing based on capacity. This is a common licensing approach today across many of the SBC vendors. Typically, capacity licensing in SBCs is handled through either one or a combination of these two constructs:

- **CPS**—Restricting the platform to a specific number of incoming call setups within a specific interval of time.
- **Concurrent calls**—Restricting the number of total concurrent calls from which a platform can handle and accept incoming call requests.

There are two main vehicles for offering these license types:

- **Perpetual**—A license is purchased only once for each instance, and it does not have a time-based expiration. Such a license typically applies for the lifetime of the intended hardware for which it is deployed. These licenses may not be able to carry over during upgrades to new software versions, and they rarely carry over to new hardware instances.
- **Subscription based**—This type of license has a terminal expiration date on the license, after which the license becomes invalid.

Subscription-based licensing may be ideal for deployments where the intended capacity is expected to significantly change over the life of the device. This model allows for purchasing a lower initial capacity and augmenting licensing purchases as the deployment grows in capacity. This model also may allow for a lower total cost of ownership over purchasing a perpetual license, based on the amount of time the SBC is expected to be in production. When there is an opportunity to leverage either licensing model for a deployment, it is wise to model the return on investment and other benefits of both types to determine which approach is more desirable for the specific deployment intention.

Tip Modern licensing schemes commonly leverage Internet connectivity to the vendor's licensing server in order to activate a license. Some implementations need Internet connectivity only for a one-time activation, and they may also offer an offline alternative for activating the license. Other licensing implementations, however, expect an always-on Internet connection to increment and decrement licensing consumption in real time. This always-on connectivity requirement is becoming more common with subscription-based licensing.

When deploying an SBC, consider the Internet connectivity needs for the vendor's licensing model and deploy appropriate connectivity to ensure that the platform will be properly licensed before pushing production traffic through the deployment.

The general licensing constructs mentioned here should assist with licensing planning for an SBC deployment, but it is important to consult the vendor on the options that are available or required, as licensing approaches vary greatly between vendors. The next portion of this chapter provides an example of an SBC licensing approach and demonstrates the licensing applicable for CUBE.

It is important to understand the service impact of exceeding licensed limits on a platform so that it does not result in service impacts during scenarios where licensed limits may be exceeded, as vendors implement licensing enforcement in various forms. Some vendors or products enforce license violations, in which case exceeding the licensed limit results in rejecting calls or features that exceed the licensed limit. Other vendor implementations may not strictly enforce the limitations and either may allow a temporary overutilization or may not systematically enforce the licensed quantity.

CUBE Licensing Models

There are two stages to CUBE licensing: The first is to license the Unified Communications (voice) feature capability on the device. A CUBE license is then applied over the top of the Unified Communications feature license.

There are two ways to consume both of these license types:

- **Single-use licensing**—This is the legacy licensing model, wherein a license is a onetime purchase that is locked to the specific device and cannot be transferred to another device when, for example, replacing changing chassis platforms to a newer hardware model.

- **Cisco ONE licensing—**This is a subscription-based licensing model, in which a license is purchased for a single instance. The license is not locked to the specific device and can be transferred to another platform when upgrading hardware platforms by only repurchasing the underlying hardware.

UC Feature Set Licensing

The feature license for Unified Communications (UC) needs to be applied to the platform, either through the single-use framework or the Cisco ONE framework.

Single-Use Technology Pack Licensing

For all modern CUBE platforms, a Cisco IOS or IOS-XE software image is a universal file that contains the superset of router features. These binaries are identified with the descriptor **universalk9** in the filename. (Images not suitable for export of cryptology are instead signified with **universalk9-npe**.)

UC (collaboration) features are then made available on the image type through the purchase of a technology package, which unlocks that set of features. All collaboration technology capabilities (including CUBE) are unavailable on the platform until the technology package is applied.

Note Some features intended to be enabled on CUBE may require security feature sets. Most features discussed in this book rely on only the UC feature set and do not require the security feature set. An example where the security feature set is needed in addition to the UC feature set, however, is when enabling RTP/SRTP interworking on CUBE. Consult the **Feature Navigator** at Cisco.com for more information on the different feature capabilities across the various feature sets.

There is no UC technology pack specific to the CSR 1000v. Instead, there are two feature licenses available that contain CUBE:

- **AppX—**Contains most CUBE features but does not contain security features to allow for running TLS/SRTP on CUBE.
- **AX—**Contains all features, including TLS/SRTP support.

On older software releases or older platforms where a **universal** or **universalk9-npe** image is not available, there are individual binary files for each of the various technology feature combinations. In these scenarios, one of the following feature sets should be used when CUBE features are desired:

- ASR Series
  - Advanced IP Services (**advipservices**)
  - Advanced Enterprise Services (**adventerprise**)

- ISR Series
  - IP Voice (**ipvoice**)
  - Enterprise Services (**entservices**)
  - SP Services (**spservices**)
  - Advanced IP Services (**advipservices**)
  - Advanced Enterprise Services (**adventerprise**)
  - Int Voice/Video (**ipvoicek9_ivs** or **adventerprisek9_ivs**)

The image binary with the descriptor that contains the descriptor noted in **bold** is contained in the filename and must be downloaded onto the router. Note that **k9** may or may not be a present feature and specified in the filename, depending on whether the image contains cryptology and whether it is suitable to export to the available country.

To obtain a UC technology license, the following procedure is followed:

Step 1. Purchase the license through identification of the Field Replaceable Unit (FRU) identifier for the desired license. The purchase of the license results in a unique Product Authorization Key (PAK) code.

Step 2. Identify the Universal Device Identifier (UDI) for the targeted device being licensed by issuing the command **show license udi**.

Step 3. Visit the Cisco License Registration Portal (https://www.cisco.com/go/license) and register the PAK to the UDI of the desired device.

Step 4. Download the resulting license file from the License Registration Portal.

Step 5. Copy the license file to the router's local storage by using the **copy** command.

Step 6. View and accept the EULA with the command **license accept end user agreement.**

Step 7. Install the license file on the router with the command **license install**, as shown in Example 8-14.

Step 8. Reload the router with the **reload** command for the licensing to take effect.

Step 9. Validate proper licensing by using the command **show license.**

Example 8-14 *UC Technology Package License Installation*

```
CUBE# license install flash0:uck9-C3900-SPE150_K9-FHH12250057.xml
Installing licenses from "uck9-C3900-SPE150_K9-FHH12250057.xml"
Installing...Feature:uck9...Successful:Supported
1/1 licenses were successfully installed
0/1 licenses were existing licenses
0/1 licenses were failed to install
```

```
CUBE# show version

!Command output abbreviated.

-------------------------------------------------
Device# PID SN
-------------------------------------------------
*0 C3900-SPE150/K9 FHH12250057


Technology Package License Information for Module:'c3900'

----------------------------------------------------------------
Technology Technology-package Technology-package
Current Type Next reboot
-----------------------------------------------------------------
ipbase ipbasek9 Permanent ipbasek9
security None None None
uc uck9 Permanent uck9
data None None None
```

An alternative to the license application approach just described is to use the Call Home functionality to apply the license. The advantage of this approach is that it doesn't require access to the License Registration Portal to download the license file. Before registering the device, Call Home must be enabled, as demonstrated by Example 8-15.

Example 8-15 *Basic Call Home Configuration*

```
ip name-server 192.0.2.99
service call-home
call-home
 sender from cube1@example.com
 contact-email-addr net-admin@example.com
 mail-server smtp.example.com
 http-proxy https://myhttpproxy.example.com port 3128
```

The **http-proxy** command is necessary only if you are downloading signatures directly from Cisco's repository when there is no direct Internet connectivity from the device. The information shown in Example 8-15 can also all be configured in a single commandlet:

```
call-home reporting contact-email-addr email-address http-proxy hostname port
port-number
```

When Call Home is enabled, the router can then be licensed with the **license call-home install pak** command, as shown in Example 8-16.

Example 8-16 *Installing a Technology Pack License by Using Call Home*

```
CUBE# license call-home install pak 4XCSL17E380
CCO User name : myCiscoComID
CCO password : myPassword
!
.....................
Pak Number : 4XCSL17E380
Pak Fulfillment type: PARTIAL
SKU Name : L-2900-LIC
SKU Type : NOMAPPING
Description : L-2900-LIC :
Ordered Qty : 1
Platform Supported : N/A
1. SKU Name : L-29-UC-K9
SKU Type : Feature
Description : L-29-UC-K9 :
Ordered Qty : 1
Available Qty : 1
Feature List :
Feature name: uck9 Count: Uncounted
Platform Supported : N/A
Select SKU to install [1-1] or Quit: 1
Selected SKU is : L-29-UC-K9
Please enter the user's detail:
First Name : John
Last Name : Smith
Title : Network Admin
Company Name : Cisco Systems Inc
Address1 : 170 West Tasman Dr
Address2 [Optional]:
City : San Jose
State : CA
Province [Optional]:
Zipcode : 95134
Country : U.S.A
Phone : (408)555-1234
Fax [Optional]:
Email : jsmith@example.com
!.
......................
Installing...Feature:uc9...Successful:Supported
1/1 licenses were successfully installed
0/1 licenses were existing licenses
0/1 licenses were failed to install
```

Cisco ONE Advanced Application Licensing

The alternative to the single-use feature license approach just discussed is to consume Cisco ONE subscription-based licenses. The advantage with this approach is that a new license does not need to be repurchased when it comes time to upgrade the underlying CUBE hardware.

Cisco ONE (C1) feature licensing is similar to single-use licensing, but the license packages have been simplified. UC capabilities are offered in the Advanced Application feature set. If additional security features are needed, a Cisco ONE Advanced Security license can also be purchased.

The following steps show an example of the procedure for purchasing an ASR 1001-X on which there is a plan to run 150 redundant CUBE sessions:

Step 1. Purchase the ASR 1001-X hardware by using SKU **C1-ASR1001-X/K9.**

Step 2. Purchase the Advanced Application + UC bundle upgrade for C1 by using SKU **C1-ASR1K-ADD** and software part code **C1AUAASR1100RK9.** This entitles the user to 100 Redundancy CUBE sessions.

Step 3. Purchase 50 additional á la carte C1 CUBE session license upgrades by using a quantity of 50 for SKU **C1-CUBEE-RED.**

With Cisco ONE, the technology pack corresponding to a feature is unlocked by connecting the device to the Cisco Smart Licensing server. This communication leverages the Call Home connectivity outlined in Example 8-16.

Tip Cisco ONE licenses use the Cisco Smart Licensing solution for continuous activation and validation. This solution generally implies that there is an active Internet connection to the Smart Licensing server from the device either directly or through a proxy/satellite server.

There are options to allow for this capability without an active Internet connection, but those approaches are subject to caveats about requiring manual monthly synchronization of data to Cisco's licensing servers. Consult the *Smart Licensing Deployment Guide* for more information on these alternative connectivity solutions.

After Call Home is configured, you can enable smart licensing by following these steps:

Step 1. Enable smart licensing with the command **license smart enable.**

Step 2. Log in to the Cisco Smart Software Manager (https://tools.cisco.com/rhodui/index#/) and generate a new token for the device.

Step 3. Install the token on the device with the command **license smart register idtoken** ***generated-token.***

Step 4. Install the UC technology license with the command **license boot suite AdvUCSuiteK9.**

Step 5. Save the configuration with **copy running-configuration startup-configuration.**

Step 6. Reload the router.

Step 7. Verify licensing with **show license status**, as shown in Example 8-17, to ensure proper communication with the licensing server.

Example 8-17 *Validating Cisco ONE Licensing*

```
CUBE# show license status
Smart Licensing is ENABLED

Registration:
 Status: REGISTERED
 Smart Account: BU Production Test
 Virtual Account: CUBE  Initial
 Registration: SUCCEEDED on Thu Jan 05 2017 15:04:18 UTC
 Last Renewal Attempt: None
 Next Renewal Attempt: Tue Jul 04 2017 15:04:18 UTC
 Registration Expires: Fri Jan 05 2018 09:25:50 UTC

License Authorization:
 Status: AUTHORIZED on Thu Jan 05 2017 15:17:04 UTC
 Last Communication Attempt: SUCCEEDED on Thu Jan 05 2017 15:17:04 UTC
 Next Communication Attempt: Sat Feb 04 2017 15:17:04 UTC
 Communication Deadline: Fri Jan 05 2018 09:25:50 UTC
```

Caution Other licensing types cannot co-reside on the same device as ONE licensing. When you enable Cisco ONE licensing, all features and functionality that are not enabled by Cisco ONE licenses are disabled.

CUBE Licenses

After the UC feature set is licensed on the platform, CUBE must then also be licensed. Cisco offers two main approaches for basic CUBE licensing:

- **Platform license**—This license type covers the right to use the CUBE feature up to the maximum that is technically supported on the platform. (Platform maximums are outlined earlier in this chapter.) This is an older licensing model and not available on the majority of the current CUBE platforms. These licenses are also not available for the Cisco ONE suite.

- **Session count license**—This license type allows for the purchase of a license for a specific number of maximum concurrent calls on the platform. A call is defined as a single end-to-end two-way call across CUBE. A single session can account for multiple media streams (for example, a call containing both voice and video, or a recorded call with forked media). When using the Cisco ONE suite, this is the only way to license CUBE capability.

Note Though media forked calls do not count against the license session limit, they still impact the platform's overall capacity limits, as discussed earlier in this chapter, in the section "CUBE Sizing."

The session count license method allows for a minimum license count to be purchased at initial deployment, with incremental additional licenses being purchased later, as the consumption of services across CUBE increase the concurrent call volume of the platform. Purchasing multiple session count licenses is permitted and will account for the sum of the multiple counts across the license files. For example, one FL-CUBEE-25 and one FL-CUBEE-100 license can be purchased separately to permit a total of 125 concurrent sessions across the node to which the license pertains.

Tip When purchasing a router, it is possible to purchase a technology bundle, which is a combination of hardware and feature licenses for common purposes. For example, if you purchase bundle ISR4431-V/K9, you obtain the ISR 4431 hardware with the UC feature set, a PVDM4-64 DSP, and 25 CUBE session licenses.

When purchasing a bundle, determine whether CUBE sessions are already included in the bundle. If the bundle includes some foundational sessions, additional á la carte session licenses need to be purchased only if you need additional sessions beyond what is included in the bundle.

In addition to CUBE licenses, the following additional features may also be licensed:

- Redundancy
- NanoCUBE

A redundancy license allows for the purchase of a single license to entitle a pair of active/standby devices for CUBE. The advantage of the redundancy license is that the price of the redundant node is offered at a discount from the full license price to license the second CUBE node. This license can also be used to license a node that is being reserved as a warm-standby node that is not part of a CUBE HA pair. An example of this would be a CUBE in a backup disaster recovery data center that would be activated only when there is failure with the primary active CUBE in the primary active data center. Single-node licenses cannot be upgraded to redundancy licenses after initial purchase.

Note CUBE HA across geographic locations or between two disparate data centers is not supported. In the scenario just mentioned where CUBE redundancy is provided as a warm standby, there would be no stateful failover upon failure of CUBE's primary side over to the other data center's CUBE.

For in-box redundancy, such as on the ASR platforms, purchasing of the redundancy license is not necessary.

NanoCUBE licenses can only be purchased for the subset of platforms that support the feature.

Table 8-9 shows the platform and session licenses currently available for the platforms. Because these license values also correlate to capacity and hence vary based on each platform model, refer to platform documentation and the available platform packages or SKUs to determine what licenses are appropriate to the specific platform model(s) of interest.

Table 8-9 *SKUs for CUBE Platform and Session Count Licenses*

License Type	Single-Use License	Redundancy License
Platform (NanoCUBE)	FL-NANOCUBE	
Session Count (ISR)	FL-CUBE-4	FL-CUBEE-5-RED
	FL-CUBEE-5	FL-CUBEE-25-RED
	FL-CUBEE-25	FL-CUBEE-100-RED
	FL-CUBEE-100	FL-CUBEE-500-RED
	FL-CUBEE-500	FL-CUBEE-1000-RED
	FL-CUBEE-1000	
Session Count (ASR)	FLASR1-CUBEE-100P	FLASR1-CUBEE-100R
	FLASR1-CUBEE-500P	FLASR1-CUBEE-500R
	FLASR1-CUBEE-1KP	FLASR1-CUBEE-1KR
	FLASR1-CUBEE-4KP	FLASR1-CUBEE-4KR
	FLASR1-CUBEE-16KP	FLASR1-CUBEE-16KR

Because CUBE licenses are not systematically enforced, there is no necessary configuration to apply the licensing once the right-to-use license is purchase.

Cisco ONE simplifies the SKUs required for CUBE. When a device or bundle is purchased under a Cisco ONE SKU, additional sessions can be added with the generic CUBE SKUs, shown in Table 8-10.

Table 8-10 *SKUs for Cisco ONE CUBE Licensing*

SKU	Description
C1-CUBEE-STD	Single CUBE session license
C1-CUBEE-RED	Single CUBE session license for redundant CUBE

Much as with the CUBE session licenses with the classic licensing models, the CUBE session licenses do not need to be installed on a platform with the Cisco ONE licensing suite.

Overload Prevention Techniques

With any network, there is a risk of exceeding the supported or intended capacity of the design. This could pose a risk to the service being provided by the call processing platform if the capacity is exceeded to a point where the platform can no longer sufficiently process calls. This condition, referred to as *overload*, is defined as a server not having "sufficient resources to process all incoming … messages" (RFC 7339, p. 4).

Overload can occur due to several different external factors, including the following:

- Current solution design not intended to meet the growth or demand of the actual call volume
- A malfunction or failure in the upstream load-balancing architecture, resulting in atypically larger volume across a subset of call paths
- A call loop triggered by a misconfiguration in call routing
- Physical world emergencies or unplanned events driving above-average call volume over what has been planned
- DoS attack on the network

Steps can be taken to prevent overload scenarios, such as appropriately sizing deployments with enough headroom for growth (as discussed in this chapter), implementing DoS prevention techniques (as discussed in Chapter 13, "Security Threat Mitigation"), and by proactively alarming (as discussed in Chapter 14, "Monitoring and Management"). Even with the preventive measures, however, it may not be adequate to protect against scenarios where a call processing platform would be at risk of degraded performance. As a result, there is a need for additional control of overload scenarios, through both the proactive mechanisms of detection and prevention. and the reactive mechanisms to refuse calls over a specific threshold.

This section outlines a number of mechanisms for controlling overload of SBCs through SIP overload specifications, as well as with CAC mechanisms such as RSVP. The approaches can be either reactive (such as rejecting calls when reaching the platform limitation) or proactive (such as with SIP overload, where guidance can be sent upstream to redirect or reduce the density of call requests to that peer).

SIP Overload Specifications

The SIP protocol can use the mechanism of sending a **503 Service Unavailable** error back to the sender when experiencing significant load (such as during a processing overload scenario). This behavior alone, though, is not enough to prevent an overload scenario. RFC 6357 suggests that responding with a 503 response in these overload conditions may actually contribute to and exacerbate the overload problem. The reasoning for this is that if there is signaling congestion, responding with additional messages such as a 503 response will add to the pile of messages; if these responses are not delivered in a timely manner, the sending client may have to retransmit the original message again, which would continue to increase the severity of the overload condition.

To help add extra protection in these scenarios, some recent RFCs have been developed to suggest and define alternative methods of using SIP signaling to detect and either prevent or recover from these overload scenarios. These controls provide a more robust architecture when external factors result in an increase in call volume that may test the capability of the platform.

RFC 6357 defines theoretical approaches for overload control, but it doesn't define specific protocols for the methods. SIP overload controls are split into two main methods of control: explicit and implicit. With explicit overload control, a server indicates to upstream peers that it is reaching its capacity limit, allowing for upstream devices to adjust their transmission rates. In contrast, implicit control uses the absence of messages from a downstream peer as an indication that overload has occurred on that device. This results in steering requests away from the overloaded device until it either hears from the device again or a timer expires. These approaches can be further split into the following defined approaches for overload control:

- **Explicit control**—This approach defines mechanisms for the receiver to indicate how much traffic it can receive.
  - **Rate based**—Communication back to the sender to limit the request rate to a maximum number of requests per second.
  - **Loss based**—Instruction sent by the receiver to the sender to reduce message transmission by a specific percentage.
  - **Window based**—Allows a sender to send a defined number of messages before requiring a response from the receiver to continue. Much as with TCP windowing, the window size here can dynamically grow to a size that will performed without notice of overload issues.
  - **Overload signal based**—The receiver transmits a **503 Service Unavailable** message during a load condition, upon which the sender reduces the transmission rate and continues to do so until the overload scenario and 503 responses are eliminated.
  - **On/off**—Allows the receiver to send a **503 Service Unavailable** message with a **Retry-After** header to define a temporary duration of time that messages should not be sent to this receiver.

- **Implicit control**—The transmission rate is decreased or stopped when a receiver indicates overload. The sender should sense this condition (such as through signaling or slow/nil responses) and then decrease the transmission rate or stop transmitting altogether for a period of time.

RFC 7339: Overload Control Communication Scheme

RFC 7339 defines a loss-based SIP overload control mechanism that is advertised through the **Via** header and defined through four parameters:

- **oc**—Indicates a reduction in the number of requests arriving at the server.
- **oc-algo**—Lists tokens corresponding to the class of overload control algorithms supported by the client. One of the algorithms is chosen and indicated in the response.
- **oc-validity**—Establishes a time limit for which overload control is in effect.
- **oc-seq**—Provides a sequence number in the form of a timestamp for overload messaging to aid in sequencing any out-of-order responses to determine the most recent overload status.

Upon first contact with a server, a client that supports SIP overload must insert the **oc** parameter without any values and must also include the **oc-algo** parameter with a list of the algorithms supported. The list of supported algorithms must always include at least the **loss** algorithm.

After negotiation of the overload algorithm to be used, an overload condition is then signaled through setting the oc parameter to a nonzero value.

> **Note** When signaling no present condition of overload, **og=0** may be used; however, it is preferred to always signal the lack of overload by setting both **og=0** and **oc-validity=0.** This approach ensures compatibility with other algorithms that may treat the condition of **og=0** as an instruction to cease all processing.

The presence of overload control can be terminated either through implicit expiration of the **oc-validity** time (the specified validity time expiring since the last message) or the subject transmitting **oc-validity=0**.

Example 8-18 shows the presence of the **oc** and **oc-algo** parameters in the **Via** header, signifying advertisement of support for overload control by using the **loss** and **rate** algorithms.

Example 8-18 *Advertisement of Overload Control in the SIP* Via *Header*

```
INVITE sips:user@example.com SIP/2.0
Via: SIP/2.0/TLS p1.example.net;branch=z9hG4bK2d4790.1;oc;oc-algo="loss,rate"
```

The receiver responds to the overload advertisement by selecting an algorithm and also setting **oc** and **oc-validity** both to **0**, as shown in Example 8-19, to indicate that it is not currently in an overload condition.

Example 8-19 *Acknowledgement of Overload Control Algorithm*

```
SIP/2.0 100 Trying
 Via: SIP/2.0/TLS p1.example.net;branch=z9hG4bK2d4790.1;
 received=192.0.2.111;oc=0;oc-algo="loss";oc-validity=0
```

In contrast, if the receiving party did not support overload control, the original parameters **oc;oc-algo="loss,A"** would be left unchanged in the **Via** header to signal that it does not support overload control.

After the overload mechanism is negotiated by the two parties, at some point, one side may experience overload. When this occurs, that side signals the condition by setting the relevant parameters. In Example 8-20, one side is requesting a **20%** reduction in message rate (that is, **500ms**).

Example 8-20 *Indication of an Overload Condition*

```
SIP/2.0 180 Ringing
Via: SIP/2.0/TLS p1.example.net;
 branch=z9hG4bK2d4790.3;received=192.0.2.111;
 oc=20;oc-algo="loss";oc-validity=500;oc-seq=1282321615.782
```

Once the overload subsides, the parameters from Example 8-20 are changed to indicate that the overload condition has been resolved, and the reduction rate is set to **0%** and for **0ms** (indefinitely), as shown in Example 8-21.

Example 8-21 *Indication of a Resolved Overload Condition*

```
SIP/2.0 183 Queued
Via: SIP/2.0/TLS p1.example.net;
 branch=z9hG4bK2d4790.4;received=192.0.2.111;
 oc=0;oc-algo="loss";oc-validity=0;oc-seq=1282321892.439
```

Supported Overload Algorithms

With the **loss** algorithm, the message rate is requested to be reduced by a specified percentage (a value between 0 and 100%), relative to the current rate of messages. The upstream party being instructed to reduce the rate then either rejects or redirects that percentage of the incoming calls for the specific time period, based on the setting in the **oc-validity** parameter. This algorithm is the default algorithm supported for overload control, and support of it is a requirement for the implementation of this overload approach defined by RFC 7339.

As defined in RFC 7415, a published alternative algorithm is the **rate** algorithm. With this algorithm, a SIP peer defines a specified value to use as the messages-per-second rate, for a defined period of time. When signaled to the sender, the sender then seeks to throttle messages for an average target of 1/(rate) seconds between message transmissions to achieve the messages-per-second target. For example, **oc=150;oc-algo="rate";oc-validity=5000;** instructs the other side to transmit at a target of 150 messages per second for a total duration of 5000 ms (5 seconds). This would be accomplished on the transmitting side by targeting a pause of 1/150 seconds between message transmissions across this period of 5 seconds.

Note The parameter of **og=0** signals that 100% of the calls should be rejected. As a result, when disabling rate limiting, the parameter **oc-validity=0** must be used.

Overload Security Considerations

A challenge with defining the ability for peers to message a desire to reduce or stop message transmission opens up potential concern for security. A malicious user could potentially signal to a critical device to reduce message transmission as a way to mount a DoS attack on the device. As a result, it is important for the device processing the overload request to trust the integrity and intent of any peer device that may signal an overload condition. This can be accomplished through standard SIP authentication schemes, such as the SIP **Authorization** header, or through S/MIME key exchange, as discussed in Section 23 of RFC 3261. Section 3.4 of RFC 7200 also defines the concept of a *trust domain*, which is a set of entities within an autonomous entity that are permitted to exchange overload filtering mechanisms.

Because it is important for overload conditions to be signaled end-to-end to prevent an overload condition from just passing the condition to a node further upstream, it is still important to be able to signal overload conditions across trust boundaries. In these scenarios, RFC 7200 suggests using a simple 503 response upstream to signal overload across a trust boundary.

It is strongly desired that TLS be employed between SIP peers and to filter processing of inbound messages to only source IP addresses of known trusted entities. This approach helps ensure that malicious users cannot spoof the source destination and trigger an unrequested overload control scenario as a way to deny service.

Additional Overload Challenges

The techniques described in this section for defending against overload conditions all require some reliance on the peer nodes in the SIP network. With explicit overload controls, the adjacent peers must typically both support the same implementation strategies for the overload control outcome to be successful. Even with implicit overload control, the local SIP node needs to have intelligence of the ability to execute the overload control when the downstream peer becomes responsive.

Call Admission Control

At the time of this writing, the SIP overload approaches described in the previous section have not become a widespread implementation and deployment. As a result, some challenges for interoperability and adoption must be overcome before these strategies can be widespread and most effective. In the meantime, other strategies can be applied locally on a device to help protect overload, which do not rely on external signaling to peers to take action. Some of these approaches that are available are discussed in this section.

Because a network has a constrained amount of bandwidth that can be used for call transmission, it is important to have controls that prevent the ability for calls to saturate these network paths. Without any control over the number of calls set up across a network segment, if the concurrent call volume exceeds what the circuit or device is capable of handling, it may result in degradation of call quality across all calls through that path.

Call Admission Control (CAC) has been defined to prevent this condition. This concept allows for a limited number of concurrent calls to be supported across a call path so administrators can control calls to a maximum concurrent volume that will not exceed the known capabilities of the network. If a call is attempted across a call path where CAC has determined that there is no additional availability to support the call, the call will be rejected or redirected along another call path to ensure integrity of call quality for the existing calls.

Note The configuration of CAC does not preclude the need for QoS to be configured within the network. Though CAC can limit the concurrent call volume to a manageable level across a network segment, it does not eliminate the possibility of packet congestion across the link causing call quality issues due to converged traffic across the network.

As a result, QoS should still be configured at any location in a network where the available link speed is reduced due to oversubscription from link convergence. Scenarios of network oversubscription may include where there is a reduction in speed from traversing different circuit types (for example, traversing from a Gigabit Ethernet LAN to a 100 Mbps WAN circuit). QoS should be applied at these egress points, at the point where the traffic is traversing from the higher speed to lower speed link, to ensure that voice and video traffic are placed in appropriate defined queues and prioritized accordingly.

Consult *End-to-End QoS Network Design: Quality of Service for Rich-Media and Cloud Networks* (Cisco Press) for more information on QoS implementations for real-time media transmission.

CAC can be accomplished through either of these two forms:

- **Local CAC**—A call processing node is restricted to allow a specific number of calls across a specific call path (for example, 20 maximum concurrent calls supported across a single SIP trunk to the service provider). This method is not intelligent enough to understand actual bandwidth consumption of the network utilization, and as a result, this is a predictive and best-guess approach to preserving bandwidth.

- **Resource-based**—The decision to permit a call is governed by the amount of available resources, such as the number of channels available for a call, maximum licensed calls, available DSP resources, or actual network utilization.

CAC on CUBE

On CUBE, CAC can be defined either at the interface or dial-peer level, or it can be configured to apply globally across the entire platform.

Interface and Dial Peer–Specific CAC

CAC on CUBE can be accomplished by simply configuring the maximum number of calls to be supported on each dial peer. This is configured by specifying the **max-conn** parameter under **dial-peer**, as shown in Example 8-22.

Example 8-22 *Configuration for Maximum Concurrent Calls on a* **dial-peer**

```
dial-peer voice 1 voip
 max-conn 10
```

With this approach of setting the maximum calls based on call counts, CUBE is not aware of the underlying bandwidth being consumed by each call leg. As a result, **max-conn 10** would support 10 maximum calls on a dial peer. Now consider a scenario in which the dial peer has a voice-class codec with G.729 and G.711 both configured. This configuration could allow for a total bandwidth consumption of 312 kbps for G.729 or 1104 kbps for G.711. This is a wide difference in bandwidth between the two scenarios, and the limitations of this approach should be considered when using this approach and determining the appropriate CAC sizes.

When a call fails due to exceeding the maximum connections defined, CUBE displays the following syslog message and then rejects the call with a **503 Service Unavailable** or Q.850 cause value 44 (requested circuit/channel not available):

```
%CALL_CONTROL-6-MAX_CONNECTIONS: Maximum number of connections reached for
dial-peer <id>
```

An alternative (or addition) to specifying the maximum call connections is to specify the maximum bandwidth permitted across the dial peer. This is done by specifying the **max-bandwidth** parameter under the dial peer with the maximum bandwidth, in Kbps, that is to be supported for the peer (see Example 8-23).

> **Tip** The **max-bandwidth** parameter is only available for SIP dial peers. H.323 dial peers cannot be configured with this parameter.

Example 8-23 *Configuration of Maximum Bandwidth CAC*

```
dial-peer voice 1 voip
 session protocol sipv2
 max-bandwidth 1024 midcall-exceed exempt-local-media
```

In this example, **dial-peer 1** is allowed to set up as many calls as it can until the total bandwidth for calls across the dial peer exceeds 1024 Kbps. The parameter **midcall-exceed** allows for already established calls to exceed the **max-bandwidth** statement if the call upgrades the codec in the middle of the call to one that consumes more bandwidth. The default action, when this command is not specified, would drop the call during such scenarios when a mid-call codec change would exceed the defined bandwidth. The **exempt-local-media** command excludes calls that are both sourced and terminate on the chassis internally to prevent them from decrementing against bandwidth counts intended for application on external interfaces, circuits, or signaling peers.

The **max-bandwidth** and **max-conn** parameters can be used individually or together on a dial peer. When combined on the same dial peer, the parameter that is first exceeded causes the call to be rejected.

When the call is rejected due to a lack of available bandwidth, no response is sent to the upstream peer. The call is ignored, and a message similar to the following is output to syslog:

```
%SIP-3-DIALPEERBWCAC: Calling number 4085551234, called number 9195551234, dial-
peer 1, used bandwidth 960, available bandwidth 0, requested bandwidth 80, call
state initial-reject
```

The cause value used during a triggered call failure due to this dial peer CAC can be changed with the following global commands, along with any SIP reason code between 400 and 699:

```
error-code-override max-conn failure SIP-code
error-code-override max-bandwidth failure SIP-code
```

Although the **max-bandwidth** command discussed earlier in this chapter is only aware at the dial peer, a call threshold can also be applied at the interface level with the **call threshold interface** command. In Example 8-24, CAC is defined for a threshold of being triggered when the interface bandwidth reaches the value of 1000 Kbps and then sustains above 800 Kbps.

Example 8-24 *Defining a per-Interface Maximum Call Bandwidth*

```
call threshold interface GigabitEthernet 0/0 int-bandwidth low 800 high 1000
```

Bursts in call setups can also be controlled at the dial-peer level with the command **call spike** along with the maximum calls desired within a specified window of time. The system takes multiple snapshots over a specified window of time to determine the current volume. The default window of measurement to determine the current incoming call number is an average of five consecutive 200 ms windows, which can be adjusted. Example 8-25 shows how to configure CUBE to reject a rate over 20 CPS by taking 5 sampling windows of 1 second (1000 ms) each.

Example 8-25 *Defining a Maximum Number of Calls per Second*

```
call spike 20 steps 5 size 1000
```

Tip You can configure call spike control globally to apply across all dial peers by applying the same command shown in Example 8-25 under the root of **configure terminal.**

Global CAC

A challenge with the **max-conn** command discussed in the previous section is that it is only dial peer aware. There is not a capability with that mechanism to be able to restrict calls when the total calls on the platform exceed a defined threshold.

For conditions where impairment from call overload needs to be controlled at an interface or platform-wide level, the global CAC functionality on CUBE can be used. This extensive CAC ability is useful for protecting against exceeding the overall platform guidelines for capacity, especially in conditions where there is a complex overlapping of dial peers distributed across several network interfaces.

In addition to total concurrent call counts on the platform, several other platform conditions can also be defined as thresholds through the **call threshold global** command. The following parameters can be defined with this CAC feature:

- **total-calls**—The total number of concurrent calls on the platform
- **cpu-5sec**—The 5-second CPU utilization
- **cpu-avg**—The average CPU utilization across 60 seconds
- **io-mem**—The amount of memory utilized for input/output of packet forwarding across the past 5 seconds
- **proc-mem**—The memory utilized for processor tasks that are not I/O related (that is, the utilized amount not used by **io-mem**) across the past 5 seconds
- **total-mem**—Total memory utilization of the platform across the past 5 seconds

Note The measurement durations for **cpu-avg** and the memory attributes can be changed with the **call threshold poll-interval** command.

A rejected call from global CAC also prints a message to the syslog; the following is an example of a string for a reject from exceeding the **total-calls** threshold:

```
%SIP-3-TOTCALLCAC: Call rejected due to CAC based on Total-calls, sent response 503
```

SIP calls have an additional configuration for defining the rejection cause value with the command **error-code-override** that is found under the **sip** section of **voice service voip**. Example 8-26 demonstrates overriding the cause value for when CAC bandwidth is exceeded to respond with a **503 Service Unavailable** message.

Example 8-26 *Overriding SIP Error Codes During CAC Conditions*

```
voice service voip
 sip
  error-code-override cac-bandwidth failure 503
```

The following parameters can be defined to override the SIP error codes with the **error-code-override** command:

- **cac-bandwidth**—Status code to be sent for **max-bandwidth** CAC
- **call spike**—Status code to be sent for call spiking
- **cpu**—Status code to be sent for all CPU thresholds
- **max-conn**—Status code to be sent for **max-conn** thresholds
- **mem**—Status code to be sent for all memory thresholds
- **total-calls**—Status code to be sent for total call thresholds

SIP error codes can also be defined under specific dial peers through the command **voice-class sip error-code-override**.

RSVP-Based CAC

An alternative that helps overcome some of the constraints with local CAC is *Resource Reservation Protocol* (*RSVP*). RSVP, as described in RFC 2205, is a protocol designed to improve admission control through reserving resources in a network for use by specific applications. RFC 2212 further leverages RSVP to allow for reservation of bandwidth resources, ensuring that QoS can be met for a data flow on a per-hop basis across the network path by controlling the maximum packet queuing delay that may be experienced. This approach ensures that the network path has the available bandwidth and resources before setting up the data session (such as a call) and then also dynamically accounts for the utilization of those resources through the life of the data session.

When a host is RSVP enabled and has a data flow that needs QoS guaranteed by RSVP, it sends an *RSVP path* message across the data path every 30 seconds. Each node that is

RSVP aware will consume the message and either ensure the needed resource reservation and forward the packet downstream or respond with a resource reservation rejection. Any hops that are not RSVP aware will simply forward the packet along the path to the next hop, without reserving resources for the flow.

The advantage of RSVP-based CAC over traditional CAC is that the entire path capable of RSVP is reserved for resources rather than just the local resources on a single node. RSVP is path aware, so if the underlying network path changes, RSVP adapts and updates each node with the new resource utilization requirements, ensuring that resource reservations are maintained and the level of expected service for the packet forwarding is upheld.

CUBE can have two layers of RSVP configuration: the general network interface RSVP commands that would be on any RSVP-aware hop in the network and the dial peer–specific RSVP configurations.

The RSVP configurations for the network need to be defined. This needs to be done on any device that is RSVP aware, regardless of whether it is an SBC or even when it isn't voice aware (that is, doesn't have **dial-peer** configurations). To define the RSVP bandwidth to be used at the network interface, the command **ip rsvp bandwidth** is used under the interface. This command specifies the amount of bandwidth to allow for reservation on RSVP-enabled flows.

If the interface is servicing multiple sensitive data flows, such as both voice and video, then a policy group can be further defined for each application type. Policy groups are created with the **ip rsvp policy** command. In Example 8-27, there is a T1 with a total reservation of bandwidth for RSVP use set to 1024 Kbps, and video is only allowed to use up 300 Kbps of that pool, but voice traffic can use up to 768 Kbps of the pool.

Example 8-27 *Interface Configuration for RSVP*

```
ip rsvp policy identity rsvp-video policy-locator .*VideoStream.*
ip rsvp policy identity rsvp-voice policy-locator .*AudioStream.*

interface Serial0/0/1:0
  ip address 192.0.2.100 255.255.255.0
  service-policy output shaper
  ip rsvp bandwidth 1024
  ip rsvp data-packet classification none
  ip rsvp resource-provider none
  ip rsvp policy local identity rsvp-voice
   maximum bandwidth group 768
   forward all
  ip rsvp policy local identity rsvp-video
   maximum bandwidth group 256
   forward all
```

The following list breaks down the information from Example 8-27:

- **ip rsvp policy identity**—Defines the regular expression to associate these request types to the application-specific **rsvp-video** and **rsvp-voice** policies defined under the interface. **VideoStream** and **AudioStream** are the application IDs that Cisco Unified Communications Manager uses as default in **System> Service Parameters> System – RSVP**. Consult vendor documentation to determine these values for other collaboration products.
- **service-policy output shaper**—Attaches the WAN QoS policy **shaper** to the interface for appropriate queuing. This is configured on interfaces where network congestion is expected to occur. The **shaper** QoS configuration is further discussed in the next section.
- **ip rsvp bandwidth 1024**—Defines the amount of bandwidth, in Kbps, to be allocated for all RSVP flows.
- **ip rsvp data-packet classification none**—Disables RSVP processing of every packet, which improves overhead and network performance.
- **ip rsvp resource-provider none**—Ensures that class-based weighted fair queueing (CBWFQ) is used for data processing, which aligns with the CBWFQ policy map that is being applied to the interface.
- **ip rsvp policy local identity rsvp-voice**—Defines a policy group called **rsvp-voice**. This is associated by RSVP application IDs with the **ip rsvp policy identity** command from earlier.
- **maximum bandwidth group 768**—Defines the portion of the overall **rsvp** bandwidth that can be reserved by applications matched for **rsvp-voice**. This specific command is reserving 768 Kbps for voice traffic flows, and video is defined as 256 Kbps. The sum of these values for all groups is allowed to exceed the total RSVP bandwidth, but in those conditions, a group may be rejected even if the utilized bandwidth for the group is under the policy limit in situations where the total RSVP bandwidth has been exceeded.
- **forward all**—Accepts and forwards all RSVP messages to the next hop.

In Example 8-27, it is important that the bandwidth defined under the interface matches the defined sizes of the appropriate queues for the QoS policy on the interface. This ensures that when the traffic is reserved for RSVP, the traffic is guaranteed to go into the appropriate queue for the circuit. The priority queue size (generally reserved for voice media) on the interface should also not be higher than the committed rate the service provider of the circuit has given.

In Example 8-27, because voice traffic should be placed in a priority queue as a best practice, the priority queue for the serial interface should match the RSVP bandwidth defined for the voice group, which in this case is 768 Kbps. Though the details of QoS configuration for collaboration media are not further covered in this book, a sample configuration to match the RSVP configuration from Example 8-27 is provided. The configuration for QoS in Example 8-28 assumes that DSCP is being trusted from the access layer through the core to this edge device.

Example 8-28 *Sample Configuration for CBWFQ for Voice/Video Traffic*

```
class-map match-any rtp-voice
  match dscp ef
class-map match-any rtp-video
  match dscp af41
 class-map match-any signaling
  match dscp cs3 af31
  match protocol mgcp
  match protocol h323
  match protocol sip
  match protocol skinny

policy-map wan-qos
 class rtp-voice
  priority 768
 class rtp-video
  priority 256
class voice-control
  bandwidth 8

class class-default
  fair-queue
  random-detect dscp-based
  set dscp 0

policy-map shaper
class class-default
  shape average 1544000
  service-policy wan-qos

interface Serial0/0/1:0
  service-policy output shaper
```

Tip It is a good practice to apply a traffic shaper (for example, **shape average**) as the parent policy-map that is shaped to the limit of the outbound committed network speed. This is essential when you are trying to control QoS on a network egress and the actual congestion point is upstream but cannot be controlled with a configuration (for example, when a WAN router with the serial interface is managed by the service provider, and it is a Gigabit Ethernet handoff to CUBE as an edge router).

Once the interface-specific configuration for RSVP has been performed, the voice-specific RSVP configuration can be performed on CUBE. Example 8-29 shows an example of RSVP configuration that would be specifically applied for a voice device such as CUBE.

Example 8-29 *RSVP Configuration for CUBE*

```
dial-peer voice 150 voip
 voice-class sip rsvp-fail-policy voice post-alert mandatory disconnect retry 2
  interval 30
 voice-class sip rsvp-fail-policy video post-alert mandatory disconnect retry 2
  interval 30
 req-qos controlled-load audio
 req-qos controlled-load video
 acc-qos controlled-load audio
 acc-qos controlled-load video
 ip qos dscp default media rsvp-fail
 ip qos dscp default video rsvp-fail
 ip qos policy-locator voice app AudioStream
 ip qos policy-locator video app VideoStream
 ip qos defending-priority 1111
```

The following list explains the information shown in Example 8-29:

- **voice-class sip rsvp-fail-policy**—This command defines the action to take when RSVP negotiation fails. This command specifies that after the alerting state of the call, if RSVP cannot reserve resources after two attempts—waiting 30 seconds and retrying—the call will be disconnected. The alternative to disconnecting is **keep-alive**, which does not disconnect the call but specifies a time interval to continue sending RSVP keep-alive messages until resources can be reserved for that call.
- **req-qos controlled-load**—The default behavior in IOS is to accept best-effort QoS, which means that an RSVP reservation is not initiated or requested by default. **req-qos** and **acc-qos** set the requested and acceptable QoS behavior, respectively. **controlled-load** requests low-delay and high-throughput QoS (by using WRED) for matches on this dial peer and is generally preferred for real-time communication. Other options for this command are **guaranteed-delay** (where RSVP guarantees bandwidth by using Weighted Fair Queuing [WFQ]) and **best-effort** (where RSVP does not reserve any bandwidth).
- **ip qos dscp default media rsvp-fail**—This command specifies that DSCP should be rewritten if an RSVP reservation has failed. Specifically, this command strips the DSCP when RSVP fails in order to avoid overloading the defined queues. The result is best-effort media transmission for any calls that come in after the defined RSVP bandwidth has been exhausted.
- **ip qos policy-locator voice app AudioStream**—This command tells the router to tag all generated voice traffic with the application ID of **AudioStream** for use with classification in RSVP policies.

- **ip qos defending-priority 1111**—This command specifies that an RSVP priority for calls matches across this dial peer. When no bandwidth is available, a call with a higher priority value can preempt an existing call that has a lower priority. This is useful in scenarios where you want to allow emergency calls to go through when a circuit may be saturated by lower-business-priority calls.

If a call is rejected due to RSVP for an SIP call, the call is rejected with a **580 Precondition Failed** message. A call rejection due to lack of RSVP bandwidth is demonstrated in Example 8-30, with **debug ccsip info** and **debug ccsip messages** enabled.

Example 8-30 *Debug Output During SIP Call Failure to Allocate RSVP Bandwidth*

```
Dec  5 05:15:19.419: //2411/1F0354C0A5FD/SIP/Info/info/133120/sipSPIBwCacIsDi-
  alPeerBwAvailable: bwcac NOP dial-peer bw available tag 102
Dec  5 05:15:19.419: //2411/1F0354C0A5FD/SIP/Info/critical/131072/sipSPIBwCacIsIn-
  terfaceBwAvailable: bwcac no interface specified!!!!
Dec  5 05:15:19.419: //2411/1F0354C0A5FD/SIP/Info/info/131072/sipSPIBwCacVerifyB-
  wThreshold: bwcac verify bw threshold, bw available allow call total bw 80000 bps
Dec  5 05:15:19.419: //2411/1F0354C0A5FD/SIP/Info/notify/133120/sipSPIGetCallQosSup-
  ported: precondition tag needed in Require  header
Dec  5 05:15:19.419: //2411/1F0354C0A5FD/SIP/Info/info/131073/sipSPIDoQoSNegotia-
  tionWithMediaLine: QOS negotiation for mline_index 1
Dec  5 05:15:19.419: //2411/1F0354C0A5FD/SIP/Info/critical/131072/sipSPIDoStreamQoS-
  Negotiation: Qos negotiation fails
Dec  5 05:15:19.419: //2411/1F0354C0A5FD/SIP/Info/critical/4096/ccsip_set_cc_cause_
  for_spi_err: Categorized cause:49, category:184
Dec  5 05:15:19.419: //-1/xxxxxxxxxxxx/SIP/Info/verbose/4096/ccsip_set_release_
  source_for_peer: ownCallId[2411], src[6]
Dec  5 05:15:19.419: //2411/1F0354C0A5FD/SIP/Info/info/4096/sipSPIContinueNewMsgIn-
  vite: ccsip_api_call_setup_ind returned: SIP_PRE_CONDITION_FAIL_ERR
Dec  5 05:15:19.419: //2411/1F0354C0A5FD/SIP/Info/verbose/4096/sipSPIUaddCcbToTable:
  Added to table. ccb=0x7F230DAB2510 key=1-8088@127.0.1.18FFE6D-38F balance 1
Dec  5 05:15:19.419: //2411/1F0354C0A5FD/SIP/Info/verbose/4096/sipSPIUaddccCallId-
  ToTable: Adding call id 96B to table
Dec  5 05:15:19.419: //2411/1F0354C0A5FD/SIP/Info/verbose/4096/sipSPISendInviteRe-
  sponse: Dialog State: [0]
Dec  5 05:15:19.419: //-1/xxxxxxxxxxxx/SIP/Info/info/1024/httpish_msg_create: cre-
  ated msg=0x7F22BFE4A070 with refCount = 1
Dec  5 05:15:19.419: //2411/1F0354C0A5FD/SIP/Info/info/8192/Session-Timer/sipSTSL-
  Main:
    SE: 0;refresher:none peer refresher:none, flags:0, posted event:E_STSL_INVALID_
  PEER_EVENT, reason:4
    Configured SE:1800, Configured Min-SE:1800
Dec  5 05:15:19.419: //2411/1F0354C0A5FD/SIP/Info/verbose/8192/sipSPIPresendProcess-
  ing: Presend Processing called for 3 event
Dec  5 05:15:19.419: //2411/1F0354C0A5FD/SIP/Info/notify/4096/sipSPI_ipip_Get-
  PassthruCopyListDataFromTdContainer: Could not get any elements from TD Container
Dec  5 05:15:19.419: //2411/1F0354C0A5FD/SIP/Info/notify/4096/sipSPI_ipip_Get-
  PassthruCopyListDataFromTdContainer: Could not get any elements from TD Container
Dec  5 05:15:19.419: //2411/1F0354C0A5FD/SIP/Info/info/4096/sipSPISendInviteRe-
  sponse: Associated container=0x7F22BF5469C8 to Invite Response 580
```

```
Dec  5 05:15:19.419: //-1/xxxxxxxxxxxx/SIP/Info/verbose/8192/sipSPIAppHandleContain-
  erBody: sipSPIAppHandleContainerBody len 0
Dec  5 05:15:19.419: //2411/1F0354C0A5FD/SIP/Info/info/2048/sipSPIGetExtensionCfg:
  SIP extension config:1, check sys cfg:1
Dec  5 05:15:19.419: //2411/1F0354C0A5FD/SIP/Info/info/2048/sipSPIGetExtensionCfg:
  SIP extension config:1, check sys cfg:1
Dec  5 05:15:19.419: //2411/1F0354C0A5FD/SIP/Info/critical/512/sentErrResDisconnect-
  ing: Sent an 3456XX Error Response
Dec  5 05:15:19.419: //2411/1F0354C0A5FD/SIP/Msg/ccsipDisplayMsg:
Sent:
SIP/2.0 580 Precondition Failed
Via: SIP/2.0/UDP 192.0.2.5:5061;branch=z9hG4bK-8088-1-0;received=192.0.2.50
From: Eleanor Rigby <sip:9195555150@192.0.2.5:5061>;tag=8088SIPpTag001
To: Mrs OLeary <sip:9195551234@192.0.2.10:5060>;tag=8FFE6D-38F
Date: Tue, 05 Dec 2017 05:15:19 GMT
Call-ID: 1-8088@192.0.2.5
CSeq: 1 INVITE
Allow-Events: telephone-event
Warning: 399 192.0.2.10 "QOS Negotiation Failure"
Reason: Q.850;cause=49
Server: Cisco-SIPGateway/IOS-15.5.3.S6
Content-Length: 0
```

Summary

This chapter covers the concepts and details involved in effectively designing and sizing for SBC integration in a collaboration deployment. The chapter first outlines the general constraints that dictate SBC scalability and sizing. General sizing guidelines that pertain to CUBE are also provided for the various supported platforms. The next section in the chapter provides an overview of licensing for an SBC and details the current licensing schemes specific to CUBE. The last section of the chapter outlines overload techniques on SBCs, covering the general SIP overload techniques as well as the concepts of CAC and RSVP.

This chapter should give you adequate knowledge to properly specify and design an SBC deployment that is suitable to support the intended call capacity, as well as defend against conditions where intended capacity is exceeded.

References

- "Troubleshooting ESX/ESXi Virtual Machine Performance Issues," https://kb.vmware.com/s/article/2001003#CPU%20constraints.
- "Ubuntu Manuals: Free.1.gz," http://manpages.ubuntu.com/manpages/xenial/en/man1/free.1.html.
- "SupportIndustry.com Research Insight: Average Speed to Answer, Wait Time and Handle Time," http://www.supportindustry.com/researchinsight_AHT.htm.
- "DSP Calculator," https://www.cisco.com/c/en/us/applications/dsp-calc.html.
- "Cisco Feature Navigator," http://cfn.cloudapps.cisco.com/ITDIT/CFN/jsp/compareImages.jsp.
- "Smart Licensing Deployment Guide," https://www.cisco.com/c/en/us/td/docs/wireless/technology/mesh/8-2/b_Smart_Licensing_Deployment_Guide.html.
- RFC 6357, "Design Considerations for Session Initiation Protocol (SIP) Overload Control," https://tools.ietf.org/html/rfc6357.
- RFC 7200, "A Session Initiation Protocol (SIP) Load-Control Event Package," https://tools.ietf.org/html/rfc7200.
- RFC 7339, "Session Initiation Protocol (SIP) Overload Control," https://tools.ietf.org/html/rfc7339.
- RFC 7415, "Session Initiation Protocol (SIP) Rate Control," https://tools.ietf.org/html/rfc7415.
- BCP 38, "Network Ingress Filtering: Defeating Denial of Service Attacks Which Employ IP Source Address Spoofing," https://tools.ietf.org/html/bcp38.
- *End-to-End QoS Network Design: Quality of Service for Rich-Media and Cloud Networks* by Tim Szigeti, Cisco Press.
- RFC 2205, "Resource ReSerVation Protocol (RSVP)—Version 1 Functional Specification," https://tools.ietf.org/html/rfc2205.
- "Cisco Unified Border Element Data Sheet," https://www.cisco.com/c/en/us/products/collateral/unified-communications/unified-border-element/data-sheet-c78-729692.html.

Chapter 9

SIP Trunking for PSTN Access Through SBCs

In the early days of real-time communications, VoIP deployments were small islands confined to the enterprise, with interconnection to other enterprises or the public switched telephone network (PSTN) provided by traditional TDM or SS7 networks. With the advent of SIP trunking, enterprises and service providers benefitted from many aspects that are inherent with end-to-end communications over IP, including low operational costs, a single path for data and multimedia, reliability, scalability, and ability to deploy services that were not possible over traditional TDM networks (for example, instant messaging and presence).

Before enabling service provider access over SIP trunking, a number of issues need to be considered, including security, QoS, monitoring, redundancy, and NAT traversal. It is also required to establish an identity with service provider networks so that they can efficiently provide break-in and break-out multimedia services to enterprises.

This chapter provides an overview of some of the best practices in deploying SIP trunking services with session border controllers (SBCs) and gets into the details of how enterprises establish an identity or a relationship with service provider networks. The following topics are covered in this chapter:

- **Best Practices for ITSP Access with SBCs**—This section outlines some of the best practices for SIP trunking from the perspective of SBCs.
- **SIP Trunk Registration**—This section provides a detailed account of the SIP **REGISTER** method. It also includes a detailed account of how an enterprise can peer with a SIP service provider network.
- **Authentication**—This section introduces the basic elements of the authentication framework and provides a detailed account of digest authentication in SIP.
- **Registration with SBCs**—This section discusses the registration of SIP trunks and endpoints with SBCs.

- **Troubleshooting—**This section provides a basic approach to troubleshooting SIP trunk registration issues from the perspective of SBCs.

By the end of this chapter, you will have an in-depth understanding of the SIP **REGISTER** method, the digest authentication framework in SIP, and how SBCs manage SIP trunking on behalf of an enterprise.

Best Practices for ITSP Access with SBCs

Chapter 1, "Laying the Groundwork," explores the benefits of SIP trunking over traditional methods of PSTN interconnection. However, while the advantages are plenty, many deployment and practical factors need to be considered before migrating communication infrastructures to IP with SIP as the call control protocol. The following are some of these considerations:

- Security and topology abstraction
- NAT traversal
- QoS for voice, video, and fax
- Monitoring and redundancy
- Scaling and Call Admission Control (CAC)
- Capability parity between enterprise and service provider networks

Most of these considerations are dealt with at the network periphery or the transit point between the enterprise and service provider/access networks. This ensures that end-to-end communications over IP provide exactly the same benefits as traditional analog/digital networks, such as guaranteed QoS, monitoring, redundancy, and reliability.

SBCs are deployed at the network edge to serve as the rendezvous point between two multimedia networks that could potentially have vastly different characteristics. The utility of having SBCs deployed at the network edge are discussed in Chapter 1 and are expanded on throughout this book. Some of the best practices for different aspects of service provider access are discussed in the following subsections.

Security

As traffic, signaling, and media are exchanged over public networks such as the Internet, data can be subject to a host of attacks, such as availability, confidentiality, and integrity attacks, all of which can be detrimental to an enterprise. When deploying IP-based service provider access through SBCs, the security practices described in the following sections help mitigate or at least minimize the impact of such attacks.

Dynamic Blacklisting

SBCs can interconnect to SIP service providers over the public Internet. In such instances, malicious entities can examine the signaling headers or Layer 3 IP headers and launch a number of attacks, from sending an unusually large number of call requests per second to sending a large number of malformed SIP messages to rob the SBC of processing cycles. These attacks are aimed at moving the SBC into an overwhelmed state, where it can no longer function productively and reliably.

To prevent such attacks, SBCs implement "blacklisting," wherein malicious entities are added to a blacklist, and subsequent requests from them are dropped without any processing. This prevents the expeditious depletion of SBC resources. If requests from a blacklisted entity cross a system-defined threshold, an SBC can generate alerts for administrators to take appropriate action.

The criteria for placement of an entity into a blacklist can vary from one SBC to another and can include factors such as the IP addresses from which requests are sourced, traffic patterns that include a large number of fuzzy or malformed requests, or spam transactions. Figure 9-1 depicts dynamic blacklisting by an SBC.

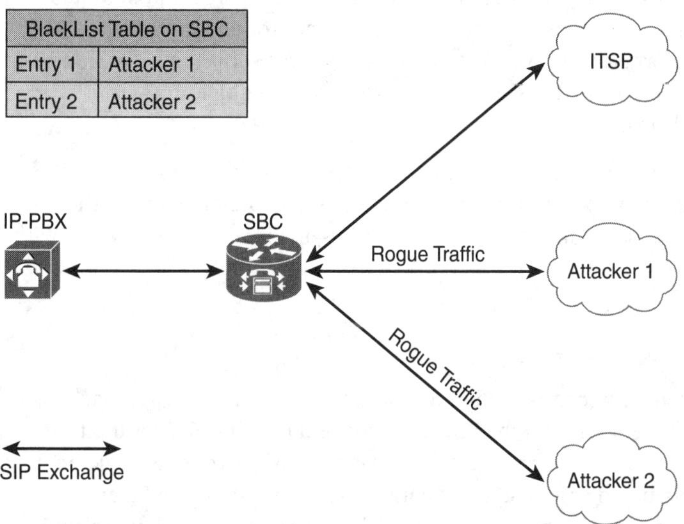

Figure 9-1 *SBC Dynamic Blacklisting*

> **Note** SIP user agents trusted by the SBC are part of a logical list known as a *whitelist*. User agents become a part of the whitelist either through configuration on the SBC or on-the-fly as they exchange signaling messages with the SBC. When user agents exchange messages with the SBC such that these messages carry certain proprietary SIP headers, they serve as identifiers for traffic sourced from trusted entities.

Secure Signaling and Media

By simply examining a call log, you can find out who is talking to whom, when a call was made, the duration of the call, and the characteristics of the call, such as the codec, the IP address and port numbers for RTP/RTCP, and so on. Even worse, if signaling is intercepted in real time, it is quite possible for the attackers to place themselves in the media and signaling path and listen in on the current conversation and future conversations by altering SIP headers and SDP bodies.

To protect against these attacks, it is generally a good idea to secure SIP signaling and media. SIP can work over Transport Layer Security (TLS) to secure the signaling channel, and the constructs of RFC 3711 can be used to secure the RTP stream. Though setting up secure SIP and RTP sessions is resource expensive, it is nonetheless recommended when signaling and media traverse untrusted networks such as the Internet. SIP over TLS and Secure RTP are discussed in detail in Chapter 6, "Secure Signaling and Media."

Topology Abstraction

Topology abstraction, or *topology hiding*, refers to limiting the amount of topology information exposed to external networks. This is required when an enterprise wants to restrict details of internal devices or IP addressing schemes to the outside world. Restricting topology information prevents attacks such as denial-of-service (DoS) attacks or distributed-denial-of-service (DDoS) attacks. It also prevents competitors from uncovering network schema.

An SBC typically performs topology abstraction by stripping off or overwriting SIP header field values that might expose topology or internal IP addressing information. While overwriting header field values, the SBC overwrites any internal IP addresses with its own IP address.

Availability

SIP trunking embodiments can choose to use a centralized or distributed approach. In either scenario, for most deployments the SBC is placed as a transit point for multimedia traffic entering or leaving the enterprise. Given that the SBC serves as a single point of failure for a site (distributed trunking) or an entire enterprise (centralized trunking), measures must be implemented to make sure the trunking services are highly scalable, reliable, and available.

The following sections discuss some of the best practices for ensuring that SIP trunking services through SBCs are highly available.

Overload Control

Overload in SIP networks refers to the inability of a SIP server to process incoming traffic due to a lack of available resources. These resources could include the components of a SIP server directly responsible for processing SIP traffic such as CPU cycles, memory, and control plane capacity or could include other components that are logically part of the SIP processing engine, such as DNS servers, databases, and RTP stacks.

SIP servers can communicate overload conditions to their neighbors implicitly or explicitly. Implicit communication of an overload condition occurs when a server fails to respond to messages or when responses are sent outside acceptable time limits, as defined within the SIP framework. Explicit overload is communicated over SIP using a **503 Service Unavailable** response with an optional **Retry-After** header. The effectiveness of such an approach has shortcomings and is known to exacerbate overload under certain conditions. The challenges of using **503 Service Unavailable** responses for overload are documented in RFC 5390. A more structured and well-designed approach to handling overload control is detailed in the RFCs compiled under the IIETF's SIP Overload Control Working group. However, these constructs often require a degree of cooperation between peer SIP servers and therefore have not found very wide adoption in the industry.

Most SBCs communicate overload conditions by using **503 Service Unavailable** responses. These responses are sent when an SBC is completely overwhelmed with incoming requests or because of administrator-defined limits on a vector of factors such the CPU usage, the memory profile, or the number of concurrent SIP sessions. Figure 9-2 diagrams a scenario in which an administrator sets threshold values for the CPU, memory, and DSP utilization on the SBC. In the course of processing calls, if any of these parameters surpasses administrator-defined thresholds, the SBC begins rejecting new requests.

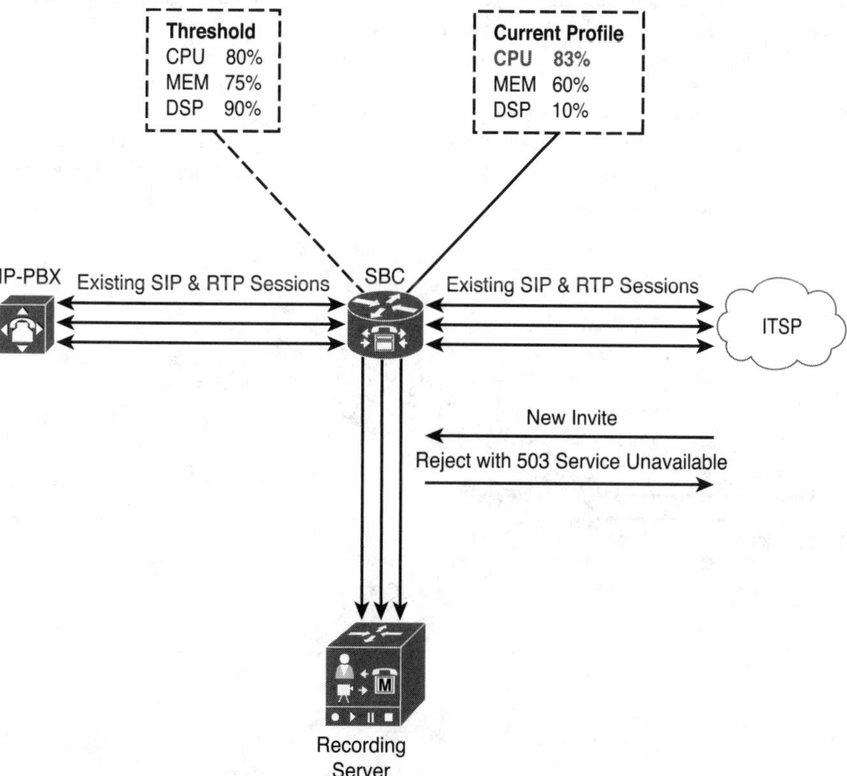

Figure 9-2 *SBC Rejecting Incoming Requests*

It should be noted that using such an approach also requires CPU cycles to be expended by the SBC in parsing requests and sending out **503 Service Unavailable** responses, which could eventually cause a severe degradation of throughput, increased retransmissions of requests, and a condition known as *congestion collapse*.

In addition, an attacker over the Internet might aim to rob the SBC of processing cycles and expeditiously move it into an overloaded state by sending a large number of malformed requests in a short span of time. For such scenarios, using 503 responses would only exacerbate the problem. A better approach for such attacks is to use the native intrusion detection/prevention systems found in many SBCs. These systems analyze traffic patterns and form a model of acceptable, legitimate traffic and malicious traffic. Malicious traffic patterns usually have signatures such as messages being malformed, not adhering to SIP standards, or being sourced from unknown IP addresses. On receiving malicious traffic, the intrusion detection/prevention systems can take corrective action such as raising high-severity alerts or dropping traffic before it is processed at the application layer.

Plurality of Entry and Exit Trunks

As with traditional ISDN or analog networks, there always exists the possibility of transient or major outages on the SIP service provider network. Such failures can greatly impact the communications infrastructure of an enterprise. To protect against such outages, an enterprise could consider the possibility of dual trunking, such that each logical trunk peers with a different service provider.

Failures in the service provider network would lead to requests either being rejected or dropped altogether. With service provider redundancy, traffic can be redirected to the failover routes to ensure that there isn't a break in uptime. Figure 9-3 depicts call failover across service provider networks.

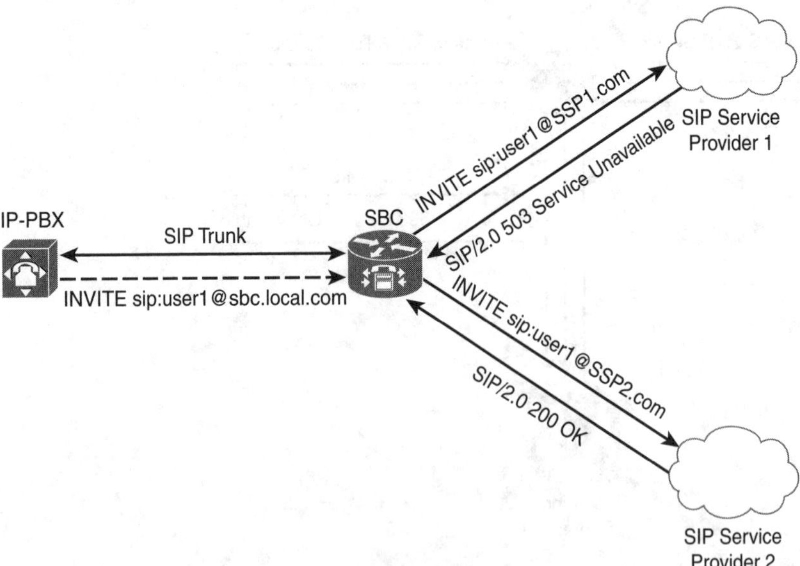

Figure 9-3 *Call Failover to a Secondary Service Provider*

SBC High Availability

To make sure SBCs are highly available, another construct used is SBC redundancy or SBC high availability, such that two physically distinct SBC units are interconnected to one another, usually over Layer 2, to form an *Active/Standby pair*. A single virtual IP address per network segment is used to send traffic to and from the high availability pair.

Signaling and media traverse only a single SBC at a time (the active SBC). There is a constant dialog between the active and passive SBC to exchange state information, such that the passive SBC can seamlessly and almost instantaneously take over call processing, if needed. If for any reason there is an issue on the active SBC, and the passive SBC has to take over call processing (as the new active SBC), the transition is seamless to call participants and devices peering with the high availability pair. Chapter 2, "SBC Deployment Models," provides details on high availability on the Cisco Unified Border Element (CUBE). Figure 9-4 diagrams a high availability pair.

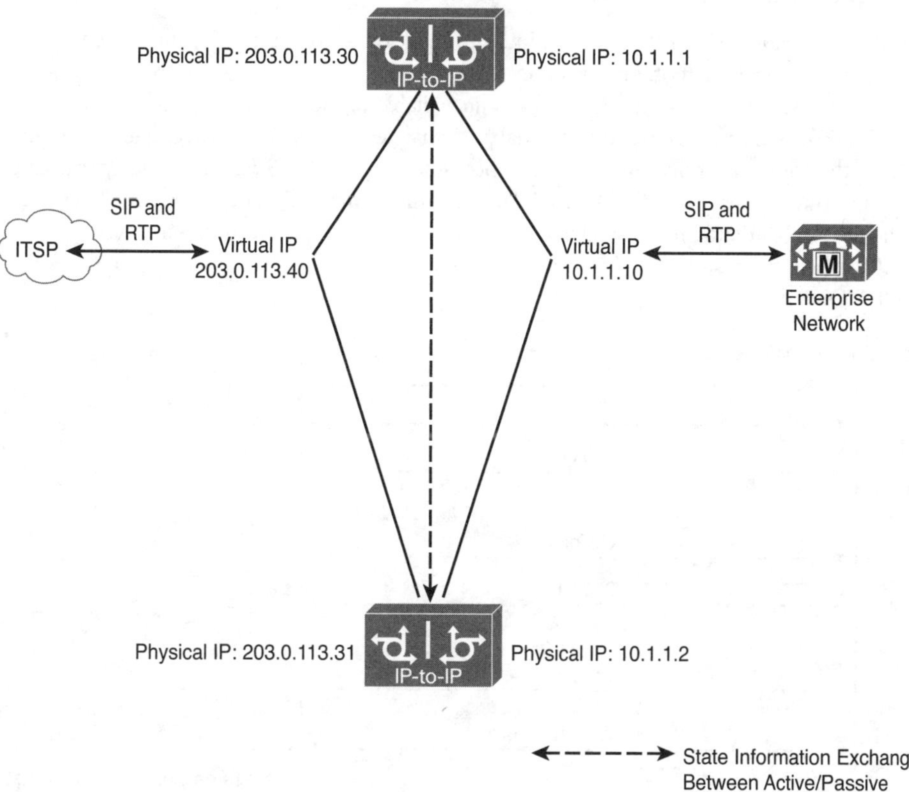

Figure 9-4 *SBC High Availability Pair*

Monitoring

Another vital aspect of SIP trunking is the ability to monitor the status of trunks and, by extension, their ability to service calls. In traditional ISDN circuits, there are protocol-specific mechanisms to advertise the status of individual bearer channels, and the call routing process can use these mechanisms to increase the efficiency between interconnected switches.

In the world of SIP trunking, a generic ICMP ping does not usually pass as a viable check for whether a remote SIP entity is capable of servicing calls. A SIP-specific method is used for probing the operational status of SIP peers—namely the SIP **OPTIONS** method, also known as SIP **OPTIONS** ping in this context. The **OPTIONS** method was introduced in RFC 3261 as a means for probing a remote SIP entity for its capabilities without actually setting up a communication session. The response codes sent to an **OPTIONS** ping request can be the same as those of a SIP **INVITE**; however, the interpretation of response codes and how these codes relate to marking the operational state of a SIP entity are currently undefined by any IETF RFC.

Different vendors use different techniques to mark the status of a SIP trunk based on responses or lack thereof. For example, a 500/503 response to an **OPTIONS** ping doesn't necessarily have to mean the SIP trunk is unavailable or incapable of servicing calls. Any 2XX/4XX/5XX may be treated as a viable exchange at the protocol layer and reason to keep the trunk in service. A lack of a response to an **OPTIONS** ping universally translates to the trunk being marked as "down." Once a trunk is marked as down or out of service, the **OPTIONS** dialog may be retried after a predefined interval to determine whether SIP services are restored at the remote peer. Figure 9-5 depicts the operation of the SIP **OPTIONS** method.

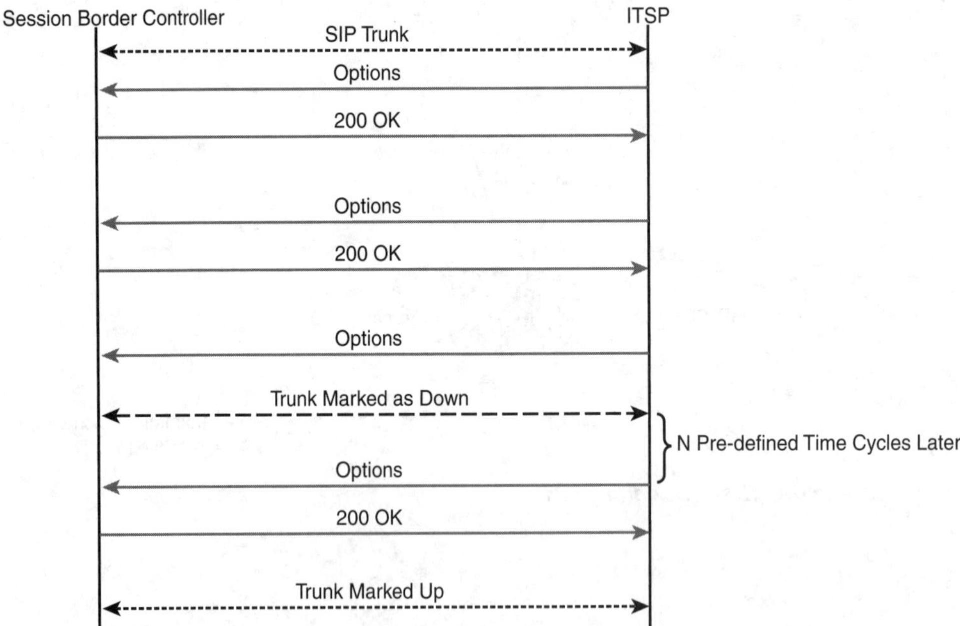

Figure 9-5 *Operation of the SIP* **OPTIONS** *Method*

Scalability

Another important aspect of SIP trunking is the number of simultaneous SIP and media sessions that can be serviced by an SBC at any given time. The number of concurrent signaling and media sessions is vendor and platform specific, and specifications are put out for "ideal" conditions, including the following:

- Basic calls without any supplementary services or midcall signaling
- G.711 calls without any transcoding or transrating
- No additional functionality such as media forking, secure calls, or NAT traversal

It is therefore critical for enterprises to do a thorough rundown of expected call patterns, call volumes, and services required of their SBCs before provisioning a SIP trunking solution. If it is required to provision more than one SBC to load balance calls, a SIP proxy would be ideal. Because of its built-in mechanisms for monitoring and load balancing, a SIP proxy can also be used for SIP message normalization before forwarding it to an SBC, thus easing operational load on the SBC.

SIP Trunk Registration

A vital aspect of SIP trunking is the process of establishing an "identity" with the SIP service provider. This is important as it enables service provider networks to determine if calls are made by authorized entities and not by malicious entities. It also enables service provider networks to obtain "lookup" details for various enterprises. This association between the SIP service provider network and enterprise is set up either by peering or by using the SIP **REGISTER** method. Both of these methods are discussed in subsequent sections, but first it is important to look at how the SIP **REGISTER** method works.

Overview of RFC 3261 for SIP REGISTER

In its simplest sense, the SIP **REGISTER** method is used to provide a mapping between a user agent's address of record (AOR) and its contact address/addresses. The SIP AOR functions as the public address of a user agent and is specified in the **To** header field of **REGISTER** requests. When the **REGISTER** transaction completes successfully, the AOR-to-Contact binding is placed in a location server, and it is later referenced whenever calls have to be sent to the user agent.

The SIP **REGISTER** request is sent to a server known as a "registrar" server that need not be a standalone SIP server and can have co-located proxy, location, and generic user agent server (UAS) capabilities. The aim of the **REGISTER** request is to create a binding between a SIP user agent's AOR and one or more URIs present in the **Contact** header field of the request. The AOR is specified in the **To** header of the **REGISTER** request.

Discovering a Registrar Server and Constructing a Request

To successfully create an address binding on the registrar, a user agent first needs to "discover" a registrar server to which the **REGISTER** request may be sent. There are three methods by which the user agent can discover a registrar:

- By static configuration
- By AOR
- By multicast

The most common method of registrar discovery is static configuration.

Before proceeding to look at different aspects of SIP trunk registration, it is important to understand the different header fields used in a **REGISTER** request and what these header field values imply:

- **Request URI:** Specifies the domain name that the **REGISTER** transaction targets. A location service is responsible for maintaining AOR-to-Contact bindings for each domain. This is first line of the **REGISTER** request and must not contain the user and @ components of a conventional request URI. For example, the following request URI is invalid for the **REGISTER** method:

  ```
  REGISTER sip:alice@sbcdomain.com:5060 SIP/2.0
  ```

  An example of a valid request URI for the **REGISTER** method is as follows:

  ```
  REGISTER sip:sbcdomain.com:5060 SIP/2.0
  ```

- **To:** The **To** header contains the actual user agent AOR for which the **REGISTER** method aims to create a binding.
- **From:** This header is exactly the same as the **To** header except when the registration of an AOR is done by an authorized third party on behalf of the user agent.
- **Call-ID:** This header field value must remain the same across all **REGISTER** messages sent from the user agent to a registrar server within the same dialog. A successful **REGISTER** transaction creates a binding between the AOR and contact address(s). This binding is not indefinite and has to be refreshed periodically. Successive **REGISTER** messages sent to refresh the binding must carry the same **Call-ID** header field value. If there is a software restart of the user agent or application, then a different **Call-ID** may be used (as it would constitute a different dialog).
- **CSeq:** The **CSeq** header field value is used on the registrar server to correctly order **REGISTER** requests coming in from a user agent. From the perspective of the user agent, for a given dialog, every new **REGISTER** request has to increment the value of this header field by one and retain the same Call-ID.
- **Contact:** The **Contact** header specifies a URI or URIs that provide reachability information for a user agent and form the second half of the entry to be placed into the location service upon successful registration. (The first half is the AOR of the user agent, as specified in the **To** header.)

Figure 9-6 illustrates the sequence of events from when a CUBE functioning as an SBC sends a **REGISTER** message to a registrar and subsequently receives a request for a communication session from a SIP proxy. The proxy, location, and registrar roles are logical and in real-world deployments can be realized by a single physical unit.

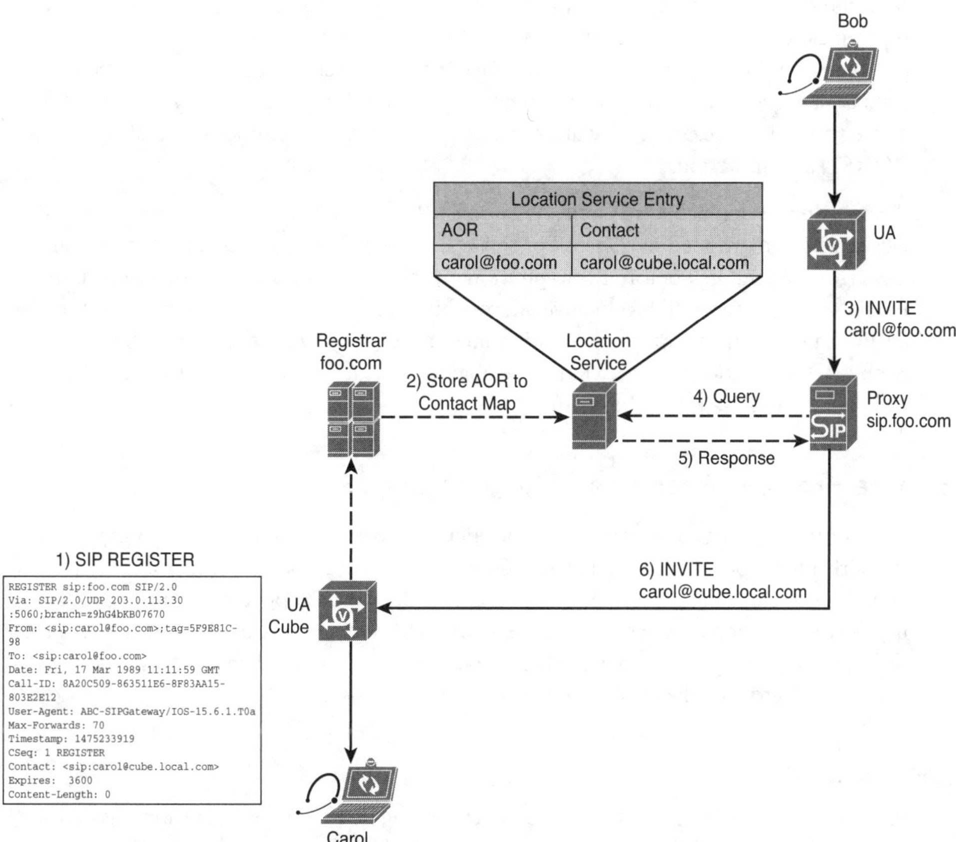

Figure 9-6 *Sequence of Events Triggered by the SIP* **REGISTER** *Message*

Refreshing Registrations

A SIP **REGISTER** message creates an AOR-to-contact binding for a user agent. This binding is then indexed from a location service whenever a new request has to be sent to the user agent. The AOR-to-contact binding created by a successful **REGISTER** transaction is bound by a time limit and does not remain valid indefinitely. The registration has to be refreshed periodically to ensure that the binding remains active. The frequency with which a registration is refreshed is dictated by the expiration interval.

A user agent can indicate the expiration interval in one of two ways:

- Using an **Expires** header field in the **REGISTER** message
- Using an **Expires** parameter in the **Contact** header field

Both the client that sources the **REGISTER** message and the registrar that responds to the request include the expiration interval. However, it is the expiration interval suggested by the registrar that always takes precedence. Failure to refresh bindings in a timely manner can lead to call break-in and break-out services being temporarily suspended. These services are restored only after the user agent initiates another successful **REGISTER** transaction.

When using an unreliable transport protocol such as UDP, it is very possible for refresh messages to be dropped in transit. For this reason, the client must ensure that refresh messages are sent well before the expiration interval, to allow for retransmissions until a final response is received. To remove address bindings, the user agent client (UAC) sends a **REGISTER** request with the expiration interval set to **0**. Once the address bindings are removed, the location service will not be able to provide a mapping between the AOR and contact address(es) of the client.

Service Provider Peering and Registration

An enterprise has two methods of establishing an identity with SIP service provider networks: by explicitly registering all AORs under its administrative control or by peering with the service provider network. In peering mode, the enterprise and service provider networks view each other as peer SIP networks and don't require an explicit **REGISTER** dialog in place. In either scenario, SBCs are usually deployed to handle registration or peering on behalf of the entire enterprise.

Registration Mode

In registration mode, all the AOR-to-contact bindings that are under the administrative control of an enterprise have to be registered with the SIP service provider. For medium to large enterprises, the number of publicly routable AORs could easily run into the thousands. It is highly impractical to initiate such a large number of independent **REGISTER** transactions and potentially overload devices along the way. Added to this is the overhead of periodically refreshing bindings for potentially thousands of location service entries. To avoid such a predicament, the following methods are generally employed by modern SIP networks:

- Implicit bulk registration
- Registration of a single AOR

Implicit Bulk Registration

With implicit bulk registration, the SIP PBX generates a special type of **REGISTER** message, following the procedures of RFC 6140. With this method, it is not required for the SIP PBX to generate a **REGISTER** transaction for every single AOR. Rather, the PBX sends a single **REGISTER** message with a specially formatted **Contact** header field. The **Contact** header field carries a URI that serves as a template of all AORs under the administrative control of the SIP PBX.

For this to work successfully, the SIP PBX and registrar must be preprovisioned with all the E.164 numbers assigned to the enterprise. Following is an operational summary of implicit bulk registration:

1. The SIP PBX and SIP service provider (which hosts the registrar server) are preprovisioned with the E.164 numbers assigned to the enterprise.
2. The SIP PBX initiates a **REGISTER** transaction with two mandatory parameters included in the **REGISTER** message: **gin** (generate implicit numbers) and **bnc** (bulk number contact).
3. The **gin** tag is placed in the **Require** and **Proxy-Require** header fields.
4. The **bnc** parameter is added in the **Contact** header field such that URI specified in this field does not include a user portion. The URI has only an IP address or domain name specified. This is in stark contrast to a normally formatted **Contact** header field.
5. On receiving the **REGISTER** message, the registrar examines the **To** header field, identifies the enterprise/SIP PBX for which registration is being requested, and authenticates the SIP PBX/enterprise.
6. On successful authentication, the registrar creates multiple AOR-to-contact bindings for the enterprise/SIP PBX and places them as distinct entries in the location service. Each entry in the location service corresponds to a unique E.164 number belonging to the enterprise.
7. Each entry in the location service is built using the template provided in the **Contact** header field value. For example, if it is required to register a block of 100 numbers with the service provider, an enterprise SBC streams a **REGISTER** message that might look like the one provided in Example 9-1.

Example 9-1 REGISTER *Message Formatted for Implicit Bulk Registration*

```
REGISTER sip:ssp.example.com SIP/2.0
Via: SIP/2.0/UDP 203.0.113.10:5060;branch=z9hG4bKnashds7
Max-Forwards: 70
To: <sip:pbx@ssp.example.com>
From: <sip:pbx@ssp.example.com>;tag=a23589
```

```
Call-ID: 843817637684230@998sdasdh09
CSeq: 1826 REGISTER
Proxy-Require: gin
Require: gin
Supported: path
Contact: <sip:203.0.113.10:5060;bnc>
Expires: 7200
Content-Length: 0
```

The **REGISTER** message provided in Example 9-1 would trigger the service provider to implicitly generate AOR-to-contact bindings for all the E.164 numbers under the administrative control of the enterprise. The entries generated would look something like the ones illustrated in Table 9-1.

Table 9-1 *Location Service Entries After Implicit Bulk Registration*

Binding Number	Entry
1	**<sip:+1333567800@203.0.113.10:5060>**
2	**<sip:+1333567801@203.0.113.10:5060>**
3	**<sip:+1333567802@203.0.113.10:5060>**
. . .	
100	**<sip:+1333567899@203.0.113.10:5060>**

Figure 9-7 provides a diagrammatic account of implicit bulk registration. It is very similar to what is seen with regular registration, except for the way the **REGISTER** message is formatted and its interpretation on a SIP registrar server.

Registration of a Single AOR

The norm followed by most service providers today is to have the enterprise register a single AOR, which results in the registration of the entire number range of the enterprise. Though logically similar to bulk implicit registration, this method does not require any specialized formatting of the SIP **REGISTER** message, nor does it have any restriction of working only on E.164-formatted numbers. Implicit bulk registration requires special formatting of the **REGISTER** message and is designed to work with only E.164 numbers.

Peering Mode

In peering mode, the enterprise and service provider networks treat one another as peer SIP networks and don't require any prior association. Each of the two peers can learn of the other's signaling address and port through configuration, DNS, or using NAPTR records.

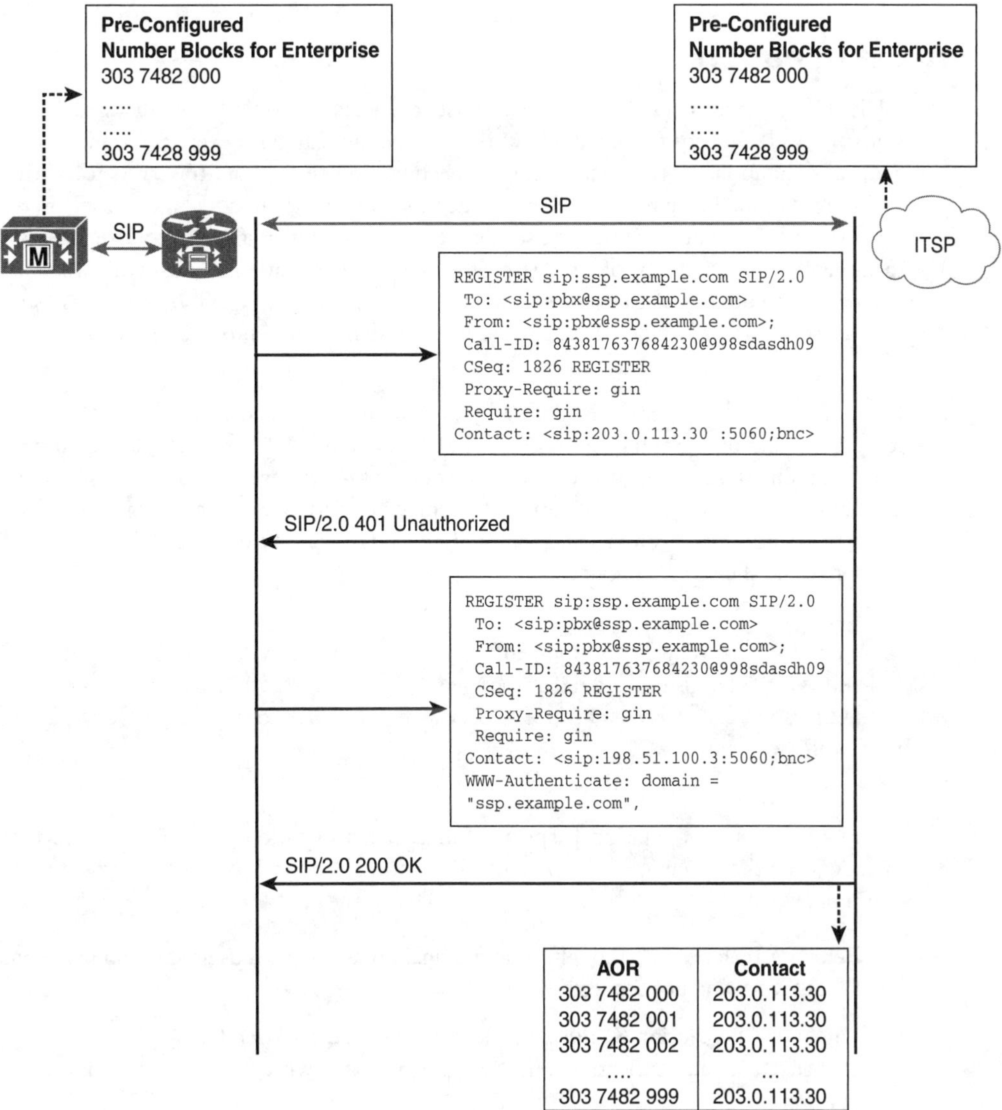

Figure 9-7 *Implicit Bulk Registration*

Though very convenient from a configuration perspective, peering mode can be subject to toll fraud attacks if a malicious party manages to spoof requests on behalf of the enterprise to make fraudulent calls. The service provider has literally no way of determining whether requests are sourced from a valid enterprise. In registration mode with digest authentication (explained in the next section), there is a pre-shared secret between the enterprise and service provider that makes validation easier.

Authentication

SIP is characterized by exchanges between user agents (and proxies) that are located across network and trust boundaries. With resources allocated for every SIP transaction and a cost component attributed to calls, it becomes imperative for SIP servers to validate the sources of incoming requests. SIP provides an authentication model that closely mirrors that of HTTP. Specifically, SIP uses digest authentication as a means for user agents to authenticate the initiator of a request. The digest authentication model in SIP is scoped to a realm or a domain. A *SIP realm*, also known as a *protection domain*, has an associated username and password that are used in the authentication process to validate the identity of the initiator of the request.

Digest authentication in SIP provides a way to avoid unauthorized access to telephony resources either on the enterprise IP PBX or SIP service provider networks. It should be noted that digest authentication does not provide message integrity and confidentiality; it only provides message authentication and replay protection. For a more comprehensive security scheme, it is recommended to use SIP over TLS for all exchanges between the enterprise and the service provider.

Note Not all service providers support SIP over TLS. For the service providers that do support SIP over TLS, it is not offered as a standard service. Enterprises wishing to secure the communication channel to and from the service provider network usually have to pay extra to avail the service.

Before looking at the operational aspects of digest authentication over SIP, it is important to understand the meaning of certain terms that form an integral part of the authentication framework:

- **Realm:** A realm can be thought of as a domain that utilizes a username and password for authentication of requests.
- **Quality of Protection (QoP):** QoP indicates whether the overarching digest exchange uses authentication (**auth**) or authentication with integrity protection (**auth-int**).

- **Nonce:** A nonce is a server-generated string that is sent to the client in the authentication challenge. The client then uses the string as one of many inputs while computing a cryptographic hash value. The main purpose of the server-generated nonce is to protect against replay attacks and ensure that responses are received in a timely manner.
- **Cnonce:** This is a client-generated string that provides protection against plaintext attacks.
- **Nonce count (nc):** This is the number of times the client sends a request with the current nonce value.
- **Response:** The response is the result of the hash function operation and ultimately determines whether the authentication process is successful.
- **Opaque:** This is a string of data provided by the server and must be returned by the client during the authentication exchange without modification. The **Opaque** header is commonly used for transporting state information. It is not always required for the server to populate this header field; it can empty.

Note The value of the realm is case sensitive. For example, the realm example.SSP.com is different from the realm Example.SSP.com.

The terms and descriptions just listed make little sense without a detailed explanation of the authentication process, which is provided in the next section. For a more granular understanding of HTTP- and SIP-based authentication, it is advisable to read the following RFCs:

- RFC 2617: HTTP Authentication: Basic and Digest Access Authentication
- RFC 7616: HTTP Digest Access Authentication
- RFC 3261: SIP: Session Initiation Protocol (Section 22)

Digest Authentication in SIP

SIP uses digest authentication to protect against unauthorized access to telephony resources. When a server receives a request, it sends a challenge to the initiator before processing the request and allocating resources in terms of RTP ports, media resources, or CPU cycles for setting up further downstream SIP sessions. On successful authentication, the request is processed as usual, inline with the established procedures of RFC 3261. If the authentication is unsuccessful, the server may re-issue the challenge or reject the request. Figure 9-8 provides the exchange between the initiator and UAS during a **REGISTER** transaction that requires authentication.

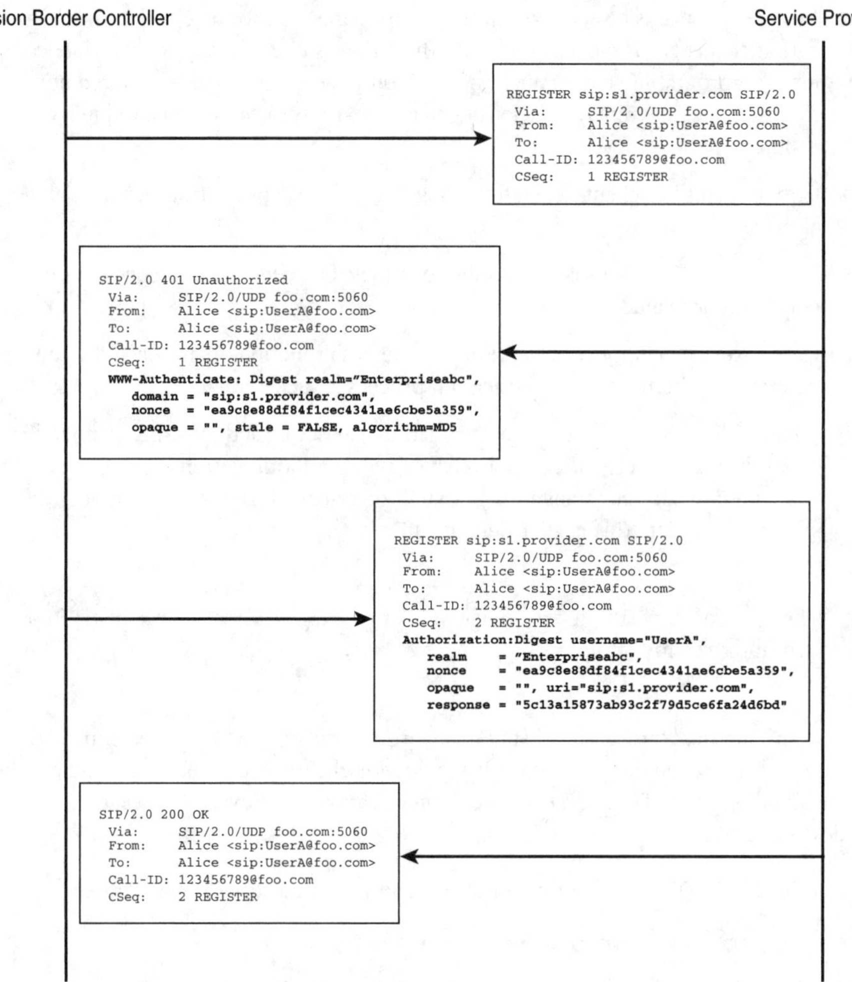

Session Border Controller
Service Provider
REGISTER sip:s1.provider.com SIP/2.0
Via: SIP/2.0/UDP foo.com:5060
From: Alice <sip:UserA@foo.com>
To: Alice <sip:UserA@foo.com>
Call-ID: 123456789@foo.com
CSeq: 1 REGISTER
SIP/2.0 401 Unauthorized
Via: SIP/2.0/UDP foo.com:5060
From: Alice <sip:UserA@foo.com>
To: Alice <sip:UserA@foo.com>
Call-ID: 123456789@foo.com
CSeq: 1 REGISTER
WWW-Authenticate: Digest realm="Enterpriseabc",
domain = "sip:s1.provider.com",
nonce = "ea9c8e88df84f1cec4341ae6cbe5a359",
opaque = "", stale = FALSE, algorithm=MD5
REGISTER sip:s1.provider.com SIP/2.0
Via: SIP/2.0/UDP foo.com:5060
From: Alice <sip:UserA@foo.com>
To: Alice <sip:UserA@foo.com>
Call-ID: 123456789@foo.com
CSeq: 2 REGISTER
Authorization:Digest username="UserA",
realm = "Enterpriseabc",
nonce = "ea9c8e88df84f1cec4341ae6cbe5a359",
opaque = "", uri="sip:s1.provider.com",
response = "5c13a15873ab93c2f79d5ce6fa24d6bd"
SIP/2.0 200 OK
Via: SIP/2.0/UDP foo.com:5060
From: Alice <sip:UserA@foo.com>
To: Alice <sip:UserA@foo.com>
Call-ID: 123456789@foo.com
CSeq: 2 REGISTER

Figure 9-8 *Digest Authentication Exchange for SIP* REGISTER

User Agent Authentication

On receiving a request, the UAS sends a challenge that sets into motion the digest authentication framework; the various operational aspects are discussed:

1. The initiator sends a request to a UAS. Dialog creating requests like the SIP **INVITE** or SIP **REGISTER** are usually the ones challenged by the UAS.

2. The UAS replies with a **401 Unauthorized** response that includes a **WWW-Authenticate** header. This header contains attributes that are used by the initiator to calculate a MD5 response. Example 9-2 shows a sample **WWW-Authenticate** header.

Example 9-2 *Sample* WWW-Authenticate *Header*

```
WWW-Authenticate: Digest
realm="biloxi.com",
qop="auth,auth-int",
nonce="dcd98b7102dd2f0e8b11d0f600bfb0c093",
opaque="5ccc069c403ebaf9f0171e9517f40e41"
```

3. On receiving the response, the originator has to supply the username and password, which are two of many components used in the calculation of the MD5 response. The username and password can be supplied with actual user intervention or by a device that has the credentials stored, such as an SBC.

4. To calculate the MD5 response, the following algorithm is used:

   - An MD5 hash of the combination of the username, password, and realm is calculated and stored as HA1.
   - An MD5 hash of the combination of the method and request URI is formed and stored as HA2; the method here refers to the actual SIP request (for example, a SIP **INVITE** or **REGISTER**).
   - An MD5 hash of the combination of HA1, nonce (sent by the server), nonce count, client nonce, quality of protection, and HA2 is calculated.
   - The result becomes the **response** attribute that is eventually sent to the server. Figure 9-9 depicts the input parameters and algorithm used in the calculation of the MD5 response.

5. When the MD5 response is successfully calculated, the UAC sends over the same request, but this time with an **Authorization** header and an increment in the CSEQ value. Example 9-3 shows a sample **Authorization** header.

Example 9-3 *Sample* Authorization *Header*

```
Authorization: Digest username="bob",
realm="biloxi.com",
nonce="dcd98b7102dd2f0e8b11d0f600bfb0c093",
uri="sip:bob@biloxi.com",
qop=auth,
nc=00000001,
cnonce="0a4f113b",
response="6629fae49393a05397450978507c4ef1",
opaque="5ccc069c403ebaf9f0171e9517f40e41"
```

6. On receiving the response, the UAS checks the value in the **response** attribute, and if it is what is expected, further processing of the SIP dialog continues, with allocation of the required resources.

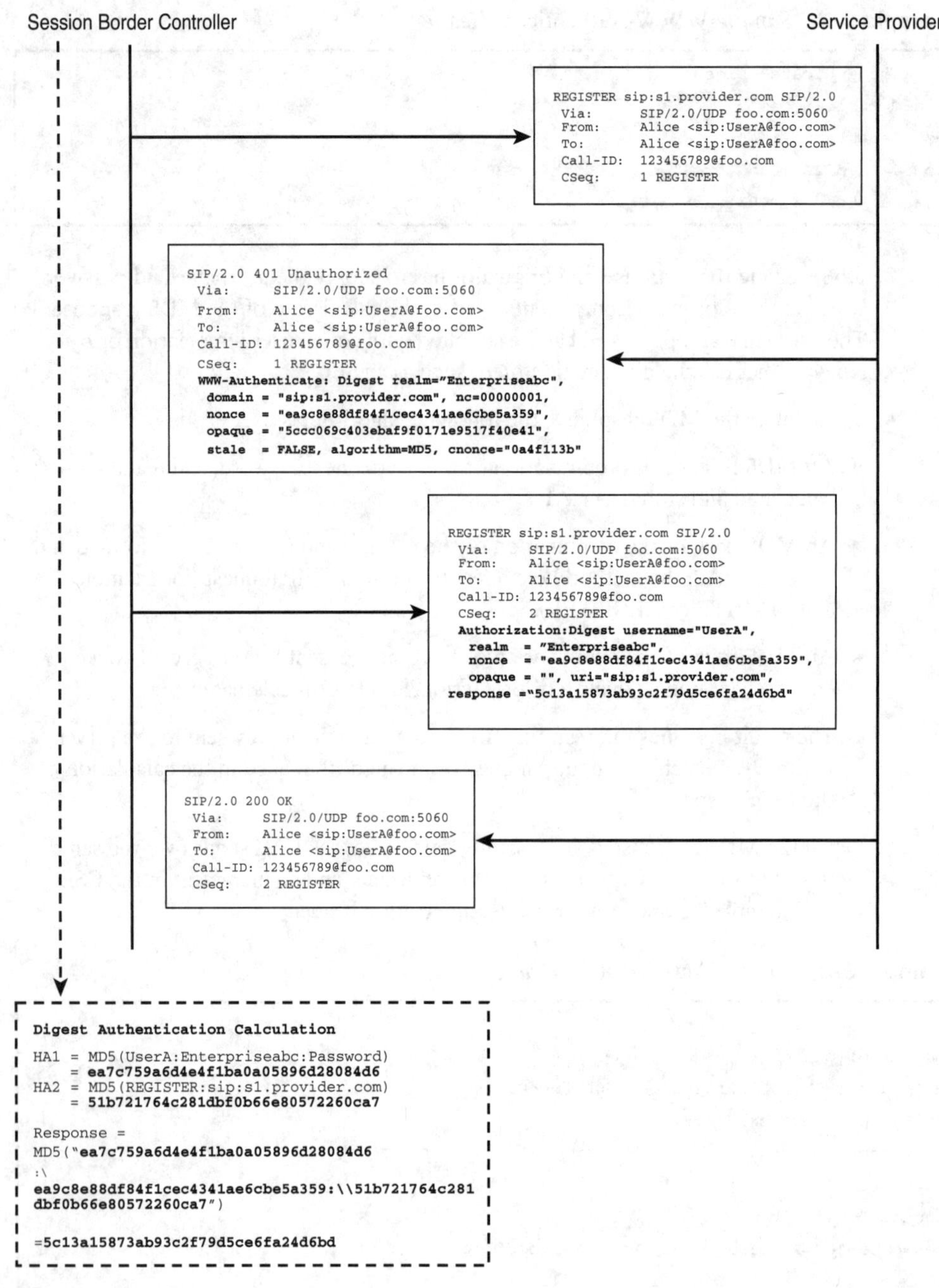
Session Border Controller
Service Provider
REGISTER sip:s1.provider.com SIP/2.0
Via: SIP/2.0/UDP foo.com:5060
From: Alice <sip:UserA@foo.com>
To: Alice <sip:UserA@foo.com>
Call-ID: 123456789@foo.com
CSeq: 1 REGISTER
SIP/2.0 401 Unauthorized
Via: SIP/2.0/UDP foo.com:5060
From: Alice <sip:UserA@foo.com>
To: Alice <sip:UserA@foo.com>
Call-ID: 123456789@foo.com
CSeq: 1 REGISTER
WWW-Authenticate: Digest realm="Enterpriseabc",
domain = "sip:s1.provider.com", nc=00000001,
nonce = "ea9c8e88df84f1cec4341ae6cbe5a359",
opaque = "5ccc069c403ebaf9f0171e9517f40e41",
stale = FALSE, algorithm=MD5, cnonce="0a4f113b"
REGISTER sip:s1.provider.com SIP/2.0
Via: SIP/2.0/UDP foo.com:5060
From: Alice <sip:UserA@foo.com>
To: Alice <sip:UserA@foo.com>
Call-ID: 123456789@foo.com
CSeq: 2 REGISTER
Authorization:Digest username="UserA",
realm = "Enterpriseabc",
nonce = "ea9c8e88df84f1cec4341ae6cbe5a359",
opaque = "", uri="sip:s1.provider.com",
response ="5c13a15873ab93c2f79d5ce6fa24d6bd"
SIP/2.0 200 OK
Via: SIP/2.0/UDP foo.com:5060
From: Alice <sip:UserA@foo.com>
To: Alice <sip:UserA@foo.com>
Call-ID: 123456789@foo.com
CSeq: 2 REGISTER
Digest Authentication Calculation
HA1 = MD5(UserA:Enterpriseabc:Password)
= ea7c759a6d4e4f1ba0a05896d28084d6
HA2 = MD5(REGISTER:sip:s1.provider.com)
= 51b721764c281dbf0b66e80572260ca7
Response =
MD5("ea7c759a6d4e4f1ba0a05896d28084d6
:\
ea9c8e88df84f1cec4341ae6cbe5a359:\\51b721764c281
dbf0b66e80572260ca7")
=5c13a15873ab93c2f79d5ce6fa24d6bd

Figure 9-9 *Calculation of the MD5 Response*

The sequence of events described here occurs when there is direct communication between a user agent client and server. However, it is often the case that requests are routed through a SIP proxy or a string of proxies. Among the different functions performed by a proxy such as targeted routing, syntax checking, load balancing and so on, one of them is message authentication. The following section details the operating principle of user-to-proxy authentication.

Proxy Authentication

Proxy authentication uses the same overarching framework described in the previous section:

1. The user agent sends a request.
2. The user agent server sends a challenge with a string of parameters.
3. The initiator uses a combination of locally stored credentials and relayed server-side parameters to calculate an MD5 hash value.
4. The MD5 hash result is sent to the server, which validates it to decide whether the request can be further processed.

Proxies do not use the 401 Unauthorized message while issuing a challenge to the user agent client and instead use a **407 Proxy Unauthorized** response with a **Proxy-Authenticate** header. The **Proxy-Authenticate** header contains the same information as the **WWW-Authenticate** header and aids in the calculation of the MD5 hash response. The MD5 response is sent to the proxy with a **Proxy-Authorization** header. (It serves the very same function as the **Authorization** header described in the previous section.)

In real-world deployments, there might be a string of proxies between the UAC and the UAS that ultimately services the request. As each proxy goes about its function of routing requests to the next hop, it may issue a challenge to the originator of the request. When the originator sends over a response (through the **Proxy-Authorization** header field), it must not be dropped or processed by any other proxy other than the one that issued the challenge.

It is also possible for a proxy to fork the request to multiple target destinations (which could be user agent servers or downstream proxy servers), such that some or all of the target destinations send either a 401/407 challenge (depending on whether the device issuing the challenge is a proxy or a user agent server). In such instances, the proxy that forked the request must aggregate all 401/407 challenges and send a single challenge to the user agent client. The resulting **407 Proxy Unauthorized** response to the client could carry a plurality of **Authenticate** or **Proxy Authenticate** headers. It is the responsibility of the user agent client to send a response for each **Authenticate/Proxy Authenticate** header. This scenario is depicted in Figure 9-10.

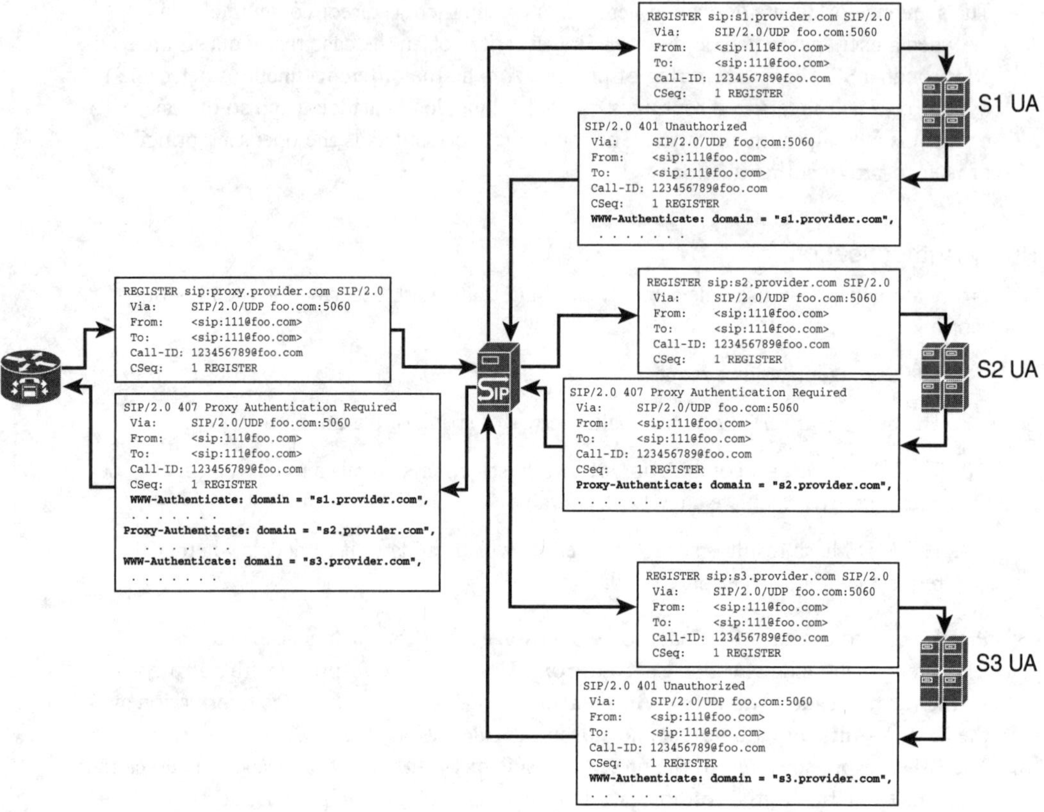

Figure 9-10 *Proxy Forking a Request to Multiple Registrars*

Digest Authentication Considerations

The previous section provides a fairly detailed overview of the digest authentication framework in SIP, which is responsible for ensuring message authentication, replay protection, and authorized access to telephony resources. However, there are sophisticated means by which the password can be obtained (by using dictionary attacks, rainbow tables, and so on). To ensure integrity and confidentiality of all signaling traffic as it transits between enterprise and service provider networks, it is recommended to use SIP over TLS.

Registration with SBCs

As discussed in the previous sections, registration of SIP trunks has a well-defined "under the hood" operation and requires a plurality of factors that need to come together to establish a relationship between service provider and enterprise networks. From the perspective of SBCs, there are broadly two registration paradigms:

- Trunk-side registration
- Line-side registration

The trunk-side registration provides call break-in and break-out services to an entire enterprise, while the line-side registration is used to provide call break-in and break-out services to a few phones; a detailed description and distinction between the two is provided in subsequent sections.

Trunk-Side Registration

Trunk-side registration involves the SBC setting in motion the registration framework with the service provider network on behalf of the enterprise. Figure 9-11 depicts a typical trunk-side registration scenario with SBCs.

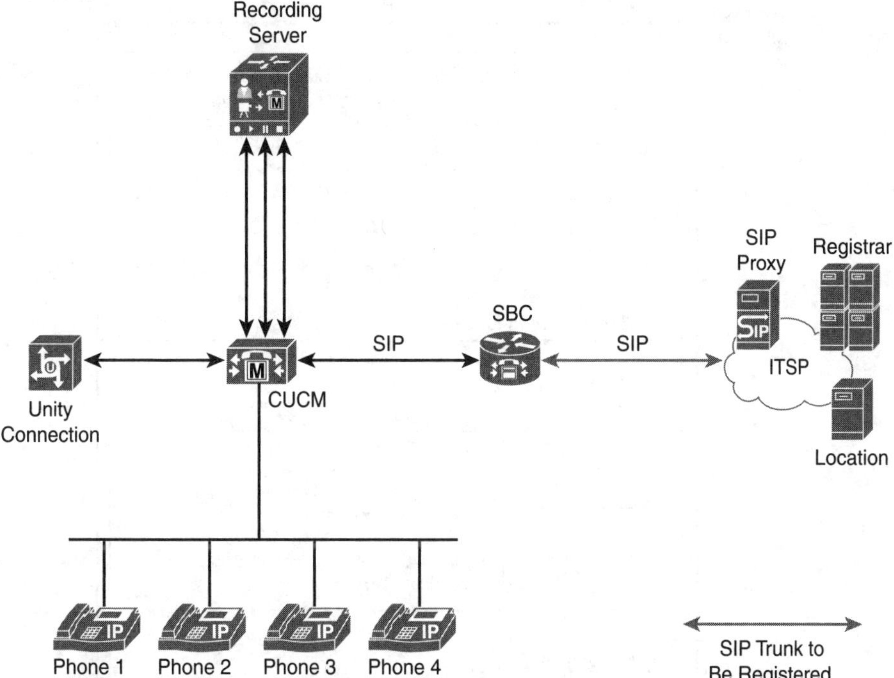

Figure 9-11 *Trunk-Side Registration with SBCs*

As mentioned earlier in this chapter, in the "Registration Mode" section, an enterprise may register a single main line number with the service provider registrar or the entire E.164 range under its administrative control. For bulk E.164 registration, the procedures of RFC 6140 may be used. However, at the time of writing this book, the adoption of RFC 6140 is not very widespread in enterprise and service provider networks and is likely not the best alternative available.

The norm is for an enterprise to register a single main line number that results in the implicit registration of the entire DID range. Though this in effect achieves the same results as RFC 6140, it lacks structure and a baseline operating framework. Figure 9-12 depicts this process.

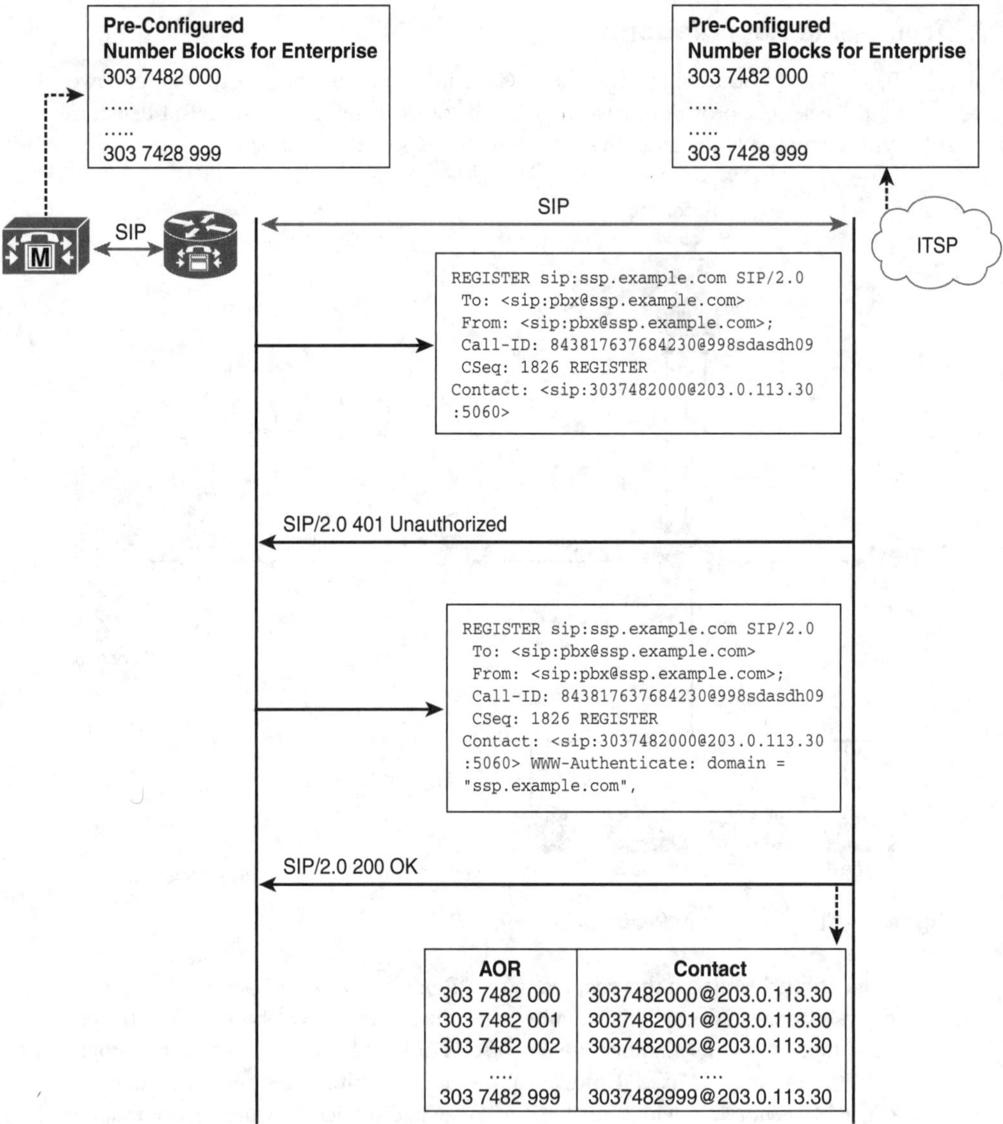

Figure 9-12 *Registration of a Single Main Line Number*

Just as with traditional digital and analog service providers, SIP service provider networks also have transient or major outages that hamper the ability of an enterprise to communicate with the outside world. Before services are restored, a significant amount of effort and time could be spent on isolating and fixing the problem, and this could translate into a loss of revenue for the enterprise. For this reason, an enterprise might provision redundancy in trunking to ensure continuity of communication services across failures. The next subsections talk about how an enterprise peers with either a single registrar or multiple registrars (for redundancy).

Single Registrar

In a single-registrar scenario, an SBC peers with a single registrar server over the service provider network. A SIP **REGISTER** message sourced from the SBC sets in motion the process of providing the AOR-to-contact binding for the enterprise. On receiving the SIP **REGISTER** message, the service provider registrar is very likely to issue an authentication challenge to validate the identity of the enterprise. On successful authentication, the registrar server places the AOR-to-contact binding for the enterprise in a location server. The location server entry is looked up whenever calls have to be sent over to the enterprise. Based on the negotiated expiration interval, the SBC is responsible for refreshing registrations to keep the binding alive.

Though peering with a single registrar simplifies the configuration significantly, this scenario lacks fallback options should there be failures on the service provider side. In most real-world scenarios, the registrar, location, and call processing services all reside on the same device. A failure on a single physical device on the service provider network can have serious repercussions for the enterprise.

The following paragraphs discuss details of configuring and peering with a single registrar from the perspective of the CUBE. The configuration, diagnostic commands, and debugging are IOS/IOS XE specific and would not be uniform across all vendors.

The following commands are required for the registration framework on the CUBE:

- **credentials**
- **registrar**
- **authentication**

The arguments to these commands are provided in Table 9-2 through 9-4.

Table 9-2 *Arguments to the* **credentials** *Command*

Command	Argument	Function
credentials {**dhcp** | **number** *number* **username** *username*} **password** [**0** | **7**] *password* **realm** *realm*	**dhcp**	(Optional) Specifies that Dynamic Host Configuration Protocol (DHCP) is to be used to send the SIP message.
	number *number*	(Optional) A string representing the DID number with which the SIP trunk will register (must be at least four characters).
	username *username*	A string representing the username for the user who is providing authentication (must be at least four characters).
	password	Specifies password settings for authentication.
	0	(Optional) Specifies the encryption type as cleartext (no encryption). This is the default.
	7	(Optional) Specifies the encryption type as encrypted.
	password	A string representing the password for authentication. If no encryption type is specified, the password will be plaintext format. The string must be between 4 and 128 characters.
	realm *realm*	(Optional) A string representing the domain where the credentials are applicable.

On configuring the **credentials** command, a SIP **REGISTER** message is sourced from the CUBE (assuming that the IP address/hostname of the registrar is already in place). The utility of the **username** and **password** arguments and how they fit into the SIP digest authentication framework will be explained shortly.

Note It is highly advisable to choose a password that cannot be obtained by using dictionary attacks.

The arguments to the **registrar** command are provided in Table 9-3.

Table 9-3 *Arguments to the* **registrar** *Command*

Command	Argument	Function
registrar {**dhcp** | [*registrar-index*] *registrar-server-address* [:*port*]} [**auth-realm** *realm*] [**expires** *seconds*] [**random-contact**] [**refresh-ratio** *ratio-percentage*] [**scheme** {**sip** | **sips**}] [**tcp**] [type] [**secondary**]	**dhcp**	(Optional) Specifies that the domain name of the primary registrar server is retrieved from a DHCP server (cannot be used to configure secondary or multiple registrars). The SIP server information is retrieved with DHCP option 120.
	registrar-index	(Optional) Allows configuration of up to six registrars. (*Note:* For configuring a single registrar, this command argument should be ignored.)
	registrar-server-address	The registrar server address, which can be specified in one of three ways. ■ **dns:***address*—The DNS address of the primary SIP registrar server. (The **dns:** delimiter must be included as the first four characters.) ■ **ipv4:***address*—The IP address of the SIP registrar server. (The **ipv4:** delimiter must be included as the first five characters.) ■ **ipv6:**[*address*]—The IPv6 address of the SIP registrar server. (The **ipv6:** delimiter must be included as the first five characters and the address itself must include opening and closing square brackets.)
	[:port]	(Optional) The SIP port number. (The colon delimiter is required.) If unspecified, it defaults to 5060.
	auth-realm	(Optional) Specifies the realm for preloaded authorization.
	realm	The realm name.
	expires *seconds*	(Optional) Specifies the expires time that is advertised in the outgoing SIP REGISTER message. The expires timer, however, is ultimately decided by the registrar.

Command	Argument	Function
	random-contact	(Optional) Specifies the random string contact header used to identify the registration session.
	refresh-ratio *ratio-percentage*	(Optional) Specifies the registration refresh ratio, in percentage. The range is 1 to 100, and the default is 80.
	scheme {**sip** |**sips**}	(Optional) Specifies the URL scheme. The options are SIP (**sip**) or secure SIP (**sips**), depending on your software installation. The default is **sip**.
	tcp	(Optional) Specifies TCP. If not specified, the default is User Datagram Protocol (UDP).
	type	(Optional) The registration type. *Note:* The **type** argument cannot be used with the **dhcp** option.
	secondary	(Optional) Specifies a secondary SIP registrar for redundancy if the primary registrar fails.

The arguments to the **registrar** command provide an administrator immense flexibility in terms of constructing the **REGISTER** message and influencing the outcome of the **REGISTER** transaction. For example, the **registrar** command can influence the transport protocol, URI scheme, **Contact** header formatting, expiration interval, and destination port number of the **REGISTER** message. As will be seen in subsequent sections, registrar server redundancy can also be specified with this command.

The arguments to the **authentication** command are provided in Table 9-4.

Table 9-4 *Arguments to the* **authentication** *Command*

Command	Argument	Function
authentication username *username* **password** [**0** | **7**] password [**realm** *realm*]	**username** *username*	A string representing the username for the user who is providing authentication (must be at least four characters).
	password	Specifies password settings for authentication.
	0	(Optional) Specifies encryption type as cleartext (no encryption). This is the default.
	7	(Optional) Specifies encryption type as encrypted.

Command	Argument	Function
	password	A string representing the password for authentication. If no encryption type is specified, the password will be cleartext format. The string must be between 4 and 128 characters.
	realm *realm*	(Optional) A string representing the domain where the credentials are applicable.

The primary purpose of the **authentication** command is to respond to authentication challenges for SIP **INVITE** or **REGISTER** messages. However, as will be explained shortly, the username/password combination in the **credentials** command may also be used. Which username/password combination is used (the authentication or credentials) depends on the **realm** of the received challenge.

The **authentication** command cannot be used to send a **REGISTER** message. The **REGISTER** message is sent only after the **credentials** command is configured, along with the appropriate registrar IP/hostname/DHCP 120 options.

Example 9-4 provides a basic configuration snippet on the CUBE for SIP trunk registration to a single registrar.

Example 9-4 *Sample Configuration Snippet for Trunk Registration*

```
sip-ua
credentials username 111111 password 7 03165A0502002C5F5A1B100B1043595F realm
  cisco.com
authentication username 111111 password 7 051907012543431A0D171E1C0C59527D realm
  cisco.com
registrar ipv4: 203.0.113.10 expires 3600
```

The configuration in Example 9-4 results in the following sequence of events:

1. The CUBE sends a SIP **REGISTER** message to the registrar IP address specified in the configuration, such that the user portions of the **From**, **To**, and **Contact** headers carry the value of the username argument specified in the **credentials** command. In this case, it is **111111**.

2. The host portions of the **From** and **To** headers carry the IP address of the registrar server. The value in the **To** header field specifies the AOR.

3. The host portion of the **Contact** header specifies an IP address configured on the CUBE. There could be several IP addresses configured on the CUBE simultaneously—some for sourcing media/signaling and some for management of the device. Which interface is ultimately used is determined by the configuration. For SIP **REGISTER** messages sent to the service provider, the **bind control source-interface** *Interface-Id* command influences the IP address populated in the **Contact** header field.

Alternatively, if SIP is not bound to a specific interface(s) (a practice that is strongly discouraged), the routing table on the CUBE decides the best available interface to source the **REGISTER** message.

4. On receiving the SIP **REGISTER** message, the service provider registrar needs to authenticate the sender of the message and issues a challenge with a "401 Unauthorized" message.

5. On receiving the challenge, the following criteria are used to determine if the username/password combination in the **authentication** or **credentials** command is picked up:

   - If the **realm** in the challenge matches the **realm** configured in the **credentials** command, then the username/password combination specified in the **credentials** command is used as two of many inputs to calculate the digest response.
   - If the **realm** in the challenge does not match the one specified in the **credentials** command, then the **realm** specified in the **authentication** command is checked to determine whether it is the same as the one specified in the challenge. If so, the username/password combination specified in the **authentication** command is used as two of many inputs to calculate the digest response.
   - If there is no match for either scenario described above, the request is terminated.

6. Once the required username/password combination is obtained, the digest response is calculated, and the **REGISTER** message is sent again with the **Authorization** header.

7. If the response is what the registrar expects, it sends over a **SIP 200 OK** that completes the registration process. Based on the value of the **Expires** header field in the **200 OK** response, the CUBE refreshes the registration by sending periodic **REGISTER** messages.

8. To verify trunk registration, the **show sip-ua register status** command is used.

Example 9-5 provides sample output of the **show sip-ua register status** command.

Example 9-5 *Sample Output of the* **show sip-ua register status** *Command*

```
CUBE# show sip-ua register status

 Line           peer    expires(sec) registered    P-Associated-URI

 ==========     =====   =========== ==========     ================

 4085551111     -1      12           yes           4085551111

                                                   4085551112

                                                   4085551113

                                                   4085551114
```

Table 9-5 describes the various fields in the **show sip-ua register status** command.

Table 9-5 *Field Descriptions for the* **show sip-ua register status** *Command*

Field	Description
Line	Indicates the user portion of the **To** header; this can either be the username or the number argument of the **credentials** command.
peer	For SIP trunk registration with the CUBE, this field is always **-1**.
expires	Specifies the duration of time after which the CUBE will refresh registration by sending a new **REGISTER** message for the same dialog. This field is dynamic, and its value changes across iterations of the command.
registered	Specifies if the SIP trunk has successfully peered/registered with the registrar; the value of this field is populated based on the SIP status code response obtained as a result of the **REGISTER** message (**yes** for **200 OK** and **no** for any other status code).
P-Associated-URI	Specifies the different numbers associated with the same AOR.

The **200 OK** responses by the service provider registrar might contain the **P-Associated-URI** header field. This header field is used to indicate all the other URIs that are associated with the AOR contained in the SIP **REGISTER** message. The UAC can use any of these URIs to populate the **From** header fields of outgoing requests.

Redundancy

To protect against outages in the service provider network and ensure continuity of call services to the outside world, SBCs can be configured to peer with a plurality of SIP registrars. In one deployment scenario, the SBC can be configured to peer with multiple registrars scoped to the same domain or service provider network simultaneously. With such a setup, if the primary registrar experiences software, hardware, or registration database access issues, the remaining registrar servers can ensure that the AOR-to-contact bindings are kept alive and provide registrar database lookup services. This particular scenario is useful only in cases where the scope of failure in the service provider network is not global and affects only a single or a few registrar servers. If there is global failure, service provider redundancy is required to ensure continued multimedia services.

Note An enterprise would expose a different DID range to registrars in different service provider networks. This is the only way call services are preserved across service provider outages.

In another deployment scenario, an SBC peers with two or more registrars such that each registrar is scoped to a different realm or service provider. This scenario provides true redundancy and protects against global failure in a given service provider network.

The CUBE can be configured to provide redundancy in one of two modes:

- Peering with a primary/secondary registrar scoped to the same domain/service provider
- Peering with multiple registrars each scoped to a different domain/service provider

Example 9-6 provides a configuration snippet on the CUBE for a primary/secondary registrar scenario.

Example 9-6 *Sample Configuration for Primary/Secondary Registrar*

```
sip-ua
credentials username 111111 password 7 03165A0502002C5F5A1B100B1043595F
realm cisco.com
authentication username 111111 password 7 051907012543431A0D171E1C0C59527D
realm sbc.cisco.com
registrar ipv4:203.0.113.10 expires 3600
registrar ipv4:203.0.113.25 expires 3600 secondary
```

A detailed explanation of all the commands seen in Example 9-7 and their respective arguments has been provided in Table 9-2 through 9-4. With the previous configuration, independent **REGISTER** transactions are initiated to the two registrars simultaneously. However, both the transactions are scoped to two different registrars within the same realm or domain (that is, the same service provider). One of the scenarios in which this design finds use is as follows:

- A **REGISTER** transaction is initiated with the service provider registrar. On successful authentication, the service provider responds with a **200 OK** (indicating a successful **REGISTER** transaction) such that the expiration interval is set to a fairly large value of **3600** seconds (1 hour).
- If during that time there were an outage on the service provider registrar, all incoming calls would likely fail until the CUBE could discover the outage with a refresh registration (which would be sent close to the 1-hour mark) and take mitigation action by peering with a backup registrar.
- When peering simultaneously with two service provider registrars, if there is a failure on the primary, the AOR-to-contact bindings for an enterprise are kept alive in the location services of the secondary.

This scenario is depicted in Figure 9-13.

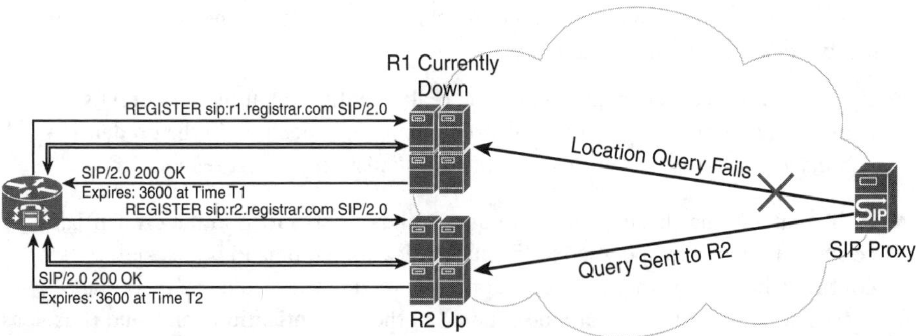

Figure 9-13 *The CUBE Registering with a Primary/Secondary Registrar*

Example 9-7 provides a configuration snippet on the CUBE for a multiple-registrar scenario such that each registrar server is scoped to a different service provider.

Example 9-7 *Sample Configuration for Multiple-Registrar Peering*

```
credentials username 1111 password 7 08701E1D5D realm services.enterpriseabc.com
credentials username 2222 password 7 0355095852 realm engineering. enterpriseabc.com
credentials username 3333 password 7 091D1C5A4D realm sales.enterpriseabc.com
credentials username 4444 password 7 040A59555B realm it. enterpriseabc.com
credentials username 5555 password 7 040A59555B realm patents. enterpriseabc.com
credentials username 6666 password 7 08701E1D5D realm standards. enterpriseabc.com
authentication username 1111 password 7 08701E1D5D realm services. enterpriseabc.com
authentication username 2222 password 7 0355095852 realm engineering.
  enterpriseabc.com
authentication username 3333 password 7 091D1C5A4D realm sales. enterpriseabc.com
authentication username 4444 password 7 040A59555B realm it. enterpriseabc.com
authentication username 5555 password 7 040A59555B realm patents. enterpriseabc.com
authentication username 6666 password 7 08701E1D5D realm standards.
  enterpriseabc.com
registrar 1 ipv4:203.0.113.10 expires 3600
registrar 2 ipv4:203.0.113.15 expires 3600
registrar 3 ipv4:203.0.113.20 expires 3600
registrar 4 ipv4:203.0.113.24 expires 3600
registrar 5 ipv4:203.0.113.28 expires 3600
registrar 6 ipv4:203.0.113.32 expires 3600
```

Example 9-7 demonstrates a configuration example of the multiple-registrar feature on the CUBE. In this example, there are six registrar servers configured. Whenever there is a challenge for an outgoing request (**INVITE** or **REGISTER**), based on the realm received in the challenge, the appropriate username and password combination is picked up from one of the **authentication** or **credentials** commands to compute the digest response.

As mentioned in the previous section, the following criteria determine which username and password combination is picked up:

- If the **realm** in the challenge matches the **realm** configured in the **credentials** command, then the username/password combination specified in the **credentials** command is used as two of many inputs to calculate the digest response.
- If the **realm** in the challenge does not match the one specified in the **credentials** command, the **realm** specified in the **authentication** command is checked to confirm whether it is the same as the one specified in the challenge. If so, the username/password combination specified in the **authentication** command is used as two of many inputs to calculate the digest response.
- If there is no match for either scenario described above, the request is terminated.

Figure 9-14 demonstrates the multiple-registrar scenario and demonstrates how the username/password combination is selected based on the response received from the registrar.

As with the primary/secondary registrar setup, the number of configured registrar servers would dictate the number of simultaneous **REGISTER** transactions sourced. With the multiple-registrar feature, it is possible to achieve true service provider redundancy as multiple **credentials** and **authentication** commands can be configured (up to 12) with different realms. However, to properly leverage this feature, the dial plan on the CUBE must implement redundancy for incoming and outgoing calls.

Note The primary/secondary registrar and multiple-registrar feature on the CUBE are mutually exclusive. That is, the administrator cannot configure these features simultaneously; only one feature can be configured at any given time.

Multitenancy

While it is extremely useful to implement service provider redundancy for continued call delivery, successfully peering SBCs with different service providers is a task in itself. This is largely because of standards being open to interpretation and having one too many loose ends. The result is the lack of a universal configuration that just "works" with different service providers. It is often necessary to attribute different feature sets to different service providers to ensure smooth interoperability.

To be able to attribute different feature sets to different service providers, there has to a clear separation of concerns wherein each service provider is treated as a completely independent entity by the SBC. In the discussion of service provider redundancy in the previous section, perhaps one limitation that was immediately apparent was the inability to attribute different session characteristics to different registrars (and, by extension, to different service provider networks).

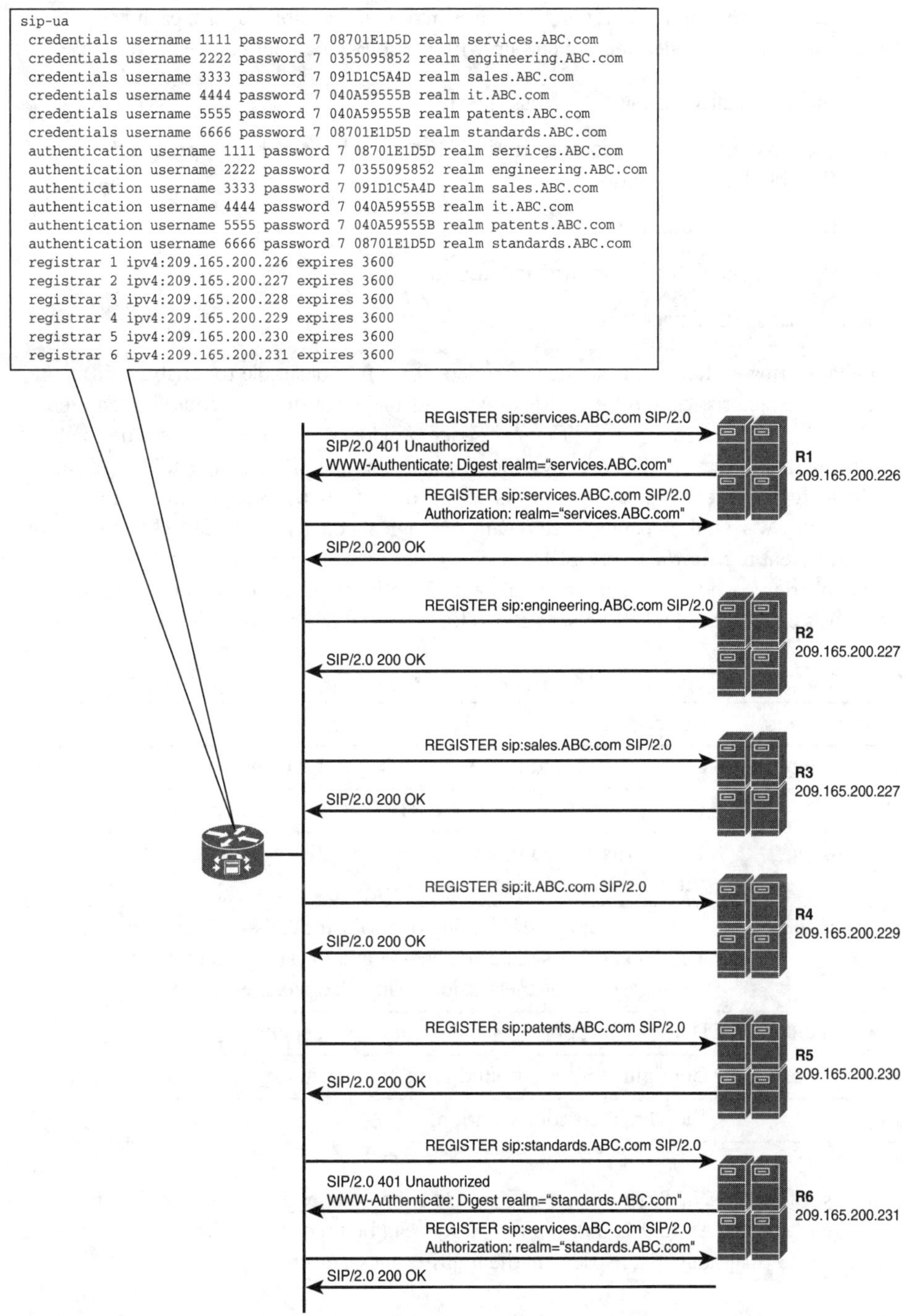
sip-ua
credentials username 1111 password 7 08701E1D5D realm services.ABC.com
credentials username 2222 password 7 0355095852 realm engineering.ABC.com
credentials username 3333 password 7 091D1C5A4D realm sales.ABC.com
credentials username 4444 password 7 040A59555B realm it.ABC.com
credentials username 5555 password 7 040A59555B realm patents.ABC.com
credentials username 6666 password 7 08701E1D5D realm standards.ABC.com
authentication username 1111 password 7 08701E1D5D realm services.ABC.com
authentication username 2222 password 7 0355095852 realm engineering.ABC.com
authentication username 3333 password 7 091D1C5A4D realm sales.ABC.com
authentication username 4444 password 7 040A59555B realm it.ABC.com
authentication username 5555 password 7 040A59555B realm patents.ABC.com
authentication username 6666 password 7 08701E1D5D realm standards.ABC.com
registrar 1 ipv4:209.165.200.226 expires 3600
registrar 2 ipv4:209.165.200.227 expires 3600
registrar 3 ipv4:209.165.200.228 expires 3600
registrar 4 ipv4:209.165.200.229 expires 3600
registrar 5 ipv4:209.165.200.230 expires 3600
registrar 6 ipv4:209.165.200.231 expires 3600
REGISTER sip:services.ABC.com SIP/2.0
SIP/2.0 401 Unauthorized
WWW-Authenticate: Digest realm="services.ABC.com"
REGISTER sip:services.ABC.com SIP/2.0
Authorization: realm="services.ABC.com"
SIP/2.0 200 OK
R1
209.165.200.226
REGISTER sip:engineering.ABC.com SIP/2.0
SIP/2.0 200 OK
R2
209.165.200.227
REGISTER sip:sales.ABC.com SIP/2.0
SIP/2.0 200 OK
R3
209.165.200.227
REGISTER sip:it.ABC.com SIP/2.0
SIP/2.0 200 OK
R4
209.165.200.229
REGISTER sip:patents.ABC.com SIP/2.0
SIP/2.0 200 OK
R5
209.165.200.230
REGISTER sip:standards.ABC.com SIP/2.0
SIP/2.0 401 Unauthorized
WWW-Authenticate: Digest realm="standards.ABC.com"
REGISTER sip:services.ABC.com SIP/2.0
Authorization: realm="standards.ABC.com"
SIP/2.0 200 OK
R6
209.165.200.231

Figure 9-14 *The CUBE Registering with Multiple Registrars*

While configuring redundancy on SBCs, it is highly undesirable to have each registrar/service provider peering end up with the following common characteristics:

- The same call signaling IP address space
- The same refresh ratios for registration (discussed later in this chapter, in the "Troubleshooting" section)
- The same SIP outbound proxy
- The same number of retry attempts for SIP messages
- The same SIP timers

When peering with multiple service providers, it is often desirable to attribute different session characteristics to different service providers. For example, it could be required to handle video differently for different service providers or exhibit different mid-call signaling behavior with different providers or use a unique SIP message normalization scheme for each service provider. This is achieved by using the *multitenancy* feature of the CUBE. With multitenancy, each tenant is a logical construct on the CUBE that maps to a different registrar/network/SIP service provider, such that unique characteristics can be applied to each tenant. The list of all characteristics that can be uniquely assigned per tenant is exhaustive; Table 9-6 lists a few selected examples.

Table 9-6 *Selected Features of Multitenancy on the CUBE*

Characteristics	Description
Authentication	The username and password for a specific realm.
Bind	The interface used to source RTP and SIP signaling.
Credentials	The username and password for a specific realm to use when authentication challenges are received.
Midcall signaling	Th specific midcall signaling behavior for calls—whether messages are blocked, passed across end-to-end or passed only when the media characteristics of the session change (codec, media type).
Options ping	Defines SIP options configuration for keepalives.
Outbound proxy	Configures SIP outbound-proxy configuration.
Video	Video-related configuration.

The list of features in Table 9-6 is by no means exhaustive and represents only a few selected features. Around 150 different features can be uniquely applied to each tenant. Figure 9-15 diagrammatically depicts the multitenancy feature.

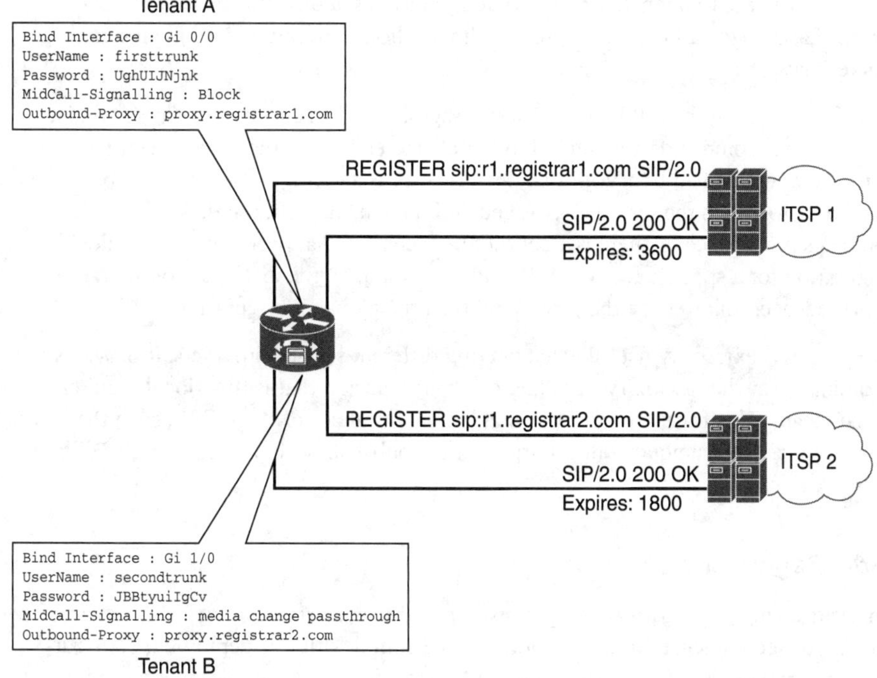

Figure 9-15 *Multitenancy on SBCs*

Configuring multitenancy on the CUBE is achieved with the **voice class tenant** command in global configuration mode. Example 9-8 provides a sample configuration for multitenancy on the CUBE.

Example 9-8 *Sample Configuration for Multitenancy*

```
voice class tenant 1
 registrar ipv4:203.0.113.10 expires 3600
 credentials username 45678 password 7 104D000A0618 realm cisco
 authentication username 45678 password 7 00071A150754 realm cisco
 bind control source-interface GigabitEthernet0/1
 bind media source-interface GigabitEthernet0/1
 outbound-proxy dns:sbc.cisco.com


voice class tenant 2
 registrar ipv4:203.0.113.30 expires 3600
 credentials username 5903 password 7 01455156085F5F realm proxy.cisco.com
authentication username 5903 password 7 014751500C5D realm
  proxy.cisco.com
 bind control source-interface GigabitEthernet0/0
 bind media source-interface GigabitEthernet0/0
 outbound-proxy dns:proxy.cisco.com
```

In Example 9-8, the two tenants have different registrars, a different IP address to source SIP and RTP traffic, and different realm, outbound proxy, and mid-call signaling characteristics.

Except for triggering the SIP **REGISTER** messages, which occurs as soon as the **registrar** and **credentials** commands are entered, other characteristics of the voice tenant take effect only when applied to a VoIP dial peer. If there is a configuration conflict between the dial peer to which the tenant is assigned and the tenant itself, the dial peer configuration takes precedence. If there is a conflict between the dial peer, tenant, and global configuration for a specific feature (SIP bind, for example), the dial peer configuration take precedence, followed by the tenant and then the global configuration.

Multitenancy is extremely useful when peering different service providers. It provides the administrator the flexibility in rolling out configuration that is functionally unique for each tenant. This feature enables several logical instances of the CUBE, such that each logical instance has a unique configuration set to enable smooth interoperability with service providers.

Line-Side Registration

With the growing popularity of off-premises, cloud-based services, organizations are beginning to see immense value in offloading the complexities of deploying, configuring, and maintaining an IP PBX to a third-party provider. In such deployments, audio and video endpoints register with call control agents hosted in the cloud. With connectivity between the endpoints and the call agents being provided over the Internet, an SBC is the perfect candidate for providing services like NAT traversal, topology abstraction, registration proxying, local authentication, and SIP message normalization. A typical line-side deployment scenario is depicted in Figure 9-16.

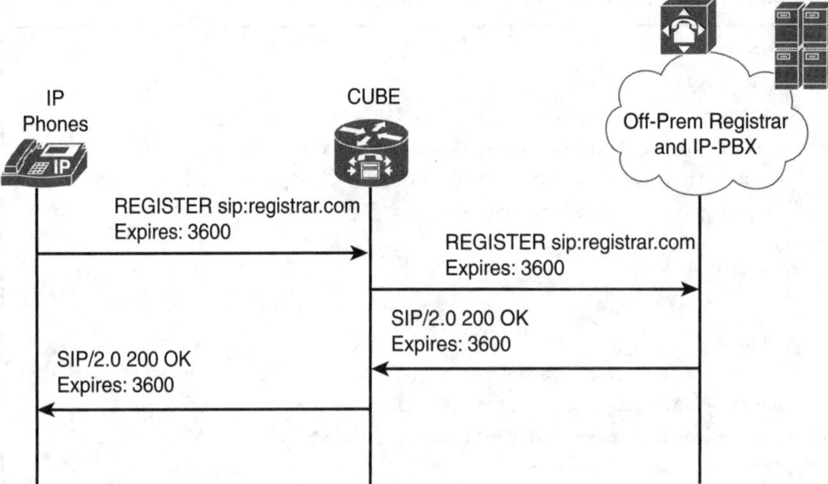

Figure 9-16 *Line-Side Deployment*

With line-side registrations, the SBC advocates registration on behalf of the endpoints. Support for line-side registration (also known as SIP Registration Proxy) is provided with the registration passthrough feature on the CUBE. Some of the benefits provided by the CUBE in registration passthrough mode include the following:

- Address hiding
- Rate limiting of traffic sent to the service provider network
- Overload protection
- Multiple-registrar support
- Authentication/authorization proxying

The registration passthrough feature in the CUBE can function in one of two modes:

- End-to-end mode
- Peer-to-peer mode

The mode of operation is chosen based on the request URI of the incoming **REGISTER** request; if it contains the IP address or hostname of the CUBE, peer-to-peer mode is activated; if the request URI of the incoming **REGISTER** request contains the IP address or hostname of the registrar in the service provider network, then end-to-end mode is activated.

Peer-to-Peer (P2P) Mode

In P2P mode, the CUBE is responsible for modifying the outgoing **REGISTER** message as per local configuration before sending it out to the service provider network; the operational aspects are as follows:

- The CUBE receives an incoming **REGISTER** request, such that the request URI contains the CUBE's IP address or domain name.
- Based on the locally configured registrar (either single or many), the CUBE sends a **REGISTER** transaction such that the IP addresses of the initiating endpoints are overwritten with the CUBE's IP address (to ensure address hiding).
- If the CUBE receives an authentication challenge from the registrar, it forms an MD5 response, using parameters that are locally configured, before sending out the challenge response.
- On successful authentication and registration with the service provider registrar, the CUBE sends a **200 OK** to the phone, indicating a successful registration.
- It is possible for CUBE to authenticate (via challenge authentication) the endpoints before processing the incoming **REGISTER** request and is activated via configuration. Though this is not the default behavior on the CUBE, endpoint authentication can be enabled with configuration.

Figure 9-17 depicts the CUBE peer-to-peer registration process.

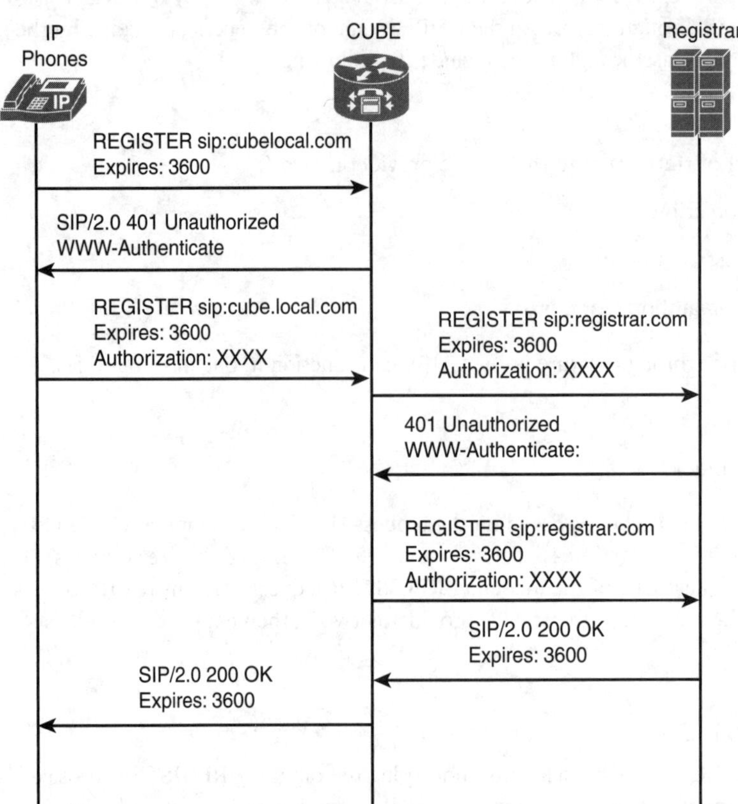

Figure 9-17 *CUBE Peer-to-Peer Registration*

End-to-End (E2E) Mode

In E2E mode, the CUBE transparently passes across the received **REGISTER** message to the registrar server specified in the request URI. All responses from the registrar (final/authentication challenges/failures) are passed back to the phone without modification. The only thing that changes is the IP address information of the phone to facilitate address hiding; the phone IP address is overwritten with the CUBE's.

Figure 9-18 depicts the CUBE end-to-end registration process.

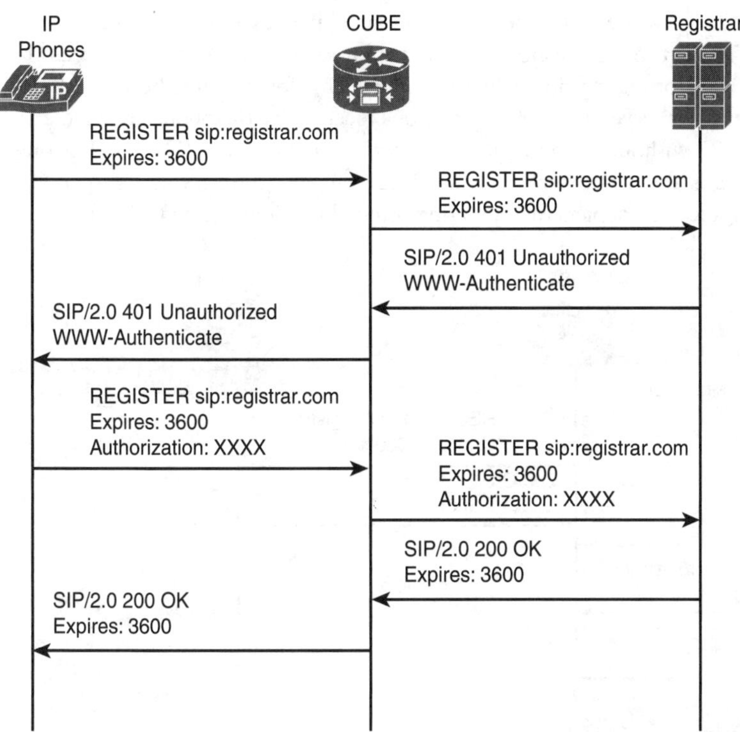

Figure 9-18 *CUBE End-to-End Registration*

Overload Protection and Registration Rate Limiting

The overload protection and registration rate limiting features are designed to decrease traffic loads traversing WAN links for registration passthrough. A sudden surge of traffic over WAN links is possible if multiple endpoints send **REGISTER** requests or try to refresh their registration bindings simultaneously; this could be really undesirable for low-capacity links and unreliable transport protocols such as UDP.

It is often desirable to configure the expiration interval between the CUBE and the phone to be of a very short duration (usually about 60 seconds). This is primarily done to keep pin holes or NAT bindings alive (as the phones might be behind a firewall or NAT device) and to ensure that the latest AOR-to-contact binding is known to the CUBE (as the phones might move from one location to another). In contrast, the expiration interval between the CUBE and the service provider registrar is usually negotiated to be of a significantly longer duration (about 600 seconds) to allow for less frequent refresh registrations and conserve WAN bandwidth. With this setup, however, the frequent refresh registrations received from the phones would have to be passed to the service provider network (either in P2P or E2E mode), leading to bandwidth chocking. To get around this, the registration rate-limiting feature can be configured on the CUBE.

With the rate-limiting feature, two timers are maintained in the CUBE: the "in-timer" and "out-timer." The in-timer corresponds to the expiration time negotiated between the phone and the CUBE for registration, while the out-timer is for the same between the CUBE and the registrar server. Refresh registrations received by the phone are handled locally by the CUBE without triggering a refresh registration on the WAN link. It is only when the out-timer is about to expire that the CUBE triggers a refresh transaction over the WAN link. Figure 9-19 depicts the operating principles of registration rate limiting.

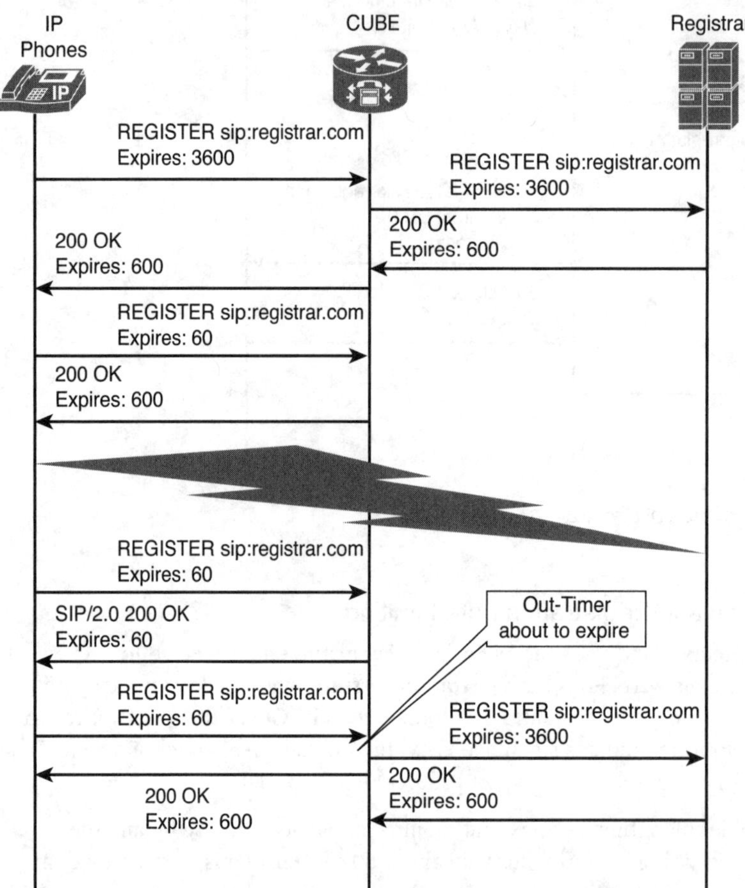

Figure 9-19 *Registration Rate Limiting*

Overload protection is a construct wherein the rate of requests is throttled down to a configured threshold. This is useful in a scenario where there is a surge of incoming requests; for example, during an avalanche restart, the CUBE receives a large number of **REGISTER** transactions simultaneously, and they have to be forwarded to the service provider registrar. This can lead to the issues highlighted in the opening paragraph of this section. To limit the number of such registrations, a threshold value can be configured on the CUBE, and if that threshold is exceeded, the CUBE sends a **503 Service Unavailable** error. Figure 9-20 depicts this scenario.

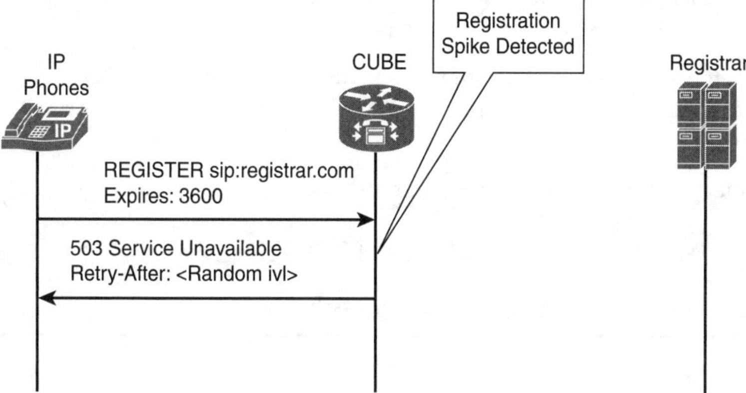

Figure 9-20 *Overload Protection for Registration*

Configuring Line-Side Registration

The line-side registration feature on the CUBE is activated using the **registration passthrough** command, which has to be applied in global configuration mode and under a dial peer. Table 9-7 describes the arguments to the **registration passthrough** command.

Table 9-7 *Arguments to the* **registration passthrough** *Command*

Command	Arguments	Description
registration passthrough [**static**] [**rate-limit** [**expires** *value*] [**fail-count** *value*]] [**registrar-index** [*index*]]	**static**	(Optional) Instructs the CUBE to look into the static registrar configuration; this command is used to override E2E mode and force it to function in P2P mode (even if the request-URI of the **REGISTER** message contains the service provider registrar's IP address or domain name).
	rate-limit	(Optional) Enables the rate-limiting feature.
	expires *value*	(Optional) Sets the expiration interval for rate limiting.
	fail-count *value*	(Optional) Sets the fail count value for rate limiting. The range is from 2 to 20. The default value is 0.
	registrar-index *index*	(Optional) Configures the registrar index that is to be used for registration pass-through.
	index	(Optional) Registration index value. The range is from 1 to 6.

The following considerations have to be taken into account while configuring this feature:

- The CUBE has to be configured as a registrar server under Voice Service VoIP and SIP. If it is not configured this way, the CUBE will fail all incoming **REGISTER** request with a **503 Service Unavailable** message.
- In P2P mode, the registrar configuration needs to be present under **sip-ua** so that the CUBE can send a **REGISTER** transaction to the registrar server(s) in the service provider network.
- A dial peer must be configured with the registration passthrough feature.

Example 9-9 provides a configuration snippet of registration passthrough on the CUBE.

Example 9-9 *Sample Configuration for Registration Passthrough*

```
!
voice service voip
sip
registrar server expires max 121 min 61

! the Expires header in all outgoing 200 OK messages from the CUBE to phone !will
  set the expiration interval to no more than 121 seconds. This range !represents in
  "in-timer" in the context of registration rate-limiting.

registration passthrough static rate-limit expires 9000 fail-count 5 registrar-index
  1 3


!The above command enforces P2P registration passthrough mode even if the !received
  REGISTER request-!URI has the registrar IP address or host name. !The expiration
  interval for the outgoing REGISTER message to the service !provider registrar is
  set to 9000 seconds. However, the expiration !interval of the REGISTER transaction
  between the CUBE and the service !provider registrar is dictated by the Expires
  header field value in the !200 OK message. This value effectively represents the
  "out-timer"


!
!
!
dial-peer voice 1111 voip
incoming called-number 1234
destination-pattern 1234
voice-class sip pass-thru content unsupp
voice-class sip registration passthrough static rate-limit expires 9000 fail-count 5
registrar-index 1 3
authentication username 1234 password 7 075E731F1A realm cisco.com
session protocol sipv2
session target registrar
```

```
!
!
sip-ua
registration spike 1000
registrar 1 ipv4:203.0.113.30 expires 3600
registrar 2 ipv4:203.0.113.20 expires 3600
registrar 3 ipv4:203.0.113.25 expires 3600
credentials username 1111 password 7 08701E1D5D realm services.enterpriseabc.com
credentials username 2222 password 7 0355095852 realm engineering.enterpriseabc.com
credentials username 3333 password 7 091D1C5A4D realm sales.enterpriseabc.com
```

Example 9-9 highlights the configuration required to enable P2P registration passthrough. The placement of the dial peer in the configuration might seem a little peculiar, but it is needed to serve as a trigger for registration passthrough on incoming **REGISTER** requests. The value in the **To** header field is matched against the incoming called-number pattern configured in the dial peer.

On successful registration, the destination pattern serves to match the calling number for calls coming in from the phone, and it matches the called number for calls going out to the phone. As the IP address of the phone can change frequently (due to endpoint mobility), it is not possible to configure the phone's IP address as the session target destination. To account for endpoint mobility, the **session target** command has been enhanced to include the **registrar** argument. With this configuration in place, the CUBE will always send calls to the latest AOR-to-contact record it has learned through a successful **REGISTER** transaction with the phone.

Troubleshooting

A three-step approach can be used to troubleshoot registration issues on the CUBE:

1. Assimilate the facts and gather information.
2. Verify the configuration and confirm whether it is in line with the functionality expected.
3. Run diagnostics.

Although the number of issues that might potentially arise is realistically innumerable, this section presents a general framework for troubleshooting SIP trunk registration issues.

SIP Trunk Not Registering with Service Provider

It is important to gather details around the problem and obtain details about the frequency of the issue and triggers that lead to the trunk deregistering (for example, configuration change or an IOS upgrade/downgrade). If deregistration is intermittent or a result of a software upgrade/downgrade, the issue most likely is not related to the configuration. It might be due to the software or externalities such as the service provider, DNS servers, or NAT devices.

If this is a day-one issue, spend time verifying the configuration; confirm that the correct registrar IP address is entered, whether DNS is used, and whether the DNS server has the appropriate records. Cross check to determine whether the credentials and authentication information are correct. Check whether the **REGISTER** message is being sent from an IP address that the service provider expects (which might require explicit SIP **bind** statements in the configuration). Any request received from an unknown IP address might be considered a DoS attack and discarded by the service provider.

Note To enable DNS lookup, the **ip domain-lookup** command is required.

Once the preceding checks—in terms of configuration, source interface for **REGISTER** messages, digest credentials, and DNS entries—have been verified and everything looks to be in place, enable the following debugs on the CUBE:

```
debug ccsip messages
debug ccsip non-call
```

Ensure that the **REGISTER** message is sent out to the service provider network. The registrar IP will feature in the first line of the **REGISTER** message (**request-URI**).

Example 9-10 shows the debug output for an outgoing **REGISTER** message, where the registrar IP is 203.0.113.30 and the local CUBE IP address is 203.0.113.31.

Example 9-10 **debug ccsip messages** *Output for a Sample Register Message*

```
Sent:
REGISTER sip:203.0.113.30:5060 SIP/2.0
Via: SIP/2.0/UDP 203.0.113.31:5060;branch=z9hG4bKB07670
From: <sip:1000@203.0.113.30>;tag=5F9E81C-98
To: <sip:1000@203.0.113.30>
Date: Fri, 17 Mar 1989 11:11:59 GMT
Call-ID: 8A20C509-863511E6-8F83AA15-803E2E12
User-Agent: Cisco-SIPGateway/IOS-15.6.1.T0a
Max-Forwards: 70
Timestamp: 1475233919
CSeq: 1 REGISTER
Contact: <sip:1000@203.0.113.31:5060>
Expires:  3600
Content-Length: 0
```

You can see in Example 9-10 that a **REGISTER** message is sent to the service provider registrar. At this point, the CUBE can expect a response with one of the following status codes:

Note Though the SIP debug output is a reliable indication of the source and destination addresses of the **REGISTER** message, for scenarios where the interface has NAT configured (which is not recommended on the CUBE) or for input queue overruns, a packet capture on the intended interface is the ultimate check of whether the request has the correct source and destination IP address.

- 5XX
- 4XX
- 200 OK

5XX responses point to an issue on the service provider network, and in most cases, changing configuration on the CUBE or further debugging would be pointless. The **5XX** responses either indicate an overload on the service provider network, which can normalize in a few minutes, or another problem all together. It is best to consult your service provider if you get such a message.

While there are many possible **4XX** response codes, the ones pertinent to trunk registration include **401 Unauthorized**, **407 Proxy Authentication Required**, **403 Forbidden**, and **423 Interval Too Brief**. If a **423 Interval Too Brief** response is received, the administrator must manually increase the value of the expiration interval such that it is larger than or equal to the one specified in the **Min-Expires** header field of the **423 Interval Too Brief** response. Example 9-11 demonstrates the sequence of events for handling a **423 Interval Too Brief** response on the CUBE.

Example 9-11 *Handling the* **423 Interval Too Brief** *response on the CUBE*

```
!
!Initial configuration on CUBE
!

sip-ua
credentials username 111111 password 7 03165A0502002C5F5A1B100B1043595F
realm cisco.com
authentication username 111111 password 7 051907012543431A0D171E1C0C59527D
realm sbc.cisco.com
registrar ipv4:203.0.113.30 expires 120


Sent:
REGISTER sip:203.0.113.30:5060 SIP/2.0
```

```
Via: SIP/2.0/UDP 203.0.113.31:5060;branch=z9hG4bKB07670
!
!Omitted for brevity
!
Expires:  120
Content-Length: 0

Received:
SIP/2.0 423 Interval Too Brief
Via: SIP/2.0/UDP 9.6.2.14:5060;branch=z9hG4bK1C12D6
!
!Omitted for brevity
!
CSeq: 21 REGISTER
Min-Expires:  500
Content-Length: 0

!
! The administrator has to manually increase the value of the expiration interval to
  reflect a value greater than or equal to 500 seconds.
!

sip-ua
credentials username 111111 password 7 03165A0502002C5F5A1B100B1043595F
realm cisco.com
authentication username 111111 password 7 051907012543431A0D171E1C0C59527D
realm sbc.cisco.com
registrar ipv4:203.0.113.30 expires 600

!
!
!
```

For the **401** and **407** response codes, the CUBE has to calculate the digest response and revert to the registrar; to ensure that the correct digest response is sent by the CUBE, first look for a subsequent **REGISTER** message sent from the CUBE that contains either the **Authorization** or **Proxy-Authorization** header (which, of course, depends on whether the CUBE received a WWW-Authenticate or a Proxy-Authenticate message). If the service provider registrar responds yet again with a **401/407** or a **403** (after the authentication response sent by the CUBE is a second **REGISTER** message), ensure that the username and password configured are what the service provider expects.

If the username and password are correctly configured on the CUBE and there is still a **401/407/403** response, make a note of the value in the **response** attribute sent by the CUBE. The value in the **response** attribute can be vetted with one of many online tools that can calculate MD5 responses for SIP. For example, SourceForge provides a downloadable SIP MD5 response calculator.

If the value is correct, the problem lies with the service provider. If, on the other hand, the value is incorrect (assuming that the username and password are correctly configured), there could be a SIP profile manipulating headers of the SIP **REGISTER** request before it is sent to the service provider network. Because the CUBE calculates the MD5 value before application of the SIP profile, there is a chance that the MD5 response will be different at the service provider. Consider a case where the initial SIP **REGISTER** message sent by the CUBE is challenged by the service provider registrar with a **401 Unauthorized** message. The **401 Unauthorized** response would contain a **WWW-Authenticate** header (refer to the section "User Agent Authentication," earlier in this chapter), which contains a plurality of fields such as **realm**, **qop**, and **nonce** (among others).

On receiving the challenge, the CUBE calculates the MD5 response and includes the **Authorization** header of the subsequent **REGISTER** message. Included in the **Authorization** header are fields such as **username, realm, nonce, uri**, and **response** (among others). A SIP profile might be configured to modify the **Authorization** header fields such as **username**, **realm**, or **response** (among others). This would certainly result in a different calculation of the **response** value on the CUBE and the service provider registrar. The CUBE calculates the response before application of the SIP profile, whereas the service provider registrar validates the response against the modified **Authorization** header. This is demonstrated in Figure 9-21.

As shown in Figure 9-21, the CUBE calculates the MD5 response before the application of the SIP profile (steps 1 and 2). On applying the SIP profile, the username is modified without a revision of the **response** field (steps 3 and 4). When the service provider registrar receives the SIP **REGISTER** message, it validates the value of the **response** header against the **Authorization** header of the modified SIP message and not the original SIP message before application of the SIP profile.

In yet another scenario, if the CUBE does not send a subsequent **REGISTER** message that contains either the **Authorization** or **Proxy-Authorization** header, then the issue is likely configuration oriented due to an incorrect **realm** being specified in the **credentials** command. If a **200 OK** response is received, it means that the trunk has successfully registered and can be verified with the command provided in Example 9-5, **show sip-ua register status.**

As mentioned earlier, the registrar always dictates the expiration interval. If the expiration interval in the **200 OK** response is too large and if it is required to refresh registration more frequently (perhaps to keep NAT bindings alive), the **refresh-ratio** command (refer to Table 9-3) on the CUBE can be used. By default it is set to 80% of the **expires** interval. Reducing its value means the refresh registrations can be more frequent.

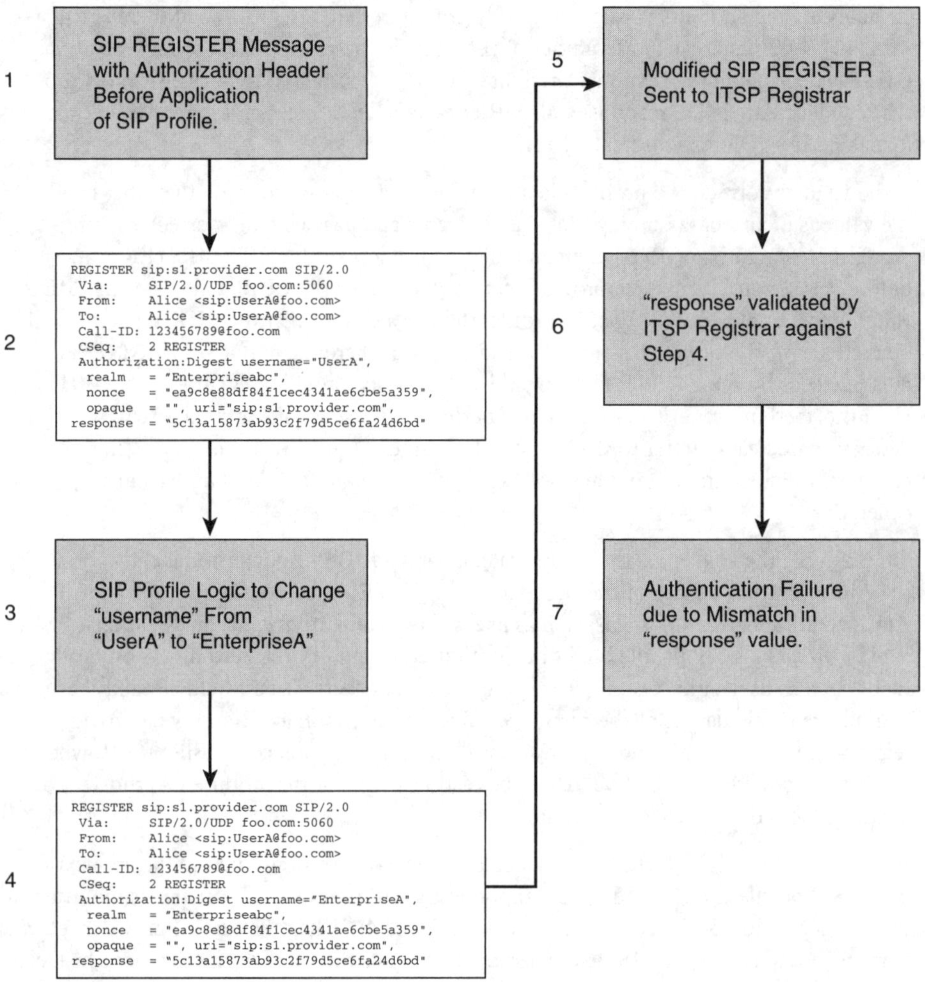

1
SIP REGISTER Message with Authorization Header Before Application of SIP Profile.
2
REGISTER sip:s1.provider.com SIP/2.0
Via: SIP/2.0/UDP foo.com:5060
From: Alice <sip:UserA@foo.com>
To: Alice <sip:UserA@foo.com>
Call-ID: 1234567890@foo.com
CSeq: 2 REGISTER
Authorization:Digest username="UserA",
realm = "Enterpriseabc",
nonce = "ea9c8e88df84f1cec4341ae6cbe5a359",
opaque = "", uri="sip:s1.provider.com",
response = "5c13a15873ab93c2f79d5ce6fa24d6bd"
3
SIP Profile Logic to Change "username" From "UserA" to "EnterpriseA"
4
REGISTER sip:s1.provider.com SIP/2.0
Via: SIP/2.0/UDP foo.com:5060
From: Alice <sip:UserA@foo.com>
To: Alice <sip:UserA@foo.com>
Call-ID: 1234567890@foo.com
CSeq: 2 REGISTER
Authorization:Digest username="EnterpriseA",
realm = "Enterpriseabc",
nonce = "ea9c8e88df84f1cec4341ae6cbe5a359",
opaque = "", uri="sip:s1.provider.com",
response = "5c13a15873ab93c2f79d5ce6fa24d6bd"
5
Modified SIP REGISTER Sent to ITSP Registrar
6
"response" validated by ITSP Registrar against Step 4.
7
Authentication Failure due to Mismatch in "response" value.

Figure 9-21 *Incorrect* response *Value Due to Application of SIP Profiles*

> **Note** For CUBE deployments that have co-located SRST functionality, SIP **REGISTER** messages are sent for configured SIP or SCCP directory numbers and destination-pattern sequences of POTS dial peers. The large number of **REGISTER** transactions sourced for unknown internal directory numbers (or patterns) is viewed as a toll fraud attack by the service provider. As a result, service providers might not honor attempts to register a valid number identifying the SIP trunk. Example 9-12 demonstrates how this behavior can be disabled on the CUBE.

Example 9-12 *Disabling Unsolicited Registration Attempts for SIP and SCCP Directory Numbers*

```
!
!Initial configuration on CUBE
!
ephone-dn 1
number 8000 no-reg
!
voice-register dn 1
no-reg

!
dial-peer voice 10 pots
Description outgoing analog dial peer for SRST
Destination-pattern 911
Port 0/0/0
No sip-register

!
!
!
```

Summary

This chapter discusses some of the best practices for SIP trunking with SBCs from the perspectives of security, availability, monitoring, and scalability. This chapter discusses the SIP **REGISTER** method in detail and its utility in establishing a relationship between an enterprise and its service provider.

The authentication framework in SIP is also described in detail, along with how SBCs assist in SIP trunking. The chapter closes by introducing a generic framework for troubleshooting SIP trunk registration.

References

- RFC 3261, "SIP: Session Initiation Protocol," https://tools.ietf.org/html/rfc3261.
- RFC 2617, "HTTP Authentication: Basic and Digest Access Authentication," https://www.ietf.org/rfc/rfc2617.
- RFC 6140, "Registration for Multiple Phone Numbers in the Session Initiation Protocol (SIP)," https://tools.ietf.org/html/rfc6140.

Chapter 10

Fax over IP (FoIP) on SBCs

Fax (short for facsimile) technology can trace its roots back to as early as the 1800s, when a Scotsman by the name of Alexander Bain came up with a very rudimentary method of transmitting data over two wires. Throughout the early 1900s, fax adoption was slow as it found application in niche areas. Over the subsequent years, however, incremental and sometimes monumental leaps in fax technology have made it the ubiquitous technology it is today.

The scope of this chapter is restricted to conceptually introducing fax over IP (FoIP) and extending the discussion to FoIP handling on SBCs. (For a more detailed understanding of FoIP, refer to the Cisco Press book *Fax, Modem, and Text for IP Telephony*.) This chapter includes the following topics:

- **Introduction to Fax**—This section provides an introduction to the phases of a fax call, a look at the common message exchange that occurs in a fax call, and a description of the different T.30 messages in a fax call. This section also provides an explanation of Super G3 (SG3) faxing and error correction mode (ECM).
- **Analyzing a Basic Fax Call**—This section explains the various timers that govern the operation of G3 faxing.
- **Fax over IP (FoIP)**—This section describes how fax-modulated data is transported over IP networks. It also provides a detailed description of the two principal methods of transporting fax data over the IP protocol: fax passthrough and fax relay.
- **SBC Handling of FoIP**—This section discusses some of the considerations that need to be taken into account for SBCs to successfully handle fax data transmission.
- **FoIP on CUBE**—This section details how CUBE handles fax data, the configuration required to enable fax functionality, and troubleshooting constructs that can be used to diagnose fax failures on CUBE.

Because fax communications are inherently different from voice communications, certain considerations are required to effectively transport fax communications over SBCs. Understanding these differences as well as FoIP fundamentals is critical to ensuring that fax calls traversing your SBCs are successful. By the end of this chapter, you will have a detailed understanding of how fax-modulated data can be transmitted over IP, how call control protocols such as SIP and H.323 are leveraged to assist in transmission of fax information, the various messages used in a fax connection, the role of SBCs in faxing, and the troubleshooting techniques available to quickly diagnose fax failures.

Introduction to Fax

With the advent of voice over IP (VoIP), existing communication infrastructures were migrated from traditional analog and digital telephony networks to IP. Among the different classes of multimedia traffic, FoIP is probably the only traffic class that requires strict supervision end-to-end for a multitude of characteristics, including the following:

- The method of fax transport over the IP network
- Jitter
- Delay
- Packet drops
- Optimal characteristics along the delivery path

Other real-time media traffic classes such as audio and video are sensitive to packet drops, jitter, and transmission delays, but audio and video communication sessions don't fail as a result of such impairments; rather, these impairments at most manifest as audio issues or blurry video. However, in the case of FoIP, such impairments almost always lead to fax transmission failures. Several constructs have been developed over the years to ensure reliable delivery of fax over IP networks. Before exploring some of these constructs, it is vital to first get a basic understanding of how fax transmission works in a traditional telephony environment without an IP transport.

Fax Group Classification

In the early days of fax technology, terminals almost always used proprietary means for communication, which resulted in interoperability problems across vendors. In an effort to improve interoperability and reliability and to provide a general structure to fax transmission, the ITU-T (International Telecommunications Union Telecommunication Standardization Sector) came up with several transmission standards over the years. The major differentiating factors among these standards were the manner in which data was transmitted and the rate of data transmission. Over the years, four groups of standards were developed, as summarized in Table 10-1.

Table 10-1 *Fax Group Classification Summary*

Group Designation	Transmission Method	Peer Specifications	Transmission Rate (per page)
G1	Analog	ITU-T Recommendation T.2	6 minutes per page
G2	Analog	ITU-T Recommendation T.3	3 minutes per page
G3	Digital	ITU-T Recommendations T.30, T.4, and T.6	Up to 1 minute per page
G4	Digital	ITU-T Recommendations T.6, T.503, T.521, T.563, T.72, T.62, T.62 bis, T.70, and F.161	Less than 1 minute per page

Note The "Transmission Rate" in the table above does not take into account the pre-transmission procedures, which include dialing the destination terminal number, negotiating fax transmission parameters, and locking in on an optimal modulation.

Group 3 (G3) fax is the most widely used group in faxing today. G3 faxing can achieve transmission speeds of up to 14,400 bps.

Phases of a Fax Call

At a high level, a fax call consists of the terminals negotiating various parameters for the communication session and, on successful negotiation of these parameters, transmission of data. The negotiation of various parameters for the call is governed by the T.30 specification, whereas the transmission of fax data is governed by the T.4 or T.6 specification. A fax call can be divided into five continuous, logical phases, such that each phase of the call has a distinct set of functions and checks before the call proceeds to the next phase. Figure 10-1 depicts the phases of a fax call:

Note The phases discussed in this section are for the T.30 specification. As shown in Table 10-1, T.30 is part of the ubiquitous G3 fax standard.

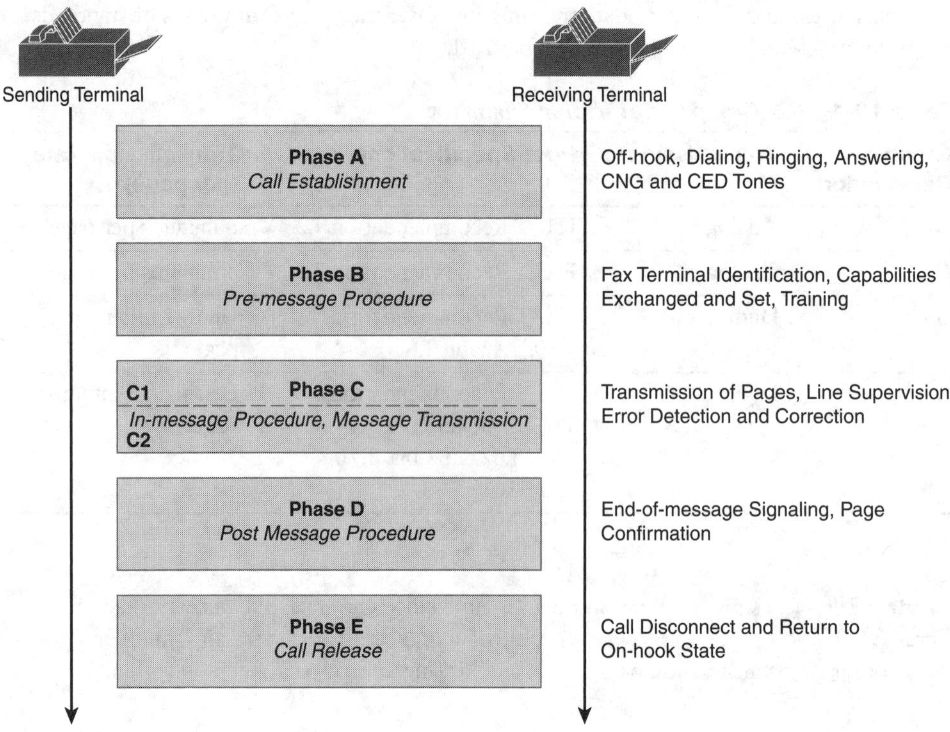

Figure 10-1 *Phases of a Fax Call*

- **Phase A:** This phase, known as the call establishment phase, involves the calling fax terminal going off-hook and dialing the destination number and transmitting a CNG, or calling, tone. The CNG tone is primarily used to distinguish the calling terminal from non-fax terminals. On answering the call, the called terminal waits 0.2 seconds and transmits a CED, or called, tone. Once these tones are exchanged bidirectionally, an assertion is made that the terminals are fax capable, and the call proceeds to Phase B. Both the CNG and CED tones are discussed in more detail in the next section.
- **Phase B:** This phase, known as the pre-message procedure phase, involves the calling and called fax terminals negotiating a myriad of characteristics for fax page transmission. Some of these characteristics include the fax page transmission speeds, the encoding algorithm used, and whether error correction mode (ECM) is enabled. (ECM is covered in more detail later in this chapter, in the section "Error Correction Mode.") Phase B involves identifying the set of characteristics that are common to the calling and called fax terminals. It also involves optional terminal identification, modulation training (discussed later in this chapter), and whether the participating fax terminals can deviate from standards-based fax transmission and use proprietary methods. As soon this phase completes, the fax page(s) is ready for transmission, and the call moves to Phase C.
- **Phase C:** This phase deals with actual fax page transmission between the participating terminals and is logically divided into two subphases, C1 and C2, that proceed in parallel with each other:

- **Phase C1:** Known as the in-message procedure, this subphase controls signaling for message synchronization, error detection, error correction, and line supervision.
- **Phase C2:** This subphase involves actual fax page transmission; the procedures for fax page transmission are covered by relevant ITU-T specifications. In the case of G3 faxes, this subphase is governed by T.4 and T.6.

- **Phase D:** This phase, known as the post message procedure phase, includes end-of-message signaling, confirmation signaling, multipage signaling, and end-of-facsimile procedure signaling. The fax call logically enters Phase D whenever there is a break in fax page transmission. From Phase D, the call can reenter Phase B or Phase C, or it can move on to Phase E.
- **Phase E:** This phase, known as the call release phase, is the last stage of a fax call, where the fax call is terminated and the calling and called fax machines go on-hook. The call can be terminated gracefully (over a T.30 DCN) or due to unexpected circumstances, such as a timeout or procedure interrupt.

Analyzing a Basic Fax Call

This section analyzes how different T.30 messages in a fax call come together to enable fax page transmission. It then explores the basic T.30 message format and provides a detailed explanation of the mandatory T.30 messages. Figure 10-2 provides an overview of the messages exchanged between participating terminals in a fax call.

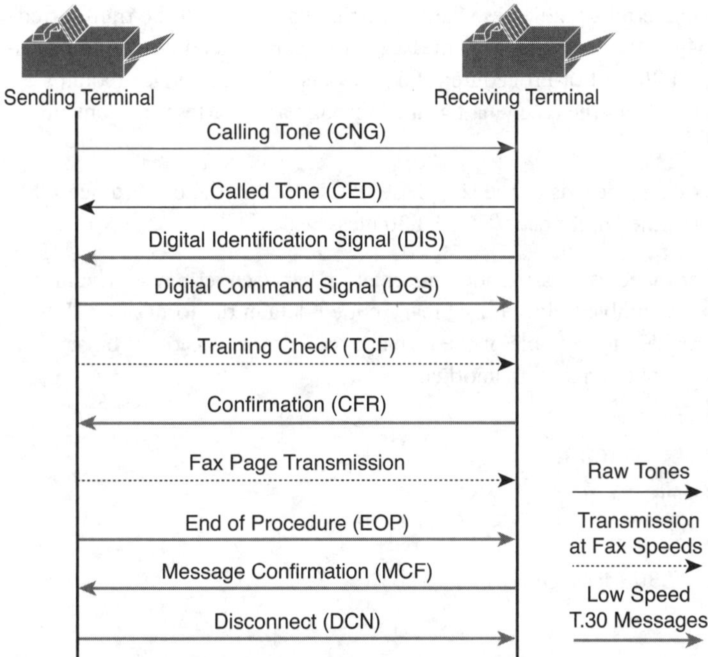

Figure 10-2 *Message Exchange in a Fax Call*

The fax call process can be summarized as follows:

1. The calling terminal goes off-hook and transmits a CNG (calling) tone, which is a 1100 Hz tone that plays for 0.5 seconds and repeats every 3 seconds.
2. The called terminal answers the call by going off-hook, followed by the transmissions of a CED (called) tone. The CED tone is 2100 Hz and plays for around 3 seconds.
3. The exchange of the CNG/CED tones is followed by both of the terminals negotiating facsimile capabilities. The capabilities negotiated include parameters such as the modulation, the encoding algorithm, and the error correction mode. Parameter negotiation is done through the exchange of the T.30 Digital Identification Signal (DIS) and Digital Command Signal (DCS) messages respectively. These messages are modulated using V.21 at 300 bps.
4. Following the exchange of the DCS message, the sending terminal transmits a Training Check (TCF) message, which is a continuous sequence of zeros transmitted using the same high-speed modulation as the proposed fax page transmission. The TCF serves as a means to check the quality of the line.
5. If the TCF message is received without any errors, the receiving terminal sends a Confirmation to Receive (CFR). This is an indication for the sending terminal to begin the transmission of the fax page.
6. The sending terminal then transmits the first fax page at the high-speed modulation negotiated during the DIS/DCS exchange and confirmed by the TCF. Once transmitted, the sending terminal indicates whether further pages need to be transmitted through a T.30 Multi-Page Signal (MPS) message or signals the end of data transmission by sending a T.30 End-of-Procedure (EOP) message. Either message requires an acknowledgment from the receiving terminal through a T.30 Message Confirm (MCF) message.
7. After this the fax call proceeds to the last phase (Phase E), and the call is gracefully terminated through the Disconnect (DCN) T.30 message.

T.30 messages are exchanged as binary-coded information between terminals. The message format includes a preamble followed by binary-coded data in the form of an HDLC frame. Figure 10-3 provides an example of the format used in transmission of binary-coded information from one terminal to another.

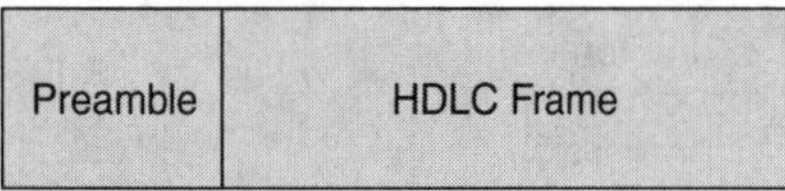

Figure 10-3 *High-Level T.30 Message Format*

The HDLC frame is further divided into several fields, as shown in Figure 10-4. The preamble is a series of repeated flag sequences that always precedes any new binary-coded data sent in either direction (from sender to receiver or vice versa). The preamble serves to condition the line and ensure that all the following data (HDLC frames) passes through, unimpeded, between the communicating terminals.

The HDLC frame that follows the preamble has several fields that serve different purposes during message transmission. Figure 10-4 shows the fields within the HDLC frame:

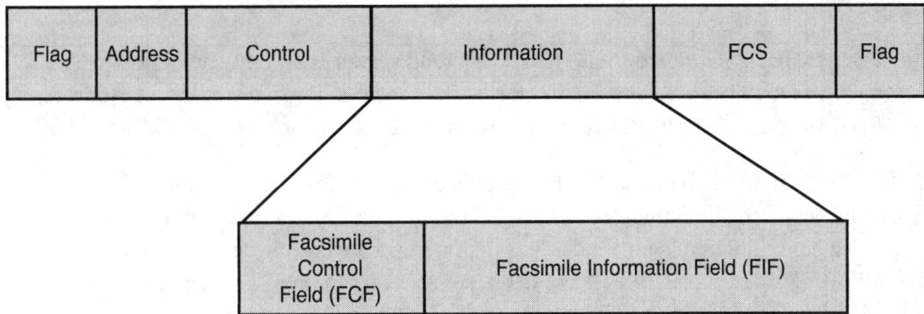

Figure 10-4 *HDLC Frame Format*

- **Flag sequence:** This 8-bit field appears at the beginning and the end of the HDLC frame. For facsimile procedures, it is used to establish bit and frame synchronization and carries the persistent bit pattern **0111 1110**.
- **Address field:** This 8-bit field is used to provide terminal identification in a multipoint communication scenario. However, in the case of fax communication over standard telephone networks, this field is hard-coded to the bit pattern **1111 1111**.
- **Control field:** This field takes the format **1100 *X*000**, where *X* = 0 for non-final frames and *X* = 1 for final frames within the procedure. A final frame is defined as the last frame transmitted prior to an expected response from the distant terminal.
- **Information field:** With the three preceding fields set to fixed formats, the Information field contains the details and the description of the various T.30 messages. The Information field is further subdivided into two fields:
  - **Facsimile Control Field (FCF):** This field is either an 8-bit or a 16-bit field, depending on whether error correction mode is used (as discussed later in this chapter). The bit pattern in this field describes the T.30 message being transmitted. For example, the bit pattern of this field is set to 0000 0001 for a DIS message. Different formats are used for different T.30 messages. A complete list of the bit pattern formats can be found in Sections 5.3.6.1.1 through 5.3.6.1.8 of the T.30 specification.

- **Facsimile Information Field (FIF):** This field provides a complete description of the T.30 message specified in the FCF field. The length of the field can vary from a few octets to several octets, depending on the level of granularity required to describe the T.30 message. Table 2 of the T.30 specification provides a detailed list of capabilities that can be advertised for the DIS/DCS messages.

Note The FIF is applicable only to select T.30 messages; for example, there is no meaningful description that can be attributed to the CFR message (among several others) through the FIF field.

- **Frame Check Sequence (FCS) field:** This field serves as an error detection mechanism and involves a binary calculation at the sender and receiver over the Address, Control, and Information fields. This 16-bit field varies for each HDLC frame.

The HDLC frame terminates with a flag sequence that serves the same purposes as the flag sequence at the beginning of the HDLC frame. The T.30 messages in Figure 10-2 represent the bare minimum set of messages that are exchanged during a successful fax call. The following section discusses some of these messages in more detail and highlights their significance in the overall T.30 exchange.

T.30 Messages

A fax call begins with the exchange of tones between the calling and called terminals; these tones include the CNG and CED tones and serve as a method to distinguish fax-capable terminals from non-fax-capable terminals. Following the transmission of the CED tone, the called terminal begins transmission of T.30 messages. The following sections explain these messages and their significance in a T.30 call. Note that several T.30 messages can be exchanged during the course of a call and lead to different behavioral subsets between the fax terminals. The ITU-T T.30 specification discusses all possible scenarios, and you are strongly advised to go through the specification to gain a more comprehensive understanding.

DIS, CSI, and NSF

On transmitting the CED tone, the called terminal may send the Called Subscriber Identification (CSI) and Non-Standard Facilities (NSF) messages, which are optional, followed by a mandatory Digital Identification Signal (DIS) message. Each message is encoded in an independent HDLC frame such that the optional CSI and NSF messages are sent before the mandatory DIS message. Because this exchange represents the transmission of new binary-coded data from the receiving terminal to the sending terminal, it is preceded by a preamble. Figure 10-5 depicts the transmission of these messages encoded as HDLC frames.

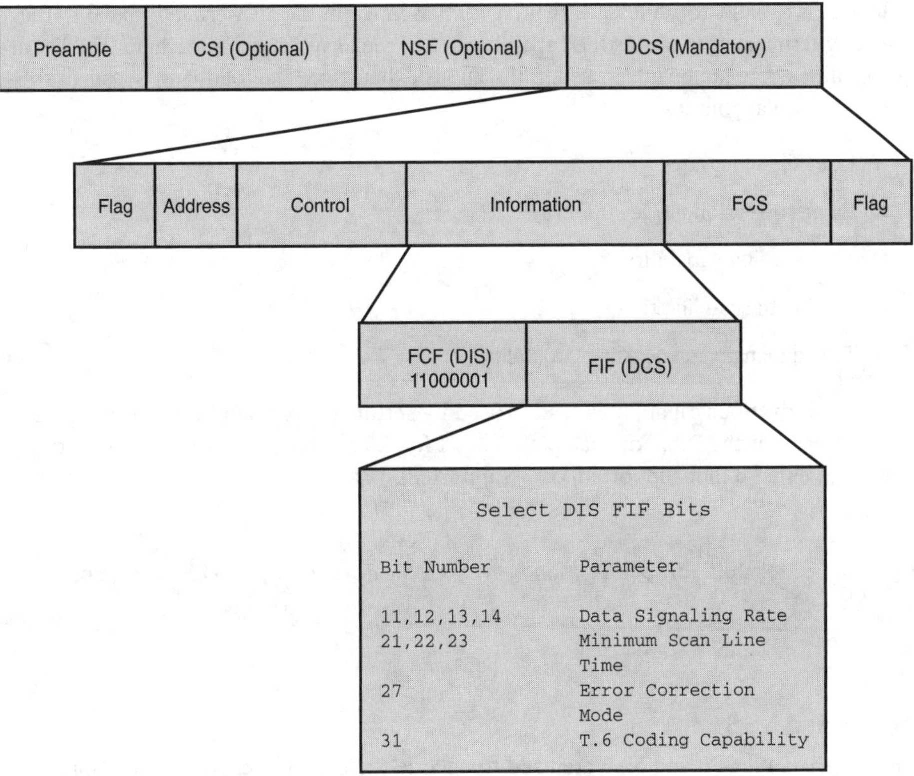

Figure 10-5 *Transmission of NSF, CSI, and DIS as HDLC-Encoded Frames*

The CSI message may be transmitted to provide the identity of the called subscriber in the form of an international telephone number. This is useful in scenarios where the number dialed for fax calls is different from the actual fax terminal number (for example, if the fax terminal is serviced by a regular voice gateway) and, alternatively, serves as a way for the caller to confirm that he or she has dialed the right number (as the value encoded in the FIF portion of the CSI message is populated on the sending fax machine display).

The NSF message, which is an optional message, is transmitted to advertise country- or vendor-specific capabilities. These capabilities might be encoded over several octets in the FIF field. If these vendor-specific capabilities are understood and supported by the transmitting fax machine, it sends an NSS (Non-Standard Signal) message, and the communicating fax machines may deviate from standards-based T.30 and use proprietary procedures for fax transmission. As discussed in subsequent sections, it is highly advisable to overwrite the NSF field and deter any vendor-specific procedures for fax transmission.

The DIS is a mandatory message that has to be sent from the answering terminal to the sending terminal as it carries the capability set of the answering fax machine. The list of capabilities that can be advertised in the DIS is exhaustive. The following is a small subset of these capabilities:

- Data signaling rate
- Error correction mode support
- T.6 encoding capability
- Minimum scan line time
- Two-dimensional encoding capability

Support for various capabilities is advertised by setting the relevant bit positions in the FIF segment of the DIS. For example, support for T.6 encoding is advertised by setting bit 31 to either 0 (not supported) or 1 (supported).

> **Note** Table 2 of the T.30 specification provides a detailed description of each bit of the FIF field.

DCS, TSI, and NSS

Just as the DIS, CSI, and NSF are used to encode the capabilities, the international number, and vendor-specific information of the answering fax machine, the DCS, TSI, and NSS are used to encode the same for the calling fax terminal. The TSI (Transmitting Subscriber Identification) is similar to the CSI and is used to encode the number of the transmitting terminal in an international format. The originating terminal transmits the NSS or NSF (Non-Standard Facilities Set-up) if it understands and supports the capabilities advertised in the NSF. The TSI and NSS are optional messages.

The DCS is a mandatory message that is used to encode the capabilities of the transmitting fax machine and must not include capabilities that aren't advertised in the DIS. This is because the DCS is essentially a command to the receiving terminal that dictates the final capability set of the fax call. Just like the DIS, the DCS contains a myriad of capabilities that are captured in the FIF portion of the DCS HDLC message. A complete list of capabilities for the DCS message can be found in Table 2 of the T.30 specification. Figure 10-6 depicts some of the FIF capabilities of the DCS message. The FIF capabilities specified in the DCS set the final parameters to be used by the sending and receiving fax machines for the session.

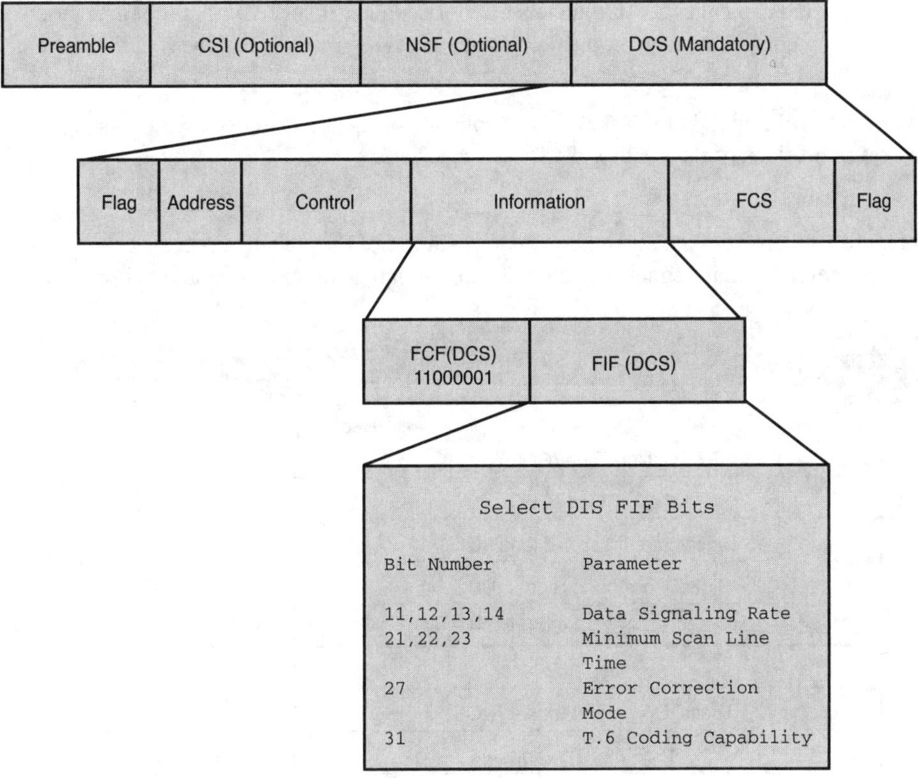

Figure 10-6 *FIF Expansion of the DCS Message*

TCF, CFR, and FTT

After the transmitting terminal sends a command through the DCS message, the viability of the data path to handle page transmission is assessed through a Training Check (TCF) message. The TCF message contains a continuous sequence of zeros and is sent for a duration of 1.5 seconds. Unlike the DIS and DCS messages, the TCF message is not encoded in an HDLC frame. The primary purpose of this message is to assess line quality by mimicking actual fax page transmission. This is why the TCF is not modulated at 300 bps and is instead transmitted at the same speed indicated in the DCS message for fax page transmission rate.

If the TCF is received reliably at the receiving terminal, a Confirmation to Receive (CFR) is sent to the transmitting terminal. This message serves as an indication for the sender to begin fax page transmission. Impairments along the transmission path can cause the TCF to be received unreliably, in which case the receiving terminal sends a Failure to Train (FTT) message to the transmitting terminal. Receipt of a FTT message is an indication for the fax call to go back to Phase B and retransmit the DCS with an updated capability set.

The updated capability set in the DCS may reflect a lower speed within the same modulation or a completely new modulation altogether. Very rarely is the DCS sent unaltered.

> **Note** The FTT and CFR messages do not contain a FIF body as these messages simply serve as indications of the quality of the training check.

Figure 10-7 provides a diagrammatic representation of the training process. This example shows several retrain sequences before an appropriate data transmission rate is chosen.

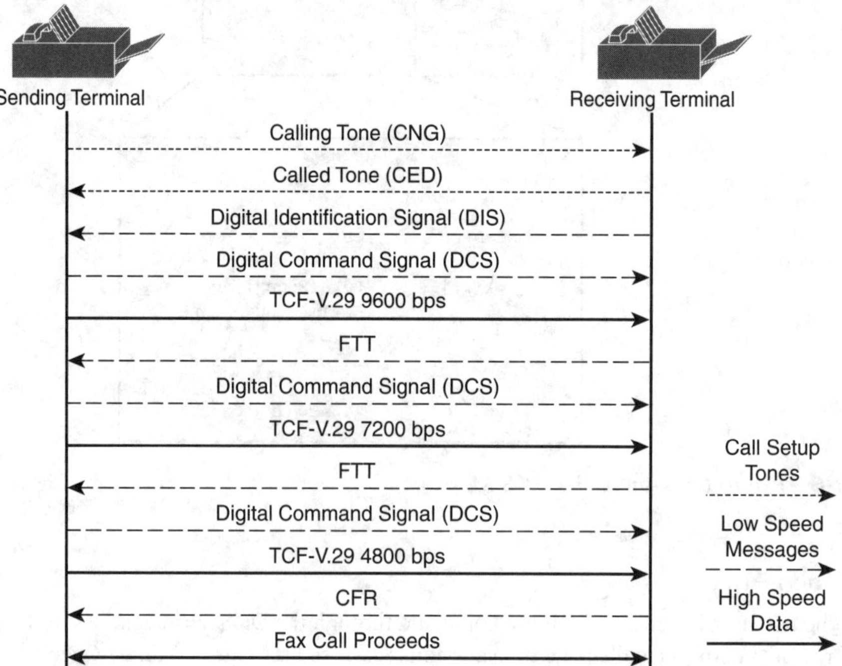

Figure 10-7 *Fax Retraining*

EOP, MCF, MPS, RTP, RTN, and DCN

After a fax page has been transmitted, the originating terminal may send an End of Procedure (EOP) message to signal the end of fax page transmission. The receiver then sends a Message Confirmation (MCF), after which the call proceeds to Phase E and gracefully disconnects.

If there are multiple fax pages to be transmitted from sender to receiver, the sender transmits a Multi-Page Signal (MPS) after each fax page. The receiver responds to each

MPS message with an MCF message. When the last fax page has been sent, an EOP is sent, as mentioned previously, to indicate that there are no more fax pages to be sent.

Over the course of a fax call, it is not uncommon for the quality of the data path to change for the worse, resulting in unreliable and error-prone fax delivery. To account for such scenarios, the receiver can either send a Retrain Positive (RTP) or a Retrain Negative (RTN) message. The RTP signal is sent when a fax page received is generally of usable, good quality with minimal errors. This serves as an indication to the sender to retrain to another speed or modulation to better ensure that transmission is impairment free. The RTN, on the other hand, is an explicit indication that the page received is unusable and has to be retransmitted. In this case, the DCS and TCF messages have to be retransmitted to reflect a slower, more reliable modulation.

Note The RTP and RTN messages are not used for an ECM-enabled call.

Note The EOP, MCF, MPS, RTP, and RTN messages are all sent at 300 bps and do not contain a FIF definition.

After a confirmation (MCF) to an EOP has been received, the sender transmits a Disconnect (DCN) to gracefully terminate T.30 procedures. After this graceful disconnect, the two fax terminals go back to an on-hook state.

Error Correction Mode

Facsimile connections are often subject to transmission impairments that lead to poor page quality. With non-ECM faxing, the error detection and error correction capabilities are inadequate to guarantee high-quality, reliable fax transmission. At most, the receiving terminal can transmit an RTN message to the sending terminal if the error rate crosses a certain threshold. However, this method is not very effective in ensuring that the sending terminal will retransmit the affected page(s) reliably and impairment free. When a non-ECM call suffers transmission impairments, it usually manifests as pages containing portions of text that are illegible. In addition, portions of the page may be blank or contain horizontal white streaks.

Error correction mode (ECM) ensures error-free, high-quality fax transmission by using a real-time, built-in error correction mechanism that provides explicit feedback between the receiver and sender. With ECM, the fax page is divided into blocks, such that each block contains several frames, with data transmitted one block at a time. The contents of a fax page might be encoded within a single block or might be encoded over several blocks, such that each block is referred to as a "partial page." A Partial Page Signal (PPS) follows the transmission of each block from the sender to the receiver and has additional definitions that are in line with the status of the block transmission. Figure 10-8 depicts a logical encoding of a fax page into blocks for ECM transmission.

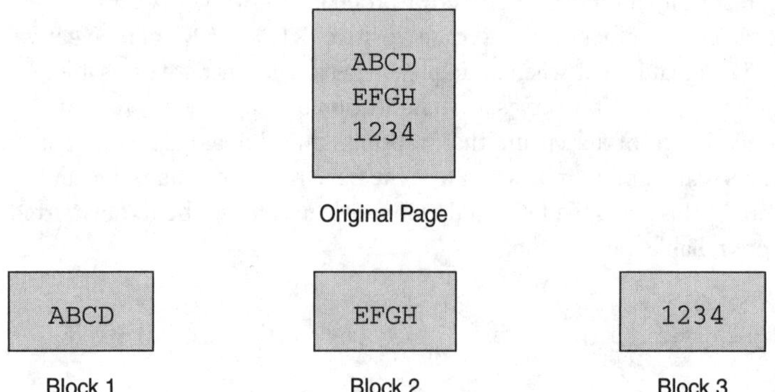

Figure 10-8 *Logical Encoding of a Fax Page for ECM Transmission*

Figure 10-9 diagrams the format of a Partial Page Signal (PPS) message. The logical formatting of a PPS message and any other T.30 message remains the same; the only difference is the presence of a secondary Fax Control Field (FCF). The FCF of the PPS message is divided into Fax Control Field 1 (FCF 1) and Fax Control Field 2 (FCF 2). The bit pattern appearing in FCF 1 remains a constant for all PPS messages, whereas the bit pattern in FCF 2 is distinct per PPS message type and serves as the distinguisher of the type of PPS message. The FCF 2 field in Figure 10-9 demonstrates possible encodings of this field and the different PPS messages they signify.

The Fax Information Field (FIF) of the PPS message is specially formatted to enable a real-time feedback mechanism between sender and receiver; the feedback mechanism will be discussed shortly. The FIF field of the PPS message includes the following subfields:

- **Page Counter (PC):** This indicates the current page number.
- **Block Counter (BC):** This indicates the block number within current page.
- **Frame Counter (FC):** This indicates the total number of frames within the block.

Fax data is transmitted in the form of HDLC frames, such that each frame could either be 64 or 256 bytes in length. The frame length is negotiated during the DIS/DCS exchange. A block can contain a maximum of 256 frames; however, if fax data overflows 256 frames, the page will have to be divided into more than one block. On the transmission of a relevant PPS message (PPS-NULL, PPS-MPS, PPS-EOP), the FC field encodes the number of frames transmitted in the preceding block.

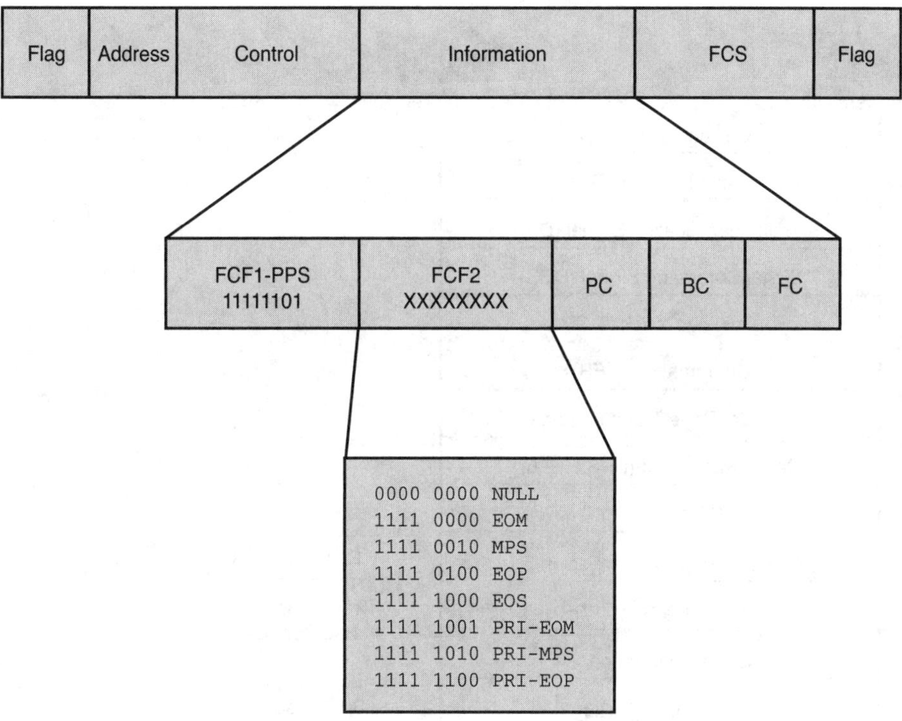

Figure 10-9 *HDLC Frame Format for an ECM PPS Message*

Figure 10-10 diagrams an ECM call. Notice the difference in the message exchange between a standard fax call without ECM as shown in Figure 10-2 and the fax call with ECM in Figure 10-10. The number of messages exchanged to and from for an ECM call is more than what would be exchanged for a standard fax call. As discussed earlier, for a fax call to proceed in ECM mode, support for ECM has to be specified by the receiving fax terminal in its DIS message and then set by the transmitting terminal through its DCS message.

As discussed earlier in this chapter, ECM fax data is sent as blocks or partial pages from the sender, and each block can contain up to 256 frames. Each frame is individually encoded as an HDLC frame that is either 64 bits or 256 bits long and has a frame number. On completing the transmission of a block, a PPS-NULL message is sent toward the receiver. If the block happens to be the last block in a page, a PPS-MPS message is sent (assuming that there is more than one page to transmit). Once data transmission completes and no more pages are to be sent, a PPS-EOP is sent instead of a PPS-MPS for the last block of a page. The PPS-NULL/MPS/EOP messages have to be acknowledged by the receiver through a Message Confirmation (MCF) message.

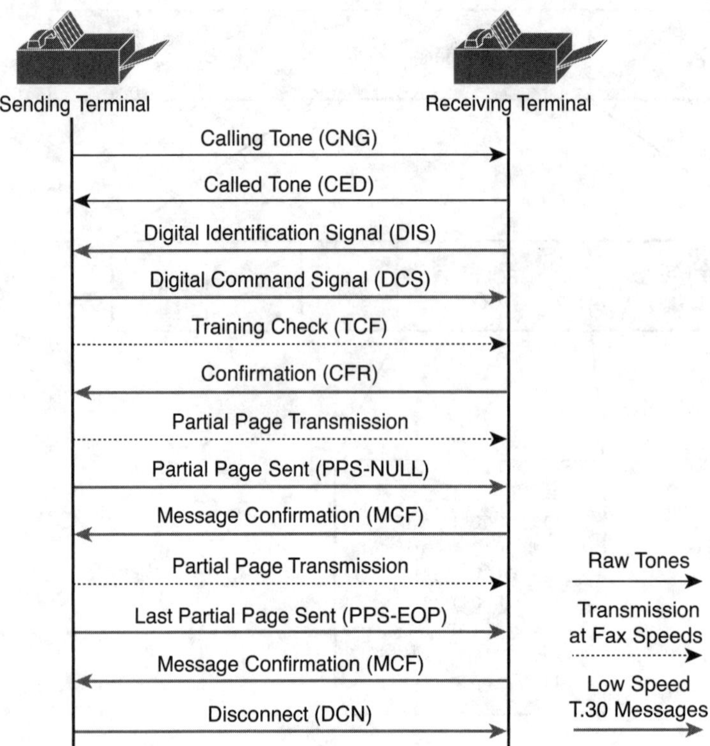

Figure 10-10 *ECM Fax Call*

The receiver constantly monitors the quality of received frames within a block by running a checksum of the FCS fields. If an error is detected, the receiver can dynamically request retransmission of the affected frame(s) within a block. This error feedback is initiated when the receiver sends a Partial Page Request (PPR) message to the sender. The structure of the PPS and PPR messages allows the receiver to correctly reference the affected frame(s). The PPR message has a standard 8-bit FCF followed by a 256-bit FIF, and each bit references one of the 256 potential frames within a block (with numbering from 0 to 255). Setting the relevant bit value to 1 references a frame that requires retransmission. Figure 10-11 diagrams the PPR message format.

Figure 10-12 depicts the precise error feedback mechanism contained in the ECM PPR message. In this scenario, there is a single fax page to be transmitted from the sender to the receiver, such that the fax data is encoded into a single block. After transmitting the block, the sender transmits a PPS-EOP message to the receiver. By running a checksum on the received frames, the receiver discovers that frames 3 and 17 contain errors. To rectify this, the receiver transmits a Partial Page Request (PPR) message to the sender, indicating that frames 3 and 17 need to be retransmitted. The sender then retransmits the affected frames, followed by a PPS-EOP. If frames 3 and 17 are received reliably and error free, the receiver replies with an MCF to confirm error-free reception of the re-sent frames. The call can now proceed to a graceful disconnect.

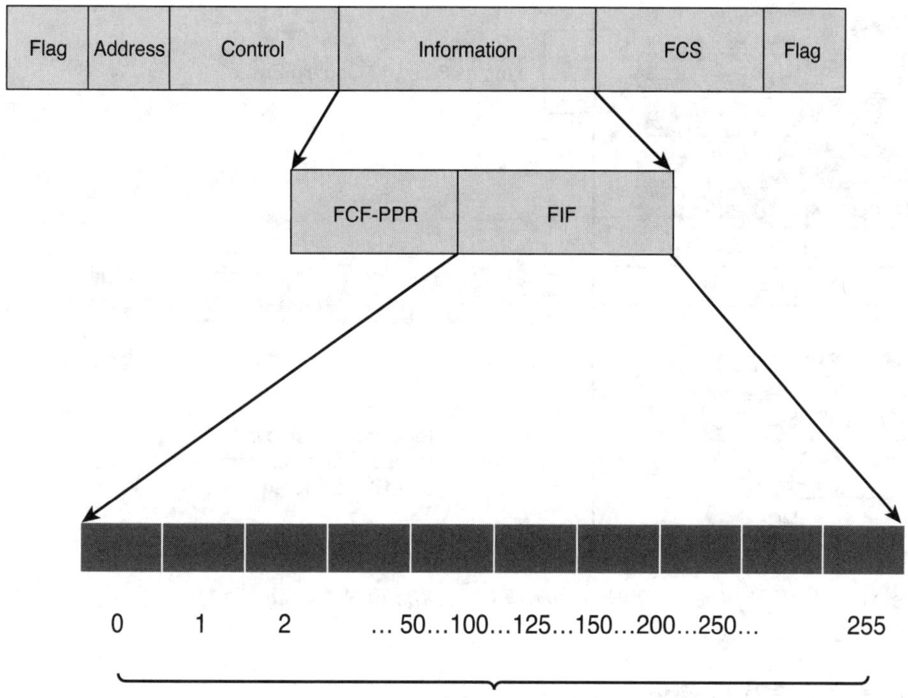

Figure 10-11 *PPR Message Format*

ECM is designed to ensure impeccable page quality for fax transmissions. However, because of the overhead of the feedback framework and the extremely tenacious nature of ECM, fax calls using ECM can take significantly longer to complete than non-ECM calls. In fact, with a large number of retransmit requests from the receiver to the sender, the transmitting terminal might ultimately give up and terminate the call before all the fax pages are sent. Transmission impairments can occur when a fax connection has one or more IP hops. In such scenarios, ECM faxing might not be the best approach as fax sessions could last several minutes or fail altogether. Ultimately, you need to decide what is best for your situation and balance the error-free reliability of ECM fax calls with longer call times and possibly more failures if impairments are encountered.

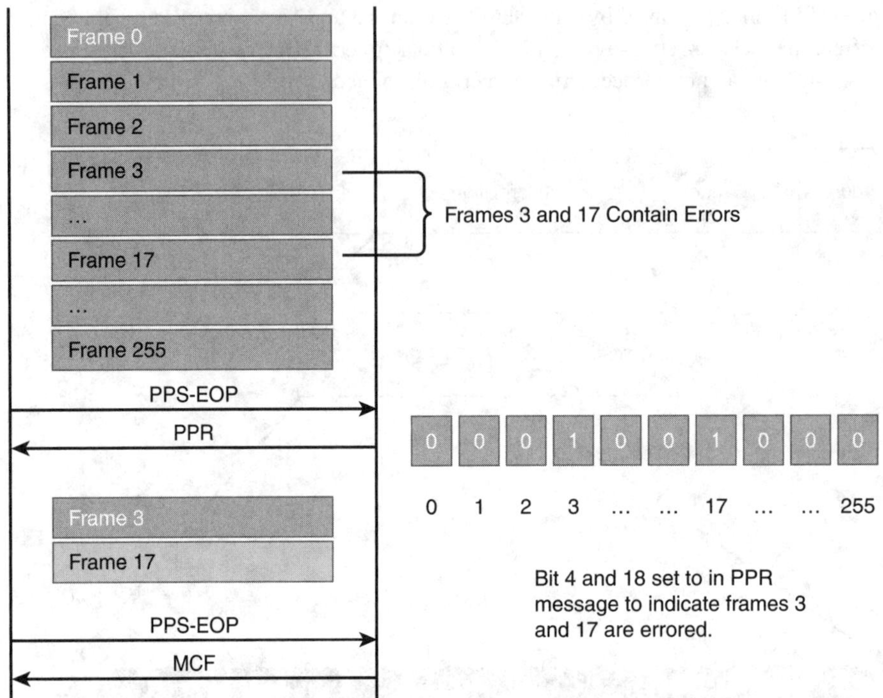

Figure 10-12 *ECM Feedback Framework Using the PPR Message*

Super G3 (SG3) Faxing

Super G3 (SG3) faxing is an enhancement to G3 that introduces two additional features:

- Mandatory support for ECM
- Transmission speeds up to 33.6 kbps

SG3 faxing is based on V.34 modulation, using the V.8 recommendation for call setup. This section discusses the procedures used in SG3 faxing and highlights the operational differences between G3 and SG3 faxing.

> **Note** This section provides a very high-level overview of SG3 faxing. For a more detailed understanding of SG3 faxing, read Annex F of the T.30 specification and the ITU V.34 specification.

A typical SG3 call is illustrated in Figure 10-13. The call begins with the transmitting terminal going off-hook and dialing the number of the destination terminal. On answering the call, the called terminal sends an ANSam tone, which is a 2100 Hz tone and phase reversed every 450 milliseconds. The ANSam tone is transmitted for a duration of 3 to 4 seconds and is used to disable any echo cancelers in the data path. You should note that this is different from the CED tone discussed previously as part of G3 faxing.

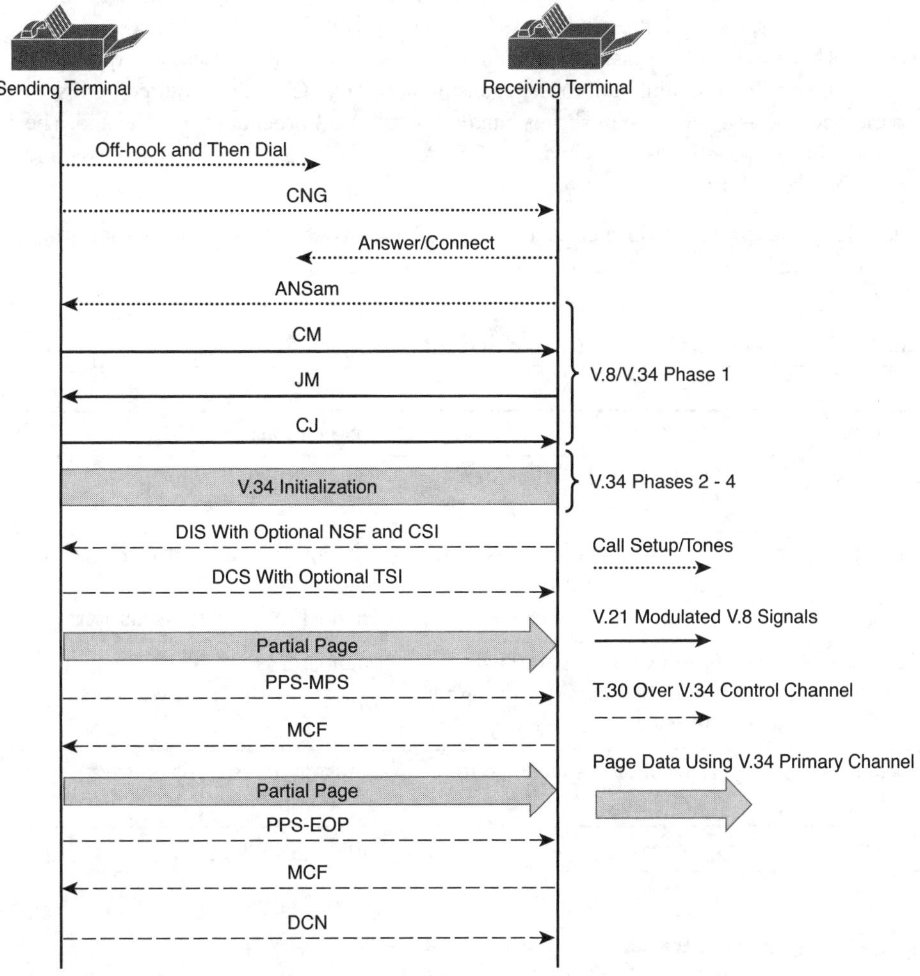

Figure 10-13 *SG3 Fax Call*

On detecting the ANSam tone, the calling terminal sends a Calling Menu (CM) message that encodes the V.34 parameters at the calling end. In response to the CM message, the called terminal sends a Joint Menu (JM) message that encodes the V.34

parameters at the called end. This concludes the V.8 procedures and is followed by a V.34 modulation scheme. An important point to note is that during the V.8 procedures, there is a control channel and a primary channel setup: The control channel is used for fax message transmission, and the primary channel is used for the exchange of fax-coded data.

After the exchange of the CM/JM and the conclusion of the V.8 procedures, the control and primary channel are established. This is followed by the exchange of the DIS and DCS messages, followed directly by the transmission of the CFR from the receiving terminal. This is in stark contrast to a G3 call, which uses the TCF to assess line quality and select the optimum modulation for fax transmission. The TCF is not required in this scenario because assessing line quality is handled by the V.34 procedures beforehand. The rest of the call progresses as a standard G3 ECM-enabled call with the same messaging sequence until Phase E.

Table 10-2 describes the differences between G3 and SG3 faxing. It is by no means an exhaustive list but provides a general, high-level overview.

Table 10-2 *Differences Between G3 and SG3 Faxing*

Property	G3	SG3
Answer tone	CED tone	ANSam tone
Initial message	Digital Identification Signal (DIS)	Calling Menu (CM)
Number of channels	Single channel for messaging and page transmission	One low-speed control channel for messaging and a high-speed primary channel for page transmission
ECM	Optional; negotiated based on terminal capability during the DIS/DCS exchange	Mandatory; an SG3 call cannot proceed without ECM
Data transmission speed	Transmission speeds up to 14,400 bps	Transmission speeds up to 33,600 bps
TCF signal	Required	Not applicable

Important Fax Timers

A standard fax call requires a detailed and structured exchange between participating terminals to ensure that pages are reliably transmitted from one end to another. Therefore, the exchanges of these messages between terminals are governed by timers which ensure that the fax call never lands into an unrecoverable state. A total of 10 timers defined in the T.30 specification supervise different scenarios of a fax call and ensure reliable state transitions between terminals.

Table 10-3 identifies some of the basic timers used in faxing.

Table 10-3 *Important Fax Timers*

Timer	Duration	Description
T0	Recommended value of 60 ± 5 s; however, it can be increased up to 120 s.	This timer defines how long a calling terminal waits for the destination terminal to answer the call. Usually a CED tone stops this timer.
T1	35 ± 5 s	This timer defines how long terminals continue to identify each other upon entering Phase B.
T2	6 ± 1 s	This is used for response/command synchronization between terminals. For example, if the receiving terminal sends an NSF+CSI+DIS and receives an NSS+TSI and not a DCS within 6 ± 1 s, this timer expires.
T3	10 ± 5 s	This timer defines how long a terminal will alert the operator if a procedure interrupt has been received.
T4	3 s ± 15%	This timer defines how long a terminal waits to receive a response. For example, if the receiving terminal sends an NSF+CSI+DIS and does not receive any response within a 3-second window, this timer expires.
T5	60 ± 5 s	Defines how long a terminal waits for a clearance of the busy condition. This is used specifically for ECM faxing.

It is worthwhile to note that from a fax failure perspective, the T4 timer is of most significance; this is especially true if terminals are communicating over links that span vast geographic distances or are unreliable with respect to end-to-end packet delivery.

Fax over IP (FoIP)

With enterprises migrating their communication infrastructures from traditional analog and digital networks to IP, the assumption that the quality of audio, video, and fax would remain exactly the same was not well founded. This is because real-time communication over IP requires multiple factors to work together flawlessly to culminate in a rich end-user experience.

Faxing over IP can be less reliable than faxing over traditional telephony networks, which is a pretty big problem for any enterprise that relies heavily on fax for sending and receiving documentation. This skew in reliability is largely due to the fact that FoIP is highly sensitive to the slightest network impairment—even more so than audio and video—and often requires networks with a higher quality of service to work well from an end-to-end perspective to maintain an acceptable transmission success rate.

Note The ITU-T T.38 standard has made a big impact in faxing reliability due to its multiple layers of redundancy that can deal with higher levels of packet loss in a network. It also is supported by most vendors and providers for increased interoperability. T.38 is discussed in more detail later in this chapter.

Another huge hindrance to FoIP is the requirement for the method of faxing (discussed next) to largely remain the same end-to-end. While there are certain service provider and enterprise-grade SBCs that allow real-time conversion from one method of faxing to another, the delay incurred in this process could lead to transmission failures.

There are two methods by which fax data is transported over IP networks:

- Fax passthrough
- Fax relay

Before these methods of faxing are explored in detail, it is useful to first understand the concept of the voice call "switchover." The following section provides a brief explanation, along with a diagrammatic representation of the process.

Switchover of Voice Calls to Fax

While it is possible for calls to establish fax connections directly, most fax calls begin as voice calls and escalate, or switch over, to fax mode on detecting specific triggers. These triggers can vary depending on the method of faxing implemented across the IP network. For instance, the trigger to switch over to a fax call from a voice call can be the detection of a V.21 preamble or the detection of a specific tone, such as the ANSam tone.

The indication to switch over and set up a fax connection is either advertised using specific call control protocol messages or RTP packets with specialized payloads in the media stream. Switching over to fax using RTP packets is antiquated and often involves proprietary techniques. Therefore, the remainder of this chapter discusses only switchover methods involving call control protocols.

Switching over from voice to fax mode is often accompanied by several changes on devices along the transmission path, such as disabling echo cancelers, turning off silence suppression, and optimizing hardware and software on the fly to decode and encode fax data. All these changes are done to ensure that the transmission path is conducive to fax transmission and to minimize the possibility of transmission impairments.

Figure 10-14 shows the switchover process, in which the voice call escalates to a fax call on detection of a stimulus.

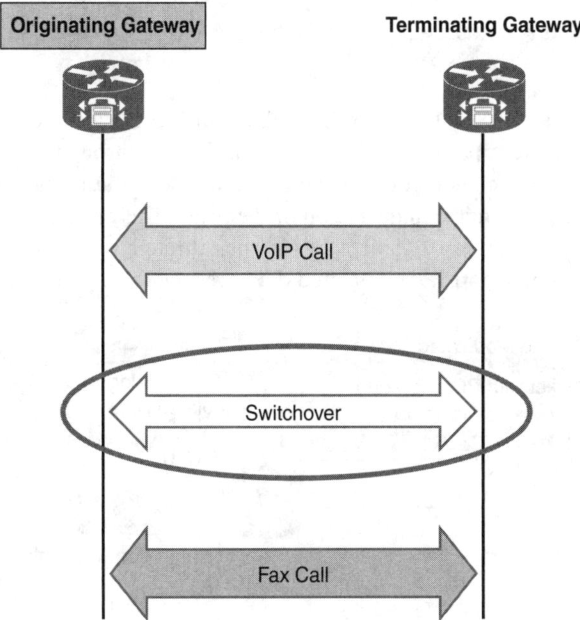

Figure 10-14 *Fax Switchover Process*

The following sections detail the operational aspects of fax passthrough and fax relay.

Fax Passthrough

Fax passthrough works on the principle of Voice Band Data (VBD), wherein certain audio codecs are used to transmit data payloads within RTP packets. The data payloads can include fax, modem, or text. From the perspective of a fax call, modulated fax data is encapsulated in standard RTP packets and transported over the IP network using the specified audio codec. VBD operation is governed by the ITU-T V.152 specification. The V.152 specification places certain restrictions on the way data can be transferred, including the following:

- The audio codec chosen must ensure that there is minimal distortion of data.
- Voice activity detection (VAD) and comfort noise generation must be disabled during VBD transfer.
- There must be appropriate use of echo cancelers along the data path to ensure reliable delivery of data.
- There must be uniform end-to-end latency to ensure fax data can be reliably reproduced at the receiving terminal.

> **Note** The terms *VBD* and *passthrough* are used and interpreted interchangeably.

The codec of choice for VBD data is often G711ulaw or G711alaw, but it could include codecs like G.723 and G.726, which are capable of reliably handling fax passthrough calls. In practice, an overwhelmingly large number of implementations use G.711 as the codec for fax passthrough. G711 ensures minimal distortion of data and helps ensure the most reliable transmission of fax data. Figure 10-15 depicts a fax passthrough scenario in which a codec like G.711 is used to transport fax-modulated data over the IP network.

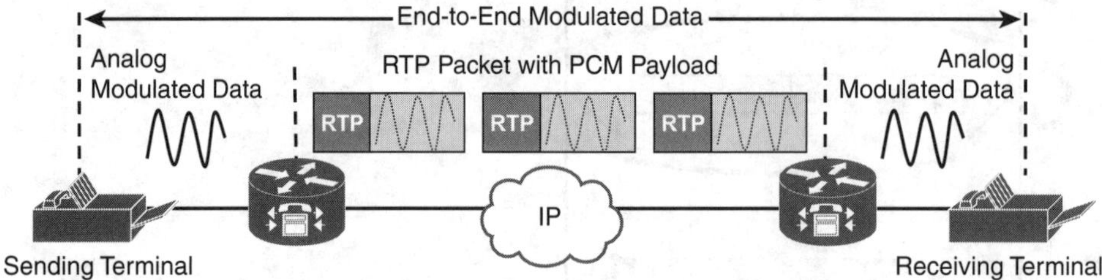

Figure 10-15 *Fax Passthrough*

High compression codecs like G.729 are not good candidates for fax passthrough because their encoding algorithms are designed to compress audio payloads and ultimately save network bandwidth. In addition, there are variants of G.729 that have built-in VAD, which adds an additional layer of unreliability to fax data transmission. VAD is a bandwidth-saving mechanism whereby RTP packets are not sent during periods of silence. VAD is known to cause signal clipping when used with fax passthrough, thus leading to loss of data and ultimately transmission failures. From the perspective of standard media gateways that interwork traditional digital/analog circuits and IP networks, several changes occur when handling a fax passthrough call, including the following:

- Codec up-speed to G.711ulaw/alaw (that is, forceful use of G.711ulaw/alaw for handling VBD or passthrough calls)
- Disabling of VAD and silence suppression
- Making the dejitter buffer static

Figure 10-16 depicts how a typical voice gateway switches over to fax mode and undergoes a codec up-speed to G.711ulaw.

SBCs tend to handle fax passthrough calls very differently than do voice gateways because they defer all switching-related decisions to the fax terminals on either end and never initiate fax switchover. They function as media relays passing across RTP packets (encoded with fax data) from one call leg to another, without any modifications to the payloads. To enhance the chance of transmission success, SBCs tend to disable VAD for fax passthrough calls.

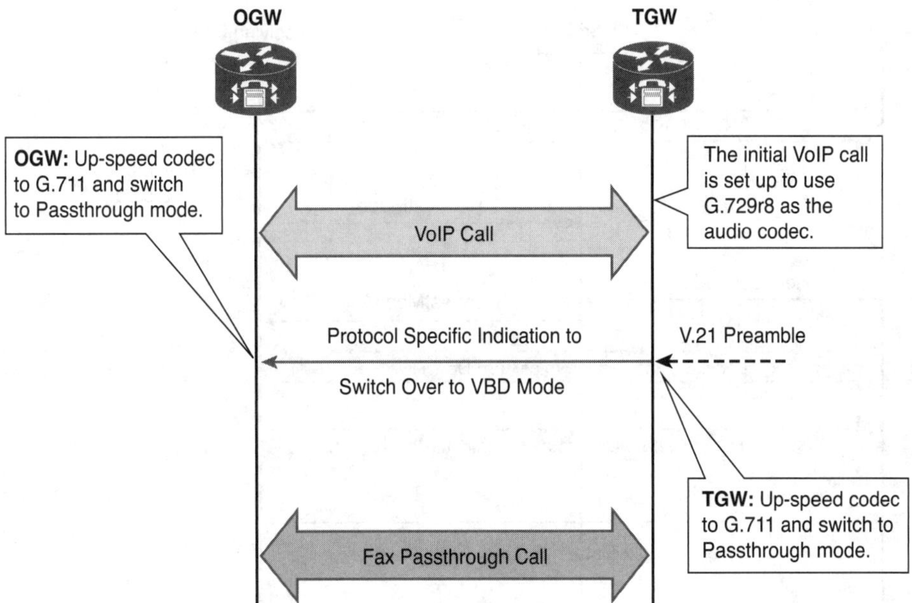

Figure 10-16 *Voice Gateway Switchover and Up-Speed*

The following subsections discuss how the call control protocols commonly deployed on SBCs (SIP and H.323) are used to indicate the transition from voice call mode to VBD mode.

Fax Passthrough over H.323

When an H.323 call is set up across an SBC, the transition to fax passthrough is initiated when one of the voice gateways detects a V.21 preamble and sends over an H.245 requestMode message. The SBC ensures that this message is propagated to the peer gateway to facilitate an end-to-end transition to fax passthrough. If the transition to fax passthrough is acceptable by the peer gateway, it sends over a requestModeAck message to the SBC. The SBC then sends the requestModeAck message to the gateway device that initiated the fax connection.

> **Note** The term *voice gateway* in this section and subsequent sections could refer to an actual voice gateway or more generically to a fax terminal like an analog telephony adapter (ATA) or fax server.

Next, the existing voice channels are torn down (remember that fax calls start out as voice calls and then "escalate" to fax), and new ones are set up for fax passthrough transmission. The logical channels set up for fax would end up using a codec that is optimized for fax passthrough transmission, which in most cases is G711. Figure 10-17 depicts the fax passthrough process with H.323.

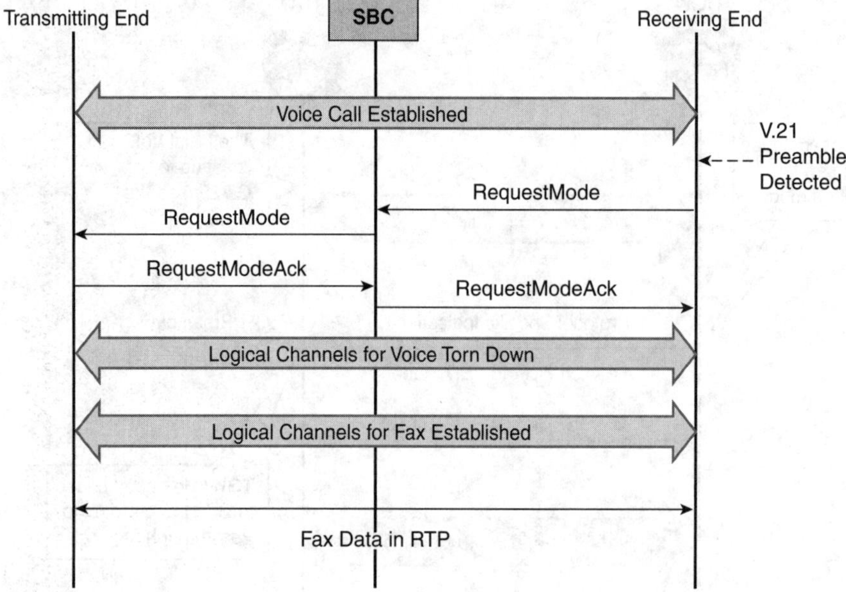

Figure 10-17 *Fax Passthrough Switchover with H.323*

For fax passthrough calls, the SBC also ensures that VAD and silence suppression are disabled. While switching over to fax passthrough, it is important to bring down the existing voice channels and set up new ones for fax transport because a voice call could have been set up to use a high-compression codec like G.729 that severely impedes fax data transmission over RTP. Notice in Figure 10-17 that once the logical channels for fax are set up, fax-modulated data is encoded within standard RTP packets and exchanged to and from the SBC. The SBC does not manipulate the RTP packet payloads in any way; rather, it just changes the IP and transport layer (IP and UDP) headers before packets are sent from one terminal to another.

Fax Passthrough over SIP

When an SBC sets up a SIP session end-to-end, the transition to fax passthrough is initiated when one of the User agents detects a V.21 preamble and sends over a SIP re-INVITE. It is worth pointing out that SIP re-INVITEs are not exclusively used to transition voice calls to fax. They are also used for a myriad of other scenarios, including the following:

- Determining session freshness
- Placing a call on hold and resuming a held call
- Changing the media characteristics of calls, such as adding a media stream, changing the media codec, or changing the media type of a call

A SIP re-INVITE used for each of the scenarios described here has a distinct signature in terms of SIP and SDP message formatting. For example, to place a call on hold, the

SDP of the re-INVITE has the connection and media direction lines set to **c=0.0.0.0** and **a=inactive**, respectively. To ensure that devices like SBCs can discern SIP re-INVITEs for fax passthrough, the SDP bodies of such re-INVITEs have typical signatures as well. A SIP re-INVITE for fax passthrough usually includes the following:

- An audio codec list that is restricted to G.711
- The presence of the **silenceSupp** attribute

Example 10-1 provides a SIP re-INVITE message snippet that is sent to set up a passthrough fax connection.

Example 10-1 **debug ccsip messages** *Snippet for Fax Passthrough Switchover*

```
INVITE sip:6473230@192.0.2.1:5060;transport=tcp SIP/2.0
Via: SIP/2.0/TCP 192.0.2.2:5060;branch=z9hG4bK3B5DCE8B
From: <sip:550956@192.0.2.2>;tag=B3DF27E8-1CDB
To: "Alice" <sip:6473230@192.0.2.1>;tag=29201101~f0b14648-6a7f-4e83-9266-
  40281d5627f6-191705821
Date: Wed, 16 Nov 2016 08:31:01 GMT
Call-ID: fabf0b80-82c1193c-ae256e-cf09640a@192.0.2.2

///Truncated for brevity///

Supported: timer,resource-priority,replaces,sdp-anat
User-Agent: Cisco-SIPGateway/IOS-15.4.3.M4
Allow: INVITE, OPTIONS, BYE, CANCEL, ACK, PRACK, UPDATE, REFER, NOTIFY, REGISTER
CSeq: 103 INVITE
Content-Type: application/sdp
Content-Length: 194

v=0
o=CiscoSystemsSIP-GW-UserAgent 2771 2656 IN IP4 192.0.2.1
s=SIP Call
c=IN IP4 192.0.2.2
t=0 0
m=audio 20368 RTP/AVP 0
c=IN IP4 192.0.2.2
a=rtpmap:0 PCMU/8000
a=sendrecv
a=silenceSupp:off - - - -
```

The codec list in Example 10-1 is restricted to G.711ulaw (though it could be G.711alaw as well). This codec selection is accompanied by the presence of the **silenceSupp** attribute, which indicates whether silence suppression needs to be enabled or disabled. For fax passthrough calls, to ensure the highest probability of transmission success, silence suppression needs to be disabled. For this reason, SIP re-INVITEs sent with the intention of establishing a fax passthrough connection always have **silenceSupp** set to **off**.

Just as with H.323, the SIP re-INVITE that indicates an attempt to set up a passthrough fax connection has to be sent by an SBC to the peer user agent. If the attempt is acceptable, the peer user agent answers with a SIP 200 OK response, with G711 as the codec to transport fax-modulated data and the **silenceSupp** attribute set to **off**. The SBC then sends the 200 OK to the initiating user agent, which results in the establishment of a fax connection. Figure 10-18 illustrates a fax passthrough switchover using SIP.

Note Unlike with H.323, there is no tearing down and reestablishment of logical channels in SIP.

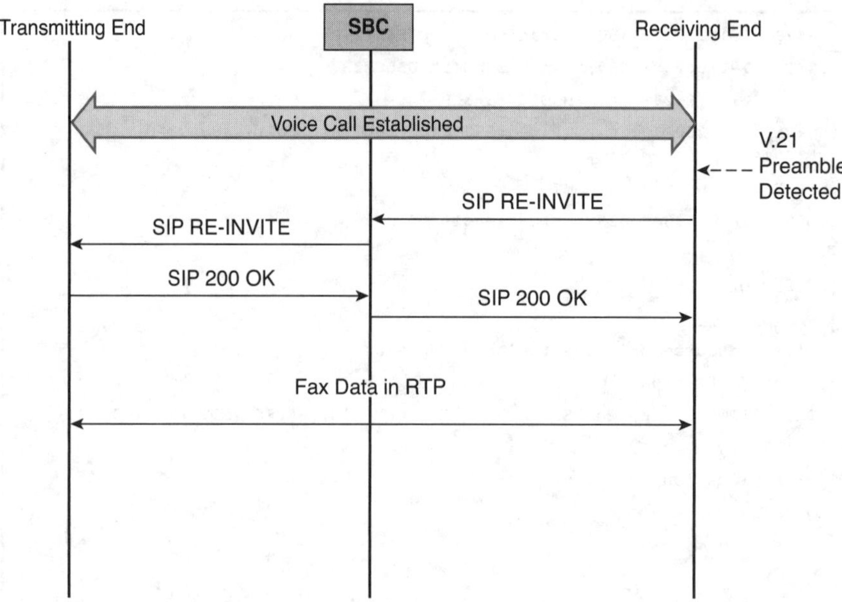

Figure 10-18 *Fax Passthrough Switchover Using SIP*

Although fax passthrough seems like a very simplified way of transporting fax-modulated data, it can be quite unreliable because the fax session is more or less viewed as a standard G.711 voice stream from the network perspective and is subject to impairments such as packet drops, jitter, and latency. While, these same impairments affect voice calls as well, with voice calls, mechanisms such as interpolation, gap fill, and silence fill minimize the effects of these impairments. Fax is data, however, and voice mechanisms do not apply.

In addition, fax passthrough does not have any native resiliency mechanism, such as the redundancy available in fax relay. General redundancy mechanisms that are applied to an RTP stream may be applied to fax passthrough calls (RFC 2198), but end-to-end support for these schemes across vendors and service providers is extremely rare.

Fax Relay

Fax relay involves the conversion of analog-modulated fax data into binary information for transport over the IP network toward the destination terminal, where the binary data is re-converted to analog-modulated fax data and played out to the fax machine. Figure 10-19 depicts the fax relay process between two voice gateways that have directly connected fax machines.

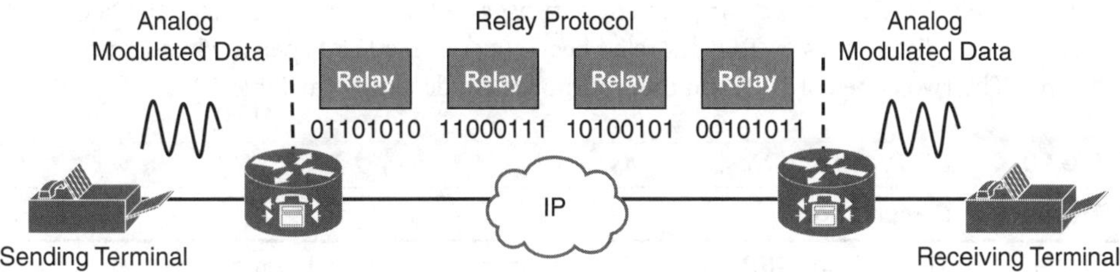

Figure 10-19 *Fax Relay over IP*

Fax relay, standardized in the ITU-T T.38 recommendation, is the most widely adopted mechanism for fax transmission over IP networks. T.38 allows for the transportation of fax over TCP, UDP, or RTP, with UDP being the most commonly used and preferred transport medium. Figure 10-20 diagrams the packet format used for T.38 fax relay over UDP. When transporting fax relay data over UDP, the UDP payload is fragmented into a UDP transport layer (UDPTL) header and payload. The UDPTL header is a 2-byte header that assists in the sequencing and ordering of information carried in the UDPTL payload. The UDPTL payload encapsulates Internet fax packets (IFPs) that are in turn used to transport T.30 messaging and fax pages.

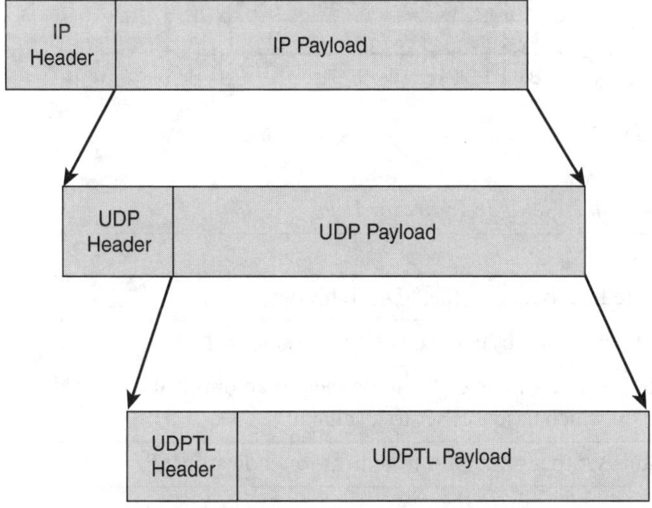

Figure 10-20 *UDPTL Packet Format*

> **Note** In addition to containing IFPs, the UDPTL payloads might also contain Forward Error Correction (FEC) information for a certain number of previously transmitted packets or might contain redundant representations of a certain number of previously transmitted packets. These methods serve as means for the receiver to detect errors and/or recover information that might have been lost or damaged during transit.

Two types of IFPs are used for different purposes and in different stages of the fax call, and further discussions of T.38 fax relay heavily use these IFP types to elucidate concepts. The two types of IFPs and their purposes are described in Table 10-4.

Table 10-4 *IFP Types and Descriptions*

IFP Type	Description
Indicator	The indicator IFP is used to transmit the CNG and CED tone indication, along with trainings for different modulations.
Data	The data IFP is used for T.30 HDLC message framing and transportation of fax pages.

The indicator IFP is 4 bytes in length and has the format depicted in Figure 10-21. The first 2 bytes that form the sequence number become the UDPTL header, which leaves 2 bytes for coding IFP-specific data. Table 10-5 describes the various fields in the indicator IFP.

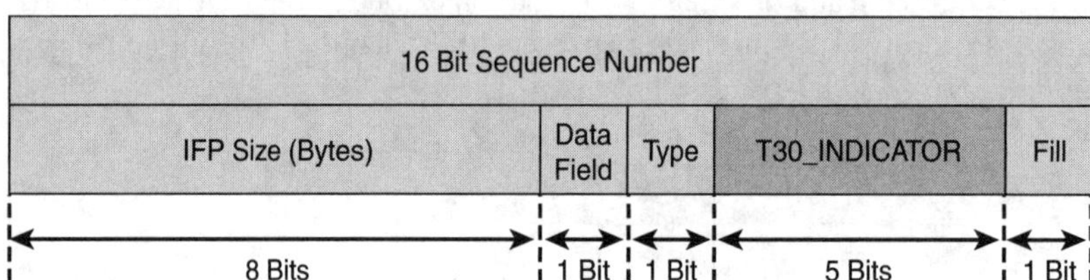

Figure 10-21 *Indicator IFP Format*

Table 10-5 *Description of Various Fields in Indicator IFPs*

Field	Description
Sequence Number	This 2-byte field becomes the UDPTL header.
IFP Size (bytes)	This field, which is 1 byte long, is set to a value of 1.
Data	This field is set to a value of 0, unless there is an optional data field included, in which case it is set to a value of 1.
Type	This field is set to a value of 0 to indicate an indicator IFP.

Field	Description
T30_Indicator	This is a 5-bit field, and the bit sequence in this field is used to designate the purpose of this indicator IFP. Remember that indicator IFPs are used to transmit the CNG and CED tone indication, along with trainings for different modulations.*
Fill Bit	This field is set to 0.

* The bit patterns of this field are used to provide a specific indication to the receiver; for example, 0X01 and 0X02 are used to indicate the CNG and CED tones, respectively, whereas 0X07 is used to indicate V.29 9600 bps training. A full list of T30_Indicator values can be found in Table 3 of the ITU-T T.30 specification.

Note In many implementations, it is the V.21 preamble that triggers a switchover to fax mode. The CNG and CED tones precede the V.21 preamble and are usually exchanged over the RTP stream. Therefore, you may not see these carried by a T.38 IFP.

A data IFP is used for HDLC framing and transmission of fax pages. The format of the data IFP is illustrated in Figure 10-22. As with the indicator IFP, the 2-byte sequence number becomes the UDPTL header. The following 2 bytes are similar to those of an indicator IFP, with the only difference being the presence of the T30_Data Type field. The bit sequence in this field identifies the modulation by which the data in ***Field-Type*** is transmitted. Table 10-6 briefly describes the various fields that appear in a data IFP.

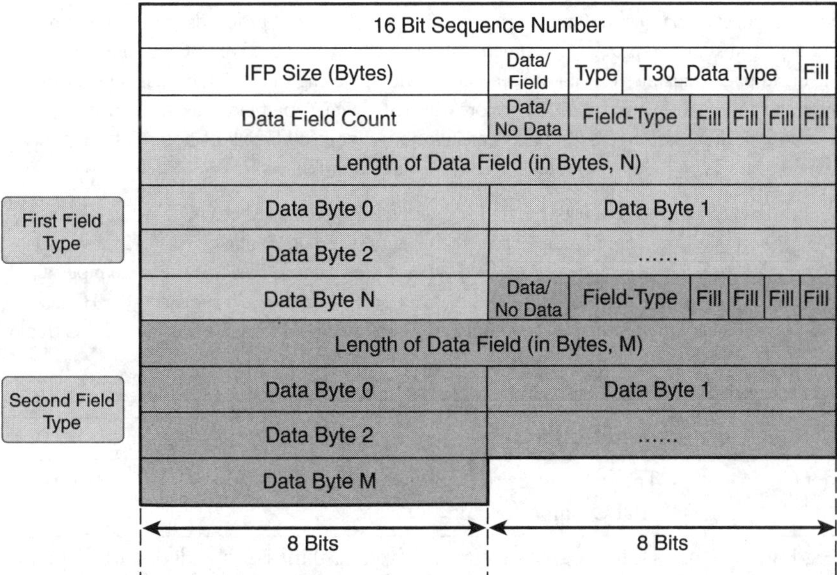

Figure 10-22 *Data IFP Format*

Table 10-6 *Description of Various Fields in Data IFPs*

Field	Description
Sequence Number	This 2-byte field becomes the UDPTL header.
IFP Size (bytes)	This is the cumulative length of all fields from the Data field to the last byte, M.
Type	This field is set to 1 for a data IFP.
T30_Data Type	The bit sequences in this field are used to specify different modulations with which the data in this IFP is transmitted.*
Fill	This bit is set to 0.
Data Field Count	This bit specifies the number of data fields that are present within an IFP. There could be a single data field or there could be multiple data fields.**
Data/No Data	This bit is set to 1 to indicate that the current data field has data and is set to 0 otherwise.
Field-Type	This is a 3-bit field whose bit sequences describe the HDLC or the T.4 characteristics of the data carried in this field type. Table 10-7 describes the different values this field can take.
4 Fill Bits	The bit values are set to 0.
Length of Data	This field is used to signify the length of data bytes for a given field type, when applicable.

* As mentioned earlier in this chapter, T.30 messaging is V.21 modulated and proceeds at 300 bps, whereas the TCF and fax page transmission proceeds at much faster rates, based on the DIS/DCS exchange. For example, the TCF and page transmission can proceed at 14,400 bps using the V.17 modulation if both machines support this modulation and speed. Therefore, the T30_Data Type field is used to encode the modulation of various T.30 messages and T.4 page transmissions. For a full listing of potential values enumerated by the T30_Data Type field, see Table 4 of the T.38 specification.

** The T.38 specification recommends the use of data IFPs with small payloads to ensure that the packets don't overrun the network MTU and are not subject to fragmentation and unreliable delivery. However, as per the specification, it is possible to include several field types within a single DATA IFP. For example, a complete T.30 message (along with data bytes, if applicable) can be sent in one field type, and the HDLC-FCS-Ok-Sig-End field type can be used in the second field type to indicate the end of the T.30 HDLC frame.

Table 10-7 *Description of the Various Field-Type Values*

Value	Description
0X0 HDLC data	The data bytes that follow encode a portion of or the entire HDLC frame for fax.
0X1 HDLC-Sig-End	HDLC signaling for the given T.30 message ended, and there are no more data bytes to follow for this field type.
0X2 HDLC-FCS-OK	Indicates the end of the HDLC frame and correct FCS; there are no more data bytes for this field type.

Value	Description
0X3 HDLC-FCS-BAD	Indicates the end of the HDLC frame and that the FCS is bad; there are no more data bytes for this field type.
0X4 HDLC-FCS-OK-Sig-End	This field type is used to combine the interpretation of the HDLC-FCS-OK and HDLC-Sig-End messages.
0X5 HDLC-FCS-BAD-Sig-End	This field type combines the interpretation of the HDLC-FCS-BAD and the HDLC-Sig-End messages.
0X6 T.4-Non-ECM	This field type indicates T.4 image data; additional data bytes will follow. This is not used for TCF or ECM data.
0X7 T.4-Non-ECM-Sig-End	This field type is used to signify the end of T.4 data.

To fully understand how data and indicator IFPs are used in fax relay over IP networks, an entire fax call is diagrammed in Figure 10-23, such that the T.30 messages/T.4 pages are interpreted from the perspective of data and indicator IFPs.

You should be able to clearly see how T.30 fax messages and fax page data are communicated using T.38 in Figure 10-23. To make sure this communication is clearly understood, let's take a closer look at this call step-by-step:

1. The fax calls begin with the answering terminal going off-hook and sending repeated V.21 flag sequences that are converted to a T.38 indicator IFP over the IP relay network. The bit pattern in the T.30 Indicator field is set to indicate the ITU-T V.21 preamble.
2. The answering terminal sends over a DIS message (note that CSI and NSF are optional) such that on the IP leg, the DIS message is encoded as a data IFP (or several data IFPs). Some of the values encoded in the data IFP are as follows:
   - T30_DATA TYPE is a bit sequence indicating V.21 modulation.
   - Field-type is HDLC.
   - Data bytes carry various DIS parameters.
3. Once the DIS message transmission is complete, either the same data IFP with a different field type or another data IFP is sent such that the T30_Data Type field is set to HDLC-FCS-OK-Sig-End.
4. Exactly the same process is followed when the transmitting terminal has to send the DCS response.
5. The next step is the transmission of the TCF. The T.38 specification provides two different ways of transmitting the TCF. The first method, known as Date Rate Management 1, only requires the appropriate indicator IFP to be sent to the peer terminal without the actual transmission of data (the continuous sequence of 0s to check line condition). The second method, known as Data Rate Management 2, requires the actual training data to be transmitted from one terminal to another. In this case, an indicator IFP is sent initially such that the T.30 Indicator field is set to the appropriate value (in this case, 14400 V.17 modulation long training). A data IFP

follows this, such that the field type is set to T.4-Non-ECM, and the data bytes are used to transport the continuous sequence of 0s.

6. A CFR from the receiving terminal is encoded as a data IFP, followed by the actual page transmission. Page transmission occurs through data IFPs with the appropriate field type values T.4-Non-ECM and T.4-Non-ECM-Sig-End when the transmission is complete.

7. The call moves to Phase E, with the exchange of the MCF from the receiver, which is a data IFP, followed by call termination after the transmission of the DCN (also through a data IFP).

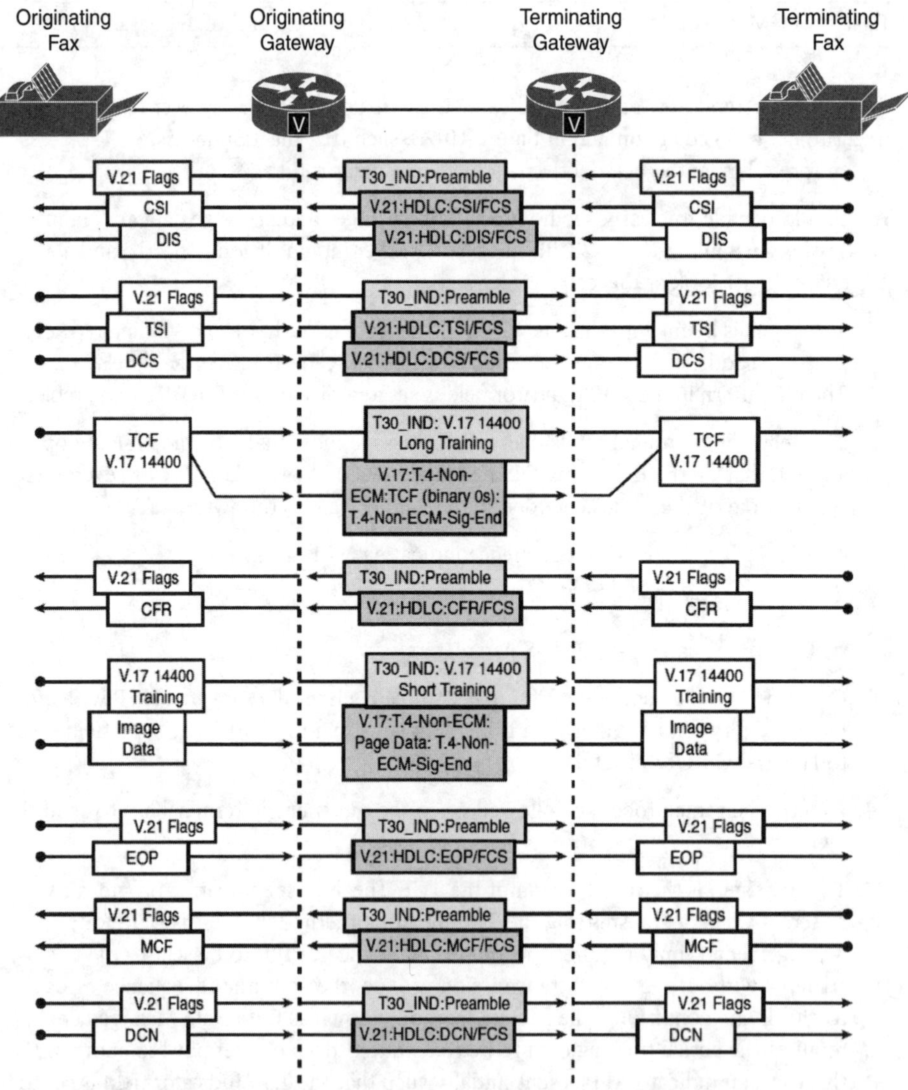

Figure 10-23 *Fax Call Flow Using T.38 Relay*

Note Whenever there is new information to be transmitted by a terminal, it is always preceded by a V.21 preamble encoded within an indicator IFP.

Note IFPs are sent over the same ports negotiated during call setup by using a protocol, such as SDP with SIP or H.245 with H.323.

T.38 over UDP is the most common method of transporting fax information over IP networks and suffers the same fate as many other data flows over UDP, such as drops, jitter, and latency. Given that fax is extremely sensitive to delay, it is mandatory to ensure timely and reliable delivery of fax data end-to-end. Unlike fax passthrough, which doesn't offer a whole lot in terms of reliable data transfer, fax relay has a built-in redundancy mechanism that is known to increase the probability of transmission success.

Redundancy provided for T.30 messaging and T.4 training/page transmission involves leveraging the sequence numbers of IFPs. Each UDPTL payload contains a primary IFP and optional redundant IFPs such that the sequence number of the primary becomes the sequence number of the UDPTL header. The sequence numbers of successive primary IFPs increase linearly, which assists the receiver in ordering IFPs correctly. If redundancy is used, a given UDPTL payload would include the primary IFP, followed by *n* prior IFPs with linearly decreasing sequence numbers.

To illustrate this concept, we can assume that the primary IFP sequence numbering began from 1 and the transmitter is currently transmitting a primary IFP with sequence number 10. If the depth of the redundancy is two (that is, two secondary IFPs), the first redundant IFP in the packet would be the IFP that had sequence number 9, and the second redundant IFP would be the IFP that had sequence number 8. This scenario is diagrammed in Figure 10-24.

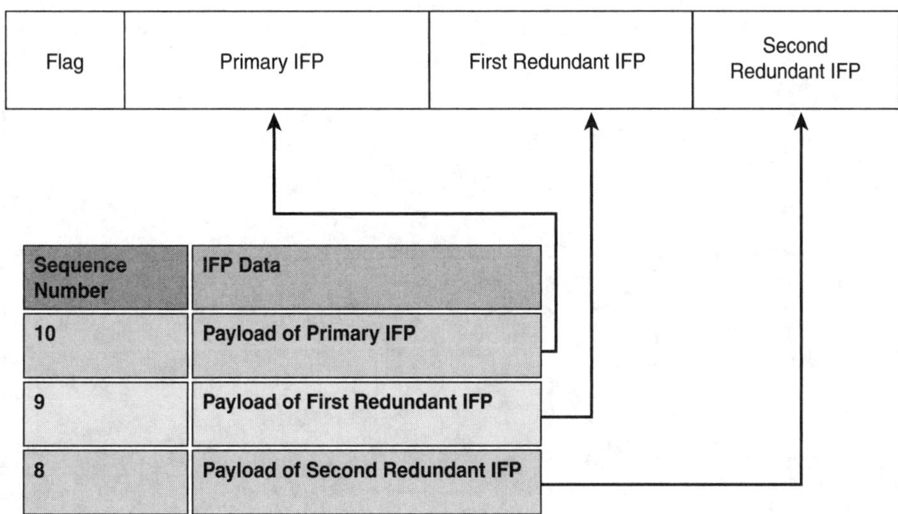

Figure 10-24 *T.38 Redundancy*

Note With this method of redundancy in place, it is not possible to send IFPs in a random manner. For example, if it is required to re-send IFP M, the transmitter must ensure that M-3, M-2, and M-1 are transmitted first.

Note If T.38 is encoded over RTP, redundancy mechanisms that are native to RTP such as Forward Error Correction (RFC 5109) and RFC 2198 are used.

Fax Relay over H.323

An H.323 terminal attempts to set up a fax call upon detecting a V.21 preamble by sending an H.245 requestMode message. Included in this message are various parameters for the T.38 session. If the T.38 connection attempt is acceptable to the receiving H.323 terminal, a requestModeAck message is transmitted. This is followed by the tearing down of logical channels set up for audio and setup of new logical channels for T.38 fax data transfer.

The requestMode message for T.38 is markedly different from the one for fax passthrough calls. To begin with, the dataType field is set to **data** as opposed to **audio**. In addition, a host of parameters are specific to T.38. Example 10-2 provides an H.245 requestMode message snippet.

Example 10-2 **debug h245 asn1** *Snippet of an H.323 requestMode Message*

```
H245 MSC INCOMING PDU ::=
value MultimediaSystemControlMessage ::= request : requestMode :
    {
      sequenceNumber 1
      requestedModes
      {
        {
          {
            type dataMode :
            {
              application t38fax :
              {
                t38FaxProtocol udp : NULL
                t38FaxProfile
```

```
            {
              fillBitRemoval FALSE
              transcodingJBIG FALSE
              transcodingMMR FALSE
              version 0
              t38FaxRateManagement transferredTCF :NULL
              t38FaxUdpOptions
              {
                t38FaxMaxBuffer 200
                t38FaxMaxDatagram 72
                t38FaxUdpEC t38UDPRedundancy : NULL
              }
            }
          }
          bitRate 144
        }
      }
    }
  }
}
```

The interpretation of all the different T.38 parameters in an H.245 requestMode message like **t38FaxMaxBuffer**, **t38FaxMaxDatagram**, and so on, is the same as specified in Table 10-8, later in this chapter.

As with T.38 calls with SIP, it is of paramount importance for the receiving gateway to ensure that the audio channels are muted while a T.38 connection is being set up.

Fax Relay over SIP

When one of the SIP user agents detects a V.21 preamble, a SIP re-INVITE is sent in an attempt to set up a fax connection. The SIP re-INVITE used for T.38 relay is in stark contrast to what is found when a fax passthrough connection is attempted. An example of a fax re-INVITE is provided in Example 10-3, followed by an explanation of the various T.38 parameters that can be a part of the SIP re-INVITE.

Example 10-3 debug ccsip messages *Snippet of a User Agent Attempting to Establish a T.38 Fax Connection*

```
INVITE sip:2222@192.0.2.1:5060 SIP/2.0
Via: SIP/2.0/UDP 192.0.2.2:5060;branch=z9hG4bK187AF
Remote-Party-ID: <sip:1111@192.0.2.2>;party=calling;screen=no;privacy=off
From: <sip:1111@192.0.2.2>;tag=2EA711B0-26D2
To: <sip:2222@192.0.2.1>;tag=A09D9F8-1567
Date: Sun, 05 Feb 2017 06:10:22 GMT
Call-ID: A27C9717-EA9B11E6-80F9EADB-AE8C6AF7@10.106.124.61
!!!
!!!Omitted for brevity
!!!
!!!
Content-Type: application/sdp
Content-Length: 321

v=0
o=CiscoSystemsSIP-GW-UserAgent 1192 1630 IN IP4 192.0.2.2
s=SIP Call
c=IN IP4 192.0.2.2
t=0 0
m=image 16480 udptl t38
c=IN IP4 10.127.239.67
a=T38FaxVersion:0
a=T38MaxBitRate:14400
a=T38FaxRateManagement:transferredTCF
a=T38FaxMaxBuffer:200
a=T38FaxMaxDatagram:320
a=T38FaxUdpEC:t38UDPRedundancy
```

The various media content types in SDP (for example, m=audio, m=video) are used to advertise and negotiate various media types for a communication session. As far as T.38 fax calls are concerned, the media type advertised and negotiated is the m=image media type. In addition to the image media type, several T.38 attributes can be included in the SDP bodies of SIP requests and responses. These attributes describe in detail the various characteristics of the impending fax call. Table 10-8 describes the various T.38 attributes that could appear in the SDP bodies of SIP requests or responses.

Table 10-8 *T.38 Attributes Used in the SDP Offer/Answer Exchange*

Name	SDP Syntax	Meaning	Optional/ Mandatory Attribute	Default Value
Version	**T38FaxVersion**	This attribute specifies the T.38 version number and indirectly specifies whether support for SG3 is present. If it is absent, the default value is used. This parameter is negotiated.	Mandatory, but if absent, it has a default interpretation	**0**
Maximum Bitrate	**T38MaxBitRate**	This attribute indicates the maximum fax transmission rate supported by an endpoint. This parameter is declarative, and the answer can be independent of the offer. This parameter is not used to determine the actual transmission speed during page transfer. It simply states the maximum supported bit rate.	Mandatory, but if absent, it has a default interpretation	14,400 bps
Fill Bit Removal	**T38FaxFillBit Removal**	This attribute indicates whether fill bits can be added and inserted for non-ECM calls to save bandwidth. This parameter is negotiated.	Optional, but if absent, it has a default interpretation	**FALSE**

Name	SDP Syntax	Meaning	Optional/ Mandatory Attribute	Default Value
MMR Transcoding	**T38FaxTranscoding MMR**	This attribute indicates support to convert from/to MMR (a page encoding scheme) to/ from another encoding. This is negotiated.	Optional, but if absent, it has a default interpretation	FALSE
JBIG Transcoding	**T38FaxTranscoding JBIG**	This attribute indicates support to convert to/from JBIG (which is a compression standard) for bandwidth savings. This parameter is negotiated.	Optional, but if absent, it has a default interpretation	FALSE
Data Rate Management Method	**T38FaxRate Management**	Indicates whether the TCF is simply advertised in an indicator IFP or is physically transferred from the emitting terminal. This is declarative, and the answer must comply with the offer.	Mandatory, but if absent, it has a default interpretation	**trans- ferredTCF** (This means the TCF is physically transferred from emit- ting terminal to receiver.)
Maximum Buffer Size	**T38FaxMaxBuffer**	This attribute indi- cates the maximum number of octets that can be stored in the buffer of an endpoint before an overflow condition occurs. Each terminal has to consider the buffer size on its peer terminal and adjust its transmitting rate accordingly. This is a declarative parameter, and the answer can be independent of the offer.	Optional, but if absent, it has a default interpretation	1800 bytes in one second

Name	SDP Syntax	Meaning	Optional/ Mandatory Attribute	Default Value
Maximum Datagram Size	**T38FaxMax Datagram**	This attribute indicates the maximum datagram size that can be accepted by an endpoint. This is declarative, and the answer can be independent of the offer. This is the combined size of the UDPTL header and payload.	Optional, but if absent, it has a default interpretation	150 bytes
Maximum IFP Size	**T38FaxMaxIFP**	This attribute indicates the maximum IFP size that can be handled by an endpoint. This is declarative, and the answer is independent of the offer.	Optional, but if absent, it has a default interpretation	40 bytes with a maximum redundancy level of 3
Error Correction	T38FaxUdpEC	Indicates the error correction scheme in place; valid values include "t38UDPFEC", "t38UDPRedundancy", "t38UDPNoEC". This is a negotiation, if the answerer supports what is offered, it indicates this in the answer. If not, this parameter is not present.	Optional, but if absent, it has a default interpretation	**t38UDPRedundancy**

Name	SDP Syntax	Meaning	Optional/ Mandatory Attribute	Default Value
Error Correction Depth	**T38FaxUdpEC Depth**	If the parameter is specified, then the **minred** value indicates that the offering endpoint wishes to receive at least that many redundancy frames per UDPTL datagram (when the answering endpoint chooses to use **t38UDP Redundancy** as the error correction mode), or that the offering endpoint wishes to receive at least that many FEC frames per UDPTL datagram (when the answering end-point chooses to use **t38UDPFEC** as the error correction mode). If **maxred** is specified, it indicates that the offering endpoint wishes to receive no more than that many redundancy frames or FEC frames per UDPTL datagram.	Optional, but if absent, it has a default interpretation	**1** for **minred** and **3** for **maxred**

Assuming that the T.38 fax connection is accepted, the answerer sends over a SIP 200 OK response with the required T.38 attributes, as depicted in Table 10-8. The m=image media type has to be included in the answer with a valid port number. A port number of 0 would indicate that the answerer is rejecting the T.38 connection.

T.38 over UDP makes use of IFPs encapsulated in UDPTL datagrams for the transport of fax messaging and data. It is imperative that the receiving gateway that is connected to the terminating fax machine mute the audio channel toward the originating gateway and the actual fax machine that is directly connected to it. Failure to do so can lead to fax-modulated data leaking into the audio stream, resulting in the terminals starting a T.30 exchange long before the T.38 fax connection has been established.

SBC Handling of FoIP

With migration to SIP trunking being in full force in enterprise and service provider networks, there are still a few technologies like fax that require special considerations. With SBCs being placed as transit devices between multimedia networks, there is often a need to optimize their configuration and functionality to reliably handle fax communication and play their part in ensuring transmission success.

Several considerations need to be taken into account while deploying SBCs that are expected to handle fax transmission. As discussed in the following sections, the main considerations include the following:

- Uniform fax handling
- QoS implementation
- Protocol mismatch handling

Uniform Fax Handling

All fax-aware devices along the IP path (including voice gateways, SBCs, and fax servers) must be able to handle the transition from voice to fax and, consequently, fax data transfer over IP in exactly the same manner. For example, in the network topology diagrammed in Figure 10-25, the fax server, SBC, and voice gateway must handle the transition from voice to fax and consequently the fax data transfer in the same way.

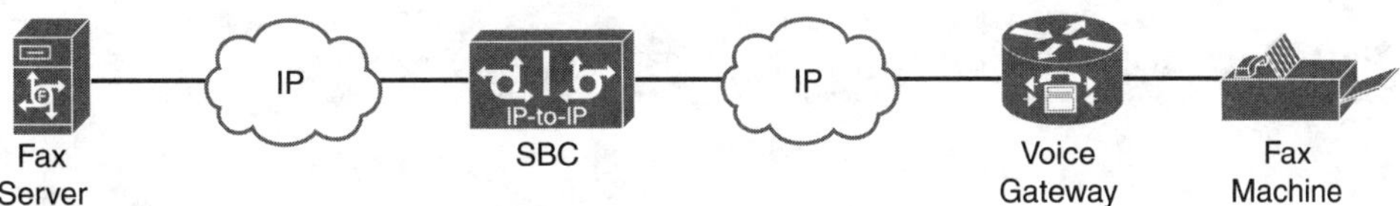

Figure 10-25 *Sample Fax Topology*

Assuming that the fax server initiates switchover from voice to fax using standards-based T.38, it is imperative that the SBC and voice gateway also support T.38 for fax transmission. If either the SBC or the voice gateway fails to support T.38, the call will most likely fail when the fax server attempts to switch over to fax.

Non-uniform fax handling end-to-end over the IP network is one of the greatest impediments to successful fax transmission and is one of the reasons fax infrastructures over IP require a lot of troubleshooting and testing before they can provide reliable fax data delivery. There are certain service provider and enterprise-grade SBCs that offset this problem by providing real-time translation between fax relay and passthrough. This transcoding almost always occurs between G.711 and T.38 because certain devices support only one fax transmission method or another. Consider the example depicted in Figure 10-26, which shows SBC peers with two enterprise networks that use different methods of faxing.

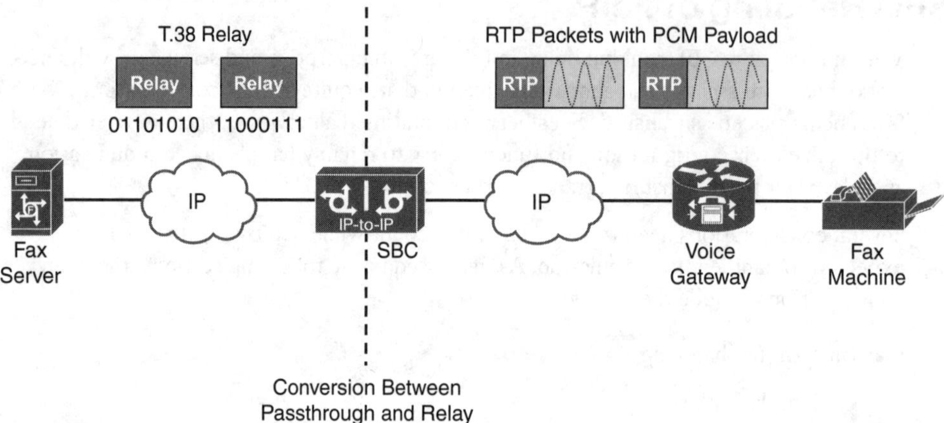

Figure 10-26 *Fax Translation in Real Time*

In addition to translating the protocol signaling in real time by adding T.38 or passthrough parameters when applicable, the SBC has to also convert modulated fax data encapsulated in RTP packets to IFPs and vice versa. To achieve this real-time translation of modulated data, a DSP is usually inserted into the call until completion. While this is an extremely useful utility provided by some SBCs, there still exist very real chances of transmission failures because of the additional complexities involved with inserting a DSP into the call path and the delay incurred while performing this translation.

Note CUBE does not support translation of fax relay and fax passthrough.

QoS Implementation

The application of QoS to ensure the preferential treatment of real-time traffic classes such as voice and video is a familiar method to ensure timely and reliable traffic transmission that is free from latency, packet drops, and jitter. The effects of packet drops, jitter, and latency can be offset to an extent for voice and video streams by prediction algorithms that are either native to software or the media codec. Unfortunately, this is simply not the case for fax because these types of algorithms are not possible with data. Therefore, a well-designed QoS scheme is highly important. In addition, SBCs are likely to be deployed to peer with different multimedia networks over WAN or MPLS networks. An improperly configured QoS policy can lead to impairments and, ultimately, fax failures.

More often than not, the QoS policies applied to service voice and video traffic classes suffice for fax as well. However, care must be taken to ensure that QoS is not simply restricted to RTP traffic. While voice and video traffic typically utilize RTP, T.38 fax relay does not. As mentioned previously, T.38 implements UDPTL instead of RTP. Therefore, voice and video QoS policies that exclusively prioritize RTP will not match T.38 traffic, and your fax data may not receive the QoS necessary for reliable fax transmissions. You should also ensure that call signaling traverses the network in a timely manner as any delays in completing a SIP transaction or a H.323 negotiation could lead to fax timers expiring, which would minimize the success of transmission.

Protocol Mismatch Handling

Coming across a protocol implementation that works differently across vendors is not uncommon because standards are largely open to interpretation and do not account for every single scenario encountered in real-world implementations. For example, it is quite possible to have two networks handle the switchover to T.38 in completely different ways or to have different interpretations of the T.38 attributes advertised and negotiated over SDP.

This break in standards interpretation can often lead to fax failures. With SBCs having several options in software and configuration at their disposal to effectively bridge this gap, fax sessions that traverse an SBC have a much better chance of success. SIP and SDP normalization is heavily used in SBCs as a means of getting rid of these protocol mismatches and improving fax transmission success rates.

FoIP on CUBE

Fax relay and passthrough are the two principal methods of fax transmission over IP, and each of these methods has several variants. Many of the variants of passthrough and relay are vendor proprietary and don't work seamlessly for all possible scenarios. For example, Cisco's proprietary NSE-based fax passthrough uses named signaling events (NSE) to switch over a call to fax mode. When this method is used with third-party devices, the NSE packets are simply ignored, and all the software/hardware optimizations required to handle fax calls don't occur, leading to almost certain call failure.

When faxing has to extend beyond an enterprise over IP, the best alternative is to use methods that have been standardized and are widely deployed due to overwhelming industry consensus over the years. Protocol-based fax passthrough and relay are standardized by the ITU-T and are the most widely adopted methods due to their ability to work seamlessly across vendors and device types. The following sections provide a detailed description of how fax passthrough and fax relay work on CUBE, the required configuration, and some of the troubleshooting considerations available to diagnose fax failure.

Fax Passthrough on CUBE

A fax passthrough call contains fax-modulated data encapsulated within standard RTP packets and appears as a G.711 call from the network perspective. Fax passthrough calls have to proceed with VAD and silence suppression disabled to ensure that none of the fax signals are clipped and to maximize the chance of transmission success.

Fax passthrough on CUBE is handled using the same principles and procedures outlined in the section "Fax Passthrough," earlier in this chapter. Although it is possible to directly set up fax passthrough calls, CUBE only supports setting up fax passthrough calls over established voice calls (see the section "Switchover of Voice Calls to Fax," earlier in this chapter). The following sections detail how fax passthrough calls are handled on CUBE, using H.323 and SIP.

Note Receiving the appropriate SIP re-INVITE or H.245 requestMode message does not guarantee that a call will switch over to fax passthrough mode. Switching from a voice call to a fax call is still a negotiation between participating endpoints, and this negotiation could fail, especially if one of the endpoints does not support fax passthrough. As an example, if a voice call is initially set up across CUBE and a SIP re-INVITE is received from one of the terminals to switch over to fax passthrough, the SBC can reject the re-INVITE with a **488 Media Unacceptable** if it is not configured to support fax passthrough. Every attempt to transition to fax passthrough over the signaling channel has to be acknowledged by either sending a SIP 200 OK or a H.245 requestModeAck.

Fax Passthrough over H.323

Figure 10-27 depicts an H.323-based fax passthrough call traversing CUBE. H.323-based fax passthrough calls on CUBE are handled using the same principles outlined in the section "Fax Passthrough," earlier in this chapter. The process works as follows:

1. On detecting a V.21 preamble, one of the H.323 terminals attempts to switch over by sending a H.245 requestMode message.
2. CUBE transmits the H.245 requestMode message to the peer H.323 terminal. If the peer H.323 terminal accepts the attempt to establish a fax passthrough call, it transmits a H.245 requestModeAck message.
3. The H.245 requestModeAck message is sent to the terminal that attempted to initiate the fax passthrough connection. This is followed by tearing down existing voice channels and setting up new ones for fax. The newly established channels then transport fax data encapsulated within standard RTP packets.

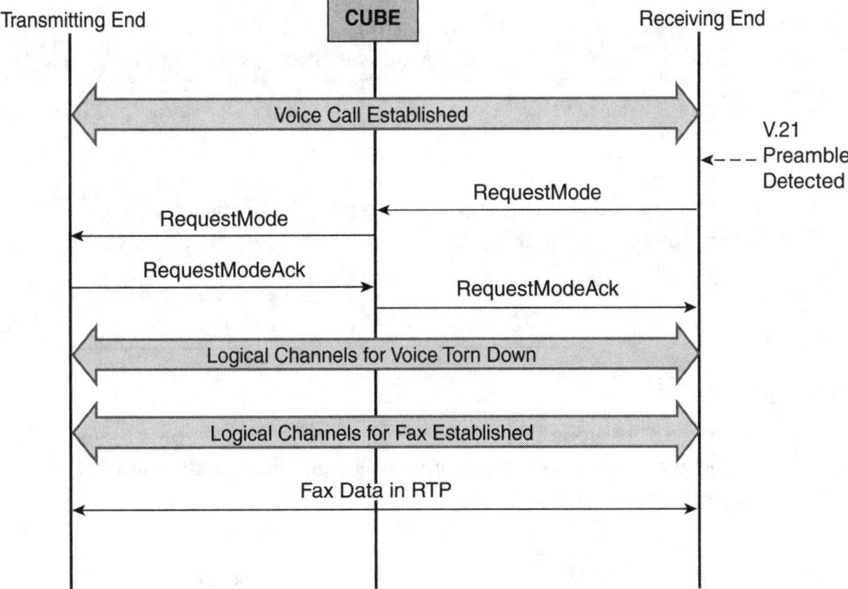

Figure 10-27 *CUBE Fax Passthrough Call over H.323*

Example 10-4 provides a snippet of the H.245 requestMode message when attempting to establish a fax passthrough call.

Example 10-4 **debug h245 asn1** *Snippet of a requestMode Message When Attempting to Switch over to Fax Passthrough*

```
Jan 1 16:00:17.191: H245 MSC INCOMING PDU ::=

value MultimediaSystemControlMessage ::= request : requestMode :
    {
      sequenceNumber 1
      requestedModes
      {


        {


          {
            type audioMode : g711Ulaw64k : NULL
          }
        }
      }
    }
```

Note The switchover to fax passthrough can fail if either the CUBE or the peer H.323 terminal (to which CUBE sends the H.245 requestMode message) is not configured to handle fax passthrough.

Note If CUBE is not configured to handle fax passthrough, it immediately sends a requestMode Reject message to the initiating terminal, without contacting the peer H.323 terminal.

Fax Passthrough over SIP

Figure 10-28 depicts a SIP-based fax passthrough call. A SIP-based fax passthrough call traversing CUBE follows the same operating principles highlighted in the section "Fax Passthrough," earlier in this chapter. The process works as follows :

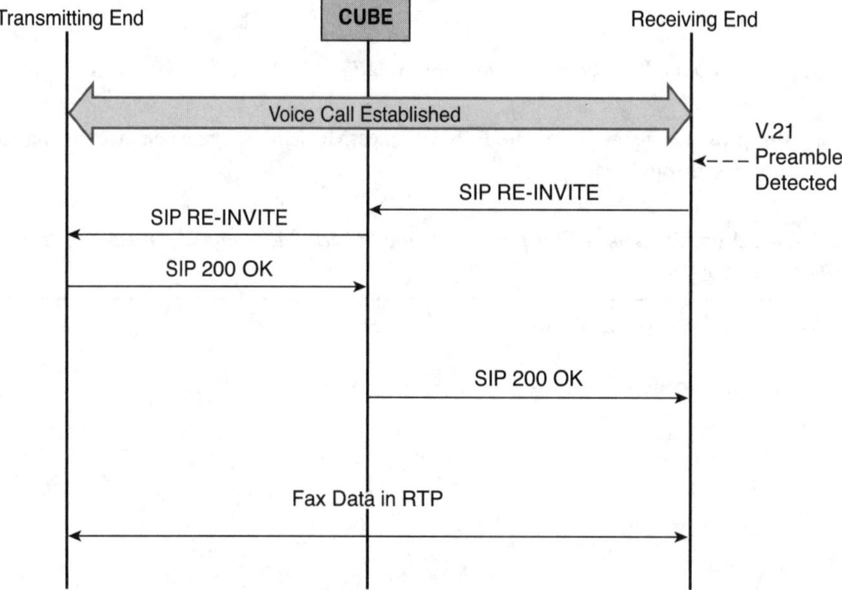

Figure 10-28 *CUBE Fax Passthrough Call over SIP*

1. On detecting a V.21 preamble, one of the SIP user agents attempts to switch over by sending a specially formatted SIP re-INVITE, like the one in Example 10-5.

2. CUBE transmits the SIP re-INVITE to the peer user agent. If the peer SIP user agent accepts the attempt to establish a fax passthrough call, it transmits a SIP 200 OK response.

3. The SIP 200 OK message is sent to the terminal that attempted to initiate the fax passthrough connection. Unlike with H.323, the existing audio channel is reused to transmit fax-encoded RTP packets.

Example 10-5 **debug ccsip messages** *Snippet for Fax Passthrough Switchover*

```
INVITE sip:6473230@192.0.2.1:5060;transport=tcp SIP/2.0
Via: SIP/2.0/TCP 192.0.2.2:5060;branch=z9hG4bK3B5DCE8B
From: <sip:550956@192.0.2.2>;tag=B3DF27E8-1CDB
To: "Alice" <sip:6473230@192.0.2.1>;tag=29201101~f0b14648-6a7f-4e83-9266-
  40281d5627f6-191705821
Date: Wed, 16 Nov 2016 08:31:01 GMT
Call-ID: fabf0b80-82c1193c-ae256e-cf09640a@192.0.2.2

///Truncated for brevity///

Supported: timer,resource-priority,replaces,sdp-anat
User-Agent: Cisco-SIPGateway/IOS-15.4.3.M4
Allow: INVITE, OPTIONS, BYE, CANCEL, ACK, PRACK, UPDATE, REFER, NOTIFY, REGISTER
CSeq: 103 INVITE
Content-Type: application/sdp
Content-Length: 194

v=0
o=CiscoSystemsSIP-GW-UserAgent 2771 2656 IN IP4 192.0.2.1
s=SIP Call
c=IN IP4 192.0.2.2
t=0 0
m=audio 20368 RTP/AVP 0
c=IN IP4 192.0.2.2
a=rtpmap:0 PCMU/8000
a=sendrecv
a=silenceSupp:off - - - -
```

Negotiating and setting up a fax passthrough call through any SBC, including CUBE, is an end-to-end exercise, and it is strongly advised that CUBE not be configured to block mid-call signaling (through the **midcall-signaling block** command). The **midcall-signaling passthru media-change** command is used to ensure that mid-call signaling is exchanged end-to-end only when there is a change in the media characteristics of an already established SIP session (such as a codec change or adding a video stream). This command could also cause fax passthrough calls to fail if the voice call was initially set up with G711ulaw/alaw, and the re-INVITE to transition to fax passthrough does not contain the **silenceSupp** attribute.

Certain vendors (typically of service provider soft switches) send fax passthrough like re-INVITEs (G711 advertisement of G.711 and disabling silence suppression) even for scenarios that have nothing to do with fax calls. This can lead to unexpected call behavior on CUBE, such as unexpected codec changes and sometimes even call failure.

Configuration of Fax Passthrough

Fax configuration can be applied on CUBE either at a global level or at the dial peer level and is done using the **fax protocol** command. The arguments to this command determine the method of faxing (relay or passthrough or both) supported on CUBE. The arguments to the **fax protocol** command in global configuration mode are specified in Table 10-9.

Table 10-9 *T.38 Arguments to the fax protocol Command in Global Configuration Mode*

Command	Argument	Meaning
fax protocol {none | pass-through {g711ulaw | g711alaw}}	**none**	All fax handling is disabled, and passthrough calls are not supported.
	pass-through	Enables fax passthrough support, and further arguments specify if VBD data will be transported over G.711ulaw or G.711alaw.

Note The same command and arguments are used for both SIP and H.323 calls.

Example 10-6 provides a configuration snippet for enabling fax passthrough globally on CUBE. Unless overridden by dial peer configuration, this would apply to all calls traversing CUBE.

Example 10-6 *Configuration Snippet of Fax Passthrough in Global Configuration Mode*

```
voice service voip
 fax protocol pass-through g711ulaw
```

If you want to enable fax passthrough for only specific calls traversing CUBE (from or to specific destinations), a more granular approach is required, involving configuring fax passthrough on specific dial peers. Table 10-10 explains the different arguments for the **fax protocol** command in dial peer mode.

Table 10-10 *T.38 Arguments to the* **fax protocol** *Command in Dial-Peer Configuration Mode*

Command	Argument	Meaning
fax protocol {none | system | pass-through {g711ulaw | g711alaw}}	none	All fax handing is disabled, and fax passthrough calls are not supported.
	system	This argument indicates that the configuration specified in global mode must apply.
	pass-through	Enables fax passthrough support, and further arguments specify if VBD data will be transported over G.711ulaw or G.711alaw.

Note The same command and arguments are used for both SIP and H.323 calls.

Example 10-7 provides a configuration snippet for fax passthrough in dial peer mode. In some conditions, CUBE might have to peer with several H.323 terminals. These terminals may have non-overlapping capability sets in terms of faxing, such as a few terminals supporting only T.38 fax relay and the others supporting fax passthrough. To segregate call characteristics such as DTMF relay, faxing, and codec classes on a per-session basis, different dial peers can be configured with different capability sets.

Example 10-7 *Configuration Snippet of Fax Passthrough in Dial Peer Configuration Mode for an H.323 Call*

```
dial-peer voice 1703 voip
 voice-class codec 10
 dtmf-relay h245-signal
 destination-pattern 4084343471
 fax protocol pass-through g711ulaw
 no vad


dial-peer voice 1803 voip
 voice-class codec 10
 dtmf-relay h245-signal
 incoming called-number 4084343471
 fax protocol pass-through g711ulaw
 no vad
```

> **Note** Adding **session protocol sipv2** transforms the dial peer to a SIP dial peer.

> **Note** When applied to the dial peer configuration mode, the incoming dial peer and the outgoing dial peer must be symmetric in terms of their ability to handle fax passthrough. If any one of the dial peers does not support fax passthrough, the call will fail.

Troubleshooting Fax Passthrough on CUBE

Troubleshooting fax passthrough calls can be a tricky proposition, depending on the stage at which the call failure is occurring. Troubleshooting typical voice call establishment failures is often trivial, as there are several debugs that can be used on CUBE to understand what needs to be fixed. Switchover failures, on the other hand, are a little more complex as there has to be a three-way check to confirm whether switchover is successful (on the initiator, CUBE, and the destination). The most difficult part of troubleshooting fax passthrough calls is when switchover is complete and there are issues with the T.30/T.4/T.6 exchange. This is because fax messaging and page transfer are encapsulated as raw modulated fax data within RTP packets, and it is impossible to discern fax information from RTP packet payloads.

While troubleshooting fax passthrough issues, the following generic approach may be used:

- **Verify the end-to-end fax configuration:** It is extremely important to ensure that the fax protocol is the same throughout the entire call flow. For example, consider the network topology depicted in Figure 10-29. The ATA 190 that has a directly connected fax machine is configured for T.38 fax relay only, while CUBE and the service provider handle the fax connection using passthrough. When either the ATA or the service provider attempts to switch over to fax, it will be unsuccessful because the method of faxing is not uniform throughout, leading to fax call failure.

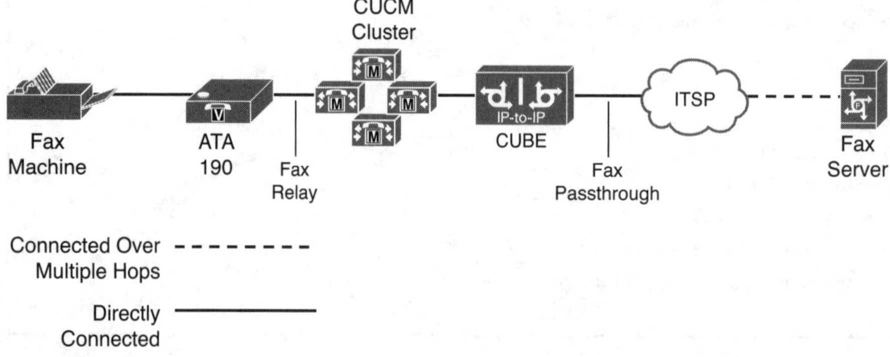

Figure 10-29 *Sample Network Topology for Fax*

While it is virtually impossible to verify how each device in the call flow is configured to handle faxing (remember that the service provider network might have several hops to the fax machine), it nonetheless is a very good practice to verify the configuration of each device on the enterprise network and ensure that the service provider supports it.

- **Voice call setup and codec restrictions:** Setting up fax calls directly over IP from the beginning is extremely rare. The norm with most vendors and devices is to first set up a voice call and then switch over to fax mode on detecting certain triggers. There are often instances where basic voice call setup fails due to misconfiguration, incorrect call routing, or other reasons. Once the configuration on devices like CUBE, call manger, fax servers, ATAs, analog gateways, and so on has been vetted, debugs or traces can be analyzed to further understand the reason for call failure.

  Since fax passthrough calls use G.711 to transport VBD data, it is essential to ensure that the choice of call codec remains dynamic and is not restricted either by bandwidth or configuration to use high-compression codecs. The configuration of regions and locations on CUCM can ensure that there is a logical restriction placed on the maximum bandwidth that is allocated for a call. By restricting fax passthrough calls to use high compression codecs, fax switchover to G.711 passthrough will fail.

- **Verify fax switchover:** On verifying the configuration and ensuring voice call setup success, the next logical step is to ensure that switchover to fax passthrough mode is successful. As mentioned earlier in this chapter, the switchover to fax passthrough can be verified by examining the call control protocol messages.

  For H.323-based calls through CUBE, the switchover to fax passthrough mode is completed by exchanging the requestMode/requestModeAck on each call leg of CUBE. Example 10-8 provides the expected message exchange when a call transitions from voice mode to fax passthrough mode. Given that CUBE has two call legs, this message sequence would have to be replicated across both call legs.

Example 10-8 **debug h245 asn1** *Snippet of Message Exchange While Transitioning to Fax Passthrough over H.323 (with Message Bodies Omitted for Brevity)*

```
021569: Feb  4 07:52:29.421: H245 MSC INCOMING PDU ::=value
  MultimediaSystemControlMessage ::= request : requestMode :


021602: Feb  4 07:52:29.421: H245 MSC OUTGOING PDU ::=
value MultimediaSystemControlMessage ::= response : requestModeAck :


021893: Feb  4 07:52:29.445: H245 MSC OUTGOING PDU ::=
value MultimediaSystemControlMessage ::= request : closeLogicalChannel :
```

```
021951: Feb  4 07:52:29.445: H245 MSC OUTGOING PDU ::=
value MultimediaSystemControlMessage ::= request : openLogicalChannel :

022011: Feb  4 07:52:29.453: H245 MSC INCOMING PDU ::=
value MultimediaSystemControlMessage ::= request : closeLogicalChannel :

022015: Feb  4 07:52:29.453: H245 MSC OUTGOING PDU ::=
value MultimediaSystemControlMessage ::= response : closeLogicalChannelAck

022104: Feb  4 07:52:29.457: H245 MSC INCOMING PDU ::=
value MultimediaSystemControlMessage ::= request : openLogicalChannel :

022182: Feb  4 07:52:29.465: H245 MSC INCOMING PDU ::=
value MultimediaSystemControlMessage ::= response : closeLogicalChannelAck :

022319: Feb  4 07:52:29.473: H245 MSC INCOMING PDU ::=
value MultimediaSystemControlMessage ::= response : openLogicalChannelAck :

022384: Feb  4 07:52:29.477: H245 MSC OUTGOING PDU ::=
value MultimediaSystemControlMessage ::= response : openLogicalChannelAck :
```

The key takeaway when analyzing the message exchange in Example 10-8 is that when the requestMode message is acknowledged, the logical channels that were in place for the voice call are torn down bidirectionally, and new logical channels are established for fax passthrough. This exchange is seen on both call legs of CUBE.

Note The order of messages after the requestMode message is acknowledged is terminal dependent and may vary. However, for a successful switchover to fax passthrough mode, the 10 messages highlighted in Example 10-8 ought to be exchanged on a per-call-leg basis.

For SIP-based calls traversing CUBE, the transition or switchover to fax passthrough completes with a re-INVITE/200 OK transaction on each call leg. As outlined earlier in this chapter, the re-INVITE to fax passthrough over SIP can be identified by the presence of a codec list that is restricted to G.711 and the presence of the **silenceSupp** attribute being set to **off**. Example 10-9 provides a **debug ccsip message** snippet of the re-INVITE/200 OK transaction that successfully transitions the call to fax passthrough mode.

Example 10-9 debug ccsip messages *Snippet of a Successful Transition to Fax Passthrough Mode over SIP*

```
INVITE sip:2222@192.0.2.1:5060 SIP/2.0
Via: SIP/2.0/UDP 192.0.2.2:5060;branch=z9hG4bK531305
Remote-Party-ID: <sip:1111@192.0.2.2>;party=calling;screen=no;privacy=off
From: <sip:1111@192.0.2.2>;tag=53BD3AC-1685
To: <sip:2222@192.0.2.1>;tag=53A7B00-628
Date: Sat, 04 Feb 2017 07:11:33 GMT
Call-ID: 5113703A-E9E911E6-815DDB64-68BBC9B8@10.127.239.66
!
!
! Omitted for brevity
!
Content-Type: application/sdp
Content-Length: 221

v=0
o=CiscoSystemsSIP-GW-UserAgent 7031 5812 IN IP4 192.0.2.2
s=SIP Call
c=IN IP4 192.0.2.2
t=0 0
m=audio 16512 RTP/AVP 0
c=IN IP4 10.106.124.61
a=rtpmap:0 PCMU/8000
a=ptime:20
a=silenceSupp:off - - - -


SIP/2.0 200 OK
Via: SIP/2.0/UDP 192.0.2.1:5060;branch=z9hG4bK531305
From: <sip:1111@192.0.2.2>;tag=53BD3AC-1685
To: <sip:2222@192.0.2.1>;tag=53A7B00-628
Date: Sat, 04 Feb 2017 08:18:37 GMT
Call-ID: 5113703A-E9E911E6-815DDB64-68BBC9B8@10.127.239.66
CSeq: 101 INVITE
!
!
! Omitted for brevity
!
Content-Type: application/sdp
```

```
Content-Length: 221

v=0
o=CiscoSystemsSIP-GW-UserAgent 4078 8993 IN IP4 192.0.2.1
s=SIP Call
c=IN IP4 192.0.2.1
t=0 0
m=audio 16456 RTP/AVP 0
c=IN IP4 10.127.239.66
a=rtpmap:0 PCMU/8000
a=ptime:20
a=silenceSupp:off - - - -
```

Another method of verifying whether the switchover has completed is to execute the **show call active voice brief** command in real time while the call is in progress. Example 10-10 demonstrates the output of the **show call active voice brief** command in two parts, the first being when the call is in voice mode and the second being when the call has transitioned to fax passthrough mode.

Example 10-10 *Output of the* **show call active voice brief** *Command Confirming Fax Passthrough Switchover*

```
Before Switchover:

133E : 71 87806830ms.1 (07:11:13.883 UTC Sat Feb 4 2017) +9260 pid:1111 Answer
  2222 connected
 !!! Omitted for brevity
 IP 10.127.239.66:16456 SRTP: off rtt:0ms pl:0/0ms lost:0/0/0 delay:0/0/0ms g729r8
  TextRelay: off Transcoded: No ICE: Off


133E : 72 87806850ms.1 (07:11:13.903 UTC Sat Feb 4 2017) +9230 pid:1111 Originate
  1111 connected
!!! Omitted for brevity
IP 10.127.239.67:16464 SRTP: off rtt:0ms pl:0/0ms lost:0/0/0 delay:0/0/0ms g729r8
  TextRelay: off Transcoded: No ICE: Off


Post Switchover:

133E : 71 87806830ms.1 (07:11:13.885 UTC Sat Feb 4 2017) +9260 pid:1111 Answer
  2222 connected
```

```
!!! Omitted for brevity
IP 10.127.239.66:16456 SRTP: off rtt:0ms pl:0/0ms lost:0/0/0 delay:0/0/0ms g711ulaw
  TextRelay: off Transcoded: No ICE: Off



133E : 72 87806850ms.1 (07:11:13.905 UTC Sat Feb 4 2017) +9230 pid:1111 Originate
  1111 connected
!!! Omitted for brevity
IP 10.127.239.67:16464 SRTP: off rtt:0ms pl:0/0ms lost:0/0/0 delay:0/0/0ms g711ulaw
  TextRelay: off Transcoded: No ICE: Off
```

- **Fax messaging and page exchange:** The most difficult aspect of troubleshooting fax passthrough calls is when there are issues with fax messaging or page transmission, as all of this is encoded as modulated data within the RTP payload and transported over the IP network.

  Fax relay encodes T.30 messaging and T.4/T.6 page transfer over IFPs that allow popular network analyzer tools like Wireshark to decode T.30 messages and give the administrator a sense of where the call fails. However, with fax passthrough calls, a packet capture is useful only if it is fed into special-purpose fax analysis software that decodes T.30 messaging and T.4/T.6 page transmission for passthrough calls. Failures in fax passthrough calls can be introduced in the negotiation of the page transfer phase due to packet drops. To determine if a given fax passthrough call is affected by packet drops, the **show call active voice brief** and **show call active voice** commands may be used. As demonstrated in Example 10-10, the **show call active voice brief** command displays the number of lost and delayed packets.

SG3 Faxing and Protocol Interworking

Super G3 faxing can achieve speeds up to 33,600 bps and greatly reduces the amount of time required to transmit pages from one terminal to another. Support for SG3 fax is available from IOS version 15.1(1)T and later and works without the need for any additional configuration for fax passthrough calls.

While H.323 is a dated call control protocol and is gradually being phased out in favor of SIP, there are still networks that use H.323 within the enterprise and SIP to peer with service provider networks. In such a scenario, CUBE ensures that there is seamless call control protocol interworking for fax passthrough. Figure 10-30 depicts CUBE interworking a fax passthrough call between SIP and H.323 networks.

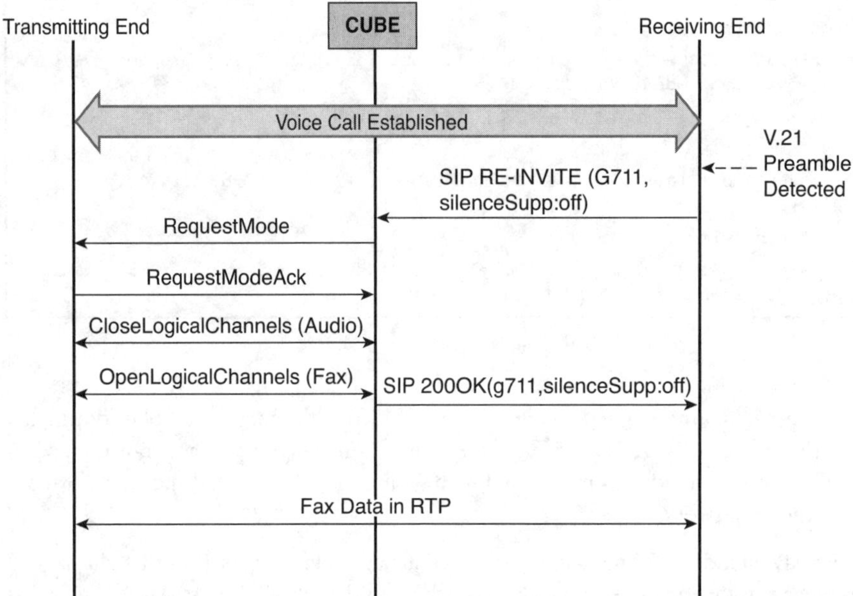

Figure 10-30 *Call Control Protocol Interworking for Fax Passthrough*

> **Note** CUBE can interwork G3 and SG3 calls between SIP and H.323 networks.

Fax Relay on CUBE

Fax relay converts analog modulated fax data into a binary sequence that is transported over the IP network in the form of IFPs. As per the T.38 specification, the encapsulation can be over UDP, TCP, or RTP. CUBE, however, only supports T.38 over UDP, which is the most widely used transport layer encapsulation. Just as with fax passthrough, the trigger to switch over to T.38 is the V.21 preamble, which results in either a SIP re-INVITE/200 OK exchange or a H.245 requestMode/requestModeAck exchange.

Fax Relay over H.323

Figure 10-31 depicts a typical T.38 fax relay call over H.323. The call is initially set up as a voice call through CUBE. When one of the H.323 terminals detects a V.21 preamble, it sends over a H.245 requestMode message with the intent to set up a T.38 fax connection. A typical H.245 requestMode message for a T.38 call is provided in Example 10-2. Assuming that CUBE is configured to handle T.38 connections, it sends another H.245 requestMode message to the peer H.323 terminal to begin end-to-end negotiations for fax.

If the peer terminal accepts the T.38 connection request, a H.245 requestModeAck message is received on CUBE, followed by the breakdown of the audio channels that were in place previously and setup of new ones for T.38 data transfer. CUBE proceeds to send the requestModeAck message to the terminal that initiated the fax connection and then builds new channels for T.38 data.

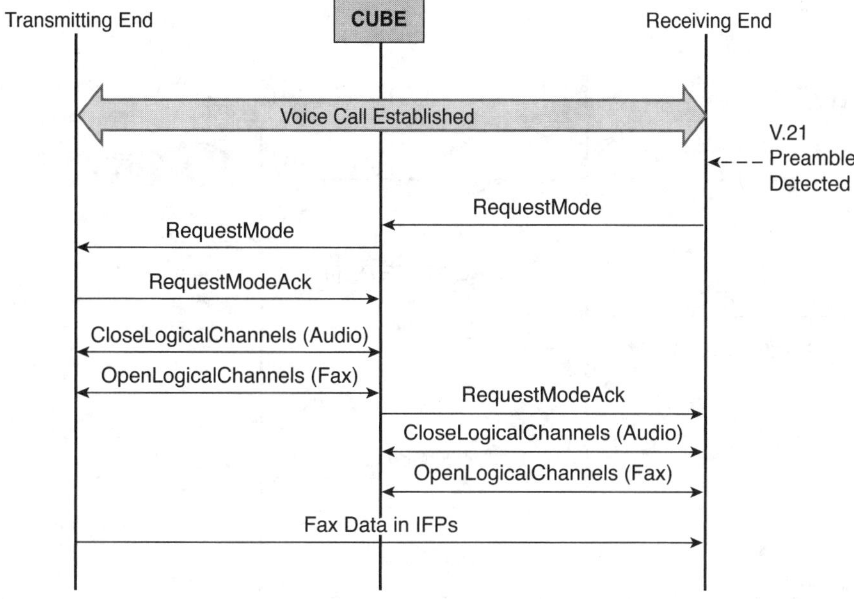

Figure 10-31 *T.38 Relay Call over H.323*

Note The switchover to fax relay can fail if either CUBE or the peer H.323 terminal (to which CUBE sends the H.245 requestMode message) is not configured to handle T.38 fax relay. If CUBE is not configured to handle fax relay, it immediately sends a requestModeReject message to the initiating terminal, without contacting the peer H.323 terminal.

Fax Relay over SIP

Figure 10-32 depicts a SIP T.38 fax relay call through CUBE. The call is initially set up as a voice call across CUBE, such that when one of the SIP user agents detects a V.21 preamble, it attempts to set up a fax connection over T.38 by sending a SIP re-INVITE. On receiving the re-INVITE, assuming that CUBE is configured to handle T.38, it sends another re-INVITE to the peer call leg to initiate an end-to-end fax connection.

If the peer user agent responds to the T.38 re-INVITE with a 200 OK, the CUBE then sends over a 200 OK to the user agent that initiated fax switchover. At this time, the call is set up as a T.38 fax relay call through CUBE, with UDPTL-encapsulated IFPs traversing the CUBE from one user agent to another. If either the CUBE or the emitting user agents are not configured to handle T.38 fax relay, they would send over a 488 Media Unacceptable message on receiving the SIP re-INVITE that attempts to set up a T.38 fax call.

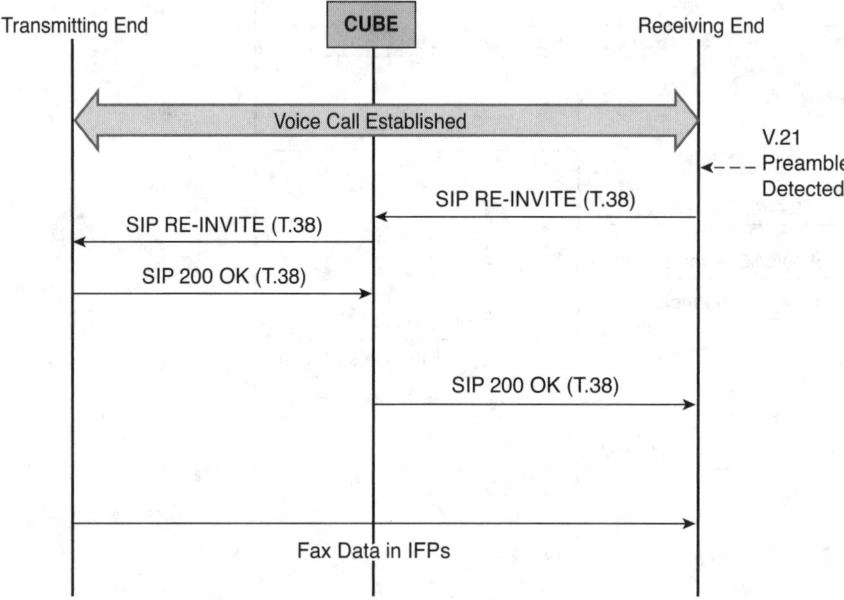

Figure 10-32 *T.38 Relay Call over SIP*

SDP bodies of SIP re-INVITEs can carry multiple media types (for example, m=audio, m=video, m=message). However, from the perspective of a T.38 connection that is attempted over an existing audio call, it makes little sense to include the audio media type along with the image media type in the SIP re-INVITE. This is because the audio stream serves no practical purpose during a T.38 connection; if anything, it can cause issues in terms of the fax tones leaking into the audio stream. The most efficient way to indicate the intent to switch over to a T.38 connection is to simply replace the audio media type with the image media type within the SDP body of the SIP re-INVITE. Example 10-11 provides a **debug ccsip message** snippet of such a scenario.

Example 10-11 **debug ccsip messages** *Snippet of the image Media Type Replacing the audio Media Type*

```
Received:
SIP/2.0 200 OK
Via: SIP/2.0/UDP 10.106.124.61:5060;branch=z9hG4bK6E8BD
From: <sip:2222@10.106.124.61>;tag=A09D9F8-1567
To: <sip:1111@10.127.239.67>;tag=2EA711B0-26D2
Date: Sun, 05 Feb 2017 06:10:02 GMT
Call-ID: A27C9717-EA9B11E6-80F9EADB-AE8C6AF7@10.106.124.61
!
! Omitted for brevity
!
Content-Length: 250

v=0
o=CiscoSystemsSIP-GW-UserAgent 1192 1629 IN IP4 10.127.239.67
s=SIP Call
c=IN IP4 10.127.239.67
t=0 0
m=audio 16480 RTP/AVP 0 101
c=IN IP4 10.127.239.67
a=rtpmap:0 PCMU/8000
a=rtpmap:101 telephone-event/8000
a=fmtp:101 0-16
a=ptime:20



Received:
INVITE sip:2222@10.106.124.61:5060 SIP/2.0
Via: SIP/2.0/UDP 10.127.239.67:5060;branch=z9hG4bK187AF
Remote-Party-ID: <sip:1111@10.127.239.67>;party=calling;screen=no;privacy=off
From: <sip:1111@10.127.239.67>;tag=2EA711B0-26D2
To: <sip:2222@10.106.124.61>;tag=A09D9F8-1567
Date: Sun, 05 Feb 2017 06:10:22 GMT
Call-ID: A27C9717-EA9B11E6-80F9EADB-AE8C6AF7@10.106.124.61
!
! Omitted for brevity
!
Content-Length: 321
```

```
v=0
o=CiscoSystemsSIP-GW-UserAgent 1192 1630 IN IP4 10.127.239.67
s=SIP Call
c=IN IP4 10.127.239.67
t=0 0
m=image 16480 udptl t38
c=IN IP4 10.127.239.67
a=T38FaxVersion:0
a=T38MaxBitRate:14400
a=T38FaxRateManagement:transferredTCF
a=T38FaxMaxBuffer:200
a=T38FaxMaxDatagram:320
a=T38FaxUdpEC:t38UDPRedundancy
```

In Example 10-11, the initial call sets up on CUBE with one of the user agents negotiating a G.711 audio connection with RTP port number 16480 (200 OK received from user agent). On detecting the V.21 preamble, the same user agent expresses intent to set up a T.38 connection by sending a re-INVITE such that the image media type in the SDP simply replaces the audio media type description.

Certain vendors indicate the intent to set up a T.38 connection by appending an image media type to the existing audio media type definition in the SDP body. Example 10-12 provides a snippet of such a scenario.

Example 10-12 debug ccsip messages *Snippet Demonstrating the image Media Type Being Appended to the audio Media Type*

```
Received:
INVITE sip:2222@10.106.124.61:5060 SIP/2.0
Via: SIP/2.0/UDP 10.127.239.67:5060;branch=z9hG4bK187AF
Remote-Party-ID: <sip:1111@10.127.239.67>;party=calling;screen=no;privacy=off
From: <sip:1111@10.127.239.67>;tag=2EA711B0-26D2
To: <sip:2222@10.106.124.61>;tag=A09D9F8-1567
Date: Sun, 05 Feb 2017 06:10:22 GMT
Call-ID: A27C9717-EA9B11E6-80F9EADB-AE8C6AF7@10.106.124.61
!
! Omitted for brevity
!
Content-Type: application/sdp

v=0
o=CiscoSystemsSIP-GW-UserAgent 1192 1630 IN IP4 10.127.239.67
```

```
s=SIP Call
c=IN IP4 10.127.239.67
t=0 0
m=audio 20368 RTP/AVP 0
c=IN IP4 10.127.239.67
a=rtpmap:0 PCMU/8000
a=inactive
m=image 16480 udptl t38
c=IN IP4 10.127.239.67
a=T38FaxVersion:0
a=T38MaxBitRate:14400
a=T38FaxRateManagement:transferredTCF
a=T38FaxMaxBuffer:200
a=T38FaxMaxDatagram:320
a=T38FaxUdpEC:t38UDPRedundancy
```

When the image media type is appended to the audio media type, the direction attribute of the audio stream is usually set to inactive to ensure that there are no RTP packets sent or received.

Another way vendors attempt to switch over is by replacing the audio media type with the image media type and re-adding the audio media type definition within the SDP body of the re-INVITE. While this is not recommended, be aware that the SDP offer/answer framework defined in RFC 3264/4566 has enough loose ends and room for interpretation to allow such an advertisement of media types. The SDP body found in such a SIP re-INVITE is provided in Example 10-13.

Example 10-13 **debug ccsip messages** *Snippet Demonstrating the audio Media Type Being Appended to the image Media Type*

```
m=image 53200 udptl t38
a=T38FaxVersion:0
a=T38MaxBitRate:14400
a=T38FaxRateManagement:transferredTCF
a=T38FaxUdpEC:t38UDPRedundancy
m=audio 53190 RTP/AVP 8 0 101
a=rtpmap:8 PCMA/8000
a=rtpmap:0 PCMU/8000
a=rtpmap:101 telephone-event/8000
a=fmtp:101 0-15
a=ptime:20
```

> **Note** A re-INVITE whose SDP body is similar to the one in Example 10-13 causes CUBE to fail to transition to T.38 fax relay. Workarounds to this include using the **pass-thru content sdp mode non-rtp** command and configuring a combination of outbound and inbound SIP profiles. At the time of this publication, SIP profiles on CUBE cannot be leveraged to modify the image media type.

> **Note** If the emitting user agent or CUBE does not support T.38 fax relay, the re-INVITE to switch over to relay gets a **488 Media Unacceptable** message response.

Fax Relay Fallback to Passthrough

Fax relay fallback to passthrough is a Cisco proprietary feature that allows calls that fail to set up a T.38 fax relay connection to fallback and re-attempts the connection by using fax passthrough. This is especially useful on SBCs like CUBE that are often required to peer with several different multimedia networks in real time, with varying capability sets for voice, video, and fax. The operational framework of the fax fallback feature for a SIP call is depicted in Figure 10-33.

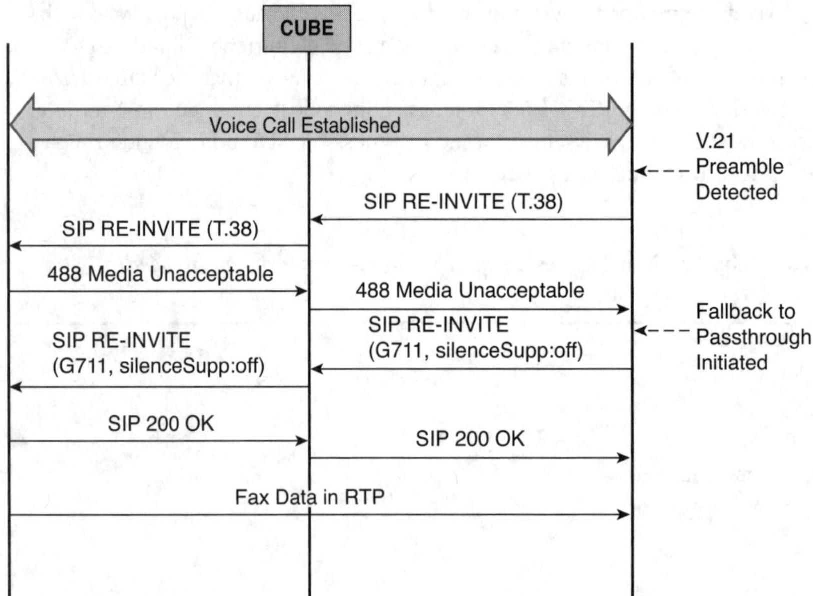

Figure 10-33 *T.38 Relay Fallback to Passthrough*

The call sets up as a standard voice call through CUBE, and one of the SIP user agents attempts to set up a T.38 fax connection on detecting a V.21 preamble. CUBE forwards the request to the peer SIP leg in an attempt to set up an end-to-end T.38 fax call. If the connection attempt is rejected with a 488 Media Unacceptable message, the response is passed back to the SIP user agent that attempted to initiate a T.38 fax connection. The initiating user agent can either terminate the call or re-attempt the connection over fax passthrough.

If a fax passthrough re-INVITE is received, CUBE forwards the requests out to the peer user agent to now attempt to set up a fax passthrough call. For this feature to work effectively, the user agent that attempts to switch over to fax and CUBE must be configured to support fallback to fax passthrough. The onus of re-trying the fax call over passthrough lies with the SIP user agent servicing the fax machine, such as a voice gateway or a call agent. The fax machine is completely unaware of the fallback process.

This fallback capability is supported if the CUBE is setting up a SIP call end-to-end or if it is interworking between H.323 and SIP.

Note If the initial voice call is set up using G.711 and an attempt to switch over to T.38 fax relay is rejected, the user agent could simply begin to encode fax-modulated data over G.711 packets without another explicit re-INVITE, indicating a fax passthrough call. If G.711 is already being used for the initial voice call, then it is essentially already set up for passthrough. Your fax success rate in this type of scenario generally parallels that of a traditional fax passthrough call that undergoes an audio codec switchover.

SG3 over Relay and Protocol Interoperability

Transmission speeds of up to 33,600 bps are possible over T.38 relay connections, as per version 3 of the ITU-T T.38 specification. Support for T.38 version 3 is advertised using the T38FaxVersion SDP attribute, such that the lowest supported common version across all devices involved in a fax connection is enforced. For example, if there are three fax terminals, A, B, and C, with terminals A and B supporting version 3 and terminal C supporting version 0, the call will end up using T.38 version 0.

Note that simply advertising version 3 of T.38 does not mean the call will end up using V.34 modulation and achieve speeds up to 33,600 bps. Advertisement of version 3 is simply an indication that the fax endpoint(s) being serviced by the SIP user agent (typically a gateway) might be SG3 capable. As with fax passthrough, support for SG3 for relay was added from IOS version 15.1(1)T onward.

Note IOS versions before 15.1(1)T did not support V.34 modulation, and SG3 calls would fail. A common workaround for this was to suppress the V.8 CM tones and force the call to fall back to G3. This works as long as there is a DSP placed in the call to identify and suppress the V.8 CM tone; this workaround was designed primarily for media voice gateways that had one POTS call leg and always required a DSP to be placed in the call. With CUBE, however, any DSP invocation is never used for fax functionality, and suppression of CM tones will not work.

Configuration of Fax Relay on CUBE

Fax relay configuration can be applied on CUBE either at the global level or the dial peer level and is done using the **fax protocol t38** command. The arguments to this command determine the method of faxing (relay or passthrough or both) supported on CUBE. The arguments to the **fax protocol t38** command in global configuration mode are specified in Table 10-11.

Table 10-11 *T.38 Arguments to the* **fax protocol t38** *Command in Global Configuration Mode*

Command	Argument	Meaning
fax protocol t38 [version { 0 | 3 }] [ls-redundancy *value* **[hs-redundancy** *value* **]] [fallback { none | pass-through { g711ulaw | g711alaw } }]**	**version**	Represents the T.38 version number that is supported on CUBE. Valid values for this argument include the following: ■ **0**: Used for G3 faxing ■ **3**: Used for SG3 faxing
	ls-redundancy	Specifies the number of redundant T.38 packets sent for low-speed V.21 messages. Examples of these messages include DIS, NSF, and CFR. This defaults to 0 and can be extended up to 5.
	hs-redundancy	Specifies the number of redundant T.38 packets sent for high-speed fax image transmission. This defaults to 0 and can be extended up to 2.
	fallback	Specifies the fallback scheme for failed T.38 calls on CUBE. Possible values include the following: ■ **none**: No fallback scheme ■ **pass-through**: Fallback to protocol-based fax passthrough using either G.711ulaw or G.711alaw.

The **fax protocol t38** command can be entered in dial peer configuration mode if further granularity is needed on a per-fax-call basis. Configurations entered at the dial peer level override the configuration at the global level. The command usage is exactly the same in the global mode and dial peer mode. Example 10-14 provides an example of a T.38 fax relay configuration snippet on CUBE.

Example 10-14 *T.38 Fax Relay Configuration on CUBE*

```
!
!
!
voice service voip
fax protocol t38 ls-redundancy 2 hs-redundancy 1 fallback none

!
!
!
dial-peer voice 1703 voip
incoming called-number 14084343471
session protocol sipv2
voice-class codec 1
no vad
dtmf-relay rtp-nte
fax protocol t38 ls-redundancy 0 hs-redundancy 0 fallback pass-through g711ulaw
!
!
dial-peer voice 1803 voip
destination-pattern 14084343471
session protocol sipv2
session target ipv4:192.0.2.1
voice-class codec 1
no vad
dtmf-relay rtp-nte
fax protocol t38 ls-redundancy 0 hs-redundancy 0 fallback pass-through g711ulaw
```

Troubleshooting Fax Relay on CUBE

Troubleshooting T.38 fax relay on CUBE is simpler than troubleshooting fax passthrough because all T.30 messaging is encapsulated over UDPTL datagrams and can be parsed by popular network analyzer tools such as Wireshark. You can thus get a good sense of where the calls fail. As a general rule, preliminary checks such as ensuring that fax relay is configured on all devices and confirming successful voice call setup are still very important.

Note Unlike with fax passthrough, the voice codec has no bearing whatsoever on fax connection failures. This is because Cisco's implementation of T.38 (and the implementations of a strong majority of other vendors) uses UDPTL datagrams for fax messaging and data. There is no requirement to up-speed the codec to G.711.

Once the configuration has been vetted and it has been confirmed that the voice calls can set up successfully, the next logical step is to verify whether the switchover to fax is successful. Examining call control protocol messages or issuing commands in real time can identify successful switchovers for T.38 fax relay calls.

The expected signaling exchange for a T.38 fax relay call over H.323 is provided in Example 10-8. Although the message sequence is exactly the same as that of a fax passthrough call, the protocol message body in the requestMode message is entirely different (refer to Example 10-2). The switchover to T.38 fax relay is complete on a given call leg with the exchange of the requestMode and requestModeAck messages.

Remember that CUBE is a back-to-back user agent and has to negotiate relay end-to-end on both call legs, regardless of the call control protocol configured. A successful switchover to fax relay from the perspective of CUBE is possible only if switchover succeeds on each call leg of the fax-call traversing CUBE. Switchover to fax relay can also be determined by running the **show call active voice brief** command in real time while the call is in progress. Example 10-15 provides the output of the **show call active voice brief** command during a fax relay call that has successfully set up.

Example 10-15 *Output of* **show call active voice brief** *Confirming Switchover to Fax Relay Mode*

```
Before switchover:

136B : 87 168417760ms.1 (05:34:44.806 UTC Sun Feb 5 2017) +-1 pid:1111 Answer
  2222 connecting
 !!! Omitted for brevity
 IP 10.127.239.66:16472 SRTP: off rtt:0ms pl:0/0ms lost:0/0/0 delay:0/0/0ms g711ulaw
  TextRelay: off Transcoded: No ICE: Off
 !!! Omitted for brevity

136B : 88 168417780ms.1 (05:34:44.826 UTC Sun Feb 5 2017) +-1 pid:1111 Originate
  1111 connected
 !!! Omitted for brevity
 IP 10.127.239.67:16480 SRTP: off rtt:0ms pl:0/0ms lost:0/0/0 delay:0/0/0ms g711ulaw
  TextRelay: off Transcoded: No ICE: Off
 !!! Omitted for brevity

Post switchover:



136B : 87 168417760ms.1 (05:34:44.806 UTC Sun Feb 5 2017) +9210 pid:1111 Answer
  2222 connected
 !!! Omitted for brevity IP 10.127.239.66:16472 SRTP: off rtt:0ms pl:0/0ms
  lost:0/0/0 delay:0/0/0ms t38 TextRelay: off Transcoded: No ICE: Off
 !!! Omitted for brevity
```

```
136B : 88 168417780ms.1 (05:34:44.826 UTC Sun Feb 5 2017) +9180 pid:1111 Originate
  1111 connected
 !!! Omitted for brevity
 IP 10.127.239.67:16480 SRTP: off rtt:0ms pl:0/0ms lost:0/0/0 delay:0/0/0ms t38
  TextRelay: off Transcoded: No ICE: Off
!!! Omitted for brevity
```

The next step in troubleshooting T.38 fax relay is to verify the T.30 messaging. Unlike with fax passthrough, where fax messaging is encoded as raw modulated tones within RTP packets, fax relay makes use of UDPTL indicator and data IFPs for fax messaging and page transfer. These IFPs can easily be decoded by packet analysis software such as Wireshark.

Note The **debug fax relay t30 all-level-1** command is incorrectly used to troubleshoot T.38 relay issues on CUBE. This command was designed to work on a Cisco IP-TDM gateway only and does not produce any output on CUBE.

A packet capture taken on CUBE can be fed into Wireshark to look into the T.30 messaging exchange to gain further insights into why a fax call has failed. Once the capture file has been opened in Wireshark, navigate to **Telephony > Voip Calls** (or, if using a Wireshark release after 1.12.X, navigate to **Telephony > SIP Flows** or **Telephony > H,225**) and select the appropriate call from the displayed list. Then click the **Flow** button. This brings up a pop-up window that provides information such as the IP addresses of the devices involved in the call, the call control protocol messages, and T.30 messages exchanged during the course of the call.

Note While taking a capture in real time, there might be several calls and call types (audio, video, fax) traversing CUBE. It is important to identify the correct call to analyze.

Note CUBE might be configured to use different interfaces to peer with different networks. If this is the case, if an end-to-end analysis of the fax call is required, a simultaneous capture on both interfaces needs to be taken.

Figure 10-34 provides a screenshot from Wireshark that displays the T.30 messaging extracted from a T.38 fax relay call between CUBE and a SIP user agent.

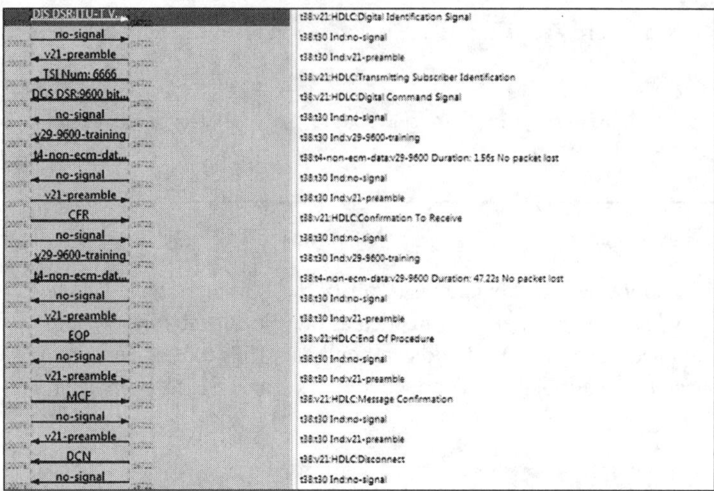

Figure 10-34 *T.30 Messaging Captured on Wireshark*

The T.30 messaging in Figure 10-34 is for a successful one-page, non-ECM, T.38 fax relay connection. The answering device sends over an NSF and a DIS, and the emitting terminal then sends over common capabilities through the T.30 DCS message. This is followed by a TCF transmitted at 9600 bps. As the TCF message has been received reliably, it is followed by a CFR. Next, there is fax page transmission that occurs at 9600bps, with the emitting terminal indicating that there are no more pages to transmit by using an EOP message. This is responded to with an MCF message from the receiving terminal, followed by a DCN.

If it is necessary to look into specific T.30 messages, such as the DIS/DCS, to get a sense of the different parameters negotiated over the fax connection, Wireshark can be used to parse the bit patterns carried in the data field bytes of T.30 data IFPs (refer to Figure 10-22) and provide a textual description. Figure 10-35 provides a screenshot from Wireshark in which the bit pattern in the DIS message is interpreted to provide a textual description.

If you go through the information in Figure 10-35, it is possible to identify important characteristics of the fax call, such as the data signaling rate, ECM support, V.8 support, and T.6 support, among several others.

If a fax call through CUBE completes successfully but has impairments in terms of page quality, such as blurry, illegible text, words interleaved with white spaces, or words appearing bunched up together, the problem most likely can be attributed to packet drops or incorrect QoS marking on CUBE or other network devices. Given that CUBE functions as a media relay for fax calls, the payload of media packets remains untouched. If CUBE introduces no packet drops or incorrect QoS marking, the issue likely lies on another device in the data path.

```
Control: Final frames within the procedure (0xc8)
⊟ .000 0001 = Facsimile Control: Digital Identification Signal (1)
    0... .... = Store and forward Internet fax- Simple mode (ITU-T T.37): Not set
    ..0. .... = Real-time Internet fax (ITU T T.38): Not set
    ...0 .... = 3rd Generation Mobile Network: Not set
    .... .0.. = V.8 capabilities: Not set
    .... ..0. = Octets preferred: 256 octets preferred
    0... .... = Ready to transmit a facsimile document (polling): Not set
    .1.. .... = Receiver fax operation: Set
    ..11 00.. = Data signalling rate: ITU-T V.27 ter and V.29 (0x0c)
    .... ..1. = R8x7.7 lines/mm and/or 200x200 pels/25.4 mm: Set
    .... ...1 = Two dimensional coding capability: Set
    00.. .... = Recording width capabilities: Scan line length 215 mm +- 1% (0x00)
    ..01 .... = Recording length capability: Unlimited (0x01)
    .... 010. = Minimum scan line time capability at the receiver: 10 ms at 3.85 l/mm: T7.7 = T3.85 (0x02)
    .... ...1 = Extension indicator: information continues through the next octet
    .0.. .... = Compress/Uncompress mode: Compressed mode
    ..0. .... = Error correction mode: Not set
    .... ..0. = T.6 coding capability: Not set
    .... ...1 = Extension indicator: information continues through the next octet
    0... .... = Field valid capability: Not set
    .0.. .... = Multiple selective polling capability: Not set
    ..0. .... = Polled Subaddress: Not set
    ...0 .... = T.43 coding: Not set
    .... 0... = Plane interleave: Not set
    .... .0.. = Voice coding with 32k ADPCM (ITU T G.726): Not set
    .... ...1 = Extension indicator: information continues through the next octet
    1... .... = R8x15.4 lines/mm: Set
    .0.. .... = 300x300 pels/25.4 mm: Not set
    ..0. .... = R16x15.4 lines/mm and/or 400x400 pels/25.4 mm: Not set
    ...0 .... = Inch based resolution preferred: Not set
    .... 1... = Metric based resolution preferred: Set
    .... .0.. = Minimum scan line time capability for higher resolutions: T15.4 = T7.7
    .... ..0. = Selective polling: Not set
    .... ...0 = Extension indicator: last octet
```

Figure 10-35 *Textual Description of Bit Pattern in Data Field Bytes of a DIS Message*

ECM, NSF, and SG3 Considerations

ECM ensures high-quality page transmission by dividing a page into blocks and making use of a real-time built-in feedback mechanism that can trigger several retransmissions to ensure impeccable page quality. The downside to ECM is that its extremely tenacious behavior can eventually lead to a high rate of transmission failures. For more details on ECM and how it works, please refer to the section on ECM earlier in this chapter.

Support for ECM is negotiated using the DIS/DCS exchange and has to be supported by both the fax terminals. However, Cisco voice gateways can influence whether ECM is advertised in the DIS message or the DCS message using the **fax-relay ecm-disable** command. For this command to work, though, a DSP is required in the fax call, which is the case for traditional IP-POTS gateways. Therefore, this command is entirely ineffective on CUBE. Aside from using the IP-TDM voice gateways, the only way to administratively override an ECM call is to manually disable ECM on one or both of the participating fax terminals.

The NSF T.30 message is used to advertise vendor-specific capabilities. If both fax machines belong to the same vendor or product family, they signal this by using specific values set in the NSF. This allows the fax machines to then deviate from standards-based T.30 and use their proprietary methods of communication. If the fax machines deviate from T.30, this presents a huge problem when troubleshooting fax failures as the message exchange no longer follows a standard, and it can be almost impossible to decode the proprietary messaging.

To ensure that fax calls always adhere to standards-based T.30, the **fax nsf 000000** command is used on traditional voice gateways so that the DSP can override any vendor encoding in the NSF. This command will not work on CUBE because it requires a DSP that cannot be invoked for a fax call.

Before the support of T.38 version 3, to allow SG3 machines to interoperate with G3 machines over T.38 fax relay, the **fax-relay sg3-to-g3** command was used in traditional

IP-POTS Cisco voice gateways. This command ensured that the V.8 CM (Calling Menu) message was squelched, thus forcing the SG3 call to fall back to a G3 call. As with the ECM and NSF commands just discussed, this command also does not work on CUBE because of the non-involvement of the DSP.

Note The **fax-rate** command that is used to alter the DIS/DCS messages with the configured data transmission rate is affected by the DSP requirement as well. Therefore, it is not applicable on CUBE either.

Given that fax relay connections traversing CUBE eventually either terminate on a fax server or a fax machine that is attached to a voice gateway, the appropriate handling for T.38 in terms of ECM, NSF, SG3 down-speeds, and fax rate can either be done on the fax server or voice gateway.

DSPs that are housed on CUBE might be invoked by CUCM and placed persistently in a fax call. This can occur if the MTP Required box is checked on the SIP trunk from CUCM to CUBE or if there is a DTMF mismatch for which CUCM invoked an IOS-based MTP on CUBE. However, these DSPs by default are not optimized to handle fax-encoded data. If DSPs are required to reliably handle fax connections, they must be configured in **codec passthrough** mode.

Summary

This chapter introduces the important concepts of fax technology and extends the discussion to elucidate the core tenets of how fax works over IP networks. The chapter discusses the two principal methods of fax data transport over IP networks: fax passthrough and T.38 fax relay. Finally, it details the role of SBCs in fax data transmission and highlights how fax is specifically handled by CUBE.

References

RFC 3261, "SIP: Session Initiation Protocol," https://tools.ietf.org/html/rfc3261.

RFC 2198, "RTP Payload for Redundant Audio Data," https://tools.ietf.org/html/rfc2198.

RFC 2833, "RTP Payload for DTMF Digits, Telephony Tones and Telephony Signals," https://tools.ietf.org/html/rfc2833.

ITU-T Recommendation H.323, "Packet-Based Multimedia Communications Systems."

ITU-T Recommendation H.225.0, "Call Signalling Protocols and Media Stream Packetization for Packet-Based Multimedia Communication Systems."

ITU-T Recommendation H.245, "Control Protocol for Multimedia Communication."

ITU-T Recommendation T.38, "Procedures for Real Time Group 3 Facsimile Communications over IP Networks."

ITU-T Recommendation T.30, "Procedures for Document Facsimile Transmission in the General Switched Telephone Networks."

Chapter 11

Network-Based Call Recording

"Your call will be recorded for training and quality purposes" You've probably heard this common message when calling a customer support center of a bank, hospital, retailer, or insurance company. This chapter discusses the business drivers, common architectures, and protocols for call recording as well as the role of SBCs in enabling this capability. It consists of the following sections:

- **The Business Need for Call Recording**—This section discusses the primary reasons for enabling call recording and how enterprises use recordings to enhance service delivery.
- **IETF SIP Recording Architecture (SIPREC)**—This section introduces basic terminologies, concepts, and call flows and provides a detailed explanation of recording metadata.
- **SIPREC Configuration**—This section provides a practical configuration example using Cisco Unified Border Element (CUBE) as a session recording client and the Quality Management (QM) component of Cisco Unified Workforce Optimization as the SIP media recorder.
- **SIPREC Troubleshooting**—This section provides a complete walk-through of a working scenario using **debug** and **show** command output and looks at troubleshooting of common issues such as recording initiation failures, missing recording metadata, and missing recording files.
- **Cisco UC Gateway Services Architecture**—This section talks about how external applications can programmatically trigger call recording in Cisco Voice gateways and SBCs running Cisco IOS and IOS XE. It also provides a high-level overview of software components such as Extended Call Control (XCC), Extended Media Forking (XMF), Extended Call Detail Record (XCDR), and Extended Serviceability (XSVC) application service providers.

- **XCC and XMF Data Model**—This section shows how the call and connection states are modeled and exchanged within the UC Gateway Services API for call-based and connection-based media forking.
- **API-Based Recording**—This section illustrates the process involved in an application registering and receiving call- and connection-related event notifications and initiating recording of specific calls of interest. It explains the parameters of UC Gateway Services API requests and responses, using real-world message examples.
- **API-Based Recording Configuration**—This section lists the step-by-step configuration tasks required to integrate CUCM with CUBE through the programmatic interface and to store the recording files in MediaSense.
- **API-Based Recording Troubleshooting**—This section explains how to use Wireshark to analyze XMF API interactions in high-call-volume environments along with **debug** walk-throughs of scenarios such as recording an IP phone call, unregistering an application, and recording initiation failures.

The Business Need for Call Recording

The need to continuously improve service delivery and compliance with regulations are the primary business reasons for enabling call recording in an enterprise.

Service Delivery Improvement

The ability to automatically record incoming calls and easily retrieve recordings is a key requirement for service operations managers. It allows them to get the right facts and insights on what happened in a customer interaction and make correct decisions when a customer reports an issue on a given interaction. The recordings also serve as real-world examples of how to deliver great service and highlight common communication-related issues to both new and existing customer support representatives as part of continuous improvement programs.

Bots, also called as virtual assistants, are starting to become popular in the services industry. The usefulness of a bot is heavily dependent on its ability to accurately understand the user's intent and perform the requested task. Bot developers use cognitive technology capabilities such as machine learning to detect the user's intent in a given text or voice message. Recordings are also of use here to provide effortless and high-quality customer experiences.

Recordings are a great source of information to identify how users typically express their intent. For example, an intent to talk to a support engineer may be expressed in a number of ways, such as "connect me to my engineer," "connect me to my case owner," and "I want to speak to an engineer handling this ticket." Data from past interactions helps bot development teams form a good training data set for every user intent and use it as training samples in the corresponding machine learning models. Development teams can also periodically update training data sets and retrain the machine learning models to adapt to new conversational requests.

SBCs are the entry and exit points for these calls in a company, and hence SBC interfaces are ideal network locations for initiating audio and video recording streams.

Regulatory Compliance

Another key business driver for call recording is proving compliance to consumer rights–related laws. In addition, companies must adhere to user privacy and data protection laws related to call recording. The applicable laws vary from industry to industry, country to country, and sometimes even state to state within a country. The websites of the Federal Trade Commission, European Commission, UK Legislation, and Consumers International are good sources of consumer rights–related information.

Following are common examples of criteria that business organizations should satisfy from a user privacy perspective:

- Inform users that a conversation is going to be recorded prior to starting the recording. This notification gives users an option to disconnect the call if they do not consent to recording.
- Inform users about the recording purpose.

Now that you understand the business needs, let's take a look at two common architectures that are widely used in SBC deployments to enable call recording functionality. The first one, IETF SIP recording architecture (SIPREC), is a standard-based approach, and the second, the UC Gateway Services architecture, is an API-based approach implemented in CUBE.

IETF SIP Recording Architecture (SIPREC)

The SIPREC working group within the Internet Engineering Task Force (IETF) organization has defined a client/server-based architecture in which clients send the recording streams and servers receive and store the recording streams. RFC 7245 and RFC 8068 provide architecture and call flow details, and RFC 7866 and RFC 7865 provide the protocol and metadata specification.

SIPREC Terminology

Let's consider a simple sample deployment to better understand basic terminology. In Figure 11-1, the inbound calls from external callers to enterprise users arrive at an SBC through the service provider network. The SBC routes a call to the call controller in the enterprise, which then sends the call to the destination IP phone. The SBC is configured to automatically trigger recording of inbound calls destined to specific called party numbers.

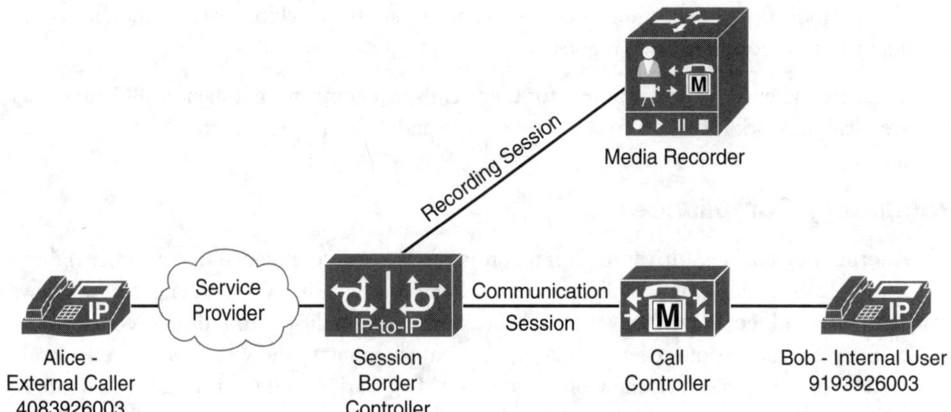

Figure 11-1 *Network Topology to Illustrate the SIPREC Architecture*

Communication Session

The term *communication session* refers to the session that is being recorded. In the sample deployment shown in Figure 11-1, the SIP session between the SBC and the call controller within the enterprise is referred to as the communication session. A communication session could be a point-to-point or multipoint conference call.

Session Recording Client

A session recording client (SRC) is a SIP device that originates media recording streams. The SBC in Figure 11-1 acts as a recording client. When inbound calls to specific directory numbers arrive at the SBC, the SBC first establishes a communication session with the IP phone. It then establishes a SIP session with the recording server and sends a copy of the communication session's media streams to the recording server. The recorded media streams contain the audio, video, or both exchanged between the PSTN caller and the enterprise user, depending on the configuration.

Session Recording Server

A session recording server (SRS) is a SIP device that receives and stores the media recording streams. The recorded media streams are made searchable and downloadable either through a graphical user interface or through application programming interfaces (APIs). The media recorder in Figure 11-1 acts as the recording server.

Media Forking

The process of copying the media streams that belong to the communication session and sending them to the recording server is called *media forking*. This task is performed by recording clients.

Recording Session

A recording session is a SIP session established between the recording client and server. For example, the SIP session between the SBC and the media recorder in Figure 11-1 is a recording session. Each recording session can be associated with zero or more communication sessions. One communication session is associated with a recording session in a point-to-point call (1:1), whereas multiple communication sessions are associated with a recording session in a conference call. Typically, the recording session is established after the communication session is set up, and it is torn down when the communication session is disconnected. If the recording session establishment gets delayed, there is a possibility of media clipping at the beginning of the call recording (that is, the first few words of the conversation in the communication session may not get recorded).

It is possible to establish a recording session even before the communication session is set up to avoid media clipping problems and continue the recording session even after the communication setup is disconnected. This is referred to as a *persistent recording session*, and in such a session, recording streams between the recording client and server are preestablished and reused for multiple communication sessions by updating the metadata of the recording streams.

The recording client assigns a label to every media stream in the recording session. This label is indicated using the **a=*label*:<*value*>** attribute in the Session Description Protocol (SDP) of the SIP **INVITE** of the recording session, as shown later in this chapter, in Example 11-12. It plays a key role in associating a media stream with its metadata.

Recording Metadata

Recording metadata contains detailed information about the communication session that is being recorded, such as directory numbers or URIs of all the participants and the media direction (send, receive, inactive) and content type of each individual media stream within the communication session. The recording client sends the metadata to the recording server initially when the recording session is established and updates the metadata whenever there is a participant or media stream change. The updates can either contain the complete metadata or just the partial metadata, with only the changes since the last update. The recording server stores the metadata along with the recording files and uses this information to find the right files when an administrator searches for past recordings.

RFC 7865 defines a framework in which recording metadata is encoded in XML format and carried within the SDP of SIP requests and responses with content-type **application/rs-metadata+xml**. Figure 11-2 provides a visual representation of the metadata data model of a sample recording session. This recording session consists of two communication sessions that are grouped together, with each session having two participants. The participants send and receive a media stream to each other.

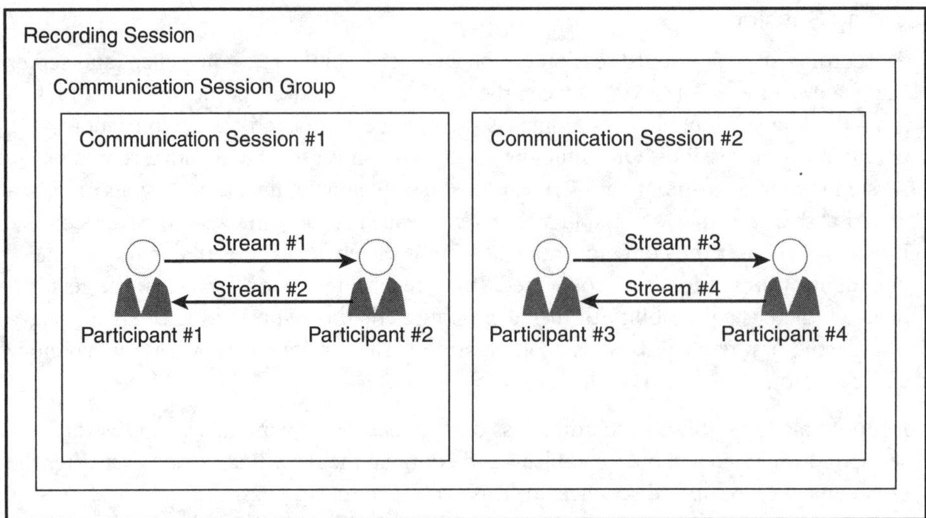

Figure 11-2 *SIPREC Recording Metadata Data Model*

The recording metadata model consists of classes that represent a recording session, a communication session, participants, a media stream, and a communication session group. Each class is defined with a set of attributes that provide information about the specific instance of a class (for example, an object). In addition, classes are defined to represent how a given object is associated to another object. For example, information about a participant and the media streams sent and received by the participant is represented as individual **participant** and **stream** objects. The **participant** object contains attributes such as the participant identifier, name, and SIP URL, and the **stream** object contains attributes such as the stream identifier. The association between the participant and its send/receive streams is stored in a **participantstreamassoc** object, which contains the participant identifier and send/receive stream identifiers as attributes. The metadata represented using this data model is exchanged between the SRC and the server in XML format. Each object maps to an XML element, and the object's attributes are stored either as XML element attributes or as child XML elements. The **participant** object maps to a **<participant>** XML element with the XML attribute **participant_id.** Other attributes, such as participant name and URL, are represented as child XML element **<Name>** with an XML attribute **aor** that contains the SIP URL value. Similarly, **stream** and **participantstreamassoc** objects map to **<stream>** and **<participantstreamassoc>** XML elements. The **<participantstreamassoc>** element contains a participant identifier as an XML attribute and send/receive stream identifiers as **<send>** and **<receive>** XML child elements.

Example 11-1 shows the metadata of a recording session that consists of a communication session between two participants, 4083926001 and 9193926003. The metadata XML contains a **<recording>** element, under which metadata objects and attributes are specified. The <**datamode>** element indicates whether this is complete metadata or partial metadata containing only the changes since the last update. If the **<datamode>** element is not present in the metadata XML, the default value **complete** is assumed (that is, the XML document represents the complete metadata). The two media streams of the communication session are identified by unique stream IDs:

- Audio stream from 4083926001 to 9193926003 (**ihKDcJPBEeeAtPH6U5qmBw==**)
- Audio stream from 9193926003 to 4083926001 (**ihKDcJPBEeeAtfH6U5qmBw==**)

Example 11-1 *Recording Metadata XML*

```
<?xml version="1.0" encoding="UTF-8"?>
<recording xmlns="urn:ietf:params:xml:ns:recording:1">
    <datamode>complete</datamode>
    <session session_id="hLOLNpPBEeeArfH6U5qmBw==">
        <sipSessionID>8c8c368da411d8df347e579968aa5507;
              remote=00004fb000105000a000000c298ea018</sipSessionID>
        <start-time>2017-09-08T11:41:42.242Z</start-time>
    </session>
    <participant participant_id="hLOLNpPBEeeArvH6U5qmBw==">
        <nameID aor="sip:4083926001@192.168.202.164"></nameID>
    </participant>
    <participantsessionassoc participant_id="hLOLNpPBEeeArvH6U5qmBw==" session_
  id="hLOLNpPBEeeArfH6U5qmBw==">
        <associate-time>2017-09-08T11:41:42.242Z</associate-time>
    </participantsessionassoc>
    <stream stream_id="ihKDcJPBEeeAtPH6U5qmBw==" session_
  id="hLOLNpPBEeeArfH6U5qmBw==">
        <label>1</label>
    </stream>
    <participant participant_id="hLOLNpPBEeeAr/H6U5qmBw==">
        <nameID aor="sip:9193926003@172.18.110.206">
        </nameID>
    </participant>
    <participantsessionassoc participant_id="hLOLNpPBEeeAr/H6U5qmBw==" session_
  id="hLOLNpPBEeeArfH6U5qmBw==">
        <associate-time>2017-09-08T11:41:42.242Z</associate-time>
    </participantsessionassoc>
    <stream stream_id="ihKDcJPBEeeAtfH6U5qmBw==" session_
  id="hLOLNpPBEeeArfH6U5qmBw==">
        <label>2</label>
    </stream>
    <participantstreamassoc participant_id="hLOLNpPBEeeArvH6U5qmBw==">
        <send>ihKDcJPBEeeAtPH6U5qmBw==</send>
        <recv>ihKDcJPBEeeAtfH6U5qmBw==</recv>
    </participantstreamassoc>
    <participantstreamassoc participant_id="hLOLNpPBEeeAr/H6U5qmBw==">
        <send>ihKDcJPBEeeAtfH6U5qmBw==</send>
        <recv>ihKDcJPBEeeAtPH6U5qmBw==</recv>
    </participantstreamassoc>
</recording>
```

Table 11-1 provides details of the key metadata objects and their attributes.

Table 11-1 *Recording Metadata*

Metadata Object	Object Description	Metadata Attribute	Metadata Description
session	Describes a communication session	session_id sipSessionID start-time stop-time reason group-ref	The **session_id** attribute indicates the unique ID assigned to each communication session in the recording session. The **sipSessionID** attribute provides the local and remote UUIDs of the end-to-end session identifier (RFC 7989) of the communication session. This attribute is not mandatory and is typically sent only by devices that support **Session**-ID. **start-time** and **end-time** are optional attributes that represent the times at which the communication session started and ended. When a communication session is terminated, the reason for the termination is provided in the SIP Reason (RFC 3326) header field value of SIP requests, such as **BYE** and **CANCEL**. This reason information is passed on to the recording session by using the **reason** metadata parameter. Recording clients can group related communication sessions together. The **group-ref** parameter references the unique group ID to which this communication session belongs.
participant	Describes a participant	nameID participant_id	The **nameID** attribute represents the name and SIP/SIPS/tel URI (also called the address of record) of each participant. The **participant_id** attribute indicates the unique ID assigned to each participant in the recording session.

Metadata Object	Object Description	Metadata Attribute	Metadata Description
stream	Describes a media stream	**stream_id** **session_id** **label** **content-type**	The **stream_id** attribute indicates the unique ID assigned to each media stream in the recording session. The **session_id** attribute is used to reference the communication session to which a given media stream belongs. The **label** metadata attribute provides the value of the **a=label** attribute assigned to this media stream in the SDP of the SIP request and responses of the recording session. It plays a key role in associating a media stream with its metadata information. **content_type** indicates the type of content carried by the media stream, such as presentation slides, image of the speaker, sign language, media from the main source, and media from an alternate source.
sessionrecordingassoc	Describes the association between a communication session and a recording session	**session_id** **associate-time** **disassociate-time**	The **session_id** attribute is used to reference the communication session associated with a given recording session. **associate_time** and **disassociate_time** indicate the times at which the given communication session was associated and disassociated with the recording session.
participantsessionassoc	Describes the association between a participant and a communication session	**participant_id** **session_id** **associate_time** **param**	**participant_id** references the unique ID assigned to the participant in the **<participant>** object. The **session_id** attribute is used to reference the participant's communication session, and the time at which the participant was associated with the communication session is indicated by **associate_time.** **param** provides the SIP participant's capability details, such as supported streaming types, events, methods, and so on.

Metadata Object	Object Description	Metadata Attribute	Metadata Description
participant-streamassoc	Describes the association between a participant and the participant's media stream	**participant_id** **send** **recv** **associate_time** **disassociate_ttime**	**participant_id** references the unique ID assigned to the participant in the **<participant>** object. The **send** attribute references the **stream_id** of the media stream sent by this participant. The **recv** attribute references the **stream_id** of the media stream received by this participant. **associate_time** and **disassociate_time** indicate the times at which the participant started and ended sending/receiving the given media stream.

Recording Session Establishment

Now that you understand the basic terminology and recording metadata, it is time to learn how the recording session is established. Figure 11-3 shows a basic SIP call flow—that is, a sequence of messages exchanged to set up a communication session and the corresponding recording session. It uses the same network topology discussed earlier, in Figure 11-1, in which Alice, an external caller, places a call to Bob, an internal enterprise user, using the SBC and back-to-back user agent (B2BUA) call controller. The SBC is configured to act as the SRC, and the media recorder is configured to act as the session recording server (SRS).

The first step is to establish the communication session required to connect Alice and Bob and enable audio and video communications between them. This is done through normal SIP **INVITE**, **200 OK**, and **ACK** message exchanges. For the sake of brevity, provisional responses such as **100 Trying** and **180 Ringing** are not shown in Figure 11-3. The **Supported** header field in the **200 OK** response from Bob has the value **record-aware**, which indicates that his endpoint is a recording-aware SIP user agent (UA). This capability enables SIP recording clients such as the SBC to use a new media or session-level attribute, **a=record**, to provide the session recording status to Bob's endpoint. The initial recording status is conveyed in the initial SIP **INVITE** or **ACK** transaction. Further status changes are informed by sending a SIP **Re-INVITE** or **UPDATE** request. In this example, the **a=record** attribute is not sent in the **ACK** request because the recording hasn't started yet.

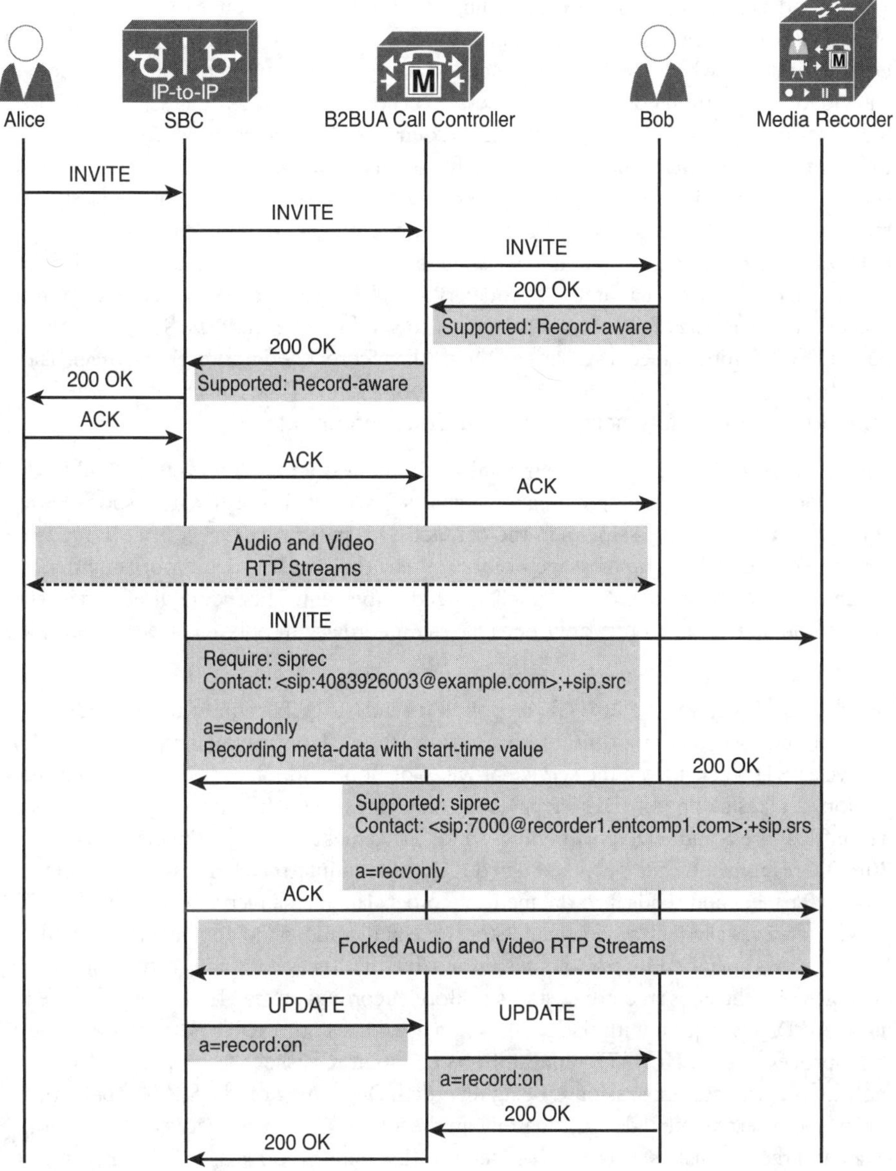

Figure 11-3 *Basic SIP Recording Session Establishment*

The second step is to establish the recording session that corresponds to the communication session between Alice and Bob. An SBC can be configured with local policies that indicate which media streams need to be recorded—audio only or both audio and video—for a given communication session. The SBC originates a new SIP **INVITE** request to the media recorder with the SIP **Require** header field value set to **siprec** and the Contact header field value set with the feature tag **+sip.src** in the contact URI. These two parameters indicate that this SIP **INVITE** request is a session recording request. This request message also contains the SDP (**application/sdp**) and recording metadata (**application/re-metadata+xml**) in its message body. SDP provides media stream details such as media type, media direction, codec type, RTP payload type, video codec profile, and so on. The media direction attribute is set to **sendonly** because the SBC will only be sending the forked media streams to the media recorder and not receiving them. The recording metadata provides the participant information and the participant-to-stream association relationship, among other information descriptors.

The media recorder processes the incoming SIP request and responds with **200 OK** if the codec of the recording media streams is supported. The **200 OK** response contains the feature tag **+sip.srs** in the contact URI, indicating that it is a SIP recording server. The SDP in the message body provides the IP address and port numbers to which the recording stream's RTP packets need to be sent. The media direction attribute in the SDP is set to **recvonly** because the recorder will only receive the recording streams.

After the SBC receives the **200 OK** response, it sends an **ACK** request to the media recorder and forks a copy of the audio and video streams toward the media recorder. As it receives a RTP packet from the service provider or Bob's endpoint for this communication session, it takes a copy of the RTP payload and creates a new RTP packet with the destination IP address and UDP port number set to the values received in the media recorder's **200 OK** response. It then puts the copied RTP payload into the UDP payload of the new RTP packet and sends it to the media recorder. The media recorder receives the RTP packet, retrieves the RTP payload, and stores the audio and video contents in a recording file format, as specified by the administrator. Now that the recording is turned on, the SBC provides the latest recording status to Bob's recording-aware SIP user agent by sending an **UPDATE** request with the **a=record:on** attribute in the SDP of the message body. After processing the **UPDATE** request, Bob's endpoint refreshes the endpoint's display to indicate that the current session is being recorded. Depending on the SBC's capabilities, it can also insert an inband recording tone in the audio RTP stream between the external caller and the internal user. The tone-based notification method is useful if either one of the two call legs managed by SBC doesn't support recording awareness at the SIP signaling level.

When the communication session between Alice and Bob terminates, the SBC disconnects the corresponding recording session by sending a SIP **BYE** request, as shown in Figure 11-4.

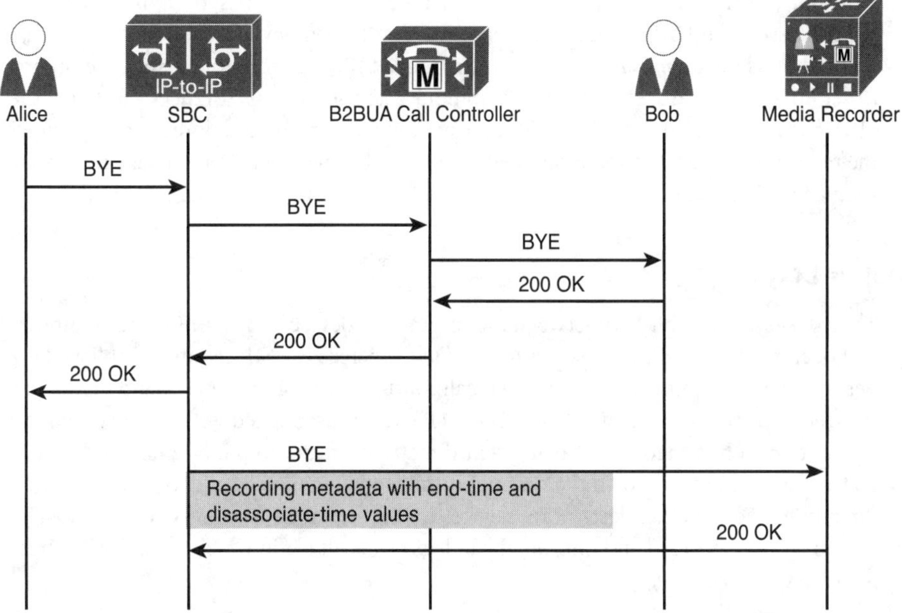

Figure 11-4 *Basic SIP Recording Session Disconnection*

The recording metadata in the SIP **BYE** request contains the communication session end time and disassociate time for participants. For conference call scenarios, the recording session is updated with media streams and recording metadata using SIP **Re-INVITE** as participants join and leave the session. The recording session is typically kept active until there is at least one associated communication session.

SIPREC Configuration

This section focuses on deploying SIPREC-based recording solutions in real-world environments with CUBE as the SBC, CUCM as the B2BUA call controller, and the QM component of Cisco Unified Workforce Optimization as the media recorder for audio streams. CUBE functions as the SRC, and QM functions as the SRS in this deployment scenario.

The first step in configuring any solution is to clearly understand the concepts behind the configuration and then select the specific configuration options that suit the business requirements. The configuration tasks to enable CUBE as a recording client are very simple once you have a good grasp of concepts such as recording dial peer, anchor legs, media recording profile, and media class.

Inbound, Outbound, and Recording Dial Peers

When a new call arrives at CUBE, it is first associated to an inbound dial peer based on called number, calling number, or URI in the From, To, or Via header field of the incoming SIP **INVITE**. Then an outbound dial peer is selected based on the called number or destination URI to route the call to the destination device. This incoming call is referred to as the *communication session* from a SIPREC protocol perspective. In order to set up a recording session for this communication session, CUBE needs to know the SIP transport method (UDP or TCP), destination number, and IP address or hostname of the recording server. The recording dial peer provides the call routing details required to send a SIP **INVITE** to the recording server and establish the recording session.

Anchor Legs

The SIP session established between the originating device and CUBE using an inbound dial peer is referred to as the *incoming call leg*, whereas the SIP session established between CUBE and the next hop in the call routing path using an outbound dial peer is referred to as the *outbound call leg*. The RTP streams associated with the incoming call leg contain audio/video received and sent directly from and to the originating device. The RTP streams associated with the outbound call leg contain audio/video sent and received directly to and from the destination device. CUBE offers the flexibility to record RTP streams of the inbound and outbound call legs. The call leg in which recording is enabled is called the *anchor leg*.

Media Recording Profiles

A media recording profile is a configuration object that is used to define which media streams needs to be recorded (audio only or audio and video) and the list of dial peers that can be used to establish recording session with the media recorder.

Media Class

The media class is a configuration object that specifies how to establish the recording session (for example, by using the SIPREC protocol) and the media recording profile to be used for the recording session.

The reference to the media class configuration object is configured under the dial peer that corresponds to the anchor leg. For example, the media class reference is configured under the incoming dial peer if the incoming call leg is enabled for recording. Similarly, the media class reference is configured under the outbound dial peer if the outgoing call leg is enabled for recording.

Audio-Only Recording

Figure 11-5 shows a deployment in which CUBE performs the role of an SBC and SRC. The endpoints used by internal enterprise users (for example, Bob) are registered to CUCM. CUBE can be configured to record incoming and outgoing calls to/from the enterprise. The incoming calls from external callers (for example, Alice) to enterprise users (for example, Bob) arrive at CUBE and are routed to CUCM, which then extends the call to the enterprise user's endpoint. After the call is established, CUBE initiates recording of this call by setting up a recording session with the QM component of the Cisco Unified Workforce Optimization server (the SRS).

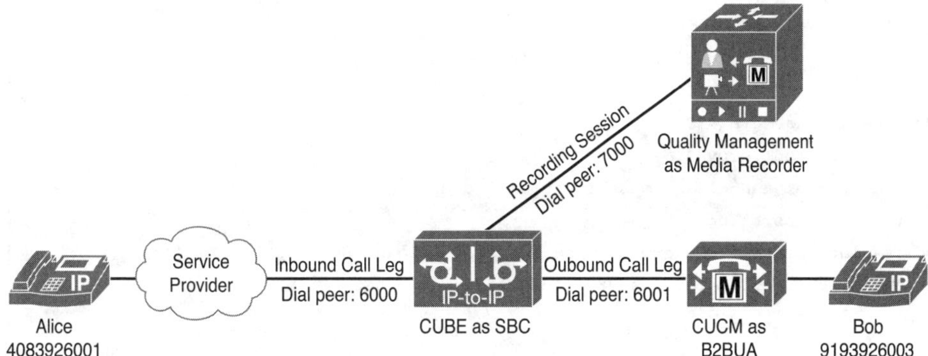

Figure 11-5 *Network Topology to Illustrate SIPREC Configuration*

Example 11-2 shows an example of the configuration for recording incoming calls to Bob (9193926003) in this deployment. The configuration consists of three dial peers:

- **6000** as the incoming dial peer
- **6001** as the outbound dial peer
- **7000** as the recording dial peer

Example 11-2 *Audio-Only Recording SIPREC Configuration*

```
media profile recorder 4001
 media-type audio
 media-recording 7000

media class 5001
 recorder profile 4001 siprec

dial-peer voice 6000 voip
 description "Inbound dial-peer for Agent phone calls"
 session protocol sipv2
 session transport tcp
 incoming called-number 9193926...
 voice-class sip bind control source-interface GigabitEthernet0/0/1
 voice-class sip bind media source-interface GigabitEthernet0/0/1
 media-class 5001
```

```
 dtmf-relay rtp-nte
 codec g711ulaw
 no vad

dial-peer voice 6001 voip
 description "Outbound dial-peer for Agent phone calls"
 preference 1
 destination-pattern 9193926...
 session protocol sipv2
 session target dns:cl2-cucm-sub1.entcomp1.com
 session transport tcp
 voice-class sip bind control source-interface GigabitEthernet0/0/2
 voice-class sip bind media source-interface GigabitEthernet0/0/2
 dtmf-relay rtp-nte
 codec g711ulaw
 no vad


dial-peer voice 7000 voip
 description "Outbound dial-peer to SIPREC based Media Recorder"
 destination-pattern 7000
 session protocol sipv2
 session target dns:recorder1.entcomp1.com
 session transport tcp
```

The **media profile recorder** command at the global configuration level defines a media recording profile named **4001**. The **media-recording** command under profile **4001** specifies dial peer **7000** to be used as recording dial peer. The **media-type audio** command restricts recording to only audio streams; that is, even if the call consists of both audio and video streams, only the audio stream is recorded.

The **media class** command at the global configuration level defines a media class configuration object named 5001. The **recorder profile 4001 siprec** command under this media class specifies **4001** as the media recording profile and SIPREC as the recording protocol.

The media class reference command **media-class 5001** under incoming **6000** enables audio-only recording on the inbound call leg and makes it an anchor leg. The dial peer **7000** serves as the recording dial peer and has **recorder1.entcomp1.com** as the media recorder's hostname and **7000** as the recording address.

When an incoming call to Bob arrives at CUBE, dial peer **6000** is matched as the inbound dial peer, and the call is routed to **cl2-cucm-sub1.entcomp1.com** through outbound dial peer **6001**. After the call is connected to Bob's phone, CUBE originates a SIP

INVITE session to **sip:7000@recorder1.entcomp1.com** with SDP, containing only the audio stream and recording metadata information. The recording session is established after the recording server sends the **200 OK** response to the SIP **INVITE** followed by **ACK** from CUBE. CUBE then forks the audio streams to/from the caller in the inbound call leg and sends a copy of the RTP packets to the media recorder. When the call to Bob ends, CUBE terminates the recording session by sending a **BYE** request with metadata information to the media recorder.

Video Recording

Video calls between internal users of an enterprise is a very common scenario, whereas video calls between external callers and internal users through the service provider SIP network is less common. Typically, enterprises have a peer-to-peer SBC connection to enable telepresence and video calls between two companies. Figure 11-6 shows one such deployment, in which two companies use CUBE to establish intercompany video calls and use a SIPREC-based media recorder that supports video recording.

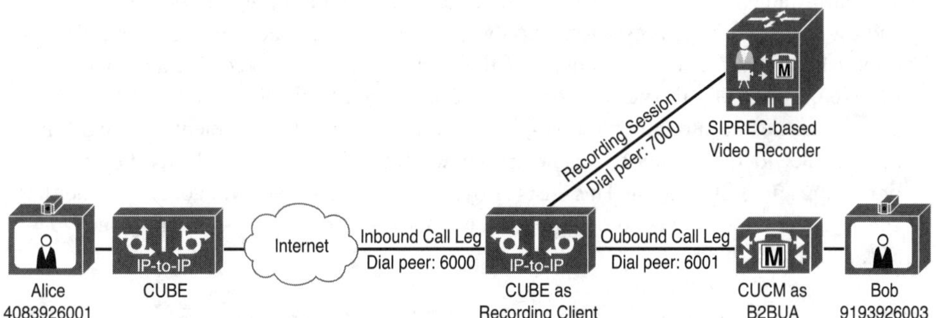

Figure 11-6 *CUBE Deployment for Video Call Flows*

From a configuration perspective, there are three key differences between audio-only recording and video recording, as shown in Example 11-3:

- Incoming and outgoing dial peers have video codecs in addition to audio codecs.
- The **media-type** command under the recording profile is set to its default value and is not limited to audio only.
- The **media profile video** command enables CUBE to send a Full Intra-Frame (FIR) request to the origination and destination video endpoints after the recording session is initiated. The FIR request can be sent either through the call signaling path using a SIP **INFO** request or through the media path using RTCP.

  The video stream within video RTP packets consists of a sequence of intra-frames (I-frames) and forward prediction frames (P-frames), as shown in Figure 11-7.

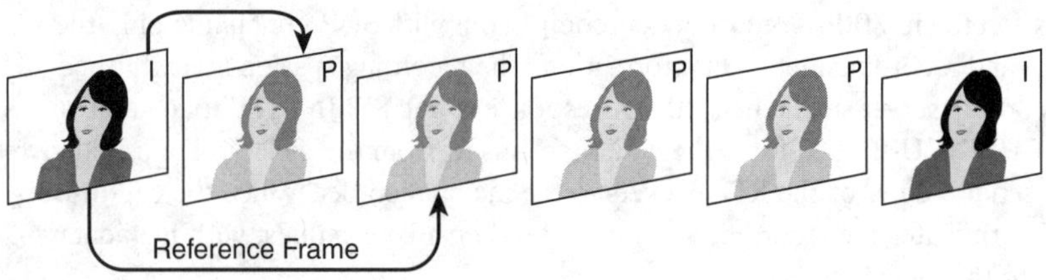

Figure 11-7 *Video Frame Types*

An I-frame contains information about all the pixels within a picture and is larger than a P-frame. The P-frames use the I-frame as a reference and contain information about only the pixel changes as the objects in the picture change over time. A video endpoint or a recorder must have the I-frame in order to correctly decode P-frames. If the I-frame is lost or not received, the decoding device cannot decode P-frames and hence cannot display the video.

In the recording call flow shown previously in Figure 11-3, Alice's and Bob's endpoints send an I-frame right after the call is established. The recording session between the SBC and the media recorder is established only after the initial call between Alice and Bob is established. This creates a possibility of the media recorder not receiving a copy of the I-frame generated by the video endpoints and hence not being able to decode the subsequent P-frames, resulting in recording loss. In order to solve this problem, the SBC can request the video endpoint to regenerate a new I-frame by sending a SIP **INFO** request or making an RTCP request. This ensures that the media recorder will get an I-frame that can be used as a reference to decode P-frames and be able to decode and play the video streams successfully.

Example 11-3 *Audio and Video Recording SIPREC Configuration*

```
media profile recorder 4002
 media-recording 7000

media profile video 4003
 ref-frame-req sip-info

media class 5002
 recorder profile 4002 siprec
 video profile 4003

dial-peer voice 6000 voip
 description "Inbound dial-peer for Agent phone calls"
 video codec h264
 session protocol sipv2
```

```
 session transport tcp
 incoming called-number 9193926...
 voice-class sip bind control source-interface GigabitEthernet0/0/1
 voice-class sip bind media source-interface GigabitEthernet0/0/1
 media-class 5002
 dtmf-relay rtp-nte
 codec g711ulaw
 no vad

dial-peer voice 6001 voip
 description "Outbound dial-peer for Agent phone calls"
 preference 1
 destination-pattern 9193926...
 video codec h264
 session protocol sipv2
 session target dns:cl2-cucm-sub1.entcomp1.com
 session transport tcp
 voice-class sip bind control source-interface GigabitEthernet0/0/2
 voice-class sip bind media source-interface GigabitEthernet0/0/2
 dtmf-relay rtp-nte
 codec g711ulaw
 no vad


dial-peer voice 7000 voip
 description "Outbound dial-peer to SIPREC based Media Recorder"
 destination-pattern 7000
 session protocol sipv2
 session target dns:recorder1.entcomp1.com
 session transport tcp
```

The **media profile recorder** command at the global configuration level defines a media recording profile named 4002. The **media-recording** command under profile **4002** specifies dial peer **7000** to be used as recording dial peer. Note that the media recorder profile does not have **media-type audio** command, and hence both audio and video streams are recorded.

The **media profile video** command at the global configuration level defines a video profile named **4003**. The **ref-frame-req sip-info** command specifies that CUBE must use SIP **INFO** to request the originating and destination video endpoints to regenerate an I-frame within the communication session.

The **media class** command at the global configuration level defines a media class configuration object named **5002**. The **recorder profile 4002 siprec** command under this media class specifies **4002** as the media recording profile with SIPREC as the recording protocol, and **video profile 4003** specifies **4003** as the video profile with SIP **INFO** used for the I-frame request.

The media class reference command **media-class 5002** under incoming dial peer **6000** enables audio and video recording on the inbound call leg. Dial peer **7000** serves as the recording dial peer and has **recorder1.entcomp1.com** as the media recorder's hostname and **7000** as the recording address.

When an incoming video call to Bob arrives at CUBE, dial peer **6000** is matched as the inbound dial peer, and the call is routed to **cl2-cucm-sub1.entcomp1.com** through outbound dial peer **6001**. After the call is connected to Bob's phone, CUBE originates a SIP **INVITE** session to **sip:7000@recorder1.entcomp1.com** with SDP, containing both the audio and video streams along with recording metadata information. The recording session is established after the recording server sends a **200 OK** response to the SIP **INVITE** followed by **ACK** from CUBE. CUBE then forks both the audio and video streams to/from the caller in the inbound call leg and sends a copy of the RTP packets to the media recorder. It is also possible for the initial call between Alice and Bob to be an audio-only call and then later escalated to video when one of the users turns on his or her camera. In this scenario, SBC sends a **Re-INVITE** on the recording session to include the video stream and corresponding recording metadata.

Note CUBE doesn't support SIPREC-based call recording for Secure RTP (SRTP) calls as of IOS XE 16.3.3.

Verification

CUBE provides a simple set of **show** commands you can use to quickly verify whether recording sessions are correctly set up and confirm that the media streams are being forked to the media recorder.

The **show** commands covered in this section correspond to the audio-only configuration shown earlier, in Example 11-2, in which CUBE is configured as the SRC and the QM component of the Cisco Unified Workforce Optimization server is configured as the SIP media recorder.

The **show call active voice brief** command is used to identify the inbound, outbound, and recording call legs associated with a given call. Example 11-4 shows an active call between external caller 4083926001 and internal IP phone 9193926003.

The inbound call leg (**56**) uses dial peer **6000**, and the outbound call leg (**57**) uses dial peer **6001** as the inbound and outbound dial peers, respectively.

Example 11-4 *Output of* **show call active voice brief** *Taken During a Recording Session*

```
CUBE1#show call active voice brief
<ID>: <CallID> <start>ms.<index> (<start>) +<connect> pid:<peer_id> <dir> <addr>
  <state>
      <output truncated for brevity>
Telephony call-legs: 0
SIP call-legs: 3
H323 call-legs: 0
Call agent controlled call-legs: 0
SCCP call-legs: 0
STCAPP call-legs: 0
Multicast call-legs: 0
Total call-legs: 3
0    : 56 49665430ms.1 (11:41:35.130 UTC Fri Sep 8 2017) +7090 pid:6000 Answer
  4083926001 active
 dur 00:01:34 tx:4712/942400 rx:4720/943240 dscp:0 media:0 audio tos:0xB8 video tos:0x0
 IP 192.168.202.119:24652 SRTP: off rtt:2ms pl:0/0ms lost:0/0/0 delay:0/0/0ms
  g711ulaw TextRelay: off Transcoded: No ICE: Off
 media inactive detected:n media contrl rcvd:n/a timestamp:n/a
 long duration call detected:n long duration call duration:n/a timestamp:n/a
 LostPacketRate:0.00 OutOfOrderRate:0.00
 LocalUUID:00004fb000105000a000000c298ea018
 RemoteUUID:8c8c368da411d8df347e579968aa5507
 VRF:
0    : 57 49671450ms.1 (11:41:41.150 UTC Fri Sep 8 2017) +1070 pid:6001 Originate
  9193926003 active
 dur 00:01:34 tx:4720/943240 rx:4712/942400 dscp:0 media:0 audio tos:0xB8 video
  tos:0x0
 IP 14.50.201.46:21762 SRTP: off rtt:2ms pl:0/0ms lost:0/0/0 delay:0/0/0ms g711ulaw
  TextRelay: off Transcoded: No ICE: Off
 media inactive detected:n media contrl rcvd:n/a timestamp:n/a
 long duration call detected:n long duration call duration:n/a timestamp:n/a
 LostPacketRate:0.00 OutOfOrderRate:0.00
 LocalUUID:8c8c368da411d8df347e579968aa5507
 RemoteUUID:00004fb000105000a000000c298ea018
 VRF:
0    : 59 49681560ms.1 (11:41:51.260 UTC Fri Sep 8 2017) +250 pid:7000 Originate
  7000 active
 dur 00:01:25 tx:4258/850840 rx:0/0 dscp:0 media:0 audio tos:0xB8 video tos:0x0
 IP 172.18.110.209:39500 SRTP: off rtt:0ms pl:0/0ms lost:0/0/0 delay:0/0/0ms
  g711ulaw TextRelay: off Transcoded: No ICE: Off
 media inactive detected:n media contrl rcvd:n/a timestamp:n/a
 long duration call detected:n long duration call duration:n/a timestamp:n/a
 LostPacketRate:0.00 OutOfOrderRate:0.00
 LocalUUID:edbc320c475c50e6820b466877e5826d
 RemoteUUID:972fdbce42ea5d8892fb977734de12cf
 VRF:
```

Note that there are three call legs in Example 11-4. What does call leg **59** represent? To answer this question, let's take a look at **show voip recmsp session**. The **recmsp** part of this command refers to *recording media service provider*, the name of an internal software component within Cisco IOS that handles recording sessions. Call leg **59**, referred to as **ForkedLeg**, is used to send forked media streams from CUBE to the SIP media recorder server. In this particular call, the media streams of the incoming call leg are being recorded, and hence the incoming call leg, **56**, is also referred to as **AnchorLeg** in the **show** command output. Call leg **58**, shown as **MSP Call-ID** in Example 11-5, is the recording call leg used by the recording media service provider (an internal software component within IOS).

Example 11-5 *Output of* show voip recmsp session

```
CUBE1#show voip recmsp session
RECMSP active sessions:
MSP Call-ID                AnchorLeg Call-ID         ForkedLeg Call-ID
58                         56                        59
Found 2 active sessions
Router
```

The MSP recording call leg ID can be used in **show voip recmsp session detail call-id** to get more details about the recording session, as shown in Example 11-6. The term **nearend** in this **show** command's context represents the calling party number, and **farend** represents the called party number.

Example 11-6 *Output of* show voip recmsp session detail call-id

```
CUBE1#show voip recmsp session detail call-id 58
RECMSP active sessions:
Detailed Information
=========================
Recording MSP Leg Details:
Call ID: 58
GUID : A99447000000

AnchorLeg Details:
Call ID: 56
Forking Stream type: voice-nearend
Participant: 4083926001

Non-anchor Leg Details:
Call ID: 57
Forking Stream type: voice-farend
```

```
Participant: 9193926003

Forked Leg Details:
Call ID: 59
Voice Near End Stream CallID 59
Stream State ACTIVE
Voice Far End stream CallID 60
Stream State ACTIVE
Found 1 active sessions
CUBE1#
```

The command in Example 11-6 verifies that recording sessions are being established. The next step in the verification process is to ensure that media streams are correctly forked and sent to the media recorder. The commands **show voip rtp connections** and **show voip rtp forking** help you accomplish this task by providing IP- and RTP-related statistics for both the media streams and recording streams of the call. The first connection shown in Example 11-7 (192.168.202.165:8088 <> 192.168.202.119:24652) represents the audio RTP connection between CUBE and the service provider, and the second connection (172.18.110.203:8090 <> 14.50.201.56:21762) represents the audio RTP connection between CUBE and the internal IP phone that answered the call from the external caller. The third and fourth streams represents the forked RTP streams, and both are destined to the media recorder's IP address, 172.18.110.209, at port numbers 39500 and 39501. These two streams are associated to the recording call leg (**58**) and ForkedLegs (**59** and **60**). The first forked stream contains RTP packets of the media stream received from the service provider (that is, the audio of the external caller to the IP phone), and the second forked stream contains RTP packets of the media stream sent to the service provider (that is, the audio of the IP phone to the external caller).

Example 11-7 *Output of* **show voip rtp connections**

```
CUBE1#show voip rtp conn
VoIP RTP Port Usage Information:
Max Ports Available: 19999, Ports Reserved: 101, Ports in Use: 4
Port range not configured
                                        Min   Max   Ports     Ports     Ports
Media-Address Range                     Port  Port  Available Reserved  In-use
------------------------------------------------------------------------------
Global Media Pool                       8000  48198 19999     101       4
------------------------------------------------------------------------------
VoIP RTP active connections :
```

```
No. CallId dstCallId LocalRTP  RmtRTP       LocalIP          RemoteIP        MPSS   VRF
1     56       57       8088     24652    192.168.202.165  192.168.202.119   NO     NA
2     57       56       8090     21762    172.18.110.203   14.50.201.46      NO     NA
3     59       58       8092     39500    172.18.110.203   172.18.110.209    NO     NA
4     60       58       8094     39501    172.18.110.203   172.18.110.209    NO     NA
Found 4 active RTP connections
CUBE1#
```

The **packets sent** counter in the command output of **show voip rtp forking** in Example 11-8 tell whether CUBE is transmitting RTP packets to the recorder. This command can be run multiple times while the recording session is active. The **packets sent** counter must increment continuously in each run. As a final step, you can check whether the recording file is correctly generated by the media recorder by accessing its web page, APIs, or the recording storage locations.

Example 11-8 *Output of* show voip rtp forking

```
CUBE1#show voip rtp forking
VoIP RTP active forks :
 Fork 1
   stream type voice-only (0): count 0
   stream type voice+dtmf (1): count 0
   stream type dtmf-only (2): count 0
   stream type voice-nearend (3): count 1
     remote ip 172.18.110.209, remote port 39500, local port 8092
       codec g711ulaw, logical ssrc 0x53
       packets sent 3052, packets received 0
   stream type voice+dtmf-nearend (4): count 0
   stream type voice-farend (5): count 1
     remote ip 172.18.110.209, remote port 39501, local port 8094
       codec g711ulaw, logical ssrc 0x55
       packets sent 3054, packets received 0
   stream type voice+dtmf-farend (6): count 0
   stream type video (7): count 0
   stream type video-nearend (8): count 0
   stream type video-farend (9): count 0
   stream type application (10): count 0
CUBE1#
```

SIPREC Troubleshooting

An effective method of troubleshooting a problem is to understand how a particular feature is expected to work and then identifying what is different in the non-working scenario. This section starts by discussing a working scenario of a successful recording session and then describes how to troubleshoot common issues such as recording not being initiated, missing recording metadata, and a recording file not being generated.

The "Verification" section, earlier in this chapter, introduces **show** commands that can be used to verify audio-only recording configuration. Now, let's walk through the corresponding debugs of the audio recording call flow, in which the call between 4083926001 (an external caller) and 9193926003 (an internal IP Phone) is recorded. The basic **debug** commands for Cisco IOS and IOS XE software components in CUBE deal with call control API (CCAPI), call control SIP (CCSIP), and recording media service provider (RECMSP), which all provide insights into the inner workings:

```
debug voip ccapi inout
debug ccsip message
debug ccsip events
debug ccsip error
debug ccsip info
debug voip recmsp event
debug voip recmsp error
debug voip recmsp inout
```

Figure 11-8 shows the end-to-end call flow shown in the IOS debug output with **A99447000000** as the call GUID value and **56**, **57**, **58**, and **59** as the call leg IDs of incoming, outgoing, and recording and forking call legs, respectively.

The following examples show debug snippets that might appear when all the debugs listed previously are enabled. For the sake of brevity, only the debug snippets that are generated after the initial call setup between **4083926001** and **9193926003** are discussed. After the call is connected from the SIP signaling perspective, the inbound call leg **56** posts a media forking start indication to its peer outbound leg **57**, which ignores this event because it is not the anchor leg (that is, the **media-class** command is configured only on the inbound dial peer **6000**). Similarly, outbound call leg **57** posts a media forking start indication to inbound call leg **56**, which processes the event and triggers the recording session creation, as shown in Example 11-9. The term **msp call ID:58** represents the recording call leg, **58**.

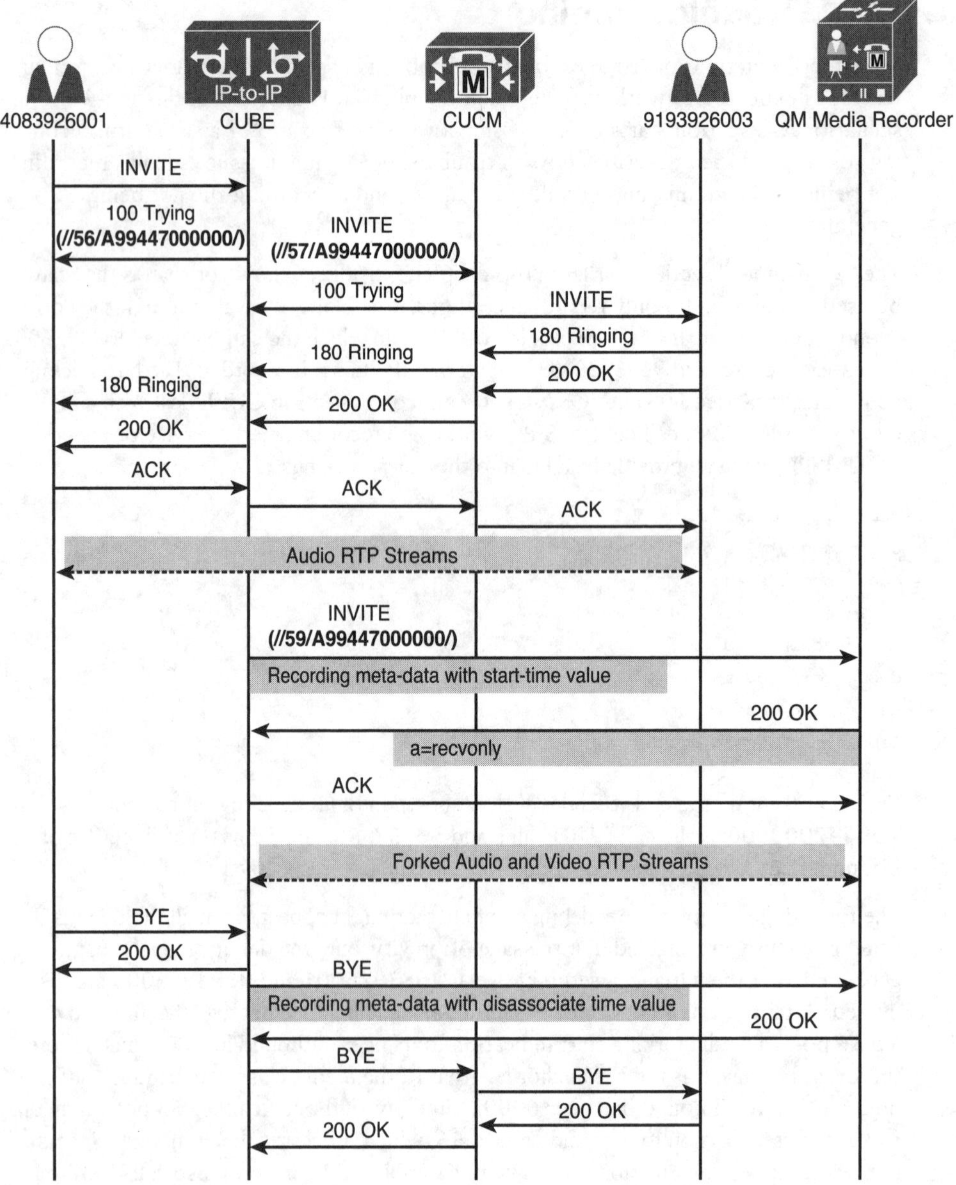

Figure 11-8 *SIPREC Call Flow Using CUBE and the QM Media Recorder*

Example 11-9 *Recording Session Creation*

```
059895: Sep  8 11:41:42.235 UTC: //56/A99447000000/SIP/Info/notify/32768/ccsip_trig-
  ger_media_forking: MF: Recv Ack & it's Anchor leg.
059896: Sep  8 11:41:42.235 UTC: //56/A99447000000/SIP/Info/info/32768/ccsip_trig-
  ger_media_forking: MF: set is_mf_start_pending flag and wait for peer leg to indi-
  cate start
059897: Sep  8 11:41:42.235 UTC: //56/A99447000000/SIP/Info/info/32768/ccsip_trig-
  ger_media_forking: MF: posting CC_EV_H245_MEDIA_FORKING_START_IND.
.....
.....
.....
059902: Sep  8 11:41:42.235 UTC: //57/A99447000000/SIP/Info/notify/32768/ccsip_event_
  handler: CC_EV_H245_MEDIA_FORKING_START_IND: peer ID 56, event = 213 type = 1
059903: Sep  8 11:41:42.235 UTC: //57/A99447000000/SIP/Info/verbose/32768/ccsip_
  event_handler: Ignoring the event on non-anchor leg
.....
.....
.....
060078: Sep  8 11:41:42.240 UTC: //56/A99447000000/SIP/Info/notify/32768/ccsip_event_
  handler: CC_EV_H245_MEDIA_FORKING_START_IND: peer ID 57, event = 213 type = 1
060079: Sep  8 11:41:42.240 UTC: //56/A99447000000/SIP/Info/verbose/32768/ccsip_
  event_handler: Peer leg has indicated start. Trigger Media Forking.
060080: Sep  8 11:41:42.240 UTC: //56/A99447000000/SIP/Info/info/32768/ccsip_ipip_
  media_forking_preprocess_event: MF: initial-call. State = 1 & posting the event
  E_IPIP_MEDIA_FORKING_CALLSETUP_IND
.....
.....
.....
060084: Sep  8 11:41:42.240 UTC: //56/A99447000000/SIP/Info/info/34816/ccsip_ipip_
  media_forking_precondition: MF: Can be started with current config.
060085: Sep  8 11:41:42.240 UTC: //-1/xxxxxxxxxxxx/Event/recmsp_api_create_session:
  Event: E_REC_CREATE_SESSION anchor call ID:56, msp call ID:58
060086: Sep  8 11:41:42.240 UTC: //-1/xxxxxxxxxxxx/Inout/recmsp_api_create_session:
  Exit with Success
```

An important step in setting up a recording session is to look up the recording dial peer configured in the media recorder profile associated with the inbound call leg. The **destination-pattern** and **session target** values under the recording dial peer are used as the recording directory number and recording server address. Example 11-10 shows that **7000** is used as the recording dial peer. The string "**Called Number = 7000**" in the debug output indicates that **7000** is the **destination-pattern** configured under the dial peer, which is used as the recording directory number.

Example 11-10 *Recording Dial Peer Lookup*

```
060145: Sep  8 11:41:42.241 UTC: //-1/xxxxxxxxxxxx/Event/recmsp_api_setup_session:
  Event: E_REC_SETUP_REQ anchor call ID:56, msp call ID:58 infunction recmsp_api_
  setup_session
060146: Sep  8 11:41:42.241 UTC: //-1/xxxxxxxxxxxx/Inout/recmsp_api_setup_session:
  Exit with Success
.....
.....
.....
060171: Sep  8 11:41:42.242 UTC: //58/A99447000000/RECMSP/Inout/recmsp_get_dp_tag_
  list: Entry recmsp_get_dp_tag_list
060172: Sep  8 11:41:42.242 UTC: //58/A99447000000/RECMSP/Inout/recmsp_get_dp_tag_
  list: RECORDER_PROFILE recmsp_get_dp_tag_list
060173: Sep  8 11:41:42.242 UTC: //58/A99447000000/RECMSP/Inout/recmsp_get_dp_tag_
  list: REC DP: = 7000
060174: Sep  8 11:41:42.242 UTC: //58/A99447000000/RECMSP/Inout/recmsp_get_dp_tag_
  list: Exit with success recmsp_get_dp_tag_list
.....
.....
.....


060187: Sep  8 11:41:42.243 UTC: //58/xxxxxxxxxxxx/CCAPI/cc_api_display_ie_sub-
  fields:
   ccCallSetupRequest:
   cisco-username=
   ----- ccCallInfo IE subfields -----
   cisco-ani=
   cisco-anitype=0
   cisco-aniplan=0
   cisco-anipi=0
   cisco-anisi=0
   dest=7000
   cisco-desttype=0
   cisco-destplan=0
   cisco-rdie=FFFFFFFFFFFFFFFF
   cisco-rdn=
   cisco-rdntype=0
   cisco-rdnplan=0
   cisco-rdnpi=0
   cisco-rdnsi=0
   cisco-redirectreason=0   fwd_final_type =0
   final_redirectNumber =
   hunt_group_timeout =0


060188: Sep  8 11:41:42.244 UTC: //58/xxxxxxxxxxxx/CCAPI/ccIFCallSetupRequestPrivate:
```

```
Interface=0x7F7BF2DF31C8, Interface Type=3, Destination=, Mode=0x0,
Call Params(Calling Number=,(Calling Name=)(TON=Unknown, NPI=Unknown,
Screening=Not Screened, Presentation=Allowed),
Called Number=7000(TON=Unknown, NPI=Unknown), Calling Translated=FALSE,
Subscriber Type Str=, FinalDestinationFlag=FALSE, Outgoing Dial-peer=7000, Call
Count On=FALSE,
Source Trkgrp Route Label=, Target Trkgrp Route Label=, tg_label_flag=0,
Application Call Id=)
```

Because the session target destination is configured as a hostname, CUBE performs DNS lookup to determine the recorder's IP address. Example 11-11 shows a **debug** snippet of the DNS lookup process for **recorder2.entcomp1.com**, which returns **172.18.110.209** as the IP address.

Example 11-11 *Recording Server DNS Lookup*

```
060243: Sep  8 11:41:42.245 UTC: //59/A99447000000/SIP/Info/verbose/5120/ccsip_call_
  setup_request: Session target or outbound proxy configured
060244: Sep  8 11:41:42.245 UTC: //-1/xxxxxxxxxxxx/SIP/Info/verbose/5120/sipSPIGet-
  OutboundHostAndDestHostPrivate: CCSIP: target_host : recorder2.entcomp1.com tar-
  get_port : 5060
.....
.....
.....
060314: Sep  8 11:41:42.247 UTC: //-1/xxxxxxxxxxxx/SIP/Info/notify/8192/sip_dns_
  type_srv_query: TYPE SRV query for _sip._tcp.recorder2.entcomp1.com and type:1
060315: Sep  8 11:41:51.250 UTC: //-1/xxxxxxxxxxxx/SIP/Info/info/8192/sip_dns_
  type_a_aaaa_query: DNS query for recorder2.entcomp1.com and type:1
060316: Sep  8 11:41:51.251 UTC: //-1/xxxxxxxxxxxx/SIP/Info/notify/8192/sip_dns_
  type_a_query: TYPE A query successful for recorder2.entcomp1.com
060317: Sep  8 11:41:51.251 UTC: //-1/xxxxxxxxxxxx/SIP/Info/info/8192/sip_dns_
  type_a_query: ttl for A records = 86400 seconds
060318: Sep  8 11:41:51.251 UTC: //-1/xxxxxxxxxxxx/SIP/Info/info/8192/sip_dns_
  type_a_aaaa_query: IP Address of recorder2.entcomp1.com is:
060319: Sep  8 11:41:51.251 UTC: //-1/xxxxxxxxxxxx/SIP/Info/info/8192/sip_dns_
  type_a_aaaa_query: 172.18.110.209
```

CUBE then builds the recording metadata XML, determines media attributes such as codecs and direction (**sendonly**), and sends a SIP **INVITE** with the message body containing both metadata using content type **application/sdp** and SDP information using content type **application/rs-medata+xml**, as shown in Example 11-12. The stream from the external caller to the IP phone user is labeled **1** and assigned the stream ID **ihKD-cJPBEeeAtPH6U5qmBw==**, whereas the stream from the IP phone user to the external caller is labeled **2** and assigned the stream ID **ihKDcJPBEeeAtfH6U5qmBw==**.

Example 11-12 *Recording a* SIP INVITE *with Metadata and Media Attributes*

```
060405: Sep  8 11:41:51.253 UTC: //59/A99447000000/SIP/Info/info/32768/ccsip_ipip_
  mf_create_xml_metadata: MF: XML metadata Len: [1731]


.....
.....
.....

060419: Sep  8 11:41:51.254 UTC: //59/A99447000000/SIP/Info/verbose/8192/sipSPI_mf_
  find_rcstream: Matched stream type = 3
060420: Sep  8 11:41:51.254 UTC: //-1/xxxxxxxxxxxx/SIP/Info/notify/1/convert_codec_
  bytes_to_ptime: Values :Codec: g711ulaw codecbytes :160, ptime: 20
060421: Sep  8 11:41:51.254 UTC: //-1/xxxxxxxxxxxx/SIP/Info/notify/1/sipSPISetMedia-
  DirectionForStream: Setting Media direction SENDONLY for stream 1
.....
.....
.....
060497: Sep  8 11:41:51.313 UTC: //-1/xxxxxxxxxxxx/SIP/Msg/ccsipDisplayMsg:
Sent:
INVITE sip:7000@recorder2.entcomp1.com:5060 SIP/2.0
Via: SIP/2.0/TCP 172.18.110.203:5060;branch=z9hG4bK46CF2
From: <sip:172.18.110.119>;tag=2F75973-167F
To: <sip:7000@recorder2.entcomp1.com>
Date: Fri, 08 Sep 2017 11:41:51 GMT
Call-ID: 84B44EB4-93C111E7-80B3F1FA-539AA607@172.18.110.203
Supported: 100rel,timer,resource-priority,replaces,sdp-anat
Require: siprec
Min-SE:  1800
Cisco-Guid: 2845067008-0000065536-0000000056-2764744896
User-Agent: Cisco-SIPGateway/IOS-16.6.1
Allow: INVITE, OPTIONS, BYE, CANCEL, ACK, PRACK, UPDATE, REFER, SUBSCRIBE, NOTIFY,
  INFO, REGISTER
CSeq: 101 INVITE
Max-Forwards: 70
Timestamp: 1504870911
Contact: <sip:172.18.110.203:5060;transport=tcp>;+sip.src
Expires: 180
Allow-Events: telephone-event
Session-ID: 972fdbce42ea5d8892fb977734de12cf;remote=00000000000000000000000000000000
Content-Type: multipart/mixed;boundary=uniqueBoundary
Mime-Version: 1.0
Content-Length: 2441

--uniqueBoundary
```

```
Content-Type: application/sdp
Content-Disposition: session;handling=required

v=0
o=CiscoSystemsSIP-GW-UserAgent 995 2743 IN IP4 172.18.110.203
s=SIP Call
c=IN IP4 172.18.110.203
t=0 0
m=audio 8092 RTP/AVP 0 101 19
c=IN IP4 172.18.110.203
a=rtpmap:0 PCMU/8000
a=rtpmap:101 telephone-event/8000
a=fmtp:101 0-16
a=rtpmap:19 CN/8000
a=ptime:20
a=sendonly
a=label:1
m=audio 8094 RTP/AVP 0 101 19
c=IN IP4 172.18.110.203
a=rtpmap:0 PCMU/8000
a=rtpmap:101 telephone-event/8000
a=fmtp:101 0-16
a=rtpmap:19 CN/8000
a=ptime:20
a=sendonly
a=label:2

--uniqueBoundary
Content-Type: application/rs-metadata+xml
Content-Disposition: recording-session

<?xml version="1.0" encoding="UTF-8"?>
<recording xmlns="urn:ietf:params:xml:ns:recording:1">
    <datamode>complete</datamode>
    <session session_id="hLOLNpPBEeeArfH6U5qmBw==">


        <sipSessionID>8c8c368da411d8df347e579968aa5507;remote=00004fb000105000a00000
  0c298ea018</sipSessionID>
        <start-time>2017-09-08T11:41:42.242Z</start-time>
    </session>
    <participant participant_id="hLOLNpPBEeeArvH6U5qmBw==">
        <nameID aor="sip:4083926001@192.168.202.164">
        </nameID>
    </participant>
```

```
    <participantsessionassoc participant_id="hLOLNpPBEeeArvH6U5qmBw==" session_
  id="hLOLNpPBEeeArfH6U5qmBw==">
        <associate-time>2017-09-08T11:41:42.242Z</associate-time>
    </participantsessionassoc>
    <stream stream_id="ihKDcJPBEeeAtPH6U5qmBw==" session_id="hLOLNpPBEeeArfH6U5qmBw==">
        <label>1</label>
    </stream>
    <participant participant_id="hLOLNpPBEeeAr/H6U5qmBw==">
        <nameID aor="sip:9193926003@172.18.110.206">
        </nameID>
    </participant>
    <participantsessionassoc participant_id="hLOLNpPBEeeAr/H6U5qmBw==" session_
  id="hLOLNpPBEeeArfH6U5qmBw==">
        <associate-time>2017-09-08T11:41:42.242Z</associate-time>
    </participantsessionassoc>
    <stream stream_id="ihKDcJPBEeeAtfH6U5qmBw==" session_id="hLOLNpPBEeeArfH6U5qmBw==">
        <label>2</label>
    </stream>
    <participantstreamassoc participant_id="hLOLNpPBEeeArvH6U5qmBw==">
        <send>ihKDcJPBEeeAtPH6U5qmBw==</send>
        <recv>ihKDcJPBEeeAtfH6U5qmBw==</recv>
    </participantstreamassoc>
    <participantstreamassoc participant_id="hLOLNpPBEeeAr/H6U5qmBw==">
        <send>ihKDcJPBEeeAtfH6U5qmBw==</send>
        <recv>ihKDcJPBEeeAtPH6U5qmBw==</recv>
    </participantstreamassoc>
</recording>

--uniqueBoundary—
```

CUBE receives a **200 OK** response from the QM media recorder and sends an **ACK**, resulting in the recording session getting established. Note that the media direction in the **200 OK** response shown in Example 11-13 is **recvonly**, which indicates that the recording server is ready to receive the forked media streams at the provided RTP IP address and port numbers, **172.18.110.209:39500** and **172.18.110.209:39501**.

When the call is terminated, the inbound call leg (**56**) initiates the disconnect process and sends a disconnect indication event to the recording call leg (**58**). CUBE sends a SIP **BYE** request along with updated metadata information to the recording server, receives a **200 OK**, and disconnects the recording session with **16** (normal call clearing) as the disconnect cause code, as shown in Example 11-14.

Example 11-13 *Recording Session Establishment*

```
060506: Sep  8 11:41:51.503 UTC: //59/A99447000000/SIP/Msg/ccsipDisplayMsg:
Received:
SIP/2.0 200 OK
CSeq: 101 INVITE
Call-ID: 84B44EB4-93C111E7-80B3F1FA-539AA607@172.18.110.203
From: <sip:172.18.110.119>;tag=2F75973-167F
To: <sip:7000@recorder2.entcomp1.com;transport=tcp>;tag=d33a9687
Via: SIP/2.0/TCP 172.18.110.203:5060;branch=z9hG4bK46CF2;rport=31334
Timestamp: 1504870911
Contact: <sip:recording@172.18.110.209:5060;transport=tcp>
Allow: INVITE, ACK, CANCEL, OPTIONS, BYE, UPDATE
Content-Type: application/sdp
Content-Length: 210

v=0
o=- 995 2743 IN IP4 172.18.110.209
s=QM_SIP_Recorder
c=IN IP4 172.18.110.209
t=0 0
m=audio 39500 RTP/AVP 0
a=rtpmap:0 PCMU/8000
a=recvonly
m=audio 39501 RTP/AVP 0
a=rtpmap:0 PCMU/8000
a=recvonly
.....
.....
.....
060676: Sep  8 11:41:51.508 UTC: //58/A99447000000/RECMSP/Inout/recmsp_api_connect:
  Entry
060677: Sep  8 11:41:51.508 UTC: //58/A99447000000/RECMSP/Event/recmsp_api_connect:
  Event: E_REC_CC_CONNECT msp call ID:58 in recmsp_api_connect
060678: Sep  8 11:41:51.508 UTC: //58/A99447000000/RECMSP/Inout/recmsp_api_connect:
  Exit with Success
.....
.....
.....
060697: Sep  8 11:41:51.509 UTC: //-1/xxxxxxxxxxxx/SIP/Info/ccsip_process_tcp_queue_
  event: Event type: send msg, connid: 36, fd: 5
060698: Sep  8 11:41:51.509 UTC: //59/A99447000000/SIP/Msg/ccsipDisplayMsg:
Sent:
```

```
ACK sip:recording@172.18.110.209:5060;transport=tcp SIP/2.0
Via: SIP/2.0/TCP 172.18.110.203:5060;branch=z9hG4bK47187C
From: <sip:172.18.110.119>;tag=2F75973-167F
To: <sip:7000@recorder2.entcomp1.com;transport=tcp>;tag=d33a9687
Date: Fri, 08 Sep 2017 11:41:51 GMT
Call-ID: 84B44EB4-93C111E7-80B3F1FA-539AA607@172.18.110.203
Max-Forwards: 70
CSeq: 101 ACK
Allow-Events: telephone-event
Session-ID: 972fdbce42ea5d8892fb977734de12cf;remote=edbc320c475c50e6820b466877e5826d
Content-Length: 0
```

Example 11-14 *Recording Session Disconnection*

```
061730: Sep  8 11:44:35.166 UTC: //56/A99447000000/SIP/Info/critical/4096/sipSPIIni-
  tiateDisconnect: Initiate call disconnect(16) for incoming call
.....
.....
.....
061738: Sep  8 11:44:35.166 UTC: //56/A99447000000/SIP/Info/verbose/32768/ccsip_
  ipip_media_forking_common_disconnect_ind: MF:
061742: Sep  8 11:44:35.166 UTC: //58/A99447000000/RECMSP/Event/recmsp_api_delete_
  session: Event: E_REC_DISCONNECT_IND anchor call ID:56, msp call ID:58 in recmsp_
  api_delete_session
061743: Sep  8 11:44:35.166 UTC: //58/A99447000000/RECMSP/Inout/recmsp_api_delete_
  session:  Exit with Success
.....
.....
.....

061911: Sep  8 11:44:35.175 UTC: //59/A99447000000/SIP/Msg/ccsipDisplayMsg:
Sent:
BYE sip:recording@172.18.110.209:5060;transport=tcp SIP/2.0
Via: SIP/2.0/TCP 172.18.110.203:5060;branch=z9hG4bK482202
From: <sip:172.18.110.119>;tag=2F75973-167F
To: <sip:7000@recorder2.entcomp1.com;transport=tcp>;tag=d33a9687
Date: Fri, 08 Sep 2017 11:41:51 GMT
Call-ID: 84B44EB4-93C111E7-80B3F1FA-539AA607@172.18.110.203
User-Agent: Cisco-SIPGateway/IOS-16.6.1
Max-Forwards: 70
Timestamp: 1504871075
CSeq: 102 BYE
Reason: Q.850;cause=16
P-RTP-Stat: PS=8162,OS=1631184,PR=0,OR=0,PL=0,JI=0,LA=0,DU=163
```

```
Session-ID: 972fdbce42ea5d8892fb977734de12cf;remote=edbc320c475c50e6820b466877e5826d
Content-Type: application/rs-metadata+xml
Content-Disposition: recording-session
Content-Length: 1099

<?xml version="1.0" encoding="UTF-8"?>
<recording xmlns="urn:ietf:params:xml:ns:recording:1">
    <datamode>complete</datamode>
    <session session_id="hLOLNpPBEeeArfH6U5qmBw==">
        <sipSessionID>8c8c368da411d8df347e579968aa5507;remote=00004fb000105000a00000
  0c298ea018</sipSessionID>
        <end-time>2017-09-08T11:44:35.172Z</end-time>
    </session>
    <participant participant_id="hLOLNpPBEeeAr/H6U5qmBw==">
        <nameID aor="sip:9193926003@172.18.110.206">
        </nameID>
    </participant>
    <participantsessionassoc participant_id="hLOLNpPBEeeAr/H6U5qmBw==" session_
  id="hLOLNpPBEeeArfH6U5qmBw==">
        <disassociate-time>2017-09-08T11:44:35.168Z</disassociate-time>
    </participantsessionassoc>
    <participant participant_id="hLOLNpPBEeeArvH6U5qmBw==">
        <nameID aor="sip:4083926001@192.168.202.164">
        </nameID>
    </participant>
    <participantsessionassoc participant_id="hLOLNpPBEeeArvH6U5qmBw==" session_
  id="hLOLNpPBEeeArfH6U5qmBw==">
        <disassociate-time>2017-09-08T11:44:35.168Z</disassociate-time>
    </participantsessionassoc>
</recording>

.....
.....
.....

062036: Sep  8 11:44:35.197 UTC: //59/A99447000000/SIP/Msg/ccsipDisplayMsg:
Received:
SIP/2.0 200 OK
CSeq: 102 BYE
Call-ID: 84B44EB4-93C111E7-80B3F1FA-539AA607@172.18.110.203
From: <sip:172.18.110.119>;tag=2F75973-167F
To: <sip:7000@recorder2.entcomp1.com;transport=tcp>;tag=d33a9687
Via: SIP/2.0/TCP 172.18.110.203:5060;branch=z9hG4bK482202;rport=31334
```

```
Timestamp: 1504871075
Content-Length: 0
.....
.....
.....
062055: Sep  8 11:44:35.197 UTC: //58/xxxxxxxxxxxx/CCAPI/cc_api_call_disconnect_
  done:
   Disposition=0, Interface=0x7F7BF2DF31C8, Tag=0x0, Call Id=58,
   Call Entry(Disconnect Cause=16, Voice Class Cause Code=0, Retry Count=0)
```

Recording Initiation Failures

The issue of recording not being initiated by CUBE is typically reported in new deployments, and the primary root cause is incorrect configuration. The following are some examples:

- There is an incorrect inbound dial peer match (that is, the selected inbound dial peer doesn't have **media-class** associated with it).
- The **destination-pattern** in the recording dial peer is a regular expression pattern instead of a simple directory number (for example, **70..** instead of **7000**).
- There is an incorrect recording server IP address or the server's hostname is not successfully resolved to an IP address.

The issue of recording not being initiated by CUBE can be easily identified by running **show call active voice brief** and observing the lack of forking call leg in the output. The same set of CCAPI, CCSIP, and RECMSP debugs shown earlier in this chapter can be enabled to troubleshoot this problem. Example 11-15 shows the debug snippets of the recording call leg (**73**) when the recording dial peer is configured with **destination-pattern 70..** (a regular expression) instead of **destination-pattern 7000** (a number). CUBE uses the value provided in the recording dial peer's destination pattern to set the **Request-URI** of the outbound recording SIP **INVITE** request. It terminates the recording session creation with cause code **28** (invalid number) because **70..** is not a valid SIP user address. The failure to initiate recording doesn't impact the actual call, and the call continues to be active until it is disconnected normally by the user.

The recording initiation failure could also be observed in post-production deployments. Most often, the root cause is related to the recording service not being available or not being reachable due to IP connectivity issues. The **debug** output shows SIP responses such as **503 Service Unavailable** and **500 Server Internal Error** from the recording server. Sometimes, there may be no response to the SIP **INVITE** sent by CUBE to the recording server. In such scenarios, it is good to add **debug ip tcp transactions** to the **debug** command list to determine whether TCP connections are getting established correctly. Example 11-16 shows the output of the forking call leg (**96**) trying to establish a

TCP connection by sending a **TCP SYN** packet to 172.18.110.210 and closing it because of receiving a TCP **RST** (reset) packet.

Example 11-15 *Recording Session Initiation Failure with Cause Code* 28

```
070436: Sep 10 13:50:44.857 UTC: //73/FCA6FF000000/RECMSP/Inout/recmsp_get_dp_tag_
  list: Entry recmsp_get_dp_tag_list
070437: Sep 10 13:50:44.857 UTC: //73/FCA6FF000000/RECMSP/Inout/recmsp_get_dp_tag_
  list: RECORDER_PROFILE recmsp_get_dp_tag_list
070438: Sep 10 13:50:44.857 UTC: //73/FCA6FF000000/RECMSP/Inout/recmsp_get_dp_tag_
  list: REC DP: = 7000
.....
.....
.....
070447: Sep 10 13:50:44.859 UTC: //73/xxxxxxxxxxxx/CCAPI/ccCallDisconnect:
   Cause Value=28, Tag=0x0, Call Entry(Previous Disconnect Cause=0, Disconnect
  Cause=0)
070448: Sep 10 13:50:44.859 UTC: //73/xxxxxxxxxxxx/CCAPI/ccCallDisconnect:
   Cause Value=28, Call Entry(Responsed=TRUE, Cause Value=28)
070451: Sep 10 13:50:44.859 UTC: //73/FCA6FF000000/RECMSP/Event/recmsp_api_discon-
  nect: Event: E_REC_CC_DISCONNECT anchor call ID:71, msp call ID:73
```

Example 11-16 *Recording Session Initiation Failure with Cause Code* 38

```
086049: Sep 10 14:24:18.409 UTC: //96/000000000000/SIP/Info/critical/32768/ccsip_
  call_setup_request: MF or SIP TDM call flow


086055: Sep 10 14:24:18.410 UTC: //96/AD1702000000/SIP/Info/verbose/5120/ccsip_call_
  setup_request: Session target or outbound proxy configured
086056: Sep 10 14:24:18.410 UTC: //-1/xxxxxxxxxxxx/SIP/Info/verbose/5120/sipSPIGet-
  OutboundHostAndDestHostPrivate: CCSIP: target_host : 172.18.110.210 target_port :
  5060
.....
.....
.....
086272: Sep 10 14:24:18.416 UTC: Reserved port 61926 in Transport Port Agent for TCP
  IP type 1
086273: Sep 10 14:24:18.416 UTC: TCP: sending SYN, seq 616483488, ack 0
086274: Sep 10 14:24:18.416 UTC: TCP0: Connection to 172.18.110.210:5060, advertis-
  ing MSS 1460
086275: Sep 10 14:24:18.416 UTC: TCP0: state was CLOSED -> SYNSENT [61926 ->
  172.18.110.210(5060)]
.....
.....
.....
```

```
086277: Sep 10 14:24:18.417 UTC: Released port 61926 in Transport Port Agent for TCP
  IP type 1 delay 240000
086278: Sep 10 14:24:18.417 UTC: TCP0: state was SYNSENT -> CLOSED [61926 ->
  172.18.110.210(5060)]
086279: Sep 10 14:24:18.417 UTC: TCP0: bad seg from 172.18.110.210 -- closing con-
  nection: port 61926 seq 0 ack 616483489 rcvnxt 0 rcvwnd 0 len 0
086280: Sep 10 14:24:18.417 UTC: TCP0: connection closed - remote sent RST
086281: Sep 10 14:24:18.417 UTC: TCB7F7BFCE6DA48 getting property TCP_VRFTABLEID
  (20)
086282: Sep 10 14:24:18.417 UTC: //-1/xxxxxxxxxxxx/SIP/Error/sip_tcp_createcon-
  nfailed_to_spi:
 TCP create conn failed to SPI (addr:172.18.110.210, port:5060)
.....
.....
.....
086290: Sep 10 14:24:18.418 UTC: //96/AD1702000000/SIP/Info/critical/4096/ccsip_set_
  cc_cause_for_spi_err: Categorized cause:38, category:186
086291: Sep 10 14:24:18.418 UTC: //96/AD1702000000/SIP/Info/verbose/4096/ccsip_set_
  release_source_for_peer: ownCallId[96], src[6]
086292: Sep 10 14:24:18.418 UTC: //96/AD1702000000/SIP/Info/critical/4096/sipSPIIni-
  tiateDisconnect: Initiate call disconnect(38) for outgoing call
```

Missing Recording Metadata

In certain situations, the initial SIP **INVITE** sent by CUBE to a SIPREC-based media recorder may not have metadata information even if the device configuration is correct. This may be observed, for example, when the recorder's hostname is given as a session target command value in the recording dial peer. If you experience this scenario, change the session target command value to the recorder's IP address to resolve the issue.

Missing Recording File

Recording file generation is the responsibility of the recording server. Before you dive into troubleshooting the media recorder and analyzing its logs, it is a good practice to quickly verify whether CUBE is sending the RTP media packets to the recording server while the recording is active. This can be accomplished by running **show voip rtp connections** and **show voip rtp forking** and ensuring that the **packets sent** counter is incrementing in each run, as shown earlier in the chapter, in Example 11-8. In some situations, the recording session might get established but the recording server may set the media stream status to be inactive (that is, it is not ready to receive media packets, and it would drop received RTP packets). Example 11-17 shows a snippet of **debug ccsip message** output containing a **200 OK** message sent in response to a SIP **INVITE** request in which the **media-direction** attribute of both media streams is set to **inactive**.

Example 11-17 *SIP 200 OK Response with Inactive Media Streams*

```
1881803: Sep  7 04:53:08.524 UTC: //300/576AFD000000/SIP/Msg/ccsipDisplayMsg:
Received:
SIP/2.0 200 OK
CSeq: 101 INVITE
Call-ID: 3B08C8AB-92BF11E7-8260D801-19F966AF@172.18.110.203
From: <sip:172.18.110.119>;tag=174F6129-1E69
To: <sip:7000@recorder2.entcomp1.com;transport=tcp>;tag=7f48a5f2
Via: SIP/2.0/TCP 172.18.110.203:5060;branch=z9hG4bKDF1CC2;rport=55540
Timestamp: 1504759988
Contact: <sip:recording@172.18.110.209:5060;transport=tcp>
Allow: INVITE, ACK, CANCEL, OPTIONS, BYE, UPDATE
Content-Type: application/sdp
Content-Length: 202

v=0
o=- 396 7598 IN IP4 172.18.110.209
s=QM_SIP_Recorder
c=IN IP4 172.18.110.209
t=0 0
m=audio 9 RTP/AVP 0
a=rtpmap:0 PCMU/8000
a=inactive
m=audio 9 RTP/AVP 0
a=rtpmap:0 PCMU/8000
a=inactive
```

Cisco UC Gateway Services Architecture

An application programming interface (API) plays a key role in network automation. It enables seamless integration between network devices and countless applications. Cisco UC network communication devices such as CUBE and TDM gateways provide APIs to subscribe for call events and to trigger call recording. External applications can leverage the APIs to invoke call recording dynamically according to policies defined in the application.

Figure 11-9 shows a high-level architectural overview of Cisco UC Gateway Services. The network communication device and external application communicate with each other by exchanging messages using Simple Object Access Protocol (SOAP).

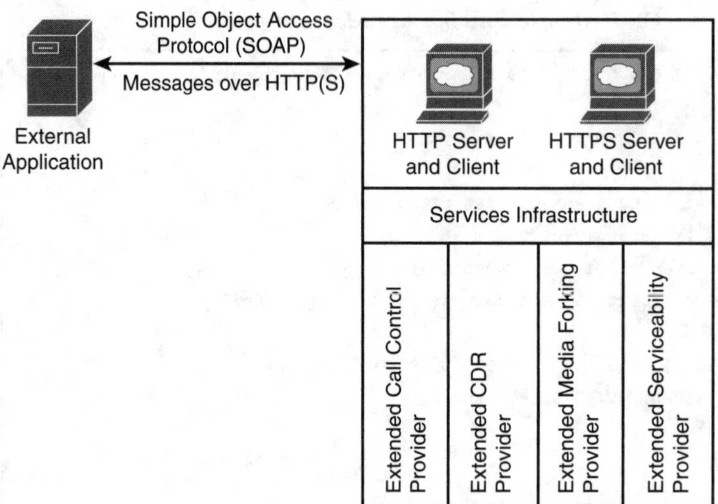

Figure 11-9 *Cisco UC Gateway Services Architecture*

SOAP enables applications to share structured and typed information in XML format. Each SOAP message consist of an **<env:envelope> xml** element, which contains two sub-elements: **<env:header>** and **<env:body>**. **<env:header>** contains metadata information, whereas **<env:body>** contains application data. The SOAP Version 1.2 Primer (see the "References" section at the end of the chapter) provides excellent transaction examples that use SOAP messages. SOAP messages can be embedded within other application-level protocols, such as Hypertext Transfer Protocol (HTTP) and Simple Mail Transfer Protocol (SMTP).

Cisco UC network communication devices and external applications use HTTP and HTTP Secure (HTTPS) to exchange SOAP messages in the UC Gateway Services architecture. HTTP and HTTPS servers running within the device take care of processing incoming HTTP **POST** requests from applications and passing the message body to the services infrastructure. The infrastructure component performs common management functions on behalf of individual UC application service providers within the network device:

- It processes the initial registration request from external applications to UC application service providers.
- It processes incoming SOAP messages and routes them to the correct UC application service provider.
- It shares UC application service provider status changes with registered applications.
- It sends probing messages (keepalive probes) to registered applications to maintain active registration.

- It sends negative probing messages when there is no response or when there is a failure response to keepalive probes.
- It unregisters an external application if there is no response to negative probe messages.

Currently, four application service providers are available:

- Extended Call Control (XCC)
- Extended Media Forking (XMF)
- Extended Call Detail Record (XCDR)
- Extended Serviceability (XSVC)

Note The Cisco Unified Communications Gateway Services API Guide (see the "References" section at the end of the chapter) provides detailed information on request and response types for all four providers.

Extended Call Control Provider

Imagine that a customer's CUBE processes all inbound calls to enterprise users, including call center agents. How would an external application request the SBC to record specific calls of interest (for example, agent calls)?

The XCC service provider enables external applications to subscribe to and get notified of call events such as call setup, connect, and disconnect and media events such as fax tone, DTMF digits, and audio-to-video transition. A call event contains information about the calling number, called number, and inbound and outbound call legs (also referred to as connections). An external application can use the event notification details to identify the call of interest and take actions such as recording the call or disconnecting a malicious call.

Extended Media Forking Provider

When an external application identifies a call of interest, it sends a SOAP request to CUBE to initiate recording by providing a reference to the connection ID of the inbound/outbound call leg and the CallID of the call. The XMF provider processes the recording request, forks the media streams of the call of interest, and sends a copy of the RTP packets to the media recorder's IP address and port number provided in the SOAP request. The status of the forking process (started or failed) is sent to the external application as a SOAP response.

Extended Call Detail Record Provider

The XCDR provider allows applications to subscribe to CDR notifications that are sent right after call termination. This helps external call accounting or monitoring applications get real-time information and quickly detect any malicious or anomalous activities such as long-duration calls from unknown numbers.

Extended Serviceability Provider

Network management applications use XSVC providers to monitor the status of VoIP trunk groups configured in CUBE. A VoIP trunk group consists of one or more SIP trunks, with each SIP trunk pointing to a remote peer such as a SIP proxy in a service provider network, a SIP call controller acting as a B2BUA, or an IP PBX. The network management application can subscribe for individual trunk status changes (such as up to down or down to up) and for trunk group configuration changes (such as a trunk being added or deleted from the group) and get notified when the change happens.

The XCC and XMF Data Model

XCC and XMF API requests and responses contain a number of parameters. The purpose and meaning of these parameters become apparent when the underlying data model is understood. The external client application and UC Gateway Service provider exchange information about overall call state, individual call leg state, and media change events. This information is represented in a simple data model called the XCC call control model.

The XCC Call Control Model

Every call processed by CUBE has an inbound call leg and an outbound call leg if the call is routed to a next-hop peer device. As shown in Figure 11-10, each call leg is referred to as a *connection* in the XCC call control model. Each connection is associated with one or more media streams. The media streams can be active or inactive, depending on the state of the call.

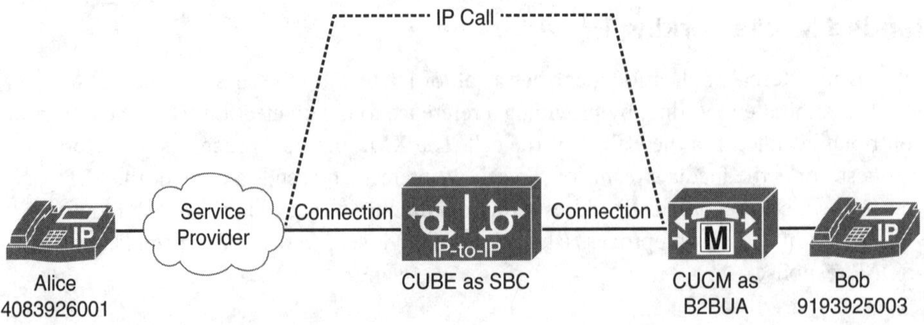

Figure 11-10 *Call Control Model*

The finite state machine of a call, illustrated in Figure 11-11, begins with the **IDLE** state during call setup time. The state changes to **ACTIVE** as the call gets connected and to **INVALID** when the call gets terminated. The call has no connections in the **IDLE** and **INVALID** states and has one or more connections in the **ACTIVE** state. Calls that are not established successfully (for example, calls to invalid called party numbers) transition from **IDLE** to **INVALID** state.

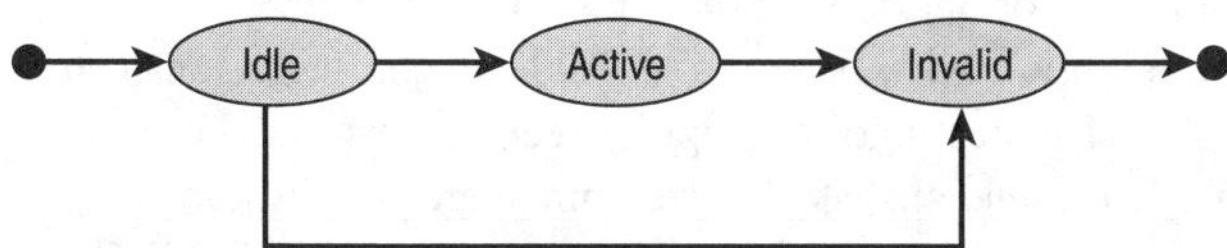

Figure 11-11 *Finite State Machine of a Call*

XCC Call Connection States

Similar to the overall call state, the XCC call control data model represents the state of inbound and outbound connections as a sequence of states. External applications can subscribe to an XCC call control provider and request to be notified when the connection reaches a specific state (for example, created or disconnected). Applications subscribe to a list of connection events of interest, referred to as a *connection events filter*. The supported connection events include **CREATED**, **AUTHORIZE_CALL**, **ADDRESS_ANALYZE**, **REDIRECTED**, **ALERTING**, **CONNECTED**, **TRANSFERRED**, **CALL_DELIVERY**, **DISCONNECTED**, **HANDOFFLEAVE**, and **HANDOFFJOIN**. Figures 11-12 and 11-13 show visual representations of inbound and outbound connection states.

An inbound connection begins at an **IDLE** state and typically transitions to the **ADDRESS_COLLECT** state, in which details about the calling and called party numbers or URIs is collected.

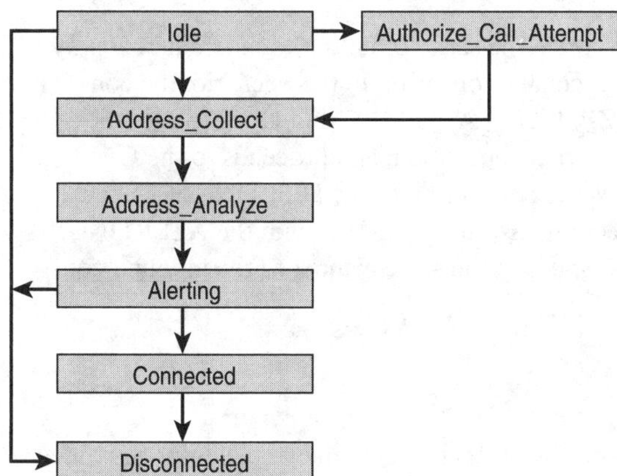

Figure 11-12 *Inbound Connection States*

The architecture allows external applications to explicitly authorize the setup of an inbound connection by subscribing to the **AUTHORIZE_CALL** connection event. In this scenario, the connection state transitions to **AUTHORIZE_CALL_ATTEMPT**, and CUBE places the call in a suspended state, notifies the external application, and proceeds to the **ADDRESS_COLLECT** state if authorized or moves the connection to the **DISCONNECTED** state if not authorized.

The calling and called party address information is analyzed in the **ADDRESS_ANALYZE** state, according to the inbound dial peer and global level configurations (for example, voice translation profiles). The destination endpoint receiving the call could answer the call after a few rings, or it could answer the call immediately or in some scenarios not answer at all. The incoming connection's state transitions to **ALERTING** and **CONNECTED**, accordingly. The connection reaches the termination state **DISCONNECTED** when the call ends.

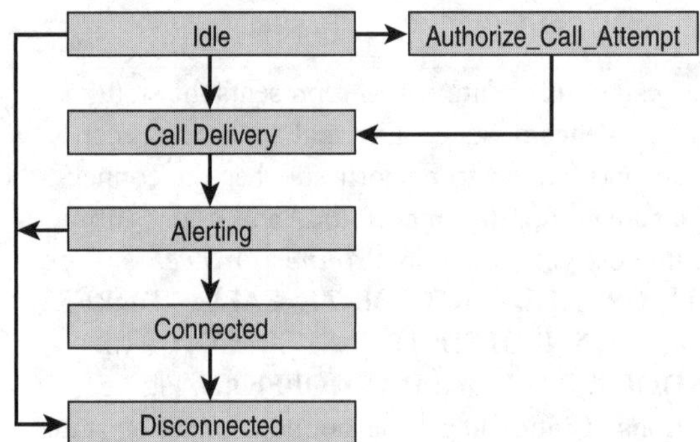

Figure 11-13 *Outbound Connection States*

An outbound connection begins at an **IDLE** state and typically transitions to the **CALL_DELIVERY** state, in which CUBE places an outbound call using an outbound dial peer.

External applications can explicitly authorize the setup of an outbound connection by subscribing to the **AUTHORIZE_CALL** connection event. In this scenario, the connection state transitions to **AUTHORIZE_CALL_ATTEMPT**, and CUBE places the call in a suspended state, notifies the external application, and proceeds to the **CALL_DELIVERY** state if authorized or moves the connection to the **DISCONNECTED** state if not authorized. The outbound connection also transitions through the **ALERTING**, **CONNECTED**, and **DISCONNECTED** states in the same manner as the inbound connection.

XCC Media Event Filter

External applications can subscribe to media events by using the media event filter in addition to the connection event filter described earlier. Media events enable an application to get visibility into the call mode, digits entered, and media stream status and to take actions such as starting call recording for audio calls and stopping recording when the call mode transitions to **FAX**. For example, an application can subscribe to call mode changes by including the **<mediaEventsFilter> MODE_CHANGE </mediaEventsFilter>** XML element in its registration request message. Table 11-2 lists the supported event filters and their corresponding event values.

Table 11-2 *XCC Media Event Filter Values*

Values for <mediaEventsFilter> XML Element	XML Element Name and Values of Detected Media Events
MODE_CHANGE Enables mode change notification	The mode change event is represented by **<modeChange>** XML element which contains two child elements: **<old>**, representing the previous call mode, and **<new>**, representing the current call mode. Each of these child elements can take one of the following **eMediaType** values: **VOICE**, **FAX**, **MODEM**, **VIDEO**, or **DATA**.
DTMF Enables inband dtmf detection	The DTMF event is represented by **<DTMF>** XML element which contains two child elements **<digit>**, which represents the detected digit, and **<dateTime>**, to indicate the time at which **DTMF** was detected.
MEDIA_ACTIVITY Enables media status change detection	The media activity is represented by **<mediaActivity>** XML element which contains two child elements: **<old>**, representing the previous media activity state, and **<new>**, representing the current media activity state. The child elements take the value of either **ACTIVE** or **INACTIVE**.
TONE_BUSY Enables busy tone detection	The busy tone event is represented by **<tone>** XML element containing the value **TONE_BUSY**.
TONE_DIAL Enables dial tone detection	The dial tone event is represented by **<tone>** XML element containing the value **TONE_DIAL**.
TONE_OUT_OF_SERVICE Enables out of service tone detection	The out of service tone event is represented by **<tone>** XML element containing the value **TONE_OUT_OF_SERVICE**.
TONE_RINGBACK Enables ringback tone detection	The ringback tone event is represented by **<tone>** XML element containing the value **TONE_RINGBACK**.
TONE_SECOND_DIAL Enables secondary dial tone detection	The secondary dial tone event is represented by **<tone>** XML element containing the value **TONE_SECOND_DIAL**.

XMF Media Forking

The XMF provider leverages the same call, connection, and event data model used by the XCC provider. In addition, it provides the ability to fork media streams for recording purposes. Media forking can be requested on a per-call or per-connection basis. The key difference between the two options is the definition of *near-end* and *far-end media streams*. The media stream from the calling party is considered the near-end media stream, and the one from the called party is considered the far-end stream in call-based media forking, as shown in Figure 11-14.

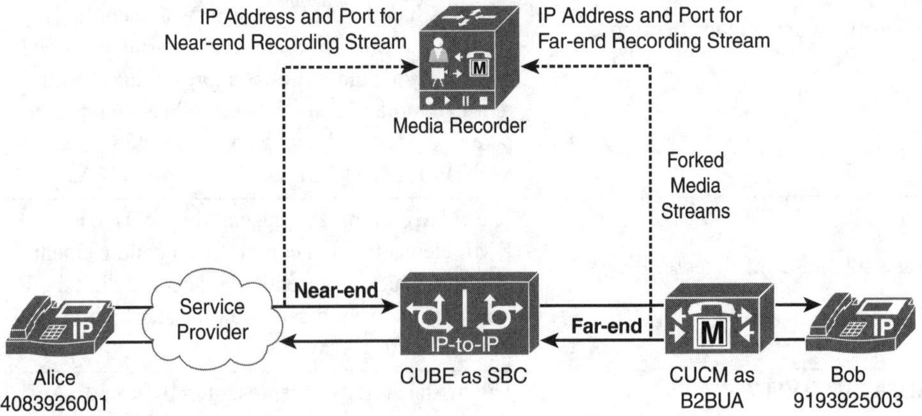

Figure 11-14 *Call-Based Media Forking*

The incoming media stream of a connection is considered a near-end stream, and the outgoing media stream of a connection is considered the far-end stream in connection-based media forking, as shown in Figure 11-15.

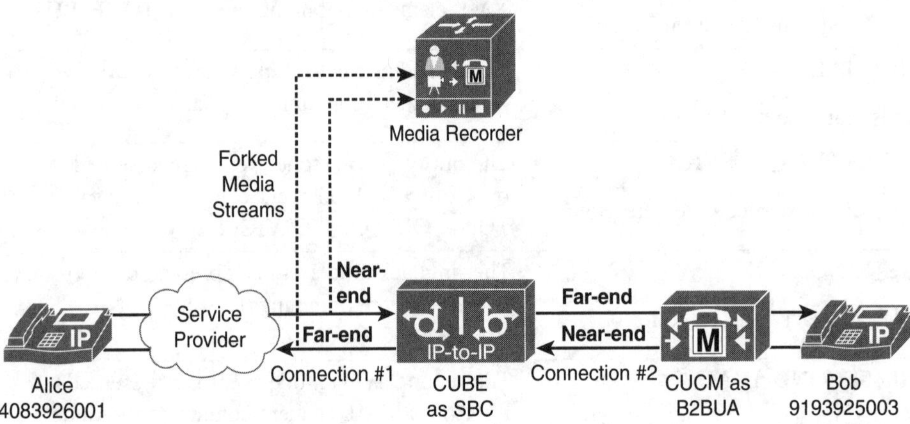

Figure 11-15 *Connection-Based Media Forking*

The architecture supports up to 32 applications to be registered with the XMF provider. Depending on the type of media forking requested by the external application using the XMF API, the XMF provider forks the corresponding near-end and far-end media streams to the recorder and sends the media forking status **FORK_STARTED** if the forking operation is successful and **FORK_FAILED** otherwise. When the XMF provider forks an SRTP stream, it extracts crypto information such as the crypto suite used for encryption and the authentication algorithm (for example, **AES_CM_128_HMAC_SHA1_80**) and the base64-encoded mastery key and salt used for encryption from the SDP of the **INVITE/200 OK** of the SIP session being recorded and passes this information along with the **FORK_STARTED** status to the external application through the API. SRTP is discussed in more detail in Chapter 6, "Secure Signaling and Media."

The XMF provider supports two important features:

- **Recording tone**—Applications can request CUBE to play a recording tone in near-end and far-end call legs or in near-end and far-end connections. The type of recording tone is represented as the data parameter **recordTone** and is set to one of the supported country tone types: **COUNTRY_USA**, **COUNTRY_AUSTRALIA**, **COUNTRY_GERMANY**, **COUNTRY_RUSSIA**, **COUNTRY_SPAIN**, or **COUNTRY_SWITZERLAND**.
- **Recording session preservation**—Applications can specify whether the media forking (that is, recording session) must be preserved even when the HTTP connection to the application is lost or when the application gets unregistered. This behavior is indicated using the data parameter **preserve**, which takes **TRUE** and **FALSE** as values.

When the recorded call or recorded connection ends, the XMF provider stops forking and informs the forking status **FORK_DONE** along with **mediaForkingReason** to the external application.

API-Based Recording

Now that you have a good understanding of call and connection data models used by XCC and XMF providers, you are ready to explore how to leverage XMF API requests to start and stop recording. An external application needs to take five main steps in order to initiate call recording:

1. Register with the XMF provider.
2. Subscribe to call or connection events.
3. Process event notifications.
4. Request media forking for the session of interest.
5. Process the response to the media forking request.

The Registration Process

As shown in Figure 11-16, an application sends a **RequestXmfRegister** message to get registered with the XMF provider. This message is embedded as a SOAP message within an HTTP **POST** request and contains **applicationData**, **providerData** and connection and media event filters.

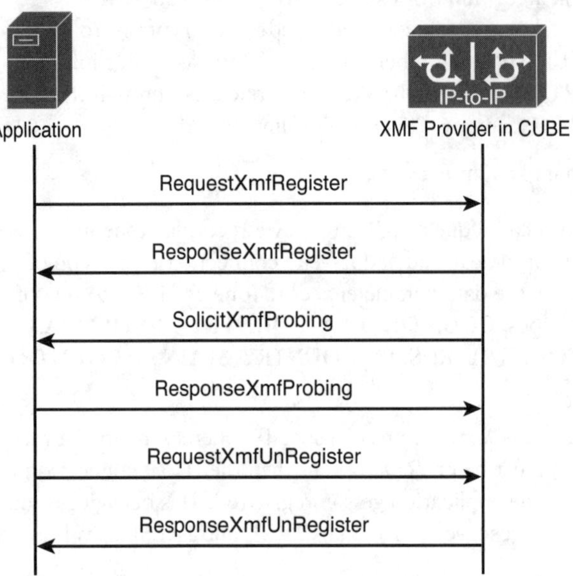

Figure 11-16 *Registration with an XMF Provider*

Example 11-18 shows a sample **RequestXmfRegister** message sent by CUCM to CUBE. The **applicationData** section contains the name and uniform resource link (URL) of the application, and the **providerData** section contains the XMF provider's URL. CUCM also specifies a subscription for **CREATED** and **DISCONNECTED** connection events within the registration request. Each request has a unique **transactionID**, which is also returned in the response message by the XMF provider and is used to associate a response to its corresponding request.

The XMF provider processes the registration request, retrieves the application URL, and verifies whether this URL is configured as a remote application URL within the CUBE device configuration. If the verification process succeeds, the XMF provider generates a unique **registrationID** and sends it within a **ResponseXmfRegister** message along with the provider status as **IN_SERVICE**. The response message contains the same **transactionID** provided in the **RequestXmfRegister** message. The **registrationID** is included in all further messages exchanged between the XMF application and the application provider. Example 11-19 shows the response message that corresponds to the request in Example 11-18.

Example 11-18 *Sample* RequestXmfRegister *Message*

```
<?xml version="1.0" encoding="UTF-8"?>
<soapenv:Envelope xmlns:soapenv="http://www.w3.org/2003/05/soap-envelope">
    <soapenv:Body>
        <RequestXmfRegister xmlns="http://www.cisco.com/schema/cisco_xmf/v1_0">
            <applicationData>
                <name>Unified CM 11.5.1.13050-1</name>
                <url>http://172.18.110.205:8090/ucm_xmf</url>
            </applicationData>
            <connectionEventsFilter>CREATED DISCONNECTED </connectionEventsFilter>
            <mediaEventsFilter></mediaEventsFilter>
            <msgHeader>
                <transactionID>Cisco:UCM:CayugaIf:4:1</transactionID>
            </msgHeader>
            <providerData>
                <url>http://cube1.entcomp1.com:8090/xmf</url>
            </providerData>
        </RequestXmfRegister>
    </soapenv:Body>
</soapenv:Envelope>
```

Example 11-19 *Sample* ResponseXmfRegister *Request*

```
<?xml version="1.0" encoding="UTF-8"?>
<SOAP:Envelope xmlns:SOAP="http://www.w3.org/2003/05/soap-envelope">
    <SOAP:Body>
        <ResponseXmfRegister xmlns="http://www.cisco.com/schema/cisco_xmf/v1_0">
            <msgHeader>
                <transactionID>Cisco:UCM:CayugaIf:4:1</transactionID>
                <registrationID>F25228ED:XMF:Unified CM 11.5.1.13050-1:12
                </registrationID>
            </msgHeader>
            <providerStatus>IN_SERVICE</providerStatus>
        </ResponseXmfRegister>
    </SOAP:Body>
</SOAP:Envelope>
```

After the initial registration is complete, it is the responsibility of the XMF provider to check whether the registered application is still active. The XMF provider periodically sends **SolicitXmfProbing** message to the application, as shown in Example 11-20.

Example 11-20 *Sample* SolicitXmfProbing *Request*

```
<?xml version="1.0" encoding="UTF-8"?>
<SOAP:Envelope xmlns:SOAP="http://www.w3.org/2003/05/soap-envelope">
    <SOAP:Body>
        <SolicitXmfProbing xmlns="http://www.cisco.com/schema/cisco_xmf/v1_0">
            <msgHeader>
                <transactionID>F253FC74:82861</transactionID>
                <registrationID>F25227B3:XMF:Unified CM 11.5.1.13050-1:10
  </registrationID>
            </msgHeader>
            <sequence>1</sequence>
            <interval>120</interval>
            <failureCount>0</failureCount>
            <registered>true</registered>
            <providerStatus>IN_SERVICE</providerStatus>
        </SolicitXmfProbing>
    </SOAP:Body>
</SOAP:Envelope>
```

The XMF provider marks the prober state as **STEADY** if it gets a **ResponseXmfProbing** message, as shown in Example 11-21.

Example 11-21 *Sample* ResponseXmfProbing *Request*

```
<?xml version="1.0" encoding="UTF-8"?>
<soapenv:Envelope xmlns:soapenv="http://www.w3.org/2003/05/soap-envelope">
    <soapenv:Body>
        <ResponseXmfProbing xmlns="http://www.cisco.com/schema/cisco_xmf/v1_0">
            <msgHeader>
                <transactionID>F253FDAD:82863</transactionID>
                <registrationID>F25228ED:XMF:Unified CM 11.5.1.13050-1:12
  </registrationID>
            </msgHeader>
            <sequence>1</sequence>
        </ResponseXmfProbing>
    </soapenv:Body>
</soapenv:Envelope>
```

If the XMF provider didn't receive **ResponseXmfProbing** messages, it sends the **SolicitXmfProbing** message with the **failureCount** value parameter incremented and the probing interval reduced from 120 to 5 seconds. This type of probe message with a nonzero **failureCount** parameter value is also called a *negative probe message*. A sample message is shown in Example 11-22. After a configured number of retries, if no response is received, the XMF provider unregisters the application. There could be multiple reasons for no application response (for example, network connectivity issues between CUBE and the application, the application being taken into maintenance mode, the application crashing). After the issue is resolved or the maintenance conditions are removed, the application re-registers with the XMF provider by sending a **RequestXmfRegister** message.

Example 11-22 *Negative* SolicitXmfProbing *Request*

```
<?xml version="1.0" encoding="UTF-8"?>
<SOAP:Envelope xmlns:SOAP="http://www.w3.org/2003/05/soap-envelope">
    <SOAP:Body>
        <SolicitXmfProbing xmlns="http://www.cisco.com/schema/cisco_xmf/v1_0">
            <msgHeader>
                <transactionID>F2C7CF13:83052</transactionID>
                <registrationID>F25228ED:XMF:Unified CM 11.5.1.13050-1:12
  </registrationID>
            </msgHeader><sequence>66</sequence>
            <interval>5</interval>
            <failureCount>1</failureCount>
            <registered>true</registered>
            <providerStatus>IN_SERVICE</providerStatus>
        </SolicitXmfProbing>
    </SOAP:Body>
</SOAP:Envelope>
```

The registered application can also gracefully unregister by sending a **RequestXmfUnRegister** message. The XMF provider accepts the unregistration and sends a **ResponseXmfUnRegister** message, as shown in Examples 11-23 and 11-24.

Example 11-23 *Sample* RequestXmfUnRegister *Request*

```
<?xml version="1.0" encoding="UTF-8"?>
<soapenv:Envelope xmlns:soapenv="http://www.w3.org/2003/05/soap-envelope">
    <soapenv:Body>
        <RequestXmfUnRegister xmlns="http://www.cisco.com/schema/cisco_xmf/v1_0">
            <msgHeader>
                <transactionID>Cisco:UCM:CayugaIf:4:2</transactionID>
              <registrationID>F25228ED:XMF:Unified CM 11.5.1.13050-1:12 </registrationID>
            </msgHeader>
        </RequestXmfUnRegister>
    </soapenv:Body>
</soapenv:Envelope>
```

Example 11-24 *Sample* ResponseXmfUnRegister *Request*

```
<?xml version="1.0" encoding="UTF-8"?>
<SOAP:Envelope xmlns:SOAP="http://www.w3.org/2003/05/soap-envelope">
    <SOAP:Body>
        <ResponseXmfUnRegister xmlns="http://www.cisco.com/schema/cisco_xmf/v1_0">
            <msgHeader>
                <transactionID>Cisco:UCM:CayugaIf:4:2</transactionID>
                <registrationID>F2511606:XMF:Unified CM 11.5.1.13050-1:7 </registrationID>
            </msgHeader></ResponseXmfUnRegister>
    </SOAP:Body>
</SOAP:Envelope>
```

The Subscription Process

There are two common methods of subscribing to interested connection- and media-related events. The first method is to embed the subscription details within a **RequestXmfRegister** message by including the parameters **connectionEventsFilter** and **mediaEventsFilter.** The recording initiating application lists the interested events within these two parameters at the time of registration. The second method is to use a specific request called **RequestXmfControlUpdate** to update the subscription details any time after the application is registered. Media event subscriptions can also be updated while updating the media attributes of a given call by including the **mediaEventsFilter** parameter in the **RequestXmfCallMediaSetAttributes** message. The sample **RequestXmfRegister** message shown in Example 11-18 leverages the first method in which CUCM subscribes to **CREATED** and **DISCONNECTED** events by listing these two values in **connectionEventsFilter.** Example 11-25 shows an example of a second subscription method in which a custom application named **Testapp** uses a **RequestXmfControlUpdate** message to subscribe for several connection and media events.

Example 11-25 *Sample* RequestXmfControlUpdate *Request*

```
<?xml version="1.0" encoding="UTF-8"?>
<soapenv:Envelope xmlns:soapenv="http://www.w3.org/2003/05/soap-envelope">
    <soapenv:Body>
        <RequestXmfControlUpdate xmlns="http://www.cisco.com/schema/cisco_xmf/v1_0">
            <connectionEventsFilter>CREATED ALERTING CONNECTED REDIRECTED TRANSFERRED
  HANDOFFLEAVE HANDOFFJOIN CALL_DELIVERY DISCONNECTED</connectionEventsFilter>
            <mediaEventsFilter>MODE_CHANGE DTMF TONE_BUSY TONE_DIAL TONE_SECOND_DIAL
  TONE_RINGBACK TONE_OUT_OF_SERVICE MEDIA_ACTIVITY</mediaEventsFilter>
            <msgHeader>
                <registrationID>55D92D4:XMF:Testapp:12</registrationID>
                <transactionID>577F538:539</transactionID>
            </msgHeader>
        </RequestXmfControlUpdate>
    </soapenv:Body>
</soapenv:Envelope></SOAP:Envelope>
```

The Media Forking Process

When the registration and subscription processes are completed, the application waits for event notifications from the XMF provider. To understand the media forking process, consider a scenario in which CUCM initiates recording of inbound calls from external callers to specific agent phones. Assume that CUCM has registered with CUBE and has been assigned registration ID **F9F3C5BE:XMF:Unified CM 11.5.1.13050-1:18**. This registration ID is used to identify all requests and responses sent to and received from CUCM. Figure 11-17 shows the messages exchanged between the recording application and the XMF provider in CUBE to register, notify call events, initiate recording, and notify about recording start and stop events.

When CUBE receives a new call from the service provider, it processes the incoming SIP **INVITE**, sets up an inbound connection, and notifies CUCM about the state of the inbound connection (**IDLE**) by sending a **NotifyXmfConnectionData** message, as shown in Example 11-26. The **callData** section of the message provides the call ID and call state, and the **connectionData** section provides the connection ID and connection state. The **event** section provides the event type and detailed information about the connection. In the message shown in Example 11-26, the **<created>** XML element represents a "created" event containing connection details such as calling address (4083926001), called address (9193925003), connection type (SIP), media data type (voice), and connection direction (incoming).

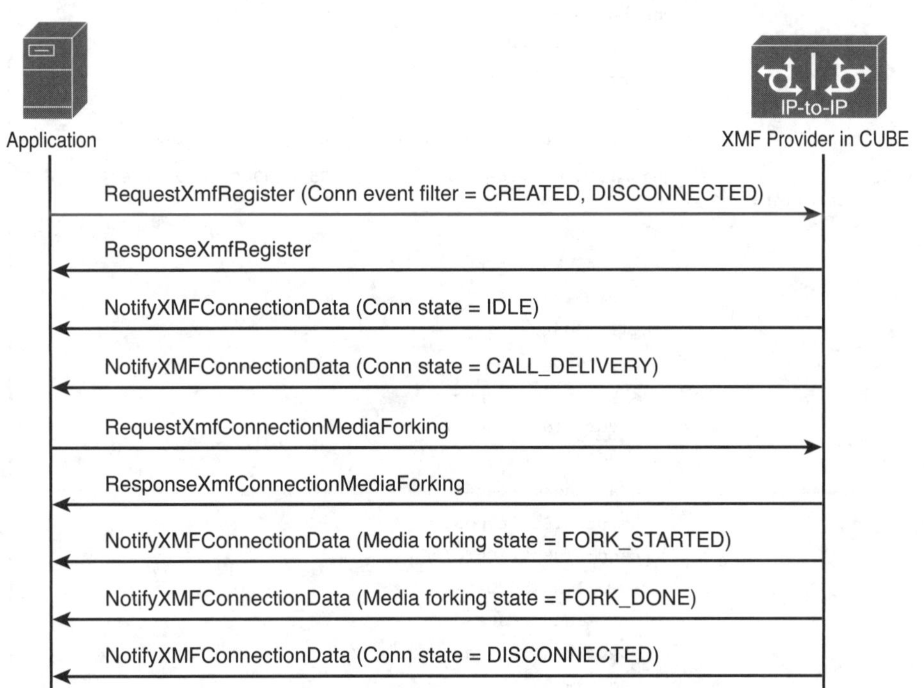

Figure 11-17 *XMF Request and Response Sequence to Initiate Media Forking*

Example 11-26 NotifyXmfConnectionData *Message with an* IDLE *Event*

```
<?xml version="1.0" encoding="UTF-8"?>
<SOAP:Envelope xmlns:SOAP="http://www.w3.org/2003/05/soap-envelope">
    <SOAP:Body>
        <NotifyXmfConnectionData xmlns="http://www.cisco.com/schema/cisco_xmf/v1_0">
            <msgHeader>
                <transactionID>F9F8ADCB:85301</transactionID>
                <registrationID>F9F3C5BE:XMF:Unified CM 11.5.1.13050-1:18
  </registrationID>
            </msgHeader>
            <callData>
                <callID>15</callID>
                <state>ACTIVE</state>
            </callData>
            <connData>
                <connID>236</connID>
                <state>IDLE</state>
            </connData>
            <event>
                <created>
                    <connDetailData>
                        <connData>
                            <connID>236</connID>
                            <state>IDLE</state>
                        </connData>
                        <guid>0x6546FB00-0x00010000-0x00000005-0xA4CAA8C0</guid>
                        <guidAltFormat>1699150592-0000065536-0000000005-2764744896
  </guidAltFormat>
                        <callingAddrData>
                            <type>E164</type>
                            <addr>4083926001</addr>
                        </callingAddrData>
                        <calledAddrData>
                            <type>E164</type>
                            <addr>9193925003</addr>
                        </calledAddrData>
                        <origCallingAddrData>
                            <type>E164</type>
                            <addr>4083926001</addr>
                        </origCallingAddrData>
                        <origCalledAddrData>
                            <type>E164</type>
                            <addr>9193925003</addr>
                        </origCalledAddrData>
                        <connIntfType>CONN_SIP</connIntfType>
```

```
                        <mediaData>
                            <type>VOICE</type>
                        </mediaData>
                        <connIntf>192.168.202.164</connIntf>
                        <connDirectionType>INCOMING</connDirectionType>
                    </connDetailData>
                </created>
            </event>
        </NotifyXmfConnectionData>
    </SOAP:Body>
</SOAP:Envelope>
```

CUBE then identifies a matching outbound dial peer, routes the call across a SIP trunk to the CUCM subscriber node, and sets up an outbound connection. It notifies CUCM about the state of the outbound connection (**CALL_DELIVERY**) by sending a **NotifyXmfConnectionData** message. The key differences between the notification messages for inbound and outbound connections are the connection ID (inbound = **236**, outbound = **237**), connection states, and connection direction, as shown in Example 11-27.

Example 11-27 NotifyXmfConnectionData *Message with a* CALL_DELIVERY *Event*

```
<?xml version="1.0" encoding="UTF-8"?>
<SOAP:Envelope xmlns:SOAP="http://www.w3.org/2003/05/soap-envelope">
    <SOAP:Body>
        <NotifyXmfConnectionData xmlns="http://www.cisco.com/schema/cisco_xmf/v1_0">
            <msgHeader>
                <transactionID>F9F8ADD1:85304</transactionID>
                <registrationID>F9F3C5BE:XMF:Unified CM 11.5.1.13050-1:18
  </registrationID>
            </msgHeader>
            <callData>
                <callID>15</callID>
                <state>ACTIVE</state>
            </callData>
            <connData>
                <connID>237</connID>
                <state>CALL_DELIVERY</state>
            </connData>
            <event>
                <created>
                    <connDetailData>
                        <connData>
                            <connID>237</connID>
                            <state>CALL_DELIVERY</state>
```

```
                        </connData>
                        <guid>0x6546FB00-0x00010000-0x00000005-0xA4CAA8C0</guid>
                        <guidAltFormat>1699150592-0000065536-0000000005-2764744896
</guidAltFormat>
                        <callingAddrData>
                            <type>E164</type>
                            <addr>4083926001</addr>
                        </callingAddrData>
                        <calledAddrData>
                            <type>E164</type>
                            <addr>9193925003</addr>
                        </calledAddrData>
                        <origCallingAddrData>
                            <type>E164</type>
                            <addr>4083926001</addr>
                        </origCallingAddrData>
                        <origCalledAddrData>
                            <type>E164</type>
                            <addr>9193925003</addr>
                        </origCalledAddrData>
                        <connIntfType>CONN_SIP</connIntfType>
                        <mediaData>
                            <type>VOICE</type>
                        </mediaData>
                        <connIntf>0.0.0.0</connIntf>
                        <connDirectionType>OUTGOING</connDirectionType>
                    </connDetailData>
                </created>
            </event>
        </NotifyXmfConnectionData>
    </SOAP:Body>
</SOAP:Envelope>
```


After the call is answered by the agent IP phone, CUCM sends a **RequestXmfConnectionMediaForking** message to initiate recording of media streams associated with the outbound connection (that is, the media stream sent from CUBE to the IP phone and vice versa). The media forking request message shown in Example 11-28 references the outbound connection using **callID** (**15**) and **connID** (**237**) parameters. The **<action>** XML element represents the media forking action and contains the media recorder's IP address and port numbers, to which near-end (incoming media stream, from IP phone to CUBE) and far-end (outgoing media stream, from CUBE to IP phone) RTP streams must be sent. CUCM also sets the **preserve** parameter to **TRUE** to indicate that the recording session should continue even if the CUBE XMF provider has lost connectivity to CUCM through the HTTP connection.

Example 11-28 RequestXmfConnectionMediaForking *Message*

```
<?xml version="1.0" encoding="UTF-8"?>
<soapenv:Envelope xmlns:soapenv="http://www.w3.org/2003/05/soap-envelope">
    <soapenv:Body>
        <RequestXmfConnectionMediaForking xmlns="http://www.cisco.com/schema/
  cisco_xmf/v1_0">
            <msgHeader>
                <transactionID>Cisco:UCM:CayugaIf:1:2</transactionID>
                <registrationID>F9F3C5BE:XMF:Unified CM 11.5.1.13050-1:18
  </registrationID>
            </msgHeader>
            <callID>15</callID>
            <connID>237</connID>
            <action>
                <enableMediaForking>
                    <nearEndAddr>
                        <ipv4>172.18.110.199</ipv4>
                        <port>54694</port>
                    </nearEndAddr>
                    <farEndAddr>
                        <ipv4>172.18.110.199</ipv4>
                        <port>59482</port>
                    </farEndAddr>
                    <preserve>true</preserve>
                </enableMediaForking>
            </action>
        </RequestXmfConnectionMediaForking>
    </soapenv:Body>
</soapenv:Envelope>
```

CUBE sends a **ResponseXmfConnectionMediaForking** message in response to the media forking request. The media forking status of the connection (**FORK_STARTED** or **FORK_FAILURE**) is conveyed to the application through a separate **NotifyXmfConnectionData** message. This message references the connection being recorded by specifying the **callID** (**15**) and **connID** (**237**) parameters and uses a **mediaForking** event to indicate media forking state. Examples 11-29 and 11-30 show the **ResponseXmfConnectionMediaForking** and **NotifyXmfConnectionData** messages sent after a successful initiation of media forking.

Example 11-29 ResponseXmfConnectionMediaForking *Message*

```
<?xml version="1.0" encoding="UTF-8"?>
<SOAP:Envelope xmlns:SOAP="http://www.w3.org/2003/05/soap-envelope">
    <SOAP:Body>
        <ResponseXmfConnectionMediaForking xmlns="http://www.cisco.com/schema/cisco_
        xmf/v1_0">
            <msgHeader>
                <transactionID>Cisco:UCM:CayugaIf:1:2</transactionID>
                <registrationID>F9F3C5BE:XMF:Unified CM 11.5.1.13050-1:18
  </registrationID>
            </msgHeader>
        </ResponseXmfConnectionMediaForking>
    </SOAP:Body>
</SOAP:Envelope>
```

Example 11-30 NotifyXmfConnectionData *Message with a* FORK_STARTED *Event*

```
<?xml version="1.0" encoding="UTF-8"?>
<SOAP:Envelope xmlns:SOAP="http://www.w3.org/2003/05/soap-envelope">
    <SOAP:Body>
        <NotifyXmfConnectionData xmlns="http://www.cisco.com/schema/cisco_xmf/v1_0">
            <msgHeader>
                <transactionID>F9F8CAD9:85305</transactionID>
                <registrationID>F9F3C5BE:XMF:Unified CM 11.5.1.13050-1:18
                </registrationID>
            </msgHeader>
            <callData>
                <callID>15</callID>
                <state>ACTIVE</state>
            </callData>
            <connData>
                <connID>237</connID>
                <state>CONNECTED</state>
            </connData>
            <event>
                <mediaForking>
                    <mediaForkingState>FORK_STARTED</mediaForkingState>
                </mediaForking>
            </event>
        </NotifyXmfConnectionData>
    </SOAP:Body></SOAP:Envelope>
```

When the call between the external caller and the IP phone ends, CUBE stops the forked media streams to the recorder and then tears down the outbound connection. The application is informed about the media forking status (**FORK_DONE**) and connection status (**DISCONNECTED**) in two **NotifyXmfConnectionData** messages. The first notification message contains the **<mediaForking>** element with the **mediaForkingState** parameter set to **FORK_DONE**, as shown in Example 11-31.

Example 11-31 NotifyXmfConnectionData *Message with a* FORK_DONE *Event*

```
<?xml version="1.0" encoding="UTF-8"?>
<SOAP:Envelope xmlns:SOAP="http://www.w3.org/2003/05/soap-envelope">
    <SOAP:Body>
        <NotifyXmfConnectionData xmlns="http://www.cisco.com/schema/cisco_xmf/v1_0">
            <msgHeader>
                <transactionID>F9FB0E8A:85309</transactionID>
                <registrationID>F9F3C5BE:XMF:Unified CM 11.5.1.13050-1:18
                </registrationID>
            </msgHeader>
            <callData>
                <callID>15</callID>
                <state>ACTIVE</state>
            </callData>
            <connData>
                <connID>237</connID>
                <state>CONNECTED</state>
            </connData>
            <event>
                <mediaForking>
                    <mediaForkingState>FORK_DONE</mediaForkingState>
                </mediaForking>
            </event>
        </NotifyXmfConnectionData>
    </SOAP:Body>
</SOAP:Envelope>
```

The second notification message references the connection ID (**237**) and state (**DISCONNECTED**) using the **connID** and **state** parameters in **the <connData>** XML element, as shown in Example 11-32. The **<event>** XML element contains detailed media information and statistics on media type, codec type, packetization interval, call duration, number of RTP packets sent and received, number of lost packets, number of early packets, number of late packets, round trip delay, and so on. These statistics can be stored as diagnostic data within the CUCM call management records for future reporting and troubleshooting purposes.

Example 11-32 NotifyXmfConnectionData *Message with a* DISCONNECTED *Event*


```
<?xml version="1.0" encoding="UTF-8"?>
<SOAP:Envelope xmlns:SOAP="http://www.w3.org/2003/05/soap-envelope">
    <SOAP:Body>
        <NotifyXmfConnectionData xmlns="http://www.cisco.com/schema/cisco_xmf/v1_0">
            <msgHeader>
                <transactionID>F9FB0E97:85315</transactionID>
                <registrationID>F9F3C5BE:XMF:Unified CM 11.5.1.13050-1:18
                </registrationID>
            </msgHeader>
            <callData>
                <callID>15</callID>
                <state>ACTIVE</state>
            </callData>
            <connData>
                <connID>237</connID>
                <state>DISCONNECTED</state>
            </connData>
            <event>
                <disconnected>
                    <mediaData>
                        <type>VOICE</type>
                        <coderType>g711ulaw</coderType>
                        <coderByte>160</coderByte>
                    </mediaData>
                    <statsData>
                        <callDuration>P0DT2M28.79S</callDuration>
                        <TxPacketsCount>7442</TxPacketsCount>
                        <TxBytesCount>1487336</TxBytesCount>
                        <TxDurationMSec>0</TxDurationMSec>
                        <TxVoiceDurationMSec>0</TxVoiceDurationMSec>
                        <RxPacketsCount>7434</RxPacketsCount>
                        <RxBytesCount>1486800</RxBytesCount>
                        <RxDurationMSec>0</RxDurationMSec>
                        <RxVoiceDurationMSec>0</RxVoiceDurationMSec>
                    </statsData>
                    <discCause>16</discCause>
                    <jitterData>
                        <roundTripDelayMSec>5</roundTripDelayMSec>
                        <onTimeRvPlayMSec>0</onTimeRvPlayMSec>
                        <gapFillWithPredictionMSec>0</gapFillWithPredictionMSec>
                       <gapFillWithInterpolationMSec>0</gapFillWithInterpolationMSec>
                        <gapFillWithRedundancyMSec>0</gapFillWithRedundancyMSec>
                        <lostPacketsCount>0</lostPacketsCount>
```

```
                    <earlyPacketsCount>0</earlyPacketsCount>
                    <latePacketsCount>0</latePacketsCount>
                    <receiveDelayMSec>0</receiveDelayMSec>
                    <loWaterPlayoutDelayMSec>0</loWaterPlayoutDelayMSec>
                    <hiWaterPlayoutDelayMSec>0</hiWaterPlayoutDelayMSec>
                </jitterData>
            </disconnected>
        </event>
    </NotifyXmfConnectionData>
</SOAP:Body></SOAP:Envelope>
```


API-Based Recording Configuration

The previous sections provide insights into the architecture, data model, and XMF APIs. This section and next one enable you to apply the learned concepts. In this section you will learn how to configure CUBE for network-based recording solutions using XMF APIs, and in the next section you will learn how to troubleshoot common issues encountered during deployment and in production environments.

HTTP Server and Client Parameters

As discussed earlier in this chapter, UC Gateway Services API service providers and applications exchange SOAP messages over HTTP. This requires HTTP server and client functionalities within CUBE to be enabled. If there are multiple interfaces in CUBE and only one of them is reachable from the recording-initiating application, then that interface can be configured to be used to source HTTP client traffic from CUBE to the external application. An example of this scenario is CUBE being able to reach the recording-initiating application only through an interface connected to the internal network.

An XMF provider uses the HTTP URL of the application as a validation mechanism to determine whether the registration request from an application is allowed. The application's URL is sent within the **RequestXmfRegister** message (refer to Example 11-18), and it should match one of the **remote-url** command values configured under the UC Web Services API (WSAPI) configuration mode, as shown in Example 11-33. The **source-address** command specifies the IP address or the hostname of the CUBE providing the UC Gateway Services API service. This value is used to derive the XMF service provider URL value (for example, http://cube1.entcomp1.com:8090/cisco_xmf) that is sent in the **NotifyXmfProviderStatus** message. This status message is sent to applications configured in the **remote-url** command whenever the XMF provider comes into service or is taken out of service (that is, shut down).

Example 11-33 *HTTP Server and Client Configuration*

```
ip http server
ip http client source-interface GigabitEthernet0/0/2

uc wsapi
 source-address cube1.entcomp1.com
 provider xmf
  no shutdown
  remote-url 1 application_url
  remote-url 2 http://172.18.110.205:8090/ucm_xmf
```

UC Web Services API Parameters

After the registration process is complete, the XMF provider sends keepalive probe messages at periodic intervals to check whether the application is still reachable. If there is no response, the XMF provider sends negative probe messages at a much shorter interval. The XMF provider unregisters the application when there is no response to three consecutive negative probes. The periodic interval for keepalive probes is set to 120 seconds, and the interval for negative probes is set to 5 seconds by default and is configurable using the **probing interval** command. The number of probes to send prior to unregistering the application is configurable using the **probing max-failures** command. The combination of the request message and the corresponding response message is defined as a message exchange. CUBE terminates the communication with the application when it experiences a configurable number of message exchange failures. This value is set to **1** by default, and you can change it to a higher value by using the **message-exchange max-failures** command, as shown in Example 11-34.

Example 11-34 *UC Web Services API Configuration*

```
uc wsapi
 message-exchange max-failures 5
 probing interval negative 5
 probing interval keepalive 120
 probing max-failures 3
```

CUCM Network-Based Recording

A network-based recording solution extends the functionality of CUBE to also aid in recording external calls in CUCM deployments. Figure 11-18 shows a typical deployment in which CUBE is used to interface with a SIP service provider and configured as a SIP trunk in CUCM. In addition, CUBE is configured as an XMF service provider, and CUCM is configured as an XMF application that registers, subscribes to connection and media events, and requests media forking for specific calls of interest.

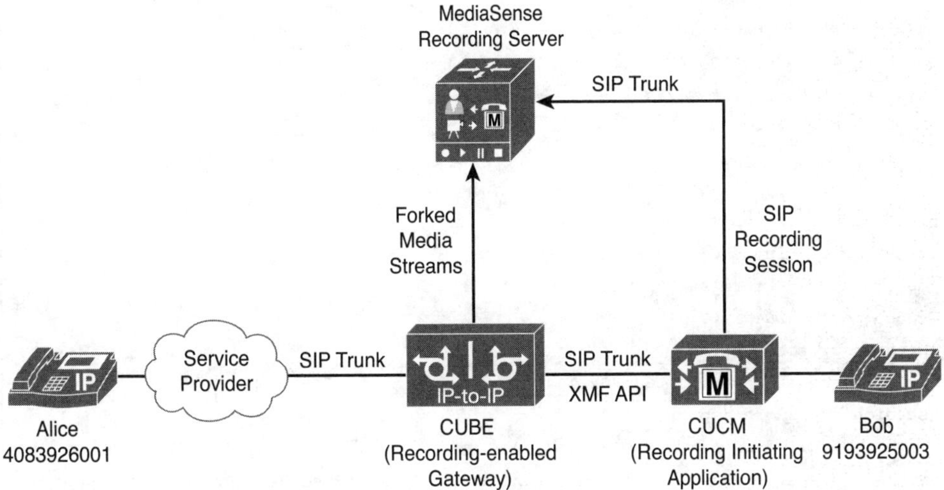

Figure 11-18 *CUCM Network-Based Recording Deployment*

CUBE Configuration

Example 11-35 shows a sample CUBE configuration for the deployment in Figure 11-18. This configuration is very similar to the ones in Examples 11-33 and 11-34. The important command to take note of is the **remote-url** command, which points to the XMF applications running on the CUCM call processing nodes. The three IP addresses 172.18.110.205, 172.18.110.206, and 172.18.110.207 are the IP addresses of the publisher, subscriber 1, and subscriber 2 in the CUCM cluster.

Example 11-35 *CUBE Configuration for Network-Based Recording Deployment*

```
ip http server
ip http client source-interface GigabitEthernet0/0/2

uc wsapi
 source-address cube1.entcomp1.com
 provider xmf
  no shutdown
  remote-url 1 http://172.18.110.205:8090/ucm_xmf
  remote-url 2 http://172.18.110.206:8090/ucm_xmf
  remote-url 3 http://172.18.110.207:8090/ucm_xmf

uc wsapi
```

```
 message-exchange max-failures 5
 probing interval negative 5
 probing interval keepalive 120
 probing max-failures 3


dial-peer voice 5000 voip
 description "Inbound dial-peer"
 destination-pattern 408392....
 video codec h264
 session protocol sipv2
 session target ipv4:192.168.202.164
 session transport tcp
 incoming called-number 9193925...
 voice-class sip bind control source-interface GigabitEthernet0/0/1
 voice-class sip bind media source-interface GigabitEthernet0/0/1
 dtmf-relay rtp-nte
 codec g711ulaw
 no vad


dial-peer voice 5001 voip
 description "Outbound dial-peer"
 preference 1
 destination-pattern 9193925...
 video codec h264
 session protocol sipv2
 session target dns:cl2-cucm-sub1.entcomp1.com
 session transport tcp
 voice-class sip bind control source-interface GigabitEthernet0/0/2
 voice-class sip bind media source-interface GigabitEthernet0/0/2
 dtmf-relay rtp-nte
 codec g711ulaw
 no vad
```

CUCM Configuration

From a CUCM perspective, there are five main configuration steps for this deployment:

1. Configure a SIP trunk to CUBE.
2. Configure a SIP trunk to the recording server.

3. Configure the route pattern for the recording directory number.
4. Configure the recording profile.
5. Configure the recording parameters at the directory number level.

SIP Trunk to CUBE

You create a SIP trunk to CUBE by selecting Device > Trunk and then setting Trunk Type to SIP Trunk and Trunk Service Type to None (Default). Associate the SIP trunk with a device pool. The call processing nodes configured in the **Cisco Unified Communications Manager Group** of the selected device pool are configured as the XMF application URL in the **remote-url** command of the CUBE configuration, as shown in Example 11-35. Figure 11-19 shows the SIP Trunk Configuration page that corresponds to the CUBE discussed in the current example (cube1.entcomp1.com).

As shown in Figure 11-20, you need to set the destination address to the IP address or hostname of CUBE and enable the option **This trunk connects to a recording-enabled gateway** in the Recording Information section.

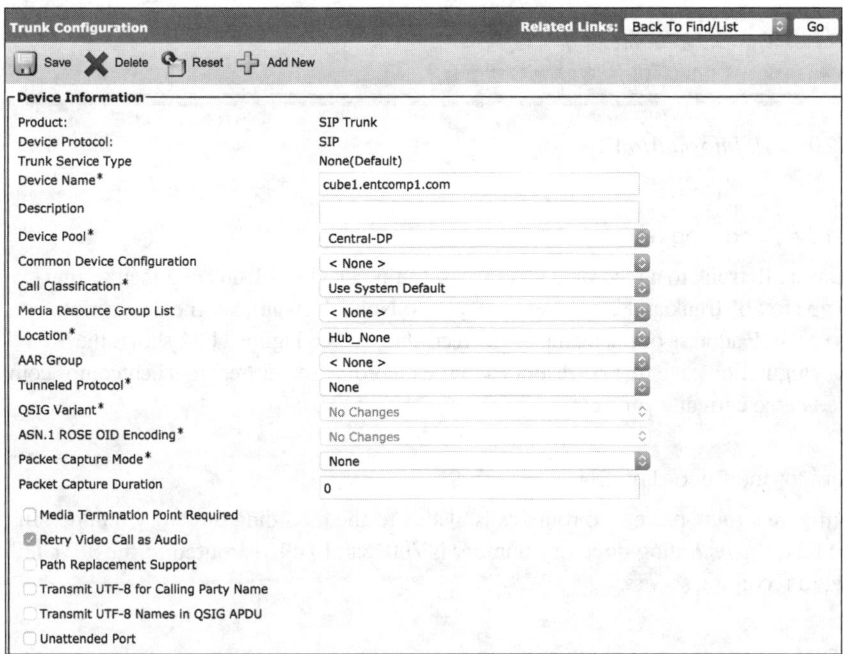

Figure 11-19 *SIP Trunk Configuration for Recording-Enabled CUBE*

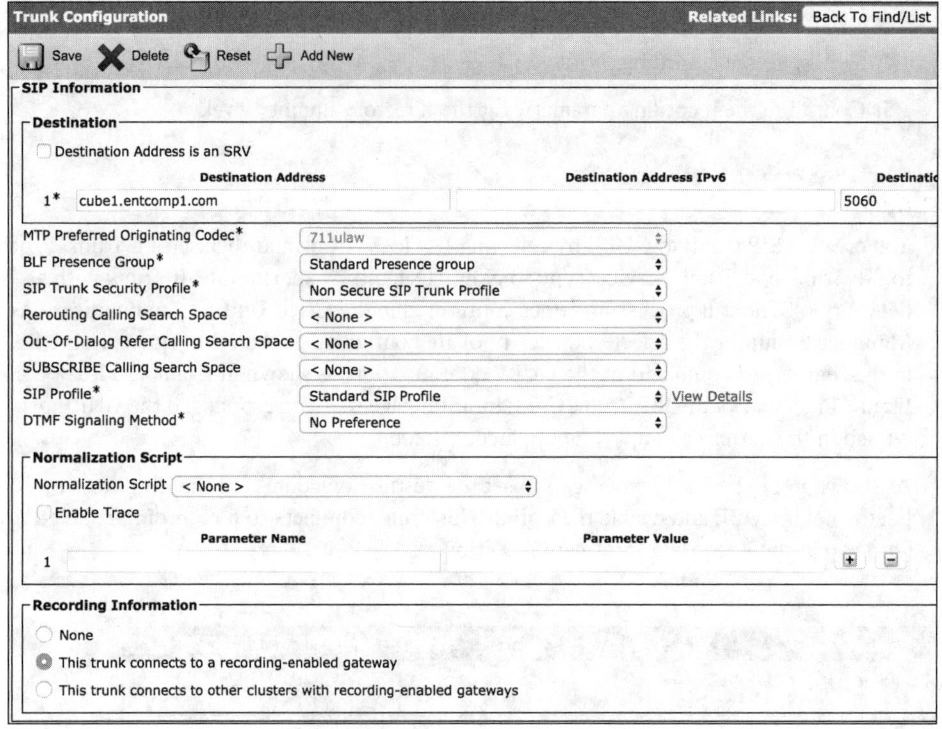

Figure 11-20 *SIP Information Section*

SIP Trunk to the Recording Server

You create a SIP trunk to a recording server by selecting Device > Trunk and then setting Trunk Type to SIP Trunk and Trunk Service Type to None (Default). Set the destination address to the IP address or hostname of the recording server. Figure 11-21 shows the SIP Trunk Configuration page that corresponds to the recording server (recorder1.entcomp1.com) discussed in the current example.

Route Pattern for the Recording DN

You configure a route pattern to route calls placed to the recording directory number. In Figure 11-22, the recording directory number is 7001, and 7001 is routed to the SIP trunk pointing to recording server.

Recording Profile

You create a recording profile by selecting Device > Device Settings > Recording Profile and then setting **Recording Destination Address** to 7001 and ensuring that **Recording Calling Search Space** contains the route partition of the route pattern configured in the previous section. Figure 11-23 shows the Recording Profile Configuration window for the directory number of the phone in the next step.

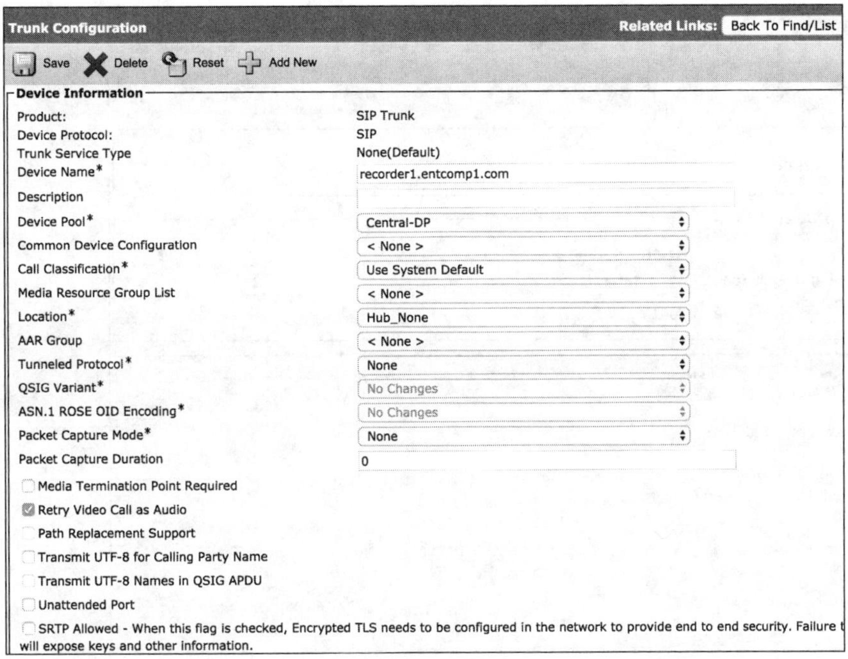

Figure 11-21 *SIP Trunk Configuration for the Media Recorder*

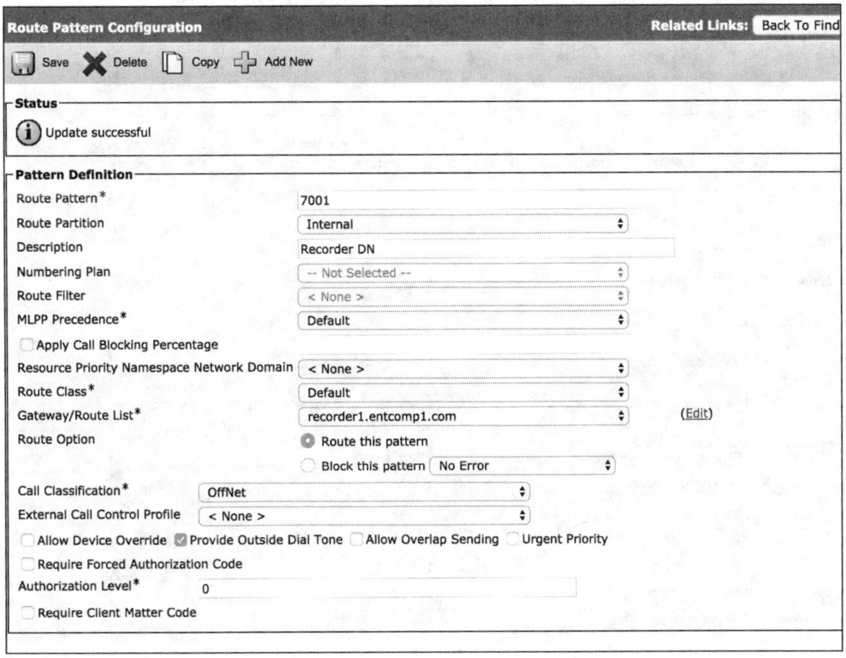

Figure 11-22 *Route Pattern Configuration for Routing Calls to the Recording Directory Number*

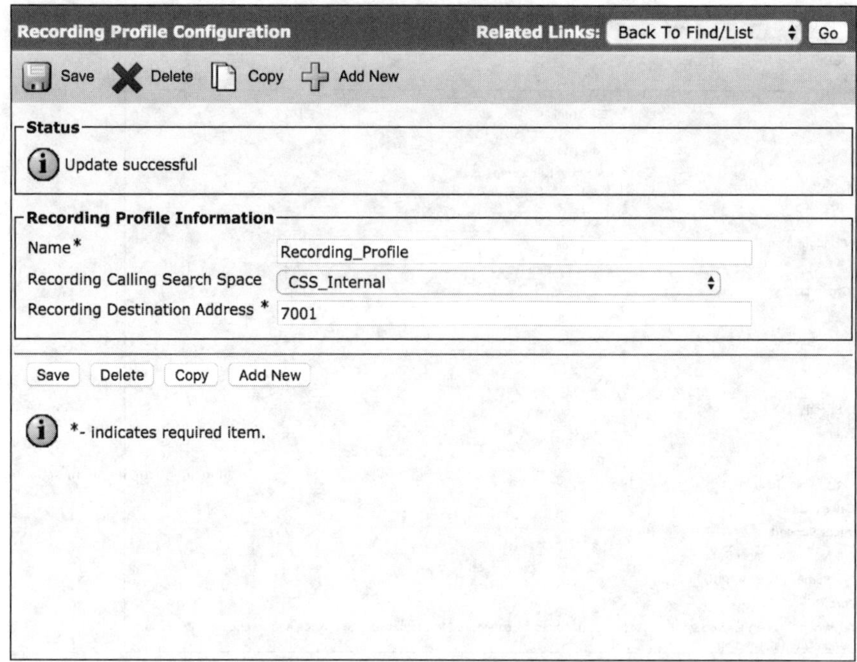

Figure 11-23 *Recording Profile Configuration*

Directory Number Configuration
Related Links: Co

Save Delete Reset Apply Config Add New

Line 2 on Device SEP1C17D340848C

Display (Caller ID)		Display text for a line appearance is intend
	instead of a directory number for calls. If you specify a number, the person receiving a call may not see the	
ASCII Display (Caller ID)		
Line Text Label		
External Phone Number Mask		
Visual Message Waiting Indicator Policy*	Use System Policy	
Audible Message Waiting Indicator Policy*	Default	
Ring Setting (Phone Idle)*	Use System Default	
Ring Setting (Phone Active)	Use System Default	Applies to this line when any line on the phone has
Call Pickup Group Audio Alert Setting(Phone Idle)	Use System Default	
Call Pickup Group Audio Alert Setting(Phone Active)	Use System Default	
Recording Option*	Automatic Call Recording Enabled	
Recording Profile	Recording_Profile	
Recording Media Source*	Gateway Preferred	
Monitoring Calling Search Space	CSS_Internal	
Log Missed Calls		

Figure 11-24 *Recording-Related Parameters for a Directory Number*

Recording Parameters at the Directory Number Level

You need to go to the directory number configuration of the phone line whose calls must be recorded. Set **Recording Option** to Automatic Call Recording Enabled, set the **Recording Profile** to the same profile name as in the previous section, and set **Recording Media Source** to Gateway Preferred. Figure 11-24 shows the Directory Number Configuration page of a phone whose second line is associated with the recording profile *Recording_Profile*, which you configured in the previous step. This enables CUCM to automatically set up a recording session to 7001 whenever the second line is used to originate or answer a call.

MediaSense Configuration

The required configuration in MediaSense is very minimal. The first step is to provision an application user account in CUCM that belongs to the Standard CCM Admin Users group and is assigned to a custom group that has the Standard AXL API Access role. MediaSense uses this account to communicate with the CUCM publisher node using the Administrative XML (AXL) API interface to retrieve call processing node details in the CUCM cluster. The username and password of the application user account are configured in the **Unified CM Configuration** section of the MediaSense administration web interface, as shown in Figure 11-25.

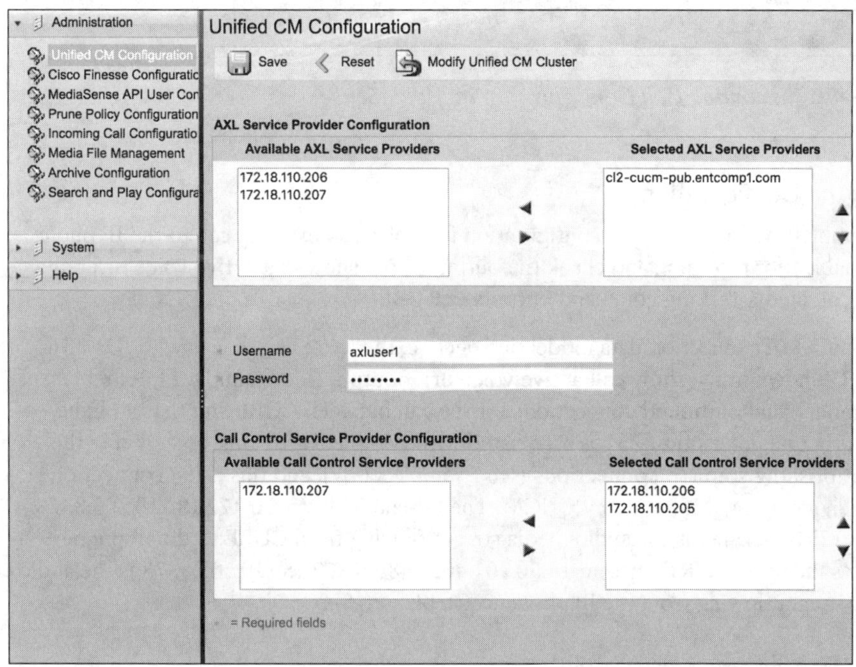

Figure 11-25 *AXL and Call Control Service Provider Configuration in MediaSense*

The next step is to navigate to Administration > Incoming Call Configuration to configure a call rule that specifies the action to be taken while processing an inbound call to the recording directory number. In Figure 11-26, MediaSense is configured to record audio streams of incoming calls to recording directory number 7001.

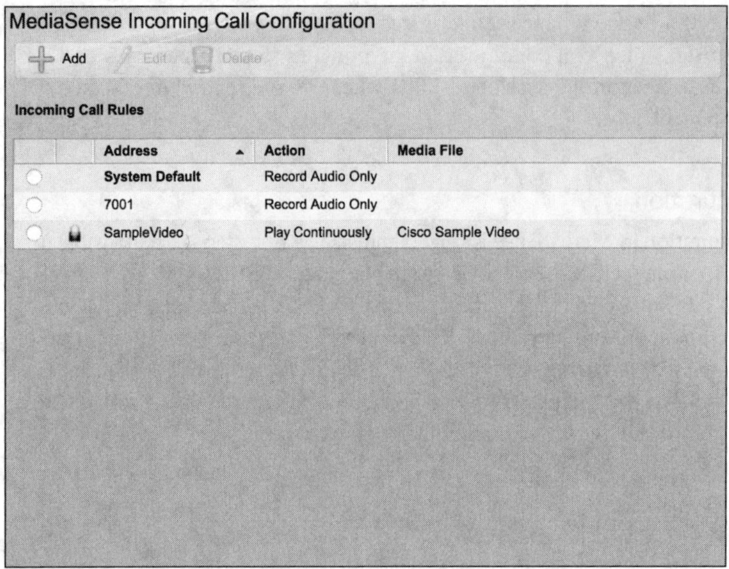

Figure 11-26 *Incoming Call Configuration in MediaSense*

Verifying the Configuration

The simplest way to verify the configuration is to place an external call to the IP phone line enabled for recording and check the output of the **show call active voice brief** and **show call media-forking** command outputs in CUBE.

From an XMF connection data model perspective, the two SIP call legs with IDs **236** and **237** shown in the **show call active voice brief** output (see Example 11-36) represent the inbound and outbound connections for the call between CUBE and the IP phone. The outbound connection **237** is associated with two media streams, as shown in the output of **show voip rtp connections** (see Example 11-37), and this is the connection in which recording is initiated by CUCM. The far-end RTP stream 172.18.110.203:8378 > 14.50.201.46:19480 is the audio media stream flowing from CUBE to the IP phone, whereas the near-end RTP stream 14.50.201.46:19480 > 172.18.110.203:8378 is the audio media stream flowing from the IP phone to CUBE.

Example 11-36 *Output of* show call active voice brief

```
CUBE1#show call active voice brief
<ID>: <CallID> <start>ms.<index> (<start>) +<connect> pid:<peer_id> <dir> <addr>
  <state>
...... <output truncated for brevity>

Telephony call-legs: 0
SIP call-legs: 2
H323 call-legs: 0
Call agent controlled call-legs: 0
SCCP call-legs: 0
STCAPP call-legs: 0
Multicast call-legs: 0
Total call-legs: 2
0 : 236 4193731230ms.1 (12:09:27.217 UTC Fri Sep 1 2017) +7070 pid:5000 Answer
  4083926001 active
 dur 00:00:18 tx:879/175800 rx:882/176248 dscp:0 media:0 audio tos:0xB8 video
  tos:0x0
 IP 192.168.202.119:24148 SRTP: off rtt:2ms pl:0/0ms lost:0/0/0 delay:0/0/0ms
  g711ulaw TextRelay: off Transcoded: No ICE: Off
 media inactive detected:n media contrl rcvd:n/a timestamp:n/a
 long duration call detected:n long duration call duration:n/a timestamp:n/a
 LostPacketRate:0.00 OutOfOrderRate:0.00
 LocalUUID:0000447200105000a000000c298ea018
 RemoteUUID:8c8c368da411d8df347e57996849aa15
 VRF:
0 : 237 4193737250ms.1 (12:09:33.237 UTC Fri Sep 1 2017) +1050 pid:5001 Originate
  9193925003 active
 dur 00:00:18 tx:882/176248 rx:879/175800 dscp:0 media:0 audio tos:0xB8 video
  tos:0x0
 IP 14.50.201.46:19480 SRTP: off rtt:2ms pl:0/0ms lost:0/0/0 delay:0/0/0ms g711ulaw
  TextRelay: off Transcoded: No ICE: Off
 media inactive detected:n media contrl rcvd:n/a timestamp:n/a
 long duration call detected:n long duration call duration:n/a timestamp:n/a
 LostPacketRate:0.00 OutOfOrderRate:0.00
 LocalUUID:8c8c368da411d8df347e57996849aa15
 RemoteUUID:0000447200105000a000000c298ea018
 VRF:
```

Example 11-37 *Output of* **show voip rtp connections**

```
CUBE1#show voip rtp connections
VoIP RTP Port Usage Information:
Max Ports Available: 19999, Ports Reserved: 101, Ports in Use: 2
Port range not configured
                                             Min   Max   Ports     Ports     Ports
Media-Address Range                          Port  Port  Available Reserved  In-use
--------------------------------------------------------------------------------
Global Media Pool                            8000  48198 19999     101       2
--------------------------------------------------------------------------------
VoIP RTP active connections :
No. CallId     dstCallId  LocalRTP  RmtRTP    LocalIP
  RemoteIP   MPSS        VRF
1     236        237        8376      24148     192.168.202.165
  192.168.202.119                           NO   NA
2     237        236        8378      19480     172.18.110.203
  14.50.201.46                              NO   NA
Found 2 active RTP connections

CUBE1#
```

The **show call media-forking** command displays the list of media forking sessions along with the recorder's IP address and port number for receiving the far-end and near-end media streams. The **Call** column value is the connection ID with which a given media forking session is associated. Example 11-38 shows that two forked sessions are associated with connection ID **ED**, which is the hexadecimal representation of the outbound connection with ID **237**. The near-end and far-end media streams are forked to the recorder at 172.18.110.199:54694 and 172.18.110.199:59482, respectively.

Another verification method is to check whether the recording file is correctly generated by the media recorder. This can be performed by logging in to the MediaSense Search and Play web page and searching for recent calls to a given called party number. Figure 11-27 shows a list of recording files available for calls destined to 9193925003, which is an IP phone line enabled for recording.

Example 11-38 *Output of* **show call media-forking**

```
CUBE1#show call media-forking
Warning: Output may be truncated if sessions are added/removed concurrently!

Session     Call     n/f  Destination (port address)
238         ED       near 54694 172.18.110.199
239         ED       far  59482 172.18.110.199

Outstanding VoIP FPI cleanups: 1
CUBE1#
```

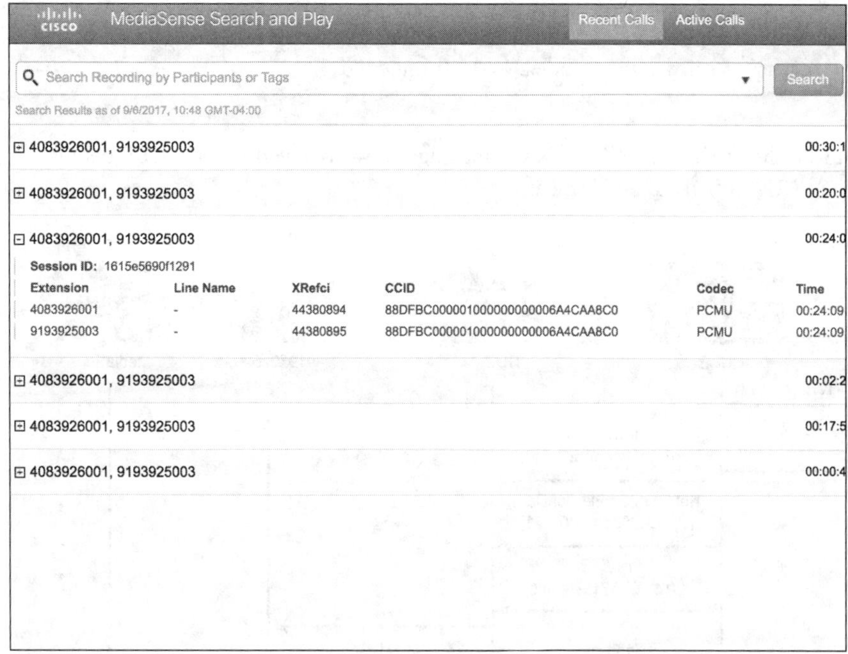

Figure 11-27 *Recording File Search in MediaSense*

API-Based Recording Troubleshooting

There are a number of tools available to troubleshoot API-based recording solutions. In addition to basic debug commands and packet capture tools, developers can also leverage test tools such as SoapUI while developing a recording application. Support engineers can enable debug commands and analyze the output to troubleshoot the API errors when the call volume is low. For high-call-volume environments, it is recommended to capture packets using the Embedded Packet Capture feature in Cisco IOS and analyze the HTTP XMF traffic by using Wireshark.

XMF application registration issues and recording initiation failures are the most commonly reported problems in CUCM network-based recording deployments. Being familiar with **debug** command outputs of a working call and knowing how to use Wireshark to analyze XMF application traffic will help troubleshoot issues faster. Let's walk through the **debug** command output of a recording session between **4083926001** and **9193935003**, shown in the sample deployment (refer to Figure 11-18) by enabling the following basic set of CCAPI, CCSIP, and WSAPI XMF **debug** commands:

```
debug voip ccapi inout
debug ccsip message
debug wsapi xmf message
debug wsapi xmf default
```

> **Tip** Enable **debug wsapi infrastructure detail** to view XMF messages in human-readable SOAP XML format, as shown in Examples 11-18 through 11-32.

Figure 11-28 shows the SIP call and XMF message flow observed in the CUBE debug output and CUCM SDL detailed traces.

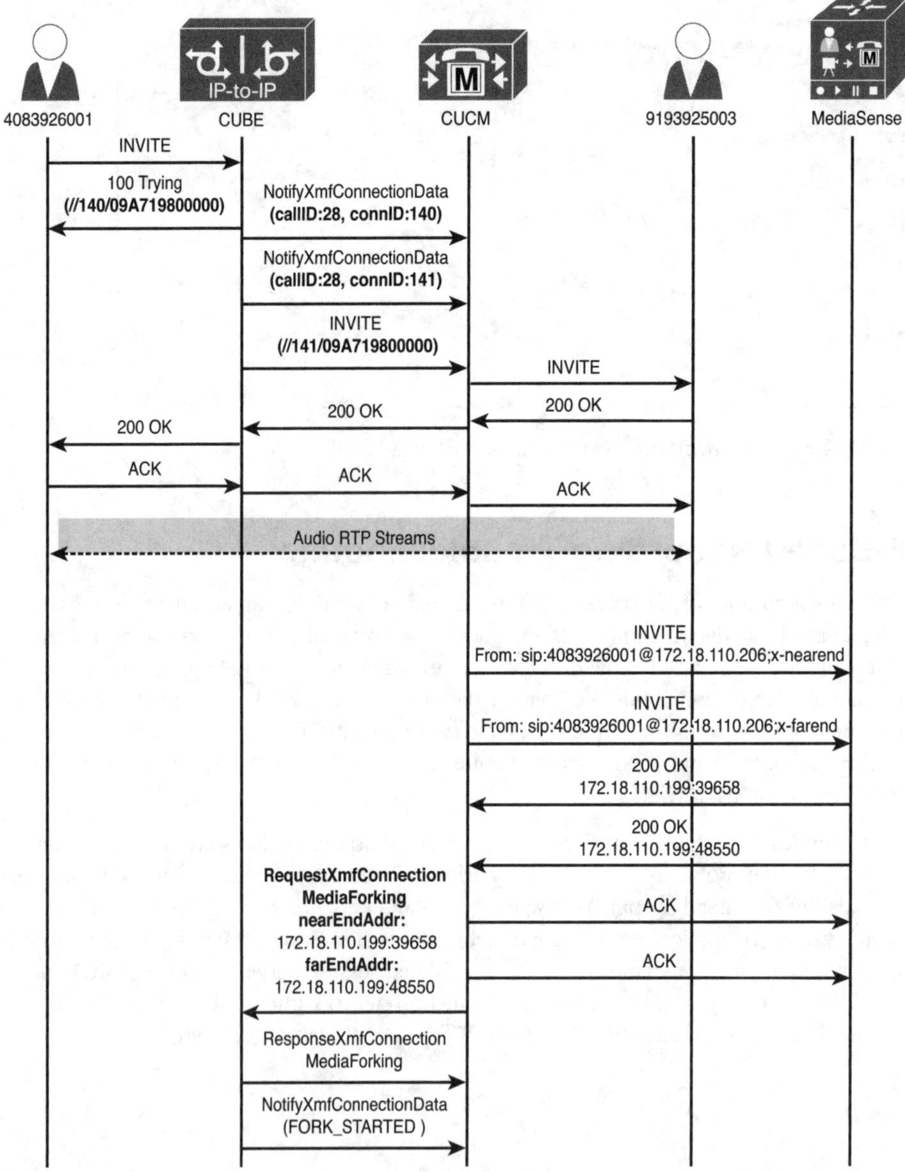

Figure 11-28 *SIP and XMF Message Flow*

Examples 11-39, 11-40 and 11-41 show CUBE debug snippets that correspond to the call flow and message sequence shown in Figure 11-28. The debug logs contain several XMF messages exchanged between CUBE and multiple CUCM nodes. The **registrationID** parameter value can be used to track messages exchanged between CUBE and a specific CUCM node. The sample output shown in Examples 11-39, 11-40, and 11-41 uses the string "**registrationID 1413028E:XMF:Unified CM 11.5.1.13050-1:5**" to identify all XMF messages exchanged between CUBE and the CUCM subscriber node at 172.18.110.206.

When the call to **9193925003** arrives at CUBE, it matches inbound dial peer **5000**, assigns connection ID **140** to the inbound connection, and identifies the outbound dial peer **5001** for routing the call. CUBE then informs CUCM about the creation of a new inbound connection by sending a **NotifyXmfConnectionData** message with **callID** set to **28**, **connID** set to **140**, and **state** set to **1** (IDLE). It sets up outbound connection **141** and informs the CUCM by sending another **NotifyXmfConnectionData** message with **callID** set to **28**, **connID** set to **141**, and **state** set to **5** (CALL_DELIVERY). The list of call, connection, and media forking states is defined in an XML Schema (XSD) file, which is available as part of UC Gateway Services API documentation.

Example 11-39 *Debug Output Showing Notifications of Inbound and Outbound Connections*

```
157997: Sep 11 19:26:00.401 UTC: //-1/09A719800000/CCAPI/cc_api_call_setup_ind_common:
   Interface=0x7F7BF2DF31C8, Call Info(
   Calling Number=4083926001,(Calling Name=)(TON=Unknown, NPI=Unknown,
  Screening=User, Passed, Presentation=Allowed),
   Called Number=9193925003(TON=Unknown, NPI=Unknown),
   Calling Translated=FALSE, Subscriber Type Str=Unknown, FinalDestinationFlag=TRUE,
   Incoming Dial-peer=5000, Progress Indication=NULL(0), Calling IE Present=TRUE,
   Source Trkgrp Route Label=, Target Trkgrp Route Label=, CLID Transparent=FALSE),
  Call Id=140
.....
.....
.....

158018: Sep 11 19:26:00.403 UTC: //140/09A719800000/CCAPI/ccIFCallSetupRequestPri-
  vate:
   Interface=0x7F7BF2DF31C8, Interface Type=3, Destination=, Mode=0x0,
   Call Params(Calling Number=4083926001,(Calling Name=)(TON=Unknown, NPI=Unknown,
  Screening=User, Passed, Presentation=Allowed),
   Called Number=9193925003(TON=Unknown, NPI=Unknown), Calling Translated=FALSE,
   Subscriber Type Str=Unknown, FinalDestinationFlag=TRUE, Outgoing Dial-peer=5001,
  Call Count On=FALSE,
   Source Trkgrp Route Label=, Target Trkgrp Route Label=, tg_label_flag=0,
   Application Call Id=)
```

```
.....
.....
.....
158037: Sep 11 19:26:00.404 UTC: //WSAPI/XMF/OUTGOING_MESSAGE:: msg_type[21]
  NotifyXmfConnectionData
158038: Sep 11 19:26:00.404 UTC: transactionID 1413C045:8682
158039: Sep 11 19:26:00.404 UTC: registrationID 1413028E:XMF:Unified CM
  11.5.1.13050-1:5
158040: Sep 11 19:26:00.404 UTC: callID: 28
158041: Sep 11 19:26:00.404 UTC: state 2
158042: Sep 11 19:26:00.404 UTC: connID: 140
158043: Sep 11 19:26:00.404 UTC: state: 1
158044: Sep 11 19:26:00.404 UTC: ConnDataOptSelector [1] [created]
158045: Sep 11 19:26:00.404 UTC: connID: 140
158046: Sep 11 19:26:00.404 UTC: state: 1
.....
.....
.....
158057: Sep 11 19:26:00.405 UTC: //141/09A719800000/CCAPI/cc_api_call_proceeding:
   Interface=0x7F7BF2DF31C8, Progress Indication=NULL(0)
.....
.....
.....
158067: Sep 11 19:26:00.408 UTC: //WSAPI/XMF/OUTGOING_MESSAGE:: msg_type[21]
  NotifyXmfConnectionData
158068: Sep 11 19:26:00.408 UTC: transactionID 1413C049:8685
158069: Sep 11 19:26:00.408 UTC: registrationID 1413028E:XMF:Unified CM
  11.5.1.13050-1:5
158070: Sep 11 19:26:00.408 UTC: callID: 28
158071: Sep 11 19:26:00.408 UTC: state 2
158072: Sep 11 19:26:00.408 UTC: connID: 141
158073: Sep 11 19:26:00.408 UTC: state: 5
158074: Sep 11 19:26:00.408 UTC: ConnDataOptSelector [1] [created]
158075: Sep 11 19:26:00.408 UTC: connID: 141
158076: Sep 11 19:26:00.408 UTC: state: 5
```

When the call is answered, CUCM initiates media forking on the outbound connection by sending a **RequestXmfConnectionMediaForking** message along with **callID**, **connID**, and the recorder's IP address and port number values. CUBE acknowledges the request by sending a **ResponseXmfConnectionMediaForking** message and forks the media streams to the recorder. When the forking is successful, CUBE provides the media forking state **FORK_STARTED** (**mediaForkingState** set to **1**) to CUCM through a **NotifyXmfConnectionData** message. Example 11-40 shows the debug output of these three messages exchanged between CUCM and CUBE.

Example 11-40 *Debug Output Showing a Media Forking Request Right After a Call Connect*

```
158147: Sep 11 19:26:07.473 UTC: //140/09A719800000/CCAPI/ccCallConnect:
   Call Entry(Connected=TRUE, Responsed=TRUE)
.....
.....
.....
158208: Sep 11 19:26:07.998 UTC: //WSAPI/XMF/INCOMING_MSG:: msg_type[13]  RequestXm-
  fConnectionMediaForking
158209: Sep 11 19:26:07.998 UTC: transactionID Cisco:UCM:CayugaIf:4:2
158210: Sep 11 19:26:07.998 UTC: registrationID 1413028E:XMF:Unified CM
  11.5.1.13050-1:5
158211: Sep 11 19:26:07.999 UTC: callID: 28
158212: Sep 11 19:26:07.999 UTC: connID: 141
158213: Sep 11 19:26:07.999 UTC: ConnMediaForkingOptSelector 1
158214: Sep 11 19:26:07.999 UTC: nearEndAddr:
158215: Sep 11 19:26:07.999 UTC: MediaAddrData:
158216: Sep 11 19:26:07.999 UTC: ipv4 172.18.110.199
158217: Sep 11 19:26:07.999 UTC: port 39658
158218: Sep 11 19:26:07.999 UTC: tone 0
158219: Sep 11 19:26:07.999 UTC: farEndAddr:
158220: Sep 11 19:26:07.999 UTC: MediaAddrData:
158221: Sep 11 19:26:07.999 UTC: ipv4 172.18.110.199
158222: Sep 11 19:26:07.999 UTC: port 48550
158223: Sep 11 19:26:07.999 UTC: tone 0
158224: Sep 11 19:26:07.999 UTC:  preserve: 1
.....
.....
.....
158225: Sep 11 19:26:07.999 UTC: //WSAPI/XMF/OUTGOING_RESPONSE:: msg_type[19]
  ResponseXmfConnectionMediaForking
158226: Sep 11 19:26:07.999 UTC: transactionID Cisco:UCM:CayugaIf:4:2.....
.....
.....
.....
158228: Sep 11 19:26:08.004 UTC: //WSAPI/XMF/OUTGOING_MESSAGE:: msg_type[21]  Noti-
  fyXmfConnectionData
158229: Sep 11 19:26:08.004 UTC: registrationID 1413028E:XMF:Unified CM
  11.5.1.13050-1:5
158230: Sep 11 19:26:08.004 UTC: callID: 28
158231: Sep 11 19:26:08.004 UTC: state 2
158232: Sep 11 19:26:08.004 UTC: connID: 141
158233: Sep 11 19:26:08.004 UTC: state: 7
158234: Sep 11 19:26:08.004 UTC: ConnDataOptSelector [10] [mediaForking]
158235: Sep 11 19:26:08.004 UTC: mediaForkingState: 1
```

When the external caller ends the call, CUBE terminates the media forking session and provides media forking state **FORKING_DONE** (**mediaForkingState** set to **3**) to CUCM. CUBE then disconnects both the inbound and outbound connections and notifies CUCM about the connection state **DISCONNECTED** (**state** set to **8**) along with the disconnect cause code and connection statistics, as shown in Example 11-41.

Example 11-41 *Debug Output Showing a Media Forking Status Change on a Call Disconnect*

```
158238: Sep 11 19:26:38.607 UTC: //140/09A719800000/CCAPI/cc_api_call_disconnected:
   Cause Value=16, Interface=0x7F7BF2DF31C8, Call Id=140
.....
.....
.....
158274: Sep 11 19:26:38.614 UTC: //WSAPI/XMF/OUTGOING_MESSAGE:: msg_type[21]  Noti-
  fyXmfConnectionData
158275: Sep 11 19:26:38.614 UTC: registrationID 1413028E:XMF:Unified CM
  11.5.1.13050-1:5
158276: Sep 11 19:26:38.614 UTC: callID: 28
158277: Sep 11 19:26:38.614 UTC: state 2
158278: Sep 11 19:26:38.614 UTC: connID: 141
158279: Sep 11 19:26:38.614 UTC: state: 7
158280: Sep 11 19:26:38.614 UTC: ConnDataOptSelector [10] [mediaForking]
158281: Sep 11 19:26:38.614 UTC: mediaForkingState: 3
.....
.....
.....
158320: Sep 11 19:26:38.616 UTC: //WSAPI/XMF/OUTGOING_MESSAGE:: msg_type[21]
  NotifyXmfConnectionData
158321: Sep 11 19:26:38.616 UTC: transactionID 14145589:8690
158322: Sep 11 19:26:38.616 UTC: registrationID 1413028E:XMF:Unified CM
  11.5.1.13050-1:5
158323: Sep 11 19:26:38.616 UTC: callID: 28
158324: Sep 11 19:26:38.616 UTC: state 2
158325: Sep 11 19:26:38.616 UTC: connID: 140
158326: Sep 11 19:26:38.616 UTC: state: 8
158327: Sep 11 19:26:38.616 UTC: type: 1
158328: Sep 11 19:26:38.616 UTC: coderType g711ulaw
158329: Sep 11 19:26:38.616 UTC: coderByte: 160
158330: Sep 11 19:26:38.616 UTC: discCause: 16
```

```
158331: Sep 11 19:26:38.616 UTC: callDuration: 31140
158332: Sep 11 19:26:38.616 UTC: TxPacketsCount: 1552
158333: Sep 11 19:26:38.616 UTC: TxBytesCount: 310400
158334: Sep 11 19:26:38.616 UTC: TxDurationMSec: 0
158335: Sep 11 19:26:38.616 UTC: TxVoiceDurationMSec: 0
158336: Sep 11 19:26:38.616 UTC: RxPacketsCount: 1555
158337: Sep 11 19:26:38.616 UTC: RxBytesCount: 310848
158338: Sep 11 19:26:38.616 UTC: RxDurationMSec: 0
158339: Sep 11 19:26:38.616 UTC: RxVoiceDurationMSec: 0
158340: Sep 11 19:26:38.616 UTC: roundTripDelayMSec: 3
158341: Sep 11 19:26:38.616 UTC: onTimeRvPlayMSec: 0
158342: Sep 11 19:26:38.616 UTC: gapFillWithPredictionMSec: 0
158343: Sep 11 19:26:38.616 UTC: gapFillWithInterpolationMSec: 0
158344: Sep 11 19:26:38.616 UTC: gapFillWithRedundancyMSec: 0
158345: Sep 11 19:26:38.616 UTC: lostPacketsCount: 0
158346: Sep 11 19:26:38.616 UTC: earlyPacketsCount: 0
158347: Sep 11 19:26:38.616 UTC: latePacketsCount: 0
158348: Sep 11 19:26:38.616 UTC: receiveDelayMSec: 0
158349: Sep 11 19:26:38.616 UTC: loWaterPlayoutDelayMSec: 0
158350: Sep 11 19:26:38.616 UTC: hiWaterPlayoutDelayMSec: 0
158351: Sep 11 19:26:38.616 UTC: ConnDataOptSelector [7] [disconnected]
.....
.....
.....
158421: Sep 11 19:26:38.620 UTC: //WSAPI/XMF/OUTGOING_MESSAGE:: msg_type[21]
  NotifyXmfConnectionData
158422: Sep 11 19:26:38.620 UTC: transactionID 1414558D:8693
158423: Sep 11 19:26:38.620 UTC: registrationID 1413028E:XMF:Unified CM
  11.5.1.13050-1:5
158424: Sep 11 19:26:38.620 UTC: callID: 28
158425: Sep 11 19:26:38.620 UTC: state 2
158426: Sep 11 19:26:38.620 UTC: connID: 141
158427: Sep 11 19:26:38.620 UTC: state: 8
158428: Sep 11 19:26:38.620 UTC: type: 1
158429: Sep 11 19:26:38.620 UTC: coderType g711ulaw
158430: Sep 11 19:26:38.620 UTC: coderByte: 160
158431: Sep 11 19:26:38.620 UTC: discCause: 16
158432: Sep 11 19:26:38.620 UTC: callDuration: 31140
158433: Sep 11 19:26:38.620 UTC: TxPacketsCount: 1555
158434: Sep 11 19:26:38.620 UTC: TxBytesCount: 310848
```

```
158435: Sep 11 19:26:38.620 UTC: TxDurationMSec: 0
158436: Sep 11 19:26:38.620 UTC: TxVoiceDurationMSec: 0
158437: Sep 11 19:26:38.620 UTC: RxPacketsCount: 1552
158438: Sep 11 19:26:38.620 UTC: RxBytesCount: 310400
158439: Sep 11 19:26:38.620 UTC: RxDurationMSec: 0
158440: Sep 11 19:26:38.620 UTC: RxVoiceDurationMSec: 0
158441: Sep 11 19:26:38.620 UTC: roundTripDelayMSec: 3
158442: Sep 11 19:26:38.620 UTC: onTimeRvPlayMSec: 0
158443: Sep 11 19:26:38.620 UTC: gapFillWithPredictionMSec: 0
158444: Sep 11 19:26:38.620 UTC: gapFillWithInterpolationMSec: 0
158445: Sep 11 19:26:38.620 UTC: gapFillWithRedundancyMSec: 0
158446: Sep 11 19:26:38.620 UTC: lostPacketsCount: 0
158447: Sep 11 19:26:38.620 UTC: earlyPacketsCount: 0
158448: Sep 11 19:26:38.620 UTC: latePacketsCount: 0
158449: Sep 11 19:26:38.620 UTC: receiveDelayMSec: 0
158450: Sep 11 19:26:38.620 UTC: loWaterPlayoutDelayMSec: 0
158451: Sep 11 19:26:38.620 UTC: hiWaterPlayoutDelayMSec: 0
158452: Sep 11 19:26:38.620 UTC: ConnDataOptSelector [7] [disconnected]
```

Collecting and analyzing network packet capture is an alternate method of viewing the API interactions. This method is useful when CUBE is handling high call volume. The method involves two tasks. The first task is to configure an access list (ACL) that matches the traffic of interest and define a monitor capture point. The second task is to start the capture, stop the capture, and export the captured traffic.

Example 11-42 shows a sample configuration of an ACL named **Recording-Traffic** that matches XMF application traffic exchanged across TCP port 8090 and all UDP traffic. The command **permit udp any any** is used to also include RTP packets of the recording session.

Example 11-42 *Access List Configuration for XMF Application and UDP Traffic*

```
ip access-list extended Recording-Traffic
 permit tcp any eq 8090 any
 permit tcp any any eq 8090
 permit udp any any
```

Example 11-43 shows a sample set of Embedded Packet Capture commands to define a monitor capture point that captures the traffic matching the access list **Recording-Traffic** in a buffer of size 50 MB. Note that the capture point is applied to the control-plane because the XMF application traffic is sourced and destined to the router itself. All the commands shown in Example 11-43 are entered in EXEC mode and not in the config mode of the router.

Example 11-43 *Embedded Packet Capture Commands Run in EXEC Mode*

```
CUBE1# monitor capture XMF access-list Recording-Traffic buffer size 50 control-
  plane both
CUBE1# monitor capture XMF start
CUBE1# monitor capture XMF stop
CUBE1# monitor capture XMF export ftp://ftp.entcomp1.com/XMF-Recording-Traffic-1.
  pcap
```

Port 8090 is not a standard HTTP application port, and hence Wireshark doesn't automatically decode XMF application traffic as HTTP. To make Wireshark decode correctly, go to Wireshark Preferences (Edit > Preferences in Windows and Wireshark > Preferences in Mac), expand the Protocols section, and select HTTP and add port 8090 to the TCP ports field, as shown in Figure 11-29.

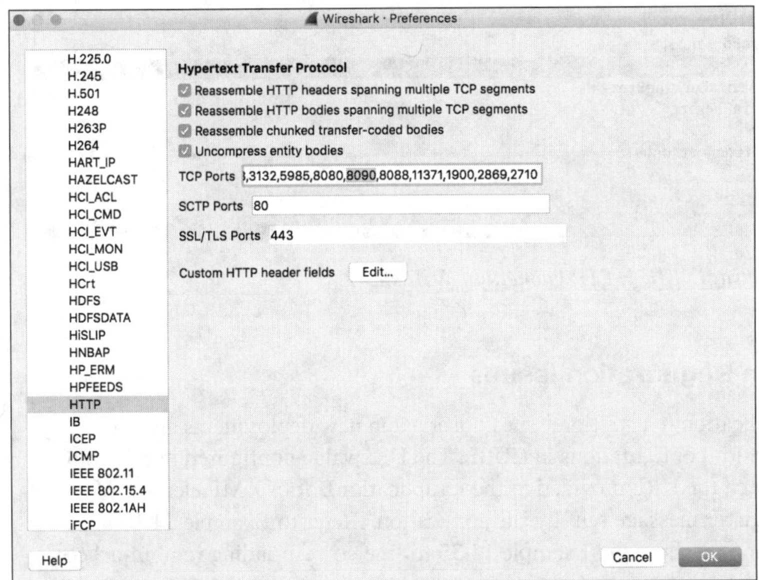

Figure 11-29 *Updating Wireshark Preferences to Decode XMF HTTP Packets*

Figure 11-30 shows an example of applying the Wireshark filter **http && ip.addr == <ip-addr of cucm node>** to display only the packets of interest from an analysis perspective. The "follow TCP stream" functionality can be used to view the request and response in a consolidated fashion. It is performed by selecting a packet, right-clicking, and selecting Follow > TCP Stream.

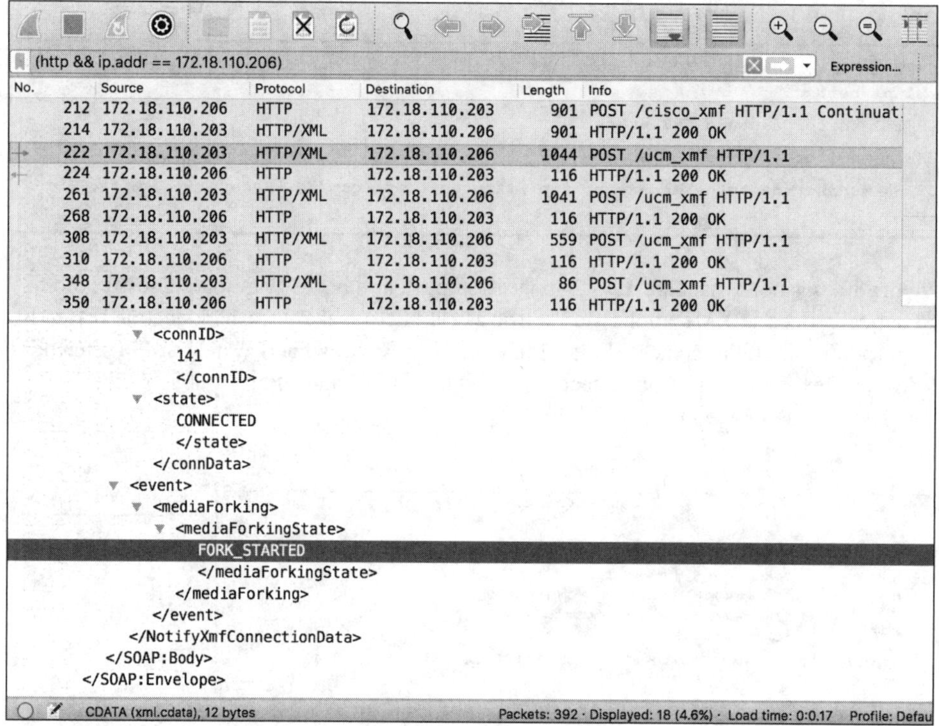

Figure 11-30 *Viewing XMF HTTP Packets in Wireshark*

XMF Application Registration Issues

Most of the application registration issues observed in new deployments are caused by incorrect **remote-url** configurations in CUBE. The URL value configured in this command should match the URL provided in the **<applicationData>** XML element of the **RequestXmfRegister** message sent by the application. (Refer to Example 11-18 for a sample registration message and Example 11-35 for the corresponding **remote-url** configuration.)

Lack of response to probes sent by CUBE from XMF applications is the primary root cause of registration issues in production environments. This could happen if the XMF application has crashed unexpectedly or is shut down for maintenance purposes or if there are IP connectivity issues. The command **show wsapi registration xmf** provides the probe status for the currently registered applications. Example 11-44 shows a scenario in which CUBE hasn't received a response for the regular probe sent every 120 seconds and hence has switched the probe status to **NEGATIVE** and decreased the probing interval to 5 seconds.

Example 11-44 *Output of* show wsapi registration xmf

```
CUBE1#show wsapi registration xmf
Provider XMF
=====================================================
registration index: 3
  id: F25228ED:XMF:Unified CM 11.5.1.13050-1:12
  appUrl:http://172.18.110.207:8090/ucm_xmf
  appName: Unified CM 11.5.1.13050-1
  provUrl: http://cube1.entcomp1.com:8090/xmf
  prober state: NEGATIVE
  connEventsFilter: CREATED|DISCONNECTED
  mediaEventsFilter:

registration index: 1
  id: F2C758A7:XMF:Unified CM 11.5.1.13050-1:13
  appUrl:http://172.18.110.205:8090/ucm_xmf
  appName: Unified CM 11.5.1.13050-1
  provUrl: http://cube1.entcomp1.com:8090/xmf
  prober state: STEADY
  connEventsFilter: CREATED|DISCONNECTED
  mediaEventsFilter:

registration index: 2
  id: F2C758FE:XMF:Unified CM 11.5.1.13050-1:14
  appUrl:http://172.18.110.206:8090/ucm_xmf
  appName: Unified CM 11.5.1.13050-1
  provUrl: http://cube1.entcomp1.com:8090/xmf
  prober state: STEADY
  connEventsFilter: CREATED|DISCONNECTED
  mediaEventsFilter:

CUBE1#
```

Example 11-45 shows sample debug output of **SolictXmfProbing** messages sent by CUBE to an application registered with **registrationID** equal to **F25228ED:XMF:Unified CM 11.5.1.13050-1:12**. CUBE doesn't get a response for the keepalive probe message with sequence number **64** and hence starts sending negative probes with sequence number **65**. After sending three negative probes—**65**, **66**, and **67**—and still not getting a response, it unregisters the application.

Example 11-45 *Output of* show wsapi registration xmf

```
1233202: Aug 31 02:36:13.960 UTC: //WSAPI//OUTGOING_MESSAGE:: type 3
  SolicitXmfProbing:
1233203: Aug 31 02:36:13.960 UTC: registrationID F25228ED:XMF:Unified CM
  11.5.1.13050-1:12
1233204: Aug 31 02:36:13.960 UTC: sequence 63
1233205: Aug 31 02:36:13.960 UTC: interval 120
1233206: Aug 31 02:36:13.960 UTC: failureCount 0
1233207: Aug 31 02:36:13.960 UTC: registered 1
1233208: Aug 31 02:36:13.960 UTC: providerStatus 1
.....
.....
.....
1233233: Aug 31 02:36:13.963 UTC: //WSAPI//INCOMING_MESSAGE:: type 4
  ResponseXmfProbing:
1233234: Aug 31 02:36:13.963 UTC: transactionID F2C5851B:83049
1233235: Aug 31 02:36:13.963 UTC: registrationID F25228ED:XMF:Unified CM
  11.5.1.13050-1:12
.....
.....
.....
1233387: Aug 31 02:38:13.964 UTC: //WSAPI//OUTGOING_MESSAGE:: type 3  SolicitXmf-
  Probing:
1233388: Aug 31 02:38:13.964 UTC: registrationID F25228ED:XMF:Unified CM
  11.5.1.13050-1:12
1233389: Aug 31 02:38:13.964 UTC: sequence 64
1233390: Aug 31 02:38:13.964 UTC: interval 120
1233391: Aug 31 02:38:13.964 UTC: failureCount 0
1233392: Aug 31 02:38:13.964 UTC: registered 1
1233393: Aug 31 02:38:13.964 UTC: providerStatus 1
.....
.....
.....
1233459: Aug 31 02:38:28.966 UTC: //WSAPI//OUTGOING_MESSAGE:: type 3
  SolicitXmfProbing:
1233460: Aug 31 02:38:28.966 UTC: registrationID F25228ED:XMF:Unified CM
  11.5.1.13050-1:12
1233461: Aug 31 02:38:28.966 UTC: sequence 65
1233462: Aug 31 02:38:28.966 UTC: interval 5
1233463: Aug 31 02:38:28.966 UTC: failureCount 0
1233464: Aug 31 02:38:28.966 UTC: registered 1
1233465: Aug 31 02:38:28.966 UTC: providerStatus 1
.....
.....
.....
```

```
1233531: Aug 31 02:38:43.967 UTC: //WSAPI//OUTGOING_MESSAGE:: type 3
  SolicitXmfProbing:
1233532: Aug 31 02:38:43.967 UTC: registrationID F25228ED:XMF:Unified CM
  11.5.1.13050-1:12
1233533: Aug 31 02:38:43.967 UTC: sequence 66
1233534: Aug 31 02:38:43.967 UTC: interval 5
1233535: Aug 31 02:38:43.967 UTC: failureCount 1
1233536: Aug 31 02:38:43.967 UTC: registered 1
1233537: Aug 31 02:38:43.967 UTC: providerStatus 1
.....
.....
.....
1233603: Aug 31 02:38:58.969 UTC: //WSAPI//OUTGOING_MESSAGE:: type 3  SolicitXmf-
  Probing:
1233604: Aug 31 02:38:58.969 UTC: registrationID F25228ED:XMF:Unified CM
  11.5.1.13050-1:12
1233605: Aug 31 02:38:58.969 UTC: sequence 67
1233606: Aug 31 02:38:58.969 UTC: interval 5
1233607: Aug 31 02:38:58.969 UTC: failureCount 2
1233608: Aug 31 02:38:58.969 UTC: registered 1
1233609: Aug 31 02:38:58.969 UTC: providerStatus 1
.....
.....
.....
1233667: Aug 31 02:39:08.969 UTC: //WSAPI/XMF/wsapi_prober_private_msg_status: Reg-
  istered Session Moving to Unregistered state
```

Recording Not Being Initiated

The CUCM alarm message **RecordingResourcesNotAvailable** is a common symptom of recording not being initiated. Example 11-46 shows an example of a CUCM SDL detailed trace snippet in which CUCM is trying to initiate network-based recording at the incoming gateway (**cube1.entcomp1.com**) that processed the call to **9193925003** but is not successful. Some of the root causes of this issue are XMF provider service in CUBE being in a shutdown state and the XMF registration not being successful due to incorrect **remote-url** configuration.

Example 11-46 *CUCM* RecordingResourceNotAvailable *Alarm Message*

```
01738185.001 |20:26:48.884 |AppInfo  |Recording::- (0000015) -processGWPreferred
  ....
01738185.002 |20:26:48.884 |AppInfo  |Recording::- (0000015) -getRecordingAnchor-
  Mode: PeerBib=[1];peerCMDevType=[8];qSigApduSupported=[0]
01738185.003 |20:26:48.884 |AppInfo  |Recording::- (0000015) -processGWPreferred: GW
  Recording - sideABibEnabled=[1]
```

```
.....
.....
.....
01738188.001 |20:26:48.884 |AppInfo  |Recording::- (0000015) -sendSsGetSharedResour-
  ceReq: BibResourceInfo=([44381127,2];[1];[cube1.entcomp1.com,StandAloneCluster]);
  requestDeviceType=[0];resPos=[2];resNum=[4083926001];tone=[64,3]


.....
.....
01738215.001 |20:26:48.886 |AppInfo  |GenAlarm: AlarmName = RecordingResourcesNo-
  tAvailable, subFac = CALLMANAGERKeyParam = , severity = 4, AlarmMsg = RecordedDe-
  viceName : SEP1C17D340848C
RecordedDeviceDN : 9193925003
RecordedDeviceCallID : 44381128
GatewayGuid : 5D5E62000001000000000051A4CAA8C0
RecordingMediaPreference : 1
CauseValue : 1114112
Reason : 1
AppID : Cisco CallManager
ClusterID : StandAloneCluster
NodeID : cl2-cucm-sub1
.....
.....
.....
01738215.004 |20:26:48.886 |AppInfo  |Recording::- (0000015) -sendRecordingStopInd-
  Local cluster only! sendStopRecording=[0]; mRecordingTrigger=[1];mRecordingAnchor=
  [1];restartRecording=[0].
```

Summary

This chapter provides a brief overview of business drivers for call recording and introduces SIP call signaling and API-based solutions for addressing call recording needs in enterprise environments. It discusses the SIPREC architecture, recording call flows, and Extended Media Forking (XMF) API requests and responses, along with configuration best practices and troubleshooting techniques.

References

RFC 3326, "The Reason Header Field for the Session Initiation Protocol (SIP)," https://tools.ietf.org/html/rfc3326

RFC 7245, "An Architecture for Media Recording Using the Session Initiation Protocol," https://tools.ietf.org/html/rfc7245

RFC 7865, "Session Initiation Protocol (SIP) Recording Metadata," https://tools.ietf.org/html/rfc7865

RFC 7866, “Session Recording Protocol,” https://tools.ietf.org/html/rfc7866

RFC 7989, “End-to-End Session Identification in IP-Based Multimedia Communication Networks,” https://tools.ietf.org/html/rfc7989

RFC 8068, “Session Initiation Protocol (SIP) Recording Call Flows,” https://tools.ietf.org/html/rfc8068

“SOAP Version 1.2 Part 1: Messaging Framework (Second Edition),” https://www.w3.org/TR/soap12-part1/

“SOAP Version 1.2 Part 0: Primer (Second Edition),” https://www.w3.org/TR/soap12-part0/

“Cisco Unified Communications Gateway Services API Guide,” https://www.cisco.com/c/en/us/td/docs/voice_ip_comm/cucme/CUCIS_API/CUCIS_API_Guide/CUCISA_OVR.html

Web Services Definition Language (WSDL) and XML Schema (XSD) files for Cisco Unified Communications Gateway Services API, https://communities.cisco.com/docs/DOC-51223

Federal Trade Commission, https://www.ftc.gov/about-ftc/bureaus-offices/bureau-consumer-protection

European Commission, https://ec.europa.eu/info/policies/consumers/consumer-protection_en

Consumer Rights Act 2015, http://www.legislation.gov.uk/ukpga/2015/15/contents/enacted

Consumers International, https://www.consumersinternational.org/

Chapter 12

Contact Center Integration

For many companies, the contact center is the lifeline that connects them directly with their customers and partners through a variety of communication channels. It is a feature-rich environment with sophisticated call flows such as interactive voice response (IVR), agent call transfers, and outbound dialer applications. SBCs are a key component of contact center architecture; they are responsible for connecting agents and applications with the external world through IP-based audio and video calls. This chapter focuses on the Cisco Unified Contact Center Enterprise (UCCE) solution and features that require integration with the CUBE SBC. For a more comprehensive look at the UCCE solution, see the *Cisco Unified Contact Center Design Guide*.

The chapter consists of the following sections:

- **Cisco UCCE Architecture**—This section provides a high-level overview of different components that form the UCCE architecture, explaining both their purposes and roles in the overall solution.
- **Inbound Calls to Agents**—This section takes a detailed look at how an inbound caller is connected to an agent in the *comprehensive call flow* model, along with the configuration required in each solution component to successfully orchestrate the call flow.
- **Call Transfers**—This section discusses the types of call transfers invoked by agents and the protocol inner workings of transfers based on SIP INVITE and SIP REFER.
- **Courtesy Callback**—This section illustrates the callback call flow and shows the interactions between a UCCE call script, CVP VXML applications, and the CUBE survivability script.
- **Call Progress Analysis (CPA)**—This section shows how CUBE assists with detection of live speech, answering machines, and fax tones in the outbound calls initiated by the SIP dialer. CPA enhances the productivity of agents by connecting them only when a call is answered by a human.

- **Troubleshooting Scenarios**—This section shares best practices for troubleshooting intermittent call disconnects and identifying reasons calls were routed to alternate destinations by the survivability script. It also lists the steps in the process of collecting and analyzing solution-level debugs for root causes of call disconnects.

Cisco UCCE Architecture

The Cisco UCCE solution is based on a highly scalable and distributed architecture. It includes a diverse set of products that work together to deliver a seamless customer experience while at the same time providing flexibility for businesses to handle customer interactions (for example, chat, email, voice, video) with agents located anywhere in the world.

SBCs are the entry point for inbound IP-based voice and video calls in a contact center. An inbound customer call is routed and connected with multiple destination devices, such as IVR applications, music-on-hold servers, and agent phones throughout the duration of the call. This chapter uses examples from UCCE version 11.6 to illustrate call flows and functionalities.

Before discussing the uses of SBCs in a UCCE environment, we first provide a high-level overview of the UCCE architecture and describe the various components that make up the solution.

UCCE Components

Figure 12-1 shows the key components of the contact center architecture, in which SIP trunks are used for inbound and outbound calls. The components of the architecture are discussed in the order in which they are used to process incoming calls to the contact center:

- Cisco Unified Border Element (CUBE)
- Cisco Unified SIP Proxy (CUSP)
- Voice browsers
- Cisco Unified Customer Voice Portal (CVP)
- Cisco Unified Contact Center Enterprise (UCCE)
- Cisco Unified Communications Manager (CUCM)
- Cisco Agent Desktop (CAD)
- Cisco Finesse Agent Desktop

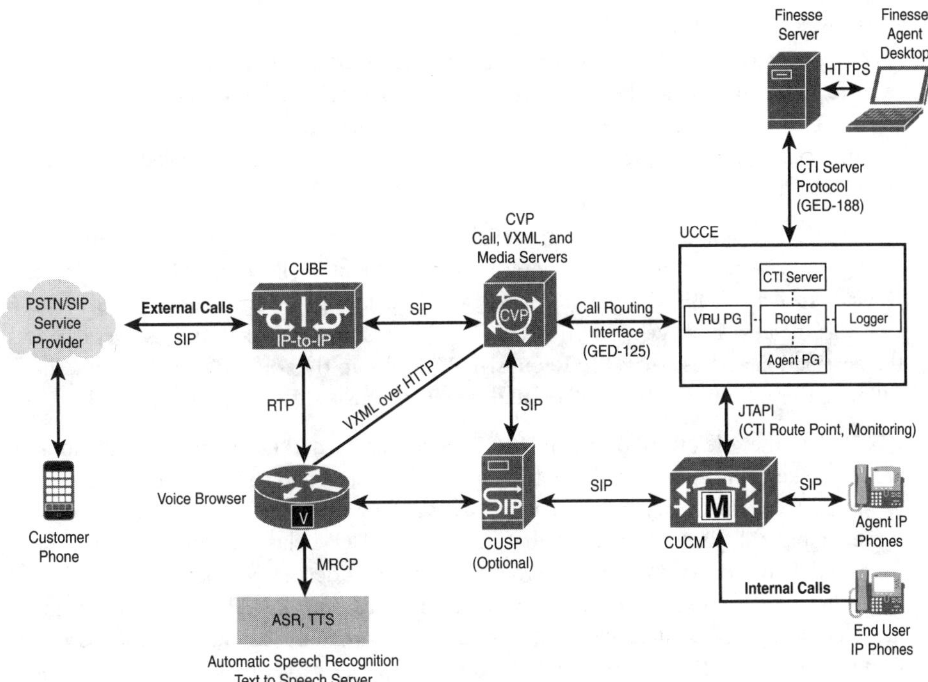

Figure 12-1 *SIP-Based UCCE Architecture*

Cisco Unified Border Element (CUBE)

CUBE Enterprise is deployed as an SBC, and it defines the demarcation point between the enterprise and service provider networks in a contact center environment. The SBC functionality runs on dedicated hardware such as the Cisco Integrated Services Router (ISR) and Aggregation Services Router (ASR) and also on virtualized routers, such as the Cloud Services Router (CSR).

In addition to performing functions such as protocol interworking, address hiding, media interworking, and DTMF interworking, CUBE also performs specialized functions such as call progress analysis for outbound calls originated from the contact center. This helps optimize the utilization of agents' time because they are assigned to a call only when the call is answered by a human and not when the call is instead answered by an answering machine, voicemail, or another automated system.

Survivability and network-based call recording are additional unique CUBE features that are used primarily in contact centers. Survivability provides the ability to reroute incoming calls to an alternate destination when the call setup with CVP is not successful. Network-based call recording allows companies to record audio and video streams of inbound and outbound contact center calls in order to meet various compliance requirements and review past interactions to continuously improve the customer experience.

Cisco Unified SIP Proxy (CUSP)

A contact center has a large number of unique directory number patterns to route calls to different destinations. These patterns, referred to as *labels*, are used to direct users' calls to VXML browsers and agents. It is a large administrative task to maintain call routing information for all these unique patterns in every device that is involved in the call signaling path.

To minimize the administration of these labels and reduce the possibility of routing configuration errors, call routing configuration can be centralized in a SIP proxy server. Devices such as CUBE, CVP, and CUCM can all be configured to point to the SIP proxy server as the next hop. When a SIP INVITE request is received, the proxy server extracts the destination address from SIP **Request-URI**, looks up the routing table by using the calling party number/URI as the key, and then forwards the INVITE to the next hop.

CUSP plays the role of SIP proxy in UCCE deployments, and it is an optional component. Two key concepts related to CUSP are server groups and route groups. A *server group* provides the ability to load balance calls across multiple elements of a cluster (for example, call processing subscriber nodes of a CUCM cluster). Route groups are used to define primary and alternate routing paths for a destination pattern. CUSP supports directory number, URI, and domain-based SIP routing. CUSP can be deployed in a Services-Ready Engine module of a Cisco ISR or as a virtual machine in a Cisco Unified Computing System (UCS) server or a Cisco UCS E-Series server module in a Cisco ISR. Newer versions of CUSP such as 9.x and higher are available only in virtualized mode.

Voice Browsers

The conversation dialog between the caller and the IVR is defined using Voice Extensible Markup Language (VXML). VXML 2.1 is an industry standard defined by the World Wide Web Consortium (W3C). VXML documents are executed in a manner that is very similar to the method used for HTML documents. Web browsers such as Firefox, Chrome, and Edge download HTML documents from web servers (for example, https://www.cisco.com) and then render a HTML page by displaying the content (text, images, and forms) in the web browser. The user then provides input to the web page and sends user data back to the server. The web browser and server are called the *HTTP client* and *server*. Similarly, VXML documents are downloaded from VXML servers and executed by VXML clients. A VXML client renders the interactive content by playing a prompt and waiting for the user's speech or DTMF input. User input is then sent back to the VXML server, where actions are performed based on the provided input. The prompts presented over VXML can either be static audio files or dynamically generated in real time, using text-to-speech (TTS) servers.

VXML clients, which are also called *voice browsers*, interact with TTS and automatic speech recognition (ASR) servers by using Media Resource Control Protocol (MRCP). MRCP messages are exchanged over Real-Time Streaming Protocol (RTSP); this protocol is referred to as MRCPv1 when sent over RTSP and MRCPv2 when sent over SIP.

Cisco Unified Customer Voice Portal (CVP)

Cisco CVP has four main components: the CVP server, CVP operations console, CVP Operations and Resource Manager (ORM), and the CVP reporting server. In addition, the CVP server has three main subcomponents:

- **CVP VXML server**—This performs the role of VXML server, with Cisco ISR and Cisco Virtualized Voice Browser (VBB) functioning as the VXML gateways or VXML clients. Developers use a graphical interface called Cisco Unified Call Studio, an integrated development environment (IDE), to define the conversation flow and save it as a voice application. The voice application is then deployed in CVP VXML server, automatically generating and serving the corresponding VXML documents out to VXML clients upon request.
- **CVP media server**—This is a web server that stores and serves both media files used as audio prompts and grammar files used to define which specific DTMF or words to consider as valid, matching user input. VXML clients send HTTP **GET** requests to the CVP media server to download audio files and cache them locally. These files are cached for a duration defined by HTTP headers, such as Cache-Control, Expires, Date, and Last-Modified in the 200 OK HTTP response. The Cisco technical article "Understanding VXML HTTP Cache for Media Files" walks through the cache time calculation process in further detail.
- **CVP call server**—This is the component that interacts with CUBE, CUSP, and CUCM, using SIP as the call signaling protocol. When an inbound external call arrives at CUBE, it is first routed to the CVP call server. The call server answers the call from the signaling perspective and consults UCCE Router to determine how to handle the call. The communication between the CVP and UCCE Router is facilitated by the voice response unit (VRU) peripheral gateway (discussed later in this chapter). Based on instructions received from UCCE, the call server acts as a SIP back-to-back user agent (B2BUA) and sets up an outbound call with the voice browser client or CUCM. The CVP call server updates the media streams of the inbound and outbound call legs such that the external caller can interact with an IVR, hear agent greetings or music on hold, or talk to an agent. The CVP call server consists of three services:
  - **SIP Service**—Handles incoming calls from CUBE and originates outbound calls to agents registered to either CUCM or other destinations in the PSTN through the use of CUBE.
  - **ICM Service**—Handles message exchanges with the UCCE peripheral gateway for routing requests and responses.
  - **IVR Service**—Handles the incoming HTTP connection from voice browsers and generates VXML documents to implement micro-applications such as Play Media, Get Speech, Get Digits, Menu, Play Data, and Capture.
- **CVP operations console**—This provides a web interface to operate, administer, manage, and provision (OAMP) the CVP server. It is used as the primary configuration interface for the CVP call server, CVP VXML server, and CVP reporting server.

- **CVP reporting server—**This stores details about the calls handled by the CVP call server and sessions processed by the CVP VXML application server in an Informix database. The reporting server is a mandatory component for the *courtesy callback* feature to work successfully. The details of the customer who requested a callback, including name and number, are stored in the CVP reporting server by the callback script.

Cisco Unified Contact Center Enterprise (UCCE)

UCCE Router is the brain of the contact center. It has full awareness of agent states and also contains the business logic regarding how to handle incoming calls. Each call is associated with a call script containing step-by-step call-handling instructions. These instructions include executing a VXML application hosted in the CVP VXML server, queueing an incoming call until an agent is available, and routing the call to an available agent.

UCCE has a number of software components, including the following:

- **Router—**A router is responsible for making routing decisions based on agent and VRU resource availability. It learns about phone, VRU port, and agents' states from the peripheral devices such as CUCM, CVP, and Finesse servers. The router interfaces with these devices via the PGs.
- **Peripheral gateway (PG)—**A PG performs the role of a message translator, providing a consistent messaging interface to the router on one side and the peripheral devices on the other side using the protocol that each device understands. Agent PGs, VRU PGs, and Media routing PGs are the most commonly deployed PGs:
  - **Agent PG—**An agent PG is used to interface with CUCM and Finesse servers. Peripheral Interface Manager (PIM) and Computer Telephony Integration (CTI) servers are two processes that run within an agent PG. CUCM uses the Java Telephony API (JTAPI) protocol to communicate with the PIM process, whereas Finesse servers use the Cisco CTI protocol to communicate with the CTI server.

    Computer telephony integration (CTI) refers to the integration of computer applications with telephone calls. For example, when a new call is received on an agent's phone, a computer application running on the agent's computer displays detailed information about the calling user and also provides the ability to answer the call directly from the computer application. The application running on the agent's computer is referred to as a *CTI client*. The server that provides call information, sends notifications of call events, processes calls, and handles agent-related requests from clients is called the *CTI server*. The list of messages exchanged between the CTI client and server using the Cisco CTI protocol is documented in the "CTI Server Message Reference Guide."
  - **VRU PG—**A VRU PG is used to interface with CVP and other devices that serve as network VRUs. The VRU devices provide IVR treatment such as playing welcome prompts and menu prompts, collecting digits, and playing music-on-hold prompts when a caller is waiting in the queue to talk to an agent.

- **Media routing PG**—A MR PG is used to interface with Outbound Dialer. It is used by the dialer to request and reserve agents prior to placing outbound calls as part of an outbound campaign.

- **Logger**—The logger stores the contact center's configuration data, such as agents, skill groups, and scripts, in a centralized database server. When the UCCE Router process starts, it reads the configuration data from the logger. Smaller UCCE deployments have the option to deploy both router and logger components in the same virtual machine, as a combined component called *rogger*. The logger also contains historical data that can be distributed to Historical Data Server (HDS).

  The logger serves as a centralized syslog feed source, consolidating events from UCCE components and sending the syslog messages to the configured syslog server. The logger receives route and termination call detail records (CDRs) from a router and stores the information in its database. The route CDR has information about the source of a routing request, the type of the routing request, and the routing result. The termination call record has information about the destination at which the call was terminated. The CDR information is periodically replicated to the administration and data server for reporting purposes.

- **Administration and data server**—The administration and data server, which interacts with the logger to update the configuration data, provides a GUI tool (Configuration Manager) for UCCE administrators to create new and update existing configuration objects within the contact center. It also contains HDS.

- **Live data server**—A live data server receives real-time call events from the router and PGs and then aggregates and publishes the data to real-time reporting applications such as Cisco Unified Intelligence Center (CUIC). Administrators and supervisors use CUIC to get real-time insights into contact center activities such as call volume.

High redundancy and availability are achieved by deploying individual UCCE application instances at two different physical locations (Side A and Side B) in order to provide geographic diversity during failure or planned maintenance. The router subcomponents in each of these instances communicate and are in sync with each other. The logger is associated with the router in the same side (for example, the logger in Side A is associated with the router in Side A, and the logger in Side B is associated with the router in Side B). The PGs also have one instance in each side, and one of them is active. Each side can continue to handle calls even if the connectivity between the two sites is interrupted for a brief period. UCCE supports several deployment models to suit business needs. UCCE solution design guides, available at Cisco.com, are the best source of information for the latest supported designs.

Cisco Unified Communication Manager (CUCM)

CUCM handles the registration and call control of IP phones and media resources such as transcoders, media termination points, music-on-hold servers, and conference bridge servers. IP phones are used by end users in the company as well as by agents in the contact center. CUCM configuration plays a key role in determining the type of audio and video codecs, the DTMF mechanism used, and the amount of bandwidth allocated for calls involving IP phones.

The communication interface between CUCM and UCCE is established through the agent PG, using the PIM process. CUCM uses JTAPI to communicate with the PIM process, conveys IP phone line status (such as on-hook, off-hook, ringing, and connected), and allows remote control of IP phone devices by external applications through this interface.

CUCM, CVP, CUBE, and CUSP interwork with each other using SIP trunks. Inbound calls to the contact center that originate from the PSTN are sent through CUBE and then are answered by CVP. When an agent becomes available, the call is sent from CVP to CUCM over a SIP trunk and routed to the agent phone.

Because CUCM also handles IP phones of non-contact center end users in the company, as shown in Figure 12-1, it is also possible for the contact center to receive calls from internal users whose endpoints are registered to CUCM. In this scenario, CUCM acts as a call routing client, requests routing instructions from the UCCE application, and routes the call according to the destination label received from UCCE. The interface used to request routing instructions is referred to as the *CTI route point*, which is an entity in the CUCM configuration. CUCM routes outbound calls either directly from the agent phones to CUBE or through CUSP in environments where CUSP is deployed.

Cisco Agent Desktop (CAD)

The CAD application is the primary tool agents use to handle contact center interactions. Agents become available by logging into the desktop application and setting their state to Ready. Agents can answer incoming calls, transfer calls, and conference other users into an existing call by using the CAD application. CAD helps increase an agent's productivity by automatically retrieving and displaying relevant information about the calling user, such as customer name, company, location, and preferences. The presentation of this information is made possible through the CTI between the CAD and CTI server component in UCCE and by using the calling party number to look up customer information in databases. CAD applications interface with the CTI OS server in order to communicate with the CTI server. The CTI OS server acts as a translator, providing access to agent, call, and skill group data through an object-oriented interface to the CTI OS clients on one side and using GED-188 to communicate with the CTI server on the other side. CTI OS client programs such as CAD use C++, Java, and .NET-based client interface libraries to read the Agent, Call, and Skill Group object parameters; set object parameters; and receive notifications when specific events of interest occur (for example, start of a call, end of call, call hold, call resume).

Finesse Agent Desktop was introduced as a next-generation agent desktop application beginning in UCCE 8.5. CAD is no longer supported in UCCE 11.6 and above, and hence it is recommended to migrate to Finesse Agent Desktop.

Cisco Finesse Agent Desktop

In the early days, Agent Desktop was a standalone Windows application. It has now evolved into a web browser–based application called Finesse Agent Desktop. Administrators no longer need to install separate applications in an agent's computer to perform this function.

The web desktop client talks to the Finesse server by using Finesse REST APIs. These APIs provide the ability to get and set agent states, make calls, perform actions such as transfer/hold/resume, and retrieve details about a given queue or team. The complete documentation of Finesse APIs is available at Cisco DevNet. A Finesse server acts as a CTI client and interfaces with the CTI server component of the UCCE application. It retrieves information about agents, calls, queues, and teams, and it makes agent state changes through this interface.

The key advantage with Finesse Agent Desktop is that it enables developers to enhance application functionality using the Finesse REST API and to add relevant custom UI gadgets within the app by using JavaScript library APIs, as shown in Figure 12-2.

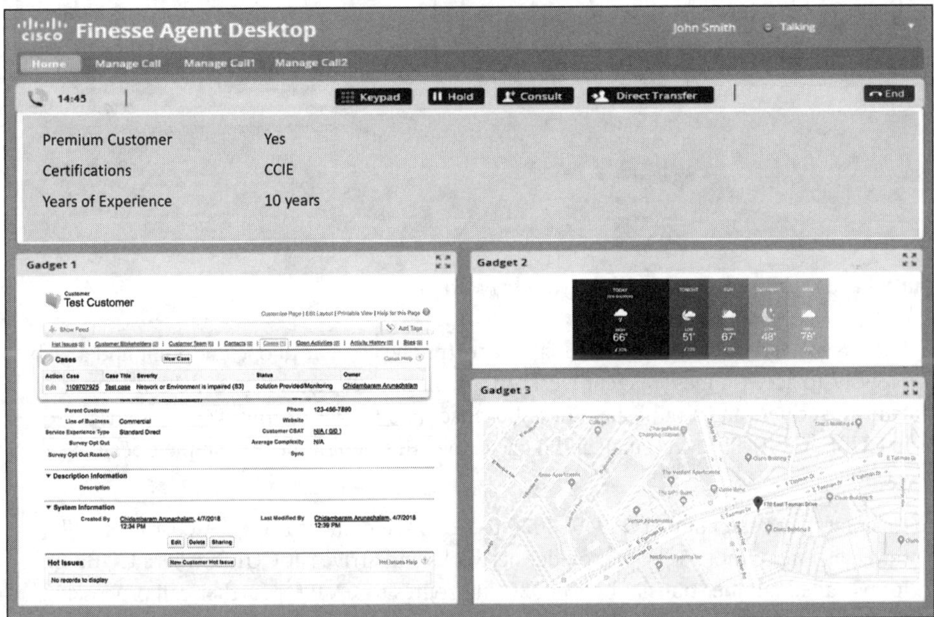

Figure 12-2 *Finesse Agent Desktop with Custom Gadgets*

Inbound Calls to Agents

The most common call flow in a contact center is connecting incoming calls to customer service representatives. The following sections describe the relevant configurations across the contact center solution components that enable the inbound call handling functionality and give a detailed walkthrough of the call flow using debug snippets and show commands.

Deployment Scenario

Figure 12-3 shows a contact center deployment example that is used in this section to explain CUBE integration concepts and configuration. For the sake of simplicity, the diagram shows only the key components of the UCCE solution that are required to understand the call signaling and media path.

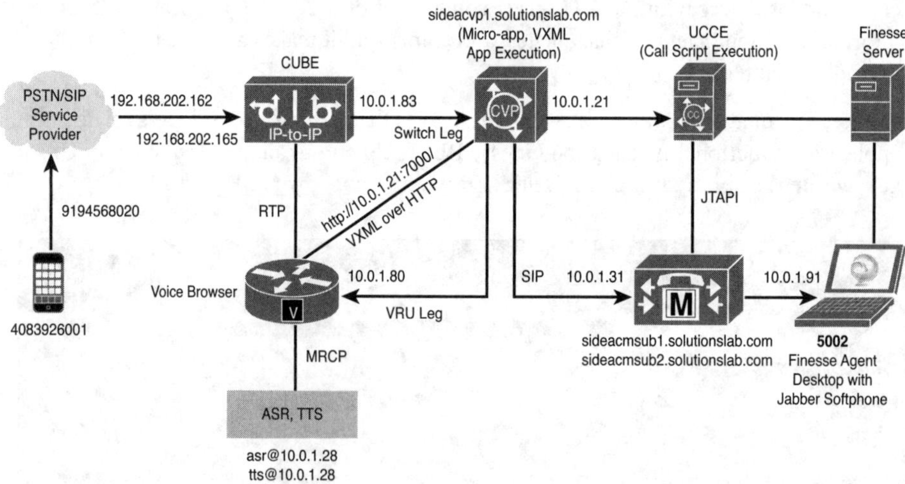

Figure 12-3 *Contact Center Deployment Example*

For this example, agents use Cisco Jabber softphone as their phone endpoint and a web browser to access Finesse Agent Desktop. Agent phones register to a CUCM cluster with two subscribers and a publisher node. Because the number of routes to be configured in CUBE, CVP, CUCM is small and manageable, this deployment example doesn't use CUSP.

Customers use the number 9194568020 to reach the contact center. A customer call traverses one or more service provider networks and arrives at CUBE, where CUBE performs called number translation to 8020 and routes to CVP for further call processing. CVP answers the call, retrieves key information, such as the calling and called party numbers, and then requests UCCE to provide routing instructions. UCCE uses the calling and called party numbers, along with time of day to look up the UCCE call script associated with this dialed number. The UCCE call script routes the call directly to an agent if one is readily available and returns the agent label in the routing response to CVP.

If no agents are available, the UCCE call script connects the incoming call leg (also known as the *switch* leg) to the VRU call leg to place the caller in a queue. UCCE sets up this connection by returning the VRU label as the routing response. CVP originates an outbound SIP call with a called number set to the VRU label. This call is routed to a Cisco IOS VXML gateway or Cisco Virtualized Voice Browser, which in turn acts as a voice browser and establishes a VXML session over HTTP with the VXML application server (10.0.1.21). CVP plays the role of a SIP B2BUA and updates media information of the switch and VRU call legs, such that the media stream traverses from CUBE to the VXML gateway or VVB.

The voice browser executes the VXML documents generated by the application named CustomHelloWorld to provide IVR treatment such as playing music-on-hold audio while the caller is waiting in the queue. Once an agent becomes available, the UCCE call script releases the VRU leg and requests the CVP routing client to connect the switch call leg to an agent by providing the agent label. This sequence completes the delivery of the call and the function of UCCE Router's responsibility. The call is then handled between the agent and the caller and disconnected accordingly. Table 12-1 lists the directory numbers and labels used in this call flow.

Table 12-1 *Directory Number and Label Used in the Inbound Call Flow*

Description	Directory Number or Label
Calling number	408-392-6001
Called number	919-456-8020
UCCE dialed number	8020
VRU label	7777777777
Agent	5002

Solution-level Configuration

This section describes the key configuration details required in different components of the contact center in order to provide a detailed understanding of how the solution components work together to handle the incoming call and deliver the intended experience to callers.

UCCE Configuration

From a UCCE configuration perspective, VRU PGs and a CUCM PG are configured to communicate with CVP and CUCM, respectively. Both CVP and CUCM are configured as routing clients so that they can solicit UCCE for routing instructions.

UCCE takes key parameters from the routing request received from the routing clients, uses the *dialed number* to find the Call Type configuration object, looks up the call script associated with the Call Type object, and executes the call routing script. The network VRU type (for example, 2, 3, 4, 5, 6, 7, 10) determines which node (for example, Translation Route to VRU, Send to VRU) in the UCCE call script is used to connect an incoming call to a network VRU external script (VXML application) or queue an incoming call at the network VRU. The network VRU type also defines how UCCE correlates the dialog handled by a given network VRU (VRU leg) with the corresponding call from the routing client (switch leg).

Unified CVP is configured as a Type 10 network VRU for *comprehensive* call flows. This configuration allows a UCCE call script to invoke CVP micro-applications and CVP VXML for IVR treatment. When the incoming call is directed to a Type 10 network VRU, UCCE forms a target label by concatenating the routing label configured for the selected network VRU and a unique correlation-ID assigned to the given call, and it returns the target label as a routing request response. Figure 12-4 shows a screenshot of the Network VRU Explorer configuration tool, containing the configuration of a Type 10 network VRU with CVP as routing client and 7777777777 as the routing label.

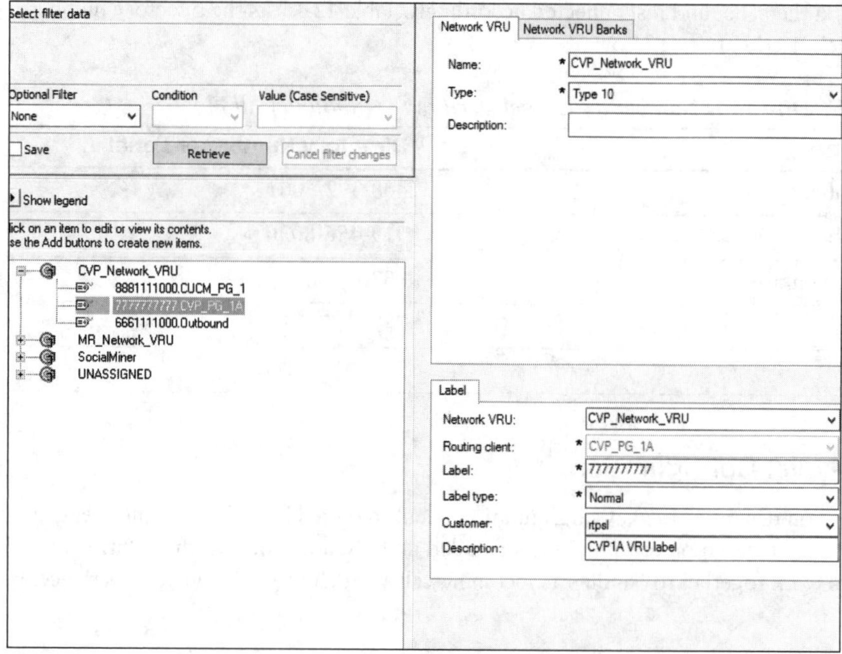

Figure 12-4 *UCCE Network VRU Explorer Showing CVP as the Network VRU*

The PG Explorer configuration tool is used to associate the network VRU CVP_Network_VRU with the VRU peripheral gateway CVP_PG_1A that is used for communication with CVP, as shown in Figure 12-5.

This configuration allows the UCCE call script to invoke the CVP network VRU to provide IVR treatment such as playing menu prompts, collecting digits, and playing music-on-hold audio prompts while a caller is waiting in a queue for agents to become available. This invocation is performed using the **Send to VRU** node within the call script. The UCCE call script that handles calls to 8020 is shown in Figure 12-6.

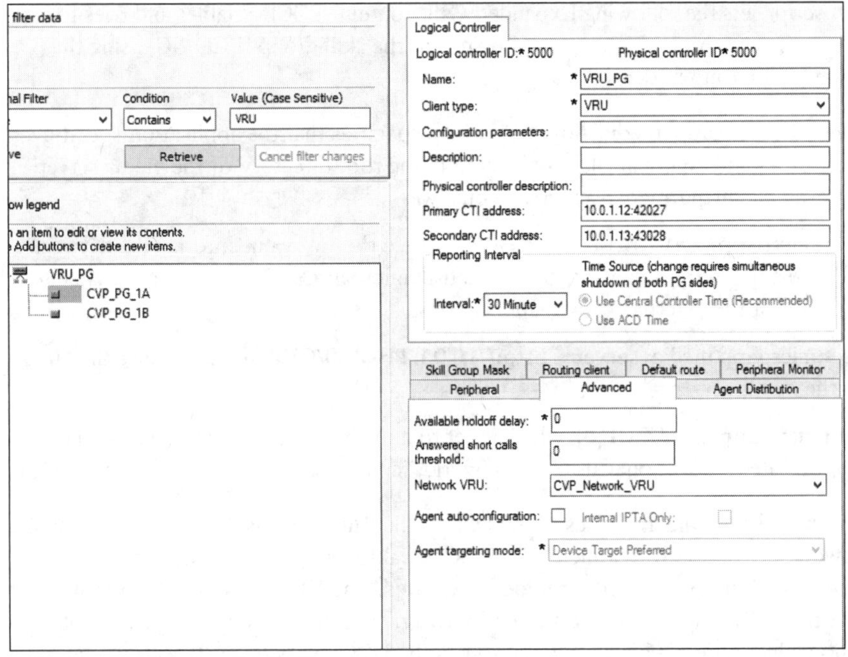

Figure 12-5 *UCCE PG Explorer Showing the PG to Network VRU Association*

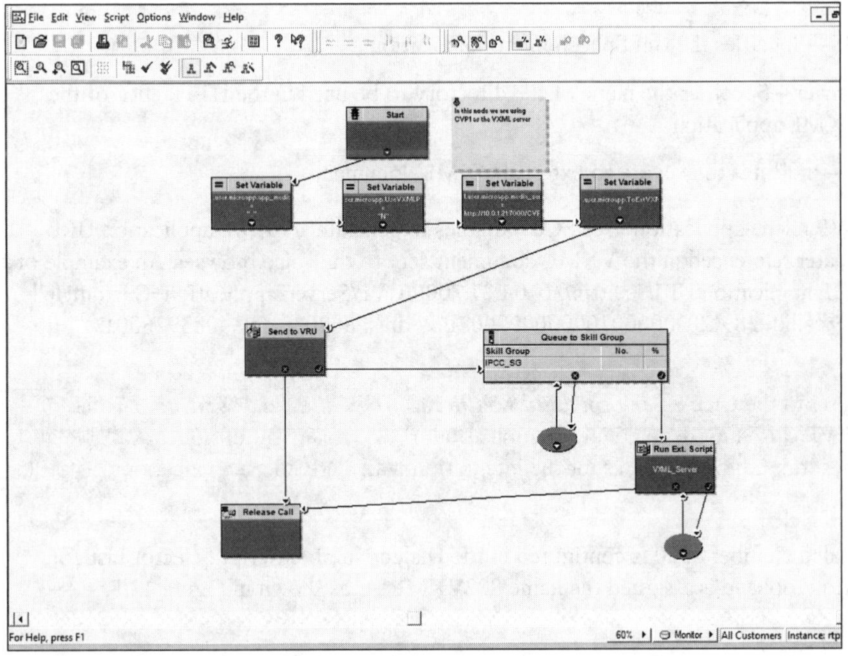

Figure 12-6 *UCCE Script Editor Call Script*

The call script sets the following Expanded Call Context (ECC) variables and tries to route the call to an available agent that belongs to the skill group IPCC_SG, using the **Queue to Skill Group** node:

- **user.microapp.app_media_lib = ".."**, which specifies that the application-specific media files and grammar files are located in the root directory of the media server; for example, http://media-server/welcome.wav
- **user.microapp.UseVXMLParams = "N"**, where the "N" value informs the network VRU to append the values provided in a user.microapp.ExtVXML array variable to the URL of the external VXML application
- **user.microapp.media_server = http://10.0.1.21:7000/CVP**, which defines the URL of the media server
- **user.microapp.ExtVXML[0]**, which is set to a dynamic value using the formula concatenate("application=CustomHelloWorld;",concatenate("callid=",Call.user.media.id))

If no agents are available, the call script executes the **Run External Script** node to invoke the network VRU for IVR treatment. The ECC variables are passed to the network VRU when the Run External Script node is executed. The VRU uses the ECC variables to select the VXML application to be run for the given call. The Run External Script node shown in Figure 12-6 is configured to run the UCCE network VRU script named VXML_Server, which is defined to execute a CVP Get Speech micro-application with the following parameters (see Figure 12-7, which is a screenshot taken from Network VRU Script List configuration tool):

- **GS**—Specifies the Get Speech micro-application
- **Server**—Specifies the name of the directory to be used in the HTTP URL of the VXML application
- **V**—Indicates to execute an external VXML document

The CVP micro-application uses ECC variables to generate a VXML application URL that is later referenced in the VXML document sent to the voice browser. An example of a VXML application URL is http://10.0.1.21:7000/CVP/Server?application=CustomHello World&callid=289C3D00000100000000007E&_dnis=8020&_ani=4083926001.

Note Refer to the *UCCE Scripting and Media Routing Guide* and *Writing Scripts for Unified CVP Guide* for detailed information about the complete set of nodes available in the UCCE script editor, as well as for the integration with CVP micro-applications.

The Dialed Number 8020 is configured in the Dialed Number/Script Selector List configuration tool and is assigned the name 802VXML1A, as shown in Figure 12-8.

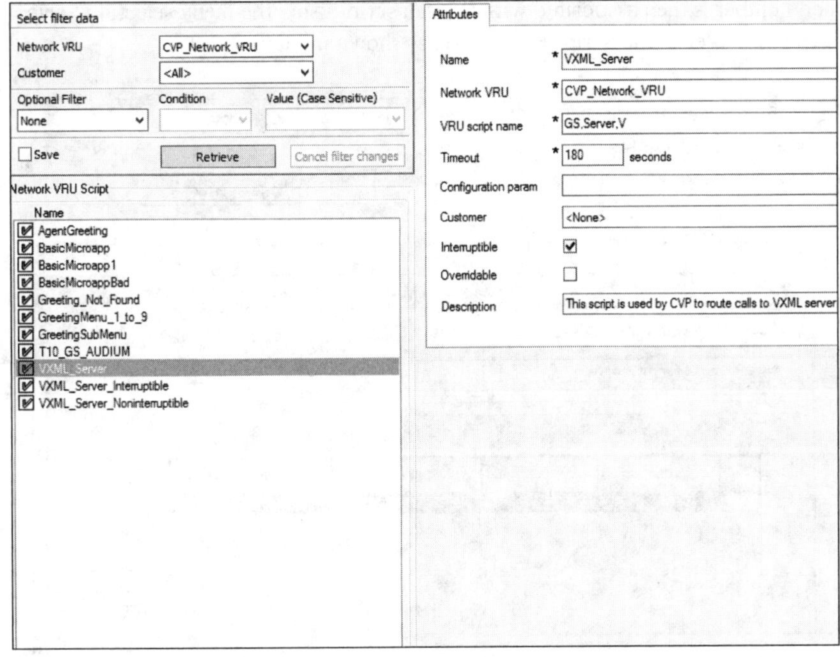

Figure 12-7 *UCCE Network VRU Script*

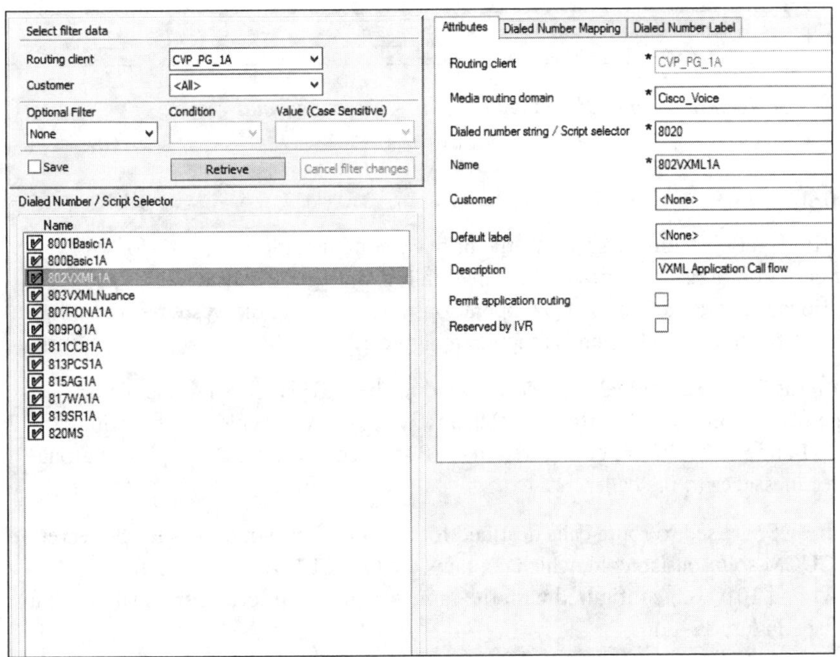

Figure 12-8 *UCCE Dialed Number/Script Selector List*

The dialed number is then associated with the call script using the menu selection **Script > Call Type Manager** in the Script Editor tool, as shown in Figure 12-9.

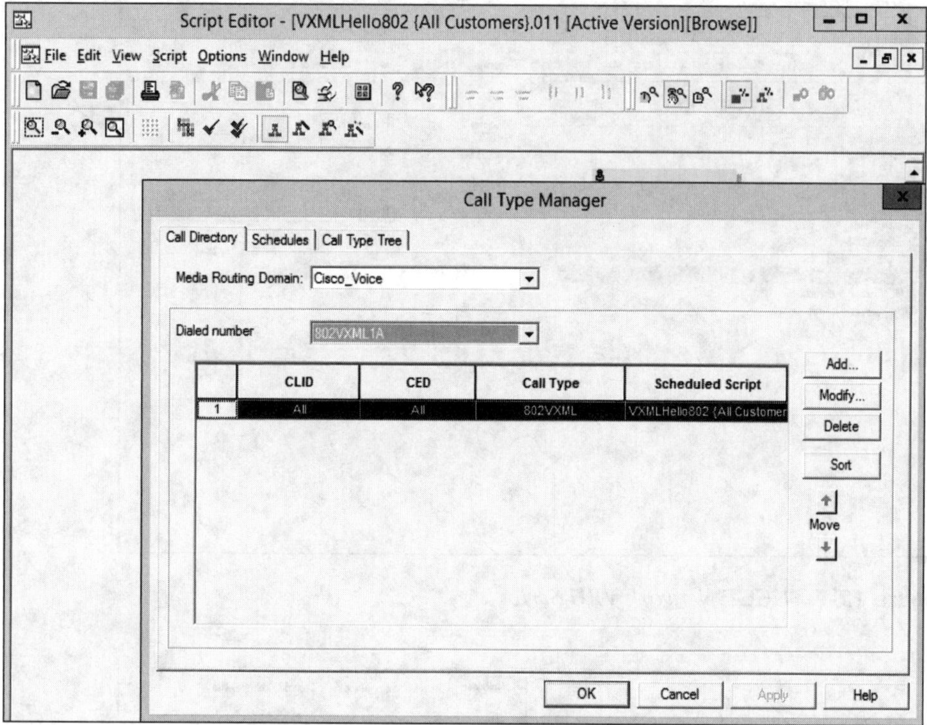

Figure 12-9 *Script Editor and Dialed Number–to–Script Association*

CVP Configuration

The CVP operations console serves as the primary administration interface for CVP-related configuration. The next-hop information for routing SIP calls to VRUs and agent destinations is configured in the CVP operations console using the **System > Dialed Number Pattern** menu selection, as shown in Figure 12-10.

The patterns 777*, 91*, and 92* that correspond to the VRU label, Ringtone, Error message playout are routed to the VXML gateway or to VVB. Typically, the strings 91919191 and 92929292 are configured in CVP as directory numbers to play ringtone and error messages to the caller.

The pattern 5* is used to route calls destined for agent directory numbers to the server group CUCM.solutionslab.com, which contains the two CUCM subscriber nodes (10.0.1.31 and 10.0.1.32) configured with the same weight and priority for equal load balancing (see Figure 12-11).

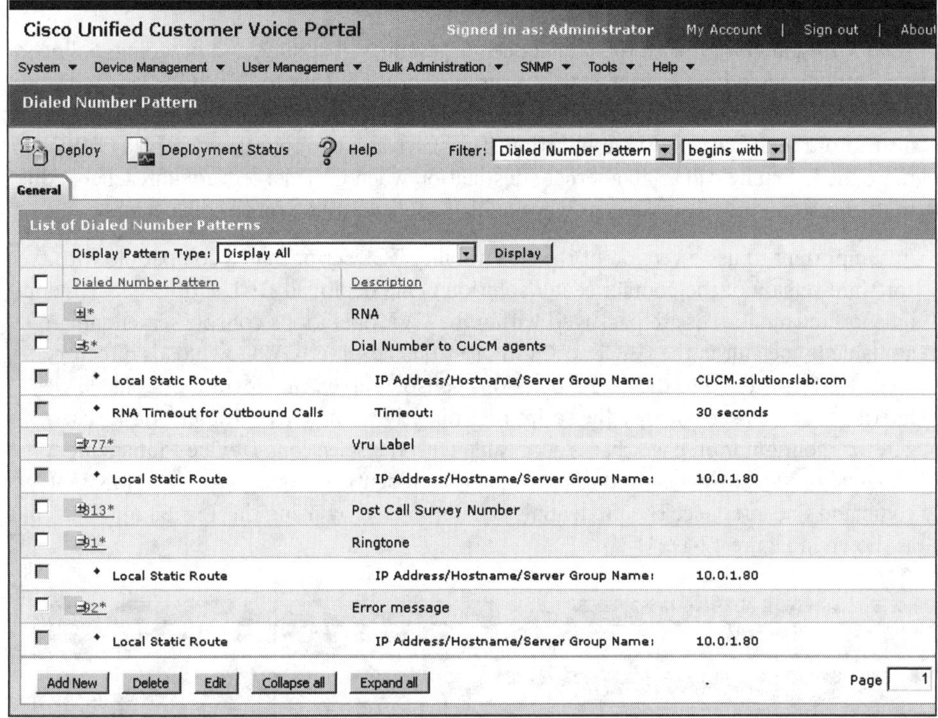

Figure 12-10 *Dialed Number Pattern Configuration in the CVP Operations Console*

Figure 12-11 *Server Group Configuration in the CVP Operations Console*

CUBE Configuration

The CUBE integration with the contact center leverages incoming and outgoing dial peer concepts discussed in Chapter 3, "Call Routing," to route calls to CVP. One key addition for UCCE applications is the inbound dial peer's use of the survivability TCL application instead of the default CCAPI application. The survivability application enables CUBE to route the incoming call to an alternate destination when CVP servers are unreachable due to network connectivity issues or when a CVP application is experiencing errors.

It is important to use a version of the survivability TCL script that is compatible with the software version of the contact center solution being deployed. TCL scripts, VXML documents, and audio files are packaged within the CVP operations console server and are available by default in the C:\Cisco\CVP\OPSConsoleServer\GWDownloads directory. Once CUBE is added to the CVP operations console server, the operations console web interface can be used to copy the script files directly to the CUBE router's flash. The gateway configuration page that is accessible with the selections **Device Management > Gateway > Add New** is used to provision the credentials required to log in to CUBE's command-line interface. The credentials can be verified by using the Test Sign-in button, as shown in Figure 12-12.

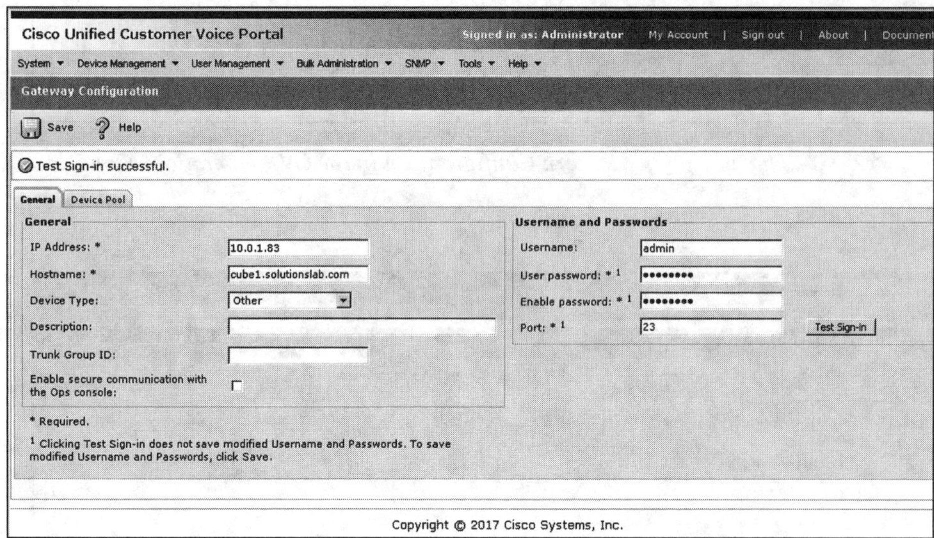

Figure 12-12 *CUBE Configuration in the CVP Operations Console*

After a CUBE instance is successfully added to the Operations Console configuration, three Task options are displayed: Statistics, IOS Command, and File Transfer. Selecting **File Transfer > Scripts and Media** displays the page shown in Figure 12-13. You select the survivability.tcl from the C:\Cisco\CVP\OPSConsoleServer\GWDownloads directory and transfer it to CUBE by clicking the Transfer button. This operation triggers the HTTP download of the TCL file into CUBE, using the Cisco IOS **copy** command through an SSH or Telnet connection.

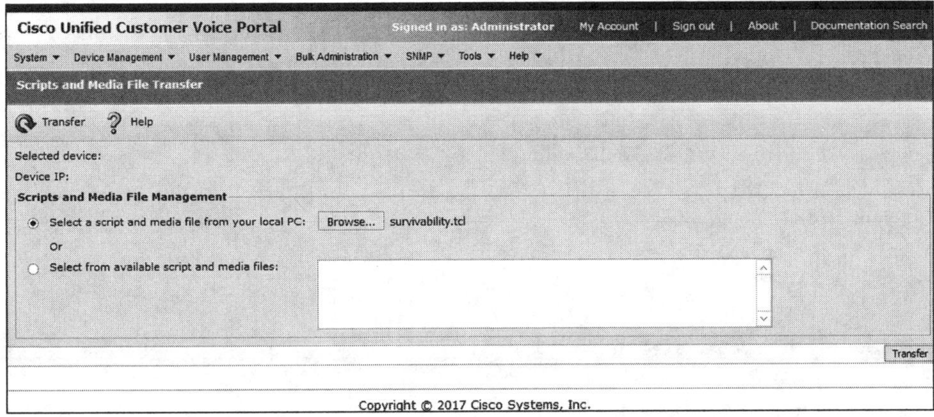

Figure 12-13 *Transferring the survivability.tcl File to CUBE*

When the TCL file is locally available within CUBE, you can define an application service named survivability that uses survivability.tcl as the application source code by associating it to the inbound VoIP dial peer 68000, using the **service** command. This is shown in Example 12-1.

Example 12-1 *CUBE Configuration for a Basic Inbound Call Flow*

```
voice service voip
 allow-connections sip to sip
 signaling forward unconditional
 mode border-element license capacity 100
 sip
  rel1xx disable
  header-passing
  options-ping 60
  midcall-signaling passthru
!
!
voice class codec 1
 codec preference 1 g711ulaw
 codec preference 2 g729r8
!
!
voice translation-rule 5
 rule 1 /919456\(....\)/ /\1/
!
!
```

```
voice translation-profile 10-digit-to-4-digit
 translate called 5

application
 service survivability flash:survivability.tcl

dial-peer voice 68000 voip
 description "Inbound dial-peer for Contact Center calls"
 service survivability
 session protocol sipv2
 incoming called-number 9194568...
 voice-class codec 1
 voice-class sip rel1xx disable
 dtmf-relay rtp-nte
 no vad
!
dial-peer voice 68001 voip
 description "Outbound dial-peer to CVP"
 translation-profile outgoing 10-digit-to-4-digit
 preference 1
 destination-pattern 9194568...
 session protocol sipv2
 session target dns:sideAcvp1.solutionslab.com
 session transport tcp
 voice-class codec 1
 voice-class sip rel1xx disable
 voice-class sip bind control source-interface GigabitEthernet0/0/3
 voice-class sip bind media source-interface GigabitEthernet0/0/3
 dtmf-relay rtp-nte
!
```

The outbound dial peer 68001 is configured to route SIP calls beginning with the called number digit string 9194568 to the CVP server using the **destination-pattern** and **session target** commands. Because contact center agents can either use G.711 or G.729 codecs, **voice-class codec** *1* is configured to advertise both options in the outbound SIP INVITE. CVP doesn't support SIP reliable provisional responses, so this behavior is disabled using the command **voice-class sip rel1xx disable** at the dial peer level.

Note The hostname sideAcvp1.solutionslab.com refers to the CVP server installed on contact center Side A. Each CVP application server functions independently and doesn't have Side A and Side B application instances, unlike other UCCE components, such as peripheral gateways, which have an application instance on each side that communicate with each other.

Tip Voice translation profiles are not applicable for dial peers associated with custom application services because the call gets handed off from the default application to the custom application before the translation profile is applied. If there is a need to translate the incoming DID number prior to routing the call to CVP, it is recommended to apply the translation profile under the outbound dial peer instead of under the inbound dial peer because it is associated with the custom survivability application service.

The commands **signaling forward unconditional** and **header-passing** configured at the global level enable better interoperability by allowing passing of application/qsig and application/x-931 SIP message bodies and SIP headers received in the inbound call leg to the outbound call leg. The command **midcall-signaling passthru** tells CUBE to forward the re-INVITE received from one SIP call leg to the other SIP call leg of the same call instead of consuming the re-INVITE message. This allows the renegotiation of codecs end to end and avoids the need to use transcoding resources where possible. For example, when the incoming call is first connected with an IVR, the codec gets negotiated to G.711. Later, when the call is connected to an agent located across a WAN, CVP sends a SIP re-INVITE to change the codec to G.729 for the media stream between CUBE and the agent phone. The **midcall-signaling passthru** command results in CUBE passing the SIP re-INVITE to the service provider and changing the codec to G.729, even on the call leg that is between CUBE and service provider.

Cisco IOS VXML Gateway Configuration

Depending on the business needs, voice browser functionality can either be configured to be co-located on the same router functioning as CUBE, or it can be configured on a separate voice gateway. The co-location deployment model is used in remote WAN sites to consolidate the unified communication functionalities into one WAN edge router.

Tip The VXML voice browser functionality is available only in the ISR 2900 and 3900 product families; it is not supported in routers that run Cisco IOS XE software such as ASR 1000, ISR 4400, and CSR Series routers. The recommendation is to use Cisco VVB, which runs as a virtual appliance, in deployments that have chosen to use ASR 1000, ISR 4400, CSR platforms for the deployment's PSTN connectivity.

Example 12-2 shows the configuration required to establish the VRU call leg (SIP-HTTP) with the VXML gateway (Cisco IOS Voice Browser). Much like CUBE, the VXML gateway also uses TCL and VXML 2.0 scripts to deliver custom call handling functionality. The following scripts and two audio files ringback.wav and critical_error.wav are transferred to the VXML gateway using the CVP operations console interface, as discussed earlier in this chapter:

- **bootstrap.tcl**—This script is associated with the inbound SIP VoIP dial peer of the VXML gateway. It answers the incoming call and extracts the called number, call GUID, and IP address of the CVP call server. The IP address of the CVP call server is extracted from the App-Info SIP header, whose value is of the format <*callserver:unsecure_port:secure_port:callserverbackup*>. For example, App-Info: <10.0.1.21:7000:7443> indicates that 10.0.1.21 is the CVP call server IP address, 7000 is the HTTP port, and 7443 is the HTTPS port. After successful extraction, it hands off the call to the bootstrap.vxml application

- **bootstrap.vxml**—This script establishes the HTTP connection to the CVP call server and initiates a new HTTP/HTTPS request, which is processed by the IVR service component of the CVP call server. The following is an example of an HTTP request URL and parameter:

```
http://10.0.1.21:7000/CVP/Server?MSG_TYPE=CALL_NEW&CALL_
DNIS=777777777760&CALL_ANI=sip:4083926001@10.0.1.21:5060&ERROR_
CODE=0&RECOVERY_VXML=flash:recovery.vxml&CLIENT_TYPE=IOS&CALL_ID=289C3D
00000100000000007EA1CAA8C0&CALL_LEGID=289C3D00000100000000007EA1CAA8C0-
152314190092728 3@10.0.1.21&CALL_UUI=&VERSION=CVP_11_6_1_0_0_0_329
```

- **ringtone.tcl**—This script plays the ringtone.wav audio file after the call gets connected.
- **cvperror.tcl**—This script plays the critical_error.wav audio file after the call gets connected.
- **handoff.tcl**—This script is used to disconnect the call with a specific Q.931 cause code, such as 38 Network out of order.

Cisco IOS Voice Browser functionality uses a separate HTTP client that is different from the default HTTP client configured using **ip http client** commands. The voice browser's recommended HTTP client settings are configured using **http client**, as shown in Example 12-2.

The VXML gateway interacts with TTS and ASR servers using MRCP version 1 or 2. In MRCP version 1 (defined in RFC 4463), the MRCP messages are embedded within RTSP requests and responses, whereas they are exchanged directly across a TCP connection in version 2 (defined in RFC 6787). The voice browser using MRCPv2 originates a SIP session with TTS and ASR servers in order to negotiate a TCP connection IP address and port number for exchanging MRCP messages.

The VXML documents generated by the CVP IVR service specify the location of the ASR and TTS using two properties, com.cisco.asr-server and com.cisco.tts-server. For example, the locations are set to rtsp://asr-en-us/recognizer and rtsp://tts-en-us/synthesizer in the case of MRCPv1 ASR and TTS servers. When these properties aren't explicitly set within the VXML document, the voice browser uses the RTSP or SIP URL defined with the **ivr asr-server** and **ivr tts-server** commands to request the ASR server to recognize digits/speech and request to play the text as defined within the VXML document. The SIP URLs sip:asr@10.0.1.28 and sip:tts@10.0.1.28 are defined as the default ASR and TTS servers in Example 12-2.

The dial peers 919191, 929292, and 9999 are used as inbound dial peers to answer the SIP calls originating from CVP. The TCL applications associated with these dial peers play ringtone, play error messages, and connect the caller to the VXML application for

IVR treatment, respectively. It is important to note that these dial peers use only the G.711 codec and RTP-NTE for DTMF relay. The URI-based call routing feature discussed in Chapter 3 is used to set up calls with ASR and TTS servers through the use of MRCPv2. The destination URI in dial peers 5 and 6 references a voice-class URI configured to match the SIP ASR and TTS URLs. These two dial peers are used as outbound dial peers for calls destined to ASR and TTS servers.

Example 12-2 *VXML Gateway Configuration for Basic Inbound Call Flow*

```
ip domain name solutionslab.com
ip host asr-en-us 10.0.1.28
ip host tts-en-us 10.0.1.28

voice service voip
 allow-connections sip to sip
 signaling forward unconditional
 sip
  bind control source-interface GigabitEthernet0/0
  bind media source-interface GigabitEthernet0/0
  rel1xx disable
  header-passing
  options-ping 60
  midcall-signaling passthru
!
!
voice class uri ASR sip
 pattern asr@10.0.1.28
!
voice class uri TTS sip
 pattern tts@10.0.1.28
!
!
http client cache memory pool 15000
http client cache memory file 1000
http client cache refresh 864000
no http client connection persistent
http client connection timeout 60
http client connection idle timeout 10
http client response timeout 30
ivr prompt memory 15000
ivr asr-server sip:asr@10.0.1.28
ivr tts-server sip:tts@10.0.1.28
!
```

```
application
 service new-call flash:bootstrap.vxml
 !
 service new-call flash:CVPSelfServiceBootstrap.vxml
 !
 service ringtone flash:ringtone.tcl
 !
 service cvperror flash:cvperror.tcl
 !
 service bootstrap flash:bootstrap.tcl
 !
 service handoff flash:handoff.tcl
 !
!
rtsp client timeout connect 20
rtsp client timeout message 20
mrcp client timeout connect 6
mrcp client timeout message 6
mrcp client rtpsetup enable
vxml tree memory 500
vxml audioerror
vxml version 2.0
!
!
dial-peer voice 919191 voip
 description CVP SIP ringtone dial-peer
 service ringtone
 incoming called-number 9191T
 voice-class sip rel1xx disable
 dtmf-relay rtp-nte
 codec g711ulaw
 no vad
!
dial-peer voice 929292 voip
 description CVP SIP error dial-peer
 service cvperror
 incoming called-number 9292T
 voice-class sip rel1xx disable
 dtmf-relay rtp-nte
 codec g711ulaw
 no vad
!
dial-peer voice 9999 voip
 description Used for VRU leg
```

```
 service bootstrap
 incoming called-number 777T
 dtmf-relay rtp-nte
 codec g711ulaw
 no vad
!

dial-peer voice 5 voip
 description Dial-peer for ARS Server
 session protocol sipv2
 session target ipv4:10.0.1.28
 session transport tcp
 destination uri ASR
 dtmf-relay rtp-nte
 codec g711ulaw
 no vad
!
dial-peer voice 6 voip
 description Dial-peer for TTS Server
 session protocol sipv2
 session target ipv4:10.0.1.28
 session transport tcp
 destination uri TTS
 dtmf-relay rtp-nte
 codec g711ulaw
 no vad
!
!

sip-ua
 retry invite 2
 retry bye 1
 timers expires 60000
 timers connect 1000
 reason-header override
!
```

Tip The combination of the **header-passing** command at the global level and an inbound dial peer with the survivability TCL script with an incoming translation profile is not supported in a Cisco IOS VXML gateway when it is co-located with CUBE (that is, the same router is configured for both VXML and CUBE functionality). The inbound calls to the contact center through CUBE may not be processed correctly in this configuration. This limitation is not applicable when the VXML gateway is configured as a standalone feature in a separate router, as shown in Example 12-2.

Cisco VVB Configuration

Voice browser functionality can be delivered by using Cisco VVB, which is deployed as a virtual machine. The configuration of VVB is very simple, as VVB comes preconfigured for the comprehensive call flow to handle SIP calls for VRU treatment, ringtone playout, and error prompt playout. The configuration for this is through the SIP Trigger Configuration, demonstrated in Figure 12-14. This configuration page is found by selecting the **Subsystems > SIP Telephony > SIP Trigger** menu options.

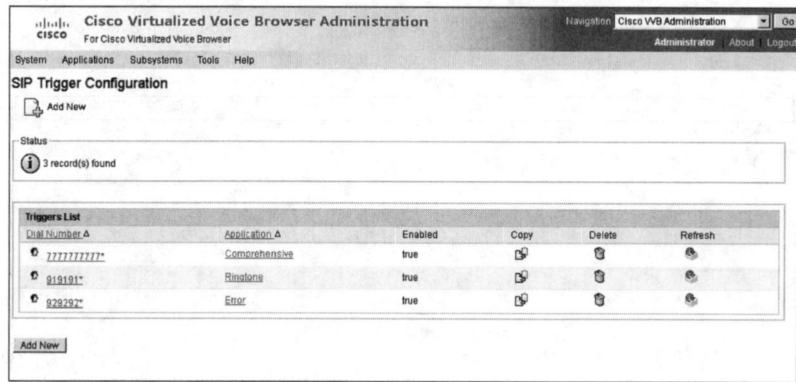

Figure 12-14 *SIP Trigger Configuration in Cisco VVB*

The CVP dialed number patterns (Figure 12-10) that are configured to route to VVB servers are associated with individual applications, as shown in Figure 12-14. When the VVB server receives the SIP call, it executes the application associated with the configured pattern (Comprehensive, Ringtone, or Error). The audio codec and the version of the MRCP protocol to be used are specified in the System parameters configuration (reached by selecting **System > System Parameters**), as shown in Figure 12-15.

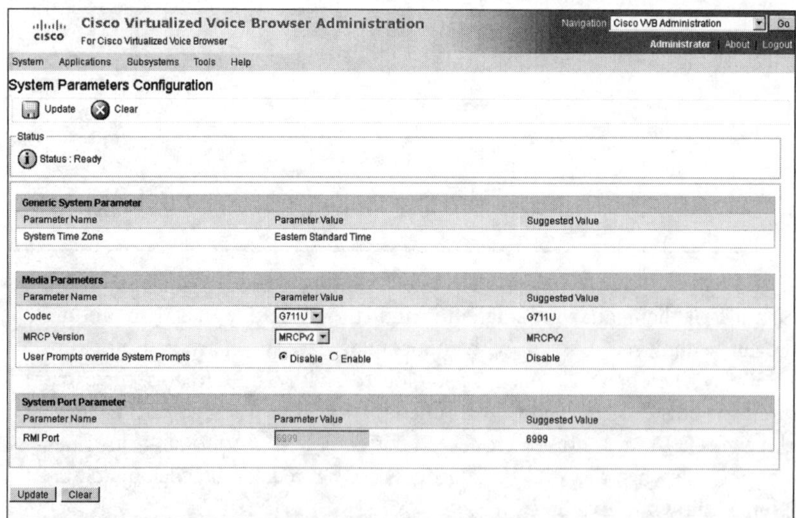

Figure 12-15 *System Parameters Configuration in Cisco VVB*

The hostname or IP address of the ASR and TTS servers are defined in the ASR Servers (**Subsystems > Speech Servers > ASR Servers**) and TTS Servers (**Subsystems > Speech Servers > TTS Servers**) configuration pages.

CUCM Configuration

A CUCM SIP trunk is used to configure key information about its SIP peers. This includes elements such as the IP address, hostname, port number, and a wide variety of protocol options for interoperability. CUCM-specific details are also configurable here, including the device pool, which maps the region with which the peer is associated. This Region setting determines the type of codec and the bandwidth negotiated for calls that get connected with the SIP peer.

CUCM is configured with one SIP trunk for each CVP call server in the contact center deployment. Even though CUBE is not CUCM's direct SIP peer for the inbound contact center call flows, it is useful to configure a SIP trunk for each CUBE in the deployment to ensure that the correct codec and bandwidth are used for the call between the external caller and the agent. CUBE is not CUCM's direct peer in UCCE deployments because calls from CUBE are sent to CVP, and CVP acts as a B2BUA, setting up the outbound call leg to CUCM as needed.

CVP uses the Call-Info header value with the purpose parameter set to **x-cisco-origIP** in the outbound SIP INVITEs to indicate the actual origination IP device (for example, CUBE, TDM gateway). For example, **Call-Info: <sip:10.0.1.83:5060>;purpose=x-cisco-origIP** indicates that 10.0.1.83 is the origination device. When CUCM receives a SIP INVITE with the value **x-cisco-origIP**, it uses the origination IP address to look up the matching SIP trunk instead of using the IP address of the SIP UDP/TCP connection in which the SIP INVITE was received.

Call Flow

CVP connects an inbound caller to two or more different destinations while executing a CVP comprehensive call flow. These destinations may be any of the following:

- An IVR that plays an audio stream and potentially places the caller in a queue until an agent is available
- A self-service IVR application that plays menu prompts and provides the information requested by the caller
- A voice browser or gateway that plays a ringtone just before the caller is connected to an agent
- An agent with whom the caller can have a conversation that pertains to the purpose of the call

Caller Placed in Queue

Figure 12-16 shows the first stage of the SIP call flow, in which CVP connects the inbound call from CUBE (the *switch leg*) to the VXML gateway. This provides IVR treatment while the caller is placed in a queue (the VRU leg). Provisional responses such as 100 Trying are not shown in the SIP call flow diagram for the sake of brevity.

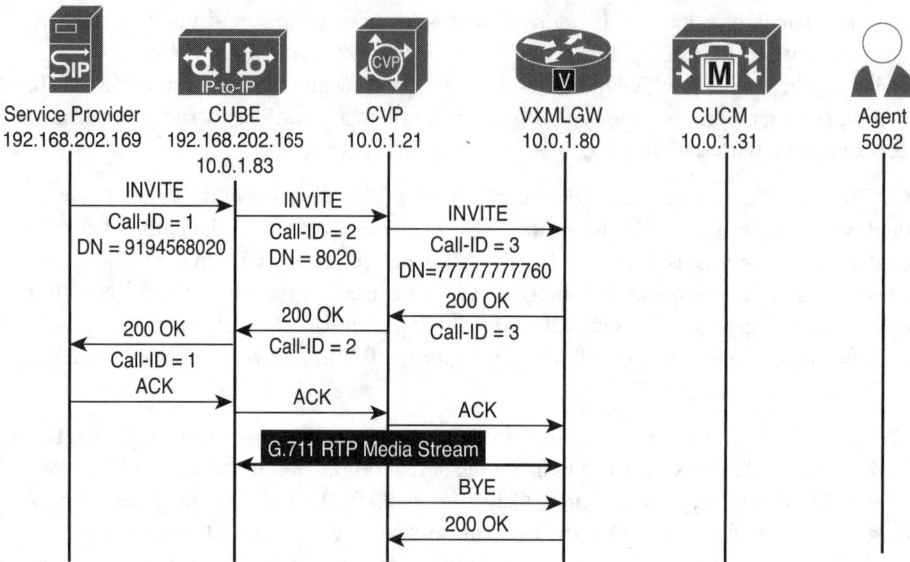

Figure 12-16 *Inbound Caller Placed in the Queue*

The following steps occur in the first stage:

Step 1. The call from 4083926001 to 9194568020 arrives at CUBE from the service provider.

Step 2. CUBE matches the dial peer 68000 as the inbound dial peer and 68001 as the outbound dial peer. The called number 9194568020 is translated to 8020 in the outbound dial peer, and a SIP INVITE is sent to CVP.

Step 3. CVP sends a 100 Trying to CUBE, retrieves the calling number (4083926001) and called number (8020) from the incoming call, and asks UCCE Router for routing instructions.

Step 4. UCCE looks up the dialed number 8020 (named 802VXML1A) and finds the associated call script VXMLHello802, configured earlier, in Figures 12-6 and 12-9.

Step 5. UCCE executes the VXMLHello802 call script and runs the Queue to Skill Group node. Because the agent isn't available, it runs another node, Run External Script.

Step 6. UCCE finds the network VRU (CVP_Network_VRU) associated with the CVP routing client, which pertains to the configuration shown in Figure 12-5, in order to execute the external script in the VRU.

Step 7. UCCE retrieves the label 7777777777 assigned to the network VRU, generates a correlation ID 60, and combines them to return 777777777760 as the temporary connect routing response to CVP.

Step 8. CVP sets up the VRU leg by originating an outbound call with the called number set to 777777777760 (Call-ID 3). It looks up its dialed number pattern table shown in Figure 12-10, determines the next hop as 10.0.1.80 (the VXML gateway), and sends a SIP INVITE to the VXML gateway.

Step 9. The VXML gateway matches the dial peer 9999 as the inbound dial peer, and the call is answered by the bootstrap.tcl application. The VXML gateway selects G.711 as the audio codec and allocates an IP address and RTP port number. It responds to CVP's SIP INVITE with a SIP 200 OK message containing the media information in the SDP.

Step 10. CVP acts as a B2BUA and sends the corresponding SIP 200 OK response to CUBE, which in turn sends it to the service provider.

Step 11. The service provider sends a SIP ACK to CUBE, which in turn sends one to CVP, and CVP sends a SIP ACK to the VXML gateway. The call is now in connected state, with RTP media streams flowing between CUBE and the VXML gateway.

Step 12. Meanwhile, the bootstrap.tcl application service on the VXML gateway retrieves key information, such as the call server's IP address, and hands off to the bootstrap.vxml application service. This VXML application service posts an HTTP connection to the IVR service of the CVP call server by sending the HTTP POST request to the URL:

```
http://10.0.1.21:7000/CVP/Server?MSG_TYPE=CALL_NEW&CALL_
DNIS=777777777760&CALL_ANI=sip:4083926001@10.0.1.21:5060&ERROR_
CODE=0&RECOVERY_VXML=flash:recovery.vxml&CLIENT_TYPE=IOS&CALL_ID=289C3D
0000010000000007EA1CAA8C0&CALL_LEGID=289C3D0000010000000007EA1CAA8C0-
1523141900927283@10.0.1.21&CALL_UUI=&VERSION=CVP_11_6_1_0_0_0_329
```

Step 13. CVP's IVR service processes the HTTP POST request and sends a routing request to UCCE for the label 777777777760. UCCE uses the correlation ID 60 to identify that this is the VRU leg of the call script executed in step 5. It requests the IVR service to run a script and passes the script name CustomHelloWorld as the value in the ECC variable user.microapp.ExtVXML[0].

Step 14. As the CustomHelloWorld VXML application is executed in the CVP VXML server, CVP generates VXML documents and sends them to the VXML gateway for execution in the voice browser.

Step 15. The VXML gateway performs tasks such as playing audio files and TTS prompts, as defined in the VXML document, and then posts the results back to the IVR server. These audio streams are sent as RTP packets to CUBE, and CUBE changes the IP header information before sending the audio to the service provider. The caller hears this audio until an agent is available.

Example 12-3 shows the SIP INVITE sent from CUBE. Note that the SDP in the SIP INVITE contains the internal IP address of CUBE (10.0.1.83), and it advertises both G.711ulaw and G.729 codecs with RTP payload types 0 and 18, respectively. CUBE adds a Session-ID header with local-uuid set to **0000664e00105000a000005056a12adc** in the outbound SIP INVITE.

Example 12-3 *Basic Inbound Call Flow: SIP INVITE from CUBE to CVP*

```
623581: Apr  7 22:58:20.989 UTC: //12446/289C3D000000/SIP/Msg/ccsipDisplayMsg:
Sent:
INVITE sip:8020@sideAcvp1.solutionslab.com:5060 SIP/2.0
Via: SIP/2.0/TCP 10.0.1.83:5060;branch=z9hG4bK2FC914FE
Remote-Party-ID: "--CVP_11_6_1_0_0_0_329"
   <sip:4083926001@10.0.1.83>;party=calling;screen=yes;privacy=off
From: sip:4083926001@192.168.202.162;tag=175F2EC1-23D3
To: <sip:8020@sideAcvp1.solutionslab.com>
Date: Sat, 07 Apr 2018 22:58:20 GMT
Call-ID: 986DC4-39EE11E8-AFE2E1BE-18C7C14D@10.0.1.83
Supported: timer,resource-priority,replaces,sdp-anat
Min-SE:  1800
Cisco-Guid: 0681327872-0000065536-0000000126-2714413248
User-Agent: Cisco-SIPGateway/IOS-16.6.1
Allow: INVITE, OPTIONS, BYE, CANCEL, ACK, PRACK, UPDATE, REFER, SUBSCRIBE, NOTIFY,
  INFO, REGISTER
CSeq: 101 INVITE
Timestamp: 1523141900
Contact: <sip:4083926001@10.0.1.83:5060;transport=tcp>
Expires: 60
Allow-Events: telephone-event
Max-Forwards: 65
X-Cisco-CCBProbe: undefined
Session-ID: 0000664e00105000a000005056a12adc;remote=00000000000000000000000000000000
Session-Expires:  1800
Content-Type: application/sdp
Content-Disposition: session;handling=required
Content-Length: 308
```

```
v=0
o=CiscoSystemsSIP-GW-UserAgent 2158 4149 IN IP4 10.0.1.83
s=SIP Call
c=IN IP4 10.0.1.83
t=0 0
m=audio 8278 RTP/AVP 0 18 101 19
c=IN IP4 10.0.1.83
a=rtpmap:0 PCMU/8000
a=rtpmap:18 G729/8000
a=fmtp:18 annexb=no
a=rtpmap:101 telephone-event/8000
a=fmtp:101 0-15
a=rtpmap:19 CN/8000
a=ptime:20
```

Tip The SIP call flow from a CVP perspective for setting up the call legs for VRU, ringtone, and error playout is exactly the same for both the Cisco IOS VXML gateway and Cisco VVB.

Example 12-4 shows the SIP INVITE sent by CVP to set up the VRU call leg through the VXML gateway. CVP acts as an SDP-modifying signaling-only B2BUA (discussed in Chapter 1, "Laying the Groundwork") and copies the SDP in the incoming INVITE, shown in Example 12-3, into the SDP of the outgoing INVITE, shown in Example 12-4. CVP also passes the Session-ID header from the incoming call leg to the outgoing call leg, enabling end-to-end call tracing functionality.

Example 12-4 *Basic Inbound Call Flow: SIP INVITE from CVP to the VXML Gateway or VVB*

```
*Apr  7 22:43:51.411: //-1/xxxxxxxxxxxx/SIP/Msg/ccsipDisplayMsg:
Received:
INVITE sip:777777777760@10.0.1.80;transport=tcp SIP/2.0
Via: SIP/2.0/TCP 10.0.1.21:5060;branch=z9hG4bKk9F7UjU8zHQ4XN9JOnRWyA~~1193
Max-Forwards: 64
To: <sip:777777777760@10.0.1.80;transport=tcp>
From: "--CVP_11_6_1_0_0_0_329" <sip:4083926001@10.0.1.21:5060>;tag=ds9f829e36
Call-ID: 289C3D00000100000000007EA1CAA8C0-1523141900927283@10.0.1.21
CSeq: 1 INVITE
Content-Length: 305
Contact: <sip:4083926001@10.0.1.21:5060;transport=tcp>
Expires: 60
User-Agent: CVP 11.6 (1) Build-329
```

```
Call-Info: <sip:10.0.1.83:5060>;purpose=x-cisco-origIP
Remote-Party-ID: "--CVP_11_6_1_0_0_0_329" <sip:4083926001@10.0.1.83>;party=calling;s
  creen=yes;privacy=off
Date: Sat, 07 Apr 2018 22:58:20 GMT
Min-SE: 1800
Cisco-Guid: 0681327872-0000065536-0000000126-2714413248
Allow: INVITE, OPTIONS, BYE, CANCEL, ACK, PRACK, UPDATE, REFER, SUBSCRIBE, NOTIFY,
  INFO, REGISTER
Allow-Events: telephone-event
X-Cisco-CCBProbe: undefined
Session-ID: 0000664e00105000a000005056a12adc;remote=00000000000000000000000000000000
Session-Expires: 1800
Content-Disposition: session;handling=required
Cisco-Gucid: 289C3D00000100000000007EA1CAA8C0
Supported: timer
Supported: resource-priority
Supported: replaces
Supported: sdp-anat
Content-Type: application/sdp
App-Info: <10.0.1.21:7000:7443>

v=0
o=Cisco-CVP-B2BUA 289844526 289844527 IN IP4 10.0.1.21
s=SIP Call
c=IN IP4 10.0.1.83
t=0 0
m=audio 8278 RTP/AVP 0 18 101 19
c=IN IP4 10.0.1.83
a=rtpmap:0 PCMU/8000
a=rtpmap:18 G729/8000
a=fmtp:18 annexb=no
a=rtpmap:101 telephone-event/8000
a=fmtp:101 0-15
a=rtpmap:19 CN/8000
a=ptime:20
```

Example 12-5 shows the SIP 200 OK response sent by the VXML gateway or the voice browser. Note that it contains the IP address of the VXML gateway (10.0.1.80), with G.711ulaw selected as the audio codec. For the sake of illustration, in this example, the VXML gateway was loaded with a Cisco IOS image that does not support the Session-ID header. As a result, the 200 OK shown in Example 12-5 does not have the Session-ID header. (At the time of this writing, Cisco VVB does not yet support Session-ID.)

Example 12-5 *Basic Inbound Call Flow: 200 OK from the VXML Gateway or VVB to CVP*

```
*Apr  7 22:43:51.427: //662596/289C3D000000/SIP/Msg/ccsipDisplayMsg:
Sent:
SIP/2.0 200 OK
Via: SIP/2.0/TCP 10.0.1.21:5060;branch=z9hG4bKk9F7UjU8zHQ4XN9JOnRWyA~~1193
From: "--CVP_11_6_1_0_0_0_329" <sip:4083926001@10.0.1.21:5060>;tag=ds9f829e36
To: <sip:777777777760@10.0.1.80;transport=tcp>;tag=DA177C34-2413
Date: Sat, 07 Apr 2018 22:43:51 GMT
Call-ID: 289C3D0000010000000007EA1CAA8C0-1523141900927283@10.0.1.21
CSeq: 1 INVITE
Allow: INVITE, OPTIONS, BYE, CANCEL, ACK, PRACK, UPDATE, REFER, SUBSCRIBE, NOTIFY,
  INFO, REGISTER
Allow-Events: telephone-event
Contact: <sip:777777777760@10.0.1.80:5060;transport=tcp>
Supported: replaces
Supported: sdp-anat
Server: Cisco-SIPGateway/IOS-15.4.3.M3
Require: timer
Session-Expires:  1800;refresher=uac
Supported: timer
Content-Type: application/sdp
Content-Disposition: session;handling=required
Content-Length: 238

v=0
o=CiscoSystemsSIP-GW-UserAgent 9649 6507 IN IP4 10.0.1.80
s=SIP Call
c=IN IP4 10.0.1.80
t=0 0
m=audio 17510 RTP/AVP 0 101
c=IN IP4 10.0.1.80
a=rtpmap:0 PCMU/8000
a=rtpmap:101 telephone-event/8000
a=fmtp:101 0-16
a=ptime:20
```

Example 12-6 shows the SIP 200 OK response sent from CVP to CUBE. CVP copies the SDP answer of the incoming 200 OK from the VXML gateway or VVB to the SDP of the outgoing INVITE, destined for CUBE. CVP also generates the local UUID a254fa8e10000162de5d5d4203430af1 on behalf of the VXML gateway or VVB and sends it in the Session-ID header.

Example 12-6 *Basic Inbound Call Flow: 200 OK from CVP to CUBE*

```
623608: Apr  7 22:58:21.026 UTC: //12446/289C3D000000/SIP/Msg/ccsipDisplayMsg:
Received:
SIP/2.0 200 Ok
Via: SIP/2.0/TCP 10.0.1.83:5060;branch=z9hG4bK2FC914FE
To: <sip:8020@sideAcvp1.solutionslab.com>;tag=ds92899e55
From: <sip:4083926001@192.168.202.162>;tag=175F2EC1-23D3
Call-ID: 986DC4-39EE11E8-AFE2E1BE-18C7C14D@10.0.1.83
CSeq: 101 INVITE
Content-Length: 235
Cisco-Guid: 0681327872-0000065536-0000000126-2714413248
Contact: <sip:10.0.1.21:5060;transport=tcp>
Date: Sat, 07 Apr 2018 22:43:51 GMT
Allow: INVITE, OPTIONS, BYE, CANCEL, ACK, PRACK, UPDATE, REFER, SUBSCRIBE, NOTIFY,
  INFO, REGISTER
Allow-Events: telephone-event
Server: Cisco-SIPGateway/IOS-15.4.3.M3
Session-Expires: 1800;refresher=uac
Content-Disposition: session;handling=required
Require: timer
Supported: replaces
Supported: sdp-anat
Supported: timer
Content-Type: application/sdp
Cisco-Gucid: 289C3D00000100000000007EA1CAA8C0
Session-ID: a254fa8e10000162de5d5d4203430af1;remote=0000664e00105000a000005056a12adc

v=0
o=Cisco-CVP-B2BUA 289844526 289844527 IN IP4 10.0.1.21
s=SIP Call
c=IN IP4 10.0.1.80
t=0 0
m=audio 17510 RTP/AVP 0 101
c=IN IP4 10.0.1.80
a=rtpmap:0 PCMU/8000
a=rtpmap:101 telephone-event/8000
a=fmtp:101 0-16
a=ptime:20
```

The Session-ID local and remote UUIDs for each call leg (12445 and 12446) in CUBE, along with RTP stream information, can be verified by using the output of **show call active voice brief** and **show voip rtp connection**, as shown in Example 12-7. The remote RTP IP address and port number of the CUBE-to-CVP call leg is 10.0.1.80:17510, which is the VXML gateway's or VVB's IP address and port number used for call queue treatment.

Example 12-7 show call active voice brief *Collected When a Caller Is in the Queue*

```
cube1# show call active voice brief
...
Telephony call-legs: 0
SIP call-legs: 2
H323 call-legs: 0
Call agent controlled call-legs: 0
SCCP call-legs: 0
STCAPP call-legs: 0
Multicast call-legs: 0
Total call-legs: 2
0   : 12445 392029150ms.1 (22:58:19.965 UTC Sat Apr 7 2018) +1080 pid:68000 Answer
  4083926001 active
 dur 00:00:12 tx:581/116200 rx:613/122600 dscp:0 media:0 audio tos:0xB8 video tos:0x0
 IP 192.168.202.162:8014 SRTP: off rtt:0ms pl:0/0ms lost:0/0/0 delay:0/0/0ms g711ulaw
  TextRelay: off Transcoded: No ICE: Off
 media inactive detected:n media contrl rcvd:n/a timestamp:n/a
 long duration call detected:n long duration call duration:n/a timestamp:n/a
 LostPacketRate:0.00 OutOfOrderRate:0.00
 LocalUUID:0000664e00105000a000005056a12adc
 RemoteUUID:a254fa8e10000162de5d5d4203430af1
 VRF:
0   : 12446 392030170ms.1 (22:58:20.985 UTC Sat Apr 7 2018) +50 pid:68001 Originate
  8020 active
 dur 00:00:12 tx:613/122600 rx:581/116200 dscp:0 media:0 audio tos:0xB8 video tos:0x0
 IP 10.0.1.80:17510 SRTP: off rtt:0ms pl:0/0ms lost:0/0/0 delay:0/0/0ms g711ulaw Tex-
  tRelay: off Transcoded: No ICE: Off
 media inactive detected:n media contrl rcvd:n/a timestamp:n/a
 long duration call detected:n long duration call duration:n/a timestamp:n/a
 LostPacketRate:0.00 OutOfOrderRate:0.00
 LocalUUID:a254fa8e10000162de5d5d4203430af1
 RemoteUUID:0000664e00105000a000005056a12adc
 VRF:

 ......
cube1# show voip rtp connection
VoIP RTP Port Usage Information:
Max Ports Available: 19999, Ports Reserved: 101, Ports in Use: 2
Port range not configured
                                        Min  Max   Ports     Ports    Ports
Media-Address Range                     Port Port  Available Reserved In-use
--------------------------------------------------------------------------------
Global Media Pool                       8000 48198 19999     101      2
--------------------------------------------------------------------------------
VoIP RTP active connections :
No. CallId dstCallId LocalRTP RmtRTP   LocalIP         RemoteIP        MPSS  VRF
1   12445  12446     8276     8014  192.168.202.165 192.168.202.162   NO    NA
2   12446  12445     8278     17510   10.0.1.83         10.0.1.80     NO    NA
Found 2 active RTP connections
```

Caller Hears Ringback Tone

Figure 12-17 shows the second stage of the call flow, during which an agent with skills matching those of the skill group IPCC_SG, as defined in the Queue to Skill Group node of the UCCE call script (shown in Figure 12-6), becomes available. CVP disconnects the call leg that provides IVR treatment for the call in the queue and connects the caller with the VXML gateway or VVB to play the ringback tone.

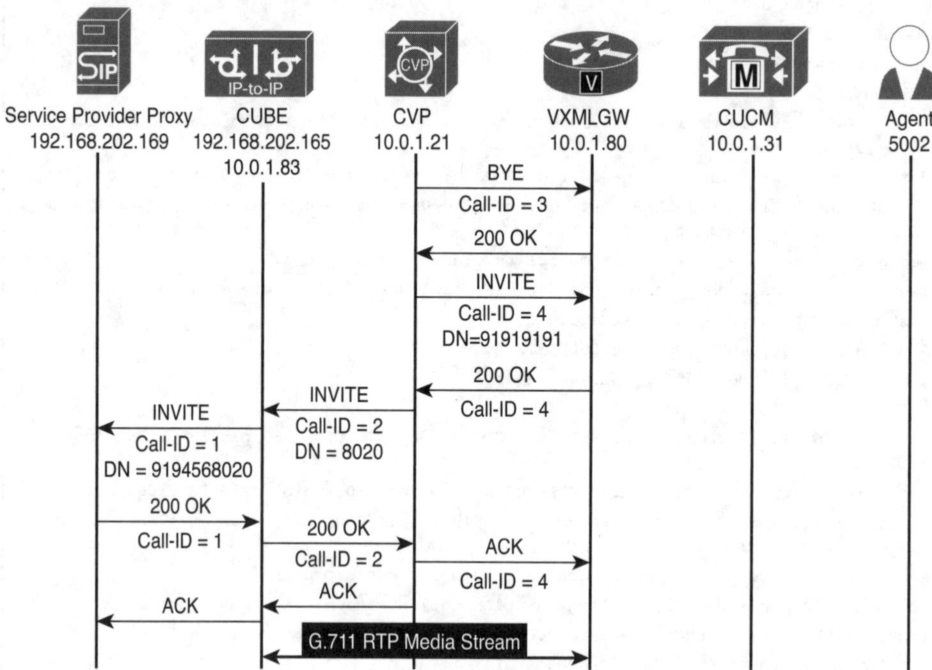

Figure 12-17 *Inbound Caller Hears Ringback Tone*

The following steps occur in the second stage:

Step 1. UCCE Router knows about the status of the agents using the information shared by CUCM via the agent PG. When an agent with the matching skill is available, UCCE Router sends the agent's directory number 5002 as the final routing response (or *label*) to CVP.

Step 2. CVP disconnects the existing VRU call leg that is connected with the VXML gateway or VVB (Call-ID 3 with called number set to 777777777760) by sending a SIP BYE request.

Step 3. CVP originates a new call leg with called number set to the value (91919191) configured for the parameter **DN on the Gateway to play the ringtone**. CVP looks up its dialed number pattern table (shown in Figure 12-10), determines that the next hop is 10.0.1.80 (the VXML gateway), and sends a SIP INVITE to the VXML gateway.

Step 4. The VXML gateway receives the SIP INVITE for 91919191 (Call-ID 4) and matches 919191 as the inbound dial peer, executing the TCL application ringtone.tcl associated with this dial peer.

The ringtone.tcl application answers the call, triggering the SIP stack in the VXML gateway to send 200 OK with the SDP containing the IP address, port number, and codec of G.711ulaw to be used for the media stream. The TCL application then extracts the filename of the ringtone audio from the App-Info header of the SIP INVITE. The following is an example of the App-Info header:

```
App-Info: <10.0.1.21:7000:7443>;ringtone=ringback.wav.
```

The ringtone.tcl application plays the audio file continuously while the call is connected to the VXML gateway.

Step 5. CVP initiates a re-INVITE to the switch call leg (the call leg between CUBE and CVP) and updates the media connections such that CUBE and the VXML gateway or VVB send media streams to each other.

Step 6. Now the caller is hearing the ringtone from the VXML gateway or VVB.

Example 12-8 shows the SIP INVITE to 91919191 received from CVP and the corresponding 200 OK response from the VXML gateway. The SDP in the 200 OK contains the same IP address and G.711ulaw codec, but the RTP port number is different from that in the previous VRU call leg set up between CVP and the VXML gateway (or VVB). The output shown in Example 12-8 is a snippet of **debug ccsip message** collected from the Cisco IOS VXML gateway.

Example 12-8 *Ringtone Play: SIP INVITE from CVP to the VXML Gateway/VVB*

```
*Apr  7 22:45:33.659: //-1/xxxxxxxxxxxx/SIP/Msg/ccsipDisplayMsg:
Received:
INVITE sip:91919191@10.0.1.80;transport=tcp SIP/2.0
Via: SIP/2.0/TCP 10.0.1.21:5060;branch=z9hG4bKk9F7UjU8zHQ4XN9JOnRWyA~~1196
Max-Forwards: 64
To: <sip:91919191@10.0.1.80;transport=tcp>
From: "--CVP_11_6_1_0_0_0_329" <sip:4083926001@10.0.1.21:5060>;tag=dsd1a82d92
Call-ID: 289C3D0000010000000007EA1CAA8C0-1523142003161284@10.0.1.21
CSeq: 1 INVITE
Content-Length: 0
Contact: <sip:4083926001@10.0.1.21:5060;transport=tcp>
Expires: 10
User-Agent: CVP 11.6 (1) Build-329
Call-Info: <sip:10.0.1.83:5060>;purpose=x-cisco-origIP
Remote-Party-ID: "--CVP_11_6_1_0_0_0_329" <sip:4083926001@10.0.1.83>;party=calling;s
  creen=yes;privacy=off
Date: Sat, 07 Apr 2018 22:58:20 GMT
Min-SE: 1800
```

```
Allow: INVITE, OPTIONS, BYE, CANCEL, ACK, PRACK, UPDATE, REFER, SUBSCRIBE, NOTIFY,
  INFO, REGISTER
Allow-Events: telephone-event
X-Cisco-CCBProbe: undefined
Session-ID: 0000664e00105000a000005056a12adc;remote=00000000000000000000000000000000
Session-Expires: 1800
Content-Disposition: session;handling=required
Cisco-Gucid: 289C3D00000100000000007EA1CAA8C0
Supported: timer
Supported: resource-priority
Supported: replaces
Supported: sdp-anat
App-Info: <10.0.1.21:7000:7443>;ringtone=ringback.wav

*Apr  7 22:45:33.719: //662609/373CD1689E35/SIP/Msg/ccsipDisplayMsg:
Sent:
SIP/2.0 200 OK
Via: SIP/2.0/TCP 10.0.1.21:5060;branch=z9hG4bKk9F7UjU8zHQ4XN9JOnRWyA~~1196
From: "--CVP_11_6_1_0_0_0_329" <sip:4083926001@10.0.1.21:5060>;tag=dsd1a82d92
To: <sip:91919191@10.0.1.80;transport=tcp>;tag=DA190BCC-1D2A
Date: Sat, 07 Apr 2018 22:45:33 GMT
Call-ID: 289C3D00000100000000007EA1CAA8C0-15231420031612840@10.0.1.21
CSeq: 1 INVITE
Allow: INVITE, OPTIONS, BYE, CANCEL, ACK, PRACK, UPDATE, REFER, SUBSCRIBE, NOTIFY,
  INFO, REGISTER
Allow-Events: telephone-event
Contact: <sip:91919191@10.0.1.80:5060;transport=tcp>
Supported: replaces
Supported: sdp-anat
Server: Cisco-SIPGateway/IOS-15.4.3.M3
Require: timer
Session-Expires:  1800;refresher=uac
Supported: timer
Content-Type: application/sdp
Content-Disposition: session;handling=required
Content-Length: 238

v=0
o=CiscoSystemsSIP-GW-UserAgent 4688 3248 IN IP4 10.0.1.80
s=SIP Call
c=IN IP4 10.0.1.80
t=0 0
m=audio 17512 RTP/AVP 0 101
c=IN IP4 10.0.1.80
a=rtpmap:0 PCMU/8000
a=rtpmap:101 telephone-event/8000
a=fmtp:101 0-16
a=ptime:20
```

Example 12-9 shows the output of **show call active voice brief** and **show voip rtp connection** collected from CUBE. Note that the local UUID in the call leg 12446 has changed from a254fa8e10000162de5d5d4203430af1 to a25689f810000162ec-886ca159506afd. The latter UUID is the new value generated by CVP on behalf of the VXML gateway or VVB for the ringtone call leg. The remote RTP IP address and port number of the CUBE-to-CVP call leg is **10.0.1.80:17512**, which is the VXML gateway or VVB's IP address and port number for the ringtone playout.

Example 12-9 show call active voice brief *Collected When the Caller Is Hearing a Ringtone*

```
cube1# show call active voice brief
...
Telephony call-legs: 0
SIP call-legs: 2
H323 call-legs: 0
Call agent controlled call-legs: 0
SCCP call-legs: 0
STCAPP call-legs: 0
Multicast call-legs: 0
Total call-legs: 2
0 : 12445 392029150ms.1 (22:58:19.970 UTC Sat Apr 7 2018) +1080 pid:68000 Answer
  4083926001 connected
 dur 00:01:42 tx:4908/981600 rx:5118/1022840 dscp:0 media:0 audio tos:0xB8 video
  tos:0x0
 IP 192.168.202.162:8014 SRTP: off rtt:0ms pl:0/0ms lost:0/0/0 delay:0/0/0ms
  g711ulaw TextRelay: off Transcoded: No ICE: Off
 media inactive detected:n media contrl rcvd:n/a timestamp:n/a
 long duration call detected:n long duration call duration:n/a timestamp:n/a
 LostPacketRate:0.00 OutOfOrderRate:0.00
 LocalUUID:0000664e00105000a000005056a12adc
 RemoteUUID:a25689f810000162ec886ca159506afd
 VRF:
0 : 12446 392030170ms.1 (22:58:20.990 UTC Sat Apr 7 2018) +50 pid:68001 Originate
  8020 connected
 dur 00:01:42 tx:5118/1022840 rx:4908/981600 dscp:0 media:0 audio tos:0xB8 video
  tos:0x0
 IP 10.0.1.80:17512 SRTP: off rtt:0ms pl:0/0ms lost:0/0/0 delay:0/0/0ms g711ulaw
  TextRelay: off Transcoded: No ICE: Off
 media inactive detected:n media contrl rcvd:n/a timestamp:n/a
 long duration call detected:n long duration call duration:n/a timestamp:n/a
 LostPacketRate:0.00 OutOfOrderRate:0.00
 LocalUUID:a25689f810000162ec886ca159506afd
 RemoteUUID:0000664e00105000a000005056a12adc
 VRF:

Telephony call-legs: 0
SIP call-legs: 2
```

```
H323 call-legs: 0
Call agent controlled call-legs: 0
SCCP call-legs: 0
STCAPP call-legs: 0
Multicast call-legs: 0
Total call-legs: 2

cube1# show voip rtp connection
VoIP RTP Port Usage Information:
Max Ports Available: 19999, Ports Reserved: 101, Ports in Use: 2
Port range not configured
                                          Min    Max    Ports      Ports     Ports
Media-Address Range                       Port   Port   Available  Reserved  In-use
-------------------------------------------------------------------------------
Global Media Pool                         8000   48198  19999      101       2
-------------------------------------------------------------------------------
VoIP RTP active connections :
No. CallId  dstCallId  LocalRTP  RmtRTP  LocalIP          RemoteIP         MPSS  VRF
1   12445   12446      8276      8014    192.168.202.165  192.168.202.162  NO    NA
2   12446   12445      8278      17512   10.0.1.83        10.0.1.80        NO    NA
Found 2 active RTP connections
```

Caller Connected to Agent

Figure 12-18 shows the third stage of the call flow, in which CVP originates a call to the available agent after setting up the call leg with the VXML gateway or VVB to play the ringtone.

The following steps occur in the third stage:

Step 1. CVP looks up the agent routing label (5002) in its dialed number pattern table (shown in Figure 12-10), determines that the next hop is the server group CUCM.solutionslab.com, and chooses 10.0.1.31 as the next hop.

Step 2. CVP sends a SIP INVITE with called number 5002 (Call-ID 5), with the SDP set to the media codec capabilities of G.711ulaw and G.729, and an RTP IP address and port number provided by CUBE of the inbound call leg (switch leg Call-ID 2). CVP passes the call signaling IP address of the actual device (CUBE) that originated the call in the Call-Info header as shown here and in Example 12-10:

```
Call-Info: <sip:10.0.1.83:5060>;purpose=x-cisco-origIP
```

Step 3. CUCM receives the SIP INVITE, extracts the originating call signaling IP address and port number from the Call-Info header, and uses it as the lookup key. This determines the corresponding SIP trunk configured for CUBE and the associated device pool–related parameters.

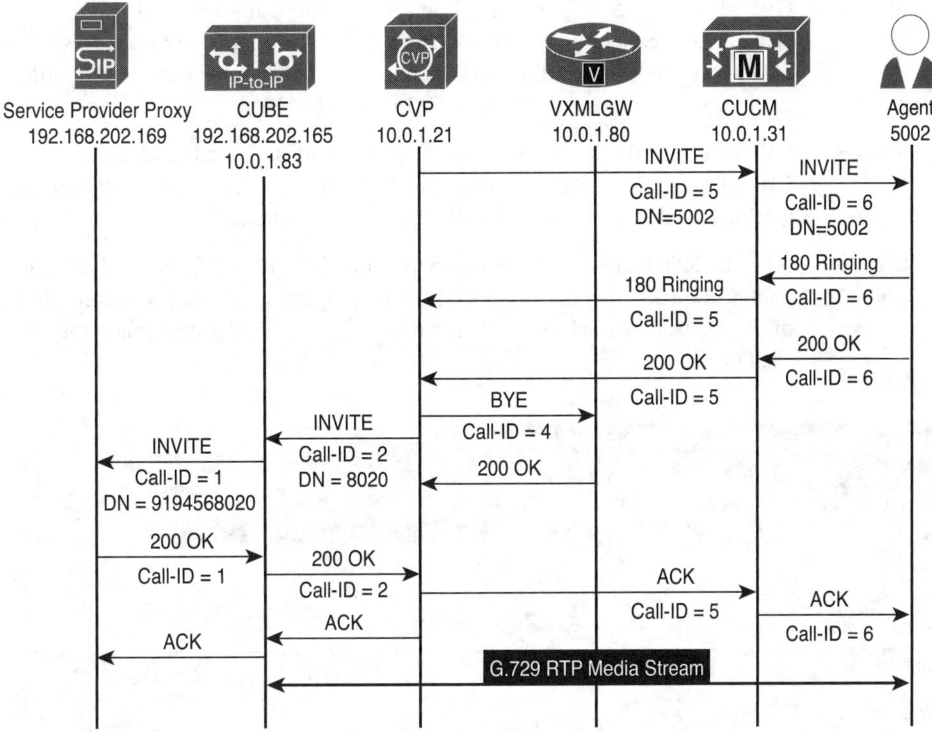

Figure 12-18 *An Inbound Caller Is Connected to an Agent*

Step 4. CUCM acts as a B2BUA and sends a SIP INVITE (Call-ID 6) to the registered agent phone. The agent phone responds with 180 Ringing response. At the same time, the Finesse client running in the agent's web browser also shows the incoming call.

Step 5. The agent answers the call from the Finesse client, which causes the agent phone to send a 200 OK response with G.729 as the selected codec, along with its IP address and port number to be used for sending and receiving RTP audio. It is important to note that several messages are exchanged among the CTI server, the Finesse server, Finesse Agent Desktop, the agent PG, CUCM, and IP phone prior to the agent phone sending a 200 OK response. (The *CTI Server Message Reference Guide* at www.cisco.com provides a high-level overview of this message flow.)

Step 6. Upon receiving the 200 OK response, CVP disconnects the ringtone call leg (Call-ID 4) established with the VXML gateway or VVB.

Step 7. CVP sends a re-INVITE to CUBE on the inbound call leg (Call-ID 2) to change the media codec from G.711ulaw to G.729. CUBE sends a corresponding re-INVITE on the call leg between itself and the service provider in order to change the audio codec from G.711ulaw to G.729.

Step 8. CVP receives 200 OK response from CUBE (Call-ID 2) and sends an ACK to CUCM (Call-ID 5) and to CUBE (Call-ID 2). This results in the end-to-end call getting established between CUBE and the agent phone.

Step 9. Now the RTP media stream is following directly between CUBE and the agent phone, and the caller is talking to the agent. Figure 12-19 shows a screenshot of Finesse Agent Desktop while the customer and agent are talking with each other.

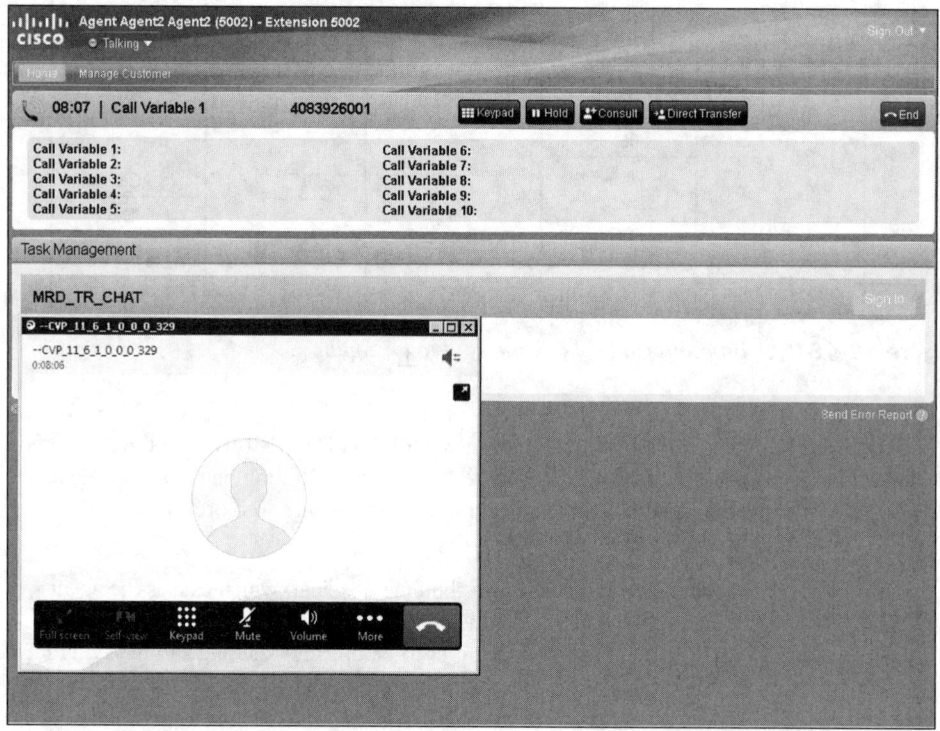

Figure 12-19 *Agent Talking to the Customer by Using Finesse Agent Desktop*

Example 12-10 shows the SIP INVITE to the agent directory number (5002) sent by CVP to CUCM. CVP passes the Session-ID header with local-uuid set to the value 0000664e00105000a000005056a12adc, which was received from CUBE in the inbound call leg (Call-ID 2). Example 12-10 through Example 12-12 show messages collected from CVP logs.

Example 12-10 *Agent Call Setup: SIP INVITE from CVP to CUCM*

```
1165133: 10.0.1.21: Apr 07 2018 19:00:03.333 -0400: %_Connection-7-com.dynamicsoft.
  DsLibs.DsUALibs.DsSipLlApi.Connection:  Sending Message (NB): INVITE sip:5002@CUCM.
  solutionslab.com;transport=tcp SIP/2.0
Via: SIP/2.0/TCP 10.0.1.21:5060;branch=z9hG4bKk9F7UjU8zHQ4XN9JOnRWyA~~1200
Max-Forwards: 64
To: <sip:5002@CUCM.solutionslab.com;transport=tcp>
From: "--CVP_11_6_1_0_0_0_329" <sip:4083926001@10.0.1.21:5060>;tag=dsae712e3e
Call-ID: 289C3D00000100000000007EA1CAA8C0-152314200333285@10.0.1.21
CSeq: 1 INVITE
Content-Length: 305
Contact: <sip:4083926001@10.0.1.21:5060;transport=tcp>
Expires: 30
User-Agent: CVP 11.6 (1) Build-329
Call-Info: <sip:10.0.1.83:5060>;purpose=x-cisco-origIP
Remote-Party-ID: "--CVP_11_6_1_0_0_0_329" <sip:4083926001@10.0.1.83>;party=calling;
  screen=yes;privacy=off
Date: Sat, 07 Apr 2018 22:58:20 GMT
Min-SE: 1800
Cisco-Guid: 0681327872-0000065536-0000000126-2714413248
Allow: INVITE, OPTIONS, BYE, CANCEL, ACK, PRACK, UPDATE, REFER, SUBSCRIBE, NOTIFY,
  INFO, REGISTER
Allow-Events: telephone-event
X-Cisco-CCBProbe: undefined
Session-ID: 0000664e00105000a000005056a12adc;remote=00000000000000000000000000000000
Session-Expires: 1800
Content-Disposition: session;handling=required
Cisco-Gucid: 289C3D00000100000000007EA1CAA8C0
Supported: timer
Supported: resource-priority
Supported: replaces
Supported: sdp-anat
Content-Type: application/sdp
App-Info: <10.0.1.21:7000:7443>

v=0
o=Cisco-CVP-B2BUA 289844526 289844527 IN IP4 10.0.1.21
s=SIP Call
c=IN IP4 10.0.1.83
t=0 0
m=audio 8278 RTP/AVP 0 18 101 19
c=IN IP4 10.0.1.83
a=rtpmap:0 PCMU/8000
a=rtpmap:18 G729/8000
a=fmtp:18 annexb=no
a=rtpmap:101 telephone-event/8000
a=fmtp:101 0-15
a=rtpmap:19 CN/8000
a=ptime:20
```

Example 12-11 shows the 180 Ringing and 200 OK responses from CUCM. The Session-ID header in the 180 Ringing response contains the local-uuid 00004ca800105000a00 000505689ea60 of the agent phone. Note that the 200 OK response has G.729 as the selected audio codec, with the RTP media stream set to the agent's phone IP address and port number (10.0.1.91:16560).

Example 12-11 *Agent Call Setup: 180 Ringing and 200 OK from CUCM to CVP*

```
1165154: 10.0.1.21: Apr 07 2018 19:00:03.396 -0400: %_TransactionManagement-7-com.
  dynamicsoft.DsLibs.DsUALibs.DsSipLlApi.TransactionManagement:  processMessage():
  Incoming message:
SIP/2.0 180 Ringing
Via: SIP/2.0/TCP 10.0.1.21:5060;branch=z9hG4bKk9F7UjU8zHQ4XN9JOnRWyA~~1200
To: <sip:5002@CUCM.solutionslab.com;transport=tcp>;tag=147253~ea04c33e-2567-47d2-
  ab0d-76daabbb8340-47714185
From: "--CVP_11_6_1_0_0_0_329" <sip:4083926001@10.0.1.21:5060>;tag=dsae712e3e
Call-ID: 289C3D0000010000000007EA1CAA8C0-1523142003333285@10.0.1.21
CSeq: 1 INVITE
Content-Length: 0
Date: Sat, 07 Apr 2018 23:00:03 GMT
Allow: INVITE, OPTIONS, INFO, BYE, CANCEL, ACK, PRACK, UPDATE, REFER, SUBSCRIBE,
  NOTIFY
Allow-Events: presence
Server: Cisco-CUCM11.0
Call-Info: <urn:x-cisco-remotecc:callinfo>;x-cisco-video-traffic-class=DESKTOP
Supported: X-cisco-srtp-fallback
Supported: Geolocation
Session-ID: 00004ca800105000a00000505689ea60;remote=0000664e00105000a000005056a12adc
P-Asserted-Identity: <sip:5002@10.0.1.31>
Remote-Party-ID: <sip:5002@10.0.1.31>;party=called;screen=yes;privacy=off
Contact: <sip:5002@10.0.1.31:5060;transport=tcp>;+u.sip!devicename.ccm.cisco
  .com="agent2"
...
1165232: 10.0.1.21: Apr 07 2018 19:00:23.427 -0400: %_TransactionManagement-7-com.
  dynamicsoft.DsLibs.DsUALibs.DsSipLlApi.TransactionManagement:  processMessage():
  Incoming message binding info: TCP local[[ port = 0 (10.0.1.21)]] remote[[ port =
  5060 (10.0.1.31) ]], Connection ID = null, network = DEFAULT, TSIP = false
1165233: 10.0.1.21: Apr 07 2018 19:00:23.427 -0400: %_TransactionManagement-7-com.
  dynamicsoft.DsLibs.DsUALibs.DsSipLlApi.TransactionManagement:  processMessage():
  Incoming message:
SIP/2.0 200 OK
Via: SIP/2.0/TCP 10.0.1.21:5060;branch=z9hG4bKk9F7UjU8zHQ4XN9JOnRWyA~~1200
To: <sip:5002@CUCM.solutionslab.com;transport=tcp>;tag=147253~ea04c33e-2567-47d2-
  ab0d-76daabbb8340-47714185
From: "--CVP_11_6_1_0_0_0_329" <sip:4083926001@10.0.1.21:5060>;tag=dsae712e3e
Call-ID: 289C3D0000010000000007EA1CAA8C0-1523142003333285@10.0.1.21
```

```
CSeq: 1 INVITE
Content-Length: 240
Date: Sat, 07 Apr 2018 23:00:03 GMT
Allow: INVITE, OPTIONS, INFO, BYE, CANCEL, ACK, PRACK, UPDATE, REFER, SUBSCRIBE,
  NOTIFY
Allow-Events: presence, kpml
Supported: replaces
Supported: X-cisco-srtp-fallback
Supported: Geolocation
Server: Cisco-CUCM11.0
Call-Info: <urn:x-cisco-remotecc:callinfo>;x-cisco-video-traffic-class=DESKTOP
Session-Expires: 1800;refresher=uas
Require: timer
Session-ID: 00004ca800105000a00000505689ea60;remote=0000664e00105000a000005056a12adc
P-Asserted-Identity: <sip:5002@10.0.1.31>
Remote-Party-ID: <sip:5002@10.0.1.31>;party=called;screen=yes;privacy=off
Contact: <sip:5002@10.0.1.31:5060;transport=tcp>;+u.sip!devicename.ccm.cisco
  .com="agent2"
Content-Type: application/sdp

v=0
o=CiscoSystemsCCM-SIP 147253 1 IN IP4 10.0.1.31
s=SIP Call
c=IN IP4 10.0.1.91
b=TIAS:8000
b=AS:8
t=0 0
m=audio 16560 RTP/AVP 18 101
a=rtpmap:18 G729/8000
a=fmtp:18 annexb=no
a=rtpmap:101 telephone-event/8000
a=fmtp:101 0-15
```

Example 12-12 shows the output of **show call active voice brief** and **show voip rtp connection** collected from CUBE. Note that the local UUID in the call leg 12446 changes from a25689f810000162ec886ca159506afd to 00004ca800105000a00000505 689ea60. This is the new UUID value generated by the agent phone when it answers the incoming call from CUCM and is passed through CUCM and CVP to CUBE. The remote RTP IP address and port number of the CUBE-to-CVP call leg changes to 10.0.1.91:16560, which is the agent's IP phone IP address and port number.

Example 12-12 show call active voice brief *Collected When the Caller Is Connected to an Agent*

```
cube1# show call active voice brief
...
Telephony call-legs: 0
SIP call-legs: 2
H323 call-legs: 0
Call agent controlled call-legs: 0
SCCP call-legs: 0
STCAPP call-legs: 0
Multicast call-legs: 0
Total call-legs: 2
0    : 12445 392029150ms.1 (22:58:19.965 UTC Sat Apr 7 2018) +1080 pid:68000 Answer
  4083926001 connected
 dur 00:02:14 tx:6486/1216000 rx:6718/1259808 dscp:0 media:0 audio tos:0xB8 video
  tos:0x0
 IP 192.168.202.162:8014 SRTP: off rtt:1ms pl:0/0ms lost:0/0/0 delay:0/0/0ms g729r8
  TextRelay: off Transcoded: No ICE: Off
 media inactive detected:n media contrl rcvd:n/a timestamp:n/a
 long duration call detected:n long duration call duration:n/a timestamp:n/a
 LostPacketRate:0.00 OutOfOrderRate:0.00
 LocalUUID:0000664e00105000a000005056a12adc
 RemoteUUID:00004ca800105000a00000505689ea60
 VRF:
0    : 12446 392030170ms.1 (22:58:20.985 UTC Sat Apr 7 2018) +50 pid:68001 Originate
  8020 connected
 dur 00:02:14 tx:6718/1259808 rx:6486/1216000 dscp:0 media:0 audio tos:0xB8 video
  tos:0x0
 IP 10.0.1.91:16560 SRTP: off rtt:8ms pl:0/0ms lost:0/0/0 delay:0/0/0ms g729r8 Tex-
  tRelay: off Transcoded: No ICE: Off
 media inactive detected:n media contrl rcvd:n/a timestamp:n/a
 long duration call detected:n long duration call duration:n/a timestamp:n/a
 LostPacketRate:0.00 OutOfOrderRate:0.00
 LocalUUID:00004ca800105000a00000505689ea60
 RemoteUUID:0000664e00105000a000005056a12adc
 VRF:

Telephony call-legs: 0
SIP call-legs: 2
H323 call-legs: 0
Call agent controlled call-legs: 0
SCCP call-legs: 0
STCAPP call-legs: 0
Multicast call-legs: 0
Total call-legs: 2
```

```
cube1# show voip rtp connection
VoIP RTP Port Usage Information:
Max Ports Available: 19999, Ports Reserved: 101, Ports in Use: 2
Port range not configured
                                         Min    Max    Ports     Ports    Ports
Media-Address Range                      Port   Port   Available Reserved In-use
-------------------------------------------------------------------------------
Global Media Pool                        8000   48198  19999     101      2
-------------------------------------------------------------------------------
VoIP RTP active connections :
No. CallId  dstCallId  LocalRTP RmtRTP    LocalIP         RemoteIP        MPSS     VRF
1   12445   12446      8276     8014   192.168.202.165 192.168.202.162  NO       NA
2   12446   12445      8278     16560     10.0.1.83        10.0.1.91     NO       NA
Found 2 active RTP connections
```

After the conversation is complete, the customer or the agent hangs up the call, and the call disconnection is triggered by CUBE or by CUCM sending a SIP BYE request to CVP, which then disconnects all the call legs associated with the call.

Call Transfers

Often, the agent assisting a customer has to transfer a call to another internal team. For example, the customer might request further assistance that is provided by another team, the customer might select an incorrect option in the IVR, or the customer might be interested in a new service. Agents use Finesse Agent Desktop to perform the transfer task using the Direct Transfer, Consult, and Conference buttons:

- **Blind Transfer**—The caller is redirected to the transfer destination directly, without the first agent talking to the new called party.
- **Consultation Transfer**—This option provides a better customer experience because the current agent keeps the customer on hold, initiates a transfer to another team with a different skill group, talks to the second agent answering the transfer call, brings the person up to speed on the customer situation, and then transfers the customer to the second agent, thereby saving the customer's time by avoiding the need to re-explain the situation.
- **Conference**—To ensure a good experience, the current agent can use this option to conference the second agent into the existing call with the customer, explain the situation with all three parties on the line, and then drop from the conference. The customer and second agent then continue with the conversation.

In addition to the internal transfers, a caller could also be transferred directly (*blind transferred*) to an external number in the PSTN. This happens when the customer's request is served by a partner company that has a dedicated PSTN number and uses its own unified communication system. PSTN service providers that are connected to the contact center via TDM trunks offer a variety of call transfer options, such as hookflash (performed on FXO trunks), two B-channel transfer (PRI trunks), and in-band DTMF mechanisms, such as transfer connect, which is triggered by dialing *8 followed by the transfer target number. SIP service providers that are connected to the enterprise through SBCs offer SIP REFER and in-band DTMF-based call transfer mechanisms. External call transfers in Cisco contact center CUBE deployments can be accomplished using in-band DTMF and hairpin mechanisms, depending on the transfer features supported by the SIP service provider:

- **In-band DTMF method**—The transfer target number is sent to the service provider as in-band DTMF digits, along with a unique prefix (for example, *8) on an existing call in order to transfer the call to an external destination. This is performed by configuring the UCCE call script to send a DTMF label (for example, *81234567890) as a routing response to CVP. CVP sends DTMF digits in SIP INFO messages to CUBE, which then sends the digits to the service provider as in-band DTMF digits, using RTP named telephony events (RTP NTE; see RFC 4733) packets. This method is also referred to as *takeback-and-transfer* (*TNT*). Chapter 7, "DTMF Interworking," discusses the SIP INFO to RTP NTE and other DTMF interworking mechanisms.
- **Hairpin method**—The SIP service provider is unaware that a call transfer is happening in the hairpin-based call transfer method. This method can either be triggered by a SIP INVITE from CUCM or by SIP REFER from CVP.

The Cisco Interoperability Portal provides validated and recommended configuration for integrating CUBE with different service providers, along with call transfer functionality. Chapter 4, "Signaling and Interworking," also discusses the different call transfer scenarios in Unified Communications deployments.

SIP INVITE–Based Call Transfer

A SIP INVITE–based call transfer is used when the call transfer is initiated by clicking the Consult button or the Direct Transfer button in Finesse Agent Desktop, as shown in Figure 12-20.

Figure 12-21 shows the call flow diagram from the time CVP originates the agent call leg to the CUCM cluster's 10.0.3.32 and 10.0.1.31 subscriber nodes to the time the call leg between CVP and CUCM is set to receive music-on-hold audio. The SDL-detailed trace files from CUCM nodes are used to generate the call flow diagram in the TranslatorX call analysis tool. The call flow diagram uses the following IP address: device mapping:

10.0.1.21: sideACVP1 server

10.0.3.32: sideAcmsub2 server

10.0.1.31: sideAcmsub1 server

10.0.1.91: agent2 IP phone

10.0.1.83: cube1 SBC

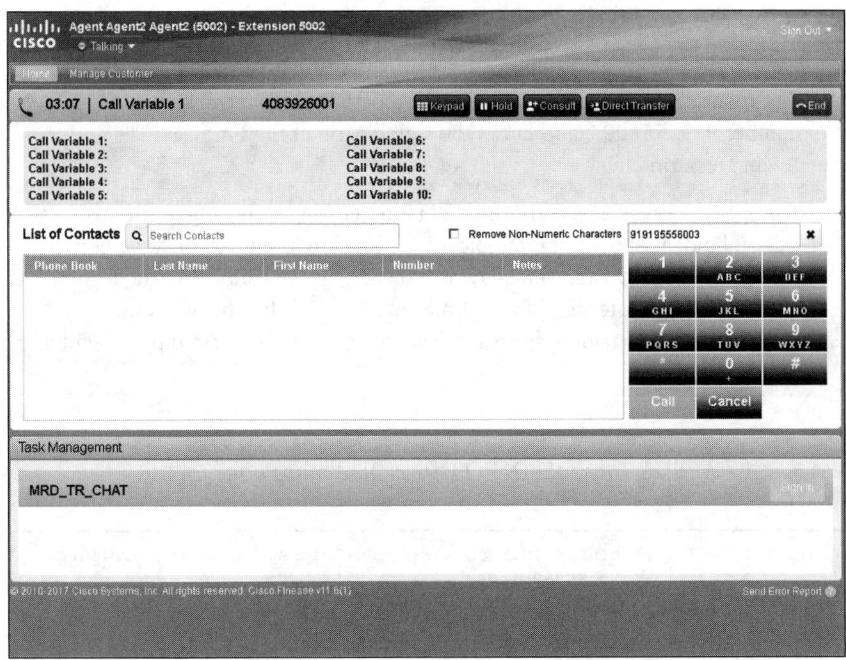

Figure 12-20 *An Agent Transferring a Caller Using the Consult Button*

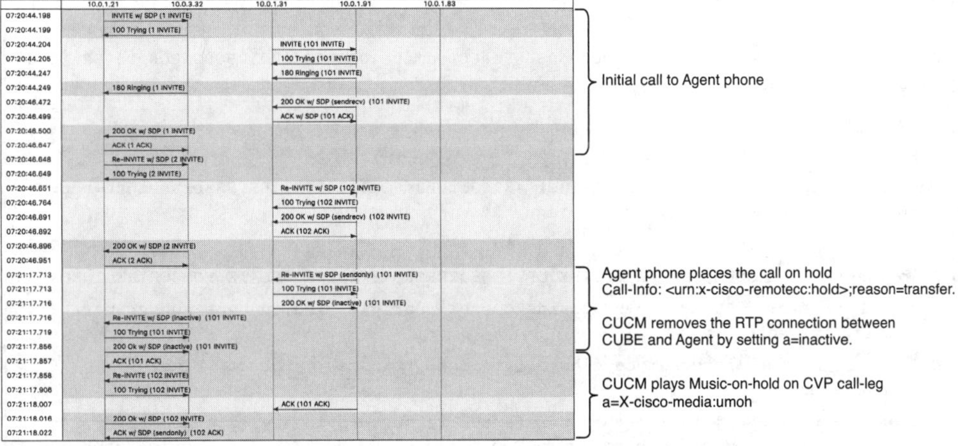

Figure 12-21 *Agent phone sends a re-INVITE to place current call on hold*

The following steps occur at this stage:

Step 1. CVP looks up the agent label 5002 in the dialed number patterns table, selects the CUCM subscriber node 10.0.1.31 as the next hop, and sends a SIP INVITE. CUCM sets up the call with the agent. The agent answers the call, and an RTP connection is established between CUBE and the agent. This step is the same as described in the section "Caller Connected to Agent," earlier in this chapter.

Step 2. The agent clicks the Consult button, enters the external transfer number 9195556003, and clicks the Call button in the Finesse Agent Desktop client.

Step 3. The agent phone sends a SIP re-INVITE requesting to put the current call on hold, as shown in Example 12-13. The key points to observe here are the call hold reason (transfer), as indicated in the Call-Info header value <urn:x-cisco-remotecc:hold>;reason = transfer, and the change in the media direction attribute from sendrecv to sendonly, indicated by a=sendonly in the SDP.

Example 12-13 *CUCM SDL Trace: Re-INVITE from an Agent Phone to Place a Call on Hold*

```
11864637.002 |07:21:17.713 |AppInfo  |SIPTcp - wait_SdlReadRsp: Incoming SIP TCP
  message from 10.0.1.91 on port 55758 index 22 with 2152 bytes:
[587759,NET] INVITE sip:4083926001@10.0.1.31:5060;transport=tcp SIP/2.0
Via: SIP/2.0/TCP 10.0.1.91:55758;branch=z9hG4bK00005551
From: <sip:5002@sideAcmsub1>;tag=00505689ea604cb800004b2f-0000028b
To: "--CVP_11_6_1_0_0_0_329" <sip:4083926001@10.0.1.31>;tag=195869~ea04c33e-2567-
  47d2-ab0d-76daabbb8340-64491462
Call-ID: 5a2c9380-ae51aa8c-39-1f01000a@10.0.1.31
Max-Forwards: 70
Session-ID: 000050ef00105000a00000505689ea60;remote=000008cc00105000a000005056a12adc
Date: Sun, 29 Apr 2018 11:20:27 GMT
CSeq: 101 INVITE
User-Agent: Cisco-CSF
Contact: <sip:04156c8d-2d7e-32d1-53ef-43168cfbb3d8@10.0.1.91:55758;transport=tcp>;
  +u.sip!devicename.ccm.cisco.com="agent2"
Accept: application/sdp
Allow: ACK,BYE,CANCEL,INVITE,NOTIFY,OPTIONS,REFER,REGISTER,UPDATE,SUBSCRIBE,INFO
Remote-Party-ID: "5002" <sip:5002@sideAcmsub1>;party=called;id-type=subscriber;
  privacy=off;screen=yes
Call-Info: <urn:x-cisco-remotecc:hold>; reason= transfer; protect= true;
  noholdreversion
Supported: replaces,join,sdp-anat,norefersub,resource-priority,extended-refer,
  X-cisco-callinfo,X-cisco-serviceuri,X-cisco-escapecodes,X-cisco-service-control,
  X-cisco-srtp-fallback,X-cisco-monrec,X-cisco-config,X-cisco-sis-7.0.0,X-cisco-
  xsi-8.5.1
Allow-Events: kpml,dialog
Recv-Info: conference
```

```
Recv-Info: x-cisco-conference
RTP-RxStat: Dur=30,Pkt=1483,Oct=30080,LostPkt=0,AvgJit=1.87593,VqMetrics="CS=0;
  SCS=0"
RTP-TxStat: Dur=30,Pkt=1469,Oct=29380

Content-Length: 641
Content-Type: application/sdp
Content-Disposition: session;handling=optional

v=0
o=Cisco-SIPUA 23060 2 IN IP4 10.0.1.91
s=SIP Call
b=AS:4000
t=0 0
a=cisco-mari:v1
a=cisco-mari-rate
m=audio 17518 RTP/AVP 114 9 104 105 0 8 18 111 101
c=IN IP4 10.0.1.91
a=rtpmap:114 opus/48000/2
a=rtpmap:9 G722/8000
a=rtpmap:104 G7221/16000
a=fmtp:104 bitrate=32000
a=rtpmap:105 G7221/16000
a=fmtp:105 bitrate=24000
a=rtpmap:0 PCMU/8000
a=rtpmap:8 PCMA/8000
a=rtpmap:18 G729/8000
a=fmtp:18 annexb=no
a=rtpmap:111 x-ulpfecuc/8000
a=extmap:14/sendrecv http://protocols.cisco.com/timestamp#100us
a=fmtp:111 max_esel=1420;m=8;max_n=32;FEC_ORDER=FEC_SRTP
a=rtpmap:101 telephone-event/8000
a=fmtp:101 0-15
a=sendonly
```

Step 4. CUCM deletes the existing RTP connection between CUBE and the agent phone by sending a re-INVITE to CVP with media direction attribute set to inactive, as indicated by a=inactive.

Step 5. CUCM sends another re-INVITE to CVP on the existing SIP call leg to set up an RTP connection between CUBE and the music-on-hold server. The re-INVITE has no SDP (a delayed media scenario), and the SDP offer and answer are exchanged in the 200 OK and ACK. Example 12-14 shows the SIP ACK message sent by CUCM, which contains the codec information of the music-on-hold stream. The caller now hears music-on-hold audio.

Example 12-14 *CUCM SDL Trace: ACK from CUCM to CVP to Stream Music-on-Hold*

```
14223160.001 |07:21:18.022 |AppInfo  |SIPTcp - wait_SdlSPISignal: Outgoing SIP TCP
  message to 10.0.1.21 on port 5060 index 32
[260999,NET] ACK sip:10.0.1.21:5060;transport=tcp SIP/2.0
Via: SIP/2.0/TCP 10.0.3.32:5060;branch=z9hG4bK2a11af01e8
From: <sip:5002@CUCM.solutionslab.com;transport=tcp>;tag=86910~ea04c33e-2567-47d2-
  ab0d-76daabbb8340-64491461
To: "--CVP_11_6_1_0_0_0_329" <sip:4083926001@10.0.1.21:5060>;tag=dsed3c45ca
Date: Sun, 29 Apr 2018 11:21:17 GMT
Call-ID: 58FB668000010000000008DA1CAA8C0-1525000844101316@10.0.1.21
User-Agent: Cisco-CUCM11.0
Max-Forwards: 70
CSeq: 102 ACK
Allow-Events: presence
Session-ID: 000050ef00105000a00000505689ea60;remote=000008cc00105000a000005056a12adc
Content-Type: application/sdp
Content-Length: 184

v=0
o=CiscoSystemsCCM-SIP 86910 4 IN IP4 10.0.3.32
s=SIP Call
c=IN IP4 10.0.3.32
t=0 0
m=audio 4000 RTP/AVP 0
a=X-cisco-media:umoh
a=ptime:20
a=rtpmap:0 PCMU/8000
a=sendonly
```

Figure 12-22 shows the call ladder diagram from the time CUCM originates a call toward the external transfer target number 919-555-6003 via CUBE (10.0.1.83) to the time when the customer is connected to the external transfer destination.

Step 6. CUCM sends a new SIP INVITE to CUBE with the called number set to 9195556003. CUBE interworks with the service provider, and the call is set up with RTP audio streams established between CUBE and the agent phone and also between CUBE and the service provider. The agent is now talking to the person at the external transfer destination.

Step 7. The agent completes the transfer by clicking the Transfer button in the panel section that corresponds to the call kept on hold, as shown in Figure 12-23.

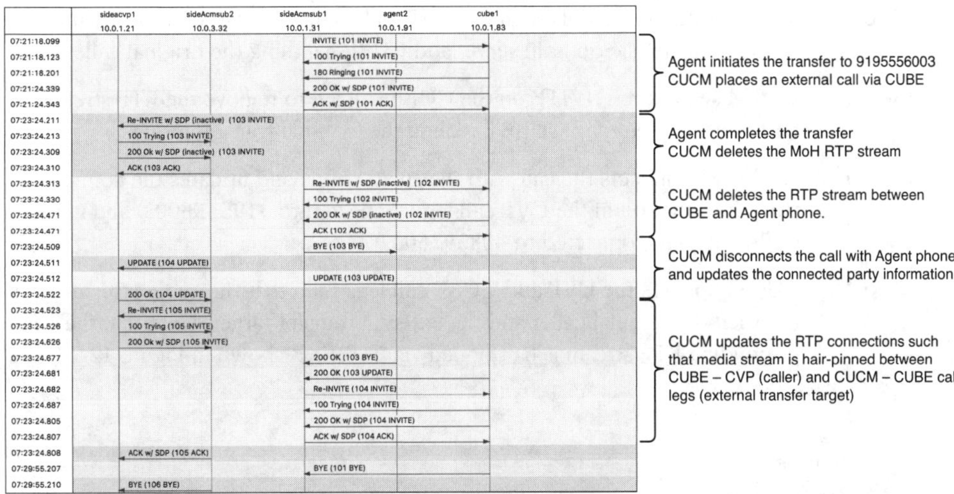

Figure 12-22 *CUCM Establishing the Call to the External Transfer Destination*

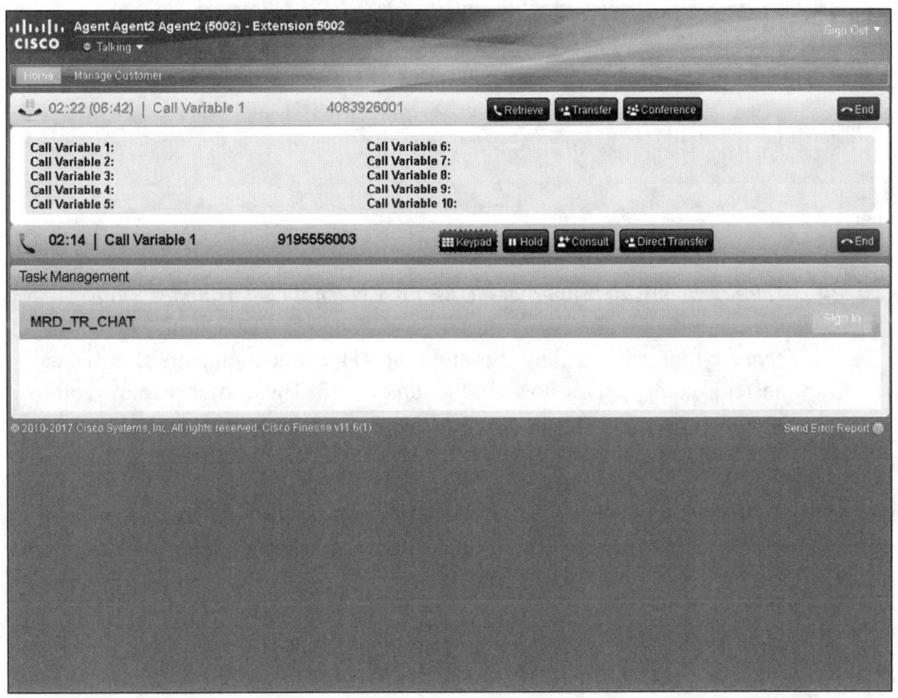

Figure 12-23 *Agent Completing the Transfer to an External Destination*

Step 8. CUCM sends a re-INVITE on the CVP call leg to remove the RTP stream between the music-on-hold server and CUBE handling the original caller.

Step 9. CUCM sends a re-INVITE on the CUBE call leg to remove the RTP stream between the agent and CUBE handling the external transfer target.

Step 10. CUCM disconnects the call with the agent phone and updates the connected party information in the CVP call leg (connected to 9195556003) and in the CUBE call leg (connected to 4083926001).

Step 11. CUCM updates the CVP and CUBE call legs such that the audio stream flows between the original caller and the external transfer target. Note that the corresponding RTP stream is hairpinned via CUBE, as shown in Figure 12-24.

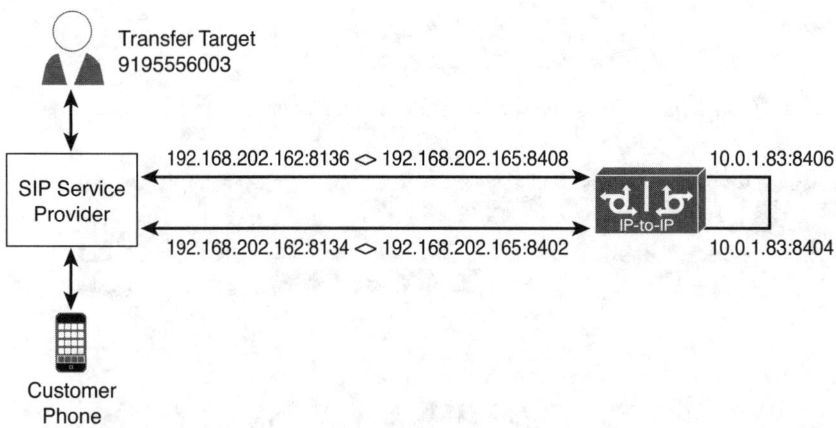

Figure 12-24 *RTP Streams Hairpinned at CUBE for External Call Transfer Flow*

There are four call signaling legs and four RTP connection pairs after the call transfer is complete, as shown in Example 12-15. The output of **show voip rtp connection** also confirms the RTP stream hairpin between the streams 10.0.1.83:8404 and 10.0.1.83:8406, as shown in Example 12-15.

Example 12-15 *SIP Call Legs After a SIP INVITE-Based Call Transfer Is Complete*

```
cube1# show call active voice brief
...
Telephony call-legs: 0
SIP call-legs: 4
H323 call-legs: 0
Call agent controlled call-legs: 0
SCCP call-legs: 0
STCAPP call-legs: 0
Multicast call-legs: 0
```

```
Total call-legs: 4
0    : 80115 2250972020ms.1 (11:20:42.837 UTC Sun Apr 29 2018) +1120 pid:68000
  Answer 4083926001 connected
 dur 00:02:53 tx:2491/281236 rx:2281/237836 dscp:0 media:0 audio tos:0xB8 video
  tos:0x0
 IP 192.168.202.162:8134 SRTP: off rtt:59ms pl:0/0ms lost:0/0/0 delay:0/0/0ms
  g711ulaw TextRelay: off Transcoded: No ICE: Off
 media inactive detected:n media contrl rcvd:n/a timestamp:n/a
 long duration call detected:n long duration call duration:n/a timestamp:n/a
 LostPacketRate:0.00 OutOfOrderRate:0.00
 LocalUUID:000008cc00105000a000005056a12adc
 RemoteUUID:0000055400105000a00000505684dea9
 VRF:
0    : 80116 2250973060ms.1 (11:20:43.877 UTC Sun Apr 29 2018) +60 pid:68001 Origi-
  nate 8020 connected
 dur 00:02:53 tx:2280/237776 rx:2498/282484 dscp:0 media:0 audio tos:0xB8 video
  tos:0x0
 IP 10.0.1.83:8406 SRTP: off rtt:11ms pl:0/0ms lost:0/0/0 delay:0/0/0ms g711ulaw
  TextRelay: off Transcoded: No ICE: Off
 media inactive detected:n media contrl rcvd:n/a timestamp:n/a
 long duration call detected:n long duration call duration:n/a timestamp:n/a
 LostPacketRate:0.00 OutOfOrderRate:0.00
 LocalUUID:0000055400105000a00000505684dea9
 RemoteUUID:000008cc00105000a000005056a12adc
 VRF:
0    : 80117 2251007290ms.1 (11:21:18.107 UTC Sun Apr 29 2018) +6230 pid:68002
  Answer 5002 connected
 dur 00:02:12 tx:6108/439748 rx:6596/479176 dscp:0 media:0 audio tos:0xB8 video
  tos:0x0
 IP 10.0.1.83:8404 SRTP: off rtt:59ms pl:0/0ms lost:0/0/0 delay:0/0/0ms g711ulaw
  TextRelay: off Transcoded: No ICE: Off
 media inactive detected:n media contrl rcvd:n/a timestamp:n/a
 long duration call detected:n long duration call duration:n/a timestamp:n/a
 LostPacketRate:0.00 OutOfOrderRate:0.00
 LocalUUID:000008cc00105000a000005056a12adc
 RemoteUUID:0000055400105000a00000505684dea9
 VRF:
0    : 80118 2251007310ms.1 (11:21:18.127 UTC Sun Apr 29 2018) +6210 pid:68003 Orig-
  inate 9195556003 connected
 dur 00:02:12 tx:6595/479116 rx:6109/439808 dscp:0 media:0 audio tos:0xB8 video
  tos:0x0
 IP 192.168.202.162:8136 SRTP: off rtt:11ms pl:0/0ms lost:0/0/0 delay:0/0/0ms
  g711ulaw TextRelay: off Transcoded: No ICE: Off
 media inactive detected:n media contrl rcvd:n/a timestamp:n/a
 long duration call detected:n long duration call duration:n/a timestamp:n/a
 LostPacketRate:0.00 OutOfOrderRate:0.00
```

```
 LocalUUID:0000055400105000a00000505684dea9
 RemoteUUID:000008cc00105000a000005056a12adc
 VRF:

Telephony call-legs: 0
SIP call-legs: 4
H323 call-legs: 0
Call agent controlled call-legs: 0
SCCP call-legs: 0
STCAPP call-legs: 0
Multicast call-legs: 0
Total call-legs: 4

cube1# show voip rtp connection
VoIP RTP Port Usage Information:
Max Ports Available: 19999, Ports Reserved: 101, Ports in Use: 4
Port range not configured
                                       Min    Max    Ports     Ports     Ports
Media-Address Range                    Port   Port   Available Reserved  In-use
-----------------------------------------------------------------------------
Global Media Pool                      8000   48198 19999      101       4
-----------------------------------------------------------------------------
VoIP RTP active connections :
No. CallId  dstCallId  LocalRTP RmtRTP    LocalIP          RemoteIP        MPSS  VRF
1   80115   80116       8402     8134   192.168.202.165   192.168.202.162  NO    NA
2   80116   80115       8404     8406     10.0.1.83          10.0.1.83     NO    NA
3   80117   80118       8406     8404     10.0.1.83          10.0.1.83     NO    NA
4   80118   80117      8408      8136   192.168.202.165   192.168.202.162  NO    NA
Found 4 active RTP connections
```

After the conversation, the caller or the transfer target ends the call. CUBE receives the SIP BYE request from the service provider and forwards it to CUCM and CVP to clear the SIP calls associated with the original caller and transfer target destination.

SIP REFER–Based Call Transfer

SIP REFER is used in two common scenarios. In the first scenario, the UCCE call script transfers the inbound caller to a target destination by executing the Label node with a string value that starts with the prefix rf followed by the transfer target number. For example, the string rf9195556003 represents a transfer to 9195556003, using the SIP REFER mechanism. When CVP receives the rf label as a routing response from UCCE router, it removes the rf prefix and sends a SIP REFER with Refer-To set to the directory number following the prefix. Figure 12-25 shows a sample script in which the caller is transferred to an external destination 9195556003 when no agents are readily available to take the incoming call.

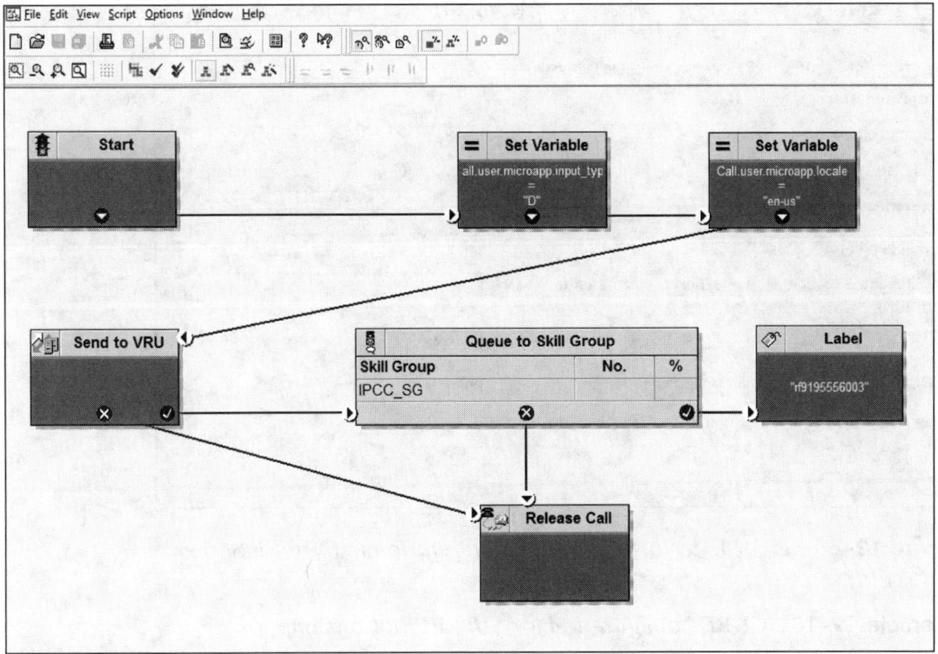

Figure 12-25 *UCCE Call Script Using the rf Label in the Transfer Node*

In the second scenario, CVP sends a SIP REFER when it experiences an application error while executing a VXML application or a call routing error while setting up a VRU call leg. The Refer-To in the SIP REFER is set to the **DN on the Gateway to play the error tone** parameter value in the CVP call server configuration. Most deployments use 92929292 as the error directory number, as shown in Figure 12-26. The call to 92929292 is handled by a VXML gateway or VVB.

In both scenarios, CUBE is configured to consume the SIP REFER and originate a new call to the transfer target number; that is, the SIP REFER received in the call leg between CVP and CUBE is not passed to the call leg between CUBE and the service provider. The command **no supplementary-service sip refer** is used to enable SIP REFER consumption behavior globally, as shown in Example 12-16. The command **refer consume** enables the SIP REFER consumption feature at a dial peer level. Inbound calls to 9194568190 match the dial peer 68000 as the inbound dial peer and are routed to CVP using dial peer 68001. CUBE translates the called number to 8190 prior to sending the SIP INVITE to CVP.

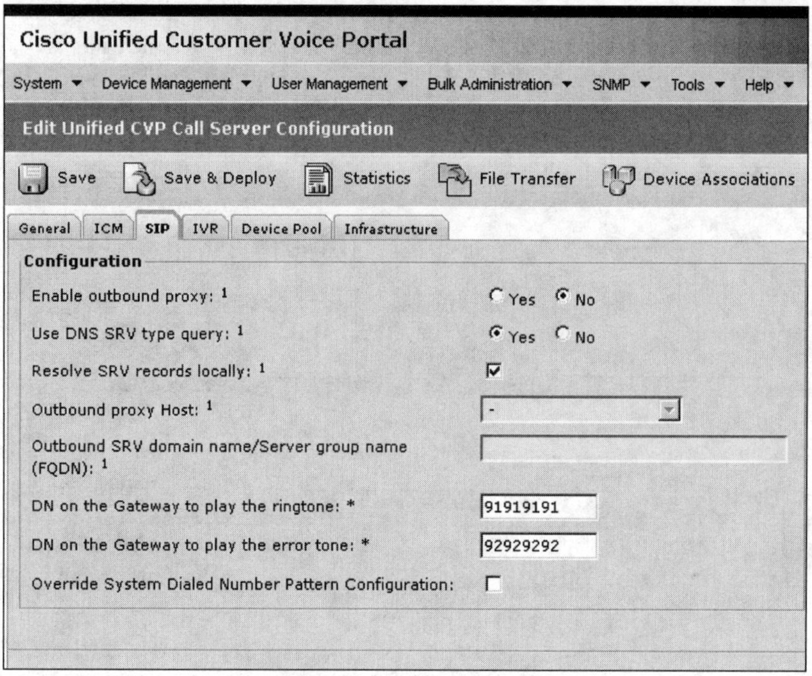

Figure 12-26 *Error Directory Number Configuration in the CVP Server*

Example 12-16 *CUBE Configuration for SIP REFER Consumption*

```
voice service voip
 no supplementary-service sip refer
 supplementary-service media-renegotiate
voice class e164-pattern-map 3
  e164 011T
  e164 [2-9].........
 !
!
dial-peer voice 68000 voip
 description "Inbound DP for contact center calls from Service provider"
 service survivability
 session protocol sipv2
 incoming called-number 9194568...
 voice-class codec 1
 voice-class sip rel1xx disable
 dtmf-relay rtp-nte
 no vad
!
```

```
dial-peer voice 68001 voip
 description "Outbound dial-peer to CVP"
 translation-profile outgoing 10-digit-to-4-digit
 preference 1
 destination-pattern 9194568...
 session protocol sipv2
 session target dns:sideAcvp1.solutionslab.com
 session transport tcp
 voice-class codec 1
 voice-class sip rel1xx disable
 voice-class sip bind control source-interface GigabitEthernet0/0/3
 voice-class sip bind media source-interface GigabitEthernet0/0/3
 dtmf-relay rtp-nte
dial-peer voice 68004 voip
 session protocol sipv2
 session target dns:p1.sp1.com
 session transport tcp
 destination e164-pattern-map 3
 voice-class codec 1
 voice-class sip bind control source-interface GigabitEthernet0/0/1
 voice-class sip bind media source-interface GigabitEthernet0/0/1
 dtmf-relay rtp-nte
 no vad
!
```

Figure 12-27 shows the SIP REFER-based call transfer call flow in a ladder diagram format. The inbound caller gets connected to the IVR, as discussed earlier in this chapter. Then CVP initiates the transfer by sending SIP REFER to CUBE.

Example 12-17 shows how CUBE accepts and processes the SIP REFER message received from the CVP server (10.0.1.21) on an existing call leg (74144) between 4083926001 and 8190. CUBE extracts the transfer target number 9195556003 from the Refer-To header, finds a matching outbound dial peer 68004, and originates a new call to the service provider (call leg 74148), with the called number set to the transfer target number (9195556003). CUBE informs CVP about the status of the call transfer by sending a SIP NOTIFY message with message body of type content/sipfrag containing the SIP response codes and text, such as SIP/2.0 100 Trying and SIP/2.0 200 OK. The output shown in Example 12-17 is a snippet from **debug ccsip message** and **debug voip ccapi inout** output collected from CUBE.

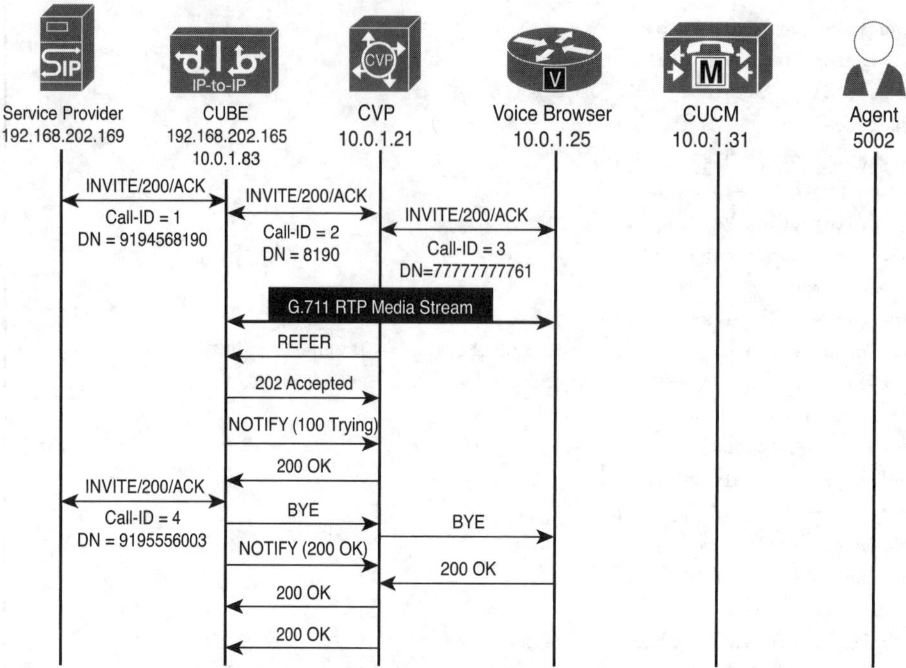

Figure 12-27 *SIP REFER-Based Call Transfer Call Flow*

Example 12-17 *SIP REFER Processing by CUBE*

```
4095619: Apr 27 22:22:20.986 UTC: //-1/xxxxxxxxxxxx/SIP/Msg/ccsipDisplayMsg:
Received:
REFER sip:4083926001@10.0.1.83:5060;transport=tcp SIP/2.0
Via: SIP/2.0/TCP 10.0.1.21:5060;branch=z9hG4bKk9F7UjU8zHQ4XN9JOnRWyA~~1299
Max-Forwards: 70
To: <sip:4083926001@192.168.202.162>;tag=7E3D68E1-D84
From: <sip:8190@sideAcvp1.solutionslab.com>;tag=ds4c333ed7
Call-ID: 4825C33B-49A011E8-999CE1BE-18C7C14D@10.0.1.83
CSeq: 1 REFER
Content-Length: 0
Contact: <sip:10.0.1.21:5060;transport=tcp>
Refer-To: <sip:9195556003@10.0.1.25;transport=tcp>
Referred-By: <sip:CVP@10.0.1.21:5060>
Session-ID: 093334221000016 3a73ef79584f00119;remote=00007fd600105000a000005056a12adc
4095620: Apr 27 22:22:20.986 UTC: //-1/xxxxxxxxxxxx/SIP/Info/verbose/4096/
  ccsip_new_msg_preprocessor: Checking Invite Dialog
4095621: Apr 27 22:22:20.986 UTC: //74144/703838000000/SIP/Info/info/4096/
  sipSPICheckFromToRequest: Found matching CB 7FAE6410C798
```

```
4095622: Apr 27 22:22:20.986 UTC: //74144/703838000000/SIP/Info/info/4096/sipSPILo-
  cateInviteDialogCCB: ****Found CCB in UAC table
4095791: Apr 27 22:22:20.992 UTC: //-1/xxxxxxxxxxxx/SIP/Msg/ccsipDisplayMsg:
Sent:
SIP/2.0 202 Accepted
Via: SIP/2.0/TCP 10.0.1.21:5060;branch=z9hG4bKk9F7UjU8zHQ4XN9JOnRWyA~~1299
From: <sip:8190@sideAcvp1.solutionslab.com>;tag=ds4c333ed7
To: sip:4083926001@192.168.202.162;tag=7E3D68E1-D84
Date: Fri, 27 Apr 2018 22:22:20 GMT
Call-ID: 4825C33B-49A011E8-999CE1BE-18C7C14D@10.0.1.83
Server: Cisco-SIPGateway/IOS-16.6.1
CSeq: 1 REFER
Content-Length: 0
Contact: <sip:4083926001@10.0.1.83:5060;transport=tcp>
4095794: Apr 27 22:22:20.992 UTC: //-1/xxxxxxxxxxxx/SIP/Msg/ccsipDisplayMsg:
Sent:
NOTIFY sip:10.0.1.21:5060;transport=tcp SIP/2.0
Via: SIP/2.0/TCP 10.0.1.83:5060;branch=z9hG4bK119DA14ED
From: <sip:4083926001@192.168.202.162>;tag=7E3D68E1-D84
To: <sip:8190@sideAcvp1.solutionslab.com>;tag=ds4c333ed7
Call-ID: 4825C33B-49A011E8-999CE1BE-18C7C14D@10.0.1.83
CSeq: 102 NOTIFY
Max-Forwards: 70
Date: Fri, 27 Apr 2018 22:22:20 GMT
User-Agent: Cisco-SIPGateway/IOS-16.6.1
Event: refer
Subscription-State: pending;expires=60
Contact: <sip:4083926001@10.0.1.83:5060;transport=tcp>
Content-Type: message/sipfrag
Content-Length: 22

SIP/2.0 100 Trying
4095809: Apr 27 22:22:20.994 UTC: //74143/703838000000/CCAPI/ccIFCallSetupRequest-
  Private:
   Interface=0x7FAE5C942DD8, Interface Type=3, Destination=, Mode=0x0,
   Call Params(Calling Number=sip:4083926001@192.168.202.162,(Calling Name=
  sip:4083926001@192.168.202.162)(TON=Unknown, NPI=Unknown, Screening=User, Passed,
  Presentation=Allowed),
   Called Number=9195556003(TON=Unknown, NPI=Unknown), Calling Translated=FALSE,
   Subscriber Type Str=Unknown, FinalDestinationFlag=TRUE, Outgoing Dial-peer=68004,
  Call Count On=FALSE,
   Source Trkgrp Route Label=, Target Trkgrp Route Label=, tg_label_flag=0, Applica-
  tion Call Id=)
```

```
4096306: Apr 27 22:22:21.079 UTC: //74148/703838000000/SIP/Msg/ccsipDisplayMsg:
Sent:
INVITE sip:9195556003@p1.sp1.com:5060 SIP/2.0
Via: SIP/2.0/TCP 192.168.202.165:5060;branch=z9hG4bK119DB8FB
Remote-Party-ID: "--CVP_11_6_1_0_0_0_329" <sip:4083926001@192.168.202.165>;party=cal
  ling;screen=yes;privacy=off
From: sip:4083926001@192.168.202.162;tag=7E3D6999-1EDC
To: <sip:9195556003@p1.sp1.com>
Date: Fri, 27 Apr 2018 22:22:21 GMT
Call-ID: 49691A93-49A011E8-999FE1BE-18C7C14D@192.168.202.165
Supported: timer,resource-priority,replaces,sdp-anat
Min-SE:  1800
Cisco-Guid: 1882732544-0000065536-0000000137-2714413248
User-Agent: Cisco-SIPGateway/IOS-16.6.1
Allow: INVITE, OPTIONS, BYE, CANCEL, ACK, PRACK, UPDATE, REFER, SUBSCRIBE, NOTIFY,
  INFO, REGISTER
CSeq: 101 INVITE
Timestamp: 1524867741
Contact: <sip:4083926001@192.168.202.165:5060;transport=tcp>
Expires: 60
Allow-Events: telephone-event
Max-Forwards: 65
X-Cisco-CCBProbe: undefined
Session-ID: 00007fd600105000a000005056a12adc;remote=00000000000000000000000000000000
Session-Expires:  1800
Content-Type: application/sdp
Content-Disposition: session;handling=required
Content-Length: 251

v=0
o=CiscoSystemsSIP-GW-UserAgent 828 5666 IN IP4 192.168.202.165
s=SIP Call
c=IN IP4 192.168.202.165
t=0 0
m=audio 8328 RTP/AVP 0 18 101
c=IN IP4 192.168.202.165
a=rtpmap:0 PCMU/8000
a=rtpmap:18 G729/8000
a=fmtp:18 annexb=no
a=rtpmap:101 telephone-event/8000
a=fmtp:101 0-16
a=ptime:20
```

Example 12-18 shows the output of **show call active voice brief** and **show voip rtp connection** after the call transfer is completed. Note that there are only two call signaling legs and two RTP connection pairs when SIP REFER is used, compared to four call signaling legs and four RTP connection pairs when SIP INVITE is used for call transfer. The call leg between CUBE and CVP (74144) has been disconnected and is no longer active after the call transfer is completed.

Example 12-18 *SIP Call Legs After the SIP REFER-Based Call Transfer Is Complete*

```
cube1# show call active voice brief
...

Telephony call-legs: 0
SIP call-legs: 2
H323 call-legs: 0
Call agent controlled call-legs: 0
SCCP call-legs: 0
STCAPP call-legs: 0
Multicast call-legs: 0
Total call-legs: 2
0 : 74143 2117867050ms.1 (22:22:17.866 UTC Fri Apr 27 2018) +3100 pid:68000 Answer
  4083926001 connected
 dur 00:00:37 tx:556/111048 rx:563/112448 dscp:0 media:0 audio tos:0xB8 video
  tos:0x0
 IP 192.168.202.162:8058 SRTP: off rtt:6ms pl:0/0ms lost:0/0/0 delay:0/0/0ms
  g711ulaw TextRelay: off Transcoded: No ICE: Off
 media inactive detected:n media contrl rcvd:n/a timestamp:n/a
 long duration call detected:n long duration call duration:n/a timestamp:n/a
 LostPacketRate:0.00 OutOfOrderRate:0.00
 LocalUUID:00007fd600105000a000005056a12adc
 RemoteUUID:000039b300105000a00000505684dea9
 VRF:
0 : 74148 2117870260ms.1 (22:22:21.076 UTC Fri Apr 27 2018) +25830 pid:68004 Origi-
  nate 9195556003 active
 dur 00:00:11 tx:563/112448 rx:556/111048 dscp:0 media:0 audio tos:0xB8 video
  tos:0x0
 IP 192.168.202.162:8060 SRTP: off rtt:3ms pl:0/0ms lost:0/0/0 delay:0/0/0ms
  g711ulaw TextRelay: off Transcoded: No ICE: Off
 media inactive detected:n media contrl rcvd:n/a timestamp:n/a
 long duration call detected:n long duration call duration:n/a timestamp:n/a
 LostPacketRate:0.00 OutOfOrderRate:0.00
 LocalUUID:000039b300105000a00000505684dea9
 RemoteUUID:00007fd600105000a000005056a12adc
 VRF:


...
cube1# show voip rtp connection
VoIP RTP Port Usage Information:
Max Ports Available: 19999, Ports Reserved: 101, Ports in Use: 2
Port range not configured
```

```
                                           Min   Max   Ports     Ports    Ports
Media-Address Range                        Port  Port  Available Reserved In-use
---------------------------------------------------------------------------------
Global Media Pool                          8000  48198 19999     101      2
---------------------------------------------------------------------------------
VoIP RTP active connections :
No. CallId  dstCallId LocalRTP RmtRTP    LocalIP           RemoteIP        MPSS  VRF
1   74143   74148     8324     8058    192.168.202.165   192.168.202.162 NO    NA
2   74148   74143     8328     8060    192.168.202.165   192.168.202.162 NO    NA
Found 2 active RTP connections
```

Courtesy Callback

Reducing customer effort is correlated with increased customer loyalty. A simple way of reducing customer effort in contact centers is to avoid or minimize the time customers wait to talk to an agent. The courtesy callback feature enables companies to free up customer time by offering customers in the call queue an option to receive a callback at their desired number without giving up their waiting position in the call queue.

Deployment and Configuration

The courtesy callback functionality is delivered using a combination of a UCCE call script, CVP VXML applications, and the survivability TCL script in CUBE (see Figure 12-28). The feature is supported in both VXML gateway and Cisco VVB deployments. VXML gateways require an additional TCL script, cvp_ccb_vxml.tcl, to be installed and configured for this function, whereas VVB doesn't require any additional configuration for courtesy callback.

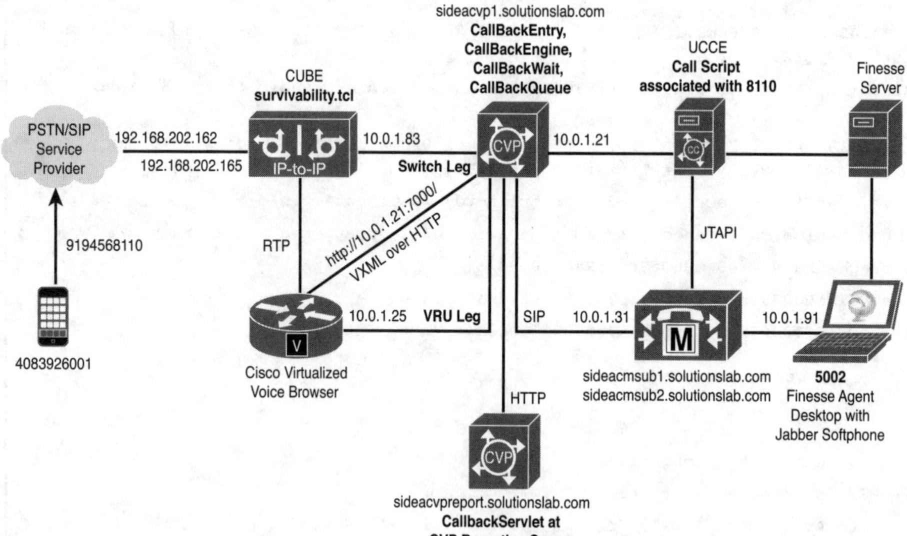

Figure 12-28 *Contact Center Deployment with the Courtesy Callback Feature*

The courtesy callback feature uses the existing dial peers configured in CUBE, as shown in Example 12-16. The dial peers 68000 and 68001 are used as inbound and outbound dial peers for the initial call from the caller to CVP through CUBE. The dial peer 68004 is used to place the outbound callback call. The survivability service application is configured with an additional parameter, ccb, as shown in Example 12-19.

Example 12-19 *CUBE Configuration for the Courtesy Callback Feature*

```
application
 service survivability flash:survivability.tcl
  param ccb id:10.0.1.83;loc:site1;trunks:25
```

The ccb parameter consists of id, loc, and trunk subparameters, which contain the IP address of CUBE (id), the site location name (loc), and the maximum number of concurrent outbound callback calls (trunks) that can be handled by CUBE. If the initial parameter values are changed, the survivability service application needs to be reloaded using the command **call application voice load** ***service-name*** in order for the new parameter values to take effect. Courtesy callback requires both detailed configuration in CVP and modifications in UCCE call scripts for successful operation. Refer to the *Cisco UCCE or PCCE Features Guide*, available at www.cisco.com, for step-by-step instructions and guidance on how to modify the UCCE call script and CVP VXML applications.

Call Flow

CUBE, CVP, and UCCE work together as described in the courtesy callback call flow:

Step 1. The inbound call from the service provider is routed to CVP through CUBE, as discussed earlier in this chapter. CVP sends a routing request to UCCE, which finds the UCCE call script associated with the dialed number. The call is then handled according to the logic defined in the script. Example 12-20 shows the inbound SIP INVITE from the service provider and the outbound SIP INIVTE to CVP with the X-Cisco-CCBProbe header carrying the CCB parameter value configured in CUBE. The outputs shown in Example 12-20 are snippets from **debug ccsip message** and **debug voip application.**

Example 12-20 *SIP Call Legs When the Caller Hears Callback Request Prompts*

```
4846078: Apr 30 23:26:55.875 UTC: //-1/xxxxxxxxxxxx/SIP/Msg/ccsipDisplayMsg:
Received:
INVITE sip:9194568110@192.168.202.165:5060;transport=tcp SIP/2.0
Via: SIP/2.0/TCP 192.168.202.169:5060;branch=z9hG4bKG5pQc+Al2l8hW28yvMt0vQ~~157
Via: SIP/2.0/TCP 192.168.202.167:5060;branch=z9hG4bKRzUwlcSQ3rMWDN01cODE+Q~~1877
Via: SIP/2.0/TCP 192.168.202.162:5060;branch=z9hG4bK24215A6
Max-Forwards: 66
Record-Route: <sip:rr$n=sp2-network@p1.example-sp2.com:5060;transport=tcp;lr>
To: <sip:9194568110@entcomp1.com>
From: <sip:4083926001@192.168.202.162>;tag=769A6575-12F1
Contact: <sip:4083926001@192.168.202.162:5060;transport=tcp>
```

```
Expires: 180
Remote-Party-ID: <sip:4083926001@192.168.202.162>;party=calling;screen=yes;privacy=off
Call-ID: C72065A7-4C0411E8-8211FA30-CAD23726@192.168.202.162
CSeq: 101 INVITE
Content-Length: 302
Date: Mon, 30 Apr 2018 23:26:43 GMT
Supported: 100rel,timer,resource-priority,replaces,sdp-anat
Min-SE: 1800
Cisco-Guid: 4142747392-0000065536-0000000181-2714413248
User-Agent: Cisco-SIPGateway/IOS-16.6.1
Allow: INVITE, OPTIONS, BYE, CANCEL, ACK, PRACK, UPDATE, REFER, SUBSCRIBE, NOTIFY,
  INFO, REGISTER
Timestamp: 1525130803
Allow-Events: telephone-event
Session-ID: 00002a1900105000a000005056a12adc;remote=00000000000000000000000000000000
Session-Expires: 1800
Content-Type: application/sdp
Content-Disposition: session;handling=required

v=0
o=CiscoSystemsSIP-GW-UserAgent 4950 6183 IN IP4 192.168.202.162
s=SIP Call
c=IN IP4 192.168.202.162
t=0 0
m=audio 8342 RTP/AVP 0 18 101
c=IN IP4 192.168.202.162
a=rtpmap:0 PCMU/8000
a=rtpmap:18 G729/8000
a=fmtp:18 annexb=no
a=rtpmap:101 telephone-event/8000
a=fmtp:101 0-15
a=ptime:20


4846558: Apr 30 23:26:56.901 UTC: //80231//TCL :/tcl_PutsObjCmd:
TCL CVP: ******* Service F6ED4F00.00010000.000000B5.A1CAA8C0 successfully registered
  ******** CallID = F6ED4F00.00010000.000000B5.A1CAA8C0


4846571: Apr 30 23:26:56.902 UTC: //80231//TCL :/tcl_PutsObjCmd:
TCL CVP: ******* Initiating transfer to CVP from ANI = sip:4083926001@192.168.202.162
  to DNIS = 9194568110 ******* CallID = F6ED4F00.00010000.000000B5.A1CAA8C0

4846701: Apr 30 23:26:56.907 UTC: //80231/F6ED4F000000/CCAPI/ccIFCallSetupRequest-
  Private:
   Interface=0x7FAE5C942DD8, Interface Type=3, Destination=, Mode=0x0,
   Call Params(Calling Number=sip:4083926001@192.168.202.162,(Calling Name=
  sip:4083926001@192.168.202.162)(TON=Unknown, NPI=Unknown, Screening=User, Passed,
  Presentation=Allowed),
```

```
  Called Number=8110(TON=Unknown, NPI=Unknown), Calling Translated=FALSE,
  Subscriber Type Str=Unknown, FinalDestinationFlag=TRUE, Outgoing Dial-peer=68001,
  Call Count On=FALSE,
  Source Trkgrp Route Label=, Target Trkgrp Route Label=, tg_label_flag=0, Application
  Call Id=)
4847292: Apr 30 23:26:56.927 UTC: //80232/F6ED4F000000/SIP/Msg/ccsipDisplayMsg:
Sent:
INVITE sip:8110@sideAcvp1.solutionslab.com:5060 SIP/2.0
Via: SIP/2.0/TCP 10.0.1.83:5060;branch=z9hG4bK134A11CC1
Remote-Party-ID: "--CVP_11_6_1_0_0_0_329" <sip:4083926001@10.0.1.83>;party=calling;scre
  en=yes;privacy=off
From: sip:4083926001@192.168.202.162;tag=8DEBA1A3-16AF
To: <sip:8110@sideAcvp1.solutionslab.com>
Date: Mon, 30 Apr 2018 23:26:56 GMT
Call-ID: CEDFE2D1-4C0411E8-B25BE1BE-18C7C14D@10.0.1.83
Supported: timer,resource-priority,replaces,sdp-anat
Min-SE:  1800
Cisco-Guid: 4142747392-0000065536-0000000181-2714413248
User-Agent: Cisco-SIPGateway/IOS-16.6.1
Allow: INVITE, OPTIONS, BYE, CANCEL, ACK, PRACK, UPDATE, REFER, SUBSCRIBE, NOTIFY,
  INFO, REGISTER
CSeq: 101 INVITE
Timestamp: 1525130816
Contact: <sip:4083926001@10.0.1.83:5060;transport=tcp>
Expires: 60
Allow-Events: telephone-event
Max-Forwards: 65
X-Cisco-CCBProbe: id:10.0.1.83;loc:site1;trunks:25
Session-ID: 00002a1900105000a000005056a12adc;remote=00000000000000000000000000000000
Session-Expires:  1800
Content-Type: application/sdp
Content-Disposition: session;handling=required
Content-Length: 308

v=0
o=CiscoSystemsSIP-GW-UserAgent 8804 3696 IN IP4 10.0.1.83
s=SIP Call
c=IN IP4 10.0.1.83
t=0 0
m=audio 8592 RTP/AVP 0 18 101 19
c=IN IP4 10.0.1.83
a=rtpmap:0 PCMU/8000
a=rtpmap:18 G729/8000
a=fmtp:18 annexb=no
a=rtpmap:101 telephone-event/8000
a=fmtp:101 0-15
a=rtpmap:19 CN/8000
a=ptime:20
```

Step 2. The UCCE call script handling the external inbound call determines whether the caller is eligible for callback functionality. This eligibility is based on business needs such as the estimated waiting time (EWT) in a call queue exceeding a given threshold (for example, 15 minutes).

> **Tip** The EWT calculation algorithm provided in the UCCE call script example that is shipped with the UCCE software requires a significant number of calls to be processed in order to statistically estimate the accurate waiting time. While testing the feature in a lab environment with slow call volume, the EWT calculated by the example algorithm could be a larger duration, and the callback will take a longer time, thereby increasing testing time. To accelerate the feature operation verification process, the EWT value can be set to a smaller static value. This can be done by setting the user.microapp.ToExtVXML[0] variable in the UCCE call script to a smaller value (for example, 300 seconds) and passing it as a parameter to the CallbackEntry VXML application. Also, the variable maxewt in the SetQueueDefaults_01.xml configuration file of the CallbackEntry VXML application in the CVP VXML server needs to be set to a smaller value. The CVP VXML application must then be restarted and redeployed, using deployApp.bat in the admin directory of the VXML application (for example, C:\Cisco\CVP\VXMLServer\applications\CallbackEntry\admin\deployApp.bat) in order to have the changed XML parameters take effect.

Step 3. If eligible, the UCCE call script executes a Run External Script node that is configured to run the CVP VXML application CallBackEntry. The CallBackEntry application can be edited to include custom prompts.

Step 4. From a SIP signaling perspective, CVP sets up a new VRU call leg with the VXML gateway or VVB and updates the switch call leg (the call leg between CUBE and CVP) such that an RTP stream is established between CUBE and the voice browser. Example 12-21 shows the two call legs 80231 with RTP streams between the service provider (192.168.202.162) and CUBE (192.168.202.165) and 80232, with RTP streams established between CUBE (10.0.1.83) and VVB (10.0.1.25). The caller is now able to interact with the IVR, powered by several CVP VXML applications discussed in subsequent steps.

Example 12-21 *SIP Call Legs When the Caller Hears Callback Request Prompts*

```
cube1# show call active voice brief
...
Telephony call-legs: 0
SIP call-legs: 2
H323 call-legs: 0
Call agent controlled call-legs: 0
SCCP call-legs: 0
STCAPP call-legs: 0
Multicast call-legs: 0
Total call-legs: 2
```

```
0    : 80231 2380945070ms.1 (23:26:55.890 UTC Mon Apr 30 2018) +1120 pid:68000
  Answer 4083926001 active
 dur 00:00:07 tx:331/66200 rx:326/65048 dscp:0 media:0 audio tos:0xB8 video tos:0x0
 IP 192.168.202.162:8342 SRTP: off rtt:0ms pl:0/0ms lost:0/0/0 delay:0/0/0ms
  g711ulaw TextRelay: off Transcoded: No ICE: Off
 media inactive detected:n media contrl rcvd:n/a timestamp:n/a
 long duration call detected:n long duration call duration:n/a timestamp:n/a
 LostPacketRate:0.00 OutOfOrderRate:0.00
 LocalUUID:00002a1900105000a000005056a12adc
 RemoteUUID:18e16cdf1000016368ed916198419d21
 VRF:
0    : 80232 2380946110ms.1 (23:26:56.930 UTC Mon Apr 30 2018) +50 pid:68001
  Originate 8110 active
 dur 00:00:07 tx:326/65048 rx:331/66200 dscp:0 media:0 audio tos:0xB8 video tos:0x0
 IP 10.0.1.25:24728 SRTP: off rtt:0ms pl:0/0ms lost:0/0/0 delay:0/0/0ms g711ulaw
  TextRelay: off Transcoded: No ICE: Off
 media inactive detected:n media contrl rcvd:n/a timestamp:n/a
 long duration call detected:n long duration call duration:n/a timestamp:n/a
 LostPacketRate:0.00 OutOfOrderRate:0.00
 LocalUUID:18e16cdf1000016368ed916198419d21
 RemoteUUID:00002a1900105000a000005056a12adc
 VRF:

...
cube1# show voip rtp connection
VoIP RTP Port Usage Information:
Max Ports Available: 19999, Ports Reserved: 101, Ports in Use: 2
Port range not configured
                                        Min  Max   Ports     Ports    Ports
Media-Address Range                     Port Port  Available Reserved In-use
------------------------------------------------------------------------------
Global Media Pool                       8000 48198 19999     101      2
------------------------------------------------------------------------------
VoIP RTP active connections :
No. CallId   dstCallId LocalRTP RmtRTP   LocalIP          RemoteIP         MPSS VRF
1   80231    80232     8590     8342   192.168.202.165  192.168.202.162  NO   NA
2   80232    80231     8592     24728    10.0.1.83        10.0.1.25        NO   NA
Found 2 active RTP connections
```

Step 5. The CallBackEntry application checks the callback eligibility criteria. If the caller is eligible, it plays a prompt that informs the caller about the EWT and asks whether the caller would like to receive a callback. If the caller isn't interested in receiving a callback, the call continues to be in the queue and is connected with an agent when one becomes available.

Step 6. If the caller opts in for callback, the CallBackEntry application asks the caller to record his or her name and provides an option to give a different callback number other than the calling party number of the current call. The callback number, the recording file containing the caller's name, and other relevant metadata are stored in the CVP reporting server. Figure 12-29 shows the DTMF between CUBE (10.0.1.83) and VVB (10.0.1.25), where the caller accepts the callback request, speaks his or her name for a recording, and then presses **#**. The call ladder diagram uses the following IP address: device mapping:

10.0.1.21: sideACVP1 server

10.0.1.25: Cisco Virtualized Voice Server

10.0.1.83: cube1 SBC

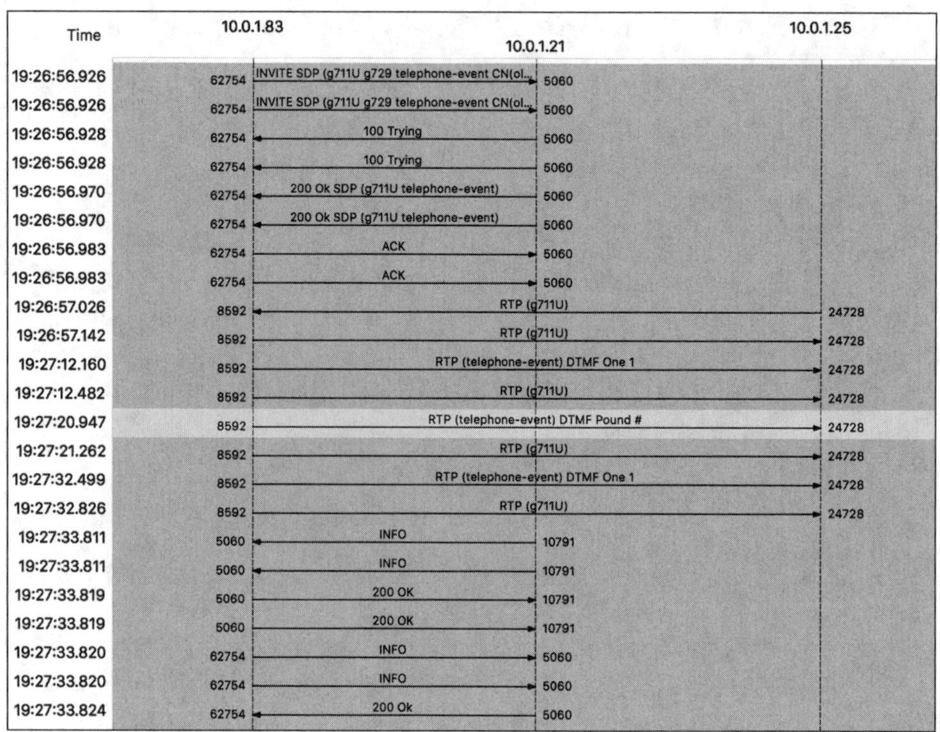

Figure 12-29 *Wireshark Call Ladder Diagram, Showing the DTMF Digits Entered*

Step 7. After successful execution of the CallBackEntry application, the UCCE call script executes another Run External Script node that is configured to run the CVP VXML application CallBackEngine.

At this time, CVP sends call handling instructions to CUBE, using SIP INFO requests containing a FACILITY message in the SIP message body. CUBE extracts the content of the FACILITY message and passes it to the survivability.tcl application, which then performs actions as specified in the FACILITY message. CVP sends call handling instructions (type=disconnect) to CUBE to disconnect the call leg between CUBE and the service provider (see Example 12-22).

Example 12-22 *SIP INFO Request from CVP to Disconnect the Inbound Call Leg*

```
4848736: Apr 30 23:27:38.471 UTC: //-1/xxxxxxxxxxxx/SIP/Msg/ccsipDisplayMsg:
Received:
INFO sip:4083926001@10.0.1.83:5060;transport=tcp SIP/2.0
Via: SIP/2.0/TCP 10.0.1.21:5060;branch=z9hG4bKk9F7UjU8zHQ4XN9JOnRWyA~~1884
Max-Forwards: 69
To: <sip:4083926001@192.168.202.162>;tag=8DEBA1A3-16AF
From: <sip:8110@sideAcvp1.solutionslab.com>;tag=ds8da98733
Call-ID: CEDFE2D1-4C0411E8-B25BE1BE-18C7C14D@10.0.1.83
CSeq: 2 INFO
Content-Length: 45
Contact: <sip:10.0.1.21:5060;transport=tcp>
Allow: INVITE, INFO, BYE, CANCEL, ACK, UPDATE
Content-Disposition: signal;handling=optional
Supported: sdp-anat
Content-Type: application/gtd

INF,
UUS,,747970653d646973636f6e6e656374
...
4848757: Apr 30 23:27:38.472 UTC: //80232/F6ED4F000000/CCAPI/cc_api_call_facility:
   Interface=0x7FAE5C942DD8, Call Id=80232
...

4848826: Apr 30 23:27:38.475 UTC: //80231//AFW_:/AFW_FSM_Drive: ACTION BEGIN: ------
  (CC_INTERCEPT[17],ev_facility[25])---[CourtesyCallback]------
...
4848848: Apr 30 23:27:38.476 UTC: //80232/F6ED4F000000/SIP/Msg/ccsipDisplayMsg:
Sent:
SIP/2.0 200 OK
Via: SIP/2.0/TCP 10.0.1.21:5060;branch=z9hG4bKk9F7UjU8zHQ4XN9JOnRWyA~~1884
From: <sip:8110@sideAcvp1.solutionslab.com>;tag=ds8da98733
To: sip:4083926001@192.168.202.162;tag=8DEBA1A3-16AF
Date: Mon, 30 Apr 2018 23:27:38 GMT
Call-ID: CEDFE2D1-4C0411E8-B25BE1BE-18C7C14D@10.0.1.83
Server: Cisco-SIPGateway/IOS-16.6.1
CSeq: 2 INFO
Session-ID: 00002a1900105000a000005056a12adc;remote=18e16cdf1000016368ed916198419d21
Contact: <sip:4083926001@10.0.1.83:5060;transport=tcp>
Content-Length: 0


...
4848850: Apr 30 23:27:38.476 UTC: //80231//TCL :/tcl_PutsObjCmd:
TCL CVP: ******* CourtesyCallback: msg from VXML gateway: type=disconnect CallID =
  F6ED4F00.00010000.000000B5.A1CAA8C0
4848851: Apr 30 23:27:38.476 UTC: //80231//TCL :/tcl_InfotagObjCmd:  infotag get
  con_ofleg 80232
...
4848961: Apr 30 23:27:38.480 UTC: //80231//TCL :/tcl_PutsObjCmd:
TCL CVP: ******* Procedure CC_DisconnectIncoming ******** CallID =
  F6ED4F00.00010000.000000B5.A1CAA8C0
4848962: Apr 30 23:27:38.481 UTC: //80231//TCL :/tcl_LegObjCmd:  leg disconnect 80231
```

Step 8. CallbackEngine invokes the CallbackWait application to keep the call active and take action when the EWT expires. The call leg between CUBE and CVP (80232), shown in Example 12-23, is kept active by CUBE sending in-dialog SIP OPTIONS keepalive messages every minute.

Example 12-23 *Output of* **show call active voice brief** *After Callback Is Scheduled.*

```
cube1# show call active voice brief
Telephony call-legs: 0
SIP call-legs: 1
H323 call-legs: 0
Call agent controlled call-legs: 0
SCCP call-legs: 0
STCAPP call-legs: 0
Multicast call-legs: 0
Total call-legs: 1
0   : 80232 2380946110ms.1 (23:26:56.921 UTC Mon Apr 30 2018) +50 pid:68001 Originate
   8110 active
 dur 00:01:00 tx:2041/404936 rx:3003/563400 dscp:0 media:0 audio tos:0xB8 video
  tos:0x0
 IP 10.0.1.25:24728 SRTP: off rtt:0ms pl:0/0ms lost:0/0/0 delay:0/0/0ms g711ulaw
  TextRelay: off Transcoded: No ICE: Off
 media inactive detected:n media contrl rcvd:n/a timestamp:n/a
 long duration call detected:n long duration call duration:n/a timestamp:n/a
 LostPacketRate:0.00 OutOfOrderRate:0.00
 LocalUUID:18e16cdf1000016368ed916198419d21
 RemoteUUID:00002a1900105000a000005056a12adc
 VRF:

...
cube1# show voip rtp connection
VoIP RTP Port Usage Information:
Max Ports Available: 19999, Ports Reserved: 101, Ports in Use: 1
Port range not configured
                                       Min   Max   Ports     Ports     Ports
Media-Address Range                    Port  Port  Available Reserved  In-use
------------------------------------------------------------------------------
Global Media Pool                      8000  48198 19999     101       1
------------------------------------------------------------------------------
VoIP RTP active connections :
No. CallId   dstCallId  LocalRTP   RmtRTP    LocalIP     RemoteIP    MPSS    VRF
1   80232    80231      8592       24728     10.0.1.83   10.0.1.25   NO      NA
Found 1 active RTP connections
```

Step 9. After the estimated wait time has expired, CVP sends call handling instructions (type=reconnect) to CUBE to place an outbound call to the callback number provided by caller earlier. The corresponding SIP INFO request message is shown in Example 12-24.

Example 12-24 *SIP INFO Request from CVP to CUBE to Place an Outbound Callback Call*

```
4849907: Apr 30 23:40:44.542 UTC: //-1/xxxxxxxxxxxx/SIP/Msg/ccsipDisplayMsg:
Received:
INFO sip:4083926001@10.0.1.83:5060;transport=tcp SIP/2.0
Via: SIP/2.0/TCP 10.0.1.21:5060;branch=z9hG4bKk9F7UjU8zHQ4XN9JOnRWyA~~1886
Max-Forwards: 69
To: <sip:4083926001@192.168.202.162>;tag=8DEBA1A3-16AF
From: <sip:8110@sideAcvp1.solutionslab.com>;tag=ds8da98733
Call-ID: CEDFE2D1-4C0411E8-B25BE1BE-18C7C14D@10.0.1.83
CSeq: 3 INFO
Content-Length: 229
Contact: <sip:10.0.1.21:5060;transport=tcp>
Allow: INVITE, INFO, BYE, CANCEL, ACK, UPDATE
Content-Disposition: signal;handling=optional
Supported: sdp-anat
Content-Type: application/gtd

INF,
UUS,,747970653d677569643d4636454434463030303030313030303030303030303042354131434141 3
  8433020747970653d7265636f6e6e65637420646e69733d343038333932363030312063 6c693d38303
  035353531323132207 26e613d3330207575693d22757575757522


...
4849997: Apr 30 23:40:44.549 UTC: //80231//TCL :/tcl_PutsObjCmd:
TCL CVP: ******* CourtesyCallback: msg from VXML gateway: type=guid=F6ED4F0000010000
  000000B5A1CAA8C0 type=reconnect dnis=4083926001 cli=8005551212 rna=30 uui="uuuuu"
  CallID = F6ED4F00.00010000.000000B5.A1CAA8C0

4850103: Apr 30 23:40:44.558 UTC: //-1/xxxxxxxxxxxx/CCAPI/ccIFCallSetupRequest
  Private:
   Interface=0x7FAE5C942DD8, Interface Type=3, Destination=, Mode=0x0,
   Call Params(Calling Number=8005551212,(Calling Name=8005551212)(TON=Unknown,
  NPI=Unknown, Screening=Not Screened, Presentation=Allowed),
   Called Number=4083926001(TON=Unknown, NPI=Unknown), Calling Translated=FALSE,
   Subscriber Type Str=, FinalDestinationFlag=FALSE, Outgoing Dial-peer=68004, Call
  Count On=FALSE,
   Source Trkgrp Route Label=, Target Trkgrp Route Label=, tg_label_flag=0,
  Application Call Id=)
4850502: Apr 30 23:40:44.591 UTC: //-1/xxxxxxxxxxxx/SIP/Msg/ccsipDisplayMsg:
Sent:
INVITE sip:4083926001@p1.example-sp2.com:5060 SIP/2.0
Via: SIP/2.0/TCP 192.168.202.165:5060;branch=z9hG4bK134B3A7B
Remote-Party-ID: <sip:8005551212@192.168.202.165>;party=calling;screen=no;
  privacy=off
From: <sip:8005551212@192.168.202.165>;tag=8DF842A7-37F
To: <sip:4083926001@p1.example-sp2.com>
```

```
Date: Mon, 30 Apr 2018 23:40:44 GMT
Call-ID: BC311AAB-4C0611E8-B25FE1BE-18C7C14D@172.18.110.203
Supported: timer,resource-priority,replaces,sdp-anat
Min-SE:  1800
Cisco-Guid: 3157214771-1275466216-2992431550-0415744333
User-Agent: Cisco-SIPGateway/IOS-16.6.1
Allow: INVITE, OPTIONS, BYE, CANCEL, ACK, PRACK, UPDATE, REFER, SUBSCRIBE, NOTIFY,
  INFO, REGISTER
CSeq: 101 INVITE
Max-Forwards: 70
Timestamp: 1525131644
Contact: <sip:8005551212@192.168.202.165:5060;transport=tcp>
Expires: 60
Allow-Events: telephone-event
Session-ID: d24d844ba2b458399f8ac4eb8393f5e6;remote=00000000000000000000000000000000
Content-Type: multipart/mixed;boundary=uniqueBoundary
Mime-Version: 1.0
Content-Length: 548
```

Step 10. When the caller answers the call, the CallBackWait VXML application plays the recorded name and asks the caller to confirm by either accepting the callback or canceling the callback. The results of the CallBackEngine application execution are passed to the UCCE call script as ECC variables.

Step 11. The UCCE call script checks ECC variable values to determine whether the user canceled or accepted the callback request. It disconnects the call if the callback request was canceled. If the callback request was accepted, it executes the Run External Script node that is configured to run CallbackQueue as the CVP VXML application.

Step 12. The CallbackQueue application places the caller in the specified call queue and plays queue music.

Step 13. When the agent is available, CVP disconnects the VRU call leg and connects the called-back caller and agent.

The core logic of the callback application resides within the CVP VXML applications and CVP reporting server. The CVP reporting server plays the role of a web server that hosts two Java servlets named CallbackServlet and DB Servlet. These two servlets are invoked by the VXML applications to store and retrieve callback-related information. When users report that callback functionality isn't working correctly, the first thing to verify is whether the CVP reporting server is up and running and able to access its database.

Example 12-25 shows the activity log snippet of the CallbackQueue VXML application in which it experiences a 500 Internal Server Error while invoking the CallbackServlet running on the CVP reporting server. The CVP reporting server isn't able to process this request because its database is offline. The activity logs of the VXML application are available in the folder C:\Cisco\CVP\VXMLServer\applications\CallbackQueue\logs\ActivityLog, and the default logs levels are sufficient for troubleshooting purposes.

Example 12-25 *Activity Log of the CallbackQueue VXML Application*

```
10.0.1.21.1518920793286.25.CallbackQueue,02/17/2018 21:26:33.286,,start,parameter,
  CallbackType=
10.0.1.21.1518920793286.25.CallbackQueue,02/17/2018 21:26:33.286,,start,parameter,
  _userCourtesyCallbackEnabled=1
10.0.1.21.1518920793286.25.CallbackQueue,02/17/2018 21:26:33.286,,start,parameter,
  qname=billing
10.0.1.21.1518920793286.25.CallbackQueue,02/17/2018 21:26:33.286,,start,parameter,
  ccError=true
10.0.1.21.1518920793286.25.CallbackQueue,02/17/2018 21:26:33.286,,start,parameter,
  callid=1442A900000100000000000101E01000A
10.0.1.21.1518920793286.25.CallbackQueue,02/17/2018 21:26:33.286,,start,parameter,
  queueapp=BillingQueue
10.0.1.21.1518920793286.25.CallbackQueue,02/17/2018 21:26:33.286,,start,parameter,
  qtime=1518920772755
10.0.1.21.1518920793286.25.CallbackQueue,02/17/2018 21:26:33.286,,start,parameter,
  _dnis=8110
10.0.1.21.1518920793286.25.CallbackQueue,02/17/2018 21:26:33.286,,start,parameter,
  _ccbServlet=http://10.0.1.20:8000/cvp/CallbackServlet
10.0.1.21.1518920793286.25.CallbackQueue,02/17/2018 21:26:33.286,,start,parameter,
  _ani=5001
10.0.1.21.1518920793286.25.CallbackQueue,02/17/2018 21:26:33.286,,start,parameter,
  _ccbServletReqTimeout=20
10.0.1.21.1518920793286.25.CallbackQueue,02/17/2018 21:26:33.286,CVP Subdialog
  Start_01,enter,
10.0.1.21.1518920793286.25.CallbackQueue,02/17/2018 21:26:33.317,CVP Subdialog
  Start_01,exit,done
10.0.1.21.1518920793286.25.CallbackQueue,02/17/2018 21:26:33.317,Decision_01,enter,
10.0.1.21.1518920793286.25.CallbackQueue,02/17/2018 21:26:33.317,Decision_01,exit,
  callbackError
10.0.1.21.1518920793286.25.CallbackQueue,02/17/2018 21:26:33.317,Announce Callback
  Error,enter,
10.0.1.21.1518920793286.25.CallbackQueue,02/17/2018 21:26:33.317,Announce Callback
  Error,interaction,audio_group,initial_audio_group
10.0.1.21.1518920793286.25.CallbackQueue,02/17/2018 21:26:33.317,Announce Callback
  Error,exit,done
10.0.1.21.1518920793286.25.CallbackQueue,02/17/2018 21:26:33.317,UpdateStatus_01,enter,
10.0.1.21.1518920793286.25.CallbackQueue,02/17/2018 21:26:33.317,UpdateStatus_01,
  custom,Callback_Update_Status,ELEMENT_ENTRY
10.0.1.21.1518920793286.25.CallbackQueue,02/17/2018 21:26:33.317,UpdateStatus_01,
  interaction,audio_group,initial_audio_group
10.0.1.21.1518920793286.25.CallbackQueue,02/17/2018 21:26:35.333,UpdateStatus_01,
  element,error,error.badfetch.http.404
```

```
10.0.1.21.1518920793286.25.CallbackQueue,02/17/2018 21:26:35.333,UpdateStatus_01,exit,
10.0.1.21.1518920793286.25.CallbackQueue,02/17/2018 21:26:35.333,,element,error,
10.0.1.21.1518920793286.25.CallbackQueue,02/17/2018 21:26:43.364,,element,warning,do
  Decision- Error while sending Callback_Update_Status request to CallbackServlet -
Error: Failed to connect to the servlet -- "HTTP/1.1 500 Internal Server Error\
```

The simplest way to verify CVP reporting server operational status is to use the CVP operations console and check the database connectivity by using the Database Administration option, as shown in Figure 12-30.

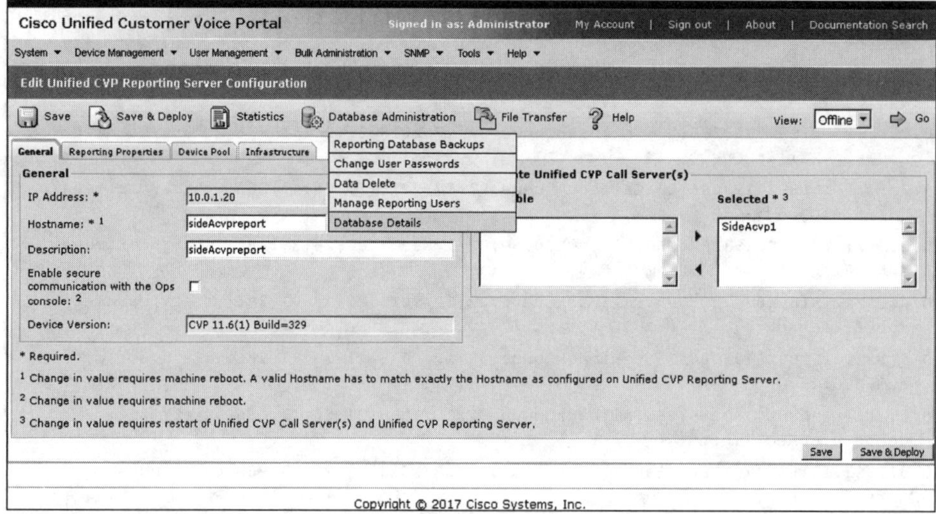

Figure 12-30 *CVP Reporting Server Configuration in the CVP Operations Console*

Call Progress Analysis (CPA)

The call flows discussed in previous sections revolve around inbound calls to a contact center. Another key aspect of a contact center is outbound engagement with customers. Several business use cases benefit from the ability to automatically dial customer phone numbers in a given list. These uses cases include marketing campaigns, tax bill and credit card payment collections, and emergency announcements. The SIP dialer component in the Cisco UCCE solution provides such automatic outbound dialing capability.

When the SIP dialer dials the phone numbers from a given list, not all calls are answered by humans. Some calls may be answered by answering machines or fax machines, and some numbers may ring busy or may no longer be valid. In order to optimize the agent workflow and to increase the productivity of the agents, the call progress analysis (CPA) feature can be enabled in the outbound calls so that only the calls that are answered by humans are connected to live agents. Other calls are instead disconnected and retried later, routed to a VRU, or removed from the list to dial in the future.

The CPA feature works by analyzing the first few seconds of the audio stream from the called party by using digital signal processors (DSPs) and detecting whether the audio is live speech, a fax/modem tone, an answering machine tone, or a special information tone (SIT). SIT is defined in ITU-T E.168/Q.35 as a sequence of three successive tones in the frequency range 950 (±50) Hz, 1400 (±50) Hz, and 1800 (±50) Hz, played by service provider networks to indicate different call failure conditions. These tones represent failures such as no circuit available and invalid or unregistered phone number. SIT tones are usually followed by a recorded announcement that provides the call failure reason.

When an outbound call from the SIP dialer is routed through CUBE to the service provider, CUBE performs CPA by invoking local DSP resources. This allows CUBE to analyze the RTP stream coming from the provider and inform the SIP dialer about the detected CPA event using a SIP UPDATE request. The SIP dialer then takes appropriate action, depending on the type of event detected, such as transferring the call to an agent or to a VRU or disconnecting the call. Table 12-2 shows a list of CPA events supported by CUBE.

Table 12-2 *Call Progress Events Detected by CUBE*

CPA Event	Description
Asm	Answering machine
AsmT	Answering machine termination tone
CpaS	Start of the CPA
FT	Fax/modem tone. Indicates detection of 2100 Hz CED/ANS tone or 2100 Hz ANSam tone with phase reversal.
LS	Live human speech
LV	Low volume or dead air call
SitIC	Operator intercept special information tone: ■ First tone frequency: 913.8 Hz (274 ms) ■ Second tone frequency: 1370.6 Hz (274 ms) ■ Third tone frequency: 1776.7 Hz (380 ms)
SitNC	No circuit special information tone: ■ First tone frequency: 985.2 Hz (380 ms) ■ Second tone frequency: 1428.5 Hz (380 ms) ■ Third tone frequency: 1776.7 Hz (380 ms)
SitVC	Vacant code (unregistered number) special information tone: ■ First tone frequency: 985.2 Hz (380 ms) ■ Second tone frequency: 1370.6 Hz (274 ms) ■ Third tone frequency: 1776.7 Hz (380 ms)

CPA Event	Description
SitRO	Reorder special information tone: ■ First tone frequency: 913.8 Hz (274 ms) ■ Second tone frequency: 1428.5 Hz (380 ms) ■ Third tone frequency: 1776.7 Hz (380 ms)
SitMT	Miscellaneous SIT tone

Deployment and Configuration

Figure 12-31 shows a sample UCCE deployment in which an agent-based campaign is configured to import contacts from the Import.txt file. The import file path is configured using the UCCE Configuration Manager tool (**Outbound Option > Import Rules**). The Campaign Manager process in the UCCE logger server processes the contact's information, reserves an agent, and asks the SIP dialer to place calls to multiple contacts for each available agent line. The SIP dialer installed on a UCCE PG server (10.0.1.15) is configured to originate outbound calls through CUBE (10.0.1.83) after adding the prefix 88 to the called party number. Note that the SIP dialer can also be configured to route calls to CUSP for call routing redundancy purposes. The first human contact to answer the call is then transferred by the SIP dialer to the reserved agent.

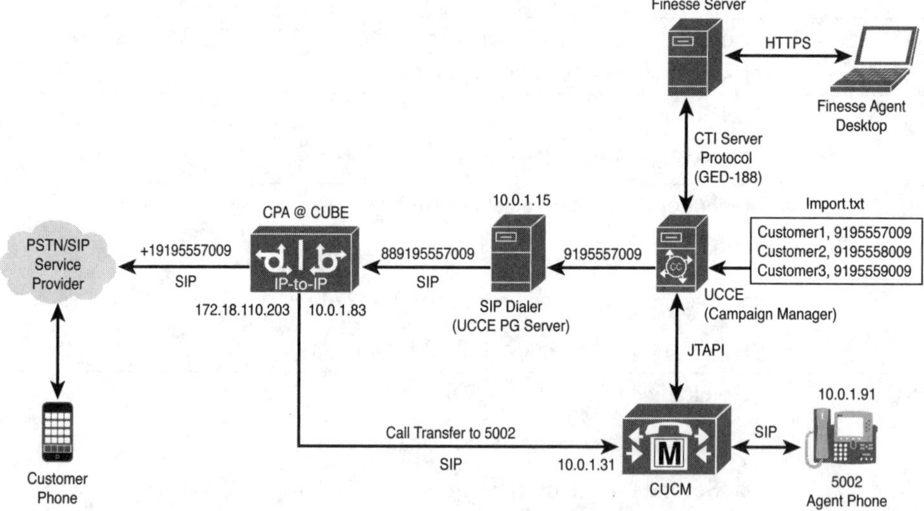

Figure 12-31 *UCCE Deployment with an Outbound SIP Dialer*

CUBE is configured with a Local Transcoding Interface (LTI)–based universal transcoder DSPFarm resource, with the command **call-progress-analysis** to perform CPA (see Example 12-26). The dial peers 68005 and 68006 are used as inbound and outbound dial peers for the call destined to 889195557009. The translation profile in the outbound dial peer removes the prefix 88 and adds +1 to make the number E.164 compliant. An important command to note is **voice-class sip rel1xx supported "100rel"**, which enables 1xx reliable provisional responses for SIP dialer calls.

When a call is answered by a human, the SIP dialer sends a SIP REFER to CUBE to transfer the customer call to the reserved agent (5002). The command **no supplementary-service sip refer** tells CUBE to consume the SIP REFER and not pass it to the service provider. CUBE uses the dial peer 68007 to route the agent (5002) call through CUCM and renegotiate the media codecs between both the CUBE–to–service provider call leg and the CUBE–to–CUCM call leg. This is because of the command **supplementary-service media-renegotiate** being present. (See the document *Outbound Option Guide for Unified Contact Center Enterprise* associated with the deployed UCCE software release for step-by-step instructions on setting up the SIP dialer and relevant UCCE configuration.)

Example 12-26 *CUBE Configuration for the CPA Feature*

```
voice service voip
 no supplementary-service sip refer
 supplementary-service media-renegotiate
 sip
  rel1xx disable
!
voice translation-rule 11
 rule 1 /^88\(.*\)/ /+1\1/
!
voice translation-profile add-plus-sign
 translate called 11
!
dspfarm profile 11 transcode universal
 codec g729abr8
 codec g729ar8
 codec g711alaw
 codec g711ulaw
 codec g729r8
 call-progress-analysis
 maximum sessions 10
 associate application CUBE
!
dial-peer voice 68005 voip
 description "Inbound dial-peer for calls from SIP Dialer"
 session protocol sipv2
 session transport tcp
 incoming called-number 88.........$
```

```
 voice-class codec 1
 voice-class sip rel1xx supported "100rel"
 dtmf-relay rtp-nte
 no vad
!
dial-peer voice 68006 voip
 description "Outbound calls to SP"
 translation-profile outgoing add-plus-sign
 destination-pattern 88.........$
 session protocol sipv2
 session target ipv4:172.18.110.59
 session transport tcp
 voice-class codec 1
 voice-class sip rel1xx supported "100rel"
 voice-class sip bind control source-interface GigabitEthernet0/0/2
 voice-class sip bind media source-interface GigabitEthernet0/0/2
 dtmf-relay rtp-nte
 no vad
!
dial-peer voice 68007 voip
 description "Outbound calls to Contact Center Agents"
 destination-pattern 5...
 session protocol sipv2
 session target ipv4:10.0.1.31
 session transport tcp
 voice-class codec 1
 voice-class sip rel1xx supported "100rel"
 voice-class sip bind control source-interface GigabitEthernet0/0/3
 voice-class sip bind media source-interface GigabitEthernet0/0/3
 dtmf-relay rtp-nte
 no vad
!
```

Tip Are you wondering why the outbound calls are prefixed with 88? The reason is that even though the SIP reliable provisional response is a key requirement for interoperation with the SIP dialer, it is unsupported by CVP and is globally disabled using the command **rel1xx disable** under **voice service voip** in the CUBE configuration. Prefixing the SIP dialer calls with 88 makes it easier to match a separate inbound dial peer that has SIP reliable provisional response enabled (**voice-class sip rel1xx supported "100rel"**) so that rel1xx is enabled only for SIP dialer calls.

Example 12-27 shows the default values for the CPA-related parameters configured under the **voice service voip** mode. The command **cpa timing live-person** defines the amount of time CUBE waits for live speech to be detected after the call is answered. The default value is 2.5 seconds, and it can be increased to 5 seconds to increase the live speech detection accuracy. Some parameters are also specified in the SIP INVITE received from the SIP dialer. The parameter values in the SIP INVITE take precedence over the configured values in CUBE. The **show dspfarm profile** *<profile ID>* command can be used to verify whether CPA is enabled on a given dspfarm profile, as shown in Example 12-27.

Example 12-27 *Default Parameter Values for the Call Progress Analysis Feature*

```
cube1# show run all | i cpa
 cpa cpa timing silent 375
 cpa timing live-person 2500
 cpa timing timeout 3000
 cpa timing noise-period 100
 cpa timing valid-speech 112
 cpa timing term-tone 15000
 cpa threshold noise-level max -50dBm0
 cpa threshold noise-level min -60dBm0
 cpa threshold active-signal 15db
 cpa threshold term-tone min-freq 300
 cpa threshold term-tone min-duration 80



cube1# show dspfarm profile 11
Dspfarm Profile Configuration

 Profile ID = 11, Service =Universal TRANSCODING, Resource ID = 6
 Profile Service Mode : Non Secure
 Profile Admin State : UP
 Profile Operation State : ACTIVE
 Application : CUBE   Status : ASSOCIATED
 Resource Provider : FLEX_DSPRM   Status : UP
 Total Number of Resources Configured : 10
 Total Number of Resources Available : 10
 Total Number of Resources Out of Service : 0
 Total Number of Resources Active : 0
 Codec Configuration: num_of_codecs:5
 Codec : g729r8, Maximum Packetization Period : 60
 Codec : g711ulaw, Maximum Packetization Period : 30
 Codec : g711alaw, Maximum Packetization Period : 30
 Codec : g729ar8, Maximum Packetization Period : 60
 Codec : g729abr8, Maximum Packetization Period : 60
 Call Progress Analysis : ENABLED
cube1#
```

Outbound Dialer Call Flow

Figure 12-32 shows the call flow of an outbound call originated from the SIP dialer (10.0.1.15) destined to 889195557009 through CUBE (10.0.1.83). CUBE transforms the called number to +19195557009 and originates an outbound SIP INVITE to the service provider. The call flow diagram is the output generated from TranslatorX, using the call IDs shown in Table 12-3.

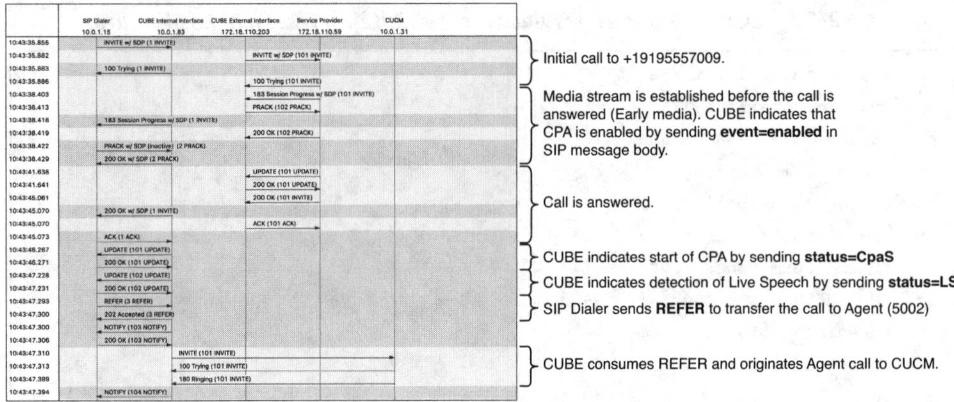

Figure 12-32 *UCCE Deployment with an Outbound SIP Dialer*

Table 12-3 *SIP Call IDs for the Outbound Dialer Call Flow*

Call Leg	Call ID
SIP Dialer–CUBE	15634e6a-37374904-fa077d2c-be0fc630
CUBE–Service provider	28491C3D-550811E8-960FE1BE-18C7C14D@172.18.110.203
CUBE–CUCM	2F1958D1-550811E8-961BE1BE-18C7C14D@10.0.1.83

The following steps occur at this stage:

Step 1. The SIP dialer sends a SIP INVITE to CUBE with the message body containing two content types, application/SDP and application/x-cisco-cpa, as shown in Example 12-28. The SDP section contains details about media capabilities, and x-cisco-cpa contains CPA-related parameters and a list of events to be detected. The SIP dialer indicates that support for reliable provisional response is mandatory by including the Require header with "100rel" as the value. The SIP dialer sets the media IP address to 0.0.0.0 in the SDP because it doesn't handle media streams.

Example 12-28 *SIP INVITE from the SIP Dialer to CUBE*

```
19587487: May 12 10:43:35.855 UTC: //-1/xxxxxxxxxxxx/SIP/Msg/ccsipDisplayMsg:
Received:
INVITE sip:889197447009@10.0.1.83 SIP/2.0
Via: SIP/2.0/UDP 10.0.1.15:58800;branch=z9hG4bK-d8754z-ff60df5c5166d862-1---d8754z-;
  rport
Max-Forwards: 70
Require: 100rel
Contact: <sip:3002@10.0.1.15:58800>
To: <sip:889197447009@10.0.1.83>
From: <sip:3002@10.0.1.15>;tag=ca364f70
Call-ID: 15634e6a-37374904-fa077d2c-be0fc630
CSeq: 1 INVITE
Session-Expires: 1800
Min-SE: 90
Allow: INVITE, ACK, CANCEL, OPTIONS, BYE, UPDATE, NOTIFY, PRACK, REFER, NOTIFY,
  OPTIONS
Content-Type: Multipart/mixed;boundary=uniqueBoundary
Supported: timer, resource-priority, replaces
User-Agent: Cisco-SIPDialer/UCCE10.0
Content-Length: 608
Remote-Party-ID: <sip:@10.0.1.83>;party=calling;screen=no;privacy=off

--uniqueBoundary
Content-Type: application/sdp
Content-Disposition: session;handling=required

v=0
o=CiscoSystemsSIP-GW-UserAgent 2884 2524 IN IP4 172.19.155.41
s=SIP Call
c=IN IP4 0.0.0.0
t=0 0
m=audio 19994 RTP/AVP 0 101
a=rtpmap:0 PCMU/8000
a=rtpmap:101 telephone-event/8000
a=fmtp:101 0-16
a=ptime:20

--uniqueBoundary
Content-Type: application/x-cisco-cpa
Content-Disposition: signal;handling=optional
```

```
Events=FT,Asm,AsmT,Sit,Piano
CPAMinSilencePeriod=608
CPAAnalysisPeriod=2500
CPAMaxTimeAnalysis=5000
CPAMaxTermToneAnalysis=30000
CPAMinValidSpeechTime=112

--uniqueBoundary--
...
19588041: May 12 10:43:35.872 UTC: //203857/2845C0C89609/SIP/Info/notify/33024/sip
  SPIupdateXcoderForCPA: Only CPA needs xcoder
19588042: May 12 10:43:35.872 UTC: //203857/2845C0C89609/SIP/Info/notify/33024/sip
  SPIupdateXcoderForCPA: XCODER needed for CPA feature
```

Step 2. CUBE processes the SIP INVITE, finds 68005 and 68006 as matching inbound and outbound dial peers, and allocates a transcoder for the CPA feature. It sends a SIP INVITE to the service provider with the Call-ID set to 28491C3D-550811E8-960FE1BE-18C7C14D@172.18.110.203.

Step 3. CUBE receives a 183 Session Progress message from the service provider and establishes early media. CUBE acknowledges receipt of the 183 Session Progress message by sending a provisional ACK (PRACK) and receives a 200 OK (CSeq: 2 PRACK) from the service provider. This establishes a bidirectional RTP connection between CUBE and the service provider.

Step 4. In parallel, CUBE also sends a 183 Session Progress message to the SIP dialer and indicates that the CPA feature is enabled for this call, by sending event=enabled in the x-cisco-cpa message body content (see Example 12-29). CUBE receives a PRACK from the SIP dialer and sends a 200 OK. Note that the SIP dialer marks the RTP stream as inactive by using a=inactive in the SDP section of the PRACK, and hence CUBE doesn't forward the RTP stream received from the service provider to the SIP dialer during this time.

Example 12-29 *SIP 183 Session Progress and PRACK Between CUBE and the SIP Dialer*

```
19590126: May 12 10:43:38.418 UTC: //203856/2845C0C89609/SIP/Msg/ccsipDisplayMsg:
Sent:
SIP/2.0 183 Session Progress
Via: SIP/2.0/UDP 10.0.1.15:58800;branch=z9hG4bK-d8754z-ff60df5c5166d862-1---d8754z-;
  rport
```

```
From: <sip:3002@10.0.1.15>;tag=ca364f70
To: <sip:889197447009@10.0.1.83>;tag=C8FD1D35-E66
Date: Sat, 12 May 2018 10:43:35 GMT
Call-ID: 15634e6a-37374904-fa077d2c-be0fc630
CSeq: 1 INVITE
Require: 100rel
RSeq: 9024
Allow: INVITE, OPTIONS, BYE, CANCEL, ACK, PRACK, UPDATE, REFER, SUBSCRIBE, NOTIFY,
  INFO, REGISTER
Allow-Events: telephone-event
Remote-Party-ID: <sip:9197447009@10.0.1.83>;party=called;screen=no;privacy=off
Contact: <sip:889197447009@10.0.1.83:5060>
Supported: sdp-anat
Server: Cisco-SIPGateway/IOS-16.6.1
Session-ID: 1c4fdaae3acf5c43842299977e4f2a50;remote=2258fb31a45c582f9ecff9488a271d3f
Content-Type: multipart/mixed;boundary=uniqueBoundary
Mime-Version: 1.0
Content-Length: 488

--uniqueBoundary
Content-Type: application/sdp
Content-Disposition: session;handling=required

v=0
o=CiscoSystemsSIP-GW-UserAgent 735 9243 IN IP4 10.0.1.83
s=SIP Call
c=IN IP4 172.18.110.203
t=0 0
m=audio 8754 RTP/AVP 0 101
c=IN IP4 172.18.110.203
a=rtpmap:0 PCMU/8000
a=rtpmap:101 telephone-event/8000
a=fmtp:101 0-16
a=ptime:20

--uniqueBoundary
Content-Type: application/x-cisco-cpa
Content-Disposition: signal;handling=optional

event=enabled
--uniqueBoundary--
```

```
19590227: May 12 10:43:38.422 UTC: //-1/xxxxxxxxxxxx/SIP/Msg/ccsipDisplayMsg:
Received:
PRACK sip:889197447009@10.0.1.83:5060 SIP/2.0
Via: SIP/2.0/UDP 10.0.1.15:58800;branch=z9hG4bK-d8754z-954e3f61645b9b6a-1---d8754z-;
  rport
Max-Forwards: 70
Contact: <sip:3002@10.0.1.15:58800>
To: <sip:889197447009@10.0.1.83>;tag=C8FD1D35-E66
From: <sip:3002@10.0.1.15>;tag=ca364f70
Call-ID: 15634e6a-37374904-fa077d2c-be0fc630
CSeq: 2 PRACK
Content-Disposition: session;handling=required
Content-Type: application/sdp
User-Agent: Cisco-SIPDialer/UCCE10.0
RAck: 9024 1 INVITE
Content-Length: 242

v=0
o=CiscoSystemsSIP-GW-UserAgent 735 9243 IN IP4 0.0.0.0
s=SIP Call
c=IN IP4 0.0.0.0
t=0 0
m=audio 8754 RTP/AVP 0 101
c=IN IP4 0.0.0.0
a=rtpmap:0 PCMU/8000
a=rtpmap:101 telephone-event/8000
a=fmtp:101 0-16
a=ptime:20
a=inactive
```

Step 5. The call gets answered, and CUBE receives a 200 OK message from the service provider. CUBE then sends a 200 OK to the SIP dialer and receives the corresponding ACK. It then sends an ACK to the service provider. Example 12-30 shows the output of **show call active voice brief**, containing two active call legs, the first one between CUBE and the SIP dialer (203856) and second one between CUBE and the service provider (203857). Note that the second call leg has "Transcoded: Yes", which indicates that a transcoder resource is invoked for this call leg. This transcoder resource performs the CPA function.

Example 12-30 *SIP Call Legs After an Outbound Call Is Answered*

```
cube1# show call active voice brief
...
Telephony call-legs: 0
SIP call-legs: 2
H323 call-legs: 0
Call agent controlled call-legs: 0
SCCP call-legs: 0
STCAPP call-legs: 0
Multicast call-legs: 0
Total call-legs: 2
27F1 : 203856 3371945050ms.1 (10:43:35.866 UTC Sat May 12 2018) +-1 pid:68005 Answer
  active
 dur 00:00:00 tx:0/0 rx:0/0 dscp:0 media:0 audio tos:0xB8 video tos:0x0
 IP 0.0.0.0:19994 SRTP: off rtt:0ms pl:0/0ms lost:0/0/0 delay:0/0/0ms g711ulaw
  TextRelay: off Transcoded: No ICE: Off
 media inactive detected:n media contrl rcvd:n/a timestamp:n/a
 long duration call detected:n long duration call duration:n/a timestamp:n/a
 LostPacketRate:0.00 OutOfOrderRate:0.00
 LocalUUID:2258fb31a45c582f9ecff9488a271d3f
 RemoteUUID:00000000000000000000000000000000
 VRF:
27F1 : 203857 3371945070ms.1 (10:43:35.886 UTC Sat May 12 2018) +-1 pid:68006
  Originate +19197447009 connected
 dur 00:00:00 tx:0/0 rx:0/0 dscp:0 media:0 audio tos:0xB8 video tos:0x0
 IP 192.168.202.11:8756 SRTP: off rtt:0ms pl:0/0ms lost:0/0/0 delay:0/0/0ms g711ulaw
  TextRelay: off Transcoded: Yes ICE: Off
 media inactive detected:n media contrl rcvd:n/a timestamp:n/a
 long duration call detected:n long duration call duration:n/a timestamp:n/a
 LostPacketRate:0.00 OutOfOrderRate:0.00
 LocalUUID:
 RemoteUUID:
 VRF:

...
```

Step 6. CUBE sends a SIP UPDATE request to the SIP dialer, indicating the start of the CPA by setting the parameter status to CpaS in the message body. This is shown in Example 12-31, where CUBE then receives the corresponding 200 OK for the UPDATE.

Example 12-31 *SIP UPDATE Request from CUBE, Indicating the Start of CPA*

```
19591196: May 12 10:43:46.267 UTC: //203856/2845C0C89609/SIP/Msg/ccsipDisplayMsg:
Sent:
UPDATE sip:3002@10.0.1.15:58800 SIP/2.0
Via: SIP/2.0/UDP 10.0.1.83:5060;branch=z9hG4bK1362F81A
From: <sip:889197447009@10.0.1.83>;tag=C8FD1D35-E66
To: <sip:3002@10.0.1.15>;tag=ca364f70
Date: Sat, 12 May 2018 10:43:45 GMT
Call-ID: 15634e6a-37374904-fa077d2c-be0fc630
User-Agent: Cisco-SIPGateway/IOS-16.6.1
Max-Forwards: 70
Supported: timer,resource-priority,replaces,sdp-anat
Timestamp: 1526121826
Allow: INVITE, OPTIONS, BYE, CANCEL, ACK, PRACK, UPDATE, REFER, SUBSCRIBE, NOTIFY,
  INFO, REGISTER
CSeq: 101 UPDATE
Contact: <sip:889197447009@10.0.1.83:5060>
Min-SE:  1800
Remote-Party-ID: <sip:9197447009@10.0.1.83>;party=called;screen=no;privacy=off
Session-ID: 9ba2ed620b0c5ad6bdf1f0c410803a52;remote=2258fb31a45c582f9ecff9488a271d3f
Content-Type: application/x-cisco-cpa
Content-Disposition: signal;handling=optional
Content-Length: 26

event=detected
status=CpaS
```

Step 7. DSP resources in CUBE detect live speech in the audio stream from the service provider, triggering CUBE to send a subsequent SIP UPDATE, indicating the detection of a live speech event. This is represented with status=LS in the message body, as shown in Example 12-32. CUBE then receives the corresponding 200 OK for this message.

Example 12-32 *SIP UPDATE Request from CUBE, Indicating Detection of Live Speech*

```
19591266: May 12 10:43:47.228 UTC: //203856/2845C0C89609/SIP/Msg/ccsipDisplayMsg:
Sent:
UPDATE sip:3002@10.0.1.15:58800 SIP/2.0
Via: SIP/2.0/UDP 10.0.1.83:5060;branch=z9hG4bK1363014F8
From: <sip:889197447009@10.0.1.83>;tag=C8FD1D35-E66
To: <sip:3002@10.0.1.15>;tag=ca364f70
Date: Sat, 12 May 2018 10:43:45 GMT
Call-ID: 15634e6a-37374904-fa077d2c-be0fc630
User-Agent: Cisco-SIPGateway/IOS-16.6.1
Max-Forwards: 70
Supported: timer,resource-priority,replaces,sdp-anat
```

```
Timestamp: 1526121827
Allow: INVITE, OPTIONS, BYE, CANCEL, ACK, PRACK, UPDATE, REFER, SUBSCRIBE, NOTIFY,
  INFO, REGISTER
CSeq: 102 UPDATE
Contact: <sip:889197447009@10.0.1.83:5060>
Min-SE:  1800
Remote-Party-ID: <sip:9197447009@10.0.1.83>;party=called;screen=no;privacy=off
Session-ID: 9ba2ed620b0c5ad6bdf1f0c410803a52;remote=2258fb31a45c582f9ecff9488a271d3f
Content-Type: application/x-cisco-cpa
Content-Disposition: signal;handling=optional
Content-Length: 167

event=detected
status=LS
pickupT=1090
maxActGlitchT=0
numActGlitch=0
valSpeechT=350
maxPSSGlitchT=0
numPSSGlitch=0
silenceP=610
termToneDetT=0
noiseTH=1000
actTh=32000
```

Step 8. Now that the call is answered by a human, the SIP dialer transfers the outbound call to the reserved agent (5002) by sending a SIP REFER to CUBE. This is shown in Example 12-33.

Example 12-33 *SIP REFER from the SIP Dialer to Initiate a Transfer of the Outbound Call to an Agent*

```
19591302: May 12 10:43:47.293 UTC: //-1/xxxxxxxxxxxx/SIP/Msg/ccsipDisplayMsg:
Received:
REFER sip:889197447009@10.0.1.83:5060 SIP/2.0
Via: SIP/2.0/UDP 10.0.1.15:58800;branch=z9hG4bK-d8754z-201a176aac27176c-1---d8754z-;
  rport
Max-Forwards: 70
Contact: <sip:3002@10.0.1.15:58800>
To: <sip:889197447009@10.0.1.83>;tag=C8FD1D35-E66
From: <sip:3002@10.0.1.15>;tag=ca364f70
Call-ID: 15634e6a-37374904-fa077d2c-be0fc630
CSeq: 3 REFER
User-Agent: Cisco-SIPDialer/UCCE10.0
Refer-To: <sip:5002@10.0.1.83>
Referred-By: sip:3002@10.0.1.15
Content-Length: 0
```

Step 9. CUBE consumes the SIP REFER, finds the dial peer 68007 as the matching outbound dial peer for the call to the agent extension 5002, and originates a SIP INVITE to CUCM. The call is answered, and an RTP connection is established between the outbound dialed customer and the agent. CUBE disconnects the call leg (203856) with the SIP dialer. Example 12-34 shows the active call legs after the call transfer is complete. The initial transcoding resource that was allocated to perform CPA function is released when the outbound dialer transfers the call to an agent. Example 12-34 shows "Transcoded: Yes" even after the transfer is complete because CUBE allocates a different transcoder resource to handle the G.711ulaw-to-G.729 codec conversion between CUBE–service provider (G.711ulaw) and CUBE–agent (G.729). The **show dspfarm dsp status** command shows the DSP transcoder resource that is associated with the two call legs.

Example 12-34 *SIP Call Legs After the Caller Is Transferred to an Agent*

```
cube1# show call active voice brief
...
Telephony call-legs: 0
SIP call-legs: 2
H323 call-legs: 0
Call agent controlled call-legs: 0
SCCP call-legs: 0
STCAPP call-legs: 0
Multicast call-legs: 0
Total call-legs: 2
27F1 : 203857 3371945070ms.1 (10:43:35.890 UTC Sat May 12 2018) +9180 pid:68006
  Originate +19197447009 connected
 dur 00:00:31 tx:1433/286600 rx:1446/289200 dscp:0 media:0 audio tos:0xB8 video
  tos:0x0
 IP 192.168.202.11:8182 SRTP: off rtt:0ms pl:0/0ms lost:0/0/0 delay:0/0/0ms g711ulaw
  TextRelay: off Transcoded: Yes ICE: Off
 media inactive detected:n media contrl rcvd:n/a timestamp:n/a
 long duration call detected:n long duration call duration:n/a timestamp:n/a
 LostPacketRate:0.00 OutOfOrderRate:0.00
 LocalUUID:9ba2ed620b0c5ad6bdf1f0c410803a52
 RemoteUUID:0000668c00105000a00000505689ea60
 VRF:
27F1 : 203865 3371956500ms.1 (10:43:47.320 UTC Sat May 12 2018) +300 pid:68007
  Originate 5002 active
 dur 00:00:29 tx:1446/87740 rx:1437/86208 dscp:0 media:0 audio tos:0xB8 video
  tos:0x0
 IP 10.0.1.91:17308 SRTP: off rtt:0ms pl:0/0ms lost:0/0/0 delay:0/0/0ms g729r8
  TextRelay: off Transcoded: Yes ICE: Off
```

```
media inactive detected:n media contrl rcvd:n/a timestamp:n/a
long duration call detected:n long duration call duration:n/a timestamp:n/a
LostPacketRate:0.00 OutOfOrderRate:0.00
LocalUUID:0000668c00105000a00000505689ea60
RemoteUUID:9ba2ed620b0c5ad6bdf1f0c410803a52
VRF:

...

cube1# show dspfarm dsp active
SLOT   DSP VERSION  STATUS CHNL USE   TYPE    RSC_ID BRIDGE_ID PKTS_TXED PKTS_RXED

0/1    1   46.2.0   UP     1    USED  xcode   1      203865    587       587
0/1    1   46.2.0   UP     1    USED  xcode   1      203857    581       584

Total number of DSPFARM DSP channel(s) 1

cube1#
```

Step 10. The customer or the agent disconnects the call when the conversation is complete.

> **Tip** CUBE tries to allocate a transcoder resource at the time of establishing media, such as right before sending a 183 Session Progress provisional response to the SIP dialer. If a transcoder resource isn't available, CUBE continues to send the 183 Session Progress response to the SIP dialer but disconnects the call with a 503 Service Unavailable response with cause code 47 (Resource Unavailable). CUBE prints the debug message "flex_dsprm_dspfm_find_dsp: not find available dsp" when **debug dsp-resource-manager flex error** is enabled during such situations.

Troubleshooting: Answering Machine Not Detected

There are a few possible reasons the CUBE CPA feature may not detect an answering machine on outbound calls initiated by the dialer. Some possible causes are as follows:

- CPA is not activated for the outbound call. This primarily occurs because of an incorrect configuration either in CUBE or in the Campaign configuration within UCCE.

The parameter Call Progress Analysis (CPA) must be enabled in the Campaign Purpose tab of the Outbound Option Campaign by using the Configuration Manager tool in UCCE (**Outbound Option > Campaign**), as shown in Figure 12-33. On the CUBE side, the command **call-progress-analysis** must be configured under the universal transcoder's configuration. If this command is not configured, CUBE sends event=disabled in the application/x-cisco-cpa message body section of the 183 Session Progress message sent to the SIP dialer, resulting in CPA not becoming activated.

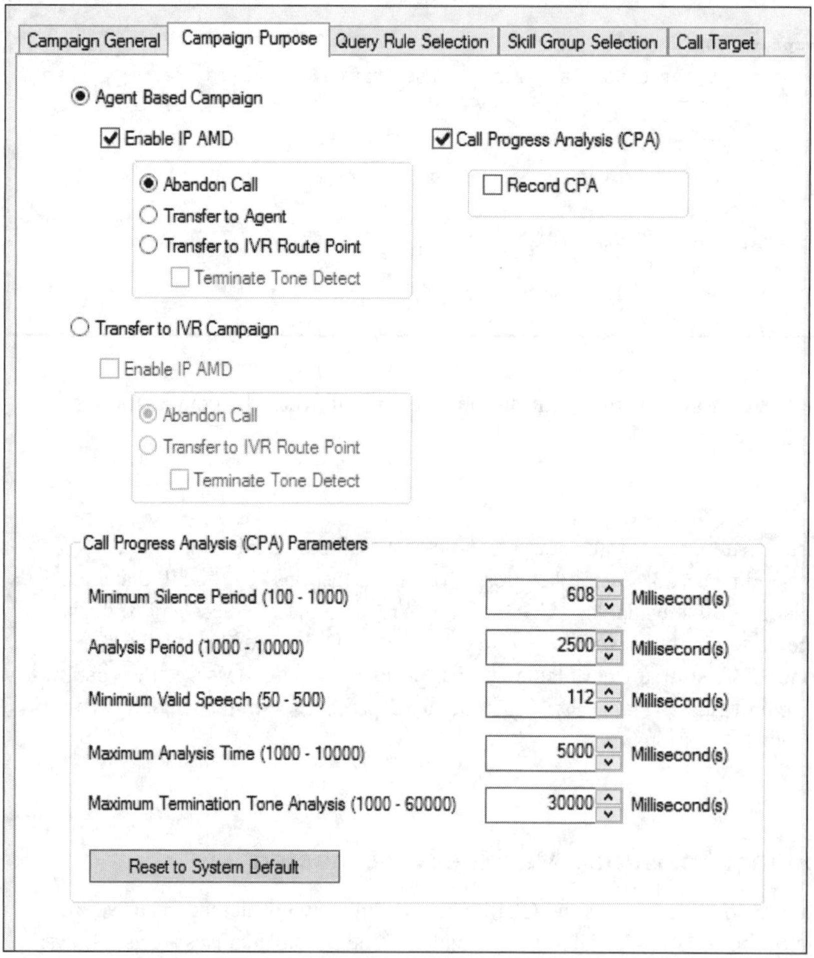

Figure 12-33 *Campaign Configuration Using the UCCE Configuration Manager Tool*

- There is no audio from the service provider, and hence the DSP in CUBE is not able to detect any tone.

  This can be confirmed by monitoring the **tx/rx** statistics of the CUBE–to–service provider call leg, as shown in **show call active voice brief** and also in **show call**

history voice brief (which shows calls that were handled by CUBE recently but are no longer active). If no RTP packets are received from the provider, the **rx** statistics counter remains as a constant and does not increment. Another verification option approach is to collect a packet capture of SIP and RTP traffic exchanged between CUBE and the service provider, decode the audio packets for the given call, and confirm the presence of silent audio. The command **media bulk-stats** must be enabled under **voice service voip** configuration mode in order to see the correct tx/rx statistics when these two **show** commands are executed in CUBE running Cisco IOS XE software.

- An answering machine termination tone is present in the audio stream but is not detected by the DSP in CUBE even when CPA is enabled for the call.

  It is possible to have the tone come after a long answering machine message. To check this possibility, collect the Wireshark capture of the call, decode the audio RTP stream, and determine the time difference between the start of the answering machine and the end of the answering machine tone. If this duration is greater than 15 seconds (the default value in CUBE), increase the time that the DSP waits to detect the answering machine tone after it detects an answering machine message using the command **cpa timing term-tone wait** *time-in-milliseconds*. For example, **cpa timing term-tone 30000** configures CUBE DSP to wait 30 seconds to detect the answering machine termination tone after the answering machine message has started.

After looking for these and other issues, if the detection problem is still not resolved, open a case with Cisco support and attach the CUBE configuration, packet capture, and output of the following debugs to the case for further analysis:

```
debug voip ccapi inout
debug ccsip message
debug ccsip info
debug ccsip error
debug dsp-resource-manager flex dspfarm
debug dsp-resource-manager flex error
debug dsp-resource-manager flex function
debug voip hpi default
```

Troubleshooting Scenarios

Troubleshooting and trying to finding the root cause of an intermittent issue in a contact center environment might seem like trying to find a needle in a haystack due to the number of products and call legs involved. The good news is the troubleshooting process can be simplified by following a consistent and systematic questionnaire-based methodology, similar to what is discussed in Chapter 3. In addition to the *what*, *who*, and *when* types of questions, it is very important to have a detailed understanding of network topology, call flows, and software versions of components deployed in the environment, as shown in Table 12-4.

Table 12-4 *Additional Questions for Contact Center–Related Issues*

Information Type	Sample Questions
Network topology	Do you have a visual network diagram showing the contact center solution deployment, including all critical components, such as routers, loggers, PGs, AW-HDS, Finesse, CUIC, CUCM, VXML gateways/VVB, CVP call servers, CVP reporting servers, CVP OAMP, CUBE, and CUSP, along with the L2 and L3 network?
	Where are the agents located? Are they in remote sites, in a centralized campus site, at home, or in a combination of these? How many agents are in each location? How many agents do you have overall, configured and also actively logged in?
	Are there multiple SIP service providers? If so, what type of calls do each of the providers handle (for example, toll-free, DID, outbound calls)?
	Is CUBE deployed in high availability mode?
	Does the deployment have a Cisco SIP proxy server?
	Does the solution use the VXML gateway or Cisco VVB for the voice browser functionality (VRU) leg?
	What agent desktop application is used by agents?
	What is the software version of the key components deployed in the solution?
Call flows	What are the most common call flows in the deployment? Examples include inbound calls to agents, SIP REFER-based transfers, outbound dialers, and transfers to external destinations.
	What type of codecs are used in the contact center solution? Do all calls use G.711, or is it a combination of G.711 and G.729 codecs?
	Are agents using softphones such as Jabber or hardphones?
	What version/model is being used?
	How are agents answering and controlling the calls?
	Are they using Finesse Agent Desktop, softphones (Jabber), or hardphones?
	How many ingress gateways do you have?
	How many CVP call servers do you have?
	How are calls being distributed across the ingress gateways?
	How are calls being distributed across the CVP call servers?
	Is there an "active" set and a "backup" set, or is everything round-robined between them?
	Do you use TCP or UDP for SIP?
	Are there any call flows in which transcoders or MTP resources are leveraged?
	What is the peak time for call volume? What is the maximum and average call volume on a business day?

The following sections cover common troubleshooting scenarios observed in Cisco Unified Contact Center solution in which the SBC (for example, CUBE) is an integral part of the call flow.

Troubleshooting Intermittent Call Disconnects

Intermittent call disconnects reported by contact center agents are classic examples of issues that require solution-level knowledge to quickly isolate the sources of problems. Answering the following questions helps obtain a detailed problem description:

- When does the call disconnect?
  - Is it while answering the call?
  - Is it while transferring the call?
  - Is it while resuming the call on hold?
  - Do you have examples, along with the calling party number and the time of the problem occurrence?
  - Is the problem observed during a specific time of the day?
- What types of calls get disconnected?
  - Are these inbound or outbound calls?
  - Are these calls from and/or to external or internal users?
  - Is there a specific set of calling party numbers in which the problem is repeatedly observed?

In addition to the listed information, you can also enable the command **voice iec syslog** in CUBE configuration to automatically generate syslog events for abnormal call disconnects.

Figure 12-34 illustrates a scenario in which an agent with extension 5002 reports intermittent call disconnects. After a discussion with the end user, it is determined that the agent sees inbound external calls in Finesse Agent Desktop and intermittently the calls drop right after he answers the call. Initially the agent wasn't aware of specific calling party numbers that experience this problem, but after being asked to track this information, he says the problem is observed with calls from 4083926010, but the problem is not observed with calls from 4083926001. Establishing working and not working scenarios for the same call flow and comparing the diagnostics data collected in both scenarios helps accelerate the root cause determination process.

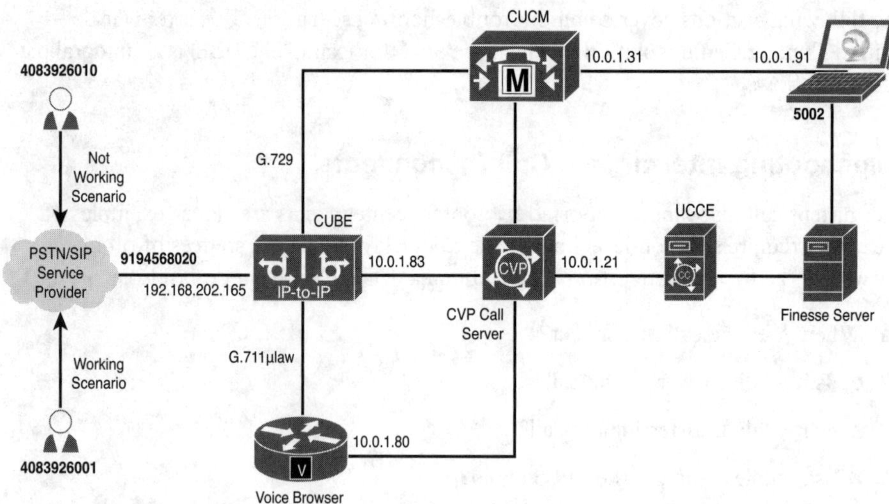

Figure 12-34 *Contact Center Topology in Which Calls Are Disconnected Intermittently*

The first step in diagnosing this problem is to collect diagnostics data from CUBE, CVP, Voice browsers and CUCM as shown in Table 12-5 in order to analyze the end-to-end SIP call signaling path and identify the reason for the call disconnect.

Table 12-5 *Diagnostics Data for End-to-End Call Trace*

Device	Diagnostics Data	Collection Method
CUBE	debug commands: **debug ccsip message** **debug cccsip error** **debug voip ccapi inout** show commands: **show version** **show run** **show call history voice brief** **show log**	SSH session
Cisco IOS VXML gateway	debug commands **debug ccsip message** **debug ccsip error** **debug voip application vxml default** show commands **show version** **show run** **show call history voice brief** **show log**	SSH session

Device	Diagnostics Data	Collection Method
Cisco VVB	Log in to the Cisco VVB Serviceability page at https://cvvb-ip-address/uccxservice/main.htm, go to **Trace > Profile**, and enable the "CallControlVVB" log profile.	Real-Time Monitoring Tool (RTMT) Collect logs of the Engine service
CVP call server	CVP SIP logs with the following settings set using the CVP Diagnostics tool in the subset of CVP call servers that are expected to handle the given calls of interest, as shown in Figure 12-35: **http://*cvp-ip*:8000/cvp/diag** Serv Mgr: **Select com.dynamicsoft.DsLibs.DsUALibs** Level: Select **Debug** and click the **Set** button. Click the "Debug/41" link to set the debug mask of ICM, IVR, and SIP subsystems within the CVP call server to the value "41".	Copy files from C:\Cisco\CVP\Logs
CUCM	CUCM SDL files containing detailed traces for Cisco CallManager and Cisco CTIManager services. Note that detailed traces are enabled by default.	RTMT

Figure 12-35 shows a snapshot of the CVP diagnostics tool. Note that com.dynamicsoft.DsLibs.DsUALibs is set to the Debug level.

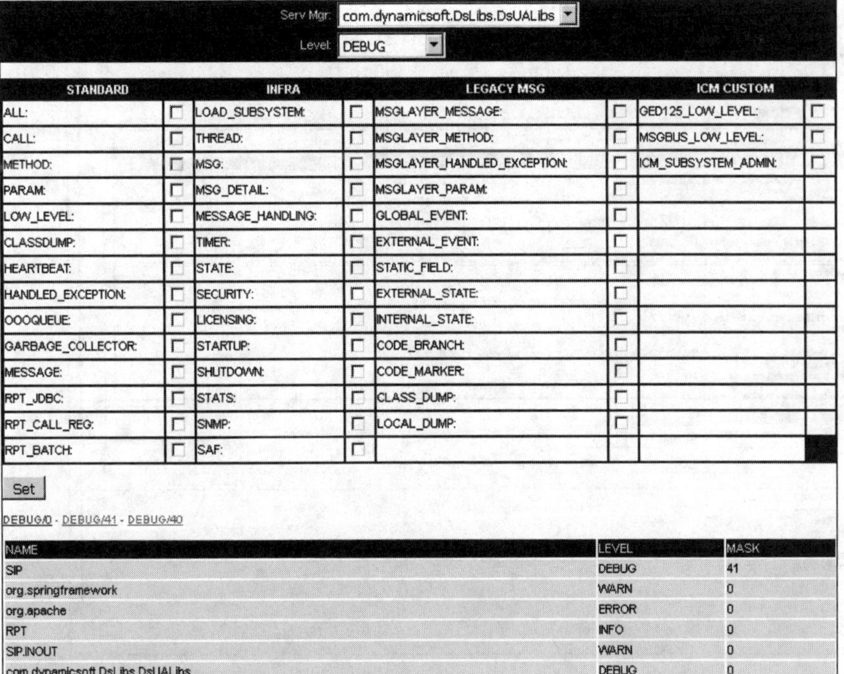

Figure 12-35 *CVP Diagnostics Tool*

An alternate way to efficiently collect data across the UCCE solution is with the Unified System CLI tool. This tool, run at a Windows command prompt, is installed by default in the CVP and UCCE servers. The tool provides the ability to set debugs using abstracted debug levels (for example, 0, 1, 2, 3, 4, 5), which are then converted to product-specific debug levels or commands and then enabled at the individual product instances. Debug level 0 is the default debug level. The higher the debug level, the more detailed the debugs will be. Configuration and log data can be retrieved across multiple devices with a single command. The *Unified System CLI Quick Reference Guide* and the "Accessing the Diagnostic Framework Through the Unified System CLI" section in the *Serviceability Guide for Cisco Unified ICM/Contact Center Enterprise* documents at www.cisco.com provide step-by-step instructions on how to set up and use the UCCE CLI. The article *How to Set Traces and Collect UCCE Logs* from www.cisco.com is also a good reference document.

The next step is to analyze the collected debug-related diagnostics data. Analyzing the CVP logs first is the quickest way to get a high-level view of how a call is handled in the contact center, since it centrally orchestrates and manages many different SIP call legs associated with the call. CVPParserG3 is a useful log analysis tool that parses the CVP log files, provides filters to focus on the specific calls of interest, and generates PDF files that shows the call flow in an easily consumable ladder diagram format.

Figure 12-36 shows the initial view of CVPParserG3 after the relevant CVP log file is dragged and dropped into the tool's graphical user interface. This view displays all the SIP messages present in the log file.

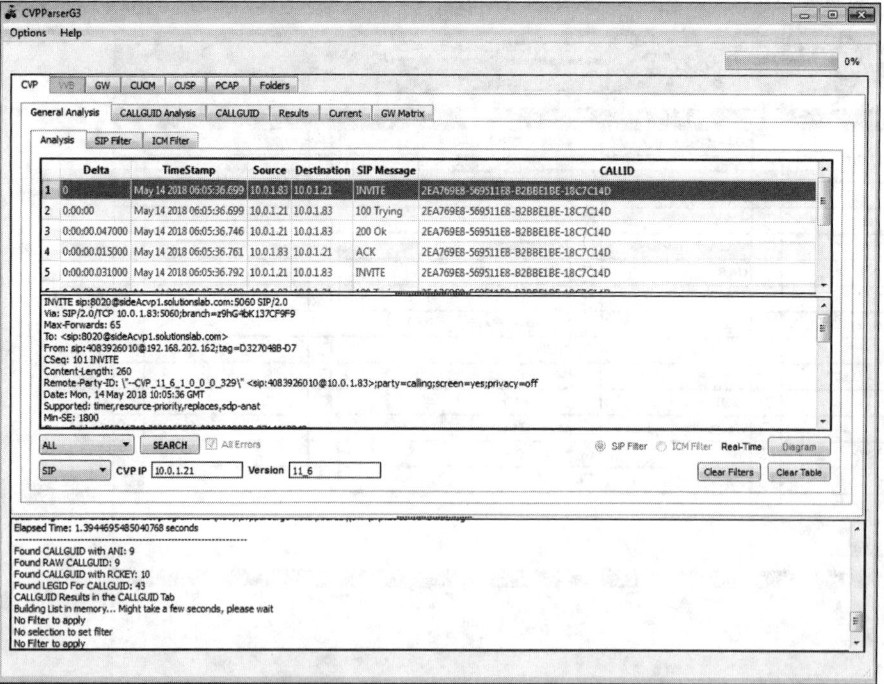

Figure 12-36 *General Analysis Tab of the CVPParserG3 Tool*

CVP assigns a unique call GUID for each call it handles. When CVP receives a new SIP INVITE from CUBE, it generates the call GUID and provides this value in the Cisco-Gucid header in the 100 Trying message as well as in all subsequent messages.

Example 12-35 shows the SIP INVITE received by CUBE from the service provider for the call from 4083926010 to 9193928020, the SIP INVITE (called number translated to 8020) sent by CUBE to CVP and the corresponding 100 Trying message with a Cisco-Gucid header set to the value 56CC070000010000000000DFA1CAA8C0 sent by CVP to CUBE.

Example 12-35 *SIP 100 Trying with the Cisco-Gucid Header Generated by CVP*

```
26756121: May 14 10:05:35.730 UTC: //-1/xxxxxxxxxxxx/SIP/Msg/ccsipDisplayMsg:
Received:
INVITE sip:9194568020@192.168.202.165:5060;transport=tcp SIP/2.0
Via: SIP/2.0/TCP 192.168.202.169:5060;branch=z9hG4bKG5pQc+Al2l8hW28yvMt0vQ~~199
Via: SIP/2.0/TCP 192.168.202.167:5060;branch=z9hG4bKRzUwlcSQ3rMWDN01cODE+Q~~2178
Via: SIP/2.0/TCP 192.168.202.162:5060;branch=z9hG4bK35474A
Max-Forwards: 66
Record-Route: <sip:rr$n=sp2-network@p1.example-sp2.com:5060;transport=tcp;lr>
To: <sip:9194568020@entcomp1.com>
From: <sip:4083926010@192.168.202.162>;tag=BBD4CDF0-494
Contact: <sip:4083926010@192.168.202.162:5060;transport=tcp>
Expires: 180
Remote-Party-ID: <sip:4083926010@192.168.202.162>;party=calling;screen=yes;privacy=
  off
Call-ID: 28D9366F-569511E8-8331FA30-CAD23726@192.168.202.162
CSeq: 101 INVITE
Content-Length: 255
Date: Mon, 14 May 2018 10:05:27 GMT
Supported: 100rel,timer,resource-priority,replaces,sdp-anat
Min-SE: 1800
Cisco-Guid: 1456211712-0000065536-0000000223-2714413248
User-Agent: Cisco-SIPGateway/IOS-16.6.1
Allow: INVITE, OPTIONS, BYE, CANCEL, ACK, PRACK, UPDATE, REFER, SUBSCRIBE, NOTIFY,
  INFO, REGISTER
Timestamp: 1526292327
Allow-Events: telephone-event
Session-ID: 00000d1800105000a000005056a12adc;remote=00000000000000000000000000000000
Session-Expires: 1800
Content-Type: application/sdp
Content-Disposition: session;handling=required

v=0
o=CiscoSystemsSIP-GW-UserAgent 2099 3699 IN IP4 192.168.202.162
s=SIP Call
```

```
c=IN IP4 192.168.202.162
t=0 0
m=audio 8534 RTP/AVP 0 101
c=IN IP4 192.168.202.162
a=rtpmap:0 PCMU/8000
a=rtpmap:101 telephone-event/8000
a=fmtp:101 0-15
a=ptime:20

26757505: May 14 10:05:36.775 UTC: //260068/56CC07000000/SIP/Msg/ccsipDisplayMsg:
Sent:
INVITE sip:8020@sideAcvp1.solutionslab.com:5060 SIP/2.0
Via: SIP/2.0/TCP 10.0.1.83:5060;branch=z9hG4bK137CF9F9
Remote-Party-ID: "--CVP_11_6_1_0_0_0_329" <sip:4083926010@10.0.1.83>;party=calling;
  screen=yes;privacy=off
From: sip:4083926010@192.168.202.162;tag=D327048B-D7
To: <sip:8020@sideAcvp1.solutionslab.com>
Date: Mon, 14 May 2018 10:05:36 GMT
Call-ID: 2EA769E8-569511E8-B2BBE1BE-18C7C14D@10.0.1.83
Supported: timer,resource-priority,replaces,sdp-anat
Min-SE:  1800
Cisco-Guid: 1456211712-0000065536-0000000223-2714413248
User-Agent: Cisco-SIPGateway/IOS-16.6.1
Allow: INVITE, OPTIONS, BYE, CANCEL, ACK, PRACK, UPDATE, REFER, SUBSCRIBE, NOTIFY,
  INFO, REGISTER
CSeq: 101 INVITE
Timestamp: 1526292336
Contact: <sip:4083926010@10.0.1.83:5060;transport=tcp>
Expires: 60
Allow-Events: telephone-event
Max-Forwards: 65
X-Cisco-CCBProbe: id:10.0.1.83;loc:site1;trunks:25
Session-ID: 00000d1800105000a000005056a12adc;remote=00000000000000000000000000000000
Session-Expires:  1800
Content-Type: application/sdp
Content-Disposition: session;handling=required
Content-Length: 260

v=0
o=CiscoSystemsSIP-GW-UserAgent 579 6732 IN IP4 10.0.1.83
s=SIP Call
c=IN IP4 10.0.1.83
t=0 0
m=audio 9024 RTP/AVP 0 101 19
c=IN IP4 10.0.1.83
```

```
a=rtpmap:0 PCMU/8000
a=rtpmap:101 telephone-event/8000
a=fmtp:101 0-15
a=rtpmap:19 CN/8000
a=ptime:20

26757518: May 14 10:05:36.778 UTC: //260068/56CC07000000/SIP/Msg/ccsipDisplayMsg:
Received:
SIP/2.0 100 Trying
Via: SIP/2.0/TCP 10.0.1.83:5060;branch=z9hG4bK137CF9F9
To: <sip:8020@sideAcvp1.solutionslab.com>
From: <sip:4083926010@192.168.202.162>;tag=D327048B-D7
Call-ID: 2EA769E8-569511E8-B2BBE1BE-18C7C14D@10.0.1.83
CSeq: 101 INVITE
Content-Length: 0
Timestamp: 1526292336
Cisco-Guid: 1456211712-0000065536-0000000223-2714413248
Contact: sip:10.0.1.21:5060;transport=tcp
Cisco-Gucid: 56CC070000010000000000DFA1CAA8C0
Session-ID: 00000000000000000000000000000000;remote=00000d1800105000a000005056a12adc
```

CVPParserG3 automatically identifies all the CallGUIDs in the log files and lists them in the CALLGUID tab, as shown in Figure 12-37.

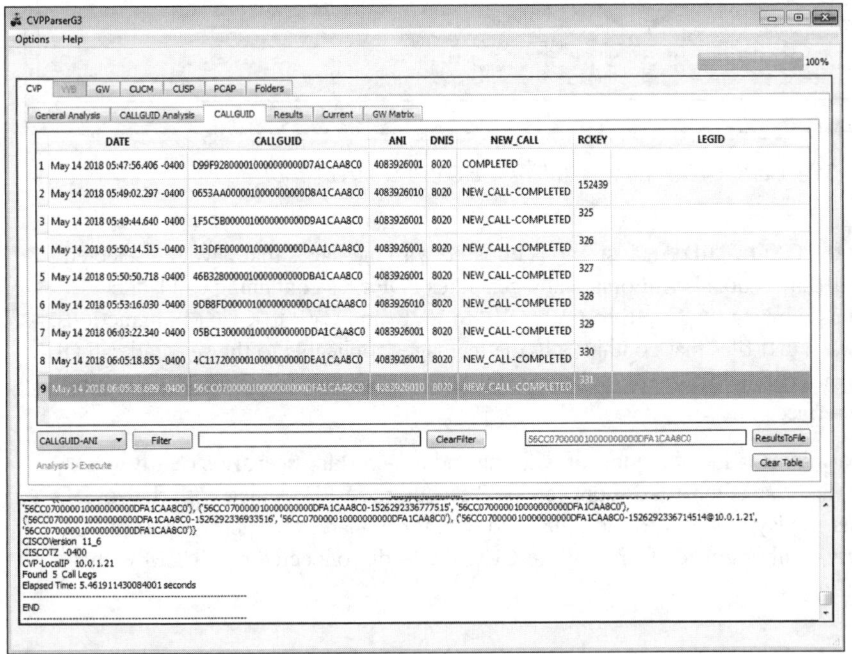

Figure 12-37 *CALLGUID Tab of the CVPParserG3 Tool*

The CALLGUID list view displays the calling number and time stamp for each identifier. The administrator selects the call of interest (that is, the call associated with the calling number of the not-working scenario 4083926010) and double-clicks the entry. The tool then displays all the SIP messages associated with this call in the CALLGUID Analysis tab, as shown in Figure 12-38.

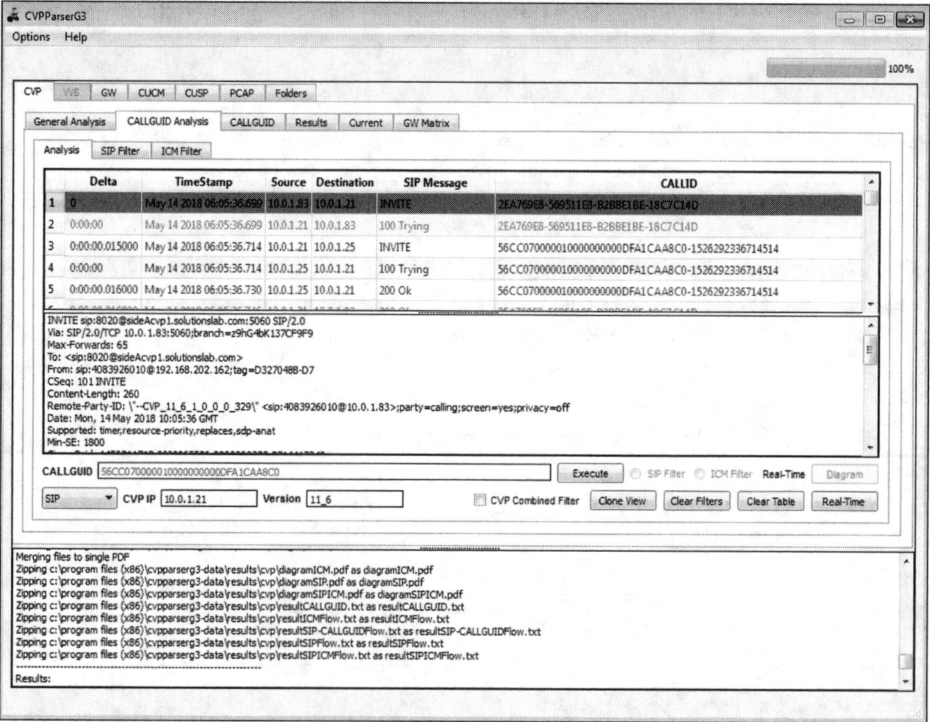

Figure 12-38 *CallGUID Analysis Tab of the CVPParserG3 Tool*

While the CALLGUID Analysis tab is updated with messages that have the selected call GUID, the tool also automatically generates PDF files containing call ladder diagrams showing the CUBE-to-CVP, CVP-to-VVB, and CVP-to-CUCM interactions, along with text files that contain only the messages applicable to the selected call GUID. The names of the PDF files are displayed in the bottom portion of the tool's graphical user interface.

Comparing the ladder diagrams of working and not-working scenarios clearly shows the reasons for call disconnect. CVP sets up the VRU call leg with the voice browser to play ringback to the caller, and then it originates the agent (5002) call. The agent call originated from CVP to CUCM gets disconnected by CUCM with

503 Service Unavailable and the cause code 47 Resources Unavailable, as shown in Figure 12-39.

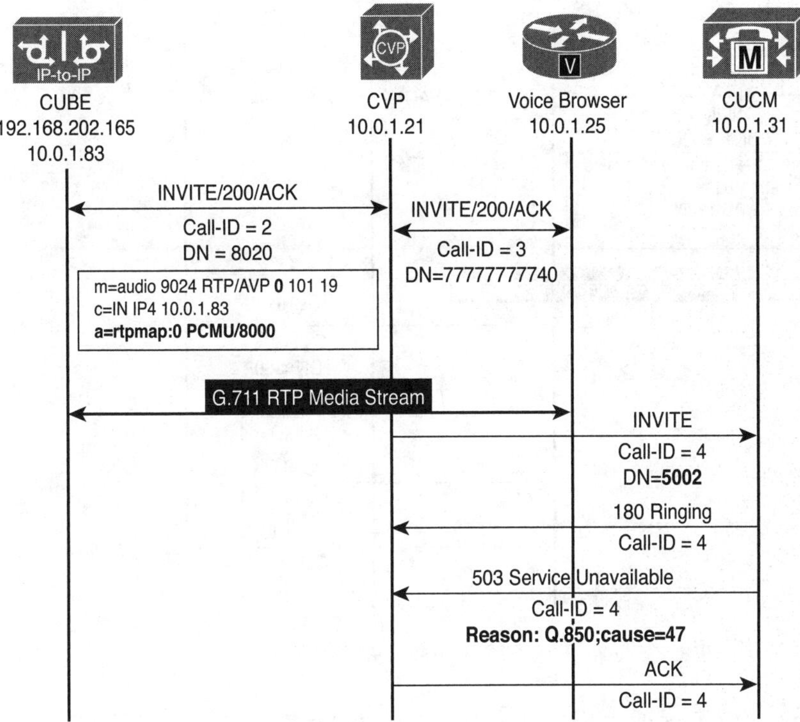

Figure 12-39 *SIP Call Ladder Diagram of a Non-working Scenario*

In the working scenario, the call to the agent is successful with a SIP 200 OK response from CUCM. This working behavior is shown in Figure 12-40.

CUCM SDL traces are analyzed to further understand the root cause. Example 12-36 shows that CUCM identifies the region of the CUBE SIP trunk (Default Region) and the agent phone (G729V6 Region) and determines that the maximum bit rate allowed for audio is only 8 Kbps. CUCM then compares the capabilities advertised in the incoming call (G.711ulaw) with the capabilities of the agent phone. The incoming call doesn't have G.729 or other codec capabilities that support 8 Kbps or less audio bandwidth. This is demonstrated in the SIP INVITE found in Example 12-35. As a result, CUCM tries to allocate a transcoder and is not successful, triggering the MediaResourceListExhausted alarm. This results in CUCM disconnecting the call with cause code 47.

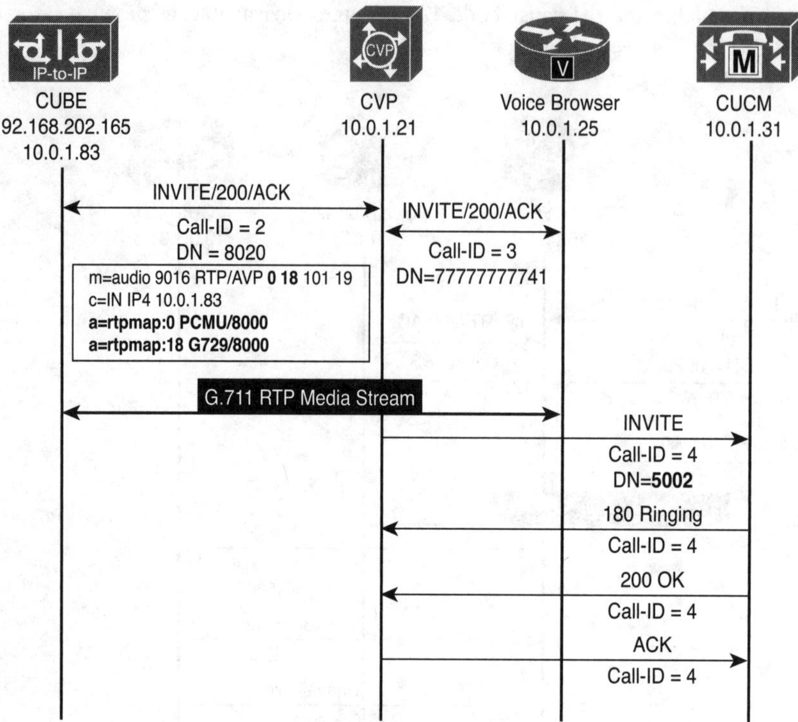

Figure 12-40 *SIP Call Ladder Diagram for a Working Scenario*

Example 12-36 *CUCM SDL Trace Snippet with the Call Disconnect Reason*

```
13948745.007 |06:05:41.232 |AppInfo  |DET-MediaManager-(80)::preCheckCapabilities,
  region1=Default, region2=G729v6, Pty1 capCount=1 (Cap,ptime)= (4,20), Pty2 cap-
  Count=8 (Cap,ptime)= (90,20) (6,20) (40,0) (41,0) (4,20) (2,20) (11,20) (12,20)
13948745.008 |06:05:41.232 |AppInfo  |DET-RegionsServer::matchCapabilities-- save-
  dOption=0, PREF_NONE, regionA=(null) regionB=(null) latentCaps(A=0, B=0) kbps=8,
  capACount=1, capBCount=8
13948745.009 |06:05:41.232 |AppInfo  |RegionsServer: applyCodecFilterIfNeeded - no
  codecs remained after filtering so restored original 0 caps
13948745.010 |06:05:41.232 |AppInfo  |DET-MediaManager-(80)::preCheckCapabilities,
  caps mismatch! Xcoder Reqd. kbps(8), filtered A[capCount=0 (Cap,ptime)=],
  B[capCount=3 (Cap,ptime)= (90,20) (11,20) (12,20)] allowMTP=0 numXcoderRequired=1
  xcodingSide=1



13948746.000 |06:05:41.232 |SdlSig |MrmAllocateXcoderResourceReq  |waiting
  |MediaResourceManager(2,100,140,1) |MediaManager(2,100,142,80)
  |2,100,14,199.4463^10.0.1.91^*             |[R:N-H:0,N:0,L:0,V:0,Z:0,D:0]
  CI=47714381 MRGLPkid=415e3b42-bb15-5a75-3897-88a8bbe6384d Kpbs=0 RegionA=Default
  CapA=1 RegionB=G729v6 CapB=8 SuppressFlag=0 Type=1 DeviceCapablity= [0x9 DETECT_2833
  PT_2833]9 MandatoryCapabilties= [0x0]0 Count=1
```

```
13948750.001 |06:05:41.232 |AppInfo  |GenAlarm: AlarmName = MediaResourceListEx-
  hausted, subFac = CALLMANAGERKeyParam = , severity = 4, AlarmMsg = MediaResource
  ListName : MediaGroupList_1
MediaResourceType : 2
AppID : Cisco CallManager
ClusterID : StandAloneCluster
NodeID : sideAcmsub1


13948779.001 |06:05:41.234 |AppInfo  |SIPTcp - wait_SdlSPISignal: Outgoing SIP TCP
  message to 10.0.1.21 on port 26969 index 77
[671542,NET]
SIP/2.0 503 Service Unavailable
Via: SIP/2.0/TCP 10.0.1.21:5060;branch=z9hG4bKk9F7UjU8zHQ4XN9JOnRWyA~~2432
From: "--CVP_11_6_1_0_0_0_329" <sip:4083926010@10.0.1.21:5060>;tag=ds283530a5
To: <sip:5002@CUCM.solutionslab.com;transport=tcp>;tag=223693~ea04c33e-2567-47d2-
  ab0d-76daabbb8340-47714379
Date: Mon, 14 May 2018 10:05:37 GMT
Call-ID: 56CC0700000100000000000DFA1CAA8C0-1526292336933516@10.0.1.21
CSeq: 1 INVITE
Allow-Events: presence
Reason: Q.850;cause=47
Server: Cisco-CUCM11.0
Session-ID: 00007d6a00105000a00000505689ea60;remote=00000d1800105000a000005056a12adc
Content-Length: 0
```

CVP selects the next CUCM subscriber node in the server group and sends the SIP INVITE to that subscriber. This time the agent is in reserved state because the previous call just got disconnected with cause code 47, so CUCM disconnects the call with 486 Busy Here. CVP has no other next hop for routing the agent call, and no more agents are available from a UCCE router perspective. Therefore, CVP disconnects the call leg to CUBE with the a 486, as shown in Example 12-37.

Example 12-37 *CUCM SDL Trace Snippet Illustrating the Call Disconnect Reason*

```
26760433: May 14 10:05:43.256 UTC: //-1/xxxxxxxxxxxx/SIP/Msg/ccsipDisplayMsg:
Received:
BYE sip:4083926010@10.0.1.83:5060;transport=tcp SIP/2.0
Via: SIP/2.0/TCP 10.0.1.21:5060;branch=z9hG4bKk9F7UjU8zHQ4XN9JOnRWyA~~2435
Max-Forwards: 70
To: <sip:4083926010@192.168.202.162>;tag=D327048B-D7
From: <sip:8020@sideAcvp1.solutionslab.com>;tag=ds9122fea
Call-ID: 2EA769E8-569511E8-B2BBE1BE-18C7C14D@10.0.1.83
CSeq: 2 BYE
Content-Length: 0
Contact: <sip:10.0.1.21:5060;transport=tcp>
Reason: SIP;cause=486
Session-ID: 5e1cd0891000016363d4a5a56198a5fa;remote=00000d1800105000a000005056a12adc
```

The call from 4083926001 to the same agent works fine because the SIP INVITE from the service provider advertises both G.711ulaw and G.729 as audio codec capabilities. This results in the SIP INVITE sent from CUBE to CVP and the subsequent SIP INVITE sent from CVP to CUCM both having G.729 in the SIP SDP. The presence of the G.729 capability assists CUCM in satisfying the 8 Kbps audio bandwidth requirement between the CUBE SIP trunk and the agent's region by setting up the codec of the agent call to be G.729. There are a couple options for resolving the call disconnect issue observed in this example scenario with callers like 4083926010:

- Work with the service provider to ensure that the SIP SBC in the network always advertises G.711ulaw and G.729 codecs for incoming calls to the contact center.
- Add a transcoder resource registered to CUCM so that it can be utilized for codec mismatch scenarios. This option requires careful design consideration as the number of required transcoder resources may be high in large contact center deployments.

The intermittent call disconnect scenario discussed previously is just one example that illustrates the troubleshooting process. Several factors contribute to call disconnect, and you can troubleshoot them by using the same process:

- Call disconnects may occur when the caller is transferred by a UCCE call script using the SIP REFER mechanism. This happens when CUBE is unable to correctly route and set up the call to the transfer destination. The following are some common reasons:
  - CUBE doesn't find a matching outbound dial peer for the transfer destination.
  - The transfer destination is no longer valid, and the call script has yet to be updated with the new number.
  - CUBE is incorrectly configured to pass through the SIP REFER to the service provider when the inbound calls are handled via dial peer with the survivability script. The command **no supplementary-service sip refer** must be explicitly configured to enable CUBE to consume SIP REFER.
- Inbound calls may intermittently disconnect with cause code 47 before or after the call connects. This could occur for several reasons:
  - Transcoder resources may not be configured to handle the codec mismatches experienced during the call flow, as discussed in the previous scenario.
  - Transcoder resources may be configured, but all the available sessions may currently be utilized and not available for new calls.
  - Rarely, this symptom can be caused when the data plane provisioning process for a new call in CUBE running on Cisco ISR 4400, ASR 1000, and CSR 1000v routers isn't successful. Even though a call may appear to get connected from a SIP signaling perspective, shortly after sending a 200 OK, CUBE disconnects the call with cause code 47. The occurrence of provisioning failures can be confirmed by using the command **show voip fpi stats**. Example 12-38 shows sample output

of **show voip fpi calls** in which CUBE has 824 successful (rsp_ok) provisioning requests and 10 failures (rsp_failed). Identifying the exact call flow that triggers the provisioning failure is critical in determining the root cause. If you are experiencing this issue, the best approach would be to check for any existing software defects with exact symptoms for the given CUBE's software in Bug Search Tool at www.cisco.com and to upgrade the software if the bug fix exists. Otherwise, you should open a case with Cisco support to get guidance on troubleshooting next steps.

Example 12-38 *CUBE Forwarding Plane Interface (FPI) Statistics*

```
cube1# show voip fpi calls
Number of Calls : 1
---------- ---------- ---------- ----------- -------------- --------------
    confID correlator    AcallID     BcallID          state          event
---------- ---------- ---------- ----------- -------------- --------------
       248        253     434396      434397      ALLOCATED  GET_STATS_RSP


cube1# show voip fpi stats
**************** VOIP FPI STATS *********************
----------- ---------- ---------- ---------- ----------
type         ReqSuccess    ReqFail RspSuccess    RspFail
----------- ---------- ---------- ---------- ----------
caps                 1          0          0          0
init                 1          0          1          0
params               1          0        N/A        N/A
config               0          0          0          0          0(skip)
deact                0          0          0          0     0(wrong state)
port add             0          0        N/A        N/A
port delete          0          0        N/A        N/A
*********************** ACTIVE *******************************
                              IDLE      ALLOCATING        ALLOCATED        MODIFYING
     CREATE_REQ                244               0                0                0
     MODIFY_REQ                  0               9              457              115
     DELETE_REQ                  0               0              243                0
  GET_STATS_REQ                  0               0            32222                2
    PROV_RSP_OK                  0             236                0              466
  PROV_RSP_FAIL                  0               8                0                0
     DELETE_RSP                  0               0                0                0
  GET_STATS_RSP                  0               0            31107                1
  STATS_TMR_EXP                  0               0                0                0
     TMR_EXPIRY                  0               0                0                0
CREATE_STRM_REQ                  9               0                0                0
```

```
MODIFY_STRM_REQ              0            0            0            0
DELETE_STRM_REQ              0            0            9            0
DETAIL_STAT_REQ              0            0            0            0
DETAIL_STAT_RSP              0            0            0            0
DT_STAT_TMR_EXP              0            0            0            0
                      DELETING  ALLOC_MOD_PEND MODIFY_MOD_PEND  DELETE_PENDING
     CREATE_REQ              0            0            0            0
     MODIFY_REQ              0            0          164            0
     DELETE_REQ              0            0            0            0
  GET_STATS_REQ              0            0            0            0
    PROV_RSP_OK              0            7          115            0
  PROV_RSP_FAIL              0            2            0            0
     DELETE_RSP            249            0            0            0
  GET_STATS_RSP              0            0            0            0
  STATS_TMR_EXP              0            0            0            0
     TMR_EXPIRY              0            0            0            0
CREATE_STRM_REQ              0            0            0            0
MODIFY_STRM_REQ              0            0            0            0
DELETE_STRM_REQ              0            0            0            0
DETAIL_STAT_REQ              0            0            0            0
DETAIL_STAT_RSP              0            0            0            0
DT_STAT_TMR_EXP              0            0            0            0
********************** END ACTIVE ****************************
...
Correlators in use:1

Corrupted table error (alloc):0

Corrupted table error (delete):0
----------- ---------- ---------- ---------- ----------
            gccb/rtpNL pr gccb NL no gccb sd badConfIds
----------- ---------- ---------- ---------- ----------
call create          0          0          0          0
            add sent T entry Fail entry insr fsm Succss
----------- ---------- ---------- ---------- ----------
                     0          0        244        244
            fsm failed ent delete       fail
----------- ---------- ---------- ---------- ----------
                     0          0          0


            entry !pre fsm failed fsm Succss
----------- ---------- ---------- ---------- ----------
call modify          0          0        745
            entry !pre entry del  fsm failed fsm Succss
----------- ---------- ---------- ---------- ----------
call delete          0          0          0        243
```

```
--------------- --------- --------- --------- ---------
                gccb/rtpNL pr gccb NL no gccb sd badConfIds
--------------- --------- --------- --------- ---------
LPBK call create         0         0         0         0
                add sent T entry Fail entry insr fsm Succss
--------------- --------- --------- --------- ---------
                         0         0         0         0
                fsm failed ent delete       fail
--------------- --------- --------- --------- ---------
                         0         0         0

                entry !pre fsm failed fsm Succss
--------------- --------- --------- --------- ---------
LPBK call modify         0         0         0
                entry !pre entry del  fsm failed fsm Succss
--------------- --------- --------- --------- ---------
LPBK call delete         0         0         0         0
--------------- --------- --------- --------- ---------

--------------- --------- --------- --------- ---------
                gccb/rtpNL pr gccb NL no gccb sd badConfIds
--------------- --------- --------- --------- ---------
STRM call create         0         0         0         0
                add sent T entry Fail entry insr fsm Succss
--------------- --------- --------- --------- ---------
                         0         0         9         9
                fsm failed ent delete       fail
--------------- --------- --------- --------- ---------
                         0         0         0

                entry !pre fsm failed fsm Succss
--------------- --------- --------- --------- ---------
STRM call modify         0         0         0
                entry !pre entry del  fsm failed fsm Succss
--------------- --------- --------- --------- ---------
STRM call delete         0         0         0         9
--------------- --------- --------- --------- ---------

          gccb !fnd entry !pre fsm failed fsm Succss
---------- --------- --------- --------- ---------
call  stats       172       4078          0     32230
```

```
            fsm failed fsm Succss  entry del
----------- --------- --------- --------- ---------
call  timer          0          0          0
            fsm failed fsm Succss
----------- --------- --------- --------- ---------
stats timer          0          0
            entry !pre     rsp ok rsp failed
----------- --------- --------- --------- ---------
provisn rsp          0        824         10
            fsm Succss fsm failed entry deld
----------- --------- --------- --------- ---------
                   834          0          0
            entry !pre     rsp ok rsp failed fsm Succes
----------- --------- --------- --------- ---------
 delete rsp          0        249          0        249
            fsm failed entry deld corr mismt inval gccb
----------- --------- --------- --------- ---------
                     0        252          0          3
type        entry !pre     rsp ok rsp failed InvGCCB
----------- --------- --------- --------- ---------
 stats  rsp          1      31114          0          1
type        fsm Succss fsm failed corr mismt
----------- --------- --------- --------- ---------
                 31114          0          0
type     entry !pre mda DN App mda UP App lpbk mda DN lpbk mda UP Cor !match InvGCCB
-------- ---------- ---------- ---------- ----------- ----------- ---------- -------
media evnt        2          18         787           0           0          0      0
```

- Active calls may disconnect around 15 and 30 minutes after being connected.
  - This is a typical symptom of interoperability issues in handling SIP session refresh in the CUBE–to–service provider, CUBE–to–CVP and CVP–to–CUCM call legs. RFC 4028 describes two SIP extensions, Session-Expires and Min-SE, that are used to negotiate the session interval for a given SIP call. At around halfway through the negotiated session interval, the SIP user agent client (UAC) performs the role of a session refresher and sends a SIP re-INVITE or UPDATE request to refresh the session. If the UAC receives no response or receives a 408 Request Timeout or a 481 Call/Transaction Does Not Exist, it disconnects the existing call. The session refresh scenarios are discussed in detail in Chapter 4.

- Sometimes call disconnects are due to user behavior. For example, when callers call in to a contact center with very long waiting time (more than 15 minutes), they tend to keep their phone on mute or drop their headsets down and start multitasking while waiting for the agent to be available. When an agent becomes available, a caller may have stepped away from her phone. An agent who does not hear any audio after answering the call may disconnect the call, thinking it is a ghost call or a call where the audio stream was not negotiated properly. Meanwhile, the caller thinks the call has dropped after the agent hangs up the call. This issue type can be mitigated by providing a callback option to callers.

Survivability: Why Did It Happen?

The survivability.tcl script that is deployed in CUBE plays a key role in rerouting inbound contact center calls to alternate destinations upon a failure condition. A common question is "Why did the call survivability event happen in the first place?" From the perspective of call detail records, calls that experienced the failure and are handled by survivability.tcl appear as normal call disconnects because these calls are disconnected with cause code **16** (normal call clearing) after they get handled by the survivability script. The occurrence of the **%IVR-4-APP_WARN** syslog message with the text **...undergoing recovery procedures due to a downstream IPCC application failure...** in CUBE signifies that survivability has occurred.

The primary contributor to call survivability event is a network connectivity error in establishing the UDP or TCP connection between CUBE and CVP to exchange SIP signaling messages. These errors may be caused by unexpected events such as an incorrect access-list configuration in the network devices along the network path between CUBE and CVP, a CVP call server application crash, a CVP call server taken out of service to perform maintenance activities, a SIP proxy device in the call signaling path dropping the SIP messages received from CUBE, or forwarding of the SIP messages after a significant delay. Sometimes the inbound calls stop working due to configuration changes in CUBE or in the service provider network that cause call establishment failures such as codec mismatches. These conditions also trigger output of survivability-related syslog messages. The quickest way to verify whether any common triggers are present is to look at the CVP operations console, which monitors CVP application servers in near real-time and check whether the CVP call servers are in the Down state. The statistics are updated every 30 seconds. Presence of this condition is demonstrated in Figure 12-41. A secondary check can be made directly on the CVP call servers in question by using the CVP Diagnostics tool. This secondary check is useful for ruling out the possibility of any communication issue between the CVP call server and the CVP operations console causing incorrect state information.

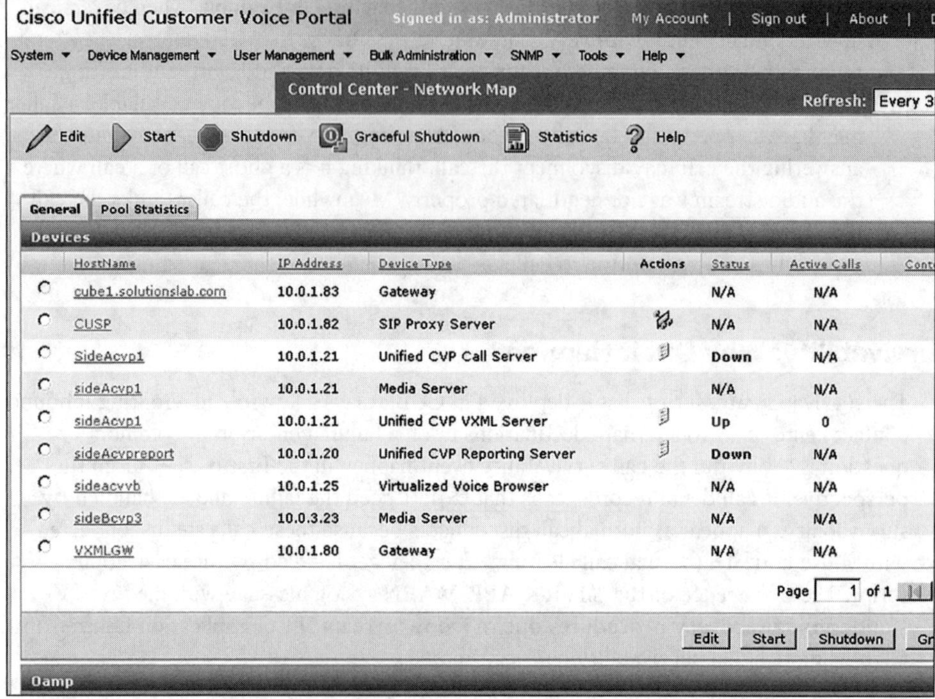

Figure 12-41 *Control Center in the CVP Operations Console*

If the services are up and running, then the following basic debugs can be enabled in CUBE to get visibility into why the calls are failing:

```
debug voip ccapi inout
debug ccsip message
debug ccsip error
debug ip tcp transaction
debug ip icmp
```

It is recommended to monitor CUBE's CPU utilization while the debugs are running and turn off the debugs when utilization reaches 75%. Automation scripts such as Embedded Event Manager applets and diagnostic signatures can be used to monitor CPU utilization and automatically disable debugs. It is also a good practice to increase CUBE's local logging buffer to 200 MB by using the command **logging buffered 200000000 debug** to capture SIP messages of interest without allowing them to be overwritten, as shown in Example 12-39.

Example 12-39 *CUBE Logging-Related Configuration*

```
service sequence-numbers
service timestamps debug datetime localtime msec
service timestamps log datetime msec
logging buffered 200000000 debug
no logging console
logging monitor error
default logging rate-limit
default logging queue-limit


event manager applet monitorCPU  auth bypass
  event snmp oid 1.3.6.1.4.1.9.2.1.56 get-type next entry-op ge entry-val 75  exit-
    time 30 poll-interval 1
  action 01 cli command "enable"
  action 02 cli command "undebug all"
  action 03 syslog msg "High CPU utilization detected. Debugs have been disabled."
```

Example 12-40 shows the sample debug output for a scenario in which CUBE isn't able to establish TCP connection with the CVP call server, resulting in the output of the voice IEC syslog message %VOICE_IEC-3-GW: SIP: Internal Error (Socket error) and an IVR APP (application) warning syslog.

Example 12-40 *Call Survivability Due to TCP Connection Establishment Failure*

```
32940054: May 20 16:42:47.641 UTC: TCP: sending SYN, seq 1575704546, ack 0
32940055: May 20 16:42:47.641 UTC: TCP0: Connection to 10.0.1.21:5060, advertising
  MSS 1460
32940056: May 20 16:42:47.641 UTC: TCP0: state was CLOSED -> SYNSENT [18016 ->
  10.0.1.21(5060)]
32940057: May 20 16:42:47.641 UTC: Released port 18016 in Transport Port Agent for
  TCP IP type 1 delay 240000
32940058: May 20 16:42:47.641 UTC: TCP0: state was SYNSENT -> CLOSED [18016 ->
  10.0.1.21(5060)]
32940059: May 20 16:42:47.641 UTC: TCP0: bad seg from 10.0.1.21 -- closing connec-
  tion: port 18016 seq 0 ack 1575704547 rcvnxt 0 rcvwnd 0 len 0
32940060: May 20 16:42:47.641 UTC: TCP0: connection closed - remote sent RST
32940061: May 20 16:42:47.641 UTC: TCB7FAE713BB630 getting property TCP_VRFTABLEID
  (20)
32940062: May 20 16:42:47.642: %VOICE_IEC-3-GW: SIP: Internal Error (Socket error):
  IEC=1.1.186.7.7.4 on callID 438374 GUID=D1A88C8000010000000000F5A1CAA8C0
32940063: May 20 16:42:47.642 UTC: TCB 0x7FAE713BB630 destroyed
32940064: May 20 16:42:47.644: %IVR-4-APP_WARN: TCL CVP: **** survivability.tcl:
  Call from ANI = sip:4083926010@192.168.202.162 to DNIS = 9194568020 is undergo-
  ing recovery procedures due to a downstream IPCC application failure **** CallID =
  D1A88C80.00010000.000000F5.A1CAA8C0
```

Example 12-41 shows the sample debug output for a scenario in which SIP UDP messages are not processed by the CVP server due to a port unreachable error (in which no application is listening on this port). CUBE outputs the voice IEC syslog message %VOICE_IEC-3-GW: SIP: Internal Error (Socket conn refused) and an IVR APP (application) warning syslog message.

Example 12-41 *Call Survivability Due to Lack of Response for a SIP INVITE Across UDP*

```
32944168: May 20 17:06:12.064 UTC: //438848/171A89000000/SIP/Msg/ccsipDisplayMsg:
Sent:
INVITE sip:8020@sideAcvp1.solutionslab.com:5060 SIP/2.0
Via: SIP/2.0/UDP 10.0.1.83:5060;branch=z9hG4bK138A8234E
Remote-Party-ID: "--CVP_11_6_1_0_0_0_329" <sip:4083926001@10.0.1.83>;party=calling;
  screen=yes;privacy=off
From: sip:4083926001@192.168.202.162;tag=F38E3BE5-1949
To: <sip:8020@sideAcvp1.solutionslab.com>
Date: Sun, 20 May 2018 17:06:12 GMT
Call-ID: EE8A5A32-5B8611E8-AD64E1BE-18C7C14D@10.0.1.83
Supported: timer,resource-priority,replaces,sdp-anat
Min-SE:  1800
Cisco-Guid: 0387614976-0000065536-0000000248-2714413248
User-Agent: Cisco-SIPGateway/IOS-16.6.1
Allow: INVITE, OPTIONS, BYE, CANCEL, ACK, PRACK, UPDATE, REFER, SUBSCRIBE, NOTIFY,
  INFO, REGISTER
CSeq: 101 INVITE
Timestamp: 1526835972
Contact: <sip:4083926001@10.0.1.83:5060>
Expires: 60
Allow-Events: telephone-event
Max-Forwards: 65
X-Cisco-CCBProbe: id:10.0.1.83;loc:site1;trunks:25
Session-ID: 0000481d00105000a000005056a12adc;remote=00000000000000000000000000000000
Session-Expires:  1800
Content-Type: application/sdp
Content-Disposition: session;handling=required
Content-Length: 308

v=0
o=CiscoSystemsSIP-GW-UserAgent 4330 1212 IN IP4 10.0.1.83
s=SIP Call
c=IN IP4 10.0.1.83
t=0 0
m=audio 9122 RTP/AVP 0 18 101 19
c=IN IP4 10.0.1.83
a=rtpmap:0 PCMU/8000
a=rtpmap:18 G729/8000
a=fmtp:18 annexb=no
```

```
a=rtpmap:101 telephone-event/8000
a=fmtp:101 0-15
a=rtpmap:19 CN/8000
a=ptime:20

32944169: May 20 17:06:12.064 UTC: ICMP: dst (10.0.1.83) port unreachable rcv from
  10.0.1.21
32944170: May 20 17:06:12.073 UTC: TCP0: ACK timeout timer expired
32944174: May 20 17:06:12.564: %VOICE_IEC-3-GW: SIP: Internal Error (Socket conn
  refused): IEC=1.1.186.7.102.1 on callID 438848 GUID=171A890000010000000000F8A1CA
  A8C0
32944175: May 20 17:06:12.566: %IVR-4-APP_WARN: TCL CVP: **** survivability.tcl:
  Call from ANI = sip:4083926001@192.168.202.162 to DNIS = 9194568020 is undergo-
  ing recovery procedures due to a downstream IPCC application failure **** CallID =
  171A8900.00010000.000000F8.A1CAA8C0
```

Summary

This chapter introduces the Cisco UCCE solution and the integration aspects for UCCE with CUBE, the Cisco SBC.

The material in this chapter provides an end-to-end view of inbound call flows, focusing both on protocol-level interworking and the configuration of solution components. Advanced functionalities such as call transfers, courtesy callback, and call progress analysis are also discussed. The detailed explanation of inbound and outbound call flows, troubleshooting methodologies, and end-to-end call analysis techniques using tools like CVPParserG3 and TranslatorX provides a foundation for administrators of CUBE in a UCCE environment to quickly isolate and resolve issues such as call disconnects. These tools and techniques aim to ensure that the business can always focus on excellent customer experience instead of issues present in the contact center.

References

"Voice Extensible Markup Language (VoiceXML)2.1," https://www.w3.org/TR/voicexml21/

RFC 4028, "Session Timers in the Session Initiation Protocol (SIP)," https://tools.ietf.org/html/rfc4028

RFC 4463, "A Media Resource Control Protocol (MRCP)," https://tools.ietf.org/html/rfc4463

RFC 4733, "RTP Payload for DTMF Digits, Telephony Tones, and Telephony Signals," https://tools.ietf.org/html/rfc4733

RFC 6787, "Media Resource Control Protocol Version 2 (MRCPv2)," https://tools.ietf.org/html/rfc6787

ITU-T Recommendation E.180/Q.35, "Technical Characteristics of Tones for the Telephone Service," https://www.itu.int/rec/T-REC-E.180-199803-I/en

"Java Telephony API (JTAPI)," http://www.oracle.com/technetwork/java/index-jsp-140696.html

"CTI Server Message Reference Guide (Protocol Version 21) for Cisco Unified Contact Center Enterprise, Release 11.6(1)," https://www.cisco.com/c/en/us/support/customer-collaboration/unified-contact-center-enterprise/products-technical-reference-list.html

"Finesse REST API Developer Guide," https://developer.cisco.com/docs/finesse/#rest-api-dev-guide

"Scripting and Media Routing Guide for Cisco Unified ICM/Contact Center Enterprise, Release 11.6(1)," https://www.cisco.com/c/en/us/td/docs/voice_ip_comm/cust_contact/contact_center/icm_enterprise/icm_enterprise_11_6_1/User/Guide/ucce_b_scripting-and-media-routing-guide1/ucce_b_scripting-and-media-routing-guide1_chapter_0110.html

"Unified Contact Center Enterprise Design Guides," https://www.cisco.com/c/en/us/support/customer-collaboration/unified-contact-center-enterprise/products-implementation-design-guides-list.html

"Cisco Packaged Contact Center Enterprise Features Guide Release 11.6(1)," https://www.cisco.com/c/en/us/td/docs/voice_ip_comm/cust_contact/contact_center/pcce/pcce_11_6_1/maintenance/Guide/pcce_b_pcce-features-guide-11-6.html

"CTI Server Message Reference Guide for Cisco Unified Contact Center Enterprise, Release 11.6(1)," https://www.cisco.com/c/en/us/td/docs/voice_ip_comm/cust_contact/contact_center/icm_enterprise/icm_enterprise_11_6_1/Reference/Guide/ucce_b_cti-server-message-reference-guide/ucce_b_cti-server-message-reference-guide_chapter_01.html

"Understanding Voice Extensible Markup Language (VXML) HTTP Cache for Media Files," https://www.cisco.com/c/en/us/support/docs/customer-collaboration/unified-customer-voice-portal/200744-Understand-Voice-Extensible-Markup-Langu.html

"How to Set Traces and Collect UCCE Logs," https://www.cisco.com/c/en/us/support/docs/customer-collaboration/unified-contact-center-enterprise-1151/212635-how-to-set-traces-and-collect-ucce-logs.html

"System CLI Quick-Reference Guide," http://docwiki.cisco.com/wiki/Unified_System_CLI_Quick-Reference_Guide

"Serviceability Guide for Cisco Unified ICM/Contact Center Enterprise, Release 11.6(1)," https://www.cisco.com/c/en/us/td/docs/voice_ip_comm/cust_contact/contact_center/icm_enterprise/icm_enterprise_11_6_1/Configuration/Guide/ucce_b_serviceability-guide-for-cisco-unified1.html

"Cisco Unified Border Element (CUBE)/SIP Trunking Solutions White Papers," https://www.cisco.com/c/en/us/solutions/enterprise/interoperability-portal/networking_solutions_products_genericcontent0900aecd805bd13d.html

CVPParserG3, http://manceradata.dynalias.com/cvpparser

TranslatorX, https://www.translatorx.org

Wireshark, https://www.wireshark.org

Chapter 13

Security Threat Mitigation

Data, as a top asset of a business, must be protected to uphold both the business's competitive advantage and reputation. Collaboration through voice and video is at the core of modern business conduct, which means the collaboration infrastructure is a fundamental carrier of sensitive information. Information security best practices must therefore be a foundational practice in the deployment and operation of the collaboration solution.

This chapter covers both policy and technical defense mechanisms for reducing the risk of attacks on collaboration systems where SBCs are deployed. The following specific topics are discussed:

- **An Overview of Security Threats to Collaboration Solutions**—This section provides a general outline of information security approaches and techniques to apply to collaboration solutions.
- **Types of Security Threats**—This section explores specific types of attacks that may be mounted against collaboration deployments and offers some solutions for defending against these attacks at the SBC edge.
- **Other SBC Security Features**—This section discusses some general threat defense functionality offered in SBCs, including CUBE, that is not specific to a single attack type but that can improve the overall security posture.
- **Designing UC Networks for Security**—This section discusses approaches and guidelines for designing protection for a collaboration network.

This chapter demonstrates the essential concepts involved in secure deployment of SBC devices. The techniques discussed here will help reduce and hopefully prevent the presence of security attacks against deployed collaboration services.

An Overview of Security Threats to Collaboration Solutions

Exploitation of the security of voice transport solutions is not a new topic. The origins can be traced back at least as far as the mid-1950s, when a young man was shopping at a national department store. Dave Condon heard a 50-cent Davy Crockett "Cat and Canary Bird Call Whistle" and was intrigued by its natural 10 Hz warbling vibrato. He purchased this toy and drilled holes in the metal resonator clip until the base pitch was tuned for a 1 kHz tone. This resulted in naturally producing the 1 kHz tone with a ±10 Hz warble, replicating a phone network's *ring-forward* signal. In the legacy phone days, this signal's function was to notify a human operator that another operator from the originating end of the call had requested another dispatcher for the connection of a long-distance call.

To test a theory on a potential weakness in the phone system, Condon suspected that if he could get legitimately patched through by a local operator to a remote site, and then get the operator at the remote dispatch to hang up, he could use this ring-forward signal to illuminate the remote site operator's switchboard. This would allow him to fake all calls coming into the remote dispatch as a peer operator, bypassing the long-distance call authentication and the required toll payment.

Condon tested this approach. He convinced his local operator to patch a call through to a remote city operator and check for a message left by another long-distance caller. (At the time, it was common practice when a called party did not answer to leave a message with an operator.) The remote operator, unable to find the message, hung up that side of the call. Condon was still connected to the distant operating center and used his whistle on the active call leg to signal a call request back to the remote site's switchboard, appearing to originate from another operator. This brought another operator at the remote city on the line, and Condon pretended to be a peer operator and requested to be patched to a long-distance number for another caller. Because the remote operators only worked with other operators to patch these calls through when their switchboard was triggered from a ring-forward indication, the call was patched through without authentication by the remote operator, and Condon had successfully circumvented the toll requirement for a long-distance call.

A similar exploit was carried out in the late 1960s, after John Draper found a toy whistle found in a Cap'n Crunch cereal box. This whistle emulated a 2600 Hz tone, generating the in-band signaling necessary to allow the dialing caller to circumvent payment for long distance calls.

Today's voice attacks are often more technical in nature than playing a note from a flute or whistle into a phone system, but the same premise of interleaving technological leverage with social engineering still makes it possible to exploit voice systems today. Due to the industry's transformation from distributed private branch exchanges (PBXs) at every remote site to converging on more centralized voice systems and trunks, there is a much larger impact when voice systems are exploited today, as an attack can target a single location and have an impact across a large user base of many physical locations.

In addition, the industry has moved toward having more external integrations, such as trunks between enterprises for business-to-business (B2B) calling or use of external cloud-hosted tools through application programming interfaces (APIs). These external integrations require an extension of trust boundaries across administrative domains and configuration of additional entry and exit points through the network. As a result of such increased risks, the need for a strong security posture with collaboration solutions has increased rapidly over the past two decades.

In the Federal Information Processing Standards (FIPS) 200, the National Institute of Standards and Technology (NIST) defines a *security threat* as a "any circumstance or event with the potential to adversely impact organizational operations (including mission, functions, image, or reputation), organizational assets, or individuals through an information system via unauthorized access, destruction, disclosure, modification of information, and/or denial of service." Security threats can either be deliberately caused by malicious users, accidental, or environmental.

This chapter primarily focuses on deliberate threats and ways to mitigate them. Controls for accidental or environmental threats (such as hardware or software failure) are mainly addressed through the deployment of high availability deployment models (see Chapter 2, "SBC Deployment Models") and monitoring (see Chapter 14, "Monitoring and Management").

Due to the increasing concerns about information security, most organizations have companywide information security policies and standards to ensure an informed and consistent approach to information security across a company. In addition, many industries have security policies that are enforced by the specific industry (for example, the Payment Card Industry Security Standards Council [PCI], or the Health Insurance Portability and Accountability Act [HIPAA]). Standards and governing bodies help define and enforce standards for information security across all technologies, including applications for collaboration solutions and SBC deployments. Some of these policies and standards are also specific to certain countries or operating regions.

To understand how to defend against voice security threats, it is important to understand the nature of these attacks. The following sections cover the targets of attacks, the origin of these attacks, and provide some common examples of current threats to voice security.

What Is the Target of an Attack?

Attacks on information security target one or more of three information attributes:

- **Confidentiality**—The privacy of data or information
- **Integrity**—The assurance that the system and information have not been altered or changed possession without authorization
- **Availability**—The notion that the intended system or service is able to be used as expected

Confidentiality attacks are attacks on privacy, exposing sensitive information to individuals that are not entitled to that information. For example, in a man-in-the-middle attack, the attacker eavesdrops on transmission of sensitive data by inserting himself in the middle of the media communication flow. Encryption, multifactor authentication, and personnel training can help thwart these types of attacks and protect sensitive data.

Threats on integrity include modification of existing data or services to perform differently than intended. These attacks may involve the sharing or destruction of important data for a business or tampering with the data to change what the data represents. Integrity threats could involve modifying a call center script or redirecting an SBC's call toward a rogue server that collects callers' Social Security numbers and personal identification numbers (PINs). An integrity attack could also spoof the identity of a caller in an attempt to gain the trust of the called party. Such an attack could result in the called party granting the malicious caller access to restricted information or data. Configuration management best practices, such as leveraging cryptographic checksums and version control, can help defend against malicious modification of asset data.

Availability attacks are attacks that threaten to reduce the availability or uptime of a service. The intent of such an attack is to take business-critical functions offline. An example of an availability attack is a denial-of-service (DoS) attack to render a sales hotline for a company unresponsive. The strongest defense against availability attacks is to design and implement dynamic and robust approaches for redundancy, resiliency, and failover capabilities.

Where Do Attacks Originate?

Security threats can be initiated from both internal and external sources. Internal threats, which are orchestrated by those from within a company, pose a greater risk because inside parties have privileged access to sensitive information such as credentials and knowledge about how the information is protected. Inside attacks may originate from disgruntled employees but also may be conducted unintentionally, such as when a victim is subject to a social engineering attack and shares sensitive information with an outside attacker.

External threats are more limited in scope, as these attacks require methods to cross the boundary of trust into the target network. In properly designed networks, external exploitation from technical attack vectors involved (for example, executing an exploit on a recent security vulnerability to gain access to the inside network of a firewall) is rare because of the complexity. As a result, many external threats rely on leveraging weaknesses in those with access inside the network to make it possible to mount an external attack.

Various studies have attempted to quantify the attacks that are internal versus external, and inadvertent versus malicious. Though there is wide variation of these percentages across the different studies, it is generally accepted in the information security industry that internal threats pose a very serious threat to the security of a business. As a result, inside attacks must be approached with a serious intent to reduce this risk, even for companies that are confident that their employees are trustworthy.

What Are the Targets of Attacks?

Most security attacks target either information or a service that is being provided. These attacks may be physical attacks, or they may be logical attacks.

Physical attacks are attacks in which physical controls are circumvented to gain material access. They include actions such as looking in trash bins for printed records, shoulder surfing (where the attacker piggybacks on a legitimate user's access to a sensitive physical area of a building) to gain access to a data center across a locked door, driving a truck through the wall of a data center to unrack and steal a server, or intentionally destroying physical infrastructure such as a power main that is being used for a hosting service.

Logical attacks are attacks that come in through the informational data plane, where physical in-person access to a device is not required. Logical attacks include attack vectors such as accessing a router through a virtual SSH session and brute-force guessing of a root account's password.

Attacks specifically against collaboration solutions target one of three areas: call signaling, call media, or the underlying network and server infrastructure that supports the collaboration solution.

Types of Security Threats

Many types of attacks target information technologies. Although this section does not aim to provide an exhaustive list of attack types, it explores some of the most common attacks in the landscape today. Your organization should consider these examples while building or assessing the governance and technical controls used as defensive mechanisms against security threats.

Social Engineering and Impersonation

Social engineering is the art of psychological manipulation of a person as a means for an attacker to circumvent existing security controls. These attacks often entail the attacker using some components of information or trickery as a way to build trust with the victim. The victim gains a level of comfort and may share confidential information such as credentials or physical/remote access to systems, and the attacker then exploits the victim's trust by stealing other company information.

Social engineering is often cited as the greatest current threat to information security, as it is the path of least resistance for an attacker. These attacks are also the most challenging for companies to put controls around, as the attacks exploit the very nature of variation in human behavior. Many networks have systematic controls around technical items such as firewall policies and vulnerability patching. These policies are feasibly reported on for compliance, but controlling human behavior and proactively assessing the information risk of employee behavior across a large company is a much bigger challenge.

Social engineering has been used for thousands of years as a mechanism of subterfuge. These attacks date back as least as far as the Trojan War, when a Greek army hid inside a horse statue presented as a gift to the Trojans. The Trojans allowed this gift to enter their city of Troy, and after nightfall, the Greek army burst from the horse and launched a surprise attack against the city of Troy—and ultimately won the war.

A modern-day example of a social engineering attack on a collaboration solution could be a phishing scam to collect users' information. An attacker might set up a rogue interactive voice response (IVR) system and trick users into thinking it is their banking system, so that they call the IVR and enter their phone numbers and PINs. These credentials would then be stored so the attacker could later authenticate as various users, potentially conducting banking tasks using different users' credentials, registering phones with users' extensions, or listening to users' voicemails.

Social engineering can occur both remotely and physically. Remote attacks can be performed over media such as email, voice/video calls, or unsolicited posts to websites such as blogs or social media sites. Physical social engineering attacks may include shoulder surfing or verbal in-person conversations to convince victims to grant access to something to which the attacker is not entitled.

Social engineering attacks often use fear or urgency as leverage to pressure victims into complying. An attacker may try to convince a victim that he knows what he is doing is wrong but that he is under a tight deadline and needs to bend the rules to accomplish the task. An attacker may also try to trick a victim into thinking that if she doesn't comply, she will get into trouble.

Mitigating Social Engineering and Impersonation

The following approaches are suggested to minimize the threat of social engineering. Consider social engineering attacks on both virtual and physical environments when developing and validating the following policies and controls:

- Develop a security policy on information protection that is easily accessible by employees and reviewed on a routine basis. It is essential to define what type of information is defined as sensitive, including items such as personal information, credentials, and information about critical systems.
- Regularly educate and assess users based on the types of social engineering attacks being used so that they can identify when a similar attack is being attempted.
- Empower the user base to be able to say "no" to divulging sensitive information, even when the request is deemed time-sensitive and under high pressure.
- Provide a trusted escalation path for employees to reach out to when suspicious inquiries come in that need to be authenticated and validated for business legitimacy. This path should include all types of workers, including internal employees (for example, IT support desk staff), customer requests for data, and external vendor access.

- Validate sources of requests for information where feasible, such as URLs and certificates for websites that are prompting for credentials. Train employees not to browse or accept connectivity to servers that are unencrypted protocols (such as HTTP), nor to those servers that have untrusted public key certificates.

Caller ID Impersonation

Historically, there were very few PSTN carriers due to the large overhead cost involved in hosting PSTN infrastructure. The small provider ecosystem allowed for providers to have mutual trust, and they would simply honor caller ID passed between carriers. Carriers did not feel the need to authenticate caller ID presented from another provider, as it could only be sent by another provider, so it was often just passed along downstream to the destination.

This inherent trust in the authenticity of caller ID resulted in many users from the legacy PSTN phone era trusting caller ID information at face value. This user mentality has now carried over into today's era of calls converged over IP networks. When a call comes in from another source, regardless of where it originated from (which today might be a small untrusted rogue SIP server spoofing caller ID), many users still inherently trust the caller ID of a call as a way to authenticate the source and identity of a user. This is a dangerous practice, as in most scenarios nothing is done to validate the authenticity of the caller ID.

For instance, an attacker could easily place a call to a victim from the calling number +1-410-872-4500, which is the current published number of the Cisco Systems headquarters. The victim might pretend to be a TAC engineer and ask a user for his or her cisco.com password. The user could do a reverse search on the number to validate that the number does indeed belong to Cisco, but that action does not validate that the person on the other end of the call is actually a Cisco employee or has the right to the requested information. The challenge here is that, whereas X.509 certificates provide for authenticity of Hypertext Transfer Protocol Secure (HTTPS) servers, there is no equivalent uniform way in the PSTN to authenticate with a root source that a call is coming from a known and trusted entity associated with that number. This presents an information security challenge because if the authenticity of the source (or destination) of a call cannot be trusted, the call could be used for social engineering or other malicious means.

Also, some voicemail systems use caller ID as the key in authenticating as the owner of a voicemail box. In these systems, if an attacker can impersonate the victim's caller ID for a call into the voicemail system, she might be able to authenticate as an owner of the voicemail inbox and listen to messages.

Attackers may also maliciously manipulate caller ID in automated calling DoS attacks to generate calls from random numbers, making it more difficult to identify and block the calls as part of the flooding attacks.

RFC 3261 defined the **From** header to be used to provide caller identity with SIP. An attacker can easily set this field to any number to test whether the upstream party honors the caller ID set. As smaller SIP carriers have become available, the values set by users for the SIP **From** header have not always been enforced. Providers often pass on whatever caller ID is sent without validating that the number is owned by the calling party. Example 13-1 shows an outbound SIP INVITE being set to the Cisco Systems headquarters number by a rogue user.

Example 13-1 *Modifying the* **From** *Header for Caller ID on a SIP INVITE*

```
INVITE sip:14085551234@192.0.2.100:5060 SIP/2.0
Via: SIP/2.0/UDP 198.52.100.1:5060;branch=z9hG4bK98e4117d52a6
From: "Cisco Systems" <sip:14108724500@198.52.100.1>;tag=25526~ffa80926-5fac-4dd6-
  b405-2dbbc56ae9a2-551664735
To: <sip:14085551234@192.0.2.100>
Date: Mon, 02 Apr 2012 18:12:31 GMT
Call-ID: 68781700-f791ec0f-2d26-e28690a@198.52.100.1
Supported: timer,resource-priority,replaces
Min-SE: 1800
User-Agent: Cisco-CUCM8.6
Allow: INVITE, OPTIONS, INFO, BYE, CANCEL, ACK, PRACK, UPDATE, REFER, SUBSCRIBE,
  NOTIFY
CSeq: 101 INVITE
Expires: 180
Allow-Events: presence, kpml
Supported: X-cisco-srtp-fallback
Supported: Geolocation
Call-Info: <sip: 198.52.100.1:5060>;method="NOTIFY;Event=telephone-
  event;Duration=500"
Cisco-Guid: 1752700672-0000065536-0000007823-0237529354
Session-Expires: 84600
Contact: <sip: +19195553456@198.52.100.1:5060>
Max-Forwards: 70
Content-Length: 0
Content-Type: application/sdp
Content-Length: 238
```

As SIP developed, a need arose to provide a mechanism to allow a caller to hide his or her identity for an outbound call, such as when calling from an unlisted number. This capability to hide caller identity has been available on the PSTN by dialing a special code to intentionally disable caller ID delivery (*67 in North America, and #31# or *31* in many other countries). RFC 3325 provided support for this scenario by overwriting the **From** header with **sip:anonymous@anonymous.invalid**. SIP servers still needed to know what number a call was coming from when hiding identity, so the **P-Asserted-Identity** header was defined for use in these scenarios as a way to pass on the caller information between trusted parties. The understanding was that this field would be stripped when the request left the trusted network and not presented to the called party.

With current implementations and Internet Telephony Service Providers (ITSP) integrations, the SIP trust boundaries have become ambiguous in some environments. Both **From** or **P-Asserted-Identity** headers are often found being honored or even passed through across a trust boundary without authentication for validity. Example 13-2 shows an example of spoofing the **P-Asserted-Identity** field to spoof caller ID; the latter part of the INVITE used by this example has been omitted for brevity.

Example 13-2 P-Asserted-Identity *Field for Caller ID on a SIP INVITE*

```
INVITE sip:+14085551212@proxy.example.net SIP/2.0
Via: SIP/2.0/TCP useragent.example.com;branch=z9hG4bK-124
Via: SIP/2.0/TCP proxy.example.com;branch=z9hG4bK-abc
To: <sip:+14085551212@example.com>
From: "Anonymous" <sip:anonymous@anonymous.invalid>;tag=9802748
Call-ID: 245780247857024504
CSeq: 2 INVITE
Max-Forwards: 69
P-Asserted-Identity: tel:+14108724500
Privacy: id
...
```

The current challenge with these attacks is that service providers rarely have the ability to validate the authenticity and integrity of this field when functioning as proxies or intermediary devices for underlying SIP calls. Some ITSPs accept inbound calls from subscribers only when the calling party number matches the direct inward dial numbers (DIDs) that the ITSP is hosting for that entity. This approach has some shortcomings, though. A company might want to send a call from a number that it owns but that is not registered with the specific ITSP the call is being sent through. This is common in call center deployments, where a company may register the main number with a specific carrier and then use that number for all agents calling outbound, even when another carrier's circuit is chosen for the outbound route. Another challenge is that the approaches only work for protecting malicious use at the first hop of the call. Intermediate service providers don't have a way to validate the upstream authenticity, and they are forced to either blindly trust and pass along the original calling party number or overwrite the number. Overwriting numbers may result in legitimate numbers being modified, and this approach is too heavy-handed to be practical for transit providers due to the major shortcomings of not validating end-to-end integrity of the caller ID. Finally, there isn't a mechanism to ensure that the original caller ID field has not been tampered with. Though SIP over TLS may help prevent message tampering within a hop, it only protects the message integrity across that single SIP hop. Given that a SIP call usually has several SIP hops between the source of the call and the final destination, SIP TLS does not protect the end-to-end integrity of caller ID as it could be modified at any of the intermediary SIP hops where the TLS connection terminates.

Mitigating Caller ID Impersonation

To protect against the type of attack mentioned earlier, where caller ID impersonation can be used to bypass voicemail authentication, voicemail systems should require PIN authentication even in scenarios where the caller ID matches a subscriber on the system.

Mitigating the manipulation of caller identity or providing authentication of a caller to the presented caller ID is a much larger challenge. The first attempt in the industry to address this was proposed in RFC 4474 in 2006, and it involved authenticating identity with a local authentication service that is permitted to represent the calling party (typically an entity that owns the domain of the calling party's URI). This authentication service then inserted an **Identity** header for a downstream verification service to validate the authenticity and integrity of the header. This header had integrity through use of a cryptographically signed digest. The approach consisted of a SIP endpoint sending calls to a local authorization proxy in charge of the domain. The authorization server would then validate the identity of the calling party (such as through SIP digest authentication), generate a hash across the desired headers (including the **From**, **To**, **Contact**, **Call-ID**, and **Date** headers) and the SIP message body for tamper prevention, and then sign the hash with the authentication proxy's private key. Another header, **Identity-Info**, was also added to allow the recipient of the message to obtain the authentication server's public certificate that was used for signing the identity. Upon receipt of the **Identity** header, a verification service would then consume the header and perform the following actions:

Step 1. Acquire the certificate that the **Identity** header was signed with, as noted by the **Identity-Info** header for the location of the public certificate of the verification service.

Step 2. Validate that the signer was an authority for the URI of the **From** header's domain.

Step 3. Validate the signature in the **Identity** field to ensure integrity.

Step 4. Validate the **Date**, **Contact**, and **Call-ID** headers.

If the validation failed, a **438 Invalid Identity Header** response was sent, and the call was not processed further. If the validation succeeded, the call was forwarded along.

The approach suggested in RFC 4474 did not take hold in the industry, as it did not account for the critical need to handle telephone number addresses instead of domain name–based/URI-based addresses. For example, a call can come in a PSTN gateway and be transmitted over SIP as coming from **sip:+17005551008@chicago.example.com** even when **chicago.example.com** is not the authoritative owner of +17005551008. Another oversight was that there was no mechanism for the recipient to validate that the authentication server signing the request owned the telephone number and was a trusted authority to define the integrity of the source. Finally, this approach attempted to provide a signature of headers that are commonly changed by SBCs and other intermediary SIP devices (such as **Call-ID**). RFC 8224 acknowledged these shortcomings, and RFC 4474 was deprecated in early 2018.

RFC 8224

To address the challenges just described, the IETF Secure Telephony Identity Revisited (STIR) workgroup proposed a new architecture of identity tokenization and called number trusts to provide secure SIP identification. As a result, this workgroup created RFC 8224 to define the use of a SIP-authenticated identity management framework and revised approach to the SIP **Identity** header, as well as new syntax for representing the identity through a personal assertion token (PASSporT). (PASSporT and the associated authentication and verification framework are covered in detail in the next section.)

The RFC 8224 approach is influenced by RFC 4474 but corrects some of the shortcomings of RFC 4474. The **CSeq**, **Call-ID**, and **Contact** fields, as well as the SIP message body, are no longer part of the **Identity** header's signature, so they can be changed by intermediary devices without the **Identity** header changing. Also, guidance on how intermediary devices such as SIP gateways should handle telephone number validation are also accounted for, to address RFC 4474's shortcomings with telephone number addresses. Furthermore, RFC 8224 allows for multiple **Identity** headers, which was not possible with the previous recommendation. Finally, the **Identity-Info** header from RFC 4474 has been deprecated in favor of including the details in the **Identity** header itself.

To provide integrity and assurance of the caller identity, the authentication service constructs a cryptographically signed JavaScript Object Notation Web Token (JWT) format, defined by RFC 7519 and updated in RFC 7797. The JWT-formatted identity token is broken down into three parts, as defined in RFC 8225, and implemented into SIP with RFC 8224. These three parts of PASSporT syntax are ***header.claims.signature***.

In this syntax, ***header*** defines the type and encryption being used in the token. The attributes **type**, **alg**, and **x5u** are the recommended minimum parameters. These parameters define the type of the token (which will always be PASSporT in this implementation), the cryptographic algorithm to be used for signature (options are outlined in RFC 7518), and a URI locator for the public X.509 certificate of the signing party.

The ***claims*** portion is essentially the important payload of the PASSporT. This contains the information about the identity of the call. The attributes outlined in Table 13-1 are used to define this information.

Table 13-1 *Claim Type Definitions*

Attribute	Claim Title	Purpose
iat	Issued At	Specifies the date and time of issuance of the JWT. This provides security against reply and cut-and-paste attacks. The format is the duration of time since epoch time (1970-01-01T00:00:00Z UTC), as defined by RFC 7519.
orig	Originator of the call	A parent object containing **tn** and/or **uri** attributes corresponding to the originator of the call. There can be only one instance of this field.

Attribute	Claim Title	Purpose
dest	Call destination	A parent object containing **tn** and/or **uri** attributes corresponding to the intended destination for the call. One or more of these fields can be present.
tn	Telephone number	Specified if the originating or destination identity is a telephone number. This number must be canonicalized into a globally routable format as specified in Section 8.3. of RFC 8224.
uri	Uniform resource identifier	Specified if any of the originating or destination identities are in the form of a URI address.

The ***signature*** portion of the JWT-formatted PASSporT is signed using the JSON Web Signature (JWS) standard defined in RFC 7515. This guarantees authenticity of the ***claims*** portion through the trust of the signing party.

Table 13-2 provides an example of the intended decoded payload for the **Identity** header and the JWT-encoded payload.

Table 13-2 *Sample PASSporT Data Syntax and JWT Encoding*

Attribute	Payload (decoded)	JWT-Encoded Payload

header	{
	"typ":"PASSporT",
	"alg":"ES256",
	"x5u":"https://cert.example.org/PASSporT.cer"
	}
		eyJhbGciOiJFUzI1NiIsInR5cCI6InBhc3Nwb3J0IiwieDV1IjoiaHR0cHM6Ly9jZXJ0LmV4YW1wbGUub3JnL3Bhc3Nwb3J0LmNlciJ9

claims	{
	"dest":{
	"tn":["19195551234"],
	"uri":["sip:alice@example.com",
	"sip:bob@example.net"]
	},
	"iat":1443208345,
	"orig":{"tn":"14085551234"}
	}
		eyJkZXN0Ijp7InRuIjpbIjE5MTk1NTUxMjM0Il0sInVyaSI6WyJzaXA6YWxpY2VAZXhhbXBsZS5jb20iLCJzaXA6Ym9iQGV4YW1wbGUubmV0Il19LCJpYXQiOjE0NDMyMDgzNDUsIm9yaWciOnsidG4iOiIxNDA4NTU1MTIzNCJ9fQ

Attribute	Payload (decoded)	JWT-Encoded Payload
signature	Not applicable, as this signature merely portrays the *header* + *claims* content, signed with the private key.	ADa7dxop6UNnN86muoQQt9gHoKVR5YEtoAVJ4LT1Ia5ticy04FpFp3tLpcyXNd53DLmhIuE-gOfhkMkL5YioQlUxAOrZ5lrxsdUzsUYj088sz_2JwtjCZO-PLIQNHGdHaqgB7tawLb1KpmZqDDAD46UR2Fje8yS3CQR_3_JRwaa2Goj7

Unlike with RC 8824, which specifies a separate **Identity-Info** header to provide the location of the certificate store, this certificate store location information is instead collapsed into the **Identity** header as a trailing attribute. Information on the algorithm selected is also added to the **Identity** header with use of the **alg** tag. If no **alg** tag is present in the **Identity** header, then ES256 is assumed. Finally, an optional tag **ppt** can be used to specify extensions to the PASSporT format if additional fields not specified in RFC 8224 are desired to be included in the ***claims*** portion.

Example 13-3 demonstrates a SIP INVITE with the presence of the full JWT-encoded and signed PASSporT **Identity** header from Table 13-2, included in the SIP **Identity** header along with the **alg** and **ppt** tags.

Example 13-3 *SIP* Identity *Header*

```
INVITE sip:14085551234@proxy.example.com;transport=UDP SIP/2.0
Via: SIP/2.0/UDP 192.0.2.100:39089;branch=z9hG4bK76ytsejam
Max-Forwards: 70
Contact: <sip:14085551234@192.0.2.100:39089;transport=UDP>
To: <sip:14085551234@proxy.example.com>
From: "14085551234"<sip: 14085551234@proxy2.example.net>;tag=1f4e4f40
Call-ID: YzR1ZDF1YzYyM2IwOTdlMzMTRmxmY3OGIzODM.
CSed: 2 INVITE
Identity: eyJhbGciOiJFUzI1NiIsInR5cCI6InBhc3Nwb3J0IiwieDV1IjoiaHR0cHM6Ly9jZXJ0Lm-
  V4YW1wbGUub3JnL3Bhc3Nwb3J0LmNlciJ9eyJkZXN0Ijp7InRuIjpbIjE5MTk1NTUxMjM0Il-
  0sInVyaSI6WyJzaXA6YWxpY2VAZXhhbXBsZS5jb20iLCJzaXA6Ym9iQGV4YW1wbGUubmV0Il-
  19LCJpYXQiOjE0NDMyMDgzNDUsIm9yaWciOnsidG4iOiIxNDA4NTU1MTIzNCJ9fQ.
  ADa7dxop6UNnN86muoQQt9gHoKVR5YEtoAVJ4LT1Ia5ticy04FpFp3tLpcyXNd53DLmhIuE-
  gOfhkMkL5YioQlUxAOrZ5lrxsdUzsUYj088sz_2JwtjCZO-PLIQNHGdHaqgB7tawLb1KpmZqDDAD46U-
  R2Fje8yS3CQR_3_JRwaa2Goj7;info=<https://cert.example.org/PASSporT.cer>;alg=ES256
Date: Fri, 25 Sep 2015 19:12:25 GMT
User-Agent: myProxy 1.0
```

The PASSporT specification also permits a *compact form* of the syntax from Table 13-2 that reduces the **Identity** header to just the third parameter. This omits redundant information and is indicated by the prefix of two periods (..) as shown in Example 13-4.

Example 13-4 *SIP* **Identity** *Header (Compact Form)*

```
INVITE sip:14085551234@proxy.example.com;transport=UDP SIP/2.0
Via: SIP/2.0/UDP 192.0.2.100:39089;branch=z9hG4bK76ytsejam
Max-Forwards: 70
Contact: <sip:14085551234@192.0.2.100:39089;transport=UDP>
To: <sip:14085551234@proxy.example.com>
From: "14085551234"<sip: 14085551234@proxy2.example.net>;tag=1f4e4f40
Call-ID: YzR1ZDF1YzYyM2IwOTdlMzMTRmxmY3OGIzODM.
CSed: 2 INVITE
Identity: ..ADa7dxop6UNnN86muoQQt9gHoKVR5YEtoAVJ4LT1Ia5ticy04FpFp3tLpcyXNd53DLmhIuE-
  gOfhkMkL5YioQlUxAOrZ5lrxsdUzsUYj088sz_2JwtjCZO-PLIQNHGdHaqgB7tawLb1KpmZqDDAD46UR2
  Fje8yS3CQR_3_JRwaa2Goj7;info=<https://cert.example.org/PASSporT.cer>;alg=ES256
Date: Fri, 25 Sep 2015 19:12:25 GMT
User-Agent: myProxy 1.0
```

The PASSporT found in the **Identity** header is then validated by both the originator's authentication service and the destination's verification service. The **Identity-Info** header previously described in RFC 4474 is no longer used in this architecture, as the certificate store location is defined in the header's **x5u** attribute as well as outside the signature with the **info** tag.

An optional attribute for PASSporT is the **mky** claim. This can also be included in the ***claims*** payload of the **Identity** header, which provides a vehicle for protecting the **a=fingerprint** attribute used in the session description protocol (SDP) for SRTP negotiation.

Figure 13-1 outlines the call flow for the authentication and verification services performed by originating and terminating service providers that support PASSporT:

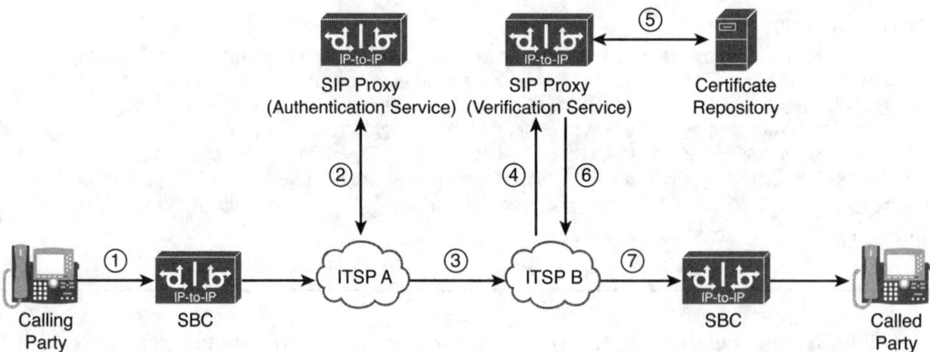

Figure 13-1 *PASSporT End-to-End Call Flow for Authentication and Verification*

Step 1. The calling party places a call to the proxy of his or her service provider (ITSP A's SIP proxy).

Step 2. ITSP A's SIP proxy authenticates the calling party, performing the function of the authentication service. It validates that it is authorized to assert the identity of the **From** field, and then an **Identity** header is constructed with the elements described earlier (PASSporT containing the ***claims*** portion for originating and destination numbers) that is signed with the applicable private key associated with the calling party.

Step 3. The INVITE with the added **Identity** header is forwarded along the SIP network to the destination, a proxy at ITSP B.

Step 4. ITSP B's SIP proxy consumes the INVITE, identifies the presence of an **Identity** header that needs to be processed, and performs the verification service role.

Step 5. The verification proxy fetches the X.509 certificate's public key from the public certificate repository.

Step 6. The proxy validates the SIP **Identity** header's signature to ensure the integrity of the **Identity** header. The time stamp is also validated for freshness. (Receipt within 60 seconds of the time stamp is desired.)

Step 7. ITSP B forwards the call to the destination called party. The validation information can then be used to make a decision about the call either by the called party's PBX or by presenting the verification status to the end user.

SHAKEN

An extension to the PASSporT format is the Signature-Based Handling of Asserted Information Using Tokens (SHAKEN) framework, documented by ATIS-1000074. When SHAKEN is being used, it is specified in the **Identity** header as **ppt=shaken**. SHAKEN improves the PASSporT framework by providing additional information on the origin of the call for further authentication and reputation building. This is done through the presence of two additional attributes in the ***claims*** payload of the **Identity** header:

- **origid**—An origination identifier that is a globally unique originating identifier to determine from what service provider network the call has originated
- **attest**—An attestation indicator for the context of how the call was originated and whether it came from a party authorized to use the number

The origination identifier is specified in a universally unique identifier (UUID) format (as defined by RFC 4122) and is assigned to a logical entity associated with the call. The UUID may represent the service provider entity itself, a specific customer, a group of devices, or otherwise logical constructs that the call has arrived from. The intent with this field is to build a reputation or traceback identification of the call origin. At the time of this publication, there is no guidance on a universal governing body for assignment of UUIDs to entities. Best practices for assigning origination identifiers are anticipated to be further developed as the standard matures.

Attestation is an assessment of the calling party's validity of the presented number, based on the origin and nature of the call. This is performed by the originating provider, which would be the closest SIP provider to the origin of the calling party. One of the three single-letter codes is used as a response for the assessment:

- **A (full attestation)**—The calling party has been authenticated and validated as authorized to use the related calling number. These are scenarios where the provider is responsible for origination of the call onto the IP network, has a direct relationship with the customer, and can establish verification of the calling number. A single origination identifier for use here is adequate, unless the service provider desires to have granularity based on region or customer class.
- **B (partial attestation)**—The origin of the call is authenticated, but the originating provider cannot validate that the source is authorized to use the calling number. These are the same requirements as with the full attestation mentioned previously, where the provider has a direct relationship with the customer originating the call but is not able to establish verification of the calling number. In such scenarios, the guidance is to use a customer-specific **origid**.
- **C (gateway attestation)**—The remote peer from which the call was received has been authenticated, but the originator of the call has not been authenticated, and the calling number also cannot be authenticated. This simply asserts the point at which the call entered the network. In this scenario, the guidance is to provide a **origid** granular enough to identify the originating node or trunk from which the call arrived into the gateway.

Coupling together the **origid** and **attest** fields provides a useful audit trail but does not guarantee full legitimacy. It is ultimately up to the authenticating service provider to determine whether it has validity to assert authorization of a number's use. Each service provider is assigned a unique **origid**, and a service provider that falsely asserts numbers will eventually erode the reputation of its **origid**, and global analytics will allow for blacklisting of calls associated with that service provider's **origid**. This is why the identifier should be more granular as the attestation becomes weaker: to prevent the reputation from degrading across large groups outside the span of influence of the device performing the attestation.

The **ppt** extension is defined in the PASSporT header in Example 13-5, and the **attest** and **origid** attributes are provided in Example 13-6.

Example 13-5 *Inclusion of SHAKEN Attributes in the PASSporT Header*

```
{
   "typ":"PASSporT",
   "alg":"ES256",
   "ppt":"shaken",
   "x5u":"https://cert.example.org/PASSporT.cer"
}
```

Example 13-6 *Inclusion of SHAKEN Attributes in the PASSporT* **claims** *Payload*

```
{
    "attest":"A",
    "dest":{"tn":["14085556789"]},
    "iat":1443208345,
    "orig":{"tn":"19195551234"},
    "origid":"123e4567-e89b-12d3-a456-426655440000"
}
```

Example 13-7 shows the inclusion of the compact format hash containing the SHAKEN extensions with the **ppt** defined for SHAKEN on the end of the **Identity** header.

Example 13-7 *Example of the SIP* **Identity** *Header with SHAKEN Enabled*

```
INVITE sip:14085551234@proxy.example.com;transport=UDP SIP/2.0
Via: SIP/2.0/UDP 192.0.2.100:39089;branch=z9hG4bK76ytsejam
Max-Forwards: 70
Contact: <sip:14085551234@192.0.2.100:39089;transport=UDP>
To: <sip:14085551234@proxy.example.com>
From: "14085551234"<sip: 14085551234@proxy2.example.net>;tag=1f4e4f40
Call-ID: YzR1ZDF1YzYyM2IwOTdlMzMTRmxmY3OGIzODM.
CSed: 2 INVITE
Identity: ..Ac_OxfRBIWxSRFZKgVsvpsy0gP0368vmX6dnxVb_WZ8R7NdXTxyKtqHl-WvddK5Xt-
   cL5OCnjQGrR-EXY3qun_RGSAf5-AHaA_4sHRFoqVxUny8qKPAyJdArdQGz1DI7-CD5kQ5pUXgfI-
   2RETwoMfvqjQ8IMnjpEwzhtPnhjOXNQxTQJ;info=<https://cert.example.org/PASSporT.
   cer>;alg=ES256;ppt=shaken
Date: Fri, 25 Sep 2015 19:12:25 GMT
User-Agent: myProxy 1.0
```

Evolving SBC Applications of PASSporT and SHAKEN

At the time of this publication, vendor implementations of PASSporT and SHAKEN have not moved past proof-of-concept testing, so no general deployment configurations of this feature on SBCs can be offered at this time. Due to the interest in improving security and integrity in caller origination and identification, upcoming adoption of these frameworks may lead to some interesting uses for SBCs.

For example, an SBC sitting at the edge of a network could review SHAKEN attestations and use machine learning or subscriptions to global blacklist repositories as a way to detect providers with poor reputation, and then either reject the calls or flag the call as having untrustworthy caller identity. This would allow for better control over calls from untrusted parties and improve the security posture by reducing calls coming from known malicious sources.

Man-in-the-Middle Attacks

With a *man-in-the-middle* (*MitM*) attack, an attacker inserts himself between two parties that believe they are communicating directly with each other. The attacker can use this approach to either passively eavesdrop on the communication or manipulate the content between the two parties. Figure 13-2 demonstrates the expected communication between two IP phones on a LAN.

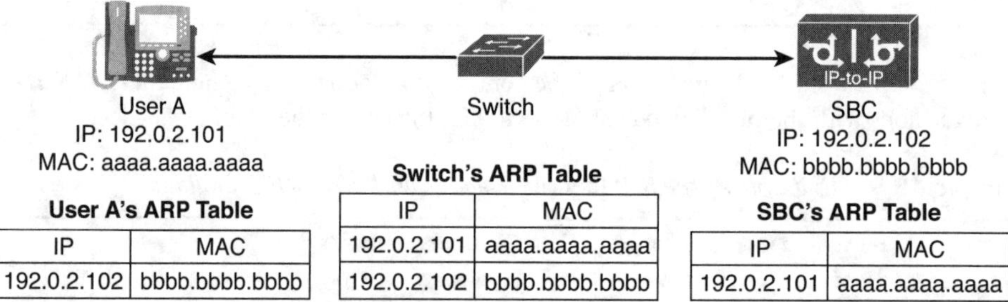

Figure 13-2 *Expected Communication Between Two Hosts*

An attacker may conduct a man-in-the-middle attack by sending gratuitous Address Resolution Protocol (ARP) responses to the switch he is targeting with the attack. A *gratuitous ARP* message is an unsolicited ARP response that instructs the switch to rewrite the switch's ARP table for the specified IP address with the destination MAC address that corresponds to the attacker's MAC address.

Figure 13-3 shows the effect of such an attack, referred to as either *ARP spoofing* or *ARP poisoning*: The switch forwards frames destined for the other user's real MAC address to the attacker's MAC address. The attacker may then choose to forward the received frames on to their originally intended destination to prevent the users from becoming aware of any disruption in the communication flow.

A MitM attack is similar to the concept of *wiretapping* in the legacy PSTN domain. A MitM attack on an IP network can tap either the media or the signaling channels or both. The attack on each type of channel will have different effects. The purposes of MitM attacks range from passively listening or modifying the underlying content of media to modifying components of the signaling channel to create undesirable effects to the call control.

The two main types of MitM attacks to be discussed in the following sections are eavesdropping and signaling hijacking.

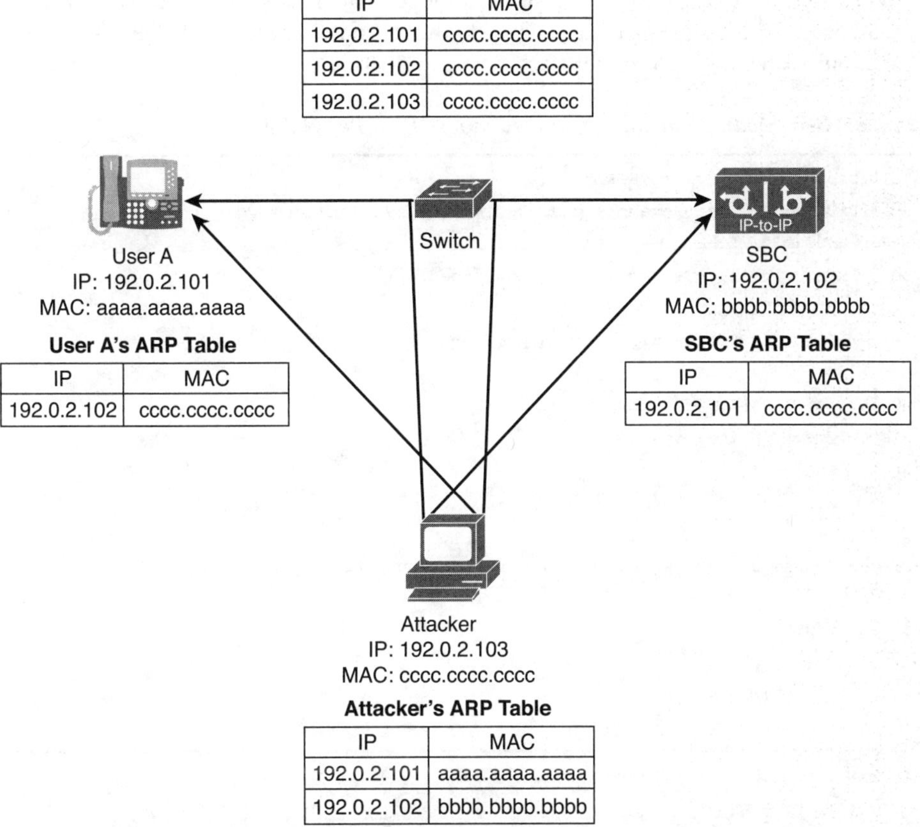

Figure 13-3 *The Effect of a Man-in-the-Middle Attack on Communication*

Eavesdropping

Eavesdropping involves an attacker inserting herself into a media stream between the two intended parties. One way this can be accomplished is through *ARP spoofing*, where the attack poisons a device's ARP cache so that the Layer 2 resolution entries for an IP destination point to the malicious device. The attacker then either terminates the packets at this malicious destination and impersonates the call destination or forwards packets on to the original destination in order to modify or passively listen to the media streams. ARP spoofing can be performed through tools such as the **ARP Poison Routing** feature in the Cain & Abel software package, which allows for modification and replay of ARP responses to poison the ARP table and insert a device in the middle of an RTP stream.

Another approach to accomplish eavesdropping is through signaling manipulation. If the attacker is able to insert herself in the middle of the signaling communication, the SIP headers or SDP can be modified to steer either further signaling or media to or through the attacker. A mid-call session refresh (that is, a SIP re-INVITE) or UPDATE is vulnerable to this type of attack, where the **Contact** header or SDP may be used to divert an active call. Example 13-8 shows an attack where both the **Contact** header and SDP destinations are manipulated to divert to the attacker at 192.0.2.101.

Example 13-8 *Manipulation of* Contact *and SDP on Re-INVITE*

```
INVITE sip:bob@example.com SIP/2.0
Via: SIP/2.0/TCP client.example.com:5060;branch=z9hG4bK74bf9
Max-Forwards: 70
From: Alice <sip:alice@example.com>;tag=9fxced76sl
To: Bob <sip:bob@example.com>
Call-ID: 3848276298220188511@example.com
CSeq: 1 INVITE
Contact: <sip:1001@192.0.2.101;transport=tcp>
Content-Type: application/sdp
Content-Length: 151

v=0
o=alice 2890844526 2890844526 IN IP4 client.example.com
s=-
c=IN IP4 192.0.2.101
t=0 0
m=audio 49172 RTP/AVP 0
a=rtpmap:0 PCMU/8000
```

Note MitM attacks such as those performed for eavesdropping can also be performed at protocol layers below the voice protocols, such as through DNS spoofing, where an attacker inserts a manipulated response to a device's DNS query in an attempt to get the device to send traffic to a different peer. Because call signaling operates below protocols such as DNS and IP entries, the vulnerabilities of these protocols can create exposure in a collaboration solution. When implementing DNS, consider the overall security of the DNS solution. Attacks such as DNS *cache poisoning*, in which an attacker sends a message to a trusted DNS server to change the IP address of a server's DNS entry, can be performed with Cain & Abel's **APR-DNS** feature by manipulating and replaying DNS responses. DNS security can be improved by implementing DNSSEC (a secure form of DNS) or by using TLS at the call signaling peers, which requires authenticity checks through the public key infrastructure (PKI) before call signaling is transmitted to ensure that the call signaling path hasn't been compromised by a DNS attack.

A third type of MitM attack that can be used for eavesdropping is performed through the life of the signaling of a call and involves the signaling being proxied through the attacker to hijack the call through the use of message suppression. In Figure 13-4, a legitimate call from a user to an IVR is established, but it is unknowingly going through the attacker (perhaps because of ARP poisoning before the presence of the initial INVITE). The call appears to behave as normal, and the user enters his banking credentials and then disconnects the call when finished. The attacker in this case suppresses the legitimate BYE message during the user's disconnection, preventing the call from being disconnected from the bank. After the caller is no longer on the call, the attacker remains connected to the authenticated IVR session of the user's bank and can perform any actions as an authenticated user, without the knowledge of the original caller.

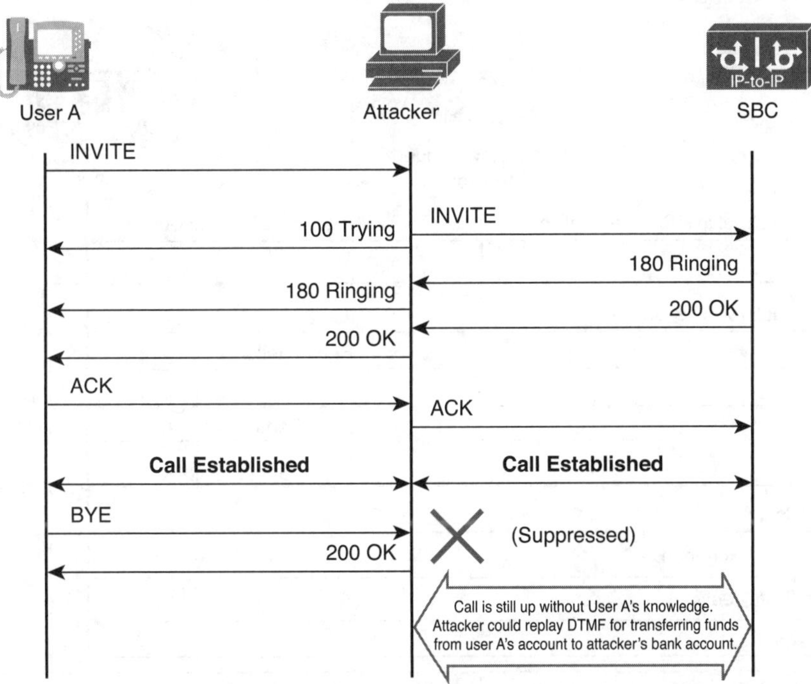

Figure 13-4 *A Man-in-the-Middle Attack with SIP BYE Suppression*

Mitigating Eavesdropping

Because RTP media have no inherent authenticity controls, a MitM attack may go unnoticed by users participating in the call. Solutions exist to help combat ARP spoofing, such as by monitoring ARP responses to detect when a response has changed and is not authentic. These tools can also be integrated into DHCP servers for increased integrity checking, comparing an ARP response against the address that originally requested the IP address to ensure that it hasn't changed.

Secure RTP (SRTP), discussed in Chapter 6, "Secure Signaling and Media," can defend against these types of MitM attacks as long as the attacker does not also have access to both the SRTP payload and the SRTP keys being used to encode and decode the encrypted RTP data. As mentioned in Chapter 6, Session Description Protocol Security Descriptions for Media Streams (SDES) and the Datagram Transport Layer Security extension for Secure Real-Time Transport Protocol (DTLS-SRTP) are two protocols used for facilitation of the SRTP key exchange.

With DTLS negotiations for SRTP, the keys are exchanged in the same path to be used by the eventual media stream. With DTLS version 1.2 and lower, several messages for the key exchange are sent in plaintext. After the key exchange, RTP is encrypted and decrypted with keys determined from the plaintext key exchange. This is demonstrated in Figure 13-5.

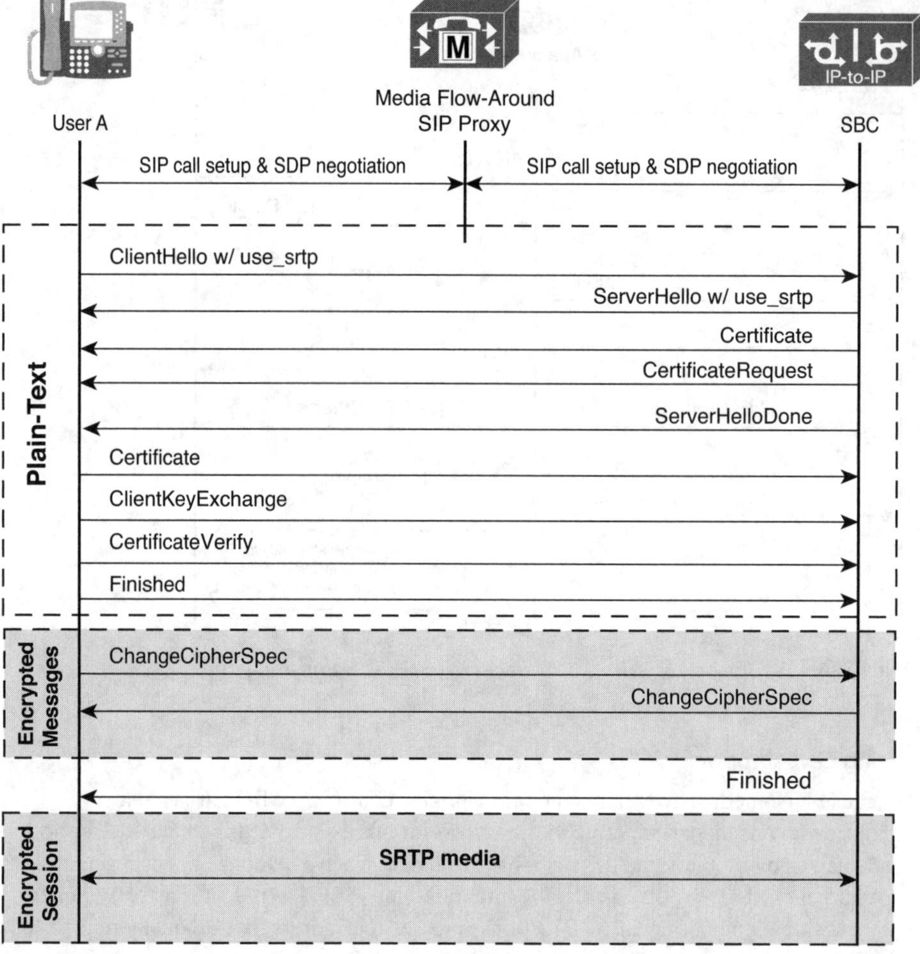

Figure 13-5 *SRTP Key Exchange over DTLS 1.2*

With DTLS 1.3, the key exchange is now protected after the **ServerHello** message, using encryption with a pre-shared key. After the key negotiation is completed across this encrypted key exchange, the media traffic is encrypted with a different key that was negotiated through the (mostly) encrypted handshake and key exchange. This provides additional security over the key exchange performed with DTLS 1.2, so any implementations of DTLS-SRTP (or even SIP over TLS) should enforce DTLS 1.3 at a minimum, as long as it doesn't pose interoperability issues with peers. For maximum compatibility, if DTLS 1.3 cannot be enforced as the only version for use, it should at least be available for use and preferred over DTLS 1.2 and lower implementations whenever possible.

Figure 13-6 demonstrates the improved signaling with DTLS 1.3.

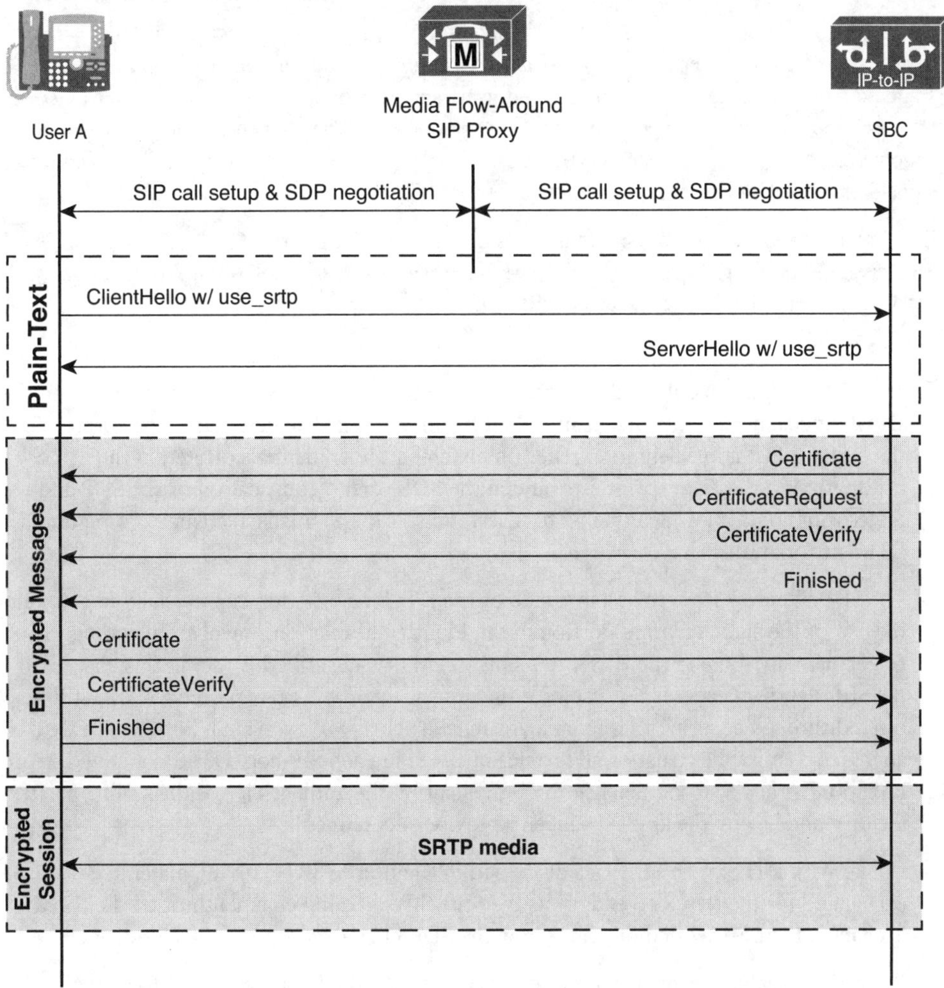

Figure 13-6 *SRTP Key Exchange over DTLS 1.3*

DTLS is robust against MitM attacks, as long as the SRTP peers can both validate that the negotiated SDP is authentic and also validate that the certificate of the peer for the DTLS connection belongs to the remote peer. As a result, it is very important that DTLS peers do not accept untrusted certificates when establishing a DTLS connection.

Caution TLS and DTLS encryption add layers of protection against MitM attacks but are not completely immune to them. A MitM attack could still be performed against (D)TLS during the time of the (D)TLS connections key exchange, but the MitM attacker would need to present a different certificate to each of the peers for the attack to be successful. Then, each SIP peer would be prompted to accept a different (and likely untrusted and/or self-signed) certificate.

As a result of this type of attack, SIP peers should be configured to reject untrusted certificates (defined as certificates not trusted through the chain of trust to an industry-standard root certificate authority), and end users and administrators should also be trained to not connect to or deploy hosts using untrusted and/or self-signed certificates. If a practice is upheld to not accept untrusted certificates, a MitM attack on TLS is very unlikely, and the signaling channel and sensitive key exchanges for SRTP are protected through SDES.

Due to vulnerabilities in the core constructs of older versions in the TLS/SSL suite such as SSL versions 1 through 3 and (D)TLS 1.0, these versions of protocols should be explicitly disabled where their absence does not pose interoperability concerns.

The DTLS framework alone does not provide protection when an attack is targeted on the signaling channel and the SDP is modified by an attacker. The negotiation performed for the DTLS-SRTP implementation relies on matching the credentials offered in the DTLS negotiation to the **fingerprint** attribute in the SDP offer. Modification of the SDP and fingerprint could allow an attacker to insert himself in the media exchange during the DTLS negotiation.

The SDP integrity from the remote side of the DTLS negotiation can be ensured through the use of the signed *claims* portion in the **Identity** header. This involves including the **fingerprint** attribute in the PASSporT's **mky** claim, as described earlier in this chapter. If the SIP **Identity** header is not used for fingerprint integrity, some protection can still be offered through securing the signaling channel (such as SIP over TLS), but this is a weaker approach as it implies trust of all proxies involved in each SIP hop. DTLS combined with PASSporT offers a strong defense through ensuring the authenticity of the calling party's identity and having the key exchange to provide secure media.

Unlike with DTLS, with SDES, as discussed in Chapter 6, SRTP keying material is exchanged for the two RTP endpoints over the SIP signaling channel through the SDP exchange. Figure 13-7 demonstrates how the SDES key exchange for SRTP occurs.

If the SIP signaling channel is not also encrypted, an attacker may be able to sniff the signaling channel to obtain SRTP keying material and subsequently eavesdrop on the SDES-negotiated SRTP conversation. Therefore, when deploying SDES, RFC 4568 strongly suggests that the SDP be protected through some means. The RFC offers suggestions such as enabling Secure/Multipurpose Internet Mail Extensions (S/MIME) or TLS/IPsec to protect the SDP and the inherent key exchange. Even with the signaling being encrypted, note that again it only allows per-hop protection. This approach requires that each hop be passed through a trusted entity, as the keys are available after decryption by each device at each termination of the SIP hop.

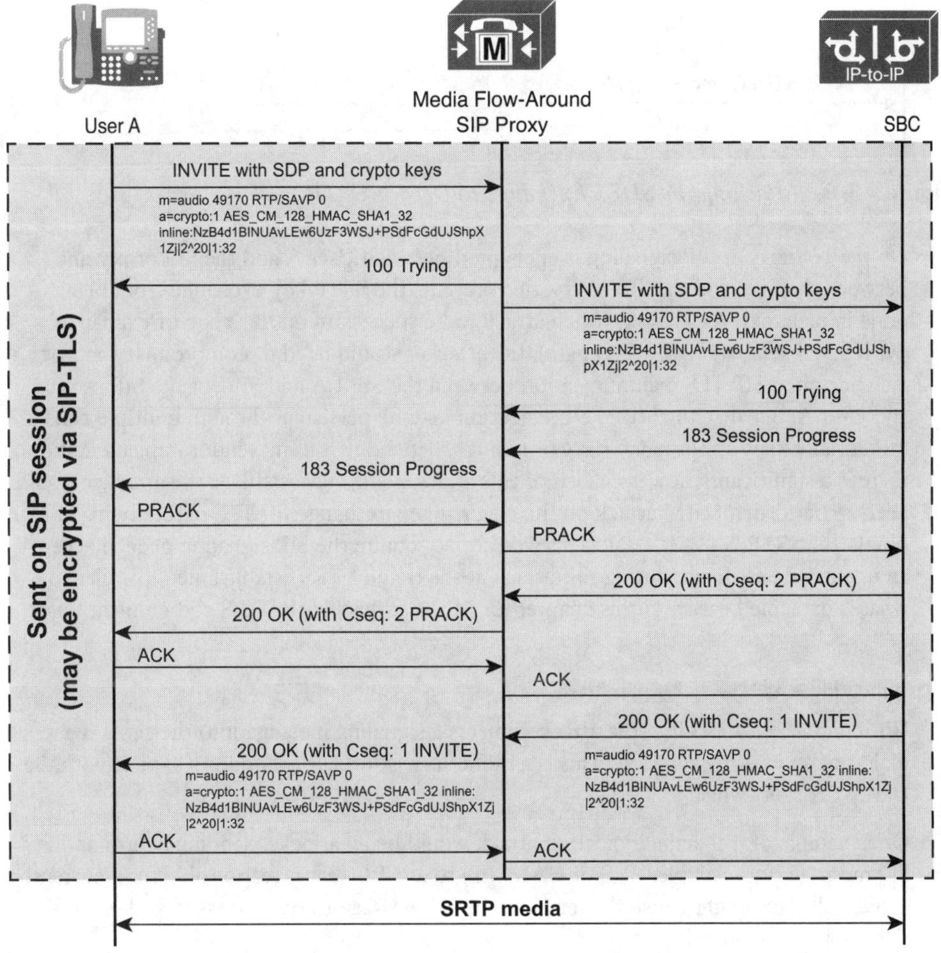

Figure 13-7 *SRTP Key Exchange over SDES*

Figure 13-8 shows an attack on SDES-exchanged SRTP keys. For this attack to be successful, the attacker must intercept the SDP within the SIP signaling of the key exchange and then also intercept the SRTP media between User A and User B. If the signaling isn't encrypted, this attack can proceed as two separate MitM attacks—one on the signaling and the other on the media communication.

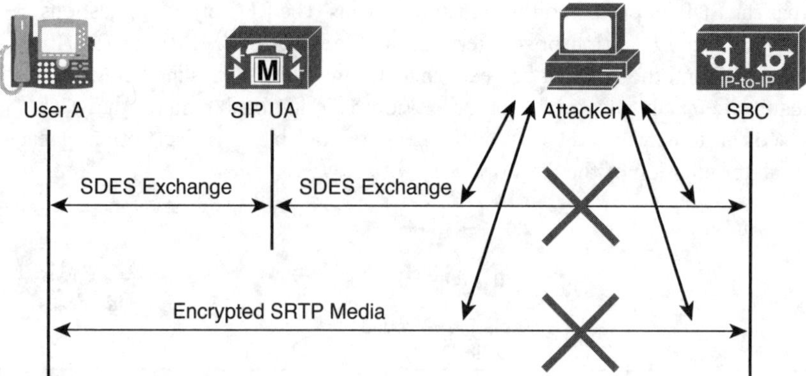

Figure 13-8 *Attacking the SDES Exchange to Decode SRTP*

On the contrary, if SIP signaling is encrypted between User A and the SIP proxy and between the SBC and the SIP proxy, this prevents the SRTP key exchange from being done in plaintext. As a result, for an attack to be successful on this type of exchange (with SDES sent over a SIP TLS path), the attacker would need to compromise the original encrypted SIP TLS communication between the SIP UA and SBC or the SIP proxy and User A. Because the SIP TLS connection may be persistent through multiple calls (potentially kept up for many days or months, depending on the vendor implementation), there is a significantly lower chance of this attack being successful, as the attacker would need to perform a MitM attack on the original key exchange for TLS before being able to obtain the SRTP keys for a call. This would also require the SIP signaling peer to accept an untrusted certificate during this attack at the time of TLS establishment (similar to what is explained earlier in this chapter for MitM attacks with DTLS communications).

Signaling Hijacking

With *signaling hijacking*, the attacker injects a signaling message into the signaling dialog of an existing call flow. This is a modern twist on Dave Condon's exploit with the Davey Crockett whistle.

One example of a signaling injection attack would be an attacker sending a terminating SIP message (for example, BYE or CANCEL) to an SBC that is responsible for a currently active call. This might cause the terminating SIP message to be processed and result in the call being dropped.

Figure 13-9 demonstrates a BYE attack, where an attacker sends a rogue BYE message on the same SIP dialog for the **Call-ID** header of the active call between User A and the SBC.

Other types of messages can be injected into call signaling in an attempt to redirect the call to or through a malicious destination. Consider the malicious intent that may be executed through the following SIP redirect messages:

- 300 Multiple Choices
- 301 Moved Permanently

- 302 Moved Temporarily
- 305 Use Proxy

These messages may be used in a *redirection attack*, instructing the calling party to redirect the SIP messages to a host in the **Contact** header. Thus, an attacker could intercept a SIP message such as an INVITE (through ARP poisoning or sniffing packets) and then respond to it with a 3xx message where the **Contact** header refers to the attacker's IP address. This would result in the upstream peer diverting the call to the IP address of the attacker instead of sending it to the intended destination. The result would be an ability to listen to or modify the media and/or signaling of the call. Such a redirect attack could be used to redirect a call from a customer to a bank to an attacker's IVR, allowing for spoofing of the banking system to get the user to enter banking account information and PIN.

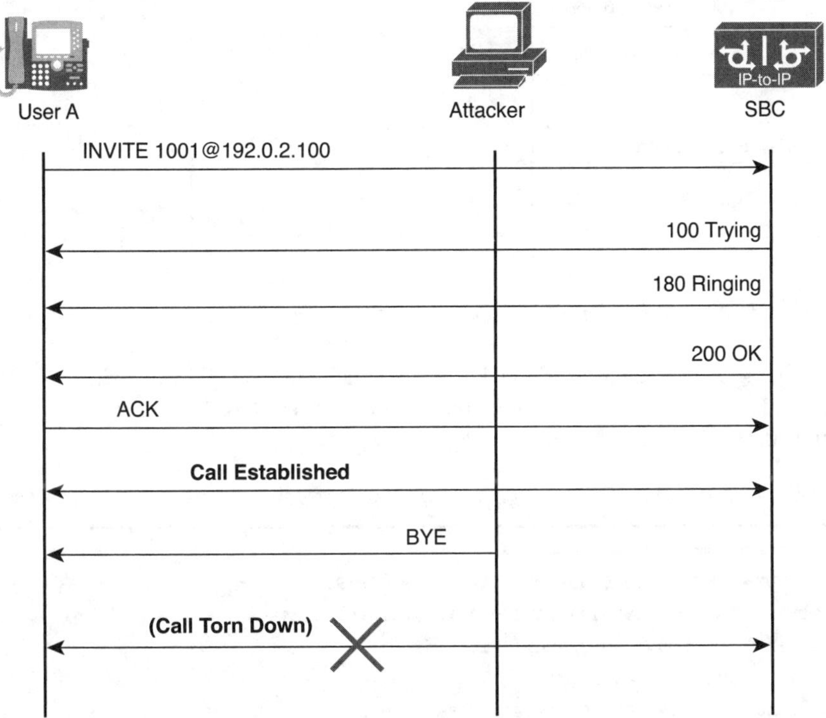

Figure 13-9 *SIP BYE Attack*

In order for such an attack to work, the 3xx message must be sent after the INVITE is transmitted but before the legitimate party responds with a **100 Trying** message. For example, in Figure 13-10, an attacker is passively listening to the network, observes an INVITE in transmission to the **SBC**, and responds with a spoofed **302 Moved Temporarily** message back to User A before the SBC has a chance to receive the INVITE and respond with the legitimate **100 Trying** message. This behavior would result in User A initiating a new dialog to **1001@192.0.2.99** for the call that was legitimately intended to **1001@192.0.2.100**.

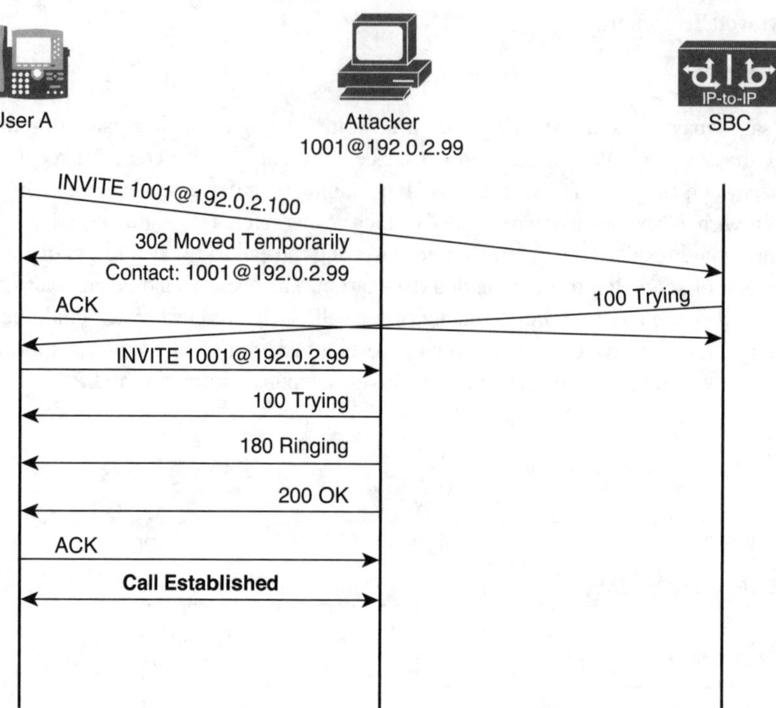

Figure 13-10 *SIP Messaging for a SIP 3xx Redirect Attack*

The malicious 3xx message for this attack is demonstrated in Example 13-9, where the **Contact** header is changed to redirect the call from **1001@192.0.2.100** to **1001@192.0.2.99**.

Example 13-9 *Using a 3xx SIP Message for a Redirect Attack*

```
SIP/2.0 302 Moved Temporarily
Via: SIP/2.0/UDP 192.0.2.100:5060;branch=z9hG4bK76661994
From: "4085551234" <sip:4085551234@192.0.2.100>;tag=DC31124-48B
To: <sip:1001@192.0.2.100>;tag=32ACC1C8-1BAB
Date: Fri, 12 Oct 2017 19:46:49 GMT
Call-ID: 9F5C6A0D-13CE11E2-B265CFEA-48AA9F88@192.0.2.100
Timestamp: 1350065293
Server: Cisco-SIPGateway/IOS-15.x
CSeq: 101 INVITE
Allow-Events: telephone-event
Contact: <sip:1001@192.0.2.99>
Content-Length: 0
```

The header from Example 13-9 could be changed to an alternate extension—for example, if the attacker has control of a local endpoint (such as with registration hijacking, as discussed in the next section).

Similarly, a redirection attack can also be performed with a SIP REFER, by modifying the **Refer-To** header as shown in Example 13-10.

Example 13-10 *Using a REFER for a Redirect Attack*

```
REFER sip:recepient@example.com SIP/2.0
Via: SIP/2.0/UDP proxy.example.com;branch=z9hG4bK2293940223
To: <sip:recepient@example.com>
From: <sip:caller@example.com>;tag=193402342
Call-ID: 898234234@proxy.example.com
CSeq: 93809823 REFER
Max-Forwards: 70
Refer-To: sip:attacker@example.org
Contact: sip:caller@example.com
Content-Length: 0
```

Mitigating Signaling Hijacking

MitM attacks can be mainly prevented through authentication mechanisms, such as those found with PKI and encrypted signaling. Authentication through PKI ensures that a device is talking to the remote peer that it expects, by validating the authenticity of the remote device with a mechanism such as a X.509 certificate that is signed by a mutually trusted certificate authority.

Encrypted communication also helps thwart MitM attacks, as it prevents the possibility of an attacker sitting in the middle of the call's signaling or media communication paths to view sensitive information about the call.

Encryption helps prevent sensitive information provided during signaling (such as the SIP **Call-ID** and **To** or **From** headers, as well as media address information) from being obtained for malicious use. The signaling channels can be encrypted by communicating the signaling over TLS. S/MIME also offers a mechanism for authentication and encryption, but it encrypts only the body of the SDP and it is end-to-end encryption that makes modification of the data difficult or impossible when needed by intermediary proxies or Network Address Translation (NAT) boundaries. S/MIME is useful for protecting media addresses and SRTP key exchanges in the SDP when there isn't a need to fix up any information in the SDP in the middle of the call path, although it does not offer any protection for the SIP headers, which are commonly targets of attacks. As a result, using S/MIME is often not a preferred approach for securing SIP signaling.

TLS offers more flexibility, as it encrypts all of the SIP signaling between two hosts. Unlike S/MIME, it does not provide an end-to-end encryption across the entire call between the calling and called parties; it just provides encryption between the immediate call signaling peers. Therefore, TLS provides security only on the signaling hop for which TLS has been enabled. Enabling TLS and SRTP at the SBC ensures that the signaling and media communication to the associated immediate peers connected inbound to and outbound from the SBC take advantage of increased security protection, but it does not ensure that upstream or downstream SIP legs are also protected.

Note An alternative to using TLS and SRTP is to encrypt the communications traffic in a tunnel between the two trusted entities (that is, between an on-premises SBC and a trusted ITSP's SBC) through an encrypted tunnel (for example, an IPsec VPN or a TLS VPN). The disadvantage here is that unlike with SIP over TLS and SRTP, the encryption is not always end-to-end encryption between the signaling endpoints. Signaling downstream of the VPN tunnel termination points would have call signaling and media sent in plaintext, providing potential target points for attackers that have access to the network at those locations (see Figure 13-11).

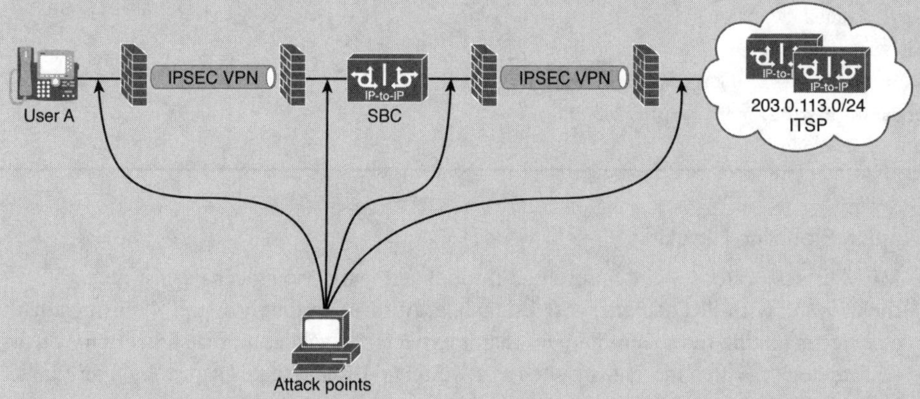

Figure 13-11 *Attack Points Outside a VPN Tunnel*

As a result, peer-to-peer encryption directly between the call signaling peers and media peers through TLS and SRTP is preferred over this approach of putting unencrypted call traffic through an encrypted tunnel.

Note that although TLS and SRTP provide additional security against malicious SIP attacks, using them does involve some disadvantages. The main challenge with encryption implementations is that they add complexity in troubleshooting issues, as traffic can't be captured in between the peers to be analyzed for troubleshooting. Implementing encryption also increases management overhead, as relevant hosts need to have PKI certificates monitored and renewed periodically to prevent unexpected disruption of communication if a certificate expires. Finally, the additional performance required for encryption may result in a lower available capacity on the platform.

Toll-Fraud Attacks

According to the yearly Communications Fraud Control Association (CFCA) Fraud Survey, toll fraud accounts for billions of dollars in losses every year. In such an attack, a malicious user attempts to place a fraudulent call to a destination number that requires a toll charge by routing a call over an Internet connection to a device that has outbound dialing connectivity to the attacker's intended destination. The goal of this type of attack is to leverage the target device's outbound dialing capability in order to make use of a call circuit that would otherwise require a toll or cost for placing the call. In a toll-fraud attack, a malicious person essentially places calls that are charged to the owner of the compromised device. Figure 13-12 provides a logical portrayal of this type of attack.

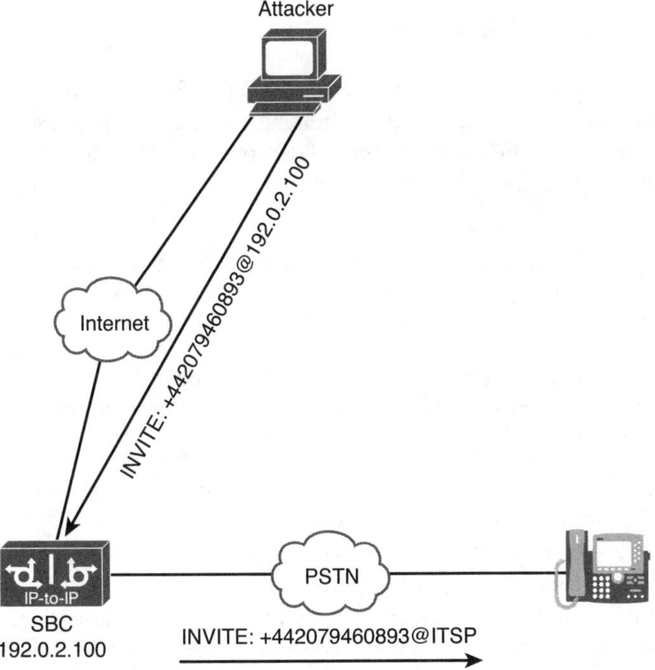

Figure 13-12 *Internet Attacker Executing Toll Fraud*

Toll fraud may be executed in the following forms:

- **IP PBX compromise**—An attacker may compromise an IP PBX that has PSTN connectivity in order to manipulate the device state (such as the call routing configuration) to open up the capability for outbound PSTN calls from Internet devices. An attacker may also brute-force SIP endpoint registration into the IP PBX to get an external device to be able to register with the capability to place an outbound toll call.

- **IVR hacking**—This type of attack leverages existing automated systems that permit outbound PSTN connectivity. For example, a voicemail system may have a dial-in number to check voicemail, and it might drop a user into a part of the system that allows for transferring or forwarding of a call back out to the PSTN.

- **Rogue call setups**—An attacker may send unsolicited call requests to devices on common ports from a public Internet connection to see if the call setup is permitted. For example, an attacker may run a port scan for Internet addresses that respond on SIP port TCP 5060 and then send a call setup attempt through this port to a destination number on the PSTN to validate whether the call will route to the destination.

Mitigating Toll-Fraud Attacks

The following are some tips to help prevent toll fraud:

- To prevent PBX compromise, employ best practices for hardening PBX devices. Ensure that default passwords are replaced and that administrative access is restricted to administrators who need to be on the system. Allow connectivity to the admin interface only from trusted IP addresses or trusted networks and disable administrative access from Internet connections where possible.
- Ensure that complex PINs and SIP registration passwords are enforced to prevent brute-force attacks against SIP endpoint registrations or IVR PIN authentications from being successful.
- Deploy temporary account lockout procedures after a defined number of failed authentication attempts to SIP registrations and IVR or voicemail systems to prevent aggressive brute-force attacks.
- Restrict call control traffic so that it is processed only when from known and trusted IP source addresses. Circuits facing outside network connections should block all call control traffic by default and should permit this connectivity only from trusted sources (such as from the local PBX addresses and any addresses for trusted ITSP's devices). A good starting point here is blocking all call signaling traffic and then allowing only ports from specific trusted source IP addresses or networks. The following call signaling ports should all be considered for restriction of general inbound traffic, even if the protocol is not in deployment:
  - **SIP**—Both TCP and UDP 5060 and TCP 5061
  - **H.323**—TCP 1719 and 1720
  - **MGCP**—UDP port 2427
  - **SCCP**—TCP to 2000
- Deploy secure call signaling to remote endpoints, through means such as TLS. This helps ensure that remote IP address spoofing isn't being performed, as TLS provides authentication through means such as an X.509 certificate.
- Restrict registration from endpoints that are outside the local LAN addresses and VPN address pools. SIP registration of devices should not be permitted from outside network connections, especially public Internet connections.

- Deploy class-of-restriction dialing, where toll calls require an authorization code to permit call routing. A more aggressive approach here could be to restrict anyone from placing calls to destinations that are at elevated risk of toll fraud. The Communications Fraud Control Association provides a list of the top countries participating in fraudulent calls in its yearly *Fraud Loss Survey* results.

In addition to the aforementioned mitigating controls for minimizing the risk of toll fraud, call detail records and ITSP billing should be regularly reviewed to identify any presence of fraudulent calls. This can be achieved by looking for a high volume of calls to and from countries that may not be regularly contacted during normal business operation. Some ITSPs now offer automated routines that monitor and baseline call behavior, detecting events such as high call volume outside business hours to highly tolled regions or to areas classified as high risk. These services can deliver alerts to customers when an account appears to have atypical call pattern behavior that may be related to toll fraud.

CUBE IP Address Trust List

CUBE has a specific feature that helps mitigate toll-fraud behavior. The out-of-the-box behavior is that CUBE will not accept call requests from any remote IP peer unless that peer has been explicitly defined in the system.

When a session target is defined in a dial peer, CUBE automatically adds to its trust list the IP address from the session target as an approved device for accepting call requests. Administrators can then add additional SIP source addresses to allow for SIP calls that may not be defined in a session target, such as IP addresses associated with SRV (DNS service) records or inbound sources for which there are no outbound dial peers configured for receiving outbound calls. Any incoming call requests from sources that aren't defined using these two approaches will then be rejected with cause value **21**.

This call rejection behavior is demonstrated in Examples 13-11 through 13-13 with the output of **debug voip ccapi inout**, **debug ccsip messages**, and **voice iec syslog**. (The IEC syslog feature is discussed further in Chapter 14.)

Example 13-11 *Output of* **debug voip ccapi inout** *During Toll-Fraud Rejection*

```
*May 28 06:47:21.326: //243802/809AFF5F6400/CCAPI/cc_process_call_setup_ind:
   >>>>CCAPI handed cid 243802 with tag 541 to app "_ManagedAppProcess_
   TOLLFRAUD_APP"
*May 28 06:47:21.326: //243802/809AFF5F6400/CCAPI/ccCallDisconnect:
   Cause Value=21, Tag=0x0, Call Entry(Previous Disconnect Cause=0, Disconnect
   Cause=0)
```

Example 13-12 *Output of* **debug ccsip messages** *During Toll-Fraud Rejection*

```
*May 28 06:47:21.415: //-1/xxxxxxxxxxxx/SIP/Error/sipSPILocateInviteDialogCCB:
Ip Trust List Authentication failed for Incoming Request, method = INVITE
```

Example 13-13 *Output of* voice iec syslog *During Toll-Fraud Rejection*

```
*May 28 06:47:21.326: %VOICE_IEC-3-GW: Application Framework Core: Internal Error
  (Toll fraud call rejected): IEC=1.1.228.3.31.0 on callID 243802 GUID=DB3F10AC61971
  1DCA7618593A790099E
```

If **voice iec syslog** is enabled, these rejected calls can also be observed without any debugs through the syslog messages demonstrated in Example 13-14.

CUBE also has another protection mechanism, called *silent discard*, which is intended to reduce the processing required of CUBE during a DoS attack from untrusted sources. This mechanism is enabled by default. When this feature is enabled, calls coming in from untrusted sources are dropped after only very minimal processing and before being passed to the CCAPI stack. With this default behavior enabled, calls are dropped before hitting the toll-fraud protection. This means that with silent discarding, rejected calls from untrusted sources do not appear at all in the call control API (CCAPI) debugs, and will not get to the point where the call disconnects with cause value **21**. This default silent response behavior can be reversed with **no silent-discard untrusted**. When silent discard is triggered, a syslog message is generated, as shown in Example 13-14.

Example 13-14 *Syslog Generated When Silent Discard Is Triggered*

```
%SIP-2-SILENT_DISCARD:  Silent Discard Request from untrusted host rejected and
  consumed,Statistics are shown:
Total untrusted request consumed: 1876
Untrusted request consumed in last 60 min: 1745
```

In some cases, legitimate call setups may come from devices that are not explicitly defined in the dial peer. This could occur in scenarios such as integrating with a service provider that uses a pool of servers. Under default behavior, these calls would be blocked by the toll-fraud prevention feature. It is possible to whitelist these peers by explicitly configuring them in a VoIP trust list. Example 13-15 demonstrates adding explicit trust for call requests to come from the single host 192.0.2.10, the entire 198.51.100/24 network, and the IPv6 network 2001:db8::/32.

Example 13-15 *Configuring Explicit Addresses for the IP Trust List*

```
voice service voip
 ip address trusted authenticate
 ip address trusted list
  ipv4 192.0.2.10
  ipv4 198.51.100.0 255.255.255.0
  ipv6 2001:db8::/32
```

Tip When using SRV records in dial peers, CUBE does not have the capability to look up the underlying IP addresses for the SRV records. As a result, when configuring SRV records, the underlying IP addresses (or range of addresses) for the corresponding SIP peers must be explicitly configured in the IP trust list. When exact IP addresses here aren't known, the administrators that reside over the DNS destination should still be able to provide at least a network range to be used for this purpose. Results from an **nslookup** of the SRV record can also help provide the IP addresses the DNS names are currently resolving toward.

The content of the IP trust list can be validated with the command **show ip address trusted list**. For instance, Example 13-16 contains a section for the implicit trusted targets resulting from configured dial peers, and it also includes what has been explicitly allowed through configuration of a network range of IP addresses through the trust list (configured in Example 13-15).

Example 13-16 *Validation of the IP Trust List with* **show ip address trusted list**

```
CUBE# show ip address trusted list
IP Address Trusted Authentication
Administration State: UP
Operation State:      UP

IP Address Trusted Call Block Cause: call-reject (21)
VoIP Dial-peer IPv4 and IPv6 Session Targets:
Peer Tag        Oper State      Session Target
--------        ----------      --------------
1001            UP              ipv4:192.0.2.50:5060

IP Address Trusted List:
 ipv4 192.0.2.10
ipv4 198.51.100.0 255.255.255.0
ipv6 2001:db8:: 0.0.0.32
```

Telephony DoS

In a telephony denial-of-service (TDoS) attack, a large number of call requests are sent to a specific call-processing destination in an attempt to disrupt the service availability of the call-processing unit and potentially render it unavailable for use. Over the past few years, TDoS attacks have been used with malicious intent against companies to trigger financial loss, or as leveraging points for extortion of the victims. As collaboration technologies have converged on IP, services have become more centralized than they were in the legacy PBX era. This poses a heightened risk for denial of service, as an attacker can target fewer destinations than in the past to starve service availability.

TDoS can be achieved through flooding of either call signaling or RTP media. The aim of call signaling flooding is either to exhaust the communications channels of the target device(s) or to cripple performance of the call processing device(s) to the point that the device(s) cannot handle processing of new or existing calls that are legitimate. RTP flooding can also be done by injecting additional RTP packets with manipulated RTP sequence numbers and time stamps into the existing media stream toward the destination, with the goal of distorting or corrupting the audio at the listener.

TDoS attacks may come from various locations (in distributed attacks), and they can be sourced either from automated systems (such as a distributed network of computers called a *botnet*) or through a large pool of people organized using social media. These attacks typically have calling numbers that are spoofed and that are often randomized and frequently changed. Attacks can come from either legacy PSTN circuits such as PRI connections, over the Internet from ITSPs such as through SIP trunks, or directly from attackers to a target SBC.

A DoS of a call system could also be performed through *protocol fuzzing*, in which case a message is manipulated in an attempt to cause unexpected behavior on the target device, such as a crash. This type of attack is discussed later in this chapter.

Mitigating Telephony DoS Attacks

The best form of defense with a TDoS signaling attack is to stop the traffic as far upstream as possible, ideally at the edge of the network. An SBC is therefore an ideal device for detecting and preventing a TDoS attack.

Simulations of DoS attacks are beneficial for measuring and understanding a network's resiliency and response to a real TDoS attack. SIP TDoS attacks can be simulated through scripting or by using tools such as the **SIP-DAS** (DoS Attack Simulator) feature in Mr. SIP, as shown in Example 13-17.

Example 13-17 *Simulating a SIP DoS Attack with Mr. SIP*

```
linux# mr.sip.py --ds --dm=invite --c 1000 --di=192.0.2.100 --dp=5060 --r
  --to=toUser.txt --fu=fromUser.txt --ua=UserAgent.txt
 m     m                    mmmm   mmmmm   mmmmm
 ##   ##   m mm            #"   "    #      #   "#
 # ## #   #"   "           "#mmm     #      #mmm#"
 # "" #   #                    "#    #      #
 #    #   #         #      "mmm#"  mm#mm    #
[!] Client Interface: en0
[!] Client IP: 192.0.2.99
Progress: ||||||||||||||||||||||||||||||||||||||||||||||||||||||||||||||||||||||||||||||||||||||||||||||||||||
  ||||||||||||||||||||||||||||||||||||||| 100.0%
[!] DoS simulation finished and 1000 packet sent to 192.0.2.100...
```

Thwarting TDoS attacks that leverage flooding of REGISTER instead of INVITE messages may be slightly more challenging, as a SIP registrar may need to be accepted from a wider range of IP addresses than would be the case with INVITEs. For instance, a registrar or proxy could be configured to accept INVITE messages only from peers that have been explicitly configured and from device IP addresses that have registered to it. In contrast, SIP registrations from endpoints may come from a variety of IP addresses and networks, so restricting the source IP address for REGISTER messages cannot be as granular. Where possible, restricting SIP and specifically REGISTER messages to only the subnets that host endpoints expected to register is ideal, but otherwise external means of DoS detection of REGISTER flooding must be employed.

DoS attacks can be detected either at the SBC or through an intrusion detection system (IDS) such as Cisco Snort. More reactive approaches employ an intrusion prevention system (IPS) that will not only detect but also take action to prevent the attack. After detection, the source(s) of the attack can be flagged for an alert or temporarily/permanently blacklisted from communication. Distributed DoS (DDoS) attacks are harder to detect, as their traffic comes from multiple sources. These attacks pose a challenge in that it is difficult to distinguish such an attack from a normal inbound traffic surge resulting from a non-malicious increase in inbound traffic. Intelligent detection devices may be used to look for other common patterns to detect DDoS attacks, such as INVITEs from multiple sources using the same destination **To** header or using the same **Call-ID** header. The more randomization that is employed by the attacker in a DDoS attack, however, the more complex the analysis needs to be to positively detect these conditions (without false positives).

Once a DoS attack is detected, the IDS needs to, at a minimum, provide an alarming mechanism to administrators. Ideally, the device should also perform as an IPS and trigger preventive mechanisms to block the DoS attack before the SBC or target device is degraded in functionality. The open source IPS tool **snortsam** has the capability to integrate with Snort and configure denial rules for the **iptables** software firewall on Linux, or ACLs to block the offending traffic on firewalls such as Cisco ASAs, and Cisco IOS devices such as CUBE.

Call Admission Control (CAC) can offer an additional minor layer of protection in DoS attacks, as it can restrict the concurrent call or bandwidth consumption to a specified limit, preventing additional calls that may be sent in from a call flood from consuming these finite resources and disrupting active calls. CAC alone is not a strong measure against DoS attacks, though, because call request flooding can still be performed without CAC's ability to suppress processing of, potentially still resulting in overwhelming the SBC's CPU resources for processing the flood of call requests.

Note Because SBCs are data devices, they are subject to classic DDoS attacks on the data plane. An organization can defend against these attacks by using the same means as for the rest of the data network.

The use of a firewall with basic threat detection may help assist in defending against DDoS attacks. The zone-based policy firewall feature, which is discussed later in this chapter, has a threat detection feature that can be enabled with the **threat-detection basic-threat** command. Refer to "Protection Against Distributed Denial of Service Attacks" in *Security Configuration Guide: Zone-Based Policy Firewall* (Cisco Systems, 2017) for more information on this feature.

Comprehensive DDoS defense strategies may be more involved than simply relying on an IDS feature in a firewall. Refer to the *Defeating DDoS Attacks* (Cisco Systems, 2017) whitepaper for a look at additional strategies for combating these situations.

Consider the RTP DoS attack mentioned earlier, in which an attacker injects additional media streams with manipulated sequences and time stamps to control the listeners' experience of the audio stream. Systematically detecting these attacks is challenging because there is not a mechanism to determine which audio packet or stream is the authentic one. Source port validation of the media stream, if available on a vendor's SBC, may help combat these attacks when the audio stream is coming from a secondary source IP address. (The source port validation feature for CUBE is discussed later in this chapter.) Otherwise, enabling SRTP is the best defense here, as doing so ensures the integrity of the media stream directly between the source and destination of the stream.

TDoS Prevention on CUBE

On CUBE, TDoS can be prevented by forcing the authentication of call signaling sources and enabling the discarding of any SIP traffic destined for CUBE that is from an untrusted source. This is done by default through the IP trust list and the default **silent-discard untrusted** setting, as discussed earlier in this chapter.

As shown in Example 13-18, it is possible to use the **show sip-ua statistics** command to see that the IP trust list and the default **silent-discard untrusted** setting successfully prevented a potential TDoS attack. This command is useful for understanding and baselining the quantity and velocity of external attacks toward this device.

Example 13-18 *Using* **show sip-ua statistics** *to Validate TDoS Information*

```
CUBE# show sip-ua statistics

!Command Output Abbreviated

SETooSmall 0/0, RequestPending 0/0,
UnsupportedResourcePriority 0/0,
Total untrusted Request Consumed 1500,
Untrusted Request Consumed in last lap 300,
Last Threshold for Untrusted Request Consumed 1000
```

The output in Example 13-18 includes the following attributes:

- **Total Untrusted Request Consumed**—The total count of untrusted messages consumed since the counters were last cleared.
- **Untrusted Request Consumed in last lap**—The count of untrusted commands within the previous 60-minute interval. This statistic is not a rolling window and is updated only once every 60 minutes.
- **Last Threshold for Untrusted Request Consumed**—The high-water mark for untrusted requests within the busiest 60-minute interval.

CUBE and other IOS or IOS XE devices performing SIP-aware NAT have an application-level inspection feature called SIP ALG, which can provide a powerful way to prevent DDoS attacks. It allows for detection and dynamic blocking of messages from sources that exceed a defined threshold. Example 13-19 provides an example of the configuration of this feature.

Example 13-19 *Configuration of SIP ALG DoS Prevention*

```
alg sip processor session max-backlog 10
alg sip processor global max-backlog 100
alg sip blacklist trigger-period 90 trigger-size 30 destination 192.0.2.1
alg sip blacklist trigger-period 90 trigger-size 30 block-time 30
alg sip timer call-proceeding-timeout 35
alg sip timer max-call-duration 90
```

Example 13-19 includes the following commands:

- **alg sip processor session max-backlog 10**—Allows a maximum of 10 SIP messages per session that are waiting for processing before being classified as a DoS attack.
- **alg sip processor global max-backlog 100**—Allows a maximum of 100 overall SIP messages waiting for processing before being classified as a DoS attack.
- **alg sip blacklist trigger-period 90 trigger-size 30 destination 192.0.2.1**—Enables the blacklist feature to be enabled for SIP traffic to the defined SIP destination 192.0.2.1. This command can be entered multiple times, with the IP address changed to allow for multiple destinations to be defined for the blacklist feature. This command sets the trigger threshold for 30 events within 90 seconds.
- **alg sip blacklist trigger-period 90 trigger-size 30 block-time 30**—Blocks the offending source of the DoS attack for 30 seconds when the threshold to define the DoS event is exceeded.
- **alg sip timer call-proceeding-timeout 35**—Sets the time at which SIP calls without a response should be terminated to 35 seconds.
- **alg sip timer max-call-duration 360**—Sets the maximum call duration for a successful SIP call to 36000 seconds (10 hours). This helps protect against DoS attacks that try to keep calls up indefinitely to exhaust resources through concurrent calls.

The status of the DoS protection feature can be observed with **show alg sip**, as shown in Example 13-20.

Example 13-20 *Output of* **show alg sip** *for Validating SIP DoS Protecting Status*

```
CUBE# show alg sip

sip timer configuration
   Type                         Seconds
   max-call-duration            380
   call-proceeding-timeout      620

sip processor configuration
   Type              Backlog number
   session            14
   global             189

sip blacklist configuration
   dst-addr            trig-period(ms)    trig-size     block-time(sec)
   192.0.2.1               1000               5              30
```

More detailed information on the blacklisting can also be observed with the command **show platform hardware qfp active feature alg statistics sip dbl**, as demonstrated in Example 13-21.

Example 13-21 *Validating Detailed SIP Blacklist Status*

```
CUBE# show platform hardware qfp active feature alg statistics sip dbl

SIP dbl pool used chunk entries number: 1

 entry_id           src_addr          dst_addr          remaining_time(sec)
 a4a051e0a4a1ebd    198.51.100.34     192.0.2.1                25
```

Protocol Fuzzing

Protocol fuzzing is a technique in which a message is modified so that its parameters contain invalid or unexpected data, in an attempt to create an unexpected condition on a call signaling device. Such an attack can cause the device to induce a memory leak or crash and disrupt the availability of the service. Both signaling and media protocols can be fuzzed. These attacks may also leverage conditions such as buffer overflows or SQL injection in an attempt to execute malicious code on the SIP server.

The following are some examples of SIP fuzzing:

- Absence of a mandatory header, such as the **To** field
- Duplicate entry of a header, such as two **CSeq** headers with different values

- Null values for mandatory fields, such as a destination URI on an INVITE message
- A negative value for a parameter, such as **Content-Length**
- Extra-long parameters, such as the following value for a **Call-ID:**
  1234567890123456789012345678901234567890-
  1234567890123456789012345678901234567890-
  1234567890123456789012345678901234567890-
  1234567890123456789012345678901234567890-
  1234567890123456789012345678901234567890-
  12345678901234567890123456789012345678901234567890123@sbc.com
- Presence of special characters or escaped UTF-8 characters in fields, such as **%s** or **\245**
- Presence of additional whitespaces in a header, such as **To: "John Smith" < sip:user@example.com >**
- Injection of SQL commands in SIP parameters, such as that provided by Example 13-22, which shows an attempt to embed a SQL command within the **Authorization** header. This SQL command rewrites a user's password to a new value, and the command is inserted for processing by forcing a semicolon (;) after the username before closing the quote (") for the username.

Example 13-22 *SQL Injection in a SIP Authorization Digest*

```
INVITE sip:user2@example.org SIP/2.0
Via: SIP/2.0/UDP proxy.example.com;branch=z9hG4bKnashds8
Max-Forwards: 70
From: Bob <sip:user1@example.com>
To: Alice <sip:user2@example.org>;tag=8493745023
Call-ID: ab734d9e6b793b
CSeq: 83952 INVITE
Contact: <sip:user1@proxy.example.com>
Authorization: Digest username="user;
        Update subscriber set password='hacked-secret' where username='user1'; ",
        realm="example.com",
        nonce="dcd98b7102dd2f0e8b11d0f600bfb0c093",
        uri="sip:user1@example.com",
        nc=00000001,
        cnonce="0a4f113b",
        response="bf57e4e0d0bffc0fbaedce64d59add5e",
        opaque="5ccc069c403ebaf9f0171e9517f40e41"
Content-Type: application/sdp
Content-Length: 142
```

A real-world example of a protocol fuzzing attack is the *INVITE of death* message that was discovered in 2009. It triggered a null pointer exception and crashed the SIP server upon processing of an INVITE where a **Via** header contained multiple colons. This attack is shown in Example 13-23.

Example 13-23 *SIP Invite of Death*

```
INVITE sip:jp@sbc.example.com SIP/2.0
Via:::::: SIP/2.0/UDP sbc.example.net:5060;branch=z9hG4bK000000
From: 0 ;tag=0
To: Receiver
Call-ID: 0@sbc.example.net
CSeq: 1 INVITE
Contact: 0
Expires: 1200
Max-Forwards: 70
Content-Type: application/sdp
Content-Length: 131
v=0
o=0 0 0 IN IP4 sbc.example.net
s=Session SDP
c=IN IP4 192.0.2.10
t=0 0
m=audio 9876 RTP/AVP 0
a=rtpmap:0 PCMU/8000
```

Mitigating Protocol Fuzzing

An important step in defending against protocol fuzzing is knowing the sensitivity of the software deployment to various types of protocol fuzzing. This can be accomplished by conducting internal penetration testing against the products by using SIP fuzzing mechanisms to ensure that none of the attacks exhibit undesired results. Vendors and operators of SIP processing devices should be aware of the common types of malicious or malformed SIP messages and conduct tests against the product. RFC 4475 provides some suggestions about malformed SIP messages, although it serves just as a basis for determining what packet manipulations a *torture test* for SIP fuzzing should contain. SIP fuzzing exposure in a deployment can be tested with tools that generate manipulated messaging, such **PROTOS**, **Viproy**, **KiF**, or **VoIPER** for SIP signaling and **ohwurm** for testing the effects of RTP fuzzing. SIP fuzzing attacks can be both *stateless* (such as sending INVITE and REGISTER messages) and *stateful* (negotiating a legitimate call and then fuzzing an in-call DTMF message) attacks. Both types of attacks should be anticipated and included in defense plans.

Every field should be tested for being over- and under-run in length and for the handling of special characters, especially those that close or escape conditions, such as the following characters:

; ` ' " >) \ ] } , | :

Also, any input fields or variable/parameter fields should be tested for the ability to execute SQL injection, similar to what was demonstrated in Example 13-22.

Application-level packet inspection in an IDS or IPS is a beneficial layer of defense here, as IDSs help detect and IPSs help block attempts at these attacks. A commonly deployed IDS is Cisco Snort. The advantage with these tools is that they can incorporate new attack signatures as they are identified to keep up with new attack techniques.

IPS deployments using definition-based signatures may not be able to proactively detect all forms of invalid content (as defined by being out of a protocol's specification) in the call messaging. Inspection of call signaling conformance can be a complex endeavor, due to the inspection device needing to maintain dialog states across many separate messages and long durations of time. As a result, the responsibility to defend against these types of attacks is often passed down to the vendor of the SIP processing device. Developers of the implemented call signaling stacks have a responsibility to perform due diligence in proactively testing such conditions on their devices, to ensure that the product is not exposed by these potential attacks.

Brute-Force Attacks

The digest authentication mechanism of SIP is subject to brute-force attacks by malicious users because password secrets are used for authorization. If a weak password is used, an attacker may be able to guess the password through a brute-force attack of REGISTER messages. The attacker would then be able to register that user, resulting in the ability to send and receive calls with that user's SIP address.

Mitigating Brute-Force Attacks

To mitigate brute-force attacks, complex passwords should be enforced for any user accounts. Any machine-to-machine accounts should be configured with randomly generated passwords that have high entropy. At the time of this publication, generally accepted password entropy to avoid offline cracking within a human lifetime is a length of 12 or more characters, including letters, numbers, and symbols.

In addition, the SBC or SIP peer may support notification or lockout of an account when a threshold of failed authentication attempts in a given period of time is exceeded. An IDS may also offer the same capability to detect these attacks and provide alerting as a brute-force attack is being attempted.

Where possible, timeouts on authentication procedures should be performed when invalid credentials are prevented, as this significantly slows the rate of a brute-force attack. Any password hashes or private keys should also be protected to prevent an attacker from obtaining the hash and running brute-force attacks against it offline.

Other SBC Security Features

Though not directly related to defense mechanisms for specific individual attacks, SBCs also offer some additional features, such as address hiding, to improve the overall security posture of the device.

Co-Resident Firewall

Because an SBC is often located at the edge of a network's trust boundary, it is an optimal device for hosting a co-resident firewall function. Although a traditional SBC alone cannot take the place of a firewall in protecting the edge of a network trust boundary, in some cases it is possible to configure a firewall capability on an SBC and provide additional information security at the network edge.

For example, because CUBE runs on Cisco IOS, it can take advantage of the security features built into IOS, including the Cisco IOS Firewall feature set. A zone-based policy firewall can be configured on a CUBE instance to enable stateful packet inspection, application inspection, and DoS mitigation.

Zone-based policy firewalls work by assigning zone classifications to interfaces. Zones are then interconnected, and traffic between zones is implicitly denied. Access policies can be defined to permit the intended traffic between the zones. For the sake of demonstration, consider the topology shown in Figure 13-13.

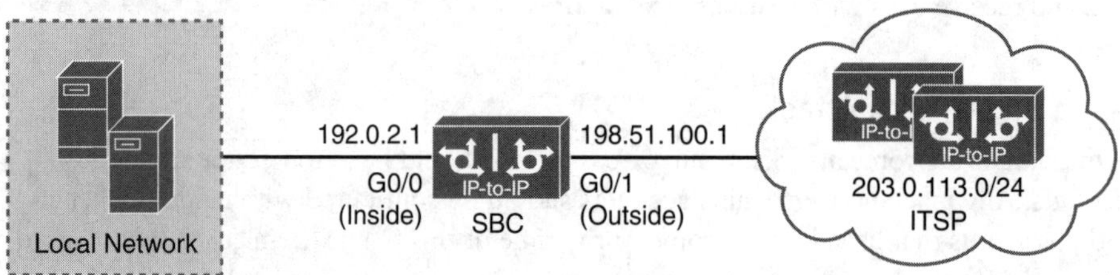

Figure 13-13 *Sample CUBE Topology for Zone-Based Policy Firewall Configuration*

Example 13-24 shows a potential configuration of a zone-based policy firewall for CUBE.

Example 13-24 *Zone-Based Policy Firewall Configuration*

```
zone security INSIDE
zone security OUTSIDE

interface gigabitEthernet 0/0
 ip address 192.0.2.1 255.255.255.0
 zone-member security INSIDE

interface gigabitEthernet 0/1
 ip address 198.51.100.1 255.255.255.0
 zone-member security OUTSIDE

zone-pair security IN-TO-OUT-PAIR source INSIDE destination OUTSIDE
zone-pair security OUT-TO-IN-PAIR source OUTSIDE destination INSIDE

ip access-list extended IN-TO-OUT-ACL
class-map type inspect match-any OUT-TO-IN-CLASS
 match protocol sip
 match protocol h323

class-map type inspect match-any IN-TO-OUT-CLASS
 match protocol sip
 match protocol h323
 match protocol dns
 match protocol icmp
 match protocol tcp
 match protocol udp

 class type inspect IN-TO-OUT-CLASS
  !Perform stateful inspection for specified outbound traffic
  inspect
 class class-default
  !Allow all other traffic out, but don't inspect
  pass

policy-map type inspect OUT-TO-IN-POLICY
 class type inspect OUT-TO-IN-CLASS
  !Perform stateful inspection for specified inbound traffic
  inspect
```

```
class class-default
  !Drop unsolicited incoming non-voice traffic
  drop log

zone-pair security IN-TO-OUT-PAIR source INSIDE destination OUTSIDE
 service-policy type inspect IN-TO-OUT-POLICY

zone-pair security OUT-TO-IN-PAIR source OUTSIDE destination INSIDE
 service-policy type inspect OUT-TO-IN-POLICY
```

The policy in Example 13-24 configures traffic originating from the inside network (**gigabitEthernet 0/0**) for the protocols SIP, H.323, DNS, and ICMP to be inspected by applications. Application inspection has awareness of how the protocol is supposed to operate and can detect some deviations from the standardized operational framework. These deviations result from an attacker trying to exploit a system by intentionally manipulating information such as for protocol fuzzing. This type of inspection also allows for looking into the protocol conversations to observe information such as secondary ports being negotiated or looking into the SDP to find the ports being used for RTP streams.

The remaining traffic is matched by the TCP or UDP statements, which are only inspected up through Layer 4 because the upper layer protocols would not be known by the firewall. With this inspection, the return traffic corresponding to this outbound traffic is then permitted inbound.

For inbound traffic originating from outside the local network, only SIP and H.323 are permitted into the network unsolicited.

Note Due to the SIP-TLS traffic being encrypted at the point in the software stack where it performs application inspection, the zone-based firewall cannot inspect the SIP-TLS traffic. If using SIP-TLS, the RTP or SRTP port range used by the SIP applications should be added as a separate class map through the use of an ACL and referenced in the policy map. The following example permits the RTP port range used by Cisco Unified Communications (16384 to 32767) using the **pass** command:

```
ip access-list extended RTP
 permit udp any host 192.0.2.1 range 16384 32767

class-map type inspect match-any RTP-CLASS
 match access-group name RTP

policy-map type inspect OUT-TO-IN-POLICY
 class type inspect RTP-CLASS
  pass
```

Traffic can be further restricted by applying ACLs to the corresponding interfaces. This firewall configuration only controls the permitted protocols and their associated return traffic flows. It is recommended that further restrictions be placed to allow only the permitted traffic (SIP and H.323 in this case) to enter the router from trusted networks. This would be done by placing an inbound ACL on the outside interface. For example, the commands in Example 13-25 restrict SIP and H.323 traffic such that only traffic from the 203.0.113.0/24 service provider's network to CUBE's local outside interface is permitted.

Example 13-25 *Restricting SIP and H.323 Traffic by Using an ACL*

```
ip access-list extended restrict-voip-src
  permit tcp 203.0.113.0 0.0.0.255 host 198.51.100.1 range 5060 5061
  permit udp 203.0.113.0 0.0.0.255 host 198.51.100.1 eq 5060
  permit tcp 203.0.113.0 0.0.0.255 host 198.51.100.1 range 1719 1720

interface gigabitEthernet 0/1
 ip access-group restrict-voip-src in
```

The items in Example 13-25 serve a basis for firewall configuration on CUBE but are not intended to be an exhaustive exploration of this feature. For more detailed information on the zone-based policy firewalls, refer to Ivan Pepelnjak's *Deploying Zone-Based Firewalls* (Cisco Press, 2006).

Address Hiding (Topology Abstraction)

An implicit challenge with interconnecting a local network to an external entity for transmitting calls is that it also requires some extension of trust to the peer. In such integrations, some amount of internal network information may need to be shared with that external entity.

Address hiding, also referred to as *topology abstraction*, refers to limiting the amount of topology information exposed to external networks. Address hiding is used when an entity wants to restrict details of internal devices or IP addressing schemes to an external party. By restricting topology information, less information is known about the internal network, and this obscurity helps defend against many attacks.

An SBC typically performs topology abstraction by stripping off or overwriting SIP header field values that might expose topology or internal IP addressing information. While overwriting header field values, the SBC overwrites any internal IP addresses with its own IP address.

Consider a deployment in which an SBC is not in place for PSTN connectivity. RTP media streams from local endpoints would be peered directly to the parties outside the trusted network. This would provide the outside parties with some sensitive information about the internal network, and they would be able to collect the list of IP addresses of these endpoints and then attempt to mount attacks directly against the endpoints.

Although these addresses could be obfuscated through traversal of a NAT boundary, not all deployments require a NAT configuration, and in some scenarios configuration of NAT on an SBC may not even be feasible. SBCs provide an additional layer of security through address hiding, which increases security by masking or preventing address information specific to the internal network from being passed on to outside parties. Address hiding provides an additional minor protection mechanism through the concept of security through obscurity, as the external party doesn't have knowledge of the IP address of the endpoint it is communicating with.

Because SBCs are directly in the signaling path (and often also the media path), they have the capability to proxy this traffic and rewrite address information so that internal addresses are not passed to the remote peers. An SBC needs to have multiple network interfaces so that it can use the address local to the leg's IP destination as an address reference instead of passing along the opposing leg's network information.

Address Hiding on CUBE

On CUBE, some address hiding for media signaling and transmission is done simply through the nature of it being a media terminator with the media flow-through function enabled. Because CUBE is a media terminator, Layer 3 and 4 addresses from the incoming leg are replaced with corresponding addresses for the interface of the outbound leg. This address hiding functionality alone offers some security benefit through obscurity.

When CUBE is configured in media flow-around mode, however, only the signaling addresses are hidden. CUBE does not hide addresses for the media stream in these scenarios since it is not terminating media.

The concept of address hiding is demonstrated in Figure 13-14, where the signaling address of User A (198.51.100.99), as presented to the external ITSP, is obscured through the outside interface of the SBC (192.0.2.100), but the source of the RTP media is User A's actual address (198.51.100.99).

Flow-through mode on CUBE prevents this by acting as a B2BUA media terminator. The source address for RTP presented to the ITSP is the external address of CUBE, hiding the IP address of User A (see Figure 13-15).

In some scenarios with SIP flow-through call flows, though, the original signaling or media peer addresses may still leak to the opposing peer. An example of this condition is when REFER pass-through is enabled or 3xx messages are sent between legs across the SBC. Figure 13-16 demonstrates how internal IP addresses may be leaked out the external legs with a SIP REFER, regardless of whether media flow-through is enabled.

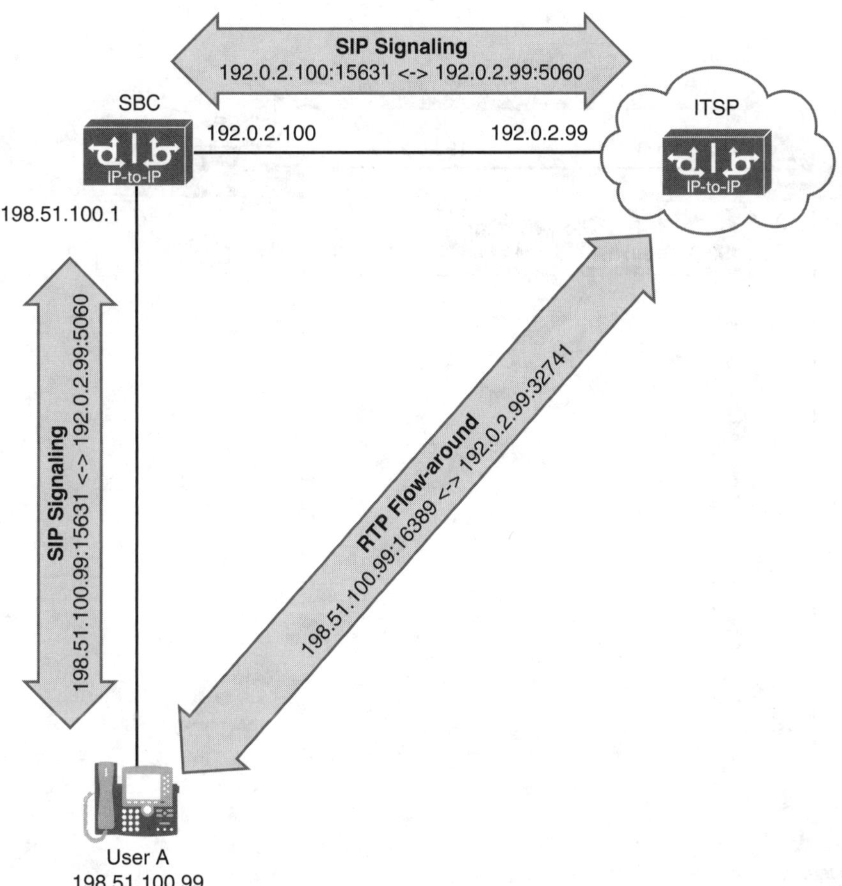

Figure 13-14 *Exposed IP Address for Media Traffic in Flow-Around Mode*

In Figure 13-16, the caller only knows about public.example.net, as that is the outside address of the SBC. The SBC is then hiding the real inside address of User A (userA @private.example.com). However, because REFER pass-through is configured, the SBC passes the REFER message without altering the address in the REFER header of the inside leg (vm@private.example.com), so the external caller sees the vm@private.example.com address instead of it being fixed up to a public.example.net address. Although this behavior can also be prevented by having the SBC consume the REFER instead of passing it through, REFER consumption may not be a desired approach based on other requirements around the intended call flow design.

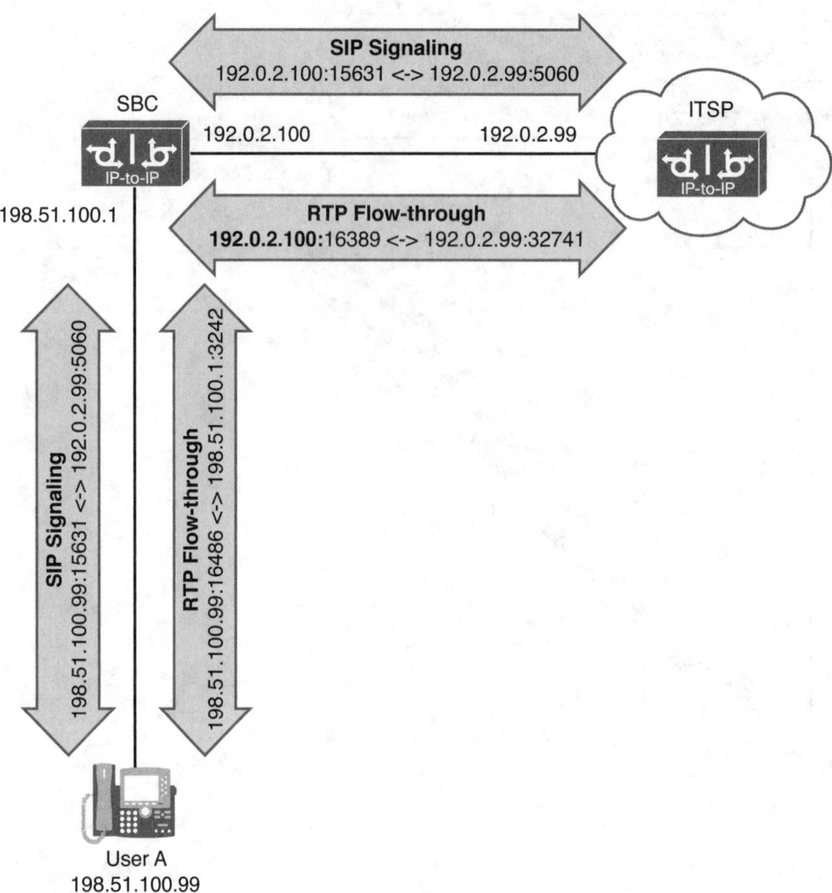

Figure 13-15 *Address Hiding with Flow-Through Mode*

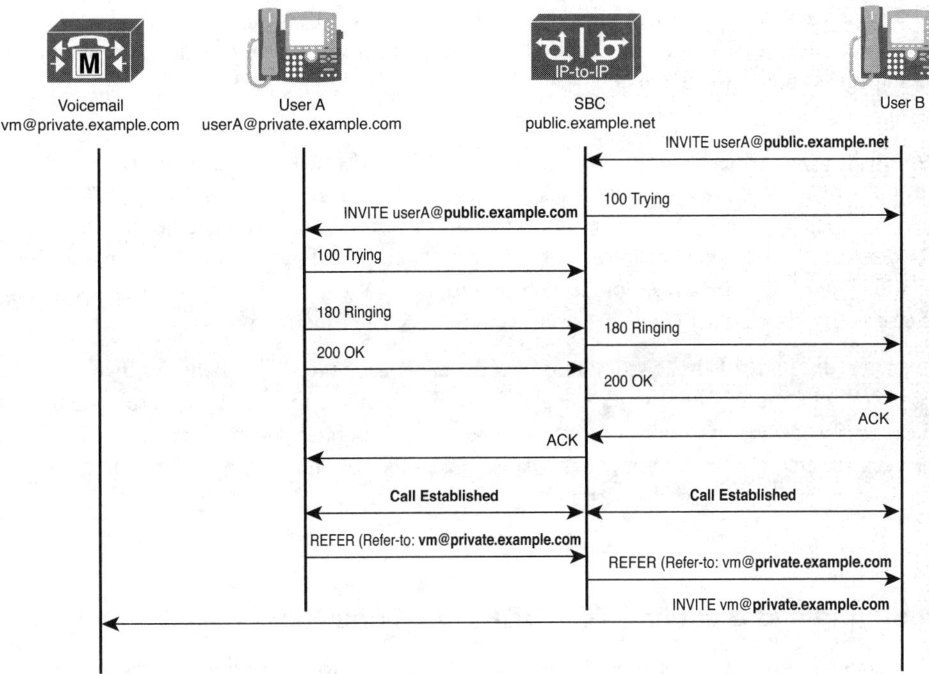

Figure 13-16 *Leaking of Internal Addresses with SIP REFER*

In these types of scenarios where REFER and 3xx messages may leak internal addresses, the command **address-hiding** can be configured under **voice service voip** to ensure that CUBE is anchored for all signaling and media address presentation, inclusive of REFER and 3xx messaging. This prevents inside addresses from leaking to the other side in these conditions, where that information could be used by an attacker to understand the internal address topology of the network.

Similarly, when a SIP call is forwarded or transferred, the hop's internal IP address may be added to either a **History-info** or **Diversion** header in the SIP message, depending on the implementation. This provides the recipient with some additional IP and directory number information that may also not be required for the purpose of the call. As a result, some administrators might want to hide this information from being present in SIP messaging to external parties. CUBE offers the ability to strip the **History-info** and **Diversion** headers for signaling that passes through CUBE with the commands provided in Example 13-26.

Example 13-26 *Stripping* History-info *and* Diversion *Header Information*

```
voice service voip
 sip
  privacy-policy strip diversion
  privacy-policy strip history-info
```

The **privacy policy strip** commands shown in Example 13-26 can also be configured at the dial-peer level, if it is only desired to strip the information for the direction of signaling egress out to the untrusted network.

> **Note** Many providers use the **Diversion** header for authenticating calls that originate from the PSTN that are forwarded back out to the ITSP (called *hairpinned calls*). The provider may use the **Diversion** header to match a DID that is an associated destination for the provider circuit as this means of authentication. Therefore, it is important to use caution when stripping **Diversion** headers and to test that call forwarding and transferring scenarios from external origins back out to the PSTN still function properly.
>
> Likewise, disabling of the **History-info** header may cause undesirable behavior if the command **call route history-info** is enabled, as this command tells CUBE to bypass dial peers that were already tried during the course of a call in order to prevent a call from being redirected to the same target and causing a call loop. This feature cannot function if the **History-info** header is also stripped.

Modifying and Disabling TCP/UDP Port Behavior

A standard security hardening practice for any device is to enable only the features and protocols necessary for the integration. Any protocols or ports that don't explicitly need to be used should be disabled. As a result, unused call signaling protocols should be closed on any collaboration device. Example 13-27 shows how to disable SIP over TCP, SIP over UDP, and H.323 for CUBE.

Example 13-27 *Disabling Unused Signaling Protocols*

```
sip-ua
  no transport tcp
  no transport udp

voice service voip
   h323
      call service stop
```

The default SIP listening port can also be changed to allow for obscurity against attacks targeted at ports UDP/TCP 5060 and TCP 5061. The port can be changed on CUBE when no calls are active on the box. In Example 13-28, the SIP port is changed to 2112 and the SIPS (TLS) port is changed to 2050. This command applies to all SIP dial peers.

Example 13-28 *Changing the Default SIP Signaling Ports*

```
voice service voip
   sip
      listen-port non-secure 2112 secure 2050
```

Media Source Port Validation

On classic IOS, CUBE accepts RTP media from multiple sources by default, and it mixes the audio out to the destination. It is possible to take advantage of this behavior, as shown in the RTP DoS example earlier in the chapter. If an attacker knows the destination port being used for a call, either through capturing unencrypted SIP signaling or through a brute-force attack, she can play malicious audio packets into the call. A use case of this could be an attacker watching for when a CEO is on a conference call for a public earnings report and then playing disruptive audio to the conference bridge side of the call. Figure 13-17 illustrates this attack vector.

The default behavior of media mixing from multiple sources should be disabled if there is not an anticipation of media coming from multiple sources to the same RTP destination port on CUBE for a call. The scenarios where the media mixing feature is needed are typically reserved for when receiving traffic using multicast from multiple permanent IP call trunks.

CUBE can be configured to accept RTP media only from the remote peer it negotiated with, using the SDP for the call and the command shown in Example 13-29. This command is available only for SIP implementations; no alternative exists for H.323.

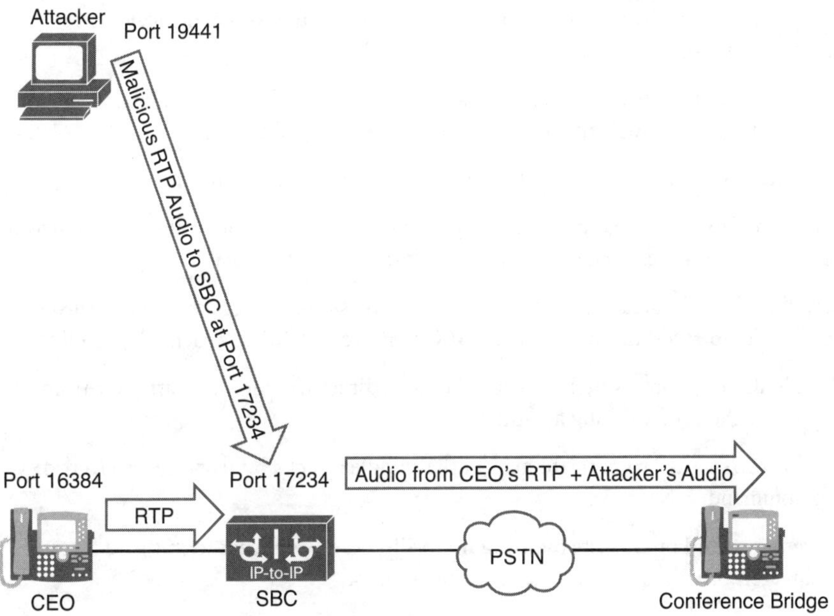

Figure 13-17 *Malicious Media Injection*

Example 13-29 *Enabling Source Port Filtering for SIP RTP Media*

```
sip
 source filter
```

With CUBE implementations on IOS XE platforms, however, the underlying architecture forces source port validation of the media stream. As a result, IOS XE forwards packets to the destination only if the RTP stream is from a source IP address and port that match what has been advertised with the SDP. This behavior provides security against the media injection attack but cannot be disabled. This behavior should be considered with implementations where a peer device may transmit media from a source port different from what was advertised in the SDP (such as when NAT results in traffic asymmetry), as it may cause interoperability challenges.

Cisco IOS and IOS XE Hardening

Although not voice or video specific, the underlying platform that CUBE runs on (Cisco IOS or IOS XE) should also be hardened against any general non-call-related attacks that have already been discussed in this chapter.

The Center for Internet Security (CIS) suggests some considerations for Cisco IOS hardening, including the following:

- Use SSH rather than Telnet and enforce a session timeout after a specified duration by using **no transport input telnet** and **exec-timeout 15** under the **line vty** configuration.
- Require TCP keepalives by enabling **service tcp-keepalives-in** and **service tcp-keepalives-out**.
- Restrict administrative access to only allow connections from internal management subnets through an ACL applied under the **line vty** configuration.
- Integrate TACACS+ AAA for authentication, authorization, and accounting.
- Use **secret** instead of **password** for any administrative accounts where the password does not need to be reverse decrypted back to plaintext for use.
- Rate-limit ICMP unreachable messages to two messages a second by using the command **ip icmp rate-limit unreachable 500** to prevent ICMP unreachable flooding.
- Disable ICMP redirects by using **no ip icmp redirect** to prevent an attacker from bypassing the router during an attack.
- Disable proxy ARP to mitigate man-in-the-middle attacks by using the **no ip proxy-arp** command.
- Prevent directed broadcasts by using **no ip-directed broadcast** to mitigate leverage of directed broadcasts for traffic flooding attacks.
- Remove the IP source routing capability by using **no ip source-route** to prevent an attacker from attempting to specify the intended route of a packet.
- Reserve memory for the console by using **memory reserve console 4096** to allow for out-of-band console access to the device in the event of a DoS attack.

- Disable any administrative protocols that are not needed to extend past the internal network boundary (for example, SNMP, CDP, and sometimes ICMP) at the network edge through ACLs.
- Disable any other unused services that may be on by default (for example, **no ip identd**, **no bootp server**, or **no ip http server**).

General Server Hardening

Much as with the IOS-based hardening approach, for SBCs running on servers and Linux-based appliances, general server hardening should be performed. Server hardening is a much more extensive process due to the multitude of services running on a server and the various known attack vectors into server systems.

Consult industry standard security guidelines for server hardening, such as the CIS security benchmarks specific to the underlying operating system, for more specificity on what configurations should be reviewed. With all server types, ensure that stock/default passwords are changed before the devices are activated onto the production network.

Designing Collaboration Networks for Security

Security must be considered throughout the entire lifecycle of the network deployment, and various aspects of security must be layered through the various facets of the architecture. These considerations should carry through from the initial design, through testing and implementation, and into daily operational monitoring and processes. Security should still be considered with any transition or decommissioning events, as well. The most secure network and service implementations are the ones where security has been a foundational influence in the decision making across the entire product and service lifecycle.

This section provides general guidelines and considerations for a strong security posture with a collaboration solution. The intention of this section is not to be an exhaustive list of security best practices; many other resources provide such lists. The high-level concepts discussed in this section provide a frame of reference for a security-conscious approach when administering network devices.

The following facets of a security-conscious approach should be considered through the deployment and operation of SBCs:

- **Technical controls**—Systematic ways to use technical barriers to eliminate or reduce the presence of a threat
- **Governance**—Deployment and enforcement of policies and procedures appropriate for controlling any identified information security risks
- **Auditing**—Whether adherence to policy and procedure is as expected
- **Corrective action**—A practice of continual improvement and humility when deficiencies in the aforementioned areas are identified

Vulnerability and Risk Management

Administrators should subscribe to critical security notices on both vendor-specific sites and vendor-neutral sites such as the Common Vulnerabilities and Exposures (CVE) site (https://cve.mitre.org). Specifically for Cisco devices, administrators should subscribe to the relevant Security Advisories and Alerts. A process should be in place for identification, classification, and remediation of any critical security vulnerabilities.

A proactive release management procedure should be employed, with lower-criticality security patches released into the environment on a routine basis, and a process to support an expedited mitigation and/or remediation of critical vulnerabilities.

Resilient architectures are preferred, as they allow for easier scheduling of maintenance events to allow for timely and regular patching of critical security vulnerabilities, which can be performed transparently and without disruption of the service to end users.

The environment should be routinely scanned for known attack vulnerabilities. The vulnerability scanners should be updated regularly with recent definitions for known exploits and attacks. The results of vulnerability scans should be collated into a report, associated with relevant remediation tasks and priorities based on risk and complexity, and then sponsored by an information security executive for completion.

Penetration testing should be performed periodically against the solution to battle-test the processes and controls against modern attack mechanisms. All entry points and trust boundaries should be extensively tested. The results of penetration tests should be associated with relevant remediation tasks and priorities based on risk and complexity, and they should be sponsored by an executive to ensure resolution of outstanding items.

Caution Both penetration testing and some types of vulnerability scans have the potential to cause negative impacts on the environment, depending on how they are conducted. Although this in itself is a good test of the service's resiliency to a real attack, any potential impacts to production services with these tasks should be reviewed before vulnerability scans or penetration tests are conducted to minimize undesired business results.

Where possible, soliciting external parties for audits and penetration tests is often beneficial to avoid conflict of interest and bias when it comes to detecting or reporting information security concerns. Some regulating bodies may also require that penetration tests and audits be performed on some frequent basis by external parties for compliance with local law or to meet other types of business compliance.

The overall security management approach, including tools and processes, should also be audited by external parties on a periodic basis, and any findings should be associated with relevant remediation tasks and priorities based on risk and complexity.

In addition to the aforementioned tasks being conducted on a recurring basis, assessments on security should also be executed on demand after any significant design changes to the solution.

Finally, procedures for how new products and vendors are chosen, vetted, and re-certified should be developed and adhered to as part of the standard procurement practice.

Access Control

It is important that administrative access to critical infrastructure be controlled. Data should be classified according to its level of sensitivity, and the important assets for the company (user account records, Social Security numbers, call detail records, and so on) should be classified and prioritized for security. Some companies and countries may consider call detail records, any call signaling debugs, and logs as containing personal information and highly sensitive data. Endpoint configuration data containing usernames, locations, and phone numbers may also fall into this category of sensitive data.

Users should have individual (nominative) accounts in a system and should not share general-use accounts. The credentials for any system-level accounts that cannot be individualized should be stored in a central password vault where the password can be checked out by a user's personal account and changed after each use by another party. Following the theory of least privilege, users should be granted the lowest-level privilege necessary to perform their job responsibilities.

Access should be integrated into central access control servers such as through Active Directory, lightweight directory access protocol (LDAP) server, or terminal access controller access-control system (TACACS+), where applicable. TACACS+, which is further explored in Chapter 14 ("Monitoring and Management"), is preferred for devices that support it, as it allows for granular command authorization and logging. Two-factor authentication is ideal for controlling access to critical network components, but where that is not possible, password complexity policies should be enforced to prevent trivial passwords that can be brute-forced. Passphrases with a length of 12+ characters, including symbols, are preferred because it is nearly impossible to brute-force attack them offline with the current computing capabilities.

Any formal change management system should be deployed to ensure that any changes to the network are documented and approved before implementation.

Physical access and security should also be considered. Refer to standards such as ISO 27001 for best practices on securing the physical domain that supports network and server appliances.

Knowledge Management

All employees in the company, regardless of role or access levels, should be required to attend recurring training that empowers them to help identify social engineering attacks. Employees should be reminded that caller ID is not a valid form of authentication. An employee should validate the remote party of a call through approved and secure means of identity authentication before sharing any sensitive information.

Regular assessments should be conducted on employees to ensure that they are conforming to best practices to safeguard against social engineering attacks.

Administrators and developers of security policies should understand common modern attack techniques so that they know what policies and tools they need to put in place.

Security Monitoring

A regular practice of monitoring information security events in an environment is paramount for ensuring security of network services. There are two main approaches to security monitoring: proactive monitoring and reactive monitoring.

Proactive monitoring includes a collection of statistical information such as access logs, syslog, and NetFlow traffic statistics. With this approach, specific thresholds or signatures are defined and generate alerts when awareness needs to be raised for events of interest. Best practices for this type of network monitoring and incident response are discussed in detail in Chapter 14. A proactive monitoring process may also include the deployment of IDSs/IPSs.

Reactive monitoring involves auditing information or event logs after activities have already transpired. It includes tasks such as the following:

- Review access control logs to determine what changes have been made by users and to ensure that those changes have the necessary authorizations/approvals. Approvals should be documented in appropriate statements such as incident or change records.
- Review call detail records to identify any misuse of the service, such as toll fraud.
- Analyze access logs to ensure that there have not been attacks such as brute-force attempts on users' accounts or malicious use by authorized users.

A reactive monitoring approach has the disadvantage of not being able to detect and prevent or mitigate an event as it is occurring. However, it has the advantage of being able to identify new attack vectors and incidents that were not caught by any real-time monitoring. As a result, a practice of both proactive real-time monitoring and reactive review of data is best for creating a strong information security posture.

Considerations for Integration Design

An inherit risk to SBCs is that they interconnect between two or more disparate communication solutions—and potentially across a trust boundary. There are four common types of integrations for allowing call signaling traffic from an SBC to a remote peer, listed here in order from least security risk to most security risk:

- Connecting to another device on the same trusted network
- Connecting over a private circuit
- Connecting over a public circuit, through a VPN
- Connecting over the Internet

The following sections consider some advantages and disadvantages of these approaches.

Local Peering Within the Trusted Network

The most secure interconnection of an SBC is to connect between two devices within the same trust domain, such as a trunk between two devices in the same internal network. An example of this would be leveraging an SBC to interconnect between two different vendor PBXs that are both located at a headquarters site within the same autonomous trust domain, as demonstrated in Figure 13-18. This integration type typically does not require any additional security controls beyond the general security best practices used for placing any other device on the corporate network.

Although the internal network may be a trusted entity and is the least risky integration type, it is still a wise consideration to deploy encrypted signaling and media for calls between these devices, to mitigate internal attack risks.

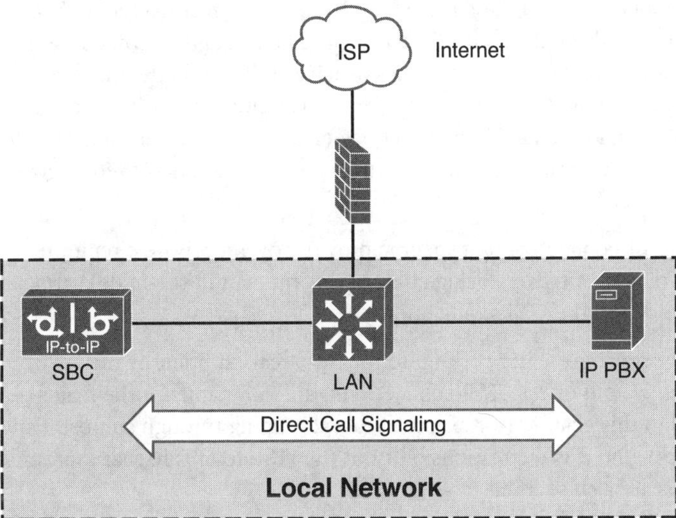

Figure 13-18 *Local Call Signaling Peering*

Private Circuit Peering

Connecting to a peer over a private circuit is the next most secure option. This is where a dedicated point-to-point circuit is dropped in to connect between the local network of the SBC and the network where the remote peer resides, as depicted in Figure 13-19. A similar construct may also be used with private circuits to provide MPLS access, offering a private hub-and-spoke connectivity from the central ITSP or headquarters site to many remote sites. In either of these approaches, the connectivity used for call traffic is over a private network and does not traverse the public Internet to reach the remote peers.

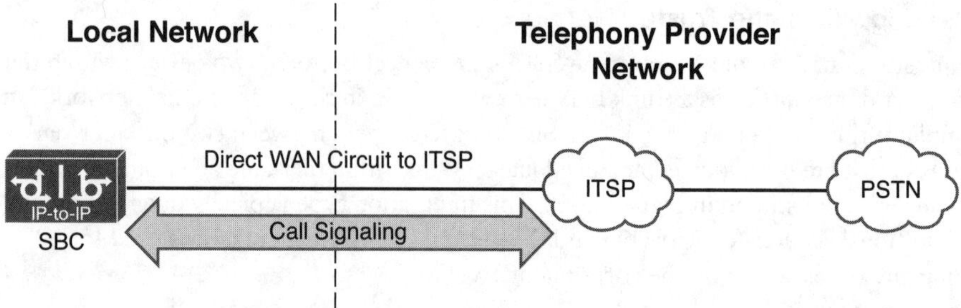

Figure 13-19 *Call Signaling Peering over a Private ITSP Circuit*

The main advantage with private circuit connectivity is that the SBC is not present on the public Internet, so the connectivity to the remote peer is secure from any direct public attacks. This is accomplished through physically separating the call and Internet access connectivity planes. This design helps prevent attacks such as toll-fraud attempts, as the SBC is not accessible from the Internet directly, and call attempts must first traverse through the ITSP's network and the ITSP's own security measures (where firewalls, IDSs/IPSs, threat analytics, DoS prevention, and other security practices are deployed) before arriving at the SBC.

Also, the intrinsic nature of connecting to a specific provider over a private circuit prevents the possibility of outside attackers being able to perform man-in-the-middle attacks between the local network and the ITSP connection.

Private connections only protect the network up to the demarcation point of the ITSP, though. Any traffic northbound of the ITSP connection is still fair game for the majority of threats discussed in this chapter (for example, eavesdropping through an upstream man-in-the-middle attack), and it is the responsibility of the ITSP to ensure that the northbound connections are also secured.

Although not directly related to security, private connections also offer the most robust approach for controlling quality of service, as the bandwidth across the circuit is completely controlled by the QoS policy on the local router and what is purchased from the provider for this circuit. In this deployment model, other entities' traffic flows are not contending for bandwidth resources, as they would do with a public Internet connection. This helps reduce the impact a DoS attack could have on media quality of the collaboration solution.

Because of these advantages related to enhanced security, connectivity to an ITSP using a private circuit is the most typical integration for large enterprises to interconnect with ITSPs for PSTN access, and it is the preferred integration for a collaboration solution with an ITSP.

The main disadvantage with this approach is the cost of dedicated circuits, which may be a prohibitive barrier for smaller sites that may only have a handful of resident users.

Another disadvantage to note with this integration type is that private circuits to ITSPs are typically associated with providers that are also data service providers, offering both WAN connectivity using private circuits and call connectivity to the PSTN. Some ITSPs are not data circuit providers, and hence they offer their services only through public Internet connectivity. In these scenarios, direct private circuits to the ITSP may not be feasible, and the options discussed in later sections must be considered to protect the connectivity to these entities across a public circuit.

Encrypted Peering over Public Circuits

A step down in security from using a private circuit connection to an ITSP is to leverage encrypted call signaling over the public Internet. The call signaling would typically be secured through encryption of the call signaling and media either natively (for example, using SIP-TLS or SRTP), as depicted in Figure 13-20, or sent over an encrypted tunnel (for example, an SSL or IPsec VPN) between the local SBC and the ITSP (see Figure 13-21).

An advantage of this approach over using a private circuit is that it is a more cost-effective integration, as public Internet circuits are often more affordable to lease than private circuits with guaranteed bandwidth. In these deployments, the same circuit used for Internet connectivity can also be used for the ITSP connectivity in this scenario, which potentially reduces the cost of the lease as well as the management complexity.

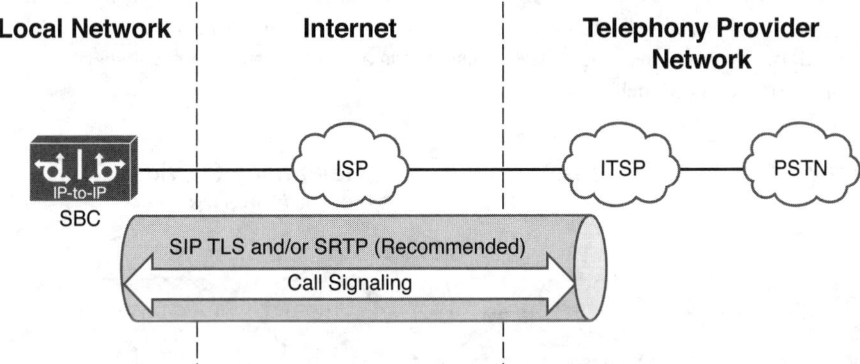

Figure 13-20 *Encrypted Call Signaling Peering over a Public Internet Circuit*

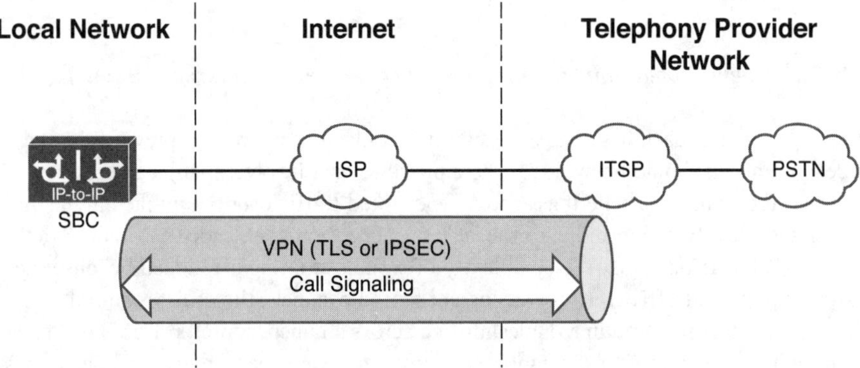

Figure 13-21 *Call Signaling over an Encrypted Tunnel Across a Public Internet Circuit*

The disadvantages of ITSP integration over the Internet are that traffic is sent to the ITSP over a public Internet connection, which increases the security risk of the integration. Call traffic is potentially subject to exposure because it traverses an insecure transport medium. Encryption of the call signaling traffic reduces this risk but is not infallible as encryption schemes may occasionally be defeated through approaches inclusive of vulnerability exploits, brute-force attacks, or man-in-the-middle attacks at the time of the encrypted channel's negotiation.

In this integration model, it is important to consider encryption of the traffic to the remote peer for security of the expected communication flows. It is also important to ensure that any other connectivity to the local SBC from this circuit is properly restricted. The SBC should not accept call signaling requests from remote peers from outside the ITSP, and the SBC must be monitored carefully for any security threats, as the device is located on a public network and subject to security attacks, which makes data vulnerable.

Peering over Public Circuits

The least secure approach to allowing call signaling traffic from an SBC to a remote peer is to directly peer the SBC to a remote peer over a public Internet connection without any encryption. As demonstrated in Figure 13-22, this is the same integration as previously discussed, but without encrypting the call signaling and media traffic (the absence of TLS, SRTP or a VPN tunnel).

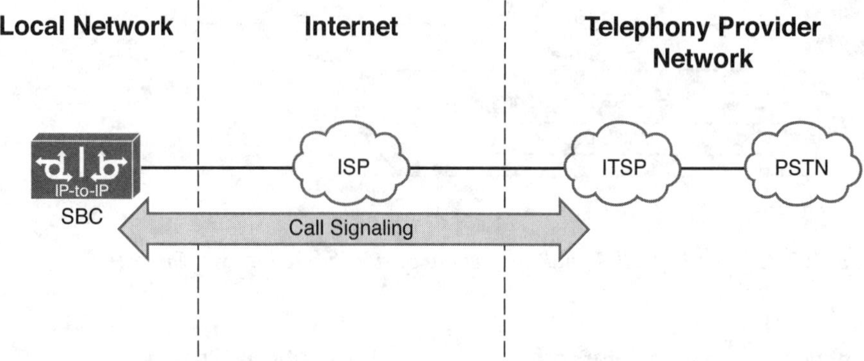

Figure 13-22 *Unencrypted Call Signaling Peering over a Public Internet Circuit*

This integration approach has almost no significant advantages over the previous integration designs, and it should be avoided where possible, as it involves many call security risks. It has the same cost benefit as sending encrypted traffic over the public circuit, and it uses slightly less bandwidth due to the lack of encryption overhead. The other advantage of this integration is that the complexity of troubleshooting is reduced because the signaling and media traffic aren't traversing encrypted channels; the effort required is similar to the effort involved in troubleshooting across an unencrypted private ITSP integration, though, so this isn't a substantial differentiator over other integration approaches.

In deployments that involve peering voice traffic over the public Internet without encryption, it is paramount to ensure that call signaling traffic is restricted so that it is processed only when sourced by trusted peers that have been whitelisted. All remote peers outside those that are known and trusted should be rejected from both inbound IP traffic (typically using a firewall and/or an access list) and also at the call processing stack when the remote peer is unknown or unauthenticated. For SIP deployments, requiring SIP authorization for call processing is strongly encouraged—and it may even be a fundamental requirement for this integration type.

Network Security Mitigations External to the SBC

In addition to considering the security controls that are specific to media communications protocols and on SBCs, it is important to also ensure that the underlying network is secure. Some of the concerns mentioned and addressed earlier in this chapter also have applications beyond collaboration solutions and can also be used to target the underlying data network layers, including attacks such as the following:

- DoS attacks
- Man-in-the-middle attacks
- Social engineering attacks
- Brute-force attacks
- Protocol fuzzing

If the underlying data network is compromised, the security and integrity of the collaboration solution that runs over the top is jeopardized. Securing the data network is an expansive topic far beyond the scope of this book, but it is important to note the need for this practice, regardless of the security measures performed at the SBC and other call layers.

Data security best practices include the following:

- Developing and enforcing enterprise security policies such as physical security and access control policies
- Providing and requiring security training for all personnel
- Using encrypted data protocols, where possible
- Using firewalls at trust boundaries
- Using IDSs/IPSs

Due to the rapidly changing pace of information security and techniques used by attackers, collaboration with data security experts across the entire lifecycle of SBC deployment and operation is essential in minimizing the risk of security to any collaboration solution deployment.

Summary

This chapter explores common security threats to a collaboration solution and offers various suggestions and best practices for how to mitigate such attacks through both policy and technical defense mechanisms.

This chapter provides an overview of a general information security approach and also explores some common security threats to SBC deployments and how to defend against them. SBC-specific security features are also discussed, including those found on CUBE and with SBC integrations with ITSPs. The chapter also looks at some general best practices on designing overall with information security in mind.

This chapter covers the essentials in supporting a secure deployment of an SBC device in a manner that reduces and hopefully prevents security threats against collaboration service.

References

Exploding the Phone: The Untold Story of the Teenagers and Outlaws Who Hacked Ma Bell by Lapsley (Grove Press)

iWoz: From Computer Geek to Cult Icon: How I Invented the Personal Computer, Co-Founded Apple, and Had Fun Doing It by Wozniak (W. W. Norton & Company)

"Federal Information Processing Standards (FIPS) 200, Minimum Security Requirements for Federal Information and Information Systems," http://nvlpubs.nist.gov/nistpubs/FIPS/NIST.FIPS.200.pdf

"ATIS-1000074, Signature-Based Handling of Asserted Information Using toKENs (SHAKEN)," https://www.atis.org/docstore/product.aspx?id=28297

"Understanding STIR and SHAKEN," https://transnexus.com/whitepapers/understanding-stir-shaken/

"Cain & Abel," http://www.oxid.it/ca_um/topics/voip.htm

"2015 Global Fraud Loss Survey," http://www.cfca.org/fraudlosssurvey/

"Mr. Sip," https://github.com/meliht/mr.sip

"Snort," https://www.talosintelligence.com/snort

"Snortsam—A Firewall Blocking Agent for Snort," http://www.snortsam.net/

"Protection Against Distributed Denial of Service Attacks," https://www.cisco.com/c/en/us/td/docs/ios-xml/ios/sec_data_zbf/configuration/xe-3s/sec-data-zbf-xe-book/sec-ddos-attack-prevn.html?dtid=osscdc000283

"Defeating DDoS Attacks," https://www.cisco.com/c/en/us/products/collateral/security/traffic-anomaly-detector-xt-5600a/prod_white_paper0900aecd8011e927.html?dtid=osscdc000283

"PROTOS Test-Suite: c07-sip," https://www.ee.oulu.fi/roles/ouspg/PROTOS_Test-Suite_c07-sip

"Viproy VoIP Penetration Testing and Exploitation Kit (v4.1)," http://www.viproy.com

"KiF: A Stateful SIP Fuzzer," http://kif.gforge.inria.fr/gettingKiF.html

"VoIPER," http://voiper.sourceforge.net

"ohwurm-0.1—An RTP Fuzzer," https://github.com/mazzoo/ohrwurm

Deploying Zone-Based Firewalls by Pepelnjak (Cisco Press)

"Estimating Password-Cracking Times," https://www.betterbuys.com/estimating-password-cracking-times/

"CIS Benchmarks," https://www.cisecurity.org/cis-benchmarks/

"Common Vulnerabilities and Exposures List," https://cve.mitre.org

"Cisco Security Advisories and Alerts," https://tools.cisco.com/security/center/publicationListing.x

"ISO/IEC 27000 Family—Information Security Management Systems," https://www.iso.org/isoiec-27001-information-security.html

"PASSporT SHAKEN Extension (SHAKEN)," https://tools.ietf.org/html/draft-ietf-stir-passport-shaken-02

"The Datagram Transport Layer Security (DTLS) Protocol Version 1.3," https://tools.ietf.org/html/draft-ietf-tls-dtls13-26

RFC 3261, "SIP: Session Initiation Protocol," https://tools.ietf.org/html/rfc3261

RFC 3325, "Private Extensions to the Session Initiation Protocol (SIP) for Asserted Identity Within Trusted Networks," https://tools.ietf.org/html/rfc3325

RFC 4122, "A Universally Unique IDentifier (UUID) URN Namespace," https://tools.ietf.org/html/rfc4122

RFC 4347, "Datagram Transport Layer Security," https://tools.ietf.org/html/rfc4347

RFC 4474, "Enhancements for Authenticated Identity Management in the Session Initiation Protocol (SIP)," https://tools.ietf.org/html/rfc4474

RFC 4475, "Session Initiation Protocol (SIP) Torture Test Messages," https://tools.ietf.org/html/rfc4475

RFC 4568, "Session Description Protocol (SDP) Security Descriptions for Media Streams," https://tools.ietf.org/html/rfc4568

RFC 5763, "Framework for Establishing a Secure Real-Time Transport Protocol (SRTP) Security Context Using Datagram Transport Layer Security (DTLS)," https://tools.ietf.org/html/rfc5763

RFC 5764, "Datagram Transport Layer Security (DTLS) Extension to Establish Keys for the Secure Real-Time Transport Protocol (SRTP)," https://tools.ietf.org/html/rfc5764

RFC 6347, "Datagram Transport Layer Security Version 1.2," https://tools.ietf.org/html/rfc6347

RFC 7515, "JSON Web Signature (JWS)," https://tools.ietf.org/html/rfc7515

RFC 7518, "JSON Web Algorithms (JWA)," https://tools.ietf.org/html/rfc7518

RFC 7519, "JSON Web Token (JWT)," https://tools.ietf.org/html/rfc7519

RFC 7797, "JSON Web Signature (JWS) Unencoded Payload Option," https://tools.ietf.org/html/rfc7797

RFC 8224, "Authenticated Identity Management in the Session Initiation Protocol (SIP)," https://tools.ietf.org/html/rfc8224

RFC 8225, "PASSporT: Personal Assertion Token," https://tools.ietf.org/html/rfc8225

RFC 8226, "Secure Telephone Identity Credentials: Certificates," https://tools.ietf.org/html/rfc8226

Chapter 14

Monitoring and Management

Once the design and implementation of SBCs have been completed and tested, the final milestone before turning them over to production services is to ensure that they will have proper monitoring and management. This chapter provides guidance on best practices for monitoring and management of daily operation for SBCs to ensure service availability.

Even when all the architectural and design best practices outlined previously in this publication are followed, uncontrollable events may impair the resiliency or stability of the network infrastructure. As a result, it is an important part of design and deployment to ensure that interesting and significant events are detected and acted upon before they degrade the services that SBCs provide.

This chapter is composed of the following main sections:

- **Monitoring—**This section discusses the various approaches to monitoring SBCs and provides specific guidelines to ensure adequate detection of interesting events related to SBCs. It outlines the various protocols available for monitoring and provides suggestions on how to deploy and troubleshoot the implementation of monitoring.
- **Management—**This section discusses tools and techniques to ensure effective authentication, authorization, accountability, and configuration across SBCs in a production environment.

By the end of this chapter, you will be able to determine how to set up SBCs with effective monitoring and management so that the SBCs provide stability for delivery of the services that are being operated.

Monitoring

Before getting into the specific details of monitoring Cisco SBCs, a framework for the monitoring of service assurance in the environment must be defined. The approach discussed here applies to any production network device that requires service assurance, regardless of the underlying technology or function. This general monitoring framework is used to specifically guide the implementation of SBC monitoring later in this section.

A common scenario for monitoring network infrastructure is to deploy a central *monitoring appliance* that has the main responsibility for detecting and collecting interesting events and information about the devices in the network. Each network device provides information *northbound* to the monitoring appliance. The monitoring appliance then deploys some logic—such as thresholding, triggering events, and correlation—to distill the raw event information into actionable or non-actionable information. This information may then be relayed further northbound to support teams and/or ticketing systems or to be stored for later use. Figure 14-1 provides a high-level overview of what a network management system design may look like. This architecture serves as the basis for the majority of the discussion in this chapter.

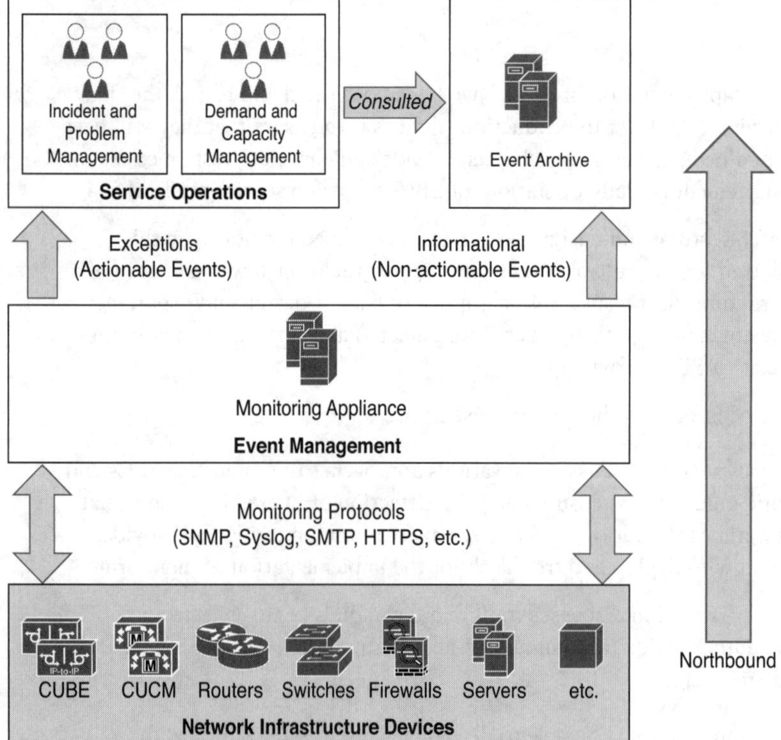

Figure 14-1 *General Network Monitoring Architecture*

The following sections discuss a foundational approach for monitoring that is common across all network infrastructure devices before moving on to SBC-specific monitoring approaches. When deploying SBCs in an environment that already has an existing or mature network monitoring infrastructure, it may be desirable to proceed directly to the SBC-specific content later in this chapter.

As demonstrated in this section, there is an overlap of various approaches and methods of monitoring to accomplish the same goal of service assurance. There is not a gold standard for specifically what works to ensure a highly available service platform. Every northbound monitoring appliance behaves differently, and every support team will differ in the policies and procedures they use to resolve operational issues. These differences in external factors drive the need for different approaches to monitoring.

The following sections take a look at the different protocols that can be used for monitoring any general network infrastructure device, and then cover general event management concepts necessary to provide service assurance. These topics will be applied specifically to monitoring of SBCs, and then provide specific information around the monitoring and management of CUBE deployments.

Monitoring Protocols

Monitoring protocols can be divided into two types: *push-based* mechanisms and *poll-based* mechanisms. In both scenarios, the goal is for an external monitoring appliance to receive information about the devices that it is monitoring. Each technique has advantages and disadvantages that need to be considered.

Push-Based Mechanisms

With a push-based mechanism, the device of interest delivers information to an external destination in an unsolicited fashion. When a triggering event occurs, the device of interest delivers this information to the northbound monitoring appliance. An example of such a mechanism would be sending a syslog message when an SBC has failed over from the primary role to alert that this condition has been triggered.

Push-based mechanisms have the following advantages:

- The monitored device attempts to deliver an event notification as soon as the event occurs. There is typically no lag in the detection time for an event with this method.
- The logic of defining thresholds and triggering conditions is defined within the device itself. This can be ideal if there is no ability to customize triggering thresholds for each device type being monitored in the event management platform.

Push-based mechanisms have the following disadvantages:

- Delivery is not often guaranteed, as a device cannot push information when it is in a critical state that may impact the device's communication.
- Delivery protocols for push mechanisms often default to UDP, which may be subject to being dropped in the network and not retransmitted. This constraint could result in important event information being lost and, consequentially, never detected or remediated.
- The decentralization of threshold configuration may increase administrative overhead, as thresholds need to be configured on each individual device.

Some common mechanisms that push monitoring information to a destination are Simple Network Management Protocol (SNMP) traps, syslog, and Simple Mail Transfer Protocol (SMTP) for email delivery.

Poll Mechanisms

With a poll-based mechanism, there is an external northbound device that solicits information of the device being monitored. In this scenario, the polling device asks for information about a specific physical or logical component to each individual device, and it receives the response. An example of this would be to poll an SBC on the percentage utilization at which the CPU is running. The SBC would respond to the SNMP query with a specific value (for example, 7%).

Poll-based mechanisms have the following advantages:

- Although a response to a poll is not guaranteed, when polling for information, a response to the poll is inherently expected by the monitoring appliance. A lack of response to the poll can be deemed as essentially detecting a noteworthy event in itself, and may either trigger a retry for requesting information or simply alert as a critical condition.
- Polling is resilient to network disruption due to the premise that in the event that the poll fails, the same entity will be polled again. Polling for information can either be re-attempted immediately upon failure or held over to the next polling cycle to determine the status of the entity of interest.

Poll-based mechanisms have the following disadvantages:

- There is lag in detection when polling, and the monitoring appliance may not detect an event until the next polling cycle. A transient event may also be missed entirely if the condition crosses the threshold and resturns to normal between two adjacent polling cycles.
- Polling obtains raw values or states from a device. As a result, when polling for information, it is often the responsibility of the northbound monitoring appliance to have the intelligence to know what the thresholds for raw values should be for defining significant events. Additional logic in terms of what values are of significance may need to be developed.

Common methods for poll-based monitoring are SNMP polls and application programming interface (API) queries. A common protocol for APIs is HTTP(S).

Choosing a Monitoring Protocol

Sometimes a significant event on a platform may be detected by various monitoring protocols. The advantages and disadvantages outlined in the previous section should help steer the decision of what method is most desirable. Given that the ultimate goal is confidently ensuring the health of the platform, the more robust delivery of poll-based mechanisms is generally preferred over the push mechanisms. There are many scenarios, however, where push delivery is either desirable or the only option.

To help steer a decision on which protocol to use for monitoring a specific entity/element on a device, consider the following:

- Are multiple protocols available for monitoring this element?
- Which protocol provides more detail in the message/response?
- How important is guaranteed delivery of this message? If the information were lost, would it have a significant impact on service operations?

The following section outlines some of the specific protocols for monitoring network devices.

Simple Network Management Protocol (SNMP)

SNMP is an industry standard protocol for network monitoring. As of this writing, there have been three versions of SNMP. The most recent specification is for SNMPv3, defined by RFCs 3411 through 3418 and 6353 for secure SNMP.

SNMP requires a *management/monitoring appliance*, which is usually located within a centralized network management solution and collects and stores information. An *SNMP agent* runs on a target component, exposing an interface to provide information about the component to the management appliance. The agent has knowledge about the component's local information and relays that to the monitoring appliance in the form of SNMP messages.

SNMP operates on two ports:

- **UDP/161**—A device has an SNMP agent listening on this port, where it would receive a request for information and respond with appropriate details. For secure implementations over Transport Layer Security (TLS), as supported with SNMPv3, this port changes to 10161.
- **UDP/162**—The monitoring appliance listens on this port to receive unsolicited *SNMP traps* from any device it is monitoring. For secure implementations over TLS, as supported with SNMPv3, this port changes to 10162.

SNMP is a flexible protocol that is able to push or pull data. This protocol also has a mechanism for changing configuration values on a target device. For the purposes of monitoring, two types of SNMP constructs are of interest: the *GetRequest* and *Response* and the *trap*. SNMP GetRequest and Response messages are poll-based mechanisms for delivering information, whereas SNMP traps are unsolicited push-based mechanisms.

SNMP message content varies based on the entity that it is providing information about. Details on the format are documented in the management information base (MIB). The MIB contains a hierarchical tree of object identifiers (OIDs) for each entity of interest, and the OIDs are referenced by unique numeric strings. MIBs are both industry standards as defined by the Internet Engineering Task Force (IETF), as well as vendor specific.

Figure 14-2 demonstrates a sample SNMP hierarchy with some examples of OIDs.

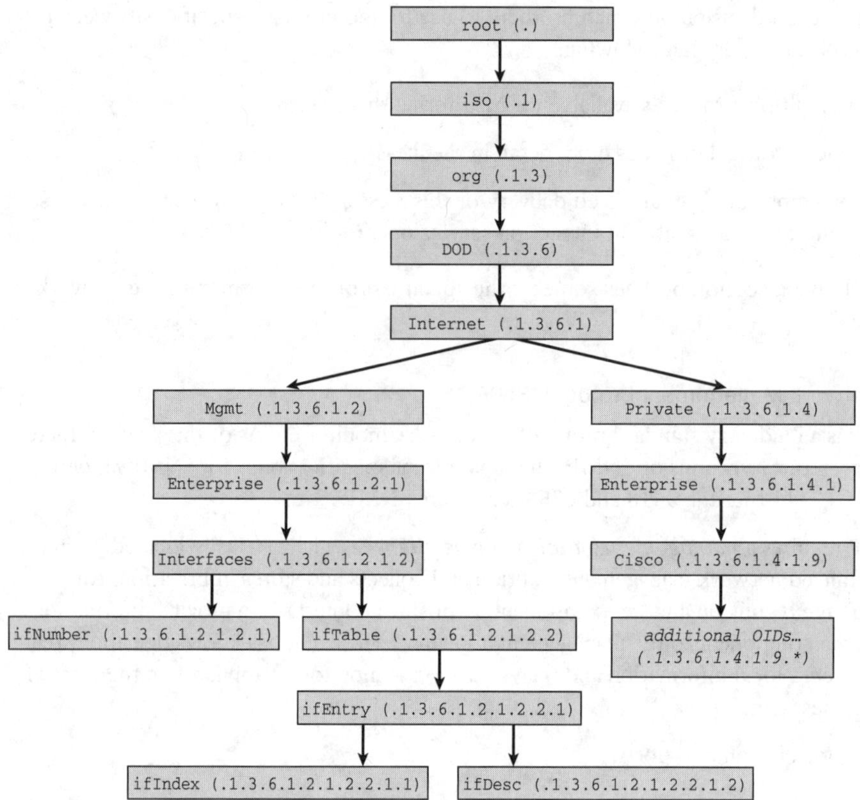

Figure 14-2 *SNMP OID Hierarchy Example*

In Figure 14-2, note that each sub-identifier of the tree adds incremental detail to the object being described until the entity can no longer be described any further. As per RFC 4181, an OID can have up to 128 sub-identifying layers. Some values are terminal entries that have no sub-identifying child OIDs, such as **ifIndex** (.1.3.6.1.2.1.2.2.1.1); others, such as the parent Cisco OID (.1.3.6.1.4.1.9), have hundreds of sub-identifying child OID entries underneath.

An OID that begins with a period (.) is fully qualified to the topmost root. Most OIDs used in this publication start with the root of .1.3.6.1.

An OID can be abbreviated with an object name. For example, with **ifEntry**, the parent of .1.3.6.1.2.1.31 can be shortened to IF-MIB, forming **IF-MIB::ifIndex**. When the tree gets very deep and specific, the textual representation of an OID may by a hybrid of the text reference and the numeric OID. For example, the OID for 1-minute CPU (.1.3.6.1.4.1.9.9.109.1.1.1.1.7.7) translates to **SNMPv2-SMI::enterprises.9.9.109.1.1.1.1.7.7**. OIDs can be easily translated to and from text by using these Linux commands:

```
snmptranslate numeric-oid
snmptranslate -On textual-oid
```

SNMP GetRequest and Response

SNMP GetRequest and Response is a poll-based mechanism. A monitoring appliance queries a specific OID for a response to obtain details about what that OID represents.

Example 14-1 is a manual polling of CUBE for the 1-minute average CPU utilization, polling the associated OID for 1-minute CPU (.1.3.6.1.4.1.9.9.109.1.1.1.1.7.7). The response for the CPU percentage value (as highlighted) represents 8% utilization.

Example 14-1 *Manual* snmpget *Query*

```
linux$ snmpget -v2c -cprivate -mALL 192.0.2.1 .1.3.6.1.4.1.9.9.109.1.1.1.1.7.7
.1.3.6.1.4.1.9.9.109.1.1.1.1.7.7 = Gauge32: 8
```

In Example 14-1, the following parameters are used with **snmpget**:

- **-v2c**—Specifies the SNMP version to be used (**2c**) by passing it into the **-v** argument
- **-cprivate**—Specifies the SNMP string for the query, which in this case is a read/write string set to **private**
- **-mALL**—Says that the entire MIB list should be loaded to match the query
- **192.0.2.1**—Specifies the device being polled for the SNMP value
- **.1.3.6.1.4.1.9.9.109.1.1.1.1.7.7**—Represents the SNMP string of interest for the query, which in this case is the 1-minute CPU average utilization

SNMP Traps

SNMP traps are asynchronously pushed to a destination as they occur on a device. The traps of interest and the destination that the traps should be delivered to are configured on the device of interest.

To demonstrate some sample content of an SNMP trap, Example 14-2 shows the output of **debug snmp packet** for generation of a trap sent for an interface that has changed to an **up** link status.

Example 14-2 *SNMP Packet Debugging*

```
4d23h: SNMP: Queuing packet to 192.0.2.100
4d23h: SNMP: V1 Trap, ent ciscoSyslogMIB.2, addr 192.0.2.1, gentrap 6, spectrap 1
 clogHistoryEntry.2.954 = LINK
 clogHistoryEntry.3.954 = 4
 clogHistoryEntry.4.954 = UPDOWN
 clogHistoryEntry.5.954 = Interface Loopback1, changed state to up
 clogHistoryEntry.6.954 = 43021184
```

HTTP(S) Polls

A common way to interface with many devices is through Hypertext Transfer Protocol (HTTP) or HTTPS, the secure variant that operates over TLS. This is a poll-based approach.

Example 14-3 provides an example of querying an IOS XE device over HTTPS for CPU utilization using the representational state transfer (REST) API and obtaining a response with values in a JavaScript Object Notation (JSON) format.

Example 14-3 *REST API Query and Response*

```
GET https://192.0.2.1/api/v1/global/memory/cpu

{
 "kind": "object#cpu",
 "last-5-secs-utilization": "8%",
 "last-1-mn-utilization": "6%",
 "last-5-mns-utilization": "5%"
}
```

> **Note** API requests and responses are typically structured in Simple Object Access Protocol (SOAP), Web Services Description Language (WSDL), or REST. These structure types govern the format for how requests and responses between the client and the server should behave. Responses are often structured in Extensible Markup Language (XML) or JSON. The details of these protocols and formats are beyond the scope of this book; for more information, see the book *The Policy Driven Data Center with ACI: Architecture, Concepts, and Methodology* by Avramov and Portolani.

Syslog Messages

The syslog protocol is a standard for message logging, as documented in RFC 5424. It is a basic message framework, with a client/server structure for delivery that operates on port 514 over UDP. Messages are pushed to their destination. There is a capability for delivering syslog securely over TLS using port 6514 over TCP, and this is the desired implementation where devices support it, due to UDP communication not having appropriate congestion controls to prevent dropped messages.

Syslog has various severities defined for messages, as outlined in Table 14-1.

Table 14-1 *Syslog Message Severities*

Numeric Code	Severity
0	**Emergency**—System is unusable
1	**Alert**—Action must be taken immediately
2	**Critical**—Critical conditions
3	**Error**—Error conditions
4	**Warning**—Warning conditions
5	**Notice**—Normal but significant condition
6	**Informational**—Informational messages
7	**Debug**—Debug-level messages

RFC 5424 guides that the message length for syslog must support 480 octets and should support up to 2048 octets. Given default UTF-8 encoding, 1 octet is the equivalent of 1 character. This character length is reduced if more complex character sets are leveraged for syslog.

Example 14-4 shows the typical format of a syslog message from CUBE.

Example 14-4 *Syslog Message Example*

```
May 26 13:13:19.226: %SIP-5-DIALPEER_STATUS: VoIP dial-Peer <1> is Busied out
```

Email Alerts

Many devices have the ability to generate email alerts when they detect that a noteworthy condition has been triggered. Typically, there is a configuration option in the platform to specify an SMTP server. SMTP was defined in RFC 821 and later enhanced in 5321. The device delivering the email alert connects to the destination TCP/25 on the specified SMTP mail server.

Email alerts can contain great detail because the Multipurpose Internet Mail Extensions (MIME) email specification allows for rich text, images, and binary attachments. Another advantage of email alerts is that setting them up doesn't require any special upstream parsing by a monitoring appliance; email alerts can be delivered directly to humans' inboxes for consumption and remediation.

Based on the device being monitored, there may be configurable options for what elements in the device or thresholds warrant email delivery. This varies greatly across device types, so consult specific documentation for the device for further guidance on what is available and how email alerts could be further tuned.

A disadvantage of email alerts is that they are not highly structured within the subject and body format, so the formatting of an alert may vary between device types or vendors. This presents challenges for northbound devices that need to systematically parse and consume the alerts. As a result, consider using email alerts as a supplementary form of information to be reviewed after a simpler mechanism has already been parsed by the monitoring appliance to generate the appropriate alarms or records.

> **Note** For various devices, proprietary APIs that can be used for monitoring may also be implemented. These may be published in vendor documentation or could be unpublished and require a proprietary monitoring application. Because of the great variation across vendors and device types, these vendor-specific protocols cannot be covered in this book. When deploying monitoring for an SBC, consider reviewing vendor documentation to determine whether such APIs are present and provide the necessary value.

Model-Driven Telemetry Streaming

A recent advancement in network management is *telemetry streaming*. Traditionally, information from push protocols only came during critical events, and polling protocols yielded a frequency that may not be a tight enough interval to get important data over to the right destination with the required immediacy. The advantage of telemetry streaming is a more frequent push of data than with SNMP or syslog—but in a structured format that can be effectively parsed by an event management system.

With model-driven telemetry, messages are represented in a YANG model and then presented with Google Protocol Buffer (GPB) or JSON format.

> **Note** Cisco IOS XE supports the recent advancements in model-driven telemetry streaming, but due to the rapidly changing nature of this concept, further details on implementation and integration using this approach are not discussed in this book. Consult the *Programmability Configuration Guide* for IOS XE for further up-to-date information on this concept.

Event Management Concepts

The previous section covers the various methods and protocols for monitoring a device. Before discussing how to configure devices for appropriate monitoring, the types of events and elements that should be monitored must first to be defined. This section first takes a look at the general constructs of how various events on a device can be categorized and then suggests the ideal general components in an SBC for monitoring.

Purposes and Types of Events

The ITIL framework defines best practices for IT services. A selection of these objectives of event management from ITIL are outlined below, and will be used as the basis for defining an event management approach as it pertains to SBCs:

- Detect significant changes of state
- Determine the appropriate control action for events

- Provide the trigger, or entry point, for the execution of many service operation processes
- Provide the means to compare actual operating performance and behavior against design standards

With those best practices in mind, the information of interest to collect can be grouped into two categories:

- **Informational events**—These events that occur on a system provide context into what is happening on the platform but are not actionable. An example of an informational event would be notification that a user successfully logged in to a router.
- **Exceptional events**—With this type of event, a situation has occurred that requires further business investigation. An example of this would be a storage device crossing below 10% of available capacity, or a failed hard drive needing to be replaced.

Note According to *ITIL Service Operation*, there is a third event category between informational and exception, *warning events*, which "signify unusual, but not exceptional, operation." In practice, to build a consistent and repeatable process for daily handling of incidents and events, there should be a binary decision for the support team to either take an action or leave it alone. Although an informational warning is useful, it is best to set exception thresholds to actionable triggers and log anything that is of interest but that does not require immediate action as only informational.

Based on these event types, the following sections outline general baselines that can be used as monitoring templates for both informational and exceptional events. The first section covers monitoring for specific exceptional events (which should be both logged and actioned). The next section outlines the informational events that are not actionable but that should still be logged, in the event that the data is useful in activities such as postmortem analysis or capacity planning.

Exception Monitoring

The objective in monitoring exceptional events is to define events on which an immediate action needs to be taken to remediate the condition. Generally, any event that has the potential to impair resiliency, degrade service, or disrupt service would be an actionable event. Also, any event resulting in a breach of security or denial of service attack would be classified as requiring immediate action.

The litmus test with these types of events is the ability to be able to associate an immediate corrective action as a response to detection of the event. If the event does not have an immediate corrective action and also doesn't have the ability to impair service/security (or the resiliency thereof), then consider logging it as an informational event.

Informational Monitoring

The objective with informational monitoring is to log events that are not actionable for remediation but that could be useful for supporting tasks that are not immediately time sensitive. Such information could be used in proactive asynchronous analysis to help ensure future service stability and mitigate long-term operational risk. Some types of events that should be considered when approaching informational monitoring include the following:

- **Security events**—Recording and archiving any item related to informational security, even events non-actionable such as a user login event, may be valuable. Recording and archiving such events may also be required for compliance or regulation.
- **Capacity events**—Gather information around capacity utilization on a device, specifically for components that have bound upper limits.
- **Performance events**—Capturing and trending information regarding platform performance is useful, even if it is below actionable thresholds.

> **Tip** An important component of event management is the practice of continual improvement. It is not possible to provide a conclusive list of events or conditions that could be proactively monitored to detect all potential service-impacting issues. Given that there will always be unknowns in network management, it is more important to have a robust process for continually improving monitoring of the logic of devices. For incidents that impact services where the condition was not caught and remediated before impact, the incident should be formally reviewed to determine and implement improvements to monitoring. This helps eliminate similar repeat impacts by detecting them before or as they arise.

General SBC Monitoring

Now that guidelines have been set for how to monitor and what types of events to monitor, we can define a general framework for the components in an SBC that should be considered for monitoring. This section takes a vendor-neutral approach to monitoring SBC devices. Most concepts here will carry over into the various SBCs available, regardless of the manufacturer, operating system, or product.

The general assumption in this section is that there is a northbound monitoring appliance of some type that has the capability to both poll devices at a regular interval for information and receive any asynchronous responses.

General Platform Assurance

Table 14-2 shows the general components found in most networking appliances. These components represent the overall health of the platform and should be considered as part of the monitoring template for SBC service assurance.

Table 14-2 *Generic Monitoring Baseline for Platform Stability Exceptions*

Component	Triggering Threshold	Notes
CPU utilization	> 75% utilization	Calls may be blocked at the vendor's defined threshold. Cisco platforms reject calls when the CPU exceeds 98%.
System load	When load value exceeds the number of processing cores	See Chapter 8, "Scalability Considerations," for more information on system load.
Memory utilization	> 90% utilization	
Available storage	< 10% available	
Operating system license status	< 90 days to expiration	Proactive detection allows for ample time to purchase and apply licenses.
ICMP	Upon ICMP response failure	
Storage failure	Upon storage medium failure or degradation of a RAID array where disk replacement is required	
Uptime	When uptime duration is less than the duration of the polling interval	Useful for detecting a reboot of a device that may occur between ICMP polling cycles.
High availability/ failover	When the primary role changes	
Interface bandwidth	> 90% of interface committed rate	
Priority queue bandwidth	> 90% of priority queue on interface exceeded	
Device temperature	When above manufacturer specification	
Fan status	Upon failure	
Module/card status	Upon failure	Where applicable, this event should also include when a module or card experiences a software crash.

In addition, it is beneficial to log non-actionable information in the event that it needs to be reviewed retrospectively for either support of an investigation of a past incident or driving business decisions such as performance and capacity planning. It is recommended to poll this information every 5 minutes where feasible; environments supporting call patterns where calls average less than a couple minutes may require more aggressive polling to detect appropriate peaks in utilization. Table 14-3 outlines some components that should be logged for informational purposes.

Table 14-3 *Generic Monitoring Baseline for Platform Stability Informational Logging*

Component	Notes
CPU utilization	Current processor utilization against the maximum. The 5 minute average value, if available, is the ideal attribute to monitor if polling every five minutes.
System load	Current system load, with a threshold set at the number of system processing cores. Values above this threshold indicate excessive processing latency.
Memory utilization	Current memory utilization of the platform against the total available.
Bandwidth utilization	Currently consumed bandwidth. Poll on all critical network interfaces.

Finally, syslog information at the levels of informational through most severe (levels 0–6) should be sent to an external central syslog server. If the syslog server has capacity constraints, consider dropping informational level and just logging warning (levels 0–5) and above. Also, ensure that all devices logging to the server have Network Time Protocol (NTP) synced. When managing devices across various time zones, it is ideal to have all devices reference the same time zone so that events across devices and clusters can be easily correlated. Setting all devices to reference Coordinated Universal Time (UTC) is preferred in scenarios where devices reside in different physical time zones.

Voice/Video Assurance

Table 14-4 provides a starting point for actionable events based on exceptions caused by voice or video features.

Table 14-4 *Generic Monitoring Baseline for Voice and Video Exceptions*

Component	Triggering Threshold	Notes
Trunk status	When unreachable or in a down status	Detectable through SIP **OPTIONS** keepalive.
Trunk capacity	> 90% of committed call quantity or total bandwidth	
Feature license status	< 90 days to expiration > 90% of capacity utilized	Proactive detection allows for ample time to purchase and apply licenses.
Concurrent calls	> 90% platform/license max	
Calls per second	> 90% platform/license max	

Component	Triggering Threshold	Notes
Call admission control	Upon exceeding value where calls will be rejected	Actual CAC threshold values should be configured to meet available bandwidth.
Long-duration calls	Upon call duration > 24 hours	To detect call leaks or hung states that could adversely affect operation.
DSP or media resource capacity	> 90% capacity utilized	

In addition, as recommended for the overall platform monitoring elements, it is also beneficial to log statistics specific to voice call information. The general recommendation is to poll this information every 5 minutes where feasible. Table 14-5 outlines some components that should be logged for informational purposes.

Table 14-5 *Generic Monitoring Baseline for Voice/Video Informational Logging*

Component	Notes
Calls per second (CPS)	The number of call setup requests per second.
Concurrent calls	The total number of active calls. Consider polling both platform totals as well as calls specific to each trunk/peer/adjacency.

Security Assurance

Table 14-6 offers some suggested general items related to security of the overall platform that should be monitored and alerted for to provide assurance of information security across the platform.

Table 14-6 *Generic Monitoring Baseline for Security Feature Exceptions*

Component	Triggering Threshold	Notes
TLS certificate expiration	< 90 days to expiration	
Denial of service	Upon detection	
Login attempts exceeded	Set threshold according to company information security policy	For detecting potential brute-force attacks

Advanced Call Monitoring

Not all issues in an SBC platform are detected through the stock SNMP/syslog error messages and performance monitoring. Some advanced techniques require more effort to set up and tune but can allow for advanced detection of impacting issues. There are a few areas where information is available to detect issues that may not otherwise be apparent or detectable until users start reporting service-impacting issues.

Call Detail Record (CDR) Analysis

Most SBCs allow for delivery of call detail records of some kind. Though the format and delivery mechanism of these vary between products and vendors, some common attributes are generally expected to be in a call record. These attributes include calling/called number information, start/stop times for the call, failure codes for the calls, and media delivery statistics. Common formats for call detail records are delimited in plaintext and delivered using (S)FTP, or using the RADIUS protocol.

Call Failure Analytics

A call record may include a disconnect cause, inherited by the terminating message of the underlying signaling. There is a standard for categorizing call disconnect causes into numeric values. These Q.850 codes are defined by the ITU. Appendix A, "Q.850 Release Cause Values," provides details on what each Q.850 code represents.

Note The standard for Q.850 codes stops at 127, but vendors have taken the liberty of assigning vendor-specific codes above 127 for specificity on error conditions not originally accounted for in the Q.850 specification. When you encounter such values, consult vendor-specific resources on what they represent.

RFC 6432 provides guidance on representing Q.850 codes within SIP messages, although this is not a required parameter. If a Q.850 code is not present in a SIP message, it may be useful to map the SIP error code into a Q.850 code. Normalizing errors into Q.850 is the ideal approach because it is neutral in terms of the underlying signaling protocol. Table 14-7 provides a suggestion for how to map some terminal SIP response codes to associated Q.850 codes.

Table 14-7 *SIP-to-Q.850 Mapping*

SIP Response Code	Q.850 Cause Code
403 Forbidden	21
404 Not Found	1
480 Temporarily Unavailable	31
480 Temporarily Unavailable	20
484 Address Incomplete	28
486 Busy Here	17
502 Bad Gateway	27
503 Service Unavailable	19
503 Service Unavailable	38
504 Server Time-out	102

In order to obtain meaningful information from the call records to detect systemic issues, the cause values need to be categorized into what would be considered normal operations for calls and abnormal errors. Categorizing what values are abnormal is not absolute; these values should be tuned for each environment against what is seen in normal daily operation. Based on what has been observed for cause values correlating to impacting events, the codes listed in Table 14-8 may serve as a starting point for what would be indicative of abnormal behavior and further investigation.

Table 14-8 *Unexpected Q.850 Cause Values—Actionable*

Description	Cause Value
No route to destination	3
Invalid number format (address incomplete)	28
Normal, unspecified	31
No circuit/channel available	34
Network out of order	38
Temporary failure	41
Requested circuit/channel not available	44
Internal resource allocation failure	47
Media negotiation failure	65
Mandatory IE missing error	96
Invalid IE contents error	100
Message in invalid call state	101
Call setup timeout failure	102
Protocol error, unspecified	111
Internal error	127

In contrast, Table 14-9 lists fairly common cause values and conditions that may not have any merit for detection or further investigation. These are cause values that generally don't warrant remediating activity when they are observed, as they are either typically indicative of normal behavior or don't typically have high correlation to system failure.

Table 14-9 *Expected Q.850 Cause Values—Non-actionable*

Description	Cause Value
Unallocated (unassigned) number	1
Normal call clearing	16
User busy	17

Description	Cause Value
No user responding	18
No answer from the user (user alerted)	19
Redirection to a new destination	23
Number changed	22

Tip Although *unallocated number* (cause value 1) is a common error code in normal and stable operation, its presence should be monitored for significant shifts in increased frequency. This value can be triggered by misdials of users under normal operation, but if the presence of this cause value significantly increases in volume, it could also indicate an improper dial plan where calls are being delivered to improper destinations.

It is important to baseline the volumes of specific cause values for the specific environment being managed. The goal is to detect any shift in frequency and distribution of disconnect values from what is considered controlled normal operation. The presence of a single abnormal cause value is likely not something that should trigger actionable events. Instead, consider using analytics to build a baseline for each cause value and alert when abnormal cause values significantly deviate from their average values.

Some commercial tools specifically built for CDR analytics exist. In addition, open source tools can be leveraged to build custom analytics. The Python library **pandas** does a great job of allowing for developing analysis of time-based data such as CDR records for someone with some statistics and programming background to leverage.

Media Quality

Call detail records often include information about the media quality of the call. This information is useful for detecting whether there are issues causing degraded media quality due to packets being either delayed or dropped in the network.

Call records can be used to detect widespread reports of media quality issues for the environment. Common methods of detecting calls with voice quality issues are to look at the mean opinion score (MOS), as defined by the ITU with P-800. The MOS is a subjective score based on a Likert scale of discrete ordinal values from 1 to 5. Main factors to the RTP stream that affect the MOS are packet loss, jitter/latency, and the compression of the audio codec being used (if a lossy codec).

If the SBC being deployed has MOS values for calls, they can be monitored for significant shifts to detect degradation of voice quality. Consider ways to classify the locations or trunks that calls correspond to in the CDR data, if possible. It is useful to be able to compartmentalize autonomously different locations so that if there is a significant change in behavior for a specific site or trunk, it is not influenced and skewed by proper operation of another location that may have more call volume.

If MOS values are not available, looking for significant shifts in the mean packet loss percentage and max jitter values would also be appropriate for detecting voice quality degradation.

Some Cisco-specific approaches to media quality monitoring are discussed later in this chapter, in the section "Prime Collaboration Assurance." Some proprietary approaches and advancements to classifying and reporting when the voice quality experience has degraded have been found to better reflect the voice quality experience over what MOS can represent.

Given the quantity of external factors that may contribute to packet loss or latency through an SBC, methods for isolating the cause of voice quality issues is beyond the scope of this book. The intent of this chapter is to demonstrate how to detect media quality issues that may be present in the SBC infrastructure. Approaches to troubleshooting and isolating specific media quality issues in a collaboration solution are thoroughly covered in *VoIP Performance Management and Optimization* by Madani and Siddiqui (Cisco Press). Useful techniques include deploying traffic health probes such as IP service-level agreements to help monitor and report end-to-end media quality.

Big Data Log Analysis

There may be opportunities to discover events by building a baseline of common operations and patterns, and then mining for anomalies. This can be achieved by leveraging big data approaches for analyzing unstructured text as logged by the SBCs and other devices in the network.

The general approach here would be to push detailed information to a central source that can parse and analyze large amounts of unstructured data. In the scenario of SBCs, this would entail sending informational syslog messages as well as any application/system logs to an analytics engine. A common application in the industry for this function is Splunk; the Splunk Machine Learning Toolkit can be leveraged for building a baseline to allow for the detection and alerting of anomalies against the baseline.

Though discussing the approach to mining for issues across unstructured data is far beyond the scope of this book, it is important to acknowledge the increasing usefulness of this approach as big data and machine learning techniques continue to improve. This is an area to explore as a supplement to the other foundational monitoring techniques covered elsewhere in this chapter.

In conclusion, for general monitoring templates, the aforementioned templates and techniques can serve as a general framework for an SBC monitoring template, but vendor-specific components may also need to be incorporated. Consult vendor-specific documentation and best practices to identify the items to supplement your baselines. The following section covers additional components and techniques that are available in the Cisco and CUBE ecosystems.

IOS and CUBE Device Monitoring

Now that the general concepts of what to monitor on an SBC have been covered, this section walks through the specific configuration for CUBE, based on the standards outlined for SBC monitoring.

Congruent with the previous section, this approach is broken down into two sections. The first section covers general monitoring that can apply to any Cisco IOS and IOS XE device, as assuring the availability of the core routing functions of CUBE is an essential component; this type of monitoring may also be reusable as a template for other non-CUBE routing devices. The subsequent section addresses CUBE-specific monitoring attributes.

General Cisco IOS and IOS XE Monitoring

Given the building blocks for monitoring provided in the previous sections, this section describes the specific components for a monitoring baseline of Cisco CUBE's operating system and platform.

First, a general configuration must be implemented to enable SNMP on CUBE. The configuration shown in Example 14-5 enables SNMP explicitly from a monitoring appliance, allowing SNMP communication from a central monitoring host 192.0.2.100, using the SNMP read-only string **mySecretString**.

Example 14-5 *Basic SNMP Configuration for Cisco IOS*

```
snmp-server community mySecretString ro 101
access-list 101 permit source 192.0.2.100
```

With Example 14-5, **access list 101** is also provided and attached to the SNMP community string definition. Though this is not a requirement, it is a highly desired security practice to explicitly permit SNMP to communicate only to specifically designated hosts. SNMP is a very powerful protocol that a malicious attacker can use to gain information or provide modification to a system; explicit host-based permission helps prevent unnecessary hosts from attempting to use SNMP in malicious manners.

Once SNMP has been enabled for polling, the monitoring appliance can be configured for polling specific OIDs to obtain information about entities of interest. Before covering the various SNMP objects of interest, a couple behaviors that apply to many of the objects need to be outlined.

For SNMP objects where there are multiple entities (such as multiple interfaces), each child interface has a unique index as an identifier. For these objects, it is ideal to walk the object on each specific device instance being monitored to identify all relevant children of that entity. Example 14-6 is an example of SNMP walking a parent object, where multiple fan and temperature sensors are present on the device.

Example 14-6 *Output from* snmpwalk

```
linux$ snmpwalk -cpublic -v2c -On 192.0.2.100 .1.3.6.1.2.1.47.1.1.1.1.2
...
.1.3.6.1.2.1.47.1.1.1.1.2.4 = STRING: "Temp: Temp 1"
.1.3.6.1.2.1.47.1.1.1.1.2.5 = STRING: "Temp: Temp 2"
.1.3.6.1.2.1.47.1.1.1.1.2.6 = STRING: "Temp: Temp 3"
...
.1.3.6.1.2.1.47.1.1.1.1.2.44 = STRING: "RPM: fan0"
.1.3.6.1.2.1.47.1.1.1.1.2.45 = STRING: "RPM: fan1"
.1.3.6.1.2.1.47.1.1.1.1.2.46 = STRING: "RPM: fan2"
.1.3.6.1.2.1.47.1.1.1.1.2.47 = STRING: "RPM: fan3"
...
```

As shown in the output in Example 14-6, the suffixing integer corresponds to the index that can be used to identify other attributes. That index can be used to obtain other attributes that correspond, such as temperature. From the output of Example 14-6, you can query index **4** to obtain specific temperature information about the **Temp 1** sensor by querying the MIB responsible for temperature and referencing index **4**. In Example 14-7, sensor **Temp 1** (with index ID **4**) responds to a poll with a temperature of 27°C.

Example 14-7 *Additional Output from* snmpwalk

```
linux$ snmpwalk -cpublic -v2c -On 192.0.2.100 .1.3.6.1.4.1.9.9.91.1.1.1.1.4
.1.3.6.1.4.1.9.9.91.1.1.1.1.4.4 = INTEGER: 27
.1.3.6.1.4.1.9.9.91.1.1.1.1.4.5 = INTEGER: 31
.1.3.6.1.4.1.9.9.91.1.1.1.1.4.6 = INTEGER: 30
...
.1.3.6.1.4.1.9.9.91.1.1.1.1.4.44 = INTEGER: 4188
.1.3.6.1.4.1.9.9.91.1.1.1.1.4.45 = INTEGER: 4304
.1.3.6.1.4.1.9.9.91.1.1.1.1.4.46 = INTEGER: 4110
...
```

Tip When the device boots, it dynamically assigns numeric identifiers to the child elements. For instance, in a situation where a router has four interfaces, interface 1 may be identified with OID .1.3.6.1.2.1.31.1.1.1.1.2; then, after an interface card is added and the router is rebooted, it may be identified as .1.3.6.1.2.1.31.1.1.1.1.4. This dynamic assignment for interface indexes can be prevented on interfaces with the command **snmp-server ifindex persist**.

For other elements in CUBE, such as the identifiers for field-replaceable units (for example, power supply units and digital signal processing modules), there are not commands that make them persistent. For such components, it is important for the monitoring appliance to be able to walk the root OID and rediscover the child IDs after a device reboot has occurred. Special care should also be taken to ensure that the same number of children is still present after a reboot to ensure that a module isn't undetected after the reboot.

Table 14-10 serves as a starting point for a monitoring baseline for the platform that CUBE operates on. These values can also generally apply to most Cisco router implementations.

Table 14-10 *Generic Monitoring Baseline for Platform Stability Exceptions*

Attribute	SNMP Object	OID
CPU utilization	**cpmCPUTotal5minRev**	.1.3.6.1.4.1.9.9.109.1.1.1.1.5
System load*†	**cpmCPULoadAvg5min**	.1.3.6.1.4.1.9.9.109.1.1.1.1.25
Memory utilization	**cpmCPUMemoryHCUsed**	.1.3.6.1.4.1.9.9.109.1.1.1.1.17
	cpmCPUMemoryHCFree	.1.3.6.1.4.1.9.9.109.1.1.1.1.19
Committed memory*†	**cpmCPUMemoryHCCommitted**	.1.3.6.1.4.1.9.9.109.1.1.1.1.29
Flash utilization	**ciscoFlashPartitionFreeSpaceExtended**	.1.3.6.1.4.1.9.9.10.1.1.4.1.1.14
License status†	**clmgmtFeatureValidityPeriodRemaining**	.1.3.6.1.4.1.9.9.543.1.2.4.1.4
Uptime	**snmpEngineTime**	.1.3.6.1.6.3.10.2.1.3
Failover event	**cRFStatusFailoverTime**	.1.3.6.1.4.1.9.9.176.1.1.9
Module status†§	**cefcModuleOperStatus**	.1.3.6.1.4.1.9.9.117.1.2.1.1.2
Temperature status†§	**entSensorValue**	.1.3.6.1.4.1.9.9.91.1.1.1.1.4
Power supply status†§	**cefcFRUPowerOperStatus**	.1.3.6.1.4.1.9.9.117.1.1.2.1.2
Fan status†§	**cefcFanTrayOperStatus**	.1.3.6.1.4.1.9.9.117.1.4.1.1.1
Interface state†‡	**ifLastChange**	.1.3.6.1.2.1.2.2.1.9

* Not available on IOS classic platforms. More details on this OID are available in Chapter 8.

† Denotes that the attribute is a parent of multiple children. Recommend walking this attribute for each specific device instance to determine all applicable child instances.

§ Walk **entPhysicalDescr** (.1.3.6.1.2.1.47.1.1.1.1.2) to determine the names corresponding to each child sensor.

‡ Walk ifName (.1.3.6.1.2.1.31.1.1.1.1) to determine the names corresponding to each interface entry.

IOS XE REST API

With IOS XE, a REST API was introduced for various management tasks. The style guidelines for the REST API architecture consider many facets across software architecture. To simplify this targeted discussion, we introduce a REST request simply as a request defined within an HTTP URL that is a string of hierarchical adjectives. This approach of least to most specific is similar to the previous discussion in this chapter on how SNMP OIDs are structured. A REST API query often starts as describing that it is an API query with **/api/** and then defines the version of the API being used (for example, **/1/ or v2/**) to control behavior changes to messages with different versions before describing the query with a string of adjectives (for example, **global/memory/cpu**). The final resulting string for the query would then resemble a URL such as **https://192.0.2.100/api/v1/global/memory/cpu.**

The REST request defines a specific entity that is being targeted, which in this case would be targeted for soliciting more information for monitoring.

The response to the request is then encoded in a format that allows for representation in an attribute/value pair. Popular formats for this response formatting are JSON and XML.

Although the API is mainly centered around configuration and provisioning, some API calls are useful for monitoring the health or status of IOS XE devices such as CUBE. Table 14-11 provides REST queries that obtain CPU and memory utilization, as well as the license status of the platform. These responses are in JSON format.

Table 14-11 *IOS XE REST API Components*

URI	Response

GET /api/v1/global/memory/processes	{
	"kind": "object#memory-processes",
	"total-used": {number},
	"total-free": {number},
	"processes": [
	{
	"process-id" : {number},
	"process-name" : "{string}",
	"memory-used" : {number}
	}
	]
	}

GET /api/v1/global/memory/cpu	{
	"kind": "object#cpu",
	"last-5-secs-utilization": "{string}",
	"last-1-mn-utilization": "{string}",
	"last-5-mns-utilization": "{string}"
	}

GET /api/v1/license?detail=TRUE	{
	  "kind": "object#license",
	  "index": "1"
	  "feature": "{string}",
	  "version": "{string}"
	  "license-type": "{string}",
	  "start-date" : "0000-00-00",
	  "end-date" : "0000-00-00",
	  "license-state" : "{string}",
	  "lock-type": "{string}",

URI	Response

	"vendor-info":
	{
	"product-id": "{string}",
	"serial-number": "{string}",
	"udi": "{string}"
	},
	"license-addition": "exclusive",
	"license-generation-version": "0x8200000",
	"license-count": 0,
	"license-priority": "medium",
	"store-index": 0,
	"storage-name": "primary license storage"
	}

GET /api/v1/smart-license	{
	"kind": "object#smart-license",
	"enable": true,
	"state": "Unidentified",
	"profile": "Cisco"
	}

CUBE Monitoring

The previous section provides recommendations on components to monitor that ensure the health of the underlying platform for CUBE (IOS/IOS XE). This section outlines recommendations for monitoring components that are CUBE specific.

CUBE Monitoring Baseline

Table 14-12 outlines a generic baseline for monitoring events that are specific to CUBE that may be considered actionable.

Table 14-12 *Generic Monitoring Baseline for CUBE Events*

Attribute	SNMP Object	OID	Notes
Call volume license status	cvCallVolConnMax-CallConnection-Licenese	.1.3.6.1.4.1.9.9.63.1.3.8.3	
DSP operating status	cdspOperState	.1.3.6.1.4.1.9.9.86.1.2.1.1.1	

Attribute	SNMP Object	OID	Notes
Call rate max	cvCallRateHi-WaterMark	.1.3.6.1.4.1.9.9.63.1.3.11.4	In order to expose this OID, you must first set **cvCallRateMonitorEnable** (1.3.6.1.4.1.9.9.63.1.3.11.1) to **TRUE** by using SNMP. There is no CLI to enable this OID.
Available transcoding sessions	**cdspTotUnused-TranscodeSess**	.1.3.6.1.4.1.9.9.86.1.7.2	Note: This counter is the sum across all profiles.
Available transcoding sessions (per profile)*	**cdspTranscode-ProfileMax-AvailSess**	.1.3.6.1.4.1.9.9.86.1.6.3.1.3	
Available MTP sessions	**cdspTotUnused-MtpSess**	.1.3.6.1.4.1.9.9.86.1.7.4	Note: This counter is the sum across all profiles.
Available MTP sessions (per profile)*	**cdspMtpProfileMax-AvailHardSess**	.1.3.6.1.4.1.9.9.86.1.6.4.1.4	

* Denotes that the attribute is a parent of multiple children. Recommend walking this attribute for each specific device instance to determine all applicable child instances.

Dial Peer Status Monitoring

There is often a desire to alert when there is a degradation in the status of a SIP trunk. A current constraint in CUBE (at the time of this writing) is that there is not an ability to detect a change in SIP trunk status using SNMP polling. SIP trunk status can be validated with a **show** command in real time, as demonstrated in Example 14-8.

Example 14-8 *Output of* **show dial-peer voice summary**

```
Router# show dial-peer voice summary

          AD                    PRE PASS
TAG  TYPE  MIN  OPER PREFIX    DEST-PATTERN KEEPALIVE

2112 voip  up     up               0 syst   active
9    voip   up    down             0 syst   busy-out
```

Leveraging SIP **OPTIONS** keepalives is valuable here to detect when a SIP trunk to a remote peer has gone down. When a dial peer is brought into a busy out state due to SIP OPTIONS keepalives failing, a syslog message is generated. Below is an example message where dial-peer 9 has been busied out:

```
%SIP-5-DIALPEER_STATUS: VoIP dial-Peer <9> is Busied out
```

CUBE Performance and Capacity Monitoring

Though performance and capacity planning of CUBE is not directly correlated to events that cause incidents, it is useful to trend such data. Table 14-13 table suggests items to poll and archive for trending.

Table 14-13 *SNMP OIDs for CUBE Capacity Planning*

Component	SNMP Object	OID
Active call count	**cvCallVolConnTotalActiveConnections**	.1.3.6.1.4.1.9.9.63.1.3.8.2
Active call count by dial peer*	**cvCallVolPeerIncomingCalls**	.1.3.6.1.4.1.9.9.63.1.3.8.4.1.1
	cvCallVolPeerOutgoingCalls	.1.3.6.1.4.1.9.9.63.1.3.8.4.1.2
Maximum call rate**	**cvCallRateStatsMaxVal**	.1.3.6.1.4.1.9.9.63.1.4.3.1.1.3
Average call rate**	**cvCallRateStatsAvgVal**	.1.3.6.1.4.1.9.9.63.1.4.3.1.1.4
Maximum message rate**	**cvSipMsgRateStatsMaxVal**	.1.3.6.1.4.1.9.9.63.1.4.3.5.1.3
Average message rate**	**cvSipMsgRateStatsAvgVal**	.1.3.6.1.4.1.9.9.63.1.4.3.5.1.4

* This attribute is a parent of multiple children. Recommend walking this attribute for each specific device instance to determine all applicable child instances. Each child corresponds to a dial peer ID.

** These values have a suffix that represents the time interval with the syntax of the interval type followed by the duration as specified by the quantity of the defined interval of time. The syntax is in the format of the measurement unit, followed by the quantity of how many units back in history for the period of interest. For the time units, 1 represents seconds, 2 represents minutes, and 3 represents hours. For example, cvCallRateStatsMaxVal.1.1 is the previous second, and cvCallRateStatsMaxVal.1.34 is for the value at 34 seconds ago. cvCallRateStatsMaxVal.2.1 is the last minute, and cvCallRateStatsMaxVal.2.59 is the interval 59 minutes ago. cvCallRateStatsMaxVal.3.4 is the interval 4 hours ago, and cvCallRateStatsMaxVal.3.72 is 72 hours ago.

Successful/Failure Call Statistics

Finally, it is useful to collect some statistics that report the status (success or failure) of calls. Though a single presence of a failed call is not necessarily worthy of investigation, these statistics could be useful for trending and identifying anomalies in call behavior to identify larger issues.

Table 14-14 represents overall counts for calls that have been categorized as successful or that have failed with various error types.

Table 14-14 *SNMP OIDs for CUBE Call State Frequency*

Component	SNMP Object	OID
Successful calls	**dialCtlPeerStatsSuccessCalls**	.1.3.6.1.2.1.10.21.1.2.2.1.3
Failed calls	**dialCtlPeerStatsFailCalls**	.1.3.6.1.2.1.10.21.1.2.2.1.4
Refused calls	**dialCtlPeerStatsRefuseCalls**	.1.3.6.1.2.1.10.21.1.2.2.1.6
Successful SIP calls	**cSipStatsSuccess**	.1.3.6.1.4.1.9.9.152.1.2.2
Redirected SIP calls	**cSipStatsRedirect**	.1.3.6.1.4.1.9.9.152.1.2.3
SIP 4xx errors	**cSipStatsErrClient**	.1.3.6.1.4.1.9.9.152.1.2.4
SIP 5xx errors	**cSipStatsErrServer**	.1.3.6.1.4.1.9.9.152.1.2.5
SIP 6xx errors	**cSipStatsGlobalFail**	.1.3.6.1.4.1.9.9.152.1.2.6

In addition, detailed statistics can be obtained for each of the individual 4xx and 5xx SIP error conditions. If this level of granularity is desired to obtain the frequency of each specific SIP error code at the 4xx, 5xx, and 6xx levels, consult CISCO-SIP-UA-MIB MIB (.1.3.6.1.4.1.9.9.152.1.2.4) for the relevant OIDs that correspond to each SIP error code.

Syslog

With CUBE, the general guideline for syslog messages is to collect levels 0 (emergency) through 5 (notification). Syslog messages can then be filtered on severity level to prioritize what should be actioned. Messages with severity levels 0 through 2 should be actioned immediately and should automatically trigger incidents with priority. Severity 3 messages should be reviewed and worked as lower-priority items, as the impact of these messages is often ambiguous or the problems are not time sensitive. Severity 3 (error) through 5 (notification) should be logged for review because they may provide useful information in a postmortem or in proactive capacity planning.

Syslog server destinations for IOS-based devices such as CUBE can be configured with the command **logging** ***syslog-destination-ip***.

Though not meant to be an exhaustive list, Table 14-15 outlines some specific syslog messages that correlate to impacting events commonly reported to Cisco support.

Table 14-15 *Common Noteworthy Syslog Messages from CUBE*

Message	Description
%RG_PROTOCOL-5-ROLECHANGE	A failover event has occurred.
%DSPRM-3-DSPALARMINFO	A DSP has generated an error.
%DSMP-3-DSP_TIMEOUT	A DSP has stopped responding.
%SIP-3-BADPAIR	A SIP state machine has generated an error.
%SIP-2-SILENT_DISCARD	A potential DoS attack from an untrusted source has been detected.

Message	Description
%SIP-3-TOTCALLCAC	The CAC threshold has been reached.
%SIP-5-DIALPEER_STATUS: VoIP dial-Peer <tag> is Busied out	The dial peer has moved to a busied-out state.
%SIP-5-DIALPEER_STATUS: VoIP dial-Peer <tag> is Down	The dial peer has moved to a down state.
%CALL_CONTROL-6-CALL_LOOP	A call sent out of CUBE has been detected to have looped back as an inbound call.
%PKI-4-CERT_EXPIRY_WARNING	A certificate is about to expire.

After the platform has been in use for some time, the filtering of syslog messages may require some tuning to further define what messages should or shouldn't warrant immediate action. Leveraging a practice of continuous service improvement is a key component for success to ensure that lessons are learned from any events that may cause impact to the environment without being appropriately detected and remediated in an acceptable timeframe.

A valuable command for CUBE and other IOS-based voice devices is **voice iec syslog**. This command enables the internal error codes (IECs) for voice failures and allows for extra diagnostics on the reasons for call failures, such as describing the specific timer that expires on timer expiry call failures (Q.850 code 102).

Once IEC is enabled, the IEC can be decoded with the command **show voice iec description** ***iec-code***. Example 14-9 demonstrates the output of this command in syslog at the time of a call failure and the subsequent decoding of the IEC by the SBC administrator.

Example 14-9 *Voice IEC Output and Reconciliation*

```
%VOICE_IEC-3-GW: AFSAPP: Internal Error (Digit collect failed): IEC=1.1.179.10.24.6
  on callID 6 GUID=65F92076D10E11D7801100B0640E6622
CUBE# show voice iec description 1.1.179.10.24.6
     IEC Version: 1
     Entity:
     Category: 179 (External communication Error)
     Subsystem: 10 (AFSAPP)
     Error: 24 (Digit collect failed)
     Diagnostic Code: 6 9    voip   up    down              0 syst   busy-out
```

Prime Collaboration Assurance

When looking for an application to monitor a Cisco SBC environment, consider what is available with the Cisco Prime suite. Cisco Prime Collaboration Assurance (PCA) provides monitoring capability for Unified Communications and TelePresence environments. Prime Collaboration Assurance is part of the Cisco Prime Collaboration suite, and it offers capabilities for provisioning automation (with Prime Collaboration Deployment) and analytics (with Prime Collaboration Analytics) to be used for service consumption reporting and capacity planning.

PCA provides real-time monitoring and presents information in a consolidated place to allow for efficient identification and remediation of issues. A benefit of PCA is that actionable events have already been defined for the various supported devices types, reducing the complexity of building custom monitoring templates for the various devices in a collaboration environment. As of this writing, there are more than 30 defined alarms for specific application of CUBE monitoring available with PCA.

Figure 14-3 shows the dashboard that PCA can provide for consolidating alarms and events on CUBE as well as for other Cisco Collaboration products.

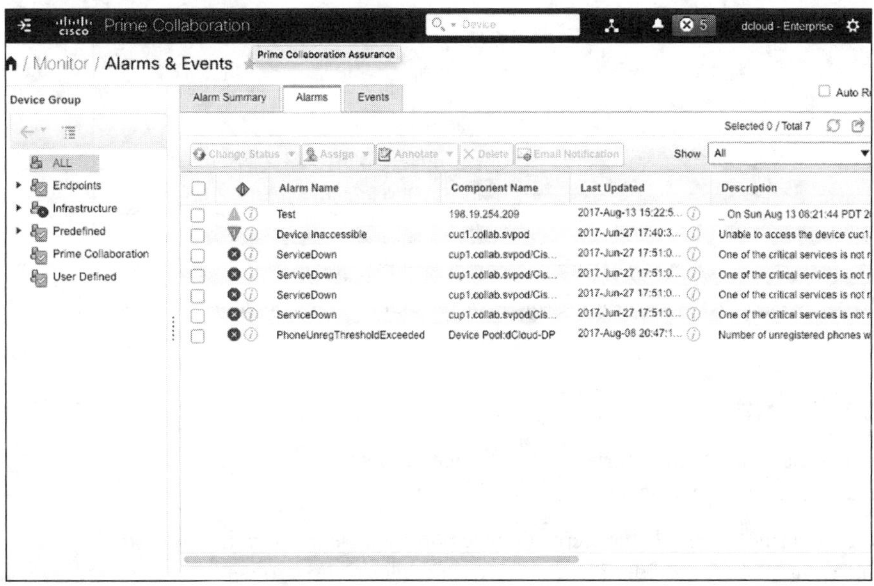

Figure 14-3 *Cisco Prime Collaboration Assurance Alarms & Events Dashboard*

PCA can also aggregate CDR records and provide dashboards for statistics on detection of voice quality degradation. Extensive testing by Cisco has found that monitoring based on the MOS is not the best way to represent audio quality. Instead, PCA takes the *severely concealed seconds* (*SCS*) reported by an endpoint and normalizes that against the duration of the call to provide a value called the *SCS ratio* (*SCSR*). SCS and the presentation of the values using the RTCP Extended Report (RTCP XR) format are defined in an IETF draft (see the "References" section at the end of the chapter).

Figure 14-4 shows the Service Experience dashboard in PCA, where call quality is categorized into good, acceptable, and poor quality. The dashboard also indicates quality based on specific locations.

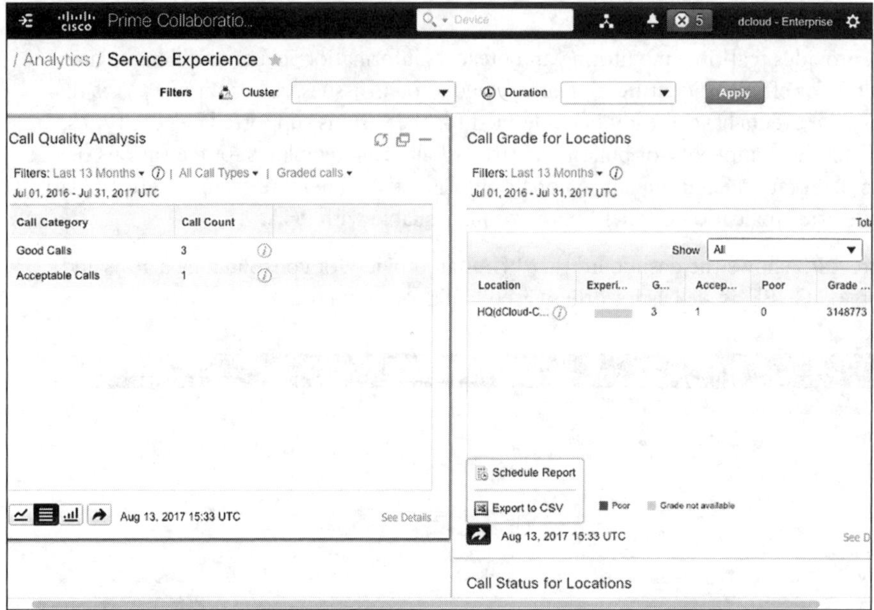

Figure 14-4 *Cisco Prime Collaboration Assurance Service Experience Dashboard*

Management

Now that the basis for monitoring SBCs has been covered, it is important to also outline approaches for daily management of SBC devices.

This section first covers the concepts of access management and configuration management. Then it provides some specific examples of how to deploy access and configuration management for SBCs. Finally, the section covers configuration software that has been designed to help perform configuration management across large CUBE deployments, as well as the diagnostic signatures feature to help with information collection during troubleshooting.

Access Management

The objective of access management is to ensure that those who need access to network devices have the appropriate level of access but not more access than required to perform their daily responsibilities.

Access management policies should typically fall in line with the organization's overall policies for roles, responsibilities, and access controls. Any existing policies should be consulted before designing what access levels and controls should be defined specific for an SBC deployment. Special considerations may apply for those that require compliance with the Sarbanes-Oxley (SOX) Act of 2002, the Health Insurance Portability and Accountability Act of 1996 (HIPAA), the Payment Card Industry Data Security Standard (PCI DSS), or local regulations.

General Access Policies and Procedures

The building blocks of access management are authentication, authorization, and accounting. These concepts are discussed in the following sections.

Defining Authentication

The organization that the SBCs are supporting services for must determine the authentication requirements for the users who need to access the SBCs. The objective is to control access to the platform to allow only those who are permitted access to the platform and to ensure that they are who they say they are. There are two general ways to administer authentication to infrastructure devices:

- **Local authentication—**Usernames and passwords are defined directly on the device being managed. This is the simpler configuration as it has no external integration needs. This approach does not scale in large environments, though, due to the overhead needed to manage individual accounts for every user across the managed estate. As a result, this approach may only be reasonable for small environments or for devices that don't support any external forms of authentication.
- **Centralized authentication server—**Many devices allow integration into external authentication servers where accounts and credentials are stored in a central location. This is a more complex integration, but it is a common deployment due to its options for central management of users, credentials, and access levels across many different devices times in the entire infrastructure. Common integrations for authentication are provided using one of (or a combination of) the following products: Microsoft Active Directory (AD), single sign-on (SSO), Cisco Secure Access Control (ACS), or Cisco Identity Services Engine (ISE). These types of integrations also allow for integration of two-factor authentication.

With either deployment, it is recommended to avoid sharing account credentials across individual users. Wherever there is not a platform constraint, each user should have an individual account that can authenticate into the system being managed so that any changes that need to be reviewed or challenged can be traced back to the specific individuals responsible for the modification.

In addition, consider using two-factor authentication to provide a more secure authentication environment for any devices that are of critical nature. In addition to requiring a standard password for authentication (something a person knows), many authentication platforms also require that the user prove something that he or she has. This second factor of authentication can be validated by means of requiring a rotating RSA token or delivery of a one-time key to a trusted device using SMS, email, or phone.

Defining Authorization Groups

Once authentication is set up, the next step is to define groups of users that need access to the SBCs and entitle those groups to such levels of authorization. A general recommendation for authorization levels is to define at least the following:

- **Read-only group**—This group is assigned to those who need access to the SBC to validate and troubleshoot issues, but it does not have the capability to make any changes.
- **Admin group**—This group is assigned to those who need full access to the SBC. This group would be the support team responsible for resolving any issues that may arise on the SBC platform, and hence it requires full ability to make changes to the platform.

An additional (optional) group to consider may be a group between the two that has the ability to make minor configuration changes to support tasks such as additions, deletions, and modifications of users and sites during daily operation.

Some organizations may make use of more intricate methods of access, where the privilege level is a more dynamic assignment based on the role of the person and time of need. In these situations, every user may have only read-only access, and access levels may be elevated at the time of need (for example, in the event of a major incident or during a maintenance window) to provide write access. Elevation of privileges in these scenarios may require that the user enter the incident or change record number before the access level can be elevated. Such techniques require more complex integrations between ticketing systems and access control servers, but they may need to be considered in order to align with any existing access policies that govern the organization.

Accounting

The final step in access management is to define accounting policies, which specify what activity on the device is logged and archived for later use. It is often beneficial to log all commands entered into a device to an external destination so that they can be reviewed in the event that a configuration change or input of a performance-intensive command causes an incident. Logging commands entered into the device also may be required for company or legal compliance.

Based on the SBC platform in use, accounting may be available using application-level logs being pushed to a destination (using SFTP or syslog), or it may be possible with TACACS+ integration.

Authentication, Authorization, and Accounting (AAA) Protocols

Two main protocols are leveraged for handling AAA across network infrastructure devices:

- **RADIUS**—A general open protocol for AAA, defined by RFC 2865 and 2866, and enhanced by several additional RFCs
- **TACACS+**—A protocol developed by Cisco and openly published as an IETF draft

TACACS+ has the benefit of allowing per-command authorization and is generally the preferred deployment in situations where the underlying device supports it.

Cisco Access Policies and Procedures for CUBE

The following sections cover how to set up appropriate access controls specific to Cisco CUBE, using local authentication and also with TACACS+ for AAA to ISE or ACS.

Local Authentication and Accounting

In very small deployments, it may be adequate to just configure users locally on the system. The commands in Example 14-10 configure local authentication and define both a standard user (**support1**) and a privileged admin (**admin2**). The **support1** user would have level 1 (user-level) privileges, and **admin2** would have additional capability, including configuration changes using level 15 (enable-level) privileges.

Example 14-10 *Local User Configuration*

```
CUBE(config)# username support1 secret mypassword
CUBE(config)# username admin2 privilege 15 secret mypassword
```

Note Encrypted passwords are used here through use of the parameter **secret** instead of **password**. This ensures that the hashed password in the configuration cannot be reversed back into plaintext by those who have access to the device configuration. The encryption used by the **password** parameter is for passwords where the hash needs to be reversed, and it is consequentially easily decoded back to the plaintext password by anyone who has access to the device's configuration.

The disadvantages with local user accounts are that the user and password configuration are decentralized and have to be done on each device. Local user configuration also doesn't offer a feasible way to manage granular command access for access groups. Regardless of those constraints, even when central TACACS+ or RADIUS is deployed, it is often still desirable to have at least a backup local user configured. The local user allows for authentication in the event that the external AAA servers are unreachable.

When using local users or not enabling AAA for accounting, consider enabling the *archive config logger* feature, which stores commands entered by users into memory.

The configuration shown in Example 14-11 stores the last 1000 commands and also delivers them using syslog to the device's defined syslog destination. Sending to an external destination helps prevent the command history from being lost during reboot or cleared by a user.

Example 14-11 *Sample Configuration for Local Configuration Accounting*

```
CUBE(config)# archive
CUBE(config-archive)# log config
CUBE(config-archive-log-cfg)# hidekeys
CUBE(config-archive-log-cfg)# logging enable
CUBE(config-archive-log-cfg)# logging size 1000
CUBE(config-archive-log-cfg)# notify syslog
CUBE(config-archive-log-cfg)# end
```

Once configured, this allows the command history to be viewed using the command shown in Example 14-12.

Example 14-12 *Output for* **show archive log config all**

```
Cube# show archive log config all
 idx   sess           user@line       Logged command
   1      1          admin@vty0      |hostname Cube1
```

This event also shows up in syslog, as shown in Example 14-13.

Example 14-13 *Local Accounting Syslog Output*

```
Aug 15 03:15:20.172: %PARSER-5-CFGLOG_LOGGEDCMD: User:admin  logged command:hostname
  Cube1
```

The logs here would be stored in the device's memory, but it is also possible to configure logging to be persistent by copying to a local or external storage destination with the command **logging persistent**. Example 14-14 demonstrates a configuration where logs are written to the router's local storage (**flash0:**), with 104857600 bytes (100 MB) of disk space allocated for log messages. Each individual file will have a maximum size of 5 MB, and after 100 MB (20 files) are written, the oldest file will be deleted and replaced by the newest file.

Example 14-14 *Local Accounting to Flash Configuration*

```
logging persistent url flash0:/logs size 104857600 filesize 5242880
```

AAA to ISE/ACS Using TACACS+

Because of the constraints of local account management, the majority of deployments containing IOS devices are integrated using either TACACS+ or RADIUS. As mentioned previously, TACACS+ is the preferred integration due to its more robust capabilities.

The most common deployment is to integrate with TACACS+ to a server such as Cisco ISE (or Cisco Access Control Server). The TACACS+ server may be further integrated to another server for authentication, such as with LDAP and a server like Microsoft Active Directory or Security Assertion Markup Language (SAML) and an SSO provider.

The ISE/ACS and AD/SSO side of the configuration for AAA integration is beyond the scope of this publication. For a look into that side of configuration for secure access and a more detailed look into best practices for enterprise AAA design, see *Cisco ISE for BYOD and Secure Unified Access* by Woland and Heary (Cisco Press).

To integrate CUBE into an external AAA server, some configuration needs to be performed on each device. The configuration is the same for both IOS and IOS XE. Example 14-15 demonstrates this configuration for TACACS+.

Example 14-15 *TACACS+ Sample Configuration*

```
CUBE(config)# aaa new-model
CUBE(config)# tacacs server ISE1
CUBE(config-server-tacacs)# address ipv4 192.0.2.50
CUBE(config-server-tacacs)# key mykey
CUBE(config-server-tacacs)# exit
CUBE(config-server)# tacacs server ISE2
CUBE(config-server-tacacs)# address ipv4 192.0.2.51
CUBE(config-server-tacacs)# key mykey
CUBE(config)# aaa authentication login default group tacacs+ local
CUBE(config)# aaa authentication enable default group tacacs+
CUBE(config)# aaa authorization exec default group tacacs+ local
```

Example 14-16 shows the alternate configuration using RADIUS.

Example 14-16 *RADIUS Sample Configuration*

```
CUBE(config)# aaa new-model
CUBE(config)# radius server RADIUS1
CUBE(config-server-radius)# address ipv4 192.0.2.150
CUBE(config-server-radius)# key mykey
CUBE(config-server-radius)# exit
CUBE(config-server)# radius server RADIUS2
CUBE(config-server-radius)# address ipv4 192.0.2.151
CUBE(config-server-radius)# key mykey
CUBE(config)# aaa authentication login default group radius local
CUBE(config)# aaa authentication enable default group radius local
```

Note Notice that RADIUS does not have any authorization commands defined because the protocol cannot provide the benefit of percommand authorization. Given this limitation, Example 14-16 just provides RADIUS authentication for login and enable modes.

Troubleshooting AAA Integrations

When troubleshooting issues with AAA, there are a few useful items to validate.

It is important to check that there is TCP or UDP connectivity to the TACACS+ or RADIUS server port from the device that is being integrated. Once that is validated, also ensure that the secret key specified on the client device matches what the server is set to use. Finally, ensure that the TACACS+/RADIUS server has been configured to accept AAA requests from this device IP address, as many servers require explicit whitelisting of device IPs.

Once these items have been validated, you can use some commands to further validate operation of AAA functions. Any connectivity issues between the device and server can be observed with the commands demonstrated in Example 14-17, depending on the implemented protocol.

Example 14-17 *Sample Output from* **show tacacs** *and* **show radius statistics**

```
CUBE1# show tacacs

Tacacs+ Server -  public  :
               Server name: ISE1
            Server address: 192.0.2.100
               Server port: 49
              Socket opens:          0
             Socket closes:          0
             Socket aborts:          0
             Socket errors:          0
           Socket Timeouts:          6913
   Failed Connect Attempts:          6913
        Total Packets Sent:          6913
        Total Packets Recv:          0

CUBE1# show radius statistics
                                  Auth.      Acct.       Both
         Maximum inQ length:         NA         NA          3
       Maximum waitQ length:         NA         NA         29
       Maximum doneQ length:         NA         NA          4
       Total responses seen:          0          0          0
     Packets with responses:          0          0          0
  Packets without responses:          0       2112       2112
```

```
  Access Rejects          :       0
 Average response delay(ms):       0          0          0
 Maximum response delay(ms):       0          0          0
  Number of Radius timeouts:       0       5150       5150
       Duplicate ID detects:       0          0          0
 Buffer Allocation Failures:       0          0          0
Maximum Buffer Size (bytes):       0       1424       1424
Malformed Responses       :       0          0          0
Bad Authenticators        :       0          0          0
Unknown Responses         :       0          0          0
```

Call Detail Records (CDRs) for CUBE

CDRs provide information about every call that is presented through CUBE. This information is very useful information for troubleshooting, as well as daily management of CUBE's capacity and health. These call details may also be required for billing or compliance requirements.

Tip In some environments, it may be possible to collect the same or similar CDR data from multiple device types in the call path. This may provide redundant information and may not be necessary. For example, consider an environment where all collaboration endpoints are registered to Cisco Unified Communications Manager (CUCM) and CUBE is used for PSTN connectivity. In this setup, it may be adequate to just collect CDR from CUCM because any calls CUCM sends out to CUBE would also be contained in the CUCM CDR, yet the CUCM CDR additionally contains the internal CUCM calls where CUBE is not involved.

There are three ways to deliver CDR records from CUBE: using RADIUS, CSV file delivery, and syslog. Each method presents different advantages and disadvantages, depending on the requirements.

RADIUS

A common deployment for CDR delivery is to transmit AAA start/stop records to an external RADIUS server, using the RADIUS protocol. Example 14-18 is the configuration for a RADIUS integration with CDR to a server with IP address 192.0.2.3.

Example 14-18 *CDR Configuration for RADIUS*

```
CUBE(config)# aaa new-model
CUBE(config)# aaa accounting connection h323 start-stop group radius
CUBE(config)# radius server cdr
CUBE(config-radius-server)# address ipv4 192.0.2.3
CUBE(config)# gw-accounting aaa
```

Note The keyword **h323** is an internally used static reference by the VoIP AAA stack, which expects an accounting connection record defined with this name. This name should not be changed, but it does not constrain to only H.323 calls; SIP calls will still be accounted with the configuration.

Troubleshooting issues with CDR delivery using RADIUS would follow the same approaches as described earlier for RADIUS authentication configuration. Again, using the **show radius statistics** command is beneficial to see if messages are being received. Example 14-19 is an example in which accounting records are timing out to the RADIUS server, signifying that there is an issue with connectivity to the RADIUS server.

Example 14-19 *Sample Output of* **show radius statistics**

```
CUBE# show radius statistics
                                  Auth.      Acct.       Both
         Maximum inQ length:         NA         NA         25
       Maximum waitQ length:         NA         NA         40
       Maximum doneQ length:         NA         NA         13
       Total responses seen:          0          0          0
     Packets with responses:          0          0          0
  Packets without responses:          0       2883       2883
  Access Rejects           :          0
 Average response delay(ms):          0          0          0
 Maximum response delay(ms):          0          0          0
  Number of Radius timeouts:          0      11568      11568
       Duplicate ID detects:          0          0          0
 Buffer Allocation Failures:          0          0          0
Maximum Buffer Size (bytes):          0       1422       1422
Malformed Responses        :          0          0          0
Bad Authenticators         :          0          0          0
Unknown Responses          :          0          0          0
 Source Port Range: (2 ports only)
 1645 - 1646
 Last used Source Port/Identifier:
 1645/0
 1646/138
```

CDR File Delivery

An alternative to sending CDR using RADIUS is to use a method that delivers CDR data in a comma-separated values (CSV) file using FTP. This allows for a common structured format for any analytics of the data, as many tools exist for parsing CSV files.

The configuration in Example 14-20 defines delivery of CDR to FTP server 192.0.2.100 and writing to the **cdr/** folder. A new file is created each day. If the FTP server isn't available, IOS writes to a local file on flash instead.

Example 14-20 *Sample CDR Configuration with FTP*

```
CUBE(config)# gw-accounting file
CUBE(config)# primary ftp 192.0.2.100/cdr username cisco password cisco
CUBE(config)# secondary ifs flash:cdr
CUBE(config)# maximum fileclose-timer 300
CUBE(config)# maximum cdrflush-timer 245
```

A disadvantage with this approach is that the accounting records are held in memory for a period of time before being appended to the file on the FTP server, defaulting to a one-hour holding. This can be changed with the command shown in Example 14-21.

Example 14-21 *CDR Flush Timer Configuration*

```
maximum cdrflush-timer minutes
```

When troubleshooting issues with CDR delivery, validate that the device can properly authenticate and write files to the FTP server. This can be observed by enabling **debug ip ftp** and then attempting to manually write a file to the FTP server.

Example 14-22 demonstrates a successful validation of proper delivery to an FTP server by redirecting **show version** output to the FTP server and path that CDR would be writing to.

Example 14-22 *Sample Output of* **debug ip ftp** *for Successful CDR Delivery*

```
CUBE# show version | redirect ftp://cisco:cisco@192.0.2.3/cdr/test.txt
Writing cdr/test.txt

Aug 26 18:39:58.598: FTP: 220 (vsFTPd 3.0.3)
Aug 26 18:39:58.598: FTP: ---> USER cisco
Aug 26 18:39:58.607: FTP: 331 Please specify the password.
Aug 26 18:39:58.607: FTP: ---> ****
Aug 26 18:39:59.248: FTP: 230 Login successful.
Aug 26 18:39:59.248: FTP: ---> TYPE I
Aug 26 18:39:59.249: FTP: 200 Switching to Binary mode.
Aug 26 18:39:59.249: FTP: ---> PASV
Aug 26 18:39:59.253: FTP: 227 Entering Passive Mode (192,0,2,3,222,198).
Aug 26 18:39:59.294: FTP: ---> STOR cdr/test.txt
Aug 26 18:39:59.318: FTP: 150 Ok to send data.
Aug 26 18:40:01.879: FTP: ---> QUIT
Aug 26 18:40:02.131: FTP: 226 Transfer complete.
Aug 26 18:40:02.131: FTP: ---> QUIT
```

A commonly encountered issue with FTP delivery is inability to open a connection to the FTP server. This is demonstrated in Example 14-23.

Example 14-23 *Sample* **debug ip ftp** *Output for FTP Timeout*

```
CUBE# show version | redirect ftp://cisco:cisco@192.0.2.5/cdr/test.txt
Writing cdr/test.txt
%Error opening ftp://cisco:cisco@192.0.2.5/cdr/test.txt (Timed out)

Aug 26 18:41:03.653: FTP: connect failed -- Connection timed out; remote host not
  responding
Aug 26 18:41:03.653: %PARSER-3-URLOPENFAIL: cannot open file for redirection
  'Timed out'
```

Another common problem is improper permissions on the FTP server for the specific account to create or write files. This condition is demonstrated in Example 14-24, in the output of **debug ip ftp**.

Example 14-24 *Sample* **debug ip ftp** *Output for FTP Permission Issue*

```
CUBE# show version | redirect ftp://cisco:cisco@192.0.2.3/cdr/test.txt
Writing cdr/test.txt
%Error opening ftp://cisco:cisco@192.0.2.3/cdr/test.txt (Permission denied)

Aug 26 18:42:18.703: FTP: 220 (vsFTPd 3.0.3)
Aug 26 18:42:18.703: FTP: ---> USER cisco
Aug 26 18:42:18.773: FTP: 331 Please specify the password.
Aug 26 18:42:18.773: FTP: ---> ****
Aug 26 18:42:19.407: FTP: 230 Login successful.
Aug 26 18:42:19.407: FTP: ---> TYPE I
Aug 26 18:42:19.437: FTP: 200 Switching to Binary mode.
Aug 26 18:42:19.437: FTP: ---> PASV
Aug 26 18:42:19.439: FTP: 227 Entering Passive Mode (192,0,2,3,141,91).
Aug 26 18:42:19.460: FTP: ---> STOR cdr
Aug 26 18:42:19.463: FTP: 553 Could not create file.
Aug 26 18:42:19.463: FTP: ---> QUIT
Aug 26 18:42:19.464: FTP: 221 Goodbye.
Aug 26 18:42:19.464: %PARSER-3-URLOPENFAIL: cannot open file for redirection
  'Permission denied'
```

CDR with Syslog

When delivering CDR records using syslog, CDR information is written to the device's local syslog, and the records are stored in memory. If there is a remote syslog destination defined (as discussed previously in this chapter), the messages will also be delivered to the remote destination using the syslog protocol.

The advantage of this approach is simplicity of configuration, as there are no external dependencies on additional tools needed for this approach. A disadvantage is that the call records in syslog are stored in memory and are not persistent if the device is rebooted. If delivering syslog to a remote device, that challenge is overcome, but note that the syslog protocol is also prone to unreliable transport, and messages may be lost.

Another challenge with this approach is that the syslog repository is a destination for many other important messages on the platform that are not related to CDR. As a result, it may be challenging to filter and discern between CDR messages, debugs, and other messages that are all writing to the same syslog destination.

Example 14-25 shows a configuration that enables CDR to syslog. It also specifies a remote destination so that messages are delivered over the network to a syslog server.

Example 14-25 *Sample CDR Configuration to Syslog*

```
router(config)# gw-accounting syslog
router(config)# logging 192.0.2.100
```

The syslog content can be viewed with the command **show logging**. An example of a CDR entry in syslog is provided in Example 14-26.

Example 14-26 *Validation of CDR in Syslog Using* **show logging**

```
CUBE# show logging
Log Buffer (100000000 bytes):
Aug 26 19:06:48.487: %VOIPAAA-5-VOIP_CALL_HISTORY: CallLegType 2, ConnectionId
  FFFFFFFF8A34CB9DFFFFFFFF89C811E7FFFFFFFF8462BF0A75842B59, SetupTime 19:06:46.327
  UTC Sat Aug 26 2017, PeerAddress sipp, PeerSubAddress , DisconnectCause 10  ,
  DisconnectText normal call clearing (16), ConnectTime 19:06:46.337 UTC Sat
  Aug 26 2017, DisconnectTime 19:06:48.487 UTC Sat Aug 26 2017, CallOrigin 2,
  ChargedUnits 0, InfoType 2, TransmitPackets 0, TransmitBytes 0, ReceivePackets 0,
  ReceiveBytes 0
Aug 26 19:06:48.487: %VOIPAAA-5-VOIP_FEAT_HISTORY: FEAT_VSA=fn:TWC,ft:08/26/2017
  19:06:46.327,cgn:sipp,cdn:4085551234,frs:0,fid:321,fcid:FFFFFFFF8A34CB9DFFFFFFFF89
  C811E7FFFFFFFF8462BF0A75842B59,legID:141,bguid:8A34CB9D89C811E78462BF0A75842B59
```

Media Quality Information in CDR

As can be observed in the output in Example 14-26, media quality statistics are not inserted in the CDR record by default. Having media quality information in the call record can be very useful for identifying and managing any issues where the media stream is becoming impaired.

Tip Consider that CUBE is in the middle of the call path, so media quality statistics may not represent the true experience of a caller, as the stats derived from the middle of the media path may be upstream of where an impacting issue may reside. When possible, obtaining RTP media statistics closest to the destination of the RTP stream is desired. This is typically the location where the RTP packet stream is terminating on a DSP to convert back to analog or a plain-old telephone system (POTS), such as a PRI. Nonetheless, having access to this data at intermediary points such as CUBE provides valuable information for identification and problem isolation when such issues around media quality arise.

For SIP-to-SIP calls, media quality statistics can be inserted in the CDR record. This data is calculated through the use of RTCP, so media flow-through must be enabled, and only calls transmitting RTCP support the reporting of these statistics.

Two useful fields are **MOS-Con**, which is the approximation of the audio quality experience based on the MOS, and **voice-quality-total-packet-loss**, which is the packet loss as a percentage.

Media information is inserted into the CDR record with the commands shown in Example 14-27.

Example 14-27 *Configuration to Enable Media Statistics in CDR*

```
voice service voip
 media statistics
```

Configuration Management

The previous section touches on the importance of accounting practices such as logging commands entered into a system, but that is often not enough to have assurance that the configuration on a device is the authorized and validated configuration that is desired for use. Accounting also does not provide a practical way to recover a full configuration in the event that the device configuration is unrecoverable. As a result, there is an important need to regularly back up device configurations and note when there are changes to configurations detected as well as any deviations from configuration compliance standards for the organization.

General Configuration Management

How the configuration for a device is stored varies greatly across device types and platforms. Some appliances retain their entire configuration in a flat text file on the device, while others have the configuration in a GUI and the underlying parameters stored in a database. These configuration databases may not always be directly accessible by a user or an administrator. As a result, it is difficult to guide the best practices for configuration management without going into vendor specifics.

General goals of configuration management, however, are as follows:

- Ensure compliance of the configuration to organization standards and regulations.
- Provide a mechanism for configuration recovery in the event of complete corruption or destruction of the device.
- Provide the ability to archive prior versions of configurations in the event that an authorized change is later found to achieve undesirable results and needs to be reverted to previous values.

Also consider the following when designing for configuration management:

- Does the device write any logs or notify upon configuration changes? If so, where is this information located? Application logs? Syslog? A database that is accessible?
- How can a full configuration snapshot be obtained?

A highly popular tool in the industry for robust configuration management across large enterprise deployments of network devices is Solarwinds Network Configuration Manager (NCM). NCM supports several IOS and CLI-based devices, and it provides configuration backups, compliance, and management. NCM is a solution to consider when shopping for a configuration management tool if there isn't a preferred tool already deployed in the environment for network configuration management.

CUBE Configuration Management

Cisco IOS and IOS XE platforms have used a basic configuration structure for many years. These platforms store an entire configuration as a single text-based configuration. As a result, the ability to pull routine backups from CUBE and other IOS-based devices is fairly straightforward. This allows for flexibility in supporting various ways for configuration files and their revisions to be maintained. If there isn't an ability to leverage specific network management tools for configuration management, though, there are also some options using native features in IOS and open source software to accomplish the same goals.

Configuration Backups Using SNMP

If there is enterprise configuration management software that supports IOS backups, SNMP backups are likely already built in to the software. To add the CUBE configuration backups, the only prerequisite before adding the CUBE IP and SNMP private string into the backup software is to define the SNMP read/write string on CUBE. This configuration is shown in Example 14-28.

Example 14-28 *Sample Configuration for an SNMP Community String*

```
snmp-server community privateString RW
```

If there is no existing configuration management software to leverage, IOS configuration collection can also be done from a Linux server, using SNMP to push the configuration to a remote network address. A combination of using the Linux **snmpset** command and setting attributes with the **CISCO-CONFIG-COPY-MIB** (.1.3.6.1.4.1.9.9.96.1.1.1.1) allows for external devices to instruct a device to transmit the configuration to an external destination such as an FTP server.

Configuration Archive

IOS has a convenient feature that allows a configuration to be routinely pushed to a destination, and this feature can be used if external software for pulling a device configuration is not possible. This feature supports writing to local file systems on the device, as well as out to external (S)FTP destinations. Each time the configuration file writes, it writes to a unique filename, with a timestamp corresponding to when the configuration was saved.

The configuration in Example 14-29 enables configuration archiving to an external FTP server.

Example 14-29 *Sample Configuration for Configuration Archiving to FTP*

```
CUBE(config)# archive
CUBE(config-archive)# path ftp://ftpUser:ftpPass@192.0.2.100/$h
CUBE(config-archive)# time-period 1440
CUBE(config-archive)# write-memory

CUBE(config-archive)# end
CUBE# archive config
```

The **$h** parameter in the **path** command is replaced by the hostname of the router. The router writes the configuration file every 1440 minutes (every day), and it triggers an automatic backup before the interval if the configuration is manually saved to memory by an administrator.

If external destinations are not available, configurations can be also saved to the local file system with a maximum retention of 14 copies before overwriting, as shown in Example 14-30.

Example 14-30 *Sample Configuration for Config Archive to* **flash**

```
CUBE(config)# archive
CUBE(config-archive)# path flash:/$h
CUBE(config-archive)# max 14
CUBE(config-archive)# time-period 1440
CUBE(config-archive)# write-memory
CUBE(config-archive)# end
CUBE# archive config
```

Validation of operation for the configuration archive feature can be performed with **show archive**, as demonstrated in Example 14-31.

Example 14-31 show archive *Output*

```
CUBE# show archive
The maximum archive configurations allowed is 14.
There are currently 3 archive configurations saved.
The next archive file will be named flash:/CUBE-<timestamp>-3
 Archive #  Name
   1        flash:/CUBE-Aug-15-02-33-41.763-0
   2        flash:/CUBE-Aug-15-02-34-10.413-1
   3        flash:/CUBE-Aug-15-02-34-15.154-2 <- Most Recent
   4
   ...
   14
```

This command is also useful for troubleshooting any connectivity issues to an external path, as it provides status and error descriptions upon failure, as shown in Example 14-32.

Example 14-32 *Example of* show archive *with a Timeout*

```
CUBE# show archive
The maximum archive configurations allowed is 14.
The next archive file will be named ftp://ftpUser:ftpPass@192.0.2.100/CUBE-
  <timestamp>-1
 Archive #  Name
   1        :Error - Timed out <- Most Recent
   2
   3
...
   14
```

Configuration Management with Arcana ManageExpress Border Manager

Comprehensive management applications such as Solarwinds NCM may not be feasible or attainable for all environments where multiple deployments of CUBE are being managed. In scenarios where a central management solution is still desired to reduce the operating expense associated with management of CUBE configuration and dial peers across many device instances, Arcana ManageExpress Border Manager is another third-party configuration management application that is supported for integration with CUBE.

ManageExpress provides central configuration deployment through the use of configuration templates. Configuration templates, which are defined using text, allow the inclusion of variables. These variables can be specified at the time of deployment, allowing for basic changes with each individual device for which the configuration is being deployed. ManageExpress manages the configuration using SSH. Figure 14-5 shows a ManageExpress configuration template with variables being specified.

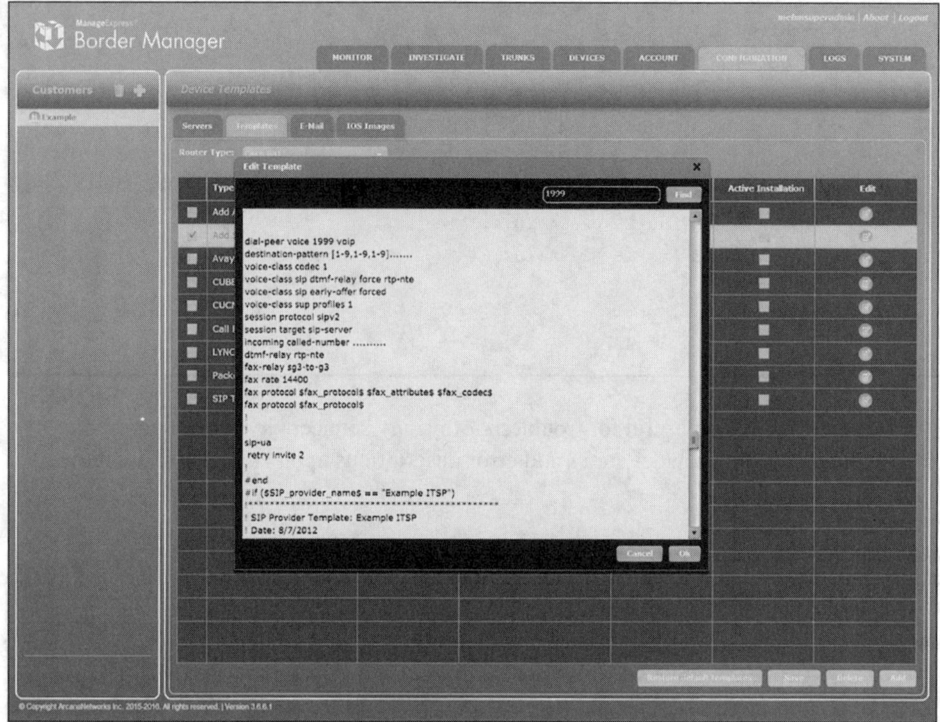

Figure 14-5 *Arcana ManageExpress Border Manager Configuration Deployment*

Much like features discussed earlier in this chapter, in the “Prime Collaboration Assurance” section, ManageExpress also allows for centralized monitoring of call quality in a dashboard format and centralized CDR collection. For environments where more comprehensive management applications cannot be deployed, ManageExpress is a potential solution to allow for centralized management of CUBE.

Diagnostic Signatures

Cisco IOS and IOS XE devices have a *diagnostic signatures* feature, which provides for a consistent way to diagnose and collect information about intermittent or transient problems on a device.

Diagnostic signatures are predefined files formatted in XML. A diagnostic signature contains a set of commands or scripts to collate information around a specific issue. This provides a simple and consistent method for collecting diagnostic information while issues are occurring. Diagnostic signatures can either be triggered on demand or executed upon detection of a specific event, such as matched text in a generated syslog message. Executing a diagnostic signature ensures that the required commands are collected as required and prevents the human error involved in collecting information. This approach allows for the information to be collected at exactly the time it is needed, based on a triggered event, ensuring that information is collected at the proper time during time-sensitive situations and then emailed to an administrator or uploaded to a Cisco support request.

Given that these signatures are executing commands on the device, the feature has been built with security in mind. The signatures are signed by Cisco to ensure the integrity of a signature and also ensure that the commands being run will not be of malicious intent. The signatures are also in plaintext, so a signature can be analyzed for validation of the actions the signature is performing.

Diagnostics use the Call Home functionality to download diagnostic signatures directly from Cisco's repository. A manual method for downloading and installing diagnostic signatures is also possible.

Diagnostic Signature Configuration

To configure diagnostic signatures, the Call Home functionality is leveraged to send alerts to administrators (see Example 14-33).

Example 14-33 *Basic Call Home Configuration*

```
ip name-server 192.0.2.99
service call-home
call-home
 sender from cube1@example.com
 contact-email-addr network-notifications@example.com
 mail-server smtp.example.com
 http-proxy https://myhttpproxy.example.com port 3128
```

The **http-proxy** command is necessary only if downloading signatures directly from Cisco's repository, when there is no direct Internet connectivity from the device. The configuration shown in Example 14-33 can also be done in a single commandlet:

```
call-home reporting contact-email-addr email-address http-proxy hostname port
port-number
```

It is possible to make signatures available for devices by logging in to the Smart Call Home portal on Cisco.com and assigning available signatures to a device by associating them to devices' hostnames and serial numbers.

Available signatures can then be obtained by loading all available signatures assigned to that device with the following command:

```
call-home diagnostic-signature download all
```

An alternative is to manually download the signature from the Diagnostic Signature Lookup Tool (https://cway.cisco.com/tools/dslt/), or if it is provided from a Cisco support engineer. The signatures can then be manually loaded with the following hidden command:

call-home diagnostic-signature load ***path***

Some signatures require that specific parameters be set up after the signature is loaded. Those signatures that require setup can be validated by viewing the output of **show call-home diagnostic-signature**, as shown in Example 14-34.

Example 14-34 *Validation of Diagnostic Signature Status*

```
CUBE1# show call-home diagnostic-signature
Current diagnostic-signature settings:
 Diagnostic-signature:  enabled
 Profile:  CiscoTAC-1 (status:  ACTIVE)
 Environment variable:Not yet set up

 Downloaded DSes:
                                                                         Last Update
 DS ID    DS Name                   Revision   Status                  (GMT-04:00)
 ----------------------------------------------------------------------------------
  -----
 12147     DS_SYS_4_FREEMEMLOW        1.0       pending               2017-07-24   10:32:16
```

If the **status** shows as **pending**, the script needs to be installed. The installation procedure allows for some dynamic parameters to be specified for the environment, and they are specific to each signature. This install process is shown in Example 14-35.

Example 14-35 *Sample Diagnostic Script Installation*

```
CUBE1# call-home diagnostic-signature install 12147
 Enter Case Number: 621487699
 Enter notification email-address: admin@example.com
 FTP Server IP Address: support-ftp.cisco.com
 FTP Username: anonymous
 FTP Password: cisco
 Free Low Memory Threshold (KB): 1000000
```

The diagnostic signature execution statistics can be viewed using **show call-home diagnostic-signature statistics**, as shown in Example 14-36.

Example 14-36 *Diagnostic Signature Execution Statistics*

```
CUBE1# show call-home diagnostic-signature statistics
                                             Triggered/      Average Run  Max Run
DS ID     DS Name                            Max/Deinstall   Time(sec)    Time(sec)
--------  ------------------------------     -------------   -----------  ---------
12147     DS_SYS_4_FREEMEMLOW                2/0/N           8.550        8.592
```

The following parameters appear in Example 14-36:

- **Triggered**—The number of times an event has been triggered
- **Max**—The maximum number of triggered events allowed
- **Deinstall**—Whether the signature should automatically uninstall itself after executing for the maximum number of times

DS 12147 has been executed twice in Example 14-36. When the **Max** value is set to zero, it runs without any maximum execution limit until it is uninstalled by the administrator using the following command:

```
call-home diagnostic-signature deinstall DS-id
```

Summary

This chapter covers monitoring and event management of SBCs. It outlines the basics of monitoring, encompassing concepts related to the various ways to monitor elements of a networking device, as well as advantages and disadvantages of the various protocols that can be used for monitoring. This chapter also covers the basic approach for general event management, including how to categorize various events as either information or actionable, as well as a baseline of items to monitor across general SBCs. This chapter presents some techniques that can be used across any vendors' SBCs to detect events that may require manual investigation to resolve potential issues. Finally, specific configuration examples and guidelines are presented that are specific to implementation on CUBE as well as techniques for troubleshooting the monitoring configuration.

The aim of this chapter's first section is to provide and empower the ability to define the service architecture all the way through to implementation of monitoring SBCs so that any issues that may arise on the platform can be reacted to and resolved in a timeframe that mitigates impact to the overlaying services.

The second section of this chapter covers management techniques for SBCs. It discusses general concepts of access management, accounting, and configuration management. It also provides specific configuration guidelines for AAA and configuration management for Cisco SBCs and briefly explores using Arcana as an alternative for CUBE configuration management as well as diagnostic signatures for increasing the consistency and efficacy of troubleshooting.

The concepts for design and implementation of effective monitoring and management techniques with SBCs should allow for maximizing the stability of the SBC services in a production operation.

References

RFC 821, "SIMPLE MAIL TRANSFER PROTOCOL," https://tools.ietf.org/html/rfc821.

RFC 2865, "Remote Authentication Dial In User Service (RADIUS)," https://tools.ietf.org/html/rfc2865.

RFC 2866, "RADIUS Accounting," https://tools.ietf.org/html/rfc2866.

RFC 3411, "An Architecture for Describing Simple Network Management Protocol (SNMP) Management Frameworks," https://tools.ietf.org/html/rfc3411.

RFC 3412, "Message Processing and Dispatching for the Simple Network Management Protocol (SNMP)," https://tools.ietf.org/html/rfc3412.

RFC 3413, "Simple Network Management Protocol (SNMP) Applications," https://tools.ietf.org/html/rfc3413.

RFC 3414, "User-based Security Model (USM) for version 3 of the Simple Network Management Protocol (SNMPv3)," https://tools.ietf.org/html/rfc3414.

RFC 3415, "View-based Access Control Model (VACM) for the Simple Network Management Protocol (SNMP)," https://tools.ietf.org/html/rfc3415.

RFC 3416, "Version 2 of the Protocol Operations for the Simple Network Management Protocol (SNMP)," https://tools.ietf.org/html/rfc3416.

RFC 3417, "Transport Mappings for the Simple Network Management Protocol (SNMP)," https://tools.ietf.org/html/rfc3417.

RFC 3418, "Management Information Base (MIB) for the Simple Network Management Protocol (SNMP)," https://tools.ietf.org/html/rfc3418.

RFC 3432, "Carrying Q.850 Codes in Reason Header Fields in SIP (Session Initiation Protocol) Responses," https://tools.ietf.org/html/rfc6432.

RFC 4181, "Guidelines for Authors and Reviewers of MIB Documents," https://tools.ietf.org/html/rfc4181.

RFC 5321, "Simple Mail Transfer Protocol," https://tools.ietf.org/html/rfc5321.

RFC 5424, "The Syslog Protocol," https://tools.ietf.org/html/rfc5424.

RFC 6020, "YANG—A Data Modeling Language for the Network Configuration Protocol (NETCONF)," https://tools.ietf.org/html/rfc6020.

RFC 6353, "Transport Layer Security (TLS) Transport Model for the Simple Network Management Protocol (SNMP)," https://tools.ietf.org/html/rfc6353.

RFC 6432, "Carrying Q.850 Codes in Reason Header Fields in SIP (Session Initiation Protocol) Responses," https://tools.ietf.org/html/rfc6432.

RFC 7159, "The JavaScript Object Notation (JSON) Data Interchange Format," https://tools.ietf.org/html/rfc7159.

"SOAP Version 1.2 Part 1: Messaging Framework (Second Edition)," http://www.w3.org/TR/soap12-part1/.

"Web Services Description Language (WSDL) Version 2," http://www.w3.org/TR/wsdl.

"Architectural Styles and the Design of Network-Based Software Architectures," https://www.ics.uci.edu/~fielding/pubs/dissertation/top.htm.

"Extensible Markup Language (XML) 1.0 (Fifth Edition)," https://www.w3.org/TR/xml/.

"Programmability Configuration Guide, Cisco IOS XE Everest 16.6.1," https://www.cisco.com/c/en/us/td/docs/ios-xml/ios/prog/configuration/166/b_166_programmability_cg/model_driven_telemetry.html.

ITIL Service Operation by Steinberg et al. (Cisco Press).

"Usage of Cause and Location in the Digital Subscriber Signalling System No. 1 and the Signalling System No. 7 ISDN User Part," ITU Recommendation Q.850.

"Cause Code Mapping," http://www.cisco.com/c/en/us/td/docs/ios-xml/ios/voice/cube/configuration/cube-book.pdf.

"pandas," http://pandas.pydata.org/index.html.

"P.800 Series P: Methods for Subjective Assessment of Quality," https://www.itu.int/rec/T-REC-P.800-199608-I/en.

VoIP Performance Management and Optimization by Ahmed et al. (Cisco Press).

"Cisco Unified Border Element (CUBE) Management and Manageability Specification," https://www.cisco.com/c/en/us/products/collateral/unified-communications/unified-border-element/white_paper_c11-613550.html.

"Supported Alarms and Events for Cisco Prime Collaboration Assurance 11.6," https://www.cisco.com/c/dam/en/us/td/docs/net_mgmt/prime/collaboration/11-6/reference_documents/Supported_Alarms_and_Events_for_Cisco_Prime_Collaboration_Assurance_Advanced_11_6.xlsx.

"RTCP XR Report Block for Concealment Metrics Reporting on Audio Applications," https://tools.ietf.org/html/draft-ietf-xrblock-rtcp-xr-loss-conceal-10.

"The TACACS+ Protocol," https://tools.ietf.org/html/draft-ietf-opsawg-tacacs-06.

Cisco ISE for BYOD and Secure Unified Access by Heary et al. (Cisco Press).

Appendix A

Q.850 Release Cause Values

Table A-1 outlines the call disconnect cause values, as defined by the International Telecom Union's standard, defined by Q.850. These numeric cause values map the reason for disconnect into a specific description for the nature of the call disconnect. These codes outline both normal disconnect scenarios, and failure or error conditions, and are common across vendors. Understanding what some of these common codes represent support the troubleshooting of issues. These codes are referenced in several chapters in this publication.

Table A-1 *Q.850 Release Cause Values*

Standard Category	Typical Scenarios	Q.850 Cause Code	Q.850 Release Cause Description
Unallocated (unassigned) number	■ The number is not in the routing table, or it has no path across the ISDN network.	1	Indicates that the destination requested by the calling user cannot be reached because the number is unassigned.
No route to specified transit network (national use)	■ The wrong transit network code was dialed. ■ The transit network does not serve this equipment. ■ The transit network does not exist.	2	Indicates that the gateway is asked to route the call through an unrecognized intermediate network.
Destination address resolution failure	■ Domain Name System (DNS) resolution failure ■ Invalid session target in configuration	3	Indicates that the called party cannot be reached because the network that the call has been routed through does not serve the desired destination.

Standard Category	Typical Scenarios	Q.850 Cause Code	Q.850 Release Cause Description
Send special information tone	■ The dialed number has a special condition applied to it.	4	Indicates that the called party cannot be reached for reasons that are of a long-term nature and that the special information tone should be returned to the calling party.
Misdialed trunk prefix (national use)	■ The wrong trunk prefix was dialed.	5	Indicates the erroneous inclusion of a trunk prefix in a called party number.
Channel unacceptable	■ Failed channel on the network	6	Indicates that the channel most recently identified is not acceptable to the sending entity for use in this call.
Call awarded and being delivered in an established channel	■ Successful call	7	Indicates that the user has been awarded the incoming call and that the incoming call is being connected to a channel already established to that user for similar calls.
Preemption	■ Emergency services	8	Indicates that the call is being preempted.
Preemption: Circuit reserved for reuse	■ Emergency services	9	Indicates that the call is being preempted and the circuit is reserved for reuse by preempting the exchange.
Normal call clearing	■ A call participant hung up.	16	Indicates that the call is being cleared because one of the users involved with the call has requested that the call be cleared.
User busy	■ The user is already using the telephone.	17	Indicates that the called party is unable to accept another call because the user busy condition has been encountered. This cause value can be generated by the called user or by the network. In the case of user-determined user busy, it is noted that the user equipment is compatible with the call.

Standard Category	Typical Scenarios	Q.850 Cause Code	Q.850 Release Cause Description
No user responding	■ The user is not answering the telephone.	18	Used when the called party does not respond to a call establishment message with either an alerting or connect indication within the time allotted. The number that is being dialed has an active D-channel, but the far end chooses not to answer.
No answer from the user (user alerted)	■ The user is not answering the telephone.	19	Used when the called party has been alerted but does not respond with a connect indication within the time allotted. This cause is not generated by Q.931 procedures but can be generated by internal network timers.
Subscriber absent	■ The user lost network connectivity or is out of range.	20	Used when a mobile station has logged off, when radio contact is not obtained with a mobile station, or if a personal telecommunication user is temporarily not addressable at any user–network interface.
Call rejected	■ The subscriber has a service constraint that does not accept this call.	21	Indicates that the equipment sending this cause code does not wish to accept this call, although it could have accepted the call because the equipment sending the cause is neither busy nor incompatible. It might also be generated by the network indicating that the call was cleared because of a supplementary service constraint. The diagnostic field might contain additional information about the supplementary service and the reason for rejection.
Number changed	■ A subscriber has changed number.	22	Returned to a calling party when the called number indicated by the calling party is no longer assigned. The new called party number might be optionally included in this diagnostic field.

Standard Category	Typical Scenarios	Q.850 Cause Code	Q.850 Release Cause Description
Redirection to a new destination	■ The call is forwarded.	23	Used by a general ISUP protocol mechanism that decides the call should be sent to a different called number.
Exchange routing error	■ The network is overloaded.	25	Indicates that the destination indicated by the user cannot be reached because an intermediate exchange has released the call due to reaching a limit in executing the hop counter procedure.
Non-selected user clearing	■ Called number failure	26	Indicates that the user has not been awarded the incoming call.
Socket failure	■ Transmission Control Protocol (TCP) socket connection failure ■ Problem sending an H.323 **SETUP** ■ Problem sending a Session Initiation Protocol (SIP) **INVITE** ■ Send or receive error on a connected socket	27	Indicates that the destination indicated by the user cannot be reached because the destination's interface is not functioning correctly. The signaling message cannot be delivered to the remote party.
Invalid number format	■ The caller is calling out using a network type number (enterprise) rather than unknown or national.	28	Indicates that the called party cannot be reached because the called party number is not in a valid format or is not complete.
Facility rejected	■ A network service is not functioning.	29	Indicates that a supplementary service requested by the user cannot be provided by the network.
Response to **STATUS ENQUIRY**	■ A STATUS message is returned.	30	Included in the **STATUS** message when the reason for generating the **STATUS** message is the prior receipt of a **STATUS ENQUIRY** message.

Standard Category	Typical Scenarios	Q.850 Cause Code	Q.850 Release Cause Description
Normal, unspecified	■ Normal operation	31	Reports a normal event only when no other cause in the normal class applies.
No circuit/ channel available	■ No B-channels are available to make the selected call.	34	Indicates that there is no appropriate circuit or channel presently available to handle the call.
Network out of order	■ Network failure	38	Indicates that the network is not functioning correctly and that the condition is likely to last for an extended period.
Permanent frame mode connection is out of service	■ Equipment or section failure	39	Included in a **STATUS** message to indicate that a permanently established frame mode connection is out of service.
Permanent frame mode connection is operational	■ Normal operation	40	Included in a **STATUS** message to indicate that a permanently established frame mode connection is operational and capable of carrying user information.
Temporary failure	■ Network failure	41	Indicates that the network is not functioning correctly and that the condition is likely to be resolved quickly.
Switching equipment congestion	■ High traffic	42	Indicates that the switching equipment generating this cause is experiencing high traffic.
Access information discarded	■ Usually reported when the far-end ISDN switch removes some piece of information before tandem-switching a call.	43	Indicates that the network could not deliver access information to the remote user as requested.

Standard Category	Typical Scenarios	Q.850 Cause Code	Q.850 Release Cause Description
Requested circuit/channel not available	■ Occurs during a glare condition when both sides are selected top-down or bottom-up. Change the allocation direction so that one end is top-down and the other is bottom-up.	44	Returned when the circuit or channel indicated by the requested entity cannot be provided by the other side of the interface.
Precedence call blocked	■ The caller is busy, and the priority level of the active call is equal to or higher than that of the incoming call.	46	Indicates that there are no preemptable circuits or that the called user is busy with a call of equal or higher preemptable level.
Internal resource allocation failure	■ Out of memory ■ Internal access to the TCP socket unavailable	47	Indicates a "resource unavailable" event.
QoS error	■ Quality of service (QoS) error	49	Indicates that the requested QoS cannot be provided.
Requested facility not subscribed	■ The caller is trying to use a service that is not permitted.	50	Indicates that the user has requested a supplementary service that the user is not authorized to use.
Outgoing calls barred within a closed user group (CUG)	■ The subscriber configuration contains this limitation.	53	Indicates that although the calling party is a member of a CUG for the outgoing CUG call, outgoing calls are not allowed for this member of the CUG.
Incoming calls barred within a closed user group (CUG)	■ The subscriber configuration contains this limitation.	55	Indicates that although the called party is a member of a CUG for the incoming CUG call, incoming calls are not allowed for this member of the CUG.
Bearer capability not authorized	■ The caller is not authorized to use the bearer capability.	57	Indicates that the user has requested a bearer capability that is implemented on the equipment but that the user is not authorized to use.

Standard Category	Typical Scenarios	Q.850 Cause Code	Q.850 Release Cause Description
Bearer capability not presently available	■ A call is placed with a bearer capacity that the service provider does not have the capacity to supply.	58	Indicates that the user has requested a bearer capability that is implemented by the equipment and is currently unavailable.
Inconsistency in designated outgoing access information and subscriber class	■ Network error	62	Indicates that there is an inconsistency in the designated outgoing access information and subscriber class.
Service or option not available, unspecified	■ Service not available	63	Reports a service or an option not available event only when no other cause in the service or option not available class applies.
Media negotiation failure	■ No codec match occurred. ■ An H.323 or H.245 problem led to a failure in media negotiation.	65	Indicates that the equipment sending this cause code does not support the bearer capability requested.
Channel type not implemented	■ Channel type match not found.	66	Indicates that the equipment sending this cause code does not support the channel type requested.
Requested facility not implemented	■ Service type match not found.	69	Indicates that the equipment sending this cause code does not support the requested supplementary service.
Only restricted digital information bearer capability is available (national use)	■ Routing error	70	Indicates that the calling party has requested an unrestricted bearer service but that the equipment sending this cause only supports the restricted version of the requested bearer capacity.
Service or option not implemented, unspecified	■ Service not implemented	79	Reports a service or option not implemented event only when no other cause in the service or option not implemented class applies.

Standard Category	Typical Scenarios	Q.850 Cause Code	Q.850 Release Cause Description
Invalid call reference value	■ The far-end switch did not recognize the call reference for a message sent by the gateway.	81	Indicates that the equipment sending the cause code has received a message with a call reference that is not currently in use on the user–network interface.
Identified channel does not exist	■ Fractional PRI error	82	Indicates a call attempt on a channel that is not configured.
A suspended call exists, but this call identity does not	■ Call ID mismatch	83	Indicates that a call resume has been attempted with a call identity which differs from that in use for any presently suspended calls.
Call identity in use	■ Equipment error	84	Indicates that the network has received a call suspended request containing a call identity that is already in use for a suspended call.
No call suspended	■ Equipment error	85	Indicates that the network has received a call resume request containing a call identity information element that does not indicate any suspended call.
Call having the requested call identity has been cleared	■ Network timeout ■ Call cleared by remote user	86	Indicates that the network has received a call identity information element indicating a suspended call that has in the meantime been cleared while suspended.
User is not a member of a closed user group (CUG)	■ The caller is not authorized.	87	Indicates that the called user for the incoming CUG call is not a member of the specified CUG.
Incompatible destination	■ The number dialed is not capable of this type of call. ■ The caller is calling a restricted line in unrestricted mode. ■ The caller is calling a POTS phone using unrestricted mode.	88	Indicates that the equipment sending this cause has received a request to establish a call that has compatibility attributes which cannot be accommodated.

Standard Category	Typical Scenarios	Q.850 Cause Code	Q.850 Release Cause Description
Nonexistent closed user group (CUG)	■ Configuration or dialing error	90	Indicates that the specified CUG does not exist.
Invalid transit network selection (national use)	■ Network error ■ Identification mismatch	91	Indicates that a transit network identification received is of an incorrect format.
Invalid message received error	■ An invalid message was received.	95	Indicates an invalid message event.
Mandatory IE missing error	■ The **Mandatory Contact** field is missing from the SIP message. ■ The Session Description Protocol (SDP) body is missing.	96	Indicates that the equipment sending this cause code has received a message that is missing an information element. This element must be present in the message before the message can be processed.
Message type non-existent or not implemented	■ Message type information is missing.	97	Indicates that the equipment sending this cause has received a message that is missing an information element which must be present in the message before the message can be processed.
Message not compatible with call state or message type non-existent or not implemented	■ ISDN protocol mismatch ■ ISDN state machine violation	98	Indicates that the equipment sending this cause has received a message such that the procedures do not indicate that this is a permissible message to receive while in this call state.
An information element or parameter does not exist or is not implemented	■ Element mismatch	99	Indicates that the equipment sending this cause has received a message that includes information elements or parameters not recognized because the information element or parameter names are not defined or are defined but not implemented by the equipment.

Standard Category	Typical Scenarios	Q.850 Cause Code	Q.850 Release Cause Description
Invalid IE contents error	■ The SIP Contact field is present, but the format is bad.	100	Indicates that the equipment sending this cause code has received an information element that it has implemented. However, the equipment sending this cause code has not implemented one or more of the specific fields.
Message in invalid call state	■ An unexpected message was received that is incompatible with the call state.	101	Indicates that a message has been received that is incompatible with the call state.
Call setup timeout failure	■ No H.323 call proceeding ■ No H.323 alerting or connect message received from the terminating gateway ■ Invite expires timer reached maximum number of retries allowed	102	Indicates that a procedure has been initiated by the expiration of a timer in association with an error-handling procedures.
Parameter nonexistent or not implemented—passed on (national use)	■ Configuration mismatch	103	Indicates that the equipment sending this cause code has received a message that includes parameters not recognized because the parameters are not defined or are defined but not implemented on the equipment.
Message with unrecognized parameter discarded	■ Unrecognized parameter	110	Indicates that the equipment sending this cause has discarded a received message that includes a parameter which is not recognized.
Protocol error, unspecified	■ Protocol error	111	Reports a protocol error event only when no other cause in the protocol error class applies.
Internal error	■ Failed to send message to Public Switched Telephone Network (PSTN)	127	Indicates that there has been interworking with a network that does not provide causes for actions it takes. The precise cause cannot be ascertained.

Index

Symbols

A

B

C

D

E

F

G

H

J

K

M

N

O

P

Q

R

S

T

U

V

W

X

Y-Z